The Flower
Ornament Scripture

The Flower
Ornament Scripture

A Translation of the *Avatamsaka Sutra*
Thomas Cleary

SHAMBHALA • BOSTON & LONDON • 1993

SHAMBHALA PUBLICATIONS, INC.
Horticultural Hall
300 Massachusetts Avenue
Boston, Massachusetts 02115
www.shambhala.com

14   13   12   11   10   9   8

Printed in the United States of America
⊚ This edition is printed on acid-free paper that meets the
American National Standards Institute Z39.48 Standard.
Distributed in the United States by Random House, Inc., and in Canada by
Random House of Canada Ltd

Library of Congress Cataloging-in-Publication Data

Tripitaka, Sūtripitaka. Buddhāvataṃsakamahāvaipulyasūtra. English.
    The Flower ornament scripture/translated by Thomas Cleary.
        p.   cm.
    ISBN 978-0-87773-940-1 (alk. paper)
    I. Cleary, Thomas F., 1949–   .   II. Title.
    BQ1622.E5T7413   1993   93-21833
    294.3'85—dc20   CIP

Contents

The Flower
Ornament Scripture

.

Introduction

THE FLOWER ORNAMENT SCRIPTURE, called *Avatamsaka* in Sanskrit and *Huayan* in Chinese, is one of the major texts of Buddhism. Also referred to as the major Scripture of Inconceivable Liberation, it is perhaps the richest and most grandiose of all Buddhist scriptures, held in high esteem by all schools of Buddhism that are concerned with universal liberation. Its incredible wealth of sensual imagery staggers the imagination and exercises an almost mesmeric effect on the mind as it conveys a wide range of teachings through its complex structure, its colorful symbolism, and its mnemonic concentration formulae.

It is not known when or by whom this scripture was composed. It is thought to have issued from different hands in the Indian cultural sphere during the first and second centuries AD, but it is written so as to embrace a broad spectrum of materials and resists rigid systematization. While standard figures and images from Indian mythology are certainly in evidence here, as in other Buddhist scriptures, it might be more appropriate to speak of its provenance in terms of Buddhist culture rather than Indian culture per se. *The Flower Ornament Scripture* presents a compendium of Buddhist teachings; it could variously be said with a measure of truth in each case that these teachings are set forth in a system, in a plurality of systems, and without a system. The integrity of Buddhism as a whole, the specificity of application of its particular elements, and the interpenetration of those elements are fundamental points of orientation of the unfolding of the scripture.

Historicity as such is certainly of little account in *The Flower Ornament Scripture*. This is generally true of the Mahayana Buddhist scriptures, although they usually present their teachings as having been revealed or occasioned by the meditations of the historical Buddha Shakyamuni. In the case of *The Flower Ornament Scripture*, most of the discourse is done by transhistorical, symbolic beings who represent aspects of universal enlightenment. The Buddha shifts from an individual to a cosmic principle and manifestations of that cosmic principle; the "Buddha" in one line might be "the Buddhas" in the next, representing enlightenment itself, the scope of enlightenment, or those who have realized enlightenment.

Certainly one of the most colorful and dramatic rehearsals of Buddhist teachings, *The Flower Ornament Scripture* became one of the pillars of

1

East Asian Buddhism. It was a source of some of the very first Buddhist literature to be introduced to China, where there eventually developed a major school of philosophy based on its teachings. This school spread to other parts of Asia, interacted with other major Buddhist schools, and continues to the present. The appreciation of *The Flower Ornament Scripture* was not, however, by any means confined to the special Flower Ornament school, and its influence is particularly noticeable in the literature of the powerful Chan (Zen) schools.

The work of translating from *The Flower Ornament Scripture* into Chinese apparently began in the second century AD, and continued for the better part of a thousand years. During this time more than thirty translations and retranslations of various books and selections from the scripture were produced. Numerous related scriptures were also translated. Many of these texts still exist in Chinese. Comprehensive renditions of the scripture were finally made in the early fifth and late seventh centuries. The original texts for both of these monumental translations were brought to China from Khotan in Central Asia, which was located on the Silk Route and was a major center for the early spread of Buddhism into China. Khotan, where an Indo-Iranian language was spoken, is now a part of the Xinjiang (Sinkiang) Uighur autonomous region in China, near Kashmir, another traditional center of Buddhist activity. The first comprehensive translation of *The Flower Ornament Scripture* was done under the direction of an Indian monk named Buddhabhadra (359–429); the second, under the direction of a Khotanese monk named Shikshananda (652–710). The latter version, from which the present English translation is made, was based on a more complete text imported from Khotan at the request of the empress of China; it is somewhat more than ten percent longer than Buddhabhadra's translation.

The Flower Ornament Scripture, in Shikshananda's version, contains thirty-nine books. By way of introduction to this long and complex text, we will focus on a comparison of *The Flower Ornament Scripture* with other major scriptures; as well as a brief glance at the main thrust of each book.

A Comparison with Other Major Buddhist Scriptures

Due to the great variety in Buddhist scriptures, analysis of their interrelation was an integral part of Buddhist studies in East Asia, where scriptures were introduced in great quantities irrespective of their time or place of origin. In order to convey some idea of the Buddhism of *The Flower Ornament Scripture* in respect to other major scriptures, as well as to summarize some of the principal features of *The Flower Ornament*, we will begin this Introduction with a comparison of *The Flower Ornament* with other important scriptures. This discussion will be based on the

"Discourse on the Flower Ornament," a famous commentary by an eighth century Chinese lay Buddhist, Li Tongxuan. What follows is a free rendering of Li's comparisons of *The Flower Ornament Scripture* to the scriptures of the lesser vehicle (the Pali Canon),[1] the *Brahmajala Scripture*, the *Prajnaparamita Scriptures*,[2] the *Sandhinirmocana Scripture*, the *Lankavatara Scripture*,[3] the *Vimalakirtinirdesa Scripture*,[4] the *Saddharmapundarika Scripture*,[5] and the *Mahaparinirvana Scripture*.[6]

The scriptures containing the precepts of the lesser vehicle are based on conceptual existence. The Buddha first told people what to do and what not to do. In these teachings, relinquishment is considered good and nonrelinquishment is considered not good. Doctrine set up this way is not yet to be considered indicative of true existence. This teaching based on existence is temporary, dealing with the delusions of ordinary feelings and the arbitrary invention of ills; this teaching is designed to stop these and enable people to live in truly human or celestial states. That is why the preface of the precepts says that if one wants to live in heavenly or human conditions one should always keep the precepts.

People's fabricated doings are unreal, and not true attainment, therefore their life in human and celestial states is impermanent, not truly real. They have not yet attained the body of reality and the body of knowledge. This teaching is not based on true existence; it is temporarily based on conceptual existence. This is the model of the lesser vehicle. As for keeping precepts in *The Flower Ornament Scripture*, it is not this way: as it says in the scripture, "Is the body religious practice? Are walking, standing, sitting, or reclining religious practice?" and so on, examining closely in search of "religious practice," ultimately finding it cannot be apprehended—this ungraspability is why it is called pure religious practice. As the scripture says, those engaged in such pure practice are said to uphold the discipline of the buddha-nature, and attain the Buddha's reality body. Therefore they attain enlightenment at the first inspiration. Because they keep the discipline of buddha-nature, they are equal to the essence of Buddha, equal in terms of noumenon and phenomenon, merging with the cosmos of reality. When they keep discipline this way, they do not see themselves keeping precepts, they do not see others breaking precepts. Their action is neither that of ordinary people nor that of saints. They do not see themselves arousing the determination for enlightenment, they do not see the Buddhas attaining enlightenment. If there is anything at all that can be grasped or apprehended—whether good or bad—this is not called enlightenment, not called pure practice. One should see in this way. Such discipline based on the essence is itself the body of reality; the body of reality is the knowledge of Buddhas; the knowledge of Buddhas is true enlightenment. Therefore this discipline of *The Flower Ornament Scripture* is not the same as the teaching of the lesser vehicle, which has choosing and rejection.

Next, the precepts for enlightening beings in the *Brahmajala Scripture* are based on presentation of both conceptual existence and real existence.

For people who have big hearts and like to practice kindness and compassion and those who seek Buddhahood, the Buddha says Vairocana is the fundamental body, with ten billion emanation bodies. To suddenly cause us to recognize the branches and return to the root, the scripture says these ten billion bodies bring innumerable beings to the Buddha. It also says if people accept the precepts of Buddha, they then enter the ranks of Buddhas: their rank is already the same as great enlightenment and they are true offspring of Buddha. This is therefore discipline based on the essence, and is thus based on reality. This scripture abruptly shows great-hearted people the discipline of the essence of the body of reality, while lesser people get it gradually. Therefore one teaching responds to two kinds of faculties, greater and lesser. The statement that the ten billion emanation bodies each bring countless beings to the Buddha illustrates giving up the provisional for the true. This is the teaching of true existence. Because in this teaching the provisional and true are shown at once, it is not the same as the lesser vehicle, which begins with impermanence and has results that are also impermanent, because the precepts of the lesser vehicle only lead to humanity and heavenly life. However, the establishment of a school of true existence in the *Brahmajala Scripture* is not the same as that expounded by Vairocana in *The Flower Ornament Scripture*. In the *Brahmajala Scripture*, by following the teaching of the emanation bodies of Buddha we arrive at the original body: in the school of the complete teaching of the *Flower Ornament*, the original body is shown all at once; the fundamental realm of reality, the body of rewards of great knowledge, cause and effect, and noumenon and phenomena are equally revealed. Also the description of the extent of the cosmos of *The Flower Ornament Scripture* is not the same as the description in the *Brahmajala Scripture*.

As for the *Prajnaparamita Scriptures*, they are based on explaining emptiness in order to show the truth. When the Buddha first expounded the teachings of the lesser vehicle to people, they stuck to principles and phenomena as both real, and therefore could not get rid of obstruction. Therefore Buddha explained emptiness to them, to break down their attachments. That is why it explains eighteen kinds of emptiness in the *Prajnaparamita Scriptures*—the world, the three treasures (the Buddha, the Teaching, and the Community), the four truths (suffering, origin, extinction, the path), the three times (past, present, and future), and so on, are all empty, and emptiness itself is empty too. This is extensively explained in these scriptures, to nullify ignorance and obstructing actions. When ignorance is totally exhausted, obstructing actions have no essence—nirvana naturally appears. This is true existence; it is not called a school of emptiness. However, though it is real true existence, many of the teachings expounded have becoming and disintegration, therefore it cannot yet be considered complete. As for *The Flower Ornament Scripture*, in it are the arrays of characteristics and embellishments that are rewards or consequences of enlightening practice—they can be empty and they can be actual. In this scripture the teachings of emptiness and existence are not applied singly—noumenon and phenomena, emptiness and existence, interpenetrate, reflecting each other. All the books of the whole *Flower Ornament Scripture* interpenetrate, all the statements intertwine. All the sayings in the scripture point to the same thing—when one becomes all become, when one disintegrates all disintegrate. In the totality, because the essence is equal, the time is equal, and the practice is equal, every part of the scripture is equal, and so the explanations of the Teaching are equal. Therefore attainment of buddhahood in the present means equality with all Buddhas of past, present, and future: consequently there is no past, present, or future—no time. In this it differs from the *Prajnaparamita Scriptures*, in which formation and disintegration take place at separate times and thus cause and effect are successive.

Now as for the *Sandhinirmocana Scripture*, this is based on nonvoidness and nonexistence. Buddha explained this teaching after having expounded teachings of existence and of emptiness, to harmonize the two views of being and nothingness, making it neither emptiness nor existence. To this end he spoke of an unalloyed pure consciousness without any defilement. According to this teaching, just as a rapid flow of water produces many waves, all of which are equally based on the water, similarly the sense consciousnesses, the conceptual consciousness, the judgmental consciousness, and the cumulative repository consciousness are all based on the pure consciousness. As the *Sandhinirmocana Scripture* says, it is like the face of a good mirror: if one thing which casts a reflection comes before it, just one image appears; if two or more things come before it, two or more images appear—it is not that the surface of the mirror changes into reflections, and there is no manipulation or annihilation that can be grasped either. This illustrates the pure consciousness on which all aspects of consciousness are based.

The *Sandhinirmocana Scripture* also says that though the enlightening being lives by the teaching, knowledge is the basis, because the teaching is a construction. The intent of this scripture is to foster clear understanding of the essence of consciousness in the medium of consciousness. Because fundamentally it is only real knowledge, it is like the stream of water, which produces waves without leaving the body of the water. It is also like a clear mirror, which due to its pure body contains many images without discrimination, never actually having anything in it, yet not impeding the existence of images. Likewise, the forms of consciousness manifested by one's own mind are not apart from essential uncontrived pure knowledge, in which there are no attachments such as self or other, inside or outside, in regard to the images manifested. Letting consciousness function freely, going along with knowledge, this breaks up bondage to emptiness or existence, considering everything neither empty nor existent. Therefore a verse of the *Sandhinirmocana Scripture* says, "The pure consciousness is very deep and subtle; all impressions are like a torrent. I do not tell the ignorant about this, for fear they will cling to the notion as 'self.' " The statement that the pure consciousness is very deep and subtle is to draw ordinary people into realization of knowledge in consciousness: it is not the same as the breaking down of forms into emptiness, which is practiced by the two lesser vehicles and the beginning enlightening beings learning the gradual method of enlightenment. It is also not the same as ordinary people who cling to things as really existent. Because it is not the same as them, it is not emptiness, not existence. What is not empty? It means that knowledge can, in all circumstances, illumine the situation and help people. What is not existent? It means that when knowledge accords with circumstances, there is no distinction of essence and characteristics, and thus there is no birth, subsistence, or extinction. Based on these meanings it is called "not empty, not existent."

While the *Sandhinirmocana Scripture* in this way lets us know, in terms of consciousness, that emptiness and existence are nondual, *The Flower Ornament Scripture* is not like this: *The Flower Ornament* just reveals the Buddha's essence and function of fundamental knowledge of the one reality, the fundamental body, the fundamental cosmos. Therefore it merges true essence and characteristics, the oceans of the reality body and the body of consequences of deeds, the reward body. It directly points out at once to people of the highest faculties the basic knowledge of the unique cosmos of reality, the qualities of Buddhahood. This is its way of teaching and enlightenment; it does not discuss such phenomena as producing consciousness according to illusion.

According to the *Saddharmapundarika Scripture*, Buddha appears in the world to enlighten people with Buddha-knowledge and purify them, not for any other religious vehicle, no second or third vehicle. Also it says that Buddha does not acknowledge the understanding of the essence and characteristics of Buddha by people of the three vehicles. Therefore the *Saddharmapundarika Scripture* says, "As for the various meanings of essence and characteristics, only I and the other Buddhas of the ten directions know them—my disciples, individual illuminates, and even nonregressing enlightening beings cannot know them." Because the *Saddharmapundarika Scripture* joins the temporary studies of the three vehicles and brings them ultimately to the true realm of reality of the Buddha-vehicle, its doctrine to some extent matches that of *The Flower Ornament Scripture*.

The Flower Ornament Scripture directly reveals the door of consummate buddhahood, the realm of reality, the fundamental essence and function of the cosmos, communicating this to people of superior faculties so that they may awaken to it: it does not set up the provisional didactic device of five, six, seven, eight, and nine consciousnesses like the *Sandhinirmocana Scripture* does. As for the *Sandhinirmocana Scripture*'s establishment of a ninth, pure consciousness, there are two meanings. For one thing, it is for the sake of those of the two lesser vehicles who have long sickened of birth and death and cultivate emptiness to annihilate consciousness, aiming directly for empty quiescence. Also, in the next phase, the *Prajnaparamita Scriptures* talk a lot about emptiness and refute the notion of existence, to turn around the minds of the two vehicles as well as enlightening beings engaged in gradual study. They also make the six ways of transcendence the vehicle of practice. Although some of those in the two vehicles are converted, they and the gradual-practice enlightening beings are predominantly inclined toward emptiness. This is because the elementary curative teachings for the gradual-study enlightening beings are similar to some extent to those for the lesser vehicles; they do have, however, a bit more compassion than the latter. They have not yet realized principles such as that of the body of reality, the buddha-nature, and fundamental knowledge. They only take the avenue of emptiness as their vehicle of salvation and the six ways of transcendence as their form of practice. Their elementary curative means are after all the same as the two vehicles—only by contemplation of impermanence, impurity, bleached bones, atoms, and so on, do they enter contemplation of emptiness. But while the two vehicles head for extinction, enlightening beings stay in life. They subdue notions of self and phenomena by means of contemplations of voidness, selflessness, and so on. Basically this is not yet fundamental knowledge of the body of reality and the buddha-nature; because their vision is not yet true, inclination toward emptiness is dominant. For this reason the *Sandhinirmocana Scripture* expediently sets up a pure consciousness distinct from the conceptual, judgemental, and cumulative consciousnesses, saying that these consciousnesses rest on the pure consciousness.

The *Sandhinirmocana Scripture* does not yet directly explain that the impressions in the cumulative or repository consciousness are the matrix of enlightenment. This is because the students are engaged in learning out of fear of suffering; if they were told that the seeds of action are eternally real, they would become afraid and wouldn't believe it, so the scripture temporarily sets up a "pure consciousness" so that they won't annihilate the conscious nature and will grow in enlightenment. For this reason the *Vimalakirtinirdesa Scripture* says, "They have not yet fulfilled buddhahood, but they don't annihilate sensation to get realization." Since sensation is not annihilated, neither are conception and consciousness. As for the *Lankavatara Scripture*, it does directly tell those whose faculties are mature that the seeds of action in the cumulative "storehouse" consciousness are the matrix of enlightenment. The *Vimalakirtinirdesa Scripture* says, "The passions which accompany us are the seeds of buddhahood."

People who practice the Way are different, on different paths, with myriad different understandings and ways of acting. Beyond the two vehicles that are called the lesser vehicles, the vehicle of enlightening beings has four types that are not the same: one is that of enlightening beings who cultivate emptiness and selflessness; second is that of enlightening beings who gradually see the buddha-nature; third is that of enlightening beings who see buddha-nature all of a sudden; fourth is those enlightening beings who, by means of the inherently pure knowledge of the enlightened, and by means of various levels of intensive practice, develop differentiating knowledge, fulfill the practice of Universal Good and develop great benevolence and compassion.

As for the *Lankavatara Scripture*, its teaching is based on five elements, three natures, eight consciousnesses, and twofold selflessness. The five elements are forms, names, arbitrary conceptions, correct knowledge, and thusness. The three natures are the nature of mere imagination, the nature of relative existence, and the nature of absolute emptiness: the imaginary nature means the characteristics of things as we conceive of them are mere descriptions, projections of the imagination; the relative nature means that things exist in terms of the relation of sense faculties, sense data, and sense consciousness; the absolute nature means that the imaginary and relative natures are not in themselves ultimately real. The eight consciousnesses are the five sense-consciousness, the conceptual consciousness, the discriminating judgemental consciousness, and the cumulative or repository "storehouse" consciousness. The twofold selflessness is the selflessness of persons and of things.

According to this scripture, there is a mountain in the south seas called Lanka, where the Buddha expounded this teaching. This mountain is high and steep and looks out over the ocean; there is no way of access to it, so only those with spiritual powers can go up there. This represents the teaching of the mind-ground, to which only those beyond cultivation and realization can ascend. "Looking out over the ocean" represents the ocean of mind being inherently clear, while waves of consciousness are drummed up by the wind of objects. The scripture wants to make it clear that if you realize objects are inherently empty the mind-ocean will be naturally peaceful; when mind and objects are both stilled, everything is revealed, just as when there is no wind the sun and moon are clearly reflected in the ocean.

The *Lankavatara Scripture* is intended for enlightening beings of mature faculties, all at once telling them the active consciousness bearing seed like impressions is the matrix of enlightenment. Because these enlightening beings are different from the practitioners of the two lesser vehicles who annihilate consciousness and seek quiescence, and because they are different from the enlightening beings of the *Prajnaparamita Scriptures* who cultivate emptiness and in whom the inclination toward emptiness is dominant, this scripture directly explains the total reality of the fundamental nature of the substance of consciousness, which then becomes the function of knowledge. So just as when there is no wind on the ocean the images of objects become clearer, likewise in this teaching of the mind ocean if you comprehend that reality is consciousness it becomes knowledge. This scripture is different from the idea of the *Sandhinirmocana Scripture*, which specially sets up a ninth "pure" consciousness to guide beginners and gradually induce them to remain in the realm of illusion to increase enlightenment, not letting their minds plant seeds in voidness, and not letting their minds become like spoiled fruitless seeds by onesidedly rejecting the world. So the *Sandhinirmocana Scripture* is an elementary gateway to entry into illusion, while the *Lankavatara* and *Vimalakirtinirdesa Scriptures* directly point to the fundamental reality of illusion. The *Lankavatara* explains the storehouse consciousness as the matrix of enlightenment, while the *Vimalakirtinirdesa* examines the true character of the body, seeing it to be the same as Buddha.

The *Lankavatara* and *Vimalakirtinirdesa Scriptures* are roughly similar, while the *Sandhinirmocana* is a bit different. *The Flower Ornament* is not like this: the body and sphere of the Buddha, the doors of teaching, and the forms of practice are far different. It is an emanation body which expounds the *Lankavatara*, and the realm explained is a defiled land; the location is a mountain peak, and the teaching explains the realm of consciousness as real; the interlocutor is an enlightening being called Great Intellect, the teaching of the emanation Buddha is temporary, and the discourse of Great Intellect is selective. As for the teaching of *The Flower Ornament Scripture*, the body of Buddha is the fundamental reality, the realm of the teaching and its results is the Flower Treasury; the teaching it rests on is the fruit of buddhahood, which is entered through the realm of reality; the interlocutors are Manjushri and Universally Good. The marvelous function of knowledge of noumenon and phenomena, the aspects of practice of five sets of ten stages, and their causes and effects, merge with each other; the substances of ten fields and ten bodies of buddhahood interpenetrate. It would be impossible to tell fully of all the generalities and specifics of *The Flower Ornament*.

Next, to deal with the *Vimalakirtinirdesa Scripture*, this is based on inconceivability. The *Vimalakirtinirdesa Scripture* and *The Flower Ornament Scripture* have ten kinds of difference and one kind of similarity. The spheres of difference are: the arrays of the pure lands; the features of the body of Buddha as rewards of religious practice or emanated phantom manifestations; the inconceivable spiritual powers; the avenues of teaching set up to deal with particular faculties; the congregations who come to hear the teachings; the doctrines set up; the activity manifested by the enlightening being Vimalakirti; the location of the teaching; the company of the Buddha; and the bequest of the teaching. The one similarity is that the teachings of methods of entry into the Way are generally alike.

First, regarding the difference in the arrays of the pure lands, in the case of the pure land spoken of in the *Vimalakirtinirdesa Scripture* Buddha presses the ground with his toe, whereupon the billion-world universe is adorned with myriad jewels, like the land of Jewel Array Buddha, adorned with the jewels of innumerable virtues. All in the assembly rejoice at this wonder and see themselves sitting on jewel lotus blossoms. But this scripture still does not speak of endless arrays of buddha-lands being in one atom. *The Flower Ornament Scripture* fully tells of ten realms of Vairocana Buddha, ten Flower Treasury oceans of worlds—each ocean of worlds containing endless oceans of worlds, interpenetrating each other again and again, there being endless oceans of worlds within a single atom. The complete sphere of the ten Buddha-bodies and the sphere of sentient beings interpenetrate without mutual obstruction; the arrays of myriad jewels are like lights and reflections. This is extensively recounted in *The Flower Ornament Scripture*; it does not speak of the purification and adornment of only one billion-world universe.

Second, regarding the difference in the features of the Buddhas' bodies, being rewards or emanations, the *Vimalakirti Scripture* is expounded by an emanation Buddha with the thirty-two marks of greatness, whereas *The Flower Ornament* is expounded by the Buddha of true reward, with ninety-seven marks of greatness and also as many marks as atoms in ten Flower Treasury oceans of worlds.

Third, the difference in inconceivable spiritual powers: according to the *Vimalakirti Scripture*'s explanation of the spiritual powers of enlightening beings, they can fit a huge mountain into a mustard seed and put the waters of four oceans into one pore; also Vimalakirti's little room is able to admit thirty-two thousand lion thrones, each one eighty-four thousand leagues high. Vimalakirti takes a group of eight thousand enlightening beings, five hundred disciples, and a hundred thousand gods and humans in his hand and carries them to a garden; also he takes the eastern buddha-land of Wonderful Joy in his hand and brings it here to earth to show the congregation, then returns it to its place. These miraculous powers are just shown for the benefit of disciples and enlightening beings who are temporarily studying the three vehicles. Why? Because disciples and enlightening beings studying the temporary teachings do not yet see the Way truly, and have not yet forgotten the distinction of self and other. The miracles shown are based on the perception of the sense faculties, and all have coming and going, boundaries and limits. Also they are a temporary device of a sage, intended to arouse those of small faculties by producing miracles through spiritual powers, to induce them to progress further. Therefore they are not spontaneous powers. *The Flower Ornament Scripture* says it is by the power of fundamental reality, because it is the natural order, the way things are in truth, that it is possible to contain all lands of Buddhas and sentient beings in one atom, without shrinking the worlds or expanding the atom. Every atom in all worlds, like this, also contains all worlds.

As *The Flower Ornament Scripture* says, enlightening beings attain enlightenment in the body of a small sentient being and extensively liberate beings, while the small sentient being does not know it, is not aware of it. You should know that it is because Buddha draws in those of lesser faculties by temporary teachings that they see Buddha outside themselves manifesting spiritual powers that come and go—in the true teaching, by means of inherent fundamental awareness one becomes aware of the fundamental mind, and realizes that one's body and mind, essence and form, are no different from Buddha, and so one has no views of inside or outside, coming or going. Therefore Vairocana Buddha's body sits at all sites of enlightenment without moving from his original place; the congregations from the ten directions go there following the teaching without moving from their original places. There is no coming and going at all, nothing produced by miraculous powers. This is why the scripture says it is this way in principle, in accord with natural law. When the scripture says time and again that is by the spiritual power of Buddha and also thus in principle or by natural law, it says "by the spiritual power of Buddha" to put forward Buddha as what is honorable, and says "it is thus in principle" or "by natural law" to put forward the fundamental qualities of reality. There is no change at all, because every single land, body, mind, essence, and form remain as they originally are and do not follow delusion—all objects and realms, great and small, are like lights, like images, mutually reflecting and interpenetrating, pervading the ten directions, without any coming or going, without any bounds. Thus within the pores of each being is all of space—it is not the same as the temporary teaching of miraculous powers with divisions, coming and going, which cause illusory views differing from the fundamental body of reality, blocking the knowledge of the essence of fundamental awareness of true enlightenment. This is why the enlightening being Vimalakirti set forth the true teaching after showing miracles. The *Vimalakirti Scripture* says, "Seeing the Buddha is like seeing the true character of one's own body; I see the Buddha doesn't come from the past, doesn't go to the future, and doesn't remain in the present."

Because those of small views studying the temporary teaching crave wonders, the enlightening being uses crude means according to their faculties to induce them to learn, and only then gives them the true teaching. One should not cling to phantoms as real and thus perpetually delude the eye of knowledge. Recognizing the temporary and taking to the true, one moves into the gate of the realm of reality.

That which is contrived can hardly accomplish adaptation to conditions, whereas the uncontrived has nothing to do. Those who strive labor without accomplishment, while nonstriving, according with conditions, naturally succeeds. In effortless accomplishment, effort is not wasted; in accomplishment by effort, all effort is impermanent, and many eons of accumulated cultivation eventually decays. It is better to instantly realize the birthlessness of interdependent origination, transcending the views of the temporary studies of the three vehicles.

Fourth is the difference in the teachings set up in relation to people of particular faculties. The *Vimalakirti Scripture* is directed toward those of faculties corresponding to the two lesser vehicles, to induce them to aim for enlightenment and enter the great vehicle. It is also directed at enlightening beings who linger in purity, whose compassion and knowledge is not yet fully developed, to cause them to progress further. Therefore, in the scripture when a group of enlightening beings from a pure land who have come here are about to return to their own land and so ask Buddha for a little teaching, the Buddha, seeing that those enlightening beings are lingering in a pure land and their compassion and knowledge are not yet fully developed, preaches to them to get them to study finite and infinite gates of liberation, telling them not to abandon benevolence and compassion and to set the mind on omniscience without ever forgetting it, to teach sentient beings tirelessly, to always remember and practice giving, kind speech, beneficial action, and cooperation, to think of being in mediative concentration as like being in hell, to think of being in birth and death as like being in a garden pavilion, and to think of seekers who come to them as like good teachers. This is expounded at length in the *Vimalakirti Scripture*.

This *Vimalakirti Scripture* addresses those of the two and three vehicles whose compassion and knowledge are not fully developed, to cause them to gradually cultivate and increase compassion and knowledge—it doesn't immediately point out the door of buddhahood, and doesn't yet say that beginners in the ten abodes realize true enlightenment, and doesn't show great wonders, because its wonders all have bounds.

Fifth is the difference in the assemblies who gather to hear the teaching. In the *Vimalakirti Scripture*, except for the great enlightening beings such as Manjushri and Maitreya and the representative disciples such as Shariputra, all the rest of the audience are students of the temporary teachings of the three vehicles. Even if there are enlightening beings therein who are born in various states of existence and bring those of their kind along, they all want to develop the temporary studies of the three vehicles, and gradually foster progress; the scripture does not yet explain the complete fundamental vehicle of the Buddhas. In the case of *The Flower Ornament Scripture*, all those who come are riding the vehicle of the Buddhas—enlightened knowledge, the virtues of realization, the inherent body of reality. They are imbued with Universally Good practice, appear reflected in all scenes of enlightenment in all oceans of lands, and attain the fundamental truth, which conveys enlightenment. There is not a single one with the faculties and temperament of the three vehicles; even if there are any with the faculties and potential of the three vehicles, they are as though blind and death, unknowing, unaware, like blind people facing the sun, like death people listening to celestial music.

Vessels of the three vehicles who have not yet consummated the power of the Way and haven't turned their minds to the vehicle of complete buddhahood are always in the sphere of Buddhas in the ocean of the realm of reality, with the same qualities and same body as Buddha, but they never are able to believe it, are unaware of it, do not know it, so they seek vision of Buddha elsewhere. As *The Flower Ornament Scripture* says, "Even if there are enlightening beings who practice the six ways of transcendence and cultivate the various elements of enlightenment for countless billions of eons, if they have not heard this teaching of the inconceivable quality of Buddha, or if they have heard it and don't believe or understand it, don't follow it or penetrate it, they cannot be called real enlightening beings, because they cannot be born in the house of the Buddhas." You should know the audiences are totally different—in the *Vimalakirti Scripture* the earthlings are not yet rid of discrimination, while the group from a pure land retain a notion of defilement and purity. Such people's views and understanding are not yet true—sticking to a pure land in one realm, though they be called enlightening beings, they are not well rounded in the path of truth and they don't completely understand the Buddha's meaning. Though they aspire to enlightenment, they want to remain in a pure land, and because they set their minds on that, they are alienated from the body of reality and the body of knowledge. For this reason the *Saddharmapundarika Scripture* says, "Even countless nonregressing enlightening beings cannot know." As for the audience of *The Flower Ornament*, their own bodies are the same as the Buddha's body, their own knowledge is the same as the Buddha's knowledge; there is no difference. Their essence and characteristics contain unity and multiplicity, and sameness and distinction. Dwelling in the water of knowledge of the realm of reality, they appear as dragons; living in the mansion of nirvana, they manifest negativity and positivity, to develop people. Principal and companions freely interreflect and integrate, teacher and student merge with one another, cause and effect interpenetrate. All of *The Flower Ornament* audience are such people.

Sixth, regarding the difference in doctrines set up, the *Vimalakirti Scripture* uses the layman Vimalakirti manifesting a few inconceivable occult displays to cause those of the two lesser vehicles to change their minds. Also Vimalakirti, in the midst of birth and death, appears to be physically ill to have people know defilement and purity are nondual. Also the scripture represents the great compassion of the enlightening being, the "enlightening being with sickness" accepting the pains of the world, and extensively sets forth aspects of nonduality. It sets up concentration and wisdom, contemplation and knowledge, which it uses to illustrate that the principle of nonseeking is most essential. Thus it says, "Those who seek truth should not seek anything." Nevertheless, it is not yet comparable to *The Flower Ornament*'s full exposition of the teachings of sameness and distinction and cause and effect of the forms of practice of five and six levels—ten abodes, ten practices, ten concentrations, ten dedications, ten stages, and equalling enlightenment.

Seventh, regarding the difference of the activity manifested by the enlightening being Vimalakirti, in order to represent great compassion Vimalakirti appears to enter birth and death and shows the actions of its ailments. In *The Flower Ornament Scripture* Vairocana, by great compassion, appears to enter birth and death and accomplish the practice of true enlightenment, illustrating great knowledge able to appear in the world.

Eighth, regarding the difference in the locations of the teachings, the expounding of the *Vimalakirti Scripture* takes place in a garden in the Indian city of Vaishali and in Vimalakirti's room; the expounding of *The Flower Ornament Scripture* takes place at the site of enlightenment in the Indian nation of Magadha, and in all worlds, and in all atoms.

Ninth, regarding the difference in the company of the Buddha, at the time of the preaching of the *Vimalakirti Scripture*, the Buddha's constant company consisted of only five hundred disciples; at the time of the preaching of *The Flower Ornament*, all the Buddha's company were great enlightening beings of the one vehicle, and there were as many of them as atoms in ten buddha-fields, all imbued with the essence and action of Universally Good and Manjushri.

Tenth, regarding the difference in the bequest of the teaching, in the *Vimalakirti Scripture*'s book on handing over the bequest it says that Buddha said to the enlightenment being Maitreya, "Maitreya, I now entrust to you this teaching of unexcelled complete perfect enlightenment, which I accumulated over countless billions of ages." Thus the teaching of this scripture is bequeathed to those who have already become enlightening beings and have been born in the family of Buddhas. In *The Flower Ornament Scripture*'s book on manifestation of Buddha, the bequest of the teaching of the scripture is made to ordinary people who as beginners can see the Way and be born in the family of Buddhas. Why? This scripture is difficult to penetrate—it can only be explained to those who can realize it by their own experience. This represents the three vehicles as temporary, because the sage exhorts cultivation and realization in the three vehicles, and anything attained is not yet real, and because the doctrines preached are not yet real either. Therefore *The Flower Ornament Scripture* says, "The treasure of this scripture does not come into the hands of anybody except true offspring of Buddha, who are born in the family of Buddhas and plant the roots of goodness, which are seeds of enlightenment. If there are no such true offspring of Buddha, this teaching will scatter and perish before long." It may be asked, "True offspring of Buddha are numberless—why worry that this scripture will perish in the absence of such people?" The answer to this is that the intent of the scripture is to bequeath it to ordinary people to awaken them and lead them into this avenue to truth, and therefore cause them to be born in the family of Buddhas and have them prevent the seed of buddhahood from dying out. Thus ordinary people are caused to gain entry into reality. If it were bequeathed to great enlightening beings, the ordinary people would have no part in it. The sages made it clear that if there were no ordinary people who study and practice, the seed of buddhahood would die out among ordinary people, and this scripture would scatter and perish. This is why the scripture is bequeathed to ordinary people, to get them to practice it; it is not bequeathed to already established great enlightening beings who have long seen the Way.

As for the similarity of means of entering the Way, the *Vimalakirti*

Scripture says, "Those who seek the truth shouldn't seek anything," and "Seeing Buddha is like seeing the true character of one's own body; I see the Buddha does not come from the past, go to the future, or remain in the present," and so on. These doors of knowledge of elementary contemplations are about the same as *The Flower Ornament Scripture*, but the forms of practice, means of access, order, and guidelines are different.

Next, to compare the *Saddharmapundarika Scripture* to *The Flower Ornament Scripture*, the *Saddharmapundarika* is based on merging the temporary in the true, because it leads people of lesser, middling, and greater faculties into the true teaching of the one vehicle, draws myriad streams back into the ocean, returns the ramifications of the three vehicles to the source. Scholars of the past have called this the common teaching one vehicle, because those of the three vehicles all hear it, whereas they called *The Flower Ornament* the separate teaching one vehicle, because it is not also heard by those of the three vehicles. The *Saddharmapundarika* induces vessels of the temporary teaching to return to the real; *The Flower Ornament* teaches those of great faculties all at once so they may directly receive it. Though the name "one vehicle" is the same, and the task of the teaching is generally the same, there are many differences in the patterns. It would be impractical to try to deal with them exhaustively, but in brief there are ten points of difference: the teachers; the emanation of lights; the lands; the interlocutors who request the teaching; the arrays of the assemblies, reality, and emanations; the congregations in the introduction; the physical transformation and attainment of buddhahood by a girl; the land where the girl who attains buddhahood lives; the inspirations of the audiences; and the predictions of enlightenment of the hearers.

First, regarding the difference in the teachers, the exposition of the *Saddharmapundarika* is done by an emanation or phantom-body Buddha; a Buddha who passed away long ago comes to bear witness to the scripture, and the Buddhas of past, present, and future alike expound it. *The Flower Ornament* is otherwise; the main teacher is Vairocana, who is the real body of principle and knowledge, truth and its reward, arrayed with embodiments of virtues of infinite characteristics. The Buddhas of past, present, and future are all in one and the same time; the characteristics realized in one time, one cosmos, reflect each other ad infinitum without hindrance. Because past and present are one time, not past, present, or future, therefore the Buddhas of old are not in the past and the Buddhas of now have not newly emerged. This is because in fundamental knowledge essence and characteristics are equal, noumenon and phenomena are not different. Thus the fundamental Buddha expounds the fundamental truth. Because it is given to those of great faculties all at once, and because it is not an emanation body, it is not like the *Saddharmapundarika*, in which there is an ancient Buddha who has passed away and a present Buddha who comes into the world and expounds the *Saddharmapundarika*.

Second, regarding the difference in emanation of lights, when expounding the *Saddharmapundarika* the Buddha emanates light of realization from between his eyebrows; the range of illumination is only said to be eighteen thousand lands, which all turn golden—there is still limitation, and it doesn't talk of boundless infinity. Therefore it only illustrates the state of result, and not that of cause. *The Flower Ornament* has in all ten kinds of emanation of light symbolizing the teaching, with doctrine and practice, cause and effect; this is made clear in the scripture.

Third, regarding the difference in the lands, when he preached the *Saddharmapundarika*, Buddha transformed the world three times, causing it to become a pure land; he moved the gods and humans to other lands, and then placed beings from other hands here, transforming this defiled realm into a pure field. When *The Flower Ornament* was expounded, this world itself was the Flower Treasury ocean of worlds, with each world containing one another. The scripture says that each world fills the ten directions, and the ten directions enter each world, while the worlds neither expand nor shrink. It also says the Buddhas attain the Way in the body of one small sentient being and edify countless beings, without this small sentient being knowing or being aware of it. This is just because the ordinary and the sage are the same substance—there is no shift. Within a fine particle self and other are the same substance. This is not the same as the *Saddharmapundarika Scripture*'s moving gods and humans before bringing the pure land to light, which is set up for those of the faculties of the temporary teaching, who distinguish self and other and linger in views.

Fourth, regarding the difference in the main interlocutors who request the teaching, in the case of the *Saddharmapundarika*, the disciple Shariputra is the main petitioner. In *The Flower Ornament*, the Buddha has Manjushri, Universally Good, and enlightening beings of every rank each expound the teachings of their own status—these are the speakers. The Buddha represents the state of result: bringing up the result as the cause, initiating compassionate action, consummating fundamental knowledge, the being of the result forms naturally, so nothing is said, because the action of great compassion arises from uncreated fundamental knowledge. Manjushri and Universally Good represent the causal state, which can be explained; Buddha is the state of result, enlightening sentient beings. The vast numbers described in the book on the incalculable can only be plumbed by a Buddha—they are not within the scope of the causes and effects of the five ranks of stages; hence this is a teaching within the Buddha's own state, and so Buddhist himself expounds it. The book on the qualities of Buddha's embellishments and lights is Buddha's own explanation of the principles of Buddhahood after having himself fulfilled cause and effect. The teachings in this book of the perpetual power of natural suchness and the lights of virtue and knowledge also do not fall within the causes and effects of the forms of practice in the five ranks of ten stages, and so the Buddha himself explains it, making it clear that buddhahood does not have ignorance of the subtle and most extremely subtle knowledge. The rest of the books besides these two are all teachings of the forms of practice of the five sets or ranks of stages, so the Buddha does not explain them himself, but has the enlightening beings in the ranks of the ten developments of faith, ten abodes, ten practices, ten dedications, and ten stages explain them: the Buddha just emanates lights to represent them. In the exposition of *The Flower Ornament Scripture* there is not a single disciple or lesser enlightening being who acts as an interlocutor—all are great enlightening beings within the ranks of fruition of buddhahood, carrying out dialogues with each other, setting up the forms of practice of the teaching of the realization of buddhahood to enlighten those of great faculties. Thus it takes the fruit of buddhahood all at once, directly taking it as the causal basis; the cause has the result as its cause, while the result has the cause as its result. It is like planting seeds: the seeds produce fruit, the fruit produce seeds. If you ponder this by means of the power of concentration and wisdom, you can see it.

Fifth, regarding the differences in the arrays of the assemblies, reality and emanations, in the assembly of the *Saddharmapundarika Scripture*, the billion-world universe is purified and adorned, with emanation beings filling it, and the Buddhas therein also are said to be emanations. In the assemblies of *The Flower Ornament Scripture*, however, the congregations all fill the ten directions without moving from their original location, filling the cosmos with each physical characteristic and land reflecting each other. The enlightening beings and Buddhas interpenetrate, and also freely pervade the various kinds of sentient beings. The bodies and lands interpenetrate like reflections containing each other. Those who come to the assemblies accord with the body of embellishment without dissolving the body of reality—the body of reality and the body of embellishment are one, without distinction; thus the forms are identical to reality, none are emanations or phantoms. This is not the same as other doctrines which speak of emanations and reality and have them mix in congregations.

Sixth, regarding the difference of the congregations in the introductions, in the assembly of the *Saddharmapundarika*, first it mentions the disciples of Buddha, who are twelve thousand in all, then the nun Mahaprajapati and her company of six thousand—she was the aunt of Buddha; then it mentions Yashodhara, who was one of the wives of Buddha, then eighty thousand enlightening beings, and then the gods and spirits and so on. *The Flower Ornament Scripture* is not like this: first it mentions the leaders of the enlightening beings, who are as numerous as atoms in ten buddha-worlds, and doesn't talk about their followers; then it mentions the thunderbolt-bearing spirits, and after that the various spirits and gods, fifty-five groups in all. Each group is different, and each has as many individuals as atoms in a buddha-world, or in some cases it simply says they are innumerable. The overall meaning of this is the boundless cosmos of the ocean of embodiments of Buddha—each body includes all, ad infinitum, without bounds. One body thus has the cosmos for its measure; the borders of self and other are entirely gone. The cosmos, which is one's own body, is all-pervasive; mental views of subject and object are obliterated.

Seventh, regarding the difference of physical transformation and attainment of buddhahood by a girl, in the *Saddharmapundarika Scripture* a girl instantly transforms her female body, fulfills the conduct of enlightening beings, and attains buddhahood in the South. *The Flower Ornament Scripture* is not like this; it just causes one to have no emotional views, so great knowledge is clarified and myriad things are in essence real, without any sign of transformation. According to the *Vimalakirti Scripture*, Shariputra says to a goddess, "Why don't you change your female body?" The goddess says to Shariputra, "I have been looking for the specific marks of 'woman' for twelve years but after all can't find any—what should I change?" As another woman said to Shariputra, "Your maleness makes my femaleness." You should know myriad things are fundamentally "thus"—what can be changed? In *The Flower Ornament Scripture*'s book on entry into the realm of reality, the teachers of the youth Sudhana—Manjushri and Samantabhadra (Universally Good), monks, nuns, householders, boys, laywomen, girls, wizards, and Hindus—fifty-three people, each are imbued with the conduct of enlightening beings, each are replete with the qualities of buddhahood; while they are seen to be physically dissimilar according to the people who perceive them, it is not said that there is transformation. If you see with the eye of truth, there is nothing mundane that is not true; if you look with the mundane eye, there is no truth that is not mundane. Because the *Saddharmapundarika* addresses those with lesser, middling, and greater faculties for the temporary teaching, whose views are not yet ended, to cause them to develop the seed of faith, it temporarily uses the image of a girl swiftly being transformed and becoming a Buddha, to cause them to conceive wonder, at which only will they be inspired to aim for true knowledge and vision. They are not ready for the fundamental truth, yet they develop roots of goodness. This illustrates inducing those in the three temporary vehicles back to the one true vehicle. Also it cuts through the fixed idea of time, the notion that enlightenment takes three eons, provoking instantaneous realization that past, present, and future are in essence fundamentally one time, without beginning or end, in accord with the equality of things. It rends the net of views of the three vehicles, demolishes the straw hut of the enlightening being, and causes them to wind up at the door of the realm of reality and enter the true abode of Buddhas. This is why it has that girl become Buddha, showing it is not a matter of long cultivation in the past; the fact that she is only eight years old also illustrates the present is not past study—the time of her transformation is no more than an instant, and she fully carries out the fruition of buddhahood without the slightest lack. Truth is fundamentally *thus*—there is no time in essence.

Those involved in temporary studies block themselves with views and miss the truth by themselves—they call it a miracle that the girl attained buddhahood, and do not know they themselves are originally thus; completely in the world, how can they point to eons of practice outside? If they don't get rid of this view, they will surely miss enlightenment forever; if they change their minds and their views vanish, only then will they realize their original abode. It would be best for them to stop the compulsion of views right now. They uselessly suffer through eons of pain and fatigue before they return.

As for *The Flower Ornament Scripture*'s doctrine of the interdependent origination of the cosmos, it makes it clear that the ordinary person and the sage are one reality; if one still retains views, one is blocked from this one reality. If one retains views one is an ordinary person; if one forgets sentiments one is a Buddha. Looking downward and looking upward, advancing and withdrawing, contracting and expanding, humility and respect, are all naturally interdependent, and are all practices of enlightening beings—there is nothing at all with transformable characteristics having birth, subsistence, and extinction. Therefore this *Flower Ornament* teaching is not the same as the *Saddharmapundarika*'s girl being physically transformed and attaining buddhahood.

Eighth, regarding the difference of the land in which the girl who becomes a Buddha dwells, in the *Saddharmapundarika Scripture* it says this is the world of nondefilement in the South, not this earth. This is interpreted to mean that nondefilement refers to the mind attaining harmony with reality, and "the South" is associated with clarity, emptiness, and detachment. However, if one abides in "the South" as a separate place, then self and other, "here" and "there" are still separate—this is still following the three vehicles to induce those with facility for the temporary teachings to develop resolution and finally come to the Buddha-vehicle. This is because the residual force of attachment to the three vehicles is hard to break. Yet there is some change of mind, and though the sense of self and other is not yet obliterated, the mind is suddenly impressed by the body of the cosmos. This is not the same as *The Flower Ornament*, in which self and other interpenetrate in each atom, standing in a universal relationship of mutual interdependence and interpenetration.

Ninth, regarding the difference in inspirations, the *Saddharmapundarika Scripture* says that when the girl attained buddhahood, all the enlightening beings and disciples on earth, seeing her from afar becoming a Buddha and preaching to the congregation of the time, were delighted and paid respects to her from afar. Subsequently it says three thousand people on earth dwelt in the stage of nonregression, and three thousand people aroused the determination for enlightenment and received predictions of their future buddhahood. When these six thousand people paid honor to the girl from afar and were inspired, their discrimination between "there" and "here" was not gone—they just pursued the created enlightenment of the temporary studies of the three vehicles, and had not attained the enlightenment of fundamental awareness of the cosmos in its universal aspect, in which self and other are one being.

The Flower Ornament is not like this: in terms of the cosmos of universality, the teaching of universal vision, the realm of absorption in the body of the matrix of enlightenment, and the teaching of the array of the cosmic net of Indra, the subtle knowledge of the interpenetration of the whirls of the oceans of worlds is all attained at once—because realization of one is realization of all, detachment from one is detachment from all. Therefore within one's own body are the arrays of oceans of lands of the ten bodies of Buddha, and within the Buddha's bodies is the realm of one's own body. They mutually conceal and reveal each other, back and forth, over and over—all worlds everywhere are naturally this way. It is like myriad streams returning to the ocean: even when they have yet entered the ocean, the nature of moisture is no different; and once they enter the ocean, they all are of the same salty flavor. The same is true of all sentient beings—though delusion and enlightenment differ, the ocean of original buddhahood is basically not different.

Tenth, regarding the difference of giving the prediction of enlightenment to the hearers, in the *Saddharmapundarika Scripture*, though the girl who becomes a Buddha reflects all at once the timelessness of the cosmos, completely revealing buddhahood, those in the temporary studies of the three vehicles, although they have faith, have not yet gotten rid of their residual tendencies and are not yet able to attain immediate realizations; because they can only ascend to enlightenment over a long period of time, they are given prediction of enlightenment in the distant future. This is not the same as *The Flower Ornament Scripture*, which teaches that when one is deluded one is in the realm of the ordinary, and when one is enlightened one is then a Buddha—even if there are residual habits, one uses the knowledge and insight of buddhahood to cure them. Without the knowledge and insight of buddhahood, one can only manage to analyze and subdue habits and cannot enter the rapids of buddhahood, but can only enter buddhahood after a long time.

Because the faculty of faith of beginners in the three vehicles is inferior, they are not able to get rid of their bondage; they are fully wrapped up in their many ties and are obsessed with the vicissitudes of mundane life. Though they seek to transcend the world, their capacities are inferior and they get stuck and regress. This is why the Buddha has them contemplate such points as birth, aging, sickness, death, impermanence, impurity, instantaneous decay, and continual instability to cause them to become disillusioned. When they develop rejection of the world, their minds dwell on the distinction between purity and defilement; for the benefit of this type of people, who, though they cultivate compassion and knowledge in quest of buddhahood, still think of a pure land as elsewhere, and because they have not obliterated their partial views characteristic of the three vehicles and so always see this world as impure, the Buddha explains cause and effect and settles their doubts, and temporarily makes the world pure, and then withdraws his mystic power so they will again see defilement.

Due to the habit of those in the three vehicles of viewing everything in terms of impermanence, selflessness, and emptiness, their minds are hard to change; though the girl in the *Saddharmapundarika* shows the Buddha-vehicle all at once, and though they believe in it, yet they cannot yet realize it immediately themselves. For this reason the predictions of full enlightenment in the *Saddharmapundarika* assembly all refer to long periods of time. The *Saddharmapundarika* gradually leads to *The Flower Ornament*, whereupon they are directly taught that the determination for enlightenment is itself buddhahood.

There are two aspects of similarity between the *Saddharmapundarika* and *The Flower Ornament Scriptures*. One is that of riding the vehicle of buddhahood directly to the site of enlightenment. The vehicle of buddhahood is the one vehicle. As *The Flower Ornament Scripture* says, among all people there are few who seek the vehicle of hearers, Buddhism disciples, even fewer who seek the vehicle of individual illumination, while those who seek the great vehicle are very few; yet it is easy to seek the great vehicle compared to the great difficulty of believing in *The Flower Ornament* teaching. The scripture also says that if there are any people who are fed up and depressed or obsessed, they are taught the path of disciples to enable them to escape from suffering; to those who are somewhat clear and sharp in mind the principle of conditioning is explained, to enable them to attain individual illumination; to those who willingly practice benevolence and compassion for the benefit of many, the path of enlightening beings is explained; if there are any who are intent on the matter of greatest importance, putting the teachings of infinite enlightenment into operation, they are taught the path of the one vehicle. This is the distinction of four vehicles in *The Flower Ornament Scripture*; as for the *Saddharmapundarika*, it sets out three temporary vehicles and finally reveals the true teaching, which is the Buddha-vehicle—there is no real second or third vehicle. The four vehicles of these two scriptures coincide in their definitions, but the manner of teaching is different.

Then again in the *Saddharmapundarika* it says that "Only this one thing is true—the other two are not real." Going by this passage, it seems to be setting up three vehicles, but actually it is four teachings: the one thing which is true is the Buddha-vehicle, while the other two refers to the great vehicle of enlightening beings and the lesser vehicles of individual illuminates and hearers, the latter being considered together because they are alike in respect to their revulsion to suffering.

Also, the girl in the *Saddharmapundarika* reflecting the nature of past, present, and future in one instant, and the statement that there is not the slightest shift from ordinary person to sage, are about the same as the teaching of the understanding and practice and entry into the Way by the youth Sudhana in the last book of *The Flower Ornament Scripture*. As for Sudhana's attainment of buddhahood in one life, within an instant he realized the nature of past, present, and future is wholly equal. This and the girl's instant transformation to buddhahood are both in accord with fundamental truth, because this is the way things are.

As for the *Nirvana Scripture*, it is based on the buddha-nature. It has ten points of difference with *The Flower Ornament Scripture*, and one similarity. The differences are as follows: the location; the arrays of the realms; the audiences; the interlocutors of the teachings; the audiences' hearing of the teaching; the purity or defilement of the lands of reward; the temporariness and reality of the Buddha-body; the patterns of birth and extinction; the forms of practice of the teachings; and the models of companionship. The one point of similarity is illustrated by the *Nirvana Scripture*'s image of an herb in the snowy mountains of such a nature that cows who eat it produce pure ghee with no tinge of blue, yellow, red, white, or black.

Regarding the first difference, that of location, the *Nirvana Scripture* is preached between the twin trees on the bank of the Hiranyavati River in Kushinagara, whereas *The Flower Ornament* is preached under a jewel enlightenment tree at the sight of enlightenment in Magadha.

Second, regarding the difference in array of the realm, when the *Nirvana Scripture* was expounded, the hallowed ground between the trees was thirty-two leagues in length and breadth, completely filled by a great congregation. At that time the places where the boundless hosts of enlightening beings and their companies sat were infinitesimal, like points: all the great enlightening beings from all buddha-lands came and assembled. Also it says that at that time, by the Buddha's power, in all the worlds in that billion-world universe the ground was soft, level, uncluttered, free from brambles, and arrayed with myriad jewels like the western paradise of the Buddha of Infinite Life. Everyone in this great assembly saw all the buddha-lands, numerous as atoms, as clearly as seeing themselves in a mirror. Also it says that the trees suddenly turned white. This is all extensively described in the scripture.

Now when *The Flower Ornament Scripture* was expounded, there were ten flower-treasury oceans of worlds, each with twenty layers above and below. On the bottom layer there are as many vast lands as atoms in one buddha-field, each with as many satellite lands as atoms in ten buddha-fields; this increases with each successive layer. All of the worlds in these oceans of worlds have adamantine soil, with trees, pavilions, palaces, mansions, lakes, seas, all adorned with precious substances. As the scripture says, "One time the Buddha was in the land of Magadha, at the site of enlightenment in a forest, having just realized true enlightenment: the ground was made of adamantine diamond, adorned with discs of exquisite jewels, flowers of myriad jewels, and clear crystals," and so on, going on to say how all the adornments of inconceivable eons of all buddha-lands were included and revealed there. This is eulogizing the adornments of the sphere of Buddha. This is also extensively described in the book on the Flower Treasury universe: these are the adornments of the Buddha's own body of true reward, not like in the *Nirvana Scripture* where Buddha uses mystic power to temporarily purify the world for the assembly. The reason for this is that in the *Nirvana Scripture* the audience is a mixture of those with the faculties of the three vehicles, so there would be no way for them to see this purity by themselves without the support of the Buddha's spiritual power. In the case of *The Flower Ornament* the audience is pure and unmixed, being only those with the faculty for the one vehicle; the disciples of the lesser vehicle who are in the crowd do not perceive these adornments of Buddha's realm, because their faculties are different. Although the scripture says "by the spiritual power of Buddha," afterwards it says, after all, that it is by the power of natural law being so, or it is so in principle. Here, "spiritual" or "mystic" means accord with reality; it doesn't mean that someone who is actually an ordinary person is given a temporary vision. *The Flower Ornament* basically shows the true reward, while the spiritual power of the *Nirvana Scripture* is a temporary measure. Also, the *Nirvana Scripture* has Buddha's pure land in the west, beyond as many buddha-lands as particles of sand in thirty-two Ganges Rivers—it is not here. This obviously is a projection, and not real.

Third, regarding the difference in the audiences, all in the audience of the *Nirvana Scripture* are human or celestial in nature, with those of the three vehicles coming together: except for the great enlightening beings, when they remember the Buddha they weep; bringing fragrant firewood for the cremation, they grieve and lament, missing the days when they attended the Buddha. All such people are suited to hearing that the Buddha passes away; except for the enlightening beings of the one vehicle who have penetrated Buddha-knowledge, all the others are like this. The audience of *The Flower Ornament Scripture* consists of enlightening beings in the ranks of fruition of buddhahood, in the ocean of knowledge of essence, all of whom are on the one vehicle. The humans, celestials, spirits, etc. are all of the same faculties and enter the stream of Buddha-knowledge. In the first assembly it says that the enlightening beings, as many of them as atoms in ten buddha-worlds, are all born from the ocean of the roots of goodness of Buddha. The ocean of roots of goodness is the ocean of knowledge of the reality body of Buddha, born of great knowledge. All Buddhas have as their basis the fundamental knowledge of the body of reality—if enlightening beings were not born from this, all their practices would be fabricated. This congregation, from the first inspiration to the entry into the ocean of Buddha-knowledge, go through six levels, cultivating ten developments of faith, ten abodes, ten practices, ten dedications, ten stages, and equaling enlightenment, from shallow to deep, the forms of practice diverse. This is not like the *Nirvana Scripture*, in which the three vehicles are alike included, and the good types of humans and celestials come to the same assembly; in *The Flower Ornament Scripture*, those of the three vehicles are not in the congregation, or even if they are, they are as though deaf, not hearing. So you should know the assembly of those of the three vehicles in the *Nirvana Scripture*—enlightening beings, Buddha's disciples, humans, celestials, etc.—is not the same as that of *The Flower Ornament Scripture*, which consists only of enlightening beings in the one vehicle, whose rank when they first set their minds on enlightenment is the same as the rank of Buddha, who enter the stream of knowledge of Buddha, share the same insight and vision as Buddha, and are true offspring of Buddha.

Fourth, regarding the difference in the interlocutors, in the *Nirvana Scripture* the main petitioners for the teaching are the enlightening being Kashyapa, the enlightening beings Manjushri and Sinhanada, and Shariputra, and so on, who are models of the teachings. The Devil, who is also a principal petitioner, urges the Buddha to pass away. As for *The Flower Ornament Scripture*, the leaders who set up the teachings are Universally Good, Manjushri, Chief in Awareness, Truth Wisdom, Forest of Virtues, Diamond Banner, Diamond Matrix, and so on. In this way there are ten "chiefs," ten "wisdoms," ten "forests," and ten "matrices," great enlightening beings within the ranks of fruition of buddhahood, who set up the teachings of forms of practice of fruition of buddhahood in several ranks. Thus because these ranks are identical to buddhahood and buddhahood is identical to these ranks, it shows that in each rank there is fruition of buddhahood.

The enlightening beings who carry on dialogues setting up the teachings in *The Flower Ornament* are all enlightening beings from the ten directions and from this world; all spiritually penetrate the source of reality, their knowledge is equal to the cosmos: appearing as reflections or responses in the ten directions, they arrive without coming or going. Their devices, in accord with the nature of things, are not accomplished by coming and going. Even in the minutest atomic particle there are infinite clusters of bodies; in a fine hair an inconceivable ocean of forms is manifest. All things in the cosmos are like this. In all places, the enlightening beings are suddenly there, without having come from anywhere; suddenly they are absent, without having gone anywhere. In all places and times, in the physical forms of living beings, the mountains, rivers, seas, and space of the environment, they appear in physical forms, freely being and not being, infinitely interpenetrating and inter-reflecting. These are all great enlightening beings, and therefore are not like the enlightening being Kashyapa or the disciple Shariputra in the *Nirvana Scripture*, who were born in human homes and appeared in the same state as ordinary people to lead the people in the three vehicles, who felt sad and wept on the passing of the Buddha.

Fifth, regarding the difference in the audiences' hearing of the teaching, the *Nirvana Scripture* is for those of the lesser vehicles and enlightening beings involved in the temporary teaching, who carry out various contemplative practices without having yet gotten rid of the obstruction of clinging, and so are obsessed with the practice and cling fast to the forms of practice, thus missing, in these forms of practice, the fundamental essence of the uncreated body of reality, which has no proof or practice; by means of practice, cultivation develops and becomes manifest, constructing realizations of the subject and object, enlightenment and nirvana: for these people the Buddha explains in this *Nirvana Scripture* that all practices are impermanent, being things that are born and perish, and that when birth and destruction die out, extinction is bliss. This is because the good conduct practiced and the realizing enlightenment are born phenomena, and the realized nirvana is the phenomenon of extinction: since the mind retains subject and object, birth and extinction do not cease, and while birth and extinction do not cease one fails to penetrate the truth. Now this *Nirvana Scripture* therefore explains that when the practices, the realizing enlightenment, and the realized nirvana all become extinct, only then does one accord with truth: so it says, "All practices are impermanent—they are born and perish. When birth and decay have passed away, silent extinction is bliss." This is why the Buddha disappeared. When the sense of subject and object is ended, that is called great nirvana.

The nirvana of the two lesser vehicles can have subject and object, and has cultivation and realization—therefore it is called created noncontamination. The nirvana of the Buddha has no subject or object: for this reason, in the *Nirvana Scripture* Cunda says to the enlightening being Manjushri, "Don't say the Buddha is the same as practices. . . . If you say the Buddha is the same as practices, then you cannot say Buddha is free." Therefore great ultimate nirvana informs those of the three vehicles that all practices, the enlightenment which realizes, and the nirvana which is realized, are all impermanent. Since that which is born is originally nonexistent, extinction is not experienced. No practice, no cultivation, is called great nirvana, and it is called complete tranquility. Therefore the *Nirvana Scripture* has those in the three vehicles who are attached to practices detach from practice and cultivation, and has those with an object of realization carry out no-realization and no-cultivation.

As for *The Flower Ornament Scripture*, the congregations from other regions and the people of this world, in the ranks of the assembly, from their very first determination for enlightenment immediately arrive at noumenal and phenomenal freedom, the merging of principle and action. Principle and action are reflected at once, without before, after, or in between. All of this is naturally so, based on the fundamental truth. If you keep thinking of beginning and end, cause and effect, before and after, this is all mundane feelings, all birth and death, having becoming and disintegration, all a matter of breaking bonds according to faculties, not a matter of the true source of fulfillment of buddhahood.

The various teachings' methods of guiding people all lead into *The Flower Ornament*'s ocean of fruition of knowledge of truth—this is their true goal. The avenues of the teaching are clear, the guiding mirror is evident; you should read through the whole scripture, with contemplative knowledge illuminating it as you go along: the mind opening up to understanding, the clouds will disperse from the sun of knowledge. Suddenly you will ascend the peak of wonder, surveying the ocean of knowledge; the two views of ordinary and holy will be washed away by the water of concentration, and the two gates of compassion and wisdom will appear through the spiritual body. This *Flower Ornament Scripture* is expounded directly to those of supremely great hearts; it is like directly bestowing monarchy on a commoner. It is like dreaming of a thousand years, all to vanish upon awakening. This is like the saying of the *Nirvana Scripture* that there is a certain herb in the snowy mountains; the cows that eat this produce pure ghee, with no tinge of blue, yellow, red, white, or black. Like this, people with the broadest minds immediately see the buddha-nature and thereupon attain true enlightenment, not coming to it gradually from lesser states. This is why we say the hearing of the audiences is different—the *Nirvana Scripture* unifies the branches and proceeds from the essence, but does not yet talk about the simultaneous operation without interference of knowledge and compassion, the real and the conventional.

Sixth, regarding the difference in purity and defilement of the lands of reward, in the *Nirvana Scripture* the Buddha's land of reward is placed in the West, past as many buddha-lands as grains of sand in thirty-two Ganges Rivers—this is said to be the land of spiritual reward of Shakyamuni Buddha. This is because those involved in the temporary studies of the three vehicles have not transcended defilement and purity and see this world as polluted, evil, and impure; the Buddha therefore temporarily points out a land of reward in the West. In the doctrine of true teaching of *The Flower Ornament*, this very world itself is pure, without defilement, and the worlds of the ten directions are pure and flawless. This is because for enlightening beings of the true teaching defilement and purity are ended, so the world is thoroughly pure; enlightening beings of the temporary teaching see defilement by themselves where there is no defilement, and therefore Buddha points out a land of reward in the West.

Seventh, regarding the difference in the temporariness and reality of the embodiment of Buddha, the Buddha in the *Nirvana Scripture* with thirty-two marks of greatness is temporary, while the true principle of complete tranquility is real. Since the measureless arrays of all marks of spiritual reward exist dependent upon the real, therefore according to *The Flower Ornament Scripture* the thirty-two marks of Vairocana Buddha enter the Buddha of nirvana—both are realm noumenon and phenomena are nondual; without destroying the body of reality, Buddha accords with the ocean of forms, measureless, endless. Forms, essence, reward, and principle interidentify; they are like lights and reflections, freely merging.

Eighth, regarding the difference in manifestations of birth and extinction, in the *Nirvana Scripture* there is set up, for the people of the vehicles of discipleship and individual awakening, Buddha's spiritual descent from Tushita heaven, birth on earth, and so on, till his entry into final nirvana. For enlightening beings of the great vehicle it says Buddha does not descend from heaven into the mother's womb; it says Buddha is eternal, blissful, self, and pure, beginningless and endless, unborn and unperishing, yet temporarily disappears. Then it posits a land of reward, which it calls Shakyamuni Buddha's land of reward, far away in the West. It makes this earth out to be a phantom land, a realm of defilement. The *Nirvana Scripture* contains these things that are different from *The Flower Ornament*, to lead those with facility for the temporary teaching. *The Flower Ornament* is otherwise: it directly points out the teaching of the fundamental body, the fundamental reality, going beyond emotional and intellectual views, without beginning or end, void of any sign of past, present, or future, one complete real reward, unborn, unperishing, not eternal, not finite, the ocean of realization in which essence and form interpenetrate freely. The emptiness of a single atom has no difference throughout the cosmos; different types of people create hindrance and bondage, their faculties and capacities are not equal, and the temporary and the true are not the same, so as a result there are myriad differences in ways of teaching. One should know the temporary and the true, one should recognize the provisional and practice the real, and not miss the true teaching by sticking to a temporary school.

Ninth, regarding the difference in the forms of practice of the teachings, according to the *Nirvana Scripture* even enlightening beings in the tenth stage do not clearly know or see the buddha-nature. So it proceeds from the ten outgrowths of faith of the ordinary person and later comes to the ten abodes, where the enlightening beings see the buddha-nature a little bit: the *Nirvana Scripture* sets up the process of ten abodes, ten practices, ten dedications, and ten stages, to be cultivated gradually— only in the stage of equally enlightenment does it clarify the fulfillment of practice producing fruition, and only the state of ineffable enlightenment is finally buddhahood. Then again, it also says there is an herb in the snowy mountains; the cows that eat this produce pure ghee with no tint of blue, yellow, red, white, or black—so it also expounds the teachings of immediate realization.

In the *Nirvana Scripture* there are after all types of teachings of five vehicles, six vehicles, seven, eight, nine, and ten vehicles. There are three kinds of vehicles of enlightening beings beyond the two vehicles of hearers and individual illuminates—altogether these make five vehicles. If we include the five precepts and ten virtues, that makes a sixth and seventh vehicle. Also, those of the three vehicles, hearing the same thing, each apprehend their own principles therein—therefore they make three times three or nine vehicles. As for the practices of the three vehicles of enlightening beings, they are: cultivating selflessness; proceeding from the ten abodes to the ten stages, gradually seeing buddha-nature; and attaining sudden realization without going through various stages.

In the *Nirvana Scripture*'s book on the buddha-nature it says that once the great enlightening beings saw the buddha-nature they all said, "We revolved in measureless births and deaths, always confused by selfless-ness." This is like the saying in *The Flower Ornament Scripture* that there are enlightening beings who practice the six ways of transcendence for countless eons, attain the six spiritual powers, and read, write, and master the canon of eighty-four thousand teachings, yet still do not believe in this deep scripture. This is an example of such enlightening beings; the spiritual powers they attain are not based on natural origina-tion, but are consequences of practicing virtues and contemplations such as selflessness. It is also like the case of people living in earthly paradise: they too are born there as a result of having practiced contemplations of the nonexistence of self or possession; their material livelihood is natu-rally abundant, but they have no teaching of enlightenment and do not realize liberation. The problem with all of these is that in the past their action and understanding were mistaken, so they could never forget what they had gained. The *Nirvana Scripture*, after having unified humans, celestials, heretics, and those of the three vehicles, returns them all to the buddha-nature, the complete tranquility of nirvana, the true principle of naturelessness: it does not yet point out that the characteristics of reward, the consequences of enlightenment, have no self or other, but include both noumenon and phenomena, with knowledge and function interpen-etrating. So it still sets up distinctions such as self-other, purity-defile-ment, and so on, and therefore says the land of reward of Shakyamuni Buddha is far away in the West. This is because the faculties of the people it addresses cannot yet bear the whole truth; the teaching is set up according to the faculties, to lead those of the three vehicles who have obstructions in connection to reality. The complete quiescence of the buddha-nature, the noumenal aspect of thusness, cannot show the inter-play of forms; blocking perception of existents, thus producing doubts, it screens the body of reality.

Thus the *Nirvana Scripture*'s teaching of the fruition of buddhahood after the ten stages is what is seen by beginners in the ten abodes in *The Flower Ornament Scripture*. The herb in the mountains from which cows produce pure ghee is like the beginners in the ten abodes in *The Flower Ornament* seeing the Way and immediately seeing that self and other, beginningless and endless, not old or new, are originally Buddha. Because body and mind, essence and forms, are originally Buddha, this door of buddhahood is considered liberation, riding the vehicle of buddhahood directly to the site of enlightenment. In the various stations and stages of enlightening beings, in each rank there is fruition of buddhahood, just as the ocean is in each drop. They carry out their practices within the buddha-nature, so there is progressive practice because of their buddha-nature. In *The Flower Ornament*, enlightening beings at the outset, in the beginning of the ten abodes, suddenly see the Buddha's body of reality, the buddha-nature, the uncreated fruit of knowledge, and carry out all the myriad practices of Universal Good, according with conditions without lingering, all of them uncontrived.

The *Nirvana Scripture* says that the buddha-nature is not a created phenomenon; but because it is covered by passions for outside objects, starting from the first of the ten abodes one uses uncontrived concentration so that one's essence accords with reality, where passions and objects have no inherent nature—there is only the essence and function of reality, which has no greed, hatred, or delusion, and is spontaneously Buddha. Therefore if you unite with it for a moment, you become Buddha in a moment; if you unite with it in a day, you become Buddha in a day—what's the need for gradual step-by-step accumulation of practice over eons to arrive at the fruit? When the mind is hooked onto quantification of ages, the vision is blocked—what end would there be to this? The teaching of the Buddhas is basically not contained in time—counting time and setting up ages or eons is not the buddha-vehicle.

Tenth, regarding the difference in patterns of companionship, in the *Nirvana Scripture* it says a youth of the snowy mountains met a demigod and was inspired by a half verse spoken by the demigod; valuing the half verse, he forfeited his life to hear the rest—"All actions are impermanent—this is the phenomenon of birth and death. When birth and death are extinguished, tranquil extinction is bliss." This is saying that the nirvana of buddha-nature cannot be cultivated by practices, because practices are fabricated and impermanent, and it cannot be realized by mind, because mind has subject and object. Thus its essence cannot be cultivated, its principle cannot be witnessed by the mind. Mind itself is the essence—there is no further subject or object. This is why Cunda said, "Don't say the Buddha is the same as practices."

As for *The Flower Ornament Scripture*, the pattern set by the youth Sudhana, from his first inspiration for enlightenment with Manjushri, till his final meeting with the Universally Good enlightening being, to each of the fifty-three teachers he met, he said, "I have aroused the determination for unexcelled complete perfect enlightenment—how would you have me learn the path of enlightening beings and carry out the practices of enlightening beings?" It does not say all practices are impermanent. Why? Because *The Flower Ornament* elucidates the teaching of the cosmos of interdependent origination, in which noumenon and phenomena are nondual. No condition is not quiescent, no phenomenon is not real. All worlds are one ocean of the essence of reality; the complete pervasion of great knowledge is the realm. The totality of everything is the ocean of essence, the one real cosmos. It is not explained according to action as sentient and insentient. Therefore, since the realm of unalloyed reality in the Flower Ornament is all knowledge, the land of the enlightening beings of the ten abodes is wisdom, the land of the enlightening beings of the ten practices is knowledge, the land of the enlightening beings of the ten dedications is wonder—it doesn't express two different views of animate and inanimate.

The *Nirvana Scripture* addresses those of the temperaments of the three vehicles; because their characters and behavior are inferior, the Buddha has then harmonized by practices, to overcome their gross ills—only then can they enter the Way. But then they conceive of the practices they are taught as absolute truths, and this screens the uncreated essence and they miss out on the truth. For this reason Buddha explains that all practices are impermanent, and the realizer and the realized are also phenomena that are born and perish. This is not the same as Sudhana's instant awakening in which there is no subject or object, intuitively becoming aware that one's own mind is fundamentally Buddha. Not attaining buddhahood, not experiencing enlightenment, the body and mind, essence and form, having no realization or cultivation, not becoming or decaying, are originally *thus*, active or still according to conditions, without destroying existence or nonexistence—the practices carried out are only products of knowledge. Therefore it doesn't say that all practices are impermanent in *The Flower Ornament Scripture*.

As for the similarity between the *Nirvana Scripture* and *The Flower Ornament Scripture*, an example of this is what is illustrated by the simile of the special herb in the snowy mountains; also the *Nirvana Scripture* says that all sentient beings have buddha-nature, and that the Buddhas have no final entry into extinction. *The Flower Ornament* says, "The Buddhas do not come forth into the world, and they have no extinction." Also, the *Nirvana Scripture* criticizes those of the two lesser vehicles for the discriminating view of Buddha as descending from heaven into the womb, living as a prince, leaving home, becoming enlightened, and passing away: this is like the notion of *The Flower Ornament* that knowledge enters past, present, and future without coming or going, and all Buddhas attain great enlightenment by the timeless essence. Instantly seeing the Way, views of past and present end, "new" and "old" do not exist at all—one attains the same enlightenment as countless Buddhas of the past, and also becomes Buddha at the same time as the Buddhas of countless ages of the future, by personally witnessing the timelessness of past, present, and future. Because there is no time, there is no coming or going.

Even if people don't see or know themselves that their own body and mind are fundamentally truly enlightened, the complete qualities of the true enlightenment of one's own body and mind fundamentally have no annihilation. And if they do themselves see and know the fundamental true enlightenment of their own body and mind, their own true enlightenment has no birth, because it is originally thus; and basically there is no one who awakens and nothing awakened to. If any awake, they after all awaken to this nonexistence of an awakening subject or an object of awakening. Thus the realm of the Buddha of fundamental awareness has no ordinary person, no sage, no concentration, no distraction; it is not cultivated, not proved, not knowledge, not ignorance, not born, not destroyed.

This outline of the perspective of *The Flower Ornament Scripture* in comparison with other important Buddhist scriptures generally follows the work of the earlier specialists in *Flower Ornament* doctrine. Li Tongxuan's work, with its emphasis on totality and immediate realization of the essential unity of being, was highly appreciated especially by students of the Chan school of Buddhism. The emphasis on the one vehicle and its totalistic perspective presented in Li's introduction to *The Flower Ornament Scripture* is particularly useful in view of the great variety and complexity of the contents of the scripture, which make it easy to get lost in detail and miss the overall meaning. While in a sense the specific principles and practices presented in the scripture are all contained in the one vehicle, they are also at once introductions into the one vehicle as well as outgrowths of the one vehicle. Once the fundamental premises and basic vocabulary of *The Flower Ornament Scripture* have been established, no further generalization is adequate to convey its contents.

A Thematic Summary of Each Book

The first book of the scripture, entitled The Wonderful Adornments of the Leaders of the Worlds, describes a symbolic assembly of various groups of beings at the site of Buddha's enlightenment. The title of this book refers to the representatives of various realms of being who appear on the scene, but it can also be read Wonderful Adornments of the Leader of the Worlds, referring specifically to the Buddha, the various states of being seen as adornments of the Buddha, their realizations representing aspects of Buddha's total enlightenment. Buddhabhadra's translation entitles this book Pure Eyes of the World, which likewise may also be read Pure Eye of the Worlds, representing the total universal awareness of the Buddha.

In this opening book a general picture of the nature of buddhahood and the general principles and scope of the teaching is built up through the various beings' eulogies and descriptions of the liberations they have realized. What is stressed is the universality and comprehensiveness of buddhahood, which is described as both physically and metaphysically coextensive with the cosmos itself. It emphasizes that Buddha expounds the truth by various means and teaches innumerable practices for the benefit of all beings: here "Buddha" refers to reality itself, and to people who are awake to reality. The various kinds of beings that appear in this book do not in this case represent their mundane aspects as such, but rather depict various facets of the Buddha's enlightenment, while also representing the potential for enlightenment inherent in all conscious beings, a fundamental theme of universalist Buddhism.

The second book, entitled Appearance of the Buddha, tells about characteristics of buddhahood, stressing the infinity and eternity of Buddha in the cosmic sense of being reality itself. The epithet of Buddha used in the title is Tathagata, which is understood in Chinese Buddhism to mean "one who comes from thusness," the term "thusness" referring to being-as-it-is, unpredicated reality. The human Buddha is considered in one sense as someone who is aware of fundamental continuity and identity with reality. In this scripture the term "Buddha" is commonly used for thusness or reality itself; in this book it is pointed out that Buddha, as reality, appears everywhere to all beings, but it is seen in accord with their perceptive capacities. It conveys the parallel messages that all experience reality according to their faculties and predilections, and that correlative to this, enlightened guides present various teachings to people in accord with their needs, potentials, and conditions. This accounts for the wide variety of doctrines in Buddhism, some of which may on the surface seem so different as to be even mutually opposed; underlying this variety is the fact that diverse aspects of a situation or levels of truth may be discussed separately, and that different ways of seeing, thinking, and acting may be recommended to different people, depending on the time and circumstances. This principle of adaptation and specific prescription is known as "skill in means" and is so basic and pervasive that it is impossible to understand Buddhism without a thorough appreciation of its premises, its purpose and implications.

The third book, called The Meditation of the Enlightening Being Universally Good, exposes the metaphysic of the bodhisattva or "enlightening being," the worker for universal enlightenment. The practical aspect of the enlightening being is here and throughout the scripture typified by a symbolic being called Universally Good, or Universal Good (Samantabhadra). The interrelatedness of all beings and the awareness of that interrelatedness on the part of enlightening beings is graphically represented in this book. By being in direct contact without "thusness" or "suchness" without the distorting influence of preconceptions and partiality, enlightening beings are, according to this book, aware of each other through being equally focused on reality. The unity of their purpose—universal liberation and enlightenment—which underlies diversity of method is emphasized strongly here. Again, it is made clear that enlightening beings may appear in virtually any form and employ a wide variety of means, according to what is useful for the liberation of people in given conditions. Universally Good, representing the enlightening work as a whole, extending throughout all places and times, therefore symbolizes a central concept of this scripture.

The fourth book, The Formation of the Worlds, presents visionary descriptions of worlds as representing the consequences of aspirations and actions. Emphasized here is the relativity of world and mind, how the features of the world depend on the states of mind and corresponding deeds of the inhabitants. A considerable portion of the contents of this and the following book consists of a series of litanies of concentration formulae, intended to convey certain impressions to the mind and to encapsulate certain aspects of the teaching to focus attention on them. It is through transformation of the vision of the world as well as the attitudes and actions connected with that vision that the world itself is transformed. This point also is an important part of the message of the scripture.

The fifth book is entitled The Flower Bank World. The so-called Flower Bank World is also referred to as the Flower Bank Array ocean of worlds, and may be translated as the world adorned by treasuries of flowers. This "world" is in the scripture represented as an "ocean of worlds," and is said to be our universe. In this scripture "flowers" generally represent practices or deeds, which produce fruits and seeds of consequent states. This book presents a visionary cosmology describing this world system or universe as purified by the vows and deeds of Vairocana Buddha, the glorified or cosmic aspect of the historical Buddha. It represents the world system as resting on an ocean of fragrant water, which symbolizes what is called the "repository consciousness," which is the mental repository or "storehouse" in which all experiential impressions are stored. It is from these impressions that images of the world develop. These images of the world are represented in the scripture as features of the world system. The land masses in the world system also contain seas of fragrant water, which symbolize virtuous qualities or wholesome factors in the mind. Many varieties of adornment are described, symbolizing not only virtues but also purely aesthetic views of the world without the contamination of emotional judgements. As a further dimension, the description of unthinkably many worlds over immensely vast reaches is calculated to foster a perspective in which any world is, as it were, reduced in size, like a pebble taken from the eye and returned to a mountain, no longer commanding the obsessive sense of unique significance that a narrow focus of attention invests in it. These elaborate descriptions allude also to the complexity of any realm, and try thereby to draw the consciousness into a broader awareness and detach it from restrictive preoccupations.

Book six, Vairocana, recounts illustrative tales of the development of the Buddha Vairocana in remote antiquity. The name "Vairocana" is interpreted in two senses, universal illuminator and specific illuminator, embodying both holistic and differentiating awareness. As noted, Vairocana is understood as another name for Shakyamuni in the cosmic, metaphysical sense, and also in the sense of the qualities or verities of buddhahood that are common to all Buddhas. This book describes a variety of realizations and attainments of Vairocana in the causal state, using mnemonic meditation formulae representing basic principles and

praxes of Buddhist teachings. These are suggested in terms of various spells, trances, psychic powers, knowledges, lights, activities, perspectives, and so on.

The seventh book, called Names of the Buddha, again emphasizes that Buddhas, enlightened people, develop profound insight into mentalities and potentials, and teach people in accord with their capacities and needs. Thus it is that all see Buddhas differently, according to their faculties and to the teachings which have been adapted to their situations. This book recites names and epithets of Buddhas to represent different perceptions or different facets of the qualities of enlightenment. Sometimes these are given from the point of view of cause, sometimes from the point of view of effect; sometimes they are explicit, sometimes they are veiled in metaphor.

The eighth book, The Four Holy Truths, is based on the same principle as the foregoing book, presenting Buddhist teaching in myriad different ways to accommodate various mentalities and understandings. Following the lead of the seventh book, The Four Holy Truths gives various names and capsule descriptions of four points that are believed to have been one of the original teaching frames of the historical Buddha. Basically, these four truths refer to the fact of suffering, the origin of suffering, the extinction of suffering, and ways to the extinction of suffering. Here again the representations of these points may be put in terms of cause or of effect. Sometimes the mundane truths—suffering and its origin—are put in terms not of conventional reality but of ultimate reality—inherent emptiness—to show a path of transition to the world-transcending truths within the mundane itself.

Book nine, entitled Awakening by Light, is an expanding vision unfolding within light issuing from Buddha's feet: the light progressively illumines greater and greater numbers of worlds as it travels further and further into space, radiating in all directions, revealing similar structures and parallel events in each world. In every world are immense numbers of Buddhas who each attract ten great enlightening beings, one from each of the ten directions, who in turn are each accompanied by countless enlightening beings. When the assemblies have all been arrayed, one of each group of ten great enlightening beings chants descriptive eulogies of the Buddha, alluding to the acts and realities of buddhahood. Here again is emphasized the identity of Buddha with truth and ultimate reality, the transcendental nature of the essence of Buddha.

The tenth book, called An Enlightening Being Asks for Clarification, follows up on the ninth, with the same interlocutors. This book goes explicitly into metaphysics, explaining the principle of the naturelessness or essenceless of all phenomena. This means that things have no individual nature, no inherent identity or essence of their own, because they are interdependent and only exist due to causes and conditions. For this reason it is repeatedly stated that the nature of things is natureless, that they have no being of their own. It points out that the seeming existence of things as discrete independent entities is in fact conceptual, a description projected by the mind on the flux of sense data; the real nature of things, it maintains, is insubstantial, and they die out instant to instant. In this book it is restated that realms or conditions of being are consequences of action, but it goes on to say that action is fundamentally baseless, or lacking in ultimate reality—it is the mind's attachment to its own constructs that provides the sense of continuity.

Also stressed in this book is the point that the teachings of Buddhas may be manifold and different according to specific circumstances, but the essential truth is one and the various teachings and practices are all part of a total effort. To clarify this point further, the different mental conditions for which particular aspects of the teaching are recommended are noted, to give some idea of the purposes of the diverse doctrines and approaches of Buddhism. This book also emphasizes the critical importance of actual application of the teachings, without which the mere description of techniques is useless. A number of classic metaphors used in Chan Buddhism to stress the need for application are taken from this particular book of *The Flower Ornament Scripture*.

Book eleven, called Purifying Practice, was translated several times, as early as the third century. It is a litany of prayers concentrating on the development of outlook and mentality of the enlightening being. It particularly focuses on the interconnectedness of all beings and the training of this awareness. It details an elaborate scheme of thought-cultivation in which consciousness of daily activities is directed to specific wishes for universal well-being and liberation. In terms of format, much of it is based on entry into monastic life, and some of the specific actions and events on which the contemplations are based are of monastic life, but many others make no necessary distinction between lay and monastic life.

The twelfth book is called Chief in Goodness, being named after the enlightening being who expounds it. This book eulogizes the aspiration or will for enlightenment, the monumental spiritual conversion by which an ordinary person becomes an enlightening being whose life and action is based on and guided by the determination for the enlightenment and liberation of all beings. The inspiration of the genuine will for enlightenment is in a sense itself transcendence of the world, as universal enlightenment becomes the reason for being, and life itself is transformed into a vehicle of enlightenment. Following this, faith is praised for its instrumental value as a means of directing the mind and focusing endeavor. Then the book goes on to describe practices and their results, in terms of both self-cultivation and assistance to others. Again versatility is emphasized, and enlightening beings are symbolically described as presenting all sorts of displays and teachings to exert edifying and liberating influences on people.

Book thirteen is entitled Ascent to the Peak of Mount Sumeru. Mount Sumeru, the polar mountain of a world, is pictured as the abode of Indra (or Shakra), the mythical king of the gods of the thirty-threefold heaven, pictured as thirty-three celestial mansions on the peaks surrounding the summit of Sumeru. This book is a brief visionary welcome of the Buddha into the palace of Indra.

Book fourteen, Eulogies on Mount Sumeru, emphasizes the metaphysical aspect of Buddha, as being absolute truth. The thrust of this approach is to counter preoccupation with forms. Buddha is said to be the very absence of inherent existence or intrinsic nature of all conditioned things. Conventional reality is called a description consisting of habitual conceptions and views. Defining the world through verbal and conceptual representations is by its very nature limiting, restricting awareness, so this chapter stresses the need to see through, see beyond conventional reality in order to become enlightened. When the nature of perceptual and conceptual organization of experience as a mere tool is forgotten or unknown, and a particular organization hardens into an exclusive view, the mind has lost its freedom. The dependence of views on social, cultural, and psychological factors attests to their nonabsoluteness; the concern of Buddhist philosophy and meditation is to see through such conditioning and restore the mind to openness and flexibility. This book states that the basis of delusion and falsehood is reality, meaning that delusion and falsehood, being themselves conditioned, do not have any inherent reality or inevitability—this very emptiness of inherent reality is what is called absolute reality or truth. What is intended by this insight is not nihilistic extinction, but seeing delusion for what it is: the term "extinction" used in this connection essentially means the extinction of conditioned views. Here the scripture says that having no views is true seeing, which sees everything because it is seeing without the restriction of predispositions of ingrained mental habits. This philosophy of the relativity of mind and world is provided as a rational basis for dissolving clinging to views and freeing the mind from the enclosure of inflexible, set ways of seeing and thinking about things.

The fifteenth book, called Ten Abodes, is a brief description of ten stations of enlightening beings. The first abode is that of initial determination, setting the mind on omniscience, to broaden its horizons. Second is preparing the ground, or cultivation; here the development of universal compassion is emphasized. Also involved is learning, from people and situations as well as from formal study. Third is the abode of practice, to clarify knowledge; here various aspects of emptiness (indefiniteness, nonabsoluteness) are emphasized. Fourth is the abode of "noble birth," which means rebirth from the enlightening teachings; here knowledge—of beings, phenomena, causality, and so on—is emphasized, as well as the knowledge, practice, and realization of the teachings of Buddhas of all times, with awareness of the essence of buddhahood, which is equal in all times. Fifth, the abode of skill in means, involves further development of knowledge and means of conveying knowledge, and working for universal salvation without attachments. Sixth, the abode of the correct state of mind, involves developing a mind that does not waver in face of apparently contradictory aspects of things; here again the inherent emptiness of things is emphasized. Seventh, the abode of nonregression, means not regressing regardless of what one may hear in regard to different aspects of things, and learning the principles of reconciliation of oppositions through relativity. Eighth, the abode of youthful nature, involves development of impeccability, of psychic freedom, and vast extension of the range of study and application of the teachings. Ninth, the abode of prince of the teaching, is a stage of development of discursive knowledge and the particular sciences of teacherhood. Tenth is the stage of coronation or anointment, referring to the accomplishment of knowledge of all sciences and means of liberation and the development of a sphere of buddhahood.

Book sixteen, entitled Religious Practice, describes detailed analytic investigations which eventually arrive at ungraspability, systematically removing the mind from fixations, dismantling the structure of a formal religious world in order to embrace formless truth. After this the book goes on to bring up the special powers of knowledge of Buddhas as realms of deep study, and concludes with exhortations to integrate compassion with the understanding of illusoriness.

The seventeenth book is called The Merit of the Initial Determination for Enlightenment. This book describes in grandiose terms the virtues of the aspiration for enlightenment. It stresses the sense of this determination transcending all limited aspirations, being directed toward omniscience and universal liberation and enlightenment. Many points or fields of knowledge are specifically mentioned in this connection, including the "mutual containment" or mutual immanence of different quanta of being and time, alluding to the interdependence of definitions, and the interrelation of elements and structural sets. Other prominent spheres of knowledge are those involved in the study of mentalities and mental phenomena, this kind of knowledge being essential to the science of liberation. The tremendous emphasis on genuine and boundless determination for complete universal enlightenment reflects its importance as the essence of the whole enterprise of enlightening beings, who do not seek enlightenment for their own personal ends. The correct orientation at the outset is deemed essential to truly transcend the limitation of self; without this transcendent resolve, the power of spiritual exercises exaggerates and bolsters the afflictions of self-seeking and can lead to harmful aberrations.

Book eighteen, entitled Clarifying Method, presents a series of lists of elements of the path of enlightening beings. First it stresses the development of the determination for omniscience, which means knowledge of all things pertinent to liberation. Then it goes on to work on nonindulgence or heedfulness, in terms of ten items; these lead to ten kinds of purity. Following this it brings up twenty things which are congenial to enlightenment, ten things whereby enlightening beings can rapidly enter the stages of enlightenment, ten things which purify their practices, ten results of purity of practice, ten vows, ten ways of fulfilling vows, and ten spiritual "treasuries" attained as a result of fulfilling vows. This book also talks about means of purifying the ten essential ways of transcendence, or perfections of enlightening beings, and about specific cures of spiritual ills.

Book nineteen, Ascent to the Palace of the Suyama Heaven, is much like book thirteen; here the Buddha is welcomed into the heaven called Suyama, without, however, leaving the foot of the enlightenment tree and the peak of the popular mountain Sumeru. This introduces the following book, in which the all-pervasiveness of Buddha is stressed.

The twentieth book is called Eulogies in the Palace of the Suyama Heaven. This book emphasizes the universality of Buddha in terms of metaphysical essence and in terms of practice. The spiritual body of Buddha is seen here as the cultivation of enlightenment potential inherent in all conscious beings in all times. The nature of Buddha, beings, and phenomena is spoken of in these terms: "Sentient and nonsentient beings both have no true reality. Such is the nature of all things—in reality they are not existent." Also, "Analyzing matter and mind, their nature is fundamentally void; because they are void they cannot be destroyed— this is the meaning of 'birthlessness.' Since sentient beings are thus, so are Buddhas—Buddhas and Buddhas' teachings in essence have no existence." And "The body is not Buddha, Buddha is not the body—only reality is Buddha's body, comprehending all things. Those who can see the Buddha-body pure as the essence of things will have no doubt about Buddha's teaching. If you see that the fundamental nature of all things is like nirvana, this is seeing Buddha, ultimately without abode." This book is also the source of the famous line often quoted in Chan Buddhism: "Mind is like an artist, depicting the worlds. . . . If one knows that the action of mind makes all worlds, one sees Buddha and realizes the true nature of Buddha."

Book twenty-one is entitled Ten Practices. These ten practices, though under different names, correspond to the ten perfections, or ways of transcendence, upon which the path of enlightening beings is based: giving, ethical conduct, forbearance, energy, concentration, wisdom, expedient methodology, power, commitment, and knowledge. The accomplishment of these is based on the relativity = emptiness equation; the first six are especially based on emptiness within relative existence, while the last four are based on relative existence within emptiness.

The twenty-second book, Ten Inexhaustible Treasuries, deals with ten sources of the development and activity of enlightening beings: faith, ethics, shame, conscience, learning, giving, wisdom, recollection, preservation of enlightening teachings, and elocution. Various items from these "treasuries" are explained in detail. The section on faith deals with the object of faith, mostly expressed in terms of absolute truth, as well as states of mind engendered by faith. The section on ethics deals with general ethical principles and orientation as well as specific articles of ethical conduct. Shame refers to being ashamed of past wrongs; conscience refers to resolve not to continue to act unwisely. The section on learning deals with specifics of interdependent origination of conditioned states, and with analytic knowledge. Giving involves "giving up" in the sense of intellectual and emotional relinquishment, such as nonattachment to past and future, as well as the act of giving itself and the frame of mind of generosity. Giving is often put in hyperbolic or symbolic terms, and has the general sense of contributing one's resources—including one's very being—to the common weal rather than to purely private aims. The section on wisdom deals with both phenomena and principles, with discursive knowledge being described as leading to insight into emptiness and independent understanding. The treasury of recollection involves recollection of every moment of awareness—represented as countless ages due to the density of experience—including changes undergone as well as contents of what has been learned. Preservation means preservation of Buddha-teachings and the sciences involved therein. Elocution refers to exposition and teaching.

Book twenty-three, entitled Ascent to the Palace of the Tushita Heaven, describes in great detail the arrays of ornaments set out to welcome Buddha to this heaven. This is on a vaster scale than the other heavens which Buddha visits in this scripture, because the Tushita heaven, the heaven of happiness or satisfaction, represents the abode of a buddha-to-be just before manifesting complete enlightenment in the world. The assembly of enlightening beings there is also depicted in terms of the practices and qualities that developed them. After this is an elaborate description of the spiritual qualities of Buddha.

Book twenty-four, Eulogies in the Tushita Palace, resembles the other comparable books of the scripture, eulogizing the universality of the awareness and metaphysical reality of Buddha, reconciling multiplicity and unity, emphasizing the relativity of the manifestation of Buddha to the minds of the perceivers.

The twenty-fifth book, called Ten Dedications, is one of the longest books of the scripture, indicative of the great importance of dedication in the life of enlightening beings. Dedication particularly reflects two essential principles of enlightening beings' practice: giving, or relinquishment; and vowing, or commitment. The basic orientation of dedication is the full development, liberation, and enlightenment of all beings. The scope of the ten dedications is beyond the capacity of an individual to fulfill personally; it is through dedication that the individual enlightening being merges with the total effort of all enlightening beings. Forms of giving which are not literally possible, for example, are presented at great length; these represent nonattachment, both material and spiritual, particularly in the sense of dedication to the service of all life. This book recites extensive correspondences between specific contributions and the results to which they are dedicated, representing the adaptation of enlightening beings' activity to particular developmental needs. This is often presented in spiritual or psychological terms, but also it is presented in material or formal terms of glorified images of Buddha symbolizing the perfection of the human being. This book again emphasizes the integration of wisdom and compassion, acting purposefully even while knowing the ultimately unreal nature of conditional existence. This skill of acting without attachment, without compulsion, without grasping or rejecting existence or emptiness, is presented as the essence of dedication and fundamental to the path of enlightening beings.

Book twenty-six is the famous book on the ten stages of enlightenment. The teaching of the ten stages is presented as the foundation of all Buddhist teachings, just as an alphabet is the foundation of all writings in its language. This book is of such significance that it was translated into Chinese no fewer than five times, three times as an individual scripture, over a period of five hundred years; it also exists in Sanskrit as an individual scripture.

The Flower Ornament Scripture is said to contain, in one form or another, all phases of Buddhist teaching; true to the scripture's basic structural principle of the parts reflecting the whole, this comprehensiveness is also to be seen clearly within the book on the ten stages. Of the various modes of teaching—sudden and gradual, explicit and implicit—it is the gradual and explicit that overtly dominate in the ten stages, thus making it one of the clearest and most straightforward of the books of the scripture.

Pursuing a theme of developmental progression, the ten stages encompass the course of the enlightening being from the first ecstasies of disentanglement and spiritual attraction to the final rain of teaching pouring from enlightened knowledge, thus completing and restarting the cycle of self- and other- enlightenment. Within this overall cycle are parallel cycles of elevation of self and others; as the enlightening beings progress from stage to higher stage, there is ongoing expansion not only of extent, depth, and precision of awareness and perception, but also of corresponding versatility and power in communicative outreach.

Throughout this progress, the development of awakening is prevented from halting at each stage by the overriding aspiration for complete, perfect enlightenment, the thoughts of the enlightening beings set ultimately on the attributes of buddhahood. The practitioner aspires to be the best of beings, not by comparison with others, but in terms of potential fulfillment, not limiting horizons or coveting personal satisfaction by acceptance of lesser goals.

The ten stages include phases of practice such as are usually associated with the so-called lesser vehicles of individual salvation, but the enlightening being does not take the annihilation or liberation from worldly concerns made available by these methods as the final realization. In the high stage wherein effortlessness and cessation of mental and physical action take place, it is external inspiration that motivates the practitioner to rise even beyond this stage of personal peace. In the highest stage the cosmic awareness whose perspective pervades the whole scripture ultimately opens up explicitly, showing the "all in one, one in all" vision of the realm of reality.

An important theme in the ten stages, one that appears here and there throughout the scripture in various guises, is the cultivation of both mundane and transmundane welfare. This is presented in concrete terms in this book, as the practitioner in a certain stage engages in the development and exercise of skills in worldly occupations. The choice of activities—whether in the arts and sciences, business, crafts, literary and cultural pursuits, entertainment, or other fields—is guided not by the personal desires of the practitioners but by the current needs of the society that they are serving, according to what will be beneficial.

The development of such occupational skills is undertaken in the same stage at which meditation is the main practice among the ten transcendent ways. The balancing of work in the world and world-transcending practices, characteristic of the ideal of comprehensive Buddhist activity, functions to promote the simultaneous benefit of self and others, preventing what is called "intoxication by the wine of meditation concentration," an obstacle in the path and an indulgence forbidden by the precepts of enlightening beings. In a later stage, these worldly occupations become effortless and can be carried on spontaneously without obstruction.

A most important concept mentioned early on in the book on the ten stages is that of the "six characteristics," as it was known in the Huayan school of Buddhism in East Asia. Not explicitly developed in the scripture but rather illustrated throughout, this idea was singled out by the founders of the Huayan school in China as a major element of their philosophy. The six characteristics are totality, distinction, sameness, difference, formation, and disintegration. In the context of stages of enlightenment, or practices, this means that all together form a single totality, while each are distinct elements of that totality; all are the same insofar as they complement each other and work together to produce the total effect, while individually they have different functions within the whole work; as elements in the same one totality, they form the whole and in it reach their individual consummation, while separately they not only do not form a whole but also are not individually perfected without the others.

The philosophy of the Huayan school, based on *The Flower Ornament Scripture*, also sees the six characteristics as aspects of all phenomena. According to this philosophy, the six characteristics are a comprehensive way of viewing things so as to overcome the tendency to lapse into partial or one-sided perceptions. Considering the phenomena and principles of Buddhism in this light, for example, produces an understanding quite different from that fostered by the notion of the multiplicity of Buddhistic teachings as representing rival schools and conflicting ideologies. In this sense the six characteristics provide a useful diagnostic aid for assessing movements that have actually hardened into exclusive schools or ideologies: seen in the Flower Ornament context, such movements become inwardly sterile by stabilization around temporary and partial teachings, yet outwardly contain a portion of nutrient in that they demonstrate this process. It is in this sense that the *Scripture on the Ultimate Extinction* states that even in the time of the extinction of the Teaching, the Teaching is not extinct, for its very demise is its demonstration of the causes thereof, for the edification of the perceptive.

Using the six characteristics, it is quite easy to get an overall perspective on the message of *The Flower Ornament Scripture*, on the activity known as the practice of the vow of Samantabhadra, the embodiment of Universal Good. Here, all workers for enlightenment are one totality, the whole effort is one totality. Within this single overall effort, different workers fulfill different functions; these may be represented, for example, as different schools, different cycles of teaching, different modes of practice. In essence, all of these workers are the same, based on the vow of Universal Good and the aspiration for universal enlightenment. All ultimately have the same essence, which is referred to as the buddha-nature, but they are different in characteristics, in the formulations and methods that they employ. The work of all the workers forms the "body" of Samantabhadra, the multitude forms the one. No individual worker completes the entire task alone; the enlightening being "enlightens all sentient beings" and "purifies all worlds" as an operative in the whole work, the vows of the enlightening being representing attunement with this totality. If different formulae, practices, or phases of the Teaching are separately held on to as dogma, absolute and complete in themselves, the total dynamic of the Universally Good work disintegrates. The characteristics of "formation" and "disintegration" could also be seen in terms of the supersession of teachings and the spatial dispersal of schools such as illustrated by the classical Chan schools in China, with formation and dispersal part of an ongoing process. The relation to the whole work is not necessarily organizational in the conventional institutional sense, but rather is organic and functional.

The twenty-seventh book, The Ten Concentrations, speaks of the enlightening being breaking through the barriers of the familiar relative world—barriers of space, time, multiplicity, solidity—by mental concentration. One aspect of this practice is the entry and exit of concentration in different domains. "Entry" is interpreted as concentration, or absorption, and "exit" as insight, or knowledge; through concentration in one domain, insight into another is awakened. This is done through numerous different mediums of concentration and is connected with the development of the Flower Ornament vision of the interpretation of principles and phenomena and the interpenetration of phenomena.

Other exercises are also presented, embedded within the imagery and descriptive narrative of the book, structured to foster the fundamental perspectives of the teaching and to guide the mental focus of development of the general and specific aspects of comprehensive knowledge for which the enlightening being strives. One characteristic of such exercises is their telescopic quality, visualizing simultaneous extension and immanence.

The Flower Ornament Scripture is like a hologram, the whole concentrated in all the parts, this very structure reflecting a fundamental doctrine of the scripture, that this is what the cosmos itself is like, everything interreflecting, the one and the many interpenetrating. In the book on the ten stages this is illustrated with the gradual mode of teaching predominant; in the book on the ten concentrations this is shown with the sudden or all-at-once mode coming strongly to the fore, paralleling the step-by-step format. Were its method unlocked, ancient research into the mental cosmos, such as reflected in *The Flower Ornament Scripture*, might have something to offer to modern investigations into the holographic nature of the brain and its linear and simultaneous modes.

An essential theme of the ten concentrations is the purpose of knowledge in the context of the life of enlightening beings; specifically, understanding the processes of development of civilizations and mentalities, and how the cycles of teaching operate in the context of these processes and their various elements.

Book twenty-eight, on the ten superknowledges, describes higher faculties, functions developed through the concentrations, said to be inconceivable to any minds except those of the fully awakened and the awakening who have attained them.

The twenty-ninth book, on the ten acceptances, deals with entry into nonconventional aspects of reality. The boundaries of conventional mental construction are penetrated but not destroyed because their ultimately illusory nature is realized. Transcendental and mundane levels of truth are both accepted: the immanence of the absolute in the relative is experienced as all-pervasive, spiritual phenomena and mundane phenomena being found to have the same phantasmagorical nature; thus the ultimate tolerance is attained whereby the mind is freed.

Book thirty, called "The Incalculable," develops the immense numbers used in the scripture. The higher numbers far exceed present estimations of the number of atoms in the universe; they are more closely approached by the numbers of potential brain operations. The Flower Ornament method of calculation includes the dimension of time as well as space, and follows the principles expounded in the scripture—for example, since everything is a series of moments, continually passing away and being renewed, each moment therefore is a new universe; also, the content of each passing moment of awareness is a universe. Furthermore, all existents are what they are in relation to all other existents; thus, in terms of the "Indra's Net" view of the Flower Ornament, the facets of existence are incalculable, interreflecting ad infinitum. This is illustrated by the progression of squares by which the incalculable numbers are developed in this book. The book concludes with a verse declaring that the cosmos is unutterably infinite, and hence so is the total scope and detail of knowledge and activity of enlightenment.

"Life Span," the thirty-first book, presents a similar progressive generation of time frames in different "worlds," culminating in the frame of reference of the prototype of enlightening beings, in which "a day and a night" is an inconceivably immense span of time in ordinary terrestrial terms, yet is still within time. Here again is illustrated the interpenetration of cosmic and mundane planes in the perspective of the enlightening being.

Book thirty-two, called "Dwelling Places of Enlightening Beings," names centers of spiritual activity, some of which can be located in India, Kashmir, Pakistan, Afghanistan, and Central and East Asian China. Whatever the historical facts behind this book may be, commentary takes it to represent the manifestations of the timeless and placeless "reality body" within time and place.

Whereas book thirty-two represents buddhas in the causal state as enlightening beings in specific domains, the thirty-third book, "Inconceivable Qualities of Buddhas," deals with buddhas in the state of effect or realization, the universal attributes of buddhas. Here the "buddhas" represent attunement to the cosmic buddha, the "reality-body." The former chapter alluded to the causal state, which is there to promote effect; the present book shows how the state of effect then extends forward into cause. Thus the Flower Ornament doctrine of interpenetration of cause and effect—cause producing effect, effect producing cause—is illustrated; this is one meaning of representing the Teaching as a wheel that continually moves forward.

Book thirty-four contains a long series of visualizations. Called "The Ocean of Physical Marks of the Ten Bodies of Buddha," it also presents the state of effect or realization, in terms of comprehensive awareness, represented by multitudes of pervasive lights revealing the phenomena of the material and spiritual worlds. "The Qualities of the Buddha's Embellishments and Lights," the thirty-fifth book, presented as spoken by Shakyamuni-Vairocana Buddha in person, refers to the causal state, that is, to the Buddha as an enlightening being, illustrating the light of awakening penetrating, breaking through, the veils of the realm of ignorance.

These expositions of the qualities of buddhahood, generally showing the emanation of the universal principles of buddhahood from the state of effect into the state of cause, are followed by the thirty-sixth book called "The Practice of Universal Good," again taking up the cycle of cause to effect. Narrated by Samantabhadra, the Universally Good enlightening being, the prototype and representation of the whole body of the practical acts of enlightening beings, this book is followed by "the appearance of Buddha," in which Samantabhadra goes on at length describing the myriad facets of the manifestation of Buddha and how it is to be perceived.

The final two books of *The Flower Ornament Scripture*, "Detachment from the World" and "Entry into the Realm of Reality," deal with the development of the enlightening being. "Detachment from the World," which commentary points out has the meaning of transcendence while in the very midst of the world, is a series of two thousand answers to two hundred questions about various aspects of the evolution of enlightening beings into buddhas.

"Entering the realm of reality," the final book of *The Flower Ornament Scripture*, is perhaps the grandest drama of the Buddhist canon. Known in Sanskrit as an individual scripture called *Gandavyuha*, this book describes the development of enlightenment through tales of a pilgrimage. The central character, a seeker of truth named Sudhana, is sent on a journey by Manjushri, the personification of wisdom. Initially directed by Manjushri, Sudhana calls on a number of spiritual guides, each of whom sends him on to another for further enlightenment. Eventually Sudhana comes to the abode of Maitreya, the imminent Buddha, and finally integrates with the total being of Samantabhadra, the representation of Universal Good, the activity of enlightenment.

The guides Sudhana encounters, referred to as spiritual benefactors or friends, are young and old, female and male, Buddhist and nonBuddhist, renunciates and householders, members of various classes, and experts in various professions, arts, and sciences. They are not organized in a perceptible formal hierarchy or institution and are not always known to the public for what they are. The spiritual friends are known to each other according to their own attainments, and it is through the successive direction of the guides themselves that Sudhana finds out who and where they are. None of them claims to hold the whole truth, and none tries to bind Sudhana to a given system of dogma or keep him as a follower. Many of them teach in surroundings and formats that are not overtly associated with what is conventionally thought of as religion.

The book begins with a symbolic description of manifestations of enlightened awareness, explaining that those who are within a fixed system have not the slightest inkling of the scope of consciousness that lies beyond the bounds of their perceptions as conditioned by their training and development. It suggests that all views that are conditioned by cultural and personal history are by definition limiting, and there is a potential awareness that cuts through the boundaries imposed by conventional description based on accumulated mental habit. According to the scripture, it is the perennial task of certain people, by virtue of their own development, to assist others in overcoming arbitrary restrictions of consciousness so as to awaken to the full potential of mind.

In order to carry out this task, it is necessary to operate partly within the field of these very restrictions. Those whose specific charge it was to write scriptures like this one, therefore, were working within the bounds of language and thought to hint at realities beyond language and thought. As has been seen in earlier books of the scripture, included in the commitments of such specially dedicated people, known here as enlightening beings, is the task of purposely bridging boundaries of culture and religion. They are also committed to bridge the boundary of secular and sacred, and part of their work involves relieving mundane suffering and anxieties that would otherwise preoccupy mental energy and hinder further awakening.

Given that the specific characters of the scripture are "fictional," the teaching indicates that in order to seek historical reflections of what the characters represent, it would be necessary to avoid being constrained by labels and definitions imposed by externalist observers. The secrecy or inaccessibility of certain aspects of spiritual teaching is due not merely to esotericism but also to the extent to which the realm and activity of the teaching is outside the system of assumptions and expectations of common convention.

Seen in this light, the scripture can foster remarkable perspectives on the history of civilization and human consciousness. Even in recorded history, there are numerous examples of people known as mystics who were also eminently practical, workers in the fields of public education, civil administration, medicine, engineering, environmental design, communications, agriculture, and so on. On the other hand, it is widely stated that many overtly religious people were in fact unregenerate worldlings; it is also on record, though less widely, that many overtly secular activities and enterprises are in fact vehicles of spiritual teaching. Given that a complete historical record is a physical impossibility, and that there is no such thing as a complete fact in itself available to the ordinary senses, it is interesting to observe how much apparently disconnected activity can be brought into coherent focus through the vision of the *Flower Ornament Scripture.*

Who were—who are—these specially dedicated and developed people whom the scripture calls enlightening beings? We have no reason to suppose that all enlightening beings are identified as such in historical records; there is more reason to suggest that their identities have in many cases been deliberately obscured. The scripture says of them:

> Some appeared in the form of mendicants, some in the form of priests, some in bodies adorned head to foot with particular emblematic signs, some in the forms of scholars, scientists, doctors; some in the form of merchants, some in the form of ascetics, some in the form of entertainers, some in the form of pietists, some in the form of bearers of all kinds of arts and crafts—they were seen to have come, in their various forms, to all villages, cities, towns, communities, districts, and nations. With mastery of proper timing, proceeding according to the time, by modification of adapted forms and appearances, modifications of tone, language, deportment,

situation, carrying out the practices of enlightening beings, which are like the cosmic network of all worlds and illumine the spheres of all practical arts, are lamps shedding light on the knowledge of all beings, are arrays of projections of all realities, radiate the light of all truths, purify the establishment of vehicles of liberation in all places, and light up the spheres of all truths, they were seen to have come to all villages, towns, cities, districts, and nations, for the purpose of leading people to perfection.

This depicts the enlightening beings coming into the world, as it were, with a purpose, using the available tools of the world to accomplish their task. The versatility of enlightening beings in their modification of appearance and activity, adapting to the specific circumstances of the time—cultural, linguistic, technological, and so on—and the needs of the people they are working with, stems from a basic freedom enlightening beings cultivate, which is sometimes referred to as being beyond the world even while in the world:

> Enlightening beings do not seek omniscience for their own sake, nor to produce mundane enjoyments and pleasures, nor in search of the various enjoyments of the realm of desire, not under the compulsion of errors of conception, thought, and view. They live and work in the world without being controlled by fetters, bonds, propensities, or obsessions, without being controlled by craving or opinions, without their minds being bound up in ideas of mundane enjoyments, without being taken with the taste of pleasure of meditation, without being blocked by mental barriers.

Of course, this does not mean to say that enlightening beings all exist in conformity with stereotyped ideals. According to the scripture, the wisdom and virtues of Buddha are in all people, but people are unaware of it because of their preoccupations. Just as the scripture points out that there are lands and beings who are a mixture of impurity and purity, there are untold incipient enlightening beings always becoming manifest in every thought, word, and deed of compassion. It is the task of the more fully developed enlightening beings in every community to contact and nurture what is best in others; whether they do it through religion or art or cooperation in ordinary activities is purely a matter of local expediency. Often it is the case that preoccupation with the external face of such activity obscures its inner purpose; over a period of time this leads to elaboration of forms without their original meaning, fragmentation of the work, and mutual misunderstanding and even intolerance and hostility among members of what have now become factions. One of the functions of *The Flower Ornament Scripture* is to present a vision of the whole underlying the parts, so as to help people offset the effects of this scattering tendency and rise above sectarianism and other forms of bigotry.

It is no secret, of course, that there have been numbers of overtly religious figures, religious leaders, who fit descriptions of enlightening beings. The potential unleashed by their appearance, however, has often been mitigated by two persistent tendencies manifested by particular types of observers. One tendency has been to absolutize even the temporal aspects of the dispensations of such leaders; the other has been to regard such people solely as products of temporal conditions. To offset the extreme view that abstracts a personality out of context, *The Flower Ornament Scripture* sometimes represents such people as kings surrounded by their retinues, showing that the activity of the teaching, which may be overtly represented by an individual, is in reality sustained by many people, who may be anonymous, and that the position and work of the king takes place within a particular context, in cooperation with a community. To counter the other extreme view of such leaders as merely the products of historical forces, the scripture uses the theme of reincarnation, depicting them as being reborn again and again in different states and circumstances, carrying out their transcendental purpose, which remains with them throughout all changes, using the means afforded by the temporal order.

Thus, while the scripture lauds the extraordinary achievements of specially dedicated individuals, it does so primarily as an inspiration to the inner sense of the potential of consciousness, and does not degenerate into personality worship or cultism. Though it recognizes the ordinarily imperative force of actions and events that continually condition the stream of existence, it also emphasizes the power of will, often referred to in terms of vows, capable of extending the awareness to reach out for latent possibilities that are not being actualized within a given set of propensities but that can become available through the exercises known as the practices of enlightening beings.

Naturally, many perceptions of the "meaning" of the scripture are possible, according to the history and condition of the interpreter. This is noted in the scripture itself and is a basic understanding of the school of hermeneutics founded on this scripture in the Far East. Each of these perceptions will have some meaning (even if it is thought of as "meaninglessness") to the perceiver, and probably to others as well, as in the case of people sharing their experience of anything, whether it is a verbalized, conceptualized, and reflective experience or an intuitive, tacitly communicative one. Whether or not particular perceptions are useful to an individual in a developmental sense is another matter; but even if they are not enlightening to the individual perceiver, they may be useful to others who observe the relation of the individual with the material. The scripture carries out its function of illustrating mentalities both directed by description and indirectly by provocation.

The provocative aspect of the scripture is not limited to bringing to light frames of mind by provoking characteristic reactions; it includes, equally if not more importantly, the evocative function of eliciting new perspectives and perceptions from the repository of potential consciousness. It is often said that Buddhism claims the world is illusory; and indeed Buddhist writings do contain statements to that effect, although it is as common to say that the world is *in* illusion or the world is *like* illusion. What this means is that the world as we know it is a description, constructed through processes of selection and organization; the illusion, or delusion, is to imagine that the description is objective reality itself. The soft sciences of modern times have come around to the recognition of the arbitrariness, or nonabsoluteness, of world views, conditioned as they are by cultural and personal history; but it is only recently that some Western workers in these sciences have begun to consider it logical to take the next step and actually experience this fact by learning how to transform or suspend the deep structures of the description at will.

It is in this endeavor, to expand capabilities of perception and understanding, that another mode of using the scripture comes into play. The traditional practice of single-minded recitation of scripture, embodying as it does meditation's twin elements of concentration and contemplation, has long been used to effect escalation of consciousness and enhancement of mental powers.

In order to attempt rational understanding of how this can work, it is important to note that the word *illusion*, which is so commonly used in Buddhism to describe the known world, also means "magic." Knowledge and awareness are referred to as magical. Thus illusion-magic has two aspects, restrictive and expansive, conservative and creative. From the point of view of the absolute, the imagined nature of things is false, but the raw material is real; so it is said in Buddhist scripture that the sense data are the matrix of enlightenment. What is constructed from this raw material depends on biological, psychological, and social conditioning, which are variable and can be consciously modified, with the result of change in perception of the world. Alterations of diet, posture, movement, breathing, thought, attention, human contacts, and physical environment are among the techniques known to have been used since ancient times for affecting the sphere of consciousness. In Buddhism, change of state is not necessarily valued in itself so much as the experiential realization of emptiness, which means nonabsoluteness of states, on the one hand, and infinitude of possibilities, on the other. What realm of awareness is beneficial for whom at what stage of development is held to be one of the sciences of enlightenment, according to which random visions, ecstasies, or insights are not productive of true spiritual maturity, though their place as incidents along the path should eventually become apparent to the sufficiently advanced.

Insofar as it tends to keep individuals and communities within certain patterns, conditioning as an ongoing process is also in a sense self-perpetuating, in that habit reinforces itself through repetition, becoming what is called "second nature." Certain conditioning operations, such as those used to inculcate patterns of behavior required to maintain the fabric of society, may be generally quite overt, though they might be given different names, such as "education." Often, however, the impacts and efforts involved in conditioning are almost entirely subliminal. Examples of this might be the practice, now prohibited in some places, of flashing pictures of refreshments on movie screens, so briefly as to be virtually unnoticed consciously, in order to induce viewers to crave these refreshments; or the familiar experience of having a tune keep running through one's mind in spite of the feeling that one is making no effort to repeat it.

To get out of the circle of habit, a reflection of what the scripture calls the "mundane whirl," Buddhist practice proposes a dual process of arresting involutionary patterns and incorporating evolutionary patterns. In the practice of spiritual recital, the focus of concentration works to halt the wandering mind and take the attention off habitual trains of thought, while the structure and imagery of the scripture that then flow into the mind, bypassing the conditioned intellect, are able to set up new patterns of perception.

It is well known that incantation practices like this can produce ecstatic states after a time if done in a concentrated fashion. The dazzle of ecstasy induced in this way is somewhat like the torrent of noise that accompanies a rush of schoolchildren as they pour out of the classroom after six hours of confinement, and is in itself of no particular value. On the contrary, it can be harmful if it becomes an obsession, as if the ecstasy itself were the goal.

Various extraordinary powers have been associated with people who spent much time in incantational practices, but these are not thought of as mechanical techniques that automatically work for everyone at all times. In fact, the concentration that is thereby generated with relative ease can have a stagnating effect as well, in that it can give a false sense of security or freedom, and can mask—and therefore perpetuate—deep-seated propensities. Furthermore, without the inclusion of other appropriate factors, concentration can turn into obsession or rigidity, and it can also degenerate and fail to produce lasting results. As scripture points out, there is no particular method of practice that is universally valid; practices are part of a coherent whole that needs all its parts to function properly. This can be seen in the doctrine of the six characteristics as applied to the ten stages. Moreover, it is held that to approach any spiritual practices in an unsuitable state, such as a state of greed for personal gain, leads not to enlightenment but to magnification of unwholesome qualities. Hence the need for proper preparation of dedication is given tremendous emphasis in this scripture.

Another traditional use of the scripture is, like that of esoteric art, as a model for visualization practice, which is similarly designed to introduce the mind to certain patterns held to be developmental. An example of this practice is made explicit in a short scripture of the Flower Ornament corpus, called "Section on Cultivation of Love from *The Flower Ornament Scripture.*" Part of the visualization involves imagining every particle of one's own body as a buddha-land, replete with such adornments as are described at great length throughout the scripture; then one visualizes all the beings in the universe entering into those buddha-lands within oneself and consciously evokes thoughts of love and wishes of well-being for them all. Another visualization practice, as evidenced in Chinese records, focuses on the lights emanated by buddhas in various scenes of the scripture.

Yet another function of the scripture, often unsuspected or considered gratuitous hyperbole, is to affirm the infinity of the path and provide ongoing challenge and inspiration. This function is hinted at in the statement of the distinguished tenth-century Chan master Yan-shou, whose mission was to demonstrate the unity of Buddhist teachings, to the effect that nine out of ten people who only practice Chan meditation and do not study scripture become conceited and lose the way. Another indication of this is found in the book on the ten stages, according to which in the eighth stage, the stage of effortlessness, where perfect comfort and tranquillity are reached, the impulse to go on to further development in the higher stages comes from *outside* the individual. Certain parts of other important scriptures such as the *Saddharmapundarika* and *Vimalakirtinirdesha* also present prime examples of this function.

The question of uses of scripture brings into relief one of the supposedly peculiar principles of Flower Ornament Buddhism, that of the mutual causation of past, present, and future. On a microscale, the experience of the present moment is in fact an edited replay of an immediately past moment of sensation; therefore, that past moment becomes present to consciousness through a process that is in its future. On a larger scale, perceptions and interpretations of the past depend on the conditions of the perceivers in the present; the legacy of the past as it bears on the present and future depends on conditions in the present. Therefore, the past, as it exists relative to the present, is not a fixed actuality, but depends on what elements of past causes are accessible and how they are perceived and experienced, what elements are in fact being acted on in a given situation, and how they are being acted on. What the past *was* is not available to ordinary perception; what the past *is*, on the other hand, is being caused by its own future, as much as it has caused its future. Various factors in the present, including understanding, expectation, and will, enter into the manner in which past causes are selected, utilized, and become operative.

This would seem to present a closed circle of determinism—the conditions of the present that determine how the past is experienced are themselves products of that past. According to the Flower Ornament teaching, however, the mutual inherence of past, present, and future does not represent unmitigated determinism, because the past, present, and future are all infinite. What is finite is the experience of being-time through the temporal capacity of a given range of consciousness; and insofar as that capacity may be altered, contracted, or expanded, it might be that many of the limitations regarded as real by any society or culture are in fact illusory, and the real potential of humanity is so much greater than imagined as to be virtually infinite, even if that infinity can never embrace the infinity of infinities.

This seems to be one of the pervasive themes of the scripture—that there are far vaster possibilities open to humankind than ordinarily suspected in the course of everyday life. However vital the impulses and activities involved in the search for survival, comfort, and stimulation may be, they have never been known to produce complete satisfaction or still the quest for something beyond, which is yet dimly sensed in the innermost recesses of the mind. The aim of the authors of the scripture in recording it and leaving it to posterity might be guessed from the contents of the scripture itself; its usefulness in the present and future, of course, depends on the use to which it is put.

On the premise that the scripture itself is a logical place to look for keys to its understanding and application, this translation is presented as a sort of raw material, with a minimum of external apparatus. A discussion of certain technical terms and concepts will be found in the introduction to Volume I, and a glossary is appended to each volume; the major explanatory material, however, is to be found in the context of the scripture itself.

There is really no way to explain all that is in the scripture, and it would seem a travesty to attempt to place it in some particular historical or intellectual context, when there is that in it which could be applied to any such context, and that which clearly transcends any such context. Immersing one's consciousness in an immense scripture like this by reading it repeatedly with judgment suspended may not recommend itself to the impatient; but supposing that the scripture, like a Zen koan, has in itself a quality that forces one to work through it on its own terms or lose the effect altogether, it might be better to leave its challenging open. As the Chan master Wu-men said, "Let another finish this poem. . . ."

Notes to Introduction

1. Translated and published by the Pali Text Society; some of the most important texts are included in the Sacred Books of the East Series, and some of these have been reprinted by Dover Publications. See *Buddhist Suttas* (New York: Dover, 1972) which contains several scriptures of the so-called "lesser vehicle."

2. See Edward Conze, *The Large Sutra on Perfect Wisdom* (Berkeley: University of California Press, 1975), as well as numerous other works by Conze on this class of scriptures.

3. D.T. Suzuki, *The Lankavatara Sutra* (Boulder: Prajna Press, 1978).

4. Translated into English from Tibetan by Robert Thurman (University Park: Pennsylvania State Press, 1976); from Chinese by Charles Luk (Boulder: Shambhala, 1972).

5. The most recent translation is by Leon Hurvitz; *Scripture of the Lotus Blossom of the Fine Dharma* (New York: Columbia University Press, 1976).

6. Translated from Japanese to English by Yamamoto Kosho (Horinkan, 1976).

BOOK ONE

The Wonderful Adornments of the Leaders of the Worlds

THUS HAVE I HEARD. At one time the Buddha was in the land of Magadha, in a state of purity, at the site of enlightenment, having just realized true awareness. The ground was solid and firm, made of diamond, adorned with exquisite jewel discs and myriad precious flowers, with pure clear crystals. The ocean of characteristics of the various colors appeared over an infinite extent. There were banners of precious stones, constantly emitting shining light and producing beautiful sounds. Nets of myriad gems and garlands of exquisitely scented flowers hung all around. The finest jewels appeared spontaneously, raining inexhaustible quantities of gems and beautiful flowers all over the earth. There were rows of jewel trees, their branches and foliage lustrous and luxuriant. By the Buddha's spiritual power, he caused all the adornments of this enlightenment site to be reflected therein.

The tree of enlightenment was tall and outstanding. Its trunk was diamond, its main boughs were lapis lazuli, its branches and twigs were of various precious elements. The leaves, spreading in all directions, provided shade, like clouds. The precious blossoms were of various colors, the branching twigs spread out their shadows. Also the fruits were jewels containing a blazing radiance. They were together with the flowers in great arrays. The entire circumference of the tree emanated light; within the light there rained precious stones, and within each gem were enlightening beings, in great hosts like clouds, simultaneously appearing.

Also, by virtue of the awesome spiritual power of the Buddha, the tree of enlightenment constantly gave forth sublime sounds speaking various truths without end.

The palace chamber in which the Buddha was situated was spacious and beautifully adorned. It extended throughout the ten directions. It was made of jewels of various colors and was decorated with all kinds of precious flowers. The various adornments emanated lights like clouds; the masses of their reflections from within the palace formed banners.

A boundless host of enlightening beings, the congregation at the site of enlightenment, were all gathered there: by means of the ability to manifest the lights and inconceivable sounds of the Buddhas, they fashioned nets of the finest jewels, from which came forth all the realms of action of the spiritual powers of the Buddhas, and in which were reflected images of the abodes of all beings.

Also, by virtue of the aid of the spiritual power of the Buddha, they embraced the entire cosmos in a single thought.

Their lion seats were high, wide, and beautiful. The bases were made of jewels, their nets of lotus blossoms, their tableaus of pure, exquisite gemstones. They were adorned with various flowers of all colors. Their roofs, chambers, steps, and doors were adorned by the images of all things. The branches and fruits of jewel trees surrounded them, arrayed at intervals.

Clouds of radiance of jewels reflected each other: the Buddhas of the ten directions conjured regal pearls, and the exquisite jewels in the topknots of all the enlightening beings all emanated light, which came and illuminated them.

Furthermore, sustained by the spiritual power of all Buddhas, they expounded the vast perspective of the Enlightened Ones, their subtle tones extending afar, there being no place they did not reach.

At that time, the Buddha, the World Honored One, in this setting, attained to supreme, correct awareness of all things. His knowledge entered into all times with complete equanimity; his body filled all worlds; his voice universally accorded with all lands in the ten directions. Like space, which contains all forms, he made no discrimination among all objects. And, as space extends everywhere, he entered all lands with equanimity. His body forever sat omnipresent in all sites of enlightenment. Among the host of enlightening beings, his awesome light shone clearly, like the sun emerging, illumining the world. The ocean of myriad virtues which he practiced in all times was thoroughly pure, and he constantly demonstrated the production of all the buddha-lands, their boundless forms and spheres of light extending throughout the entire cosmos, equally and impartially.

He expounded all truths, like spreading great clouds. Each of his hairtips was able to contain all worlds without interference, in each manifesting immeasurable spiritual powers, teaching and civilizing all sentient beings. His body extended throughout the ten directions, yet without coming or going. His knowledge entered into all forms and realized the emptiness of things. All the miraculous displays of the Buddhas of past, present, and future, were all seen in his light, and all the adornments of inconceivable eons were revealed.

There were great enlightening beings numerous as the atoms in ten buddha-worlds surrounding him. Their names were: Universally Good

(Samantabhadra), Light of the Supreme Lamp of Universal Virtue, Lion Banner of Universal Light, Subtle Light of Flames of Universal Jewels, Banner of Oceans of Qualities of Universal Sounds, Realm of Enlightenment of Radiance of Universal Knowledge, Banner of Flowers of a Topknot of Universal Jewels, Pleasing Voice of Universal Awareness, Light of Inexhaustible Virtue of Universal Purity, Mark of Universal Light, Great Brilliance of the Light of the Moon Reflected in the Ocean, Undefiled Treasury of Light of Oceans of Cloudlike Sounds, Born of Wisdom and Adorned with Virtue, Great Light of Sovereign Virtue, Brave Lotus Topknot, Sun Banner of Clouds of Universal Knowledge, Greatly Persevering with Indestructible Courage, Light Banner of Fragrant Flames, Deep Beautiful Sound of Great Enlightened Virtue, Born of Wisdom with the Light of Great Virtue. These and others were the leaders—there were as many as there are atoms in ten buddha-worlds.

These enlightening beings had all in the past accumulated roots of goodness along with Vairocana Buddha, and were all born from the ocean of roots of goodness of the Buddha. They had already fulfilled the various means of transcendence, and their wisdom eye was thoroughly clear. They observed all times with impartiality. They were thoroughly purified in all states of concentration. Their eloquence was oceanic, extensive and inexhaustible. They possessed the qualities of buddhahood, were dignified and honorable. They knew the faculties of sentient beings, and taught them according to potential and necessity. They entered into the matrix of the cosmos, their knowledge was nondiscriminatory; they experienced the liberation of the Buddhas, exceedingly deep and immensely vast. They were able to enter into one stage, according to technical expediency, yet maintain the virtues of all stages, supported by the ocean of all vows, always accompanied by wisdom, throughout the future. They had thoroughly comprehended the rarely-attained, vast secret realm of all Buddhas. They were familiar with the equal teachings of all Buddhas. They were already treading the Buddhas' ground of universal light. They entered the doors of boundless oceans of concentrations. They manifested bodies in all places and participated in worldly activities. Their memory power was enormous, and they assembled the ocean of all the teachings. With intelligence, eloquence, and skill they turned the wheel which never turns back. The vast ocean of virtuous qualities of all Buddhas entered entirely into their bodies. They went willingly to all the lands in which there were Buddhas. They had already made offerings to all Buddhas, over boundless eons, joyfully and tirelessly. In all places when the Buddhas attained enlightenment, they were always there, approaching them and associating with them, never giving up. Always, by means of the vows of universal goodness and wisdom, they caused the wisdom-body of all sentient beings to be fulfilled. They had perfected innumerable such virtues.

There were also present thunderbolt-bearing spirits, as numerous as atoms in a buddha-world, known as Demigod of Wonderful Form, Banner of Swiftness of the Sun, Light of the Flowers of the Polar Mountain, Pure Sound of Clouds, Sublime Faculties, Delightful Light, Sound of Thunder in Great Trees, Lion King Light, Auspicious Eye of Intense Flames, Jewel Topknot of Lotus Light; these were the leaders, and there were as many of them as there are atoms in a buddha-world. All of them had constantly invoked great vows over countless past eons, vowing to always draw near to and serve the Buddhas. Their practices in accord with their vows had already reached fulfillment, and they had reached the other shore. They had accumulated boundless pure good works. They had clearly arrived at all the realms of meditative absorption, and had attained spiritual powers. They dwelled wherever a Buddha was, and entered into the realm of inconceivable liberation; taking their place in the assembly, their dignified light stood out. They manifested their bodies according to the needs of sentient beings and thereby pacified them. Wherever there were manifestations of Buddhas, they all went there magically. Wherever the Buddhas dwelt, they always diligently guarded and protected the place.

There were also multiple-body spirits, numerous as atoms in a buddha-world, known as Flower Topknot Adornment, Light Illumining All Directions, Oceanic Sound Conquering, Pure Flower Adorned Topknot, Infinite Dignified Postures, Array of Supreme Light, Fragrant Clouds of Pure Light, Guardian Sustainer, Ubiquitious Shepherd, Immutable Light. These were the leaders; there were as many as there are atoms in a buddha-world. They had all in the past fulfilled great vows and had provided for and served all the Buddhas.

Also there were footstep-following spirits, numerous as atoms in a buddha-world. Their leaders were known as Precious Symbol, Lotus Light, Topknot of Pure Flowers, Embodying All Beautiful Visions, Exquisite Gem Star Banner, Joyfully Uttering Sublime Sounds, Sandalwood Tree Light, Lotus Luminosity, Subtle Light, Collection of Fine Flowers, and so on. Over innumerable past ages they had all associated with Buddhas, always following them.

There were also sanctuary spirits, as numerous as atoms in a buddha-world. Their leaders were known as Banner of Pure Adornments, Polar Mountain Jewel Light, Sign of the Thunder Banner, Wonderful Eyes Raining Flowers, Garland Light Topknot, Raining Jewel Arrays, Courageous Fragrant Eye, Diamond-Colored Cloud, Lotus Light, Radiance of Ineffable Light, and so on. All of them had in the past met innumerable Buddhas, perfected their will power, and brought forth extensive offerings.

There were also city spirits, as numerous as atoms in a buddha-world. Their leaders were known as Jewel Peak Radiance, Beautifully Adorned Palace, Jewel of Pure Joy, Sorrowless Purity, Flower Lamp Flame Eyes, Flame Banner Clearly Showing, Light of Virtue, Pure

Light, Fragrant Topknot Adornment, Beautiful Jewel Light, and so on. All of them had, over innumerable, inconceivable eons, adorned the mansions in which the Buddhas stayed.

There were also earth spirits, as numerous as atomic particles in a buddha-world. Their leaders were known as Pure Flower of Universal Virtue, Adornment of Stable Blessings, Beautiful Flower Adorned Tree, Universal Distributor of Treasures, Pure Eye Observing the Season, Beautiful Supreme Eye, Fragrant Hair Emitting Light, Pleasing Sound, Curled Topknot of Beautiful Flowers, Diamond-Adorned Body, and so on. They had all in the past made profound, grave vows, vowing to always associate with the Buddhas and cultivate the same virtuous acts.

There were also innumerable mountain spirits, led by such as Jewel Peak Blooming Flower, Flower Forest Beautiful Topknot, Lofty Banner Shining Everywhere, Undefiled Jewel Topknot, Light Illumining All Directions, Light of Great Power, Awesome Light Conquering All, Light-Orb of Subtle Intensity, Universal Eye Clearly Seeing, Adamantine Eye of Mystery. They had all attained pure eyes in regarding all things.

There were also an inconceivable number of forest spirits, led by such spirits as Spreading Flowers Like Clouds, Outstanding Trunk Unfolding Light, Bearing Branches Emitting Radiance, Auspicious Pure Leaves, Draped Flame Treasury, Pure Light, Pleasant Thunder, Light and Fragrance All-Pervading, Subtle Light Shining Far, Flowers and Fruits Savoring of Light, and so on. They all had infinite pleasing glows.

There were also innumerable herb spirits, led by such as Auspicious, Sandalwood Forest, Pure Light, Universal Renown, Radiant Pores, Universal Purifier, Roarer, Banner of Light Outshining the Sun, Seeing in All Directions, Energy-Augmenting Clear Eyes, and so on. Their natures were all free from defilement, and they helped beings with kindness and compassion.

There were also innumerable crop spirits, led by such spirits as Gentle Superb Flavor, Pure Light of Seasonal Flowers, Physical Strength Courage and Health, Increasing Vitality, Everywhere Producing Roots and Fruits, Wonderfully Adorned Circular Topknot, Moistening Pure Flowers, Developing Wonderful Fragrance, Liked by All Who See, Undefiled Pure Light. All of them had attained perfection of great joyfulness.

There were also innumerable river spirits, led by such spirits as Everywhere Producing Swift Currents, Universally Purifying Springs and Streams, Dustfree Pure Eye, Roaring Everywhere, Rescuing Sentient Beings, Heatless Pure Light, Universally Causing Joy, Supreme Banner of Extensive Virtue, Light Shining on All Worlds, Light of Oceanic Virtues. All of them diligently concentrated on benefiting living beings.

There were also innumerable ocean spirits, led by such spirits as

Producing Jewel Light, Diamond Banner, Undefiled, Palaces in All Waters, Auspicious Jewel Moon, Beautiful Flower Dragon Topknot, Everywhere Holding the Flavor of Light, Jewel Flame Flower Light, Beautiful Diamond Topknot, Thunder of the Ocean Tide. They had all filled their bodies with the great ocean of virtues of the Buddhas.

There were also innumerable water spirits, led by such spirits as Ubiquitous Cloud Banner, Cloudlike Sound of the Ocean Tide, Beautiful Round Topknot, Whirlpool of Skills, Store of Undefiled Fragrance, Virtue Bridge Light Sound, Freedom of Contentment, Good Sound of Pure Joy, Everywhere Manifesting Awesome Light, Roaring Sound Filling the Sea. They always diligently strived to rescue and protect all beings.

There were also countless fire spirits, led by such spirits as Repository of Flames of Universal Light, Banner of Universal Assembly of Light, Great Light Shining Everywhere, Palace of Wonders, Inexhaustible Light Topknot, Eyes of Various Flames, Palaces in All Directions Like Polar Mountains, Sovereign of Awesome Light, Light Destroying the Darkness, Thunder and Lightning. All of them manifested various kinds of light, causing the irritations of sentient beings to vanish.

There were also innumerable wind spirits, led by such spirits as Unimpeded Light, Everywhere Manifesting Courageous Action, Wind Striking Cloud Banner, Arrays of Light, Power Able to Dry Up Water, Great Voice Howling Everywhere, Tree Branch Hanging Topknot, Unimpeded Wherever It Goes, Various Mansions, Great Light Shining Everywhere. They all worked to dispel the mentality of conceit.

There were also innumerable space spirits, led by such spirits as Pure Light Shining All Around, Traveling Everywhere Deeply and Extensively, Producing Auspicious Wind, Abiding Securely Beyond Obstruction, Broad Steps and Beautiful Topknot, Unhindered Light Flames, Unobstructed Conquering Power, Spotless Light, Deep and Far-Reaching Sublime Sound, All-Pervading Light. Their minds were all free from defilement, broad, vast, clear, and pure.

There were also innumerable direction spirits, led by such spirits as Dwelling Everywhere, Ubiquitous Light, Array of Light Beams, Traveling Everywhere Unhindered, Forever Ending Confusion, Roaming Everywhere in Pure Space, Great Sound of Cloud Banners, Topknot and Eyes Undisturbed, Universally Observing the Doings of the Worlds, Traveling Everywhere Watching. They were able, by means of their skills, to emanate light in all directions, always illuminating the ten directions continuously without interruption.

There were also innumerable night spirits, led by such spirits as Pure Light of Universal Virtue, Observing the World with Joyful Eyes, Everywhere Manifesting Auspicious Omens, Everywhere Causing Tree Flowers to Bloom, All Senses Always Joyful, Producing Pure Bounty. They all practiced diligently, taking delight in the truth.

There were also innumerable day spirits, led by such as Displaying

Palaces, Bringing Forth the Fragrance of Wisdom, Delighting in Superb Adornments, Exquisite Light of Fragrant Flowers, Collecting All Wonderful Herbs, Liking to Make Joyful Eyes, Appearing In All Places, Light of Great Compassion, Radiance of Goodness, Garlands of Beautiful Flowers. They all had certain faith in the sublime truth and always strived diligently in concert to adorn the palace.

There were also innumerable titan kings, led by such as Rahula, Bhimacitta, Skillful Magical Arts, Great Following, Great Strength, Universal Shining, Wonderful Adornment of Firm Action, Vast Causal Wisdom, Manifesting Superior Qualities, Sublime Voice. They had all worked energetically to conquer pride and other afflictions.

There were also an inconceivable number of kinnara kings, led by such as Heaven of Light of Refined Intellect, Exquisite Flower Banner, Various Adornments, Pleasing Sound, Jewel Tree Light, Delight to the Beholder, Adornment of Supreme Light, Delicate Flower Banner, Earth-Shaking Power, Conquering Evil Beings. They all made diligent efforts, contemplating all things, their minds always blissful, roaming freely.

There were also innumerable garuda kings, led by such as Power of Great Swiftness, Unbreakable Jewel Topknot, Pure Speed, Nonregressing Mind, Sustaining Power in the Ocean, Steady Pure Light, Artistically Decorated Crown Topknot, Immediate Manifestation Everywhere, Surveying the Ocean, Universal Sound and Broad Eyes. They had already perfected the power of great skill in expedient methods of liberation and were able to rescue all beings.

There were also innumerable mahoraga kings, led by such as Beneficent Wisdom, Pure Dignified Sound, Adornment of Supreme Wisdom, Lord of Sublime Eyes, Lamplike Banner, Refuge of the Masses, Supreme Light Banner, Lion Guts, Sound Adorned by Myriad Subtleties, Stable as a Polar Mountain, Delightful Light. They all diligently cultivated great and extensive skills in method to cause sentient beings to forever tear apart the net of ignorance.

There were also innumerable yaksha kings, led by such as Vaishravana, Independent Sound, Solemn Weapon Bearer, Great Wisdom, Lord of Flaming Eyes, Adamantine Eye, Arm of Courage and Strength, Bravely Resisting General, Rich in Material Goods, Power to Smash High Mountains. They all strived to guard and protect all living beings.

There were also innumerable great naga kings, led by such as Virupaksha, Shakra, Subtle Banner of Cloud Sounds, Flaming Mouth Ocean Light, Ubiquitous High Cloud Banner, Unbounded Steps, Pure Form, Great Sound Traveling Everywhere, No Heat or Torment; they all worked hard making clouds and spreading rain to cause the heat and afflictions of all beings to vanish.

There were also innumerable kumbanda kings, led by such as Increase, Dragon Lord, Banner of Adornments of Goodness, Universally Beneficial Action, Most Fearsome, Handsome with Beautiful Eyes, High Peak Intellect, Brave and Strong Arms, Boundless Pure Flower Eyes,

Enormous Godlike Face with Titan's Eyes. They all diligently practiced and studied the teachings of freedom from impediment, and emitted great light.

There were also innumerable gandharva kings, led by such as Sustaining the Nation, Tree Light, Clear Eyes, Flower Crown, Universal Sound, Joyously Moving Beautiful Eyes, Wondrous Sound Lion Banner, Diamond Tree Flower Banner, Joyfully Causing Adornments to Appear Everywhere. They all had deep faith and appreciation of the great teaching, rejoiced in it and respected it, and diligently practiced it tirelessly.

There were also innumerable moon deities, led by such as Moon Godling, Flower King Topknot Halo, Myriad Sublime Pure Lights, Pacifying the Hearts of the World, Luminosity of Tree King Eyes, Manifesting Pure Light, Immutable Light Traveling Everywhere, Sovereign Monarch of Constellations, Moon of Pure Awareness, Great Majestic Light. All strived to bring to light the mind-jewel of living beings.

There were also innumerable sun deities, led by such as Sun Godling, Eyes of Flames of Light, Awesome Light, Undefiled Jewel Arrays, Nonregressing Courage, Light of Beautiful Flower Garlands, Supreme Banner Light, Universal Light of a Jewel Topknot, Eyes of Light. All of them diligently learned and practiced to benefit living beings and increase their roots of goodness.

There were also innumerable kings of the thirty-three heavens, led by such as Shakra-Indra, Everywhere Intoning Fulsome Sound, Kind Eyes Jewel Topknot, Jewel Light Banner Fame, Joy-Producing Topknot, Admirable Right Mindfulness, Supreme Sound of the Polar Mountain, Perfect Mindfulness, Pleasing Flower Light, Eye of the Sun of Knowledge, Independent Light Able to Enlighten. All of them strived to bring forth great works in all worlds.

There were also innumerable kings of the Suyama heavens, led by such as Timely Portion, Delightful Light, Banner of Inexhaustible Wisdom and Virtue, Skilled in Miraculous Displays, Great Light of Memory Power, Inconceivable Wisdom, Circular Navel, Light Flames, Illumination, Greatly Famed for Universal Observation. All of them diligently cultivated great roots of goodness, and their minds were always joyful and content.

There were also an inconceivable number of kings of the Tushita heavens, led by such as Contented, Ocean of Bliss Topknot, Supreme Virtue Banner, Still and Silent Light, Pleasing Beautiful Eyes, Clear Moon on a Jewel Peak, Supreme Courage and Strength, Subtle Diamond Light, Constellation Array Banner, Pleasing Adornments. All of them diligently kept in mind the names and epithets of all the Buddhas.

There were also innumerable kings of the heavens of enjoyment of emanations, led by such as Skillful Transformation and Emanation, Light of Silent Sound, Light of the Power of Transformation and Emanation, Master of Adornment, Light of Mindfulness, Supreme Cloud Sound, Supreme Light of Myriad Subtleties, Exquisite Topknot

Light, Perfect Joy and Intellect, Flower Light Topknot, and Seeing in All Directions. All of them worked diligently to tame living beings and enable them to attain liberation.

There were also countless kings of the heavens of free enjoyment of others' emanations, led by such as Sovereign Freedom, Sublime Eye Lord, Beautiful Crown Banner, Courageous Intelligence, Wonderful Sound Phrases, Subtle Light Banner, Gate of the Realm of Peace, Array of Splendid Discs Banner, Flower Grove Independent Intellect, and Light of Beautiful Adornments of the Power of Indra. All of them diligently practiced and studied the vast and great teaching of independent skill in means of liberation.

There were also uncountable kings of the great brahma heavens, led by such as Shikhin, Light of Wisdom, Radiance of Benificent Wisdom, Sound of Ubiquitous Clouds, Independent Observer of the Sounds of Speech of the Worlds, Eyes of Still Light, All-Pervading Light, Sound of Magical Displays, Eyes of Shining Light, and Pleasing Ocean Sound. All of them had great compassion and took pity on living beings; unfolding light that illumined everywhere, they caused them to be joyful and blissful.

There were also innumerable kings of the heavens in which light is used for sound, led by Pleasing Light, Pure Subtle Light, Sound of Freedom, Supreme Awareness and Knowledge, Delightful Pure Subtle Sound, Sound of Skillful Meditation, Universal Sound Illumining Everywhere, Most Profound Light-Sound, Pure Name Light, and Supreme Pure Light. All of them dwelt in the unhindered state of great peace, tranquility, joy, and bliss.

There were also innumerable kings of the heavens of universal purity, led by such as Pure Reputation, Supreme Vision, Virtue of Tranquility, Sound of the Polar Mountain, Eye of Pure Mindfulness, Light Flame Sovereign, Enjoyer of Meditation on the Truth and Creating Demonstrations, Banner of Miraculous Displays, and Exquisite Array of Constellation Sounds. They were all already abiding securely in the great teaching, and worked diligently to benefit all worlds.

There were also innumerable kings of the heavens of vast results, led by such as Banner of the Delightful Light of Truth, Ocean of Pure Adornments, Light of Supreme Wisdom, Independent Wisdom Banner, Delight in Tranquility, Eye of Universal Knowledge, Delight in Use of Intellect, Light of Intellect Sown with Virtue, Undefiled Tranquil Light, and Vast Pure Light. They all dwelt at peace in the palace of tranquility.

There were also countless kings of the heavens of great freedom, led by such as Sea of Subtle Flames, Light of the Name of Freedom, Eye of Pure Virtues, Enjoyable Great Intelligence, Freedom of Immutable Light, Eyes of Sublime Adornments, Light of Skillful Meditation, Delightful Great Knowledge, Universal Sound Array Banner, and Light of Fame of Extreme Exertion. All of them diligently contemplated the truth of formlessness, and their actions were all equanimous and impartial.

At that time the oceanic hosts at the Buddha's site of enlightenment had assembled: the unlimited types and species were all around the Buddha, filling everywhere. Their forms and companies were each different. From wherever they came, they approached the World Honored One, wholeheartedly looking up to him. These assembled masses had already gotten rid of all afflictions and mental defilements as well as their residual habits. They had pulverized the mountains of multiple barriers, and perceived the Buddha without obstruction. They were like this because Vairocana Buddha in past times, over oceans of eons, cultivating the practices of enlightening beings, had received them and taken care of them with the four saving practices of generosity, kind words, beneficial action, and cooperation, and while planting roots of goodness in the company of each Buddha in those eons, had already taken good care of them and had taught and developed them by various means, establishing them on the path of omniscience, where they sowed innumerable virtues, gained great merits, and had all entered completely into the ocean of skill in liberative means and undertaking of vows. The actions they carried out were fully pure, and they had well embarked on the way to emancipation. They always saw the Buddha, clearly illumined, and by the power of supreme understanding entered into the ocean of the qualities of buddhahood. They found the doors of liberation of all Buddhas, and roamed freely in spiritual powers.

That is to say, Ocean of Subtle Flames, a king of a heaven of great freedom, found the door of liberation through the tranquility and practical power of the realm of space and the cosmos. The celestial king Light of the Name of Freedom gained the door of liberation through freely observing all things. The celestial king Eye of Pure Virtues found the door of liberation of effortless action knowing that all things are not born, do not perish, and do not come or go. The celestial king Enjoyable Great Intelligence found the door of liberation through the ocean of wisdom directly perceiving the real character of all things. The celestial king Freedom of Immutable Light found the door of liberation through the great practical concentration of bestowing boundless peace and happiness on living beings. The celestial king Eye of Sublime Adornments found the door of liberation through causing observation of the truth of nullity and annihilating all ignorance and fear. The celestial king Light of Skillful Meditation found the door of liberation through entering infinite realms without producing any activity of thought about existents. The celestial king Delightful Great Knowledge found the door of liberation by going everywhere in the ten directions to preach the truth, yet without moving and without relying on anything. The celestial king Universal Sound Array Banner found the gate of liberation by entry into the Buddhas' realm of tranquility and everywhere manifesting great light. The celestial king Light of Fame of Extreme Exertion found the gate of liberation by abiding in his own enlightenment, yet having an infinitely broad perspective.

At that time the celestial king Ocean of Subtle Flames, imbued with the spiritual power of the Buddha, surveyed the whole host of celestial beings of the heavens of great freedom, and said in verse,

The buddha body extends throughout all the great assemblies:
It fills the cosmos, without end.
Quiescent, without essence, it cannot be grasped;
It appears just to save all beings.

The Buddha, King of the Teaching, appears in the world
Able to light the lamp of sublime truth which illumines the world;
His state is boundless and inexhaustible:
This is what Name of Freedom has realized.

The Buddha is inconceivable, beyond discrimination,
Comprehending forms everywhere as insubstantial.
For the sake of the world he opens wide the path of purity:
This is what Pure Eyes can see.

The Buddha's wisdom is unbounded—
No one in the world can measure it.
It forever destroys beings' ignorance and confusion:
Great Intelligence has entered this deeply and abides there in
    peace.

The Buddha's virtues are inconceivable;
In beings who witness them afflictions die out.
They cause all worlds to find peace:
Immutable Freedom can see this.

Sentient beings, in the darkness of ignorance, are always deluded;
The Buddha expounds for them the teaching of dispassion and
    serenity.
This is the lamp of wisdom that illumines the world:
Sublime Eyes knows this technique.

The Buddha's body of pure subtle form
Is manifest everywhere and has no compare;
This body has no essence and no resting place:
It is contemplated by Skillful Meditation.

The voice of the Buddha has no limit or obstruction;
All those capable of accepting the teaching hear it.
Yet the Buddha is quiescent and forever unmoving:
This is the liberation of Delightful Knowledge.

Serene, emancipated, master of the celestial and the human,
There is nowhere in the ten directions he does not appear.
The radiance of his light fills the world:
This is seen by Majestic Banner of Unimpeded Truth.

The Buddha sought enlightenment for the sake of all beings
Over boundless oceans of eons;
With various spiritual powers he teaches all:
Light of Fame has realized this truth.

Furthermore, the celestial king Banner of the Delightful Light of Truth found the door of liberation in observing the faculties of all beings, expounding the truth for them, and cutting off their doubts. The celestial king Ocean of Pure Adornments found the door of liberation causing vision of Buddha whenever brought to mind. The celestial king Light of Supreme Wisdom found the door of liberation realizing the body of adornments that have no basis and are equal in terms of phenomenal nature. The celestial king Banner of Independent Wisdom found the door of liberation of comprehending all mundane things and in a single instant setting up oceans of inconceivable adornments. The celestial king Delight in Tranquility found the door of liberation of manifesting inconceivable buddha-lands in a single pore without hindrance. The celestial king Eye of Universal Knowledge found the door of liberation of all-sided observation of the universe. The celestial king Delight in Use of Intellect found the door of liberation producing all kinds of displays for the benefit of all beings, always appearing eternally. The celestial king Light of Intellect Sown with Virtue found the door of liberation observing all objects in the world and entering into the truth of inconceivability. The celestial king Undefiled Tranquil Light found the door of liberation showing all beings the essential ways of emancipation. The celestial king Vast Pure Light found the door of liberation of observing all teachable beings and guiding them into the way of enlightenment.

At that time the celestial king Banner of the Delightful Light of Truth, imbued with the Buddha's power, surveyed all the hosts of the heavens of minor vastness, infinite vastness, and vast results, and said in verse,

The realm of the Buddhas is inconceivable:
No sentient being can fathom it.
The Buddhas cause their minds to develop faith and resolution
And great enjoyment without end.
If any beings can accept the teaching,

The Buddha, with spiritual powers, will guide them,
Causing them to always see the Buddha before them:
Ocean of Adornments sees in this way.

The nature of all things has no resting place—
The Buddhas' appearance in the world is the same way—
They have no resting place in any state of being:
Supreme Wisdom can contemplate the meaning of this.

Whatever be the heart's desire of sentient beings,
The Buddhas' spiritual powers can manifest.
Each different, they are inconceivable:
This is Wisdom Banner's ocean of liberation.

All lands existing in the past
They can show in a single pore:
This is the great spiritual power of the Buddhas:
Delight in Tranquility can expound this.

The inexhaustible ocean of all teachings
Is assembled in the sanctuary of one teaching.
Such is the nature of truth explained by the Buddhas:
Eye of Knowledge can understand this technique.

In all lands in all quarters
Expounding the truth in each in every one,
The Buddha's body has no coming or going:
This is the realm of Delight in Use of Intellect.

The Buddha sees things of the worlds as like reflections of light;
He enters into their most recondite mysteries
And explains that the nature of all things is always quiescent:
Intellect Sown with Virtue can see this.

The Buddha knows all phenomena
And rains the rain of truth according to beings' faculties
In order to open the inconceivable gate of emancipation:
Tranquil Serenity can understand this.

The World Honored One always, with great kindness and
    compassion,
Appears in order to benefit sentient beings,
Equally showering the rain of truth to the fill of their capacities:
Pure Light can expound this.

Furthermore, the celestial king Repute of Pure Wisdom found the door of liberation comprehending the ways and means of emancipation of all sentient beings. The celestial king Supreme Vision found the door of liberation of shadowlike demonstration according to the wishes of all celestial beings. The celestial king Virtue of Tranquility found the door of liberation of great skill in means adorning the realms of all Buddhas. The celestial king Sound of the Polar Mountain found the door of liberation of following all sentient beings into the eternally flowing cycle of birth and death. The celestial king Eye of Pure Mindfulness found the door of liberation remembering the Buddhas' ways of taming and pacifying sentient beings. The celestial king Delightful Universal Illumination found the door of liberation that flowed forth from the ocean of universal memory and concentration power. The celestial king Sovereign Lord of the World found the door of liberation of ability to cause sentient beings to meet the Buddha and produce the treasury of faith. The celestial king Light Flame Sovereign found the door of liberation of ability to cause all beings to hear the truth, to believe and rejoice, and become emancipated. The celestial king Enjoyer of Meditating on the Truth and Creating Demonstrations found the door of liberation entering into the civilizing activities of all enlightening beings, boundless and inexhaustible as space. The celestial king Banner of Miraculous Displays found the door of liberation observing the infinite afflictions of sentient beings with universal compassion and wisdom.

At that time the celestial king Repute of Pure Wisdom, imbued with the power of the Buddha, surveyed the hosts of celestial beings of the heavens of little purity, boundless purity, and ubiquitous purity, and said in verse,

> He who realizes that the nature of things is without solidity
> Appears in all the boundless lands of the ten directions:
> Expounding the inconceivability of the realm of buddhahood,
> He causes all to return to the ocean of liberation.
>
> The Buddha is in the world without a resting place—
> Like a shadow or reflection he appears in all lands.
> The nature of things is ultimately nonorigination:
> This is the entry way of the king Supreme Vision.
>
> Cultivating skill in means over countless ages,
> Purifying all lands in the ten directions,
> The suchness of the universe never moves:
> This is the realization of Virtue of Tranquility.
>
> Sentient beings are shrouded and veiled by ignorance;
> Blind, in the dark, they remain always in birth-and-death.

The Buddha shows them the path of purity:
This is the liberation of Polar Mountain Sound.

The unexcelled path that the Buddhas traverse
Cannot be plumbed by any sentient being.
It is shown by various expedient methods:
Pure Eye, clearly observing, can comprehend them all.

The Buddha, by means of concentration formulae
Numerous as the atoms in oceans of lands
Teaches sentient beings, covering everything:
Universal Illumination can enter this.

The appearance of a Buddha is hard to encounter;
It may be met once in countless eons;
It is capable of inducing faith in sentient beings:
This is the realization of the celestial Sovereign.

The Buddha explains that the nature of things is natureless;
Profound, far-reaching, it is inconceivable.
He causes all beings to engender pure faith:
Light Flame can comprehend this.

The Buddhas of all times are replete with virtue;
They teach sentient beings inconceivably.
Contemplating this produces joy:
Enjoyer of Truth can teach in this way.

Sentient beings are sunk in the ocean of afflictions:
Their ignorance and pollution of views are much to be feared.
The great teacher pities them and frees them forever:
This is the realm of contemplation of Banner of Miracles.

The Buddha constantly emits great beams of light;
In each light beam are innumerable Buddhas.
Each makes displays of sentient beings' affairs;
This is the entry way of Wonderful Sound.

Furthermore, the celestial king Pleasing Light found the door of liberation of always experiencing the bliss of tranquil serenity yet being able to appear in order to eliminate the sufferings of the world. The celestial king Pure Subtle Light found the door of liberation of the ocean of great compassion, the mine of joy and happiness of all sentient beings. The celestial king Sound of Freedom found the door of liberation manifesting in a single instant the power of virtue of all sentient beings of boundless eons. The celestial king Supreme Awareness and Knowledge found the door of liberation causing all becoming, existing, and disintegrating worlds to be as pure as space. The celestial king Delightful Pure Subtle Sound found the door of liberation of joyfully believing and accepting the teachings of all sages. The celestial king Sound of Skillful Meditation found the door of liberation of ability to spend an eon expounding the meanings and methods of all stages of enlightenment. The celestial king Adornment Explaining Sound found the door of liberation of methods of making great offerings when all enlightening beings descend from the palace of the Tushita heaven to be born in the world. The celestial king Profound Light-Sound found the door of liberation of contemplation of the inexhaustible ocean of spiritual power and wisdom. The celestial king Great Fame found the door of liberation of techniques for appearing in the world, having fulfilled the ocean of virtues of all Buddhas. The celestial king Supreme Pure Light found the door of liberation of the mine of faith and delight produced by the power of the Buddha's ancient vows.

Then the celestial king Pleasing Light, imbued with the power of the Buddha, surveyed all the celestial hosts from the heavens of little light, infinite light, and intense light, and said in verse,

> I remember the past practice of the Buddha,
> Serving and providing offerings for innumerable Buddhas:
> His pure deeds, in accord with his original faith,
> Are now all visible, through the Buddha's spiritual power.

> The Buddha's body is formless, free from all defilement;
> Always abiding in compassion and pity,
> He removes the distress of all worlds:
> This is the liberation of Subtle Light.

> The Buddha's teaching is vast and boundless;
> It is manifest in all fields,
> According to their becoming and decay, each different:
> This is the power of liberation of Sound of Freedom.

> The Buddha's spiritual power is incomparable;
> It appears everywhere, in the vast fields of all directions,
> And makes them all pure, always manifest:
> This is the technique of liberation of Supreme Mindfulness.

> Respectfully serving all the Buddhas,
> Numerous as atoms in oceans of lands,
> Hearing the teaching, getting rid of defilement, not acting in vain,
> This is Subtle Sound's application of the teaching.

The Buddhas have, for immeasurable eons,
Expounded the techniques of the stages, without peer.
What they have explained is boundless and inexhaustible:
Sound of Skillful Meditation knows the meaning of this.

The infinite scenes of the Buddha's miraculous displays
Appear in all places in a single instant,
Great techniques for conquering spirits and attaining enlightenment:
This is the liberation of Adorning Sounds.

Sustained by awesome power, able to explain
And to demonstrate the deeds of spiritual powers of the Buddhas,
Purifying all according to their faculties:
This is the liberation door of Light-Sound.

The Buddha's wisdom is boundless—
It has no equal in the world, it has no attachment;
Compassionately responding to beings, it manifests everywhere:
Great Fame has realized this path.

The Buddha, in the past, cultivated enlightening practices,
Made offerings to all the Buddhas of the ten directions—
The vows made in the presence of each Buddha
Supreme Light hears and greatly rejoices.

Furthermore, the brahma king Shikhin found the door of liberation abiding in all sites of enlightenment everywhere and preaching the truth while being pure and free of attachments in all actions. Brahma king Light of Wisdom found the door of liberation inducing all sentient beings to enter meditative absorption and stay there. Brahma king Radiance of Beneficent Wisdom found the door of liberation entering everywhere into all inconceivable truths. Brahma king Sound of Ubiquitous Clouds found the door of liberation entering into the ocean of all utterances of the Buddhas. Brahma king Independent Observer of the Sounds and Speech of the Worlds found the door of liberation of ability to remember all the techniques used by enlightening beings in teaching all sentient creatures. Brahma king Eyes of Still Light found the door of liberation showing the individual differences in characteristics of results of actions of all beings. Brahma king All-Pervading Light found the door of liberation of appearing before all sentient beings to guide them according to their various types. Brahma king Sound of Magical Displays found the door of liberation dwelling in the realm of tranquil and serene action of the pure aspect of all things. Brahma king Eyes of Shining Light found the door of liberation of always diligently appearing with no attachments, no boundaries, and no dependence in the

midst of all existence. Brahma king Pleasing Ocean Sound found the
door of liberation of constant contemplation and investigation of the
inexhaustible truth.

At that time the great brahma king Shikhin, imbued with the spiritual power of the Buddha, surveyed all the celestial hosts of the heavens of brahma bodies, brahma assistants, brahma masses, and great brahmas, and said in verse,

> The Buddha-body is pure and always tranquil;
> The radiance of its light extends throughout the worlds;
> Signless, patternless, without images,
> Like clouds in the sky, thus is it seen.

> This realm of concentration of the Buddha-body
> Cannot be assessed by any sentient being;
> It shows them inconceivable expedient doors:
> This is the enlightenment of Wisdom Light.

> The ocean of teachings, numerous as atoms in a buddha-land,
> Are expounded in a single word—all without remainder.
> They can be expounded this way for oceans of eons without ever
>   being exhausted:
> This is the liberation of Light of Beneficent Wisdom.

> The complete sound of the Buddhas is equal to the worlds;
> Sentient beings each obtain understanding according to their
>   kind,
> Yet there is no difference in the sound:
> Such is the understanding of the brahma king Universal Sound.

> The methods for entering enlightenment
> Of the Buddhas of all times
> Are all apparent in the Buddha-body:
> This is the liberation of Sound of Freedom.

> The activities of all sentient beings are different;
> According to the causes, the effects are various.
> In this way do the Buddhas appear in the world:
> Silent Light can understand this.

> Master of countless media of teaching,
> Civilizing sentient beings everywhere in all quarters,
> Yet not making distinctions therein:
> Such is the realm of Universal Light.

The Buddha-body is like space, inexhaustible—
Formless, unhindered, it pervades the ten directions.
All of its accommodational manifestations are like conjurations:
Sound of Magical Displays understands this way.

The appearances of the Buddha-body are boundless,
And so are the knowledge, wisdom, and voice—
Being in the world, manifesting form, yet without attachment:
Shining Light has entered this door.

The King of Truth reposes in the Palace of Sublime Reality—
The light of the reality-body illumines everything.
The nature of reality is incomparable and has no marks:
This is the liberation of king Ocean Sound.

Furthermore, the celestial king Sovereign Freedom had found the door of liberation of the treasury of freedom manifestly developing and maturing innumerable sentient beings. Celestial king Sublime Eye Lord found the door of liberation examining the pleasures of all sentient beings and causing them to enter the pleasure of the realm of sages. Celestial king Beautiful Jewel Banner Crown found the door of liberation causing all sentient beings to initiate practices according to their various inclinations and understandings. Celestial king Courageous Intelligence found the door of liberation holding together all the doctrines preached for the benefit of sentient beings. Celestial king Wonderful Sound Phrases found the door of liberation remembering the compassion of the Buddha and increasing progress in his own practice. Celestial king Subtle Light Banner found the door of liberation of manifesting the door of great compassion and smashing down the banner of all pride and conceit. Celestial king Realm of Peace found the door of liberation conquering the malicious attitudes of all people. Celestial king Array of Splendid Discs Banner found the door of liberation of all the infinite Buddhas of the ten directions coming whenever they are remembered. Celestial king Flower Light Wisdom found the door of liberation of everywhere manifesting perfect enlightenment according to the minds and thoughts of sentient beings. Celestial king Sublime Light of Indra found the door of liberation of independence of great awesome power to enter all worlds.

At that time the celestial king Sovereign Freedom, imbued with the majestic power of the Buddha, surveyed all the celestial hosts of the heavens of freedom and said in verse,

The Buddha body is all-pervasive, equal to the cosmos.
It manifests in response to all sentient beings;

With various teachings he is always guiding:
Master of Teaching, he is able to enlighten.

Of the various pleasures of the world,
The pleasure of holy tranquility is supreme;
Abiding in the vast essence of reality:
Sublime Eye sees this.

The Buddha appears throughout the ten directions
Universally responding to all hearts, teaching the truth—
All doubting thoughts are cut off:
This is the door of liberation of Beautiful Banner Crown.

The Buddhas speak the wondrous sound throughout the world;
The teachings spoken over countless ages
Can all be expounded in a single word:
This is the liberation of Courageous Intelligence.

All the great kindness in the world
Cannot equal a hairtip of the Buddha's.
The Buddha's kindness is inexhaustible as space:
This is the realization of Wonderful Sound.

Completely demolishing in all quarters
The mountains of pride of all beings,
This is the function of the great compassion of the Buddha:
This is the path traveled by Subtle Light Banner.

The light of wisdom, pure, fills the world;
Any who see it are relieved of ignorance
And caused to leave the evil ways:
Realm of Peace realizes this truth.

The light of a hair pore is able to expound
Buddha names as numerous as sentient beings.
According to their pleasure, they all can hear it:
This is Splendid Disc Banner's liberation.

The Buddha's freedom cannot be measured—
It fills the cosmos and all space.
All the congregations see it clearly:
This liberation door Flower Intellect enters.

Over oceans of eons, infinite, boundless,
Manifesting everywhere and preaching the truth,
Never has a Buddha been seen to have any going or coming:
This is the enlightenment of Wonderful Light.

Furthermore, the celestial king Skillful Transformation found the door of liberation of the power of magical displays demonstrating all actions. Celestial king Light of Silent Sound found the door of liberation of relinquishing all clinging to objects. Celestial king Light of the Power of Transformation and Emanation found the door of liberation annihilating the ignorant muddled minds of all beings and causing their wisdom to become fully complete. Celestial king Master of Adornments found the door of liberation manifesting unlimited pleasing sounds. Celestial king Light of Mindfulness found the door of liberation knowing the infinite virtuous characteristics of all Buddhas. Celestial king Supreme Cloud Sound found the door of liberation knowing the process of becoming and decay of all past ages. Celestial king Supreme Light found the door of liberation of knowledge to enlighten all beings. Celestial king Exquisite Topknot found the door of liberation shedding light swiftly filling space in all directions. Celestial king Joyful Wisdom found the door of liberation of the power of energy whose deeds cannot be ruined by anyone. Celestial king Flower Light Topknot found the door of liberation knowing the rewards of actions of all sentient beings. Celestial king Seeing in All Directions found the door of liberation showing inconceivable differences in form and kind of sentient beings.

At that time the celestial king Skillful Transformation, imbued with the majestic power of the Buddha, surveyed the whole host of celestial beings of the heavens of enjoyment of emanations and said in verse,

> The essence of the doings of the world is inconceivable—
> The Buddha teaches all about it for the confused,
> Skillfully explaining the true principle of causality
> And the different doings of all sentient beings.
>
> Looking at the Buddha in various ways, there's nothing there;
> Seeking him in all directions, he can't be found.
> The manifestations of the reality-body have no true actuality:
> This truth is seen by Silent Sound.
>
> The Buddha cultivated many practices over oceans of eons
> In order to extinguish the ignorance and confusion of the world.
> Therefore his purity is the most radiant light:
> This is the realization of the mind of Light Power.
>
> Of the sublime sounds and voices in the world,
> None can compare to the Buddha's sound.
> The Buddha pervades the ten directions with a single sound:
> Entering this liberation is the Master of Adornment.

All the power of wealth in the world
Is not equal to a single characteristic of the Buddha—
The virtues of the Buddha are like space:
This is perceived by Mindful Light.

The infinite ages of past, present, and future,
The various aspects of their becoming and decay,
The Buddha can show in a single pore:
Supreme Cloud Sound can comprehend this.

The extent of all space may be known,
But the extent of a pore of Buddha cannot be apprehended.
Such nonobstruction is inconceivable:
Exquisite Topknot has been able to realize this.

The Buddha, in countless past ages
Fully cultivated the far-reaching transcendent means,
Working diligently with nonflagging vigor:
Joyful Intelligence knows this teaching.

The causes and conditions of the nature of actions are inconceivable—
The Buddha explains them all for the world.
The nature of things is fundamentally pure, with no defilements:
This is the entryway of Flower Light.

You should gaze on a pore of the Buddha—
All sentient beings are therein,
And they neither come nor go:
This is the understanding of Universal Sight.

Furthermore, the celestial king Contented found the door of liberation of all Buddhas bringing forth a complete, fully rounded teaching in the world. Celestial king Ocean of Joy and Bliss Topknot found the door of liberation of the body of pure light extending throughout the realm of space. Celestial king Banner of Supreme Virtues found the door of liberation of the ocean of pure vows to extinguish the sufferings of the world. Celestial king Still and Silent Light found the door of liberation of physical manifestation everywhere to expound the truth. Celestial king Pleasing Eyes found the door of liberation purifying the realms of all sentient beings. Celestial king Jewel Peak Moon found the door of liberation of the inexhaustible store of eternal manifestation teaching all worlds. Celestial king Courage and Strength found the door of liberation showing the realm of true awakening of all Buddhas. Celestial king Subtle Diamond Light found the door of liberation fortifying and solidifying all sentient beings' will for enlightenment, making it unbreakable.

Celestial king Constellation Banner found the door of liberation of techniques for associating with all Buddhas that appear, meditative investigation, and harmonization of sentient beings. Celestial king Pleasing Adornments found the door of liberation of instantaneously knowing the minds of sentient beings and appearing according to their potentials.

At that time celestial king Contented, imbued with the awesome power of the Buddha, surveyed all the hosts of the heavens of contentment and spoke in verse,

> The Buddha is vast, extending throughout the cosmos,
> Equal toward all sentient beings—
> Universally responding to all hearts, he opens the door of wonder,
> Causing them to enter the inconceivable pure truth.

> The Buddha-body manifests everywhere in the ten directions;
> Free from attachment and obstruction, it cannot be grasped.
> In various forms it is seen by all worlds:
> This is the entry of Topknot of Joy.

> The Buddha cultivated various practices in the past,
> His pure great vows deep as the sea;
> All enlightening ways he causes to be fulfilled:
> Supreme Virtue knows these techniques.

> The Buddha's body is inconceivable;
> Like reflections it shows separate forms, equal to the cosmos,
> Everywhere clarifying all things:
> This is the liberation door of Silent Light.

> Sentient beings are bound and covered by habitual delusion—
> Conceited, careless, their minds run wild.
> The Buddha expounds for them the way to calm:
> Pleasing Eyes, aware of this, rejoices at heart.

> The true guide of all worlds,
> He appears to rescue, to provide refuge,
> Showing all beings the abode of peace and happiness:
> Jewel Peak Moon enters deeply into this.

> The state of the Buddhas is inconceivable—
> It extends throughout all universes,
> Entering all things, reaching the other shore:
> Courageous Intellect, seeing this, rejoices.

If any sentient beings can accept the teaching,
And, hearing the virtues of Buddha, strive for enlightenment,
He causes them to dwell in the ocean of bounty, forever pure:
Subtle Light is able to observe this.

Gathering around all the Buddhas,
Numerous as the atoms of the lands of the ten directions,
Reverently making offerings and hearing the teaching:
This is the vision of Constellation Banner.

The ocean of sentient beings' minds is inconceivable;
It has no rest, no motion, no place of abode—
The Buddha can see it all in an instant:
This Beautiful Array well comprehends.

Furthermore, the celestial king Timely Portion had found the door of liberation of inspiring virtue in all sentient beings and causing them to be forever free from anxiety and torment. Celestial king Sublime Light found the door of liberation entering into all realms. Celestial king Banner of Inexhaustible Wisdom and Virtue found the door of liberation of the wheel of great compassion destroying all afflictions. Celestial king Skilled in Miraculous Displays found the door of liberation comprehending the mentalities of all sentient beings of the past, present, and future. Celestial king Great Light of Memory Power found the door of liberation of the light of the gates of concentration formulae holding in memory all teachings without forgetting. Celestial king Inconceivable Wisdom found the door of liberation of inconceivable methods of skillfully entering into the nature of all actions. Celestial king Circular Navel found the door of liberation of methods of activating the cycles of the teaching and developing sentient beings to maturity. Celestial king Light Flame found the door of liberation of the vast eye observing all sentient beings and going to civilize them. Celestial king Illumination found the gate of liberation, getting beyond all barriers of habit and not going along with bedeviling doings. Celestial king Greatly Famed for Universal Observation found the door of liberation of skillfully guiding all celestial beings and inducing them to undertake actions with a pure heart.

At that time the celestial king Timely Portion, imbued with the power of the Buddha, surveyed all the hosts of the Suyama heavens of good timely portion and spoke in verse, saying,

The Buddha, for innumerable long eons,
Has dried up the sea of troubles of the world:
Opening wide the road of purity out of defilement,
He causes to shine eternally the lamp of beings' wisdom.

The Buddha's body is exceedingly vast—
No borders can be found in the ten directions.
His expedient means are unlimited:
Subtle Light's knowledge has access to this.

The pains of birth, aging, sickness, death, and grief
Oppress beings without relief.
The Great Teacher takes pity and vows to remove them all:
Inexhaustible Wisdom Light can comprehend this.

Unhindered is the Buddha's knowledge that all is illusory;
He clearly comprehends all things in all times,
Delving into the mental patterns of all sentient beings:
This is the realm of Skillful Teaching.

The bounds of his total recall are not to be found;
The ocean of his eloquence is also unlimited.
He is able to turn the wheel of the pure subtle truth:
This is the liberation of Great Light.

The nature of actions is vast and inexhaustible—
His knowledge comprehends it and skillfully explains;
All his methods are inconceivable:
Such is the entry of Wisdom.

Turning the wheel of inconceivable truth,
Demonstrating and practicing the way of enlightenment,
Forever annihilating the suffering of all sentient beings:
This is the level of technique of Circular Navel.

The real body of the Buddha is fundamentally nondual;
Yet it fills the world according to beings and forms—
Sentient beings each see it before them:
This is the perspective of Flames of Light.

Once any sentient beings see the Buddha,
It will cause them to clear away habitual obstructions
And forever abandon all devilish actions:
This is the path traveled by Illumination.

All the hosts of beings are vast as oceans—
Among them the Buddha is most majestically glorious.
Everywhere he rains the rain of truth to enrich sentient beings:
This liberation door Greatly Famed enters.

Furthermore, the celestial king Shakra-Indra had found the liberation door of great joy remembering the appearance in the world of the Buddhas of past, present, and future, and clearly seeing the becoming and distintegration of the lands. Celestial king Full Sound of Universal Fame found the door of liberation of ability to cause the form body of the Buddha to be most pure and vast, without compare in the world. Celestial king Kind Eyes Jewel Topknot found the door of liberation of clouds of compassion covering all. Celestial king Jewel Light Banner Fame found the door of liberation of always seeing the Buddha manifesting various forms of majestic bodies to all the leaders of the worlds. Celestial king Joy-Producing Topknot found the door of liberation knowing from what virtuous actions the cities and buildings of all sentient beings came to be. Celestial king Admirable Mindfulness found the door of liberation showing the deeds of the Buddhas developing sentient beings. Celestial king Lofty Supreme Sound found the door of liberation of knowledge of the becoming and decay of all worlds and the signs of change of the ages. Celestial king Perfect Mindfulness found the door of liberation of calling to mind the acts of future enlightening beings in civilizing people. Celestial king Pure Flower Light found the door of liberation of knowledge of the cause of happiness in all heavens. Celestial king Sun of Wisdom Eye found the gate of liberation showing the acceptance and production of roots of goodness of all celestial beings, removing ignorance and illusion. Celestial king Independent Light found the door of liberation enlightening all celestial beings, causing them to cut off all sorts of doubts forever.

At that time celestial king Shakra-Indra, imbued with the power of the Buddha, surveyed all the hosts of celestial beings of the thirty-three heavens, and spoke in verse, saying,

> I am conscious of the spheres of all Buddhas
> In all times being all equal
> As their lands form and disintegrate:
> They see all by enlightened spiritual powers.

> The Buddha body is vast and all-pervasive;
> Its ineffable form, incomparable, aids all beings,
> The radiance of its light reaching everywhere:
> This path Universal Fame can observe.

> The Buddha's great compassionate ocean of techniques
> Has been utterly purified by past eons of practice
> And guides sentient beings without bound:
> Jewel Topknot has realized this.

I contemplate the ocean of virtues of the King of Truth,
Supreme in the world, having no peer,
Producing an immense sense of joy:
This is the liberation of Jewel Light.

The Buddha knows the sea of sentient beings' good works,
Various excellent causes producing great blessings;
All these he causes to be manifest:
This is seen by Topknot of Joy.

The Buddhas appear in the ten directions,
Everywhere throughout all worlds,
Observing the minds of beings and showing how to tame them:
Right Mindfulness realizes this path.

The vast eye of the Buddha's wisdom-body
Sees every particle of the world
And reaches in the same way throughout the ten directions:
This is the liberation of Cloud Sound.

The enlightening practice of all Buddhists
The Buddha shows in a single hair pore,
Infinite as they are, all complete:
This is seen clearly by Mindfulness.

All the pleasant things of the world
Are born of the Buddha—
The virtues of the Buddhas are supreme, unequalled:
This liberation Flower King enters.

If one thinks of a bit of the Buddha's virtue,
The mind concentrating on it for even a moment,
The fears of the evil ways will be banished forever:
Wisdom Eye profoundly realizes this.

Great spiritual powers within the state of tranquility
Universally respond to all minds, extending everywhere,
Causing all doubt and confusion to be cut off:
This is the attainment of Light.

Furthermore, Sun Godling had found the door of liberation of pure light shining on the sentient beings of the ten directions, always benefiting them forever and ever. The deity Light Flame Eyes found the door of liberation enlightening sentient beings through the agency of all corresponding bodies, causing them to enter the ocean of wisdom. The deity Polar Mountain Light Joy Banner found the door of liberation of being the leader of all sentient beings and having them diligently cultivate boundless pure qualities. The deity Pure Jewel Moon found the door of liberation of the joy of profound determination cultivating all ascetic practices. The deity Nonregressing Courage found the door of liberation of unhindered light shining everywhere causing all beings to increase in purity and clarity. The deity Light of Beautiful Flower Garlands found the door of liberation of pure light illumining the bodies of all sentient beings and causing them to produce oceans of joy and faith. Supreme Banner Light found the door of liberation of light illumining all worlds, causing them to perfect various wonderful qualities. The deity Universal Light of a Jewel Topknot found the door of liberation of the ocean of great compassion manifesting jewels of various forms and colors of boundless realms. The deity Eyes of Light found the door of liberation purifying the eyes of all sentient beings, causing them to see the matrix of the cosmos. The deity Virtue Bearing found the door of liberation developing pure continuous attention, never letting it be lost or broken. The deity Universal Light found the door of liberation carrying the palace of the sun all over, shining on all sentient beings of the ten directions, allowing them to accomplish their work.

At that time Sun Godling, imbued with the Buddha's power, surveyed all the sun deities and said in verse,

The Buddha's great light of knowledge
Illumines all lands in the ten directions:
All sentient beings can see the Buddha's
Various disciplines and manifold techniques.

The forms of the Buddha are boundless,
Appearing to all according to their inclinations,
Opening up the ocean of knowledge for all worlds:
Flame Eyes beholds the Buddha in this way.

The Buddha-body is peerless, it has no compare;
Its light shines throughout the ten directions,
Transcending all, supremely unexcelled:
Such a teaching has Joyful attained.

Practicing austerities to benefit the world,
Traversing all realms of existence for countless ages,
His light is everywhere as pure as space:
Jewel Moon knows these techniques.

The Buddha speaks the wondrous sound without obstacle—
It pervades all lands in the ten directions,

Benefiting the living with the flavor of truth:
Courageous knows this technique.

Emanating inconceivable nets of light,
Everywhere purifying all conscious beings,
He causes them to engender profound faith:
This is the way Flower Garland has entered.

All the lights in the world
Cannot match the light of a single pore of the Buddha—
This is how inconceivable the Buddha's light is:
This is the liberation of Supreme Banner Light.

The way of all Buddhas is thus:
They all sit under the tree of enlightenment
And bring the errant to the right path:
Jewel Topknot Light sees in this way.

Sentient beings are blind, ignorant, and suffering—
The Buddha wants to make them produce a pure eye,
And so lights the lamp of wisdom for them:
Good Eye looks deeply into this.

Honored master of liberating techniques—
If any see him and make an offering,
He causes them to cultivate practice and reach the result:
This is Virtue's power of means.

In one teaching there are many aspects—
For countless ages he teaches this way.
The far-reaching meanings of the teachings expounded
Are comprehended by Universal Light.

Furthermore, Moon Godling found the door of liberation of pure light illuminating the universe, edifying all sentient beings. The deity Flower King Topknot Halo found the door of liberation observing the worlds of all sentient beings and causing them to enter the boundless truth. The deity Myriad Subtle Pure Lights found the door of liberation knowing the various operations of clinging to objects in the ocean of the minds of all sentient beings. The deity Pacifying the Hearts of the World found the door of liberation bestowing inconceivable happiness on all sentient beings, causing them to dance with joy. The deity Luminosity of Tree King Eyes found the door of liberation protecting agricultural work, the seeds, sprouts, stalks, etc., according to the season, causing it to be successfully accomplished. The deity Manifesting Pure Light found the door of liberation compassionately saving and protecting all sentient beings, causing them to witness the facts of experiencing pain and pleasure. The deity Immutable Light Traveling Everywhere found the door of liberation able to hold the pure clear moon and show it throughout the ten directions. The deity Sovereign Monarch of Constellations found the door of liberation showing all things to be illusory and like empty space, formless and without inherent nature. The deity Moon of Pure Awareness found the door of liberation performing great works for the benefit of all beings. The deity Great Majestic Light found the door of liberation universally cutting off all doubt and confusion.

At that time Moon Godling, imbued with the spiritual power of the Buddha, surveyed all the celestial hosts in all the moon palaces, and said in verse,

> The Buddha radiates light pervading the world,
> Illumining the lands in the ten directions,
> Expounding the inconceivable, far-reaching teaching
> To destroy forever the darkness of ignorance and delusion.

> His sphere is infinite and inexhaustible—
> He teaches eternally through countless eons,
> Edifying beings through various powers:
> Flower Topknot looks upon Buddha this way.

> The ocean of sentient beings' minds varies from moment to moment;
> The Buddha's knowledge is so broad it comprehends all this,
> Expounding the truth for them all, making them glad:
> This is the liberation of Subtle Light.

> Sentient beings have no holy tranquility;
> Sunk in evil ways, they suffer many pains—
> The Buddha shows them the nature of things:
> Peaceful Meditation sees in this way.

> The Buddha, with unprecedented great compassion,
> Enters all states of existence to help sentient beings,
> Explaining truth, encouraging virtue, promoting fulfillment:
> This is known to Eye Light.

> The Buddha opens up the light of truth,
> Analyzing the natures of the acts of all worlds,
> Their good and their evil, without a mistake:
> Pure Light, seeing this, gives rise to joy.

The Buddha is the basis of all blessings,
Like the earth supporting all buildings;
He skillfully shows the peaceful way out of distress:
Immutable knows this technique.

The bright glow of his fire of knowledge pervades the universe—
He manifests countless forms, equal to all beings,
Exposing true reality for the benefit of all:
Monarch of Constellations realizes this path.

The Buddha is like space, with no inherent nature;
Appearing in the world to benefit the living,
His features and refinements are like reflections:
Pure Awareness sees in this way.

The pores of the Buddha's body emit sounds everywhere:
The clouds of the teaching cover all worlds;
All those who hear are joyful and glad:
Such is the realization of Liberation Light.

Furthermore, the gandharva king Sustaining the Nation found the door of liberation of independent techniques for saving all sentient beings. The gandharva king Tree Light found the door of liberation seeing the array of all virtues. The gandharva king Clear Eyes found the door of liberation cutting off forever the grief and suffering of all sentient beings, producing a treasury of joy. The gandharva king Flower Crown found the door of liberation forever cutting off the confusion of all sentient beings' erroneous views. The gandharva king Universal Sound of Joyful Steps found the door of liberation like clouds overspreading, shading and refreshing all sentient beings. The gandharva king Joyously Moving Beautiful Eyes found the door of liberation manifesting an enormous beautiful body, causing all to obtain peace and bliss. The gandharva king Wondrous Sound Lion Banner found the door of liberation scattering all famous jewels in all directions. The gandharva king Universal Emanation of Jewel Light found the door of liberation manifesting the pure body of all great joyous lights. The gandharva king Diamond Tree Flower Banner found the door of liberation causing all trees to richly flourish, causing all who see them to be delighted. The gandharva king Universal Manifestation of Adornments found the door of liberation skillfully entering into the sphere of all Buddhas and bestowing peace and happiness on all living beings.

At that time the gandharva king Sustaining the Nation, imbued with the power of the Buddha, looked over all the hosts of gandharvas and said in verse,

The innumerable doors to the realm of the Buddhas
Cannot be entered by any sentient beings.
The Buddha is like the nature of space, pure;
He opens the right path for all worlds.

In each one of the Buddha's pores
Is an ocean of virtues, all replete—
All words are benefited and pleased by them:
This is what Tree Light can see.

The vast ocean of sorrow and suffering of the world
The Buddha can evaporate entirely.
The Buddha, compassionate, has many techniques:
Clear Eyes has deep understanding of this.

The ocean of lands in the ten directions is boundless—
The Buddha illumines them all with the light of knowledge,
Causing them to wash away all wrong views:
This is where Tree Flower enters.

The Buddha, over countless eons in the past
Cultivated great compassion and skill in means,
To pacify all the worlds:
This path Universal Sound can enter.

The Buddha body is pure—all like to see it.
It can produce endless enjoyment in the world
As the causes and effects of liberation are successively fulfilled:
Good Eyes skillfully demonstrates this.

Sentient beings are confused, always going in circles—
Their barriers of ignorance are most firm and dense.
The Buddha expounds the great teaching for them:
This Lion Banner is able to expound.

The Buddha manifests everywhere a body of wondrous form,
With innumerable differentiations, equal to sentient beings,
By various means enlightening the world:
Wondrous Sound looks upon the Buddha this way.

The infinite doors of knowledge and means
The Buddha opens all for sentient beings,
To enter the true practice of supreme enlightenment:
This Diamond Banner well observes.

Within an instant, millions of eons—
The Buddha's power can show this, with no effort,
Bestowing peace and comfort equally on all living beings:
This is the liberation of Pleasant Adornment.

Furthermore, the kumbanda king Increase found the door of liberation of the power to eliminate all maliciousness. The kumbanda king
Dragon King found the door of liberation cultivating a boundless ocean
of practices. The kumbanda king Adornment found the door of liberation knowing what is pleasing to the minds of all sentient beings. The
kumbanda king Beneficial Action found the door of liberation of work
perfecting pure radiance. The kumbanda king Fearsome found the door
of liberation showing all sentient beings the safe path free from fear.
The kumbanda king Sublime Adornment found the door of liberation
evaporating the ocean of cravings of all sentient beings. The kumbanda
king High Peak Intellect found the door of liberation manifesting clouds
of light in all realms of being. The kumbanda king Brave Strong Arms
found the door of liberation shedding light everywhere, destroying
mountain-like barriers. The kumbanda king Boundless Pure Flower
Eyes found the door of liberation revealing the treasury of nonregressing
great compassion. The kumbanda king Enormous Face found the door
of liberation everywhere manifesting bodies transmigrating in the various states of being.
At that time the kumbanda king Increase, imbued with the power of
the Buddha, looked over all the assembled kumbandas and said in
verse,

Perfecting the power of patience, the Guide of the World
Cultivated practice for the sake of beings for countless eons,
Forever leaving the confusion of worldly pride—
Therefore his body is most majestically pure.

In the past the Buddha cultivated oceans of practices,
Edifying innumerable beings in all quarters,
Benefiting the living by all sorts of means:
This liberation door Dragon King has found.

The Buddha saves sentient beings with great knowledge,
Clearly understanding all of their minds
And taming them with various powers:
Adornment Banner, seeing this, gives rise to joy.

Spiritual powers appear responsively, like reflections of a light;
The wheel of teaching in reality is like space,

Being thus in the world for incalculable eons:
This is realized by the Beneficent King.

Sentient beings are blinded by ignorance, always confused;
The light of Buddha illumines the path of safety
To rescue them and cause suffering to be removed:
Fearsome contemplates this teaching well.

Floating and sinking in the ocean of desire, full of all pains;
The all-illumining light of wisdom annihilates this all,
And having removed pain, then expounds the truth:
This is the realization of Splendid Arrays.

The Buddha body responds to all—none do not see it.
With various techniques it teaches the living,
Sound like thunder, showering the rain of truth:
This teaching High Intellect enters.

The pure light is not shone in vain—
Any who meet it, it will cause to dissolve heavy barriers;
It expounds Buddha's virtues without any bounds:
Grave Arms can clarify this profound principle.

To give peace and comfort to all sentient beings,
He practiced great compassion for innumerable ages,
Removing all pains by various means:
This is the vision of Pure Flower.

Spiritual powers independent and inconceivable,
That body appears throughout the ten directions,
Yet nowhere does it come or go:
This is what Enormous Face understands.

Furthermore, the naga king Virupaksha found the door of liberation extinguishing all the burning pains of the state of nagas. Shakra found the door of liberation of instantaneously transforming his own naga form and manifesting the forms of countless beings. The naga king Cloud Sound Banner found the door of liberation speaking the boundless ocean of Buddha-names with a pure clear voice in all realms of being. The naga king Flaming Mouth found the door of liberation showing the differences in arrangements of boundless buddha worlds. The naga king Cloud Banner found the door of liberation showing all sentient beings the ocean of great joy and virtue. The naga king Takshaka found the door of liberation destroying all fears with the pure voice of salvation. The naga king Boundless Steps found the door of liberation showing the form bodies of all Buddhas and the succession of their eons. The naga king Pure Form found the door of liberation producing the ocean of great delight and joy of all sentient beings. The naga king Great Sound Traveling Everywhere found the door of liberation manifesting the pleasing, unobstructed sound that is equal to all. The naga king No Heat or Torment found the door of liberation annihilating all the sufferings of the world with the cloud of great compassion that covers all.

At that time, naga king Virupaksha, imbued with the power of the Buddha, looked over all the hosts of nagas, and said in verse,

> See how the Buddha's teaching is always thus:
> It helps and benefits all sentient beings;
> It can, by the power of great compassion and pity,
> Rescue those who have fallen into fearful ways.
>
> The various differences of all sentient beings
> The Buddha shows all on the tip of a hair,
> Filling the world with spiritual demonstrations:
> Shakra sees the Buddha this way.
>
> The Buddha, by means of unlimited spiritual power,
> Tells of his names and epithets, as many as all beings—
> He makes them all hear whichever they like:
> Thus can Cloud Sound understand.
>
> The beings of infinite, boundless lands
> The Buddha can make enter a single pore
> While sitting at rest among those hosts.
> This is the vision of Flaming Mouth.
>
> The irascible minds of all sentient beings,
> Their bondage and ignorance, are deep as the sea;
> The Buddha compassionately removes it all:
> Flame naga, observing this, can see it clearly.
>
> The virtuous powers of all sentient beings
> Appear clearly in the Buddha's pores—
> Having shown this, he returns all to the ocean of blessings:
> This is the vision of High Cloud Banner.
>
> The pores of the Buddha's body radiate the light of wisdom;
> That light intones a sublime sound everywhere—
> All who hear it are free from worry and fear:
> Takshaka realizes this way.

The lands, adornments, and succession of ages
Of all the Buddhas of all times
Appear as they are in the Buddha's body:
Broad Steps sees this spiritual power.

I observed the Buddha's practice in the past,
Making offerings to the ocean of all Buddhas,
Increasing his joy with all of them:
This is the entry of naga Swift.

The Buddha, by means of expedient sound adapted to type,
Expounds truth for the masses, making them rejoice.
That sound is pure and sublime, enjoyed by all who hear:
Going Everywhere, hearing this, joyfully awakens.

Sentient beings are oppressed in all states of existence,
Whirled about by habitual delusion, with no one to rescue them;
The Buddha liberates them with great compassion:
No Heat or Torment realizes this.

Furthermore, the yaksha king Vaishravana found the door of liberation saving evil beings by means of boundless skill in means. The
yaksha king Independent Sound found the door of liberation examining
all sentient beings, saving them with appropriate techniques. The yaksha
king Solemn Weapon Bearer found the door of liberation of ability to
give sustenance to all emaciated evil sentient beings. The yaksha king
Great Wisdom found the door of liberation extolling the ocean of
virtues of all sages. The yaksha king Lord of Flaming Eyes found the
door of liberation observing all sentient beings and engendering great
compassion and knowledge. The yaksha king Adamantine Eye found
the door of liberation aiding and comforting all sentient beings by
various appropriate means. The yaksha king Arm of Courage and
Strength found the door of liberation entering into the meanings of all
teachings. The yaksha king Bravely Resisting General found the door
of liberation guarding all sentient beings, causing them to abide in the
Way, with none living in vain. The yaksha king Rich in Material Goods
found the door of liberation increasing all beings' stores of blessings
and virtues and causing them to always feel blissful. The yaksha king
Power to Smash High Mountains found the door of liberation producing
the light of wisdom and power of the Buddhas whenever called to
mind.

At that time the great yaksha king Learned, imbued with the power
of the Buddha, looked over all the assembly of yakshas and said in
verse,

The evils of sentient beings are extremely fearsome—
They do not see the Buddha for hundreds, thousands of eons.
Drifting through life and death, they suffer myriad pains—
To rescue them, the Buddhas appear in the world.

The Buddha saves and protects all worlds,
Appearing before all sentient beings
To put a stop to the pains of transmigration in fearsome realms:
Independent Sound enters this gate of teaching.

Sentient beings' evil deeds create multiple barriers;
The Buddha demonstrates sublime principles to break through
    them,
While lighting up the world with a bright lamp:
This truth Weapon Bearer can see.

The Buddha cultivated practices over oceans of eons past,
Praising all the Buddhas in the ten directions—
Therefore he has a lofty, far-reaching fame:
This is what is understood by Wisdom.

His wisdom is like space, unbounded;
His reality-body is immense, inconceivable—
Therefore he appears in all ten directions:
Flaming Eyes can observe this.

Intoning the wondrous sound in all realms of being,
He expounds the truth to benefit the living;
Wherever his voice reaches, all pains vanish:
Delving into this technique is Adamant Eye.

All profound, vast meanings
The Buddha can expound in one phrase;
Thus the principles of the teaching are equal to the worlds:
This is the realization of Courageous Wisdom.

All sentient beings are on false paths—
Buddha shows them the right path, inconceivable,
Causing all worlds to be vessels of truth:
This Brave General can understand.

All virtuous activities in the world
Come from the Buddha's light;
The ocean of Buddha's wisdom is immeasurable:
Such is the liberation of Materially Rich.

Recall the countless eons of the past
When the Buddha cultivated the ten powers,
Able to fulfill all the powers:
This is comprehended by High Banner.

Furthermore, the mahoraga king Beneficent Wisdom found the door
of liberation of using all spiritual powers and techniques to cause
sentient beings to amass virtues. The mahoraga king Pure Dignified
Sound found the door of liberation causing all sentient beings to get rid
of afflictions and attain the joy of coolness. The mahoraga king Adornment of Supreme Wisdom found the door of liberation causing all
sentient beings, having good or bad thoughts and consciousness, to
enter into the pure truth. The mahoraga king Lord of Sublime Eyes
found the door of liberation comprehending the equality of all virtuous
powers without any attachments. The mahoraga king Lamp Banner
found the door of liberation edifying all sentient beings and causing
them to leave the dark, fearsome states. The mahoraga king Supreme
Light Banner found the door of liberation knowing the virtues of all the
Buddhas and giving rise to joy. The mahoraga king Lion Guts found
the door of liberation of the courage and strength to be the savior
and guardian of all beings. The mahoraga king Sound Adorned by
Myriad Subtleties found the door of liberation causing all sentient
beings to give rise to boundless joy and pleasure whenever brought
to mind. The mahoraga king Polar Mountain Guts found the door of
liberation of certain unshakability in the face of all objects, finally
reaching the other shore. The mahoraga king Pleasing Light found
the door of liberation of showing the path of equality to all unequal
beings.
At that time the mahoraga king Dignified Light of Beneficent Wisdom,
imbued with the power of the Buddha, surveyed the assembly of all the
mahoragas and said in verse,

Observe the purity of the essence of the Buddha;
Manifesting everywhere a majestic light to benefit all kinds,
Showing the Path of Elixir, making them clear and cool,
All miseries vanishing, having no basis.

All sentient beings dwell in the sea of existence
Binding themselves with evil deeds and delusions—
He shows them the way of serenity he practices:
Pure Dignified Sound can well understand this.

The Buddha's knowledge is peerless, inconceivable;
He knows the minds of all beings, in every respect,

And clarifies for them the pure truth:
This Adorned Topknot can comprehend.

Innumerable Buddhas appear in the world,
Being fields of blessings for all sentient beings—
Their ocean of blessings is vast and immeasurably deep:
Sublime Eyes can see all of this.

All sentient beings suffer grief and fear—
Buddhas appear everywhere to rescue them,
Extending everywhere through the space of the cosmos:
This is the sphere of Lamp Banner.

The virtues in a single pore of the Buddha
Cannot be assessed by all beings combined—
They are boundless, infinite, the same as space:
Thus does Vast Light Banner perceive.

The Buddha comprehends all things,
Is aware of the nature of all things,
Unshakable as the Polar Mountain:
Entering this approach to the truth is Lion Gut.

The Buddha in vast eons past
Amassed an ocean of joy, endlessly deep;
Therefore all who see him are glad:
This truth Adorned Sound has entered.

Realizing the real cosmos has no formal characteristics,
The ocean of transcendent ways completely fulfilled,
His great light saves all sentient beings:
Mountain Gut knows this technique.

Observe the independent power of the Buddha
Appearing equally in the ten directions
Illuminating and awakening all sentient beings:
This Subtle Light can well enter into.

Furthermore, the kinnara king Heaven of Light of Refined Intellect found the door of liberation universally producing all joyous actions. The kinnara king Exquisite Flower Banner found the door of liberation able to produce the unexcelled joy of truth and cause all beings to experience comfort and happiness. The kinnara king Various Adornments found the door of liberation of the vast store of pure faith replete with all virtues. The kinnara king Pleasing Sound found the door of liberation always producing all pleasing sounds, causing those who hear to be free from distress and fear. The kinnara king Jewel Tree Light found the door of liberation of compassionately establishing all sentient beings in enlightened understanding of mental objects. The kinnara king Delight to the Beholder found the door of liberation manifesting all bodies of exquisite form. The kinnara king Supreme Light Array found the door of liberation knowing the works by which are produced all the most excellent adornments. The kinnara king Subtle Flower Banner found the door of liberation observing the results produced by the activities of all worlds. The kinnara king Earth-Shaking Power found the door of liberation always doing all things to benefit living beings. The kinnara king Fierce Lord found the door of liberation thoroughly knowing the minds of all kinnaras and skillfully controlling them.

At that time the kinnara king Heaven of Light of Refined Intellect, imbued with the power of the Buddha, looked over all the masses of kinnaras and said in verse,

> All the pleasant things in the world
> Arise from seeing the Buddha.
> The Guide benefits all living beings,
> Being the savior and refuge of all.
>
> He produces all joys and delights
> Which beings receive without end;
> He causes all who see not to waste:
> This is the enlightenment of Flower Banner.
>
> The ocean of Buddha's virtue is inexhaustible;
> No bounds or limits to it can be found.
> Its light shines in all ten directions:
> This is the liberation of Adornment King.
>
> The Buddha's great sound is always spoken,
> Showing the real true way out of distress;
> All beings who hear it are happy and glad:
> Pleasing Sound is capable of believing this way.
>
> I see the Buddha's sovereign powers
> All stem from practices cultivated in the past;
> With great compassion he saves beings and makes them pure:
> This Jewel Tree King can understand.
>
> It is difficult to get a chance to see a Buddha;
> Beings may encounter one in a million eons,

Adorned with the marks of greatness all complete:
This is the view of Beholder's Delight.

Observe the great knowledge and wisdom of Buddha,
Responding to the desires of all sentient beings,
Expounding to all the path of omniscience:
Supreme Adornments can comprehend this.

The ocean of deeds is inconceivably vast—
Beings' suffering and happiness all come from it;
All this the Buddha can show:
This is what Flower Banner knows.

The Buddha's mystic powers are uninterrupted—
In all directions the earth constantly quakes,
Though no sentient beings are aware of it:
This Immense Power ever clearly sees.

Manifesting spiritual powers while among the masses,
He radiates light to make them wake up,
Revealing the realm of all the enlightened:
This Fierce Lord capably observes.

Furthermore, the garuda king Power of Great Swiftness had found the door of liberation of the nonattached, unobstructed eye observing everything in the worlds of sentient beings. The garuda king Unbreakable Jewel Topknot found the door of liberation abiding in the realm of reality and teaching sentient beings. The garuda king Pure Speed found the door of liberation of the power of energy to perfect all means of transcendence. The garuda king Nonregressing Mind found the door of liberation of bold power entering the realm of enlightenment. The garuda king Steady Pure Light found the door of liberation fully developing knowledge of the boundless differences in sentient beings. The garuda king Beautifully Adorned Crown Topknot found the door of liberation adorning the citadel of the Buddha teaching. The garuda king Immediate Manifestation Everywhere found the door of liberation perfecting the power of unbreakable equanimity. The garuda king Ocean Surveyor found the door of liberation knowing the physical forms of all sentient beings and manifesting forms for them. The garuda king Dragon Sound Great Eye Energy found the door of liberation of the knowledge entering into the acts of all sentient beings in death and life.

At that time the garuda king Power of Great Swiftness, receiving the power of the Buddha, looked over all the garudas and said in verse,

The Buddha-eye is vast and boundless,
Seeing all the lands in the ten directions.
Sentient beings therein are innumerable:
Showing great spiritual powers, he conquers them all.

The Buddha's spiritual powers are unhindered;
He sits under all the enlightenment trees in the ten directions
And expounds the truth like a cloud filling everywhere:
Jewel Topknot, hearing this, does not oppose.

The Buddha did various practices in the past,
Universally purifying great means of transcendence,
Giving offerings to all the enlightened:
This the Swift king deeply believes.

In each pore of the Buddha
Boundless practices are shown in an instant;
Such is the realm of Buddhahood:
Adorned by Nonregression clearly sees all.

The Buddha's boundless wisdom light
Can destroy the net of ignorance and illusion,
Saving all beings in all worlds:
This is the teaching held by Stable Light.

The citadel of truth is immense, endless;
Its gates are various and uncountable—
The Buddha, in the world, opens them wide:
Here Beautiful Crown Topknot clearly enters.

All the Buddhas are one reality body—
True suchness, equal, without distinctions;
The Buddha always abides through this power:
Immediate Manifestation Everywhere can fully expound this.

The Buddha in the past saved beings in all realms,
Shining light throughout the world,
Teaching and taming by various means:
This supreme teaching Ocean Surveyor realizes.

The Buddha sees all lands
All resting on the ocean of doing,
And rains the rain of truth on them all:
Dragon Sound's liberation is like this.

Furthermore, the titan king Rahula found the door of liberation of appearing as the honored leader of the masses. Bhimacitta found the door of liberation making countless eons manifest. The titan king Skillful Magical Arts found the door of liberation extinguishing the sufferings of all sentient beings and purifying them. The titan king Great Following found the door of liberation of self-adornment by cultivation of all ascetic practices. The titan king Bhandhi found the door of liberation causing boundless realms in the ten directions to quake. The titan king Universal Shining found the door of liberation of securely establishing all sentient beings by various techniques. The titan king Wonderful Adornment of Firm Action found the door of liberation of everywhere gathering unbreakable roots of goodness and clearing away all attachments. The titan king Vast Causal Wisdom found the door of liberation of leadership with great compassion free from confusion. The titan king Manifesting Supreme Virtue found the door of liberation causing all to see the Buddhas, serve, make offerings, and cultivate roots of goodness. The titan king Good Sound found the door of liberation of the practice of sure equanimity entering into all states of being.

At that time the titan king Rahula, imbued with the power of the Buddha, looked over all the titans and said in verse,

> In all the great masses in the ten directions,
> The Buddha is most unique among them.
> The radiance of his light is equal to space,
> Appearing before all sentient beings.

> Billions of eons' buddha-lands
> Clearly appear in an instant;
> Shedding light, he edifies beings everywhere:
> This Bhimacitta praises with joy.

> The realm of Buddhahood has no compare—
> With various teachings he is always giving aid,
> Annihilating beings' pains of existence:
> King Kumara can see this.

> Practicing austerities for countless eons,
> He aids sentient beings and purifies the worlds;
> Thereby is the Sage's wisdom universally perfected:
> Herein does Great Following see the Buddha.

> Unhindered, incomparable great mystic powers
> Move all lands in the ten directions
> Without causing sentient beings to fear:
> Great Power can understand this.

The Buddha appears in the world to save the living,
Revealing the way of complete knowledge,
Causing all to give up suffering and attain peace and bliss:
This teaching Universal Shining expounds.

The ocean of blessings in the world
Buddha's power can produce and purify;
Buddha can show the realm of liberation:
Adornment of Firm Action enters this door.

Unequaled is the Buddha's body of compassion,
Extending everywhere, unhindered, causing all to see,
Like a reflection appearing in the world:
Causal Wisdom can express this quality.

Rare, incomparable great mystic powers
Manifest bodies everywhere throughout the cosmos,
Each sitting under a tree of enlightenment:
Superior Qualities can explain the meaning of this.

The Buddha has cultivated practices for all times,
Having passed through every state of existence.
Liberating sentient beings from distress.
This is praised by the King Good Sound.

Furthermore, the day spirit Displaying Palaces found the door of liberation entering into all worlds. The day spirit Bringing Forth the Fragrance of Wisdom found the door of liberation observing all sentient beings, helping and benefiting them all, causing them to be happy and content. The day spirit Delighting in Superb Adornments found the door of liberation emanating boundless pleasing light beams. The day spirit Exquisite Light of Fragrant Flowers found the door of liberation arousing the pure faith and understanding of boundless sentient beings. The day spirit Everywhere Collecting Marvelous Herbs found the door of liberation of power to assemble and array all-pervading lights. The day spirit Liking to Make Joyful Eyes found the door of liberation universally enlightening all sentient beings whether they be suffering or happy, and causing them to realize the enjoyment of truth. The day spirit Observing the Directions and Appearing Everywhere found the door of liberation of different bodies of the worlds in the ten directions. The day spirit Majestic Power of Great Compassion found the door of liberation saving all sentient beings and making them peaceful and happy. The day spirit Radiance of Goodness found the door of liberation of the power to produce the virtues of joy and contentment in

every way. The day spirit Garland of Beautiful Flowers found the door
of liberation of universal renown and bringing benefit to all who see.

At that time the day spirit Displaying Palaces, imbued with the
power of the Buddha, surveyed all the day spirits and said in verse,

> The Buddha's knowledge is like space; it has no end.
> His light shines throughout the ten directions.
> He knows the mental patterns of all sentient beings.
> There is no world he does not enter.

> Knowing what pleases all sentient beings,
> He expounds an ocean of teachings, according to suitability;
> The expressions and meanings, great and far-reaching, are not the
>   same:
> Complete Wisdom can perceive them all.

> Buddha radiates light illumining the world;
> Those who see it rejoice without fail—
> It shows the vast, profound realm of pure peace:
> Delight in Pleasing Adornments understands this.

> The Buddha showers the rain of truth without bound,
> Able to make witnesses greatly rejoice;
> Supreme roots of goodness are born from this.
> Such is the realization of Exquisite Light.

> Entering into all aspects of teaching with enlightening power,
> Ages of cultivation and discipline thoroughly pure—
> All this is for the salvation of beings:
> This is what Wonderful Herbs understands.

> Edifying sentient beings by various means,
> All who see or hear receive benefit,
> Causing them all to dance for joy:
> Joyful Eyes sees in this way.

> Appearing responsively throughout the world,
> Throughout indeed the entire cosmos,
> Buddha's substance and nature neither exist nor do not:
> This the Direction Observer enters into.

> Sentient beings wander through difficulty and danger—
> Buddha appears in the world out of pity for them,
> Making them get rid of all suffering:
> In this liberation Compassion Power dwells.

Sentient beings are shrouded in darkness, sunk in eternal night;
Buddha preaches truth for them, bringing the dawn,
Allowing them to find happiness, getting rid of distress:
Light of Goodness enters this door.

The extent of Buddha's blessings is like that of space—
All blessings in the world arise therefrom.
Whatever he does is not in vain:
This liberation Flower Garland gains.

Furthermore, the night spirit Pure Light of Universal Virtue found the door of liberation of great courage and strength in the bliss of tranquil meditation. The night spirit Observing the World with Joyful Eyes found the door of liberation characterized by great pure delightful virtues. The night spirit World-Protecting Energy found the door of liberation appearing everywhere in the world taming sentient beings. The night spirit Sound of a Tranquil Sea found the door of liberation accumulating a spirit of immense joy. The night spirit Everywhere Manifesting Splendor found the door of liberation of the sound of profound independent pleasing speech. The night spirit Everywhere Causing Flower Trees to Bloom found the door of liberation of a vast store of joy full of light. The night spirit Egalitarian Protector and Nourisher found the door of liberation enlightening sentient beings and causing them to develop roots of goodness. The night spirit Sporting Happily found the door of liberation of boundless compassion rescuing and protecting sentient beings. The night spirit All Senses Always Joyful found the door of liberation everywhere manifesting the magnificent gates of great compassion. The night spirit Producing Pure Bounty found the door of liberation causing all sentient beings' desires to be fulfilled.

At that time the night spirit Pure Light of Universal Virtue, imbued with the power of the Buddha, looked over all the night spirits and said in verse,

You all should observe the Buddha's action,
Its vastness, serenity, and space-like character;
The shoreless sea of craving he purifies completely,
His undefiled majesty illumining all quarters.

All beings like to see the Buddha,
Met with but once in countless eons,
Compassionately mindful of all beings, extending to all:
This liberation door World Observer sees.

The Guide saves and protects all worlds;
All beings see him before them,
Able to purify all realms of existence:
This World Guardian ably observes.

In the past Buddha cultivated an ocean of joy—
Vast, boundless, beyond all measure;
Therefore those who see are all delighted:
This is realized by Silent Sound.

The realm of the Buddha is immeasurable—
Tranquil yet able to preach throughout all quarters,
Causing all beings' minds to be pure:
The night spirit Splendor, hearing, rejoices.

Among sentient beings who have no blessings,
Buddha's arrays of great blessing majestically shine,
Showing them the way of serenity, beyond the dusts of the world:
Causing Flowers to Bloom Everywhere realizes this way.

Displaying great mystic powers everywhere,
Taming all sentient beings,
He makes them see various physical forms:
This the Guardian Nourisher perceives.

In the past, Buddha spent every moment
Purifying the ocean of means and compassion
To save all beings in all of the worlds:
This is the liberation of Blissful Happiness.

Sentient beings are ignorant, always muddled—
The stubborn poisons of their minds are much to be feared.
The Buddha appears for their sake, out of pity:
This Enemy Destroyer realizes with joy.

The Buddha's past practice was for sentient beings,
To let them satisfy their aspirations;
Because of this he has developed virtuous characteristics:
This is what Bounty Producer enters into.

Furthermore, the direction spirit Dwelling Everywhere found the door of liberation of the power of universal salvation. The direction spirit Ubiquitous Light found the door of liberation perfecting the practice of mystic powers to edify all sentient beings. The direction spirit Array of Light Beams found the door of liberation destroying all barriers of darkness and producing the great light of joy and happiness. The direction spirit Traveling Everywhere Unhindered found the door of liberation appearing in all places without wasted effort. The direction Forever Ending Confusion found the door of liberation revealing names and epithets of Buddha equal in number to all sentient beings, producing virtue and merit. The direction spirit Roaming Everywhere in Pure Space found the door of liberation continuously producing exquisite sound causing all who hear to be pleased. The direction spirit Great Sound of Cloud Banner found the door of liberation bringing rain everywhere, like a naga, causing sentient beings to rejoice. The direction spirit Topknot and Eyes Undisturbed found the door of liberation of the independent power to show the doings of all sentient beings without discrimination. The direction spirit Universally Observing the Doings of the Worlds found the door of liberation examining the various actions of beings in all realms of existence. The direction spirit Traveling Everywhere Watching found the door of liberation fulfilling all tasks and bringing happiness to all sentient beings.

At that time the directions spirit Dwelling Everywhere, imbued with the power of the Buddha, looked over all the direction spirits and said in verse,

> The Buddha freely appears in the world
> To teach all living beings,
> Showing the ways to truth, having them understand and enter,
> Putting them in a position to realize highest wisdom.
>
> His spiritual powers are as boundless as beings,
> Displaying various forms according to their desires;
> And all who see are freed from suffering:
> This is Ubiquitous Light's power of liberation.
>
> Buddha, in the ocean of beings hindered by darkness,
> Manifests the great light of the lamp of truth for them,
> That light shining everywhere, so none do not see:
> This is the liberation of Light Beam Arrays.
>
> Commanding the various languages of all worlds,
> Buddha teaches so that all can understand,
> And the afflictions of his hearers disappear:
> This is the realization of Traveling Everywhere.
>
> As many names as there are in all worlds,
> Buddha names emerge in equal numbers,
> Causing all beings to be free from ignorance:
> This is the sphere of Ending Confusion.

If any sentient beings come before the Buddha
And hear the Buddha's sublime sound,
They will all be greatly delighted:
Traveling Throughout Space understands this truth.

The Buddha, in every single instant,
Everywhere showers the boundless rain of truth,
Causing all beings' afflictions to perish:
This is known to Cloud Banner.

The ocean of doings of all worlds
The Buddha equally shows,
Causing all beings to be rid of delusion by actions:
This is what Undisturbed Eyes understands.

The stage of omniscience has no bounds;
All the various mentalities of beings
The Buddha perceives with complete clarity:
This immense door the World Observer enters.

Buddha cultivated various practices in the past,
Completely fulfilling infinite transcendent ways,
Compassionately aiding all sentient beings:
This is the liberation of Universal Traveler.

Furthermore, the space spirit Pure Light Shining All Around found the door of liberation knowing the mentalities of sentient beings in all realms of existence. The space spirit Traveling Everywhere Deeply and Extensively found the door of liberation entering everywhere into the cosmos of reality. The space spirit Producing Auspicious Wind found the door of liberation comprehending the physical forms of boundless objects. The space spirit Abiding Securely Beyond Obstruction found the door of liberation able to remove all beings' obstructions by delusions caused by actions. The space spirit Broad Steps and Beautiful Topknot found the door of liberation observing and contemplating the vast ocean of practical application. The space spirit Unhindered Light Flames found the door of liberation of the light of great compassion rescuing all sentient beings from danger. The space spirit Unobstructed Conquering Power found the door of liberation entering into the power of all virtues free from attachment. The space spirit Spotless Light found the door of liberation able to cause the minds of all beings to remove their veils and become pure. The space spirit Deep and Far-Reaching Sublime Sound found the door of liberation of the light of knowledge seeing everywhere. The space spirit All-Pervading Light found the door of liberation manifesting everywhere without moving from its own place.

At that time the space spirit Pure Light Shining All Around, imbued with the power of the Buddha, surveyed all the space spirits and spoke the following verses,

> The vast eye of the Buddha
> Is pure and clear as space,
> Seeing all beings
> With complete clarity.

> The great light of the Buddha body
> Illumines the ten directions,
> Manifesting in every place:
> Traveling Everywhere sees this way.

> The Buddha body is like space;
> Unborn, it clings to nothing,
> It is ungraspable and without inherent nature:
> This is seen by Wind of Good Omen.

> The Buddha, for countless eons,
> Has expounded all holy paths,
> Destroying barriers for all beings:
> Sphere of Perfect Light understands this.

> I observe the enlightenment practices
> Accumulated by the Buddha in the past,
> All to make the world at peace:
> Beautiful Topknot works in this sphere.

> The realms of all sentient beings
> Whirl in the sea of birth and death.
> Buddha emits a pain-killing light:
> The Unhindered spirit can see this.

> His treasury of pure virtues
> Is a field of blessings for the world,
> Appropriately enlightening with knowledge:
> The spirit Power understands this.

> Sentient beings are veiled by ignorance,
> Wandering on dangerous paths;
> The Buddha emanates light for them:
> Spotless Light realizes this.

Knowledge and wisdom have no bounds,
Appearing in every land,
With light illumining the world:
Sublime Sound sees Buddha here.

Buddha, to liberate beings,
Cultivates practices everywhere;
This grandiose will
Universal Manifestation can observe.

Furthermore, the wind spirit Unimpended Light found the door of liberation entering into all the Buddha teachings and all worlds. The wind spirit Everywhere Manifesting Courageous Action found the door of liberation providing extensive offerings to all the Buddhas appearing in innumerable lands. The wind spirit Wind Striking Cloud Banner found the door of liberation eliminating the sickness of all sentient beings with a fragrant wind. The wind spirit Arrays of Pure Light found the door of liberation producing roots of goodness in all sentient beings and causing them to pulverize the mountains of multiple barriers. The wind spirit Power to Dry Up Water found the door of liberation able to defeat boundless armies of malicious demons. The wind spirit Great Voice Howling Everywhere found the door of liberation annihilating the fears of all sentient beings. The wind spirit Tree Branch Hanging Topknot found the door of liberation of the ocean of powers of elucidation, entering into the real character of all things. The wind spirit Going Everywhere Unimpeded found the door of liberation of the treasury of techniques to harmonize and civilize all sentient beings. The wind spirit Various Mansions found the door of liberation entering into still, serene meditative poise and destroying the extremely deep darkness of folly and ignorance. The wind spirit Great Light Shining Everywhere found the door of liberation of unhindered power to go along with all sentient beings.

At that time the wind spirit Unimpeded Light, imbued with the power of the Buddha, looked over all the wind spirits and said in verse,

The teachings of all Buddhas are most profound,
With unhindered means by which all may enter,
Appearing always in all worlds,
Signless, formless, without image.

Observe how the Buddha in the past
Gave offerings to endless Buddhas in a single instant—
Such bold enlightenment practice
Everywhere Manifesting can comprehend.

Buddha saves the world inconceivably;
None of his methods are used in vain—
All cause action to be free from distress:
This is the liberation of Cloud Banner.

Beings have no blessings, they suffer many pains,
With heavy veils and dense barriers always deluding them.
Buddha makes them all attain liberation:
This is known to Pure Light.

The Buddha's vast mystic power
Conquers all armies of demons;
All his methods of subduing
Healthy Power is able to observe.

Buddha emanates subtle sound from his pores
Which extends everywhere throughout the world
Causing all misery and fear to end:
This is understood by Howling Everywhere.

Buddha, in all oceans of lands,
Always preaches, over unthinkable eons.
This wonderful elucidation power of buddhahood
Tree Branch Topknot can comprehend.

Buddha's knowledge enters all avenues of means,
Completely free of hindrance therein—
His realm is boundless and without any equal:
This is the liberation of Going Everywhere.

The Buddha's state is without bounds—
By expedient means he shows it everywhere,
Yet his body is tranquil and has no form:
This is the liberation door of Various Mansions.

The Buddha cultivated practices for oceans of eons
And has completely fulfilled all powers
And can respond to beings in accord with worldly norms:
This is the view of Shining Everywhere.

Furthermore, the fire spirit Repository of Flames of Universal Light found the door of liberation removing the darkness of all worlds. The fire spirit Banner of Universal Assembly of Light found the door of liberation able to end all sentient beings' delusions, wanderings, and pains of irritating afflictions. The fire spirit Great Light Shining Everywhere found the door of liberation of the treasury of great compassion with the immutable power of enriching. The fire spirit Topknot of Inexhaustible Light found the door of liberation of light beams illuminating the boundless reaches of space. The fire spirit Eyes of Various Flames found the door of liberation of silent, serene lights in various magnificent arrays. The fire spirit Palace of Wonders found the door of liberation observing the Buddha's spiritual powers appearing without bound. The fire spirit Palaces in All Directions Like Polar Mountains found the door of liberation able to extinguish the blazing torments of all beings in all worlds. The fire spirit Sovereign of Awesome Light found the door of liberation able to freely enlighten all beings. The fire spirit Light Shining in All Directions found the door of liberation destroying forever all ignorant, attached opinions. The fire spirit Thunder and Lightning found the door of liberation of the great roar of power to fulfill all undertakings.

At that time, the fire spirit Repository of Flames of Universal Light, imbued with power from the Buddha, looked over all the fire spirits and said in verse,

> Observe the Buddhas' power of energy—
> For vast, inconceivable millions of eons
> They have appeared in the world to help sentient beings,
> Causing all barriers of darkness to be destroyed.

> Sentient beings, in their folly, create various views;
> Their passions are like torrents, like fires blazing;
> The Guide's techniques remove them all:
> Banner of Universal Assembly of Light understands this.

> Blessings and virtues like space, unending—
> No bounds to them can ever be found;
> This is the Buddha's immutable power of compassion:
> Light Shining, realizing this, conceives great joy.

> I observe the Buddha's practices
> Over the eons, without bound,
> Thus manifesting spiritual powers:
> Palace of Wonders understands this.

> Practice perfected over billions of eons, inconceivable,
> To which no one can find any bound or limit,
> Buddha expounds the real character of things, causing joy:
> This is perceived by Inexhaustible Light.

> All the vast masses in the ten directions
> Behold the Buddha present before them,

The tranquil light clearly lighting the world:
This Subtle Flames can comprehend.

The Sage appears in all worlds,
Sitting in all their palaces,
Raining the boundless great teaching:
This is the perspective of All Directions.

The Buddhas' wisdom is most profound;
Free in all ways, they appear in the world,
Able to clarify all genuine truths:
Awesome Light, realizing this, rejoices at heart.

The folly of views is a dark veil;
Beings, deluded, eternally wander;
For them Buddha opens the gate of sublime teaching:
Illumining All Quarters can understand this.

The gate of Buddhas' vows is vast, inconceivable—
Their powers and transcendent ways are developed and purified;
All appear in the world according to their ancient vows:
This is what Thunder and Lightning understands.

Furthermore, the water spirit Ubiquitous Cloud Banner realized the door of liberation of compassion equally benefiting all beings. The water spirit Cloudlike Sound of the Ocean Tide found the door of liberation adorned with boundless truths. The water spirit Beautiful Round Top-knot found the door of liberation observing those who could be taught and dealing with them with appropriate techniques. The water spirit Whirlpool of Skills found the door of liberation everywhere expounding the most profound realm of the Buddhas. The water spirit Store of Undefiled Fragrance found the door of liberation everywhere manifesting pure, bright light. The water spirit Virtue Bridge Light Sound found the signless, essenceless door of liberation of the pure realm of truth. The water spirit Freedom of Contentment found the door of liberation of the inexhaustible ocean of great compassion. The water spirit Good Sound of Pure Joy found the door of liberation being a mine of great joy among the hosts of enlightening beings at sites of enlightenment. The water spirit Everywhere Manifesting Awesome Light found the door of liberation appearing everywhere by means of the unimpeded, immensely vast power of virtue. The water spirit Roaring Sound Filling the Sea found the door of liberation observing all sentient beings and producing infinite techniques for harmonizing and pacifying them.

At that time the water spirit Ubiquitous Cloud Banner, imbued with power from the Buddha, looked over all the water spirits and said,

Gates of pure compassion, as many as atoms in all lands,
Together produce a single sublime feature of the Buddha.
Other features also are each like this:
Therefore beholders of Buddha never become jaded.

When the Buddha cultivated practice in the past,
He went to visit all of the Buddhas,
Cultivating himself in various ways, never lax:
These methods Cloud Sound enters.

The Buddha, in all ten directions,
Is still, unmoving, not coming or going,
Yet teaches beings appropriately, causing them all to see:
This is what Round Topknot knows.

The realm of the Buddha is boundless, immeasurable—
All sentient beings cannot comprehend it.
The preaching of his wondrous voice fills all directions:
This is Technique Whirlpool's sphere.

The light of the Buddha has no end;
It fills the cosmos, inconceivably,
Teaching, edifying, liberating beings:
This Pure Fragrance watches and sees.

The Buddha is pure as space,
Signless, formless, present everywhere,
Yet causing all beings to see:
This Light of Blessings well observes.

Of old Buddha practiced great compassion,
His mind is broad as all of life.
Therefore he is like a cloud appearing in the world:
This liberation Contentment knows.

All lands in the ten directions
See the Buddha sitting on his seat
Becoming clearly enlightened with great realization:
This is where Joyful Sound enters in.

Buddha's sphere of action is free from hindrance—
He goes to all lands in the ten directions,

Everywhere showing great mystic powers:
Manifesting Awesome Light has realized this.

He cultivates boundless expedient practices,
Equal to the worlds of sentient beings, filling them all,
The subtle action of his mystic power never ceasing:
Roaring Sound Filling the Sea can enter this.

Furthermore, the ocean spirit Producing Jewel Light found the door of liberation impartially bestowing an ocean of blessings on all beings. The ocean spirit Unbreakable Diamond Banner found the door of liberation preserving the good roots of all sentient beings by skillful means. The ocean spirit Undefiled found the door of liberation able to evaporate the ocean of all sentient beings' afflictions. The ocean spirit Always Dwelling in the Waves found the door of liberation causing all sentient beings to depart from evil ways. The ocean spirit Auspicious Jewel Moon found the door of liberation everywhere destroying the darkness of great ignorance. The ocean spirit Beautiful Flower Dragon Topknot found the door of liberation extinguishing the sufferings of all states of being and bestowing peace and happiness. The ocean spirit Everywhere Holding the Flavor of Light found the door of liberation purifying all sentient beings of their opinionated, ignorant nature. The ocean spirit Jewel Flame Flower Light found the door of liberation producing the will of enlightenment which is the source of all nobility. The ocean spirit Beautiful Diamond Topknot found the door of liberation of the ocean of virtues of the unshakable mind. The ocean spirit Thunder of the Ocean Tide found the door of liberation entering everywhere into absorption in the cosmos of reality.

At that time, the ocean spirit Producing Jewel Light, imbued with power from the Buddha, looked over all the ocean spirits and spoke these verses,

Over an ocean of inconceivably vast eons
He made offerings to all the Buddhas,
Distributing the merit to all living beings—
That is why his dignity is beyond compare.

Appearing in all worlds,
Knowing the capacities and desires of all beings,
Buddha expounds for them the ocean of truths:
This is joyfully realized by Indestructible Banner.

All sentient beings are shrouded by afflictions,
Roaming in all conditions, subject to all miseries—

For them he reveals the state of buddhahood:
Palace in All Waters enters this door.

Buddha, in unthinkable oceans of eons,
Cultivated all practices endlessly,
Forever cutting the net of beings' confusion:
Jewel Moon can clearly enter this.

Buddha sees beings always afraid,
Whirling in the ocean of birth and death;
He shows them the Buddha's unexcelled Way:
Dragon Topknot, comprehending, gives rise to joy.

The realm of the Buddhas cannot be conceived—
It is equal to the cosmos and space—
It can clear away beings' net of delusion:
This Flower Holding is able to expound.

The Buddha-eye is pure and inconceivable:
Comprehensively viewing all things,
He points out to all the excellent paths:
This Flower Light understands.

The army of demons, huge, uncountable,
He destroys in the space of an instant,
His mind undisturbed, unfathomable:
This is Diamond Topknot's technique.

Speaking a wondrous sound in the ten directions,
That sound pervades the entire universe—
Such is the Buddha's meditation state:
This is the realm of Ocean Tide Thunder.

Futhermore, the river spirit Everywhere Producing Swift Currents
found the door of liberation everywhere raining the boundless rain of
truth. The river spirit Universally Purifying Springs and Streams found
the door of liberation appearing before all sentient beings and causing
them to be forever free from afflictions. The river spirit Dustfree Pure
Eye found the door of liberation by compassion and appropriate techniques washing away the dust of delusions from all sentient beings. The
river spirit Roaring Everywhere found the door of liberation constantly
producing sounds beneficial to all sentient beings. The river spirit
Rescuing Sentient Beings Everywhere found the door of liberation
always being nonmalevolent and kind toward all sentient beings. The
river spirit Heatless Pure Light found the door of liberation showing all

pure and cool roots of goodness. The river spirit Universally Causing Joy found the door of liberation cultivating complete generosity, causing all sentient beings to forever give up stinginess and attachment. The river spirit Supreme Banner of Extensive Virtue found the door of liberation being a field of blessings giving joy to all. The river spirit Light Shining on All Worlds found the door of liberation able to cause all defiled beings to be pure, and all those poisoned with anger to become joyful. The river spirit Light of Oceanic Virtues found the door of liberation able to cause all sentient beings to enter the ocean of liberation and always experience complete bliss.

At that time the river spirit Everywhere Producing Swift Currents, imbued with power from the Buddha, looked over all the river spirits and spoke in verse,

> Of old the Buddha, for the sake of all beings,
> Cultivated boundless practices of the ocean of truths;
> Like refreshing rain clearing blazing heat,
> He extinguishes the heat of beings' afflictions.

> Buddha, in uncountable past eons,
> Purified the world with the light of his vows,
> Causing the mature to realize enlightenment:
> This is the realization of Universal Purifier.

> With compassion and methods numerous as beings
> He appears before all, always guiding,
> Clearing away the dirt of afflictions:
> Pure Eyes, seeing this, rejoices profoundly.

> Buddhas speak of wondrous sound, causing all to hear—
> Sentient beings, delighted, have hearts full of joy,
> Causing them to wash away innumerable pains:
> This is the liberation of Everywhere Roaring.

> The Buddha cultivated enlightenment practice
> To aid sentient beings for innumerable ages—
> Therefore his light fills the world:
> The spirit Guardian, remembering, is happy.

> Buddha cultivated practices for the sake of beings,
> By various means making them mature,
> Purifying the ocean of blessings, removing all pains:
> Heatless, seeing this, rejoices at heart.

> The gate of generosity is inexhaustible,
> Benefiting all sentient beings,

Causing witnesses to have no attachment:
This is the enlightenment of Universal Joy.

Buddha cultivated genuine methods of enlightenment,
Developing a boundless ocean of virtues,
Causing witnesses all to rejoice:
This Supreme Banner happily realizes.

He clears away the defilements of beings,
Equally compassionate even to the vicious,
Therefore acquiring radiance filling all space:
Light Shining on All Worlds sees and rejoices.

Buddha is the field of blessings, ocean of virtues,
Able to cause all to abandon evil
And even fulfill great enlightenment:
This is the liberation of Ocean Light.

Furthermore, the crop spirit Gentle Superb Flavor found the door of liberation bestowing rich flavor on all sentient beings, causing them to develop a buddha-body. The crop spirit Pure Light of Seasonal Flowers found the door of liberation able to cause all sentient beings to experience great joy and happiness. The crop spirit Physical Strength Courage and Health found the door of liberation purifying all realms by means of all round, complete teachings. The crop spirit Increasing Vitality found the door of liberation seeing the boundless mystical powers compassionately used by the Buddha for edifying demonstrations. The crop spirit Everywhere Producing Roots and Fruits found the door of liberation everywhere revealing the Buddha's field of blessings and causing seeds planted there not to spoil. The crop spirit Wonderfully Adorned Circular Topknot found the door of liberation causing the flower of pure faith of sentient beings everywhere to bloom. The crop spirit Moistening Pure Flowers found the door of liberation compassionately saving sentient beings and causing them to increase in blessings and virtue. The crop spirit Developing Wonderful Fragrance found the door of liberation extensively demonstrating all methods of enlightening practice. The crop spirit Liked by All Who See found the door of liberation able to cause all sentient beings in the universe to abandon such ills as sloth and anxiety and to become pure in all ways. The crop spirit Pure Light found the door of liberation observing the good roots of all sentient beings, explaining the truth to them in appropriate ways, bringing joy and fulfillment to the masses.

At that time the crop spirit Gentle Superb Flavor, imbued with power from the Buddha, looked over all the crop spirits and said,

The Buddha's ocean of unexcelled virtues
Manifests a lamp which illumines the world:
Saving and protecting all sentient beings,
He gives them all peace, not leaving out one.

The Buddha's virtues are boundless—
No beings hear of them in vain—
He causes them to be free from suffering and always happy:
This is what Seasonal Flowers enters into.

The powers of the Buddha are all complete—
His array of virtues appears in the world
And all sentient beings are harmonized:
To this fact Courageous Power can witness.

The Buddha cultivated an ocean of compassion,
His heart always as broad as the whole world;
Therefore his spiritual powers are boundless:
Increasing Vitality can see this.

Buddha always appears throughout the world;
None of his methods are employed in vain,
Clearing away beings' delusions and torments:
This is the liberation of Universal Producer.

Buddha is the great ocean of knowledge in the world,
Emanating pure light which reaches everywhere,
Whence is born all great faith and resolution:
Thus can Adorned Topknot clearly enter.

Buddha, observing the world, conceives kind compassion,
Appearing in order to aid sentient beings,
Showing them the supreme way of peace and joy:
This is the liberation of Pure Flowers.

The pure practices cultivated by Buddha
Are fully expounded under the tree of enlightenment,
Thus edifying everyone in all quarters:
This Wonderful Fragrance can hear.

Buddha, in all worlds,
Brings freedom from sorrow, creating great joy;
All potentials and aspirations he purifies:
The spirit Pleasing understands this.

The Buddha appears in the world,
Observes the inclinations of all beings,
And matures them by various means:
This is the liberation of Pure Light.

Furthermore, the herb spirit Auspicious found the door of liberation observing the mentalities of all sentient beings and striving to unify them. The herb spirit Sandalwood Forest found the door of liberation embracing all sentient beings with light and causing those who see it not to waste the experience. The herb spirit Pure Light found the door of liberation able to annihilate the afflictions of all sentient beings by pure techniques. The herb spirit Universal Renown found the door of liberation able to increase the boundless ocean of good roots by means of a great reputation. The herb spirit Radiant Pores found the door of liberation hurrying to all sites of illness with the banner of great compassion. The herb spirit Darkness Destroying Purifier found the door of liberation able to cure all blind sentient beings and cause their eye of wisdom to be clear. The herb spirit Roarer found the door of liberation able to expound the verbal teaching of the Buddha explaining the different meanings of all things. The herb spirit Banner of Light Outshining the Sun found the door of liberation able to be the advisor of all sentient beings, causing all who see to produce roots of goodness. The herb spirit Seeing in All Directions found the door of liberation of the mine of pure compassion able to make beings give rise to faith and resolve by means of appropriate techniques. The herb spirit Everywhere Emanating Majestic Light found the door of liberation causing beings to remember Buddha, thereby eliminating their sicknesses.

At that time the herb spirit Auspicious, imbued with power from the Buddha, looked over all the herb spirits and said,

The Buddha's knowledge is inconceivable—
He knows the minds of all sentient beings,
And by the power of various techniques
Destroys their delusions and infinite pains.

The Great Hero's skills cannot be measured;
Nothing he does is ever in vain,
Unfailingly causing the suffering of beings to vanish:
Sandalwood Forest can understand this.

Observe the Buddha's teaching like so:
He practiced for innumerable eons
And has no attachment to anything:
This is the entry of Pure Light.

A Buddha is hard to meet, in a million ages;
If any can see one or hear one's name,
It will unfailingly bring benefit:
This is the understanding of Universal Renown.

Each of the Buddha's hair pores
Emits light annulling distress,
Causing wordly afflictions to end:
This is the entry of Radiant Pores.

All sentient beings are blinded by ignorance,
With an infinite variety of miseries from deluded acts—
Buddha clears it all away and opens the radiance of wisdom:
This Darkness Breaker can see.

One tone of the Buddha has no limiting measure—
It can open up the ocean of all teachings
So that all who hear can comprehend:
This is the liberation of Great Sound.

See how Buddha's knowledge is inconceivable—
Appearing in all realms he saves beings there,
Able to make those who see follow his teaching:
This Outshining the Sun deeply understands.

Buddha's ocean of compassionate means
Is produced to help the world,
Opening the right path wide to show beings:
This Seeing in All Directions can comprehend.

Buddha emits great light all around
Illumining all in the ten directions,
Causing virtue to grow as the Buddha's remembered:
This is the liberation door of Majestic Light.

Furthermore, the forest spirit Spreading Flowers like Clouds found the door of liberation of the repository of the vast, boundless sea of knowledge. The forest spirit Outstanding Trunk Unfolding Light found the door of liberation of great cultivation and universal purification. The forest spirit Bearing Branches Emitting Radiant Light found the door of liberation increasing the growth of all sorts of sprouts of pure faith. The forest spirit Auspicious Pure Leaves found the door of liberation arrayed with all pure virtues. The forest spirit Draped Flame Treasury found the door of liberation of universal wisdom always viewing the entire cosmos. The forest spirit Pure Arrays of Light found the door of liberation knowing the ocean of all sentient beings' activities and producing and spreading clouds of teaching. The forest spirit Pleasant Thunder found the door of liberation enduring all unpleasant sounds and producing pure sounds. The forest spirit Light and Fragrance All-Pervading found the door of liberation showing the vast realm of practices cultivated and mastered in the past. The forest spirit Subtle Light Shining Far found the door of liberation benefiting the world by means of all virtuous qualities. The forest spirit Flowers and Fruits Savoring of Light found the door of liberation able to cause all to see the Buddha appearing in the world, to always remember with respect and never forget, and adorn the mine of virtues.

At that time the forest spirit Spreading Flowers like Clouds, imbued with power from the Buddha, looked over all the forest spirits and said,

> In the past Buddha cultivated enlightening practices;
> His virtue and wisdom are thoroughly complete,
> He has all powers fully in command—
> Emitting great light, he appears in the world.
>
> The aspects of his compassion are as infinite as beings—
> Buddha purified them all in eons past,
> And therefore is able to bring aid to the world:
> This is the understanding of Outstanding Trunk.
>
> Once sentient beings see the Buddha,
> He'll plunge them into the ocean of faith,
> Showing to all the enlightening way:
> This is the liberation of Wonderful Branches.
>
> The virtues amassed in a single pore
> Could not be all told of in an ocean of eons—
> The Buddha's techniques are inconceivable:
> Pure Leaves can understand this teaching.
>
> I recall the Buddha in the past
> Made offerings to infinite numbers of Buddhas,
> His knowledge gradually becoming clearer with each:
> This is what Store of Flames understands.
>
> The ocean of actions of all sentient beings
> The Buddha knows in an instant of thought;
> Such vast unhindered knowledge
> Beautiful Adornments can begin to realize.

Always intoning the Buddha's serene, sublime sound
Produces incomparable joy everywhere,
Causing all to awaken according to their understanding and
    inclination:
This is the principle of Thunder Sound's practice.

The Buddha shows great mystic powers
All throughout the ten directions,
Causing all his past deeds to be seen:
This is where All-Pervading Light and Fragrance enters.

Sentient beings are dishonest and don't practice virtue—
Lost and deluded, they sink and flow in birth and death;
For them he clearly opens the paths of knowledge:
This is seen by Subtle Light.

Buddha, for the sake of beings blocked by habits,
Appears in the world after millions of eons,
Causing them to see always for the rest of time:
This is observed by Savor of Light.

Furthermore, the mountain spirit Jewel Peak Blooming Flowers found
the door of liberation entering the light of absorption in great quiescence.
The mountain spirit Flower Forest Topknot found the door of liberation cultivating and collecting good roots of kindness and developing
an inconceivable number of beings to maturity. The mountain spirit
Lofty Banner Shining Everywhere found the door of liberation looking
into the inclinations of all sentient beings and purifying their senses. The
mountain spirit Undefiled Jewel Topknot found the door of liberation
of boundless eons of diligent striving without becoming weary or
remiss. The mountain spirit Light Illumining All Directions found the
door of liberation awakening all with lights of infinite qualities. The
mountain spirit Light of Great Power found the door of liberation of
capability of self-development and causing sentient beings to give up
deluded behavior. The mountain spirit Awesome Light Conquering All
found the door of liberation removing all pains so that none are left. The
mountain spirit Light-Orb of Subtle Intensity found the door of liberation
spreading the light of the teachings, showing the virtues of all Buddhas.
The mountain spirit Universal Eye Clearly Seeing found the door of
liberation causing all sentient beings to make their roots of goodness
grow even in dreams. The mountain spirit Adamantine Eye of Mystery
found the door of liberation bringing forth a great ocean of meaning.
   At that time, the mountain spirit Blooming Flowers All Over the
Earth, imbued with power from the Buddha, surveyed all the hosts of
mountain spirits and said in verse,

Having cultivated excellent practices without bound,
Now he has attained mystic powers, also infinite.
His gates of teaching are wide open, numerous as atoms,
Causing all sentient beings to deeply understand and rejoice.

His body, adorned in many ways, is omnipresent,
The lights from his pores are all pure;
With compassionate techniques he teaches all:
Flower Forest Topknot understands this.

The Buddha-body appears everywhere—it's boundless,
Filling all worlds in the ten directions,
All faculties pure, a joy to all beholders:
This truth High Banner can understand.

For eons practicing diligently without flagging,
Unaffected by worldly things, like empty space,
By various means he edifies beings:
Realizing this is Jewel Topknot.

Sentient beings blindly enter dangerous paths;
Pitying them, Buddha emits shining light,
Causing all beings thereby to awake:
Awesome Light, understanding this, rejoices.

Extensively cultivating practices in all states of being,
He made offerings to innumerable Buddhas,
Causing beings who saw to make great vows:
This Great Power can clearly enter.

Seeing beings' sufferings in transmigration,
Always enshrouded by barriers of doing,
He extinguishes all with the light of wisdom:
This is the liberation of Conquering All.

Each of his pores emits subtle sound
Praising the Buddhas in accord with beings' mentalities,
Pervading all quarters, for uncounted ages:
This is the door by which Light Orb has entered.

Buddha appears throughout the ten directions
Expounding the subtle truth by various means,
With an ocean of practices aiding all beings:
This is what Clearly Seeing has understood.

> The gates of the teaching are boundless as the sea—
> He expounds it with one voice, making all understand,
> Preaching forever, with never an end:
> Delving into this technique is Diamond Eye.

Furthermore, the earth spirit Pure Flower of Universal Virtue found the door of liberation constantly watching all sentient beings with an attitude of kindness and compassion. The earth spirit Adornment of Stable Blessings found the door of liberation manifesting the power of blessings and virtues of all sentient beings. The earth spirit Beautiful Flower Adorned Tree found the door of liberation entering into all things and producing adornment for all buddha-fields. The earth spirit Universal Distribution of Treasures found the door of liberation cultivating and producing various states of meditation and causing sentient beings to get rid of obstructing defilements. The earth spirit Pure Eye Observing the Season found the door of liberation causing all sentient beings to sport happily. The earth spirit Beautiful Golden Eyes found the door of liberation manifesting all pure bodies and harmonizing sentient beings. The earth spirit Fragrant Hair Emitting Light found the door of liberation of great power comprehending the ocean of virtues of all Buddhas. The earth spirit Silent Pleasing Sound found the door of liberation holding the ocean of speech-sounds of all sentient beings. The earth spirit Curled Topknot of Beautiful Flowers found the door of liberation of the undefiled nature pervading all Buddha-fields. The earth spirit Indestructible All-Sustainer found the door of liberation revealing all that is contained in the cycles of teaching of all Buddhas.

At that time, the earth spirit Pure Flower of Universal Virtue, imbued with power from the Buddha, looked over all the earth spirits and said,

> The doors of compassion opened by the Buddha
> In every moment of the past cannot be all told of;
> He cultivated such practice unceasingly,
> Therefore he has an indestructible body.

> The store of blessings of all
> Sentient beings in all times, as well as enlightening beings,
> All appear in the Buddha's pores:
> Adornment of Blessings, seeing this, rejoices.

> His vast state of serene absorption
> Is unborn, imperishable, has no coming or going;
> Yet he purifies lands to show sentient beings:
> This is the liberation of Flowered Tree.

Buddha cultivated various practices
To make sentient beings dissolve all barriers;
Universal Distributor of Treasure
Sees this liberation and rejoices.

The sphere of the Buddha is boundless—
He appears every moment throughout the world:
Observing the Season with Pure Eyes,
Seeing Buddha's realm of action, is joyful.

His sublime voice is limitless and inconceivable—
He destroys afflictions for all sentient beings:
Diamond Eye can realize this,
Seeing Buddha's boundless supreme virtues.

He appears in disguise in all kinds of forms,
All throughout the universe:
Fragrant Hair Emitting Light always sees Buddha,
Thus teaching all sentient beings.

His sublime voice extends everywhere,
Explaining for beings for infinite eons:
Pleasing Sound earth spirit comprehends this,
And, hearing it from the Buddha, is reverently joyful.

Buddha's pores emit clouds of fragrant flames
Filling the world according to the mentalities of beings;
All who see this develop maturity:
This is what Flower Swirl observes.

Stable and unbreakable as diamond,
More unshakable than the polar mountain,
The Buddha's body is in the world this way:
All-Sustainer, able to see, gives rise to joy.

Furthermore, the city spirit Jewel Peak Radiance found the door of liberation benefiting sentient beings by appropriate means. The city spirit Beautifully Adorned Palace found the door of liberation knowing the faculties of sentient beings and teaching and maturing them. The city spirit Jewel of Pure Joy found the door of liberation always joyfully causing all sentient beings to receive various blessings. The city spirit Sorrowless Purity found the door of liberation of the mine of great compassion saving those in fear. The city spirit Flower Lamp Flame Eyes found the door of liberation of universally clear great wisdom and knowledge. The city spirit Flame Banner Clearly Showing found the door of liberation appearing everywhere with appropriate means. The city spirit Light of Virtue found the door of liberation observing all sentient beings and causing them to cultivate the vast ocean of virtue. The city spirit Body of Pure Light found the door of liberation awakening all sentient beings from the darkness of ignorance. The city spirit Eyes of Light of a Mountain of Jewels found the door of liberation able to pulverize the mountains of obstructions hindering sentient beings, by means of a great light.

At that time the city spirit Jewel Peak Radiance, imbued with power from the Buddha, surveyed all the hosts of city spirits and said in verse,

> The Guide is so inconceivable,
> With light illumining the ten directions:
> All sentient beings see Buddha before them,
> Teaching and developing countless numbers.

> The faculties of sentient beings are each different;
> The Buddha knows them all.
> The spirit Beautifully Adorned Palaces
> Enters this gate of teaching with joy.

> The Buddha cultivated practices for boundless eons,
> Maintaining the teachings of the Buddhas of past ages,
> His mind always happily accepting them:
> Jewel of Joy realizes this way.

> Buddha in the past was already able to remove
> The fears of all sentient beings
> And always exercise kindness and compassion toward them:
> This the spirit Sorrowless comprehends with joy.

> Buddha's knowledge is vast and boundless;
> Like space, it cannot be measured.
> Flower Eyes, realizing this, is pleased:
> He can study the Buddha's ineffable wisdom.

> The Buddha's physical forms are equal to sentient beings—
> He causes them to see him according to their inclinations;
> Flame Banner Clearly Showing understands this in his heart
> And practices this technique, producing joy.

> Buddha cultivated an ocean of myriad blessings—
> Pure, vast, without any bounds:
> Light of Virtue Banner, taking this approach,
> Contemplates, comprehends, and is happy in mind.

Sentient beings ignorantly wander through various states of
  existence;
Like people born blind, after all they cannot see.
Buddha appears in the world to help them:
Pure Light enters this door.

The Buddha's powers are boundless,
Like clouds covering all the world;
He appears even in dreams to teach:
This is what Fragrant Banner perceives.

Sentient beings are foolish and ignorant, as though blind and deaf,
They are shrouded by all kinds of obstructing veils;
Buddha's light penetrates them, making them open up:
Such is the entry way of Mountain of Jewels.

Furthermore, the sanctuary spirit Banner of Pure Adornments found
the door of liberation of the power of commitment to produce vast
adornments to offer to the Buddha. The sanctuary spirit Polar Mountain Jewel Light found the door of liberation appearing before all
sentient beings perfecting the practice of great enlightenment. The
sanctuary spirit Sign of the Thunder found the door of liberation
causing all sentient beings to see the Buddha in dreams teaching them
according to their mentalities and inclinations. The sanctuary spirit
Wonderful Eyes Raining Flowers found the door of liberation able to
rain all precious adornments that are hard to part with. The sanctuary
spirit Form of Pure Flowers found the door of liberation able to
manifest beautifully adorned sanctuaries, teach many beings, and cause
them to develop to maturity. The sanctuary spirit Garland Light Topknot found the door of liberation teaching the truth according to
beings' faculties, causing them to develop right awareness. The sanctuary spirit Raining Jewel Arrays found the door of liberation able to
eloquently rain everywhere boundless joyous truths. The sanctuary
spirit Courageous Fragrant Eye found the door of liberation extensively
praising the virtues of the Buddhas. The sanctuary spirit Diamond
Colored Cloud found the door of liberation causing arrays of trees of
boundless colors and forms to appear. The sanctuary spirit Lotus Light
found the door of liberation being still and unmoving under the tree of
enlightenment yet being present everywhere. The sanctuary spirit Radiance of Ineffable Light found the door of liberation demonstrating the
various powers of a Buddha.

At that time the sanctuary spirit Banner of Pure Adornments, imbued
with power from the Buddha, looked over all the sanctuary spirits and
said,

I recall the Buddha in former times,
The practices he performed for countless eons,
Making offerings to all the Buddhas who appeared—
So he has virtues vast as all space.

The Buddha practiced unlimited generosity
In infinite lands, numerous as all atoms;
Thinking of the well-faring Buddha,
Polar Mountain Light's heart is glad.

The physical forms of Buddha have no end;
His transformations pervade all lands,
Always appearing, even in dreams:
Thunder Banner, seeing this, gives rise to joy.

He practiced relinquishment for countless ages,
Able to give up eyes, hard to part with, enough to fill a sea—
This practice of relinquishment was for the sake of all beings:
This Wonderful Eyes happily understands.

Boundless forms, like blazing clouds of jewels,
Appear in sanctuaries throughout the world:
The spirit Form of Pure Flames rejoices
Upon seeing the mystical power of Buddha.

The ocean of sentient beings' activities is shoreless;
The Buddha fills it with the rain of truth,
Removing doubt and confusion according to potential:
Flower Garland, realizing this, is pleased.

The different meanings of innumerable teachings
Are delved into by his oceanic eloquence:
The spirit Raining Precious Adornments
Is always thus in mind.

In unspeakably many lands
He praised the Buddhas in all languages,
And therefore has great fame and virtue:
Courageous Eye can keep this in mind.

Infinite trees of various forms
Appear beneath the king, tree of enlightenment:
Diamond Colored Cloud realizes this,
And always watches the tree with delight.

Bounds to the ten directions cannot be found—
Likewise the knowledge of Buddha on the site of enlightenment:

Lotus Light's pure mind of faith
Enters this liberation and profoundly rejoices.

Everything at the site of enlightenment produces exquisite sound
Extolling the pure, inconceivable powers of the Buddha
As well as the perfected causal practices:
This can be heard by Ineffable Light.

Furthermore, the footstep-following spirit Precious Symbol found the door of liberation raining jewels all over, producing bountiful joy. The footstep-following spirit Lotus Light found the door of liberation showing the Buddha seated on a lotus throne of lights of all colors, causing delight to those who see. The footstep-following spirit Supreme Flower Topknot found the door of liberation setting up the sanctuaries and assemblies of all Buddhas in every moment of thought. The footstep-following spirit Embodying All Beautiful Visions found the door of liberation pacifying and harmonizing countless sentient beings at every step. The footstep-following spirit Exquisite Gem Star Banner found the door of liberation in every moment of thought magically producing various lotus-like webs of light, everywhere raining showers of jewels producing marvelous sounds. The footstep-following spirit Joyfully Uttering Sublime Sounds found the door of liberation producing boundless oceans of joy. The footstep-following spirit Sandalwood Tree Light found the door of liberation awakening the assemblies at all sites of enlightenment with a fragrant breeze. The footstep-following spirit Lotus Light found the door of liberation emanating light from every pore intoning the subtle sounds of truth. The footstep-following spirit Subtle Light found the door of liberation producing from the body webs of various lights illumining everywhere. The footstep-following spirit Collection of Fine Flowers found the door of liberation enlightening all beings and causing them to develop oceans of virtues.

At that time the footstep-following spirit Precious Symbol, imbued with the Buddha's power, surveyed all the assembled footstep-following spirits and said in verse,

Buddha practiced for innumerable eons,
Making offerings to all the Buddhas,
His mind always joyful, never wearied,
His joy as deep and vast as the sea.

His spiritual powers, active every moment, are immeasurable—
He produces lotuses of various fragrances,
With Buddhas sitting on them, traveling all over:
Lotus Light sees it all.

The teaching of the Buddhas is *thus*:
The vast assemblies fill all directions;
They show mystic powers which can't be assessed:
This Supreme Flower clearly perceives.

In all places in the ten directions,
With every step he takes
He can develop all beings:
This Beautiful Visions understands.

He manifests bodies numerous as beings;
Each of these bodies fills the universe,
All shedding pure light and showering jewels:
This liberation Star Banner enters into.

The realm of the Buddha has no bounds;
He showers the rain of truth, filling all—
Seeing the Buddha, the masses rejoice:
This is what's seen by Sublime Sound.

The Buddha's voice is equal in extent to space—
All sounds and voices are contained therein;
It tames sentient beings, extending to all:
Thus can Sandalwood hear.

All his pores emit magical sounds
Extolling the names of Buddhas of all times;
All who hear these sounds are delighted:
Thus does Lotus Light see.

The disguised appearances of the Buddha are inconceivable—
His physical forms are like the ocean,
Causing all to see according to mentality:
This is what Suble Light apprehends.

Displaying great mystic powers everywhere,
He enlightens all beings:
Fine Flowers, seeing this truth,
Becomes joyful at heart.

Furthermore, the multiple-body spirit Realm of Pure Joy found the door of liberation remembering the ocean of Buddha's ancient vows. The multiple-body spirit Light Illumining All Directions found the door of liberation of light shining everywhere on boundless worlds. The multiple-body spirit Oceanic Sound Conquering found the door of liberation of a great sound awakening all beings and causing them to be happy and harmoniously tranquil. The multiple-body spirit Pure Flower Adorned Topknot found the door of liberation of a body like space, omnipresent. The multiple-body spirit Infinite Dignified Postures found the door of liberation showing all sentient beings the realm of the Buddhas. The multiple-body spirit Array of Supreme Light found the door of liberation causing all famished sentient beings to be physically healthy and strong. The multiple-body spirit Fragrant Clouds of Pure Light found the door of liberation clearing away all sentient beings' defiling afflictions. The multiple-body spirit Guardian Sustainer found the door of liberation overturning all sentient beings' ignorant, foolish, maniacal actions. The multiple-body spirit Ubiquitous Shepherd found the door of liberation manifesting adornments in the palaces of all world leaders. The multiple-body spirit Immutable Light found the door of liberation embracing all sentient beings and causing them to produce pure roots of goodness.

At that time the multiple-body spirit Realm of Pure Joy, empowered by the Buddha, looked over all the multiple-body spirits and said,

I remember, countless eons ago,
A Buddha, Sublime Light, appeared in the world;
This World Honored One, in the presence of that Buddha,
Vowed to attain enlightenment, and served all Buddhas.

Buddha's body emits great light,
Which fills the entire cosmos;
When beings encounter it, their minds are subdued:
This is seen by Illumining All Directions.

Buddha's voice makes all countries tremble;
Every sphere of sound
Awakes all beings without exception:
Conqueror, hearing, rejoices at heart.

The Buddha body is pure, ever calm,
Manifesting all forms, yet without any signs,
Abiding this way everywhere in the world:
This is the approach of Pure Flowers.

The Guide is so inconceivable,
Causing all to see according to their minds—
Sometimes sitting, or walking, or standing:
Infinite Dignified Postures understands this.

A Buddha is hard to meet even in a million eons—
He appears in the world to give help freely,
Causing beings to be free from the pains of destitution:
Here is where Supreme Light Array enters.

Each of the Buddha's teeth
Emits blazing clouds of light, as from a fragrant lamp
Destroying the illusions of all sentient beings:
Undefiled Clouds sees in this way.

Beings' attachments and delusions are multiple barriers—
They follow demons in their ways, always involved in routines;
Buddha shows them the way to liberation:
Guardian Sustainer can understand this.

I see the independent power of Buddha,
His light filling the universe;
In royal palaces he edifies beings:
This is the realm of the Ubiquitous One.

Beings are deluded, full of miseries—
Buddha is in their midst, always saving,
Causing delusions to vanish and joy to abound:
This is what's seen by Immutable Light.

Furthermore, the thunderbolt-bearing spirit Demigod of Wonderful Form found the door of liberation seeing the Buddha manifest a body of infinite physical forms. The thunderbolt-bearing spirit Banner of Swiftness of the Sun found the door of liberation of each hair of the buddha-body radiating clouds of various light beams, like the sun. The thunderbolt-bearing spirit Light of the Flowers of the Polar Mountain found the door of liberation of great mystic powers manifesting innumerable bodies. The thunderbolt-bearing spirit Pure Sound of Clouds found the door of liberation of infinite sounds corresponding to all species. The thunderbolt-bearing spirit Great-Armed God found the door of liberation appearing as the leader in all worlds and awakening sentient beings. The thunderbolt-bearing spirit Delightful Light found the door of liberation revealing all the different aspects of the Buddha's teachings. The thunderbolt-bearing spirit Sound of Thunder in Great Trees found the door of liberation bringing together all the tree spirits with delightful ornaments. The thunderbolt-bearing spirit Lion King Light found the door of liberation fulfilling and clearly understanding the Buddha's vast array of blessings. The thunderbolt-bearing spirit Auspicious Eye of Intense Flames found the door of liberation observing the minds of sentient beings on dangerous paths and manifesting a magnificently adorned body for them. The thunderbolt-bearing spirit Lotus Jewel Topknot found the door of liberation showering everywhere the jewel topknots adorning all enlightening beings.

At that time the thunderbolt-bearing spirit Demigod of Wonderful Form, empowered by the Buddha, said in verse,

> Observe the King of Truth—
> The teaching of the King of Truth is *thus*.
> His physical forms have no bounds,
> Manifesting throughout the world.
>
> Each of the Buddha's hairs
> Is an inconceivable act of light,
> Like the clear orb of the sun
> Illuminating all lands.
>
> The spiritual powers of the Buddha
> Pervade the entire cosmos—
> In the presence of all sentient beings,
> He manifests infinite bodies.
>
> The sound of the Buddha's teaching
> Is heard in all quarters;
> According to the type of being,
> He satisfies all their minds.
>
> The masses see the honored sage
> In the palace in the world
> For the sake of all the living
> Expounding the great teaching.
>
> In the whirlpool of the ocean of truth,
> With all kinds of different doctrines,
> Various appropriate techniques,
> He teaches without end.
>
> Those boundless great techniques
> Respond to all the lands;
> Those who meet the Buddha's light
> All see the Buddha-body.
>
> Having served all the Buddhas,
> Many as atoms in a billion lands,
> His virtue is as vast as space,
> Looked up to by all.

His mystical power is impartial,
Appearing in all lands;
While sitting at rest in the sublime enlightenment site
He appears before all sentient beings.

Blazing clouds illumining all
With various spheres of light
Extending throughout the universe,
Showing where the Buddha acts.

Furthermore, the enlightening being Universally Good entered into
the ocean of techniques of inconceivable doors of liberation, and entered into the ocean of virtues of the Buddha. That is to say, there was
a door of liberation called purifying all buddha-lands, pacifying the
sentient beings and causing them all to be ultimately emancipated.
There was a door of liberation called going to all realms of complete
virtues cultivated by all the Buddhas. There was a door of liberation
called the great ocean of vows defining the stages of all enlightening
beings. There was a door of liberation called everywhere manifesting
infinite bodies, numerous as atoms in the cosmos. There was a door of
liberation called explaining an inconceivable number of different names
throughout all lands. There was a door of liberation called showing all
the boundless realms of enlightening beings' psychic powers in all
atoms. There was a door of liberation named showing the events of the
formation and decay of the ages of past, present, and future, in the
space of an instant. There was a door of liberation named showing the
oceans of faculties of all enlightening beings, each entering their own
spheres. There was a door of liberation named ability to make various
bodies appear by mystic powers all throughout the boundless cosmos.
There was a door of liberation called showing the processes of all
enlightening beings' practices, entering into the great techniques of
universal knowledge.

At that time, the enlightening being Universally Good, by virtue of his
own accomplishment, and also receiving the spiritual power of the
Buddha, having looked over the ocean of all the assemblies, spoke these
verses,

The immense, vast fields adorned by the Buddha
Are equal in number to all atoms;
Pure children of Buddha fill them all,
Raining the inconceivable, most sublime teaching.

As in this assembly we see the Buddha sitting,
So it is also in every atom;

The Buddha-body has no coming or going,
And clearly appears in all the lands there are.

Demonstrating the practices cultivated by enlightening beings,
The various techniques of innumerable approaches to their stages,
Expounding as well the inconceivable truth,
He causes the Buddha-children to enter the realm of reality.

Producing phantom buddhas numerous as atoms,
Corresponding to the inclinations of all beings' minds,
The expedient doors into the profound realm of truth,
Boundlessly vast, all he expounds.

The Buddha's names are equal to the worlds,
Filling all lands in the ten directions;
None of his methods are employed in vain:
He tames sentient beings and purifies all.

The Buddha, in every atom,
Displays infinite great mystic powers—
Sitting in each on the enlightenment site,
He speaks of past Buddhas' enlightening deeds.

All immense eons of past, present, and future,
Buddha reveals in every instant—
All the events of their formation and decay
His inconceivable knowledge comprehends.

The congregation of Buddha's children is endlessly vast;
But though they try together to fathom Buddha's state,
The teachings of the Buddhas have no bounds—
To thoroughly know them all is most difficult.

Buddhas like space, without discrimination,
Equal to the real cosmos, with no resting place,
Phantom manifestations circulate everywhere,
All sitting on enlightenment sites attaining true awareness.

Buddha teaches widely, with wonderful voice—
All stages of enlightenment are thoroughly clear.
Appearing before each sentient being,
He gives all the Buddha's equal truth.

Furthermore, the enlightening being Sublime Light of Pure Virtue,
the great spiritual hero, found the door of liberation going to all

assemblies of enlightening beings in the ten directions and adorning the sites of enlightenment. The enlightening being Light of the Supreme Lamp of Universal Virtue found the door of liberation in a single instant showing endless entrances to attainment of true awakening, teaching and developing inconceivable worlds of sentient beings. The enlightening being Lion Banner of Universal Light found the door of liberation cultivating the enlightening beings' adornments of blessings and virtue, producing all buddha-lands. The enlightening being Subtle Light of Flames of Universal Jewels found the door of liberation observing the realms of the Buddha's mystic powers, without confusion. The enlightening being Banner of Oceans of Qualities of Universal Sounds found the door of liberation showing the adornments of all buddha-fields in one congregation at a site of enlightenment. The enlightening being Light of Universal Knowledge Illumining the Realm of Buddhahood found the door of liberation following the Buddha investigating the most profound and enormously vast matrix of the cosmos. The enlightening being Light of Inexhaustible Virtue of Universal Purity found the door of liberation entering into all mundane activities and producing the boundless practices of enlightening beings. The enlightening being Universal Supreme Light found the door of liberation able to manifest the spheres of all Buddhas within the formless realm of truth.

At that time the enlightening being Sublime Light of Pure Virtue, the spiritual hero, empowered by the Buddha, looked over the ocean of liberation doors of all the enlightening beings and said in verse,

> All lands there be in the ten directions
> Are beautified and purified, all in an instant,
> By the sublime voice turning the wheel of truth
> Throughout the world, without an equal.
>
> The realm of the Buddha has no bounds—
> In an instant the cosmos is filled;
> In every atom he sets up an enlightenment site,
> Proving enlightenment in all, creating mystic displays.
>
> Buddha cultivated practices in the past
> Extending through countless eons
> Adorning all buddha-fields,
> Appearing unhindered, like space.
>
> The Buddha's spiritual powers are unlimited,
> Filling the boundless reaches of all time—
> Even if one spent countless eons constantly
> Observing, one would never be wearied or jaded.

Observe the realms of Buddha's mystic power—
All lands in all quarters are beautifully pure:
He appears therein, in every one,
Instantaneously changing, in infinite forms.

If you observe the Buddha for countless ages
You won't apprehend even the extent of one hair—
The Buddha's boundless doors of techniques
Illumine inconceivably many fields.

Buddha, in past ages in the world,
Served an infinite ocean of Buddhas;
Therefore all beings are like river rapids
Coming to make offerings to the World Honored One.

The Buddha appears everywhere,
In infinite lands in each atom,
The realms therein being all infinite too;
In all he abides for endless eons.

Buddha of yore for the sake of all beings
Cultivated an ocean of boundless compassion,
Entering birth and death along with all beings,
Teaching the masses, making them pure.

Buddhas abide in the matrix of the cosmos of real thusness—
Signless, formless, free from all taints.
When beings observe Buddha's various bodies,
All their troubles and pains then dissolve.

Furthermore, the enlightening being Great Brilliance of the Moon Reflected in the Ocean, the great spiritual hero, found the door of liberation producing the means of transcendence pertaining to each stage of enlightenment, thereby edifying sentient beings and purifying all buddha-lands. The enlightening being Undefiled Treasury of Light of Oceans of Cloudlike Sounds found the door of liberation in every instant of awareness entering into the various distinctions of all objective realms. The enlightening being Topknot Born of Wisdom found the door of liberation revealing pure great virtues to all sentient beings when they first arrive at the site of enlightenment. The enlightening being Brave Lotus Topknot found the door of liberation revealing all the Buddha teachings to sentient beings in accord with their infinite faculties and understandings. The enlightening being Sun Banner of Clouds of Universal Knowledge found the door of liberation developing the knowledge of buddhahood, abiding forever. The enlightening

being Greatly Persevering with Indestructible Courage found the door
of liberation of power to enter into all the boundless symbols of the
teachings. The enlightening being Banner of Light of Fragrant Flames
found the door of liberation showing how all the present Buddhas first
began enlightening practice, and on through to their final consummation of the body of knowledge and wisdom. The enlightening being
Deep Beautiful Sound of Great Enlightened Virtue found the door of
liberation peacefully abiding in the ocean of all the great vows of
Vairocana, the Illuminator. The enlightening being Born of Wisdom
with the Light of Great Virtue found the door of liberation revealing
the most profound realm of the Buddha, which pervades the cosmos.

At that time the enlightening being Great Brilliance of the Moon
Reflected in the Ocean, empowered by the Buddha, observed the ocean
of arrays of all the hosts of enlightening beings and said in verse,

The transcendent means and the stages of enlightenment,
Vast, inconceivable, are all fulfilled:
Infinite sentient beings subdued and harmonized,
All buddha-lands are pure.

As Buddha teaches in the worlds of beings,
All lands in the ten directions are filled:
In an instant of thought he turns the wheel of truth,
Accommodating it to all states of mind.

Buddha, over countless vast eons,
Has appeared everywhere before sentient beings;
According to his past cultivation,
He shows his purified realm of action.

I see everywhere in all directions
And see the Buddhas showing mystic powers,
All sitting in sanctuaries realizing enlightenment,
Surrounded by listening crowds.

The immense radiance of Buddha's reality body
Can appear in the world through expedient means,
According with the inclinations of all beings' minds,
Raining the teachings to suit their faculties.

The impartial, signless body of true suchness,
The pure reality-body of untainted light;
With knowledge and calm, with innumerable bodies,
He preaches the truth, adapting to all.

The powers of the King of Truth are all pure,
His knowledge and wisdom like space, unbounded;
He reveals all without any concealment,
Causing all beings to be enlightened.

In accord with what Buddha cultivated
Up to his perfection of all knowledge,
Now he radiates light through the cosmos
Showing it all therein.

Buddha shows mystic powers through his original vow,
Illuminating all in the ten directions;
What the Buddha practiced of yore,
All is expounded in these networks of light.

There is no end of worlds in all directions—
No equals, no bounds, each one distinct.
Buddha's unhindered power emits a great light
Clearly revealing all of those lands.

At that time the Buddha's lion seat, its round platform of exquisite flowers of many jewels, its base, steps, doors, and all its embellishments, each produced as many great enlightening beings as there are atoms in a buddha-land. Their names were Oceanic Wisdom, Sovereign King of Occult Powers; Thunder Shaking All; Topknot of Lights of Many Jewels; Bold Intelligence of the Sun of Knowledge; Seal of Knowledge Made of Jewels of Inconceivable Qualities; Hundred Eye Lotus Topknot; Light Spheres of Golden Flames; Universal Sound of the Cosmos; Cloud Sound Pure Moon; Banner of Light of Benevolent Courage: these were the leaders, and there were as many of them as atoms in many buddha-lands.

At the same time as they appeared, these enlightening beings each produced clouds of various offerings: for example, clouds of flowers of all jewels, clouds of all subtle fragrances of lotus blossoms, clouds of orbs of jewel lights, clouds of fragrant flames of boundless realms, clouds of jewel-like light spheres from the treasury of the sun, clouds of all pleasing musical sounds, clouds of flames of light from all jewel lamps, with boundless colors and forms, clouds of branches, flowers, and fruits from trees of many jewels, clouds of regal jewels with inexhaustible pure radiance, clouds of all the finest decorative gems; there were as many such clouds of various offerings as there are atoms in a buddha-world. Each of those enlightening beings produced such clouds of offerings unceasingly, raining on the oceanic assemblies at all enlightenment sites.

Having manifested these clouds, they circled the Buddha to the right, circling him countless hundreds and thousands of times. In whatever direction they came from, there, not far from the Buddha, they magically produced innumerable lotus lion seats of various jewels, and each sat crosslegged thereon.

The spheres of actions of these enlightening beings were pure and vast as the sea. They had attained the state of universality of illumination of knowledge and wisdom. Following the Buddhas, they were unhindered in their actions. They were able to enter the ocean of all principles of discernment and elucidation, and had mastered the teaching of inconceivable liberation. They dwelt in the state of all-sidedness of the Buddhas. They had already mastered all techniques of concentration formulae, and were able to contain the ocean of all the teachings. They dwelt in the stage of equanimous knowledge of past, present, and future. They had attained the immense joy of profound faith. Their boundless stores of blessings were most pure. They observed everywhere in space throughout the cosmos. They diligently made offerings to all Buddhas appearing in any land in all worlds.

At that time, the enlightening being Oceanic Wisdom, Sovereign King of Occult Powers, the great spiritual hero, empowered by the Buddha, surveyed the oceans of masses at the scene of enlightenment and said in verse,

> Buddha knows what all Buddhas have realized—
> Unhindered as space, he illumines all,
> His light pervading countless lands everywhere.
> He sits amidst the hosts, all magnificently pure.
>
> The Buddha's virtues cannot be measured;
> They fill all the cosmos in every direction.
> Sitting under every enlightenment tree,
> All the great powers assemble like clouds.
>
> Buddha has such spiritual powers,
> Manifesting infinite forms at once.
> The Buddha's sphere is beyond bounds—
> Individuals see according to their liberation.
>
> Buddha passed oceans of eons
> Working in all realms of being
> Teaching creatures by various means,
> Having them accept and practice enlightening ways.
>
> Vairocana, replete with magnificent refinements,
> Sits on a lotus-bank lion seat.
> All the assembled hosts are pure;
> Silently all gaze in respect.

The banks of jewels radiate light,
Emitting boundless clouds of fragrant flames;
Countless flower garlands are draped around:
On such a seat does the Buddha sit.

Various adornments decorate its glorious facades;
Constantly emitting lamp-light clouds of fragrant flames,
Immensely vast, blazing, illumining all:
The Sage sits upon supreme embellishments.

Beautiful windows of various jewels,
Draped with lotuses of exquisite gems,
Always producing sublime sounds delighting all hearers:
Thereon Buddha sits, most radiant of all.

A jewel crescent supports the seat, shaped like a half-moon;
Diamond is its pedestal, its color blazing bright;
Enlightening beings constantly circle it:
Buddha is most radiant among them.

His various mystic displays fill the ten directions,
Expounding the far-reaching vows of the Enlightened One:
All reflected images appear therein;
It is on such a seat the Buddha calmly sits.

At that time the great enlightening being Thunder Shaking All, empowered by the Buddha, looked over all the assembled hosts and said,

Buddha accumulated enlightenment practices,
Making offerings to infinite Buddhas everywhere.
Sustained by the power of the Enlightened One,
None do not see him on his seat.

Jewels of fragrant flames, fulfilling all wishes,
Encrust the Buddha's flower lion throne;
Various adornments, all appearing as reflections,
Are clearly seen by all the hosts.

Buddha's throne displays magnificent forms;
Instant to instant their colors and types each differ.
According to the differences in beings' understandings
Each sees the Buddha thereupon.

Jewel branches hanging down, webs of lotus flowers,
As the flowers open, enlightening beings emerge,
Each producing sublime, pleasing voices
Praising the Buddha on his throne.

Buddha's virtues are extensive as space—
All adornments are born from them.
The embellishing features of each particular state
No sentient beings can comprehend.

Diamond is the ground, indestructible—
Vast, pure, level, and even.
Nets of pearls hang in the sky,
All around the enlightenment tree.

The infinite colors of the ground are all distinct;
Gold dust is spread all around,
Flowers and jewels strewn about,
All beautifying Buddha's throne.

Earth spirits dance with joy,
With infinite manifestations in an instant,
Creating clouds of adornments everywhere,
While remaining reverently gazing at Buddha.

Jewel lamps, immensely large, shining extremely bright,
Fragrant flames and swirling light never ending,
These manifestations differ according to the time;
Earth spirits make offerings of these.

All the adornments existing
In every single land
Appear at this enlightenment scene
By the mystic power of Buddha.

Then the great enlightening being Jewel Light Topknot, empowered by the Buddha, surveyed the oceanic masses at the site of enlightenment and said,

When the Buddha was cultivating practice in the past,
He saw the various buddha-lands, all fully complete.
The lands he saw this way were endless:
All of them appear at this enlightenment scene.

The Buddha's enormous spiritual power
Sheds light showering gems everywhere:
This treasury of jewels is scattered over the site,
Beautifying the ground all around.

Buddha's blessings and mystical powers
Adorn everywhere with precious gemstones;
The ground and the enlightenment tree
Alternately emit light and sound expressing the truth.

Precious lamps, infinite, rain from the sky,
Studded with regal sapphires,
All emitting subtle sounds speaking truth:
This the earth spirits cause to appear.

The jewel ground manifests ubiquitous clouds of light,
Jewel lamps blaze bright as lightning,
Jewel nets hung afar cover above,
Jewel boughs variously draped make decorations.

Look over the entire ground—
Adorned with various beautiful jewels,
It shows beings the ocean of actions,
Causing them to comprehend the real nature of things.

The enlightenment trees in all the spheres
Of all the Buddhas everywhere
All appear at the enlightenment site,
Expounding the Buddha's pure teaching.

In accord with the inclinations of beings' minds
The ground produces wonderful sounds,
Conforming to what the Buddha would preach at his seat,
Each of the teachings fully explained.

The ground constantly produces subtle, fragrant light;
In the light are chanted pure clear sounds:
If any beings are able to receive the teaching,
It causes them to hear, and their afflictions vanish.

Each adornment is fully complete
And could not be described in a million years.
The Buddha's mystic power extends everywhere:
That's why the ground is beautifully pure.

Then the great enlightening being Bold Intelligence of the Sun of
Knowledge, empowered by the Buddha, looked over all the multitudes
assembled on the scene and said in verse,

Buddha sits in the hall of truth with steady gaze,
Brilliantly lighting up the palace.
In accordance with the dispositions of all beings
His body appears throughout all lands.

The Buddha's palace is beyond conception,
Adorned with stores of precious jewels,
Each decoration shining with light;
Sitting there, the Buddha is most conspicuous of all.

With pillars of jewels of various hues,
Chimes of real gold hanging like clouds,
Jewel stairways in rows on four sides,
The gates open in every direction.

Arrays of banners of flowery silk,
Jewel trees with decorated branches and boughs,
Garlands of pearls draped on all sides;
The Ocean of Wisdom sits calmly therein.

Nets of jewels, exquisite fragrant banners,
Brilliant lamps hung like clouds;
Covered with various decorations,
The world-transcending true knower sits within.

Everywhere he manifests clouds of mystic displays,
Those clouds teaching throughout the world,
Harmonizing and calming down all sentient beings:
All this appears from the Buddha's palace.

Trees of gems bloom with fine flowers
Having no peer in all the world;
The embellishments of the lands of all times
Reveal their reflections therein.

Everywhere there are heaps of jewels;
Their light blazes in countless hues.
Gates and doors open at intervals all around;
The beams and ceiling are especially beautiful.

The Buddha's palace is inconceivable;
Its pure radiance contains every form—

In it appear all palaces,
A Buddha sitting in each.

The Buddha's palace is boundless;
The Naturally Awakened One abides therein.
All the masses from all ten directions
Come gather around the Buddha.

Then the great enlightening being Seal of Knowledge Made of Jewels
of Inconceivable Qualities, empowered by the Buddha, looked over all
the oceans of beings gathered at the scene of enlightenment and said in
verse,

The Buddha cultivated an ocean of blessings,
Many as the atoms in all lands;
Produced by the powers of his mind and will,
The enlightenment site is pure, without any taint.

Wish-fulfilling jewels are the roots of the trees,
Diamond are their trunks;
Nets of jewels cover them
And a rich fragrance surrounds.

The tree branches are adorned by all kinds of gems,
The limbs are of precious stone, soaring high;
The branches and twigs hang thickly, like heavy clouds:
Underneath sits Buddha on the enlightenment site.

The site of enlightenment is unthinkably vast:
The trees surround it, covering all;
The dense foliage and luxurious flowers mutually cover and
   reflect,
While in the flowers grow gemstone fruits.

From among all the branches emanate beautiful lights
Illuminating the whole enlightenment scene;
Pure, bright, inexhaustible,
This appears by the power of Buddha's vows.

Banks of precious stones are the flowers,
Reflections shining like patterned clouds;
The encircling trees perfume all around:
The enlightenment site's adorned everywhere.

See in the site of the Buddha's enlightenment
Lotuses and jewel nets, all pure;
Flames of light in whorls appear from here,
Music of bells and chimes comes from the clouds.

All the wonderfully adorned trees
Existing in all lands
Appear in the enlightenment tree;
Buddha, beneath it, sheds all defilement.

The site of enlightenment is made of vast blessings;
The tree branches rain jewels without end.
In the jewels appear enlightening beings,
Going everywhere to serve the Buddhas.

The realm of the Buddhas is inconceivable;
They cause all the trees there to produce music—
In accord with the enlightened way developed by Buddha,
The hosts of beings, hearing the music, can see it all.

Then the great enlightening being Hundred Eyes Lotus Topknot,
empowered by the Buddha, surveyed all the assemblies at the scene of
enlightenment and said,

All the jewels emit wondrous sounds
Extolling the names of Buddhas of all times.
The deeds of those Buddhas' mystical powers
Can all be viewed in this enlightenment scene.

Flowers bloom in profusion, like parti-colored cloth;
Clouds of light flow in all directions:
The spirits of enlightenment trees bring these to the Buddha,
With single-minded devotion making offerings of them.

Flames of jewel light all form banners;
From the banners burst forth sublime fragrances,
The fragrances perfuming all the congregations—
Therefore the place is all beautifully pure.

Lotuses hang down, with light of golden hue,
The light intoning clouds of Buddha's wondrous voice,
Covering all the lands in all directions,
Extinguishing the fires of sentient beings' torments.

The independent power of Enlightenment Tree King
Constantly radiates light extremely pure;
The assembled masses in the ten directions have no bounds,
Yet all of them appear reflected in the enlightenment scene.

The light flames of the jewel branches are like bright lamps;
Their light emanates sound declaring the great vow—
What the Buddha practiced of yore in all states of being
Is fully expounded therein.

Under the tree are spirits, as many as atoms in the land,
All staying together at this enlightenment site,
Each before the Buddha's enlightenment tree
Continuously expounding the liberation doors.

Buddha practiced many deeds of yore,
Making offerings to all the enlightened:
His practices as well as his fame
All appear within the jewels.

Everything in the scene produces wonderful sound—
The sound is vast, pervading the ten directions;
If any beings can hear the teaching,
It civilizes them and makes them pure.

The Buddha in the past cultivated
Infinite embellishments, all;
All the adornments, innumerable kinds,
Of every enlightenment tree.

Then the great enlightening being Light Spheres of Golden Flames,
empowered by the Buddha, looked over all the assemblies at the scene
of enlightenment and said,

Buddha cultivated enlightening practices,
Comprehending all things,
Clarifying the true and the false;
This is the Buddha's first power of knowledge.

As in the past he observed the nature of all things equally,
He clarified the ocean of all doings:
Thus now in the nets of light
He can tell it all, throughout all quarters.

In past eons he developed great techniques
For guiding beings according to their faculties,
Causing all their minds to be pure;
Thus was Buddha able to perfect the knowledge of potentials.

As the understanding of sentient beings is not the same,
And their inclinations and actions are different,
He teaches them according to their needs:
Buddha can do this by his powers of knowledge.

Comprehending the oceans of lands in all directions,
All the worlds of beings they contain,
Buddha's knowledge is equanimous, like space:
All he can show within a pore.

Buddha knows the outcome of all acts,
Comprehending past, present, and future instantly;
The lands, ages, beings, and times of all regions:
All he can reveal and make clear.

Meditation states, liberations, and powers are boundless,
And so are trances and other techniques:
Buddha shows them all to beings, gladdening them,
Causing all to wash away the darkness of afflictions.

Buddha's knowledge is unhindered, comprehending all times;
All he shows in an instant, in his hair pores:
The Buddhas' teachings, lands, and sentient beings:
All these appear from his recollective power.

Buddha's eye is as vast as space;
He sees the entire cosmos.
In the unimpeded state, with unequalled function,
All Buddhas can tell of this eye.

All sentient beings are totally bound;
All their intoxications and habits
Buddha causes to be removed by his methods,
Appearing throughout the world.

Then the great enlightening being Universal Sound of the Cosmos, empowered by the Buddha, looked over the assembled beings at the site of enlightenment and said,

The Buddha's awesome spiritual powers pervade the ten directions,
Their grandiose displays making no discrimination;
The transcendent means, enlightening practices
Fulfilled in the past—all they show.

Of old he conceived compassion for beings
And practiced transcendent generosity,
Wherefore his body is most sublime,
Gladdening all who see.

In boundless eons past
He cultivated transcendent self-control,
So acquired a pure body all-pervading,
Extinguishing the various torments of the world.

He cultivated patience and tolerance, pure,
Faithful to truth, without discrimination;
So his physical form is perfect,
Shedding light in all directions.

He strove for boundless eons past,
Able to overthrow the barriers of sentient beings;
Therefore he can emanate bodies in all directions,
All appearing under enlightenment trees.

Buddha practiced, for long, long eons,
Oceans of meditations, all of them pure:
Thus he delights his beholders,
Removing all taint of afflictions.

Buddha mastered the ocean of practices,
Fulfilling transcendent wisdom;
Therefore he sheds light illumining all,
Destroying the darkness of ignorance.

Edifying beings by various means,
He causes their practice to succeed;
Traveling everywhere in the ten directions
For endless eons, he never rests.

Buddha practiced for boundless eons
Purifying and mastering transcendent vows;
Therefore he appears throughout the world
Saving beings forever and ever.

Buddha cultivated extensively for countless eons
Transcendent power to deal with all truths;

Thus he has perfected natural power,
Appearing throughout all lands.

Buddha cultivated all-sided knowledge;
The nature of his omniscience is like space:
Therefore he has unhindered power
Illuminating all lands in the ten directions.

Then the great enlightening being Cloud Sound Pure Moon, empowered by the Buddha, looked over all the beings gathered at the enlightenment site and said,

The realm of his spiritual powers is equal to space—
No beings do not perceive them.
The stages he perfected in his past practice
Are fully explained in the jewels.

Striving purely for countless eons,
He entered the first stage, that of extreme joy;
Producing the vast knowledge of the cosmos,
He saw countless Buddhas of the ten directions.

In the stage of purity amidst all things
He observed standards of purity numerous as beings;
Having practiced extensively for many eons,
He served the boundless ocean of Buddhas.

Accumulating virtue in the stage of radiance,
His store of calm was firm and enduring;
The vast cloud of teachings he had already learned:
So it is told in the gemstone fruits.

The incomparable stage of clear intellect like an ocean of flames—
Comprehending situations, he gave rise to compassion,
With an equal physical presence in all lands:
These accomplishments of the Buddha are all expounded.

Universal store of equanimity—the difficult to conquer stage;
According with action and stillness, without contradiction,
The realm of the Buddhist teaching is completely impartial;
How the Buddha purified it, the jewels can tell.

Far-reaching practice—the stage of oceanic wisdom,
Totally comprehending all aspects of the teachings,

Appearing in all lands like space:
The voice of these teachings comes from the trees.

The body of space, pervading the cosmos,
The lamp of wisdom, shining on all beings,
All practical methods completely purified:
His past long journey he causes to be told.

Adorned by execution of all vows,
Infinite oceans of lands are all pure;
Undisturbed by any discrimination,
This peerless stage is fully explained.

Mystic powers of infinite scope
Enter the illumining power of the teachings;
This pure stage of beneficent wisdom
And its eons of practice are fully revealed.

The far-reaching tenth stage of clouds of teaching
Engulfs everything, pervading all space;
The realm of the Buddha is told in the voice,
This voice is the Buddha's spiritual power.

Then the great enlightening being Banner of Light of Benevolent Courage, empowered by the Buddha, surveyed the ten directions and said,

Innumerable sentient beings are in the congregation;
Their various minds of faith are all pure;
All can enter into understanding of Buddha's wisdom,
And understand all states which adorn it.

Each initiates pure vows and puts them into practice;
All have made offerings to innumerable beings.
They are able to see the real true body of Buddha
As well as all his mystical displays.

Some can see the Buddha's reality-body,
Incomparable, unhindered, pervading everywhere:
The nature of all the infinity of things
Is in that body completely.

Some see the Buddha's sublime body of form,
Its boundless physical characteristics blazing with light;

According to the different understandings of various beings,
It transforms into various appearances, everywhere.

Some see the body of unobstructed knowledge,
Equal in all times, like space;
According to the changes in beings' inclinations,
It causes them to see all kinds of differences.

Some can understand the Buddha's voice
Pervading all lands in the ten directions;
According to sentient beings' abilities to understand,
It produces verbal sounds for them, without any hindrance.

Some see the Buddha's various lights,
Variously shining throughout the world;
And some see too, in the Buddha's light,
Buddhas displaying their mystic powers.

Some see Buddha's oceans of clouds of light
Issuing from his pores, of radiant hues,
Showing the paths he practiced of yore,
Causing beings to deeply believe and enter Buddha's knowledge.

Some see the Buddha's adorning marks and blessings
And see where the blessings come from—
The oceans of transcendent means he practiced of old
Are clearly seen in the Buddha's marks.

Buddha's qualities cannot be measured;
They fill the cosmos, without any bounds.
These and the ranges of psychic powers
These beings can expound through Buddha's power.

Then the ocean of worlds of arrays of flower banks, by the power of the Buddha, all shook in six ways, in eighteen manners: that is, they trembled, trembled all over, trembled all over in all directions; they welled up, welled up all over, welled up all over in all directions; they surged, surged all over, surged all over in all directions; they quaked, quaked all over, quaked all over in all directions; they roared, roared all over, roared all over in all directions; they crashed, crashed all over, crashed all over in all directions.

These various world leaders each caused clouds of inconceivable offerings to appear, raining on the ocean of beings at the site of enlightenment: clouds of ornaments of all fragrant flowers; clouds of decorations of all precious stones; clouds of flower nets of all jewel flames; clouds of spheres of light of jewels of boundless varieties; clouds of treasuries of pearls of all colors; clouds of all precious sandalwood scents; clouds of umbrellas made of all kinds of precious substances; clouds of diamonds with pure resonance; clouds of necklaces of jewels shining like the sun; clouds of banks of lights of all gemstones; clouds of all sorts of decorations. These clouds of adornments were infinite, inconceivably numerous. These world leaders each produced such clouds of offerings, showering upon the ocean of beings at the Buddha's site of enlightenment, all reaching everywhere.

As in this world the world leaders joyfully produced such offerings, so did all the world leaders in all worlds of the ocean of worlds of arrays of flower banks make such offerings. In each of their worlds there was a Buddha sitting on the site of enlightenment. The individual world leaders' various resolutions of faith, foci of concentration, methods of meditation, practice of methods assisting enlightenment, accomplishments, joys, approaches, understandings of the teachings, access to the realm of Buddha's spiritual powers, access to the realms of Buddha's abilities, entryways into the Buddha's liberation, were the same as in the flower bank ocean of worlds in all the oceans of worlds in the entire space of the whole cosmos.

BOOK TWO

Appearance of the Buddha

AT THAT TIME the enlightening beings and the leaders of all the worlds formed these thoughts: "What are the stages of the Buddha? What are the vistas of the Buddha? What are the empowerments of the Buddha? What are the acts of the Buddha? What are the powers of the Buddha? What are the fearlessnesses of the Buddha? What are the meditations of the Buddha? What are the invincibilities of the Buddha? What are the sense organs of the Buddha? What are the minds of the Buddha? What are the lights of the Buddha's body? What are the halos of the Buddha? What are the voices of the Buddha? What are the knowledges of the Buddha? O please, World Honored One, pity us and explain to us. Also, all the Buddhas of all oceans of worlds in the ten directions explain to the enlightening beings the oceans of worlds, the oceans of sentient beings, the oceans of Buddhas' liberations, the oceans of Buddhas' mystical displays, the oceans of Buddhas' teachings, the oceans of Buddhas' names, the oceans of Buddhas' life spans, as well as the oceans of vows of all enlightening beings, the oceans of approaches of all enlightening beings, the oceans of aids to the Way of all enlightening beings, the oceans of all vehicles of enlightening beings, the oceans of activities of all enlightening beings, the oceans of emancipations of all enlightening beings, the oceans of psychic powers of all enlightening beings, the oceans of ways of transcendence of all enlightening beings, the oceans of stages of all enlightening beings, and the oceans of knowledge of all enlightening beings—please, O Buddha, Enlightened One, World Honored One, explain these for us too."

Then the enlightening beings, by mystical power, produced sound issuing spontaneously from the clouds of offerings, speaking verses:

> Countless eons of practice complete,
> You've become truly awake under the enlightenment tree:

You appear universally to liberate beings,
Like clouds filling all to the end of time.

When beings have doubts, you put an end to them,
Causing all to develop great faith and resolution;
Everywhere removing unlimited suffering,
You make all experience the peace of the Buddhas.

An infinite number of enlightening beings
Have all come here to behold you:
Please explain the truth, eliminate doubt,
According to our capacities to receive.

How can we know the stages of the Buddhas?
How can we observe the Buddha's sphere?
The empowerment of the Buddha has no bounds:
Please show us this truth and purify us.

What is the Buddha's realm of action
That can be entered by wisdom?
Buddha's power is pure and unlimited:
Please show it to us enlightening beings.

What are your vast meditation states?
How do you purify fearlessness?
Your mystic powers cannot be measured:
Please explain in accord with beings' dispositions.

The Buddhas, kings of truth, are like the world leaders—
Free wherever they go, none can constrain them:
This and other great teachings
Please expound for the benefit of all.

How are the Buddha's eyes innumerable,
As also are the other organs of sense?
And how are the minds also countless?
Please show us a way to know about this.

As are the oceans of worlds and oceans of beings,
All oceans of arrangements in the cosmos,
So are the oceans of Buddhas—unbounded:
Please tell all to the children of Buddha.

The ocean of transcendent ways, forever beyond conception,
The ocean of techniques for universal liberation,
The ocean of all the aspects of the teaching,
Please expound at this enlightenment site.

At that point the Buddha, knowing what the enlightening beings were thinking, emitted a multitude of light rays from his teeth. Those light rays were as numerous as atoms in a buddha-field: they included, for example, light rays of flowers of jewels illumining everywhere; light rays producing various sounds adorning the universe; light rays draping subtle clouds; light rays showing the Buddhas of the ten directions sitting on their sites of enlightenment making mystical displays; light rays of umbrellas of clouds of flames of all jewels; light rays filling the universe without impediment; light rays adorning all buddha-fields; light rays setting up banners of pure diamonds; light rays adorning the scenes of enlightenment where hosts of enlightening beings were assembled; light rays with subtle vibrations intoning the names and epithets of all the Buddhas. There were as many such light rays as there are atoms in a buddha-field, and each individual ray had as many light beams accompanying it. Those lights all contained all exquisite jewellike hues, and they each illumined oceans of worlds as numerous as atoms in a billion buddha-lands. The congregations of enlightening beings in all the other oceans of worlds could see this Lotus Bank Array ocean of worlds within those lights. By the spiritual power of the Buddha, those lights, in the presence of all those enlightening beings, intoned these verses:

Cultivating oceans of practices over countless eons,
Making offerings to oceans of Buddhas everywhere,
Teaching and liberating the oceans of all beings,
Now fulfilling sublime enlightenment—The Universal Illuminator.

From his pores come magic clouds
With light shining through all quarters,
Awakening those able to receive the teaching,
Causing them to approach enlightenment, pure, unhindered.

Buddha traversed all paths of existence,
Teaching and developing the living beings;
The mystic powers at his command are infinite:
Instantly he causes all to be freed.

The enlightenment tree of precious gems
Is embellished with the finest adornments;
Buddha truly awakes under it,
Emanating light, majestically shining.

The roar of his great voice fills all quarters,
Preaching for all the way to great peace.
According to the mental dispositions of beings,
He wakes them by various means.

He practiced transcendent ways and fulfilled them,
As many as atoms in a thousand lands.
All the powers he has already attained;
You all should go and pay him respect.

Buddha-children of all quarters, as many as atoms of lands,
All come together, with joy;
Having showered clouds of offerings,
Now they stand before Buddha with single-minded gaze.

One tone of the Buddha contains an infinity,
Able to expound the deep ocean of scriptures,
Raining the sublime teaching in accord with all minds;
That most honored human you all should go see.

The vows of Buddhas of all times
Are told under the enlightenment tree;
All appear in an instant:
Hurry to the Buddha's spot.

Vairocana's great ocean of knowledge
Shines from his face for all to see.
Now, awaiting the gathering of the masses, he's about to speak:
Go see him and hear what he says.

At that time, all the masses in the oceans of worlds in the ten
directions, awakened by the Buddha's light, all went to Vairocana
Buddha's place and made offerings. For example, to the east of this
Flower Bank Array ocean of worlds there is an ocean of worlds called
Array of Lotuses of Pure Light: among its world systems is a land
called Diamond Mine of Jewel Necklaces; the Buddha there was called
Infinite King Awakening Space with the Water of Truth; among that
Buddha's vast congregation was a great enlightening being named
Lotus Banner Contemplating the Supreme Teaching who came to the
Buddha with a group of enlightening beings as numerous as atoms in
an ocean of worlds; each produced ten kinds of clouds of forms of
enlightening beings, filling space and not dissolving. They also manifested ten kinds of clouds of jewel mountains, ten kinds of clouds of
spheres of sunlight, ten kinds of clouds of jewel flower ornaments, ten
kinds of clouds of music containing all tones, ten kinds of clouds of
powder incense trees, ten kinds of clouds of myriad forms of perfume
and incense, and ten kinds of clouds of trees of all kinds of fragrances.
Clouds of offerings such as these, as many as atoms in an ocean of
worlds, filled all of space, not dispersing. Having caused these clouds to
appear, the enlightening beings bowed to the Buddha and offered them

to him. They then magically produced in the eastern quarter lion seats of banks of lights of various flowers and sat crosslegged on those seats.

South of this Flower Bank ocean of worlds is an ocean of worlds called Mine of Ornaments of Radiance of Moons Made of All Jewels. Among its world systems is a land called Array of Boundless Light Spheres. The Buddha there was named Polar Mountain King with the Virtues of the Light of Universal Knowledge. Among that Buddha's immense congregation was an enlightening being named Wisdom Universally Illumining the Ocean of Truths, who came to the Buddha along with a group of enlightening beings as numerous as atoms in an ocean of worlds; each produced ten kinds of clouds of jewels from mines of lights of all adornments, filling space without dispersing. They also manifested ten kinds of clouds of all-illumining regal jewels, raining all kinds of ornaments, ten kinds of clouds of blazing jewels intoning the names and epithets of the Buddhas, ten kinds of clouds of jewels expounding all the Buddhas' teachings, ten kinds of clouds of jewel trees adorning the scene of enlightenment, ten kinds of jewel clouds of precious light projecting myriad phantom buddhas, ten kinds of jewel clouds displaying the forms of the adornments of all sites of enlightenment, ten kinds of jewel clouds of lamps of intense flames expounding the realm of the Buddhas, ten kinds of jewel clouds of forms of the palaces of infinite lands, and ten kinds of jewel clouds showing images of the Buddhas of past, present, and future. Jewel clouds such as these, as many as atoms in an ocean of worlds, all pervaded space without dispersing. Having caused these clouds to appear, the enlightening beings bowed to the Buddha and offered them to him; then each produced in the southern quarter lotus bank lion seats of sapphires and rose gold, then sat crosslegged on the seats.

To the west of this Flower Bank ocean of worlds there is an ocean of worlds named Pleasant Jewel Light. Among the world systems therein is a land called Producing the Best Life-Supports. The Buddha there was named Array of Quality Jewels of Fragrant Flowers. Among the vast congregation of that Buddha was a great enlightening being called Universal Arrays of Moonlight's Fragrant Flames, who, together with as many enlightening beings as atoms in an ocean of worlds, came to the Buddha, each producing ten kinds of clouds of mansions of all kinds of precious fragrant flowers, filling all space without dispersing. They also produced ten kinds of clouds of mansions of precious stones of boundless colors and forms, ten kinds of clouds of mansions of fragrant flames from precious lamps, ten kinds of clouds of mansions of all pearls, ten kinds of clouds of mansions of all precious flowers, ten kinds of clouds of mansions decorated with jewel ornaments, ten kinds of clouds of mansions manifesting the treasuries of lights of all adornments in the ten directions, ten kinds of clouds of mansions of all kinds of embellishments from throughout the ten directions, ten kinds of clouds of mansions studded with all kinds of precious stones, and ten kinds of clouds of mansions with gates of flowers and networks of chimes. These mansion clouds, as numerous as atoms in an ocean of worlds, all filled space without dispersing. Having caused these clouds to appear, the enlightening beings bowed to the Buddha and presented them as offerings; then they produced in the western quarter lion seats of great treasuries of gold leaves, and then sat crosslegged on these seats.

To the north of this Flower Bank ocean of worlds there is an ocean of worlds called Treasuries of Light Spheres of Lapis Lazuli Lotuses. Among the world systems therein is a land called Array of Blue Lotuses. The Buddha's name was King of Sound of the Banner of Universal Knowledge. Among that Buddha's vast congregation was a great enlightening being named Lion Stretch Light, who, with a group of enlightening beings as numerous as atoms in an ocean of worlds, came to the Buddha, each manifesting ten kinds of clouds of beautiful trees of all kinds of fragrant jewels, which filled space without dispersing. They also produced ten kinds of clouds of trees displaying arrays of all trees of infinite colors and forms, ten kinds of clouds of trees adorned with all flowers, ten kinds of clouds of trees adorned with spheres of light of the radiance of all jewels, ten kinds of clouds of trees adorned with physical forms of enlightening beings, perfumed with all kinds of sandalwood, ten kinds of clouds of trees inconceivably adorned with scenes of past sites of enlightenment, ten kinds of clouds of trees of sunlike light from treasuries of clothes made of all kinds of jewels, and ten kinds of clouds of trees emanating all kinds of pleasing sounds. Clouds such as these, numerous as atoms in an ocean of worlds, extended throughout space without dispersing. Having caused these clouds to appear, the enlightening beings bowed to the Buddha and presented them as offerings; then they each magically produced in the northern quarter lion seats of banks of lotuses with jewel lamps, and sat crosslegged on those seats.

Northeast of this Flower Bank ocean of worlds there is an ocean of worlds called Rose Gold and Lapis Lazuli Banner. Among the world systems there is a land called Array of Jewels. The Buddha there was called Fearless Lamp of All Truths. Among that Buddha's vast congregation was a great enlightening being called Inexhaustible Mine of Virtues of the Lamp of Supreme Light, who came, with as many enlightening beings as there are atoms in an ocean of worlds, to the Buddha, each producing ten kinds of clouds of lion thrones of stores of jewel lotuses of boundless forms, which filled space without dispersing. They also produced ten kinds of clouds of lion thrones of stores of lights of diamonds, ten kinds of clouds of lion thrones adorned with all kinds of decorations, ten kinds of clouds of lion thrones of banks of flames of lamps ringed with jewels, ten kinds of clouds of lion thrones showering jewel ornaments all over, ten kinds of clouds of lion thrones of treasuries of precious ornaments of all fragrant flowers, ten kinds of clouds of lion thrones of mines of regal jewels showing the adornments of the seats of all Buddhas, ten kinds of clouds of lion thrones of treasuries of jewel branches and stems of trees of all kinds of precious stones, ten kinds of clouds of lion thrones of all arrays of ornaments, steps, and doors, and ten kinds of clouds of lion thrones of banks of lights adorned with gems and perfumes. Such clouds as these, as many as atoms in an ocean of worlds, all filled space without dispersing. Having caused these clouds to appear, the enlightening beings bowed to the Buddha and presented them to him as offerings. Then, in the northeast direction each magically produced a lion seat of jewel lotuses with banners of lights of precious stones and sat crosslegged thereon.

Southeast of this Flower Bank ocean of worlds is an ocean of worlds called Gold Embellished Lapis Lazuli Light Shining Everywhere. Among its world systems is a land called Pure Fragrant Light. The Buddha there was named King of Profound Faith and Universal Joy. Among the Buddha's vast congregation was a great enlightening being called Universal Light of the Lamp of Wisdom, who came to the Buddha along with a group of enlightening beings as numerous as atoms in an ocean of worlds, each producing ten kinds of clouds of drapes of all kinds of wish-fulfilling jewels, which filled all of space without dispersing. They also caused to appear ten kinds of clouds of drapes adorned with all flowers of sapphires, ten kinds of clouds of drapes of all fragrant jewels, ten kinds of clouds of drapes of lamps with jewel flames, ten kinds of clouds of drapes of regal jewels displaying the Buddhas' spiritual powers expounding the teachings, ten kinds of clouds of drapes of gems in the forms of all clothing adornments, ten kinds of clouds of drapes of lights of masses of all jewels, ten kinds of clouds of drapes of sounds of chimes on jewel nets, ten kinds of clouds of drapes on jewel pedestals with lotus nets, and ten kinds of clouds of drapes displaying the forms of all inconceivable adornments. Clouds of drapes of jewels such as these, as many as atoms in an ocean of worlds, all filled space without dispersing. Having caused these clouds to appear, the enlightening beings bowed to the Buddha and presented them as offerings. Then, to the southeast, each magically produced a lion seat of banks of jewel lotuses and sat crosslegged thereon.

Southwest of this Flower Bank ocean of worlds is an ocean of worlds called Sunlight Shining Everywhere; among its world systems is a land called Lion Sunlight. The Buddha there was called Sound of Light of Universal Knowledge. Among that Buddha's vast congregation was a great enlightening being named Topknot of Flames of Radiant Flower Lights, who came to the Buddha with a group of enlightening beings, as many as there are atoms in an ocean of worlds, each manifesting ten kinds of clouds of parasols of beautiful ornamental jewels, filling space without dispersing. They also produced ten kinds of clouds of parasols of flowers of arrays of light beams, ten kinds of clouds of parasols of treasures of pearls of boundless colors, ten kinds of clouds of parasols of diamonds emanating the sounds of compassion of all enlightening beings, ten kinds of clouds of parasols of blazing garlands of jewels, ten kinds of clouds of parasols draped with nets of chimes embellished with precious stones, ten kinds of clouds of parasols decorated with branches of jewel trees, ten kinds of clouds of parasols of diamonds like the sun shining everywhere, ten kinds of clouds of parasols of all kinds of perfume and incense, ten kinds of clouds of parasols of stores of sandalwood, and ten kinds of clouds of parasols of arrays of universal lights of the vast sphere of buddhahood. Such clouds of parasols of precious substances, numerous as atoms in an ocean of worlds, all filled space without dispersing. Having caused these clouds to appear, the enlightening beings bowed to the Buddha and presented them as offerings. Then, to the southwest, they each magically produced a lion seat of banks of adornments of flames of sapphire light and sat crosslegged thereon.

Northwest of this Flower Bank ocean of worlds is an ocean of worlds called Precious Light Radiance. Among its world systems is a land called Array of Myriad Fragrances. The Buddha there was called Light of the Ocean of Infinite Virtues. Among that Buddha's congregation was a great enlightening being called Jewel King of Inexhaustible Light, who, together with as many enlightening beings as there are atoms in an ocean of worlds, came to the Buddha, each producing ten kinds of clouds of light spheres of radiance of all jewels, filling space without dispersing. They also produced ten kinds of clouds of light spheres of all beautiful flowers, ten kinds of clouds of light spheres of all phantom buddhas, ten kinds of clouds of light spheres of the buddha-lands of the ten directions, ten kinds of clouds of light spheres of the jewel trees and thunderous sound of the realm of the Buddhas, ten kinds of clouds of light spheres of all regal gems, ten kinds of clouds of light spheres instantaneously displaying the forms of infinite beings, ten kinds of clouds of light spheres of the voice of the Buddha's great vow, and ten kinds of clouds of light spheres of diamonds emanating sounds edifying all sentient beings. Such clouds of light spheres, numerous as atoms in an ocean of worlds, all filled space without dispersing. Having produced these clouds, the enlightening beings bowed to the Buddha and presented them as offerings. Then, to the northwest, they each produced a lion seat of treasuries of awesome qualities of infinite light and sat crosslegged thereon.

Below this Flower Bank ocean of worlds there is an ocean of worlds called Treasury of Exquisite Qualities of Lotus Blossom Fragrance. Among its world systems is a land called Radiance of Light of a Jewel Lion. The Buddha there was named Light of the Cosmos. In the vast congregation of that Buddha was a great enlightening being named Wisdom Flaming with the Light of the Universe, who, together with as many enlightening beings as there are atoms in an ocean of worlds, came to the Buddha, each producing ten kinds of clouds of light beams of mines of all jewels, filling space without dispersing. They also produced ten kinds of clouds of light beams of all fragrances, ten kinds of clouds of light beams producing the sounds of all Buddhas explaining the truth, ten kinds of clouds of light beams revealing the arrays of all buddha-lands, ten kinds of clouds of light beams of palaces of all beautiful flowers, ten kinds of clouds of light beams displaying the work of the Buddhas of all ages teaching sentient beings, ten kinds of clouds of light beams of flower buds of all inexhaustible treasures, and ten kinds of clouds of light beams of all kinds of decorated thrones. Clouds of light beams such as these, numerous as atoms in an ocean of worlds, filled all space without dispersing. Having caused these clouds to appear, the enlightening beings bowed to the Buddha and presented them as offerings. Then each created, in the nadir, a lion seat of lotuses with lamps with jewel flames, and sat crosslegged thereon.

Above this Flower Bank ocean of worlds is an ocean of worlds called Radiant Arrays of Precious Stones. Among the world systems there is a land called Formless Subtle Light. The Buddha there was called Unimpeded Light of Virtue. Among that Buddha's vast congregation was a great enlightening being called Vigorous Intellect with Unhindered Power, who, along with as many enlightening beings as atoms in an ocean of worlds, came to the Buddha, each producing ten kinds of clouds of light-flames of jewels of boundless physical forms, filling space without dispersing. They also produced ten kinds of clouds of light-flames of webs of precious stones, ten kinds of clouds of light-flames of the ornaments of all the vast buddha-lands, ten kinds of clouds of light-flames of all exquisite fragrances, ten kinds of clouds of light-flames of all adornments, ten kinds of clouds of light-flames of the mystical displays of the Buddhas, ten kinds of clouds of light-flames of all beautiful tree-flowers, ten kinds of clouds of light-flames of all diamonds, ten kinds of clouds of light-flames of jewels bespeaking the practices of infinite enlightening beings, and ten kinds of clouds of light-flames of lamps of all pearls. Clouds of light flames like these, as numerous as atoms in an ocean of worlds, all filled space without dispersing. Having caused these clouds to appear, the enlightening beings bowed to the Buddha and presented them as offerings. Then, at the zenith, they each produced a lion seat of lotus banks of light intoning the voices of the Buddhas and sat crosslegged thereon.

In this way, in as many oceans of worlds as there are atoms in ten billion buddha-fields, there were as many great enlightening beings, each surrounded by a group of enlightening beings as numerous as atoms in an ocean of worlds, who came to the gathering. These enlightening beings each produced clouds of offerings of various adornments, as numerous as atomic particles in an ocean of worlds, which all filled space without dispersing. And having produced these clouds, they bowed to the Buddha and presented them as offerings; then, in the direction from which they had come, all magically pro-

duced lion seats with various precious adornments and sat crosslegged
on them.

After having thus seated themselves, those enlightening beings each
produced, from the hair pores of their bodies, light rays of the various
colors of all jewels, as many as atoms in ten oceans of worlds; in each
light ray there appeared as many enlightening beings as there are atoms
in ten oceans of worlds, all sitting on lion seats of banks of lotuses.
These enlightening beings all could enter into every atom of the oceans
of structures in all universes. In each individual atom were vast fields,
as many as atoms in ten buddha-worlds; in each field were all the past,
present, and future Buddhas. These enlightening beings were all able to
go to all these Buddhas, associate with them, and provide them with
offerings, and in each and every thought-instant, by means of mastery
of dream-power, demonstrated teachings enlightening as many sentient
beings as there are atoms in an ocean of worlds; in every instant, by the
teaching showing how celestial beings die and are born, they enlightened as many sentient beings as atoms in an ocean of worlds; in every
instant, by explaining the teaching of the acts and practices of enlightening beings, they enlightened as many sentient beings as atoms in an
ocean of worlds; in every instant, by the teaching of the Buddha's
virtues and mystical displays which stir all lands, they enlightened as
many sentient beings as atoms in an ocean of worlds; in every instant,
by the teaching of beautifying and purifying all buddha-lands, revealing
the ocean of all great vows, they enlightened as many sentient beings
as atoms in an ocean of worlds; in every instant, by the teaching of the
Buddha's voice which contains the languages of all sentient beings, they
enlightened as many sentient beings as atoms in an ocean of worlds; in
every instant, by the teaching which can shower the rain of all Buddha
teachings, they enlightened as many sentient beings as atoms in an
ocean of worlds; in every instant, by the teaching of light illuminating
everywhere in the ten directions, pervading the cosmos and showing
mystical demonstrations, they enlightened as many beings as atoms in
an ocean of worlds; in every instant, by the teaching of all Buddhas'
power of liberation manifesting the body of Buddha everywhere, filling
the cosmos, they enlightened as many sentient beings as atoms in an
ocean of worlds; in every instant, by the teaching of the universally
good enlightening being setting up the ocean of all sites of enlightenment with all assemblies of beings, they enlightened as many sentient
beings as atoms in an ocean of worlds.

In this way, throughout all universes, adapting to the mentalities of
sentient beings, they caused them all to awaken. In every instant they
each caused as many sentient beings as atoms in a polar mountain who
had fallen into miserable states to be forever relieved of their sufferings;
each caused that many sentient beings stuck in wrong concentrations to
enter right concentration; each caused that many sentient beings to be
born in celestial spheres according to their inclinations; each caused that

many sentient beings to rest secure in the states of Buddhas' disciples or self-enlightened ones; each caused that many sentient beings to serve good teachers and act virtuously; each caused that many sentient beings to set their minds on supreme enlightenment; each caused that many sentient beings to head for the enlightening being's stage of nonregression; each caused that many sentient beings to attain the eye of pure wisdom and see all things impartially, as does the Buddha; each caused that many sentient beings to abide securely in the powers and the oceans of vows, and to purify the buddha-lands by means of inexhaustible knowledge; each caused that many sentient beings to dwell in the vast ocean of Vairocana's vows and be born in the family of the Buddhas.

At that time the enlightening beings simultaneously raised their voices within the lights and spoke in verse, saying,

> In the light rays wondrous sounds are produced,
> Pervading all lands in the ten directions,
> Expounding the virtues of the Buddha's children,
> Able to enter the wondrous path of enlightenment.

> Cultivating practices for oceans of eons, never wearied,
> Enabling suffering beings to realize liberation,
> Spirits never downcast, never worn out:
> Buddha children can well enter these techniques.

> Cultivating appropriate means for oceans of eons,
> Infinite, boundless, leaving out none,
> Entering into all the aspects of the teachings,
> They constantly teach, yet their essence is silent and tranquil.

> The vows of the Buddhas of past, present, and future,
> All have they mastered, all consummated;
> Then do they thereby benefit all beings
> As their own pure practical work.

> In the congregations of all the Buddhas,
> Going everywhere throughout the ten directions,
> All, by the ocean of profound knowledge and wisdom,
> Enter the Buddha's way of ultimate peace.

> Each of the light rays, boundless,
> Enters inconceivable lands;
> The eye of pure knowledge can see it all:
> This is enlightening beings' sphere of action.

Enlightening beings can, resting on a single hairtip,
Stir all lands in the ten directions
Without causing fear in the beings there:
This is their stage of pure skill in means.

Infinite bodies in each individual atom
Furthermore manifest lands variously arrayed;
Instantaneous death and birth, all do they show:
Those who've attained the unhindered mind.

All ages in the past, present, and future
They can show in a single instant;
Knowing the body is illusory, without substance or sign
Are those who realize the nature of things unimpeded.

They're all able to enter the supreme practice of the universally
    good,
So all sentient beings like to see them,
Buddha children can abide by this teaching,
With a great sound roaring within their lights.

Then the Buddha, wishing to enable all the enlightening beings to realize the spiritual power of the boundless realm of the Enlightened One, emitted a light from between his brows. That light was called Treasury of the Light of Knowledge of All Enlightening Beings Illumining the Ten Directions. Its form was like a cloud of lamps with jewellike light. It shone throughout all buddha-fields in the ten directions, revealing all the lands and beings therein. It also caused all networks of worlds to tremble. In every single atom it revealed innumerable Buddhas showering the teachings of all the Buddhas of all times, in accord with the differences in character and inclination of the various sentient beings. It clearly showed the Buddha's ocean of transcendent ways, and also rained infinite clouds of various emancipations, causing the sentient beings to forever cross over birth and death. It also showered clouds of the great vows of the Buddhas, and clearly showed, in all worlds in the ten directions, the universally good enlightening beings' congregations at the sites of enlightenment. Having done all this, the light swirled around the Buddha, circling to the right, then went in under his feet.

Then an immense lotus blossom suddenly appeared before the Buddha. That lotus had ten kinds of adornments, unmatched by any other lotuses. That is to say, its stem was a mixture of various gems; its bud was of diamond; its petals were all the jewels in the universe; its pistils were of fragrant gems; rose gold adorned its base; exquisite nets covered it above; its radiant color was pure; it instantaneously displayed the boundless miracles of the Buddhas; it could produce all kinds of sounds;

its diamonds reflected the body of Buddha. In its sounds it could expound all the practical undertakings cultivated by enlightening beings.

When this flower had sprung up, in an instant there was, in the curl of white hair on the Buddha's brow, a great enlightening being named Supreme Sound of All Truths, together with a group of enlightening beings, as numerous as atoms in an ocean of worlds: they all came forth together and circled the Buddha to the right innumerable times; then, having bowed to the Buddha, Supreme Sound of All Truths sat on the flower dais, while the other enlightening beings sat on the pistils.

This enlightening being Supreme Sound of All Truths comprehended the profound realm of reality, gave rise to great joy, and entered the sphere of action of the Buddha, his knowledge unobstructed. He entered the unfathomable ocean of the Buddha's reality-body, and went to where the Buddhas were in all lands. In each hair pore of his body he showed mystical powers. In every moment of thought he contemplated the entire cosmos. The Buddhas of the ten directions all bestowed their power on him, causing him to rest in all meditation states, forever seeing the Buddhas' body of the ocean of qualities of the boundless cosmos, including all meditations and liberations, mystic powers and miraculous displays. Then, in the midst of the assembly, empowered by the Buddha, he looked over the ten directions and said in verse,

> The Buddha's body fills the cosmos,
> Appearing before all beings everywhere—
> In all conditions, wherever sensed, reaching everywhere,
> Yet always on this seat of enlightenment.

> In each of the Buddha's pores
> Sit Buddhas many as atoms in all lands,
> Surrounded by masses of enlightening beings
> Expounding the supreme practice of the universally good.

> Buddha, sitting at rest on the enlightenment seat,
> Displays in one hair oceans of fields;
> The same is true of every single hair,
> Thus pervading the cosmos.

> He sits in each and every land,
> Pervading the lands one and all;
> Enlightening beings from everywhere gather,
> All coming to the enlightenment scene.

> Oceans of enlightening beings with virtues and lights
> Numerous as atoms in all lands

All are in the congregation of the Buddha,
Filling the entire cosmos.

In lands numerous as atoms in the cosmos
He appears in every congregation;
This realm of knowledge of body-distribution
Can be established in the practice of universal goodness.

In the congregations of all the Buddhas
Enlightening beings of supreme knowledge sit,
Each hearing the teaching, conceiving joy,
Cultivating themselves in every situation for boundless ages.

Having entered the far-reaching vows of the universally good,
Each produces the teachings of the Buddhas,
In the ocean of Vairocana's teachings,
They practice and master buddhahood.

What the enlightening being Universally Good is awake to
All Buddhas alike praise with joy:
Having attained the great mystic powers of the Buddhas,
He circulates throughout the whole cosmos.

In all lands, as many as atomic particles,
He manifests clouds of bodies, filling them all,
Radiating light for beings everywhere,
Each raining teachings suited to their minds.

At that time there was another great enlightening being in the assembly,
named King of Lotus Light Wisdom Contemplating All Supreme Truths,
who, empowered by the Buddha, looked over the ten directions and
said in verse,

The profound knowledge of the Buddha
Enters everywhere in the cosmos:
Able to operate in accord with all times,
It is a clear guide for the world.

The Buddhas have the same reality-body—
It depends on nothing, is without distinction;
It causes beings to see Buddha in physical form
According to their intellects.

Replete with all knowledge,
Buddha knows all things:

In all lands,
Everything is evident.

Buddha's bodies, lights, and physical forms
Are all inconceivable.
Sentient beings who believe
He causes to see them according to potential.

In one Buddha-body
He produces infinite Buddhas,
Thunderous sound pervading all lands
Expounding the teaching, the deep ocean of thusness.

In each hair pore
Are webs of light pervading all quarters,
Intoning the sublime voices of Buddha,
Taming the hard to tame.

From the Buddha's light
Issues deep and wondrous sound
Extolling the Buddha's ocean of virtues
And the practices of enlightening beings.

Buddha turns the wheel of true teaching,
Which is infinite and has no bounds;
The truth taught is beyond compare:
The shallow cannot fathom it.

In all worlds he manifests,
Fulfilling true enlightenment,
In each displaying miracles
Which fill the whole cosmos.

Each of the Buddha's bodies
Manifests Buddhas equal to the number of beings,
In every one of the numberless lands
Showing spiritual powers.

At that time there was another enlightening being in the assembly, called Light of Wisdom of Joy in the Truth; empowered by the Buddha, he looked over the ten directions and said,

Buddha's body is always apparent,
Filling the entire cosmos,

Always intoning far-reaching sound
Shaking all lands in all quarters.

Buddha manifests bodily everywhere,
Entering into all worlds,
Revealing occult spiritual power
According to the inclinations of beings.

Buddha appears before all beings
In accordance with their minds;
What the sentient beings see
Is the Buddha's mystic power.

His radiance has no bounds
And his teaching too is infinite;
Buddha children can enter and observe
According to their knowledge.

The Buddha's body has no birth
Yet can appear to be born.
The nature of reality is like space:
Therein do the Buddhas dwell.

No abiding, yet no departing:
Everywhere the Buddha's seen;
His light reaches everywhere,
His fame is heard afar.

No substance, no abode,
And no origin that can be found;
No signs, no form:
What appears is like reflections.

Buddha raises clouds of teachings
Suited to beings' minds;
With various forms of expedient means
He enlightens them and calms them down.

In all worlds is Buddha seen
Sitting on the enlightenment site,
Surrounded by a great congregation,
Illumining all lands.

The bodies of all Buddhas
All have infinite forms;
Though their manifestations be innumerable,
Their forms are never exhausted.

At that time another great enlightening being in the assembly, named Wisdom like Fragrant Flame Light Illumining Everywhere, empowered by the Buddha, looked over the ten directions and said in verse,

The enlightening beings in this assembly
Enter the Buddha's inconceivable state,
Each able to see
All the Buddha's spiritual powers.

The body of knowledge can enter
The atoms of every land,
Perceiving bodies therein,
Seeing all the Buddhas.

Like reflections appearing in all worlds
Where all the Buddhas are,
In each and every one
They reveal miraculous deeds.

The practice of vows of Universally Good
They have developed, clear and pure;
They are able to see in all lands
Buddha's miracles everywhere.

They physically dwell in all places,
Equanimous in all;
With knowledge capable of such action,
They enter the Buddha's realm.

Having realized enlightened knowledge,
They illumine the cosmos equally,
Fitting into the Buddha's pores
The oceans of all worlds.

In all buddha-lands
They manifest mystic powers,
Appearing in various bodies,
With various names as well.

They can, in an instant's time,
Show miracles everywhere:
Truly awakening at the site of enlightenment
And turning the wheel of truth.

All lands, wide and vast,
Billions of ages, inconceivable,

Can be shown in a moment's span
In the enlightening beings' concentration.

Each and every enlightening being
In all the buddha-lands
Is in the Buddha-body,
Boundless, without limit.

Then another great enlightening being in the assembly, named Lion Stretch Wisdom Light, empowered by the Buddha, looked over the ten directions and said,

Vairocana Buddha
Can turn the wheel of truth
In all the lands of the cosmos,
Filling it like clouds.

In all the great oceans of worlds
In all the ten directions
Buddha's power of mind and will
Turns the wheel of truth.

In the vast assemblies of beings
In all lands
His names are not the same;
He expounds the truth according to need.

Buddha's majestic powers
Were made by the vows of universal goodness and wisdom;
In all lands
That wondrous sound reaches everywhere.

Buddha's bodies are numerous as atoms in lands,
Showering the rain of truth everywhere;
Unborn, without distinction,
Appearing in all worlds.

What he practiced in the past
Over countless billions of eons
In all lands, many as atoms,
That wondrous sound can fully tell.

Nets of lights pervade
All the numberless lands;

In the lights are Buddhas
Teaching all beings everywhere.

The Buddha-body, without distinction,
Fills the cosmos,
Able to manifest physical forms,
Teaching according to potentials.

Different are the various names
Of all the guides
In all worlds of all times;
They are spoken so all may see.

The cycles of sublime teachings
Of all the Buddhas
Of past and present
All gathered here can hear.

Then another great enlightening being in the assembly, named Treasury of Qualities of Wisdom of the Ocean of Truth, empowered by the Buddha, looked over the ten directions and said,

Buddha children in this assembly
Cultivate all knowledge and wisdom;
These people can enter
Such gates of means.

In each and every land
They speak the great sound
Telling of the Buddha's sphere
Making it heard through all quarters.

In each mental moment
They observe all things
Abiding in the state of true thusness;
They comprehend the ocean of all phenomena.

In every buddha-body
For billions of ages, inconceivable,
They practiced ways of transcendence
And purified all the lands.

In each atom
They can witness all things;

Thus without obstruction
They go to all lands.

To every buddha-field
They go without exception;
Seeing the Buddhas' mystic power,
They enter the Buddhas' realm.

The far-reaching sound of the Buddhas
Is heard throughout the cosmos;
Enlightening beings can understand,
And enter the ocean of sound.

Intoning subtle sounds through the eons,
Those sounds equal, without distinction,
Those with knowledge of sounds
Can completely comprehend.

Reaching stage after stage,
Dwelling in the stage of power,
They diligently worked for eons,
And such is their attainment.

Then another great enlightening being in the assembly, named Universal Light of the Lamp of Wisdom, empowered by the Buddha, looked over the ten directions and said,

All the Buddhas
Are beyond all forms;
Who can understand this truth
Sees the Guide of the World.

Enlightening beings in meditation,
The light of wisdom illumining all,
Can know the independent essence
Of all the Buddhas.

Seeing the Buddha's real body,
They awake to the profound truth;
Observing everywhere the cosmos,
They assume bodies at will.

Born from the sea of blessings,
Abiding in the stage of wisdom,

They investigate all things
And cultivate the supreme path.

In all buddha-lands
Where all Buddhas are,
Thus throughout the cosmos,
They see the real true body.

In immense lands in all quarters,
For billions of eons diligently practicing,
They are able to roam in true knowledge
Of the sea of all phenomena.

There is only one indestructible immanent body
Seen in all particles:
Unborn, signless,
It's manifest in all lands.

According to the mentalities of beings
It appears everywhere before them;
Showing various means of training,
It turns them to the Buddha-way.

By the spiritual power of the Buddha
Are enlightening beings born;
Sustained by the strength of the Buddha,
They see all enlightened ones.

All the guides
With boundless spiritual powers
Awaken enlightening beings
Throughout the entire cosmos.

Then there was another great enlightening being in the assembly,
named Flower Flame Topknot with Universally Illumining Knowledge,
who, empowered by the Buddha, looked over the ten directions and said,

In all lands
Uttering subtle sounds
Extolling Buddha's virtues,
The cosmos is all filled.

Buddha has reality for his body,
Pure as space itself;

All the physical forms that appear
He includes in this reality.

If anyone has deep faith and joy
And is accepted by the Buddhas,
Know that such a person
Can engender knowledge comprehending Buddha.

Those with little knowledge
Cannot know these truths;
Those whose wisdom eye is pure
Alone are able to see.

By the Buddha's power
They examine all phenomena;
As they enter, abide, and leave,
All they see is clear.

In all things
Boundless are the aspects of teaching;
Developing omniscience,
One enters the deep ocean of reality.

Abiding in the buddha-land
Appearing in all places,
No coming and no going:
All Buddha's teachings are thus.

In the ocean of sentient beings
The buddha-body appears like a reflection;
According to the differences in their understandings
Thus do they see the Guide.

In each and every hair pore
He manifests mystical powers;
The pure ones who practice the vow
Of universal wisdom can see.

Buddha, with each of his bodies,
Teaches in every place,
Pervading the whole cosmos,
Beyond the reach of thought.

Then another great enlightening being in the congregation, named Inexhaustible Light of Majestic Wisdom, empowered by the Buddha, surveyed the ten directions and said,

In each and every buddha-land
Sits Buddha on all enlightenment sites,
Surrounded by assembled groups,
Conquering the armies of demons.

The Buddha's body radiates light
Filling the ten directions;
Appearing in accord with need,
In forms that are not the same.

Every single atom
Is filled with light;
It's seen in all lands in the ten directions,
Variously, different in each.

The countless various lands
In the oceans of lands of all quarters
All are level and pure,
Made of royal sapphires.

Some inverted, some sideways,
Some like lotus buds,
Some round, some square:
They are of various forms.

Traveling unimpeded to all lands
Throughout the universe,
In all groups of beings
Buddha always teaches.

The buddha-body is inconceivable;
All lands exist therein:
In all places there
He guides the worlds, teaching truth.

In the subtle teaching he expounds
The essence of things is undifferentiated;
Based on the one real truth,
He expounds various characteristics of things.

Buddha, with a round, complete sound,
Exposes the genuine truth;
According to differences in understanding,
He manifests infinite teachings.

In all lands we see
Buddha sitting on the enlightenment site;
Buddha's body appears like reflections:
Its birth or death cannot be found.

Then another great enlightening being in the assembly, named Wisdom Illumining the Universe, empowered by the Buddha, looked over the ten directions and said,

Inconceivable is the form
Of the Buddha's subtle body;
Those who see it rejoice,
Respecting and believing the teaching.

All the features of the Buddha's body
Each manifest innumerable Buddhas
Entering all worlds everywhere,
Into each atom therein.

The infinite, boundless Buddhas
Of all oceans of lands
Each, in every instant,
Display their spiritual powers.

Enlightening beings of great knowledge
Enter deeply into the ocean of truth;
Sustained by the power of the Buddha,
They can know his techniques.

If any be already established
In the practical vows of universal goodness and wisdom,
They see in all those lands
The mystic powers of all Buddhas.

If anyone has certain faith
As well as great determination,
They'll have profound wisdom
And comprehend all things.

Able to observe
All the Buddhas' bodies,
Form and sound unhindered,
They'll understand all realms.

Able to abide in the sphere of knowledge
Of all buddha bodies,
They'll plunge into buddhahood
Embracing the whole cosmos.

As many as atoms in buddha-lands,
This many lands
They can cause in an instant
To appear in every atom.

All lands
And deeds of mystic power
All appear in a single land:
Such is the power of enlightening beings.

Then another great enlightening being in the assembly, named Unobstructed Wisdom with Vigorous Power, empowered by the Buddha,
looked over the ten directions and said,

Buddha speaks one subtle sound
Heard throughout the cosmos;
Containing all sounds,
The rain of truth fills everywhere.

With the ocean of all languages,
In all sounds according to type,
In all buddha-lands,
He expounds the pure teaching.

In all lands are seen
The miracles of the Buddha;
Hearing the Buddha preach the truth,
They head for enlightenment.

In each atom
Of all lands in the cosmos
Buddha, by the power of liberation,
Manifests physically therein.

The reality-body is like space;
Unobstructed, without differentiation.
Physical forms appear like reflections,
Manifesting myriad appearances.

Reflections have no location;
Like space, they've no substantial nature:
Those whose wisdom is great
Will comprehend their equality.

The buddha-body is ungraspable;
Unborn, uncreated,
It appears in accord with beings,
Equanimous as empty space.

All Buddhas in the ten directions
Enter into a single pore,
Each showing mystic powers
That the eye of wisdom can see.

The power of Vairocana Buddha's vows
Pervades the entire cosmos,
In all lands
Always expounding the unexcelled teaching.

The miracles shown in a single hair,
Even if told of by all the Buddhas
For innumerable eons,
Could not be completely defined.

As in this world, at the site of enlightenment, by virtue of the
Buddha's spiritual power, there were in each of the ten directions as
many enlightening beings as atoms in a billion oceans of worlds who
came and gathered, so you should know that in each world of all oceans
of worlds the same thing took place at all the enlightenment sites.

BOOK THREE

The Meditation of the Enlightening Being Universally Good

THE ENLIGHTENING BEING Universally Good, the great being, sat on a lion throne made of a bank of lotus flowers, and, imbued with the psychic power of the Enlightened One, entered into concentration. This concentration is called the immanent body of the illuminator of thusness, which is in all enlightened ones. It enters everywhere into the equal essence of all enlightened ones, and is capable of manifesting myriad images in the cosmos, vastly and immensely, without obstruction, equal to space. All the whirling oceans of universes flow along into it; it produces all states of concentration, and can contain all worlds in all directions. The oceans of lights of knowledge of all the enlightened ones come from here; it can reveal all the oceans of all conditions everywhere. It contains within it all the powers and liberations of the enlightened ones and the knowledge of the enlightening beings. It can cause the particles of all lands to be universally able to contain boundless universes. It develops the ocean of virtuous qualities of all Buddhas, and reveals the ocean of great vows of these enlightened ones. All the cycles of teaching of the Buddhas flow through it and are guarded and maintained by it, and kept without interruption or end.

As in this world the enlightening being Universally Good entered this concentration in the presence of the World Honored One, thus in the same way throughout the realm of space of the cosmos, in all directions and all times, in a subtle, unhindered, vastly expansive light, in all lands visible to the Buddha's eye, within reach of the Buddha's power, manifested by the Buddha's body, and in each atom of all those lands, there were Buddhas as numerous as atoms in an ocean of worlds, and in front of each Buddha were Universally Good enlightening beings numerous as atoms in an ocean of worlds, each also entering into this concentration in the immanent body of the illuminator of thusness in enlightened ones.

At that time each of the Universally Good ones saw the Buddhas of the ten directions appearing before them; those Buddhas praised Universally Good in the same voice: "Good! You are able to enter this enlightening beings' concentration in the immanent body of the illuminator of thusness in all Buddhas; this is fostered in you by all the Buddhas everywhere together, by means of the power of the original vow of the illuminating realized one Vairocana Buddha, and it is also because you cultivate the power of the practices and vows of all Buddhas: that is to say, because you can activate all the cycles of the enlightening teaching, revealing the ocean of knowledge and wisdom of all enlightened ones, universally illumine all the oceans of distinctions everywhere, without exception, cause sentient beings to clear away confusion and affliction and attain purity, universally accept all lands without attachment, deeply enter the sphere of all enlightened ones without impediment, and universally expound the virtues and qualities of all enlightened ones; because you are able to enter into the true character of all things and develop knowledge and wisdom, analyze all the media of the teachings, comprehend the faculties of all living beings, and because you are able to hold the ocean of written teachings of all the Buddhas."

At that time all the Buddhas of the ten directions then bestowed on the great enlightening being Universally Good the knowledge that enters into the power inherent in omniscience, the knowledge that enters into the infinity of the cosmos, the knowledge that perfects the realization of the sphere of all enlightened ones, the knowledge of the becoming and decay of all oceans of worlds, the knowledge of the full extent of the worlds of all sentient beings, the knowledge that abides in the extremely profound liberation of all enlightened ones and the nondiscriminating knowledge of all meditation states, the knowledge that enters into the ocean of all faculties of enlightening beings, the knowledge of elocution to turn the wheel of the teaching in the ocean of languages of all sentient beings, the knowledge that enters in all ways into the bodies of all oceans of worlds in the cosmos, and the knowledge that comprehends the voices of all Buddhas.

As in this world in the presence of the Buddha the enlightening being Universally Good experienced the Buddhas bestowing such knowledge, so in all oceans of worlds, as well as in each atom of all those worlds, so did all the enlightening beings Universally Good there experience this. Why? Because they had realized that state of mental focus in this way.

Then the Buddhas of the ten directions each extended his right hand and patted Universally Good on the head. Their hands were each adorned with the marks of greatness, being finely webbed, emanating light, fragrance, and flames. They also produced the various wondrous tones of all Buddhas. And within it were manifested the phenomena of mystical powers, the ocean of vows of universal goodness of all enlightening beings of past, present, and future, the cycles of pure teachings of all enlightened ones, as well as the images of the Buddhas of past, present, and future.

As in this world Universally Good was patted on the head by all the Buddhas of the ten directions, so in all the oceans of worlds, and in each atom of those worlds, the enlightening beings Universally Good there were patted on the head by the Buddhas of the ten directions.

Then the enlightening being Universally Good arose from this concentration; when he did so, he rose from media of oceans of concentrations numerous as atoms in all oceans of worlds. For example, he rose from the medium of concentration of skillful knowledge realizing that the worlds of past, present, and future have no distinction in the succession of instants; he rose from the medium of concentration of knowledge of all the subtlest and most minute constituents of all universes in all times; he rose from the medium of concentration on the manifestation of all buddha-fields of past, present, and future; he rose from the medium of concentration revealing the dwelling places of all living beings; he rose from the medium of concentration of knowledge of various differences in locations of the universes of the ten directions; he rose from the medium of concentration of knowledge of boundlessly vast clouds of buddha-bodies existing in every atom; he rose from the medium of concentration of explanations of the ocean of inner principles in all things.

When the enlightening being Universally Good rose from such media of concentration, all the enlightening beings each found oceanic clouds of concentrations, numerous as atoms in an ocean of worlds, found oceanic clouds of spells, oceanic clouds of techniques to teach everything, oceanic clouds of ways of felicitous expression, oceanic clouds of practices, oceanic clouds of lights from the knowledge of the treasury of virtues of all who realize thusness, oceanic clouds of nondiscriminating techniques of the powers, knowledges, and wisdom of all enlightened ones, oceanic clouds of Buddhas each manifesting myriad lands in each and every pore, oceanic clouds of enlightening beings one by one manifesting descent from the palace of the Tushita heaven to be born on earth and become an enlightened Buddha, turn the wheel of the teaching, and enter into ultimate extinction, all as numerous as atoms in an ocean of worlds.

As when in this world the enlightening being Universally Good rose from concentration all the hosts of enlightening beings received such blessings, so in all the oceans of worlds, as well as in each atom of each world, the same thing occurred.

At that time, by the spiritual power of all the Buddhas and the power of Universally Good's concentration, all oceans of worlds in the ten directions trembled. Each world was arrayed with precious elements and gave forth wondrous sound, explaining all things. And on each Buddha, in the ocean of sites of enlightenment where the masses gathered, everywhere there rained ten kinds of clouds of regal jewels:

clouds of beautiful gold star jewels, jewels like precious discs descending, shining light jewels, jewels of the treasury manifesting the images of enlightening beings, jewels extolling the names of Buddhas, jewels of brilliant light illuminating the sites of enlightenment in buddha-fields everywhere, jewels whose light reflects the various miracles everywhere, jewels praising the virtues of all enlightening beings, jewels with a light that shines like the sun, jewels whose delightful music is heard everywhere.

After the universal rain of these ten kinds of clouds of jewels, all the Buddhas emitted lights from their pores, and in the light rays spoke verses:

Universally Good is present in all lands
Sitting on a jeweled lotus throne, beheld by all;
He manifests all psychic powers
And is able to enter infinite meditations.

The Universally Good always fill the universe
With various bodies flowing everywhere,
With concentration, psychic power, skill and strength,
In a universal voice teaching extensively without hindrance.

In every land, in the presence of all the Buddhas,
Various states of concentration revealing psychic powers,
Each psychic power pervades everywhere
In all lands of the ten directions.

As with the Buddhas of all lands,
So it is in all the atoms of the lands as well;
The phenomena of concentration and mystic powers
Are the will power of the illuminator.

Universally Good physically is like space,
Abiding by reality, not a land,
According to the heart's desires of all beings
Manifesting all kinds of embodiments, equal to all.

Universally Good, abiding at peace in great determination,
Thus attained these infinite spiritual powers,
In any lands of all buddha bodies
Manifesting his form going there.

All the myriad oceans are boundless:
He reproduces his body infinitely and dwells there;
All lands of his manifestation are purified,
And in an instant are seen many eons.

Universally Good lives peacefully in all lands:
The spiritual powers he displays are incomparable;
The trembling extending everywhere
Causes those who look to be able to see.

The knowledge, virtue, and powers of all Buddhas,
Their various great qualities, he has all fulfilled;
By the medium of techniques of all meditations
He shows his past enlightening acts.

Such independence, inconceivable,
Is manifest in the lands of the ten directions
To reveal the universal entrance of all meditations;
In the clouds of buddha light his praises are sung.

Then all the hosts of enlightening beings turned to Universally Good, joined their palms and gazed respectfully at Universally Good; imbued with the psychic power of the Enlightened, they sang in praise with the same voice,

Born from the teachings of the Enlightened,
Also originating from the will power of the Buddha,
The womb of space, the equality of real thusness:
You have purified this body of reality.

In the congregations of all buddha-fields
Universally Good is omnipresent there;
The light of the oceans of universal virtue and wisdom
Equally illumine everywhere, so all are visible.

The immensely vast oceans of virtues of Universally Good
Goes everywhere to approach the enlightened;
To the lands within all atoms
He can travel and clearly appear there.

O Child of Buddha, we always see you
Associating with all the enlightened ones,
Abiding in the real state of concentration
For eons numerous as atoms in all lands.

The child of Buddha, with an all-pervading body,
Can go to the lands in all directions,
Liberating all the oceans of living beings,
Entering into all the parts of the cosmos.

Entering into all particles of the cosmos,
The body is endless and undifferentiated;
Omnipresent as space,
It expounds the great teaching of the realization of thusness.

The light of all virtue,
Immense like clouds, power surpassing,
Traveling to all oceans of living beings
Expounding the incomparable way practiced by all Buddhas.

Cultivating and learning the supreme practice of universal goodness
In order to liberate sentient beings for oceans of eons,
Expounding all truths, like a great cloud,
The voice is tremendous, none do not hear.

How can the land be established?
How do the Buddhas appear?
And how about beings?
Please explain truthfully the truth as it is.

BOOK FOUR

The Formation of the Worlds

THEN THE GREAT enlightening being Universally Good, by means of the spiritual power of the Buddha, looked over the oceans of all worlds, the oceans of all sentient beings, the oceans of all Buddhas, the oceans of all elemental realms, the oceans of all sentient beings' actions, the oceans of all sentient beings' faculties and inclinations, the oceans of all teaching cycles of all Buddhas, the oceans of all time periods, the oceans of all powers of vows of the Buddhas, and the oceans of all the Buddhas' miracles.

Having thus observed and examined all these, he declared to all the enlightening beings in the ocean of congregations at all scenes of enlightenment, "Children of Buddha, the Buddhas' pure knowledge of the formation and disintegration of all oceans of worlds is inconceivable. Their knowledge of the oceans of actions of all sentient beings is inconceivable. Their knowledge of the oceans of structures of all elemental realms is inconceivable. Their knowledge which can tell of the oceans of all inclinations, understandings, and faculties is inconceivable. Their instantaneous knowledge of all the past, present, and future is inconceivable. Their knowledge revealing the boundless ocean of vows of all enlightened ones is inconceivable. Their knowledge demonstrating the oceans of miracles of all Buddhas is inconceivable. Their knowledge operating the cycles of teaching is inconceivable. Their knowledge of how to construct explanations is inconceivable. Their pure buddhabodies are inconceivable. Their oceans of boundless forms illumining everywhere are inconceivable. Their marks and subsidiary refinements, all pure, are inconceivable. Their ocean of boundless auras, fully pure, is inconceivable. Their ocean of clouds of light of various colors is inconceivable. Their ocean of extraordinary jewel radiance is inconceivable. Their ocean of perfect languages is inconceivable. Their ocean of powers of magical displays to civilize and develop sentient beings is inconceivable. Their oceans of courageous taming of all sentient beings, letting none go to ruin, is inconceivable. Their abode in the state of buddhahood is inconceivable. Their entry into the realm of realization of thusness is inconceivable. Their protective and sustaining power is inconceivable. Their examination of all spheres of enlightened knowledge is inconceivable. Their spheres of power, which none can overcome, are inconceivable. Their quality of fearlessness, which none can surpass, is inconceivable. Their abiding in undifferentiated concentration is inconceivable. Their miraculous displays are inconceivable. Their pure independent knowledge is inconceivable. All the enlightening teachings, which none can destroy, are inconceivable.

"All these things I shall, with the power of the Buddha and of all enlightened ones, fully expound, to cause all sentient beings to enter the ocean of knowledge and wisdom of the Buddha, to cause all enlightening beings to abide securely in the ocean of virtues of the Buddha, to cause all oceans of worlds to be adorned by the freedom of the Buddhas, to cause the lineage of the enlightened ones to continue unbroken throughout all ages, to cause the real true nature of all things to be pointed out in all oceans of worlds, to cause all sentient beings to be taught in accordance with their understandings, to cause the expedient methods according to the ocean of all beings' faculties to induce them to engender the qualities of buddhahood, to cause the mountains of all obstructions to be smashed, according to the inclinations of all beings, to cause all sentient beings to purify and master the essential ways of emancipation in accordance with their mentalities, and to cause all enlightening beings to abide in the ocean of vows of universal goodness and wisdom."

Now the enlightening being Universally Good, because he wished to gladden the innumerable beings at the site of enlightenment, to increase their appreciation of all truths, to cause them to conceive an ocean of great true faith and resolve, to cause them to purify the all-sided cosmic matrix body, to cause them to establish the ocean of vows of the Universally Good, to cause them to purify the eye of equanimous knowledge, which enters equally into past, present, and future, to cause them to increase the ocean of great wisdom illumining the repository of all worlds, to cause them to develop memory power to hold all the teaching cycles, to cause the whole realm of buddhahood to be manifested in all enlightenment sites, to cause all the Buddha teachings to be brought forth, to increase the nature of vast, profound all-knowledge of the cosmos, he spoke these verses:

The exceedingly profound ocean of virtues of wisdom
Appears in innumerable lands throughout the ten directions,
Its light shining everywhere, turning the wheel of the teaching
In accord with what the various sentient beings need to see.

The ocean of lands of the ten directions is inconceivable:
Buddha has purified them all, over immeasurable eons;
In order to edify beings and cause them to mature
He appears in all lands.

The Buddha's realm is most profound, inconceivable;
He shows it to all beings, letting them enter:
But their minds like the petty and are attached to existents,
So they cannot understand what the Buddha has realized.

If any have pure faith and unshakable minds
And are always able to associate with good teachers,
All the Buddhas will give their power
So they can enter enlightened knowledge.

Beyond flattery and deception, hearts pure,
Always gladly kind and compassionate, of joyful natures,
Determination broad and great, faith profound:
Such people, hearing this teaching, are glad.

Dwelling on the ground of universally good vows,
Cultivating the pure ways of enlightening beings,
Regarding the cosmos like space:
These people can know the Buddha's sphere.

Such enlightening beings gain true benefit
Seeing the Buddha's mystical powers;
None who practice other paths can know:
Only those of universally good practice can understand.

Sentient beings are infinite
Yet Buddha guards them all in his thoughts;
Teaching the truth, reaching all:
The power of Vairocana's realm.

All lands are in my body
And so are the Buddhas living there;
Watch my pores,
And I will show you the Buddha's realm.

The practice and vows of Universally Good are boundless;
I have already fully cultivated them.
The vast body of the realm of the universal eye
Is the Buddha's sphere: listen clearly.

Then the great enlightening being Universally Good said to the great
masses, "O Children of Buddha, there are ten things about the world
oceans which the Buddhas of past, present, and future have explained,
do explain, and will explain. What are these ten? They are the causes
and conditions of the origination of the world oceans, the bases of the

world oceans, the forms of the world oceans, the substances and natures of the world oceans, the adornments of the world oceans, the purity of the world oceans, the appearance of Buddhas in the world oceans, the eons of subsistence of the world oceans, the differences in changes over the ages of the world oceans, and the aspects of the world oceans that have no differences. If expressed in brief there are these ten things, but if they are fully expounded, there are as many as atoms in an ocean of worlds, which the Buddhas of past, present, and future have, do, and will explain.

"Children of Buddha, if explained in brief, there are ten kinds of causes and conditions by which all oceans of worlds have been formed, are formed, and will be formed. What are the ten? They are: because of the Buddhas' mystical powers, because they must be so by natural law, because of the acts of all sentient beings, because of what is realized by all enlightening beings developing omniscience, because of the roots of goodness accumulated by both enlightening beings and all sentient beings, because of the power of the vows of enlightening beings purifying lands, because enlightening beings have accomplished practical undertakings without regressing, because of the enlightening beings' freedom of pure resolve, because of the independent power flowing from the roots of goodness of all enlightened ones and the moment of enlightenment of all Buddhas, and because of the independent power of the vows of the Universally Good. This is a summary explanation of ten kinds of causes; if I were to explain in full, there are as many as atoms in an ocean of worlds."

Then the great enlightening being Universally Good, in order to reiterate the meaning of what he had said, receiving the power of the Buddha, looked over the ten directions and spoke these verses:

The boundless ocean of myriad lands explained
Vairocana Buddha has all beautifully purified.
The World Honored One's realm is inconceivable;
Such are his knowledge, wisdom, and mystic powers.

Enlightening beings cultivate the practice of oceans of vows,
Universally adapting to the inclinations of sentient beings.
The mentalities of sentient beings are boundless;
The enlightening beings' lands extend throughout all ten directions.

Enlightening beings aim for omniscience,
Diligently cultivating various spiritual powers,
Generating oceans of infinite vows,
Developing vast, expansive lands.

Cultivating oceans of practices, without bound,
They enter the realm of buddhahood, also infinite;
In order to purify the lands in the ten directions,
They spend countless eons in each land.

Sentient beings are muddled by afflictions,
Their conceptions and inclinations are not the same;
According to their mental states they perform inconceivably many
    acts,
Thereby forming the oceans of all lands.

The treasury of adornments of the lands of Buddha-children
Is made of jewels of undefiled light;
This depends on a mind of vast resolute faith.
Their dwelling places in all quarters are all like this.

Enlightening beings can cultivate the universally good practice,
Traveling paths as numerous as atomic particles in the cosmos,
In each atom revealing countless lands
Pure and vast as space.

They manifest mystic powers equal in extent to space
And go to enlightenment sites where the Buddhas are;
Upon their lotus seats they reveal many forms,
In each and every body containing all lands.

In a single instant they reveal past, present, and future,
Where all oceans of lands are formed.
Buddha, by appropriate techniques, enters them all:
This is what Vairocana has purified.

Then the enlightening being Universally Good said to the congregation,
"O Children of Buddha, each of the oceans of worlds has bases of
support as numerous as atoms in an ocean of worlds. That is to say,
they may rest on all adornments, or in space, or on the lights of all
jewels, or on the lights of all Buddhas, or on the lights of the colors of
all jewels, or on the voices of all Buddhas, or on illusory actions, or on
thunderbolt bearers in the form of powerful titans, or on the bodies of
all the leaders of the worlds, or on the bodies of all enlightening beings,
or on the ocean of all different embellishments produced by the power
of the vows of the universally good enlightening beings. The oceans of
worlds have such bases as these, as many as atoms in an ocean of
worlds." Then, in order to reiterate the meaning of this, Universally
Good, receiving the power of the Buddha, surveyed the ten directions
and said in verse,

All the various lands there are
Filling space in the ten directions
Sustained by Buddha's mystic power
Appear in all places, so all can see.

There are some varieties of lands
All made of undefiled jewels,
Pure gems, the most exquisite,
Radiating everywhere oceans of light.

Then there are lands of pure light
Which rest in the realm of space;
Some are in oceans of jewels,
Some rest in mines of light.

Buddha, in the midst of this ocean of groups,
Expounds teachings, all skillful and subtle;
The realm of the Buddhas is boundlessly vast:
Beings who see it are gladdened at heart.

Some are embellished with precious stones
Shaped like flower lamps in vast arrays,
Their clouds of fragrant flame-light blazing with color,
Covered with webs of jewel lights.

Some lands have no boundaries;
They rest in the deep, immense lotus sea,
Broad, pure, unique among worlds,
Because they're adorned by Buddhas' goodness.

Some world-oceans revolve,
Stabilized by Buddha's power;
Enlightening beings are everywhere there,
Always seeing immeasurably vast treasures.

Some rest in thunderbolt hands,
Some on celestial leaders' bodies;
The supremely honored Vairocana
Is always here actively teaching.

Some rest evenly on jewel trees,
Or likewise on clouds of fragrant flames;
Some rest on great bodies of water,
Some in the ocean of indestructible diamond.

Some rest on thunderbolt banners,
Some are in flower seas;
Vast mystic powers all-pervading,
Vairocana here can appear.

Some long, some short, there are innumerable kinds;
Different too are the rings they form.
Their stores of beautiful adornments are extraordinary:
Only the purified and cultivated can see.

Thus each of them are different,
But all rest on the ocean of vows.
Some lands are always in space,
With Buddhas like clouds filling them.

Some hang upside-down in space,
Sometimes existing, sometimes not;
Some lands are extremely pure,
Resting in enlightening beings' precious crowns.

The great spiritual powers of the Buddhas everywhere
All are seen herein;
The voices of the Buddhas fill them all,
Produced by the power of deeds.

Some lands fill the universe,
Pure, undefiled, arising from mind,
Like reflections, illusions, boundlessly vast,
Each different, like in Indra's net.

Some show stores of various adornments
Set up in empty space.
Realms of actions are inconceivable:
Buddha's power reveals them for all to see.

Inside the particles of each land
Constantly revealing the Buddha-lands,
Their numbers infinite, equal to beings:
Such is the action of the Universally Good.

In order to fully develop beings
He cultivated practice here for infinite eons,
Producing great miraculous displays
Extending everywhere through the cosmos.

In each atom of the lands of the cosmos
Rest the vast oceans of worlds;
Clouds of Buddhas equally cover them all,
Filling every place.

Like the free action in one atom
So it is in all atoms;
All the great occult powers of Buddhas and enlightening beings
Vairocana can cause to appear.

All the vast lands
Are like reflections, illusions, or flames:
Nowhere is their origin seen,
Nor where they go or whence they came.

Disintegration and formation recur in cycles
Without pause, in the midst of space;
All depends on pure vows
Sustained by the vast power of action.

Then the enlightening being Universally Good said further to the great
congregation, "Children of Buddha, the oceans of worlds have various
different forms and characteristics. That is to say, some are round,
some square, some neither round nor square. There are infinite
distinctions. Some are shaped like whirlpools, some like mountains of
flames, some like trees, some like flowers, some like palaces, some like
living creatures, some like Buddhas. There are as many forms such as
these as there are atoms in an ocean of worlds."

Then, to review this point, Universally Good, imbued with the
power of the Buddha, looked over the ten directions and said,

The oceans of lands are variously different:
Various adornments, various supports;
Different forms, all beautiful, pervade the ten directions:
You should together all observe them.

Some are round, some are square,
Some triangular, some octagonal;
Gemstone-wheel shaped, lotus blossoms, and so on:
All are different, according to deeds.

Some have arrays of pure flames,
Mixed with gold, most rarely fine,

All doors open, with no resistance:
This is from deeds broadminded and pure.

The store of boundless differences of the oceans of worlds
Is like clouds draped in the sky,
Jewel discs spread on the ground in wonderful arrays,
The lights of the Buddhas shining therein.

All lands, distinctions of mind,
Appear reflected in various lights;
In these oceans of worlds
Buddhas each manifest mystical powers.

Some lands are dirty, some are pure;
Pleasant or painful, each is different.
This comes from the inconceivable ocean of acts:
Cyclic phenomena are always like this.

Inside a single hair pore, inconceivable lands
With various bases, many as atoms:
In each of them a universal illuminator
Expounds the truth in the midst of the crowd.

In a single atom, great and small lands,
Variously different, as numerous as atoms;
Level, high and low, each is different:
Buddha goes to all to operate the teaching.

The lands manifested in a single atom
Are all the occult power of the original vow:
According to the various differences in inclination of mind
All can be made, in the midst of space.

In all atoms of all lands
Buddha enters, each and every one,
Producing miracle displays for sentient beings:
Such is the way of Vairocana.

Then the enlightening being Universally Good also said to the great assembly, "Children of Buddha, know that the oceans of worlds have various substances. Some have bodies of arrays of all jewels, some are of various ornaments made of all precious substances, some are of lights of all jewels, some are of lights of various colors, some are of lights of various adornments, some are composed of Buddhas' powers, some are of characteristics of fine gems, some are made of miraculous displays of

Buddhas, some are of jewel sun discs, some are of extremely minute, fine jewels, some are made of radiance of all jewels, some are of various fragrances, some are made of crowns of precious flowers, some are of all jewel reflections, some are made of what is manifested by all adornments, some are made of an instant of mind manifesting the whole cosmos, some are made of jewels in the forms of enlightening beings, some are made of jewel flower pistils, some are made of the spoken sounds of the Buddhas." Then, to repeat this, Universally Good surveyed the ten directions by the Buddha's power and said,

> There are some oceans of worlds
> Compounded of jewels,
> Solid and unbreakable,
> Resting on precious lotus blossoms.
>
> Some are pure light beams
> Of unknowable origin;
> These arrays of all light beams
> Rest in empty space.
>
> Some are made of pure light
> And also rest on light rays
> Embellished with clouds of light
> Where enlightening beings roam.
>
> There are some oceans of lands
> Born of the power of vows,
> Existing like reflections:
> They can't be grasped or explained.
>
> Some are made of precious stones
> Emitting sunlike light;
> Discs of pearls adorn the ground,
> And enlightening beings abound.
>
> Some lands are made of jewel flames,
> Covered with clouds of flames,
> The radiance of the jewels superb;
> All comes from results of acts.
>
> Some are born of subtle forms,
> With various features adorning the ground,
> Like crowns holding all jewels;
> These come from the Buddha's work.

Some are born from the ocean of minds,
Existing according to what the minds understand.
Like illusions, they have no locus:
All are mental constructions.

Some are made of the precious light
Of the Buddha's aura;
All the Buddhas appear therein,
Each producing miracles.

Some universally good enlightening beings
Produce various oceans of lands,
Adorned by the power of their vows,
All exceptionally sublime.

Then the enlightening being Universally Good also said to the great congregation, "Know that the oceans of worlds have various adornments. Some are adorned by all ornaments producing beautiful clouds, some by explanations of the virtues of all enlightening beings, some by explanations of the rewards of actions of all sentient beings, some by revelations of the ocean of vows of all enlightening beings, some by representations of the images of all Buddhas of past, present, and future, some by the spheres of occult powers revealing boundless eons in a single moment, some by production of all buddha-bodies, some by production of fragrant clouds of all jewels, some by radiant lights showing the wonderful things in all enlightenment scenes, some by illustration of the practices and vows of all universally good ones. There are as many such adornments as atoms in an ocean of worlds."

Then, to repeat, Universally Good, imbued with the power of the Buddha, looked over the ten directions and said,

The vast oceans of lands are boundless;
All are made from pure action,
With various adornments and various abodes,
They fill all ten directions.

Clouds of jewel flames of boundless forms,
Vast arrays of adornments, not the same,
Always appear in all oceans of lands,
Radiating subtle sounds expounding the truth.

Adorned by the various great vows
Of the enlightening beings' boundless sea of virtues,

These lands simultaneously produce sublime sounds
Shaking the network of the lands of the ten directions.

The ocean of beings' acts is vast, immeasurable;
According to the results they effect, the lands are each different.
The adornments in all places
Can tell of this, by the Buddha's powers.

The spiritual powers of Buddhas past, present, and future
Appear throughout the oceans of lands;
In each phenomenon all the Buddhas appear:
Thus do they purify—you should observe.

Past, future, and present eons,
All lands in the ten directions,
And all the adornments therein,
All appear in each land.

In all phenomena are countless Buddhas:
As many as beings, filling the world;
In order to teach they produce mystic effects
Whereby they adorn the oceans of lands.

All the adornments emit beautiful clouds
Of various flowers and fragrant flames,
With clouds of jewels appearing as well:
The oceans of worlds are embellished with these.

All sites of enlightenment in the ten directions
Are complete with all kinds of adornment;
Flowing lights spread afar, like clouds of color:
All are shown in this ocean of lands.

The practice of the vows of the universally good
Buddha children have practiced for eons as many as beings;
Boundless lands have they all adorned,
All appearing in all places.

Then Universally Good also said to the congregation, "Know that in
the oceans of worlds there are oceans of purifying techniques as many
as atoms in an ocean of worlds. That is to say, the enlightening beings
associate with all good teachers to cultivate the same roots of goodness;
they cause great clouds of virtues to grow, extending throughout
the universe; they clarify all their great beliefs; they contemplate the
spheres of all enlightening beings and abide therein; they cultivate all

means of transcendence and fulfill them; they contemplate all stages of enlightenment and enter them; they produce the ocean of all pure aspirations; they cultivate all practices essential for emancipation; they enter into the ocean of all adornments; they perfect the power of purifying methods. There are as many of these and others as there are atoms in an ocean of worlds."

Then, to reiterate, Universally Good looked over the ten directions by the power of the Buddha invested in him, and said,

> The adornments of all oceans of worlds
> Are born from countless techniques, vows, and powers;
> All the oceans of lands always shine,
> Produced by the power of countless pure deeds.

> Forever associating with good teachers,
> Together doing good works, all pure,
> With great compassion extending to all beings,
> Thereby are world-oceans adorned.

> Concentration on all the teachings,
> Meditation, liberation, and skill in means
> Are all purified with the Buddha:
> Thus are the world-oceans born.

> Developing boundless certainty,
> Able to understand like the Buddha,
> Having purified patience and skill in means,
> Thus can boundless lands be purified.

> Cultivating supreme practices to aid sentient beings,
> Virtue great and always growing,
> Like clouds spreading as far as space:
> Thus are world-oceans perfected.

> The transcending means are infinite, many as beings;
> All have the Buddhas practiced to perfection;
> Transcendent vow-taking has no end:
> Pure world-oceans are born from here.

> Purely practicing all peerless truths,
> Developing boundless liberating practices,
> Edifying beings by various means:
> Thus are beautified oceans of worlds.

> Practicing techniques of adornment,
> Entering the ocean of teachings of enlightened virtues,

Causing all beings to dry up the source of suffering:
Thus are vast lands perfected.

The ocean of powers is peerlessly great,
Causing all beings to plant roots of good,
Making offerings to all the enlightened:
Thus are boundless lands all purified.

Then Universally Good addressed the masses again: "Buddha children, know that in each ocean of worlds there are differences in the manifestation of the Buddhas, as many as atomic particles in an ocean of worlds. That is, some manifest small bodies, some large bodies, some manifest short lives, some long lives, some only adorn and purify a single buddha-land, some adorn and purify innumerable buddha-lands, some only reveal one vehicle of teaching, some reveal inconceivably many vehicles of teaching, some appear to tame a few sentient beings, some tame boundless sentient beings. Such differences as these are as many as atomic particles in an ocean of worlds."

Then Universally Good, to review, looked over the ten directions by the power he received from the Buddha, and said,

Various accommodating methods of the Buddhas
Appear in all the oceans of worlds,
All adapted to the inclinations of sentient beings:
This is the Buddhas' power of skillful expedients.

The reality-body of the Buddhas is inconceivable:
Colorless, formless, beyond any image,
Yet able to manifest myriad forms for sentient beings,
Causing them to see, according to their inclinations.

Some manifest short lives for beings,
Some appear to live for countless eons;
The reality-body manifests throughout the ten directions,
Appearing in the world according to suitability.

Some there are who beautify and purify all
The inconceivable oceans of worlds in all directions;
And some only purify one single land,
Yet showing all within that one.

Some, according to the mentalities of sentient beings,
Reveal inconceivably many various vehicles of liberation;

Some only expound one vehicle of teaching,
Yet within that one are revealed innumerable methods.

Some there are who, naturally enlightened,
Cause a few beings to abide in the Way;
Some can in a single instant
Awaken countless deluded ones.

Some produce mystical clouds from their pores
Which manifest countless, boundless Buddhas
Appearing in all worlds,
Liberating beings by various means.

Some there are whose spoken sounds pervade everywhere
Explaining truth in accord with mental inclinations of beings,
Through inconceivably many eons
Taming oceans of countless beings.

Some have infinite beautified worlds,
Their congregations pure, sitting solemnly,
Buddhas like clouds spreading over,
Filling the oceans of worlds in the ten directions.

The techniques of the Buddhas are inconceivable,
All appearing in accord with beings' minds,
Abiding in various beautified fields,
Extending throughout all lands.

Then Universally Good again addressed the great assembly: "Buddha-children, know that the oceans of worlds have as many spans of existence as there are atoms in an ocean of worlds. That is, some abide for an incalculable eon, some abide for an infinite eon, some abide for a boundless eon, some abide for an incomparable eon, some abide for an uncountable eon, some abide for an unspeakable eon, some abide for an inconceivable eon, some abide for an immeasurable eon, some abide for an inexplicable eon. There are as many such spans as atoms in an ocean of worlds."

Then, to review, Universally Good, looking over the ten directions by the power received from the Buddha, said,

Among the oceans of worlds are various ages,
Adorned by vast, extensive technical skills;
Observing all the lands in the ten directions,
The differences in the measures of their ages become clear.

I see that the eon lengths in the world-oceans of the ten directions
Are innumerable, same as sentient beings:
Some long, some short, some are without bounds;
I now tell of them, by the Buddha's voice.

I see the oceans of lands in the ten directions:
Some abide for eons numerous as atoms,
Some for one eon, some for numberless;
Each is different, due to the variety of vows.

Some are wholly pure, some wholly defiled;
Then again, in some purity and defilement are mixed.
The structures of the oceans of vows vary,
Abiding in the conceptions of sentient beings.

Having cultivated practices for eons as many as atoms in a
    land
And attained vast and pure oceans of worlds,
The Buddhas' realm is fully adorned,
Abiding forever, through boundless eons.

Some eons are called Light of Various Jewels,
Some, Mind of Radiant Eyes, or Equal Sound,
Undefiled Light, or Eon of Virtue;
These pure eons contain all eons.

There are pure eons where one Buddha appears,
Or in one eon countless Buddhas may appear.
With inexhaustible skill in means and great will power,
They enter into all the various ages.

Infinite eons may enter one eon,
Or one eon may enter many eons:
The various aspects of the ocean of all eons
Clearly appear in the lands of the ten directions.

The adornments of all eons
May all appear in one eon;
Or the adornments of one eon
May enter all boundless eons.

From the first moment to the completion of the eon,
All is born from the conceptions of beings' minds.
All oceans of lands, their eons boundless,
Are purified by one technique.

Then Universally Good also said to the masses, "Children of Buddha, you should know that the oceans of worlds have as many differences in changes in the ages as there are atoms in an ocean of worlds. That is, as a consequence of natural law, the oceans of worlds have innumerable changes of the ages, forming and disintegrating; because defiled beings live in them, the oceans of worlds have changes in the ages, becoming defiled; as a result of having sentient beings who cultivate great virtues living in them, the oceans of worlds have changes in the ages coming to have some purity in the midst of their defilements; as a result of enlightening beings with faith and understanding living there, world oceans have changes in the ages, coming to have more purity than defilement; as a result of innumerable beings there conceiving the will for enlightenment, the oceans of worlds have changes in their ages, becoming totally pure; as a result of enlightening beings traveling in the various worlds, the oceans of worlds have changes in the ages, becoming beautified with boundless adornment; as a result of the enlightening beings of all the world-oceans in the ten directions gathering, world-oceans have changes in the ages, becoming beautified with infinite great adornments; because of the Buddhas passing away into nirvana, world oceans have changes in the ages, their adornments dying out; because of Buddhas appearing in the worlds, oceans of worlds have changes in the ages, becoming extensively beautified and purified; because of the mystic powers and edifying miracles of the Buddhas, world-oceans have changes in the ages, becoming pure all over. There are as many such changes as atoms in an ocean of worlds."

Then, to reiterate, the enlightening being Universally Good, looking over the ten directions by the power received from the Buddha, said in verse,

> All lands are born
> According to the power of actions;
> You all should observe
> The forms of changes as they are.
>
> Defiled sentient beings are bound
> By habitual confusions, to be feared;
> Their minds cause oceans of worlds
> To all become defiled.
>
> If any have pure hearts
> And cultivate virtuous deeds,
> Their minds will cause oceans of worlds
> To have purity mixed with defilement.

If enlightening beings of faith and understanding
Are born in the age,
According to what's in their minds
Purity mixed with defilement will show.

When infinite sentient beings
Determine on enlightenment,
Their minds will cause world-oceans
To be pure for that age.

When boundless billions of enlightening beings
Travel to all quarters,
Adornments, all of them equal,
Are variously seen through the age.

When in each and every atom
Of Buddha-lands as many as atoms
Enlightening beings gather together,
All the lands are pure.

When a Buddha passes away
That land's adornments perish;
If no beings are vessels of truth,
That land becomes defiled.

If a Buddha appears in the world
Everything is marvelous;
In accord with the purity of mind,
All adornments are complete.

The spiritual powers of the Buddhas
Are shown in inconceivable numbers;
Then the ocean of lands
Are all totally pure.

Then Universally Good again addressed the assembly: "Children of
Buddha, know that there are many ways in which the oceans of worlds
are not different, as many as atoms in an ocean of worlds. That is, there
is no difference in the number of worlds in each ocean of worlds, being
as many as atoms in an ocean of worlds; there is no difference in the
powers of the Buddhas appearing in each ocean of worlds; there is no
difference in that all enlightenment sites in each ocean of worlds pervade the cosmos in all directions; there is no difference in the assemblies
at the enlightenment sites of all the Buddhas in each ocean of worlds;
there is no difference in the auras of all the Buddhas in each ocean of

worlds pervading the cosmos; there is no difference in the miracles and epithets of all Buddhas in each ocean of worlds; there is no difference in the voices of all the Buddhas in each ocean of worlds pervading the ocean of worlds and abiding forever. There is no difference in the techniques of the teaching cycles in each ocean of worlds; there is no difference in that in each ocean of worlds all oceans of worlds everywhere enter into the individual atom; there is no difference in that in each and every atom of each ocean of worlds are manifest the vast realms of all the Buddhas of the past, present, and future. The aspects of the oceans of worlds which are not different are, briefly stated, thus; if they are fully told, there are as many as atoms in an ocean of worlds."

Then the enlightening being Universally Good, to recapitulate, looked over the ten directions by the power of the Buddha and said in verse,

> In each atom are many oceans of worlds,
> Their locations each different, all beautifully pure;
> Thus does infinity enter into one,
> Yet each unit's distinct, with no overlap.

> Within each atom are inconceivably many Buddhas
> Appearing everywhere in accord with beings' minds,
> Reaching everywhere in all oceans of worlds:
> This technique of theirs is the same for all.

> In each and every atom are enlightenment trees,
> All draped with various adornments
> In which all lands alike appear;
> In this all are no different.

> In each atom are congregations numerous as atoms,
> All surrounding the leader of humanity,
> Going beyond all, pervading the worlds,
> Yet with no crowding or confusion.

> In each atom are innumerable lights
> Pervading the lands of the ten directions,
> All showing the Buddhas' enlightening practices,
> The same in all oceans of worlds.

> In each atom are infinite bodies
> Transforming like clouds, circulating everywhere;
> By mystic buddha-powers they guide all beings,
> No different in all ten directions' lands.

In each atom are expounded many teachings;
Those teachings are pure and revolve like wheels.
The gates of freedom by various means
Are all told of, without discrimination.

One atom emanates all Buddhas' voices,
Filling those beings who are receptors of truth;
Omnipresent in the oceans of worlds for countless eons,
These voices too have no difference.

The countless beautiful adornments of oceans of worlds
All enter inside a single atom;
Such mystic powers of the Buddhas
All arise from the nature of action.

In each atom the Buddhas of all times
Appear, according to inclinations;
While their essential nature neither comes nor goes,
By their vow power they pervade the worlds.

BOOK FIVE

The Flower Bank World

THEN THE ENLIGHTENING BEING Universally Good again addressed the great assembly, saying, "Children of Buddha, this Flower Bank Array ocean of worlds was adorned and purified by Vairocana Buddha as in the remote past he cultivated enlightening practices for as many eons as atoms in an ocean of worlds, in each eon associating with as many Buddhas as there are atoms in an ocean of worlds, in the presence of each Buddha purely practicing great vows as numerous as atoms in an ocean of worlds.

"This Flower Bank Array ocean of worlds is supported by as many atmospheres as there are atoms in the polar mountain. The bottommost atmosphere is called Impartial Abode; it holds arrays of blazing flames of all jewels above it. The next atmosphere is called Producing Various Precious Adornments; it holds diamond banners radiant with pure light above it. The next higher atmosphere is called Precious Power; it holds chimes of all jewels above it. The next higher atmosphere is called Impartial Flavor; it holds diamond orbs of the appearance of sunlight above it. The next higher atmosphere is called Various Universal Adornments; it holds flowers of light discs above it. The next higher atmosphere is called Universal Purity; it holds flaming lion thrones of all flowers above it. The next higher atmosphere is called Sound Pervading the Ten Directions; it holds banners of all regal pearls above it. The next higher atmosphere is called Light of All Jewels; it holds all diamond tree flowers above it. The next higher atmosphere is called High Velocity Universal Support; it holds mountainous clouds of all fragrant gems above it. The next higher atmosphere is called Various Mansions in Motion; it holds clouds of pedestals of all precious colors and fragrances above it. The uppermost of those atmospheres as numerous as atoms in a mountain is called Repository of Supreme Light; it holds an ocean of fragrant water, adorned by radiant diamonds. In this ocean of fragrant water is an enormous lotus blossom, called Banner of Fragrance, with pistils of all kinds of lights; this Flower Bank Array ocean of worlds rests therein. This ocean of worlds is square and level, pure and stable, surrounded by diamond circular mountains. Its lands, seas, and trees each have distinct boundaries."

Then Universally Good, to recapitulate, looked over the ten directions with the power of the Buddha and said in verse,

> In the past the Buddha, in all states of being,
> Cultivated pure deeds with Buddhas as many as atoms;
> Thus he attained the Flower Bank Array ocean of worlds
> With all kinds of jewel lights.

> His vast clouds of mercy cover all;
> He has given up his body innumerable times.
> Because of the power of his past eons of practice,
> This world now has no defilements.

> It emanates great light, which abides throughout space;
> Held by atmospheric power, it doesn't tremble or quake.
> It is adorned everywhere by jewels of Buddha's treasury;
> The power of Buddha's vows has made it pure.

> Strewn about are flowers of beautiful mines of jewels,
> Resting in the sky through the power of ancient vows.
> Over an ocean of various adornments, stable and strong,
> Clouds of light spread, filling the ten directions.

> In all the jewels are clouds of enlightening beings
> Traveling to all quarters, blazing with light;
> Rimmed with glowing flames, beautiful flower ornaments
> Circulate throughout the universe, reaching everywhere.

> From all the jewels emanates pure light
> Which totally illumines the ocean of all beings;
> Pervading all lands in the ten directions,
> It frees them from pain and turns them to enlightenment.

> The Buddhas in the jewels are equal in number to all beings;
> From their hair pores they emanate phantom forms:
> Celestial beings, world rulers, and so on,
> Including forms of all beings as well as Buddhas.

> Their magical light beams are as many as all things;
> In the light they intone the names of all Buddhas.
> By various means they teach and civilize,
> Accommodating all the various minds everywhere.

In each atom of the Flower Bank world
Is seen the universe of the elemental cosmos;
Jewel lights display Buddhas like masses of clouds:
This is the Buddha's freedom in his field.

The vast cloud of his vows extends throughout the cosmos,
Edifying all beings throughout all time.
Having completed the practice of the state of knowledge of universal good,
All the adornments there are emerge from here.

Then Universally Good again addressed the great congregation: "Children of Buddha, the surrounding mountains of this Flower Bank Array ocean of worlds rest on lotus blossoms of sun-pearls. Their mass is made of sandalwood crystals, their peaks of majestic diamonds. Their curves are made of precious stones of exquisite fragrance. They are composed of fiery diamonds. Rivers of all perfumes flow between them. Their forests are made of all kinds of jewels. They are covered with beautiful flowers and fragrant herbs, and studded with bright pearls. Nets of precious stones are draped all around. There are as many such beautiful adornments as there are atoms in an ocean of worlds."

Then, to recapitulate, Universally Good, the enlightening being, receiving spiritual power from the Buddha, looked over the ten directions and said in verse,

The great ocean of worlds has no bounds;
Its circumference of jewels is pure and multicolored.
All the adornments it has are of rare beauty;
This comes from the spiritual power of the Buddha.

Rings of jewels, rings of exquisite incense,
As well as rings of pearls and lamp flames—
Various beautiful treasures adorn it,
Whereon rest a pure ring of mountains.

Their mines are of solid jewels,
They're decorated with rose gold,
Their light blazes throughout the ten directions;
Inside and out they shine, all pure and clear.

Made of masses of diamonds,
Also raining beautiful jewels,
Their jewel atmospheres are unique and different,
Radiating pure light beautifying everywhere.

The fragrant rivers divide into streams of infinite hues,
Scattering flower-jewels and sandalwood,
With lotuses thickly blooming, like clothing spread,
And rare plants abundantly growing, all of them aromatic.

Countless jewel trees adorn everywhere,
The colors of their blooming flowers radiantly bright;
Various kinds of fine raiment are placed thereon,
With clouds of light shining everywhere, all round and full.

Countless, boundless great enlightening beings
Holding canopies, burning incense, fill the universe,
Each producing all wonderful voices
Everywhere expounding the Buddhas' true teaching.

The trees of precious elements have branches of jewels,
Each jewel branch emitting light;
Vairocana's pure body
Enters therein, causing all to see.

In all the adornments are manifest buddha-bodies
Of boundless forms and countless numbers,
All going to all quarters, reaching everywhere,
The beings they teach also being limitless.

All the adornments emit sublime sounds
Expounding the circle of the Buddha's original vows—
Buddha's independent power causes them to pervade
All the pure oceans of lands there are.

Then Universally Good also said, "The land within the surrounding mountains of this ocean of worlds is all made of diamond. Its stable, strong adornments cannot be broken. It is clean and level. It is fringed by precious stones and contains repositories of jewels. It is arrayed at intervals with all kinds of gems in the various forms of all sentient beings. It is strewn with jewel dust and spread with lotus blossoms, with jewels from fragrant mines placed among them. The various adornments fill everywhere, like clouds. It is decorated with all the embellishments of all the buddha-lands of past, present, and future. It is webbed with beautiful precious stones, which reflect the states of all the Buddhas like the net of Indra, emperor of the heavens, hanging there. The ground of this ocean of worlds has adornments such as these, as many as atoms in an ocean of worlds."

Then, to recapitulate, Universally Good, receiving spiritual power from the Buddha, looked over the ten directions and said,

That ground is level and utterly pure,
Firmly abiding, indestructible;
It is adorned with jewels everywhere,
With various gemstones interspersed.

The diamond earth is most delightful,
Embellished with jewel rings and nets,
Spread with lotus blossoms in full bloom,
With exquisite raiment covering all.

Enlightening beings' celestial crowns and jewel necklaces
Are spread all over the ground as decorations;
Sandalwood-scented jewels are strewn about,
All radiating pure, exquisite light.

Jewel flowers flame, producing subtle light;
Flames of light, like clouds, illuminate all.
These flowers, and myriad jewels,
Are strewn over the ground for adornment.

Dense clouds rise and fill the ten directions
With tremendous rays of light that have no end,
Reaching all lands in the ten directions
Expounding the Buddha's vivifying teaching.

All the Buddha's vows are in the jewels
Revealing boundless, vast eons;
What the Supreme Knower did in days gone by
Is all seen within these jewels.

Into all the jewels of this ground
Come and enter all the Buddha-fields—
And into each atom of those buddha-fields
Also enter all lands.

In the Flower Bank world, adorned with wondrous jewels
Enlightening beings travel throughout the ten directions,
Expounding the universal vows of the Great Hero:
This is their power of freedom in enlightenment sites.

The ground arrayed with beautiful precious stones
Radiates pure light replete with all adornments
Filling the cosmos, equal to space;
Buddha's power naturally manifests like this.

Those who master the vows of universal good,
Those of great knowledge who enter the Buddha's realm,
Can know, in this ocean of lands,
All such mystic transformations as these.

Then Universally Good also said to the assembly, "In the land masses of this ocean of worlds are seas of fragrant waters, as numerous as atoms in unspeakably many buddha-fields. All beautiful jewels adorn the floors of those seas; gems of exquisite fragrances adorn their shores. They are meshed with luminous diamonds. Their fragrant waters shine with the colors of all jewels. Flowers of all kinds of gems swirl on their surfaces. Sandalwood powder settles on the bottom of the seas. They emanate the sounds of Buddhas' speech. They radiate jewellike light. Boundless enlightening beings, holding various canopies, manifest mystic powers causing the adornments of all worlds to appear therein. Stairways of ten kinds of precious substances are set out in rows, with balustrades of ten kinds of jewels surrounding them. White lotuses ornamented with jewels, as many as atoms in four continents, are spread over the waters, in full bloom. There are unspeakable hundreds of thousands of billions of trillions of banners of ten precious elements, banners of belled gauze of raiments of all jewels, as many as sand grains in the Ganges river, jewel flower palaces of boundless forms, as many as sand grains in the Ganges river, a hundred thousand billion trillion lotus castles of ten precious substances, forests of jewel trees as many as atoms in four continents, networks of flaming jewels, as many sandalwood perfumes as grains of sand in the Ganges, and jewels of blazing radiance emitting the sounds of Buddhas' speech; unspeakable hundreds of thousands of billions of trillions of walls made of all jewels surround all of them, adorning everywhere."

Then, to reiterate, Universally Good, spiritually empowered by the Buddha, looked over the ten directions and said,

On the land masses of these worlds
Are seas of fragrant water, adorned by jewels;
Pure beautiful gems line the sea floors,
Resting on diamond, indestructible.

Heaps of jewels of fragrant mines form the shores,
Orbs of sun-flame pearls are spread like clouds;
Garlands of lotuses and exquisite jewels
Adorn everywhere, pure, without taint.

The fragrant waters are clear and contain all colors;
Precious flowers swirl, radiating light.

Sounds that cause all to quake are heard far and near,
Expounding the subtle truth by the Buddha's mystic powers.

The arrays of stairways contain all jewels
And are studded at intervals with pearls;
The surrounding balustrades are all made of jewels
With nets of lotuses and pearls draped like clouds.

Gemstone trees stand in rows,
Flower buds blossom, their luster bright;
Various music is always playing:
Buddha's mystic power makes it so.

White lotuses of various superb jewels
Are spread in arrays on the fragrant water seas.
Rays of fragrant flames never cease:
Their vast auras fill everywhere.

Banners of bright pearls, ever radiant,
Drapes of fine clothing ornamenting,
Nets of crystal bells intone the sound of truth,
Causing hearers to head for buddha-knowledge.

Lotuses of jewels form castles
Adorned with multicolored gems,
While clouds of pearls shade the four corners,
Thus adorning the seas of fragrant waters.

Walls surround everything
With facing towers arrayed on them.
Countless lights are always shining,
Variously adorning the pure clear seas.

Vairocana, in ancient times,
Beautified and purified various oceans of lands
Like this, vast, broad, without bounds:
All is the Buddha's sovereign power.

   Then Universally Good went on to say to the great congregation,
"Each one of the fragrant seas has as many rivers of fragrant waters as
there are atoms in four continents, circling them to the right. All of
them have diamond banks adorned with crystals of pure light, always
manifesting clouds of jewel color lights of the Buddhas, as well as the
speech sounds of all sentient beings. The causal practices cultivated by
the Buddhas, their various forms and characteristics, all emerge from

the swirls in the rivers. There are networks of crystals and chimes of many jewels, wherein appear the adornments of all the oceans of worlds. Clouds of jewels cover them above: those clouds show all the phantom Buddhas emanated in the ten directions by Vairocana of the Flower Bank world, as well as the deeds of psychic power of all Buddhas; they also produce miraculous sounds extolling the names of the enlightened and enlightening beings of past, present, and future. From those fragrant waters constantly emerge clouds of light with the radiance of all jewels, continuing uninterrupted. If the full story be told, each river has as many adornments as atoms in an ocean of worlds."

Then, to reiterate, Universally Good, with the psychic power he received from the Buddha, looked over the ten directions and said,

> Currents of pure fragrance fill the great rivers,
> Beautiful diamonds form their banks.
> Rings of jewel dust are spread on the ground;
> The various ornaments are all rare and fine.

> Jewel stairways arrayed in rows, beautifully adorned,
> Balustrades surrounding, all extremely fine,
> Flower decorations, with stores of pearls,
> And various garlands draped all around.

> The fragrant waters' jewellike luster is pure,
> Always spewing crystals in rushing currents;
> The flowers undulate with the ripples,
> All producing music intoning sublime truths.

> The mud is made of sandalwood powder,
> All splendid jewels swirl together;
> Aromas of stores of scent spread therein,
> Emitting flames circulating fragrance everywhere.

> In the rivers are produced wonderful jewels,
> All emitting lights of blazing color;
> The lights cast reflections forming terrace seats
> Complete with canopies and garlands of pearls.

> In the diamonds appear bodies of Buddhas,
> Their lights illumining the ten directions' lands;
> Circles of them decorate the river beds,
> Always full of fragrant water, clear.

> Crystal nets, bells of gold,
> Cover the rivers, broadcasting Buddha's voice,

Preaching all ways to enlightenment
And the sublime practice of universal good.

The crystals of the jewel banks are extremely pure,
And always produce the tones of the Buddhas' original vows,
Telling of and showing
The past deeds of all Buddhas.

From the whirls of those rivers enlightening beings
Constantly emerge, like clouds,
All traveling in the vast, extensive lands,
Till all the universe is filled.

Pure pearls are spread like clouds
Covering all the fragrant rivers;
Those pearls are as many as the appearances from Buddha's brow,
Clearly showing the images of all enlightened ones.

Then Universally Good also said to the great assembly, "The land in between these rivers of fragrant waters is all variously adorned with beautiful jewels. Each land space has as many white lotuses decorated with jewels as there are atoms in four continents, surrounding and filling everywhere. Each has as many forests of jewel trees as atoms in four continents, standing in orderly rows, with each tree constantly producing clouds of all ornaments, diamonds shining within them. The fragrances of all kinds of flowers fill everywhere. Those trees also produce subtle sounds, speaking of the great vows practiced by all the Buddhas in all ages. They also scatter various kinds of diamonds all over the ground: diamonds with lotus auras, fragrant flame light cloud diamonds, variously embellished diamonds, diamonds reflecting the colors of inconceivably many adornments, diamonds like stores of raiment of sunlight, diamonds draping clouds of webs of light throughout the ten directions, diamonds reflecting the spiritual metamorphoses of all Buddhas, diamonds reflecting the ocean of consequences of actions of all sentient beings. There are as many of such as these as there are atoms in an ocean of worlds. The lands in between the fragrant rivers all have such adornments."

Then, to reiterate, Universally Good, receiving spiritual power from the Buddha, looked over the ten directions and said,

The land is level and thoroughly pure,
Garnished with gold and jewels.
Trees in rows shade the land,
With soaring trunks hung with branches and flowers like clouds.

The twigs and stems are adorned with gems,
The glow of their flowers make auras illumining all around;
Their fruits, of crystal, hang like clouds,
Making all in the ten directions visible.

Diamonds are spread over the ground,
Adorning together with jewel pollen from the flowers.
There are also crystal palaces,
Showing the reflected images of all beings.

Diamonds reflecting the images of Buddhas
Are scattered all over the ground;
Their luster pervades the ten directions,
Revealing Buddhas in each and every atom.

Arrays of exquisite jewels are distributed well,
Interspersed with networks of pearl lamps.
Everywhere are crystal orbs
Each showing the Buddhas' powers.

The arrays of jewels radiate light
In which appear the phantom buddhas,
Each one traveling everywhere
And teaching with the ten powers.

White lotuses of jewels
Fill all the waters,
Their blooms all various,
Each shining endless light.

All adornments of all ages
Appear in the crystal fruits;
Their essential nature, unborn, cannot be grasped:
This is the sovereign power of Buddha.

All the adornments on this ground
Manifest the vast body of Buddha:
It neither comes nor goes,
But causes all to see by the power of Buddha's ancient vows.

In each atom of this ground
All Buddha-children cultivate the Way;
All see the lands predicted for their futures,
All of them pure according to their wishes.

Then Universally Good went on to declare, "The adornments of the ocean of worlds of the Buddha are inconceivable. Why? Each object in this Flower Bank Array ocean of worlds is adorned by as many pure qualities as there are atoms in an ocean of worlds."

Then, to reiterate this point, Universally Good, imbued with spiritual power from the Buddha, surveyed the ten directions and said,

> Every place in this ocean of lands
> Is embellished with myriad jewels,
> Their flames leaping into the sky, spreading like clouds,
> Their light penetrating, always covering all.

> Jewels spew clouds without end
> Wherein appear images of all Buddhas;
> Their mystic powers and metamorphoses never stop,
> And all enlightening beings come and gather.

> All the jewels broadcast Buddha's voice,
> The sound exquisite, inconceivable;
> What Vairocana did in the past
> Is always heard and seen within these jewels.

> The universal illuminators with pure auras
> All show their forms reflected in the ornaments;
> Transforming, distributing their bodies, surrounded by congregations,
> They reach throughout all oceans of lands.

> Buddha's independent deeds of spiritual powers
> All pervade the lands of the ten directions;
> Thereby are the oceans of lands purely adorned:
> All of this is seen within the jewels.

> The mystic displays in the ten directions
> Are all like images in a mirror;
> They just come from the spiritual will power
> Exercised by the Buddha in the past.

> If any can practice the deeds of universal goodness
> And enter the enlightening beings' ocean of supreme knowledge,
> They can, in a single atom,
> Manifest their bodies everywhere and purify many lands.

> For inconceivable billions of eons
> Having associated with all the Buddhas,

Everything they practice
Can be shown in a single instant.

The Buddhas' lands are like space,
Peerless, unborn, without any signs—
To aid living beings, they beautify and purify lands,
Dwelling therein by the power of their original vows.

Then Universally Good went on to say, "What worlds are there herein? I'll tell you. In these seas of fragrant waters, numerous as atoms in unspeakably many buddha-fields, rest an equal number of world systems. Each world system also contains an equal number of worlds. Those world systems in the ocean of worlds have various resting places, various shapes and forms, various substances and essences, various locations, various entryways, various adornments, various boundaries, various alignments, various similarities, and various powers of maintenance.

"Some of these world systems rest on seas of gigantic lotuses, some rest on seas of jewel flowers of boundless forms, some rest on seas of ornaments of treasures from repositories of all pearls, some rest on seas of perfume, some rest on seas of all flowers, some rest on seas of crystal webs, some rest on seas of swirling light, some rest on seas of enlightening beings' jewelled crowns, some rest on seas of the bodies of all the various living beings, some rest on diamonds emanating the sounds of the voices of all Buddhas. There are as many of these, if fully expounded, as atoms in an ocean of worlds.

"Some of these world systems are shaped like high mountains, some like rivers, some like whorls, some like whirlpools, some like wheel rims, some like altars, some like forests, some like palaces, some like mountain banners, some like all geometric figures, some like wombs, some like lotus blossoms, some like baskets, some like bodies of sentient beings, some like clouds, some like the distinguishing features of Buddhas, some like spheres of light, some like webs of various pearls, some like all doors, some like various ornaments. Their shapes, if fully told of, number as many as atoms in an ocean of worlds.

"As for the substances of these world systems, some are made of clouds of jewels of all quarters, some of multicolored flames, some of light beams, some of flames of precious scents, some of cotton flowers adorned by all jewels, some of images of enlightening beings, some of auras of Buddhas, some of physical forms of Buddhas, some of the light of one precious element, some of the lights of many precious elements, some of the sounds of the sea of blessings and virtues of all living beings, some of the sounds of the sea of actions of all living beings, some of the pure sounds of the sphere of all Buddhas, some of the sounds of the sea of great vows of all enlightening beings, some of the sounds of the formation and disintegration of the adornments of all lands, some of the sounds of the methods and techniques of all Buddhas, some of the sounds of the voices of boundless Buddhas, some of the voices of goodness of all sentient beings, some of the sounds of the mystical demonstrations of all Buddhas, some of the pure sounds of the ocean of virtue of all Buddhas. If fully told, there as many of these as atoms in an ocean of worlds."

Then Universally Good, to reiterate what he meant, looked over the ten directions by the power bestowed on him by the Buddha and said in verse,

> The stable, marvelous adornments of the systems of worlds,
> Vast, pure treasuries of light,
> Rest on seas of lotus blossom jewels
> Or on perfume seas, and so on.
>
> Shaped like mountains, cities, trees, altars,
> The world systems extend in all directions,
> Their various adornments and shapes different,
> Each set out in arrays.
>
> Pure light is the substance of some;
> Some, flower banks, and some, clouds of jewels;
> Some world systems are made of flames,
> Resting in indestructible mines of jewels.
>
> Clouds of lamps, colored lights of flames, and more:
> Various, boundless forms, all pure;
> Some are composed of sound,
> Of the inconceivable teachings of Buddha.
>
> Some are sound produced by the power of vows,
> Some of sounds of miraculous displays,
> Some are those of beings' virtues,
> Or the sounds of Buddhas' qualities.
>
> The individual different aspects of the world systems
> Are inconceivable, without end.
> The ten directions are filled with them,
> Their vast adornments manifesting spiritual powers.
>
> All the immense lands of the ten directions
> Enter into this system of worlds;
> Though we see all in the ten directions enter,
> Really there is no coming and no entry.

One world system enters all,
And all completely enter one;
Their substances and characteristics remain as before, no different:
Incomparable, immeasurable, they all pervade everywhere.

In the atoms of all lands
Are seen Buddhas existing there;
The voices of their oceans of vows are like thunder,
Subduing all sentient beings.

The Buddha's body pervades all lands,
Which are also filled by countless enlightening beings;
The Buddha's freedom has no equal,
Edifying all conscious creatures.

Then Universally Good said, "These seas of fragrant waters, numerous as atoms in unspeakably many buddha-fields, are in the Flower Bank Array ocean of worlds, spread out like the net of Indra, king of the gods. The sea of fragrant water in the very center is called Boundless Light of Beautiful Flowers. Its floor is made of diamond banners reflecting the forms of all enlightening beings. It produces huge lotuses called Diamond Adornments of All Scents. There is a system of worlds resting on it called Blazing Light Illuming the Ten Directions; composed of all ornaments, it contains as many worlds as atoms in unspeakably many buddha-fields, arrayed therein. In the nadir is a world called Supreme Light Shining Everywhere, adorned by all kinds of diamonds, bounded by a circle of light, resting on flowers of many jewels, shaped like a crystal, covered with clouds of arrays of flowers of all gems, surrounded by worlds as numerous as atoms in a buddha-field, with various structures and various adornments. The Buddha of this world is called Undefiled Lamp of the Eye of Purity.

"Above this, past worlds as numerous as atoms in a buddha-field, is a world called Beautiful Array of Lotus Flowers of Various Scents, bounded by all kinds of ornaments, resting on a network of jewel lotus blossoms, shaped like a lion throne, covered with nets of pearls of the colors of all jewels, surrounded by as many worlds as atoms in two buddha-fields. The Buddha is called Supreme Radiance of Lion Light.

"Above this, past worlds as numerous as atoms in a buddha-field, is a world called All-Illuminating Light of Ornaments of All Jewels, bounded by an atmosphere of perfume, resting on garlands of various gems, octagonal in shape, covered by clouds of solar discs of crystals with subtle light, surrounded by as many worlds as atoms in three buddha-fields. The Buddha is called Banner of Supreme Knowledge Like Pure Light.

"Above this, past worlds as numerous as atoms in a buddha-field, is a world called Array of Flowers of Various Lights, bounded by all the finest jewels, resting on a sea of pure banners of multicolored diamonds, shaped like a crystal lotus blossom, covered by clouds of diamond light, orbited by worlds as numerous as atoms in four buddha-fields, all thoroughly pure. The Buddha is called Diamond Light with Infinite Energy Skillfully Producing Manifestations.

"Above this, past worlds as numerous as atoms in a buddha-field, is a world called Radiating Light of Beautiful Flowers, bounded by nets adorned with bells of all jewels, resting on a sea of networks of jewel spheres adorned with forests of all trees, geometric in shape, with many angles and sides, covered by clouds of diamonds with pure resonance, surrounded by worlds as many as atoms in five buddha-fields. The Buddha is called Ocean of Joyful Power of Fragrant Light.

"Above this, past worlds as numerous as atoms in a buddha-field, is a world called Pure Subtle Light, bounded by banners decorated with diamonds, resting on a sea of diamond palaces, square in shape, covered by clouds of drapes of crystal orb topknots, surrounded by as many worlds as atoms in six buddha-fields. The Buddha is called Banner of Sovereignty with Universal Light.

"Above this, past worlds as numerous as atoms in a buddha-field, is a world called Array of Radiance of Myriad Flowers, bounded by decorations of all kinds of flowers, resting on a sea of flames of the colors of all jewels, shaped like a palace, covered by clouds of robes of the colors of all jewels and railings of pearls, surrounded by worlds as numerous as atoms in seven buddha-fields, all uniformly pure. The Buddha is called Ocean of Joy with the Light of Virtue, Fame, and Freedom.

"Above this, past as many worlds as atoms in a buddha-field, is a world called Producing the State of Awesome Power, bounded by ornaments of diamonds that produce all sounds, resting on a sea of spheres of lotus thrones of the colors of various jewels, shaped like Indra's net, covered by clouds of flower webs of boundless colors, surrounded by as many worlds as atoms in eight buddha fields. The Buddha is called Renowned Banner of the Ocean of Knowledge.

"Above this, past as many worlds as atoms in a buddha-field, is a world called Producing Wondrous Sounds, bounded by spherical arrays of mind-jewels, resting on a sea of diamonds in cloudlike arrays constantly producing all wonderful sounds, shaped like the body of a celestial king of the Brahma heaven, covered by clouds of lion thrones adorned with countless jewels, surrounded by as many worlds as there are atoms in nine buddha-fields. The Buddha is called Invincible Radiance like Pure Moonlight.

"Above this, past as many worlds as atoms in a buddha-field, is a world called Diamond Banner, bounded by garlands of gems from pearl treasuries of boundless adornments, resting on a crystal sea of jewel lion thrones with all adornments, spherical in shape, covered by mountainous clouds of jewel flowers of all fragrances, as numerous as atoms in ten gigantic mountains, and surrounded by as many worlds as atoms in ten buddha-fields, all uniformly pure. The Buddha is called Supreme King of the Ocean of All Truths.

"Above this, past worlds as many as atoms in a buddha-field, there is a world called Constantly Producing Sapphire Light, bounded by arrays of indestructible diamonds, resting on a sea of various different flowers, shaped like the half moon, covered by clouds of drapes of celestial jewels, surrounded by worlds as many as atoms in eleven buddha-fields. The Buddha is called Boundless Virtues.

"Above this, past worlds as many as atoms in a buddha-field, is a world called Light Shining, bounded by arrays of radiant lights, resting on a sea of perfume of flower swirls, shaped like a wreath, covered by clouds of various garments, surrounded by worlds as numerous as atoms in twelve buddha-fields. The Buddha is named Transcending the Gods.

"Above this, past worlds as many as atoms in a buddha-field, we come to this world, called Endurance, bounded by ornaments of diamonds, held by atmospheres of various colors, resting on a network of lotus flowers, shaped like space, covered by space adorned with spherical celestial palaces, surrounded by worlds as numerous as atoms in thirteen buddha-fields. The Buddha is this Vairocana.

"Above this, past worlds as numerous as atoms in a buddha-field, is a world called Tranquil Undefiled Light, bounded by adornments of all jewels, resting on a sea of various kinds of precious raiment, shaped like a thunderbolt-bearer, covered by clouds of diamonds of boundless colors, surrounded by worlds as numerous as atoms in fourteen buddha-fields. The Buddha is called Supreme Sound Pervading the Cosmos.

"Above this, past as many worlds as atoms in a buddha-field, is a world called Lamp of Many Beautiful Light Beams, bounded by drapes of all ornaments, resting on a sea of webs of pure flowers, shaped like a fylfot, covered by clouds of seas of crystal trees and perfumed waters, surrounded by as many worlds as atomic particles in fifteen buddha-fields, all uniformly pure. The Buddha is called Universally Illuminating Banner of Invincible Strength.

"Above this, past as many worlds as atoms in a buddha-field, is a world called Pure Light Shining Everywhere, bounded by diamonds from inexhaustible clouds of jewels, resting on a sea of lotus flowers with various fragrant flames, shaped like a tortoise shell, covered by sandalwood clouds of radiant crystal orbs, surrounded by as many worlds as atoms in sixteen buddha-fields. The Buddha is called Eyes with the Qualities of Pure Suns.

"Above this, past as many worlds as atoms in a buddha-field, is a world called Mine of Jewel Ornaments, bounded by diamonds in the forms of all living beings, resting on a sea of diamonds from mines of light, octagonal in shape, covered by webs of flower trees adorned by jewels from all the surrounding mountains, surrounded by as many worlds as atoms in seventeen buddha-fields. The Buddha is called Light of Unhindered Knowledge Illumining the Ten Directions.

"Above this, past as many worlds as atoms in a buddha-field, is a world called Dustless, bounded by ornaments of all kinds of exquisite forms, resting on a sea of lion thrones of myriad beautiful flowers, shaped like a pearl necklace, covered by clouds of auras of diamonds with all precious fragrances, surrounded by as many worlds as atoms in eighteen buddha-fields, all uniformly pure. The Buddha is called Supreme Banner of Infinite Means.

"Above this, past as many worlds as atoms in a buddha-field, is a world called Pure Light Illumining Everywhere, bounded by diamonds producing inexhaustible clouds of jewels, resting on a sea of mountains of fragrant flames of infinite colors, shaped like a wreath of jewel flowers, covered by diamond clouds of light of boundless colors, surrounded by as many worlds as atoms in nineteen buddha-fields. The Buddha is called Light Illumining All the Space of the Cosmos.

"Above this, past as many worlds as atoms in a buddha-field, is a world called Beautiful Jewel Flames, bounded by jewels like the sun and moon illuming everywhere, resting on a sea of diamonds in the shapes of all celestial beings, shaped like jewel arrays, covered by clouds of banners of all precious robes and networks of banks of crystal lamps, surrounded by as many worlds as atoms in twenty buddha-fields, all uniformly pure. The Buddha is called Shining with Signs of Virtue.

"This world system, Blazing Light Illumining the Ten Directions, has as many such vast worlds as there are atoms in unspeakably many buddha-fields, each with their individual resting places, shapes, substances and natures, aspects, entrances, adornments, boundaries, arrays, similarities, and powers of maintenance, all revolving around it: that is, there are as many spiral-shaped worlds as atoms in ten buddha-fields, a like number of river-shaped worlds, the same number of whirlpool-shaped worlds, the same number of wheel-rim-shaped worlds, the same number of altar-shaped worlds, the same number of forest-shaped worlds, the same number of tower-shaped worlds, the same number of forest-shaped worlds, the same number of pennant-shaped worlds, the same number of womb-shaped worlds, the same number of geometrically shaped worlds, the same number of lotus-blossom-shaped worlds, the same number of basket-shaped worlds, the same number of worlds shaped like living creatures, the same number of Buddha-shaped worlds, the same number of light aura-shaped worlds, the same number of cloud-shaped worlds, the same number of net-shaped worlds, the same number of door-shaped worlds—there are as many such as atoms in unspeakably many buddha-fields. Each of these worlds has as many enormous worlds as atoms in ten buddha-fields surrounding it, each one also having as many worlds, the same as explained above. All of these worlds are in this Boundless Light of Beautiful Flowers sea of fragrant waters, or in the rivers of fragrant water surrounding it."

Then the enlightening being Universally Good also said to the great assembly, "East of this Boundless Light of Beautiful Flowers sea of fragrant water is another sea of fragrant water called Repository of Undefiled Flames. It produces huge lotuses called Beautiful Adornments of Diamonds with All Scents. There is a world system resting on it called Vortex of Lands Shining Everywhere. Its substance is the roaring sound of deeds of enlightening beings. At its bottom is a world called Palace Decoration Banner, square in shape, resting on a sea of ornaments of all precious stones, covered by clouds of webs of lotus light, surrounded by worlds as many as atoms in a buddha-field, all uniformly pure. The Buddha is named Brow-Light Illumining Everywhere.

"Above this, past worlds as many as atoms in a buddha-field, is a world called Repository of Flowers of Virtue, spherical in shape, resting on a sea of flower pistils made of all kinds of pearls, covered by clouds of lion thrones with pearl banners, orbited by as many worlds as atoms in two buddha-fields. The Buddha is called Wisdom of the Ocean of All Boundless Truths.

"Above this, past as many worlds as atoms in a buddha-field, is a world called Fragrant Circle of Miracles, shaped like a diamond, resting on a sea of nets of chimes adorned with all kinds of jewels, covered by clouds of auras of all kinds of ornaments, orbited by as many worlds as atoms in three buddha-fields. The Buddha is named Light of Virtuous Characteristics Shining Everywhere.

"Above this, past as many worlds as atoms in a buddha-field, is a world called Light of Sublime Color, shaped like a crystal orb, resting on a perfume sea of jewels of boundless colors, covered by clouds of palaces of radiant pearls, surrounded by as many worlds as atoms in four buddha-fields, all uniformly pure. The Buddha is named Ubiquitous Illumination Producing Good Company.

"Above this, past as many worlds as atoms in a buddha-field, is a world called Good Cover, shaped like a lotus blossom, resting on a perfume sea of diamonds, covered by perfume clouds of undefiled light, orbited by as many worlds as atoms in five buddha-fields. The Buddha is called Inexhaustible Wisdom of Delight in Truth.

"Above this, past as many worlds as atoms in a buddha-field, is a world called Wreath of Light of Pure Flowers, triangular in shape, resting on arrays of all unbreakable jewels, covered by light beams from the jeweled crowns of enlightening beings, surrounded by as many worlds as atoms in six buddha-fields. The Buddha is called Pure Universal Light.

"Above this, past as many worlds as atoms in a buddha-field, is a world called Array of Jewel Lotus Blossoms, shaped like a half moon, resting on a sea of arrays of all kinds of lotuses, covered by clouds of flowers of all jewels, orbited by as many worlds as atoms in seven buddha-fields, all uniformly pure. The Buddha is called Pure Eye of Flowers of Virtue.

"Above this, past worlds as many as atoms in a buddha-field, is a world called Repository of Undefiled Flames, shaped like a row of jewel lamps, resting on a sea of banks of jewellike flames, covered by clouds of various bodies constantly raining perfume, surrounded by as many worlds as atoms in eight buddha-fields. The Buddha is called Invincible Power Of Wisdom.

"Above this, past worlds as many as atoms in a buddha-field, is a world called Sublime Pure Sound, shaped like a fylfot, resting on a sea of jewel raiment, covered with clouds of drapes adorned with all flowers, surrounded by as many worlds as atoms in nine buddha-fields. The Buddha is called Enormous Eyes like the Clear Moon in the Sky.

"Above this, past as many worlds as atoms in a buddha-field, is a world called Sounds as Numerous as Atoms, shaped like the net of Indra, resting on a sea of waters of all precious elements, covered by clouds of jeweled canopies of all musical sounds, surrounded by as many worlds as atoms in ten buddha-fields. The Buddha is called Golden Mountain Lamp.

"Above this, past as many worlds as atoms in a buddha-field, is a world called Array of Jewel Colors, shaped like a fylfot, resting on a sea of gems shaped like the king of the gods, covered by clouds of flowers radiant as the sun, surrounded by many worlds as atoms in eleven buddha-fields. The Buddha is called Radiant Knowledge Illuminating the Cosmos.

"Above this, past as many worlds as atoms in a buddha-field, is a world called Golden Light, shaped like a huge castle, resting on a sea of ornaments made of all jewels, covered by clouds of jewel flowers from scenes of enlightenment, surrounded by as many worlds as atoms in twelve buddha-fields. The Buddha is called Banner of Precious Lamps Lighting All.

"Above this, past as many worlds as atoms in a buddha-field, is a world called Sphere of Light Illumining Everywhere, shaped like a wreath of flowers, resting on a sea of whirlpools of jewel raiment, covered by clouds of palaces made of diamonds emanating the sound of Buddha's voice, surrounded by as many worlds as atoms in thirteen buddha-fields. The Buddha is called Lotus Flower Illumining Everywhere.

"Above this, past as many worlds as atoms in a buddha-field, is a world called Jewel Mine Ornaments, shaped like four continents, resting on a mountain of jewel necklaces, covered by clouds of blazing jewels, surrounded by as many worlds as atoms in fourteen buddha-fields. The Buddha is called Blooming Flowers of Inexhaustible Blessings.

"Above this, past as many worlds as atoms in a buddha-field, is a world called Appearing Everywhere like Reflections in a Mirror, shaped like the body of a titan, resting on a sea of diamond lotuses, covered by clouds of light rays from jeweled crowns, surrounded by as many worlds as atoms in fifteen buddha-fields. The Buddha is called Elixir Sound.

"Above this, past as many worlds as atoms in a buddha-field, is a world called Sandalwood Moon, octagonal in shape, resting on a sea of indestructible precious sandalwood, covered by clouds of pearl flowers, surrounded by as many worlds as atoms in sixteen buddha-fields, all uniformly pure. The Buddha is called Peerless Knowledge of the Supreme Truth.

"Above this, past as many worlds as atoms in a buddha-field, is a world called Untainted Light, shaped like a whirlpool of fragrant water, resting on a sea of jewel light of boundless colors, covered by clouds of exquisitely aromatic light, surrounded by as many worlds as atoms in seventeen buddha-fields. The Buddha is called Sound of Light Illumining All Space.

"Above this, past as many worlds as atoms in a buddha-field, is a world called Array of Beautiful Flowers, spiral shaped, resting on a sea of all flowers, covered by crystal clouds of all musical sounds, surrounded by as many worlds as atoms in eighteen buddha-fields. The Buddha is called Everywhere Manifesting Supreme Light.

"Above this, past as many worlds as atoms in a buddha-field, is a world called Array of Supreme Sounds, shaped like a lion throne, resting on a sea of golden lion thrones, covered by clouds of banks of lotuses of all colors, surrounded by as many worlds as atoms in nineteen buddha-fields. The Buddha is called Universal Light of Renown for Boundless Virtue.

"Above this, past as many worlds as atoms in a buddha-field, is a world called Supremely High Lamp, shaped like the Buddha's palm, resting on a sea of banners of perfume of precious raiment, covered by clouds of palaces made of jewels radiant as the sun, surrounded by as many worlds as atoms in twenty buddha-fields, uniformly pure. The Buddha is called Lamp Illuminating Space.

"South of this Repository of Undefiled Flames sea of fragrant waters is another sea of fragrant waters, called Sphere of Inexhaustible Light, with a world system called Array of Banners of Buddhas, composed of the sounds of the ocean of virtues of all Buddhas. At the bottom of this world system is a world called Lovely Flower, shaped like a jewel disc, resting on a sea of diamonds from a mine of diamond trees, covered by clouds of jewel mines projecting reflections of forms of enlightening beings, surrounded by as many worlds as atoms in a buddha-field, all uniformly pure. The Buddha there is called Joyful Countenance of Lotus Light.

"Above this, past as many worlds as atoms in a buddha-field, is a world called Sublime Sound; the Buddha there is called Wonderfully High Jewel Lamp.

"Above this, past as many worlds as atoms in a buddha-field, is a

world called Light of Arrays of Myriad Jewels; the Buddha there is called Banner of Sounds of the Cosmos.

"Above this, past as many worlds as atoms in a buddha-field, is a world called Diamond Treasury of Fragrance; the Buddha there is called Sound of Light.

"Above this, past as many worlds as atoms in a buddha-field, is a world called Pure Sound; the Buddha there is called Supreme Energy.

"Above this, past as many worlds as atoms in a buddha-field, is a world called Array of Jewel Lotus Blossoms; the Buddha there is called Thunder of Clouds of Castles of Truth.

"Above this, past as many worlds as atoms in a buddha-field, is a world called Peace and Bliss; the Buddha there is called Renowned Lamp of Wisdom.

"Above this, past as many worlds as atoms in a buddha-field, is a world called Undefiled Net; the Buddha there is called Ocean of Virtues with Invincible Light.

"Above this, past as many worlds as atoms in a buddha-field, is a world called Flowering Grove Banner Illumining Everywhere; the Buddha there is called Light of the Lotus of Great Knowledge.

"Above this, past as many worlds as atoms in a buddha-field, is a world called Innumerable Adornments; the Buddha there is called Banner of the Real Sphere of the Universal Eye.

"Above this, past as many worlds as atoms in a buddha-field, is a world called Array of Jewels of Radiant Light; the Buddha there is called Great Caravan Leader of Supreme Knowledge.

"Above this, past as many worlds as atoms in a buddha-field, is a world called Flower King; the Buddha there is called Moonlight Banner.

"Above this, past as many worlds as atoms in a buddha-field, is a world called Undefiled Treasury; the Buddha there is called Pure Awareness.

"Above this, past as many worlds as atoms in a buddha-field, is a world called Jewel Light; the Buddha there is called Lamp of the Space of Omniscience.

"Above this, past as many worlds as atoms in a buddha-field, is a world called Producing Jewel Necklaces; the Buddha there is called Light of the Forms of the Ocean of Virtues of the Ways of Transcendence.

"Above this, past as many worlds as atoms in a buddha-field, is a world called Sublime Circles Covering All; the Buddha there is called Subduing All Attached Minds and Causing Joy.

"Above this, past as many worlds as atoms in a buddha-field, is a world called Jewel Flower Banner; the Buddha there is called Great Fame of Extensive Virtues.

"Above this, past as many worlds as atoms in a buddha-field, is a world called Infinite Adornments; the Buddha there is called Ocean of Qualities of Light of Impartial Knowledge.

"Above this, past as many worlds as atoms in a buddha-field, is a

world called Banner of Arrays of Infinite Lights, shaped like a lotus blossom, resting on a sea of webs of all jewels, covered by webs of lotus light crystals, surrounded by as many worlds as atoms in twenty buddha-fields, all uniformly pure. The Buddha there is called Pure Light of the Cosmos.

"Turning the right of this Sphere of Inexhaustible Light sea of fragrant water, there is a sea of fragrant water called Diamond Flame Light, with a system of worlds called Repository of Arrays of Buddha Halos, composed of voices extolling the names of all Buddhas. At the bottom of this world system is a world called Jewel Flame Lotus, shaped like a curl of hair, the color of crystal, resting on a sea of whirlpools of the colors of all jewels, covered by clouds of palaces of all adornments, surrounded by as many worlds as atoms in a buddha-field, all uniformly pure. The Buddha there is called Undefiled Jewel Light.

"Above this, past as many worlds as atoms in a buddha-field, is a world caled Repository of Flames of Light; the Buddha there is called Light of Unhindered Independent Wisdom.

"Above this, past as many worlds as atoms in a buddha-field, is a world called Beautiful Array of Jewel Discs; the Buddha there is called Light of All Jewels.

"Above this, past as many worlds as atoms in a buddha-field, is a world called Sandalwood Tree Flower Banner; the Buddha is called Light of Pure Knowledge.

"Above this, past as many worlds as atoms in a buddha-field, is a world called Exquisite Array of Buddha-Fields; the Buddha is called Great Sound of Joy.

"Above this, past as many worlds as atoms in a buddha-field, is a world called Array of Subtle Lights; the Buddha is called Independent Knowledge of the Cosmos.

"Above this, past as many worlds as atoms in a buddha-field, is a world called Boundless Forms; the Buddha is called Unimpeded Knowledge.

"Above this, past as many worlds as atoms in a buddha-field, is a world called Flame Cloud Banner; the Buddha is called Nonregressive Teaching.

"Above this, past as many worlds as atoms in a buddha-field, is a world called Pure Circle of Jewel Ornaments; the Buddha is called Pure Flower Light.

"Above this, past as many worlds as atoms in a buddha-field, is a world called Great Emancipation; the Buddha is called Eye of the Sun of Unhindered Knowledge.

"Above this, past as many worlds as atoms in a buddha-field, is a world called Beautifully Adorned Diamond Throne; the Buddha is called Great Light of Knowledge of the Cosmos.

"Above this, past as many worlds as atoms in a buddha-field, is a

world called Everywhere Adorned by Knowledge and Wisdom; the Buddha there is called King of the Light of the Torch of Knowledge.

"Above this, past as many worlds as atoms in a buddha-field, is a world called Deep Wonderful Sound of a Lotus Pond; the Buddha there is called Omniscience Illumining Everywhere.

"Above this, past as many worlds as atoms in a buddha-field, is a world called Varicolored Light Beams; the Buddha there is called Radiant Flower King Cloud.

"Above this, past as many worlds as atoms in a buddha-field, is a world called Exquisite Jewel Banner; the Buddha there is called Light of Virtue.

"Above this, past as many worlds as atoms in a buddha-field, is a world called Crystal Flower Light; the Buddha there is called Cloud of Universal Sound.

"Above this, past as many worlds as atoms in a buddha-field, is a world called Extremely Deep Ocean; the Buddha there is called Leader of All Beings in the Ten Directions.

"Above this, past as many worlds as atoms in a buddha-field, is a world called High Mountain Light; the Buddha there is called Sound of Universal Knowledge of the Cosmos.

"Above this, past as many worlds as atoms in a buddha-field, is a world called Golden Lotus; the Buddha there is called Universal Light of the Repository of Virtue.

"Above this, past as many worlds as atoms in a buddha-field, is a world called Mine of Jewel Ornaments, shaped like a fylfot, resting on a sea of trees of all scents adorned by crystals, covered by clouds of pure light, surrounded by as many worlds as atoms in twenty buddha-fields, all uniformly pure. The Buddha is called Web of Light of Great Mystical Displays.

"Turning to the right of this Diamond Flame Light sea of fragrant water, there is another sea of fragrant water called Sapphire Array, with a world system called Light Illumining the Ten Directions, resting on clouds of scent of lotus blossoms of all beautiful adornments, composed of the voices of boundless Buddhas. At the bottom of this system is a world called Wheel Containing Infinite Colors of All Quarters, shaped like a spiral with an infinite number of turns, resting on a sea of treasuries of jewels of unlimited colors, covered by the net of Indra, surrounded by as many worlds as atoms in a buddha-field, all uniformly pure. The Buddha there is called Lotus Eyes with All-Illuminating Light.

"Above this, past worlds as numerous as atoms in a buddha-field, is a world called Mine of Pure Exquisite Ornaments; the Buddha there is called Great Lion of Unexcelled Wisdom.

"Above this, past worlds as numerous as atoms in a buddha-field, is a world called Producing Lotus Thrones; the Buddha is called King of of Light Illumining the Cosmos.

"Above this, past as many worlds as atoms in a buddha-field, is a world called Jewel Banner Sound; the Buddha there is called Universal Repute of Great Virtue.

"Above this, past as many worlds as atoms in a buddha-field, is a world called Diamond Ornament Treasury; the Buddha there is called Lotus Sun Light.

"Above this, past as many worlds as atoms in a buddha-field, is a world called Indra Flower Moon; the Buddha there is called Banner of Independent Knowledge of Truth.

"Above this, past as many worlds as atoms in a buddha-field, is a world called Treasury of Beautiful Globes; the Buddha there is called Pure Sound of Great Joy.

"Above this, past as many worlds as atoms in a buddha-field, is a world called Mine of Wonderful Sounds; the Buddha there is called Good Caravan Leader of Great Power.

"Above this, past as many worlds as atoms in a buddha-field, is a world called Pure Moon; the Buddha there is called Power of Knowledge with Monumental Light.

"Above this, past as many worlds as atoms in a buddha-field, is a world called Boundless Adorning Marks; the Buddha there is called Pure Moonlight of Means and Vows.

"Above this, past as many worlds as atoms in a buddha-field, is a world called Beautiful Flower Sound; the Buddha there is called Sound of Great Vows of the Ocean of Truth.

"Above this, past as many worlds as atoms in a buddha-field, is a world called Array of All Jewelry; the Buddha there is called Supreme Heaven of Beautiful Sound.

"Above this, past as many worlds as atoms in a buddha-field, is a world called Indestructible Ground; the Buddha there is called Form of Jewel Light of Virtue.

"Above this, past as many worlds as atoms in a buddha-field, is a world called Universal Light Readily Transforming; the Buddha there is called Calm Intellect with Great Energy.

"Above this, past as many worlds as atoms in a buddha-field, is a world called Protective Adorning Action; the Buddha there is called Gladdening to See.

"Above this, past as many worlds as atoms in a buddha-field, is a world called Sandalwood Jewel Flower Treasury; the Buddha there is called All-Illumining Light of Extremely Profound Immutable Wisdom.

"Above this, past as many worlds as atoms in a buddha-field, is a world called Sea of Various Colors and Forms; the Buddha there is called Radiating Sovereign Light of Inconceivable Ultimate Truth.

"Above this, past as many worlds as atoms in a buddha-field, is a world called Producing Great Lights in All Directions; the Buddha there is called Incomparable Majestic Light of Supreme Virtue.

"Above this, past as many worlds as atoms in a buddha-field, is a world called Mountain Cloud Banner; the Buddha there is called Eyes of Ultimately Pure Light.

"Above this, past as many worlds as atoms in a buddha-field, is a world called Radiant Lotus, round in shape, resting on a sea of crystals of boundless colors and many wonderful fragrances, covered by clouds of ornaments of all vehicles, surrounded by as many worlds as atoms in twenty buddha-fields, all uniformly pure. The Buddha there is called Energetic Sun of Liberation.

"Turning to the right of this Sapphire Array sea of fragrant water there is another sea of fragrant water, called Diamond Orb Adorned Floor, with a world system called Indra's Net Studded with Wonderful Jewels, composed of sounds produced by the knowledge of universal virtue. At the bottom of this world system is a world called Lotus Blossom Net, shaped like the polar mountain, resting on a sea of banners of mountains of beautiful flowers, covered by clouds of Indra's nets of diamonds from the sphere of buddhahood, surrounded by as many worlds as atoms in a buddha-field, all uniformly pure. The Buddha there is called Wisdom Universally Aware of the Body of Reality.

"Above this, past as many worlds as atoms in a buddha-field, is a world called Endless Sunlight; the Buddha there is called Mind of Supremely Great Awareness.

"Above this, past as many worlds as atoms in a buddha-field, is a world called Radiating Subtle Light in All Directions; the Buddha there is called Endless Power of Clouds of Great Virtue.

"Above this, past as many worlds as atoms in a buddha-field, is a world called Tree Blossom Banner; the Buddha there is called Sound of the Cosmos of Boundless Knowledge.

"Above this, past as many worlds as atoms in a buddha-field, is a world called Pearl Canopy; the Buddha there is called Transcendental Lion Stretch.

"Above this, past as many worlds as atoms in a buddha-field, is a world called Boundless Sound; the Buddha there is called Omniscient Awareness.

"Above this, past as many worlds as atoms in a buddha-field, is a world called Forested Peak Visible Everywhere; the Buddha there is called Appearing before All Beings.

"Above this, past as many worlds as atoms in a buddha-field, is a world called Invincible Light of Indra's Net; the Buddha is called Clouds of Flames of Golden Light from a Spotless Sun.

"Above this, past worlds as many as atoms in a buddha-field, is a world called Jewel Studded; the Buddha there is called Supreme Wisdom.

"Above this, past as many worlds as atoms in a buddha-field, is a world called Ground of Undefiled Light; the Buddha there is called Pure Moon With All Powers.

"Above this, past worlds as many as atoms in a buddha-field, is a world called Constantly Emitting Sounds Praising Buddhas' Virtues; the Buddha there is called Spacelike Mind of Universal Awareness.

"Above this, past as many worlds as atoms in a buddha-field, is a world called High Bank of Flames; the Buddha there is called Great Cloud Banners Majestically Appearing in All Quarters.

"Above this, past as many worlds as atoms in a buddha-field, is a world called Sanctuary Adorned with Light; the Buddha there is called Incomparable Knowledge Illumining Everywhere.

"Above this, past as many worlds as atoms in a buddha-field, is a world called Producing Ornaments of All Jewels; the Buddha there is called King of Mystic Powers Widely Liberating Sentient Beings.

"Above this, past as many worlds as atoms in a buddha-field, is a world called Beautiful Palace Adorned With Light; the Buddha there is called Vast Intellect Establishing All Truths.

"Above this, past as many worlds as atoms in a buddha-field, is a world called Undefiled Tranquility; the Buddha there is called Not Appearing In Vain.

"Above this, past as many worlds as atoms in a buddha-field, is a world called Banner of Crystal Flowers; the Buddha there is called Auspicious Sound Delighting the Mind.

"Above this, past as many worlds as atoms in a buddha-field, is a world called Repository of Universal Clouds, shaped like a palace, resting on a perfume sea of various palaces, covered by clouds of lamps of all jewels, surrounded by as many worlds as atoms in twenty buddha-fields, all uniformly pure. The Buddha there is called King of Mystic Powers of Supreme Awareness.

"Turning to the right of this Diamond Orb Adorned Floor sea of fragrant water is another sea of fragrant water, called Lotus Blossom Indra Net, with a world system called Everywhere Showing Reflections of the Ten Directions, resting on a lotus blossom adorned with jewels, with all kinds of scents, composed of the sounds of the light of knowledge of all Buddhas. At the bottom of this world system is a world called Jewel Light of the Ocean of Living Beings, shaped like a treasury of pearls, resting on a sea of garlands of all jewels, covered with clouds of crystals of the luster of water, surrounded by as many worlds as atoms in a buddha-field, uniformly pure. The Buddha there is called All-Illumining Moon of Inconceivable Virtue.

"Above this, past as many worlds as atoms in a buddha-field, is a world called Wreath of Wonderful Fragrance; the Buddha there is called Banner of Infinite Power.

"Above this, past as many worlds as atoms in a buddha-field, is a world called Sphere of Subtle Light; the Buddha there is called Enlightening Wisdom with the Sound of the Light of the Cosmos.

"Above this, past as many worlds as atoms in a buddha-field, is a

world called Roaring Crystal Banner; the Buddha there is called Lotus Light with Beautiful Arms Always Hanging Down.

"Above this, past as many worlds as atoms in a buddha-field, is a world called Sphere of Extreme Stability; the Buddha there is called Light of the Sea of Nonregressive Virtue.

"Above this, past as many worlds as atoms in a buddha-field, is a world called Array of Light Beams; the Buddha is called Omniscient All-Conquerer.

"Above this, past as many worlds as atoms in a buddha-field, is a world called Lion Throne Illumining Everywhere; the Buddha is called Infinitely Powerful Enlightened Wisdom with Inconceivable Light.

"Above this, past as many worlds as atoms in a buddha-field, is a world called Array of Jewel Flames; the Buddha is called Pure Knowledge of All Things.

"Above this, past as many worlds as atoms in a buddha-field, is a world called Immeasurable Lamp; the Buddha is called No Sign of Distress.

"Above this, past as many worlds as atoms in a buddha-field. is a world called Hearing Buddha's Voice; the Buddha is called Supremely Magnificent Natural Light.

"Above this, past as many worlds as atoms in a buddha-field, is a world called Pure Metamorphoses; the Buddha is called Golden Lotus Light.

"Above this, past as many worlds as atoms in a buddha-field, is a world called Entering All Quarters; the Buddha is called Expanding Mind Observing the Cosmos.

"Above this, past as many worlds as atoms in a buddha-field, is a world called Blazing Flames; the Buddha is called Light Flame Tree Kinnara King.

"Above this, past as many worlds as atoms in a buddha-field, is a world called All-Illumining Aromatic Light; the Buddha is called Skillfully Teaching Fragrant Lamp.

"Above this, past as many worlds as atoms in a buddha-field, is a world called Wreath of Innumerable Flowers; the Buddha is called Everywhere Manifesting Buddhas' Virtues.

"Above this, past as many worlds as atoms in a buddha-field, is a world called Universal Purity of All Subtleties; the Buddha is called King of Psychic Powers Equanimous toward All Things.

"Above this, past as many worlds as atoms in a buddha-field, is a world called Sea of Golden Light; the Buddha is called Freely Manifesting Any Form in Any Place.

"Above this, past as many worlds as atoms in a buddha-field, is a world called Pearl Flower Treasury; the Buddha there is called Inconceivable Wisdom with Cosmic Jewel Light.

"Above this, past as many worlds as atoms in a buddha-field, is a

world called Lofty Lion Throne of the Gods; the Buddha is called Light of Supreme Power.

"Above this, past as many worlds as atoms in a buddha-field, is a world called Boundless Jewel Illumining Everywhere, square in shape, resting on a sea of flowered forests, covered by an imperial net raining diamonds everywhere, surrounded by as many worlds as atoms in twenty buddha-fields, all uniformly pure. The Buddha there is called Supreme Sound Illumining the Whole World.

"Turning to the right of this Lotus Blossom Indra Net sea of fragrant water is another sea of fragrant water, called Treasury of Accumulated Precious Incense, with a world system called Array of All Virtues, composed of the sounds of the teachings of all Buddhas. At the bottom of this system is a world called Various Products, shaped like a thunderbolt, resting on various diamond mountain banners, covered by clouds of diamond light, surrounded by as many worlds as atoms in a buddha-field, uniformly pure. The Buddha there is named Lotus Blossom Eyes.

"Above this, past as many worlds as atoms in a buddha-field, is a world called Gladdening Sound; its Buddha is Producer of Joy and Bliss.

"Above this, past as many worlds as atoms in a buddha-field, is a world called Jewel Ornament Banner; its Buddha is Omniscience.

"Above this, past as many worlds as atoms in a buddha-field, is a world called Radiant Cotton Flowers; its Buddha is Subtle Sound of Pure Calm.

"Above this, past as many worlds as atoms in a buddha-field, is a world called Light of Transformation and Production; its Buddha is Moon of Knowledge in Pure Space.

"Above this, past as many worlds as atoms in a buddha-field, is a world called Exquisite Arrays; its Buddha is Showing the Forms of Dense Clouds of the Sea of Virtues.

"Above this, past as many worlds as atoms in a buddha-field, is a world called Subtle Sound of All Ornaments; its Buddha is Clouds of Joy.

"Above this, past as many worlds as atoms in a buddha-field, is a world called Lotus Pond; its Buddha is Banner of Renown.

"Above this, past as many worlds as atoms in a buddha-field, is a world called Array of All Jewels; its Buddha is Expanding Observant Eye.

"Above this, past as many worlds as atoms in a buddha-field, is a world called Pure Flower; its Buddha is called Inexhaustible Indestructible Knowledge.

"Above this, past as many worlds as atoms in a buddha-field, is a world called Lotus-Adorned City; its Buddha is Universal Light of Eyes like a Mine of Suns.

"Above this, past as many worlds as atoms in a buddha-field, is a

world called Mountain Peak with Innumerable Trees; its Buddha is Thunder of All Truths.

"Above this, past as many worlds as atoms in a buddha-field, is a world called Sunlight; its Buddha is Demonstrating Infinite Knowledge.

"Above this, past as many worlds as atoms in a buddha-field, is a world called Resting on Lotus Leaves; its Buddha is Mountain of All Virtues.

"Above this, past as many worlds as atoms in a buddha-field, is a world called Universally Supporting Atmosphere; its Buddha is Senses Shining like the Sun.

"Above this, past as many worlds as atoms in a buddha-field, is a world called Evident Light; its Buddha is Body Glow Illumining Everywhere.

"Above this, past as many worlds as atoms in a buddha-field, is a world called All-Illuminating Diamond Reverberating with Fragrant Thunder; its Buddha is Form of Supreme Flowers Blooming.

"Above this, past as many worlds as atoms in a buddha-field, is a world called Imperial Net Adornment, shaped like a balustrade, resting on a sea of all ornaments, covered by clouds of palaces of flames of light, surrounded by as many worlds as atoms in twenty buddha-fields, uniformly pure. The Buddha there is named Manifesting Clouds of Fearlessness.

"Turning to the right of this Treasury of Accumulated Precious Incense sea of fragrant water is another sea of fragrant water, called Jewel Array, with a world system called Everywhere Undefiled, composed of sounds of spiritual metamorphoses of buddha-fields within all atoms. At the bottom of this system is a world called Pure Refinement, flat in shape, like a jewel, resting on a sea of light spheres of all jewels, covered by clouds of various sandalwood crystals and pearls, surrounded by as many worlds as atoms in a buddha-field, uniformly pure. The Buddha there is called Peerless Banner of Invincibility.

"Above this, past as many worlds as atoms in a buddha-field, is a world called Bright Beautiful Adornments; its Buddha is Lotus Mind King of Mystical Powers.

"Above this, past as many worlds as atoms in a buddha-field, is a world called Banner of Rings of Subtle Forms; its Buddha is Endless Light of Universal Renown.

"Above this, past as many worlds as atoms in a buddha-field, is a world called Marvelous Arrays of Crystals from Mines of Flames; its Buddha is Great Wisdom and Knowledge Delightful to All Who See or Hear.

"Above this, past as many worlds as atoms in a buddha-field, is a world called Array of Exquisite Flowers; its Buddha is Supreme Knowledge of Infinite Power.

"Above this, past as many worlds as atoms in a buddha-field, is a

world called Producing Pure Particles; its Buddha is Transcending the Gods.

"Above this, past as many worlds as atoms in a buddha-field, is a world called Scent of Metamorphic Productions of Universal Light; its Buddha is Scented Elephant of Unbreakable Power.

"Above this, past as many worlds as atoms in a buddha-field, is a world called Vortex of Light; its Buddha is Good Reputation of Proven Logic.

"Above this, past as many worlds as atoms in a buddha-field, is a world called Sea of Jewel Necklaces; its Buddha is Incomparable Light Shining Everywhere.

"Above this, past as many worlds as atoms in a buddha-field, is a world called Banner of Lamps of Beautiful Flowers; its Buddha is Lamp of Unhindered Wisdom with Ultimate Virtues.

"Above this, past as many worlds as atoms in a buddha-field, is a world called Array of Skillful Techniques; its Buddha is Transcendence of the Sun of Wisdom.

"Above this, past as many worlds as atoms in a buddha-field, is a world called Radiant Light of Sandalwood Flowers; its Buddha is Sound of the Cosmos of Boundless Wisdom.

"Above this, past as many worlds as atoms in a buddha-field, is a world called Imperial Net Banner; its Buddha is Lamplight Shining Far.

"Above this, past as many worlds as atoms in a buddha-field, is a world called Pure Flower Wreath; its Buddha is Light of the Cosmic Sun.

"Above this, past as many worlds as atoms in a buddha-field, is a world called Great Awesome Radiance; its Buddha is Sound of the Cycles of Teaching of Boundless Virtue.

"Above this, past as many worlds as atoms in a buddha-field, is a world called Jewel Lotus Pond Abode of Common Peace; its Buddha is Showing Knowledge Entering into the Inconceivable.

"Above this, past as many worlds as atoms in a buddha-field, is a world called Level Ground; its Buddha is King of Light of Jewels of Virtue.

"Above this, past as many worlds as atoms in a buddha-field, is a world called Mass of Aromatic Crystals; its Buddha is Exquisite Adornments of the Sea of Inexhaustible Virtue.

"Above this, past as many worlds as atoms in a buddha-field, is a world called Subtle Light; its Buddha is Pervasive Sound of Incomparable Power.

"Above this, past as many worlds as atoms in a buddha-field, is a world called Radiance of Adornments Solid and Stable Everywhere, octagonal in shape, resting on a sea of mind-king crystal globes, covered by clouds of drapes adorned by all precious stones, surrounded by as many worlds as atoms in twenty buddha-fields, uniformly pure. The Buddha there is called Great Luminous Lamp of the Universal Eye.

"Turning to the right of this Jewel Array sea of fragrant water, there is another sea of fragrant water, called Mass of Diamonds, with a world system called Cosmic Action, composed of the enunciation of the principles of the methods pertaining to all of the stages of development of enlightening beings. At the bottom of this system is a world called Radiance of Pure Light, shaped like a string of pearls, resting on a sea of necklaces of pearls of all colors, covered by clouds of crystals of light from the pearl topknots of enlightening beings, surrounded by as many worlds as atoms in a buddha-field, uniformly pure. The Buddha there is called Light of Supreme Virtue.

"Above this, past as many worlds as atoms in a buddha-field, is a world called Wonderful Canopy; its Buddha is Mind Free in All Things.

"Above this, past as many worlds as atoms in a buddha-field, is a world called Jewel Adorned Lion Throne; its Buddha is called Great Dragon Abyss.

"Above this, past as many worlds as atoms in a buddha-field, is a world called Producing Diamond Thrones; its Buddha is called Ascending the Lotus Platform of a Lion Throne.

"Above this, past as many worlds as atoms in a buddha-field, is a world called Supreme Lotus Sound; its Buddha is All-Enlightening Light of Knowledge.

"Above this, past as many worlds as atoms in a buddha-field, is a world called Good Customs; its Buddha is King of Sublime Light Holding the Earth.

"Above this, past as many worlds as atoms in a buddha-field, is a world called Sound of Happiness; its Buddha is King of the Lamp of Truth.

"Above this, past as many worlds as atoms in a buddha-field, is a world called Jewel Treasury Indra's Net; its Buddha is Not Seen in Vain.

"Above this, past as many worlds as atoms in a buddha-field, is a world called Myriad Wonderful Mines; its Buddha is Flame Body Banner.

"Above this, past as many worlds as atoms in a buddha-field, is a world called Wheel of Golden Light; its Buddha is Purifying the Acts of Living Beings.

"Above this, past as many worlds as atoms in a buddha-field, is a world called Adornments of the Polar Mountains; its Buddha is Clouds of All Virtues Shining Everywhere.

"Above this, past as many worlds as atoms in a buddha-field, is a world called Shapes of Myriad Trees; its Buddha is Awareness like a Pure Moon like a Jewel Flower.

"Above this, past as many worlds as atoms in a buddha-field, is a world called No Fear; its Buddha is Torch of Supreme Golden Light.

"Above this, past as many worlds as atoms in a buddha-field, is a

world called Dragon King Banner of Great Renown; its Buddha is Seeing All Things as Equal.

"Above this, past as many worlds as atoms in a buddha-field, is a world called Displaying Crystal Colors; its Buddha is Sun of Metamorphic Production.

"Above this, past as many worlds as atoms in a buddha-field, is a world called Array of Light Flame Lamps; its Buddha is Jewel Canopy Light Illumining All.

"Above this, past as many worlds as atoms in a buddha-field, is a world called Fragrant Light Cloud; its Buddha is Contemplative Wisdom.

"Above this, past as many worlds as atoms in a buddha-field, is a world called No Enmity; its Buddha is Ocean of Energetic Supreme Intellect.

"Above this, past as many worlds as atoms in a buddha-field, is a world called Banner of Lights of All Adornments; its Buddha is Sovereign King Able to Produce Delightful Lotuses Anywhere.

"Above this, past as many worlds as atoms in a buddha-field, is a world called Hair-Curl Adornments, shaped like a half-moon, resting on a sea of crystal flowers from the polor mountain, covered by clouds of radiant diamonds of all kinds of ornaments, surrounded by as many worlds as atoms in twenty buddha-fields, all uniformly pure. Its Buddha is called Pure Eye.

"Turning to the right of this Diamond Mass sea of fragrant water, there is another sea of fragrant water, called Jewel Ramparts of Celestial Cities, with a world system called Lamp Flame Light, composed of the sounds of all impartial teachings. At the bottom of this system is a world called Ring of Jewel Moonlight Flowers, shaped like all kinds of ornaments, resting on a sea of flowers embellished with all kinds of jewels, covered by clouds of lion thrones the color of lapis lazuli, surrounded by as many worlds as atoms in a buddha-field. The Buddha there is called Free Light of Sun and Moon.

"Above this, past as many worlds as atoms in a buddha-field, is a world called Polar Mountain Jewel Light; its Buddha is Banner of Inexhaustuble Jewels of Truth.

"Above this, past as many worlds as atoms in a buddha-field, is a world called Myriad Beautiful Light Beams; its Buddha is Great Mass of Flowers.

"Above this, past as many worlds as atoms in a buddha-field, is a world called Crystal Light Flower; its Buddha is Most Independent of Humans.

"Above this, past as many worlds as atoms in a buddha-field, is a world called Universal Sound; its Buddha is Omniscience Illumining Everywhere.

"Above this, past as many worlds as atoms in a buddha-field, is a world called Great Tree Kinnara Sound; its Buddha is Independent Dragon with Infinite Virtues.

"Above this, past as many worlds as atoms in a buddha-field, is a world called Boundless Pure Light; its Buddha is Light of Jewel Flowers of Virtue.

"Above this, past as many worlds as atoms in a buddha-field, is a world called Supreme Sound; its Buddha is Array of All Knowledge.

"Above this, past as many worlds as atoms in a buddha-field, is a world called Decorated with Many Jewels; its Buddha is Jewel Flame Polar Mountain.

"Above this, past as many worlds as atoms in a buddha-field, is a world called Pure Wonderfully High Sound; its Buddha is Manifesting the Light of All Practices.

'Above this, past as many worlds as atoms in a buddha-field, is a world called Perfume Canopy; its Buddha is Unobstructed Ocean of All Transcendent Ways.

"Above this, past as many worlds as atoms in a buddha-field, is a world called Lion Flower Net; its Buddha is Jewel Flame Banner.

"Above this, past as many worlds as atoms in a buddha-field, is a world called Lamp of Beautiful Diamond Flowers; its Buddha is Light of All Great Vows.

"Above this, past as many worlds as atoms in a buddha-field, is a world called Stage of Illumination of All Things; its Buddha is Vast True Meaning of All Things.

"Above this, past as many worlds as atoms in a buddha-field, is a world called Level Ornaments of Pearl Dust; its Buddha is Net of Light of Supreme Wisdom.

"Above this, past as many worlds as atoms in a buddha-field, is a world called Lapis Lazuli Flowers; its Buddha is called Jewel Cluster Banner.

"Above this, past as many worlds as atoms in a buddha-field, is a world called Sphere of Immeasurable Subtle Lights; its Buddha is Oceanic Treasury of Great Powerful Knowledge.

"Above this, past as many worlds as atoms in a buddha-field, is a world called Clearly Seeing the Ten Directions; its Buddha is Banner of Pure Cultivation of All Virtues.

"Above this, past as many worlds as atoms in a buddha-field, is a world called Pleasing Pure Sound, shaped like Buddha's hand, resting on a sea of networks of jewel lights, covered by clouds of all adornments of enlightening beings' bodies, surrounded by as many worlds as atoms in twenty buddha-fields, all uniformly pure. The Buddha there is called Unimpeded Light Illumining the Entire Cosmos."

The enlightening being Universally Good also said to the great congregation, "East of the Repository of Undefiled Flames sea of fragrant water is another sea of fragrant water, called Subtle Body of Mystic Emanation. In this sea is a system of worlds called Well-Arrayed Different Quarters. Next to that is a sea of fragrant water called Adamantine Eye Banner, with a world system called Bridges

Adorning the Universe. Next to that is a sea of fragrant water called
Beautiful Arrays of Various Lotuses, with a world system called Constantly Producing Emanations in the Ten Directions. Next to that is a
sea of fragrant water called Gapless Diamond Wheel, with a world
system called Dense Clouds of Jewel Lotus Stems. Next to that is a sea
of fragrant water called Flames of Wonderful Fragrance Adorning
Everywhere, with a world system called Vairocana's Acts of Metamor-
phosis and Emanation. Next to that is a sea of fragrant water called
Gold Banner of Jewel Dust, with a world system called Realm of the
Buddhas' Protection. Next to that is a sea of fragrant water called
Blazing Lights of All Colors, with a world system called Supreme
Light Shining Everywhere. Next to that is a sea of fragrant water called
Realm of All Embellishments, with a world system called Jewel Flame
Lamp.

"There are as many such seas of fragrant waters as atoms in unspeakably many buddha-fields. The sea of fragrant water closest to the
perimeter mountains is called Crystal Ground, with a world system
called Always Radiating Light, composed of the sounds of the pure eons
of the ocean of worlds. At the bottom of this world system is a world
called Banner of Pleasing Pure Light, surrounded by as many worlds as
atoms in a buddha-field, uniformly pure; the Buddha there is called
Energetic Wisdom with Supreme Concentration. Above this, past as
many worlds as atoms in ten buddha-fields, level with the world
Diamond Banner, the world on the tenth level of the world system of
the sea of fragrant water in the center, is a world called Banner of
Arrays of Fragrances, surrounded by as many worlds as atoms in ten
buddha-fields, uniformly pure; the Buddha there is called Unobstructed
Lamp of the Cosmos. Above this, past as many worlds as atoms in
three buddha-fields, parallel to the world Endurance, is a world called
Radiant Treasury of Light; its Buddha is Unimpeded Light of Wisdom
Pervading the Cosmos. Above this, past as many worlds as atoms in
seven buddha-fields, at the top of this world system, is a world called
Supreme Body Fragrance, surrounded by as many worlds as atoms in
twenty buddha-fields, uniformly pure. The Buddha there is called
Flowers of the Branches of Enlightenment.

"Beyond the sea of fragrant water called Sphere of Inexhaustible
Light is another sea of fragrant water, called Full of Subtle Light, with a
world system called Everywhere Undefiled. Next to that is a sea of
fragrant water called Canopy of Radiance, with a world system called
Boundless Adornments. Next to that is a sea of fragrant water called
Array of Exquisite Jewels, with a world system called Parametric Form
of Aromatic Crystals. Next there is a sea of fragrant water called
Producing the Sounds of Buddha's Voice, with a world system called
Well-Structured Array. Next is a sea of fragrant water called Polar
Mountain Treasury of Banners of Fragrance, with a world system
called Light Filling Everywhere. Next is a sea of fragrant water called

Subtle Light of Sandalwood, with a world system called Wreath of Flower Radiance. Next is a sea of fragrant water called Atmospheric Power Sustaining, with a world system called Banner of Clouds of Aromatic Flames. Next is a sea of fragrant water called Adornments of the Body of the King of Gods, with a world system called Pearl Treasury. Next is a sea of fragrant water called Level and Pure, with a world system called Various Adornments of Lapis Lazuli Dust.

"There are as many such seas of fragrant water as atoms in unspeakably many buddha-fields; the one closest to the surrounding mountains is called Beautiful Tree Blossoms, having a world system called Producing Vast Lands, composed of the sounds of all Buddhas vanquishing demons. At the bottom of this system is a world called Flaming Torch Banner; its Buddha is called Ocean of Wordly Virtues. Above this, past as many worlds as atoms in ten buddha-fields, parallel to the world Diamond Banner, is a world called Producing Jewels; its Buddha is Jewel Clouds of Invincible Power. Above this, parallel to the world Endurance, is a world called Raiment Banner; its Buddha is King of the Ocean of Omniscience. At the top of this world system is a world called Jewel Necklace Lion Light; its Buddha is called Lotus Banner of Skillful Transformation and Emanation.

"Beyond the sea of fragrant water called Diamond Flame Light is another sea of fragrant water, called Banner Brightly Decorated with All Adornments, with a world system called Adorned by Pure Actions. Next to that is a sea of fragrant water called Sea of Radiance of Flowers of All Jewels, with a world system called Adorned by Virtuous Characteristics. Next is a sea of fragrant water called Lotus Blooming, with a world system called Crown Jewels of Enlightening Beings. Next is a sea of fragrant water called Raiment of Exquisite Jewels, with a world system called Pure Pearl Orbs. Next is a sea of fragrant water called Lovely Flowers Illumining Everywhere, with a world system called Radiance of Clouds of a Hundred Lights. Next is a sea of fragrant water called Great Light Pervading Space, with a world system called Jewel Light Shining Everywhere. Next is a sea of fragrant water called Banner Adorned with Beautiful Flowers, with a world system called Gold Moon Eye Necklace. Next is a sea of fragrant water called Fragrant Ocean Treasury of Pearls, with a world system called Buddha Halo. Next is a sea of fragrant water called Jewel Disc Light, with a world system called Light Easily Displaying the Realm of Buddhahood.

"There are as many such seas of fragrant waters as atoms in an unspeakable number of buddha-fields; the one nearest to the surrounding mountains is called Boundless Discs Adorning the Floor. It has a world system called Distinctions of Innumerable Regions, composed of the sounds of the languages of all countries. At the bottom of the system is a world called Diamond Flower Canopy; the Buddha there is called Universal Sound of Light of Inexhaustible Features. Above this, past as many worlds as atoms in ten buddha-fields, is a world, parallel to the world Diamond Banner, called Banner Producing Precious Raiment; its Buddha is called Great Power of Clouds of Virtue. Above this, parallel to the world Endurance. is a world called Beautiful Array of Implements of Myriad Jewels; its Buddha is Ocean of Supreme Wisdom. At the top of this world system is a world called Banner of Raiment of Sunlight; its Buddha is Lotus Cloud of the Sun of Knowledge.

"Beyond the Sapphire Array sea of fragrant water is another sea of fragrant water, called Titan Palace, with a world system called Supported by Scented Light. Next to that is a sea of fragrant water called Jewel Lion Array, with a world system called Revealing All the Jewels in All Regions. Next is a sea of fragrant water called Palace Color Light Clouds, with a world system called Beautiful Array of Jewel Globes. Next is a sea of fragrant water called Producing Gigantic Lotuses, with a world system called Beautiful Ornaments Lighting Up the Universe. Next is a sea of fragrant water called Wonderful Eye of Lamp Flames, with a world system called Overseeing All Transformations in the Ten Directions. Next is a sea of fragrant water called Sphere of Inconceivable Adornments, with a world system called Universal Renown of the Light of the Ten Directions. Next is a sea of fragrant water called Jewel Heap Adornment, with a world system called Lamp Light Radiance. Next is a sea of fragrant water called Pure Jewel Light, with a world system called Unobstructed Wind. Next is a sea of fragrant water called Balustrade Draped with Precious Raiment, with a world system called Light of Buddha's Body.

"There are as many such seas as atoms in unspeakably many buddha-fields. Closest to the surrounding mountains is a sea of fragrant water called Banner Decorated with Trees, with a world system called Resting Peacefully in the Imperial Net, composed of the sounds of the stages of knowledge of all enlightening beings. At the bottom of this system is a world called Golden; its Buddha is called Supremely Majestic Light of Aromatic Flames. Above this, past as many worlds as atoms in ten buddha-fields, parallel to the world Diamond Banner, is a world called Crystal Tree Flowers; its Buddha is called Unhindered Appearance Anywhere. Above this, parallel to the world Endurance, is a world called Beautiful Adornments of Lapis Lazuli; its Buddha is called Stable Intellect Mastering All Principles. At the top of this world system is a world called Sublime Array of Pure Sounds; the Buddha is called King of Light of Lotuses Blooming.

"Beyond the sea of fragrant water Diamond Orb Adorned Floor is another sea of fragrant water, called Realm of Magical Production of Lotus Blossoms, with a world system called Equality and Justice in the Land. Next to that is a sea of fragrant water called Crystal Light, with a world system called No Confusion throughout the Universe. Next is a sea of fragrant water called Sun Crystal of Many Wonderful Scents, with a world system called Appearing in All Quarters. Next is a sea of fragrant water called Eternally Admitting Jewel Rivers, with a world system called Sounds of Buddha's Speech Carried Out Everywhere. Next is a sea of fragrant water called Boundless Deep Wondrous Sound, with a world system called Boundless Distinctions in Location. Next is a sea of fragrant water called Solid Mass, with a world system called Distinctions in Innumerable Places. Next is a sea of fragrant water called Pure Sound, with a world system called Everywhere Pure Adornments. Next is a sea of fragrant water called Sandalwood Balustrade Treasury of Sound, with a world system called Egregious Banner. Next is a sea of fragrant water called Adornment of Light of Diamonds of Wonderful Fragrance, with a world system called Power of Light Appearing Everywhere.

"Beyond the Lotus Blossom Indra Net sea of fragrant water is another sea of fragrant water, called Beautiful Ornaments of Silver Lotus Flowers, with a world system called Universal Action. Next is a sea of fragrant water called Cloud of Intense Radiance of Lapis Lazuli Bamboo, with a world system called Everywhere Producing the Sounds of All Quarters. Next is a sea of fragrant water called Mass of Light Flames of the Ten Directions, with a world system called Always Producing Metamorphic Displays Distributed Throughout the Ten Directions. Next is a sea of fragrant water called Gold-Producing Crystal Banner, with a world system called Form of Diamond Banners. Next is a sea of fragrant water called Great Equal Adornments, with a world system called Circle of Bravery. Next is a sea of fragrant water called Endless Light of Jewel Flower Groves, with a world system called Boundless Pure Light. Next is a sea of fragrant water called Gold Banner, with a world system called Expounding Mysteries. Next is a sea of fragrant water called Light Beams Shining Everywhere, with a world system called Everywhere Adorned. Next is a sea of fragrant water called Tranquil Sound, with a world system called Appearing Hanging Down.

"There are as many such seas as atoms in unspeakably many buddha-fields. The one closest to the surrounding mountains is called Intense Flame Cloud Banner; its world system, called Array of All Lights, is composed of the sounds of the beings assembled at the enlightenment sites of all Buddhas. At the bottom of this system is a world called Pure Eye Adornment; its Buddha is called Diamond Moon Illumining the Ten Directions. Above this, past as many worlds as atoms in ten buddha-fields, parallel to the world Diamond Banner, is a world called Qualities of Lotus Blossoms, with a Buddha called Greatly Energetic Well-Aware Mind. Above this, parallel to the world Endurance, is a world called Dense Arrays of Diamonds, with a Buddha called Shala King Banner. Above this, past as many worlds as atoms in seven buddha-fields, is a world called Pure Ocean Adornments, with a Buddha called Incomparable Virtue which None Can Conquer.

"Beyond the sea of fragrant water Treasury of Accumulated Precious Incense is another sea of fragrant water, called Light of All Jewels

Shining Everywhere, with a world system called Adornment of Unde-filed Reputation. Next is a sea of fragrant water called Flowers of Many Jewels Blooming, with a world system called Form of Space. Next is a sea of fragrant water called Tent of Glory Shining Everywhere, with a world system called Everywhere Adorned with Unimpeded Light. Next is a sea of fragrant water called Sandalwood Tree Blossoms, with a world system called Whirl Appearing Everywhere. Next is a sea of fragrant water called Producing Jewels of Exquisite Colors, with a world system called Supreme Banner Traveling Everywhere. Next is a sea of fragrant water called Everywhere Producing Diamond Flowers, with a world system called Displaying Inconceivable Adornments. Next is a sea of fragrant water called Mind King Crystal Wheel Ornaments, with a world system called Manifesting the Unobstructed Light of Buddha. Next is a sea of fragrant water called Necklace of Masses of Jewels, with a world system called Clearing Away Doubt. Next is a sea of fragrant water called Everywhere Adorned with Rings of Pearls, with a world system called Flowing from the Vows of the Buddhas.

"There are as many such seas as atoms in unspeakably many buddha-fields. The one closest to the surrounding mountains is called Circle of Jewel Mines, with a world system, called Universal Sound Banner, composed of the sounds of enunciation of ways of entry into omniscience. At the bottom of this world system is a world called Flower Pistil Flames, with a Buddha called Energetic Generosity. Above this, past as many worlds as atoms in ten buddha-fields, parallel to the world Diamond Banner, is a world called Lotus Light Banner, with a Buddha called Supreme Mind King with All Virtues. Above this, past as many worlds as atoms in three buddha-fields, parallel to the world Endurance, is a world called Ten Directions Adorned, with a Buddha called King Skillfully Manifesting Innumerable Virtuous Qualities. At the top of this world system is a world called Crystal Fragrance Mountain Banner, with a Buddha called Vast Benevolent Eyes Removing Doubt.

"Beyond the sea of fragrant water Jewel Array is a sea of fragrant water called Treasury of Light Supporting the Polar Mountain, with a world system called Producing Immense Clouds. Next to that is a sea of fragrant water called Variously Adorned Realm of Great Power, with a world system called Adornments of Unobstructed Purity. Next is a sea of fragrant water called Thickly Spread Jewel Lotus Blossoms, with a world system called Supreme Lamp Array. Next is a sea of fragrant water called Resting on Adornments of All Jewels, with a world system called Treasury of Sunlight Webs. Next is a sea of fragrant water called Manifold Beatification, with a world system called Resting Place of Jewel Flowers. Next is a sea of fragrant water called Exercise of Extremely Brilliant Intellect, with a world system called Array of Superlative Forms. Next is a sea of fragrant water called Mountain Peak Holding Beautiful Precious Stones, with a world system called Universally Pure Treasury of Space. Next is a sea of fragrant water called Great Light Illumining Everywhere, with a world system called Sapphire Torch Light. Next is a sea of fragrant water called Filled with Delightful Jewels Illuminating Everywhere, with a world system called Ubiquitous Roar.

"There are as many such seas as atoms in unspeakably many buddha-fields. The one closest to the surrounding mountains is called Producing Sapphires, with a world system called Everywhere Undifferentiated composed of the booming voices of all enlightening beings. At the bottom of this system is a world called Exquisite Treasury, with a Buddha called Supremely Virtuous Mind. Above this, past as many worlds as atoms in ten buddha-fields, parallel to the world Diamond Banner, is a world called Embellishments, with a Buddha called Great Transcendental Light. Above this, parallel to the world Endurance, is a world called Everywhere Adorned with Lapis Lazuli Globes, with a Buddha called Polar Mountain Lamp. At the top of this world system is a world called Flower Banner Sea, with a Buddha called Cloud of Sublime Wisdom Capable of Endless Transmutations and Productions.

"Beyond the sea of fragrant water Mass of Diamonds is another sea of fragrant water, called Reverently Adorned Jewel Parapets, with a world system called Outstanding Jewel Banner. Next to that is a sea of fragrant water called Array of Jewel Banners, with a world system called Manifesting All Lights. Next is a sea of fragrant water called Cloud of Sublime Jewels, with a world system called Universally Shining Light. Next is a sea of fragrant water called Adorned with Jewel Tree Blossoms, with a world system called Decorated with Beautiful Flowers. Next is a sea of fragrant water called Array of Raiment of Wonderful Jewels, with a world system called Ocean of Light. Next is a sea of fragrant water called Jewel Tree Peak, with a world system called Jewel Flame Cloud. Next is a sea of fragrant water called Displaying Light, with a world system called Entering Diamond with No Resistance. Next is a sea of fragrant water called Lotuses Adorning Everywhere, with a world system called Oceanic Abyss with Boundless Shores. Next is a sea of fragrant water called Array of Beautiful Jewels, with a world system called Treasury Displaying All Lands.

"Such seas are as numerous as atoms in unspeakably many buddha-fields. The one nearest to the surrounding mountains is called Indestructible Sea, with a world system called Lotus Blossom Setting Decorated With Beautiful Discs composed of the sounds produced by all the powers of Buddhas. At the bottom of this system is a world called Most Sublime Fragrance, with a Buddha called Producing Innumerable Light Beams. Above this, past as many worlds as atoms in ten buddha-fields, parallel to the world Diamond Banner, is a world called Ornamental Gates of Inconceivably Many Distinctions, with a Buddha called Immeasurable Knowledge. Above this, parallel to the world Endurance, is a world called Beautiful Flower Treasury of the Light of the Ten Directions, with a Buddha called Lion Eye Light Flame Cloud. At the top of this world system is a world called Ocean Sound, with a Buddha called Gate of Light Flames of the Heaven of Waters.

"Beyond the sea of fragrant water Jewel Ramparts of Celestial Cities is another sea of fragrant water, called Brilliant Light of a Wheel of Flames, with a world system called Unspeakably Many Adornments of All Kinds. Next to that is a sea of fragrant water called Jewel Dust Road, with a world system called Everywhere Entering Infinite Spirals. Next is a sea of fragrant water called Containing All Ornaments, with a world system called Jewel Light Shining Everywhere. Next is a sea of fragrant water called Spreading Jewel Nets, with a world system called Arrayed Deep and Thick. Next is a sea of fragrant water called Beautiful Jewel Array Banners, with a world system called Sound of Clear Understanding of the Ocean of Worlds. Next is a sea of fragrant water called Pure Reflection of the Palace of the Sun, with a world system called Entering Everywhere in Indra's Net. Next is a sea of fragrant water called Beautiful Sound of Music of All Drums, with a world system called Round and Full, Level and Straight. Next is a sea of fragrant water called Various Beautiful Adornments, with a world system called Cloud of Flames of Pure Intense Light. Next is a sea of fragrant water called Lamp With All-Pervasive Jewel Flames, with a world system called Various Forms According to the Original Vows of the Buddha.

"Such seas of fragrant waters are as numerous as atoms in unspeakably many buddha-fields. The one nearest to the surrounding mountains is called Raiment of Assembled Ornaments; its world system, called Magically Produced Beautiful Raiment, is composed of the sound of the voices of all the Buddhas of past, present, and future. At the bottom of this system is a sea of fragrant water called Indra Flower Treasury, with a world called Producing Joy, surrounded by as many worlds as atoms in a buddha-field, all uniformly pure. The Buddha is called Stable Enlightened Knowledge. Above this, past as many worlds as atoms in ten buddha-fields, parallel to the world Diamond Banner, is a world called Adorned with Jewel Nets, surrounded by as many worlds as atoms in ten buddha-fields, all uniformly pure. The Buddha is called Light of Infinite Joy. Above this, past as many worlds as atoms in three buddha-fields, parallel to the world Endurance, is a world called Jewel Lotus Lion Throne, surrounded by as many worlds as atoms in thirteen buddha-fields. The Buddha is called Most Pure Unwasteful Learning. Above this, past as many worlds as atoms in seven buddha-fields, at the top of this world system is a world called Jewel Lotus Dragon Light, surrounded by as many worlds as atoms in twenty buddha-fields, uniformly pure. The Buddha there is called All-Illumining Light Pervading the Cosmos.

"In these seas of fragrant water, as many as atomic particles in ten unspeakably large numbers of buddha-fields, are an equal number of world systems, all resting on lotus blossoms adorned with diamond

banners in the forms of all enlightening beings, each with unbroken
boundaries of ornaments, each radiating lights of jewel colors, each
covered by clouds of lights, each with their particular adornments,
particular time period differences, particular Buddhas appearing, particular oceans of teachings being expounded, particular beings filling their
particular entries in the ten directions, particular supports by the spiritual powers of all Buddhas. All of the worlds in each of these systems
rest on various adornments, connecting with each other, forming a
network of worlds, set up, with various differences, throughout the
Flower Bank Array ocean of worlds."

Then, to recapitulate, the enlightening being Universally Good, receiving power from the Buddha, said in verse,

> The Flower Bank ocean of worlds
> Is equal to the universe.
> Its adornments are extremely pure,
> Resting peacefully in space.
>
> In this ocean of worlds
> Are inconceivably many world systems;
> Each one independent,
> They are not all mixed up.
>
> In the Flower Bank world-ocean
> The world systems are well arrayed
> With different shapes and adornments
> Varying in appearance.
>
> The sounds of Buddhas' displays
> Are the substance of various systems;
> Seeing according to the power of acts,
> The world systems are finely adorned.
>
> Polar Mountain city networks,
> Circular shapes of whirlpools,
> Immense lotus flowers blooming,
> They circle one another.
>
> Mountain banner palace shapes,
> Whirling diamond shapes:
> Like this are the inconceivable
> Vast systems of worlds.
>
> Flames of pearls from the ocean,
> Inconceivable nets of light:

The world systems like this
All rest on lotus blossoms.

The webs of light of each system
Cannot be fully described:
In the lights appear all the lands
Throughout the seas in ten directions.

Into the ornaments adorning
All the systems of worlds
Enter all the lands,
Making all visible everywhere.

The world systems are inconceivable,
The worlds are boundless;
Their various fine embellishments
Derive from the Great Sage's power.

In each of the systems of worlds
The worlds are inconceivably many;
Some forming, some decaying,
Some have already crumbled away.

Like leaves in a forest,
Some growing and some falling,
So too in these systems thus
Do worlds form and decay.

Like according to the forest
The various fruits are different,
In these world systems too
Do various beings live.

Just as when seeds are different
So are the fruits they produce,
Because of differences in the force of acts
Living beings' lands are not the same.

Just as the mind-king jewel
Appears in different colors to different minds,
When beings' minds are pure
They can see pure lands.

Like great dragon kings
Creating clouds filling the sky,
So does the power of Buddhas' vows
Produce the various lands.

Just as the magicians' arts
Can make various things appear,
Due to the force of beings' acts
The number of realms is inconceivable.

Just like pictures
Drawn by an artist,
So are all worlds
Made by the painter-mind.

Beings' bodies' differences
Arise from the mind's discriminations;
Thus are the lands varied
All depending on acts.

Just as the Guide is seen
In various different forms,
So do beings see the lands
According to their mental patterns.

The borders of all the worlds
Are draped with lotus nets;
Their various features different,
Their adornments are all pure.

In those lotus nets
Rest networks of lands
With various adornments,
Inhabited by various beings.

Some lands
Are dangerous and uneven;
Because of beings' afflictions
They see them in this way.

Innumerable kinds of worlds,
Defiled as well as pure,
Develop according to beings' minds,
Maintained by enlightening beings' power.

In some lands
Is purity as well as defilement;
This arises from the force of deeds
Under the influence of enlightening beings.

Some lands are made of pure jewels
Radiating light,

With various fine adornments
Purified by the Buddhas.

In each system of lands
Are eonic fires, inconceivable;
While it appears disastrous,
The places always remain secure.

By the force of beings' acts
Are many lands produced,
Supported by wind atmospheres,
Or resting on water spheres.

The phenomena of the worlds
Are thus variously seen;
Yet they really have no origination
And also no disintegration.

In each moment of mind
Are infinite lands produced;
By the Buddha's spiritual power
All are seen as pure.

Some lands are made of dirt,
Their substance very hard;
Dark, with no light shining,
They're inhabited by evildoers.

Some lands are made of thunderbolts,
Mixed up and terrifying,
With much misery and little happiness,
The abodes of those of scant virtue.

Some are made of iron,
Some of ruddy copper,
With stone mountains, steep and fearsome,
Full of animals.

Among the lands are hells
Where beings cannot be saved from pain:
Always in the dark,
Burnt by seas of flame.

Some, again, have animals
Of various wretched forms;
Because of their own evil deeds
They always suffer affliction.

Some see a nether-world,
Oppressed by hunger and thirst;
Climbing great mountains of fire,
They suffer extreme pain.

There are also some lands
Composed of precious elements,
With various kinds of mansions;
These are realized by pure deeds.

You should observe these worlds,
The humans and celestials therein:
Developed by results of pure deeds,
They feel happiness all the time.

In each and every pore
Are unthinkable billions of lands,
Adorned in various ways,
With never any cramp.

By the individual acts of beings
These worlds are infinite in kind:
Therein are born attachments
And differences of misery and happiness.

Some lands are made of jewels
Always radiating boundless light;
Diamond lotus flowers
Adorn them, totally pure.

Some lands are made of light
Resting too on spheres of light:
Golden, with sandalwood scent,
Flaming clouds illumining all.

Some lands are made of lunar discs,
Draped with fragrant robes,
In a lotus blossom,
Filled with enlightening beings.

Some lands are made of many jewels,
Their colors without impurities,
Like the imperial net of Indra,
Always shining with light.

Some lands are made of fragrance,
Some are diamond flowers;
Their forms of crystal light
Are most pure when looked into.

There are also inconceivably many lands
Made of flower wreaths,
Filled with phantom Buddhas
And radiance of enlightening beings.

There are some pure lands
All of flowering trees,
Beautiful boughs spread over sanctuaries,
Shaded by crystal clouds.

Some lands are made
Of diamond flowers with pure light;
Some are sounds of Buddhas teaching,
Forming boundless networks of arrays.

Some lands are like the jeweled crowns
Of enlightening beings;
Some are shaped like thrones
Issuing from magical light.

Some are sandalwood powder,
Some like emanated light,
Some the sounds in Buddha's aura
Formed into a wondrous land.

Some see pure lands
Adorned with a single light;
Some see many ornaments,
All variously superb.

Some have for adornments
The marvelous things of ten lands;
Some are adorned with everything
In a thousand lands.

Sometimes one land is embellished
With the things of a billion lands,
Their various features unlike,
All appearing as reflected images.

The things of unspeakably many lands
Adorn a single land,

Each radiating light,
Produced by the Buddhas' vows.

There are some lands
Purified by the power of vows;
In each of their adornments
Are seen all oceans of worlds.

The pure lands realized by those
Who practice the vows of universal good
Manifest within themselves the adornments
Of past, present, and future lands.

You should observe, O Children of Buddha,
The spiritual power in the systems of worlds:
The worlds of the future, all
They'll show you, like in a dream.

The worlds of the ten directions,
The oceans of lands of the past,
All within a single land
Show their forms, like phantoms.

All Buddhas of past, present, and future,
As well as their lands,
Can all be observed
In a single world system.

The spiritual power of all Buddhas
Shows many lands in an atom:
Of various kinds, all clearly seen,
Like reflections, they have no true reality.

There are many lands
Whose forms are like oceans;
And lands like polar mountains
Are inconceivable in number.

Some lands are well disposed,
Formed like Indra's net;
Some are shaped like forests,
With Buddhas filling them.

Some are shaped like jewel discs,
Some like lotus blossoms,

Or octagonal, with all decorations;
They're various, and all pure.

Some are shaped like seats,
Some again are triangular;
Some are like pure jewels,
Castle walls, or celestial bodies.

Some are like gods' topknots,
Some like the half-moon;
Some are like crystal mountains,
Some like the solar orb.

The shape of some of the worlds
Is like whirlpools in a fragrant sea;
Some are spheres of light,
Purified by Buddhas past.

Some are shaped like wheel rims,
Some are altar-shaped;
Some are like Buddha's hair curl,
His flesh topknot, or large long eyes.

Some are like Buddha's hand,
Some like thunderbolts,
Some are like mountains of flames;
Enlightening beings fill them all.

Some are shaped like lions,
Some like seashells;
Of infinite colors and forms,
Their substances are each distinct.

In one system of worlds
Are endless forms of lands;
All depend on Buddhas' vow power
For protection and stability.

Some lands last an eon,
Some exist for ten eons,
Or for more eons than atoms
In a hundred thousand lands.

In a single eon
Lands are seen to dissolve;

Measureless or countless,
Or inconceivably many of them.

Some lands have a Buddha,
And some lands do not;
Some have just one Buddha,
And some have countless Buddhas.

If a land has no Buddha,
Then a Buddha from another world
Will mystically appear there
To manifest the works of Buddhas—
Dying in heaven and descending in spirit,
Residing in a womb and being born,
Vanquishing demons and becoming enlightened,
Turning the wheel of the unexcelled teaching;
According to the inclinations of beings' minds
Buddha manifests various forms,
Teaching them the sublime truth
In accord with each of their faculties.

In each buddha-field
A Buddha appears in the world,
Spending billions of years
Expounding unexcelled truths.

If beings are not vessels of truth,
They cannot see the Buddhas;
If any have the will,
They see Buddha everywhere.

In each individual buddha-field
Is a Buddha appearing in the world;
The Buddhas in all lands
Are inconceivable in number.

Herein each and every Buddha
Shows countless mystic transformations,
Pervading the entire universe,
Taming the ocean of beings.

Some lands have no light;
They're dark and full of fear,
With pains like knives and swords:
Those who see them suffer by themselves.

Some have heavenly lights;
Some, lights of palaces;
Some have sun and moon lights:
Inconceivable are the networks of lands.

Some lands are inherently luminous,
In some the trees emit pure light;
There has never been suffering there,
Due to the power of beings' virtue.

Some have lights of mountains,
Some have crystal lights,
Some are lit by lamps:
All the force of beings' deeds.

Some have Buddhas' auras,
Filled with enlightening beings;
Some are lotus blossom lights
With magnificent blazing colors.

Some lands are lit by flower lights,
Some by the sheen of fragrant waters,
Or by perfumes and burning incense;
All comes from the force of pure vows.

Some are lit by cloud lights,
Some by jewel oysters' lights;
The light of Buddhas' mystic power
Can intone gladdening sounds.

Some are lit by jewel lights,
Some by diamond flames.
Their pure sounds can shake far-off realms;
Wherever they reach there are no pains.

Some have crystal lights
Or lights from ornaments
Or from enlightenment scenes
Shining in the crowds.

Buddha emanates a great light
Filled with phantom Buddhas;
That light touches all with its glow,
Pervading the whole cosmos.

Some lands are terrifying,
With great howls of pain,
Those voices most bitter and harsh,
Frightening all who hear.

The realms of hells and beasts
As well as the netherworlds:
These are polluted, evil worlds,
From which always come cries of pain and distress.

There are some lands
That always produce enjoyable sounds,
Pleasing, in accord with the teaching;
This is attained by pure deeds.

In some lands are always heard
Heavenly sounds of various gods,
Pure sounds of celestial realms,
Or the voices of leaders of the worlds.

There are some lands
That produce wonderful sounds from clouds;
They're filled with jewel seas,
Crystal trees, and music.

In the auras of the Buddhas
Are endless magical voices
And those of enlightening beings
Heard throughout all lands:
The voices expounding the teaching
In inconceivably many lands,
The voices produced by the ocean of vows,
The wondrous tales of practical action.

The Buddhas of past, present, and future,
Are born in the various worlds,
Fulfilling all their epithets,
Their voices without any end;

In some lands is heard
The voice of all Buddhas' powers;
The stages, the transcendent ways, and such
Teachings are all expounded.

The power of the vows of universal good
Intones wondrous sayings in billions of worlds,

That sound like thunder shaking,
Remaining for endless ages.

The Buddhas in pure lands
Manifest independent speech
Heard by one and all
Throughout the cosmos, everywhere.

BOOK SIX

Vairocana

THEN THE ENLIGHTENING BEING Universally Good went on to say to the great assembly, "Children of Buddha, in the remote past, as many eons ago as atoms in a world— nay, even twice as long ago as that, there was an ocean of worlds called All-Sided Pure Light. In that ocean of worlds was a world called Supreme Sound, which rested on a sea of nets of crystal flowers, and had as many satellite worlds as atoms in the polar mountain. It was perfectly round in shape, and its ground was replete with innumerable adornments. It had around it three hundred circles of surrounding mountains, forested with trees of myriad precious substances. It was covered by clouds of all kinds of gems. It was illumined by pure shining light. Its cities and mansions were like great high mountains. Food and clothing appeared whenever thought of. The age then was called Variously Adorned.

"In that world Supreme Sound was a sea of fragrant water called Pure Light. From the midst of that sea rose a great polar mountain of lotus flowers, called Banner Adorned All Over with Flowery Flames. It was surrounded by balustrades made of ten kinds of precious elements. On the mountain was a great forest, called Circle of Branches with Jewel Flowers. Arrayed all around it were innumerable flower towers and jewel terraces. Everywhere was richly embellished with innumerable banners of exquisite fragrances, jewel mountain pennants, and jewel lotus blossoms. Innumerable nets of aromatic crystal lotus blossoms were draped all around. There was music, harmonious and pleasing. Fragrant clouds shone. All of these were countless, impossible to fully record.

"There were a million billion trillion cities all around the forest, with various beings living in them. East of this forest was a huge city called Flame Light, the capital city of a human king, surrounded by a million billion trillion cities, all made of pure, beautiful jewels, each one seventy leagues long and seventy leagues wide, with walls made of seven kinds of precious substances. The armory towers to repel attackers were all high and beautifully adorned, with moats made of jewels and precious metals filled with fragrant water, with blue, red, and white lotuses, all of jewels, spread here and there as ornaments. Seven layers of jewel trees also surrounded the city. The palaces and mansions were all adorned with jewels, draped with various beautiful nets, and graced within with perfumes and scattered flowers. There were a million billion trillion gates, all decorated with jewels, with forty-nine jewel banners in front of each gate, arrayed in ranks. There were also a million billion gardens and groves all around, with various mixed scents and the fragrances of crystal trees wafting through them and perfuming everything. Myriad birds sang in harmony, a delight to the hearer.

"The inhabitants of this great city had all perfected the bases of mystic power as a result of what they had done. They could travel through the sky like celestial beings. Whatever they wanted came to them when they thought of it.

"Just south of that city was a celestial city called Adorned with Tree Blossoms. To the right of that was a great dragon city called Ultimate. Next to that was a yaksha city called Supreme Banner of Diamonds. Next was a gandharva city called Beautiful Palace. Next was a titan city called Jewel Wheel. Next was a garuda city called Array of Beautiful Jewels. Next was a royal Brahma heaven city called Various Wonderful Adornments. There were a million billion trillion such cities, each surrounded by a million billion trillion palaces, each with innumerable adornments.

"In this great forest Circle of Branches with Jewel Flowers was a sanctuary called Jewel Flowers Illumining Everywhere, arrayed with many huge jewels, with wreaths of crystal flowers blooming everywhere, blazing with fragrant lamps, covered by flaming clouds containing the colors of all jewels, with webs of light shining everywhere. All the ornaments constantly produced exquisite jewels, and all kinds of music played with elegant sounds. Diamonds showed the bodies of enlightening beings. There were various exquisite flowers everywhere.

"In front of that sanctuary was an ocean called Fragrant Diamonds, which produced a huge lotus flower called Flaming Circle of Flower Pistils. That flower was a hundred billion leagues across; its stem, leaves, pistils, and base were all of wonderful jewels. It was surrounded by unspeakable hundreds of thousands of billions of trillions of lotuses, constantly radiating light and emanating beautiful sound filling all directions.

"In the first eon of that world Supreme Sound as many Buddhas as atoms in ten mountains appeared in the world. The first Buddha was called Supreme Clouds on the Mountain of All Virtues. A hundred years before that Buddha was to appear in the world, all the adornments in the great forest Circle of Branches with Jewel Flowers all became pure. That is to say, they produced inconceivable numbers of clouds of jewel flames emanating voices praising the virtues of Buddhas;

radiant nets of light intoning the voices of countless Buddhas covered all quarters; the palaces and mansions reflected each other in their glow; lights from jewel flowers clustered into clouds and produced sublime sounds telling of the extensive roots of goodness practiced by all living beings in past times, telling of the names of the Buddhas of past, present, and future, telling of the ultimate path of the vows and deeds carried out by all the enlightening beings, telling of the sublime teachings of the enlightened ones. The manifestation of such magnificent signs revealed that the Buddha was about to appear in the world.

"Because the kings in that world all saw those signs, their roots of goodness became mature and they all came to the site of enlightenment desirous of seeing the Buddha. Then the Buddha Supreme Cloud on the Mountain of All Virtues suddenly appeared on a big lotus blossom in that sanctuary. His body was everywhere, equal to the cosmos, appearing to be born in all buddha-fields, going to all sites of enlightenment. His boundless pure form was thoroughly pure and could not be outshone by any being in any world, replete with all noble characteristics, each one distinctly clear. His image appeared in all palaces, and all living beings could witness it with their own eyes. Boundless phantom Buddhas emanated from his body, with auras of various colors filling the universe.

"As on the top of the mountain Banner Adorned with Flowery Flames in this sea of fragrant water Pure Light, in the midst of the great forest Circle of Branches with Jewel Flowers, that Buddha appeared bodily sitting there, so did he appear and sit atop every one of the sixty-eight trillion high mountains in the world Supreme Sound.

"At that point the Buddha emitted a great light beam from between his brows. That light beam was called Producing the Sounds of All Roots of Goodness, and was accompanied by as many light rays as atoms in ten buddha-fields. That light filled all lands in the ten directions, and if there were any sentient beings with the potential to be harmonized, that light touched them with its radiance and they immediately awoke on their own, ending all feverish confusion, sundering the web of obstruction, smashing the mountains of barriers, clearing away all pollution, developing great faith and resolution, producing excellent roots of goodness, forever leaving the fears of the various difficulties, annihilating all the miseries of mind and body, conceiving the will to see the Buddha and head for omniscience. At that time, all the world leaders and their retinues, countless hundreds of thousands, having been awakened by Buddha's light, all went to the Buddha and prostrated themselves before him.

"In the great city Flame Light was a king called Benevolent Mind a Joy to Behold. He reigned over a million billion trillion cities. He had thirty-seven thousand wives and concubines, the principal one being Auspicious Sign of Blessings. He had five hundred sons, the eldest being Light of Great Power, who himself had a thousand wives, the principle one being Exquisite Sight. At that time, the prince Light of Great Power, having seen the Buddha's light, due to the power of the roots of goodness he had cultivated, immediately realized ten kinds of teachings: he realized the concentration of the spheres of the virtues of all Buddhas; he realized all-sided memory power of all Buddha teachings; he realized transcendent knowledge containing a vast store of skillful techniques; he realized the great culture of kindness harmonizing and pacifying all living beings; he realized great compassion whose reverberations are like clouds extending everywhere; he realized the great joy of the supreme mind which gives birth to boundless virtues; he realized the great equanimity which is aware of all things as they really are; he realized the great spiritual power of the impartial treasury of extensive skill in means of liberation; he realized the great aspiration which increases power of faith; he realized the gate of brilliant intellectual powers entering into omniscience.

"Then Prince Light of Great Power, having attained illumination of these teachings, receiving mystic power from the Buddha, looked over the great masses and spoke some verses, saying,

The Buddha sits on the site of enlightenment;
Pure and clear is his great radiant light,
Like a thousand suns emerging
Illumining all over space.

After countless billions of ages
Does the Guide appear;
Now the Buddha's come into the world,
Beheld and attended by all.

Observe the Buddha's light,
Its inconceivable phantom Buddhas,
In every single palace
Reposed in true absorption.

See the Buddha's mystic powers
Producing clouds of flames from his pores,
Illuminating the world
With light that has no end.

Behold the Buddha's body,
With webs of light most pure,
Manifesting forms equal in number to all beings,
Filling the ten directions.

His wondrous voice pervades the world
And all who hear rejoice;
In the languages of all living beings
They praise the Buddha's virtues.

Illumined by Buddha's light,
All beings are peacefully happy;
All pains of existence cleared away,
Their minds are filled with joy.

See the hosts of enlightening beings
Gathering from the ten directions,
All emitting crystal clouds
Extolling the praises of Buddha.

The enlightenment site produces wondrous sound,
Extremely deep and far reaching,
Able to eliminate the suffering of sentient beings;
This is the Buddha's spiritual power.

Everyone's paying reverent respect,
All greatly joyful at heart,
Together before the World Honored One,
Gazing at the King of Truth.

"When the prince, Light of Great Power, spoke these verses, his voice pervaded the world Supreme Sound, by the mystic power of the Buddha. The king, Benevolent Mind a Joy to Behold, heard these verses and was greatly pleased; he looked at his retinue and said in verse,

You should quickly assemble
All the various kings,
Their princes and great ministers,
Their governors, and the rest.

Announce in all the cities
They should beat the great drum
Gathering all the people
To go and see the Buddha.

At every single crossroad
Jewel bells should be rung:
Let wives, children, households,
Together go to see the Buddha.

All the city castles
Should be ordered cleaned:
Raise beautiful banners everywhere
Decorated with jewels.

Myriad skeins of jewel gauze,
Music wafting like clouds,
Beautifully arrayed in the sky:
Let everywhere be filled.

Let the streets be cleaned,
Showered with beautiful cloth;
Adorn your jeweled chariots
And see the Buddha with me.

Each, according to his power
Shower ornaments everywhere,
All like clouds spreading
Filling the whole sky.

Lotus canopies of fragrant flames,
Half-moon jewel necklaces,
And countless fine garments:
You should dispense them all.

Seas of the greatest perfumes,
Discs of finest crystal,
As well as purest sandalwood:
All should fill the skies.

Garlands of many jewels,
Ornaments pure and flawless,
As well as crystal lamps:
Set all of them in the air.

Bring them all to the Buddha
With hearts full of joy;
Wives, children, retinue, all
Go see the World Honored One.

"Then the king, together with his thirty-seven thousand wives and
concubines, five hundred sons, and sixty thousand great ministers, of
whom the chief was Power of Wisdom, as well as others, a company
totalling seventy-seven million billion trillion, went out of the city of
Flame Light, all of them traveling through the sky by the power of the

king, their various offerings filling the sky. Coming to the Buddha's place, they prostrated themselves at his feet, then sat to one side.

"There was also the celestial king Banner of Good Influence from the city Beautiful Flowers, with a company of ten billion trillion. There was also the dragon king Pure Light from the city Ultimate Greatness, with a company of twenty-five billion. There was also the yaksha king Fierce Strength from the city Supreme Diamond Banner, with a company of seventy-seven billion. There was also the gandharva king Gladdening Sight from the city Undefiled, with a company of ninety-seven billion. There was also the titan king Contemplation of Pure Form from the city Beautiful Sphere, with a company of fifty-eight billion. There was also the garuda king Exercise of Ten Powers, from the city Exquisite Array, with a company of ninety-nine billion. There was also the kinnara king Indestructible Qualities from the city Playful Enjoyment, with a company of eighteen billion. There was also the mahoraga king Banner of Noble Repute from the city Diamond Banner, with a company of three billion hundred thousand trillion. There was also the brahma king Supreme from the city Pure Adornments, with a company of eighteen billion. The kings from a million billion trillion such cities, along with their retinues, all went together to the Buddha Supreme Cloud on the Mountain of All Virtues, prostrated themselves at his feet, then sat to one side.

"Then that Buddha, in order to harmonize and pacify the sentient beings, expounded the scripture Universal Collection of Methods of Freedom of All Buddhas of Past, Present, and Future, along with subsidiary scriptures as numerous as atoms in the world, causing all beings to receive benefit according to their mentalities.

"At that point the enlightening being Light of Great Power, having heard this teaching, attained the lights of the ocean of teachings collected in former ages by the Buddha Supreme Cloud on the Mountain of All Virtues. That is to say, he attained the light of knowledge of concentration on the equality of all groups of things; the light of knowledge of all truths entering and abiding in the mind in its initial determination for enlightenment; the light of knowledge of the pure eye of the repository of the omnipresent light of all the universes of the ten directions; the light of knowledge contemplating the ocean of great vows of all Buddhas; the light of knowledge of pure action entering the boundless sea of virtue; the light of knowledge of the storehouse of immensely powerful speed heading for the stage of nonregression; the light of knowledge of the sphere of emancipation with the power to appear in any form anywhere in the universe; the light of knowledge certainly entering the ocean of fulfillment of all virtuous qualities; the light of knowledge of the ocean of perfection of the adornment of certain understanding of all Buddhas; the light of knowledge of the ocean of spiritual power by which the boundless Buddhas of the cos-

mos appear before all sentient beings; the light of knowledge of the
states of the powers and fearlessness of all Buddhas.

"Then the enlightening being Light of Great Power, having attained
innumerable such lights of knowledge, imbued with power from the
Buddha, spoke these verses:

I've heard the Buddha's wondrous teachings
And attained the light of knowledge,
Whereby I see the World Honored One's
Deeds in days of yore.

All the places he was born,
His different names and physical forms,
And his offerings to the Buddhas:
All of this I see.

In the past he served
All the enlightened ones,
Practicing for innumerable eons,
Purifying oceans of worlds.

Giving up his body
Without any bound or limit,
Cultivating supreme action,
He purified oceans of lands.

Ears, nose, head, and limbs,
As well as his dwelling places:
All he gave up, numberless,
To purify all worlds.

Able in every land
Through unthinkable eons
To practice enlightening acts,
He purified oceans of lands.

By the power of the vow of universal good
In all oceans of Buddhas,
He cultivated innumerable practices
Purifying oceans of worlds.

As by the light of the sun
We can see the solar orb,
By the light of Buddha knowledge I see
The path the Buddha traveled.

I see the great pure light
Of Buddha's ocean of worlds
Calmly realizing enlightenment
Pervading the whole cosmos.

I will, like the World Honored One,
Purify oceans of lands,
And by the Buddha's spiritual power
Practice enlightening ways.

"At that time the enlightening being Light of Great Power, because he saw the Buddha Supreme Clouds on the Mountain of All Virtues and had served him and provided him with offerings, was able to attain understanding there, and, for the sake of all beings, revealed the ocean of the Buddha's past practices, revealed the techniques he employed in the past as an enlightening being, revealed the ocean of virtues of all Buddhas, revealed the independent power of attaining buddhahood at all sites of enlightenment, revealed the pure knowledge which enters into all phenomena, revealed the impartial knowledge of the power and fearlessness of Buddhas, revealed the universal manifestation of the Buddha, revealed the inconceivable mystical metamorphoses of the Buddha, revealed the adornment of innumerable buddha-lands, revealed all the practical vows of universally good enlightening beings, causing as many sentient beings as atoms in a mountain to awaken the determination for enlightenment, causing as many sentient beings as atoms in a buddha-field to perfect the pure land of the enlightened.

"Then the Buddha Supreme Clouds on the Mountain of All Virtues spoke these verses for the enlightening being Light of Great Power:

Excellent, magnificent Light!
Mine of blessings, of wide renown!
For the purpose of aiding all beings
You set forth on the road of enlightenment.

You've attained the light of knowledge
Filling the universe;
Your virtue and wisdom are both great,
You shall attain the deep ocean of knowledge.

Cultivating practices in a land
For as many eons as atoms:
As you have seen me doing thus,
So you'll attain such knowledge.

It is not those of base deeds
Who are able to know these techniques:
Only by determined effort
Can one purify an ocean of worlds.

In each and every atom
Cultivating for countless eons,
Only such a one is able
To adorn the buddha-lands.

Spending eons in transmigration
For the sake of every being
Without weariness of mind,
One will then become a guide of the world.

Offering support to every Buddha
Until the end of time,
Never getting tired of it,
One will attain the highest path.

All Buddhas of all times
Will together fulfill your hopes;
You will attend in person
The congregations of all Buddhas.

Boundless are the vows
Of all the enlightened ones;
Those who have great knowledge
Are able to know their means.

Great Light, you've given me offerings
And thereby attained great power,
Causing beings as many as atoms
To mature and turn toward enlightenment.

The great enlightening beings
Who cultivate the practice of universal good
Adorn the Buddhas' oceans of worlds
Throughout the universe.

"In that eon of Great Adornment there were as many small eons as
grains of sand in the Ganges River; the human life span was two small
eons. That Buddha Supreme Clouds on the Mountain of All Virtues lived
for fifty billion years; after he passed away, there appeared in the world
another Buddha, named King of Adornments of the Good Eye of the

Transcendent Ways, who also attained true awakening in that great forest Circle of Branches with Jewel Flowers. At that time, the youth Light of Great Power, seeing that Buddha attain perfect enlightenment and manifest the power of spiritual awareness, thereupon attained absorption in buddha-remembrance, called gate of the boundless oceanic treasury, attained a concentration formula spell called depths of truth of the power of great knowledge, attained great kindness called expediently pacifying and liberating all living beings, attained great compassion called cloud covering all realms, attained great joy called treasury of power of the ocean of virtues of all Buddhas, attained great equanimity called spacelike equality and purity of the real essence of all things, attained transcendent knowledge called pure body of the real cosmos inherently free from defilement, attained psychic power called unhindered light appearing anywhere, attained analytic power called entering the pure depths, and attained light of knowledge called pure treasury of all enlightening teachings. He comprehended a thousand gates of teaching like these.

"Then the youth Light of Great Power, imbued with the power of the Buddha, spoke these verses for the benefit of his retinue:

> Even in inconceivably many billions of eons
> An enlightened guide of the world is hard to meet;
> The beings of this land are very fortunate
> That now they can see their second Buddha.

> The Buddha's body emanates great light
> With physical forms boundless and totally pure,
> Filling all lands like clouds,
> Everywhere extolling the Buddha's virtues.

> All illumined by the light rejoice,
> Beings in distress are all relieved,
> All are induced to respect and kindness:
> This is the work of the Buddha's power.

> Producing inconceivable clouds of mystic displays,
> Emanating networks of lights of infinite colors
> Filling all lands in the ten directions:
> These are manifestations of Buddha's psychic powers:

> From each hair pore appear clouds of light
> Filling all space, emitting great sound:
> All dark places are illumined,
> Causing the pains of hells to disappear.

Buddha's wondrous voice pervades everywhere,
Fully producing all sounds of speech,
According to the power of beings' standing goodness:
This is a function of the Teacher's mystic power.

Measureless, boundless, the oceans of communities:
Buddha appears within each one,
Expounding the inexhaustible truth for all of them,
Harmoniously pacifying all sentient beings.

Buddha's mystic powers have no end,
Appearing in every single land;
Such is the Buddha's knowledge, unimpeded:
He attains enlightenment to benefit all beings.

You should all be joyful;
Dance, delight, and pay respect.
I will go with you there:
If one sees the Buddha, all miseries will cease.

Arouse your minds to seek enlightenment,
Kindly care for all living beings,
Abide by the great vows of universal goodness,
And you'll attain freedom like the King of Truth.

"When the youth Light of Great Power spoke these verses, by the power of the Buddha his voice was unimpeded and could be heard in all worlds; innumerable sentient beings aroused the will for enlightenment. Then the prince Light of Great Power, together with his parents and their company, surrounded by countless millions of billions of trillions of beings, with jeweled canopies like clouds filling the skies, went together to the Buddha King of Adornments of the Good Eye of Transcendent Ways. That Buddha expounded for them the scripture The Pure Adornments of the Essential Nature of the Cosmos of Realities, with as many subsidiary scriptures as atoms in an ocean of worlds.

"Having heard these scriptures, that great congregation attained pure knowledge called entry into all pure techniques of enlightenment, attained a stage called undefiled light, attained a sphere of transcendence called showing delightful adornments in all worlds, attained a sphere of expanding action called pure vision with boundless light entering all worlds, attained a sphere of purposeful activity called banner of light of clouds of pure virtue, attained a sphere of constant realization called vast light of the ocean of all verities, attained ever-deepening progressive practice called adornment of great knowledge, attained an ocean of knowledge of high initiates called extremely refined effortless vision,

attained an obvious great light called universal shining of light characterized by the ocean of virtues of the enlightened, and attained pure
knowledge productive of will power called treasury of faith and resolution of immeasurable will power.

"Then that Buddha spoke these verses for the enlightening being
Light of Great Power:

> Excellent, O sea of virtue and wisdom,
> Is your resolve for great enlightenment;
> You shall attain inconceivable buddhahood
> And be a reliance for all living beings.
>
> You've produced a great ocean of knowledge
> Able to fully comprehend all things;
> With inconceivable subtle skills
> You'll enter buddhahood's endless realm.
>
> Having seen the Buddhas' clouds of virtues
> And entered the stage of infinite wisdom,
> The ocean of all transcendent means
> You will fulfill, o glorious one.
>
> Having attained command of methods
> And inexhaustible expressive powers,
> Practicing various active vows
> You'll realize the peerless knowledge.
>
> Having produced a sea of vows
> And entered the ocean of concentration,
> You'll fulfill great spiritual powers
> And all the inconceivable qualities of Buddhas.
>
> The ultimate realm of truth is inconceivable;
> Your vast, deep faith is already pure;
> You see the oceans of lands, purely adorned,
> Of all the Buddhas in the ten directions.
>
> You've entered into my enlightenment practices,
> The ocean of means I employed in the past;
> That which my practices purified,
> This sublime action, you understand.
>
> I gave various offerings to oceans of Buddhas
> In countless individual lands;

As the fruit realized by that practice
Such adornments all you see.

Over an inexhaustible ocean of immense eons
Cultivating pure practice in all lands
With firm aspiration, inconceivable,
You'll attain this mystic power of Buddhas.

Giving offerings to all the Buddhas,
Adorning the lands, all pure,
Cultivating mystic practices in all ages,
You'll fulfill the great virtues of Buddhas.

"When the Buddha King of Adornments of the Good Eye of Transcendent Ways had entered extinction, the king Benevolent Mind a Joy to Behold also subsequently passed away, and his son Light of Great Power inherited the position of great monarch, in that great forest Circle of Branches with Jewel Flowers a third Buddha appeared in the world, by the name of Ocean of Supreme Virtue. At that time, when the sovereign Light of Great Power saw the signs of that Buddha's realization of enlightenment, he went, together with his family and courtiers, his armies, and the populace of the cities, towns, and villages, all carrying seven kinds of jewels and precious metals, to that Buddha and presented a great mansion adorned with all kinds of aromatic crystals. Then that Buddha, there in the forest, expounded the scripture The Illuminating Activity of the Enlightening Being with the Universal Eye, along with subsidiary scriptures as numerous as atoms in a world. Then the enlightening being Light of Great Power, having heard this teaching, attained a contemplative focus called universal light of great virtue. And because he had attained this state of mental focus, he was able to know the past, present, and future seas of good and evil of all enlightening beings and all sentient beings.

"Then that Buddha spoke these verses for the enlightening being Light of Great Power:

Excellent, O virtuous Light of Great Power,
That you all have come to me;
With sympathy for all living beings
You've conceived the supreme will for enlightenment.

For the sake of all suffering beings
You exercise great compassion to liberate them.
You'll be a reliance for all who are lost;
This is called the skillful enlightening work.

If enlightening beings can, with firm strength,
Carry out supreme practices unflagging,
The highest supreme unhindered understanding
And subtle knowledge they will attain.

O light of virtue, banner of blessings,
Abode of virtue, sea of blessings,
All vows of universal good enlightening
Your great light can enter.

With these great vows you can enter
The inconceivable ocean of Buddhas.
The sea of Buddhas' blessings has no bounds:
You can see all by sublime understanding.

In the lands of the ten directions
You see infinite, boundless Buddhas;
The ocean of past practices of those Buddhas
You can see, all as they were.

Any who dwell in this ocean of means
Can enter the stages of knowledge;
This is following the Buddhas to learn,
Surely leading to omniscience.

In all oceans of worlds you performed
Various practices for oceans of eons;
The ocean of practices of all enlightened ones
You having learned, you'll become a Buddha.

As you see in the ten directions
All oceans of lands are extremely pure;
Your land will also be pure like that,
Attained by one with boundless vows.

The oceanic masses at this sanctuary,
Having heard your vows, all rejoice;
All enter the great vehicle of universal goodness,
Inspired and dedicated to enlightenment.

In each of the boundless lands,
All enter practice for oceans of eons,
By the power of vows able to fulfill
All the practices of the enlightening being Universally Good.

"O Children of Buddha, in that great forest Circle of Branches with Jewel Flowers there appeared yet another Buddha, called Universally Renowned Lotus Eye Banner. At this time the life of Light of Great Power came to an end, and he was reborn in the celestial city Jewel Palace of Tranquility, atop the polar mountain, where he became a celestial king called Banner of Undefiled Virtue. He went with the heavenly hosts to see that Buddha, showering clouds of jewel flowers as offerings. Then the Buddha expounded for them the scripture Extensive Skill in Means of Liberation with All-Sided Approaches Universally Illuminating, along with subsidiary scriptures as numerous as atoms in an ocean of worlds. The celestial king and his company, having heard these scriptures, attained a state of contemplation called all-sided treasury of joy, and by the power of this contemplation were able to enter the ocean of the real character of all things. Having attained this benefit, they left the sanctuary and went back to their place."

End of the first assembly.

BOOK SEVEN

Names of the Buddha

AT THAT TIME the World Honored One had just attained true awakening in a forest sanctuary in the country of Magadha. Sitting on a lotus bank lion throne in the hall of universal light, he fulfilled ineffable enlightenment, forever cutting off mundane ideas of transmigration and extinction; arriving at truth without form, he dwelt in the abode of buddhahood, attained the equanimity of the enlightened, reached the state of immutability, in the realm where there are no barriers; unhindered in action, he established the inconceivable, perceiving all in the past, present, and future.

He was together with as many enlightening beings as atoms in ten buddha-fields, all of whom were qualified to attain buddhahood in their next lifetime. They had all gathered here from different regions. They skillfully observed the realms of sentient beings, the realm of the elemental cosmos, the realm of extinction, the consequences of all actions, the processes of mental behavior, the meanings of all statements, the mundane and the transmundane, the compounded and the uncompounded, the past, the present, and the future.

At that time the enlightening beings formulated these thoughts: "If the World Honored One looks upon us with compassion, may he, in accord with our inclinations, reveal to us the buddha-fields, the Buddhas' abodes, the adornments of the buddha-fields, the nature of buddhahood, the purity of buddha-lands, the teachings expounded by the Buddhas, the substances and natures of the buddha-lands, the powers and qualities of the Buddhas, the formation of the buddha-fields, the great enlightenment of the Buddhas. Just as the Buddhas of all worlds in the ten directions, in order to develop all enlightening beings, to cause the family of the enlightened ones to continue uninterrupted, to rescue all sentient beings, to cause all living beings to be forever free from all afflictions, to comprehend all actions, to expound all truths, to clear away all defilements, and to forever cut through all webs of doubt, explain the enlightening beings' ten abodes, ten practices, ten dedications, ten treasuries, ten stages, ten vows, ten concentrations, ten powers, and ten peaks, and explain the sphere of buddhahood, the mystic forces of Buddhas, the actions of Buddhas, the powers of Buddhas, the fearlessness of Buddhas, the meditations of Buddhas, the psychic abilities of Buddhas, the freedom of Buddhas, the nonobstruction of Buddhas, the sense faculties of Buddhas, the powers of analysis and articulation of Buddhas, the knowledge and wisdom of Buddhas, and the transcendence of Buddhas, so also may the Buddha, the World Honored One, explain this for us.''

Then the Buddha, knowing what the enlightening beings were thinking, manifested mystic powers to them, according to their particular types. When he had done that, there came, from a world called Golden, whose Buddha was called Immutable Knowledge, which was to the East, past as many worlds as atoms in ten buddha-fields, an enlightening being of that world, named Manjushri, along with as many enlightening beings as atoms in ten buddha-lands. When they arrived, they bowed, and then produced lotus bank lion seats to the east and sat crosslegged on them.

In the South, past as many worlds as atoms in ten buddha-lands, was a world called Sublime Color, with a Buddha called Unhindered Knowledge. There was an enlightening being there named Chief of the Awakened, who, together with as many enlightening beings as atoms in ten buddha-lands, came to the Buddha, bowed, and the to the south produced lotus bank lion seats and sat crosslegged on them.

In the West, past as many worlds as atoms in ten buddha-lands, was a world called Lotus Blossom Color, with a Buddha called Darkness-Destroying Knowledge. There was an enlightening being there, named Chief in Riches of Truth, who, along with as many enlightening beings as atoms in ten buddha-lands, came to the Buddha, bowed, produced lotus bank lion seats to the west and sat crosslegged on them.

In the North, past as many worlds as atoms in ten buddha-lands, was a world called Golden Flower Color, with a Buddha called Knowledge of Dignified Conduct. There was an enlightening being there, named Chief of the Precious, who, with as many enlightening beings as atoms in ten buddha-lands, came to the Buddha, bowed, produced lotus bank lion seats to the north and sat crosslegged on them.

In the northeast, past as many worlds as atoms in ten buddha-lands, was a world called Blue Lotus Color, with a Buddha called Knowledge of Characteristics. There was an enlightening being there, called Chief of the Virtuous, who, with as many enlightening beings as atoms in ten buddha-lands, came to the Buddha, bowed, produced lotus bank lion seats to the northeast and sat crosslegged on them.

In the southeast, past as many worlds as atoms in ten buddha-lands, was a world called Gold Color, with a Buddha called Ultimate Knowledge. There was an enlightening being there called Chief in Vision, who, with as many enlightening beings as atoms in ten buddha-lands, came to the Buddha, bowed, produced lotus bank lion seats to the southeast and sat crosslegged on them.

In the southwest, past as many worlds as atoms in ten buddha-lands, was a world called Jewel Color, with a Buddha called Supreme Knowledge. There was an enlightening being there called Chief in Effort, who, with as many enlightening beings as atoms in ten buddha-lands, came to the Buddha, bowed, produced lotus bank lion seats to the southwest and sat crosslegged on them.

In the northwest, past as many worlds as atoms in ten buddha-lands, was a world called Diamond Color, with a Buddha called Independent Knowledge. There was an enlightening being there called Chief in Doctrine, who, with as many enlightening beings as atoms in ten buddha-lands, came to the Buddha, bowed, produced lotus bank lion seats to the northwest and sat crosslegged on them.

In the nadir, past as many worlds as atoms in ten buddha-lands, was a world called Crystal Color, with a Buddha called Pure Knowledge. There was an enlightening being there called Chief in Knowledge, who, with as many enlightening beings as atoms in ten buddha-lands, came to the Buddha, bowed, produced lotus bank lion seats in the nadir and sat crosslegged on them.

In the zenith, past as many worlds as atoms in ten buddha-lands, was a world called Equal Color, with a Buddha called Observing Knowledge. There was an enlightening being there called Chief in Goodness, who, with as many enlightening beings as atoms in ten buddha-lands, came to the Buddha, bowed, produced lotus bank lion seats in the zenith and sat crosslegged on them.

Then the great enlightening being Manjushri, empowered by the Buddha, looked over all the congregations of enlightening beings, and spoke these words: "These enlightening beings are most rare. O Children of Buddhas! The Buddhas' lands are inconceivable. The Buddhas' abodes, the adornments of their fields, the nature of buddhahood, the purity of buddha-lands, the teachings of the Buddhas, the manifestation of the Buddhas, the formation of the buddha-lands, and the complete perfect enlightenment of the Buddhas are all inconceivable. Why? Because all the Buddhas in the worlds in the ten directions know that the inclinations of sentient beings are not the same, and so they teach and train them according to their needs and capacities. The extent of this activity is equal to the realm of space of the cosmos.

"Children of Buddhas, in the four quarters of this world Endurance, the Buddha, with various bodies, names, forms, sizes, life spans, situations, faculties, birth places, languages, and observations causes all living beings to individually perceive and know differently. In these four quarters, the Buddha is sometimes called Fulfiller of All Aims, sometimes called The Full Moon, sometimes called The Lion Roarer, sometimes called Shakyamuni, sometimes called The Seventh Sage, sometimes called Vairocana, sometimes called Gautama, sometimes called The Great Mendicant, sometimes called The Supreme, sometimes called The Guide; there are ten thousand such names, individually letting beings know and see in various ways.

"East of this region is a world called Good Protection: there the Buddha may be called Adamantine, or Free, or Possessor of Knowledge and Wisdom, or Invincible, or King of Sages, or Noncontention, or Capable Leader, or Joyful Heart, or Incomparable, or Beyond Philosophy; there are ten thousand such names, individually letting sentient beings know and see in various ways.

"South of this region is a world called Difficult to Endure: there the Buddha may be called King of the Gods, or Precious Name, or Undefiled, or Truth Teller, or Tamer, or Joyful, or Great Renown, or Giver of Aid, or Infinite, or Supreme; there are ten thousand such names, individually letting people know and see in various ways.

"West of this region is a world called Personal Wisdom: there the Buddha may be called God of Waters, or Gladdening Sight, or Supreme Monarch, or Celestial Tamer, or Real True Wisdom, or Arrived at the Ultimate, or Joyous, or Objective Knowledge, or Done with All Tasks, or Abiding in Goodness; there are ten thousand such names, letting beings know and see in various ways.

"North of this region is a world called Lion of Existence: there the Buddha may be called Great Sage, or Ascetic, or World Honored One, or Supreme Field, or Omniscient, or Good Mind, or Pure, or Master of Universal Sound, or Supreme Giver, or Attained by Difficult Practice; there are ten thousand such names, individually letting beings know and see in various ways.

"Northeast of this region is a world called Subtle Observation: there the Buddha may be called Demon Queller, or Completed, or Dispassionate, or Celestial Virtue, or Free from Greed, or Supreme Wisdom, or Equanimity of Mind, or Unconquerable, or Sound of Wisdom, or Rarely Appearing; there are ten thousand such names, letting beings know and see in various ways.

"Southeast of this region is a world called Joy and Happiness: there the Buddha may be called Ultimate Dignity, or Mass of Light Flames, or Universal Knower, or Secret Mystery, or Liberation, or Inherently Secure, or Acting According to Truth, or King of Pure Eyes, or Great Courage, or Energetic Power; there are ten thousand such names, causing beings to individually know and see in various ways.

"Southwest of this region is a world called Extremely Solid and Firm: there the Buddha may be called Peaceful Abiding, or King of Knowledge, or Complete, or Immutable, or Subtle Eye, or Supreme Monarch, or Sound of Freedom, or Giver of All, or Sages of the Masses, or Supreme Mountain; there are ten thousand such names, letting beings know and see in various ways.

"Northwest of this region is a world called Wonderful Ground; there the Buddha may be called Universal, or Flames of Light, or Jewel

Topknot, or Worthy of Remembrance, or Unexcelled Meaning, or Always Joyful, or Inherently Pure, or Sphere of Light, or Long Arms, or Abiding in the Fundamental; there are ten thousand such names, letting beings know and see in various ways.

"Below this region is a world called Radiant Wisdom: the Buddha there may be called Collecting Roots of Goodness, or Lionlike, or Razorlike Intellect, or Golden Flames, or All-Knower, or Ultimate Sound, or Benefactor, or Arrived at the Ultimate, or God of Truth, or Universal Conqueror; there are ten thousand such names, letting beings know and see in various ways.

"Above this region is a world called Holding the Ground: there the Buddha may be called Possessor of Knowledge and Wisdom, or Pure Face, or Conscious Wisdom, or Leader, or Adorned by Conduct, or Gladdener, or Wish Fulfilled, or Blazelike, or Ethical, or The One Path; there are ten thousand such names, letting beings know and see in various ways.

"In this world Endurance there are a hundred billion regions, wherein the Buddha has a million billion various names, letting all sentient beings know and see in various ways.

"East of this world Endurance is another world, called Secret Teaching: there the Buddha may be called Impartial, or Excellent, or Soother, or Enlightening Mind, or Speaker of Truth, or Attainer of Freedom, or Supreme Body, or Great Courage, or Peerless Knowledge; there are a million billion such diverse names, letting beings know and see in various ways.

"South of this world Endurance is another world, called Abundance: there the Buddha may be called Original Nature, or Diligent Intellect, or Unexcelled Honored One, or Great Torch of Knowledge, or Nonreliant, or Treasury of Light, or Treasury of Wisdom, or Treasury of Virtue, or God of Gods, or Great Independent One; there are a million billion such names, letting beings know and see in various ways.

"West of this world Endurance is a world called Undefiled: there the Buddha may be called Wish Fulfilled, or Knower of the Way, or Resting in the Fundamental, or Able to Untie Bonds, or Comprehending Truth, or Easily Discerning, or Supreme Insight, or Pacifying Action, or Ascetic Practicer, or Replete with Power; there are a million billion such various names, letting beings know and see in varous ways.

"North of this world Endurance is a world called Inclusion: there the Buddha may be called Forever Free from Suffering, or Universal Liberation, or Great Hidden Treasury, or Knowledge of Liberation, or Storehouse of the Past, or Jewel Light, or Detached from the World, or State of Nonobstruction, or Treasury of Pure Faith, or Imperturbable Mind; there are a million billion such names, letting sentient beings know and see in various ways.

"Southeast of this world Endurance is a world called Beneficial: there the Buddha may be called Manifesting Light, or Knowledge of Extinction, or Beautiful Sound, or Supreme Faculties, or Ornamental Canopy, or Energetic Faculties, or Arrived at the Other Shore beyond Discrimination, or Supreme Stability, or Simple Speech, or Ocean of Wisdom; there are a million such diverse names, letting beings know and see in various ways.

"Southwest of this world Endurance is a world called Rarefied: there the Buddha may be called Master among Sages, or Possessor of All Treasures, or Liberated from the World, or Faculty of Universal Knowledge, or Excellent Speech, or Clear Sight, or Freedom of the Senses, or Great Immortal Teacher, or Guiding Work, or Adamantine Lion; there are a million billion such names, letting beings know and see in various ways.

"Northeast of this world Endurance is a world called Joy: there the Buddha may be called Mass of Beautiful Flowers, or Sandalwood Canopy, or Lotus Treasury, or Transcendent beyond All Things, or Jewel of Truth, or Reborn, or Pure Exquisite Canopy, or Immense Eye, or Possessor of Good Qualities, or Concentrated on the Truth, or Network Treasury; there are a million billion such names, letting beings know and see in various ways.

"Below this world Endurance is a world called Door Bolt: there the Buddha may be called Producing Flames, or Poison Queller, or Bow of the King of Gods, or No Constant Location, or Aware of the Fundamental, or Stopping Increase, or Great Speed, or Always Gladly Giving, or Discerning the Way, or Banner of Victory; there are a million billion such names, letting beings know and see in various ways.

"Above this world Endurance is a world called Shaking Sound: there the Buddha may be called Banner of Courage, or Infinite Treasure, or Glad Magnanimity, or Celestial Light, or Appearance of Good Omen, or Transcending Objects, or Master of All, or Nonregressing Wheel, or Beyond All Evil, or Omniscient; there are a million billion such names, letting beings know and see in various ways.

"As in this world Endurance, so in the eastern direction, in hundreds of thousands of billions, countlessly, innumerably, boundlessly, incomparably, incalculably, unrecountably, unthinkably, immeasurably, unspeakably many worlds, throughout the entire space of the cosmos, the names and epithets of the Buddhas are variously different; the same is true of the South, West, and North, the four intermediate directions, and the zenith and the nadir. Just as when the Buddha was an enlightening being, by means of various discussions, various speeches, various words, various actions, various consequences, various situations, various techniques, various faculties, various beliefs, and various stations, attained maturity, so he causes sentient beings to perceive in this way, teaching them thus."

BOOK EIGHT

The Four Holy Truths

THEN THE GREAT ENLIGHTENING BEING Manjushri said to the enlightening beings, "Children of Buddhas, the holy truth of suffering, in this world Endurance, is sometimes called wrongdoing, or oppression, or change, or clinging to objects, or accumulation, or thorns stabbing, or dependence on the senses, or deceit, or the place of cancer, or ignorant action.

"The holy truth of the (cause of) the accumulation of suffering, in this world Endurance, may be called bondage, or disintegration, or attachment to goods, or false consciousness, or pursuit and involvement, or conviction, or the web, or fancified conceptualizing, or following, or awry faculties.

"The holy truth of the extinction of suffering, in this world Endurance, may be called noncontention, or freedom from defilement, or tranquility and dispassion, or signlessness, or deathlessness, or absence of inherent nature, or absence of hindrance, or extinction, or essential reality, or abiding in one's own essence.

"The holy truth of the path to the extinction of suffering, in this world Endurance, may be called the one vehicle, or progress toward serenity, or guidance, or ultimate freedom from discrimination, or equanimity, or putting down the burden, or having no object of pursuit, or following the intent of the saint, or the practice of sages, or ten treasuries.

"In this world there are four quadrillion such names to express the four holy truths in accord with the mentalities of sentient beings, to cause them all to be harmonized and pacified.

"What in this world is called the holy truth of suffering is, in that world Secret Teaching, called the sense of striving and seeking, or not being emancipated, or the root of bondage, or doing what shouldn't be done, or contending and struggling in all manner of situations, or total lack of power to analyze, or being depended on, or extreme pain, or hyperactivity, or things with form. What is called the holy truth of the accumulation of suffering is, in that world Secret Teaching, called following birth and death, or habitual attachment, or burning, or continuous revolving, or corrupt senses, or continuing existences, or evil behavior, or emotional attachment, or the source of illness, or categorization. What is called the holy truth of the extinction of suffering is, in that world Secret Teaching, also called the ultimate truth, or emancipation, or praiseworthy, or peace, or the place good to enter, or docility, or singleness, or faultlessness, or freedom from greed, or resolution. What is called the holy truth of the path to extinction of suffering is, in that world Secret Teaching, also called bold generalship, or superior action, or transcendence, or having skill in means, or impartial eye, or detachment from extremes, or comprehensive understanding, or inclusion, or supreme eye, or contemplating the four truths. In the world Secret Teaching, there are four quadrillion such names to explain the four holy truths, to cause sentient beings to be harmonized and pacified according to their mentalities.

"What is, in this world Endurance, called the holy truth of suffering, is, in the world Abundance, also called fear, or individual mortality, or disgusting, or what should be worked on, or change, or ensnaring enemy, or deceptive usurper, or hard to work with, or false discrimination, or possessor of power. What is called the holy truth of the accumulation of suffering is, in that world Abundance, called corruption, or ignorance, or great enemy, or sharp blade, or taste of destruction, or revenge, or not one's own thing, or bad guidance, or increasing darkness, or ruining goodness. What is called the holy truth of the extinction of suffering is, in that world Abundance, called great meaning, or benefit, or goal of goals, or infinity, or what should be seen, or detachment from discrimination, or supreme pacification, or constant equanimity, or worthy of living together, or nonfabrication. What is called the holy truth of the path to extinction of suffering is, in that world Abundance, called able to burn up, or the highest class, or certitude, or unbreakable, or profound techniques, or emancipation, or not mean or base, or mastery, or essence of liberation, or capable of setting free. In that world Abundance there are four quadrillion such names to explain the four holy truths, to cause sentient beings to be harmonized and pacified according to their mentalities.

"What is, in this world Endurance, called the holy truth of suffering, is, in the world Undefiled, also called regret, or dependency, or aggravation, or dwelling within walls, or one flavor, or untruth, or living at home, or abode of deluded attachment, or false views, or innumerable. What is called the holy truth of the accumulation of suffering is, in the world Undefiled, also called no real thing, or only having words, or not pure, or place of birth, or grasping, or baseness, or increase, or heavy burden, or producer, or roughness. What is called the holy truth of the extinction of suffering is, in the world Undefiled, also called incomparable, or thoroughly cleared, or removal of defilement, or supreme faculties, or harmony, or independence, or extinction of confusion, or most excellent, or the ultimate, or breaking the seal.

What is called the holy truth of the path to the extinction of suffering is, in that world Undefiled, called something indestructible, or the part of appropriate means, or the basis of liberation, or reality of basic nature, or the blameless, or the most pure, or the boundary of all existences, or maintaining what is received complete, or producing the ultimate, or pure discernment. In the world Undefiled there are four quadrillion such names to explain the four holy truths, to cause all sentient beings to be harmonized and pacified according to their mentalities.

"What is, in this world Endurance, called the holy truth of suffering, is, in the world Rich Pleasure, also called the place of emotional attachment, or root of danger and harm, or the sectors of the ocean of existence, or made by accumulation, or discriminating senses, or aggravation, or origination and destruction, or hindrance, or base of sword blades, or made of sets. What is called the holy truth of the accumulation of suffering is, in the world Rich Pleasure, called detestable, or names, or endless, or different sets, or not to be loved, or able to grab and bite, or crude things, or emotional attachment, or receptacle, or stirring. What is called the holy truth of the extinction of suffering is, in that world Rich Pleasure, called end of continuation, or revelation, or no label, or nothing to practice, or no object of vision, or nondoing, or extinction, or already burnt out, or casting off the heavy burden, or purged. What is called the holy truth of the path to extinction of suffering is, in that world Rich Pleasure, called serene action, or emancipating action, or diligent practice and experience, or gone to tranquility, or infinite life, or comprehensive knowledge, or the ultimate path, or difficult to practice, or reaching the other shore, or invincible. In the world Rich Pleasure there are four quadrillion such names to explain the four holy truths, to cause all sentient beings to be harmonized and pacified according to their mentalities.

"What is in this world Endurance, called the holy truth of suffering, is, in the world Inclusion, also called able to plunder and usurp, or not a good friend, or full of fear, or various fancies, or the nature of hell, or untruth, or the burden of covetousness, or roots of deep gravity, or changing with moods, or fundamental vanity. What is called the holy truth of the accumulation of suffering is called, in that world Inclusion, greedy attachment, or wrong accomplishment, or the evil of excess, or nothing that can be explained, or nothing that can be apprehended, or continuous revolving in circles. What is called the holy truth of the extinction of suffering is, in the world Inclusion, called nonregression, or beyond speech, or formlessness, or enjoyable, or stability, or supreme wonder, or freedom from folly, or extinction, or detachment from evil, or escape. What is called the holy truth of the path to extinction of suffering is, in the world Inclusion, called beyond words, or noncontention, or teaching and guidance, or good dedication, or great skill, or a variety of techniques, or spacelike, or serene action, or supreme knowledge, or ability to understand truth. In the world Inclusion there are four quadrillion such names to explain the four holy truths, to cause sentient beings to be harmonized and pacified according to their mentalities.

"What is, in this world Endurance, called the holy truth of suffering, is, in the world Beneficial, also called the heavy burden, or instability, or like a robber, or aging and death, or made of craving, or transmigration, or fatigue, or bad condition, or growth, or the sharp blade. What is called the holy truth of the accumulation of suffering is, in the world Beneficial, called decay, or confusion, or regression, or powerlessness, or loss, or opposition, or disharmony, or doing, or grasping, or wishing. What is called the holy truth of the extinction of suffering is, in the world Beneficial, also called escape from prison, or real truth, or freedom from troubles, or protection, or detachment from ill, or docility, or the fundamental, or abandoning the cause, or nonstriving, or noncontinuation. What is called the holy truth of the path to the extinction of suffering is, in that world Beneficial, also called arriving at nonexistence, or the seal of the totality, or the treasury of meditation, or attainment of light, or the nonregressive state, or ability to put an end to being, or the wide great road, or ability to tame, or having peace and security, or nonroutinized faculties. In the world Beneficial there are four quadrillion such names to explain the four holy truths, to cause sentient beings to be harmonized and pacified according to their mentalities.

"What is, in this world Endurance, called the holy truth of suffering, is, in the world Rarefied, also called dangerous desires, or place of bondage, or misguided action, or receptivity, or shamelessness, or rooted in greed, or the ever-flowing river, or constant disintegration, or of the nature of torch fire, or full of stress and anxiety. What is called the holy truth of the accumulation of suffering is, in that world, called broad ground, or tendency, or distance from wisdom, or obstruction, or fear, or laxity, or taking in, or attachment, or ignorance being master of the house, or continuous bonds. What is called the holy truth of the extinction of suffering is, in that world, also called fulfillment, or immortality, or selflessness, or absence of inherent nature, or end of discrimination, or abode of peace and happiness, or infinitude, or cutting off transmigration, or cutting off compulsive mental activity, or nonduality. What is called the holy truth of the path to extinction of suffering is, in that world, also called great light, or ocean of explanation, or analyzing meaning, or the way of harmony, or freedom from attachment, or breaking the continuum, or the broad highway, or the basis of impartiality, or pure methods, or supreme insight. In that world Rarefied are four quadrillion such names to explain the four holy truths, to cause sentient beings to be harmonized and pacified according to their mentalities.

"What is, in this world Endurance, called the holy truth of suffering, is, in the world Joy, called continuous revolving, or birth, or loss of benefit, or habitual attachment, or the heavy load, or discrimination, or inward danger, or gathering, or wrong abode, or of the nature of misery and affliction. What is called the holy truth of the accumulation of suffering is, in that world, also called the ground, or conveniences, or wrong timing, or untruth, or bottomless, or possessiveness, or departure from morality, or afflictions, or narrow views, or accumulation of defilement. What is called the holy truth of the extinction of suffering is, in that world, called destroying dependency, or not indulging, or truth, or equality, or purity, or freedom from sickness, or undistorted, or formless, or free, or birthless. What is called the holy truth of the path to extinction of suffering is, in that world, called entering the supreme realm, or cutting off accumulation, or transcending comparison, or vast nature, or end of discrimination, or the path of spiritual power, or multitude of appropriate techniques, or practice of right mindfulness, or the ever quiet road, or embracing liberation. In that world Joy there are four quadrillion such names to explain the four holy truths, to cause beings to be harmonized and pacified according to their mentalities.

"What is, in this world Endurance, called the holy truth of suffering, is, in the world Door Bolt, also called decaying form, or like a broken vessel, or the product of ego, or embodiment of various tendencies, or numerous routines, or the gate of the multitude of ills, or inherent pain, or that which should be abandoned, or flavorlessness, or coming and going. What is called the holy truth of the accumulation of suffering is in that world called activity, or the poison of anger, or conglomeration, or sensation, or selfishness, or mixed poison, or empty names, or opposition, or imitation, or astonishment. What is called the holy truth of the extinction of suffering is in that world called no accumulation, or ungraspable, or wonder medicine, or incorruptible, or nonattachment, or immeasurable, or vast, or the sphere of awakening, or freedom from addiction, or absence of obstruction. What is called the holy truth of the path to extinction of suffering is in that world called peaceful action, or detachment from craving, or ultimate reality, or entry into truth, or the essential ultimate, or manifestation of purity, or concentration, or heading for liberation, or salvation, or supreme action. In that world Door Bolt there are four quadrillion such names to express the four holy truths, to cause sentient beings to be harmonized and pacified according to their mentalities.

"What is, in this world Endurance, called the holy truth of suffering, is, in the world Shaking Sound, also called hidden sickness, or the mundane, or the dwelling place, or conceit, or the nature of habitual attachment, or the torrent, or unenjoyable, or hypocrisy, or the evanescent, or difficult to control. What is called the holy truth of the accumulation of suffering is in that world called that which must be controlled, or mental tendencies, or that which binds, or arising in every thought, or extending to the future, or combination, or discrimination, or the gateway, or blown by the wind, or concealment. What is called the holy truth of the extinction of suffering is in that world called no reliance, or ungraspable, or returning, or freedom from conflict, or small, or great, or pure, or inexhaustible, or broad, or priceless. What is called the holy truth of the path to extinction of suffering is in that world called analytic observation, or ability to destroy the enemy, or seal of knowledge, or ability to enter the essence, or unopposable, or limitless meaning, or able to enter knowledge, or the path of harmony, or eternal imperturbability, or the highest truth. In that world Shaking Sound there are four quadrillion such names to explain the four holy truths, to cause sentient beings to be harmonized and pacified according to their mentalities.

"Just as in this world Endurance there are four quadrillion names to express the four holy truths, so in all the worlds to the east—hundreds of thousands of billions, countlessly, innumerably, boundlessly, imcomparably, incalculably, unspeakably, inconceivably, immeasurably, inexplicably many worlds, in each there are an equal number of names to express the four holy truths, to cause the sentient beings there to all be harmonized and pacified in accordance with their mentalities. And just as this is so of the worlds to the east, so it is with all the infinite worlds in the ten directions.''

BOOK NINE

Awakening by Light

THEN THE BUDDHA, from beneath the wheel-marks on his feet, emitted a hundred billion light beams, illuminating this billion-world universe, with its four hundred billion continents, hundred billion oceans, hundred billion surrounding mountain ranges, hundred billion enlightening beings being born, hundred billion enlightening beings leaving home, hundred billion Buddhas realizing true enlightenment, hundred billion Buddhas teaching, hundred billion Buddhas passing away, a hundred billion polar mountain kings, a hundred billion heavens of hosts of celestial kings, a hundred billion heavens of thirty-three celestial realms, a hundred billion heavens of timely portion, a hundred billion heavens of satisfaction, a hundred billion heavens of enjoyment of emanations, a hundred billion heavens of free enjoyment of others' emanations, a hundred billion heavens of pure hosts, a hundred billion light-sound heavens, a hundred billion heavens of purity, a hundred billion heavens of vast rewards, a hundred billion heavens of the ultimate of form; everything therein was all clearly manifest.

As in this place the Buddha, the World Honored One, was seen sitting on a lotus bank lion throne, surrounded by as many enlightening beings as atoms in ten buddha-lands, so also sat the hundred billion Buddhas in a hundred billion continents. In each case, because of the spiritual force of the Buddhas, in each of the ten directions was a great enlightening being, each with a company of as many enlightening beings as atoms in ten buddha-lands, who came to the Buddha. Their names were Manjushri, Chief of the Awakened, Chief in Riches of Truth, Chief of the Precious, Chief of the Virtuous, Chief in Vision, Chief in Effort, Chief in Doctrine, Chief in Knowledge, and Chief in Goodness. The lands from whence these enlightening beings came were respectively called Golden World, Sublime Color World, Lotus Color World, Saffron Flower Color World, Blue Lotus Color World, Gold Color World, Jewel Color World, Diamond Color World, Crystal Color World, and Equal Color World. These enlightening beings had each cultivated pure practice in the company of Buddhas—the Buddha of Immutable Knowledge, the Buddha of Unhindered Knowledge, the

Buddha of Knowledge of Liberation, the Buddha of Knowledge of Dignified Conduct, the Buddha of Knowledge of Characteristics, the Buddha of Ultimate Knowledge, the Buddha of Supreme Knowledge, the Buddha of Independent Knowledge, the Buddha of Pure Knowledge, and the Buddha of Observing Knowledge.

Then the Manjushris in all places, in the presence of each of the Buddhas, spoke up simultaneously and said in verse,

> If any see the Truly Awake
> As becoming liberated and divorced from taints
> And not attached to any world,
> They have not realized the eye of the Way.
>
> If any know the Buddha's
> Substance and form have no existence,
> And by cultivation gain clear understanding,
> Such people will soon be Buddhas.
>
> Who can see this world
> Unstirred in mind,
> And likewise Buddha's body,
> Will attain supreme knowledge.
>
> If, regarding the Buddha and truth,
> One understands that they are equal,
> Having no thought of duality,
> One will walk on the inconceivable plane.
>
> If one sees the Buddha and oneself
> Resting in equality,
> Without abode, entering nowhere,
> One will become one of the Rare.
>
> Form and feeling have no sets:
> Nor do conception, action, consciousness;
> Any who can know this way
> Will become great sages.
>
> Whether mundane or transmundane views,
> Having risen beyond them all
> While well able to know the truth,
> One will become a great illuminate.
>
> If, toward omniscience,
> One engenders dedication,

Seeing mind without origination,
One will gain the greatest name.

Living beings have no birth,
Nor either any decay;
If one attains such knowledge as this,
One will realize the unexcelled way.

In one understanding infinity,
Within infinity, one:
Realizing their origin's interdependent
One will attain to fearlessness.

Then the light beams passed this world and illuminated ten lands in the eastern direction, also doing likewise in the South, West, North, the four intermediate directions, and the zenith and nadir. In all of those worlds were a hundred billion continents called Jambudvipa, and so on, including a hundred billion heavens of the ultimate of form—everything in all those realms was clearly revealed. In each of the Jambudvipa continents the Buddha was seen sitting on a lotus bank lion throne surrounded by as many enlightening beings as atoms in ten buddha-lands; and in each one, due to the spiritual force of the Buddha, ten great enlightening beings from the ten directions, each accompanied by as many enlightening beings as atoms in ten buddha-lands, came to the Buddha; those enlightening beings were called Manjushri, etc., the lands they came from were called Golden, etc., and the Buddhas they served were called Immutable Knowledge, etc. Then the Manjushris in all those places, each in the presence of the Buddha in that place, all simultaneously spoke out, saying these verses:

Sentient beings lack wisdom,
Wounded and poisoned by the thorns of craving;
For their sake we seek enlightenment:
Such is the law of all Buddhas.

Seeing all things,
Giving up extremes,
Once enlightened, never regressing,
They turn the incomparable wheel of truth.

For inconceivable eons
Cultivating various practices vigorously
In order to liberate beings:
This is the power of the great sages.

The Guide conquers demons
Bravely and invincibly,
Preaching subtle truths in his light
Because of kind compassion.

By knowledge and wisdom
Breaking the barriers of afflictions,
In an instant seeing all:
This is the spiritual power of Buddhas.

Beating the drum of the great teaching,
Awakening all lands in the ten directions,
Making all turn toward enlightenment:
Independent power can act like this.

Without breaking the infinite boundaries,
Traveling through the billions of lands
Without attachment to any existent:
Such is freedom like the Buddhas'.

The Buddhas are like space,
Ultimately forever pure;
Those who rejoice in remembering this
Will fulfill all of their vows.

In each and every one of the hells
They pass innumerable eons;
In order to liberate sentient beings
They're able to bear these pains.

Without begrudging body or life,
Always preserving the Buddhas' teachings,
With egoless mind harmonious,
One can attain the enlightened way.

Then the light beams passed ten worlds and illuminated a hundred lands in the eastern direction, also doing likewise in every other direction. In all of those worlds were a hundred billion continents called Jambudvipa, and so on, including a hundred billion heavens of the ultimate of form—everything in all those realms was clearly revealed. In each of the Jambudvipa continents the Buddha was seen sitting on a lotus bank lion throne surrounded by as many enlightening beings as atoms in ten buddha-lands; and in each one, due to the spiritual force of the Buddha, ten great enlightening beings, from the ten directions, each accompanied by as many enlightening beings as atoms in ten buddha-lands, came to the Buddha; those enlightening beings were called Manjushri, etc., the lands they came from were called Golden, etc., and the Buddhas they served were called Immutable Knowledge, etc. Then the Manjushris in all those places, each in the presence of the Buddha in that place, all simultaneously spoke out, saying these verses:

> Buddha understands things are like phantoms;
> Comprehending, he is unhindered.
> His mind is pure and free from attachments;
> He harmonizes and pacifies all beings.

> Some see him first born,
> His color like a mountain of gold;
> Living in his final body,
> He's forever a moon of humanity.

> Some see him walking around,
> Replete with boundless virtues;
> Attention and intellect well employed,
> The Great Man walks like a lion.

> Some see his violet eyes
> Gazing in the ten directions;
> Sometimes he shows a smile,
> To accommodate beings' wishes.

> Some see his lion roar,
> His supreme, incomparable body
> Manifesting his last incarnation,
> Speaking naught but the truth.

> Some see him leaving home,
> Shedding all bonds,
> Practicing the acts of Buddhas,
> Always contemplating extinction.

> Some see him sitting on the enlightenment site
> Awakening knowledge of all things,
> Reaching the other shore of all virtues,
> Darkness and affliction ended.

> Some see the supreme man
> Full of great compassion
> Turning the wheel of teaching
> Liberating numberless beings.

> Some see the lion roar,
> Its awesome light unique,
> Transcending all the worlds
> With peerless mystic power.
>
> Some see the mind at peace,
> Like a lamp gone out forever;
> Variously manifesting spiritual mastery,
> The ten-powered one can be like this.

Then the light beams passed a hundred worlds and illumined a thousand worlds in each of the ten directions. In all of those worlds were a hundred billion continents called Jambudvipa, and soon, including a hundred billion heavens of the ultimate of form—everything in all those realms was clearly revealed. In each one of the Jambudvipa continents the Buddha was seen sitting on a lotus bank lion throne surrounded by as many enlightening beings as atoms in ten buddha-lands; and in each one, due to the spiritual force of the Buddha, ten great enlightening beings from the ten directions, each accompanied by as many enlightening beings as atoms in ten buddha-lands, came to the Buddha; those enlightening beings were also called Manjushri, etc., the lands they came from were also called Golden, etc., and the Buddhas they served were also called Immutable Knowledge, etc. Then the Manjushris in all those places, simultaneously spoke up, saying these verses:

> The Buddha comprehends, without peer,
> The exceedingly profound truth;
> Sentient beings cannot understand,
> So he reveals it step-by-step.
>
> The nature of self has never existed,
> And possessions of self are also nil;
> So how come the enlightened ones
> Are able to have their bodies?
>
> The liberated ones, with knowledge and conduct,
> Are beyond category or compare;
> All the logic and reasoning of the world
> Cannot find any fault in them.
>
> The Buddhas are not worldly clusters,
> Elements, senses, born and dying things;

Phenomenal sets cannot produce them:
Thus they're called human lions.

Their nature is fundamentally empty and inactive,
They're liberated within and without;
Detached from all delusive ideas:
Such is the peerless state.

Their substance and nature never moves,
Selfless, no coming or going;
Yet they can awaken the worlds,
Pacifying all, without bound.

They always enjoy contemplating extinction,
Uniform, without duality;
Their minds do not increase or decrease,
Yet manifest boundless powers.

They do not do the deeds
That cause results for sentient beings,
Yet can understand unhindered:
Such is the enlightened way.

All kinds of living beings
Transmigrate through all realms;
Buddhas, not discriminating,
Liberate the boundless kinds.

The Buddhas' golden color
Is not existent, yet pervades all existences;
According to the inclinations of beings,
They teach them ultimate peace.

Then the light beams passed a thousand worlds and illumined ten
thousand worlds in all directions; in all of those worlds were a hundred
billion continents called Jambudvipa, and so on, including a hundred
billion heavens of the ultimate of form—everything in all those realms
was clearly revealed. In each one of the Jambudvipa continents the
Buddha was seen sitting on a lotus bank lion throne surrounded by as
many enlightening beings as atoms in ten buddha-lands; and in each
one, due to the spiritual force of the Buddha, a great enlightening being
from each of the ten directions, each accompanied by as many enlightening beings as atoms in ten buddha-lands, came to the Buddha; those
enlightening beings were also called Manjushri, etc., the lands they
came from were also called Golden, etc., and the Buddhas they served

were also called Immutable Knowledge, etc. Then the Manjushris in all those places, each in the presence of the Buddha in that place, all simultaneously spoke out, saying these verses:

Developing great compassion
To save and protect all sentient beings,
Forever leaving human and celestial realms:
This is what work should be done.

Always with faith in the Buddha,
The mind never regressing,
Associating with the enlightened ones:
This is what work should be done.

Intent on the virtues of buddhahood,
The will never receding,
Abiding in pure cool wisdom:
This is what work should be done.

In all manner of activities,
Always remembering the Buddhas' virtues,
Without ever a lapse day or night:
This is what work should be done.

Observing the boundless past, present, and future,
Studying enlightened virtues
Without ever tiring of it:
This is what work should be done.

Observing the real characteristics of the body,
All being void and nil,
Detaching from self, with no egotism:
This is what work should be done.

A mind seeing beings as equal,
Not creating discrimination,
Entering the realm of real truth:
This is what work should be done.

Lifting up boundless worlds,
Drinking up all the oceans:
This power of knowledge of psychic attainment
Is the kind of work that should be done.

Contemplating the various lands,
Their material and immaterial aspects,

Able to know them all:
This is what work should be done.

The atoms of all lands everywhere
Are, each and every one, a Buddha;
To be able to know their number:
This is what work should be done.

Then the light beams passed ten thousand worlds and illuminated a hundred thousand worlds in all directions. In all of those worlds were a hundred billion continents called Jambudvipa, and so on, including a hundred billion heavens of the ultimate of form—everything in all those realms was clearly revealed. In each of the Jambudvipa continents the Buddha was seen sitting on a lotus bank lion throne surrounded by as many enlightening beings as atoms in ten buddha-lands; and in each one, due to the spiritual force of the Buddha, a great enlightening being from each of the ten directions, each accompanied by as many enlightening beings as atoms in ten buddha-lands, came to the Buddha; those enlightening beings were called Manjushri, etc., the lands they came from were called Golden, etc., and the Buddhas they served were called Immutable Knowledge, etc. Then the Manjushris in all those places, each in the presence of the Buddha in that place, all simultaneously spoke out, saying these verses:

If one sees the Human Tamer
In terms of form or family,
These are diseased eyes, perverted views:
They can't know the supreme truth.

The various formal characteristics of the Buddha
Cannot be assessed by any being;
Though billions and trillions together calculate,
Those features and virtues are yet more boundless.

The Buddha does not have forms as substance:
It's just the formless, quiescent state:
Yet the physical forms and dignities are complete,
Seen by worldlings in accord with their wishes.

The Buddhas' reality is subtle and hard to fathom;
No words or speech can reach it.
It is not compounded or uncompounded;
Its essential nature is void and formless.

Buddha's body is unborn, beyond imagination;
It is not a cluster of diverse elements.
Having the power of freedom and certain insight,
He travels the fearless, inexpressible path.

Body and mind equanimous,
Liberated within and without,
Abiding forever in true awareness,
He has no attachment, no bondage.

The illumined one whose mind is pure
Acts without habituation;
With the eye of knowledge reaching everywhere
He greatly aids living beings.

One body is infinite,
And the infinite too are one;
Understanding all the worlds,
He manifests forms everywhere.

This body comes from nowhere
And accumulates nothing either;
It is due to beings' discrimination
That they see various bodies of Buddha.

Mind discriminates worlds,
But that mind has no existence;
The enlightened know this truth,
And thus see the Buddha-body.

Then the light beams passed a hundred thousand worlds and illumined a million worlds, in each of the ten directions. In all of those worlds with a hundred billion continents called Jambudvipa, and so on, including a hundred billion heavens of the ultimate of form—everything in all those realms was clearly revealed. In each of the Jambudvipa continents the Buddha was seen sitting on a lotus bank lion throne surrounded by as many enlightening beings as atoms in ten buddha-lands; and in each one, due to the spiritual force of the Buddha, ten great enlightening beings from the ten directions, each accompanied by as many enlightening beings as atoms in ten buddha-lands, came to the Buddha; those enlightening beings were called Manjushri, etc., the lands they came from were called Golden, etc., and the Buddhas they served were called Immutable Knowledge, etc. Then the Manjushris in all those places, each in the presence of the Buddha in that place, all simultaneously spoke out, saying these verses:

The enlightened one most free,
Transcending the world, relying on nothing,
Replete with all virtues,
Liberates creatures from all states of being.

Unaffected, unattached,
Without conceptions, resting nowhere,
Substance and essence immeasurable:
Those who see all praise.

Light pervasive, clear and pure,
Clearing away mundane afflictions,
Immutable, beyond extremes:
This is enlightened knowledge.

Any who see the enlightened
Free from discrimination in body and mind
Will have no more doubts or hesitation
In regard to anything.

In all worlds, everywhere
Turning the wheel of teaching,
Natureless, with nothing turned,
The Guide expounds expedients.

Having no doubt as to truth,
Forever ending mental fabrication,
Not producing a discriminating mind:
This is awareness of enlightenment.

Comprehending different things,
Not sticking to verbal explanations,
With no "one" or "manifold":
This is following Buddha's teaching.

In many there's no oneness;
Neither has one plurality:
Abandoning both of these,
Comprehensively enter the qualities of buddhahood.

Sentient beings and their lands
Are all completely null;
With no reliance or discrimination
One can enter Buddha's enlightenment.

Of sentient beings and lands
Unity or difference cannot be found;
Insightfully seeing like this
Is called knowing the meaning of Buddha's teaching.

Then the light beams passed a million worlds and illuminated a billion worlds in each of the ten directions. In all of those worlds were a hundred billion continents called Jambudvipa, and so on, including a hundred billion heavens of the ultimate of form—everything in all those realms was clearly revealed. In each of the Jambudvipa continents the Buddha was seen sitting on a lotus bank lion throne surrounded by as many enlightening beings as atoms in ten buddha-lands; and in each one, due to the spiritual force of the Buddha, a great enlightening being from each of the ten directions, each accompanied by as many enlightening beings as atoms in ten buddha-lands, came to the Buddha; those great enlightening beings were called Manjushri, etc., the lands they came from were called Golden, etc., and the Buddhas they served were called Immutable Knowledge, etc. Then the Manjushris in all those places, each in the presence of the Buddha in that place, all simultaneously spoke out, saying these verses:

Wisdom peerless, teaching boundless,
Gone beyond the sea of existences, reaching the other shore,
Life span and radiance without compare:
This is the power of the Virtuous One's skill.

Clearly understanding all the Buddhas' teachings,
Always observing all times tirelessly,
Even when perceiving objects, not discriminating:
This is the power of the Inconceivable One's skill.

Contemplating sentient beings without any concept thereof,
Observing all existences without such ideas,
Always abiding in meditative stillness yet not binding the mind:
This is the power of skill of unhindered wisdom.

Skillfully comprehending all things,
With right mindfulness diligently cultivating the path of nirvana,
Enjoying liberation, divorcing partiality:
This is the power of skill of the peaceful, dispassionate one.

If any can exhort to complete enlightenment,
Heading for all-knowledge of the cosmos,

And influence beings to enter into truth:
This is the power of skill of dwelling in the Buddha-mind.

Able to enter into all truths the Buddhas teach
With vast knowledge and wisdom unobstructed,
Able to arrive at every destination:
This is the power of skill of cultivation of freedom.

Always abiding in nirvana, like empty space,
Able to transform and appear anywhere at will:
This is creating form based on the formless,
The power of skill of the one who reaches the hard to reach.

Day and night, day and month, year and era,
The signs of the beginning and end, formation and disintegration
   of the worlds:
Remembering and thoroughly knowing these
Is the power of skill of knowledge of measures of time.

All living beings have birth and death;
Material and immaterial, thinking or unthinking:
Knowing all the various names
Is the power of skill of abiding in the inconceivable.

Of past, present, and future times,
Understanding all that's said,
Yet knowing all times are equal:
This is the power of skill of incomparable understanding.

Then the light beams passed a billion worlds and illuminated ten billion worlds in each of the ten directions. In all of those worlds were a hundred billion continents called Jambudvipa, and so on, including a hundred billion heavens of the ultimate of form—everything in all those realms was clearly revealed. In each of the Jambudvipa continents the Buddha was seen sitting on a lotus bank lion throne surrounded by as many enlightening beings as atoms in ten buddha-lands; and in each one, due to the spiritual force of the Buddha, ten great enlightening beings from the ten directions, each accompanied by as many enlightening beings as atoms in ten buddha-lands, came to the Buddha; those great enlightening beings were called Manjushri, etc., the lands they came from were called Golden, etc., and the Buddhas they served were called Immutable Knowledge, etc. Then the Manjushris in all those places, each in the presence of the Buddha in that place, all simultaneously spoke out, saying these verses:

Having cultivated extensive difficult practices,
Diligently working day and night,
Having crossed the hard to cross, with a lion's roar,
Teaching all beings—this is *the* practice.

Sentient beings whirl in the sea of craving and greed,
Shrouded by the web of ignorance, terribly oppressed;
The Most Benevolent bravely cuts it all away,
We vow to also do so—this is *the* practice.

Worldlings have no control, attached to sense desires;
Falsely discriminating, they suffer myriad pains.
Practicing the Buddhas' teaching, always control the mind,
Vowing to cross over this—this is *the* practice.

Sentient beings, attached to self, enter birth and death;
Looking for a limit to this, none can be found.
Serving all the enlightened to obtain the wondrous teaching,
Explain it to others—this is *the* practice.

Living beings are helpless, wrapped up in sickness,
Forever sunk in evil ways, producing the three poisons,
The fierce flames of a great fire always burning them;
With a pure heart to rescue them, this is *the* practice.

Sentient beings, confused, have lost the right path;
Always going the wrong way, they enter the house of darkness.
For their sake lighting the lamp of truth,
To be a light forever—this is *the* practice.

Sentient beings bob and sink in the ocean of existences;
Their troubles are boundless, they have no place to rest.
To make for them an ark of truth
To ferry them over—this is *the* practice.

Sentient beings are ignorant and don't see the fundamental;
Confused, foolish, crazed, in the midst of danger and difficulty.
Buddhas pity them and set up a bridge of teaching
With right awareness, to let them climb—this is *the* practice.

Seeing beings on perilous paths,
Oppressed by the pains of age, illness, and death,
Develop unlimited skill in means
And pledge to save them all—this is *the* practice.

Hearing the truth, believing without doubt,
Comprehending essential emptiness without shock or fear,
Appearing in all realms in appropriate forms,
Teach all the deluded—this is *the* practice.

Then the light beams passed ten billion worlds and illumined in all
ten directions a hundred billion worlds, a trillion worlds, a hundred
trillion worlds, a quadrillion worlds, a hundred quadrillion worlds, a
quintillion worlds, a hundred quintillion worlds; in this way countless,
unquantifiable, boundless, imcomparable, uncountable, unaccountable,
unthinkable, immeasurable, unspeakable numbers of worlds, to the
utmost extent of the realm of space of the cosmos, in all ten directions,
were likewise illumined. In all of those worlds were a hundred billion
continents called Jambudvipa, and so on, including a hundred billion
heavens of the ultimate of form—everything in all those realms was
clearly revealed. In each of the Jambudvipa continents the Buddha was
seen sitting on a lotus bank lion throne surrounded by as many enlightening beings as atoms in ten buddha-lands; and in each one, due to the
spiritual force of the Buddha, a great enlightening being from each of
the ten directions, each accompanied by as many enlightening beings as
atoms in ten buddha-lands, came to the Buddha; those great enlightening beings were called Manjushri, etc., the lands they came from were
called Golden, etc., and the Buddhas they served were called Immutable Knowledge, etc. Then the Manjushris in all those places, each in the
presence of the Buddha in that place, all simultaneously spoke out,
saying these verses:

In one instant observing measureless eons
Without going, coming, or dwelling,
Thus comprehending the events of past, present, and future,
Buddhas transcend expedients and fulfill ten powers.

With incomparable good repute in all quarters,
Forever out of trouble, always rejoicing,
They go to all lands
To explain such a teaching for all.

For the benefit of beings, they supported the enlightened,
Attaining a comparable result, according to their will;
Readily acknowledging all truths,
They reveal spiritual powers everywhere.

From their first offerings to the enlightened their minds were
   flexible and patient;

They entered deep meditative concentration and observed the
nature of things.
Exhorting all beings to aspire to enlightenment,
Through this they speedily attained the unexcelled reward.

Who seeks truth everywhere with undivided mind
To cultivate virtues to full maturity,
Eliminating all duality of being and nonbeing:
Such people truly see the Buddha.

Going to all lands in all directions,
Expounding the sublime teaching for the welfare of the many,
Abiding in reality without any wavering:
Such people's virtues are the same as Buddha.

The cycles of wondrous teaching turned by the Buddhas
Are all aspects of enlightenment;
If one, having heard, can realize the nature of things,
Such a person will always see Buddha.

If one does not see the Ten Powered as empty, phantomlike,
Though one sees one sees not, as though blind.
Discriminating and grasping forms one does not see Buddha;
Having finally divorced attachment, then can one see.

Sentient beings are variously different, according to their actions;
In the ten directions, inside and out, it's hard to see them all:
The Buddha-body's unhindered, pervading all directions,
And cannot be completely seen, in just the same way.

Like unto the infinite worlds in space,
Without coming or going, pervading the ten directions,
Becoming and disintegrating having no resting place,
So does Buddha pervade space in the same way.

BOOK TEN

An Enlightening Being Asks for Clarification

THEN THE ENLIGHTENING BEING Manjushri asked the enlightening being Chief of the Awakened, "Since the nature of mind is one, what is the reason for seeing the existence of various differences, such as going to good or bad tendencies, having complete or imperfect faculties, differences in birth, beauty and ugliness, pain and pleasure, suffering and happiness? Why is it that activity doesn't know mind, mind doesn't know activity, reception doesn't know consequence, consequence doesn't know reception, mind doesn't know reception, reception doesn't know mind, cause doesn't know condition, condition doesn't know cause, knowledge doesn't know object, object doesn't know knowledge?"

Chief of the Awakened answered in verse, saying,

> Benevolent One, you ask the meaning of this
> To awaken all the ignorant.
> I will answer according to the essence:
> Listen clearly, Benevolent One.
>
> Phenomena have no function
> And have no individual nature;
> Therefore all of them
> Do not know one another.
>
> Like the waters in a river,
> Their rushing flow races past,
> Each unaware of the others:
> So it is with all things.
>
> It's also like a mass of fire,
> Blazing flames shoot up at once,

Each not knowing the others:
Phenomena are also thus.

Also like a continuous wind
Fanning and drumming whatever it hits,
Each unaware of the other:
So also are all things.

Also like the various levels of earth,
Each based on another,
Yet unaware of the others:
Thus are all phenomena.

Eye, ear, nose, tongue, body,
Mind, intellect, the faculties of sense:
By these one always revolves,
Yet there is no one, nothing that revolves.

The nature of things is fundamentally birthless,
Yet they appear to have birth;
Herein there is no revealer,
And nothing that's revealed.

Eye, ear, nose, tongue, body,
Mind, intellect, the faculties of sense:
All are void and essenceless;
The deluded mind conceives them to exist.

Seen as they truly are,
All are without inherent nature.
The eye of reality is not conceptual:
This seeing is not false.

Real or unreal,
False or not false,
Mundane or transmundane:
There's nothing but descriptions.

Then Manjushri asked Chief in Riches of Truth, "Since all sentient beings are not sentient beings, why does the Buddha appear in their midst for their sake and teach them according to the time, according to their lives, according to their species, according to their actions, according to their understandings, according to their philosophies, according to their inclinations, according to their expedients, according to their thoughts, according to their observations?" Chief in Riches answered him in verse:

This is the realm of the learned
Who delight in ultimate peace.
I will explain for you;
Now please listen clearly.

Analyze the body within:
Who herein is the "self"?
Who can understand this way
Will comprehend the existence or not of the self.

This body is a temporary set-up
And has no place of abode;
Who understands this body
Will have no attachment to it.

Considering the body carefully,
Everything will be clearly seen:
Knowing all the elements are unreal,
One will not create mental fabrications.

Based on whom does life arise,
And based on whom does it disappear?
Like a turning wheel of fire,
Its beginning and end can't be known.

The wise can observe with insight
The impermanence of all existents;
All things are empty and selfless,
Forever apart from all signs.

All consequences are born from actions;
Like dreams, they're not truly real.
From moment to moment they continually die away,
The same as before and after.

Of all things seen in the world
Only mind is the host;
By grasping forms according to interpretation
It becomes deluded, not true to reality.

All philosophies in the world
Are mental fabrications;
There has never been a single doctrine
By which one could enter the true essence of things.

By the power of perceiver and perceived
All kinds of things are born;
They soon pass away, not staying,
Dying out instant to instant.

Then Manjushri asked Chief of the Precious, "All sentient beings equally have four gross physical elements, with no self and nothing pertaining to self—how come there is the experience of pain and pleasure, beauty and ugliness, internal and external goodness, little sensation and much sensation? Why do some experience consequences in the present, and some in the future? And all this while there is no good or bad in the realm of reality." Chief of the Precious answered in verse:

According to what deeds are done
Do their resulting consequences come to be;
Yet the doer has no existence:
This is the Buddha's teaching.

Like a clear mirror,
According to what comes before it,
Reflecting forms, each different,
So is the nature of actions.

And like a skillful magician
Standing at a crossroads
Causing many forms to appear,
So is the nature of actions.

Like a mechanical robot
Able to utter various sounds,
Neither self nor not self:
So is the nature of actions.

And like different species of birds
All emerging from eggs,
Yet their voices not the same:
So is the nature of actions.

Just as in the womb
All organs are developed,
Their substance and features coming from nowhere:
So is the nature of actions.

Also like being in hell—
The various painful things
All come from nowhere:
So is the nature of actions.

Also like the sovereign king
With seven supreme treasures—
Their provenance cannot be found:
So is the nature of actions.

And as when the various worlds
Are burnt by a great conflagration,
This fire comes from nowhere:
So does the nature of actions.

Then Manjushri asked Chief of the Virtuous, "Since that which the
Buddhas realize is but one truth, how is it that they expound countless
teachings, manifest countless lands, edify countless beings, speak in
countless languages, appear in countless bodies, know countless minds,
demonstrate countless mystic powers, are able to shake countless worlds,
display countless extraordinary adornments, reveal boundless different
realms of objects, whereas in the essential nature of things these different characteristics cannot be found at all?" Chief of the Virtuous answered in verse:

The meaning of what you ask
Is deep and hard to fathom.
The wise are able to know it,
Always delighting in Buddha's virtues.

Just as the nature of earth is one
While beings each live separately,
And the earth has no thought of oneness or difference,
So is the truth of all Buddhas.

Just as the nature of fire is one,
While able to burn all things
And the flames make no distinction,
So is the truth of all Buddhas.

Just as the ocean is one
With millions of different waves
Yet the water is no different:
So is the truth of all Buddhas.

And as the nature of wind is one
While able to blow on all things
And wind has no thought of oneness or difference:
So is the truth of all Buddhas.

Also like great thunderheads
Raining all over the earth,
The raindrops make no distinctions:
So is the truth of all Buddhas.

Just as the element earth, while one,
Can produce various sprouts,
Yet it's not that the earth is diverse:
So is the truth of all Buddhas.

Just as the sun without clouds overcast
Shines throughout the ten directions,
Its light beams having no difference:
So is the truth of all Buddhas.

And just as the moon in the sky
Is seen by all in the world
Yet the moon doesn't go to them:
So is the truth of all Buddhas.

Just as the king of the gods
Appears throughout the universe
Yet his body has no change:
So is the truth of all Buddhas.

Then Manjushri asked the enlightening being Chief in Vision, "Buddhas as fields of blessings are one and the same to all—how is it that when sentient beings give alms to them, the resulting rewards are not the same—various forms, various families, various faculties, various property, various masters, various followers, various official positions, various virtuous qualities, various kinds of knowledge—and yet the Buddhas are impartial toward them, not thinking of them as different?" Chief in Vision answered in verse:

Just as the earth is one
Yet produces sprouts according to the seeds
Without partiality toward any of them,
So is the Buddhas' field of blessings.

And just as water is uniform
Yet differs in shape according to the vessel,
So is the Buddhas' field of blessings:
It differs only due to beings' minds.

And just as a skilled magician
Can make people happy,
So can the Buddhas' field of blessings
Cause sentient beings joy.

As a king with wealth and knowledge
Can bring gladness to the masses,
So can Buddhas' field of blessings
Bring peace and happiness to all.

Like a clear mirror
Reflecting images according to the forms,
So from Buddhas' field of blessings
Rewards are obtained according to one's heart.

Like a panacea
Which can cure all poisoning,
So does Buddhas' field of blessings
Annihilate all afflictions.

And just as when the sun comes up
It illuminates the world,
Thus does Buddhas' field of blessings
Clear away all darkness.

Like the clear full moon
Shining over the earth,
So is Buddhas' field of blessings
Equal in all places.

Just as a great conflagration
Can burn up all things,
So does Buddhas' field of blessings
Burn up all fabrication.

Just as a violent wind
Can cause the earth to tremble,
So does Buddhas' field of blessings
Move all living beings.

Then Manjushri asked Chief in Effort, "The Buddhas' teaching is one, which all beings can see—why don't they all immediately cut off all the bonds of afflictions and win emancipation? Furthermore, in their clusters of material form, clusters of sensation, conception, coordination-activity, and consciousness, the realms of desire, form, and formlessness, as well as ignorance and craving, they are no different—this is the Buddha's teaching; why is it of benefit to some and not to others?" Chief in Effort answered in verse:

> Listen well and clearly
> And I will answer truly.
> Some are quickly freed,
> And some can hardly escape.
>
> If one wishes to eliminate
> The countless faults and ills,
> One should work with diligence
> On the Buddha-teaching.
>
> For example, a little bit of fire
> Moisture in the kindling will extinguish;
> So it is with those who're lazy
> About the Buddha-teaching.
>
> Just as when you drill for fire
> And stop before the fire appears
> The heat will immediately disappear:
> So it is with the indolent.
>
> When a man with a magnifying glass
> Doesn't focus the sun's rays on anything,
> Fire can never be obtained:
> So it is with the lazy.
>
> Like when the dazzling sun shines
> A child shuts its eyes
> And complains "Why can't I see?":
> So too are the lazy like this.
>
> Like a man lacking hands and feet
> Wanting to shoot all over the earth
> With arrows made of reeds:
> So too are the lazy ones.
>
> Like using a single hair
> To take the ocean water

Trying to drain the ocean:
So also are the slothful.

Like when the eon fire flares
Trying to put it out with a little water:
So are those who are lazy
About the Buddha's teaching.

Like someone who sees space
While sitting still, unmoving,
And says he is traveling through it:
So is the lazy one.

Then Manjushri asked Chief in Doctrine, "According to what the Buddha says, if any sentient beings accept and hold the true teaching, they can cut off all afflictions. Why then are there those who accept and hold the true teaching and yet do not cut off afflictions, who go along with anger and resentment, go along with jealousy and stinginess, go along with deception and flattery, compelled by the power of these things, having no will to detach from them? If they are able to accept and hold the true teaching, why then do they still produce afflictions in their mental actions?" Chief in Doctrine answered in verse:

Listen well and clearly
To the true meaning of what you ask.
It is not only by much learning
That one can enter the Buddhas' teaching.

Like a man floating in water
Who dies of thirst, afraid of drowning:
So are those who are learned
Who do not apply the teaching.

Like a person skilled in medicine
Who can't cure his own disease:
So are those who are learned
But do not apply the teaching.

Like someone counting others' treasures
Without half a coin of his own:
So is the one who is learned
Who doesn't practice the teaching.

Like one who's born in a royal palace
Yet who freezes and starves:
So are those who are learned
But do not practice the teaching.

Like a deaf musician
Who pleases others, not hearing himself:
So is the one who is learned
Who does not apply the teaching.

Like a blind embroiderer
Who shows others but cannot see:
So are those who are learned
But do not practice the teaching.

Like a ship's captain
Who dies at sea:
So are those who are learned
But do not apply the teaching.

Like someone on a corner
Saying all kinds of fine things,
While having no real inner virtue:
So are those who don't practice.

Then Manjushri asked Chief in Knowledge, "In the Buddha teaching, knowledge is chief—so why do the Buddhas, in dealing with people, sometimes praise generosity, sometimes praise self-control, sometimes praise tolerance, sometimes praise effort, sometimes praise meditation, sometimes praise wisdom, or again sometimes praise kindness, compassion, joy, and equanimity, yet all the while there is ultimately but one truth whereby to attain emancipation and realize complete perfect enlightenment?" Chief in Knowledge answered in verse:

Son of Buddha, most rare
Is the ability to know beings' minds.
As for what you ask,
Listen well and I'll explain.

Of the past, future,
And present guides,
None expounds just one method
To become enlightened.

Buddhas know beings' minds,
Their natures each different;
According to what they need to be freed,
Thus do the Buddhas teach.

To the stingy they praise giving,
To the immoral they praise ethics;
To the angry they praise tolerance,
To the lazy they praise effort.

To those with scattered minds they praise meditative concentration,
To the ignorant, they praise wisdom;
To the inhuman, they praise kindness and sympathy,
To the malicious, compassion.

To the troubled they praise joy,
To the devious they praise equanimity.
Thus practicing step-by-step,
One gradually fulfills all Buddha teachings.

It's like first setting up a foundation
Then building the room:
Generosity and self-control, like this,
Are bases of enlightening beings' practices.

Just like building a castle
To protect all the people:
So are tolerance and effort
Protecting enlightening beings.

And just as a universal monarch
Can bestow all felicities:
So can kindness, compassion, joy and equanimity
Give enlightening beings happiness.

Then Manjushri asked Chief in Goodness, "The Buddhas, the World
Honored Ones, attain emancipation by means of one path alone; why
then are the things in the Buddha-lands we see now various and not
the same? That is to say, the worlds, the realms of beings, the teaching and training, the life span and auras of light, the miracles, the
congregations, the modes of teaching and doctrinal bases, each have
differences, yet all include all the truths of the Buddhas, whereby
complete perfect enlightenment is attained." Chief in Goodness answered
in verse:

Manjushri, truth is always thus:
The Kings of Truth have just one truth.
People unhindered by anything,
They leave birth and death by one road.

All the Buddha bodies
Are just one reality-body:
One in mind, one in wisdom,
The same in power and fearlessness.

According to their dedications
When originally starting out for enlightenment,
They developed such lands,
Congregations, and teachings.

The adornments of all buddha-lands
Are totally complete;
According to differences in beings' actions
They seem to be unalike.

The buddha-lands and buddha-bodies,
The congregations and explanations:
Such Buddhist teachings as these
No sentient beings can see.

When their minds are purified
And their vows fulfilled,
Such illuminated people
Then are able to see.

According to beings' mental inclinations
And the force of the fruits of their deeds,
There seem to them to be differences;
This is due to Buddhas' mystic powers.

Buddha-lands have no discrimination,
No hatred and no attachment:
But according to beings' minds
They seem to have differences.

Because of this, in the worlds
What is seen is different:
This is not the fault
Of the enlightened sages.

In all worlds
Those who are fit to receive the teaching
Always see the Hero of humanity:
Such is the Buddhas' teaching.

Then these enlightening beings said to Manjushri, "Son of Buddha, we have each spoken of our understanding. We ask you, benevolent one, to use your wonderful powers of elucidation to expound the realm of the enlightened—what is the sphere of the Buddhas, what are the causal bases of the sphere of the Buddhas, what are the methods of liberation in the sphere of the Buddhas, what are the entries into the states of the Buddhas, what is the wisdom in the realm of the Buddhas, what are the laws of the realm of the Buddhas, what are the explanations of the states of the Buddhas, what is the knowledge of the sphere of the Buddhas, what is the realization of the realm of the Buddhas, what are the manifestations of the states of the Buddhas, what is the extent of the sphere of the Buddhas?" Manjushri answered in verse:

The profound realm of the Buddhas
Is equal in extent to space;
All beings enter it,
Yet really nothing's entered.

The sublime causes
Of the Buddhas' profound states
Could not be fully told
In a billion eons of talk.

According to beings' minds and wisdom,
Buddhas lead them on and aid them;
This is the realm of the Buddhas,
Liberating beings this way.

Able to enter all lands
In the world,
The body of knowledge is formless
And cannot be seen by others.

The Buddhas' knowledge is free,
Unhindered in all times;
This realm of wisdom
Is equanimous as space.

The realms of beings of the cosmos
Ultimately have no distinction;
Thoroughly knowing all of them
Is the sphere of the enlightened ones.

All languages and sounds
There are in the worlds
Buddhas' knowledge can comprehend
Without discrimination.

Not perceptible to sense consciousness
And not the sphere of mind,
Its nature fundamentally pure,
Buddhas' knowledge teaches living beings.

Not action, not affliction,
With no thing and no abode,
No looking and no object,
Their realization's equanimous throughout the world.

The minds of all sentient beings
In the past, present, and future,
The enlightened, in one instant,
Can thoroughly comprehend.

Then all the differences in state, activity, realm, body, faculties, birth, results of keeping precepts, results of breaking precepts, and in resulting lands of all sentient beings in this world Endurance, by the Buddha's spiritual power all became clearly manifest. In the same way all these various differences of all sentient beings in the infinite worlds throughout the space of the cosmos in all directions were all clearly revealed by the Buddha's mystic power.

BOOK ELEVEN

Purifying Practice

THEN THE ENLIGHTENING BEING Chief in Knowledge asked the enlightening being Manjushri, "How can enlightening beings attain faultless physical, verbal, and mental action? How can they attain harmless physical, verbal, and mental action? How can they attain blameless physical, verbal, and mental action? How can they attain invulnerable physical, verbal, and mental action? How can they attain nonregressive physical, verbal, and mental action? How can they attain unshakable physical, verbal, and mental action? How can they attain excellent physical, verbal, and mental action? How can they attain pure physical, verbal, and mental action? How can they attain unpolluted physical, verbal, and mental action? How can they attain physical, verbal, and mental action that is guided by wisdom? How can they attain birth in appropriate places, among good people, physically complete, with full mindfulness, understanding, completeness in conduct, fearlessness, and awareness? How can they attain excellent discernment, foremost discernment, supreme discernment, immeasurable discernment, incalculable discernment, inconceivable discernment, incomparable discernment, unfathomable discernment, inexpressible discernment? How can they attain causal power, will power, skill power, the power of proper conditions and objects of attention, faculty power, powers of observation, the power to stop the mind, powers of analytic insight, and power of contemplative thought? How can they attain skill in analyzing the psychophysical elements and organs, skill in analyzing interdependent origination, skill in analyzing the realms of desire, form, and formlessness, and skill in understanding the past, present, and future? How can they cultivate well the branches of enlightenment—mindfulness, discernment, effort, joy, well-being, concentration, relinquishment? How can they attain emptiness, signlessness, wishlessness? How can they fulfill the means of transcendence—generosity, self-control, tolerance, effort, meditation, and wisdom? How can they fulfill kindness, compassion, joy, and equanimity? How can they attain the power of knowledge of what is so and what is not, the power of knowledge of consequences of past, future, and present acts, the power of knowledge of superiority and inferiority of faculties, the power of knowledge of various realms, the power of knowledge of various understandings, the power of knowledge of where all paths lead, the power of knowledge of defilement or purity of meditations, liberations, and trances, the power of knowledge of past lives, the power of knowledge of unhindered clairvoyance, and the power of knowledge of having cut off all taints? How can they always gain the protection, respect, and support of celestial kings, dragon kings, yaksha kings, gandharva kings, titan kings, garuda kings, kinnara kings, mahoraga kings, human kings, and brahma kings? How can they be a reliance and savior, a refuge and resort, a lamp and a light, an illuminator and a guide, a supreme and universal leader for all sentient beings? How can they be foremost and greatest, excellent and supreme, sublime and most wonderful, highest and unexcelled, incomparable and peerless among all sentient beings?"

Manjushri said to Chief in Knowledge, "Excellent, O Child of Buddha! You have asked this out of a desire to benefit many, to bring peace to many, out of pity for the world, to profit and gladden celestial and human beings. Child of Buddha, if enlightening beings use their minds properly, they can attain all supreme qualities, can have a mind unhindered in regard to all enlightening teachings, can remain on the Path of the Buddhas of past, present, and future, never leaving it even while living in the midst of sentient beings, can comprehend the characteristics of all things, cut off all evil and fulfill all good. They will be physically most excellent, like Universally Good; all of their practical vows they will be able to fulfill, and will be free in all ways, and will be guides for all sentient beings. How can they use their minds so as to attain all supreme sublime qualities?

> Enlightening beings at home
> Should wish that all beings
> Realize the nature of "home" is empty
> And escape its pressures.
>
> While serving their parents,
> They should wish that all beings
> Serve the Buddha,
> Protecting and nourishing everyone.
>
> While with their spouses and children,
> They should wish that all beings
> Be impartial toward everyone
> And forever give up attachment.

When attaining desires,
They should wish that all beings
Pull out the arrow of lust
And realize ultimate peace.

On festive occasions
They should wish that all beings
Enjoy themselves with truth
And realize amusement's not real.

If in palace rooms,
They should wish that all beings
Enter the sanctified state,
Forever rid of defiled craving.

When putting on adornments,
They should wish that all beings
Give up phony decoration
And reach the abode of truth.

When climbing up in balconies,
They should wish that all beings
Ascend the tower of truth
And see through everything.

When they give something,
They should wish that all beings
Be able to relinquish all
With hearts free of clinging.

When in gatherings or crowds,
They should wish that all beings
Let go of compounded things
And attain to total knowledge.

If in danger and difficulty,
They should wish that all beings
Be free,
Unhindered wherever they go.

When they give up home life,
They should wish that all beings
Have no hindrance in leaving home,
And that their minds be liberated.

Entering a monastery
They should wish that all beings
Expound various principles
Of noncontention.

Going to tutors and teachers,
They should wish that all beings
Skillfully serve their teachers
And practice virtuous ways.

Seeking initiation,
They should wish that all beings
Reach the nonregressing state,
Their minds without impediment

Shedding lay clothing,
They should wish that all beings
Cultivate roots of goodness
And abandon the yoke of transgressions.

When shaving off their hair,
They should wish that all beings
Forever divorce all afflictions
And pass on to ultimate tranquility.

Putting on religious garb,
They should wish that all beings
Be undefiled in mind
And fulfill the Way of the Great Sage.

When they formally leave home,
They should wish that all beings
Leave home with the Buddha
And rescue one and all.

Taking refuge in the Buddha,
They should wish that all beings
Continue the lineage of Buddhas,
Conceiving the unexcelled aspiration.

Taking refuge in the Teaching,
They should wish that all beings
Enter deeply into the scriptures
And their wisdom be deep as the sea.

Taking refuge in the Community,
They should wish that all beings
Order the masses,
All becoming free from obstruction.

When receiving the learners' precepts,
They should wish that all beings
Learn self-control well
And not do any wrong.

Receiving a mentor's instruction,
They should wish that all beings
Bear themselves with dignity
And that their actions be truthful.

Receiving a teacher's guidance,
They should wish that all beings
Enter the knowledge of birthlessness
And reach the state of independence.

Receiving the full set of precepts,
They should wish that all beings
Fulfill all means of liberation
And master the supreme teaching.

When entering a hall,
They should wish that all beings
Ascend to the unexcelled sanctuary
And rest there secure, unshakable.

When setting out a seat,
They should wish that all beings
Cause good principles to bloom
And see their true character.

Sitting up straight,
They should wish that all beings
Sit on the seat of enlightenment,
Their minds without attachment.

Sitting cross-legged,
They should wish that all beings
Have firm and strong roots of goodness
And attain the state of immovability.

Cultivating concentration,
They should wish that all beings
Conquer their minds by concentration
Ultimately, with no remainder.

When practicing contemplation,
They should wish that all beings
See truth as it is
And be forever free of opposition and contention.

When uncrossing the legs,
They should wish that all beings
Observe that all acts and all things
Return to dispersal and extinction.

When lowering the feet and resting,
They should wish that all beings
Attain liberation of mind,
Resting at peace, unstirred.

When raising the legs,
They should wish that all beings
Leave the sea of birth and death
And fulfill all good qualities.

When putting on lower garments,
They should wish that all beings
Wear the foundations of goodness
And have a sense of shame and conscience.

When putting on a belt,
They should wish that all beings
Bundle roots of goodness
And not let them be lost.

When putting on an outer garment,
They should wish that all beings
Attain supreme bases of goodness
And reach the Other Shore of the teaching.

Putting on monastic robes,
They should wish that all beings
Enter the foremost rank
And attain imperturbability.

Taking a toothstick in hand,
They should wish that all beings
Attain the wonderful teaching
And be ultimately pure.

When chewing on the toothstick,
They should wish that all beings
Be harmonious and pure in mind,
Biting through all afflictions.

When going to the toilet,
They should wish that all beings
Reject greed, hatred, and folly,
And clean away sinful things.

When going to wash thereafter,
They should wish that all beings
Speedily go
To the transmundane.

When washing off the body's filth,
They should wish that all beings
Be pure and harmonious
And ultimately without defilement.

When washing the hands with water,
They should wish that all beings
Have pure clean hands
To receive and hold Buddha's teaching.

When washing the face with water,
They should wish that all beings
Attain the pure teaching
And be forever free from defilement.

Picking up a staff,
They should wish that all beings
Establish great works of charity
And point out the road of truth.

Taking up a bowl,
They should wish that all beings
Perfect the vessel of truth
And receive human and divine support.

Setting out on a road,
They should wish that all beings
Go where the Buddha goes,
Into the realm of nonreliance.

When on the road,
They should wish that all beings
Tread the pure realm of reality,
Their minds without obstruction.

Seeing a road uphill,
They should wish that all beings
Forever leave the world,
Their minds free from weakness.

Seeing a road downhill,
They should wish that all beings
Be humble in mind
And develop enlightened bases of virtue.

Seeing a winding road,
They should wish that all beings
Abandon false paths
And forever purge wrong views.

Seeing a straight road,
They should wish that all beings
Be straight and true in mind,
Without flattery or deceit.

Seeing a dusty road,
They should wish that all beings
Get rid of dust and dirt
And attain the state of purity.

Seeing a dust-free road,
They should wish that all beings
Always practice great compassion,
Their hearts refreshing and nourishing.

Seeing a dangerous road,
They should wish that all beings
Abide in the realm of truth
And avoid the troubles of wrongdoing.

Seeing a group of people,
They should wish that all beings
Expound the most profound teaching,
That all be harmoniously united.

If they see a big tree,
They should wish that all beings
Divorce egotistic contentiousness
And be free of anger and resentment.

If they see a grove,
The should wish that all beings
Be worthy of the respect
Of celestials and humans.

If they see high mountains,
They should wish that all beings'
Roots of goodness stand out,
Their peak beyond anyone's reach.

If they see thorny trees,
They should wish that all beings
May quickly cut away
The thorns of the three poisons.

Seeing trees with luxuriant foliage,
They should wish that all beings
Make a canopy of light
With stability and liberation.

If they see flowers blooming,
They should wish that all beings'
Mystic spiritual powers
Be like blossoming flowers.

If they see blossoms on trees,
They should wish that all beings'
Features be like flowers,
With all marks of distinction.

If they see fruits,
They should wish that all beings
Attain the supreme teaching
And realize the way of enlightenment.

If they see a big river,
They should wish that all beings
Gain entry into the stream of truth
And enter the ocean of Buddha-knowledge.

If they see a reservoir,
They should wish that all beings
Quickly awaken to
The truth of the oneness of the Buddhas.

If they see a pond,
They should wish that all beings
Be fully accomplished in speech
And be skillful in preaching.

If they see a well,
They should wish that all beings
Have full powers of elucidation
To explain all things.

If they see a spring,
They should wish that all beings'
Skill in means increases
And their good roots be inexhaustible.

If they see a bridge,
They should wish that all beings
Carry all across to freedom
Like a bridge.

If they see flowing water,
They should wish that all beings
Develop wholesome will
And wash away the stains of delusion.

Seeing a garden cultivated
They should wish that all beings
In the garden of sense desires
Clear away the weeds of craving.

Seeing a forest of "sorrowless" trees
They should wish that all beings
Forever divorce greed and lust
And not produce anxiety and fear.

If they see a park,
They should wish that all beings
Diligently cultivate the practices
Leading to Buddhas' enlightenment.

Seeing people wearing ornaments
They should wish that all beings
Be adorned with a Buddha's
Thirty-two marks of distinction.

Seeing the unadorned
They should wish that all beings
Give up decorations
And practice austerity.

Seeing people attached to pleasure
They should wish that all beings
Delight themselves with truth,
Not abandoning love for it.

Seeing the unattached
They should wish that all beings
Have no care in their minds
For fabricated things.

Seeing happy people
They should wish that all beings
Always be peaceful and happy,
Gladly supporting the Buddhas.

Seeing people suffer
They should wish that all beings
Attain fundamental knowledge
And eliminate all misery.

Seeing people with no maladies
They should wish that all beings
Enter true wisdom
And never have sickness or afflictions.

Seeing people sick
They should wish that all beings
Know the body is empty and null
And divorce opposition and conflict.

Seeing handsome people
They should wish that all beings
Always have pure faith
In the enlightened and enlightening ones.

Seeing ugly people
They should wish that all beings
Not become attached
To anything not good.

Seeing grateful people
They should wish that all beings
Be able to know the blessings
Of the Buddhas and enlightening beings.

Seeing ungrateful people
They should wish that all beings
Not increase the punishment
Of those who are bad.

If they see mendicants,
They should wish that all beings
Be harmonious and tranquil,
Ultimately conquering themselves.

Seeing brahmins
They should wish that all beings
Always maintain pure conduct,
Getting rid of all evil.

Seeing ascetics
They should wish that all beings
By austere practices
Reach the ultimate state.

Seeing self-disciplined people
They should wish that all beings
Strongly maintain their will in practice
And not give up the Buddhas' path.

Seeing people wearing armor
They should wish that all beings
Always wear the armor of virtue,
Heading for the teacherless state.

Seeing the unarmed
They should wish that all beings
Be forever rid of all
Doings that are not good.

Seeing people debate
They should wish that all beings
Be able to refute
All erroneous doctrines.

Seeing people of proper livelihood
They should wish that all beings
Succeed in pure livelihood
Without improper behavior.

If they see a king,
They should wish that all beings
Become kings of truth,
Always expounding the right teaching.

If they see a prince,
They should wish that all beings
Be reborn from the truth
And be children of Buddha.

If they see an elder,
They should wish that all beings
Be able to clearly cut off
And not practice evil ways.

If they see a great minister,
They should wish that all beings
Always maintain right mindfulness
And practice all virtues.

If they see a castle,
They should wish that all beings
Gain strong and firm bodies
And indefatigable minds.

If they see a capital,
They should wish that all beings
Collect all virtuous qualities
And always be joyful and blissful.

Seeing someone in a forest,
They should wish that all beings
Be worthy of praise and honor
Of celestials and humans

Entering a village to beg,
They should wish that all beings
Enter the profound realm of truth,
Their minds without impediment.

Coming to someone's door,
They should wish that all beings
Enter into all
Doors of Buddha's teaching.

Having entered a house,
They should wish that all beings
Might enter the vehicle of buddhahood
Which is equal in all times.

Seeing someone who doesn't give
They should wish that all beings
Never ever give up
Supremely virtuous ways.

Seeing those who give
They should wish that all beings
Forever abandon
The three evil paths and their miseries.

If they see an empty bowl,
They should wish that all beings
Be pure of heart
And empty of afflictions.

If they see a full bowl,
They should wish that all beings
Completely fulfill
All virtuous ways.

If they receive respect,
They should wish that all beings
Respectfully practice
All the Buddha's teachings.

If they get no respect,
They should wish that all beings
Not act in any ways
That are not good.

Seeing people with conscience
They should wish that all beings
Act with discretion
And cover their organs.

Seeing the shameless
They should wish that all beings
Give up shamelessness
And abide in the way of kindness.

If they get fine food,
They should wish that all beings
Should fulfill their aspirations
And be free from envy and longing.

If they get poor food,
They should wish that all beings
Should not fail to obtain
The taste of all meditations.

Getting soft food
They should wish that all beings
Be imbued with compassion,
Their minds becoming gentle.

Getting coarse, dry food
They should wish that all beings
Have no attachments
And cut off mundane craving.

When they eat,
They should wish that all beings
Feed on the joy of meditation
And be sated by delight in truth.

When tasting flavor,
They should wish that all beings
Attain the supreme savor of buddhahood
And be filled with the elixir of immortality.

When the meal is finished,
They should wish that all beings
Accomplish all their tasks
And fulfill the Buddha's teachings.

When they explain the teaching,
They should wish that all beings
Attain inexhaustible eloquence
And widely expound the essentials of the teaching.

When they leave a place,
They should wish that all beings
Deeply enter enlightened knowledge,
Forever leaving the triple world.

When they enter a bath,
They should wish that all beings
Enter omniscient knowledge,
Knowing past, present, and future are equal.

While washing their bodies,
They should wish that all beings
Be undefiled in body and mind,
Radiantly pure inside and out.

In the blistering heat of the day
They should wish that all beings
Cast off myriad afflictions,
Putting an end to them all.

When the heat subsides and begins to cool,
They should wish that all beings
Experience the highest truth
And be ultimately cool.

When reciting scripture,
They should wish that all beings
Accord with the Buddha's teachings,
Remembering without forgetting.

If they get to see a Buddha,
They should wish that all beings
Be all like Universally Good,
Handsome and well adorned.

When seeing a Buddha's tomb,
They should wish that all beings
Be honored as the shrine
And receive the offerings of celestials and humans.

Reverently gazing at the shrine,
They should wish that all beings
Be looked up to by all
Celestials and humans.

Bowing their heads to the shrine,
They should wish that all beings
Be exalted beyond the view
Of gods and men.

Circumabulating the shrine,
They should wish that all beings
Act without offense
And develop omniscience.

Circling the shrine thrice,
They should wish that all beings
Diligently see the Buddha's path
Without indolence of mind.

Praising the Buddha's virtues,
They should wish that all beings
Fulfill all virtues
Extolled endlessly.

Praising the Buddha's distinguishing marks,
They should wish that all beings
Develop the buddha-body
And realize formless truth.

When washing their feet,
They should wish that all beings
Fulfill the bases of spiritual powers,
Unhindered wherever they go.

When going to sleep at night,
They should wish that all beings
Attain physical ease
And undisturbed minds.

Awakening from sleep,
They should wish that all beings
Awaken omniscience,
Perceiving in all directions.

"Child of Buddha, if enlightening beings use their minds in this way, they will attain all supremely wonderful qualities, which cannot be dislodged by any gods, demons, monks, brahmins, gandharvas, titans, etc., or by any Buddhist followers or self-enlightened ones."

BOOK TWELVE

Chief in Goodness

THEN THE ENLIGHTENING BEING Manjushri, having explained the great virtues of unpolluted, undistorted pure activity, wanted to bring out the virtues of the aspiration for enlightenment, so he asked the enlightening being Chief in Goodness,

Now I have, for the sake of the enlightening beings,
Explained the purifying practices cultivated by Buddhas in the past;
Benevolent One, you too, in this assembly should
Expound the supreme virtues of practical application.

Then Chief in Goodness responded in verse:

Very good, Benevolent One—you should listen clearly.
Those virtues and merits cannot be measured:
I will now tell a little, as well as I can,
But it will be but as a drop of the ocean.

When an enlightening being first determines on the Way,
Vowing to seek and realize Buddhas' enlightenment,
The virtues therein are boundless,
Immeasurable, beyond compare.

How much the more so, through countless, boundless eons,
To fully practice the virtues of the stages and transcendent ways;
Even all the Buddhas of the ten directions
Together could not fully expound them all.

Of such boundless great virtues
I will now tell a little bit,

Like the space trod by a bird's feet,
Or like a mote of dust of the earth.

When enlightening beings determine to seek enlightenment,
This is not without cause, not without conditions;
Engendering pure faith in the Buddha, Teaching, and Community,
By this they produce a broad, magnanimous mind.

Not seeking objects of desire or positions of authority,
Wealth, personal enjoyment, or fame,
It is only to forever annihilate creatures' miseries
And to benefit the world that they rouse their will.

Always wanting to profit and gladden all beings,
They adorn lands and make offerings to Buddhas.
Accepting the right teaching, they cultivate its knowledges;
To realize enlightenment they arouse their minds.

Deep faith, belief, and resolution always pure,
They honor and respect all Buddhas,
As well as their Teachings and Communities;
Making offerings with ultimate sincerity, they rouse their will.

Deeply believing in the Buddha and the Buddha's teaching,
They also believe in the Way traversed by buddhas-to-be,
And believe in unexcelled great enlightenment:
Thereby do enlightening beings first rouse their will.

Faith is the basis of the Path, the mother of virtues,
Nourishing and growing all good ways,
Cutting away the net of doubt, freeing from the torrent of passion,
Revealing the unsurpassed road of ultimate peace.

When faith is undefiled, the mind is pure;
Obliterating pride, it is the root of reverence,
And the foremost wealth in the treasury of religion,
Being a pure hand to receive the practices.

Faith is generous, the mind not begrudging;
Faith can joyfully enter the Buddha's teaching;
Faith can increase knowledge and virtue;
Faith can assure arrival at enlightenment.

Faith makes the faculties pure, clear and sharp;
The power of faith is strong and indestructible.

Faith can annihilate the root of affliction,
Faith can turn one wholly to the virtues of buddhahood.

Faith has no attachment to objects:
Transcending difficulties, it reaches freedom from trouble.
Faith can go beyond the pathways of demons,
And reveal the unsurpassed road of liberation.

Faith is the unspoiled seed of virtue,
Faith can grow the seed of enlightenment.
Faith can increase supreme knowledge,
Faith can reveal all Buddhas.

Therefore I'll explain in steps practicing in accord:
Faith is most powerful, very difficult to have;
It's like in all worlds having
The wondrous wish-fulfilling pearl.

If one can always faithfully serve the Buddhas,
Then one can keep the precepts and cultivate studies;
If one always keeps the precepts and practices what one learns,
Then one can embody all virtuous qualities.

Self-control can develop the basis of enlightenment,
Study the foundation of cultivating virtues;
Always acting in accord with discipline and study,
One will be praised for excellence by all enlightened ones.

If one always faithfully serves the Buddhas,
Then one can assemble great offerings.

If one can assemble great offerings,
One's faith in Buddha is beyond conception.

If one always faithfully serves the honorable Teaching,
Then one will tirelessly listen to the Buddha's teaching.

If one hears the Buddha's teaching without tiring of it,
One's faith in the Teaching is inconceivable.

If one always faithfully serves the pure Community,
Then one's faith will never regress.

If one's faith never regresses,
One's power of faith is unshakable.

If nothing can shake one's power of faith,
Then one gains purity, clarity, and sharpness of sense.

If one has purity, clarity, and sharpness of sense,
One can avoid bad associates.

If one can avoid bad associates,
Then one can approach good associates.

If one can be with good associates,
Then one can cultivate great goodness.

If one can cultivate great goodness,
One can perfect great causal power.

If one perfects great causal power,
Then one can attain supremely certain understanding.

If one attains supremely certain understanding,
Then one will be protected by the Buddhas.

If one is protected by the Buddhas,
Then one can arouse the will for enlightenment.

If one can arouse the will for enlightenment,
Then one can diligently cultivate the virtues of buddhahood.

If one can diligently cultivate the virtues of buddhahood,
Then he can be born in the family of the enlightened.

If one gets to be born in the family of the enlightened,
Then one can practice skillful liberative techniques.

If one can develop skill in means of liberation well,
Then one can reach purity of the faithful mind.

If one gains purity of the faithful mind,
Then one can increase supreme will.

If one can increase supreme will,
Then one can always practice the transcendent ways,

If one always practices the transcendent ways,
Then one can fulfill the Great Vehicle.

If one can fulfill the Great Vehicle,
Then one can give offerings to Buddhas in the right way.

If one can make offerings to Buddhas in the right way,
Then one can remember Buddha with unwavering mind.

If one can remember Buddha with unwavering mind,
Then one can always see infinite Buddhas.

If one always sees infinite Buddhas,
Then one sees the essence of the enlightened is eternal.

If one sees the essence of the enlightened is eternal,
Then one can know the truth never dies.

If one can know the truth never dies,
Then one attains unhindered powers of elucidation.

If one attains unhindered powers of elucidation,
Then one can expound boundless teachings.

If one can expound boundless teachings,
Then one can compassionately liberate beings.

If one can compassionately liberate beings,
Then one can attain a mind of unshakable compassion.

If one can attain a mind of unshakable compassion,
Then one can appreciate the most profound truth.

If one can appreciate the most profound truth,
Then one can abandon the errors of fabrication.

If one can abandon the errors of fabrication,
Then one can divorce conceit and indulgence.

If one can get rid of conceit and indulgence,
Then one can benefit all beings together.

If one can benefit all beings,
Then one can be in birth-and-death unwearied.

If one can be in birth-and-death unwearied,
Then one can be invincibly brave and strong.

If one can be invincibly brave and strong,
Then one can bring forth great spiritual powers.

If one can bring forth great spiritual powers,
One will know the activities of all sentient beings.

If one knows the activities of all sentient beings,
Then one can mature and perfect living beings.

If one can mature and perfect living beings,
One will attain the knowledge to save all beings.

If one attains the knowledge to save all beings,
Then one can perfect the means of salvation.

If one can perfect the means of salvation,
One then will give beings unlimited benefit.

If one gives beings unlimited benefit,
One will fulfill the techniques of supreme knowledge.

If one fulfills the techniques of supreme knowledge,
One will remain on the heroic unexcelled path.

If one remains on the heroic unexcelled path,
One can crush the power of all demons.

If one can crush the power of all demons,
One can get beyond the realm of the four demons.

If one can get beyond the realm of the four demons,
Then one can reach the stage of nonregression.

If one can reach the stage of nonregression,
One attains profound acceptance of the nonorigination of things.

If one attains deep acceptance of the nonorigination of things,
One will receive the Buddhas' prediction of enlightenment.

If one's enlightenment is foretold by the Buddhas,
Then all the Buddhas will appear in one's presence.

If all the Buddhas appear in one's presence,
One will comprehend the profound, mystic use of spiritual
  powers.

If one comprehends the deep mystic function of spiritual powers,
One will be remembered by all the Buddhas.

If one is remembered by the Buddhas,
Then one will adorn oneself with the qualities of buddhahood.

If one adorns oneself with the qualities of buddhahood,
One will attain a splendid body of felicity.

If one attains a splendid body of felicity,
One's body will be radiant as a mountain of gold.

If one's body is radiant as a mountain of gold,
It will be adorned with the thirty-two marks of distinction.

If one is adorned with the thirty-two marks,
One will be adorned with accompanying refinements.

If one is adorned with the accompanying refinements,
The light of one's aura will be unlimited.

If one's aura light is infinite,
One will be adorned with inconceivable light.

If one is adorned with inconceivable light,
That light will produce lotus blossoms.

If the light produces lotus blossoms,
Innumerable Buddhas will sit on the blossoms,
Appearing everywhere in the ten directions,
Able to pacify all sentient beings.

If able to harmonize beings this way,
One manifests infinite mystical powers.

If one manifests infinite mystical powers,
One dwells in inconceivable lands,
Expounding inconceivable teachings,
Gladdening inconceivably many beings.

If one explains inconceivable teachings
Gladdening inconceivably many beings,
Then with wisdom and power of elucidation
One guides in accord with being's minds.

If one uses wisdom and powers of elucidation
To guide in accord with beings' minds,
Then one will never lose
Action guided by wisdom.

If one never loses
Action guided by wisdom,

Then one's will power will be sovereign,
And one will appear physically in any state of being.

If one's will power attains the freedom
To manifest a body in any state of being,
Then one will be able, when teaching,
To accord with any language, inconceivably.

If one can, when teaching,
Adopt any language, according to the congregation,
Then one will instantly know all
The minds of all sentient beings.

If one can instantly know
The minds of all sentient beings,
One will know afflictions arise from nowhere
And will not sink and drown in birth and death.

If one knows afflictions come from nowhere
And will never drown in birth and death,
Then one attains the body of the essence of truth
And appears in the world by the power of truth.

If one attains the virtuous body of the essence of truth
And appears in the world by the power of truth,
One will attain all the stages and freedoms of enlightenment,
Practice the ways of transcendence and be supremely liberated.

If one attains the stages and freedoms of enlightenment,
Practices the transcendent ways and is supremely liberated,
One will attain the great spiritual powers of the anointed
And abide in the most supreme meditations.

If one attains the great spiritual powers of the anointed
And abides in the most supreme meditations,
Then in the presence of the Buddhas
One will be annointed and ascend to that rank;
One will be anointed with the elixir of deathlessness
By all the Buddhas in the ten directions.

If one is anointed with elixir
By the Buddhas of the ten directions,
One's body will be all-pervasive as space,
Abiding at rest, immovable, filling the ten directions.

If one's body is pervasive as space,
Abiding at rest, immovable, filling all directions,
One's action will be beyond compare,
Unknowable to gods and men.

Enlightening beings practice acts of great compassion,
Vowing to liberate all successfully;
Those who see, hear, listen, accept, or make offerings,
They cause all to attain peace and happiness.

Those great beings have magnificent spiritual powers;
Their eye of reality is always complete, without any lack;
The wonderful practices of virtuous ways and other such paths
Are supreme jewels which they cause to appear.

Just like clusters of diamonds in the ocean,
By their mystic powers they produce many jewels;
Without decrease or increase, and inexhaustible:
Such is the mass of enlightening beings' virtues.

Where there are lands with no Buddha,
There they appear to attain enlightenment;
Where there are lands where the Teaching's unknown,
They expound there the treasury of sublime doctrines.

Without discrimination, without effort,
They reach everywhere in a single instant,
Like the moonlight extending everywhere,
Teaching beings by innumerable techniques.

In the worlds of the ten directions
Constantly they show the way of Buddhahood:
Turning the wheel of the true teaching and entering extinction,
Down to the distribution of their relics.

Sometimes they show the paths of followers or self-enlightened
    ones;
Sometimes they show the universal adornment of full buddhahood;
Thus they open up the teachings of the three vehicles,
Widely liberating beings for infinite eons.

They may manifest the forms of dragon girls or boys,
Or celestial dragons, or titans too,
Down to mahoragas and so on:
They let everyone see according to desire.

Living beings' forms and features are unalike,
Their behaviors and sounds are also countless;
All of these enlightening beings can make appear
By the mystic power of the oceanic reflection meditation.

Beautifully purifying inconceivable lands,
Making offerings to all enlightened ones,
Emanating great light without bound,
They liberate sentient beings without limit too.

Their knowledge and wisdom is independent and inconceivable,
Their speech in explaining truth is unhindered,
Their generosity, self-control, tolerance, energy, and meditation,
Wisdom, skill in means, spiritual powers, and such,
Are all likewise free,
By the power of Buddha's flower garland meditation.

They enter concentration on one atom
And accomplish concentration on all atoms,
And yet that particle doesn't increase:
In one are manifest inconceivable lands.

Of the many lands in that one atom,
Some have Buddhas, some do not;
Some are polluted, some are pure;
Some are large, some are small;
Some are forming, some disintegrating;
Some are upright, some are sideways;
Some are like heat-mirages on a vast plain,
Some are like Indra's net in the heavens.

What in one atom is manifest
Is also manifest in all atoms;
This is the mystic power of concentration and liberation
Of these sages of great renown.

If they want to make offerings to all Buddhas,
They enter into concentration and produce mystic transformations,
Able to reach throughout the universe with one hand
To give offerings to all the enlightened ones.

The most beautiful flowers in all realms,
Perfumes, incense, and priceless jewels:
Such as these all emerge from their hands
To present to the Conquerors under the trees of enlightenment.

Priceless jewel raiment, with mixed perfumes,
Precious banners and canopies, all finely adorned,
With flowers of gold and curtains of jewels:
All of these rain from their palms.

Whatever wonderful things there be in all realms
That may be worthy to offer to the Supreme Honored One,
All shower from their palms, all complete,
And they bring it to the enlightenment trees to offer to the
    Buddhas.

All the artful music of the ten directions:
Bells and drums, harps and lyres, various different kinds,
All played harmoniously, with beautiful tones,
All emerges from the enlightening beings' palms.

All eulogies that be in the ten directions,
Praising the virtues of the enlightened ones,
All of their various wonderful words
Are intoned from within their palms.

The enlightened beings' right hands radiate pure light:
Within the light is fragrant water raining from the sky,
Sprinkling the buddha-lands of the ten directions,
As offerings to all the Lamps that Light the Worlds.

Also they emit wondrous arrays of light beams
Producing countless jewel lotus blossoms;
The colors and forms of the flowers are all superb,
And these they present to the Buddhas.

They also emit flower garlands of light
With all kinds of flowers bunched into drapes,
Scattered all over the lands everywhere
As presents to all the Honored Ones of great virtue.

They also emit lights adorned with perfumes,
Various wonderful scents massed into drapes,
Scattered all throughout the lands everywhere
As presents to the Honored Ones of great virtue.

They also emit lights adorned with powdered incense,
Various incenses collected into drapes,
And distribute them throughout all worlds
As gifts to the Honored Ones of great virtue.

They also emanate lights adorned with raiment,
Various fine robes gathered into drapes,
And distribute them throughout all worlds
As offerings to the Honored Ones of great virtue.

They also emit lights adorned with jewels,
Various beautiful jewels massed into drapes,
And distribute them throughout all worlds
As presents to the Honored Ones.

They also produce lights adorned with lotuses,
Various lotuses assembled into drapes,
And distribute them throughout all worlds
As gifts to the Honored Ones.

They also emit lights necklace adorned;
Various fine necklaces gathered into drapes
They distribute throughout all worlds
To offer to the Honored Ones.

They also emanate lights adorned with pennants
Radiant with multicolored patterns,
Of all kinds, innumerable, all superbly fine:
With these they decorate the buddha-lands.

Canopies adorned with melanges of jewels,
Draped with finely embroidered flags,
And crystal chimes intoning Buddhas' voices :
These they take to offer the enlightened ones.

Their hands producing such inconceivable gifts,
They present them to a Guide,
And do the same to all the Buddhas,
With their great psychic powers of concentration.

Enlightening beings dwell in concentration,
Dealing with beings by various abilities,
All of them guiding by innumerable means,
By the virtuous principles they practice.

Some use the approach of offerings to Buddhas,
Some use the approach of inconceivable generosity,
Some use the approach of austerity and discipline,
Some use the approach of unshakable tolerance,
Some use the approach of ascetic effort,
Some use the approach of tranquil meditation,

Some use the approach of certain, thorough knowledge,
Some use the teaching of practical expedients,
Some use the teachings of the pure abodes and psychic powers,
Some use the approach of the benefits of the means of salvation,
Some use the approach of the adornments of knowledge and
    virtue,
Some use the teaching of conditioning and liberation,
Some use the teachings of faculties, powers, and the right path,
Some use the teaching of followers' liberation,
Some use the teaching of purity of self-awakened ones,
Some use the teaching of the freedom of the Great Vehicle,
Some use the teaching of the miseries of impermanence,
Some use the teaching of no self and no life,
Some use the teaching of impurity and detachment from desire,
Some use the approach of extinctive concentration.

According to the differences in beings' ailments
They all use teaching-medicines to cure them.
According to the inclinations of beings' minds
They all use expedients to satisfy them.

According to the differences in sentient beings' behaviors
They all use adaptive skills to perfect them.
The characteristics of such spiritual powers of concentration
Cannot be fathomed by any gods or men.

Having a wondrous concentration called according to actions,
Enlightening beings abide in this and observe everywhere,
Appearing as appropriate to liberate sentient beings,
Causing them to gladly change according to the truth.

Where there is famine and disaster in the age,
They give means of comfort to all in the world,
Causing them to be satisfied according to their desires,
Creating benefit for all sentient beings.
They may give away fine food and drink,
Sumptuous clothing, garlands of jewels,
And even a royal throne,
To cause those who like generosity to accord with the teaching.

Adorned with flower garlands, anointed with perfume,
With dignified behavior, they liberate beings,
Liked and esteemed by all in the world.
Their appearance and their garb
They adopt as is appropriate to please
And cause those who like form to follow the Path.

With exquisite voices like songs of birds,
Wondrous tones in harmony,
Complete with all kinds of pure voice,
They preach to beings according to their likes.

Eighty-four thousand gates of teaching
Do the Buddhas use to liberate beings:
And according to the different teachings
They use what's appropriate to liberate.

Sentient beings' pains and pleasures, gains and losses, etc.,
Whatever things are done by beings of the world,
Enlightening beings can appear to do the same things,
Whereby to liberate all living beings.

The suffering of all worldly beings
Is deep and wide and boundless like the sea;
Enlightening beings, sharing their tasks, can tolerate it all,
To cause them to benefit and gain peace and happiness.

If any do not know the way to emancipation
And do not seek liberation, to leave turmoil behind,
Enlightening beings show them relinquishment of nation and
    wealth,
Satisfaction in detachment and peace of mind.

If the home is a place of bondage by attachments,
In order to cause sentient beings to all escape trouble
They show home-leaving and attainment of liberation,
Without craving for any pleasures.

Enlightening beings manifest the practice of ten kinds of action
And also practice the ways of great people,
Including the practices of seers and sages,
Because they want to benefit sentient beings.

If there are beings whose life span is immeasurable,
Whose afflictions are slight and pleasures complete,
Enlightening beings, being free in their midst,
Show the suffering of the ills of age, sickness, and death.

In the cases of those with greed, hatred, and ignorance,
The raging fires of these afflictions always blazing,
Enlightening beings manifest aging, sickness, and death for them,
To cause those sentient beings to all be tamed.

The Buddhas' ten powers and fearlessness,
As well as their eighteen unique qualities,
All their countless virtues,
Are manifested to liberate beings.

Knowledge of others' minds, appropriate teaching, and ability to
    appear anywhere
Are all free functions of the enlightened ones;
The great enlightening beings manifest them all,
Able to cause sentient beings to all be tamed.

Enlightening beings' various methods and techniques
Adapt to worldly conditions to liberate beings:
Just like lotus blossoms, to which water does not adhere,
In the same way they are in the world, provoking deep faith.

With extraordinary thoughts and profound talent, as cultural
    kings,
Song and dance, and conversation admired by the masses,
All the various arts and crafts of the world
They manifest, like magicians.

Some become grandees, city chiefs,
Some become merchants, caravan leaders;
Some become physicians and scientists,
Some become kings and ministers.

Some become great trees in the plains,
Some become medicines or jewel mines;
Some become pearls that fulfill all wishes,
Some show the right path to sentient beings.

If they see a world just come into being,
Where the creatures don't yet have the tools for livelihood,
Enlightening beings become craftsmen
And teach them various skills.

They do not make anything that will oppress or afflict living
    beings:
They only explain things that will be of benefit to the world;
Various fields of knowledge, such as incantational arts and medici-
    nal herbs,
And all contained therein they can explain.

The excellent practices of all the sages
Faithfully looked up to by humans and divines,

Such difficult practices and austerities
Enlightening beings can perform according to need.

Some become non-Buddhist mendicants,
Some practice asceticism alone in the forest;
Some go naked, without any clothes,
Being teachers and leaders of such groups.

Some show various practices of wrong livelihood,
Practicing incorrect principles as supreme;
Some manifest the postures of brahmin ascetics,
Becoming leaders of such groups.

Some expose themselves to the heat of fire and sun,
Some practice cults imitating animals,
Some put on filthy clothing and worship fire:
In order to transform such cultists, they become their teachers.

Some make a show of visiting shrines of various deities,
Some make a show of entering the water of the Ganges River,
Some eat roots and fruits, all making a show of these practices,
While always contemplating the truth that transcends them.

Some show themselves kneeling or standing on one foot,
Some lie on thorns or in dust and dirt;
Some lie on pounding stones, seeking release,
And become teachers and leaders of such groups.

Of such followers of heretical paths
They observe the minds and understandings, and do the same
    things;
The ascetic practices they demonstrate, worldlings cannot bear:
They cause them to be tamed after seeing them.

Sentient beings are deluded and accept false teachings;
Sticking to wrong views, they suffer many pains:
For them are expediently taught wonderful principles
To cause them to understand the genuine truth.

The four truths may be explained in local magical language,
Or the four truths may be told in skillful esoteric language,
Or the four truths may be spoken in direct human speech,
Or the four truths may be told in the language of divine mystery;
The four truths are explained through analysis of words,
The four truths are explained through ascertainment of principles,
The four truths are explained skillfully refuting others,

The four truths are explained undisturbed by outsiders;
The four truths may be explained in several languages,
Or they may be explained in all languages.
In whatever languages beings understand
The four truths are explained for them, to liberate them.
All the teachings of all Buddhas
Are thus explained exhaustively,
Knowing the realm of language is inconceivable:
This is called the power of concentration of expounding the truth.

There is a supreme concentration called peace and bliss
Which can universally save and liberate all sentient beings,
Radiating a great light, inconceivable,
Causing those who see it to all be pacified.
This light emanated is called "good manifestation"—
If any sentient beings encounter this light,
It will cause them to benefit, without fail:
By this way they can attain unsurpassed knowledge;
It first shows the Buddhas,
Shows the Teaching, shows the Community, shows the Right
    Path,
And also shows the Buddhas' tombs and images—
By this the light is formed.

It also emits a light called "shining"
Which outshines the lights of all the gods,
Removing all barriers of darkness,
Benefiting all living beings.
This light awakens all sentient beings,
Inducing them to offer lamps to the Buddhas;
Because they present lamps to the Buddhas,
They can become supreme lamps in the world.
Burning oil lamps and butter lamps,
As well as various bright torches,
And lamps of finest jewels with fragrant herbs,
And presenting them to the Buddhas, they attain this light.

It also emits a light called "salvation":
This light can awaken all beings
And cause them to develop great determination
To liberate the living from the sea of desire.
If one can universally produce this determination
To liberate the living from the sea of desire,
Then one can cross over the torrents of afflictions
And lead the way to the sorrowless citadel of freedom.
By building bridges and rafts

Wherever there is water on the roads,
Criticizing fabrication and praising dispassionate calm,
Thereby is this light attained.

It also emanates a light called "annihilating attachment":
This light can awaken all beings,
Causing them to give up objects of desire
And concentrate on the savor of the sublime teaching of liberation.
If one can give up objects of desire
And concentrate on the subtle true savor of liberation,
One can, with the Buddha's rain of sweet dew,
Extinguish all the cravings in the world.
By charitably giving ponds, wells, and springs,
Only seeking the unsurpassed way of enlightenment,
Criticizing desires and praising meditation,
It is possible to produce this light.

It also radiates a light called "joy":
This light can awaken all beings,
Causing them to long for perfect enlightenment
And determine to realize the teacherless path.
Making statues of the Buddha of Great Compassion,
Adorned with all distinguishing marks, sitting on a flower,
And by always praising Buddha's supreme virtues
Can this light thereby be produced.

It also emits a light called "appreciation":
This light can awaken all beings,
Causing their minds to appreciate the Buddhas
As well as their Teaching and Community.
If they always appreciate the Buddhas,
Their teachings and communities,
Then in the congregations of the Buddhas
They'll attain acceptance of the profound truth of the emptiness of
   things.
Enlightening sentient beings without number,
Making them always remember the Buddha, Teaching, and
   Community,
Is whereby this light is attained.

It also emanates a light called "collection of virtues":
This light can awaken all beings,
Inducing them to practice unlimited giving in various forms,
Aspiring thereby to the unexcelled Path.
Establishing great charitable functions without imposing limits,
Satisfying the needs of all who come,

Not letting their hearts feel any lack,
Is whereby this light is made.

It also emits a light called "full knowledge":
This light can awaken all beings,
Causing them to instantly, in one principle,
Understand innumerable teachings.
Analyzing teachings for sentient beings
And determining the real true meaning,
Skillfully expounding the meanings of the teachings, without
    lack,
Is how this light is made.

It also radiates a light called "lamp of wisdom":
This light can awaken all beings
And cause them to know sentient beings are inherently empty and
    at rest,
And that all things have no existence.
Explaining that all things are empty, with no controller, no self,
Like illusions, like flames, like the moon reflected in the water,
And also like dreams or reflected images,
Is how this light is made.

It also emits a light called "mastery of the teachings":
This light can awaken all beings
And cause them to attain inexhaustible mnemonic command
To retain all the teachings of the Buddhas.
Honoring and supporting the holders of the teachings,
Serving and protecting the sages and saints,
Handing on various teachings to beings,
Is how this light is produced.

It also emanates a light called "able to relinquish":
This light can awaken miserly people,
Making them realize all wealth is impermanent,
And enjoy giving, without attachment.
Able to subdue stubborn stinginess,
Understanding wealth is like dreams or floating clouds,
Causing the pure mind of generosity to grow,
Is how this light is attained.

It also radiates a light called "removing heat":
This light can awaken the immoral
And cause them to maintain pure precepts
And determine to realize the teacherless path.
Inducing sentient beings to accept moral precepts

And to purify the practice of virtuous actions
And causing them to be inspired to seek enlightenment
Is how this light is made.

It also emits a light called "adornment of tolerance":
This light can awaken bad-tempered beings,
Causing them to get rid of anger and divorce conceit,
And gladly be tolerant and harmonious.
When the violence of beings is hard to endure,
To be unmoved in mind, for the sake of enlightenment,
Always happily extolling the virtues of tolerance,
Is how this light's produced.

It also radiates a light called "intrepitude":
This light can awaken the lazy,
Causing them always to respect and support
The Buddha, Teaching, and Community, without weariness.
If they always support and respect
The Buddha, the Teaching, and the Community,
They can get beyond the realms of the four demons
And quickly attain unsurpassed enlightenment.
Exhorting sentient beings to progress,
Always diligently supporting the Buddha, Teaching, and Community,
Wholeheartedly guarding the Teaching when it's about to perish,
Is how this light can be made.

It also emanates a light called "tranquility":
This light can awaken the scatter-minded,
Causing them to detach from greed, anger, and folly,
With their minds unstirring and properly stabilized.
Abandoning all bad associates,
Meaningless talk and impure action,
Praising meditation and solitude:
Thus is this light produced.

It also radiates a light called "adornment of wisdom":
This light can awaken the ignorant and deluded,
Causing them to realize the truth and understand conditional origination,
Their faculties, knowledge, and wisdom penetrating thoroughly.
If they can realize the truth and understand conditioned origination,
Their faculties, knowledge, and wisdom penetrating,
They'll attain the state of "sun-lamp" mental focus
With the light of wisdom and perfect the fruit of buddhahood.
Being able to give away country and wealth

For the sake of enlightenment, seeking the right teaching,
Then, having heard it, single-mindedly applying it and explaining
to others,
Is how this light may be made.

It also emits a light called "buddha-wisdom":
This light can awaken all conscious creatures,
Causing them to see innumerable, boundless Buddhas,
Each sitting on jewel lotus flowers.
Praising the Buddhas' powers and liberation,
Telling of the Buddhas' freedom without bound,
Manifesting Buddhas' powers and mystic abilities,
Is how this light may be produced.

It also emanates a light called "fearlessness":
This light shines on those in fear
And causes the speedy annihilation
Of all inhuman harmful things.
Being able to give beings freedom from fear,
Exhorting the ceasing of all affliction and injury encountered,
Rescuing those in danger, the orphaned and the helpless,
Is how this light can be made.

It also radiates a light called "peace":
This light can illumine those who are ill
And cause all pains to be relieved
So all can gain the bliss of right concentration.
Dispensing medicine to cure afflictions,
Anointing with precious life-prolonging perfume,
Giving butter, oil, honey, and milk for nourishment,
Is how this light can be made.

It also emits a light called "seeing Buddha":
This light can awaken those about to die,
Causing them to see any Buddha they think of,
So when their life ends they can be born in that Buddha's pure
    land.
To exhort the dying to remembrance of Buddha,
And show them icons for them to behold,
Causing them to take refuge in the Buddha,
Is how this light can be made.

It also emanates a light called "delight in the Teaching":
This light can awaken all beings,
Causing them to always delight in the true teaching,
Listening to it, expounding it, writing and copying it.

Being able to expound the teaching when it's about to perish,
Causing those who seek the teaching to be fulfilled,
Appreciating the teaching and striving to practice it,
Is how this light can be made.

It also radiates a light called "wondrous sound":
This light can awaken enlightening beings
And cause all voices heard in the world
To be to the hearer the voice of Buddha.
Praising the Buddha out loud,
And presenting music like bells and chimes,
And causing all creatures to hear the sound of Buddha,
Is how this light can be made.

It also emits a light called "dispensing elixir":
This light can awaken all beings,
Causing them to give up all indulgence
And fully practice all virtues.
Explaining the instability of created things
And how they're filled with countless vexations,
Always happily extolling the bliss of dispassionate tranquility
Is how this light can be made.

It also emanates a light called "supreme":
This light awakens all beings,
Causing them to hear from the Buddhas,
The supreme teachings of discipline, concentration, and knowledge.
Always gladly praising all Buddhas'
Supreme self-control, concentration, and knowledge,
In this way seeking the unexcelled Path,
Is how this light is attained.

It also radiates a light called "jewel adornment":
This light can awaken all beings,
Causing them to attain an inexhaustible treasury of jewels
To offer to the enlightened ones.
Presenting various excellent jewels
To the Buddhas and Buddhas' shrines,
Also giving them generously to the poor,
Is how this light can be made.

It also emits a light called "adornment of fragrance":
This light can awaken all beings,
Causing those who sense it to be pleased
And assured of fulfilling enlightened virtues.
Spreading the ground with exquisite incense

To offer to the supreme Guides,
And also therewith making shrines and icons,
Is how this light can be made.

It also emanates a light called "various adornments"
With jewel pennants and canopies beyond number,
Burning incense, scattering flowers, playing music,
Filling cities, inside and out.
Having originally presented the Buddhas with various adornments:
Wonderful dancing and music,
Perfumes, flowers, pennants, canopies, and such,
Is how this light was made.

It also radiates a light called "purification"
Which causes the ground to be flat as a palm.
Adorning the Buddhas' shrines and their surroundings
Is how this light can be made.

It also emits a light called "great clouds"
Which can produce fragrant clouds and rain fragrant water.
Sprinkling the shrines and their precincts
Is how this light is made.

It also emanates a light called "adornments"
Which can cause the naked to be clothed.
Giving fine things to adorn the body
Is how this light is made.

It also radiates a light called "excellent savor"
Which can cause the hungry to get fine food.
Giving various delicacies
Is how this light is made.

It also radiates a light called "great wealth"
Which causes the poor to gain treasure.
Giving unlimited things to the Buddha, Teaching, and Community,
Is how this light can be made.

It also emits a light called "clarity of eye"
Which can cause the blind to see all forms and colors.
Giving lamps to Buddhas or their shrines
Is how this light is made.

It also emanates a light called "clarity of ear"
Which can cause the deaf to be able to hear.

Playing music for Buddhas or at their shrines
Is how this light is made.

It also radiates a light called "clarity of nose"
By which one can smell scents hitherto unnoticed.
Giving incense to the Buddhas and their shrines
Is how this light is made.

It also emits a light called "purity of tongue"
Able to praise the Buddhas in beautiful tones.
Forever getting rid of coarse, unwholesome speech
Is how this light is made.

It also emits a light called "purity of body"
Which causes the impaired to be fully restored.
Prostrating the body to Buddhas and their shrines
Is how this light is made.

It also radiates a light called "purity of mind"
Causing the absent-minded to gain right mindfulness.
Practicing concentration till totally mastered
Is how this light is made.

It also emanates a light called "purity of form"
Causing one to see the inconceivable forms of Buddhas.
Adorning shrines in various beautiful forms
Is how this light is made.

It also emits a light called "purity of sound"
Causing knowledge of the basic emptiness of the nature of sound.
Contemplating the dependent origination of sound, like echoes in
  a valley
Is how this light is made.

It also radiates a light called "purity of scent"
Causing all bad odors to be sweetly purified.
Washing the shrines and enlightenment trees with fragrant water
Is how this light is made.

It also emits a light called "purity of taste"
Which can eliminate all poisons in food.
Continued support of the Buddha, Community, and parents
Is how this light is made.

It also emanates a light called "purity of feeling"
Able to soften what's unpleasant to touch;

Though spears and swords rain from the sky,
It can change them all to flower garlands.
By having in the past spread the roads
With perfumes, scattered flowers, and robes
For the Buddhas to walk upon
Is how such a light was attained.

It also radiates a light called "purity of phenomena"
Able to cause all hair pores to expound
Inconceivable wonderful teachings
So all who hear joyfully understand.
What originates from causes and conditions has no origination;
The reality-body of the Buddhas is not a body;
The nature of things is eternally like space:
By explaining these meanings is there light like this.

Such incomparable gateways of lights
Are innumerable, like sand grains of the Ganges River;
All emerge from the Great Sage's pores,
Each performing a distinct function.
As the lights emanated from a single pore
Are countless, innumerable as the Ganges' sands,
So are those of each and every pore:
This is the power of the Sage's concentration.
According to the lights attained by past practice,
Those who practice likewise, according to their affinities,
Now radiate lights therefore like this:
This is the freedom of the Sage's knowledge.
Those who practiced virtuous deeds like the Buddha
And had appreciation and rejoiced in accord,
Who saw what he did and then did likewise,
They are all able to see this light.
If any practice virtuous deeds themselves
And make offerings to innumerable Buddhas,
Always aspiring to the virtues of buddhahood,
They are awakened by this light.

Just as when those born blind don't see the sun
It is not because there's no sun appearing in the world—
All those who have eyes can clearly see it,
Each doing their work according to their occupations,
So it is with the lights of the Great Being—
Those who have wisdom all can see,
While ordinary folk with false beliefs and low understanding
Cannot perceive these lights at all.

Crystal palaces and chariots
Painted with precious ethereal scents
Are naturally supplied to those with virtue:
They cannot be occupied by the virtueless ones;
So it is with the Great Being's lights:
Those of deep knowledge are all illumined,
While the ignorant, with false beliefs and poor understanding
Are not able to see these lights at all.

If any who hear of the varieties of these lights
Can develop pure and profound faith and resolution,
They'll sunder forever the web of all doubts
And promptly complete the banner of virtue.

There's a supreme concentration that can produce
Arrays of retinues, all free,
Incomparable assemblies of Buddha-children
Of all buddha-lands in the ten directions:
There is a lotus blossom, adorned with lights,
Of equal extent to a billion world galaxy,
On which the enlightening being sits, completely filling it—
This is the mystic power of this concentration.
There are also lotus blossoms surrounding,
As many as atoms in ten lands,
On which the hosts of Buddha-children sit,
Abiding in the spiritual power of this concentration.
Having fully developed good causes in the past
And fully practiced the virtues of buddhahood,
Such people surround the enlightening being,
All joining their palms and gazing tirelessly.
Like the bright moon among the stars
Is the enlightening being in the midst of the congregation.
Such is the practice of the great being
Entering the spiritual power of this concentration.
As manifested in one region
Surrounded by hosts of Buddha-children,
So it is in all regions,
Abiding in this spiritual power of concentration.

There's a supreme concentration called "network of loci"—
The enlightening being dwelling in this teaches widely,
Appearing bodily in all quarters,
Sometimes entering concentration, sometimes emerging:
Sometimes entering right concentration in the East
And emerging from concentration in the West,
Sometimes entering right concentration in the West

And emerging from concentration in the East,
Sometimes entering right concentration in other directions
And emerging from concentration in still others,
Sometimes entry and emergence pervade all ten directions:
This is called the enlightening being's concentration power.

Appearing before and associating with
All the countless Buddhas
In the lands throughout the East
While dwelling in this concentration, silent and unmoving,
And emerging from concentration
In the presence of all the Buddhas
Of the worlds in the West,
Making unlimited offerings to all of them;
Appearing before and associating with
All the countless Buddhas
In the lands throughout the West
While remaining in concentration, silent and unmoving,
And emerging from concentration
In the presence of all the Buddhas
Of the worlds in the East,
Making unlimited offerings to all of them,
Thus does the enlightening being enter
All the worlds of the ten directions,
Sometimes manifesting concentration, silent and unmoving,
Sometimes manifesting respectful offering to the Buddhas.

Entering right concentration in the eye-organ,
Emerging from concentration in the field of form,
Showing the inconceivability of the nature of form,
Unknowable to all gods and men;
Entering right concentration in the field of form
And emerging from concentration in the eye, without disturbing
    the mind,
Explaining the eye is birthless and has no origin,
By nature empty, null, and doing nothing;

Entering right concentration in the ear faculty
And emerging from concentration in the field of sound,
Distinguishing the sounds of all languages,
Unknowable to gods and men,
Entering right concentration in the field of sound,
Emerging from concentration in the ear, the mind undisturbed,
Explaining the ear is birthless and has no origin,
By nature empty, null, and doing nothing;

Entering right concentration in the nose faculty
And emerging from concentration in the field of scent,
Discovering all the most excellent fragrances,
Unknowable to gods and men,
Entering right concentration in the field of scent,
Emerging from concentration in the nose, mind undisturbed,
Explaining the nose is birthless and has no origin,
Empty by nature, null, and doing nothing;

Entering right concentration in the tongue faculty,
Emerging from concentration in the field of flavor,
Discovering all the most exquisite flavors
Unknowable to gods and men,
Entering right concentration in the field of flavor,
Emerging from concentration in the tongue, mind undisturbed,
Explaining the tongue is birthless and has no origin,
By nature, empty, null, and doing nothing;

Entering right concentration in the faculty of the body,
Emerging from concentration in the field of touch,
Able to clearly distinguish all textures,
Unknowable to gods and men,
Entering right concentration in the field of touch,
Emerging from concentration in the body, mind undisturbed,
Explaining the body is birthless and has no origin,
By nature empty, null, and doing nothing;

Entering right concentration in the mental faculty,
Emerging from concentration in the field of phenomena,
Discerning the characteristics of all things,
Unknowable to gods and men,
Entering right concentration in the field of phenomena,
Emerging from concentration in the mental organ, mind undis-
    turbed,
Explaining the mind is birthless and has no origin,
By nature empty, null, and doing nothing;

Entering right concentration in the body of a youth,
Emerging from concentration in the body of an adult,
Entering right concentration in the body of an adult,
Emerging from concentration in the body of one aged,
Entering right concentration in the body of one aged,
Emerging from concentration in the body of a devout woman,
Entering right concentration in the body of a devout woman,
Emerging from concentration in the body of a devout man,
Entering right concentration in the body of a devout man,

Emerging from concentration in the body of a nun,
Entering right concentration in the body of a nun,
Emerging from concentration in the body of a monk,
Entering right concentration in the body of a monk,
Emerging from concentration in the body of a learner or nonlearner,
Entering right concentration in the body of a learner or nonlearner,
Emerging from concentration in the body of a self-enlightened
one,
Entering right concentration in the body of a self-enlightened one,
Emerging from concentration in the body of a fully enlightened
one,
Entering right concentration in the body of an enlightened one,
Emerging from concentration in the body of a celestial being,
Entering right concentration in the body of a celestial being,
Emerging from concentration in the body of a dragon,
Entering right concentration in the body of a dragon,
Emerging from concentration in the body of a yaksha,
Entering right concentration in the body of a yaksha,
Emerging from concentration in the body of a ghost,
Entering right concentration in the body of a ghost,
Emerging from concentration in a hair pore,
Entering right concentration in one hair pore,
Emerging from concentration in all hair pores,
Entering right concentration in all pores,
Emerging from concentration on a hairtip,
Entering right concentration on a hairtip,
Emerging from concentration in an atom,
Entering right concentration in an atom,
Emerging from right concentration in all atoms,
Entering right concentration in all atoms,
Emerging from concentration in diamond ground,
Entering right concentration in diamond ground,
Emerging from concentration on a crystal tree,
Entering right concentration on a crystal tree,
Emerging from concentration in Buddha's aura,
Entering right concentration in Buddha's aura,
Emerging from concentration in rivers and seas,
Entering right concentration in rivers and seas,
Emerging from concentration in the element fire,
Entering right concentration in the element fire,
Emerging from concentration in the wind, mind undisturbed,
Entering right concentration in the element wind,
Emerging from concentration in the element earth,
Entering right concentration in the element earth,
Emerging from concentration in the mansion of heaven,
Entering right concentration in the mansion of heaven,

Emerging from concentration in space, mind undisturbed:
This is called the inconceivable freedom of concentration
Of the one with infinite virtues,
Which all the Buddhas of the ten directions
Could not thoroughly expound even in countless eons.

All the enlightened ones together explain
That the consequences of beings' actions are unthinkably many.
The metamorphic emanations of the dragons, the masteries of the
    Buddhas,
And the spiritual powers of enlightening beings are also inconceiv-
    able.
Though one try to illustrate this by metaphor,
After all there is no metaphor that can be likened to this;
However, people of wisdom and intelligence
Understand their meaning by means of similitudes.

Buddha's followers' minds dwell in the eight liberations
And the transformations they display are all freely done:
They can manifest many bodies by one body
And can make one body of many bodies.
They can enter fire-concentration in space,
Walking, standing, sitting, and lying, all in the sky,
Producing water from the upper body and fire from the lower,
Or fire from the upper body and water from the lower.
In this way, in the moment of one thought,
They can transform freely in innumerable ways.
They do not fully have great compassion
And do not seek buddhahood for the sake of all beings,
Yet still they can manifest such inconceivable things—
How much more is the power of the great benefactors, enlighten-
    ing beings:
Like sun and moon traveling through space,
Their lights' reflections appearing in all places,
In springs, ponds, reservoirs, and water in vessels,
In jewellike rivers and seas—they reflect everywhere:
So it is with the forms of enlightening beings—
They appear everywhere, inconceivably;
This is all the freedom of concentration,
Which only the enlightened can completely realize.
Like the images of four armies in the ocean water,
Each distinct, not merging or mixing,
Their swords, spears, bows and arrows, are many and diverse,
Their armor, helmets, and chariots are not the same:
Whatever the differences in the forms they have,

All are reflected in the water,
Yet the water itself does not discriminiate—
The concentration of enlightening beings is also like this.

In the ocean are spirits called "good at sound"
Whose voices universally adapt to all creatures of the sea,
And who completely understand all their languages
And make them all joyful and happy:
Those spirits have greed, malice, and folly,
Yet they can still understand all sounds—
How much more the enlightening beings' power of mental
    command—
Can they not cause all beings joy?

There is a woman named Explanatory Ability
Who was born through her parents' supplication to heaven:
If one can divorce evil and delight in truth,
One can enter her body and engender wondrous eloquence.
She still has desire, aversion, and ignorance,
Yet can bestow elucidating powers in accord with practice—
How much the more so can enlightening beings full of wisdom
Bestow benefits on sentient beings.

Like a magician who knows the ways of magic
Can produce any number of various things,
Make an instant seem a day, a month, a year,
Produce a city rich and very happy;
The magician has greed, anger, and ignorance still,
Yet can delight the world with magic ability—
How much the more so can the power of meditation and liberation
Bring all creatures joy.

When the gods and titans fought,
The titans lost and ran away;
Their armaments, chariots, and soldiers
They hid at once where none could see.
They have greed, malice, and folly,
Yet are still capable of inconceivable transformations;
How much the more can dwelling in fearlessness of supernormal
    powers
Now manifest independent freedom.

Indra, king of gods, has a royal elephant—
When it knows the king wants to go somewhere,
It transforms itself, creating thirty-three heads,
Each head having six tusks,

With the waters of seven ponds on each tusk,
Clean and fragrant, pure, still and full;
In the water of each pure pond
Are seven lotuses in beautiful array;
On each of those adorning lotus blossoms
Are seven celestial jadelike maidens
Skillfully dancing and playing music
Entertaining Indra, king of gods.
That elephant can also lose its original form
And transform its body to be like that of the gods,
Completely the same in bearing and action—
It has this miraculous power of transformation.
It still has greed, anger, and ignorance,
Yet nonetheless can manifest such miraculous powers—
How much the more is one replete with skill and knowledge
Free in all states of concentration.

Like the metamorphosed phantom body of a titan
Walking on the diamond stratum, standing in the ocean,
The water at the deepest part of the ocean only reaching its
    midriff
While its head is level with the soaring polar mountain—
It has greed, anger, and ignorance,
Yet still can display such great wonders—
How much the more does the demon-quelling Lamp that Lights
    the World
Have awesome mystic powers at his command.

When the gods and the titans warred
King Indra's magic power was inconceivable—
However many the troops of titans were,
Indra manifested as many bodies to oppose them.
The titans had the idea
"Indra is coming at us
And will surely capture and bind us,"
So they were all anxious and scared.
Indra manifested a body with a thousand eyes,
Holding thunderbolts, throwing flames,
Armored, armed, and awesomely majestic;
The titans, seeing this, all retreated.
Indra, with the power of a little virtue
Still could defeat a great enemy—
How much more is the savior of all
Replete with virtues, all at his command.

In the heaven of happiness is a celestial drum
Produced as a consequence of deeds of the gods;
It knows when the gods are indulging themselves,
And spontaneously produces this sound in the sky:
"All objects of desire are transient,
Like bubbles, foam—empty, unreal;
All existents are like dreams, like mirages,
Like floating clouds, the moon in the water.
Indulgence is an enemy, a torment and a pain—
It's not the immortal way, but the path of birth and death.
Any who act indulgently
Will enter the mouth of the shark of death.
As the root of all the miseries in the world,
All wise people shun it.
The qualities of objects of desire are perishable—
You should take pleasure in what's real and true."
When the gods of the thirty-three heavens hear this sound,
They all go up into the hall of good teaching
And Indra preaches for them the subtle teaching,
Making them docile and tranquil, removing greed and craving.
That sound is formless and cannot be seen,
Yet it can benefit the celestial beings—
How much the more, manifesting bodies adapting to inclinations,
Can enlightening beings rescue and liberate the living.

When the gods and titans warred,
By the superior power of the gods' virtue
The celestial drum sounded, telling the hosts,
"You should not worry or fear,"
And the gods, hearing this declaration,
Were rid of fear and increased in strength.
Then the titans' hearts trembled with fright
And their troops all retreated and fled.
The wonderful ambrosial concentration is like that heavenly drum:
It always produces the sound of dispassion, conquering demons;
Great compassion mercifully rescues all,
Causing all beings to end their afflictions.

Indra has intercourse with all the goddesses,
Ninety-two trillion in number,
Causing each to think to herself
That the king is amusing her alone.
As he responds to all the goddesses' bodies,
So it is in the hall of good teaching—
He can instantly manifest supernatural powers
And go to everyone to preach to them.

Indra, who has greed, anger, and ignorance,
Can cause all in his retinue to be happy—
How much the more is skillful spiritual power
Able to cause all to rejoice.

The king of the heaven of access to others' enjoyments
Has sovereignty in the realm of desire;
With habitual confusion for a snare,
He captures and binds all ordinary folk.
He has greed, anger, and ignorance,
Yet has mastery over sentient beings—
How much the more is the possessor of the ten independent powers
Able to cause beings to act in accord.

The great brahma king of the billion world galaxy
Can appear in all the abodes
Of the brahma gods and sit with them,
Speaking in the subtle, pure brahma voice.
He abides in the worldly brahma path,
Yet still commands concentration and supernatural powers—
How much the more so does the transcender of the world,
    unexcelled,
Have mastery of meditation and liberation.

The god Maheshavara's knowledge is sovereign:
When the dragons of the sea shower rain,
He can count distinctly every drop,
Discerning them all in a single instant:
If one has diligently practiced and learned for countless eons
And attained the supreme knowledge of enlightenment,
How would such a one not be able
To instantly know the minds of all beings?

The consequences of sentient beings' actions are inconceivably
    many,
Being as a great wind power, producing the worlds:
Vast oceans, mountains, celestial palaces,
Radiance of jewels, and all sorts of things;
They also can produce clouds and bring rain,
And can disperse and dissolve all cloudiness,
And can ripen all grains,
And comfort the living.
The wind cannot learn transcendent wisdom,
Or learn the qualities of buddhahood,
Yet still can perform inconceivable deeds—
How much the more so one who fulfills all vows.

The various voices of men and women,
The calls of birds and beasts,
The sounds of oceans, rivers, and thunder,
Can all delight sentient beings' minds—
How much the more one who knows the nature of sound is like echoes,
Who attains to unhindered, wonderful eloquence,
And teaches the truth as appropriate to each,
Is able to bring joy to the creatures of the world.

The ocean has a special extraordinary quality—
It can be an equal reflector of all;
Sentient beings, precious things, rivers and streams—
All it contains, prohibiting none.
One with inexhaustible meditation, concentration, and liberation,
Can also be a seal of equanimity, equally reflecting, like this;
The wonderful practices of virtue and knowledge
This one cultivates all without tiring.
When the dragon kings of the ocean roam about,
They are free wherever they may be,
Producing clouds covering the earth,
Those clouds of various decorative colors:
In the sixth heaven, of access to others' enjoyments,
The clouds are the color of gold;
In the heaven of enjoyment of emanations they're the color of ruddy pearls;
In the heaven of happiness, they're the color of frost and snow;
In the heaven of timely portion they're the color of lapis lazuli;
In the heaven of thirty-three celestial realms they're opal colored;
In the heaven of the four kings they're crystal colored;
Over the oceans, they're diamond colored;
Among kinnaras they're incense colored;
In the dragons' abodes they're lotus colored;
Where yakshas live, the color of white geese;
Among titans, the color of mountain rocks;
In the region of Uttara, the color of golden flames;
In Jambudvipa, the color of sapphire;
In the other continents, their adornments are mixed—
These are given according to the likes of the creatures.

Also in the heaven of access to others' enjoyments
Lightning in the clouds shines like sunlight;
In the heaven of enjoyment of emanations, it's like moonlight;
In the heaven of happiness, like rose gold;
In the timely portion heaven, it's the color of jadelike snow;
In the thirty-threefold heaven, the color of golden flames;

In the four kings' heaven, the color of all jewels;
In the ocean, the color of red pearls;
In the realm of the kinnaras, the color of lapis lazuli;
In the abode of dragons, the colors of a mine of jewels;
Where the yakshas live, the color of crystal;
Among the titans, the color of onyx;
In the realm of Uttara, the color of fiery pearls;
In Jambudvipa, the color of sapphires;
In the other continents, the embellishments are mixed—
As are the colors of the clouds, so is the lightning.

In the heaven of access to others' enjoyments, thunder is like the
    voice of Brahma;
In the heaven of enjoyment of emanations, it's like the sound of
    great drums;
In the heaven of happiness it's like the sound of singing;
In the heaven of timely portion it's like the voices of goddesses;
In the heaven of thirty-three celestial regions
It's like the various sounds of kinnaras;
In the heaven of the four world-guarding kings
It's like the sounds produced by grandharvas;
In the ocean it sounds like mountains crashing together;
Among the kinnaras, it's the sound of pipes,
In the castles of the dragons, it sounds like the call of kalavinka
    birds;
In the yakshas' abode it's like the voices of dragon maidens;
Among the titans, it sounds like a celestial drum;
Among humans, it's like the sound of the surf.

In the heaven of free access to others' enjoyments rain perfumes
With various mixed flowers as embellishments;
In the heaven of enjoyment of emanations rain cotton flowers,
Mandarava flowers, and rich perfumes;
In the heaven of happiness rain crystals
Complete with adornments of various jewels;
The jewels in the topknots there are like moonlight,
The exquisite clothes worn there are the color of gold;
In the heaven of time rain banners and canopies,
Garlands, perfumes, and beautiful decorations,
As well as excellent raiment the color of pearl
And various kinds of music;
In the heaven of thirty-three realms rain wish-fulfilling jewels,
Solid black aloes and sandalwood fragrance,
Various perfumes of heavenly flowers
Raining down intermingled with each other;
In the citadels of the world guardians rain delicacies

With color, aroma, and flavor with strengthening power;
It also rains inconceivable beautiful jewels,
All made by the dragon kings.
Also in the oceans
It rains increasingly, like a whirl,
And rains inexhaustible treasuries of jewels,
And rains various jewel ornaments as well.
In the world of kinnaras it rains necklaces,
Lotuses of many colors, robes, and jewels,
Flowers that grow in the rains, and golden colored flowers,
With various kinds of music all included therein.
In the castles of the dragon kings rain ruddy pearls;
Among the titans it rains weapons
Conquering all enemies.
In the continent Uttara it rains necklaces
And also rains innumerable exquisite flowers;
In the continents Purvavideha and Aparagodaniya
It rains various ornamental articles;
In the continent Jambudvipa it rains pure water,
Fine, refreshing, always at appropriate times,
Nourishing flowers, fruits, and herbs,
Ripening all the crops.
Innumerable such beautiful adornments,
Various clouds, lightning, thunder, and rain,
The dragon kings can freely make
Without moving their bodies, without discrimination
In their world, the ocean, they dwell,
Yet can manifest this inconceivable power—
How much the more those who enter the ocean of truth and
    embody virtue
Can produce great mystical transformations.

The doors of liberation of the enlightening beings
Cannot be revealed by any similes,
But I have, with these metaphors,
Said something of their free power.

Foremost knowledge, vast wisdom,
True knowledge, boundless wisdom,
Extraordinary wisdom, supreme wisdom—
Such a teaching has now been explained.
This teaching is rare and most extraordinary;
If people who have heard it can accept,
Can believe, absorb, praise, and explain it,
This accomplishment is to be considered most difficult.
Of all the ordinary people in the world

It's hard to find one with faith in this teaching.
If any diligently cultivate pure virtues,
By the power of past cause they can believe.
Among the creatures of all worlds
Are few who want to seek the vehicle of Buddha's followers;
Those who seek solitary enlightenment are even fewer,
And those who aim for the Great Vehicle are very hard to find.
But striving for the Great Vehicle is still easy
Compared to the greater difficulty of believing this teaching.
Even more difficult it is to retain, recite, and explain it for others,
To practice according to the teaching and truly understand it.
To hold a galaxy on one's head
Without moving, for one eon,
Is not to be considered difficult
Compared to believing this teaching.
To pick up ten buddha-lands in the hand
And stand in space through an eon
Is not to be considered hard
Compared to believing this teaching.
If one provides comforts for an eon
To the homes of beings numerous as atoms in ten lands,
His merit is not to be considered supreme—
One who believes this teaching is most excellent.
Even spending an eon serving
Buddhas as many as atoms in ten lands,
One's merit will be greater, supreme,
If one can recite and hold this book.

When the enlightening being Chief in Goodness had spoken these verses, the worlds in the ten directions quaked in six ways, the palace of demons was shrouded, the realms of ill ceased; the Buddhas of the ten directions appeared before him and each patted him on the head with his right hand and praised him, saying, "Excellent! You incisively explain this teaching, and we all accordingly rejoice."

End of the second assembly.

BOOK THIRTEEN

Ascent to the Peak of Mount Sumeru

THEN, BY THE SPIRITUAL POWER of the Enlightened One, in the Jambudvipa continent of all worlds in the ten directions there was seen the Enlightened One sitting under a tree, in each place with enlightening beings receiving the Buddha's spiritual power and expounding the teaching, all thinking they were at all times facing the Buddha in person. At that time the Buddha, without leaving the foot of the enlightenment tree, ascended Mount Sumeru and headed for the palace of Indra; then Indra, king of gods, in front of the Hall of Surpassing Wonder, seeing Buddha coming from afar, adorned this palace by means of his supernatural power. He put in it a lion throne of banks of radiant lights, all made of exquisite jewels, with ten thousand levels of dazzling ornaments and ten thousand nets of gold covering it, ten thousand kinds of curtains and ten thousand levels of canopies arrayed all around, with ten thousand embroidered silks as curtain sashes, ten thousand strings of pearls joined together, and ten thousand robes spread on the throne. Ten thousand godlings and ten thousand Brahma kings surrounded it in front and behind, while ten thousand light beams illumined it.

Then Indra, having set up this throne for the Enlightened One, bowed and joined his palms, reverently facing the Buddha, and said, "Welcome, World Honored One; welcome, Blissful One; welcome, Realized One, Perfectly Enlightened One: please be so compassionate as to sojourn in this palace." Then the Buddha, accepting his invitation, entered the Hall of Surpassing Wonder. This also took place in the same way in all the worlds of the ten directions. Then, due to the Buddha's spiritual power, all the music in the palaces spontaneously ceased, and Indra recalled to himself how he had planted roots of goodness with Buddhas of the past; he spoke in verse, saying,

> Kashyapa Buddha had great compassion,
> Supreme among the auspicious.

That Buddha has come into this palace,
Hence this place is most auspicious.

Kanakamuni's vision was unobstructd,
Supreme among the auspicious.
That Buddha has come into this palace,
Hence this place is most auspicious.

Krakucchanda was like a mountain of gold,
Supreme among the auspicious.
That Buddha has come into this palace,
Hence this place is most auspicious.

Vishvabhu Buddha was undefiled,
Supreme among the auspicious.
That Buddha has come into this palace,
Hence this place is most auspicious.

Shikhin Buddha was free from discrimination,
Supreme among the auspicious.
That Buddha has come into this palace,
Hence this place is most auspicious.

Vipashin Buddha was like a full moon,
Supreme among the auspicious.
That Buddha has come into this palace,
Hence this place is most auspicious.

Pushya clearly realized the ultimate truth,
Supreme among the auspicious.
That Buddha has come into this palace,
Hence this place is most auspicious.

Tishya Buddha's eloquence was unhindered,
Supreme among the auspicious.
That Buddha has come into this palace,
Hence this place is most auspicious.

Padma Buddha was utterly pure,
Supreme among the auspicious.
That Buddha has come into this palace,
Hence this place is most auspicious.

Dipankara Buddha was effulgent,
Supreme among the auspicious.
That Buddha has come into this palace,
Hence this place is most auspicious.

As in this world the king of the thirty-threefold heaven, Indra, by the spiritual power of the Buddha, extolled the virtues of ten Buddhas, so did all the Indras in the worlds of the ten directions also praise the Buddhas' virtues. Then the World Honored One entered the Hall of Surpassing Wonder and sat crosslegged: this hall suddenly became vastly spacious, like the dwelling places of all the celestial hosts. The same thing happened in all worlds in the ten directions.

BOOK FOURTEEN

Eulogies on Mount Sumeru

THEN, DUE TO THE SPIRITUAL POWER of the Buddha, there came and gathered great enlightening beings from each of the ten directions, each accompanied by as many enlightening beings as atoms in a buddha-land, coming from worlds far away, beyond lands as numerous as atoms in a hundred buddha-lands. Their names were Wisdom of Truth, Total Wisdom, Supreme Wisdom, Virtuous Wisdom, Vigorous Wisdom, Good Wisdom, Knowing Wisdom, True Wisdom, Unexcelled Wisdom, and Stable Wisdom. The worlds they came from were called Indra Flower, Red Lotus, Jewel Flower, Blue Lotus, Diamond Flower, Fragrant Flower, Delightful Flower, Rosy Dawn Flower, Adorning Flower, and Space Flower. They had each cultivated pure practice with Buddhas; the Buddhas were called Extraordinary Moon, Infinite Moon, Imperturbable Moon, Wind Moon, Water Moon, Liberation Moon, Unexcelled Moon, Constellation Moon, Pure Moon, Comprehending Moon. When the enlightening beings had reached the Buddha, they prostrated themselves at the Buddha's feet, and then magically produced luminous lion seats in the direction from which they had come. In the same way as the enlightening beings gathered atop Mount Sumeru in this world, so it was in all worlds; their names, worlds, and the names of their Buddhas were all like this.

At that juncture the Buddha emitted a hundred thousand billion light beams of sublime hue from the toes of his feet, illumining all the worlds in the ten directions, so that the Buddhas and congregations in the palaces of the Indras atop Mt. Sumerus were all revealed. Then the enlightening being Wisdom of Truth, infused with spiritual power from the Buddha, looked over the ten directions and said in verse,

> Buddha emits a pure light
> Showing all the Guides of the worlds
> Sojourning in the Halls of Wonder
> On the peaks of Mt. Sumerus.

All of the kings of gods
Invited the Buddhas into the palace,
All with ten beautiful verses
Praising the enlightened ones.

Among those great assemblies
The groups of enlightening beings
Have come from the ten directions
And sit calmly on the seats they made.

The enlightening beings in those congregations
All have the same names as we
And the names of the lands they come from
Are also the same as ours.

The Buddhas of their own lands
Also have the same names as ours;
Each one has, with a Buddha,
Purely cultivated unexcelled practices.

Buddha-children, you should observe
The Buddha's power of freedom:
In all the Jambudvipas
All think the Buddha's there.

We now see the Buddha
On top of Sumeru:
It's the same in the ten directions,
By the Buddha's power of freedom.

In each world
They determine to seek the Buddha-way,
And based on such a vow
Practice enlightening deeds.

Buddha, with various bodies,
Travels throughout the worlds,
Unhindered in the cosmos,
Beyond the ken of anyone.

The light of his wisdom always shines everywhere,
Removing all the darkness of the world;
It has no compare at all:
How can it be comprehended?

Then the enlightening being Total Wisdom, infused with the power of the Buddha, looked over the ten directions and said in verse,

> Even if one always looked at Buddha
> For a hundred thousand eons,
> Not according to the absolute truth
> But looking at the savior of the world,
> Such a person is grasping appearances
> And increasing the web of ignorance and delusion,
> Bound in the prison of birth and death,
> Blind, unable to see the Buddha.

> Observing all things
> To be without inherent existence,
> Whatever their appearances of origin and disappearance,
> Being just provisional descriptions,
> All things are unborn,
> All things are imperishable:
> To one who can understand this
> The Buddha will always be manifest.

> The nature of things is fundamentally empty and null,
> With no grasping and no vision.
> The emptiness of inherent nature is Buddha;
> It cannot be assessed in thought.
> If one knows the inherent nature
> Of all things is like this,
> This person will not be affected
> By any afflictions.

> Ordinary people seeing things
> Just pursue the forms
> And don't realize things are formless:
> Because of this they don't see Buddha.

> The Sage is detached from the realms of time,
> Replete with the marks of greatness,
> Dwelling in nondwelling,
> Omnipresent without moving.

> I observe all things
> And clearly understand them;
> Now I see the Buddha
> With certainty, free from doubt.

Wisdom of Truth has already explained
The real nature of the Enlightened;
From him I have understood
That enlightenment's inconceivable.

Then the enlightening being Supreme Wisdom, receiving power
from the Buddha, looked over the ten directions and said in verse,

The Enlightened One's great wisdom
Is rare, beyond compare;
All beings in the worlds
Cannot reach it in their thoughts.

Ordinary people's deluded views
Grasp forms and are not veritable.
Buddha is beyond all forms,
So not within their view.

The deluded and unknowing
Wrongly grasp the forms of the five clusters,
Not understanding their true nature;
Such people don't see Buddha.

Knowing that all things
Have no inherent being of their own,
Understanding the nature of things this way
One will see Vairocana.

Caused by the preceding five clusters,
Succeeding clusters arise in continuum;
Comprehending this nature,
One sees Buddha, inconceivable.

Just like a jewel in the dark
Cannot be seen if there is no lamp,
With no one to explain Buddha's teaching
Even the intelligent cannot comprehend it.

And like an eye with cataracts
Cannot see pure beautiful colors,
So too the impure mind
Cannot see the Buddha's teaching.

And as the bright clear sun
Cannot be seen by the blind,
Those who have no wisdom
Can never see the Buddhas.

If one can remove the eye's cataracts
And abandon the concept of form
And not see in terms of things,
Then one can see the Buddha.

Total Wisdom has explained
The enlightenment of the Buddhas;
I, having learned from him,
Have gotten to see Vairocana.

Then the enlightening being Virtuous Wisdom, imbued with power
from the Buddha, looked over the ten directions and said in verse,

Things have no true reality;
Because of wrongly grasping them as real
Do ordinary people therefore
Revolve in the prison of birth and death.

Things expressed by words
Those of lesser wisdom wrongly discriminiate
And therefore create barriers
And don't comprehend their own minds.

If one doesn't comprehend one's own mind,
How can one know the right path?
Based on misconstrued intellect
They increase all evils.

Not seeing all things are empty,
Always suffering the pains of birth and death,
This is because such people
Cannot yet have the pure objective eye.

In the past I experienced suffering
Because I didn't see Buddha.
So one should clarify the eye of reality
And see what is to be seen.

If one can see the Buddha,
One's mind will have no grasping;
Such a person can then perceive
Truth as the Buddha knows it.

If one can see Buddha's real teaching,
One is said to have great knowledge;
This person has pure eyes
And can see into the world.

No view is seeing
Which can see all things;
If one has any views about things,
This is not seeing anything.

The nature of all things
Has no origin and no end.
How wonderful the Great Guide:
Awakened himself, he can awaken others.

Supreme Wisdom has explained
The truth realized by the Buddhas;
We, having learned from him,
Can know the Buddha's true nature.

Then the enlightening being Vigorous Wisdom, receiving power from
the Buddha, looked over the ten directions and said in verse,

If one dwells on discrimination,
One ruins the eye of purity;
Ignorant, false views increase,
And one never sees the Buddha.

If one can understand falsehood
As it is, without delusion,
And know the basis of delusion is itself reality,
One's perception of Buddha will be pure.

If there are views, this is defilement;
This is not yet to be considered seeing.
By dismissing all views
Can one thus see Buddha.

Things spoken of in conventional terms
People wrongly conceptualize;
Knowing the world is all birthless:
This is seeing the world.

If one sees seeing the world,
This seeing is a feature of the world;
In reality they're equal, no different:
This is called true insight.

If one sees they're equal, no different,
One won't discriminate among things.
Such vision is free from delusions:
Without indulgence, it's free.

All the different things
Pointed out by the Buddhas
Are impossible to apprehend
Because their nature's pure.

The nature of things is fundamentally pure;
Like space, it has no marks.
Nothing at all can explain it:
This do the wise observe.

Divorcing the concept of things,
Not indulging in anything,
And not even cultivating this,
One can see the great Sage.

As Virtuous Wisdom explained,
This is called one who sees Buddha;
All the actions there be
Are all inherently nil.

Then the enlightening being Good Wisdom, infused with Buddha's power, looked over the ten directions and said in verse,

Extraordinary, the great beings,
The countless enlightened ones
Are free from taint, their minds are free;
Self-liberated, they can liberate others.

I see the Lamps of the Worlds
As they are, without delusion,
As one who has accumulated knowledge
Over eons can see.

The acts of ordinary people
All soon pass away;
Their nature is like space,
So said to be without end.

When the wise speak of endlessness,
This is still not saying anything;
Because inherent nature is endless,
It can have an inconceivable end.

In the endlessness spoken of
There are no beings to be found;
Knowing the nature of things is thus,
One will see the Honored One.

No view is called seeing,
The birthless is called beings;
Whether views or beings,
Knowing they've no substantial nature,
The seer dismisses entirely
The subject and object of seeing;
Not destroying reality,
This person knows the Buddha.

If one knows the Buddha
And the truth the Buddha tells,
One can illumine the world
Like Buddha Vairocana does.

The truly enlightened point out well
The pure road of one truth;
The great being Vigorous Wisdom
Expounds innumerable teachings:
Whether of existence or nonexistence,
His conceptions are all removed:
Thus he can see the Buddha
And abide in reality.

Then the enlightening being Knowing Wisdom, imbued with power from the Buddha, looked over the ten directions and said in verse,

Hearing the supreme teaching,
I produce the light of wisdom
Illumining all worlds everywhere,
Seeing all the Buddhas.

Herein there's not the slightest thing:
Only provisional names;
Those who think there's self and person
Enter a dangerous path due to this.

People who grasp and cling
Think the body really exists:
The Buddha is not something grasped,
So they never get to see.

These people lack the eye of wisdom
And cannot see the Buddha,
Circulating in the sea of birth and death
Through uncountable eons.

Contention is called birth-and-death,
Noncontention is nirvana:
Birth-and-death and nirvana
Both cannot be grasped.

If one pursues provisional names
And grasp these two things
One is not in accord with reality
And doesn't know the Sage's subtle path.

If one produces such conceptions—
"This is Buddha, this is supreme"—
One is deluded—this is not real truth;
Thus one cannot see true awakening.

If one can know this real body's
Quiescent character of true thusness,
One can see the truly enlightened
Transcending the path of speech.

Things expressed in words
Cannot disclose the character of reality;
Only through equanimity can one see
Things, including the Buddha.

The Truly Enlightened in the past
The future, and the present,
Forever sever the root of discriminiation—
That's why they're called Buddha.

Then the enlightening being True Wisdom, empowered by the Buddha, looked over the ten directions and said in verse.

I'd rather suffer the pains of hell
While able to hear the name of Buddha
Than to experience boundless pleasure
Without hearing the name of Buddha.

The reason for suffering in the past
Over countless eons
Revolving within birth and death
Is due to not hearing the name of Buddha.
Not deluded about things,
Realizing them as they truly are,
Detached from all compounded forms:
This is called unsurpassed awakening.

The present is not compounded,
Nor are the past and future;
All things have no signs:
This is the real body of Buddha.

If one can see this way
The profound truth of things,
Then one can see all Buddhas'
Reality-body in its true aspect.

Seeing what's true as true
And what's not true as untrue:
Such ultimate understanding
Is the reason for the name of Buddha.

Buddha's truth cannot be perceived;
Realizing this is called perceiving truth.
The Buddhas practice this way:
Nothing can be grasped.

Knowing they are many because one
And one because many,

Realize all things have no basis
And only arise from compounding.

There is no creator or created:
They only arise from habitual conceptions.
How can we know it is so?
Because other than this naught is.

All things have no abode:
No definite locus can be found;
The Buddhas abide in this,
Ultimately unwavering.

Then the enlightening being Unexcelled Wisdom, receiving Buddha's power, looked over the ten directions and said in verse,

The unexcelled great beings
Dismiss the concept of creatures.
None can surpasss them,
That's why they're called unexcelled.

The sphere attained by the Buddhas
Has no fabrication and no discrimination;
The gross has no existence,
And neither does the fine.

The realms accessible to Buddhas
Are innumerable therein;
True awareness is detached from numbers:
This is the Buddhas' true teaching.

Buddha's light shines everywhere,
Destroying all darkness and gloom;
This light neither has radiance
Nor does not have radiance.

It has no attachment to things,
No thought and no defilement,
No abode and no location,
And does not destroy the nature of things.

Herein there is no dualism,
Yet neither is there oneness;

One who sees well with great knowledge
Skillfully abides according to truth.

No mean and no duality,
And not even any nonduality:
All in the worlds is void—
This is the vision of the Buddhas.

People with no awakened understanding
Buddha makes abide in the truth.
All things have no abode—
Understanding this, one sees one's own body
Is not a body, yet said to be so;
Is not born yet manifests birth:
No body and no view—
This is the unexcelled Buddha-body.
Thus has True Wisdom explained
The nature of Buddhas' subtle teaching;
Any who hear this teaching
Will attain the pure eye.

Then the enlightening being Stable Wisdom, empowered by the Buddha, looked over the ten directions and said in verse,

How grand, the Great Light,
The vigorous Unsurpassed Hero,
Who appears in the world
To help the confused.

The Buddha observes all beings
With a heart of great compassion,
Seeing them in the three realms of existence
Suffering over and over.

Except for the Truly Enlightened,
The honored Guide, full of virtue,
There is none who can rescue
All human and heavenly beings.

If the Buddhas and enlightening beings
Did not appear in the world,
There would not be a single creature
Who could have peace and ease.

The Buddha, rightly awakened,
As well as the sages and saints,
Appear in the world,
Able to bestow happiness on beings.

If someone sees the Buddha,
That is gaining great benefit;
Hearing the name Buddha and developing faith
Is a monument in the world.

We see the World Honored Ones
And consider it a great boon;
Hearing such a wonderful teaching,
We all shall attain enlightenment.

The enlightening beings, in the past,
By the spiritual power of Buddha,
Attained the pure eye of wisdom
And perceived the realms of the Buddhas.

Now we see Vairocana
And grow doubly in pure faith.
Buddha's knowledge is boundless
And cannot be fully explained.

Even if the enlightening beings
Such as Supreme Wisdom, and I, Stable Wisdom,
Were to speak for countless eons,
We could not tell it all.

BOOK FIFTEEN

The Ten Abodes

THEN THE ENLIGHTENING BEING Truth Wisdom, empowered by the Buddha, entered into the concentration of infinite techniques of enlightening beings; by the power of concentration there appeared before him Buddhas as numerous as atoms in a thousand buddha-fields from each of the ten directions beyond as many worlds as atoms in a thousand buddha-fields: all of those Buddhas had the same name, Truth Wisdom. They said to the enlightening being Truth Wisdom, "Excellent! Excellent, good man, that you are able to enter this enlightening being's concentration of infinite techniques. Good man, in each of the ten directions as many Buddhas as atoms in a thousand buddha-fields all together empower you with their spiritual force, and this is also the spiritual power of the force of Vairocana Buddha's ancient vows, as well as the power of the roots of goodness you have cultivated, whereby you enter this concentration, allowing you to expound the teaching, for growth in enlightened knowledge, to enter deeply into the realm of reality, to comprehend well the worlds of sentient beings, to be unhindered in whatever is entered into, to be unobstructed in all activities, to attain incomparable skill in means, to enter the essence of omniscience, to be aware of all things, to know all faculties, to be able to hold and expound all the teachings; that is to say, bringing forth the ten abodes of enlightening beings. Good man, you should receive the spiritual power of the Buddhas and expound this teaching."

Then the Buddhas gave the enlightening being Truth Wisdom unhindered knowledge, unattached knowledge, unbroken knowledge, knowledge free from ignorance, unvarying knowledge, knowledge without loss, immeasurable knowledge, unexcelled knowledge, unremitting knowledge, and knowledge that cannot be taken away. Why? Because the power of this concentration is naturally this way in principle.

Now the Buddhas all extended their right hands and rubbed Truth Wisdom's head; then the enlightening being Truth Wisdom emerged from concentration and declared to the enlightening beings, "Children of Buddhas, the abode of enlightening beings is vast, as vast as the space of the cosmos. Enlightening beings dwell in the house of the

Buddhas of past, present, and future. The abodes of enlightening beings I shall now explain. Buddha-children, there are ten kinds of abodes of enlightening beings, which the past, future, and present Buddhas have explained, will explain, and do explain. What are the ten? They are the abode of initial determination; the abode of preparing the ground; the abode of practice action; the abode of noble birth; the abode of fulfillment of skill in means; the abode of the correct state of mind; the abode of nonregression; the abode of youthful nature; the abode of prince of the teaching; the abode of coronation. These are called the ten abodes of enlightening beings, expounded by the Buddhas of past, future, and present.

"What is the enlightening beings' abode of initial determination? The enlightening beings, seeing the magnificence of the Buddhas, which people like to see, rarely encountered, having great power; or seeing their spiritual powers, or hearing predictions of enlightenment, or listening to their teachings and instructions, or seeing sentient beings suffering severe pains, or hearing the far-reaching teaching of enlightenment of the Buddhas, develop the determination for enlightenment, to seek omniscience. The enlightening beings arouse determination with ten difficult-to-attain objectives: the knowledge of what is so and what is not; knowledge of consequences of good and bad actions; knowledge of superiority and inferiority of faculties; knowledge of the differences of various understandings; knowledge of the differences of various realms; knowledge of where all paths lead; knowledge of all meditations, liberations, and concentrations; knowledge of past lives; clairvoyance; knowledge of the universal end of indulgence for all time. Here the enlightening beings should encourage and study ten things: diligently making offerings to the Buddhas; gladly remaining in the world; guiding worldly people to reject evil deeds; always carrying on instruction by means of the most sublime teaching; praising the unexcelled teaching; learning the virtues of buddhahood; being born in the presence of Buddhas and always being received into their company; expediently expounding tranquil concentration; extolling detachment from the cycle of birth and death; being a refuge for suffering beings. What is the reason? To cause enlightening beings' minds to broaden in the Buddha's teaching and to be able to understand whatever teaching they hear without depending on another's instruction.

"What is the enlightening beings' abode of preparing the ground? Here the enlightening beings develop ten attitudes toward all living beings: altruism; compassion; wish to give happiness; wish to give security; pity; care; protecting; identification; considering them as teachers; considering them as guides. Here the enlightening beings should encourage and study ten things: study and learning; uncluttered tranquility; association with the wise; gentle, pleasing speech; speech appropriate to the occasion; fearlessness; understanding; acting in accord with the teaching; avoiding folly and delusion; stability. What is the reason? To cause enlightening beings to increase great compassion toward sentient beings, and to immediately understand whatever teachings they hear without relying on the instruction of another.

"What is the enlightening beings' abode of practice? Here enlightening beings contemplate all things through ten practices: observing that all things are impermanent, all things are painful, all things are empty, all things are selfless, all things have no creation, all things are flavorless, all things do not correspond to the names, all things have no locus, all things are apart from discrimination, all things lack stable solidity. Here the enlightening beings should encourage and study ten things: observing the realms of sentient beings, the realms of phenomena and principles, and the realms of the world; observing the elements of earth, water, fire, and air; observing the realms of desire, form, and formlessness. What is the reason? To cause enlightening beings' knowledge to be perfectly clear, so they can immediately understand any teaching they hear without depending on the instruction of another.

"What is the enlightening beings' abode of noble birth? Here the enlightening beings are born from the wise teaching and perfect ten things: never regressing from the presence of the Buddhas; profoundly engendering pure faith; carefully examining things; thoroughly knowing living beings, lands, worlds, actions, consequences, birth and death, and nirvana. Here the enlightening beings should encourage and study ten things: knowing all past, future, and present Buddhas' teachings; practicing and accumulating all past, future, and present Buddhas' teachings; fulfilling all past, future, and present Buddhas' teachings; and knowing that all Buddhas are equal. What is the reason? To cause progress in equanimity in respect to past, present, and future, and to be able to understand any teaching heard without relying on the instruction of another.

"What is the enlightening beings' abode of fulfilling skill in means? Here the roots of goodness cultivated by the enlightening beings are all to save all sentient beings, to benefit all sentient beings, to cause all sentient beings to be free from calamities and difficulties, to cause all sentient beings to leave the miseries of birth and death, to cause all sentient beings to develop pure faith, to cause all sentient beings to be harmonized and pacified, to cause all sentient beings to experience nirvana. Here the enlightening beings should encourage and learn ten things: to know sentient beings are boundless, to know sentient beings are infinite, to know sentient beings are countless, to know sentient beings are inconceivable, to know sentient beings' infinite forms, to know sentient beings are immeasurable, to know sentient beings are empty, to know sentient beings create nothing, to know sentient beings possess nothing, to know sentient beings have no identity. What is the reason? To cause the mind to increase in mastery and have no attachments, and to immediately understand any teaching heard without depending on the instruction of another.

"What is the enlightening beings' abode of the correct state of mind? Here the enlightening being's mind is steady and unwavering even when hearing these ten things: hearing the Buddha praised or reviled, the mind is steady and unwavering in regard to the Buddha's teaching; hearing the teaching praised or reviled, the mind is steady and unwavering in regard to the Buddha's teaching; hearing enlightening beings praised or reviled, the mind is steady and unwavering in regard to the Buddha's teaching; hearing the practices of enlightening beings praised or reviled, the mind is steady and unwavering in regard to the Buddha's teaching; hearing it said that living beings are finite or infinite, the mind is steady and unwavering in regard to the Buddha's teaching; hearing it said that sentient beings are defiled or undefiled, the mind is steady and unwavering in regard to the Buddha's teaching; hearing it said that sentient beings are easy to liberate or difficult to liberate, the mind is steady and unwavering in regard to the Buddha's teaching; hearing it said that there is becoming or disintegration of the universe, the mind is steady and unwavering in regard to the Buddha's teaching; hearing it said that the universe exists or does not exist, the mind is steady and unwavering in regard to the Buddha's teaching. Here the enlightening being should study and encourage the study of ten things: that all things are signless; all things are insubstantial; all things cannot be cultivated; all things have no existence; all things have no true reality; all things are empty; all things lack inherent nature; all things are like illusions; all things are like dreams; all things have no discrimination. What is the reason? To cause the mind to progress further to attain nonregressing acceptance of the nonorigination of things, and immediately understand whatever teaching is heard, without depending on the instruction of another.

"What is the enlightening beings' abode of nonregression? Here the enlightening being remains firm and doesn't regress even when hearing these ten things: hearing that Buddhas do or do not exist, the mind does not regress in the Buddha's teaching; hearing that truth exists or does not exist, the mind does not regress in the Buddha's teaching; hearing that enlightening beings do or do not exist, the mind does not regress in the Buddha's teaching; hearing that enlightening beings' practices do or do not exist, the mind does not regress in the Buddha's teaching; hearing that enlightening beings do or do not attain emancipation through their practices, the mind does not regress in the Buddha's teaching; hearing that there were or were not Buddhas in the past, the mind does not regress in the Buddha's teaching; hearing that there will or will not be Buddhas in the future, the mind does not regress in the Buddha's teaching; hearing there are or are not Buddhas in the present, the mind does not regress in the Buddha's teaching; hearing that a Buddha's knowledge is finite or infinite, the mind does not regress in the Buddha's teaching; hearing that past, present, and future are uniform or not uniform, the mind does not regress in the Buddha's teaching.

Here the enlightening being should encourage and study ten far-reaching principles: explaining one is many; explaining many are one; literary expression according with meaning; meaning according with literary expression; nonexistence is existence; existence is nonexistence; formless is form; form is formlessness; nature is natureless; naturelessness is nature. What is the reason? To progress further, to be able to gain emancipation from all things, to understand any teaching without relying on another's instruction.

"What is the enlightening beings' abode of youthful nature? Here the enlightening being abides in ten kinds of activity: physically acting without error; verbally acting without error; mentally acting without error; being born at will; knowing the various desires of sentient beings; knowing the various understandings of sentient beings; knowing the various realms of sentient beings; knowing the various activities of sentient beings; knowing the becoming and decay of the world; going anywhere freely by psychic projection. Here the enlightening being should encourage and study ten kinds of things: knowing all buddha-lands; activating all buddha-lands, maintaining all buddha-lands; observing all buddha-lands; visiting all buddha-lands; traveling in countless worlds; receiving innumerable teachings of Buddhas; manifesting a body with freedom to metamorphose; producing a far-reaching, universal voice; serving and providing for countless Buddhas in a single instant. What is the reason? To advance in skillfulness in applying teachings, to be able to understand any teaching without depending on another's instructions.

"What is the enlightening beings' abode as the prince of the teaching? Here enlightening beings know ten things well: they know how sentient beings are born; they know the origin of afflictions; they know the continuation of habit energy; they know what techniques are to be employed; they know innumerable teachings; they understand all modes of dignified behavior; they know the differentiations of the world; they know past and future events; they know how to explain conventional truth; they know how to explain ultimate truth. Here the enlightening beings should study and encourage the study of ten things: the skills proper to a king of the teaching; the regulations and manners proper to a king of the teaching; the abode of a king of the teaching; that which a king of the teaching enters into; the contemplations proper to a king of the teaching; the coronation of a king of the teaching; the power and sustenance of a king of the teaching; the fearlessness of a king of the teaching; the repose of a king of the teaching; the praise of a king of the teaching. What is the reason? To promote progress in nonobstruction of mind, to understand any teaching spontaneously without relying on the instruction of another.

"What is the enlightening beings' abode of coronation? Here the enlightening being perfects ten kinds of knowledge: shaking countless worlds; illuminating countless worlds; supporting countless worlds; traveling to countless worlds; purifying countless worlds; teaching countless sentient beings; observing countless sentient beings; knowing the faculties of countless sentient beings; causing countless sentient beings to strive to enter enlightenment; causing countless sentient beings to be harmonized and pacified. This enlightening being's body and physical activities, various manifestations of spiritual powers, past, future, and present knowledge, development of a buddha-land, state of mind, and realm of knowledge are all unknowable: even an enlightening being in the station of prince of the teaching cannot know them. Here the enlightening being should promote and study ten kinds of knowledge proper to Buddhas: knowledge of past, present, and future; knowledge of enlightening teachings; knowledge of the harmony of the universe; knowledge of the boundlessness of the universe; knowledge filling all worlds; knowledge illumining all worlds; knowledge supporting all worlds; knowledge of all sentient beings; knowledge of all things; knowledge of the infinite Buddhas. What is the reason? To increase in knowledge of all particulars and all means of liberation and spontaneously understand any teaching without depending on the instruction of another."

Then, due to the spiritual power of the Buddha, in each of the ten directions as many worlds as atoms in ten thousand buddha-lands quaked in six ways; there rained celestial flowers, celestial incense powder, celestial garlands, celestial perfumes, celestial jewel raiment, celestial jewel clouds, celestial ornaments; celestial music spontaneously played, with radiant lights and exquisite sounds. As in this world on the peak of Mt. Sumeru, in the palace of King Indra, the ten abodes were expounded and supernatural manifestations appeared, so also did the same thing transpire in all worlds. And due to the spiritual power of the Buddha, in the ten directions, past as many worlds as atoms in ten thousand buddha-lands, there were as many enlightening beings as atoms in ten buddha-lands who came here, filling the ten directions, and said these words: "Excellent, excellent! O Child of Buddha, you have explained this teaching well. We too all have the same name, Truth Wisdom, and the lands we come from are all called Truth Cloud, and the Buddhas in those lands are all named Sublime Truth. In the presence of our Buddhas we too expound the ten abodes, and the congregations and followings, the words and phrases, the doctrines and principles, are all like this, with no addition or omission. Receiving spiritual power from the Buddha, we have come into this assembly to be witnesses for you. As it is in this assembly, so it is in all the worlds there are in the ten directions."

Then the enlightening being Truth Wisdom, imbued with the power of the Buddha, looked over the ten directions, throughout the cosmos, and spoke these verses:

Seeing the subtle body of the Supremely Wise,
Replete with adorning marks and refinements,
So honorable and rare to meet,
Enlightening beings boldly make their resolve.

Seeing incomparable great spiritual powers,
Hearing tell of mind-reading and appropriate teaching,
And the immeasurable sufferings of mundane beings,
Enlightening beings thereby first become determined.

Hearing the Enlightened Ones, universally supremely honored,
Have perfected all meritorious and virtuous qualities,
Like space, not discriminating,
Thereby do enlightening beings develop resolve.

The causes and effects of past, present, and future are called what
    is so;
The inherent nature of self and phenomena is called what is not
    so.
Wanting to know the genuine truth
Do enlightening beings therefore arouse their will.

All the good and evil deeds there be
In past, future, and present worlds
Do they want to know completely;
Therefore enlightening beings are determined.

All meditations, liberations, and concentrations,
Defiled and pure, of countless kinds,
They want to know all—entry, abiding, and exit;
Therefore do enlightening beings arouse their aspiration.

According to the sharpness or dullness of beings' faculties,
So are their powers of effort also various;
Wanting to understand and know them all distinctly,
Do enlightening beings therefore arouse determination.

Sentient beings have various understandings
And their mental inclinations are each different:
Wanting to know all these innumerable inclinations
Do enlightening beings therefore arouse their will.

The realms of sentient beings are each different;
There is no measure to all the worlds there are:
Wanting to know completely their substance and nature
Do enlightening beings rouse their aspiration.

The paths of all fabricated actions
Each have a destination;
Wanting to know the true nature of all
Do enlightening beings rouse their determination.

The sentient beings of all worlds
Bob and flow according to their deeds, without cease;
Wanting to attain the celestial eye to see them all
Do enlightening beings rouse their will.

Such constitutions and such characteristics
As there were in past ages
They want to know, as former lives,
So enlightening beings arouse aspiration.

The continuity, appearance, and habit energy
Of the binding delusions of all sentient beings
They want to know thoroughly and finally,
So enlightening beings thus rouse their will.

Of all the various philosophies and theories
Which sentient beings may set up
They want to know the worldly truth,
So enlightening beings thus rouse determination.

All things are beyond speech—
Their nature is empty, null, and creates nothing:
Wishing to clearly arrive at this truth
Do enlightening beings therefore rouse their will.

Wanting to shake the worlds of the ten directions
And overturn all the oceans,
Fulfilling the great spiritual powers of the Buddhas,
Do enlightening beings rouse determination.

Wanting to emit lights from a single pore
That will illumine infinite lands in the ten directions,
In each light awakening all,
Do enlightening beings therefore rouse aspiration.

Wanting to take inconceivably many buddha-lands
And put them in their palms, without moving,
Comprehending all is like magic illusions,
So enlightening beings rouse their determination.

Wanting to take the beings of innumerable lands
And put them on a hairtip without crowding,
Knowing all have no person and no self,
Therefore do enlightening beings arouse their will.

Wanting to take drops from the ocean on a hair
So as to dry up all the oceans
While specifically knowing the number of drops,
Therefore do enlightening beings rouse their aspiration.

Reducing entirely to dust
Inconceivable numbers of worlds,
Wanting to know distinctly the number of particles
Do enlightening beings arouse their will.

Wanting to comprehend exhaustively
The signs of becoming and decay of all worlds
In countless eons past and future
Do enlightening beings rouse their aspiration.

Wanting to know all the teachings
Of all the Buddhas of all times,
All self-enlightened ones and Buddhas' disciples,
Do enlightening beings rouse their determination.

Wanting to pick up with a single hair
Countless, boundless worlds
And know their substances and forms as they are,
Do enlightening beings rouse their will.

Wanting to put in a pore
Countless mountain chains
And know their sizes as they are
Do enlightening beings rouse their aspiration.

Wanting to preach appropriately to all kinds of beings everywhere
With the single subtle voice of tranquility and peace
And cause them all to purely, clearly comprehend,
Do enlightening beings rouse their determination.

To utter in a single word
What is spoken by all sentient beings:
Wanting to know all their inherent natures
Do enlightening beings rouse their will.

Producing all spoken sounds of the worlds
To make all realize peaceful dispassion:
Wanting to attain such a marvelous tongue
Do enlightening beings rouse their aspiration.

Wanting to cause all to see
The signs of becoming and decay of all worlds
And know they are born of conceptions
Do enlightening beings rouse their determination.

All worlds in the ten directions
Are filled with countless Buddhas;
Wanting to know all the teachings of those Buddhas
Do enlightening beings arouse their will.

Countless bodies of various transformations,
Numerous as atoms in all worlds:
Wanting to comprehend they all come from mind
Do enlightening beings rouse this determination.

Wanting to know in a single thought
The measureless, countless Buddhas
Of past, future, and present worlds
Do enlightening beings rouse this aspiration.

Wanting to expound the one phrase teaching
For incalculable eons without exhausting it
Yet have the expressions and nuances be each different
Do enlightening beings therefore arouse this will.

Wanting to know in a single thought
The signs of cylic births and deaths
Of all sentient beings everywhere
Do enlightening beings rouse their aspiration.

Wanting to go everywhere unhindered
Through physical, verbal, and mental action
And comprehend all times are empty and null
Do enlightening beings rouse determination.

Having thus determined to become enlightened
They should be made to go to all lands
To honor and provide for the Enlightened Ones,
Whereby to cause them not to regress.

Enlightening beings bravely seeking the Buddha-way
Stay in birth and death unwearied
For others extolling what will make them follow the way
And thus cause them never to regress.

Being honorable leaders in countless lands
In the worlds of the ten directions,
Teach like this for the enlightening beings
Whereby to cause them not to regress.

The supreme, the highest, the foremost,
Profound and subtle purest teaching,
Urge enlightening beings to teach to people
Whereby to cause them to be rid of afflictions.

The unshakable realm of victory,
Peerless in all the worlds,
Always extols for other enlightening beings
To cause them not to regress.

Buddha is the great powerful leader of the world,
Replete with all merits and virtues,
Causing enlightening beings to abide herein,
Thereby teaching them to be superior people.

To countless, boundless Buddhas' places
They can go and draw near,
Always taken in to the company of Buddhas,
Thus causing them not to regress.

To destroy the wheels of birth and death
And turn the wheel of the pure wonderous teaching
Without attachment to any world:
Such is the teaching for enlightening beings.

All sentient beings fall into evil ways
Bound and oppressed by measureless pains:
To be saviors and reliances for them
Is the teaching for enlightening beings.

This is enlightening beings' abode of initial determination:
With single-minded will seeking the unexcelled path;
As is the teaching of which I speak,
So is the teaching of all the Buddhas.

In the second abode, of preparing the ground,
Enlightening beings should form this thought:
"All sentient beings everywhere
I vow to induce to follow the Buddhas' teaching."

With a mind to aid them, with compassion, to give them peace
   and ease,
To establish them securely, with sympathy and acceptance,
Protecting sentient beings, looking upon them as the same as
   themselves,
As teachers and as guides—
Once abiding in these sublime states of mind
Next they are directed to study and learn,
To always enjoy peace and quiet and right meditation,
And draw near to all good associates.

Speaking gently, with no roughness or harshness,
Always speaking appropriately to the situation, without fear,
Comprehending the meaning of the teaching and acting in accord,
Leaving ignorance and delusion behind, the mind unmoving:
This is the practice of beginning study for enlightenment;
Those who can do these things are true children of the Buddhas.

I now explain what they should practice;
Thus should Buddha-children diligently study:
In the third abode of enlightening beings, practice,
They should earnestly contemplate, according to Buddha's teaching,
The impermanence, painfulness, and emptiness of all things,
The absence of self, person, and activity.
All things cannot be enjoyed,
None accord with their names, they have no location,
There's nothing of what is conceived, no true reality in them:
Those who contemplate thus are called enlightening beings.

Next they are made to observe the realms of sentient beings
And urged to contemplate the elemental cosmos:
All the various differentiations of the worlds
They all should be urged to contemplate and observe.

The worlds of the ten directions, and space,
Their earth, water, fire, and air,
The realms of desire, form, and formlessness,
They are exhorted to investigate thoroughly.

Examining the individual distinctions of those realms,
Their substances and natures, exhaustively,

Receiving this teaching, diligently cultivating its practice,
Is what is called being true Buddha-children.

Enlightening beings in the fourth abode, noble birth,
Are born from the teachings of the sages;
Comprehending that existents have no existence,
They transcend things and are born in the realm of reality.

Their faith in Buddha is firm and unbreakable,
Their dispassionate mind contemplating things is at peace.
Whatever beings there be, they comprehend all
Are essentially false, without true reality.

Worlds, lands, actions and rewards,
Birth, death, and nirvana are all like this:
Buddha-children, contemplating things this way,
Are born from Buddha-parents and called Buddha-children.

To know the accumulation and fulfillment
Of all the Buddhas' teachings
In past, present, and future worlds,
Thus they study, to the ultimate end.

All the enlightened ones of past, present, and future
They can contemplate, all equal,
In which various distinctions cannot be found:
Those who meditate thus comprehend the three time frames.

If any can practice diligently, according to the teaching,
The virtues of this fourth abode
Such as I am now extolling,
They will soon accomplish unsurpassed enlightenment.

From here, enlightening beings of the fifth abode,
Called the abode of fulfilling skill in means,
Enter deeply into infinite expedient skills,
Developing ultimate virtuous action.

The virtues produced by enlightening beings
Are all to rescue living beings:
Dedicated to aiding and comforting them,
They wholeheartedly pity them and liberate them.

Removing difficulties for all beings,
Drawing them out of existences, making them happy,

They pacify all, leaving none out,
Making them all turn to nirvana, full of virtue.

Sentient beings are boundless,
Incalculable, countless, inconceivably many,
And cannot be told of or measured:
Enlightening beings accept this teaching of the Buddha.

These Buddha-children in the fifth abode
Develop skillful means to liberate sentient beings;
The Saint of Great Knowledge, with all virtues,
Enlightens them with teachings like this.

In the sixth abode, the fulfillment of right mindfulness,
There is no confusion about the inherent nature of things;
Meditating with right mindfulness, detaching from discrimination,
One cannot be moved by any god or man.

Hearing praise or slander of the Buddhas or their teachings,
Of enlightening beings and the practices they perform,
Or that sentient beings are finite or infinite,
Defiled or undefiled, easy or hard to liberate,
Or that the cosmos is great or small, becomes or decays,
Or exists or does not, the mind is unmoved:
Past, future, and present,
Thinking clearly, always sure;
All things are signless,
Insubstantial, without inherent nature, empty, unreal,
Like illusions, like dreams, beyond conception:
They always delight in hearing such doctrines.

Enlightening beings of the seventh abode of nonregression
Never regress in spite of whatever they hear
About Buddhas, the Teaching, or enlightening beings—
Whether or not they exist, whether or not they escape,
Whether or not there are Buddhas
Past, present, and future,
Whether Buddha-knowledge is finite or infinite,
Whether the past, present, and future are uniform or various.
One is many, many are one;
Expression follows meaning, meaning follows expression;
Thus do all interdependently become:
This is what those who don't regress should explain.
Whether things have signs or are signless,
Whether they have inherent nature or not;

Various distinctions subsume each other:
These people, hearing this, attain the ultimate.

Enlightening beings in the eight abode, youthful nature,
Fulfill physical, verbal, and mental actions
All pure, without mistakes;
They are freely born as they will
And know the inclination of sentient beings,
Their various understandings, each different,
And all the factors involved therein
And the signs of becoming and decay of all lands.
Attaining to wondrous psychic powers of swiftness,
They go anywhere as soon as they think of it:
Listening to the teachings from various Buddhas,
They praise and practice unflagging.
They comprehend all Buddha-lands,
Shaking, supporting, and contemplating,
Going beyond incalculable buddha-lands,
They travel in worlds without number,
To ask about innumerable principles;
Free to take on any physical form,
Their skill in speech pervades everywhere
As they serve countless Buddhas.

Enlightening beings in the ninth abode, of the prince,
Can see the difference in births of sentient beings;
Knowing their afflictions and habits,
They understand which techniques to employ.
Individual differences in teachings and in modes of bearing,
Dissimilarities of worlds, past and future times,
In accord with their conventional and ultimate realities,
All they know completely, leaving none out.
The skillful set-ups of kings of the teaching,
The doctrines they establish according to the situation,
The palaces of kings of teaching and their entries
As well as what is seen therein,
The laws of coronation of the kings of teaching,
Their spiritual capacities, empowerments, and fearlessnesses,
Their rooms of repose, as well as their praises—
With these they instruct the princes of the teaching,
Explaining all this for them, exhaustively,
And causing their minds to have no attachments;
As they comprehend this and cultivate right mindfulness,
All the Buddhas appear before them.

True Buddha-kings of the tenth abode of coronation
Fulfill the unexcelled, foremost teaching.
All the countless worlds in the ten directions
They can cause to quake, and illumine with their light,
Maintaining and traveling to all without exception,
Fully purifying and adorning them all.
They teach sentient beings without number,
Observing and knowing their faculties completely,
Inspiring and training boundless beings too,
Causing them all to turn to great enlightenment.
Observing all phenomenal realms,
They travel to all lands in the ten directions:
Their embodiments and physical actions there,
Their spiritual powers and metamorphoses, are unfathomable.
The realms of lands of the Buddhas of all times
Even the princes of the teaching cannot understand:
The knowledge of all times of the all-seeing,
Knowledge understanding all Buddhas' teachings,
Unhindered, boundless knowledge of the realm of realities,
Knowledge filling all worlds,
Supporting knowledge illumining the world,
Knowledge comprehending the states of all beings,
And the boundless knowledge of true awakening
The Buddhas explain for them, so they will consummate them.
Thus the enlightening beings of the ten abodes
Are all born by transformation from the teachings of the enlightened;
Their practices according to the virtues they have
No humans or gods are able to fathom.

In past, future, and present worlds, boundless are those
Who set their minds to attain buddhahood;
They fill all lands in the ten directions,
All determined to become omniscient.

Boundless is the totality of all lands;
Boundless too are the states of worlds and beings,
Their delusions, actions, and inclinations each different:
Due to them enlightening beings aspire to enlightenment.

The very first thought to seek buddhahood
Worldlings, or even those
Of the two vehicles cannot know—
Much less the other virtuous practices.

If one can lift with a single hair
All the worlds in the ten directions,

One can know these Buddha-children's
Progression toward the wisdom of the enlightened ones.

If one can drain by drops with a hair
The waters of all oceans in the ten directions,
One can know the virtuous deeds
Practiced by these Buddha-children in a single instant.

If one can reduce all worlds to dust
And know the specific number of each mote,
Such a person alone can see
The path traversed by these Buddha-children.

The Buddhas of all places and times,
All self-enlightened ones and Buddhas' disciples,
All with various powers of elucidation
Illustrate the mind first bent on enlightenment.

The virtues of this aspiration cannot be measured:
If all the knowledges filling all realms of beings
Were to explain together, they could not exhaust it,
Much less the rest of the wondrous practices carried out.

BOOK SIXTEEN

Religious Practice

THEN THE GODLING Right Mindfulness said to the enlightening being Truth Wisdom, "In all worlds, enlightening beings, following the teaching of the Enlightened Ones, dye their clothing and leave home to become mendicants: how can they attain purity of religious practice, and from the state of enlightening reach the path of unexcelled enlightenment?"

Truth Wisdom said, "Great enlightening beings, when performing religious practice, should attentively contemplate ten things objectively: the body, physical action, speech, verbal action, mind, mental action, Buddha, the Teaching, the religious community, and the precepts. They should contemplate in this way: Is the body religious practice? And so on, down to: Are precepts religious practice? If the body were religious practice, then religious practice would be not good, it would not be the true teaching, it would be defiled, it would be impure, it would be foul, it would be unclean, it would be disgusting, it would be intractable, it would be defined, it would be a corpse, it would be a mass of microbes. If physical action were religious practice, then religious practice would be walking, standing, sitting, lying down, looking around, up and down. If speech were religious practice, then religious practice would be sound and breath, chest, tongue, lips, exhalation and inhalation, constriction and relaxation, high and low, clear and unclear. If verbal activity were religious practice, then religious practice would be greetings, summary explanations, extensive explanations, metaphorical explanations, direct explanations, praise, criticism, definitions, explanations accommodated to conventions, clear explanations. If the mind were religious practice, then religious practice would be consideration and pondering, discrimination, various discriminations, conception, various conceptions, thought, various thoughts, acts of illusion and dreams. If mental activity were religious practice, then religious practice would be ideas, cold and heat, hunger and thirst, pain and pleasure, sorrow and joy. If Buddha is religious practice, is material form to be considered Buddha? Is sensation Buddha? Is conception Buddha? Is action Buddha? Are spiritual powers Buddha? Are works Buddha? Are resulting consequences Buddha? If the Teaching is religious practice, is extinction the Teaching? Is nirvana the Teaching? Is nonbirth the Teaching? Is nonorigination the Teaching? Is inexplicability the Teaching? Is nondiscrimination the Teaching? Is nonaction the Teaching? Is nonconjunction the Teaching? If the Community is religious practice, is heading for stream-entering the Community? Is the fruit of stream-entering the Community? Is heading for the state of once-returner the Community? Is the fruit of once-returner the Community? Is heading for the state of nonreturner the Community? Is the fruit of nonreturner the Community? Is heading for sainthood the Community? Is the fruit of sainthood the Community? Are those with the three super-knowledges the Community? Are those with the six paranormal powers the Community? If the precepts are religious practice, is the ordination altar the precepts? Is asking about purity the precepts? Is teaching proper manners the precepts? Is the threefold repetition the precepts? Is the instructor the precepts? Is the tutor the precepts? Is shaving off the hair the precepts? Is putting on the monastic garb the precepts? Is begging the precepts? Is right livelihood the precepts?

"Having contemplated thus, having no attachment to the body, no clinging to practice, no dwelling on doctrine, the past gone, the future not yet arrived, the present empty, there is no doer, no receiver of consequences; this time doesn't move, another time doesn't shift—what thing is therein to be called religious practice? Where does religious practice come from? Where is it? Who is the body? By whom is it performed? Does it exist? Does it not exist? Is it form? Is it not form? Is it sensation? Is it not sensation? Is it conception? Is it not conception? Is it action? Is it not action? Is it consciousness? Is it not consciousness? Contemplating in this way, because the reality of religious practice cannot be apprehended, because the things of past, present, and future are all empty, because the intellect has no attachment, because the mind has no obstruction, because the sphere of operation is nondual, because expedient means are free, because of acceptance of formless truth, because of contemplation of formless truth, because of knowing the Buddha's teaching is equanimous, because of fulfilling all qualities of Buddhahood, is such practice called pure religious practice.

"Ten things should also be cultivated: knowledge of what is so and what is not; knowledge of past, present, and future consequences of actions; knowledge of all meditations, liberations, and concentrations; knowledge of superiority and inferiority of faculties; knowledge of all kinds of understandings; knowledge of all kinds of realms; knowledge of where all paths lead; unhindered clairvoyance; unhindered knowledge of past lives; knowledge of the eternal cancellation of habit energy. Contemplating each of these ten powers of the enlightened, in each power are innumerable meanings; one should ask about them, and after having heard about them should arouse a mind of great kindness and compassion and observe sentient beings without abandoning them, reflect on the teachings unceasingly, carry out superlative deeds without seeking rewards, comprehend that objects are like dreams, like illusions, like reflections, like echoes, and like magical productions. If enlightening beings can unite with such contemplations, they will not entertain a dualistic understanding of things and all enlightening teachings will become evident to them: at the time of their first determination they will immediately attain complete perfect enlightenment, will know all things are the mind's own nature, and will perfect the body of wisdom and understand without relying on another."

BOOK SEVENTEEN

The Merit of
The Initial Determination
for Enlightenment

THEN INDRA, king of gods, said to the enlightening being Truth Wisdom, "Son of Buddha, what is the extent of the merit attained when the enlightening being first determines to become enlightened?"

Truth Wisdom said, "The truth of this is extremely deep, difficult to explain, difficult to know, difficult to discern, difficult to believe, difficult to experience, difficult to practice, difficult to master, difficult to think of, difficult to assess, difficult to approach and enter. Even so, by the power of the Buddha I will explain for you.

"O Child of Buddha, suppose someone were to provide all comforts for all the beings of incalculable worlds in the eastern direction for a whole eon, and after that teach them to keep the five precepts with purity, and were to do the same thing in the southern, western, and northern directions, the four intermediate directions, and the zenith and nadir as well—do you think this person's merit would be much?"

Indra said, "Only a Buddha could know this person's merit—no one else could be able to assess it."

Truth Wisdom said, "This person's merit, compared to the merit of an enlightening being who has just determined to realize enlightenment, does not amount even to a hundredth, not even a thousandth, a hundred thousandth, a millionth, a hundred millionth, a billionth, a hundred billionth, a trillionth, a hundred trillionth, a quadrillionth, a quintillionth—that merit does not amount to the smallest imaginable fraction of the merit of determination for enlightenment.

"Setting aside that example for the moment, suppose someone provided all the beings of ten infinities of worlds with medicines for a hundred eons, and then taught them to practice the path of ten virtues, serving them thus for a thousand eons; then teaching them to dwell in the four meditations for a hundred thousand eons, then teaching them to dwell in the four immeasurable states of mind for a hundred million eons, then teaching them to dwell in the four formless concentrations for ten billion eons, then teaching them to dwell in the state of stream-enterer for a hundred billion eons, then teaching them to dwell in the state of once-returner for ten trillion eons, then teaching them to dwell in the state of nonreturner for a quadrillion eons, then teaching them to dwell in sainthood for a quintillion eons, then teaching them to dwell in the path of the self-enlightened; do you think this person's merit would be great?"

The king of gods said, "Only a Buddha could know the merit of such a person."

Truth Wisdom said, "This person's merit, compared to the merit of an enlightening being who has just determined to realize enlightenment, does not amount to a hundredth part, not even a thousandth, a hundred thousandth, or even the smallest imaginable fraction thereof. Why? Because when the Buddhas first set their minds on enlightenment, they do not do so just to provide the beings of innumerable worlds in all directions with all comforts for a hundred eons or a hundred thousand quadrillion eons. They do not set their minds on enlightenment just to teach that many beings to cultivate morality and goodness, just to teach them to abide in the four meditations, four immeasurable minds, and four formless concentrations, just to teach them to attain the states of stream-enterer, once-returner, nonreturner, saint, and independently enlightened one. Rather, they set their minds on enlightenment to cause the lineage of the enlightened ones not to die out, to pervade all worlds, to liberate the sentient beings of all worlds, to know the formation and disintegration of all worlds, to know the defilement and purity of beings in all worlds, to know the inherent purity of all worlds, to know the inclinations, afflictions, and mental habits of all sentient beings, to know where all sentient beings die and are born, to know expedient means appropriate to the faculties of all sentient beings, to know the mentalities of all sentient beings, to know all sentient beings' knowledge of past, present, and future, and to know all realms of Buddhas are equal.

"Again, setting this example aside for the moment, suppose someone could, in a single instant, pass incalculably many worlds to the east, and did this instant after instant for an incalculable eon—no one could determine a limit to those worlds. Then suppose there were another person who could pass in a single instant all the worlds that the former person passed in an incalculable eon, and also went on thus for an incalculable eon. Then suppose there were yet another person, and another and another, up to ten, each of whom could pass in an instant all the worlds that the preceding one passed in an incalculable eon, and went on thus for an incalculable eon. Then suppose there were also such people in all the other nine directions. Thus in the ten directions there would be one hundred people, each successively passing in each and every instant of an eon as many worlds as the preceding passed in an eon: the limit of these worlds might be known, but the limit of the roots of goodness in the enlightening being's initial determination on enlightenment cannot be known. Why? Because enlightening beings do not set their minds on enlightenment just to go to and gain knowledge of a limited number of worlds; they set their minds on enlightenment to know all worlds in the ten directions. That is to say, they want to know subtle worlds are gross worlds, gross worlds are subtle worlds, upward facing worlds are downward facing worlds, downward facing worlds are upward facing worlds, small worlds are large worlds, large worlds are small worlds, wide worlds are narrow worlds, narrow worlds are wide worlds, one world is unspeakably many worlds, un-speakably many worlds are one world, one world enters unspeakably many worlds, unspeakably many worlds enter one world, defiled worlds are pure worlds, pure worlds are defiled worlds; they want to know the differentiations of all worlds in a single hair, and the unity of a single hair in all worlds. They want to know the production of all worlds in a single world. They want to know the insubstantiality of all worlds. They want to be able to know all vast worlds in a single moment of thought without any hindrance. This is why they set their minds on unexcelled complete perfect enlightenment.

"Again, setting this example aside, suppose there is someone who can in a single thought know the number of eons of becoming and decay of innumerable worlds in the eastern direction, and does this for an incalculable eon; no one can determine the bounds of those numbers of eons. Then suppose there is a second person who can know in a single thought all the numbers of eons known by the first person over an incalculable eon. Again, continue this up to ten persons, then extend it to all ten directions. The limit of the number of eons of becoming and decay of all these incalculable worlds of the ten directions may be known, but the limit of the virtues of the enlightening being setting the mind on perfect enlightenment cannot be known. Why? Because en-lightening beings do not set the mind on unexcelled complete perfect enlightenment just to know the number of eons of becoming and decay of a certain limited number of worlds. It is to completely know the eons of becoming and decay of all worlds that they set their minds on unexcelled complete perfect enlightenment. That is, to know that long eons and short eons are equal; short eons and long eons are equal; one eon is equal to countless eons; countless eons are equal to one eon; eons with Buddhas are equal to eons without Buddhas; eons without Buddhas are equal to eons with Buddhas; in an eon with one Buddha there are unspeakably many Buddhas; in an eon with unspeakably many Buddhas there is one Buddha; finite eons are equal to infinite eons; infinite eons are equal to finite eons; eons that end are equal to endless eons; endless eons are equal to eons that end; unspeakably many eons are equal to one instant; one instant is equal to unspeakably many eons; all eons enter the noneon; the noneon enters all eons.★ They want to know instantly the eons of becoming and decay of all worlds of the entire past, present, and future—that is why they set their minds on unexcelled complete perfect enlightenment. This is called the initial determination's adornment of great vows, the spiritual knowledge of all eons.

"Again, setting aside this example, suppose someone could, in the time of a single instant, know the various different understandings of all the sentient beings in incalculably many worlds in the eastern direction, and went on like this instant after instant for a whole incalculable eon; now suppose a second person can know in a single instant all the differences in sentient beings' understandings known by the first person in an incalculable eon, and also went on like this (knowing more and more each instant) for an incalculable eon. Now apply this pattern successively up to the tenth person, and also to the other nine directions: the limit of the various different understandings of these sentient beings in the ten directions may be known, but the limit of the virtues of the enlightening being's first determination on enlightenment cannot be known by anyone. Why? Because enlightening beings do not set their minds on unexcelled complete perfect enlightenment just to know the understandings of a particular limited number of sentient beings. They set their minds on unexcelled complete perfect enlightenment to know the various different understandings of all sentient beings in all worlds. That is, they want to know different understandings are boundless, and that one sentient being's understanding is equal to countless sentient beings' understandings; they want to attain the light of knowledge of liberative techniques appropriate to unspeakably many different understandings; they want to know all the individual different understandings in the ocean of sentient beings; they want to know all the infinite various understandings, good and bad, of past, present, and future; they want to know all understandings which resemble each other and those which don't; they want to know all understandings are one understanding, one understanding is all understandings; they want to attain the enlightened ones' power of understanding; they want to know the differences between understanding that can be surpassed and understanding that is unexcelled, understanding which has remainder and understanding without remainder, equal understandings and unequal understandings; they want to know the differences between dependent and independent understanding, common understanding and unique understanding, bounded understanding and boundless understanding, differentiated understanding and undifferentiated understanding, good understanding and bad understanding, mundane understanding and trans-mundane understanding; they want to attain the unhindered knowledge of liberation of the enlightened in respect to all subtle understanding, great understanding, infinite understanding, and understanding of the

★That is, "eon" is a division that is ultimately arbitrary.

true state; they want to know, by means of infinite appropriate means, the pure understandings and defiled understandings, broad understandings and summary understandings, fine understandings and coarse understandings, of each and every sentient being in all realms of sentient beings in the ten directions; they want to know deeply secret understandings, expedient understandings, discriminating understandings, spontaneous understandings, understandings that arise according to causes, understandings that arise according to conditions, the networks of all understandings—to know these they set their minds on unexcelled complete perfect enlightenment.

"Again, setting aside this example, suppose there is someone who can in one instant know the differences in faculties of all sentient beings in countless worlds in the eastern direction, and continues in this way for an incalculable eon; then suppose there is a second person who could know in one instant all the differences in faculties known by the first person, in each instant of an incalculable eon; extend this to the tenth person and apply it also to the other nine directions—the limit of the various differences in faculties of the sentient beings of the worlds of the ten directions might be known, but no one can know the limit of the virtues of the enlightening being's initial determination for unexcelled complete perfect enlightenment. Why? Because enlightening beings do not set their minds on unexcelled complete perfect enlightenment just to know the faculties of sentient beings in a given limited number of worlds. It is to know all the various differences in faculties of all beings in all worlds, wanting to know the network of all faculties, that they set their minds on unexcelled complete perfect enlightenment.

"Again setting this example aside, suppose there is someone who can in a single instant know the inclinations of all the sentient beings in countless worlds in the eastern direction, thus knowing more and more instant after instant for an incalculable eon. Extend this as before to ten people, and to all ten directions: the limit of the inclinations of these sentient beings of the ten directions might be known, but a limit to the virtues of the enlightening being's first determination for unexcelled complete perfect enlightenment cannot be known by anyone. Why? Because the enlightening being's determination for enlightenment is not limited to just the purpose of knowing the inclinations of a limited number of sentient beings. It is to know all the inclinations of all beings in all worlds, wanting to know the network of all inclinations, that they set their minds on unexcelled complete perfect enlightenment.

"Again, setting this example aside, suppose there is someone who can in a single instant know the techniques of all the sentient beings in countless lands in the eastern direction, and extend this example as before to ten people and to all ten directions: the extent of the various techniques of these sentient beings of the ten directions may be known, but the extent of the virtues of the enlightening being's initial determination for enlightenment cannot be known by anyone. Why? Because enlightening beings do not set their minds on unexcelled complete perfect enlightenment just to know the various techniques of beings of a limited number of worlds. It is to know all the techniques of all beings of all worlds, wanting to know the network of all techniques, that they set their minds on unexcelled complete enlightenment.

"Again, setting this example aside, suppose there is someone who can in a single instant know the various different mentalities of sentient beings in countless worlds in the eastern direction, and extend this example as before to ten people and to all ten directions: the bounds of the various different mentalities of the sentient beings in all these worlds of the ten directions may be known, but the bounds of the virtues of the enlightening being's first determination for unexcelled complete perfect enlightenment cannot be known to anyone. Why? Because enlightening beings do not set their minds on unexcelled complete perfect enlightenment just to know the mentalities of a limited number of sentient beings; it is to know the various mentalities of the boundless sentient beings of the whole realm of space of the cosmos, wanting to completely know the network of all minds, that they set their minds on unexcelled complete perfect enlightenment.

"Again, setting this example aside, suppose there is someone who can in a single instant know the various different actions of the sentient beings in countless worlds in the eastern direction; as before, extend this to the tenth person and to the ten directions: the bounds of the various different actions of these sentient beings of the ten directions may be known, but the bounds of the virtues of the enlightening being's initial determination for unexcelled enlightenment cannot be known. Why? Because enlightening beings do not set their minds on unexcelled complete perfect enlightenment only to know the actions of the sentient beings of a limited number of places. They want to know the actions of all sentient beings of past, present, and future, and want to know the network of all actions—this is why they set their minds on unexcelled complete perfect enlightenment.

"Again, leaving this example aside, suppose there is someone who can in one instant know the various afflictions of the sentient beings of countless worlds in the eastern direction, and thus knows more and more instant by instant for an entire incalculable eon; no one could know the bounds of the various differences of these afflictions. Now suppose there is a second person who can in one instant know all the differences in afflictions of sentient beings known by the first person in an incalculable eon, and also went on like this knowing more and more instant by instant for an incalculable eon. Again, extend this to the tenth person and the ten directions: the bounds of the differences of afflictions of these sentient beings of the ten directions may be known, but the limits of the virtues of the enlightening being's initial determination on enlightenment cannot be known. Why? Because enlightening beings do not set their minds on unexcelled complete perfect enlighten-

ment just to know the afflictions of sentient beings in a limited number
of worlds; they set their minds on unexcelled complete perfect enlightenment to know all the differences in afflictions of all beings in all
worlds. In other words, they want to thoroughly know light afflictions
and heavy afflictions, afflictions of sleep and afflictions of waking, the
various differences in the innumerable afflictions of each and every
sentient being, and their various musings and ruminations, to clear
away all their confusions and defilements; they want to thoroughly
know all afflictions based on ignorance and afflictions connected with
affection, to cut off all bonds of afflictions in all realms of being; they
want to thoroughly know all afflictions of greed, all afflictions of
hatred, all afflictions of folly, and all afflictions of greed, hatred, and
folly in equal measure, to sever the root of all afflictions; they want to
thoroughly know all afflictions of ego, afflictions of possessions, and
afflictions of conceit, to be totally aware of all afflictions; they want to
thoroughly know all basic and concomitant afflictions arising from
misconceptions, and the sixty-two views arising from the idea of a real
body existing, to vanquish all afflictions; they want to know thoroughly the afflictions of mental shrouds and hindrances; to develop a
heart of great compassion to rescue and protect, to sunder the web of
all afflictions and cause the nature of omniscience to be utterly pure—
this is why they set their minds on unexcelled complete perfect
enlightenment.

"Again, leaving this example aside, suppose there is someone who in
the space of an instant presents countless Buddhas as well as sentient
beings of innumerable worlds in the eastern direction with various fine
foods and drinks, fragrant flowers and raiment, banners, pennants,
canopies, parasols, sanctuaries with beautiful chambers, jeweled curtains and enclosures of nets, lion seats with various adornments, as well
as all kinds of exquisite jewels, reverently honoring them, bowing to
them and lauding them, humbly looking up to them, and continues
thus unceasingly for countless eons, and also urges other sentient beings
to make such offerings to the Buddhas, and after the Buddhas die sets
up a monument for each one, the monuments high and wide, made of
all kinds of precious substances from countless worlds, variously
decorated, with countless statues of Buddhas in each monument, with
radiance illuminating countless worlds, continuing this work for countless eons; and suppose the person did the same in the South, West, and
North, the four intermediate directions, the zenith and the nadir: Do
you think this person's merit would be great?"

The king of gods said, "Only a Buddha could know this person's
merit—no one else could assess it."

"Child of Buddha, this person's merit, compared to the merit of the
enlightening being's initial determination for enlightenment, does not
amount to a hundredth part, a thousandth, a hundred thousandth part,
not even the smallest fraction.

"Again setting this example aside, suppose there is a second person who can in a single instant perform all the acts of almsgiving performed by the first person in countless worlds, to the beings therein, for countless eons; and suppose this person went on like this, instant after instant, presenting innumerable kinds of offerings to countless Buddhas as well as the sentient beings of innumerable worlds, for innumerable eons; and suppose that a third person, up to a tenth person, could each perform in an instant all the almsgiving performed by the preceding person, and did so instant after instant, presenting boundless, incomparably many, uncountable, unaccountably many, unthinkably many, immeasurably many, unspeakably many, unspeakably unspeakably many offerings to infinite, untold Buddhas as well as to all the sentient beings in as many worlds, for unspeakably unspeakably many eons, and then after the passing of each Buddha, built a monument for each one, high and wide, as previously described. This merit too would not amount to even the smallest fraction of the virtue of the enlightening being's initial determination for enlightenment. Why? Because enlightening beings do not set their minds on unexcelled complete perfect enlightenment just to make offerings to a certain number of Buddhas. They set their minds on unexcelled complete perfect enlightenment to make offerings to all the innumerable, unspeakably unspeakably many past, present, and future Buddhas of the entire space of the whole cosmos in all directions.

"Having aroused this determination, they are able to know the first attainment of true awakening as well as the final release of all Buddhas of the past, are able to believe in the roots of goodness of all Buddhas of the future, and are able to know the knowledge and wisdom of all Buddhas of the present. The virtues of those Buddhas, these enlightening beings can believe in, can accept, can cultivate, can attain, can know, can witness, and can perfect; they can be equal, of the same nature, as the Buddhas. Why? Because these enlightening beings arouse their aspiration in order not to let the lineage of all enlightened ones die out; they arouse their aspiration in order to pervade all worlds; they arouse their determination in order to liberate the beings of all worlds; they arouse their aspiration in order to completely know the formation and disintegration of all worlds; they arouse their determination in order to completely know the defilement and purity of all beings; they arouse their minds in order to know the purity of the realms of desire, form, and formlessness in all worlds; they arouse their determination in order to completely know the inclinations, afflictions, and mental habits of all living beings; they arouse their aspiration in order to completely know the faculties and means of all beings; they arouse their determination in order to completely know the mental activities of all beings; they arouse their aspiration in order to know all beings' knowledge of past, present, and future. Because they have set their minds on enlightenment, they are always remembered by all the Buddhas of past, present, and future, and will attain the unsurpassed enlightenment of all Buddhas of all times. Then they will be given the sublime teachings of all Buddhas of all times, and will be actually and essentially equal to all Buddhas of all times. Having cultivated the methods of fostering the Path used by all Buddhas of all times, consummated the powers and fearlessnesses of all Buddhas of all times, and adorned themselves with the unique qualities of all Buddhas of all times, they will thoroughly attain the knowledge and wisdom to explain the truth of all Buddhas of the cosmos. Why? Because by means of this determination they will attain Buddhahood.

"Know that such a person is thereupon the same as the Buddhas of all times, thereupon equal in perspective to the Buddhas of all times, thereupon equal in virtue to the Buddhas of all times, and attains the true knowledge of the ultimate equality of one body and infinite bodies of the Enlightened.

"As soon as one sets the mind on complete enlightenment, one is praised by all the Buddhas of all quarters and can thereupon expound the teaching, edify and purify the beings of all worlds, and can thereupon shake all worlds, and can thereupon illumine all worlds, and can thereupon extinguish the pains of the states of misery in all worlds, and can thereupon beautify and purify all lands, and can thereupon manifest attainment of Buddhahood in all worlds, and can thereupon cause all living things to rejoice, and can thereupon enter into the essence of all reality realms, and can thereupon maintain the lineage of all enlightened ones, and can thereupon attain the light of wisdom of all Buddhas.

"This enlightening being who has just aspired to enlightenment does not apprehend anything in the past, present, or future—whether Buddhas, Buddhas' teachings, enlightening beings, principles of enlightening beings, solitary awakened ones, principles of solitary awakened ones, listeners, principles of listeners, the world, worldly things, the transmundane, transmundane things, sentient beings, or norms of sentient beings—the enlightening being only seeks omniscience and has no mental attachment to anything."

At that point, by the spiritual power of the Buddha, worlds as numerous as the atoms in ten thousand buddha-lands in each of the ten directions all quaked in six ways, rained celestial flowers, perfumes, incenses, garlands, robes, jewels, and ornaments, produced celestial music and radiated celestial lights and sounds. Now in each of the ten directions, beyond as many worlds as atoms in ten buddha-lands, were as many Buddhas as atoms in ten thousand buddha-lands, all named Truth Wisdom; each of them appeared bodily before the enlightening being Truth Wisdom and said these words: "Good, good! Truth Wisdom, you are now able to expound this teaching; we Buddhas, as many in each of the ten directions as atoms in ten thousand buddha-lands, also expound this teaching. All Buddhas teach in this way. As you expounded this teaching, there were as many enlightening beings as atoms in ten thousand buddha-lands who were inspired with the determination for enlightenment: we now give them all the prediction of enlightenment, that in the future, after ten unspeakable numbers of boundless eons, they will alike attain buddhahood in the same eon, and, appearing in the world, will all be called Pure Mind Buddha. The worlds they live in will each be different. We will all protect and keep this teaching, so that all the enlightening beings of the future who have not heard it will be able to hear it."

As in this world Endurance, atop the Mt. Sumerus of the four quarters, this teaching was spoken, to cause them to accept the teaching once they have heard it, so also was it spoken in all the countless worlds throughout the universe, to edify living beings. All those who expounded it were called Truth Wisdom. They spoke such a teaching by the spiritual power of the Buddhas, by the power of the Buddhas' original vow, in order to reveal the Buddhas' teaching, to illumine all with the light of knowledge, to expose the truth, to cause beings to realize the essence of things, to cause all congregations to rejoice, to reveal the causal basis of the Buddhas' teaching, to realize the equality of all Buddhas, to comprehend the nonduality of the realm of reality.

Then the enlightening being Truth Wisdom looked over all the congregations in all lands in the ten directions of the entire realm of space, and because he desired to perfect the living beings, because he wanted to purify all actions, results, and consequences, because he wanted to reveal the realm of reality, because he wanted to extirpate the roots of defilement, because he wanted to increase great faith and resolution, because he wanted to cause all to know the faculties of infinite sentient beings, because he wanted to cause all to know the equality of past, present, and future phenomena, because he wanted to cause all to contemplate the realm of nirvana, and because he wanted to increase inherently pure roots of goodness, he spoke these verses by the power of Buddha:

> To benefit the world enlightening beings make a great resolution,
> That resolution extending everywhere throughout the ten directions:
> Living beings, lands, the phenomena of past, present, and future,
> Enlightened as well as enlightening beings, supreme oceans,
> To the limits of space, equal to the cosmos,
> And all the worlds there are therein:
> In accord with Buddhas' teachings, they go to every one;
> Arousing their minds this way, they never regress.
> They think of living beings with compassion, never abandoning
>   them;
> They reject all that is harmful, benefiting all.
> Their light illumines the world, being as a refuge,
> Guarded by the Ten Powered inconceivably.

They enter all lands in the ten directions,
Manifesting all kinds of physical forms.
In accord with Buddhas' virtue and knowledge, boundless,
They cultivate the appropriate causes, without any attachment.

Some lands face upward, some sideways or inverted;
Coarse, subtle, wide and vast—there are innumerable kinds:
Once enlightening beings have roused the supreme aspiration,
They can travel to all of them, unobstructed.
Enlightening beings' supreme practices cannot be all told:
All they cultivate diligently without dwelling anywhere.
Seeing all Buddhas, they're always joyful,
And enter everywhere into the ocean of profound truths.
Pitying beings living in mundane dispositions,
They cause them to clear away defilements, to be thoroughly
    pure;
Succeeding to the lineage of Buddhas, they do not let it die out:
They devastate the palace of demons, completely destroying them.
Dwelling in the equanimity of the Enlightened,
They skillfully cultivate subtle techniques.
Developing aspiration for the realm of buddhahood,
They are anointed by the Buddhas, their minds without attach-
    ment.
Remembering to requite their debt to the Most Honorable Human,
Their minds are incorruptible, like diamond.
Able to clearly comprehend the sphere of Buddhas' action,
They naturally cultivate and practice enlightening deeds.

The different thoughts of the various realms of beings are infinite—
Their acts, their results, and their minds are also not one—
Everything down to their various different faculties and natures
Are all clearly seen once the great mind is developed.
That mind is far-reaching, as vast as the cosmos;
Without reliance, unchanging, like space—
Heading for Buddha-knowledge without grasping anything,
It clearly comprehends the realm of truth, apart from discrimina-
    tory thought.
Knowing the minds of living beings without the concept of beings,
Comprehending all things without the concept of things,
Though discriminating all, yet free from discrimination,
It goes to all lands, billions and trillions.
Following, contemplating, able to enter all
The wondrous troves of teachings of countless Buddhas,
Knowing all the faculties and behaviors of living beings,
Those who have reached this point are like the Buddha.
Always in accord with the pure great vow,

Gladly supporting the enlightened without turning back,
Always pleasing to the sight of humans and celestials,
Always protected mindfully by the Buddhas,
Their minds are pure, free from dependence;
Though they contemplate the profound teaching, they do not
    cling,
Meditating thus for countless eons
Without any attachments in the past, present, or future.
Their minds are firm and sure, impossible to overcome;
They proceed to Buddhas' enlightenment without obstruction.
Determined to seek the wondrous Way, they get rid of infantile
    ignorance;
Traversing the whole cosmos, they do not complain of weariness.
They know the phenomena of speech and language are all null and
    void;
Only entering into true thusness, they cut off different interpreta-
    tions.
Harmoniously observing all the spheres of the enlightened,
They comprehend all frames of time, their minds without
    obstruction.
When enlightening beings first develop the vastly great mind,
They can go to all lands in the ten directions:
Aspects of truth beyond number or explanation
Their light of knowledge illumines clearly.
Liberating many with great compassion, utterly beyond compare,
Their kindness extends everywhere, like space.
And yet they do not discriminate in regard to living beings;
Thus being pure, they roam through the world.
Giving solace and comfort to living beings everywhere,
Everything they do is true and genuine.
Always with a pure heart, they don't contradict themselves;
They are always strengthened and protected by all the Buddhas.
They remember everything that was in the past,
And discern everything in the future.
They enter all worlds in the ten directions
To liberate beings, causing them to be detached.
Enlightening beings have the light of sublime knowledge
And understand causes and conditions beyond any doubt.
They do away with all confusion and delusion,
And in this way roam the reality-realm.
All the palaces of demons they smash;
All the blinders of living beings they destroy.
Free from discrimination, minds undisturbed,
They understand well the realm of the enlightened.
They have removed the webs of doubt of all time
And aroused faith in those who have realized thusness.

By faith they've attained immutable knowledge,
And because their knowledge is pure their understanding is true.
In order to allow living beings to attain emancipation,
And to benefit them universally throughout all time,
They undergo long toils and hardships unflagging,
Calmly enduring even the pains of the hells.
Replete with boundless virtue and wisdom,
They know all the faculties and inclinations of beings;
They see all, including their works and deeds,
And teach them in accord with their tendencies.
They understand all is empty and selfless,
Yet think kindly of beings, never abandoning them;
With one subtle, sublime voice of great compassion
They enter all worlds to teach.
Emanating great lights of various colors,
They shine on all beings, removing the darkness;
In the lights are enlightening beings sitting on lotus blossoms
Bringing forth the pure teaching for all beings.
In a single pore they manifest many lands,
With great enlightening beings filling them all.
The knowledge of the congregation is different for each,
While all can understand the minds of living beings.
To unspeakably many lands in the ten directions
They can go in an instant, to all of them,
Aiding beings, giving offerings to Buddhas.
From the Buddhas they ask the profound truth;
They think of the enlightened ones as parents,
And perform enlightening practices to benefit sentient beings.
With wisdom and flexible means they penetrate the treasury of
     truths,
Entering the profound realm of knowledge without any attachment.
Meditating in accord with truth, they explain the reality-realm
For countless eons, without being able to exhaust it.
Though their knowledge skillfully penetrates, it has no location;
They are not tired or wearied, have no attachment to anything.
Born in the house of the Buddhas of past, present, and future,
They experience the subtle reality-body of the enlightened ones.
Manifesting various forms for all living beings,
Like magicans there's nothing they can't make:
Some manifest the beginning of practice of excellent action,
Some manifest birth, up to leaving home,
Some manifest fulfilling enlightenment under a tree,
And some show extinction, for the benefit of beings.
The rare truth in which enlightening beings abide
Is only the realm of Buddhas, not the two vehicles.
They are rid of concepts of body, speech, and thought,

But can manifest them variously, according to the occasion.
The Buddha-teachings attained by enlightening beings
Sentient beings go crazy when thinking of.
The knowledge of enlightening beings enters reality, their minds
  unhindered;
Everywhere they manifest the independent powers of the Enlight-
  ened;
In this they have no compare in all the world:
How much the more when their excellent practices are added.
Though they have not yet completely fulfilled omniscience,
They have already attained the independent power of the enlight-
  ened.
Already they abide on the ultimate path of the One Vehicle
And enter deeply into the subtle highest truth.
They know beings well, and appropriate and inappropriate times;
For beings' benefit they reveal spiritual powers:
Multiplying their bodies, they fill all lands,
Emanating pure light to remove the darkness of the world.
Like dragon kings producing great clouds,
They shower wonderful rains, filling and refreshing all.
They see sentient beings as like illusions and dreams,
Always revolving in circles from the force of their acts;
With compassion and pity they rescue them all,
Explaining to them the uncreated, pure nature of things.
The infinity of Buddhas' powers is also like this:
Like space, it has no bounds.
In order to enable sentient beings to attain liberation,
They diligently practice for eons untiring.
Pondering in various ways upon wondrous virtues,
They skillfully cultivate the unsurpassed foremost of works;
Never giving up the transcendent practices,
They concentrate on developing omniscience.
With one body they manifest innumerable bodies,
Omnipresent throughout all worlds,
Their minds pure, with no discrimination;
Such is their instantaneous inconceivable power.
They do not discriminate among worlds,
They have no illusions about any thing;
While they contemplate the teachings, they do not grasp them,
And though they are always rescuing beings none are delivered.
All worlds are only mental images:
Therein are various distinctions:
Knowing the realms of ideation are dangerous and deep,
Enlightening beings manifest spiritual powers to rescue and liberate.
Like the powers of a magician
Are the spiritual metamorphoses of enlightening beings;

Their bodies fill the cosmos and space
For all to see according to their mentalities.
Both distinctions of subject and object they have left behind:
Whether defiled or pure, nothing do they grasp;
Cognition of bondage or of liberation they entirely forget,
Only vowing to grant bliss to all sentient beings.
All worlds being only the force of ideation,
They enter them by knowledge with minds free from fear.
Their contemplation of all things is also thus:
Investigating their past, present, and future, they cannot be
      apprehended.
Able to enter into the whole of the past,
Able to enter into the whole of the future,
Able to enter into all places in the present,
They always observe diligently how nothing exists.
According with the dispassionate state of nirvana,
They abide in noncontention and nonreliance.
Their minds, like ultimate reality, have no compare:
They are turned wholly to enlightenment, never to regress.
Cultivating supreme practice without backsliding or weakening,
They rest on enlightenment, unwavering.
Buddhas, enlightening beings, and the worlds
Throughout the cosmos, they all clearly understand.
If you want to attain the supreme, foremost of paths,
And be an omniscient sovereign of liberty,
You should quickly develop the determination for enlightenment,
Forever end indulgence and help sentient beings;
Proceeding to enlightenment, mind pure,
Your virtues will be vast and great beyond telling.
I am setting this forth for the benefit of beings:
Those of intelligence should listen well.
Infinite worlds are all atoms:
In each atom are infinite lands;
The Buddhas in each are infinite:
Enlightening beings see all clearly without any grasping;
They know living beings without having such a concept,
They know spoken words with no idea of speech.
Their minds are unhindered in any world:
They comprehend all without attachments.
Their minds are broad and vast as space,
They comprehend all things in all times.
They annihilate all doubt and confusion,
And correctly perceive the Buddhas' teachings without clinging.
To infinite lands in the ten directions
They instantly go, their minds without attachment.
Understanding the reasons for suffering in the world,

They all dwell in the uncreated sphere of reality.
To the assemblies of infinite Buddhas
They go to call on them;
Always being leaders, they ask the Buddhas
About the vows and practices cultivated by enlightening beings.
Their minds always remember the Buddhas of the ten directions,
Yet without depending on or grasping anything.
They constantly urge living beings to plant roots of goodness,
Adorning their lands, making them pure.
All sentient beings in all realms of existence
They observe with unobstructed eyes:
Their habits, natures, faculties, and understandings,
Countless and boundless, all they clearly see.
Aware of all defilement and purity,
They cause them to cultivate themselves and enter the Way.
Measureless, countless meditation concentrations
Enlightening beings can enter in a single instant:
Their perceptions, knowledges and objects therein
They all know thoroughly and attain mastery.
Enlightening beings, attaining this great knowledge,
Immediately direct it to enlightenment, unhindered.
Because they want to help and benefit living beings,
Wherever they are they expound the principles of great people.
They know the long and short eons of the worlds,
A month, a fortnight, a day and a night,
In each land are different, but equal in essence.
Always diligently observing, they are not lax or indulgent;
Going to all worlds in the ten directions,
Yet they do not cling to place or location;
Adorning and purifying all lands with exception,
Yet they never produce the concept of purity.
Sentient beings' rights and wrongs,
The differences in their deeds and the consequences,
They accordingly reflect upon, entering the Buddha's power
And comprehending all of this.
The various natures in all worlds,
Various courses of action, and their realms of being,
Sharp faculties as well as the middling and inferior—
All such things do they observe and examine.
Various understandings, pure and impure,
Superior, inferior, and middling, all they clearly see.
The acts of all beings and where they lead,
The continuity of realms of being—all they can explain.
Meditations, concentrations, liberations, trances,
Defiled and pure, their causes and origins each different:
These, plus the differences of pain and pleasure of past lives,

Purely cultivating Buddha-power, all they can see.
Sentient beings' habitual delusions continue the various states of
    being—
By cutting off these tendencies and states they attain peace and
    dispassion,
Various tainted states do not arise anymore:
All this, and the seeds of those habits, enlightening beings know.
The afflictions of the Enlightened are all extinguished:
Their light of great knowledge illumines the world.
Though enlightening beings have not yet attained
Buddhas' ten powers, yet they do not have doubt.
Enlightening beings, in a single pore,
Manifest the infinite lands of the ten directions:
Some are defiled, some are pure,
Made by various deeds—all do they comprehend.
In a single atom, infinite lands,
With infinite Buddhas and their offspring;
The lands are each distinct, not mixed up:
As of one, all they clearly see.
In one pore they see all the worlds
In the space of the ten directions.
There is not a single place where there is no Buddha;
Thus are the buddha-lands all pure.
In a pore they see buddha-lands
And also see all sentient beings:
The three times and six dispositions are not the same—
Day and night, month and hour, bondage and freedom.
Thus do enlightening beings of great knowledge
Single-mindedly head for the sovereignty of truth.
Meditating on the abode of the Enlightened,
They obtain boundless great joy.
Enlightening beings multiply their bodies into countless billions
To make offerings to all the enlightened ones;
The manifestations of their spiritual powers are supreme, incom-
    parable—
They can abide in all the spheres of action of the Buddhas.
They praise and look up to all the countless Buddhas
And deeply savor the treasuries of all their teachings.
Seeing the Buddhas, hearing their teachings, they diligently prac-
    tice them,
Their hearts joyful, as if they were drinking ambrosial elixir of
    immortality.
Having attained the supreme concentration of the enlightened,
They delve into all truths and their knowledge grows.
Their faith is unshakable as a great mountain,
Being a treasury of virtues for all living beings.

Their compassion is great, extending to all living creatures:
All they hope will soon develop universal knowledge.
Yet they are always without attachment or dependence;
Shedding afflictions, they've attained freedom.
Vast in knowledge, with pity for sentient beings,
They embrace all as the same as themselves.
With awareness of emptiness, signlessness, and unreality,
Yet they act, their minds unflagging.
The virtues of enlightening beings' determination for enlightenment
Could not be exhaustively told even in a billion eons,
Because it produces all the Enlightened Ones,
And the bliss of the self-enlightened and Buddhas' disciples.
To give peace for countless eons
To all the beings of the lands of the ten directions,
Urging them to keep the five precepts and ten virtues,
The four meditations, four equipoises, and such concentrations,
And also giving them bliss for many eons,
Causing them to cut off delusions and become saints,
Amasses virtue which may be immeasurable,
But cannot compare to the virtue of the will for enlightenment.
Also, to cause millions to achieve individual awakening
And attain the subtle path of noncontentious action,
Does not amount to anything much at all
Compared to the determination for enlightenment.
If one could pass billions of lands in an instant
And did so for immeasurable eons,
The number of these lands might be assessed,
But the virtues of the will for enlightenment cannot be known.
The number of eons past, future, and present
Is boundless, yet still might be known;
But the virtue of rousing the mind to enlightenment
Cannot be measured by anyone.
This is because the determination for enlightenment extends
    everywhere,
Knowing all discernments that exist,
Comprehending past, present, and future in an instant,
Benefiting innumerable sentient beings.
The desires, understandings, means, and mental patterns
Of the sentient beings of the worlds of the ten directions,
As well as the bounds of space, might be measured,
But the virtues of the aspirations for enlightenment cannot be
    assessed.
Enlightening beings' aspiration is equal to the ten directions;
Their kindness universally nourishes all living beings,
Causing all to cultivate the virtues of buddhahood:
That's why their power has no bounds.

Sentient beings' desires, understandings, inclinations,
Faculties, devices, and practices are all different;
Enlightening beings know them all instantly,
Same as the mind of omniscience.
The deluded actions of living beings
Continue through time without interruption,
Yet their bounds still might be known;
But the virtues of will for enlightenment are inconceivable.
Will for enlightenment can divorce afflictions of action
And provide offerings to all the Enlightened:
Once habitual delusions are divorced, their continuity's broken,
And liberation is attained for all time.
If one gives offerings to boundless Buddhas in an instant,
And also gives to countless sentient beings,
Fragrant flowers and garlands,
Precious banners, canopies, and raiment,
Fine food, excellent seats, and places to walk around,
Various palaces, all finely adorned,
Luminous, wonderful pearls,
Wish-fulfilling jewels, radiating light,
And brings such offerings moment after moment
Over countless eons, beyond the power of speech,
Though such a person's accumulation of merit would be great,
It does not equal the magnitude of the virtue of aspiring to
    enlightenment.
None of the various examples told
Can match the determination for enlightenment,
Because the most honorable people of all times
Have all been born from this aspiration.
The will for enlightenment is unhindered, unlimited:
No measure can be found for it.
Vowing to fulfill omniscience,
To forever deliver all beings,
That aspiration is vast as space,
Producing virtues equal to the cosmos.
Their share of action extending everywhere, as though there were
    no difference,
Forever leaving all attachments, equal to the Buddhas,
Entering all gates of truth,
Able to travel to all lands,
Arriving at all spheres of knowledge,
Perfecting all virtues,
Able to relinquish everything, always consistent,
Purifying behavior, free from attachment,
Fulfilling unsurpassed virtues,
Always persevering without regression,

Entering deep concentration, always meditating,
Uniting with vastly great knowledge and wisdom:
This is the supreme stage of enlightening beings,
Producing the path of all the Universally Good.
All the Enlightened Ones of past, present, and future
Protect the initial aspiration,
Adorning it with spiritual powers and mystic transfiguration,
With concentrations and spells.
The living beings of the ten directions are infinite,
As are the worlds and space:
But the infinity of the enlightenment aspiration surpasses these:
Hence it can give birth to all Buddhas.
The will for enlightenment is the basis of the ten powers
As well as the four special knowledges and fearlessnesses.
The same is true of the eighteen unique qualities:
All of them are attained from the aspiration for enlightenment.
The Buddhas' physically adorned bodies,
As well as their equal body of reality,
Their knowledge, wisdom, and nonattachment, worthy of honor,
All can exist because of the determination for enlightenment.
All the vehicles of individual illuminates and Buddhist disciples,
The pleasures of the meditation states of the realm of form,
As well as the trances of the formless realm,
All have the will for enlightenment as their basis.
The free pleasures of humans and gods,
As well as the various pleasures of the other states of being,
And the pleasures of progress, concentration, religious faculties
    and powers, and so on,
All depend on the first aspiration to enlightenment.
Based on the production of this far-reaching determination
Can one practice the six ways of transcendence:
Urging sentient beings to carry out right practice,
Experiencing peace and happiness in the three realms,
Abiding in the Buddhas' unhindered true knowledge,
Revealing all the wonderful actions there are,
Able to cause countless living beings
To cut off deluded actions and turn to nirvana,
Making vows of boundless virtues
To give happiness to all living beings,
Carrying out these vows forever and ever,
Always working so as to liberate beings,
The infinite great vows inconceivable,
Vowing to purify all living beings—
Though empty, signless, wishless, without reliance,
By the power of will, enlightening beings can reveal them.
Understanding the inherent nature of things is like space;

That all are quiescent, all equal,
The gates of the teaching, countless, unspeakable,
They expound to beings, without attachment.
All Enlightened Ones of the worlds of the ten directions
All praise the first aspiration for enlightenment;
This inspired mind is adorned by infinite virtues
And can arrive at the other shore, same as the Buddhas.
Were those virtues to be expounded for as many eons
As there are living beings, they could not be all told.
Because this mind dwells in the vast house of the Enlightened,
Nothing of the world can compare it or explain it.
If you want to know all the truths of the Buddhas,
You should quickly develop the determination for enlightenment.
This determination is the most excellent of virtues,
Assuring attainment of the unhindered knowledge of the enlight-
    ened.
The mental activities of living beings might be counted,
And so might the number of atoms in a land;
The extent of space might be assessed,
But the virtues of the will for enlightenment cannot be measured:
It produces all the Buddhas of all times,
And perfects happiness in all worlds,
Increases all excellent virtues,
Extirpates all confusion,
Reveals all wondrous realms,
Eliminates all obstacles,
Develops all pure lands,
Produces all enlightened knowledge.
If you want to see all the Buddhas of the ten directions,
And want to disburse from the inexhaustible treasury of virtue,
If you want to extinguish the afflictions of beings,
Quickly arouse the will for enlightenment.

BOOK EIGHTEEN

Clarifying Method

THEN THE ENLIGHTENING BEING Vigorous Wisdom said to the enlightening being Truth Wisdom: "O Child of Buddha: when great enlightening beings first arouse the mind to seek all-knowledge, they fulfill such infinite virtues, are replete with great adornments, climb up into the vehicle of omniscience, enter the correct state of enlightening beings, give up all worldly things and attain the transmundane truths of the Buddhas, are taken into the company of all the Buddhas of past, present, and future, and will certainly reach the ultimate point of unexcelled enlightenment: how should those enlightening beings practice the Buddha-teachings so as to cause all the Enlightened Ones joy, enter the abode of all enlightening beings, attain purity of all great actions, fulfill all great vows, obtain the vast treasuries of enlightening beings, always teach according to necessity and potential for edification without ever giving up the transcending practices, cause all sentient beings under their care to attain deliverance, and continue the lineage of the three treasures unbroken, that their good roots and adaptive skills not be wasted? O Child of Buddha, by what techniques can they cause these things to be fulfilled? Please extend your compassion to explain for us—everyone in this assembly wants to hear.

"Furthermore, if great enlightening beings always diligently practice, to annihilate all the darkness of ignorance, conquer demons and enemies and control heretics, forever wash away all afflictions defiling the mind, they will all be able to perfect all roots of goodness, forever escape the difficulties of all miserable realms of being, purify all spheres of great knowledge, accomplish all the stages of enlightenment and their pure virtues—the transcending practices, mnemonic mastery, concentration, the six superknowledges, and the four fearlessnesses—adorning all Buddha-lands; their physical refinements as well, their bodily, verbal, and mental actions will all be perfectly complete. They will know well all the powers, fearlessnesses, unique qualities, omniscience, and spheres of action of all the Enlightened Ones, the Buddhas. In order to develop and mature all living beings according to their mentalities, they will take appropriate buddha-lands and expound the truth as necessary in accord with beings' faculties and in accord with the time and situation. They will fulfill various immeasurable great Buddha-works, as well as innumerable other virtuous things, various practices, paths, and realms, and soon be equal to the enlightened ones. They can maintain and protect all the treasuries of truths assembled by the perfectly enlightened ones over their hundreds and thousands of immeasurable eons of cultivating enlightening practices, and can expound them unhindered and undisrupted by demons or heretics. They will hold the true teaching forever, and in all worlds when they teach they will be protected by celestial beings, yaksha kings, gandharva kings, titan kings, garuda kings, kinnara kings, mahoraga kings, human kings, Brahma kings, and enlightened kings of truth. All worlds will respect and support them, alike crowning them. They will always be under the care of the Buddhas, and will also be loved and respected by all enlightening beings. Attaining the power of roots of goodness, they will increase virtuous ways, expound the treasury of profound teachings of the Enlightened, and hold the true teaching, wherewith they will adorn themselves. Please expound the process of enlightening beings' practices."

Then the enlightening being Vigorous Wisdom, wanting to reiterate his intention, spoke these verses:

O famous one, well do you expound
The virtues accomplished by enlightening beings,
Deeply entering boundless great action
Fulfilling pure teacherless knowledge.
If enlightening beings, at their first inspiration,
Accomplish the practice of virtue and wisdom,
Enter the rank of freedom from birth, transcending the world,
Universally attaining the principle of true enlightenment,
Then how should they, in the Buddha-teaching,
Stably and strongly practice with diligence, to progress further,
To cause all the Enlightened Ones to rejoice,
To be able to quickly enter the state of the Buddhas,
Fulfill all the pure vows they carry out,
And attain the vast treasury of knowledge and wisdom,
And also be able to teach the truth to liberate beings
Without their minds relying on or attached to anything,
Fulfill all the transcendent ways of enlightening beings,
Rescue and liberate all beings under their care,
Forever maintain the lineage of Buddhas unbroken,
So all they do is sure and not in vain,
And they accomplish all tasks and win emancipation.
Please explain this pure path,
In accord with what all the Victors practice,

To forever destroy the darkness of ignorance,
Overthrow all demons and heretics,
Wash away all defilements,
To be able to approach the great knowledge and wisdom of the
   Enlightened
And forever leave the dangers of the evil ways,
To purify the extraordinary spheres of great knowledge,
Attain the powers of the sublime way, next to the Supreme
   Honored One,
To fulfill all virtues,
Realize the supreme knowledge of the Enlightened,
· Live in innumerable lands
And expound the truth according to the mentalities of the beings
   there,
And perform the various great deeds of Buddhas.
How can they attain the wonderful paths
And expound the treasury of true teachings of the Enlightened,
Always able to accept and hold the Buddha-teachings,
Unsurpassable and incomparable?
How can they be fearless like lions,
Their acts pure as the full moon?
How can they cultivate the Buddhas' virtues,
Like lotuses to which water does not adhere?

Then the enlightening being Truth Wisdom said to the enlightening being Vigorous Wisdom, "Very good, Child of Buddha; you have asked about the pure practice cultivated by enlightening beings, out of compassion for the world, because you wish that many be aided and comforted, that many be benefited. Child of Buddha, you abide by the truth, you activate great vigor, increasing without recession; having already attained liberation, you are able to pose this question, the same as an enlightened one. Listen clearly, think well upon this; now, by the spiritual power of Buddha, I will explain a little of it for you.

"Child of Buddha, once enlightening beings have developed the determination for omniscience, they should leave the darkness of ignorance and diligently guard themselves from indulgence and laxity. If enlightening beings abide by ten things, that is called nonindulgence: one is to keep the behavioral precepts; second is to abandon folly and purify the will for enlightenment; third is to like straightforwardness and reject flattery and deception; fourth is to earnestly cultivate virtues without regressing; fifth is to continually reflect on one's aspiration; sixth is not to enjoy association with ordinary people, whether they be householders or monks; seventh is to do good deeds without hoping for worldly rewards; eighth is to forever leave lesser vehicles and practice the path of enlightening beings; ninth is to gladly practice what is good, not letting goodness be cut off; tenth is to always examine one's own power of perseverance. If enlightening beings practice these ten things, this is called abiding in nonindulgence.

"When enlightening beings persist in nonindulgence, they attain ten kinds of purity: (1) acting in accord with what they say; (2) consummation of attention and discernment; (3) abiding in deep concentration without torpor or agitation; (4) gladly seeking Buddha-teachings without flagging; (5) contemplating the teachings heard according to reason, fully developing skillfully flexible knowledge; (6) entering deep meditation and attaining the psychic powers of Buddhas; (7) their minds are equanimous, without sense of high or low status; (8) in regard to superior, middling, and inferior types of beings, their minds are unobstructed, and like the earth, they benefit all equally; (9) if they see any beings who have even once made the determination for enlightenment, they honor and serve them as teachers; (10) they always respect, serve, and support their preceptors and tutors, and all enlightening beings, wise friends, and teachers. These are called the ten kinds of purity of enlightening beings persisting in nonindulgence.

"Enlightening beings abide in nonindulgence, evoke great vigor, produce correct mindfulness, engender supreme aspiration, and work unceasingly. Their minds are free from dependence on any thing. They are able to diligently cultivate the most profound teaching, and enter the gate of noncontention. Broadening their minds, they are able to accordingly comprehend boundless Buddha-teachings, causing the Enlightened Ones to all rejoice.

"There are ten more things by which enlightening beings can cause the Buddhas to rejoice: (1) persevering without regression; (2) not begrudging their physical life; (3) not seeking profit or support; (4) knowing all things are like space; (5) being skillful at contemplation, entering into all realms of reality; (6) knowing the definitive marks of all things; (7) always invoking great vows; (8) developing the light of pure tolerant knowledge; (9) examining one's own virtues without exaggeration or underestimation; (10) cultivating pure practices in accord with the way of nonstriving. This is called enlightening beings persisting in ten things whereby they are able to bring joy to all the Enlightened Ones.

"There are ten more things by which they can make all Buddhas joyful: abiding securely in nonindulgence; abiding securely in acceptance of nonorigination; abiding securely in great kindness; abiding securely in great compassion; abiding securely in the fulfillment of the transcendent ways; abiding securely in the enlightening practices; abiding securely in great vows; abiding securely in skillful means; abiding securely in dauntless power; abiding securely in knowledge and wisdom, observing all things have no abode, like empty space. If enlightening beings abide in these ten things, they can cause all Buddhas joy.

"There are ten things which cause enlightening beings to quickly enter the stages: (1) skillfully fulfilling the twin practices of virtue and knowledge; (2) ability to greatly adorn the path of the transcendent practices; (3) knowledge clearly comprehending, not following others' words; (4) serving good friends, never abandoning them; (5) always practicing perseverance, without laziness; (6) skillful ability to abide in the psychic powers of Buddhas; (7) cultivating roots of goodness without growing wearied; (8) with a deep mind and incisive knowledge, adorning oneself with the teaching of the Great Vehicle; (9) the mind not dwelling on the teachings of each stage; (10) being of the same essential nature as all Buddhas of all times in virtue and liberative means. These ten things cause enlightening beings to quickly enter the stages.

"Furthermore, when enlightening beings are in the first stage, they should carefully investigate all the principles and knowledge pertaining to it, the causes cultivated there, the effects realized, the spheres, functions, manifestations, distinctions, and attainments pertaining to it. They should carefully examine and realize that all things are one's own mind, and have no attachments to anything; with this knowledge they enter the stages of enlightening beings and can steadfastly continue therein.

"Those enlightening beings formulate these thoughts: 'We should quickly enter the stages. Why? If we sojourn in stage after stage, we will develop such great virtuous qualities; being replete with virtue, we will gradually enter the stage of buddhahood; once we are in the stage of buddhahood, we can perform boundless great buddha-works. Therefore we should always practice diligently and unremittingly, without wearying, adorning ourselves with great virtues and enter the stages of enlightening beings.'

"There are ten things which cause the practices of enlightening beings to be pure: (1) giving up all possessions to satisfy the wishes of sentient beings; (2) adhering to pure morality, not transgressing; (3) being inexhaustibly gentle and tolerant; (4) cultivating practices diligently without regressing; (5) being free from confusion and mental disturbance, through the power of correct mindfulness; (6) analyzing and comprehending the innumerable teachings; (7) cultivating all practices without attachment; (8) being mentally imperturbable, like a great mountain; (9) extensively liberating living beings, like a bridge; (10) knowing that all living beings are in essence the same as the Buddhas. These ten things make enlightening beings' practices pure.

"Once enlightening beings have attained purity in practice, they also attain ten even greater things: (1) the Buddhas of other realms always protect them; (2) their roots of goodness increase, going beyond any comparison; (3) they are able to receive the boosting power of the Buddhas; (4) they always find good people and are relied on by them; (5) they remain diligent and are never heedless; (6) they know all things are equal and not different; (7) their minds always abide in unexcelled great compassion; (8) they observe things as they really are, producing sublime wisdom; (9) they are able to practice skillful techniques of liberation; (10) they are able to know the Enlightened Ones' power of skill in liberative means. These are the ten excellent qualities of enlightening beings.

"Enlightening beings have ten pure vows: (1) they vow to develop living beings to maturity, without wearying; (2) they vow to fully practice all virtues and purify all worlds; (3) they vow to serve the Enlightened, always engendering honor and respect; (4) they vow to keep and protect the true teaching, not begrudging their lives; (5) they vow to observe with wisdom and enter the lands of the Buddhas; (6) they vow to be of the same essence as all enlightening beings; (7) they vow to enter the door of realization of thusness and comprehend all things; (8) they vow that those who see them will develop faith and all be benefited; (9) they vow to stay in the world forever by spiritual power; (10) they vow to fulfill the practice of Universal Good, and master the knowledge of all particulars and all ways of liberation. These are the ten pure vows of enlightening beings.

"Enlightening beings can successfully fulfill their great vows by abiding by ten principles: (1) never wearying in mind; (2) preparing great adornments; (3) remembering the superlative will power of enlightening beings; (4) when hearing about the Buddha-lands, vowing to be born in them all; (5) keeping their profound determination everlasting; (6) vowing to develop all living beings fully; (7) staying through all ages without considering it troublesome; (8) accepting all suffering without aversion; (9) having no craving for or attachment to any pleasures; (10) always diligently protecting the unexcelled teaching.

"When enlightening beings fulfill such vows, they attain ten inexhaustible treasuries: perception of the Buddhas; perfect memory power; certain understanding of all the teachings; compassionate salvation; various states of concentration; extensive blessings and virtues satisfying the hearts of all beings; profound knowledge to expound all truths; spiritual powers gained as a consequence of practice; subsistence for immeasurable eons; entry into boundless worlds. These are enlightening beings' ten inexhaustible treasuries.

"When enlightening beings have attained these ten treasuries, their virtue is complete, their knowledge is pure; they explain the truth to sentient beings according to their needs and capacities. How do enlightening beings explain the truth to sentient beings according to their needs and capacities? They know what beings do; they know their causes and conditions; they know their mental behavior; they know their inclinations. To those with much greed and desire they expound impurity; to those with much anger and hatred they expound magnanimity and kindness; to those with much ignorance and delusion they teach diligent contemplation; to those in whom these poisons of greed, hatred, and ignorance are equal, they expound the teaching of the development of the knowledge to overcome them. Those who like birth and death they teach about the three kinds of suffering. To those who are attached to where they are, they teach the empty nullity of places. To those who are lazy they talk of great vigor. To those who harbor conceit they explain the equality of things. To flatterers and deceivers they tell of the simple honesty of the hearts of enlightening beings. To those who like silence and tranquility they expound the Teaching extensively, so that they will accomplish it. Thus do enlightening beings teach according to what is necessary and appropriate.

"When they expound the Teaching, their expressions interlink, the meanings are free from contradiction and confusion. They observe the context of the teachings, analyze them wisely, determine right and wrong, accord with the definitive marks of things—impermanence, dispassion, and selflessness—and progressively set up boundless practical approaches, to cause all sentient beings to cut off all doubt. They know all faculties well, enter into the teachings of the enlightened, experience true reality, know things are equal, cut off all attachment to things, eliminate all clinging, and always remember the Buddhas, their minds never leaving them for a moment. They know the substance and essence of sounds are equal, and have no attachment to verbalizations. They can skillfully expound examples and allegories, without any contradiction, to make everyone able to realize the impartial body of wisdom which all the Buddhas manifest everywhere according to need and suitability.

"When enlightening beings expound the Teaching to sentient beings in this way, they practice it themselves, increasing its benefit, not giving up the ways of transcendence, fully setting out the path of the transcendent practices. At this time, enlightening beings give up everything external and internal, without attachment, to satisfy the hearts of sentient beings—thus they can purify the transcendent practice of giving. They keep ethical precepts without attachment, forever divorcing conceit—thus they can purify the transcendent practice of morality. They are able to tolerate all evils, with minds equanimous toward all beings, without disturbance or wavering, just like the earth, able to bear all—thus they can purify the transcendent practice of forbearance. They undertake all practices without laziness, never regressing in what they do, with indomitable courage and energy, not grasping or rejecting all virtues, but able to fulfill all aspects of knowledge—thus they can purify the transcendent practice of vigor. They have no attachment or greed for any objects of desire, are able to consummate the successive degrees of concentration, always meditate correctly, neither dwelling in or leaving concentration, yet able to dissolve all afflictions, produce innumerable facets of concentration, develop boundless great psychic powers, going back and forth successively from meditation state to meditation state, in one meditation enter boundless meditations, knowing all spheres of meditation, not discordant with the seal of knowledge of all concentrations and trances, able to quickly enter the stage of omniscience—thus they can purify the transcendent practice of meditation. Hearing the Teaching from the Buddhas and accepting and keeping it, associating with wise companions, serving them tirelessly, always glad to hear the teaching, never growing weary of it, thinking about what is heard according to the true principle, entering genuine concentration, divorcing all biased views, observing all things well, apprehending the definite mark of the character of reality, comprehending the effortless path of the Enlightened, riding on universal wisdom, entering the gate of the knowledge of all knowledge, attaining eternal rest—thus can they purify transcendent wisdom.

"Manifesting all worldly occupations to teach living beings, never getting tired of it, appearing to them in forms pleasing to them, having no attachments to anything done, sometimes manifesting the acts of ordinary people, sometimes manifesting the acts of sages, sometimes manifesting birth and death, sometimes manifesting nirvana, able to keenly observe all doings and manifest all adornments without covetousness, entering all realms of existence to liberate sentient beings—thus can they purify the transcendent practice of skill in means.

"Thoroughly developing all living beings, thoroughly adorning all worlds, making offerings to all Buddhas, completely arriving at the state of nonobstruction, thoroughly cultivating practice extending throughout the universe, physically remaining throughout all times, knowing the thoughts of all minds, being fully aware that all cyclic transformations return to extinction, appearing in all lands, completely realizing the knowledge and wisdom of the enlightened—thus they can purify the transcendent practice of vows.

"Replete with the power of profound will, being without defilement, replete with the power of profound faith, being invincible, replete with the power of great compassion, never being wearied, replete with the power of great kindness, being impartial in action, replete with memory power, being able to skillfully retain all meanings, replete with the power of elucidation, causing all beings to be happy and fulfilled, replete with the power of transcendent practices, adorning the great vehicle, replete with the power of vows, never ceasing, replete with the power of spiritual abilities, producing innumerable miracles, replete with the power of strengthening and sustaining, able to induce faith and acceptance—thus can they purify the transcendent practice of power.

"Knowing those who act on covetousness, knowing those who act on anger, knowing those who act on folly, knowing those who act equally on all of these, knowing those who cultivate learning, in a single thought knowing the actions of boundless sentient beings, knowing the minds of boundless sentient beings, knowing the truth of all things, knowing the powers of all enlightened ones, being aware of all aspects of the cosmos of reality—thus can they purify the transcendent practice of knowledge.

"Child of Buddha, when enlightening beings thus purify the transcendent practices, fulfill the transcendent practices, do not give up the transcendent practices, they abide in the magnificently adorned vehicle of enlightening beings, and expound the Teaching to all sentient beings who come to their attention, causing them to increase pure conduct and attain liberation. Those who have fallen into evil ways they cause to aspire to enlightenment, those in difficulty they cause to diligently persevere. To the greedy they teach desirelessness. The wrathful they induce to practice equanimity. To those attached to views they explain interdependent origination. Beings in the realm of desire they teach to divorce unwholesome things like craving and hatred. To beings in the realm of form they teach analytic insight. To beings in the formless realm they expound subtle wisdom. To people of the two lesser vehicles they teach the practice of dispassion and tranquility. To those who like the great vehicle they expound the great adornment of the ten powers.

"As in the past when they first aspired to enlightenment they saw innumerable beings fallen into evil ways, they made the great lion's roar and said, 'I should by means of various teachings appropriate to their needs and potentials rescue and liberate them'; enlightening beings, replete with such knowledge and wisdom, are able to liberate all sentient beings.

"Child of Buddha, enlightening beings, endowed with such knowledge and wisdom, cause the lineage of the three treasures never to end. How? Great enlightening beings teach creatures to awaken the will for enlightenment, and therefore are able to cause the lineage of Buddhas not to be broken off. They always expound the treasury of the Teaching for sentient beings, and therefore are able to cause the lineage of the Teaching not to be cut off. They maintain the principles of the Teaching well, without opposition or violation, and therefore can cause the lineage of the religious community not to be cut off. Furthermore, they are able to praise all great vows, and therefore are able to cause the lineage of Buddhas not to be cut off. They analyze and explain the aspects of causality, and are therefore able to cause the lineage of the Teaching not to be cut off. They always earnestly practice the six principles of harmony and respect and therefore are able to cause the lineage of the religious community not to be cut off. Also, they plant the seeds of buddhahood in the field of sentient beings, and therefore are able to cause the lineage of Buddhas not to be cut off; they protect and keep the Teaching unreservedly, and therefore are able to cause the lineage of the Teaching not to be cut off; they unify and order the great community tirelessly, and therefore are able to cause the lineage of the religious community not to be cut off. Also, they serve and uphold the teachings spoken and the precepts established by the Buddhas of past, present, and future, and therefore are able to cause the lineage of the Buddha, Teaching, and Community to never be cut off.

"Thus enlightening beings succeed to the Three Treasures, free from error in all they do: all of their actions they dedicate to omniscience, and therefore their physical, verbal, and mental actions are free from flaws; being free from flaws, all the good deeds they do, all the practices they carry out, edifying beings, teaching them according to their needs, are never in error even for a moment; all are in consonance with skill and knowledge, all are dedicated to omniscient knowledge, none passing in vain.

"Cultivating and practicing good ways like this, enlightening beings fulfill ten kinds of adornments moment after moment: adornment of bodies—they appear as appropriate to beings who can be taught; adornment of speech—they cut off all doubts and cause everyone to rejoice; adornment of mind—they enter all meditations in a single instant; adornment of buddha-lands—all are pure, free from afflictions; adornment of auras—they radiate boundless light, illumining sentient beings everywhere; adornment of community—they unify communities and gladden them all; adornment of spiritual powers—they can appear freely, adapting to the minds of sentient beings; adornment of true teaching—they are able to attract all intelligent people; adornment of the state of nirvana—becoming enlightened in one place, they pervade the whole universe; adornment of skillful explanation—they teach in accord with the place, the time, the faculty, and capacity.

"Perfecting these adornments, the physical, verbal, and mental actions of enlightening beings, moment after moment, are never wasted; all they dedicate to entering into omniscience. If any sentient beings see these enlightening beings, know that this also will not be in vain, for they will surely attain unexcelled complete perfect enlightenment. Any who hear their names, or make offerings to them, or live with them, or remember them, or leave home to follow them, or listen to them preach, or rejoice in their virtues, or respect them from afar, or even praise their names, will all attain unexcelled complete perfect enlightenment.

"For example, it is as though there were a medicine, called 'good to see,' which removed all toxins from those who saw it; so it is with enlightening beings who have accomplished this teaching—if sentient beings see them, all the poisons of afflictions will be destroyed, and wholesome states will increase.

"Enlightening beings, abiding by this teaching and earnestly applying it, destroy the darkness of ignorance by means of the light of wisdom; they conquer the armies of demons by the power of compassion; they check heretics by means of great knowledge and the power of virtue; they wipe out all afflictions staining the mind by means of adamantine concentration; they gather roots of goodness by the power of diligence; they avoid the difficulties of evil ways by means of the power of virtues of purifying buddha-lands; they purify their spheres of knowledge by the power of nonattachment; by the power of skill in means and knowledge they produce the transcendent practices of the stages of enlightening, as well as the various concentrations, six superknowledges, and four fearlessnesses, making them all pure; by the power of all virtues they fully develop the pure lands of all Buddhas, their boundless distinguishing marks and refinements, and complete physical, verbal, and mental adornments; by the power of observation with independent knowledge they know the powers, fearlessnesses, and unique qualities of all enlightened ones are equal; by the power of vast knowledge they comprehend the realm of omniscience; by the power of their past vows they manifest buddha-lands according to the needs of those to be taught, turn the wheel of the great teaching, and liberate innumerable living beings.

"Great enlightening beings diligently practice these things, gradually accomplishing all the deeds of enlightening beings, till they attain equality with the Buddhas, become great teachers in boundless worlds, maintaining the true teaching, protected by all the Buddhas, guarding and upholding the vast treasury of truth. Attaining unhindered intellect, they enter deeply into the facts of the teaching, and in boundless worlds among the great masses they manifest different physical forms, according to type, replete with supremely excellent features; with unhindered powers of elucidation they skillfully explain the profound teaching. The spheres of their speech, well rounded, skillfully reach everyone, therefore are able to cause those who hear to enter the gate of inexhaustible knowledge. Knowing the afflictions current in the minds of beings, they teach them accordingly; because the sounds of the speech they utter are completely pure, they can, preaching with 'one sound,' cause all to become joyful. They are physically well formed, and have great strength, so among the masses none can surpass them. Because they know sentient beings' minds well, they are able to appear in any way. Because they explain the truth skillfully, their voice is unhindered. Because they have freedom of mind, they explain the great teaching adaptively, and no one can obstruct them. Because they have attained fearlessness, their hearts are free from cowardice. Because they are masters of teaching, none can excel them. Because they are masters of knowledge, none can surpass them. Because they are masters of transcendent wisdom, the teachings they expound are not contradictory. Because they are masters of powers of elucidation, they teach continuously with eloquence. Because they are masters of mental command, they definitively disclose the real character of all things. Because they are masters of elocution, whenever they speak they can bring forth all sorts of examples and metaphors. Because they are masters of great compassion, they diligently teach sentient beings without flagging. Because they are masters of great kindness, they emanate a great web of lights pleasing all hearts. Thus do enlightening beings, on the high and wide lion throne, expound the Great Teaching; aside from the Enlightened Ones and the great enlightening beings of surpassing will and knowledge, no other beings can excel them, none can see their crowns, none can outshine them, and no one can stump them with difficult questions.

"Child of Buddha, once enlightening beings have attained such independent power, even if there were a vast sanctuary the size of unspeakably many worlds filled with beings, each of whom had the majesty of a lord of a billion worlds, as soon as any of the enlightening beings showed themselves, they would outshine the whole crowd of such beings. With great kindness and compassion they would give them security where they were afraid and weak, and with profound wisdom they would examine their inclinations and teach them with fearless eloquence, causing joy to all. Why? Because great enlightening beings have developed the sphere of immeasurable knowledge and wisdom; because they have developed immeasurable skillful discernment; because they have developed vast power of right mindfulness; because they have developed infinitely flexible intellect; because they have developed the total mental command to ascertain the true character of all things; because they have developed a boundless determination for enlightenment; because they have developed unerring powers of elucidation; because they have developed profound faith and resolve boosted by the Buddhas; because they have developed the power of knowledge to enter the assemblies of all Buddhas; because they have developed the pure mind that knows the Buddhas of all times are of the same essential nature; because they have developed the knowledge of enlightened ones of all times, and the great will and knowledge of all enlightening beings, and are able to be teachers of the truth, to open up the treasury of the true teaching of the Buddhas, and to protect and keep it."

Then, to restate what he meant, the enlightening being Truth Wisdom, by the spiritual power of the Buddha uttered these verses:

> Mind dwelling on enlightenment, gathering myriad virtues,
> Never self-indulgent, planting unshakable wisdom,
> Always mindful of the aspiration for enlightenment—
> At this all Buddhas rejoice.
>
> Mindfulness and will firm, self-motivated,
> Relying on nothing in the world, and never shrinking in fright,
> Entering the profound truth by the practice of noncontention—
> At this the Buddhas all rejoice.
>
> Once the Buddhas rejoice, enlightening beings are firm in effort—
> They cultivate virtue and wisdom, and all that assists the Path.
> Entering into the pure practices of all the stages,
> They fulfill the aspiration spoken of by the Enlightened.

Practicing this, they attain the wondrous truth,
And having attained to truth, they pass it on to others—
According to mentalities, faculties, and natures,
They teach in accord with whatever is fitting.

Enlightening beings expound the Teaching for others
Without giving up their own transcendent practices:
Once they have accomplished the transcendent ways,
They remain forever in the sea of existence, rescuing living beings.

They practice diligently day and night, never flagging,
Causing the seeds of the three treasures not to perish.
All the pure practices they carry out
They dedicate to the stage of enlightenment.

The virtuous acts performed by enlightening beings
Are all to develop and complete the living,
To have them destroy obscurity and annihilate affliction,
Subdue the demon armies and fulfill true awakening.

Thus practicing, they attain Buddha-knowledge,
Entering deeply into the treasury of truth of the Enlightened.
As great teachers they expound the subtle truth,
Like sweet elixir refreshing all.

Their compassion and pity extends to all—
They know the mind of every sentient being
And expound to them in accord with their predilections
Infinite, boundless enlightening teachings.

Their deportment is calm as a majestic elephant,
Their fearless courage is like that of a lion:
Imperturbable as a mountain, their knowledge is like an ocean,
And like a great rain, removing all heat.

When Truth Wisdom had spoken these verses, the Buddha was delighted, and everyone reverentially put them into practice.

BOOK NINETEEN

Ascent to the Palace of the Suyama Heaven

THEN, BY THE SPIRITUAL POWER of the Enlightened One, in all worlds of the ten directions, in the Jambu continent of each of the four quarters, and on the peak of their polar mountains, the Enlightened One was seen in the midst of an assembly, wherein the enlightening beings, due to the spiritual power of the Buddha, expounded the Teaching, each one having the sense of facing the Buddha at all times.

At that time the World Honored One, without leaving the foot of the enlightenment trees and the peaks of the polar mountains, headed for the jewel-adorned hall of the palace of the Suyama heaven. The king of the Suyama heaven, seeing from afar the Buddha coming, produced by magical powers a jewel lotus bank lion throne in his palace, with a million tiers of decorations, wrapped in a million golden nets, covered with a million drapes of flowers, a million drapes of garlands, a million drapes of perfumes, and a million drapes of jewels, surrounded by a million canopies each of flowers, garlands, perfumes, and jewels; a million lights illumined it. A million celestial kings of the Suyama heaven bowed in respect, a million Brahma kings danced for joy, a million enlightening beings sang praises. A million heavenly symphonies each played a million tones of truth, continuing endlessly; a million clouds of various flowers, a million clouds of various garlands, a million clouds of various ornaments, and a million clouds of various robes, covered all around; a million clouds of various wish-fulfilling jewels shone with light. The throne was born from a million kinds of roots of goodness, protected by a million Buddhas, augmented by a million kinds of virtues, dignified and purified by a million kinds of faith and a million kinds of vows, produced by a million kinds of action, established by a million kinds of truths, conjured up by a million kinds of spiritual powers, always producing a million kinds of sounds revealing all truths.

Then that celestial king, having set out this throne, turned to the Buddha, the World Honored One, bowed and joined his palms with reverence and respect and said, "Welcome, O World Honored One; welcome, Felicitous One; welcome, Enlightened One; welcome, O Worthy; welcome, O Truly Awakened One. Please be so gracious as to sojourn in this palace." Then the Buddha, accepting the invitation, ascended to the precious hall. This also took place in the same way everywhere in the ten directions.

Then the celestial king, reflecting on the roots of goodness he had planted with past Buddhas, spoke these verses with the aid of the Buddha's spiritual powers:

> The Buddha Renown, famed throughout the ten directions,
> Supreme among the Auspicious,
> Has been in this hall of jewels;
> Therefore this place is most auspicious.

> The Buddha Jewel King, lamp of the world,
> Supreme among the Auspicious,
> Has been in this pure hall;
> Therefore this place is most auspicious.

> The Buddha Joyful Eye, with unhindered vision,
> Supreme among the Auspicious,
> Has been in this adorned hall;
> Therefore this place is most auspicious.

> The Buddha Burning Lamp, lighting the world,
> Supreme among the Auspicious,
> Has been in this magnificent hall;
> Therefore this place is most auspicious.

> The Buddha Benefactor, aid of the world,
> Supreme among the Auspicious,
> Has been in this undefiled hall;
> Therefore this place is most auspicious.

> The Buddha Well Aware, who had no teacher,
> Supreme among the Auspicious,
> Has been in this hall of precious fragrance;
> Therefore this place is most auspicious.

> The Buddha Surpassing the Gods, a lamp in the world,
> Supreme among the Auspicious,
> Has been in this hall of sublime fragrance;
> Therefore this place is most auspicious.

The Buddha No Departure, hero of philosophy,
Supreme among the Auspicious,
Has been in this hall of the universal eye;
Therefore this place is most auspicious.

The Buddha Unsurpassed, replete with all virtues,
Supreme among the Auspicious,
Has been in this well-adorned hall;
Therefore this place is most auspcious.

The Buddha Ascetic, benefiting the world,
Supreme among the Auspicious,
Has been in this hall of universal embellishment;
Therefore this place is most auspicious.

Just as the king of the Suyama heaven in this world, graced with the occult power of the Buddha, recalled the virtues of Buddhas of ancient times and extolled them, so did all the kings of the Suyama heavens in the ten directions laud the virtues of Buddhas.

Then the World Honored One entered the jewel-adorned hall and sat crosslegged on the jewel lotus flower bank lion throne; the hall suddenly expanded vastly. The same thing happened in all worlds of the ten directions as happened in the abodes of the gods.

BOOK TWENTY

Eulogies in the Palace of the Suyama Heaven

THEN, DUE TO THE SPIRITUAL FORCE of the Buddha, a great enlightening being from each of the ten directions, each accompanied by as many enlightening beings as atoms in a buddha-land, came from beyond as many lands as atoms in a hundred thousand buddha-lands, and gathered in an assembly. The names of those great enlightening beings were: Forest of Virtues; Forest of Wisdom; Forest of Victory; Forest of Fearlessness; Forest of Conscience; Forest of Energy; Forest of Power; Forest of Practice; Forest of Awareness; Forest of Knowledge. The lands which these enlightening beings came from were called: Intimate Wisdom; Symbolic Wisdom; Jewel Wisdom; Supreme Wisdom; Lamp Wisdom; Adamantine Wisdom; Peaceful Wisdom; Sun Wisdom; Clear Wisdom; Pure Wisdom. These enlightening beings had each purely cultivated religious practice in the company of a Buddha; the names of those Buddhas were: Eternal Eye; Invincible Eye; Nondwelling Eye; Imperturbable Eye; Divine Eye; Eye of Liberation; Eye Comprehending Truth; Eye Understanding Forms; Supreme Eye; Violet Eye.

Having come to the Buddha, these enlightening beings bowed at the Buddha's feet, then each made jewel bank lion seats in their respective directions and sat thereupon. As in this world enlightening beings gathered this way in the Suyama heaven, so did this also take place in all worlds; the names of the enlightening beings, their worlds, and the Buddhas they associated with, were all the same.

Then the World Honored One emanated from the top of his feet ten trillion beams of light of wonderful hues, illumining the ten directions; the Buddhas and congregations in the palaces of the Suyama heavens in all worlds were made clearly visible. Then the Enlightening being Forest of Virtues, imbued with power from the Buddha, looked over the ten directions and said in verse,

441

Buddha emanates great light
Illumining the ten directions;
All see the Honored One of heaven and earth
Freely, without obstruction.

Buddha sits in the Suyama palace
Yet pervades all worlds in the cosmos;
This phenomenon is most extraordinary,
Wondered at by the world.

The king of the Suyama heaven
Has praised ten Buddhas in verse;
What is seen in this assembly
Is all the same everywhere.

Those groups of enlightening beings
All have the same names as ours:
In every place in the ten directions
They expound the unsurpassed teaching.

The worlds from which they come
Are also the same in name as ours:
Each of them have, with their Buddhas,
Perfected religious practice.

The names of each of those Buddhas
Are also the same as of ours;
Their countries are rich and happy,
Their spiritual powers are autonomous.

Everywhere in the ten directions
They think the Buddha's there;
Some see him in the human world,
Some see him in heaven.

The Buddha abides everywhere
In all the various lands:
We now see the Buddha
In this celestial court.

He made a vow of enlightenment
That extended to every world in the cosmos;
This is why Buddha's power
Pervades all inconceivably.

Leaving behind worldly desires
He fulfilled boundless virtue;
Therefore he gained spiritual power
And is seen by all beings.

He traverses all worlds in the cosmos
Like space, with no obstruction;
One body, infinite bodies:
His form cannot be grasped.

Buddha's virtues are boundless;
How could they be measured?
Neither abiding nor leaving,
He permeates the cosmos.

Then the enlightening being Forest of Wisdom, empowered by the Buddha, looked over the ten directions and said in verse,

The great leader of the world,
Supreme honored one, free from defilement,
Is hard to get to meet
Even in countless eons.

Buddha emits great light
Visible to all the world;
Preaching extensively for the multitudes,
He benefits all living beings.

Buddha appears in the world
Removing the darkness of ignorance;
Such a lamp of the world
Is rare and hard to get to behold.

Having cultivated generosity, self-control, and patience,
Diligence and meditation,
And ultimate transcendent wisdom,
With them he lights the world.

The Buddha has no peer;
None comparable can be found.
Without comprehending real truth
No one can perceive him.

Buddha's body and psychic powers
Are inconceivably free:
Neither going nor coming,
He speaks the truth to liberate.

If any can see and hear
The pure Teacher of humans and gods,
They'll leave forever the states of woe
And cast off all miseries.

For measureless, countless eons
He cultivated enlightening practice;
Who cannot know the meaning of this
Cannot attain buddhahood.

If one can know this meaning,
One's virtues will surpass
One who makes offerings to countless Buddhas
For inconceivable eons.

Even if one gives to a Buddha
Countless lands full of jewels,
If one knows not this meaning,
One never attains enlightenment.

Then the enlightening being Forest of Victory, imbued with power
from the Buddha, looked over the ten directions and said in verse,

As in the summer months
With the sky clear and cloudless,
The radiant sun blazes with light
Filling the ten directions,
That light boundless,
Impossible to measure
Even by those with eyes,
Let alone the blind—
So are the Buddhas—
Their virtues are boundless;
Even in inconceivable eons
No one can know them in detail.

All things have no provenance
And no one can create them:

There is nowhere whence they are born,
They cannot be discriminated.

All things have no provenance,
Therefore they have no birth;
Because there is no birth,
Neither can extinction be found.

All things are birthless
And have no extinction either;
Those who understand in this way
Will see the Buddha.

Because things have no birth,
Their inherent nature is nonexistent;
One who analyzes and knows this
Will arrive at the profound truth.

Because things have no inherent nature
No one can comprehend them;
When understanding things in this way,
Ultimately nothing is understood.

That which is said to have birth
Is to manifest lands—
If one can know the nature of lands
One's mind will not be confused:
Examining according to truth
The nature of the world and lands,
If one is able to know this,
One can explain all things.

Then the enlightening being Forest of Fearlessness, by the power of the Buddha, looked over the ten directions and said in verse,

The Buddha's immense body
Reaches the extremities of the cosmos;
Without leaving this seat
It pervades all places.

Whoever, hearing this teaching,
Respects and has faith in it,
Shall forever escape all the miseries
Of the states of woe.

Even going to many worlds,
Uncountably numerous,
Single-mindedly desiring to hear
Of the powers of the Buddha,
And such qualities of Buddhas,
Their unexcelled enlightenment,
Even wanting to hear for a moment,
None is able to do so.

If any in the past
Believed this aspect of Buddha,
They have already become Buddhas
And are lamps of the world.

If any will get to hear
Of the Buddha's free powers,
And having heard will believe,
They too will become Buddhas.

If any in the present
Can believe this teaching of Buddha,
They will also become Buddhas
And expound the teaching fearlessly.

This teaching is hard to encounter
Even in countless eons:
If any get to hear it,
Know it is the power of past vows.

If any can accept and hold
Such teachings of Buddha,
And, upholding them, spread them too,
They will become Buddhas.

How much the more so those who work diligently,
Firm of mind, not giving up:
You should know such people
Will certainly attain enlightenment.

Then the enlightening being Forest of Conscience, empowered by
the Buddha, looked over the ten directions and said in verse,

If people get to hear
This rare teaching of freedom

And can produce a joyful mind
They'll soon remove the webs of doubt.

The one who knows and sees all
Speaks these words himself;
There's nothing the Buddha knows not,
Therefore he's inconceivable.

Never from lack of wisdom
Has wisdom ever been born:
Worldlings are always in the dark,
And therefore none can produce it.

Just as form and nonform
Are two and not one,
So are knowledge and ignorance:
They are essentially different.

As signs and signlessness,
Birth-death and nirvana,
Are distinct and not the same,
So are knowledge and nescience.

When a world first comes to be
There's no sign of decay:
So it is with knowledge and ignorance:
Their characteristics are not simultaneous.

Like the enlightening beings' first state of mind
Does not coexist with their final state of mind,
So it is with knowledge and nescience:
These two minds do not coexist.

Just as bodies of consciousness
Are individual and don't combine,
So also knowledge and ignorance
Ultimately have no communion.

Just as a panacea
Can eliminate all toxins,
So also can knowledge
Extinguish all ignorance.

The Enlightened is unexcelled
And also has no peer;
He has no compare at all
And is therefore hard to meet.

Then the enlightening being Forest of Energy, empowered by the Buddha, looked over the ten directions and said in verse,

All things have no differentiation;
No one can know them:
Only among Buddhas are they known,
Because Buddhas' knowledge is ultimate.

Just as gold and gold color
Are in essence no different,
So also phenomena and nonphenomena
Are in essence no different.

Sentient beings and not sentient beings
Are both without reality:
In this way the natures of all things
In truth are nonexistent.

Just as the future
Has not the marks of the past,
So also do all things
Not have any marks at all.

Just as the signs of birth and death
Are all unreal,
So also are all things
Void of intrinsic nature.

Nirvana cannot be grasped,
But when spoken of there are two kinds,
So it is of all things:
When discriminated, they are different.

Just as based on something counted
There exists a way of counting,
Their nature is nonexistent:
Thus are phenomena perfectly known.

It's like the method of counting,
Adding one, up to infinity;
The numbers have no substantial nature:
They are distinguished due to intellect.

Just as the worlds have an end
When burnt in the final holocaust

Yet space is not destroyed:
So is the Buddha's knowledge.

These sentient beings of the universe
Each grasp characteristics of space:
So it is of the Buddhas;
Worldlings conceive of them arbitrarily.

Then the enlightening being Forest of Power, by the Buddha's power, looked over the ten directions and said in verse,

All realms of living beings
Are in the past, present, or future:
The living beings of past, present, and future
All dwell in the five clusters.

The five clusters are based on actions,
Actions are based on mind:
Mental phenomena are like phantoms,
And so indeed is the world.

The world doesn't make itself,
Nor is it made by another:
Yet it has a formation
And also has a disintegration.

Though the world has a formation
And a disintegration,
One who understands the world
Would not speak this way.

What is the world,
What is not a world?
World and not world
Are only distinctions of name.

The three times and five clusters
Are called the world,
Their extinction is "not the world":
Thus they are just temporary names.

How are the clusters explained?
What nature do they have?

The nature of the clusters is indestructible,
So it is called unborn.

Analyzing these clusters,
Their nature is fundamentally empty and nil;
Because it is empty, it cannot be destroyed:
This is the meaning of birthlessness.

Since sentient beings are thus,
So also are the Buddhas;
Buddhas and Buddha-teachings
Intrinsically have no existence.

If any can know these things
Truly, without delusion,
The one who knows and sees all
Will always be before them.

Then the enlightening being Forest of Practice, empowered by the Buddha, looked over the ten directions and said in verse,

As in all worlds
All the solid elements
Have no independent existence
Yet are found everywhere,
So also does the Buddha-body
Pervade all worlds,
Its various physical forms
Without abode or origin.

Just because of activities
Do we say the name "living beings"—
And there is no action to be found
Apart from living beings.

The nature of action is fundamentally empty and nil,
But is that on which beings are based,
Everywhere producing all physical forms,
And yet coming from nowhere.

This is the active power of forms,
Impossible to conceive:
If one comprehends the basis,
Therein no object is seen.

The Buddha-body is also like this:
It cannot be conceived;
Its various physical forms
Appear in all lands in the cosmos.

The body is not the Buddha,
Nor is Buddha a body:
Only reality is the body,
Permeating all things.

If one can see the Buddha-body
Pure as the nature of reality,
Such a one has no doubt
Or confusion about the Buddha.

If one sees all things
As in essence like nirvana,
This is seeing the Enlightened
Ultimately without abode.

If one cultivates right awareness
And clearly sees true awakening,
Signless, without discrimination,
This is an inheritor of truth.

Then the enlightening being Forest of Awareness, imbued with the power of Buddha, looked over the ten directions and said in verse,

It's like a painter
Spreading the various colors:
Delusion grasps different forms
But the elements have no distinctions.

In the elements there's no form,
And no form in the elements;
And yet apart from the elements
No form can be found.

In the mind is no painting,
In painting there is no mind;
Yet not apart from mind
Is any painting to be found.

That mind never stops,
Manifesting all forms,
Countless, inconceivably many,
Unknown to one another.

Just as a painter
Can't know his own mind
Yet paints due to the mind,
So is the nature of all things.

Mind is like an artist,
Able to paint the worlds:
The five clusters all are born thence;
There's nothing it doesn't make.

As is the mind, so is the Buddha;
As the Buddha, so living beings:
Know that Buddha and mind
Are in essence inexhaustible.

If people know the actions of mind
Create all the worlds,
They will see the Buddha
And understand Buddha's true nature.

Mind does not stay in the body,
Nor body stay in mind:
Yet it's able to perform Buddha-work
Freely, without precedent.

If people want to really know
All Buddhas of all times,
They should contemplate the nature of the cosmos:
All is but mental construction.

Then the enlightening being Forest of Knowledge, receiving power
from the Buddha, looked over the ten directions and said in verse,

The grasped cannot be grasped,
The seen cannot be seen,
The heard cannot be heard:
The one mind is inconceivable.

The finite and the infinite
Are both ungraspable;
If any want to apprehend them,
Ultimately they apprehend nothing.

To say what should not be said
Is self-deception;
When one's own task is not complete,
One cannot gladden others.

Those who wish to laud the Buddha's
Boundless body of wondrous form
Could not express it fully
Even in countless eons.

Just as the wish-fulfilling jewel
Can manifest all colors,
Being colorless yet manifesting color,
So are all the Buddhas.

Also like clear space
Is formless and invisible
And though it shows all forms
None can see space,
So it is with the Buddhas;
They manifest infinite forms everywhere
Yet are not in the province of mental activity
So no one is able to see them.

Though the Buddha's voice is heard,
The sound is not the Buddha;
And yet not apart from sound
Can the Truly Awake be known.

Enlightenment has no coming or going;
It's apart from all discriminations:
How then can one
Say he is able to see it?

The Buddhas have no doctrine:
How could Buddha have any explanation?
It is just in accord with one's own mind
One thinks Buddha expounds such a doctrine.

BOOK TWENTY-ONE

Ten Practices

THEN THE ENLIGHTENING BEING Forest of Virtues, imbued with the Buddha's power, entered into absorption in the skillful meditation of enlightening beings; when he had entered this absorption, there appeared before him Buddhas from beyond as many lands as atoms in ten thousand buddha-lands from each direction, and all were named Forest of Virtues. They said to the enlightening being Forest of Virtues, "Very good it is, O Child of Buddha, that you are able to enter this concentration in skillful meditation. Good man, it is the collective empowerment of the Buddhas of the same name, as many as atoms in ten thousand buddha-lands from each of the ten directions, and also the power of the past vows and the spiritual force of Vairocana Buddha, as well as the power of the virtues of the enlightening beings, that enables you to enter this concentration and expound the teaching, for the sake of increasing in enlightened knowledge, deep entry into the realm of reality, comprehension of the realms of sentient beings, nonobstruction in what is entered into, nonhindrance in the realm of activity, attainment of infinite skill in means, embracing of the essence of all knowledge, conscious realization of all truths, knowledge of all faculties, and ability to uphold and explain all the teachings; in other words, it is for initiating ten kinds of practice of enlightening beings. Good man, you should receive the spiritual power of the Buddhas to expound this teaching."

Then the Buddhas bestowed on the enlightening being Forest of Virtues unobstructed knowledge, unattached knowledge, uninterrupted knowledge, teacherless knowledge, knowledge without folly, unvarying knowledge, unerring knowledge, immeasurable knowledge, invincible knowledge, unflagging knowledge, and knowledge that cannot be taken away. Why? Because the power of this concentration is naturally thus.

Then the Buddhas each extended their right hands and patted the enlightening being Forest of Virtues on the head, whereupon he rose from concentration and addressed the enlightening beings, saying, "O Buddha Children, the practice of enlightening beings is inconceivable, equal to the space of the cosmos. Why? Because enlightening beings cultivate practice in emulation of the Buddhas of past, present, and future. Buddha-Children, great enlightening beings have ten kinds of practices, which are expounded by the Buddhas of past, present, and future. What are the ten? (1) The practice of giving joy; (2) beneficial practice; (3) the practice of nonopposition; (4) the practice of indomitability; (5) the practice of nonconfusion; (6) the practice of good manifestation; (7) the practice of nonattachment; (8) the practice of that which is difficult to attain; (9) the practice of good teachings; (10) the practice of truth.

"What is the great enlightening being's practice of giving joy? Here the enlightening beings are magnanimous givers, bestowing whatever they have with an equanimous mind, without regret, without hoping for reward, without seeking honor, without coveting material benefits, but only to rescue and safeguard all living beings, to include all living beings in their care, to benefit all living beings, and to emulate the original practice of all Buddhas, recall the original practice of all Buddhas, delight in the original practice of all Buddhas, purify the original practice of all Buddhas, further develop the original practice of all Buddhas, make manifest the original practice of all Buddhas, and expound the original practice of all Buddhas, to cause all sentient beings to be relieved of pain and suffering and attain comfort and happiness.

"When great enlightening beings cultivate this practice, they cause all living beings joy and delight. In any place there is poverty and want, they go there by the power of will to be born noble and wealthy, so that even if every single moment countless beings come to the enlightening beings and say, 'O benevolent one, we are poor and in need, without sustenance, hungry and weak, worn out and miserable, on the brink of death; please pity us and give us your flesh to eat so that we may live,' the enlightening beings would immediately give it to them, to gladden and satisfy them. Even should countless hundreds of thousands of beings come begging this way, the enlightening beings would not shrink back, but would rather increase even more in kindness and compassion. Indeed, because sentient beings all come seeking, the enlightening beings, seeing them, would become more joyful, and think, 'I have gained a fine boon; these beings are my field of blessings, they are my good friends and benefactors—without my asking them, they come to cause me to enter into the Buddha's teaching. I should now cultivate learning in this way, not controverting the wishes of sentient beings.' They also form this thought: 'May all the good that I have done, do, and will do, cause me in the future, in all worlds, among all beings, to receive an immense body, so as to satisfy all starving beings with the flesh of this body, and may I not die so long as even a single tiny creature is still not filled, and may the flesh I cut off be inexhaustible. By this virtue may I attain unexcelled complete perfect enlightenment, and experience great nirvana; and may those who eat my flesh also attain perfect enlightenment, attain impartial knowledge, fulfill all Buddha teachings, extensively perform Buddha work until entering extinction without remainder. If the heart of even one sentient being is unfulfilled, I will not attain unexcelled perfect enlightenment.'

"Thus do enlightening beings benefit the living, yet without any concept of self or any concept of sentient beings, or any concept of existence, or any concept of life, without various concepts—no concept of personality, no concept of person, no concept of human being, no concept of doer or receiver—they only observe the infinity of the realm of reality and the realm of sentient beings, their emptiness, absence of existents, signlessness, insubstantiality, indeterminacy, nondependence, and noncreation.

"When they perform this contemplation, they do not see themselves, they do not see anything given, they do not see a receiver, they do not see a field of blessings, they do not see a deed, they do not see any reward, they do not see any result, they do not see a great result, they do not see a small result.

"Then the enlightening beings observe that all the bodies taken on by living beings in the past, future, and present eventually perish; then they form this thought: 'How remarkable it is how foolish and ignorant sentient beings are; within birth and death they receive countless bodies, which are perishable and transient, soon returning to decay and extinction: having already passed away, now passing away, and yet to pass away, they still cannot use the destructible body to seek the indestructible body. I should learn all that the Buddhas learn, to realize omniscience, know all truths, and explain to sentient beings the indestructible nature of reality, which is equal in past, present, and future, and which accords with utmost tranquility and serenity, to cause them to permanently attain peace and happiness.'

"This is called the great enlightening beings' first practice, of giving joy.

"What is the great enlightening beings' beneficial practice? Here enlightening beings maintain pure self-control, and their minds have no attachment to color or form, sound, fragrance, flavor, or feeling. Also they preach this to sentient beings. They do not seek power, social status, wealth, appearance, or dominions. They have no attachment to anything, but just firmly uphold pure conduct, thinking, 'As I maintain pure discipline, I shall surely get rid of all bondage, the torment of craving, oppression, slander, and disturbance, and will attain the impartial truth praised by the Buddhas.'

"When enlightening beings maintain pure discipline in this way, even if countless devils should come to them in a single day, each bringing countless goddesses all well versed in the arts of pleasure, beautiful and alluring, with various amusing things, in order to disturb the enlightening beings' attention on the Way, the enlightening beings think, 'These desires are hindrances to the Way and obstruct unexcelled enlightenment.' Therefore they do not conceive even a single thought of lust; their minds are as pure as Buddha. The only exception is in terms of expedient means to teach and transform sentient beings—yet they still do not relinquish the determination for omniscience.

"Enlightening beings do not afflict a single sentient being in pursuit of their own desires; they would rather die themselves than to do anything which would afflict a single being.

"After enlightening beings have gotten to see the Buddha, they never arouse a single thought of desire, much less act upon desire.

"At this point, enlightening beings think, 'All sentient beings, throughout the long night of ignorance, think of desires, pursue desires, and are attached to desires; their minds are set in their ways and they are addicted to desires, whirling along with them, not having any freedom. I should cause these devils and these goddesses, and all sentient beings, to abide by the unexcelled precepts; once they abide in pure discipline, their minds will never turn back from the direction of universal knowledge, and eventually they will attain unexcelled complete perfect enlightenment, and finally enter complete extinction with no remainder. Why? This is the work we ought to do. We should follow the Buddhas in cultivating this learning, and having done so, divorce all bad actions and get rid of the ignorance of the idea of self, enter all Buddha-teachings by means of knowledge, and explain them to sentient beings, to rid them of delusion, all the while knowing, however, that there is no delusion apart from sentient beings and there are no sentient beings apart from delusion, that there are no sentient beings within delusion and no delusion within sentient beings, and also that it is not that delusion is sentient beings or that sentient beings are a delusion—delusion is not something inside or outside, and sentient beings are not something inside or outside. They know all things are unreal, suddenly arising and suddenly perishing, having no solidity or stability, like dreams, like reflections, like phantoms, like illusions, fooling the ignorant. Those who understand in this way will be able to comprehend all actions, to master birth and death as well as nirvana, to realize enlightenment, to save themselves and cause others to gain salvation, to liberate themselves and enable others to gain liberation, to conquer themselves and cause others to be tamed, to become tranquil themselves and enable others to become tranquil, to be secure themselves and enable others to be secure, to be free from defilement themselves and cause others to be free from defilement, to be pure themselves and cause others to be pure, to be dispassionate themselves and cause others to be dispassionate, to be happy themselves and cause others to be happy.

"Here enlightening beings also form this thought: 'I should follow all the enlightened ones, detach from all worldly actions, fulfill all qualities of buddhahood, abide in supreme equanimity, be impartial toward all beings, clearly understand the objective realm, get rid of all error, cut off all conceptualizations, abandon all attachments, and skillfully engineer emancipation, to ever abide mentally in unexcelled, inexplicable, independent, immutable, measureless, boundless, inexhaustible, formless, most profound wisdom.'

"This is called the great enlightening beings' second practice, of beneficial action.

"What is the great enlightening beings' practice of nonopposition? Here enlightening beings always practice tolerance and forbearance, being humble and respectful, not harming self, others, or both; not stealing or causing others to steal, not being attached to themselves, to others, or to both; not seeking fame or profit. They only think, 'I should always expound the Teaching to sentient beings, to cause them to divorce all evils, to cut off greed, anger, folly, pride, hypocrisy, stinginess, jealousy, obsequiousness, and dishonesty, and cause them to always abide peacefully in forbearance and harmony.'

"When enlightening beings achieve this forbearance, even if countless beings should come to them and each being should produce countless mouths and utter countless words—unpleasant words, unwholesome words, displeasing words, undesirable words, words which are not those of the benevolent or the virtuous, words which are not those of wisdom, words which are not in accord with sagacity, words which sages do not approach, detestable words, and unbearable words—even if they abuse and revile the enlightening beings with such speech, and, furthermore, if they all had countless hands, bearing countless cudgels, with which they attacked and injured the enlightening beings, without relenting, for immeasurable eons, should enlightening beings encounter such torture, their hair standing on end, their life about to end, they form this thought: 'If my mind is disturbed by this suffering, then I have not mastered myself, I am not self-possessed, I do not understand myself, I am uncultivated, I am not properly stabilized, I am not at peace, I am careless, I give rise to attachments—how can I enable others to attain purity of mind?'

"Then the enlightening beings also think, 'Since beginningless time I have dwelt in birth and death and experienced its pains and vexations,' and thus reflecting, they redouble their efforts, purify their minds, and attain joy. They skillfully tune and concentrate themselves, and, themselves able to abide in the Buddha-teaching, they also enable sentient beings to attain the same condition. They further reflect, 'This body is empty and null, it has no self or possessions, it has no reality—it is void by nature, with no duality. Neither pain nor pleasure has any existence, because all things are empty. I should expound this teaching for people, to enable all sentient beings to do away with their views. Therefore, though I meet with suffering today, I should accept it with patience, out of compassion for beings, to benefit beings, to pacify beings, out of pity for beings, to take care of beings and not abandon them, to attain enlightenment myself and also to enable others to attain enlightenment, so that my mind will never regress, and so that I may progress on the way of Buddhahood.'

"This is called the enlightening beings' third practice, of nonopposition.

"What is great enlightening beings' practice of indomitability? Here the enlightening beings cultivate various forms of energy—foremost energy, great energy, excellent energy, outstanding energy, supreme energy, sublime energy, exalted energy, unsurpassed energy, unequalled energy, comprehensive energy. They become naturally free from the three poisons of greed, hatred, and delusion, naturally free from pride and conceit, naturally not hypocritical, naturally not stingy or jealous, naturally not deceitful, naturally conscientious. Ultimately they do not make any effort that would afflict a single living being. They only make efforts to cut off all afflictions, to pull out the roots of all confusion, to get rid of all force of habit, to know all realms of living beings, to know where all beings die and are born, to know the afflictions of all sentient beings, to know the inclinations of all sentient beings, to know the perspectives of all sentient beings, to know the superiority and inferiority of faculties of all sentient beings, to know the mental activities of all sentient beings, to know all realms of phenomena, to know the basic nature of all Buddha qualities, to know the equal nature of all Buddha qualities, to know the equal nature of all time frames, to attain the light of knowledge of all Buddha-teachings, to experience the knowledge of all Buddha-teachings, to know the unique true character of all Buddha-teachings, to know the infinity of all Buddha-teachings, to attain far-reaching decisive knowledge of techniques of all Buddha-teachings, and to attain the knowledge to analyze and expound the expressions and meanings of all Buddha-teachings.

"Once enlightening beings have perfected these practices of energetic effort, if someone should say to them, 'Can you pass countless eons enduring the pains of uninterrupted hell for the sake of each and every being in countless worlds, cause those beings to each meet countless Buddhas in the world, and through seeing Buddhas attain felicity and finally enter extinction without remainder, after which you yourself attain unexcelled complete perfect enlightenment?' They would answer 'I can.' Then again if someone should say, 'There are countless oceans—you should drain them drop by drop with a hairtip; there are countless worlds—you should shatter them to atoms, and count each and every drop of the oceans and atoms of the worlds, and for that number of eons endure incessant suffering for the sake of living beings,' the enlightening beings would not have a moment of regret or resentment on hearing such words—they would only be more joyful, feeling profoundly happy and fortunate that they had attained such a great benefit that they could by their power enable sentient beings to be forever liberated from suffering. Enlightening beings, by these means which they employ, enable all beings in all worlds to eventually reach ultimate release without remainder.

"This is called the enlightening beings' practice of indomitability.

"What is great enlightening beings' practice of nonconfusion? Here enlightening beings perfect right mindfulness, their minds free from distraction and disturbance, firm and imperturbable, consummately pure, immeasurably vast, without any delusion or confusion. By virtue of this right mindfulness they well understand all worldly speech and are able to remember the verbal explanations of transmundane laws. That is to say, they can remember the explanations of material and immaterial phenomena; they can remember the explanations of the definition of the intrinsic nature of sensation, perception, conditioning, and consciousness, without any confusion in their minds. In the world they die in one place and are born in another without confusion in their minds. They enter the womb and leave the womb without confusion in their minds. They arouse the will for enlightenment without confusion in their minds. They attend teachers without confusion in their minds. They earnestly practice the Buddhas' teachings without confusion in their minds. They notice the doings of demons without confusion in their minds. They divorce demonic activity without confusion in their minds. They cultivate enlightening practice for countless eons without confusion in their minds. The enlightening beings, having developed this immeasurable right mindfulness, spend countless eons listening to truthful teachings from enlightened and enlightening guides—profound teachings relating to emptiness, vast teachings relating to activity in the relative world, teachings relating to adornment by virtuous qualities, teachings of all kinds of arrays of the qualities of the cosmos, all interrelated, teachings expounding various bodies of words, phrases, and sentences, teachings of the embellishments of enlightening beings, teachings of the supremacy of the spiritual power and radiance of the Buddhas, teachings of the purity of correct seeking of certain understanding, teachings of nonattachment to any world, teachings which define all worlds, teachings of extremely broad scope, teachings of removing the blinders of ignorance and understanding all beings, teachings of what is common and what is not, teachings of the excellence of enlightening knowledge, teachings of the independence of omniscience.

"Having heard these teachings, enlightening beings keep them constantly in mind for an incalculable period of time. Why? When great enlightening beings cultivate practices over countless eons, they never afflict a single sentient being, which would cause loss of right mindfulness; they do not ruin the right teaching, and do not cut off roots of goodness—their minds are always expanding knowledge. Furthermore, these enlightening beings cannot be confused or disturbed by any kind of sound—loud sounds, coarse and garbled sounds, terrifying sounds, pleasing sounds, displeasing sounds, ear-shattering sounds, sense-debilitating sounds. When the enlightenings hear such countless good or bad sounds, even though the sounds fill countless worlds, they are never disturbed or distracted for a moment. That is to say, their right

mindfulness is undisturbed, their state is undisturbed, their concentration is undisturbed, their entry into emptiness is undisturbed, their
practice of enlightening acts is undisturbed, their determination for
enlightenment is undisturbed, their recollection of the Buddhas is
undisturbed, their contemplation of truth is undisturbed, their knowledge to civilize sentient beings is undisturbed, their knowledge to
purify sentient beings is undisturbed, their certain understanding of the
meaning of profundity is undisturbed.

"Because they do no evil, they have no obstruction of evil habits;
because they do not produce afflictions, they have no obstruction by
afflictions; because they do not slight the teaching, they have no barrier
to the teaching; because they do not slander and repudiate the truth,
they have no obstruction by retribution.

"Even if the aforementioned sounds should each fill countless worlds
ceaselessly for countless eons, each able to devastate the faculties, bodies
and minds of sentient beings, they still could not damage the minds of
these enlightening beings. Enlightening beings enter concentration, abide
in the teaching of the Sage, and meditate on and investigate all sounds,
becoming thoroughly familiar with the characteristics of origin, existence,
and disappearance of all sounds, and come to know the nature of the
origin, existence, and disappearance of all sounds: having heard them,
they do not give rise to covetousness or aversion, and don't lose
mindfulness—they apprehend their characteristics precisely without being
influenced by or attached to them. They know all sounds have no
existence and are in reality ungraspable, that they have no creator and
no origin, that they are equal to nirvana and have no differentiations.

"Thus do enlightening beings perfect tranquil, peaceful physical,
verbal, and mental action, never regressing, till they reach omniscience.
They skillfully enter all manner of meditative concentrations and know
that all concentrations are of the same one essence. They comprehend
that all things have no bounds and attain true knowledge of all things.
They attain profound concentration detached from all sounds. They
attain countless kinds of concentration. They increasingly develop a
boundlessly vast mind of great compassion.

"At this point enlightening beings attain countless concentrations in a
single instant, and, hearing such sounds, are not disturbed—they gradually increase and broaden their concentration. They form this thought:
'I should get all beings to abide peacefully in unsurpassed pure
mindfulness, so they may attain nonregression on the way to omniscience,
and ultimately attain to nirvana without remainder.'

"This is called the enlightening beings' fifth practice, leaving confusion behind.

"What is the great enlightening beings' practice of good manifestation?
Here the enlightening beings are pure in thought, word, and deed; they
abide in nonacquisition, and demonstrate nonacquisitive thought, word,
and deed. They know that physical, verbal, and mental actions have no

absolute existence. Because they are free from falsehood, they are free from bondage. What they demonstrate is without inherent nature and depends on nothing. They abide in mental accord with reality. They know the intrinsic nature of infinite minds. They know the inherent nature of all things is ungraspable, formless, exceedingly profound and difficult to penetrate. They abide in the absolute state, true thusness, the essence of things; they appear in life by way of expedients, yet have no retribution for actions. Unborn and undying, they abide in the dispassionate, tranquil nature of the realm of nirvana. They abide in the nature of true reality, absence of inherent reality or own-being. They are beyond the power of speech to fully describe, they transcend all worlds and do not depend on anything. They enter into the truth that is free from discrimination, bondage, and attachment. They enter the true principle of supreme knowledge. They enter the transcendental truth which cannot be understood or known by any worldlings. Such are the characteristics of the enlightening beings' expedient manifestations of life.

"These enlightening beings formulate this thought: 'The nature of all sentient beings is naturelessness; the nature of all phenomena is uncreated; the form of all lands of formlessness—in all worlds there only exists verbal expression, and verbal expression has no basis in facts. Furthermore, facts have no basis in words.' Thus do enlightening beings understand that all things are void, and all worlds are silent: all the Buddha teachings add nothing—the Buddha teachings are no different from the phenomena of the world, and the phenomena of the world are no different from the Buddha teachings. The Buddha teachings and worldly phenomena are neither mixed up nor differentiated. Knowing that the nature of elements is equal, entering everywhere into the triple world, never giving up the determination for great enlightenment, never retreating from the will to transform sentient beings, ever expanding and increasing the heart of great compassion, they are a reliance for all living beings.

"Then enlightening beings also form this thought: 'If I do not develop and mature sentient beings, who will? If I do not pacify and civilize sentient beings, who will? If I do not teach and renew sentient beings, who will? If I do not awaken sentient beings, who will? If I do not purify sentient beings, who will? This is my duty, my task.' They also form this thought: 'If I alone understand this profound teaching, then only I will attain liberation in unexcelled complete perfect enlightenment, while all sentient beings, being blind, will enter perilous paths, bound by afflictions, like people seriously ill constantly suffering pains. In the prison of craving and attachment, they are unable to get out by themselves. They will not leave the realms of hells, hungry ghosts, animals, or the netherworld; they cannot extinguish suffering or abandon evil deeds. Forever in the darkness of ignorance, they do not see reality. Revolving in birth and death, they have no means of emancipation. Living in the eight difficult situations, encrusted by all sorts of defilements, all manner of afflictions cover their minds. Deluded by false views, they do not travel the right path.' Thus observing sentient beings, enlightening beings think, 'It would not be proper for me to abandon these sentient beings while they are still undeveloped, immature, and unruly, and myself attain unexcelled complete perfect enlightenment. I should first transform these sentient beings, practicing enlightening deeds for unspeakably many eons, first developing the undeveloped, and taming the unruly.'

"When these enlightening beings abide by this practice, if gods, demons, ascetics, priests, or inhabitants of any worlds—cherubim, titans, etc.—should get to see them, or sojourn with them for awhile, and honor and respect them, serve them and give them offerings, or even hear of them, once having crossed their minds these deeds will not be in vain—they shall surely attain perfect enlightenment.

"This is called the great enlightening beings' sixth practice, the practice of good manifestation.

"What is the great enlightening beings' practice of nonattachment? These great enlightening beings, with minds free from attachment, can in every successive instant enter into countless worlds and adorn and purify these countless worlds, their minds free from attachment to anything in these worlds. They visit countless Buddhas, pay their respects, wait on them, and present them with offerings of countless flowers, perfumes, garlands, fragrant ointments, powdered incenses, clothes, jewels, banners, parasols, and various other adornments, all without number. These offerings are for the sake of the ultimate uncreated truth, for the sake of abiding in the inconceivable truth. In every instant they see countless Buddhas; their minds are free from attachment to the Buddha's places, and they have no attachment to the buddha-lands either. They also have no attachment to the distinguishing marks of the Buddhas, and while they see the Buddhas' auras of light and hear the Buddha's sermons, yet they have no attachment. They also have no attachment to the congregations of the Buddhas and enlightening beings of the worlds of the ten directions.

"Having heard the Buddhas' teachings, their minds are joyful, and the power of their will is greatly increased, so that they are able to encompass and carry out the practices of enlightening beings; yet they have no attachments.

"These enlightening beings, through unspeakably many eons, see untold Buddhas appear in the world; they attend and supply each Buddha for untold eons, never wearying of this. Seeing the Buddhas, hearing their teachings, and seeing the magnificent arrays of the assemblies of enlightening beings, they are unattached to any of them. And when they see impure worlds, they have no aversion. Why? Because these enlightening beings observe according to the Buddha teachings. In the teaching of the Buddhas, there is neither defilement nor purity,

neither darkness nor light, neither difference nor unity, neither truth
nor falsehood, neither security nor danger, no right path and no wrong
path.

"Thus do enlightening beings enter deeply into the realm of reality,
teaching and transforming sentient beings without forming attachments
to sentient beings. They accept and hold the teaching, yet they do not
form attachments to the teaching. They arouse the will for enlightenment and abide in the abode of the Buddhas, yet they do not form
attachments to the abode of Buddhas. Though they speak, their minds
have no attachment to speech. They enter the various realms of life
with minds unattached to those realms. They comprehend concentration,
can enter and can dwell in concentration, but they have no attachment
to concentration. Going to visit countless buddha-lands, they may
enter, see, or sojourn therein, but their minds have no attachment to
buddha-lands, and when they leave they do not miss them.

"Because great enlightening beings are able to be without attachment
in this way, their minds have no barriers to the Buddha teaching. They
comprehend the enlightenment of Buddhas, they realize the discipline
of the teaching, they abide by the right teaching of the Buddhas and
cultivate the practices of enlightening beings, they contemplate the
enlightening beings' methods of liberation. Their minds are free from
attachment to the dwelling places of enlightening beings, and they also
have no attachments to the practices of enlightening beings. They clear
the way of enlightening beings and receive the prediction of enlightenment
which is given to enlightening beings. Having received the prediction,
they reflect, 'Sentient beings are foolish and ignorant, without knowledge
or vision, without faith or understanding, lacking in intelligent action,
greedy and dishonest, covetous and grasping, revolving in the flow of
birth and death—they do not seek to see the Buddha, they do not
follow enlightened guides, they do not trust the Buddha; they are lost
in error, mistakenly entering dangerous paths; they do not respect the
Soviereign of the Ten Powers, they do not realize the benevolence of
the enlightening beings. They are attached to their dwelling places, and
when they hear that all things are empty, their minds are startled and
frightened, and they shy away from the true teaching and abide in false
teachings; they abandon the level, even path and enter perilous, difficult
paths. They reject the ideas of the Buddha and pursue the ideas of
demons. They are firmly and relentlessly attached to existents'. Thus
observing sentient beings, enlightening beings increase in great compassion and develop roots of goodness—and yet they are unattached.

"At this point enlightening beings also think, 'I should, for the sake
of a single sentient being, in each land in the worlds in the ten directions,
spend countless eons teaching and developing, and should do the same
for all sentient beings, without on this account wearying or giving up.'

"Furthermore, measuring the entire universe with a hairtip, at a
single point they pass unspeakably many unspeakable numbers of eons

teaching, edifying, and civilizing all beings, and also do likewise at each and every point in the universe. Never for a moment do they cling to self or entertain any conception of self or possession. At each point they cultivate enlightening practice throughout the eons of the future, not attached to the body, not attached to phenomena, not attached to recollection, not attached to vows, not attached to concentration, not attached to contemplation, not attached to tranquil stabilization, not attached to spheres or objects, not attached to teaching and training sentient beings, and not attached to entering the realm of reality.

"Why? The enlightening beings form this thought: 'I should look upon all objective realms as like phantoms, all Buddhas as like reflections, enlightening practices as like dreams, Buddhas' sermons as like echoes; all worlds are like illusions, because they are upheld by the consequences of actions; differentiated bodies are like apparitions, because they are produced by the power of deeds; all sentient beings are like mind, because they are defiled by various influences; all things are like the limit of reality, because they cannot change.'

"They also form this thought: 'I should carry on enlightening practices in all lands, in all worlds throughout space, moment after moment clearly realizing all truths taught by the Buddha, with precise presence of mind, free from attachments.'

"Thus do enlightening beings observe that the body has no self, and they see the Buddha without hindrance. In order to transform sentient beings, they expound various teachings, to cause them to have unlimited joy and pure faith in the Buddha's teaching. They rescue all without weariness of mind. Because they are unwearied, if there are any sentient beings in any world who are not mature or unruly in any way, they go there and employ expedient methods to transform and liberate them. By virtue of great commitment and will they remain secure among those beings' various kinds of speech, deeds, attachments, devices, associations, routines, activities, perspectives, births, and deaths, and teach them, not letting their minds be disturbed or discouraged, and never for a moment forming any thought of attachment. Why? Because they have attained nonattachment and independence. Their own benefit and the benefit of others is fulfilled with purity.

"This is called the great enlightening beings' seventh practice, of nonattachment.

"What is the great enlightening beings' practice of that which is difficult to attain? Here the enlightening beings perfect roots of goodness which are difficult to attain, invincible roots of goodness, supreme roots of goodness, indestructible roots of goodness, unsurpassable roots of goodness, inconceivable roots of goodness, inexhaustible roots of goodness, independently powered roots of goodness, greatly influential roots of goodness, roots of goodness which are of the same essence as all Buddhas.

"When these enlightening beings carry out their practice, they attain supreme understanding of the Buddha-teaching, they attain broad understanding of the Buddhas' enlightenment. They never give up the vows of enlightening beings, and for all ages their minds never weary. They do not shrink from suffering, and they cannot be moved by any demons. Under the care of all Buddhas, they fully carry out all the difficult undertakings of enlightening beings. In cultivating enlightening practices, they are diligent and energetic, never lazy. They never retreat from the vow of universal salvation.

"Once the enlightening beings abide in these difficult to accomplish practices, they are able to transmute immeasurable ages of birth and death in every instant, without giving up the great vow of enlightening beings. If any sentient beings serve and support them, or even see or hear of them, they all will attain nonregression on the way to unexcelled complete perfect enlightenment.

"Though the enlightening beings understand that sentient beings are not existent, yet they do not abandon the realms of sentient beings. They are like ship captains, not staying on this shore, not staying on the other shore, not staying midway, yet able to ferry sentient beings from this shore over to the other shore, because they are always traveling back and forth. In the same way enlightening beings do not stay in birth and death, do not stay in nirvana, and also do not stay in midstream of birth and death, while they are able to deliver sentient beings from this shore to the other shore, where it is safe and secure, without sorrow or trouble. And they have no attachment to the numbers of sentient beings—they do not abandon one being for attachment to many beings, and do not abandon many beings for attachment to one being. They neither increase nor decrease the realms of sentient beings; they neither exhaust nor perpetuate the realms of sentient beings; they neither discriminate nor bifurcate the realms of sentient beings. Why? Enlightening beings enter deeply into the realms of sentient beings as the realm of truth; the realms of sentient beings and the realm of truth are nondual. In the nondual there is no increase or decrease, no origination or destruction, no existence or nonexistence, no grasping and no reliance, no attachment and no duality. Why? Because enlightening beings realize that all things and the realm of truth are nondual.

"Thus do enlightening beings, by means of appropriate techniques, enter into the profound realm of truth and abide in formlessness while adorning their bodies with pure forms. They understand that things have no intrinsic nature, yet they are able to distinguish the characteristics of all things. They do not grasp sentient beings, yet they are able to know the numbers of sentient beings. They are not attached to worlds, yet they appear physically in Buddha-lands. They do not discriminate principles, yet they enter skillfully into the Buddha teachings; they profoundly understand their meanings and principles and extensively expound the verbal teachings. They comprehend the dispassionate reality of all things, yet do not cease the path of enlightening. They do not withdraw from enlightening, they always diligently cultivate inexhaustible practice. They freely enter the pure realm of reality.

"It may be likened to drilling wood to produce fire: fires may be unlimited but the fire doesn't go out. In the same way do enlightening beings liberate people without end, yet they remain in the world forever without becoming extinct. They neither do nor do not reach an ultimate end; neither do nor do not grasp, neither do nor do not rely, are neither worldlings or Buddhists, neither ordinary people nor realized people.

"When enlightening beings accomplish this difficult-to-attain state of mind, and cultivate enlightening practice, they do not preach the doctrines of the two vehicles, they do not preach buddhism, they do not talk about the world, they do not expound worldly doctrines, they don't explain sentient beings, they don't say there are no sentient beings, they don't talk about purity or defilement. Why? Because enlightening beings know all things have no defilement and no grasping, do not proceed and do not recede.

"When enlightening beings practice this dispassionate, subtle, extremely deep and all-surpassing teaching, they do not think 'I am cultivating this practice, have cultivated this practice, will cultivate this practice.' They are not attached to physical or mental elements, or to sense faculties, sense consciousness, or sense data, or to inner or outer worlds. The great vows they undertake, their transcendent ways, and all their methods are without attachments. Why? Because in the realm of truth there are no names corresponding to reality; in the vehicle of listeners and the vehicle of the self-awakened there are no real names; in the vehicle of enlightening beings there are no real names; in perfect enlightenment there are no real names; in the world of ordinary people there are no real names, nor in purity or impurity, in birth and death or nirvana. Why? Because all things are nondual, yet none are not dual. They are like space, which anywhere in the universe, whether past, present, or future, cannot be apprehended, yet it is not that there is no space. Thus do enlightening beings observe all things to be ungraspable, yet not nonexistent. They see things as they are, without neglecting their tasks, everywhere demonstrating the practices of enlightening activities; they do not give up their great vows, civilizing sentient beings, turning the wheel of true teaching. They do not violate cause and effect and do not deny it, and do not deviate from the impartial truth. Equal to the Buddhas of all times, they do not cut off the lineage of buddhahood, they do not violate the character of reality. Entering deeply into the teaching, their expository ability is endless. They hear the teaching without attachment; reaching the profound depths of the teaching, they are able to expound it skillfully, hearts without fear. They do not give up the abode of Buddhas, but they do not violate natural laws; they appear throughout the world, yet are not attached to the world.

"Thus do enlightening beings achieve the mind of wisdom which is difficult to attain. Cultivating various practices, they free sentient beings from the three woeful states of hell, ghosthood, and animality, teaching and enlightening, taming and civilizing, placing them on the Way of the Buddhas of all times, making them unshakable.

"Furthermore, they form this thought: 'Beings in the world are ungrateful and even hostile to one another; with false views and clinging attachments, illusions and delusions, they are ignorant and unwise; having no faith, they follow bad associates, and develop various kinds of perverse cleverness. They are full of various afflictions, like craving and ignorance. This is where I am to cultivate the practice of enlightening beings. If people who are grateful, intelligent, wise and knowing filled the world, I would not cultivate the practices of enlightening beings therein. Why? I have no attraction or opposition to sentient beings, I seek nothing from them, I do not seek even so much as a single word of praise.' Cultivating enlightening practices forever and ever, they never have a single thought of doing it for themselves—they only want to liberate all sentient beings, to purify them so that they attain eternal emancipation. Why? Because those who would be enlightened guides must be thus—not grasping, not seeking, just practicing the enlightening Way for the sake of beings, to enable them to reach the peaceful, secure other shore and attain complete perfect enlightenment.

"This is called the great enlightening beings' eighth practice, that which is difficult to attain.

"What is the great enlightening beings' practice of good teachings? Here the enlightening beings act as pure, cool reservoirs of truth for the sake of beings of all worlds—celestial and human beings, devils and gods, ascetics and priests, etc. Maintaining true teaching, they do not let the seed of buddhahood be cut off. Because they attain the spell of pure light, in teaching and predicting enlightenment their intellectual powers are inexhuastible. Because they attain the spell of complete meaning their comprehension of meanings is inexhaustible. Because they attain the spell of realization of true principles, their comprehension of principles is inexhaustible. Because they attain the spell of explanatory expression, their comprehension of words is inexhaustible. Because they attain the spell of nonobstruction of inexhaustible meanings of boundless words and phrases, their unimpeded comprehension is inexhaustible. Because they attain the spell of nonobstruction of inexhaustible meanings of boundless words and phrases, their unimpeded comprehension is inexhaustible. Because they are anointed by the spell of the Buddhas' coronation, their delightful eloquence is inexhaustible. Because they attain the spell of enlightenment without relying on another, their illuminating discourse is inexhaustible. Because they attain the spell of adaptive explanation, their adaptive discourse is inexhaustible. Because they attain the spell of elucidation and analysis of all kinds of bodies of words, phrases, and sentences, their explanatory eloquence is inexhaustible. Because they attain the spell of boundless versatility, their boundless elucidation is inexhaustible.

"The great compassion of these enlightening beings is strong and steadfast, extending to all creatures. Throughout the universe they change their bodies to a golden color and carry out the deeds of Buddhas time and time again; adapting to the faculties, natures, and inclinations of sentient beings, with a universal tongue within one voice they manifest unlimited sounds, teaching as appropriate to the occasion, bringing joy to all. Even if there were countless beings in innumerable conditions, all in the same assembly, that assembly so vast it fills untold worlds, and each had innumerable mouths each capable of producing billions of sounds, and each should ask the enlightening beings different questions all at once, the enlightening beings would be able to take on all the questions instantly and reply to them and cause their doubts to be removed. As this is true of one assembly, so it is also of countless assemblies.

"Furthermore, even if every single spot as big as a hairtip should in every successive moment produce unspeakably many unspeakable numbers of congregations, throughout the eons of the future—those eons may be exhausted, but the congregations are infinite—and all of them should every moment ask different questions in different words, enlightening beings could receive them all in a single instant, without fear or timidity, without doubt or error, thinking, 'Even if all sentient beings come and question me, I will expound the truth to them ceaselessly, endlessly, causing them all to rejoice and dwell in the path of virtue, and also cause them to understand all words and expressions and be able to explain various principles to sentient beings, yet without discrimination in regard to language. Even if they come and ask difficult questions in countless various ways of speaking, I will receive them all at once and answer them all in one voice, causing them all to understand, without omitting anything.' This is because they have been anointed with omniscience, because they have found the unobstructed treasury of the potential of enlightenment, because they have attained the sphere of light of all truths, and because they are replete with universal knowledge.

"Once the enlightening beings abide in the practice of good teachings, they can purify themselves, and also can benefit all sentient beings by appropriate means without attachments, not seeing that there are any sentient beings that attain emancipation.

"As they do in this universe, so in countless universes do they turn golden, and, fully equipped with the wondrous voice, with no barrier to any truth, perform Buddha work.

"These enlightening beings develop ten kinds of body: the transcendent body which enters into boundless realms, due to annihilating all worldliness; the immanent body which enters into boundless realms, due to birth in all worlds; the unborn body, due to abiding in the impartiality of birthlessness; the undying body, due to all expression of extinction being ungraspable; the nonreal body, due to attainment of accord with reality; the nonfalse body, due to adaptive appearance; the unchanging body, being removed from death in one place and rebirth in another; the nondisintegrating body, the nature of the realm of reality being indestructible; the uniform body, being beyond all manner of speaking, past, present, or future; the formless body, due to ability to observe the characteristics of things.

"Developing these ten bodies, enlightening beings are a house for all sentient beings, because they raise all roots of goodness; they are saviors for all sentient beings, because they enable them to attain great peace; they are a refuge for all sentient beings, because they act as a great reliance for them; they are guides for all sentient beings, because they enable them to attain unsurpassed emancipation; they are teachers of all sentient beings, because they cause them to enter into the truth; they are lamps for all sentient beings, because they cause them to see clearly the consequences of actions; they are lights for all sentient beings, because they cause the extremely profound wondrous truth to be illuminated; they are a torch for all in all times, because they cause them to clearly understand the truth; they are illumination for all worlds, because they cause them to enter the state of radiant light; they are clarifiers for all realms of being, because they reveal the powers of the enlightened.

"This is called the great enlightening beings' ninth practice, of good teachings. When enlightening beings abide in this practice, they are a pure cool reservoir of truth for all sentient beings, because they can plumb the source of all the Buddha teachings.

"What is the great enlightening beings' practice of truth? Here the enlightening beings perfect true speech—they can act in accord with what they say, and can speak according to what they do. These enlightening beings study the true words of the Buddhas of all times, they enter the nature of the lineage of the Buddhas of all times, they equal the roots of goodness of the Buddhas of all times, they apprehend the nondual speech of the Buddhas of all times. Learning from the enlightened ones, their knowledge and wisdom is consummate.

"These enlightening beings develop the knowledge of what is so and what is not so in regard to sentient beings, the knowledge of consequences of past, future, and present actions, the knowledge of sharpness and dullness of all faculties, the knowledge of various realms, the knowledge of various understandings, the knowledge of where all paths lead, the knowledge of defilement or purity and proper or improper timing of all meditations, liberations, and concentrations, the knowledge of past abodes in all worlds, the knowledge of clairvoyance, and the knowledge of the end of all taints—yet they don't give up carrying out all the practices of enlightening beings. Why? Because they want to teach and enlighten all living beings and purify them.

"The enlightening beings also conceive this overwhelming determination: 'If I attain complete perfect enlightenment first without having established all sentient beings on the path of unsurpassed liberation, I would be violating my original vow—that would never do, so I should first cause all sentient beings to attain unexcelled enlightenment and nirvana without remainder, and then after that fulfill buddhahood. Why? Sentient beings have not asked me to set my mind on enlightenment—I of my own accord act as an unsolicited friend to sentient beings, wishing to first cause all beings to fully develop their good potential and attain omniscience. This is why I am supreme—because I am not attached to any world. I am highest, because I dwell in the state of unsurpassed self-control. I am free from all blindness, because I understand that sentient beings are boundless. I am done, because my original vow is accomplished. I am versatile, because of the adornment of virtues of enlightening beings. I am reliable, because of the acceptance of the Buddhas of all times.'

"Because the enlightening beings do not give up their fundamental vow, they gain entry to the adornment of unexcelled knowledge and wisdom. They benefit living beings, causing them all to be fulfilled; they attain final consummation of their original vow. Their knowledge has free access to all truths. They cause all sentient beings to attain to purity. Instant to instant they travel throughout the worlds of the ten directions, instant to instant visiting countless buddha-lands, instant to instant seeing countless Buddhas and the pure lands the Buddhas adorned. They show the independent spiritual power of the Enlightened pervading the space of the cosmos.

"These enlightening beings manifest innumerable bodies, entering all worlds without relying on anything. In their bodies they manifest all lands, all beings, all phenomena, and all Buddhas. These enlightening beings know the various thoughts, desires, understandings, results of actions, and roots of goodness of all living beings, and appear to them in accordance with their needs, in order to civilize and tame them. They look upon the enlightening beings as like phantoms, all things as like magic tricks, the appearance of Buddhas in the world as like reflections, all worlds as like dreams. They attain the inexhaustible treasury of bodies of meanings and expressions. They are in command of right mindfulness, and they have certain knowledge of all truths. Their wisdom is supreme and they enter into the true character of all concentrations, and abide in the state of nonduality of one essence.

"Because sentient beings all cling to duality, great enlightening beings abide in great compassion; cultivating this teaching to annihilate afflictions, they attain the ten powers of buddhahood and enter the reality realm which is like the net of Indra. Accomplishing the unhindered liberation of the enlightened, they are valiants among humans; roaring the lion's roar, they attain fearlessness, and are able to turn the wheel of the unimpeded pure teaching. Attaining liberation of intellect, they know thoroughly all objects in the world. Stopping the whirlpool of birth and death, they enter the ocean of wisdom. Preserving the right teachings of the Buddhas of past, present, and future for the sake of all sentient beings, they reach the fountainhead of the real character of the ocean of all Buddha teachings.

"Once enlightening beings dwell in this practice of truth, any beings who associate with them are caused to open up in understanding, be full of joy and completely pure. This is called the great enlightening beings' tenth practice, of truth."

Then, because of the spiritual power of the Buddha, in each of the ten directions as many worlds as atoms in a buddha-land quaked in six ways, moving, moving everywhere, moving equally everywhere, rising, rising everywhere, rising equally everywhere, surging, surging everywhere, surging equally everywhere, shaking, shaking everywhere, shaking equally everywhere, roaring, roaring everywhere, roaring equally everywhere, crashing, crashing everywhere, crashing equally everywhere. It rained beautiful celestial flowers, celestial perfumes and incense, celestial garlands and raiment, celestial jewels and ornaments. Heavenly music played and celestial lights shone, conveying the subtle voices of all celestial beings. The miracles that appeared when the ten practices were expounded in the Suyama heaven of this world also appeared likewise in all the worlds of the ten directions.

Also, due to the spiritual power of the Buddha, from each of the ten directions as many enlightening beings as atoms in a hundred thousand buddha-lands came to this world from beyond worlds as numerous as atoms in a hundred thousand buddha-lands; filling the ten directions, they said to the enlightening being Forest of Virtue, "Excellent, O Child of Buddha; you can skillfully expound the practices of enlightening beings. We are all similarly named Forest of Virtues and the worlds we live in are all called Banner of Virtue, and the Buddhas of those lands are all named Universal Virtue. At our Buddhas' places this teaching is also expounded—the assembly, words, and principles are all the same, nothing more and nothing less. Child of Buddha, we have all come to this assembly through the power of the Buddhas to be witnesses for you. This is also true of all the worlds in the ten directions."

Then the enlightening being Forest of Virtues, by the spiritual power of the Buddha, looked over all the congregations in the ten directions, throughout the cosmos. Because he wanted to cause the lineage of Buddhas to continue, to cause the family of enlightening beings to be pure, to cause those who undertake vows not to regress, to cause practitioners to persevere, to cause all peoples in all times to be equal, to contact all the strains of Buddhas of all times, to expound roots of goodness that have been cultivated, to observe and analyze all faculties, inclinations, understandings, afflictions, habits, and mental activities, and to clarify the enlightenment of all Buddhas, said in verse:

Wholehearted honor to the Lords of Ten Powers,
Undefiled, totally pure, the unobstructed seers;
Their realm is profound and far-reaching, beyond compare,
They abide in the spacelike Path.

The supreme among humans in the past,
With immeasurable virtue, free from attachments,
Foremost in valor, without any peer:
Those beyond the dusts travel this Path.

Now in the lands of the ten directions
The ultimate truth is ably explained:
Free from all faults, utterly pure,
The independent travel this path.

The future lions among humans
Travel everywhere throughout the cosmos;
Having evoked the Buddhas' mind of compassion,
The benefactors travel this path.

The incomparable honored ones of all times
Naturally destroy the darkness of ignorance,
Equanimous toward all things;
Those of great power travel this path.

They see countless, boundless worlds everywhere,
All their beings and conditions,
Yet having seen do not discriminate falsely;
The impertubable travel this path.

Understanding everything in the cosmos,
Most clear about the ultimate truth,
They forever destroy anger, pride, and folly:
The virtuous travel this path.

Accurately distinguishing sentient beings,
They enter into the true nature of all phenomena,
Spontaneously understanding without relying on others;
The spacelike travel this path.

To all lands throughout space
They go and teach, through many examples,
What they teach pure and irrefutable;
The supreme sages travel this path.

Throughly stable, unregressing,
They accomplish the noble, supreme teaching;
Will power inexhaustible, they reach the other shore:
Good practitioners travel this path.

All stages, infinitely boundless,
Their vast, most deep and subtle realms,
All they know and see, without exception;
The lions of philosophy travel this path.

Understanding the meanings of all expressions,
Crushing all disputes,
They are certain of the truth, without a doubt;
The great sages travel this path.

Getting rid of the errors and ills of the world,
Giving peace and happiness to all beings,
They can be peerless great guides;
Those of excellent virtue travel this path.

They always give impartially to beings,
Causing them all to rejoice,
Their minds pure, free from all taint;
The peerless ones travel this path.

Their mental actions are pure and well tuned;
Divorcing sophistry, they speak without fault.
Their magnificent aura's admired by all;
The supreme travel this path.

Entering truth, reaching the other shore,
Abiding in virtue, minds forever at rest,
The Buddhas always protect them;
Those who extinguish being travel this path.

Detached from self, free from affliction,
Always proclaiming the truth aloud,
They reach all lands in the ten directions;
The incomparable travel this path.

Having fulfilled transcendent generosity.
Adorned by a hundred marks of blessing,
All who see them are joyful;
The supremely wise travel this path.

The state of knowledge, hard to enter,
They can abide in by subtle wisdom,
Their minds ultimately impertubable;
Those firm in practice travel this path.

Able to enter all realms of being in the cosmos
And find the ultimate wherever they enter,
Their spiritual powers free and all-embracing;
Those illumined by truth travel this path.

The incomparably great sages
Cultivate the nonduality of concentration,
Their minds always in equipoise, enjoying tranquility;
The all-seers travel this path.

The interpenetration and distinction
Of minute and great lands
They know all in their proper spheres;
The mountain-kings of knowledge travel this path.

Their intellects are always clear and clean,
Without attachments in the world;
Keeping the precepts, they reach the other shore:
The pure-minded travel this path.

Knowledge and wisdom boundless, inexpressible,
Pervading the space of the cosmos,
They ably learn to abide therein;
Those of indestructible wisdom travel this path.

Their knowledge enters and pervades
The realms of all Buddhas of all times,
Never for a moment growing tired or wearied:
The supreme travel this path.

Well able to discern the elements of the ten powers,
They know where all paths lead;
Their actions are unhindered and they are free:
Those embodying virtue travel this path.

All the sentient beings there are
In the infinite worlds in the ten directions
They will rescue without forsaking:
The fearless travel this path.

Earnestly practicing the Buddha teachings,
Their minds ever vigorous and indefatigable,
They purify all the worlds:
The great dragon kings travel this path.

Knowing the dissimilarities in beings' faculties
And the countless differences in inclination and understanding,
They clearly comprehend all kinds of realms:
Those who go everywhere travel this path.

To infinite lands in the worlds of the ten directions
They go and are born, countless times,
With never a thought of weariness or disdain:
The joyful ones travel this path.

Radiating nets of countless lights
Illuminating all worlds,
They enter the nature of reality wherever the light shines:
The good-minded travel this path.

Causing the lands of the ten directions to tremble—
Countless billions of trillions,
They do not cause the beings to fear:
This is the path traveled by benefactors of the world.

Understanding all principles of language,
They are consummately skilled in dialogue,
Their brilliant discursive intellect knowing all:
This is the path traveled by the fearless.

They understand the various lands with various orientations,
Discerning, thinking, finding the ultimate,
Causing all to abide in the state of inexhaustibility:
This is the path traveled by those of superior intellect.

Their virtues are infinitely numerous—
They cultivate them all in search of the Buddha way,
And reach the other shore of them all:
This is the path traveled by the inexhaustible workers.

The world-transcending philosophers
With supreme eloquence roar the lion's roar,
Causing all living beings to reach the other shore;
This is the path traveled by the pure-minded.

They have already been crowned
With the supreme teaching of the Buddhas;
Their minds always dwell in the truth:
The broadminded travel this path.

Sentient beings have innumerable differences;
They comprehend their minds thoroughly,
Maintaining with certainty the treasury of Buddha teachings:
Those like polar mountains travel this path.

They are able to reveal countless sounds
In each and every word
Enabling beings to understand in accord with their kind:
The unhindered seers travel this path.

Their knowledge has impartial access
To all rules of language,
While they dwell in the realm of real truth;
This is the path traveled by those who see the essence.

Abiding at peace in the deep ocean of truth,
Able to verify all actualities
They understand the true aspect of signlessness of things:
This is the path traveled by those who see the truth.

They travel to every buddha-land
Over countless, boundless eons,
Observing and meditating ceaselessly:
This is the path traveled by the indefatigable.

Infinite, countless Buddhas,
Their names each different,
They clearly see in the space of a point:
This is the path traveled by those of pure virtue.

They see Buddhas in the space of a point,
Their number beyond measure or speech,
The same true for every phenomenon:
The children of Buddhas travel this path.

Measureless, boundless, countless eons
They clearly see in an instant,
And know their length has no fixed characteristics:
This is the path traveled by the liberated.

They can cause all who see them to benefit,
All planting affinities with the Buddha-teaching—
Yet they have no attachment to their deeds:
This is the path traveled by the most excellent.

Meeting Buddhas for billions of eons
With never a thought of weariness,
The joy in their hearts increases more and more:
This is the path traveled by those who don't see in vain.

Observing the realms of all beings
Over countless, boundless eons,
They've never seen that a single being exists:
This is the path of the steadfast heroes.

Cultivating boundless stores of virtue and knowledge,
They are pure, cool universal reservoirs of virtue
Benefiting all beings:
The foremost of humans travel this path.

The various species in the universe,
Filling space, uncountable,
They know all exist in terms of words:
This is the path traveled by lion roarers.

Able in each individual concentration
To enter countless concentrations,
They arrive at the recondite depths of the teaching:
The expounders of the moon travel this path.

With the power of acceptance they practice earnestly and reach the
    other shore,
Able to accept the supreme teaching of dispassionate extinction,
Their minds equanimous and imperturbable:
This is the path traveled by those of boundless knowledge.

At one seat in one world
Their bodies are unmoving, ever tranquil,
Yet they manifest their bodies in everything;
Those of boundless bodies travel this path.

Countless, boundless lands
They cause to enter at once into one atom,
Which is able to contain all unhindered:
Those of boundless thought travel this path.

Comprehending what is so and what is not,
They are able to enter the realm of all the ten powers
And accomplish the supreme powers of the enlightened:
This is the path traveled by the foremost in power.

Countless, boundless consequences of acts
In past, future, and present ages,
They always comprehend by knowledge:
This is the path traveled by those of consummate understanding.

Understanding right and wrong timing in the world,
They civilize beings according to necessity,
In every case adapting to their needs;
This is the path traveled by those who comprehend.

Guarding well their action, speech, and thought,
Always making them apply the teaching in practice,
They divorce all attachments and conquer all demons;
This is the path traveled by the wise.

Able to skillfully adapt the teachings,
And able to enter the impartiality of true thusness,
Their eloquent exposition is inexhaustible:
This is the path of Buddha practice.

Having fulfilled the method of mental command,
Able to rest in the treasury of nonobstruction,
They comprehend all realms of reality:
This is the path of those who delve deeply.

Equal in mind, same in knowledge
As all Buddhas of all times,
They are of one nature and one character:
This is the path of the unimpeded.

Having removed all veils of ignorance
And entered deeply into the ocean of knowledge,
They bestow pure eyes on all sentient beings:
This is the path of those with eyes.

Having fulfilled the impartial, nondual practice of spiritual powers
Of all the Guides,
They attain the independent power of the Enlightened:
This is the path of the well-cultivated.

They travel through all worlds
Showering everywhere the boundless rain of wondrous teaching,
Causing all to gain certain understanding of the meaning:
This is the path of the Clouds of Teaching.

Able to produce nonregressing pure faith
In the Buddhas' knowledge and liberation,
They produce the roots of knowledge and wisdom by faith:
This is the path traveled by those who learn well.

Able to know in a single instant
All living beings, without exception,
They comprehend the intrinsic nature of beings' minds:
This is the path of those who realize naturelessness.

To all lands in the cosmos, countless,
They can travel by projection,
Their bodies most subtle, beyond comparison:
This is the path of peerless action.

Buddha-lands are boundless and countless;
There are infinite Buddhas therein:
Enlightening beings appear before them all,
Attending, providing, engendering respect.

Enlightening beings can, with a single body,
Enter concentration, become poised in stillness,
And cause that body to appear as countless bodies
Each rising from concentration.

The abode of enlightening beings is most profound and subtle;
Their practices and deeds are free from nonsense,
Their minds are pure, always happy,
Able to cause all beings joy.

The differences in faculties and expedients
Are clearly apparent to their knowledge,
Yet they realize all faculties have no basis:
This is the path of the tamers of the intractable.

Able to expediently distinguish with skill
They are versatile masters of all teachings.
The worlds of the ten directions are each different:
They live therein and perform Buddha work.

Their faculties are subtle, so are their deeds;
They are able to expound the truth broadly to beings:
Who would not rejoice on hearing them?
This is the path traveled by those equal to space.

Their eye of knowledge is pure, without peer,
They see all things clearly,
This knowledge expediently distinguishing them:
This is the path traveled by the peerless.

All inexhaustible great virtues
They have cultivated to consummation,
To cause all beings to be pure:
This is the path traveled by the incomparable.

Urging all to cultivate the aids to the Path,
Causing all to dwell on the ground of method,
They liberate beings without number
Without ever forming a concept of beings.

They observe all opportunities and affinities,
First protecting others' minds, making them noncontentious,
Showing all sentient beings the place of peace;
This is the path traveled by the skillful.

Perfecting highest, ultimate knowledge,
Replete with measureless, boundless knowledge,
They are fearless among all groups of people:
This is the path of the knowers of means.

All worlds and all phenomena
They can enter into with freedom;
They also enter all congregations
And liberate countless beings.

In all lands in the ten directions
They beat the great drum of truth and awaken the living;
As givers of teaching they are unsurpassed:
This is the path traveled by the unperishing.

With one body sitting crosslegged upright
They fill countless worlds in the ten directions
Yet cause their bodies not to be crowded:
This is the path of those with the body of reality.

In one doctrine, one statement,
They can explain boundless principles,
And no limit to them can be found:
This is the path traveled by those of boundless knowledge.

They learn the Buddhas' liberations well,
Attain Buddha-knowledge without obstruction,
Develop fearlessness and become valiants of the world:
This is the path traveled by the skillful.

They know the oceans of worlds in the ten directions
And also know the oceans of all buddha-lands,
And comprehend the oceans of knowledge and truth;
All who see them are filled with joy.

Sometimes they show entering the womb, sometimes birth,
Sometimes the attainment of enlightenment—
Thus they cause all worldlings to see:
This is the path traveled by the unbounded.

In countless billions of lands
They manifest themselves entering nirvana
But really they don't give up their vows for extinction:
This is the path of the heroic philosophers.

The indestructible, esoteric unique subtle body
Is equal to the Buddhas', no different,
But all sentient beings each see it differently:
This is the path of the one true body.

The real cosmos is all equal, without distinction,
Containing infinite, boundless meanings;
They enjoy contemplating oneness, minds unmoving:
This is the path of knowers of all times.

In terms of sentient beings and enlightening teachings,
Their constructions and empowerments are consummate;
Their supporting power is the same as the Buddhas:
The supreme upholders of teaching travel this path.

Their power of psychic travel is unimpeded, like Buddhas',
Their clairvoyance is unhindered and utterly pure,
Their auditory faculties, unobstructed, can hear well:
This is the path of those with unhindered minds.

All their spiritual powers are fully complete,
All developed according to their knowledge;
They know all, without peer:
This is the path traveled by the wise.

Their minds are rightly concentrated, unwavering,
Their knowledge is boundlessly vast,
They comprehend all realms:
This is the path traveled by the all-seers.

Having already arrived at the shore of all virtue
They can deliver beings one after another,
Their minds ultimately never wearying:
This is the path traveled by the constantly diligent.

They know and see the teachings
Of the Buddhas of all times,
And are born in the family of the enlightened:
The Buddha-children travel this path.

They have fully developed adaptive speech
And skillfully refute all opposition,
And always can proceed toward enlightenment:
This is the path of those with boundless wisdom.

One light illumines boundlessly,
Filling all lands in the ten directions,
Causing all worlds to gain great brightness:
This is the path of the darkness destroyers.

According to what should be seen and supported
They manifest the pure body of the enlightened,
Teaching and edifying billions of beings
And adorning buddha-lands the same way.

In order to enable sentient beings to transcend the world
They cultivate all the sublime practices;
This activity is boundlessly great:
How could anyone be able to know?

Even if the body were reproduced to an unspeakable number,
Equal to the space of the cosmos,
And all should together laud their virtues,
They could not finish them in a billion eons.
Enlightening beings' virtues have no bounds;
They have fulfilled all cultivation:

Even countless, boundless Buddhas
Could not tell of them all in measureless eons,
How much less could mundane gods and humans,
Listeners and self-illumined ones,
Be able in unlimited eons
To sing their praises exhaustively.

BOOK TWENTY-TWO

Ten Inexhaustible
Treasuries

THEN THE ENLIGHTENING BEING Forest of Virtues also said to the enlightening beings, "Children of Buddhas, great enlightening beings have ten kinds of treasury, which have been, will be, and are explained by the Buddhas of past, future, and present. What are the ten? They are the treasury of faith, the treasury of ethics, the treasury of shame, the treasury of conscience, the treasury of learning, the treasury of giving, the treasury of wisdom, the treasury of recollection, the treasury of preservation, and the treasury of elocution.

"What is the great enlightening being's treasury of faith? The enlightening beings believe all things are empty, they believe all things are signless, they believe all things are wishless, they believe all things are noncreative, they believe all things are without discrimination, they believe all things have no basis, they believe all things cannot be measured, they believe all things have nothing beyond, they believe all things are hard to transcend, they believe all things are uncreated.

"If enlightening beings are able in this way to engender pure faith in accord with all things, when they hear all Buddha teachings are inconceivable, their minds are not intimidated; when they hear all Buddhas are inconceivable, their minds are not intimidated; when they hear the realms of sentient beings are inconceivable, their minds are not intimidated; when they hear the realm of reality is inconceivable, their minds are not intimidated; when they hear the realm of space is inconceivable, their minds are not intimidated; when they hear the realm of nirvana is inconceivable, they are not intimidated; when they hear the past, present, and future times are inconceivable, their minds are not intimidated; when they hear entry into all eons is inconceivable, their minds are not intimidated.

"Why? The enlightening beings have wholehearted, firm faith in the Buddhas; they know the knowledge and wisdom of the Buddhas are boundless and inexhuastible. In each of the countless worlds in the ten directions are innumerable Buddhas who have attained, will attain, or

485

now are attaining unexcelled complete perfect enlightenment, who have appeared, now are appearing, or will appear in the world, who have entered, are now entering, or will enter nirvana—the knowledge and wisdom of those Buddhas neither increase nor decrease, are unborn and imperishable, neither advance nor regress, are not near or far, have neither concern nor indifference. The enlightening beings enter into the Buddhas' knowledge and wisdom and develop boundless, inexhaustible faith.

"Once they have attained this faith, their minds do not regress, their minds do not become confused; they cannot be broken down, they have no attachments. They always have a fundamental basis, they follow the sages, they dwell in the house of the enlightened, they maintain the lineage of all Buddhas, they increase the faith and resolution of all enlightening beings, they conform to the virtues of all enlightened ones, they set forth the enlightening techniques of the Buddhas. This is called the treasury of faith of great enlightening beings. When enlightening beings abide in this treasury of faith, they can hear and retain all the Buddha teachings, explain them to sentient beings, and cause them all to awaken to understanding.

"What is the enlightening beings' treasury of ethics? Enlightening beings perfect the ethic of universal benefit, the ethic of not accepting wrong precepts, the ethic of nondwelling, the ethic of no regret or resentment, the ethic of noncontention, the ethic of noninjury, the ethic of nondefilement, the ethic of noncovetousness, the ethic of impeccability, and the ethic of nontransgression of moral precepts.

"What is the ethic of universal benefit? The enlightening beings accept and uphold pure ethics fundamentally for the sake of benefiting all living beings. What is the ethic of not accepting false precepts? The enlightening beings do not accept or practice precepts of cultists; they only exert themselves naturally in maintaining the impartial, pure precepts of the Buddhas of past, present, and future. What is the ethic of nondwelling? When the enlightening beings accept and keep ethical precepts, their minds do not dwell in the realm of desire, they don't dwell in the realm of form, they don't dwell in the formless realm. Why? Because they don't keep precepts in hopes of being born there in those realms. What is the ethic of no regret or resentment? The enlightening beings always abide peacefully in a state of mind free from regret and resentment. Why? Because they don't commit serious wrongdoings, they don't practice flattery or deception, and they don't break the pure precepts. What is the ethic of noncontention? The enlightening beings do not deny what has been previously established, and do not innovate— their minds always follow the precepts which are directed toward nirvana, keeping them without transgression. They do not afflict other beings by their keeping of precepts—they keep ethical precepts with the sole desire that all beings be joyful. What is the ethic of noninjury? The enlightening beings do not harm sentient beings on account of their precepts, or by learning charms, or by making drugs. They only keep ethical precepts for the purpose of saving and protecting all living beings. What is the ethic of nondefilement? The enlightening beings do not cling to extreme or biased views, they do not keep impure precepts: they only contemplate interdependent origination and keep emancipating precepts. What is the ethic of noncovetousness? The enlightening beings do not display extraordinary signs to make a show of virtue; they only keep ethical precepts for the purpose of fulfilling the way to emancipation. What is the ethic of impeccability? The enlightening beings do not boast of themselves as upholding precepts, and when they see those who break the precepts they do not scorn or shame them. They only make their minds single and keep the ethical precepts. What is the ethic of nontransgression? The enlightening beings forever cease killing, stealing, sexual misconduct, lying, two-faced talk, slander, meaningless talk, greed, anger, and false views: they fully accept the precepts of ten kinds of virtuous actions. When enlightening beings observe this ethic of nontransgression, they think, 'Sentient beings' transgressions of pure morality are all due to delusion. Only a Buddha is able to know why sentient beings become deluded and transgress pure morality. I should accomplish supreme enlightenment and extensively explain the truth to sentient beings, to free them from delusion.' This is called the great enlightening beings' second treasury, of ethics.

"What is the great enlightening beings' treasury of shame? The enlightening beings remember the wrongs they committed in the past and conceive shame. That is, they think, 'Since beginningless past all sentient beings and I have been parents and children, brothers and sisters to each other: being full of greed, hatred, and ignorance, pride, conceit, dishonesty, deception, and all other afflictions, we have therefore harmed each other, plundering, raping, and killing, doing all manner of evil. All sentient beings are like this—because of passions and afflictions they do not respect or honor each other, they don't agree with or obey each other, they don't defer to each other, they don't edify or guide each other, they don't care for each other—they go on killing and injuring each other, being enemies and malefactors to each other. Reflecting on myself as well as other sentient beings, we act shamelessly in the past, future, and present, while the Buddhas of past, future, and present see and know it all. Now if I don't stop this shameless behavior, the Buddhas of all times will also see me. Why do I still not stop such conduct? This will never do. I should therefore concentrate on eliminating evil and realizing complete perfect enlightenment, to expound the truth for all beings.' This is called great enlightening beings' third treasury, of shame.

"What is the great enlightening beings' treasury of conscience? The enlightening beings are ashamed of their insatiable desires of the past and consequent increase of all afflictions, such as greed, anger, folly, etc., and resolve that they should not act this way anymore. Also they think, 'Sentient beings are unwise; developing afflictions, they do all sorts of bad things. They do not respect or honor each other and develop into enemies and malefactors to each other. They have committed all such evils, and are happy about it, pursuing and approving of them. Blind, having no eye of wisdom, they enter wombs in mother's bellies and undergo birth, becoming impure corporeal beings, finally to become grey and wrinkled. Those of wisdom observe this to be simply something impure born of lust. The Buddhas of past, present, and future see and know all: if I now were to still act in these ways, I would be trying to fool the Buddhas. Therefore I should cultivate conscience, quickly attain complete perfect enlightenment, and explain the truth to all beings.' This is called great enlightening beings' fourth treasury, of conscience.

"What is the great enlightening beings' treasury of learning? The enlightening beings know that something exists because something else exists, and that something does not exist because something else does not exist; they know that something comes to be because something else comes to be, and that something passes away because something else passes away; they know what is mundane and what is transmundane, what is compounded and what is uncompounded, what is meaningful and what is pointless.

"What does it mean that something exists because something else exists? It means that when there is ignorance there is conditioning. What does it mean that because something does not exist something else does not exist? It means that when there is no discriminating consciousness there is no name and form. What does it mean that something comes to be because something else comes to be? It means that when craving comes to be suffering comes to be. What does it mean that something passes away because something else passes away? It means that when becoming passes away birth passes away.

"What are mundane phenomena? Material form, sensation, perception, conditioning, and consciousness. What are transmundane phenomena? Discipline, concentration, wisdom, liberation, and the knowledge and insight of liberation. What are compounded things? The realm of desire, the realm of form, the formless realm, and the realm of sentient beings. What are uncompounded things? Space, nirvana, extinction by analysis, extinction because of lack of conditions, and the subsistence of the nature of things, interdependent origination.

"What are things with meaning? The four holy truths, the four fruits of ascesis, the four special knowledges, the four fearlessnesses, the four points of mindfulness, the four right efforts, the four bases of spiritual powers, the five faculties and five powers, the seven branches of enlightenment, and the eightfold path of sages.

"What are pointless issues? Whether the world is finite or infinite, or both, or neither; whether the world is permanent or impermanent, or both, or neither; whether a Buddha exists after nirvana or not, whether a Buddha both does and does not exist or neither does nor does not exist after nirvana; whether oneself and sentient beings exist or not, whether they both do and do not exist, whether they neither do nor do not exist; how many Buddhas attained final nirvana in the past, how many listeners and individual illuminates attain final nirvana, how many Buddhas, listeners, individual illuminates, and sentient beings there are presently existing; what Buddhas appeared first, what listeners and individual illuminates appeared first; what Buddhas will appear last, what listeners and individual illuminates will appear last; where the world came from, where the world will go; how many worlds have come to be, how many worlds have perished, where did the worlds come from, where did the worlds go; what the very beginning of birth and death is, what the very end of birth and death will be—these all are called pointless issues. Great enlightening beings form this thought: 'Sentient beings haven't much learning in regard to birth and death and are not capable of knowing all these things. I should determine to sustain the treasury of learning, realize unexcelled complete perfect enlightenment, and expound the truth to sentient beings.' This is called great enlightening beings' fifth treasury, of learning.

"What is the great enlightening beings' treasury of giving? The enlightening beings practice ten kinds of giving: partial giving, exhaustive giving, inside giving, outside giving, inside and outside giving, total giving, past giving, future giving, present giving, and ultimate giving.

"What is enlightening beings' partial giving? They are benevolent and kind by nature and are very generous. If they receive fine food, they don't take it all themselves—they want to share it with others, and only then will they eat. The same applies to everything they may receive. When they eat, they think. 'There are countless microorganisms in my body whose life depends on me. If my body is satisfied, so are they. If my body is hungry or in pain, so are they. May this food which I now receive enable all beings to be satisfied; I myself eat this in order to distribute it to them, without greed for the taste.' They also think, 'Throughout the long night of ignorance I have been attached to this body and want to satisfy it, so I take food and drink. Now I bestow this food on living beings, so that I may forever end covetousness and attachment.' This is called partial giving.

"What is enlightening beings' exhaustive giving? They get various kinds of fine food, incense, flowers, clothes, and other necessities of life—if they use them themselves, they can live out their years in comfort; if they give them up and pass them on to others, they will suffer want and die. Sometimes there may be people who come and say, 'You should give me everything you have'—the enlightening beings think to themselves, 'Since beginningless past I have died of starvation countless times without having the benefit of being able to help anyone at all. Now I shall again give up my life as I have in the past, so I should do it for the sake of helping sentient beings.' So they give away all they have, even to the point of ending life. This is called exhaustive giving.

"What is enlightening beings' inside giving? When the enlightening beings are young vigorous, and good looking, adorned with scents, flowers, and clothing, and have just received coronation as universal sovereigns, having all the seven treasures of universal monarchs, reigning over the four quarters, if someone should come and say, 'O great sovereign, know that I am old and feeble, seriously ill, alone and helpless, worn out, not far from death: if I were to receive the hands and feet, blood and flesh, head, eyes, bones, and marrow from the king's body, my life would be saved. Please don't deliberate further and do not begrudge me this—just look upon me with compassion and give them to me.' At such a time the enlightening beings would think, 'This body of mine will in the end surely die, without any benefit. I should take the opportunity to give it away early to save a living being.' With this thought they give without regret. This is called inside giving.

"What is enlightening beings' outside giving? When enlightening beings are in full maturity and physical well being, replete with all marks of dignity, adorned with fine flowers and excellent clothing, having been crowned as universal monarchs regining over the four quarters, having all the seven treasures, should someone come and say, 'I am poor and oppressed by all kinds of miseries; please be so kind and compassionate as to give up your rank to me, so that I may reign and experience the felicities of sovereignty,' the enlightening beings think, 'All flourishing and prosperity must inevitably decline and end. When it does decline and end, it is no longer possible to benefit sentient beings. I should satisfy this person as he requests.' And having formed this thought, they give up the throne without regret. This is called outside giving.

"What is enlightening beings' inside and outside giving? When the enlightening beings are in the position of universal monarch, as explained before, if someone comes and says, 'You have been in the rank of universal monarch for a long time, and I have never been. Please abdicate in my favor, and be my attendant.' At that time the enlightening beings think, 'My body, wealth, and rank are all impermanent. I am now in my prime, wealthy, in possession of the whole world. Now a beggar appears before me; I should, through these perishable things, seek the imperishable truth.' And so thinking, they abdicate, personally work respectfully as servants, without regret. This is called inside and outside giving.

"What is the enlightening beings' total giving? The enlightening beings are in the rank of universal monarchs, as described before, and countless poor people come and say, 'The fame of the monarch is heard throughout the world, and we have come here because of your reputation. We each have requests which we hope you will compassionately fulfill.' Then those poor people variously ask the monarch for the land, for his wife and children, for his hands and feet, blood, flesh, heart, lungs, head, eyes, marrow, and brains. At such a time, the enlightening beings think, 'All who love must eventually part, with no benefit to sentient beings. Now I want to give up all clinging, and fulfill the wishes of sentient beings with these things which I must in any case eventually lose.' Having thus reflected, they give all, without regret or resentment, and without looking down on sentient beings. This is called total giving.

"What is the enlightening beings' past giving? The enlightening beings, having heard of the accomplishments and virtues of the Buddhas and enlightening beings of the past, are not attached to them, realizing they are not existent. They do not create discrimination, do not covet, crave, or seek them. They depend on nothing. They see things as like dreams, without solidity. They do not conceive of roots of goodness as existent, and they do not rely on them; however, they fulfill the teachings of Buddhas and expound them in order to teach and edify grasping, clinging sentient beings. Also they contemplate all things of the past, searching them out everywhere to find they cannot be apprehended. Having reflected thus, they ultimately relinquish all things of the past. This is called past giving.

"What is enlightening beings' future giving? When enlightening beings hear of the practices of Buddhas of the future, they realize they are not existent; they do not grasp their characteristics, they do not particularly delight in going to be born in the Buddhas' lands, they do not indulge, do not cling, and yet do not disdain them; they do not dedicate virtues there, yet they do not withdraw from virtue on their account—they always cultivate practice diligently, never giving up, just wanting to include sentient beings in those realms, explain the truth to them, and cause them to master the qualities of buddhahood. And yet these qualities have no locus, yet are not without location; they are not inside or outside, not near or far. They also think that since things are not existent they cannot but be relinquished. This is called future giving.

"What is enlightening beings' present giving? When the enlightening beings hear of the virtues of all the beings of various heavenly states, of Buddhist disciples and individual illuminates, their minds are not confused or absorbed, not concentrated or scattered: they only observe all actions as like dreams, unreal—they have no craving or attachment, but in order to cause sentient beings to divorce evil dispositions, they practice the enlightening path without discrimination, fulfill the Buddha teachings, and expound them. This is called present giving.

"What is enlightening beings' ultimate giving? If innumerable sentient beings, some lacking eyes, some lacking ears, some lacking noses or tongues, or hands or feet, should come and say to the enlightening beings, 'We are unfortunate, physically handicapped—please be so kind as to give up your organs so as to make us complete,' the enlightening beings, hearing this, immediately give them; even if because of this they should be physically handicapped for incalculable eons, they would never have a single throught of regret. They just observe this body from its first conception, its various organs an unclean little mass of cells, which is born, ages, gets sick, and dies. They also contemplate this body as having no true reality, being shameless, lacking in sagacity, foul and unclean, held up by bones and joints, covered with blood and flesh, with nine apertures constantly flowing, despised by people. Having thus contemplated, they do not conceive a single thought of attachment. They also reflect that this body is fragile and unstable and not to be clung to, that it should be given to satisfy the wishes of others, and that this deed will guide all sentient beings and cause them to be unattached to body or mind, enabling them to develop the pure body of knowledge. This is called ultimate giving. This is the enlightening beings' sixth treasury, of generosity.

"What is the great enlightening beings' treasury of wisdom? The enlightening beings know form as it really is, know the assemblage of form as it really is, know the extinction of form as it really is, know the path to extinction of form as it really is; they know sensation, perception, conditioning, and consciousness as they really are, know the assemblage of sensation, perception, conditioning, and consciousness as it really is, know the extinction of sensation, perception, conditioning, and consciousness as it really is, and know the path to extinction of sensation, perception, conditioning, and consciousness as it really is. They know ignorance as it really is, know the accumulation of ignorance as it really is, know the extinction of ignorance as it really is, know the path to extinction of ignorance as it really is. They know craving as it really is, they know the accumulation of craving as it really is, they know the extinction of craving as it really is, they know the path to the extinction of craving as it really is. They know Buddhist discipleship as it really is, they know the principles of discipleship as they really are, they know the development of discipleship as it really is, they know the nirvana of Buddhist disciples as it really is. They know individual enlightenment as it really is, they know the principles of individual enlightenment as they really are, they know the development of individual enlightenment as it really is, they know the nirvana of individual illuminates as it really is. They know enlightening beings as they really are, they know the principles of enlightening beings as they really are, they know the development of enlightening beings as it really is, they know the nirvana of enlightening beings as it really is.

"In what way do they know these things? They know that actions resulting from past deeds, productions of causes and conditions, are all unreal and empty, are not self, are not substantial—there is not a single thing that can be established. Wishing to cause sentient beings to know their true nature, they explain it extensively for them. What do they explain to them? They explain that all things cannot be destroyed. What things cannot be destroyed? Material form cannot be destroyed, sensation, perception, conditioning, and consciousness cannot be destroyed; ignorance cannot be destroyed; the principles of discipleship, self-enlightenment, and universal enlightenment cannot be destroyed. Why? Because all things are uncreated, have no creator, have no explanation and no location, are unborn and unoriginated, not given and not taken, have no motion and no function.

"Enlightening beings developing such a measureless treasury of wisdom, understand all things by a minimum of devices, spontaneously comprehending them clearly and not depending on another for enlightenment.

"This inexhaustible treasury of wisdom is said to be inexhaustible because it has ten kinds of inexhaustibility: because the skills of learned enlightening beings are inexhaustible; because association with wise people is inexhaustible; because appropriate analysis of expressions and meanings is inexhaustible; because entry into the profound realm of reality is inexhaustible; because adornment with uniform knowledge is inexhaustible; because indefatigably accumulating all virtues is inexhaustible; because entering the gates of all concentration formulae is inexhaustible; because ability to distinguish the sounds of languages of all sentient beings is inexhaustible; because the ability to cut off the doubt and confusion of all sentient beings is inexhaustible; because manifesting all spiritual powers of Buddhas for all sentient beings to teach and civilize them and cause them to practice the teaching without interruption is inexhaustible.

"This is called the great enlightening beings' seventh treasury, of wisdom: those who abide in this treasury attain inexhaustible knowledge and wisdom, and are able to enlighten all sentient beings."

"What is great enlightening beings' inexhaustible treasury of recollection? The enlightening beings cast off ignorance and confusion and attain full mindfulness. They remember one lifetime, two lifetimes, even ten lifetimes, a hundred, a thousand, a hundred thousand, countless hundreds of thousands of lifetimes in the past, their ages of formation, ages of decay, and ages of both formation and decay. And not just one age of formation, not just one age of decay, not just one age of formation and decay—a hundred ages, a thousand ages, a hundred thousand trillion ages, even up to countless, measureless, boundless, incomparable, uncountable, incalculable, unthinkable, immeasurable, inexplicable, unspeakably unspeakable numbers of Buddhas' names. They remember the appearance in the world and forecasting of one Buddha up to an unspeakably unspeakable number of Buddhas. They remember the emergence in the world and discourses of one up to an unspeakably unspeakable number of Buddhas—as they remember the discourses, so also they remember the recapitulative verses, predictions, poems, stories, extemporaneous expositions, tales of past events, tales of past lives, extensive and universal teachings, miracles, metaphors, and analytic philosophy of the Buddhas. They remember one assembly, up to an unspeakably unspeakable number of assemblies. They remember the exposition of one teaching, up to an unspeakably unspeakable number of teachings. They remember the various natures of one faculty, up the various natures of an unspeakably unspeakable number of faculties. They remember the innumerable various natures of one up to an unspeakably unspeakable number of faculties. They remember the various natures of one affliction, up to the various natures of an unspeakably unspeakable number of afflictions. They remember the various natures of one up to an unspeakably unspeakable number of afflictions. This recollection is of ten kinds: dispassionate, serene recollection; pure, clear recollection; unmuddled recollection; thoroughly lucid recollection; recollection apart from defilement; recollection apart from various defilements; untainted recollection; radiant recollection; pleasant recollection; unhindered recollection.

"When enlightening beings dwell in this recollection, no one from any world can disturb them, no different philosophies or arguments can change or move them. Their roots of goodness from the past are all purified. They are not influenced by or attached to mundane things. Demons and outsiders cannot harm them. They can be reborn in different forms without forgetting anything. Their teaching in past and future is inexhaustible. They live together with sentient beings in all worlds with never any faults or misdeeds. They enter the congregation at the sites of enlightenment of all Buddhas without impediment, and are able to associate with all Buddhas. This is called the great enlightening beings' eighth treasury, of recollection.

"What is great enlightening beings' treasury of preservation? The enlightening beings preserve the discourses of the Buddhas, their expressions, meanings, and principles, without forgetting or losing them, for one lifetime, up to an unspeakably unspeakable number of lifetimes. They hold the name of one Buddha up to an unspeakably unspeakable number of Buddhas. They preserve the reckoning of one age up to an unspeakably unspeakable number of ages. They preserve the predictions of one Buddha up to an unspeakably unspeakable number of Buddhas. They preserve one scripture, up to an unspeakably unspeakable number of scriptures. They hold one assembly, up to an unspeakably unspeakable number of assemblies. They preserve the explanation of one doctrine, up to the explanations of an unspeakably unspeakable number of doctrines. They keep in mind the countless various natures of one up to an unspeakably unspeakable number of faculties. They keep in mind the countless various natures of one, up to an unspeakably unspeakable number of afflictions. They keep in mind the countless various natures of one, up to an unspeakably unspeakable number of concentrations. This treasury of preservation is boundless and hard to fill; it is hard to reach its depths, hard to approach. No one can conquer it. It is measureless and boundless, inexhaustible, and has great power. This is in the realm of Buddhas and can only be completely comprehended by a Buddha. This is called the great enlightening beings' ninth treasury, of preservation.

"What is great enlightening beings' treasury of elocution? The enlightening beings have profound knowledge and wisdom and know reality. They extensively explain all things for sentient beings without contradicting the scriptures of all the Buddhas. They explain one doctrine, up to an unspeakably unspeakable number of doctrines. They explain one Buddha-name, up to an unspeakably unspeakable number of Buddha-names. In this way they explain one world, one Buddha's predictions, one scripture, one assembly, one teaching, countless various natures of one faculty, countless various natures of one affliction, countless various natures of one concentration, up to an unspeakably unspeakable number of all of these. They may speak for a day, for a fortnight, for a month, for a century, for a millennium, a hundred millennia, an eon, a hundred eons, a thousand eons, a hundred thousand eons, a hundred thousand billion trillion eons, or for countless, innumerable eons, up to unspeakably unspeakable numbers of eons—the number of eons might be exhausted, but the meanings and principles in a single sentence or phrase can hardly be exhausted. Why? Because the enlightening beings have developed these ten inexhaustible treasuries, and can comprehend all things; the method of concentration formulae is obvious to them, containing incalculable millions of concentration spells. Once they have attained mental command of this concentration formula, they can extensively explain things to sentient beings by the light of truth. When they preach, with a universal tongue they produce marvelous sounds which fill all worlds in the ten directions, satisfying all according to their faculties and natures, so that their minds are happy and freed from the entangling taints of all afflictions.

"The intellectual and interpretative powers of the enlightening beings, able to enter into all linguistic expression, spoken and written, causes all sentient beings to continue the lineage of Buddhas. Their purity of mind is continuous, and they expound the truth endlessly by the light of the teaching, without becoming weary. Why? Because these enlightening beings have developed boundless bodies as extensive as space, pervading the cosmos.

"This is called the enlightening beings' tenth treasury, of elocution. This treasury is inexhaustible, unbroken, uninterrupted, unchanging, unhindered, never receding. It is extremely deep, and indeed bottomless. It is hard to enter. It goes into the doors of all the Buddha teachings.

"These ten inexhaustible treasuries have ten kinds of inexhaustibility which enable enlightening beings to ultimately achieve unexcelled enlightenment. What are they? They benefit all sentient beings; they skillfully dedicate their original vows; they have no end throughout all time; throughout the realm of space all become enlightened, their minds unbounded; their dedication involves striving but they are not attached; the phenomena in the realm of an instant of thought are infinite; the mind of great vows never changes; they skillfully take in all concentration formulae; they are guarded by all the Buddhas; they comprehend all things are like phantoms. These are the ten inexhaustible things which can enable deeds in all worlds to attain the ultimate inexhaustible great treasuries."

BOOK TWENTY-THREE

Ascent to the Palace of the Tushita Heaven

THEN, BY THE SPIRITUAL POWER of the Buddha, in each continent Jambu of every world in the ten directions was seen the Buddha sitting under a tree, at each of which were enlightening beings imbued with spiritual power from the Buddha expounding the teaching, each thinking themselves to be always face to face with the Buddha.

At that time the Buddha, again by spiritual power, went to the palace adorned by all exquisite jewels in the Tushita heaven of satisfaction and happiness, yet without leaving the foot of the enlightenment tree and the palace of the Suyama heaven on the peak of Mt. Sumeru. The celestial king of the Tushita heaven, seeing from afar the Buddha's advent, set up a jewel mine lion seat in the palace; that lion throne was made of a collection of celestial jewels obtained from roots of goodness cultivated in the past, made manifest by the spiritual powers of all Buddhas, born of countless hundreds of thousands of millions of billions of roots of goodness, created by the pure teachings of all enlightened ones, adorned by the power of infinite virtue. Resulting from pure actions, it was indestructible, endlessly delightful to all beholders. Its transcendental qualities were not influenced by the world. Though all sentient beings come to gaze on it, none could exhaustively fathom its glories. There were a hundred trillion tiers all around it, with a hundred trillion gold webs, a hundred trillion flower curtains, a hundred trillion jewel curtains, a hundred trillion garland curtains, and a hundred trillion incense curtains hung above it. Garlands of flowers hung down, their scent perfuming everywhere. A hundred trillion canopies of flowers, a hundred trillion canopies of garlands, and a hundred trillion canopies of jewels were held by various celestial beings arrayed in rows on all four sides. A hundred trillion precious robes were spread on it. A hundred trillion balconies radiantly adorned it, with a hundred trillion nets of pearls and a hundred trillion nets of jewels covering above, while a hundred trillion nets of necklaces hung down on all four sides. A hundred trillion nets of ornaments, a hundred trillion nets of canopies, a hundred trillion nets of robes, and a hundred trillion nets of jewel tapestries were hung above. A hundred trillion nets of jewel lotuses in full bloom with glorious light, a hundred trillion nets of incense with exquisite fragrance delighting everyone, a hundred trillion curtains of jewel chimes moving gently producing harmonious elegant sounds, a hundred trillion curtains of precious sandalwood, its fragrance perfuming the air, a hundred trillion curtains of precious flowers in full bloom, a hundred trillion curtains of raiment of various subtle hues, rare in the world, a hundred trillion curtains showing enlightening beings, a hundred trillion multicolored curtains, a hundred trillion gold curtains, a hundred trillion lapis lazuli curtains, and a hundred trillion curtains of various jewels, were all hung above.

A hundred trillion curtains of all jewels, adorned by huge wish-fulfilling gems, and a hundred trillion flowers of exquisite jewels surrounded in glorious arrays. A hundred trillion reflecting hangings, of superb beauty, were placed at intervals. A hundred trillion garlands of jewels and a hundred trillion garlands of fragrances hung down on all four sides. A hundred trillion celestial fragrant resins perfumed everywhere. A hundred trillion ornaments of celestial decorations, a hundred trillion ornaments of jewel flowers, a hundred trillion ornaments of jewels from the finest mines, a hundred trillion ornaments of wish-fulfilling jewels, and a hundred trillion ornaments of wish-fulfilling pearls from the ocean, adorned the body of the throne. A hundred trillion embroidered tapestries of exquisite jewels trailed down like streamers. A hundred trillion cosmic nets of diamonds, a hundred trillion wish-fulfilling jewels, and a hundred trillion beautiful gold treasure troves were placed at intervals as embellishments.

A hundred trillion luminous jewels and a hundred trillion sapphires blazing with light and a hundred trillion indestructible celestial gems formed the windows: a hundred trillion jewels of pure qualities, giving forth sublime colors, and a hundred trillion jewels from pure beautiful mines formed the doorways. A hundred trillion crescent jewels, finest in the world, a hundred trillion mind-king wish-fulfilling jewels, a hundred trillion rose gold jewels, a hundred trillion jewels from pure troves, and a hundred trillion jewels symbolic of sovereignty, all radiating light, covered the top. A hundred trillion jewels set in pure silver and a hundred trillion jewels emblematic of the polar mountain adorned its lotus blossom bank.

A hundred trillion pearl ornaments, a hundred trillion lapis lazuli ornaments, a hundred trillion ruby ornaments, a hundred trillion wish-fulfilling jewel ornaments, a hundred trillion ornaments of jewel lights, a hundred trillion ornaments of jewels of various mines, a hundred trillion red pearls, extremely pleasing to the sight, a hundred trillion ornaments of jewels from treasuries of boundless colors and forms, a hundred trillion ornaments of incomparable jewels of extreme purity, and a hundred trillion ornaments of jewels of superlative brilliance were hung all around as adornments.

A hundred trillion unusually beautiful decorations made of jewels, a hundred trillion jewels in the exquisite forms of celestial beings, a hundred trillion subtle perfumes from the ten directions, a hundred trillion black sandalwood incenses, a hundred trillion fragrances from inconceivable realms, a hundred trillion most excellent scents, and a hundred trillion extremely pleasing incenses all emitted fragrant airs, perfuming the ten directions. A hundred trillion special incenses were scattered in all ten directions; a hundred trillion scents of pure light perfumed sentient beings; a hundred trillion incenses of boundless various colors perfumed all the buddha-lands, never fading away; a hundred trillion perfumes, a hundred trillion scents, a hundred trillion burning incenses perfumed everything. A hundred trillion aloe perfumes from lotus blossom banks producing great sound, a hundred trillion wafting fragrances with the power to transform the minds of sentient beings, and a hundred trillion perfumes with the power to enlighten pervaded everywhere, causing all the senses of those who noticed them to become dispassionate and tranquil. There were also a hundred trillion various arrays of peerless perfumes, kings among fragrances.

There rained a hundred trillion clouds of celestial flowers, a hundred trillion clouds of celestial perfumes, a hundred trillion clouds of heavenly incense powders, a hundred trillion clouds of celestial blue lotuses, a hundred trillion clouds of celestial red lotuses, a hundred trillion clouds of heavenly white lotuses, a hundred trillion clouds of heavenly mandarava flowers, a hundred trillion clouds of all kinds of celestial flowers, a hundred trillion clouds of celestial garments, a hundred trillion clouds of jewels, a hundred trillion clouds of celestial canopies, a hundred trillion clouds of celestial banners, a hundred trillion clouds of celestial crowns, a hundred trillion clouds of celestial ornaments, a hundred trillion clouds of celestial garlands, a hundred trillion clouds of necklaces of heavenly jewels, a hundred trillion clouds of celestial sandalwood incense, and a hundred trillion clouds of celestial aloe incense.

There were set up a hundred trillion jewel banners, there were hung a hundred trillion jewel pennants, there were draped a hundred trillion jewel streamers, there were lit a hundred trillion incense braziers, there were spread a hundred trillion jewel garlands, there were held a hundred trillion jewel fans, there were taken up a hundred trillion gold whisks, there were draped a hundred trillion nets of jewel chimes producing exquisite sounds when stirred by the breeze. A hundred trillion jewel balustrades surrounded the throne, a hundred trillion jewel palm trees were arrayed in rows. A hundred trillion windows framed with gorgeous gems made magnificent adornments. A hundred trillion jewel trees provided shade all around. A hundred trillion jewel turrets adorned north to south and east to west. A hundred trillion jeweled doorways were draped with garlands. A hundred trillion golden chimes produced sublime music. A hundred trillion ornaments in the form of auspicious symbols were draped in splendid arrays. There were a hundred trillion jewel talismans able to get rid of all evils, a hundred trillion gold treasuries woven of golden thread, a hundred trillion jewel umbrellas with handles of precious elements held in rows, and a hundred trillion nets of all kinds of precious ornaments arrayed at intervals.

A hundred trillion luminous jewels radiated various kinds of light; a hundred trillion light beams illumined everywhere. There were a hundred trillion sun-treasury orbs and a hundred trillion moon-treasury orbs, all made of collections of jewels of infinite colors. A hundred trillion fragrant flames shone with crystal clear light. A hundred trillion banks of lotuses burst into glorious bloom. A hundred trillion nets of jewels, a hundred trillion nets of flowers, and a hundred trillion nets of incenses covered above.

A hundred trillion jewel robes, a hundred trillion sapphire robes, a hundred trillion celestial yellow robes, a hundred trillion celestial red robes, a hundred trillion celestial robes of unusual colors, a hundred trillion extraordinary celestial robes of various precious substances, a hundred trillion various perfumed robes, a hundred trillion robes made of all precious substances, and a hundred trillion pure white robes, were all carefully spread, delightful to all observers.

A hundred trillion banners of celestial chimes and a hundred trillion banners of golden mesh produced subtle tones. There were a hundred trillion banners of heavenly embroideries, containing all colors. A hundred trillion fragrant banners were draped with webs of perfume. A hundred trillion flower banners showered all kinds of flowers. A hundred trillion banners of raiment trailed exquisite robes. There were a hundred trillion celestial jewel banners, studded with all sorts of gems, a hundred trillion celestial ornament banners, decorated with all manner of embellishments, a hundred trillion celestial garland banners, garlands of various kinds of flowers arrayed on four sides, a hundred trillion celestial canopy banners, with jewel bells harmoniously ringing, pleasing all hearers.

There were a hundred trillion celestial conches producing wonderful sounds, a hundred trillion celestial bass drums producing great booms, a hundred trillion celestial pipes producing subtle sounds, a hundred trillion celestial drums producing loud beautiful sounds, a hundred trillion orchestras playing all at once, a hundred trillion independent celestial musicians producing sublime sounds filling all buddha-lands, a hundred trillion celestial magical music sounding like echoes, responding to all things, a hundred trillion celestial drums producing wonderful sounds when struck, a hundred trillion kinds of miraculous celestial music which produced spontaneous harmony, and a hundred trillion various celestial assemblies producing wonderful music extinguishing all afflictions.

A hundred trillion pleasing sounds sang praises of giving offerings; a hundred trillion far-reaching sounds sang praises of service; a hundred trillion extremely deep sounds sang praises of practical application; a hundred trillion sounds of myriad subtleties sang praises of the fruits of the Buddhas' deeds; a hundred trillion delicate sounds sang praises of principles in accord with reality; a hundred trillion unimpeded sounds of truth sang praises of Buddha's past practices; a hundred trillion pure sounds sang praises of past offerings to the Buddhas; a hundred trillion sounds of teachings sang praises of the supreme fearlessness of the Buddhas; a hundred trillion infinite sounds sang praises of the infinity of enlightening beings' virtues; a hundred trillion sounds of the stages of enlightening beings sang praises of revealing the practices appropriate to all the stages of enlightening; a hundred trillion uninterrupted sounds sang praises of the endlessness of the Buddha's virtues; a hundred trillion conformative sounds sang praises of practices by which Buddha is seen; a hundred trillion sounds of extremely profound teaching sang praises of principles corresponding to unhindered knowledge of all things. A hundred trillion great sounds filled all buddhalands; a hundred trillion sounds of unimpeded purity caused all to rejoice in accord with their inclinations; a hundred trillion sounds of nondwelling in the triple world caused all hearers to enter deeply into the nature of reality; a hundred trillion sounds of joy caused the minds of all hearers to be unobstructed, with deep faith and respect; a hundred trillion sounds of the realm of buddhahood revealed the meanings of all things; a hundred trillion sounds of concentration formulae expounded the distinctions of all doctrines, definitively comprehending the esoteric treasury of the Enlightened Ones; a hundred trillion sounds of all truths, gentle and pleasant, harmonized all the music.

There were a hundred trillion newly inspired enlightening beings who, as soon as they saw this throne, doubly increased their determination for omniscience; a hundred trillion enlightening beings preparing the ground, their minds pure and joyful; a hundred trillion practicing enlightening beings, their understanding pure and clear; a hundred trillion nobly born enlightening beings, abiding in supreme zeal; a hundred trillion enlightening beings equipped with skill in means, activating the great vehicle; a hundred trillion enlightening beings in the abode of right mindfulness, diligently cultivating the path of all enlightening beings; a hundred trillion nonregressing enlightening beings, purifying all stages of enlightenment; a hundred trillion enlightening beings of youthful nature, attaining the light of concentration of all enlightening beings; a hundred trillion prince of teaching enlightening beings, entering the inconceivable sphere of all Buddhas; a hundred trillion coronated enlightening beings, able to manifest the ten powers of infinite enlightened ones; a hundred trillion enlightening beings with mastery of spiritual powers; a hundred trillion enlightening beings with pure understanding; a hundred trillion enlightening beings with determined minds; a hundred trillion enlightening beings with profound, unbreakable faith; a hundred trillion enlightening beings expounding the meanings of the teachings, causing knowledge to be sure; a hundred trillion enlightening beings with undisturbed correct recollection; a hundred trillion enlightening beings of certain knowledge; a hundred trillion enlightening beings with the power to retain what they hear, holding all the Buddha teachings; a hundred trillion enlightening beings producing infinitely vast great awareness and understanding; a hundred trillion enlightening beings abiding in the faculty of faith; a hundred trillion enlightening beings who had attained transcendent self-control and fully kept all the moral precepts; a hundred trillion enlightening beings who had attained transcendent generosity and were able to give everything; a hundred trillion enlightening beings who had attained transcendent forbearance whose minds did not wander and who were able to accept all the Buddha teachings; a hundred trillion enlightening beings who had attained transcendent vigor and were capable of carrying out infinite efforts for emancipation; a hundred trillion enlightening beings who had attained transcendent meditation and were imbued with the shining light of infinite meditations; a hundred trillion enlightening beings who had attained transcendent wisdom, the light of their wisdom able to illumine everywhere; a hundred trillion enlightening beings who had perfected great vows, all pure; a hundred trillion enlightening beings who had attained the lamp of knowledge, clearly illumining the teachings; a hundred trillion enlightening beings illuminated by the light of truth of the Buddhas of the ten directions; a hundred trillion enlightening beings expounding the way to get rid of folly throughout the ten directions; a hundred trillion enlightening beings who entered the fields of all Buddhas; a hundred trillion enlightening beings whose body of reality reached all buddha-lands; a hundred trillion enlightening beings who had attained the voice of Buddhas and were capable of enlightening many; a hundred trillion enlightening beings who had attained the means of producing all knowledge; a hundred trillion enlightening beings who had accomplished all aspects of the teaching; a hundred trillion enlightening beings who had attained true knowledge, like jewel banners, able to make plain all Buddha teachings; and a hundred trillion enlightening beings able to fully reveal the realm of enlightenment.

A hundred trillion celestial kings of the various heavens prostrated themselves reverently; a hundred trillion naga kings gazed fixedly; a hundred trillion yaksha kings joined their palms above their heads; a hundred trillion gandharva kings developed pure minds of faith; a hundred trillion titan kings cut off their pride; a hundred trillion garuda kings held streamers in their mouths; a hundred trillion kinnara kings danced joyfully; a hundred trillion mahoraga kings gazed with delight; a hundred trillion world leaders bowed with respect; a hundred trillion kings of the heavens of thirty-three celestial realms gazed unblinking; a hundred trillion kings of the Suyama heavens joyfully sang praises; a hundred trillion kings of Tushita heavens prostrated their bodies; a hundred trillion kings of the heavens of enjoyment of emanations bowed their heads to the ground in respect; a hundred trillion kings of the heavens of command of others' emanations joined their palms reverently; a hundred trillion kings of the Brahma heavens watched single-mindedly; a hundred trillion celestial kings of great power reverently made offerings; a hundred trillion enlightening beings sang eulogies aloud; a hundred trillion goddesses single-mindedly made offerings; a hundred trillion deities with the same aspirations danced with joy; a hundred trillion deities who had lived in the same place in antiquity sang hymns of praise with beautiful voices; a hundred trillion Brahma-body deities prostrated themselves in respect; a hundred trillion Brahma-assistant deities joined their palms at their crowns; a hundred trillion Brahma-group deities circled around as guardian attendants; a hundred trillion great Brahma deities sang eulogies of infinite virtues; a hundred trillion deities of the heavens of light threw themselves on the ground; a hundred trillion deities of the heavens of little light sang eulogies of the difficulty of meeting with an age when a Buddha is in the world; a hundred trillion deities of the heavens of infinite light bowed to the Buddha from afar; a hundred trillion deities of the heavens of light-sound sang of the rarity of getting to see a Buddha; a hundred trillion deities of the heavens of purity came here along with their mansions; a hundred trillion deities of the heavens of minor purity bowed their heads with pure hearts; a hundred trillion deities of the heavens of infinite purity descended, wishing to see the Buddha; a hundred trillion deities of the heavens of universal purity approached with reverence and respect and made offerings; a hundred trillion deities of the heavens of vastness reflected on past roots of goodness; a hundred trillion deities of the heavens of minor vastness contemplated the rarity of the enlightened; a hundred trillion deities of the heavens of infinite vastness, with sure respect, initiated all good actions; a hundred trillion deities of the heavens of vast results bowed reverently; a hundred trillion deities of the heavens of no troubles bowed respectfully, their faith firm and enduring; a hundred trillion deities of the heavens of no heat joined their palms and remembranced the Buddha tirelessly; a hundred trillion deities of the heavens of good sight bowed their heads to the ground; a hundred trillion deities of the heavens of good manifestation meditated constantly on honoring and serving the Buddhas; a hundred trillion deities of the heaven of the ultimate of form bowed reverently.

A hundred trillion deities of various heavens sang praises with great joy; a hundred trillion deities each carefully considered and made adornments; a hundred trillion enlightening deities guarded the Buddha's throne, ceaselessly embellishing it; a hundred trillion flower-bearing enlightening beings showered all kinds of flowers; a hundred trillion incense-bearing enlightening beings showered all kinds of fragrances; a hundred trillion garland-bearing enlightening beings showered all kinds of garlands; a hundred trillion elightening beings bearing powdered incense showered all kinds of powdered incenses; a hundred trillion perfume-bearing enlightening beings showered all kinds of perfumes; a hundred trillion raiment-bearing enlightening beings showered all kinds of raiment; a hundred trillion parasol-bearing enlightening beings showered all kinds of parasols; a hundred trillion banner-bearing deities showered all kinds of banners; a hundred trillion pennant-bearing enlightening beings showered all kinds of pennants; a hundred trillion gem-bearing enlightening beings showered all kinds of jewels; a hundred trillion ornament-bearing enlightening beings showered all kinds of ornaments.

A hundred trillion godlings came forth from their celestial palaces to the site of the throne; a hundred trillion godlings with pure faithful minds came with their palaces; a hundred trillion nobly born godlings supported the throne with their bodies; a hundred trillion consecrated godlings held the throne with their whole bodies.

A hundred trillion meditating enlightening beings contemplated respectfully; a hundred trillion nobly born enlightening beings gave rise to purity of mind; a hundred trillion enlightening beings became joyful and blissful in all senses; a hundred trillion enlightening beings' profound minds of faith were purified; a hundred trillion enlightening beings' faith and resolve were purified; a hundred trillion enlightening beings' actions were purified; a hundred trillion enlightening beings were enabled to take on birth freely; a hundred trillion enlightening beings glowed with the light of truth; a hundred trillion enlightening beings consummated the stages of enlightenment; a hundred trillion enlightening beings became well able to teach and influence all sentient beings.

Born of a hundred trillion roots of goodness, protected by a hundred trillion Buddhas, perfected by a hundred trillion virtues, purified by a hundred trillion sublime aspirations, beautified by a hundred trillion great vows, produced by a hundred trillion good actions, stabilized by a hundred trillion virtuous qualities, made manifest by a hundred trillion spiritual powers, developed by a hundred trillion meritorious achievements, eulogized for a hundred trillion praiseworthy qualities—as in the world the king of the Tushita heaven reverently set up a throne like this for the Enlightened One, so did the kings of the Tushita heavens in all worlds likewise set up such thrones, with such adornments, with such ceremonies, with such faith, with such purity of mind, with such delight, with such joy, with such respect, with such appreciation of rarity, with such dancing, with such yearning—all were the same.

Then the king of the Tushita heaven, having set up the throne for the Enlightened One, respectfully greeted the Buddha together with countless godlings of the Tushita heaven; with pure hearts they showered clouds of flowers of innumerable colors, clouds of incenses of inconceivable colors, clouds of garlands of various colors, vast clouds of pure sandalwood, clouds of innumerable various parasols, clouds of fine celestial raiment, clouds of boundless beautiful jewels, clouds of celestial ornaments, clouds of innumerable incenses of all kinds, and clouds of all kinds of sandalwood and aloe. When the godlings each produced these clouds from their bodies, a hundred trillion incalculable numbers of godlings of the Tushita heaven, as well as the other godlings in the assembly, were overjoyed and bowed reverently. Countless goddesses danced with joyful anticipation, gazing at the Enlightened One. In the Tushita palace a host of unspeakably many enlightening beings hovered in the air, and with diligence and single-mindedness produced offerings surpassing all the heavens and presented them to the Buddha, bowing respectfully, while countless forms of music played all at once.

At this point, because of the great spiritual power of the Buddha, because of the effluence of past roots of goodness, and because of his inconceivable mystic powers, all the gods and goddesses in the Tushita palace saw the Buddha from afar as though he were right before them. They all had the same thoughts: "The appearance of an Enlightened One in the world is rarely encountered—now we are getting to see an omniscient one, who has unimpeded true awareness of all things." Thus thinking, thus observing, together with the other groups they all welcomed the Buddha, each heaping celestial robes with all kinds of flowers, fragrances, jewels, ornaments, heavenly sandalwood and aloe incense, celestial jewel incenses, flowers of all heavenly fragrances, and mandarava flowers from all the heavens, and spread them as offerings to the Buddha.

Hundreds of trillions of infinities of Tushita deities hovered in the air; all considering the Buddha the realm of wisdom and knowledge, they burnt all kinds of incenses, producing aromatic clouds, adorning the sky. Also, thinking of the Buddha with joy, they showered clouds of celestial flowers, adorning the sky. Also, thinking of the Buddha with respect, they showered clouds of celestial canopies, adorning the sky. Also, desirous of making offerings to the Buddha, they scattered clouds of all kinds of celestial garlands, adorning the sky. Also, engendering resolute faith in the Buddha, they cast countless nets of gold through the sky, with chimes of all kinds of jewels continuously producing beautiful tones. Also, considering the Buddha the supreme field of blessings, they adorned the sky with countless drapes and showered clouds of all kinds of jewelry endlessly. Also, conceiving profound faith in the Buddha, they adorned the sky with countless celestial mansions, playing all manner of celestial music, producing subtle, melodious tones. Also, considering how rare it is to meet a Buddha, they adorned the sky with clouds of celestial raiment of all kinds of colors, showering various incomparably beautiful robes. Also, their hearts leaping with boundless joy at the Buddha, they adorned the sky with countless celestial jewel crowns, raining countless celestial crowns forming great clouds. Also, conceiving great joy in regarding the Buddha, they adorned the sky with countless jewels of various colors, ceaselessly raining clouds of all kinds of jewelry.

Hundreds of trillions of infinities of celestial beings, all conceiving pure faith in the Buddha, scattered countless heavenly flowers of various colors and burned various celestial incenses as offerings to the Buddha. Also, thinking of the Buddha as a magnificent miraculous appearance, they brought celestial sandalwood incenses of innumerable various colors and reverently scattered them before the Buddha. Also, their hearts leaping with joy in regarding the Buddha, they followed the Buddha holding countless precious celestial robes of various colors and spread them on the roads as offerings to the Buddha. Also, regarding the Buddha with purity of mind, they greeted the Buddha carrying countless banners of celestial jewels of various colors. Also, conceiving supreme joy at the thought of the Buddha, they brought countless celestial adornments of various colors to present to the Buddha. Also, engendering unbreakable faith in the Buddha, they brought countless garlands of celestial jewels to present to the Buddha. Also, incomparably joyful at the thought of the Buddha, they brought countless pennants of celestial jewels of various colors to offer to the Buddha. A hundred trillion infinities of celestial beings, with tamed, tranquil minds free from indulgence, brought countless celestial musical instruments of various forms producing sublime tones to present to the Buddha.

A hundred trillion infinities of enlightening beings already living in the palace of the Tushita heaven, with offerings surpassing those of all the gods, produced by the teaching transcending the worlds of desire, form, and formlessness, produced by infinitely broad knowledge, developed by steadfast pure faith, produced by action free from afflictions, produced by the all-pervading unobstructed mind, produced by the profound principle of adaptable methodology, produced by inconceivable roots of goodness, perfected by countless displays of skill in means, revealed by the will to make offerings to the Buddha, stamped by the teaching of noncreation, made gifts of these offerings to the Buddha. They presented to the Buddha canopies of all precious substances born in the transcendent ways, drapes of all kinds of flowers born of pure understanding of the realm of all Buddhas, all kinds of garments born of acceptance of the nonorigination of things, all kinds of nets of chimes born of the unimpeded mind entering into the state of indestructibility, all kinds of solid fragrance born of the mind understanding all things are like apparitions, beautiful thrones of myriad precious substances of all Buddhas, born of the mind omnipresent at the thrones of Buddhas in all realms of enlightenment, banners of all jewels, born of the mind tirelessly make offerings to the Buddhas, palaces of all jewels, dwelt in by the Buddhas, born of the joyful mind that understands that all things are like dreams, clouds of lotus blossoms of all jewels, born of roots of goodness without attachment and uncreated roots of goodness, clouds of all solid incenses, clouds of boundless flowers of all colors, clouds of exquisite raiment of all various colors, clouds of infinite pure sandalwood incenses, clouds of precious canopies with all kinds of embellishments, clouds of all burning incenses, clouds of all kinds of beautiful garlands, clouds of all kinds of pure decorations, all filling the cosmos, going beyond all the heavens.

Those enlightening beings each produced from their bodies unspeakable hundreds of trillions of infinities of enlightening beings, filling the space of the cosmos, their minds all equal to the Buddhas of all times; by means of development from the delusion-free teaching and strengthening by the power of infinite enlightened ones, they revealed to sentient beings the path of peace; equipped with unspeakably many meaningful expressions, they entered into the seeds of all concentration formulae containing infinite teachings, and produced inexhaustible treasuries of intellectual powers; their minds without fear, they conceived great joy, and with unspeakable infinities of points of truthful praise they tirelessly eulogized the Enlightened One.

Then all the celestial beings and all the enlightening beings saw the Buddha, the perfectly enlightened one, the inconceivable hero of humanity, his bodies infinite, uncountable, manifesting inconceivably many different varieties of mystical transfigurations, causing the minds of countless sentient beings to be full of joy, pervading all universes throughout space, adorned with the embellishments of buddhahood, causing all sentient beings to abide in roots of goodness, displaying infinite spiritual powers of the Buddhas, beyond all manners of speaking, admired and respected by all great enlightening beings, causing them all to rejoice in accord with what they need to be taught, abiding in the immense body of the Buddhas, all virtues and roots of goodness purified, most excellent in appearance, not to be outshone by anyone.

The sphere of the Buddha's knowledge was inexhaustible, born of incomparable concentration. His body was boundless, omnipresent in the bodies of all sentient beings. He caused great joy to infinite beings. He caused the lineage of omniscient ones to continue unbroken. Dwelling in the ultimate abode of the Buddhas, born in the family of the Buddhas of past, present, and future, he caused the faith of countless sentient beings to be purified, and caused the knowledge and wisdom of all enlightening beings to be perfected. All his senses were joyful. The clouds of his teaching covered all universes in space, teaching and taming without omission, fulfilling all sentient beings according to their mentalities, causing them to abide in nondiscriminatory knowledge. He was beyond all sentient beings.

Having attained omniscience, he radiated a great light. Causing his roots of goodness of past ages to be clearly manifest, he inspired great determination in everyone and caused all sentient beings to abide in the indestructible knowledge of universal good. Abiding everywhere in all lands of sentient beings, born of the nonregressing true teaching, he dwelt in the totally impartial realm of reality. Clearly understanding what was appropriate to the minds of sentient beings, he manifested unspeakably many different buddha-bodies, beyond the power of worldly speech to extol, able to cause all to always think of the Buddha, filling the cosmos, liberating vast numbers of living beings. According to the aid they required, he bestowed the teaching on them, causing them to be pacified and their faith to be pure, manifesting inconceivable physical forms.

Regarding all living beings impartially, his mind had no attachments. He dwelt in the abode of nonobstruction and had attained the ten powers of buddhahood without impediment. His mind was always quiet and stable, never distracted or disturbed. Abiding in omniscience, he was able to express all kinds of truths. Able to enter completely into the boundless ocean of knowledge, he produced infinite treasuries of virtue and wisdom. With the sun of enlightenment he constantly illumined the entire cosmos.

In accord with the power of his original vows, he was always manifest, never disappearing, always dwelling in the realm of reality, abiding in the abode of Buddhas, without change. He had no attachment to self or to possessions. He dwelt in the transmundane state and was not affected by mundane things. In all worlds he set up the banner of knowledge and wisdom, his knowledge vast and great, transcending the world, with no attachments. He rescued sentient beings from the mire, placing them on the highest ground of wisdom. All his blessings and virtues benefited sentient beings yet were never exhausted.

He was fully aware of the knowledge and wisdom of all enlightening beings, their faith and direction certain, sure to attain enlightenment. By great compassion he manifested infinite adornments of the buddha-body. With a wondrous voice he expounded infinite teachings, satisfying sentient beings according to their mentalities. In the past, future, and present, his mind was always pure. He caused all sentient beings to be unattached to objects. He constantly forecast the enlightenment of all the enlightening beings, causing them to enter the family of Buddhas to be born in the house of Buddhas, and attain the coronation of Buddhas.

He always traveled throughout the ten directions, never resting, never craving for or clinging to anything. Able to live in all buddha-lands in the cosmos, he knew the minds of all sentient beings. All his virtues were unworldly and pure. He did not dwell in birth and death, yet appeared throughout the world, like a reflection. He illumined the whole cosmos by the moon of knowledge and realized that everything is ungraspable. By his wisdom he was constantly aware that all worlds are like illusions, like reflections, like dreams, like magic tricks, that all have mind as their inherent nature. Abiding in this way, he manifested buddha-bodies in accord with the dissimilarities of the actions and consequences of sentient beings, the distinctions in their mental inclinations, and the individual differences in their faculties.

The Enlightened One was always relating to countless sentient beings, explaining to them that everything in the world derives from conditional, interdependent origination. He knew that the signs of all things are signless, this being their sole characteristic, the basis of wisdom. He wanted to cause all sentient beings to detach from all signs, forms, and characteristics. He showed clearly all natures and characteristics of the world, thus traversing the world; to reveal to them unexcelled enlightenment, desiring to rescue all sentient beings, he appeared in the world and showed the way of the enlightened. He caused them to perceive the features of the body of the enlightened one, to concentrate on them and meditate on them, to diligently cultivate and develop themselves to annihilate mundane afflictions, cultivate enlightening practice with unwavering minds, and attain fulfillment of all aspects of the Great Vehicle, attaining the rewards of the Buddhas.

He was able to observe the roots of goodness of sentient beings, and did not allow the results of their pure deeds to die out. His knowledge was clear and complete entering into all times, forever detached from all mundane discrimination. He radiated networks of light beams, fully illuminating all worlds in the ten directions.

Those who saw him never tired of beholding the sublime refinements of his physical form. By means of great virtue, knowledge, wisdom, and spiritual power, he produced all kinds of enlightening practices. The spheres of his senses were free and complete, round and full. He did Buddha-work, and when he finished doing it he disappeared.

He was able to show the path of all knowledge of past, present, and future. For the enlightening beings he showered a rain of innumerable concentration formulae, causing them to develop great rapture, to take them up, hold them, and practice them, and perfect the virtues of all Buddhas, in their full glory, with boundless wonderful forms, to adorn their beings.

He saw everything in all worlds, and was forever rid of all obstruction. He had attained the pure true meaning of all verities. He had attained mastery of virtuous qualities, and was a great king of truth, like the sun illumining everywhere. Being a field of blessings for the world, he had great dignity, influence, and virtue.

He manifested emanation bodies in all worlds, radiating the light of wisdom, causing all to be enlightened. Wanting to cause all sentient beings to know the boundless virtues possessed by the Buddha, he took the turban of nonobstruction, tied it on his head, and assumed the rank of Budhahood. Adapting to the world, he guided by means of expedient methods, comforting beings with the hand of wisdom. As a great physician, he skillfully cured all sickness, able to go to all the countless lands in all worlds, without rest.

His clear, pure eye of wisdom was free from all obstructions, able to clearly see all. Evil-doing sentient beings he tamed in various ways, causing them to enter the Path, skillfully seizing appropriate opportunities to civilize and teach them, never ceasing. If sentient beings developed equanimous, impartial minds, he would then show them the consequences of impartial deeds. In accord with their inclinations and in accord with their actions and results thereof, he manifested various spiritual powers of the buddha-body for them, to expound the truth and enlighten them, that they may attain the knowledge and wisdom of the teaching, and that their minds be joyful and their senses ecstatic, that they see innumerable Buddhas, develop profound faith, and produce roots of goodness, never regressing.

All sentient beings, in accord with their involvement and entrapment by actions, sleep forever in birth-and-death; the Enlightened One, appearing in the world, can awaken them all, comfort their minds, and cause them to be without anxiety or fear. Any who see him he causes to realize independent knowledge of truth. With knowledge and skill in means he comprehends the objective world. His embellishing marks and adornments cannot be overshadowed. His mountain of wisdom and talons of teaching are all purified.

Sometimes he manifests as an enlightening being, sometimes he appears as a Buddha, causing all sentient beings to arrive at the realm of sorrowlessness. Adorned by countless virtues, developed by practical action, he appears in the world. The adornment and purity of all Buddhas are accomplished by the works of omniscience.

Always keeping his original vow, he does not abandon the world, being a steadfast benefactor of sentient beings. His supreme pure light makes itself visible to all sentient beings. By means of spiritual power, the Buddha always follows the sentient beings of the six realms of mundane existence, boundless and countless, never abandoning them. If there are any who have planted similar roots of goodness in the past, he causes them all to be purified, yet without giving up his original vow with regard to all sentient beings of the six paths of mundane existence. He deceives no one, appropriately dealing with them in virtuous ways, causing them to practice pure acts and break up demonic conflicts.

From the realm of nonobstruction he produces great power. Nothing blocks his supreme treasury of light. He manifests reflections in the realm of pure minds, which all worlds see. He bestows many various teachings on sentient beings. Buddha is a boundless treasury of light; his powers, knowledge, and wisdom are all fully complete. He constantly illumines all sentient beings with great light, causing them all to be fulfilled in accordance with their aspirations. Beyond all enmity, he is the highest field of blessings, relied upon by all sentient beings; if any give anything, he causes them to be pure, and to receive boundless blessings from doing a little bit of good. He causes all to be able to enter the stage of inexhaustible knowledge. He is the pure-minded master, planting roots of goodness for all sentient beings. He is the most excellent fertile field producing blessings and merit for sentient beings.

His knowledge and wisdom is exceedingly deep; with skill in means he can rescue all from the pains of the woeful states of greed, anger, and ignorance.

Thus believing, thus observing, thus entering the depths of knowledge, thus sporting in the ocean of virtues, thus arriving at spacelike wisdom, thus cognizing sentient beings' field of blessings, thus contemplating with presence of mind, thus observing the deeds, marks and embellishments of Buddha, thus observing the Buddha appearing throughout the world, thus observing the Buddha's mystical power, the great congregation at that time saw each pore of the Buddha's body emit a hundred trillion infinities of light beams, each beam of light having countless hues, countless purities, countless radiances, causing countless beings to watch, countless beings to rejoice, countless beings to be happy, countless beings to grow in faith, countless beings' aspiration to be pure, countless beings' senses to be pure and cool, and causing countless beings to develop respect and honor.

Then the great assembly all saw the Buddha's body emit a hundred trillion infinities of inconceivable great lights, each light with inconceivably many hues and inconceivable many beams illumining inconceivably many realms of phenomena, by the Buddha's spiritual power producing great subtle sound conveying infinites of eulogies in words transcending all worlds, perfected by transmundane virtues. He also manifested hundreds of trillions of quadrillions of inconceivable numbers of subtle adornments, which could never be fully described even in a hundred trillion quadrillion inconceivable number of eons, all of them produced by the inexhaustible spiritual power of the Buddha. He also manifested unspeakably many enlightened ones arising in the world and leading sentient beings into the door of wisdom to understand the most profound truth. He also manifested the docetic metamorphoses of the enlightened ones throughout the space of the cosmos, causing all worldly beings to be impartial and purified. All of this sprung from the unhindered omniscience in which the Buddha dwelt. It was also born of the inconceivable superlative virtues which the Buddha cultivated. He also manifested a hundred trillion quadrillion inconceivable numbers of beautiful jewel light flames, originating from the good roots of his ancient great vows. He did so because he had presented offerings to and served countless enlightened ones, because he had cultivated pure practices without slacking, because his omniscient mind, without impediment, produced roots of virtue, in order to reveal the universality of the powers of the enlightened, to cut off the doubts of all sentient beings, to cause all of them to be able to see the enlightened one, to cause infinite sentient beings to abide in virtue, to show the enlightened one's spiritual powers cannot be outshone, to cause all sentient beings to be able to enter into the ocean of the ultimate, to cause the enlightening beings of all buddha-lands to assemble, and because he wanted to reveal the inconceivable teachings of the Buddha.

Then the Enlightened One, his great compassion covering all, showed the adornments of omniscience, wanting to cause the sentient beings in innumerable worlds who had no faith to have faith, to cause those with faith to develop, to cause the developed to become pure, to cause the pure to become mature, to cause the mature to conquer their minds and contemplate the profound truth, be filled with the boundless light of knowledge and wisdom, develop an immeasurably broad mind, an omniscient mind, never regressing, not going against the essential nature of things, not fearing ultimate reality, to realize genuine truth, fulfill all transcendent practices, purify all transmundane virtues, like Universally Good, attain the freedom of buddhahood, leave the realm of demons and enter the realm of Buddhas, comprehend the profound teaching and attain inconceivable knowledge, never regressing from the vows of universal salvation, to always see the Buddhas, never abandoning them, to perfect experiential knowledge, realize infinite truths, be filled with the boundless power of the treasury of virtue, develop a joyous mind, enter the realm where there is no doubt, divorce evil and be pure, see things unperturbed due to omniscience, gain entry to the congregations of all enlightening beings, and always be born in the family of the enlightened ones of past, present, and future.

These adornments manifested by the Buddha were all made by roots of goodness accumulated in the past, for the purpose of harmonizing and civilizing all sentient beings, to reveal the great powerful virtue of the enlightened, to light up the treasury of unobstructed knowledge and wisdom, to show the extreme radiance of the boundless supreme virtues of the enlightened, to show the inconceivable great spiritual displays of the enlightened, to manifest the buddha-body in all realms of being by means of spiritual powers, to show the boundlessness of the mystic powers and magical transfigurations of the enlightened, to fulfill all his original aspirations, to show that the dauntless knowledge and wisdom of the enlightened can go everywhere, to become the king of truth free in all ways, to produce all avenues of knowledge, to manifest the purity of the body of the enlightened, and also to reveal the supreme splendor of his body, to manifest the realization of the equal state of the Buddhas of all times, to reveal the pure treasury of roots of goodness, to manifest the most sublime form, to which nothing in the world may be likened, to show the characteristics of full command of the ten powers, to cause beholders never to tire, to be the sun of the world, illumining past, present, and future. All the virtuous qualities of the sovereign king of truth were manifested by roots of goodness of the past; even if all enlightening beings were to eulogize and tell of them throughout all time, they never would be exhaustively told.

Then the king of the Tushita heaven, having prepared all the offerings for the Buddha, together with countless deities of the Tushita heaven, joined his palms in a gesture of respect toward the Buddha and said, "Welcome, World Honored One; welcome, Felicitous One;

welcome, Enlightened One, Worthy, Truly Awakened One! Please look upon us with compassion and sojourn in this place."

Then the World Honored One, adorning himself with the adornments of Buddhahood, replete with magnificent virtues, in order to gladden all beings, in order that all enlightening beings develop profound understanding, so that all the celestial beings of the Tushita heaven increase in determination, so that the king of the Tushita heaven never tires of generosity and service, so that countless beings focus their attention on the Buddha and become inspired to seek enlightenment, so that countless types of beings see the endlessness of the Buddha's roots of goodness, blessings, and virtues, so that they always be able to arouse pure faith, so that, seeing a Buddha, they serve without seeking anything, so that all of their aspirations be pure, so that they diligently amass roots of goodness without flagging, and so that they would vow to seek omniscience, the Buddha accepted the invitation of the celestial king and entered the palace adorned by all jewels. Just as in this world, the same thing transpired in all worlds in the ten directions.

At that point the hall adorned by all jewels naturally had wonderfully fine decorations, surpassing all the heavens, and atop the decorations were nets of all jewels covering all over, showering clouds of all the finest gems all over, showering clouds of all kinds of ornaments, clouds of all kinds of precious raiment, clouds of all kinds of sandalwood incenses, clouds of all kinds of solid fragrances, clouds of canopies adorned by all jewels, and clouds of bunches of inconceivably many flowers, producing everywhere inconceivable music praising the Enlightened One's knowledge of all means of liberation, all in accord with the sublime truth. All these offerings were beyond those of the celestial beings.

Then in the Tushita palace rich music and singing continued ceaselessly. By the spiritual power of the Buddha, the mind of the king of Tushita was made imperturbable; his past roots of goodness all reached complete fulfillment, his good qualities became more firm and stable, he increased in pure faith, he aroused great vigor, conceived great joy, purified profound aspiration, made the determination for enlightenment, and placed his unwavering attention on the teaching, keeping it firmly in mind. Then the king of the Tushita heaven, empowered by the Buddha, recalled the roots of goodness he had planted with past Buddhas and said in verse,

> There once was a Buddha, Unobstructed Moon,
> Most auspicious among the auspicious;
> He once entered this hall of adornment,
> Therefore this place is most auspicious.

> There once was a Buddha called Broad Knowledge,
> Most auspicious among the auspicious;

He once entered this golden hall,
Therefore this place is most auspicious.

There once was a Buddha called Universal Eye,
Most auspicious among the auspicious;
He once entered this hall of adornment,
Therefore this place is most auspicious.

There once was a Buddha called Coral,
Most auspicious among the auspicious;
He once entered this jewel mine hall,
Therefore this place is most auspicious.

There once was a Buddha, Lion of Philosophy,
Most auspicious among the auspicious;
He once entered this mountain king hall,
Therefore this place is most auspicious.

There once was a Buddha called Sunlight,
Most auspicious among the auspicious;
He once entered this hall of flowers.
Therefore this place is most auspicious.

There once was a Buddha called Boundless Light,
Most auspicious among the auspicious;
He once entered this tree-adorned hall,
Therefore this place is most auspicious.

There once was a Buddha called Banner of Truth,
Most auspicious among the auspicious;
He once entered this jewel palace hall,
Therefore this place is most auspcious.

There once was a Buddha called Lamp of Knowledge,
Most auspicious among the auspicious;
He once entered this fragrant mountain hall,
Therefore this place is most auspicious.

There once was a Buddha called Light of Virtue,
Most auspicious among the auspicious;
He once entered this crystal hall,
Therefore this place is most auspicious.

As in this world the king of the Tushita heaven, by the power of the Buddha, eulogized Buddhas of the past, so also did the kings of the Tushita heavens in all worlds praise the virtues of Buddhas.

Then the World Honored One sat crosslegged on the jewel treasury lion throne in the hall adorned by all jewels. His body of reality was pure, his inconceivable action was free. He was in the same realm as all Buddhas of all times, abiding in omniscience, entering into the same one essence with all the Buddhas. His enlightened eye was perfectly clear, and he saw all things without hindrance. He had great mystic powers, coursing everywhere throughout the cosmos unceasingly. He had great occult powers, able to go anywhere there might be beings who could be taught. His body was adorned with the unobstructed embellishments of all Buddhas. He was well aware of appropriate timing in expounding teachings to people.

Unspeakably many enlightening beings came from various lands in other regions and assembled; the congregation was pure, their reality-body nondual; they rested on nothing, and were freely able to perform the actions of Buddhas.

When the Buddha had sat on this throne, in the hall there spontaneously appeared countless adornments surpassing all the offerings of the celestials. That is, flower garlands, robes, perfumes, incense, jeweled parasols, banners, pennants, music, and singing. Each of these was uncountable. With great reverence and respect these were offered to the Buddha. The same thing took place in all the Tushita heavens in the ten directions.

BOOK TWENTY-FOUR

Eulogies in the Tushita Palace

THEN, DUE TO THE SPIRITUAL FORCE of the Buddha, a great enlightening being from each of the ten directions, each accompanied by as many enlightening beings as atoms in ten thousand buddha-lands, came to where the Buddha was, from worlds beyond lands as numerous as atoms in ten thousand buddha-lands. Their names were Diamond Banner, Banner of Steadfastness, Banner of Bravery, Banner of Light, Banner of Knowledge, Jewel Banner, Banner of Energy, Banner of Purification, Constellation Banner, and Banner of Truth. The worlds they came from were called Fine Jewel World, Fine Music World, Fine Silver World, Fine Gold World, Fine Crystal World, Fine Diamond World, Fine Lotus World, Fine Blue Lotus World, Fine Sandalwood World, and Fine Fragrance World. They each purified and cultivated religious practice with Buddhas, the names of which Buddhas were Banner of Inexhaustibility, Wind Banner, Banner of Liberation, Banner of Dignity, Banner of Understanding of Characteristics, Banner of Eternity, Banner of Supreme Excellence, Banner of Freedom, Banner of Purity, and Banner of Observation.

When those enlightening beings arrived at the Buddha's spot, they prostrated themselves before the Buddha; then, by the Buddha's mystic power he magically produced lion seats of masses of beautiful jewels covered with nets of jewels all around, and the hosts of enlightening beings, according to the direction from which they had come, sat on those seats, Their bodies all emanated countless beams of pure light. This boundless light all came from the enlightening beings' pure mind-jewels, their great vows which were free from all evils. They revealed the pure phenomena of the powers of all Buddhas. By the power of the impartial vision of all enlightening beings they were able to universally save all sentient beings. They were a gladdening sight in all worlds; those who saw them did not do so in vain—all attained harmony and tranquility.

Those enlightening beings had all already perfected innumerable virtues:

for example, they traveled to all buddha-lands without hindrance; they saw the pure body of reality which rests on nothing; with the body of knowledge they manifested countless bodies going everywhere in the ten directions to serve the Buddhas; they entered into the Buddhas' innumerable, boundless, inconceivable powers; they dwelt in the medium of omniscience; by the light of knowledge they comprehended all things; they had attained fearlessness in all respects; they taught wherever they were, their powers of elucidation forever inexhaustible; with great knowledge and wisdom they opened the gate of concentration spells; with the eye of wisdom they entered the profound realm of truth; the realm of their knowledge was boundless and ultimately pure, like space itself.

As in the palace of the Tushita heaven in this world the hosts of enlightening beings gathered like this, the same thing transpired in all the Tushita heavens in the ten directions; the names of the enlightening beings who gathered, the names of their countries, and the Buddhas there were all the same.

Then the World Honored One emanated countless beams of light from the wheel marks on his knees, illuminating the entire space of the cosmos in the ten directions. The enlightening beings in all worlds all saw this miraculous display of the Buddha, and the enlightening beings here saw the miraculous displays of all the Buddhas in other worlds. These enlightening beings had all similarly planted roots of goodness in the distant past along with Vairocana Buddha, cultivating enlightening practice; they all had awakened to and entered the free, extremely profound liberation of the Buddhas, and had attained the undifferentiated cosmic body, entering all lands without dwelling anywhere. They saw countless Buddhas and went to serve them all. In a single mental instant they traversed the cosmos, freely and without hindrance. Their minds and intellects were pure, like priceless jewels. Innumerable Buddhas always guarded them mindfully, sharing their power with them. They reached the ultimate, supreme other shore; by pure mindfulness they continually dwelt in highest awareness; in every moment of thought they continually entered into the realm of omniscience; they put the small in the large and the large in the small, free in all ways, with no obstruction whatsoever. They had already attained the buddha-body and dwelt in the same abode as the Buddhas; they had attained omniscience and produced their bodies from omniscience. They were able to enter the spheres of action of all enlightened ones. They opened up innumerable gates of knowledge and wisdom. They reached the other shore of indestructible great knowledge, attained adamantine concentration, and cut off all doubts and confusion. They had attained the autonomous spiritual powers of Buddhas, teaching and taming countless numbers of sentient beings in the lands of the ten directions. Though they had no attachments to any categories or phenomena, they were were able to learn and develop ultimate skill in use of doctrines and to establish all teachings conducive to enlightenment.

Hosts of enlightening beings with such infinite treasuries of all inexhaustible pure virtues of past, present, and future all came and assembled at the Buddha's place; the same thing occurred at the places of all the Buddhas revealed by the light.

Then the enlightening being Diamond Banner, empowered by the Buddha, looked over the ten directions and said in verse,

The Buddha does not appear in the world
And has no extinction either:
By the power of his great original vow
He demonstrates his freedom.

This truth is inconceivable—
It is not in the sphere of mind:
When knowledge reaches the other shore
One then sees the realm of the Buddhas.

The physical body is not the Buddha,
Neither is the audible voice:
Yet not apart from form and sound
Can Buddha's mystic power be perceived.

Those of little knowledge cannot know
The true realm of the Buddhas;
After long cultivation of purifying action
Will one be able to comprehend.

The Truly Awake comes from nowhere
And also goes nowhere:
The pure, refined physical body
Appears through spiritual power.

Manifesting the body of an enlightened one
In innumerable worlds,
Widely expounding the subtle teachings,
His mind has no attachments.

His knowledge, being boundless,
Comprehends all things;
Entering everywhere in the universe,
He manifests autonomous powers.

Sentient beings and all phenomena
He comprehends unhindered;
Everywhere manifesting physical forms,
He is omnipresent in all lands.

If you want to see omniscience
And soon attain highest awareness,
You should, with pure clear mind,
Cultivate enlightening practice.

If any see such mystic powers
Of the Enlightened One,
They should serve the Supreme Honored One
And not give rise to doubt.

Then the enlightening being Banner of Steadfastness, empowered by the Buddha, looked over the ten directions and said in verse,

The Enlightened One is incomparable,
Most profound, inexplicable,
Beyond all manner of speech,
Pure as space itself.

Behold the Human Lion's
Autonomous mystic power,
Beyond discrimination,
Yet causing distinct perceptions.

In order to expound
The profound and subtle teaching
The Guide, for this reason,
Manifests this peerless body.

This is great knowledge,
The realm of all the Buddhas;
If any want to know,
Let them approach the Enlightened.

With mental action always pure,
Making offerings to the Buddhas
With never any weariness,
One can enter the Buddha Way.

Filled with endless virtues,
Steadfast in the will for enlightenment,
Thereby the net of doubt is removed
And one gazes tirelessly on the Buddha.

By comprehending all things
Does one become a true child of Buddha:
Such a person can know
The Buddhas' autonomous power.

As explained by those of vast knowledge,
Will is the root of the teachings;
One must develop supreme aspiration,
Determined to seek highest awakening.

If any respect the Buddha
And want to requite the Buddha's grace,
They will never leave
The abode of all the Buddhas.

How can intelligent people
Who've seen and heard the Buddha
Not carry out pure vows
And tread the path the Buddha traversed?

Then Banner of Bravery, empowered by the Buddha, looked over the ten directions and said in verse,

Just as a clear eye
Can see colors due to the sun,
So too can a pure heart
See the Enlightened by Buddha's power.

As by the power of effort
One can plumb the depths of the sea,
So too can the power of knowledge
See innumerable Buddhas.

As in a fertile, watered field
Whatever's planted will grow,
So does the ground of a pure mind
Produce enlightened qualities.

As a man who's found a jewel mine
Is forever freed from poverty,
An enlightening being finding the Buddha teaching
Is free from defilement, pure in mind.

Just as a true panacea
Can eliminate all toxins,
Buddha's teaching too is like this:
It annihilates all afflictions.

Truly genuine teachers
Are praised by the enlightened:
Through their spiritual power
We get to hear the Buddha teachings.

Even if for countless cons
One gave precious things to Buddha,
If one doesn't know the real nature of Buddha
This is not called giving.

Infinite physical characteristics
Adorn the Buddha's body;
Yet it is not in physical form
That the Buddha can be seen.

The Enlightened One, Truly Awake,
Is peaceful, never moving,
Yet can manifest his body
Throughout all worlds in the ten directions.

Just as space itself
Is unborn and unperishing,
So is the truth of the Buddhas
Ultimately birthless and deathless.

Then Banner of Light, empowered by the Buddha, looked over the
ten directions and said in verse,

In the human and celestial realms
In all the worlds there are
They see everywhere the Enlightened One's
Body of pure wondrous form.

Just as the power of one mind
Can produce various minds,
So can one buddha-body
Manifest all Buddhas everywhere.

Enlightenment is nondual
And also has no marks:
Yet in the realm of duality
He manifests a glorified body.

Comprehending the nature of things is empty,
Their origination like apparitions,
His realm of action's inexhaustible:
Thus does the Guide appear.

Pure is the reality-body
Of all Buddhas of all times;
They manifest sublime physical forms
Wherever and however people need to be taught.

The enlightened do not think
"I'll produce such a body":
They manifest spontaneously
Without discriminating.

The realm of reality is undifferentiated
And also has no basis:
And yet in the world
It manifests countless bodies.

The Buddha's bodies are not emanations
And yet not other than emanations:
In the reality where there are no emanations
He appears to have emanated forms.

True awareness cannot be measured,
The reality-realm's equal to space;
Profound, vast, without bound or bottom,
Utterly beyond the power of speech.

The Enlightened One has mastered
The road leading everywhere:
Through the myriad lands of the cosmos
He goes without obstruction.

Then Banner of Knowledge, empowered by the Buddha, looked over the ten directions and said in verse,

If one can believe and accept
Omniscience without obstruction,
And practice enlightening ways,
One's mind will be immeasurable.

In all lands
Buddha manifests countless bodies,
Yet the bodies stay in no place,
And he dwells not in the real.

Each one of the Enlightened
Manifest bodies by spiritual powers:
Even in unthinkable eons
They never could be fully counted.

The number of all living beings
Of all times may be known,
But the number of Buddhas' manifestations
Cannot ever be found.

Sometimes they show one or two,
Up to countless bodies—
Appearing everywhere, in all lands,
Yet really with no duality.

Just as the clear full moon
Appears in all bodies of water
And while the reflections are numberless
The real moon is not two,
So does the one of unimpeded knowledge
With perfect true enlightenment
Universally appear in all lands:
Yet the Buddha-body is nondual.

It is not one, and yet not two,
And also not immeasurable:
According to the needs of the taught
Do countless bodies appear.

The buddha-body is not past
And also not future:

In a single instant he appears to be born,
To become enlightened, and pass away.

As forms produced by magic
Have no birth and no origination,
So too is the buddha-body thus—
Appearing without any birth.

Then Jewel Banner, empowered by the Buddha, looked over the ten
directions and said in verse,

The buddha-body is infinite
Yet can manifest finite bodies:
According to what needs to be seen
Does the Guide appropriately appear.

The buddha-body has no location,
Yet fills all places;
Like space, it's boundless:
Such is its inconceivability.

It is not in the province of mental function,
And mind does not arise therein:
In the realm of the Buddhas
Ultimately there's no birth or death.

Like what is seen by clouded eyes
Is neither internal nor external,
So also, you should know,
Is the worlds' vision of the Buddhas.

In order to benefit living beings
Do the Enlightened Ones appear in the world:
Sentient beings see them as coming forth,
But in reality there is no such thing.

A Buddha cannot be seen
In terms of a land, or day or night,
Nor indeed can one be seen
In terms of years, months, or moments.

Sentient beings say
Buddha was enlightened on a certain day;

But enlightenment in reality
Is not bound to time.

The Enlightened are beyond discrimination:
Not of the world, they transcend all accounts—
All Guides of past, present, and future
Appear in this way.

Just as the pure orb of the sun
Doesn't conjoin with the dark night,
Yet we speak of such and such a day and night,
So is the principle of the Buddhas;
Though the ages of past, present, and future
Do not conjoin with the Enlightened,
Yet we speak of the Buddhas of past, present, and future:
Such is the principle of the Guides.

Then Banner of Energy, empowered by the Buddha, looked over the ten directions and said in verse,

All the Guides'
Bodies are the same, as are their meanings;
Throughout the lands of the ten directions
They appear variously according to needs.

Observe the Honored Sage:
His activity is most unique;
He fills the entire cosmos
And everything that's in it.

The buddha-body is not within
And also not outside:
It manifests by spiritual power;
Such is the teaching of the Guide.

According to deeds accumulated in former times
By the various species of living beings,
Such various different bodies
Appear, each one dissimilar.

Thus the bodies of the Buddhas
Are infinite, uncountable:
Except for the great enlightened one
No one can conceive of them.

Just as the self, being inconceivable,
Cannot be grasped by mentation,
So too the inconceivability of Buddhas
Is not manifested by mentation.

Just as all things
Originate due to multiple conditions,
So also does seeing Buddha
Necessarily depend on many good works.

Just as the wish-fulfilling jewel
Can satisfy beings' hearts,
So can the teachings of the Buddhas
Completely fulfill all aspirations.

In infinite lands
The Guides appear in the world;
In accord with the power of their vows
They respond in every place.

Then Banner of Purification, empowered by the Buddha, looked over the ten directions and said in verse,

The light of great knowledge of the Enlightened
Universally purifies all worlds;
Once the worlds are purified,
He reveals the enlightening teachings.

Even if people want to see
Buddhas as numerous as sentient beings,
The Buddha responds to their wishes—
Yet really comes from nowhere.

With Buddha as the object,
Concentrating continuously,
One can see Buddhas
As many as thoughts.

Carrying out pure ways,
Fulfilling virtues,
One can concentrate unremittingly
On omniscience.

The Guides expound teachings
To beings in accord with their needs;
Wherever any can be taught
He manifests the supreme incarnation.

The bodies of Buddha and the worlds' beings
Are all without self:
Realizing this, he attains true awakening
And also explains it to others.

All the Human Lions,
With boundless powers of freedom,
Manifest bodies equal to thoughts,
Those bodies each being different.

As are the bodies of the beings of the worlds,
So too are the bodies of Buddhas:
When one really knows their inherent nature,
That is called Buddhahood.

The Enlightened see and know all,
Clearly comprehending all things:
Buddhahood and enlightenment
Are both ungraspable.

The Guide has no coming or going
And also no place of abode:
Departing from all delusions
Is called true perfect enlightenment.

Then Constellation Banner, empowered by the Buddha, looked over
the ten directions and said in verse,

The Realizer of Thusness, without dwelling anywhere,
Abides in all lands,
Going to all lands,
Seen in all places.

Buddha manifests all bodies
According to sentient beings' minds,
Attaining the Way, teaching the truth,
And finally passing utterly away.

The Buddhas are inconceivable:
Who can conceive of the Buddhas?
Who can see the Truly Awake?
Who can manifest the Supreme?

All things are *thus*,
And so are the states of the Buddhas;
There's not a single thing in *thusness*
That has birth or death.

Sentient beings erroneously discriminate:
"This is Buddha," "this is the world."
For one realizing the true nature of things
There's no Buddha and no world.

The Realizer of Thusness appears before all
Causing sentient beings to believe and rejoice.
But the essence of Buddha is ungraspable,
And they are not seeing anything either.

If one can, in the world,
Depart from all attachments,
With unimpeded mind, joyful,
One will awaken to the truth.

That manifested by spiritual power
Is what is called Buddha:
Though one search in all times, past, present, or future,
It has no existence at all.

If one can know in this way
The mind and all things,
One will know and see all
And soon become enlightened.

In words are expressed
The powers of Buddhas;
But true enlightenment transcends words,
Though it be provisionally explained by words.

Then Banner of Truth, empowered by the Buddha, looked over the
ten directions and said in verse,

It's better to always experience
All the pains of the world

Than to be apart from the Buddha
And not see Buddha's mystic powers.

If there are any sentient beings
Who have not yet set their minds on enlightenment,
If they once hear the name of Buddha
They'll surely attain enlightenment.

People with knowledge and wisdom,
Once they set their minds on enlightenment,
Will surely become supreme Buddhas:
Have no doubt of that.

The mystic power of the enlightened
Is rarely encountered even in countless ages;
If you engender a single thought of faith
You'll soon ascend to the highest path.

Even if in every instant
You give offerings to countless Buddhas,
If you don't know the real truth
This is not to be called offering.

If you hear such a teaching,
The Buddhas are born from this;
Though you experience countless pains
You'll not quit enlightening practices.

Once having heard of great knowledge,
The state entered by the Buddhas,
Everywhere in the universe
You'll become a guide of all times.

Though one pass the whole future
Traveling to all buddha-lands,
If one doesn't seek this wondrous truth
One will never become enlightened.

Sentient beings, from beginningless past,
Have long revolved in birth and death;
They do not know the real truth,
So Buddhas come forth in the world.

Truths cannot be destroyed,
And no one can destroy them:
The great light of mystic power
Is revealed throughout the world.

BOOK TWENTY-FIVE

Ten Dedications

THEN THE ENLIGHTENING BEING Diamond Banner, empowered by the Buddha, entered absorption in the light of knowledge of enlightening beings. When he had entered this absorption, there appeared before him as many Buddhas as atoms in a hundred thousand buddha-lands from beyond as many worlds as atoms in a hundred thousand buddha-lands in each of the ten directions. Those Buddhas, who were all alike named Diamond Banner, praised him, saying, "Good! Good man, it's very good that you can enter this absorption in the light of knowledge of enlightening beings. Good man, this is the spiritual power of Buddhas as numerous as atoms in a hundred thousand buddha-lands in each of the ten directions bolstering you, and also the spiritual power of the force of Vairocana Buddha's past vows, and it is also due to the purity of your knowledge and wisdom, and to the growing supremacy of the bases of goodness of enlightening beings, enabling you to enter this absorption and expound the teaching, in order to enable enlightening beings to attain pure fearlessness, to have unimpeded powers of elucidation, to enter the state of unobstructed knowledge, to abide in the great mind of omniscience, to perfect innumerable virtues, to fulfill unhindered pure ways, to enter into the all-sided realm of reality, to manifest the spiritual freedom of all Buddhas, to maintain previous awareness and knowledge, to gain all Buddhas' protection of all faculties, to extensively expound myriad principles by means of countless approaches, to understand and keep in memory the teachings heard, to embrace all the foundations of goodness of enlightening beings, to accomplish the aids to the path transcending the world, to prevent omniscient knowledge from dying out, to develop great vows, to interpret true meanings, to know the realm of reality, to cause all enlightening beings to rejoice, to cultivate the equal roots of goodness of all Buddhas, to protect and maintain the lineage of all enlightened ones; that is, you expound the ten dedications of enlightening beings.

"Child of Buddha, you should receive the spiritual power of the Buddha and expound this teaching, to gain the protection of the Buddhas, to dwell in the house of the Buddhas, to increase transcendental virtues, to attain the light of concentration, to enter the unobstructed state of the Buddha, to illumine the realm of reality with great light, to assemble faultless pure ways, to abide in the realm of great knowledge, to attain the unimpeded light of truth."

Then the Buddhas bestowed on Diamond Banner boundless knowledge and wisdom, unhalting, unimpeded eloquence, skill in distinguishing expressions and meanings, unhindered light of the teaching, the equal body of wisdom of the enlightened, a pure voice with infinite distinct tones, the inconceivable concentration of enlightening beings' skillful observation, the knowledge of dedication of indestructible foundations of all goodness, consummate skill in analytic observation of all things, and uninterrupted power of elucidation to explain all things in all places. Why? Because of the power of the virtue of entry into this absorption.

Then the Buddhas each patted the enlightening being Diamond Banner on the head with their right hands, after which Diamond Banner rose from absorption and declared to the enlightening beings, "Children of Buddhas, great enlightening beings have inconceivable great vows, filling the cosmos, able to save all sentient beings. That is, to learn and practice the dedications of all Buddhas of past, present, and future. How many kinds of dedication have the great enlightening beings? Great enlightening beings have ten kinds of dedication, which are expounded by the Buddhas of past, present, and future. What are they? (1) Dedication to saving all sentient beings without any mental image of sentient beings. (2) Indestructible dedication. (3) Dedication equal to all Buddhas. (4) Dedication reaching all places. (5) Dedication of inexhaustible treasuries of virtue. (6) Dedication causing all roots of goodness to endure. (7) Dedication equally adapting to all sentient beings. (8) Dedication with the character of true thusness. (9) Unattached, unbound, liberated dedication. (10) Boundless dedication equal to the cosmos. These are the ten kinds of dedication of great enlightening beings, which the past, future, and present Buddhas have, will, and do expound.

"What is the great enlightening beings' dedication to saving all sentient beings? Here the enlightening beings practice transcendent giving, purify transcendent discipline, cultivate transcendent forbearance, arouse transcendent energy, enter transcendent meditation, abide in transcendent wisdom, great compassion, great kindness, great joy, and great equanimity. Cultivating boundless roots of goodness such as these, they form this thought: 'May these roots of goodness universally benefit all sentient beings, causing them to be purified, to reach the ultimate, and to forever leave the innumerable pains and afflictions of the realms of hells, ghosts, and animals, and so on.' When the great enlightening beings plant these roots of goodness, they dedicate their own roots of goodness thus: 'I should be a hostel for all sentient beings, to let them escape from all painful things. I should be a protector for all sentient beings, to let them all be liberated from all afflictions. I should be a refuge for all sentient beings, to free them from all fears. I should be a goal for all sentient beings, to cause them to reach universal knowledge. I should make a resting place for all sentient beings, to enable them to find a place of peace and security. I should be a light for all sentient beings, to enable them to attain the light of knowledge to annihilate the darkness of ignorance. I should be a torch for all sentient beings, to destroy all darkness of nescience. I should be a lamp for all sentient beings, to cause them to abide in the realm of ultimate purity. I should be a guide for all sentient beings, to lead them into the truth. I should be a great leader for all sentient beings, to give them great knowledge.' Enlightening beings dedicate all foundations of goodness in this way, to equally benefit all sentient beings and ultimately cause them all to attain universal knowledge.

"The enlightening beings' protection of and dedication to those who are not their relatives or friends are equal to those for their relatives and friends. Why? Because enlightening beings enter the equal nature of all things, they do not conceive a single thought of not being relatives or friends. Even if there be sentient beings who have malicious or hostile intentions toward the enlightening beings, still the enlightening beings also regard them with the eye of compassion and are never angered. They are good friends to all sentient beings, explaining the right teaching for them, so that they may learn and practice it. Just as the ocean cannot be changed or destroyed by all poisons, so too are enlightening beings—the various oppressive afflictions of all the ignorant, the unwise, the ungrateful, the wrathful, those poisoned by covetousness, the arrogant and conceited, the mentally blind and deaf, those who do not know what is good, and other such evil sentient beings, cannot disturb the enlightening beings.

"Just as the sun, appearing in the world, is not concealed because those who are born blind do not see it, and is not hidden by the obstruction of such things as mirages, eclipses, trees, high mountains, deep ravines, dust, mist, smoke, or clouds, and is not concealed by the change of seasons, so also are the enlightening beings—they have great virtues, their minds are deep and broad, they observe with true mindfulness, without boredom; because they want ultimate virtue and knowledge their minds aspire to the supreme truth; the light of truth illumines everywhere and they perceive the meanings of everything. Their knowledge freely commands all avenues of teaching, and in order to benefit all sentient beings they always practice virtuous ways, never mistakenly conceiving the idea of abandoning sentient beings. They do not reject sentient beings and fail to cultivate dedication because of the meanness of character of sentient beings, or because their erroneous views, ill will, and confusion are hard to quell. The enlightening beings just array themselves with the armor of great vows of enlightening beings, saving sentient beings without ever retreating; they do not withdraw from enlightening activity and abandon the path of enlightenment just because sentient beings are ungrateful, they do not get sick of sentient beings just because ignoramuses altogether give up all the foundations of goodness which accord with reality, or because they repeatedly commit excesses and evils which are hard to bear. Why? Just as the sun does not appear in the world for just one thing, so too the enlightening beings do not cultivate roots of goodness and dedicate them to complete perfect enlightenment just for the sake of one sentient being—it is in order to save and safeguard all sentient beings everywhere that they cultivate roots of goodness and dedicate them to unexcelled complete perfect enlightenment. In the same way, it is not to purify just one buddha-land, not because of belief in just one Buddha, not just to see one Buddha, not just to comprehend one doctrine, that they initiate the determination for great knowledge and dedicate it to unexcelled complete perfect enlightenment—it is to purify all buddha-lands, out of faith in all Buddhas, to serve all Buddhas, to understand all Buddha teachings, that they initiate great vows, cultivate the foundations of goodness, and dedicate them to unexcelled complete perfect enlightenment.

"Enlightening beings, focusing on all the Buddha teachings, develop a broad mind and great determination, a determination never to retreat, and through measureless eons cultivate and collect rare, hard to obtain mental jewels, all equal to those of all Buddhas. Thus observing the bases of goodness, enlightening beings' mind of faith is pure, their great compassion is firm and enduring; they truly and genuinely dedicate them to sentient beings with a most profound intent, a joyful mind, a pure mind, a mind conquering all, a gentle mind, a kind, compassionate mind, a mind of pity and sympathy, with the intention to protect, to benefit, and to give peace and happiness to all sentient beings—they do this sincerely and in reality, not just in words.

"When great enlightening beings dedicate roots of goodness, they think in these terms: 'By my roots of goodness may all creatures, all sentient beings, be purified, may they be filled with virtues which cannot be ruined and are inexhaustible. May they always gain respect. May they have right mindfulness and unfailing recollection. May they attain sure discernment. May they be replete with immeasurable knowledge. May all virtues of physical, verbal, and mental action fully adorn them.' They also think, 'By these roots of goodness I'll cause all sentient beings to serve all Buddhas, to their unfailing benefit. I'll cause their pure faith to be indestructible; I'll cause them to hear the true teaching, cut off all doubt and confusion, remember the teaching without forgetting it and practice in accord with the teaching. I will cause them to develop respect for the Enlightened, to act with purity, to rest securely on innumerable great foundations of goodness, to be forever free of poverty, to be fully equipped with the seven kinds of wealth—faith, self-control, shame, conscience, learning, generosity, and wisdom—to always learn from the Buddhas, to perfect innumerable supreme roots of goodness, to attain impartial understanding, to abide in omniscience, to look upon all sentient beings equally with unobstructed eyes, to adorn their bodies with all marks of greatness, without any flaws, to have pure, beautiful voices replete with all fine qualities, to have control over their senses, to accomplish the ten powers, to be filled with good will, to dwell or depend on nothing, to cause all sentient beings to attain the enjoyments of buddhahood, attain infinite spiritual stations, and abide in the abode of Buddhas.

"When enlightening beings see sentient beings doing all sorts of bad things and suffering all sorts of misery and pain, and being hindered by this from seeing the Buddha, hearing the teaching, and recognizing the community, the enlightening beings think, 'I should, in those states of woe, take on the various miseries in place of the sentient beings, to liberate them.' When enlightening beings suffer pain in this way, they become even more determined—they do not give up or run away, are not shocked or frightened, are not discouraged or intimidated, and are unwearied. Why? Because according to their vows they are determined to carry all sentient beings to liberation. At such a time, enlightening beings think in these terms: 'All sentient beings are in the realm of the pains and troubles of birth, old age, sickness, and death, revolving in repeated routines according to the force of their acts, ignorant, with erroneous views, bereft of qualities of goodness—I should save them and enable them to attain emancipation.'

"Also, sentient beings are wrapped up in the web of attachments, covered by the shroud of ignorance, clinging to all existents, pursuing them unceasingly, entering the cage of suffering, acting like maniacs, totally void of virtue or knowledge, always doubtful and confused; they do not perceive the place of peace, they do not know the path of emancipation, they revolve in birth and death without rest, always submerged in the mire of suffering. Enlightening beings, seeing this, conceive great compassion and desire to help them, wanting to enable sentient beings to all attain liberation; to this end they dedicate all their virtues, dedicating them with a great, magnanimous heart, in conformity with the dedication practiced by the enlightening beings of all times, in accord with dedication as explained in the scriptures, praying that all sentient beings be thoroughly purified and ultimately accomplish knowledge of all means of liberation. They also think, 'What I practice is in order to enable sentient beings to all become supreme sovereigns of knowledge; I am not seeking liberation for myself, but only to serve all sentient beings, to cause them to all attain the omniscient mind, to cross over the flow of birth and death, and be freed from all suffering.'

"They also form this thought: 'I should accept all sufferings for the sake of all sentient beings, and enable them to escape from the abyss of immeasurable woes of birth and death. I should accept all suffering for the sake of all sentient beings in all worlds, in all states of misery, forever and ever, and still always cultivate foundations of goodness for the sake of all beings. Why? I would rather take all this suffering on myself than to allow sentient beings to fall into hell. I should be a hostage in those perilous places—hells, animal realms, the nether world, etc.—as a ransom to rescue all sentient beings in states of woe and enable them to gain liberation.'

"They also form this thought: 'I vow to protect all sentient beings and never abandon them. What I say is sincerely true, without falsehood. Why? Because I have set my mind on enlightenment in order to liberate all sentient beings; I do not seek the unexcelled Way for my own sake. Also I do not cultivate enlightening practice in search of pleasure or enjoyment. Why? Because mundane pleasures are all suffering, the realm of maniacs, craved by ignorant people but scorned by Buddhas; all misery arises from them. The anger, fighting, mutual defamation, and other such evils of the realms of hells, ghosts, animals, and the nether world are all caused by greedy attachment to objects of desire. By addiction to desire one becomes estranged from the Buddhas and hindered from birth in heaven, to say nothing of unexcelled complete perfect enlightenment.' Observing thus how worldlings, because of greed for a little taste of what they desire, experience immeasurable suffering, enlightening beings after all do not seek unexcelled enlightenment and cultivate enlightening practice for the sake of those pleasures of the senses; it is only to bring peace and comfort to all sentient beings that they set their minds on enlightenment and practice to fulfill their great vows to cut sentient beings' halter of miseries and enable them to attain liberation.

"Great enlightening beings also form this thought: 'I should dedicate roots of goodness in this way to enable all sentient beings to attain ultimate bliss, beneficial bliss, the bliss of nonreception, the bliss of dispassionate tranquility, the bliss of nondependence, the bliss of imperturbability, immeasurable bliss, the bliss of not rejecting birth and death yet not regressing from nirvana, undying bliss, and the bliss of universal knowledge.'

"They also think, 'I should be for all sentient beings as a charioteer, as a leader, holding the torch of great knowledge and showing the way to safety and peace, freeing them from danger, using appropriate means to inform them of the truth; and also, in the ocean of birth and death, be as a skillful ship's captain who knows all, to deliver sentient beings to the other shore.'

"In this way do great enlightening beings dedicate all their basic virtues—that is, they save all sentient beings by employing means appropriate to the situation to cause them to emerge from birth and death, serve and provide for all the Buddhas, attain unhindered, omniscient knowledge, abandon all maniacs and bad associates, approach all enlightening beings and good associates, annihilate all error and wrongdoing, perfect pure behavior, and fulfill the great practical vows and innumerable virtues of enlightening beings.

"When great enlightening beings have properly dedicated their roots of goodness, they form this thought: 'Many suns do not appear because of the multitude of sentient beings in the four continents—only one sun appears, yet it can shine on all sentient beings. Also, sentient beings do not know the day and night, or travel, or see, or carry out their work by the light of their own bodies—the accomplishment of these things all depends on the emergence of the sun; yet the sun is only one, not two.' In the same way, great enlightening beings, cultivating and amassing roots of goodness, thinking as they dedicate them, 'Sentient beings cannot save themselves—how can they save others? Only I alone have this unique determination,' they cultivate and amass roots of goodness and dedicate them in this way—that is to liberate all sentient beings, to illumine all sentient beings, to guide all sentient beings, to enlighten all sentient beings, to watch over and attend to all sentient beings, to take care of all sentient beings, to perfect all sentient beings, to gladden all sentient beings, to bring happiness to all sentient beings, and to cause all sentient beings to become freed from doubt.

"Great enlightening beings also think, 'I should be like the sun, shining universally on all without seeking thanks or reward, able to take care of all sentient beings even if they are bad, never giving up my vows on this account, not abandoning all sentient beings because one sentient being is evil, just diligently practicing the dedication of roots of goodness to cause all sentient beings to attain peace and ease. Even if my roots of goodness be few, I embrace all sentient beings and make a great dedication with a joyful heart. If one has roots of goodness but does not desire to benefit all sentient beings, that's not called dedication. When every single root of goodness is directed toward all sentient beings, that is called dedication.'

"They cultivate dedication to place sentient beings in the true nature of things where there is no attachment, dedication seeing that the intrinsic nature of sentient beings doesn't move or change, dedication without depending on or grasping dedication, dedication without attachment to the appearances of roots of goodness, dedication without false ideas about the essential nature of consequences of actions, dedication without attachment to the characteristics of the five clusters of material and mental existence, dedication without destroying the characteristics of the five clusters, dedication without grasping action, dedication without seeking reward, dedication without attachment to causality, dedication without imagining what is produced by causality, dedication without attachment to reputation, without attachment to location, dedication without attachment to unreal things, dedication without attachment to images of sentient beings, the world, or mind, dedication without creating delusions of mind, delusions of concepts, or delusions of views, dedication without attachment to verbal expression, dedication observing the real true nature of all things, dedication observing the aspects in which all sentient beings are equal, dedication stamping all roots of goodness with the seal of the realm of truth, dedication observing all things dispassionately; they understand that all things have no propagation and that roots of goodness are also thus; they observe that things are nondual, unborn, and unperishing, and that so is dedication.

"Dedicating such roots of goodness, they cultivate and practice pure methods of curing spiritual ills. All of their roots of goodness are in accord with transcendental principles, but they do not conceive of them dualistically: it is not in their deeds that they cultivate omniscience, yet it is not apart from deeds that they are dedicated to omniscience; omniscience is not identical to action, but omniscience is not attained apart from action either. Because their action is pure as light, the consequences are also pure as light; because the consequences are pure as light, omniscience is also pure as light. Detached from all confusions and thoughts of self and possession, they know perfectly in this way and skillfully dedicate all roots of goodness.

"When enlightening beings practice dedication in this way, liberating sentient beings ceaselessly, they do not dwell on appearances; but though they know that in all things there is no action and no consequence, yet they can skillfully produce all deeds and consequences, without opposition or contention. In this way they expediently practice dedication. When enlightening beings practice dedication in this way, they are free from all faults and are praised by all Buddhas. This is called the great enlightening beings' first dedication, saving all sentient beings without any image or concept of sentient beings."

Then the enlightening being Diamond Banner looked over all the assemblies in the ten directions, throughout the cosmos; entering into the meanings and expressions of the profundities, cultivating supreme action with a boundless mind, covering all beings with great compassion, maintaining the lineage of the enlightened ones of past, present, and future, entering the treasury of virtuous qualities of all Buddhas, producing the verity body of all Buddhas, able to discern the mentalities of all sentient beings, knowing the roots of goodness he had planted were ripe, while abiding in the reality body he manifested pure physical embodiment for them and, empowered by the Buddha, said in verse,

> Cultivating the Way over inconceivable eons,
> Vigor firm, mind unobstructed,
> Always seeking the virtuous qualities of Buddhas
> To benefit living beings,
> The peerless tamers of the world

Thoroughly purify their minds;
Determining to save all conscious creatures,
They can enter well into the treasury of dedication.

Their courageous power of energy complete,
Their knowledge clear, their minds pure,
They rescue all beings everywhere,
Their minds enduring, unperturbed.

Their hearts can rest peacefully, without compare;
Their minds are ever pure and full of joy.
Earnestly striving thus for the sake of the living,
They are like earth, accepting all.

They do not seek pleasure for themselves:
They only want to rescue sentient beings;
Thus developing a heart of great compassion,
They quickly gain entry to the unhindered state.

They are able to accept all beings
In all worlds in the ten directions;
They stabilize their minds to save those beings,
This way cultivating the dedications.

They practice generosity most gladly
And preserve pure conduct, without transgression;
Their intrepid, vigorous mind unstirred,
They dedicate this to enlightened omniscience.

Their mind is boundlessly broad,
Their forbearance is stable, unshakable;
Their meditation is most profound, always illumining,
Their wisdom's inconceivably subtle.

In all worlds in the ten directions
They fully cultivate pure practices:
All these virtues they dedicate
To the peace and happiness of all conscious beings.

The great heroes diligently practice good works,
Measureless, boundless, uncountable:
All these they use to benefit sentient beings
And cause them to abide in inconceivable supreme knowledge.

To act for the benefit of all sentient beings
They spend inconceivably many eons in hells;

This they do without wearying or shrinking back,
Always practicing dedication with courage and decision.

They do not seek form, sound, smell or taste,
And they do not seek nice feelings:
It is just to liberate all living beings
That they always seek supreme knowledge.

Their knowledge and wisdom are pure as space,
They pratice boundless enlightening acts;
The practical methods the Buddhas carry out
Those people always practice and learn.

The great heroes, traveling through all worlds,
Are able to give peace and safety to all beings,
Causing all to rejoice,
Tirelessly cultivating enlightening practice.

Destroying all mental poisons,
Contemplating and cultivating highest knowledge,
They do not seek comfort for themselves:
They only wish that sentient beings be freed from pain.

These people's dedication is ultimate—
Their hearts are always pure and free from poison:
Entrusted by the Buddhas of all times,
They dwell in the citadel of the loftiest teaching.

They're never attached to forms
Or to sensations, perceptions, habits, or consciousness;
Their minds have forever transcended existence,
While all their virtues they dedicate to others.

All the sentient beings seen by the Buddhas
They take into their care, without exception,
Vowing to enable them all to be liberated;
For them do they strive, with great joy.

Their minds are constantly stable,
Their knowledge and wisdom's incomparably vast.
Truly mindful, free from ignorance, they're always calm,
And all their deeds are totally pure.

Those enlightening beings, while in the world,
Are not attached to any internal or external phenomena;

Like the wind traveling unhindered through the sky
Is the function of the great beings' mind.

Their physical actions are all pure,
All their speech is without error;
Their minds always take refuge in the Buddha,
And they can please all the Buddhas.

In the infinite worlds of the ten directions,
Wherever there are Buddhas, they go;
There, seeing the lords of great compassion,
They all gaze with reverent respect.

Their minds are always pure and faultless,
Entering all worlds without fear;
Already in the Enlightened Ones' unexcelled Path,
They act as great reservoirs of truth for all beings.

Diligently observing and examining all phenomena,
They contemplate existence and nonexistence accordingly:
Thus they pursue the truth
And gain entry to the most profound realm of noncontention.

With this they cultivate the steadfast Way
Which no sentient beings can break down;
Well able to comprehend the nature of all things,
They have no attachments in any world.

Thus they are dedicated to reaching the other shore,
Enabling all beings to be free from defilements;
Forever rid of all dependency,
They enter the realm of ultimate independence.

In the languages of all sentient beings
In accord with the differences in their types,
Enlightening beings can distinctly explain
While their minds are unattached and unhindered.

Thus do enlightening beings practice dedication:
Unspeakably many are their virtues and their methods;
They earn the praise of all the Buddhas
In all worlds of the ten directions.

"What is the indestructible dedication of great enlightening beings?
These great enlightening beings attain indestructible faith in the Enlight-

ened Ones of past, future, and present, because they serve all Buddhas. They attain indestructible faith in enlightening beings, even those who have just resolved on the search for omniscience for the first time, because they vow to tirelessly cultivate all foundations of goodness of enlightening beings. They attain indestructible faith in all the Buddha qualities, because they conceive profound aspiration. They attain indestructible faith in all Buddha teachings, because they abide by them and maintain them. They attain indestructible faith in all sentient beings, because they look upon them impartially with the eye of compassion and dedicate roots of goodness to their universal benefit. They attain indestructible faith in all pure ways, because everywhere they amass boundless roots of goodness. They attain indestructible faith in the path of dedication of enlightening beings, because they fulfill their noble aspirations. They attain indestructible faith in all teachers of the ways of enlightening beings, because they think of the enlightening beings as Buddhas. They attain indestructible faith in the spiritual powers of all Buddhas, because they deeply believe in the inconceivability of the Buddhas. They attain indestructible faith in the practice of skill in expedient means exercised by all enlightening beings, because they include countless various realms of activity.

"When great enlightening beings abide in indestructible faith, they plant roots of goodness, innumerable and boundless, in various realms, such as those of Buddhas, enlightening beings, disciples of Buddhas, individual illuminates, of Buddhist doctrines, and of sentient beings, causing the determination for enlightenment to grow more and more. Their kindness and compassion broad and great, they observe impartially. They accord with and practice the deeds of the Buddhas, embracing all pure foundations of goodness. Entering the truth, they assemble virtuous practices, carry out great works of charity, and cultivate meritorious qualities, looking upon the past, present, and future as equal.

"Great enlightening beings dedicate such virtues to omniscience, aspiring to always see the Buddhas. They associate with good companions and live among enlightening beings. Constantly keeping their minds on omniscience, they accept and hold the Buddhist teachings, conscientiously protecting them, and educate and develop all sentient beings, their minds always dedicated to the path of emancipation from the world. They provide for and serve all teachers of truth. Understanding the principles of the teachings, they retain them in memory; they cultivate and practice great vows, causing them all to be fulfilled.

"Thus do enlightening beings amass roots of goodness, accomplish roots of goodness, develop roots of goodness, contemplate roots of goodness, concentrate on roots of goodness, analyze roots of goodness, delight in roots of goodness, cultivate roots of goodness, and abide in roots of goodness.

"Once enlightening beings have amassed various roots of goodness in this way, they cultivate the practices of enlightening beings by means of the results of these roots of goodness. In every successive moment they see innumerable Buddhas, and serve and provide for them in accordance with their needs. They provide innumerable jewels, flowers, garlands, garments, parasols, banners, pennants, adornments, servants, beautified places, perfumes, powdered incenses, mixed scents, burning incenses, profound faith, aspiration, pure minds, respect, praise, honor, jeweled seats, flower seats, incense seats, seats of garlands, sandalwood seats, cloth seats, diamond seats, crystal seats, precious streamer seats, jewel-colored seats, bejeweled parks, flowered parks, perfumed parks, parks hung with garlands, parks spread with robes, jewel-studded parks, parks decorated with streamers of all jewels, parks with trees of all precious substances, parks with balustrades of all precious substances, parks covered with nets of chimes of all jewels, palaces with all precious substances, palaces with all kinds of flowers, palaces with all kinds of incenses, palaces with all kinds of garlands, palaces of all kinds of sandalwood, palaces with stores of all kinds of aromatic resins, palaces of all kinds of diamonds, palaces of all kinds of crystals, all extraordinarily fine, surpassing those of the heavens; innumerable trees of mixed jewels, trees of various fragrances, trees of precious raiment, trees of music, trees of fascinating jewels, trees of gem-studded streamers, trees of precious rings, trees adorned with banners, pennants, and canopies with the fragrances of all flowers—such trees, with luxuriant foliage interreflecting, adorn the palaces; the palaces also are adorned with countless lattices, windows, doors, balconies, crescents, and drapes, countless nets of gold covering them, countless perfumes wafting throughout them scenting everything, and countless robes spread on the ground.

"Enlightening beings reverently present these offerings with pure-minded respect to all Buddhas for countless, incalculable eons, never retreating, never ceasing; and after each Buddha dies they also respectfully make similar offerings to all their relics, in order to induce all sentient beings to develop pure faith, to embody all foundations of goodness, to be freed from all suffering, to have broad understanding, to be arrayed with great adornments, to be arrayed with infinite adornments, to consummate all their undertakings, to know how rare it is to meet a Buddha in the world, to fulfill the immeasurable power of the enlightened, to adorn and make offerings to the tombs and shrines of Buddhas, and to maintain the teachings of all Buddhas.

"Their offerings to living Buddhas and to their relics after death could never be fully told of even in an incalculable period of time. Such cultivation and accumulation of immeasurable virtue is all to develop and mature sentient beings, without retreating, without ceasing, without wearying, without clinging, free from all mental images, without stopping anywhere, forever beyond all dependence, detached from self and anything pertaining to a self. They seal all aspects of their activities with the stamp of truth, realize the birthlessness of things, abide in the

abode of buddhahood, and observe the nature of birthlessness definitively marking all objects. In the care of the Buddhas, they set their
minds on dedication—dedication in accord with the essential nature of
things, dedication entering into the uncreated truth yet perfecting created
expedient methods, dedication of techniques discarding attachments to
concepts of phenomena, dedication abiding in countless enlightening
skills, dedication forever departing from all realms of existence, dedication of expedient application of practices without sticking to forms,
dedication embracing all foundations of goodness, great dedication
purifying the acts of all enlightening beings, dedication rousing the will
for enlightenment, dedication living with all bases of goodness, dedication fulfilling supreme faith.

"When enlightening beings dedicate such roots of goodness, though
they go along with birth and death they are not changed: they seek
omniscience without ever retreating; while being in the various realms
of existence, their minds are undisturbed; they are able to liberate all
sentient beings; they are not stained by compounded things; they do
not lose unimpeded knowledge; their fulfillment of causes and conditions of enlightening beings' practices and stages is inexhaustible; worldly
things cannot change or move them; they fulfill the pure ways of
transcendence; they are able to accomplish all knowledge and power.
Thus do enlightening beings get rid of the darkness of ignorance and
folly, develop the will for enlightenment and reveal its light, increase
pure ways, dedicated to the supreme Way, fulfilling all its practices.

"With clear, pure intellect they are able to skillfully analyze and
comprehend all things as appearing according to the mind; they know
deeds are like illusions, results of deeds are like paintings, all activities
are like magic tricks, things born of causes and conditions are all like
echoes, and the practices of enlightening beings are all like reflections.
They produce the clear, pure eye of reality, seeing the vast realm of the
uncreated; realizing their null essence, they understand the nonduality of
things and discover the true aspect of things. They fulfill the practices
of enlightening beings without attachment to any forms. They are able
to carry out all commonplace acts without ever abandoning pure principles and practices. Free from all attachments, they remain unattached in
action.

"Thus do enlightening beings think flexibly, without confusion or
delusion, without contradicting facts, without destroying active causes,
dedicating as is appropriate, with clear perception of real truth. They
know the inherent nature of things, yet by the power of skill in means
they accomplish results of action and reach the other shore. With
knowledge and wisdom they examine all things and attain knowledge
of spiritual faculties. The virtues of their deeds are carried out without
striving, in accordance with their free will.

"Enlightening beings dedicate roots of goodness in this way because
they want to liberate all sentient beings, keep the lineage of Buddhas

unbroken, be forever rid of demonic activity, and see omniscience. Their boundless aspiration is never discarded; they detach from mundane objects and cut off all mixup and defilement. They also wish for sentient beings to attain pure knowledge, enter deeply into the techniques of liberation, depart from the state of birth and death, attain the bases of virtues of buddhahood, forever end all delusive activities, stamp all actions with the seal of equanimity, determine to enter knowledge of all ways of liberation, and accomplish all transmundane qualities. This, O Child of Buddha, is called enlightening beings' second dedication, indestructible dedication.

"When enlightening beings abide in this dedication, they get to see all the countless Buddhas and master innumerable pure, sublime teachings. They attain impartiality toward all sentient beings, and have no doubt about anything. Strengthened by the spiritual power of all Buddhas, they overcome all demons and forever get rid of their influence. They achieve noble birth and fulfill the will for enlightenment. Attaining unhindered knowledge, they can expound the meanings of all doctrines without relying on another for understanding. They are able, following the power of imagination, to enter all lands; illumining sentient beings everywhere, they cause them all to become purified. Great enlightening beings, by the power of this indestructible dedication, embody all foundations of goodness and dedicate them in this way."

Then Diamond Banner, spiritually empowered by Buddha, looked over the ten directions and said in verse,

Enlightening beings, having attained indestructible will,
Carry out all good works;
Therefore they're able to make the Buddhas rejoice:
Those who are wise dedicate this.

Making offerings to infinite Buddhas,
Giving charity, with self-control, they subdue their senses,
Out of desire to benefit all sentient beings,
To cause them all to be purified.

All sorts of beautiful, fragrant flowers,
Innumerable different splendid robes,
Jeweled canopies and adornments,
They present to all the Buddhas.

Thus do they make offerings to Buddhas
For countless, unthinkable eons;
Reverent, respectful, always rejoicing,
They never have a thought of weariness.

They concentrate their thought on the Buddhas,
The Great Bright Lamps of all worlds:
All the Enlightened Ones of the ten directions
Appear before them, as though face to face.

For inconceivably infinite eons
They give in all ways, their minds never weary:
For hundreds of millions of eons
They practice good principles in the same way.

After the Buddhas become extinct,
They make offerings to their relics, tirelessly:
With various fine adornments for each
They set up inconceivably many shrines.

Built in incomparably excellent forms,
Adorned with jewels and gold,
The shrines are magnificent, big as mountains,
Their number countless billions.

Having made offerings with pure minds, with respect,
They also conceive the will to gladden and benefit others;
For inconceivable eons they stay in the world,
Rescuing sentient beings and liberating them.

They know that sentient beings are illusory
And do not discriminate among them,
Yet can differentiate the faculties of beings
And act for the benefit of all the living.

Enlightening beings cultivate and build up virtues
Vast, extensive, incomparably supreme;
Understanding they're essentially not existent,
In this way they dedicate them all with certainty.

Observing all things with supreme knowledge,
There's not a single thing that's born;
Thus do they provisionally cultivate dedication,
Virtue infinite, inexhaustible.

By this means they purify the mind,
Equal to all the Buddhas—
This power of skill in means is inexhaustible;
Therefore felicitous results have no limit.

Initiating the will for unsurpassed enlightenment,
Without depending on anything in the world,
They go to all worlds in the ten directions
And are not hindered by anything at all.

All Buddhas appear in the world
Because they want to guide beings' minds;
They examine the true natures of their minds
And discover they ultimately cannot be found.

All phenomena, without exception,
Are included in thusness, with no essential nature;
Dedicating with this pure eye
They open the prison of birth and death in the world.

Though they purify all existences,
Yet they do not have a notion of existences;
They know the nature of existents has no existence
And purify the joyful mind.

They depend on nothing in one buddha-land,
Or in any buddha-lands,
And they are not attached to conditioned things,
Knowing their phenomenality has no basis.

Hereby they cultivate omniscience;
Hereby highest knowledge adorns them;
Hereby the Buddhas all rejoice;
This is enlightening beings' work of dedication.

Enlightening beings focus their minds on the Buddhas,
Their supreme knowledge, wisdom, and means.
Like Buddhas, they depend on nothing at all:
May we accomplish these virtues.

Concentrating on saving all,
They cause them to abandon evil deeds;
Thus benefiting sentient beings,
They contemplate attentively without abandoning them.

Abiding in the state of knowledge and guarding the teaching,
They do not take nirvana by other vehicles—
They only vow to attain the Buddhas' unexcelled Way;
This is the dedication of enlightening beings.

They do not grasp the fabricated unrealities
Spoken of by sentient beings,
But though they do not rely on speech
Still they don't cling to wordlessness.

All the enlightened ones in the ten directions
Comprehend all things without exception;
But though they know all things are empty, void,
They don't produce a notion of voidness.

With one adornment they adorn all
Yet don't discriminate phenomena—
They enlighten all living beings:
All is without inherent nature, without objectivity.

"What is great enlightening beings' dedication equal to all Buddhas? Here the enlightening beings follow and cultivate the path of dedication of the Buddhas of the past, future, and present. When they practice and learn the path of dedication in this way, when they perceive any objects of sense, whether pleasant or unpleasant, they do not conceive like or dislike—their minds are free, without faults, broad, pure, joyful, blissful, free from all sorrows and troubles. Their minds are flexible, their senses are pure and cool.

"When great enlightening beings gain such peace and bliss, they become even more determined, dedicating their determination to the Buddhas, with these thoughts: 'With the roots of goodness I am now planting I vow to cause the bliss of the Buddhas to increase more and more—that is, the bliss of the inconceivable abode of Buddhas, the bliss of the peerless concentration of Buddhas, the bliss of unlimited compassion, the bliss of liberation of all Buddhas, the bliss of vast, ultimate, immeasurable power, the bliss of tranquility detached from all cognition, the bliss of abiding in the state of nonobstruction, always rightly concentrated, the bliss of carrying out the practice of nondualism without change.'

"Once the great enlightening beings have dedicated their roots of goodness to the Buddhas, they also dedicate these virtues to the enlightening beings: that is, to cause those who have not fulfilled their vows to fulfill them, to cause those whose minds are not yet pure to attain purity, to cause those who have not fulfilled the ways of transcendence to fulfill them, to settle them in the indestructible will for enlightenment, that they not regress on the way to omniscience, not give up great effort, preserve all the foundations of goodness of the gates of enlightenment, and be able to cause sentient beings to give up conceit, set their minds on enlightenment, fulfill their aspirations, abide in the abode of all enlightening beings, attain the clear, sharp senses of enlightening beings, cultivate roots of goodness, and realize omniscience.

"Having thus dedicated their roots of goodness to enlightening beings, the great enlightening beings then dedicate them to all sentient beings, wishing that the roots of goodness of all sentient beings, even the slightest—even seeing a Buddha, hearing teaching, or respecting holy mendicants, for but the time of a fingersnap—all be free from obstruction, that they reflect on the completeness of Buddhas, on the techniques of the teaching, and on the nobility and importance of the community, that they not be separated from vision of the Buddha, that their minds become pure, that they attain the qualities of buddhahood, build up immeasurable virtue, purify spiritual powers, give up doubts about the truth and live according to the teaching. As they make such dedication to sentient beings, they also make such dedication for the Buddhist disciples and the individual illuminates.

"Also they pray that all sentient beings forever leave all miserable places like hells, ghosthood, and animality, the nether world, and so on, that they further develop the supreme will for enlightenment, concentrate their minds on the earnest search for knowledge of all means of liberation, never repudiate the true teaching of the Buddhas, attain the peace of the Buddhas, be pure in body and mind, and realize omniscience.

"The foundations of goodness of great enlightening beings are all correctly initiated, built up, and developed by great vows, causing them all to expand and to be completely fulfilled.

"When great enlightening beings live at home with spouses and children, they never for a moment give up the determination for enlightenment; with correct mindfulness they meditate on the realm of all knowledge, liberating themselves and others, enabling them to reach the ultimate. Using appropriate means they transform the members of their own households, causing them to enter the knowledge of enlightening beings and causing them to develop to maturity and attain liberation. Though they live together, their minds have no attachments. By their basic great great compassion they remain in home life, and because of their kindness they harmonize with their spouses and children, with no hindrance to the pure Way of enlightening beings.

"Though great enlightening beings be in home life and work at various occupations, they never for a moment give up the will for omniscience; that is, whether they are dressing, eating, taking medicine, washing, looking around, walking, standing still, sitting, reclining, speaking, thinking, asleep or awake, whatever they are doing their minds always dedicate it to the path of omniscience. They concentrate and contemplate unremittingly, because they want to aid all sentient beings and settle them in enlightenment; with immeasurable great vows they embody countless great roots of goodness, diligently cultivating virtues to save everyone. They forever divorce arrogance and indulgence and proceed surely toward the state of omniscience, never conceiving any intention of turning to another path. Always contemplating the enlightenment of all Buddhas, they forever abandon all impure ways. Cultivating practice of what all enlightening beings learn, they encounter no obstruction on the path of omniscience and stand on the ground of knowledge. They are devoted to recitation and learning, and collect roots of goodness by means of immeasurable knowledge. Their minds have no affection for any mundane realm, nor are they obsessed with what they practice. They wholeheartedly accept and hold the principles of the Buddhas' teachings. Thus enlightening beings living at home cultivate and internalize roots of goodness in every way, cause them to grow, and dedicate them to the unsurpassed enlightenment, which is the essence of the Buddhas.

"At such a time, enlightening beings, even when they are feeding domestic animals, all make this vow: 'I should cause these creatures to leave the realm of animality, to be helped and comforted and ultimately be liberated, having forever crossed over the ocean of suffering, eternally annihilating painful sensations, forever removing suffering physical and mental elements, eternally cutting off painful feeling, accumulation of pain, painful actions, the causes of pain, the root of suffering, and painful situations. May these sentient beings all be able to leave these behind.' Thus do enlightening beings focus their thoughts on all sentient beings; with their roots of goodness in the forefront, they dedicate them to knowledge of ways of liberation for all beings.

"When enlightening beings first engender the determination for enlightenment, they include all sentient beings, cultivating the foundations of goodness and dedicating them to causing all sentient beings to leave the plain of birth and death forever, to attain the unhindered bliss of the enlightened, emerge from the ocean of afflictions, practice the path of the Buddha teachings, to fill everywhere with kindness, to have vast powers of compassion, cause all to attain pure bliss, preserve foundations of goodness, draw near to the qualities of Buddhahood, leave the realms of demons and enter the realm of Buddhas, to cut off the seeds of mundanity and plant the seeds of enlightenment, to abide in the truth which is equal in all times.

"Enlightening beings dedicate all the roots of goodness they have collected, will collect, and are collecting in this way, and form this thought: 'As the Buddhas and enlightening beings of the past have practiced—respectfully serving all enlightened ones, liberating sentient beings so that they be forever emancipated, diligently cultivating and practicing all roots of goodness and dedicating them all without attachment, without depending on form, without attachment to sensation, without erroneous conceptions, without creating fixed patterns, without grasping consciousness, detached from the senses, not dwelling on things of the world, delighting in transcendence, knowing that all things are empty as space, come from nowhere, are unborn and not perishing, and have no true reality; having no attachments, they avoided all discriminatory views, were imperturbable and unaffected by anything, never lost awareness or calm, abiding in reality without form, detached from all appearances, all being one; thus they entered deeply into the nature of all things, always happily practiced all-sided virtues, and saw the congregation of all Buddhas—just as all those enlightened ones of the past dedicated roots of goodness in this way, I, too, should practice dedication in this way, understand these principles, actualize these principles, and, based on these principles determine to learn and act, not violating the specifics of the teachings, knowing that what is practiced is like illusions, like shadows, like the moon's image in the water, like reflections in a mirror, manifested by the combination of causes and conditions, proceeding thus up to the ultimate stage of enlightenment.'

"Great enlightening beings also form this thought: 'Just as the Buddhas of the past, when cultivating enlightening practice, dedicated roots of goodness in this way, and so do and will the Buddhas of the present and future, so too should I arouse my will and dedicate roots of goodness like those Buddhas—with foremost dedication, excellent dedication, supreme dedication, superior dedication, unexcelled dedication, peerless dedication, unequalled dedication, incomparable dedication, honorable dedication, sublime dedication, impartial dedication, straightforward dedication, virtuous dedication, far-reaching dedication, good dedication, pure dedication, dedication free from evil, dedication not going wrong.'

"Once enlightening beings have dedicated roots of goodness in this way, they accomplish pure action of body, speech, and mind, and abide in the abode of enlightening beings without any faults. Practicing good works, they get rid of evils of action and speech. Their minds are without flaw or defilement; they cultivate omniscience, abide in an immeasurably broad mind, and know all phenomena create nothing. They abide in transmundane states and are not influenced by things of the world. They analyze and comprehend innumerable actions and fully develop skill in means of dedication, extirpating the root of grasping and attachment forever. This is the great enlightening beings' third dedication, dedication equal to all Buddhas.

"When great enlightening beings abide in this dedication, they enter deeply into the acts of all the enlightened ones, proceed toward the supremely wonderful qualities of the enlightened, enter into the profound realm of pure knowledge, do not depart from the works of enlightening beings, are able to distinguish skillful, subtle means of liberation, enter the profound realm of truth, know well the process of practice of enlightening beings, enter the family of the Buddhas, and with skill in means analyze and comprehend all things. Though they appear physically, born in the world, yet their minds have no attachment to things of the world."

Then the enlightening being Diamond Banner, spiritually empowered by the Buddha, looked over the ten directions and said in verse,

Those great enlightening beings
Practice the ways of dedication of past Buddhas,
And also cultivate the practices
Of all the Guides of future and present.

They attain peace and ease in all realms,
Praised by all the enlightened ones;
Their expansive light and pure eyes
They dedicate all to the great Brilliant Sages.

Blissful are the bodies of enlightening beings,
And so are all their senses;
Such immeasurable, supremely wonderful bliss
They all dedicate to the Supreme.

All the good ways in the world
And those the Buddhas have accomplished,
All they foster, excepting none,
Whereby they joyfully benefit the living.

Their joys in the world are infinite:
These they dedicate to sentient beings,
Vowing to cause them all to be filled
With the bliss of the Human Lion.

The various raptures known and perceived
By the Buddhas of all lands
They vow to foster in sentient beings
And become great lamps lighting the world.

The supremely refined pleasure of enlightening beings
They dedicate to all sentient beings:
Though they are dedicated to the benefit of the living,
Yet they have no attachment to dedication.

Enlightening beings, practicing this dedication,
Produce a mind of infinite compassion;
The virtues of dedication practiced by the Buddhas
They vow to cultivate and fulfill the same way.

The subtle bliss of the vehicle of omniscience
Such as attained by the Supreme,

As well as the infinite bliss of enlightening practice
Carried out while they're in the world,
The bliss of peace while appearing to be in the world,
The bliss of tranquility, always guarding the senses,
All they dedicate to sentient beings
To cause all to develop unexcelled knowledge.

Their work is not physical, verbal, or mental,
Yet doesn't exist apart from this;
They just destroy ignorance by expedient means
And thus develop supreme knowledge.

The deeds practiced by enlightening beings
Build up immeasurable excellent virtues;
Following the Enlightened, born in the family of Buddhas,
Dispassionate and calm, they dedicate aright.

They take care of all beings there are
In all worlds of the ten directions,
Dedicating all roots of goodness to them,
Vowing to fill them with the bliss of peace.

They do not seek benefit for themselves;
They want to cause all to be at ease.
They have never entertained arbitrary conceptions:
They only observe all things to be empty and selfless.

To all the true children of Buddhas
Seen by the innumerable Supreme Ones in the ten directions
They dedicate all roots of goodness,
Vowing to hasten their ultimate enlightenment.

The conscious creatures in all worlds
They embrace impartially, without exception;
With the good works they do themselves
They cause those beings to soon become Buddhas.

The countless, boundless great vows
Expounded by the unexcelled Guides
Vow that all Buddha-children become pure
And fulfill all their aspirations.

Observing all worlds in the ten directions,
Donating all their virtues to them,
They vow to cause them all to be wonderfully adorned:
Thus do enlightening beings practice dedication.

Their minds do not weigh dualistic things;
They only constantly realize the nonduality of things.
In all things, whether dual or nondual,
They ultimately have no attachments.

All the worlds in the ten directions
Are sentient beings' conceptualizations;
Not apprehending anything in conception or nonconception,
Thus are conceptions understood.

The enlightening beings' bodies are purified,
So their minds are pure, without blemish:
Their speech being already pure and faultless,
Know that their minds are pure, without attachment.

Single-mindedly they think of the past Buddhas
And also of the Guides of the future,
As well as the Honored Ones of the present:
They study the teachings they all expound.

All enlightened ones of past, present, and future
Have clear penetrating knowledge, their minds unobstructed;
Because they want to help sentient beings
They dedicate myriad works to enlightenment.

Those of foremost wisdom, vast wisdom,
Wisdom free from falsehood, without delusion,
Impartial, true wisdom, pure wisdom,
And supreme wisdom, explain this way.

"What is the great enlightening beings' dedication reaching all places? Here when the enlightening beings cultivate all roots of goodness, they think, 'May the power of virtue of these roots of good reach all places, just as reality extends everywhere without exception, reaching all things, all worlds, all living beings, all lands, all phenomena, all space, all time, all that is compounded and uncompounded, all speech and sound; may these roots of goodness in the same way reach the abodes of all enlightened ones, and be as offerings to all those Buddhas, the past Buddhas whose vows are all fulfilled, the future Buddhas, fully adorned, and the present Buddhas, their lands, sites of enlightenment, and congregations, filling all realms throughout the entirety of space. I aspire, by virtue of the power of faith, by virtue of great knowledge without obstruction, by virtue of dedication of all roots of goodness, to present offerings like those of the celestials, filling infinite worlds.'

"Great enlightening beings also form this thought: 'The Buddhas pervade all realms in space, the worlds of all the unspeakably many world systems in the ten directions produced by various actions—unspeakably many buddha-lands, buddha-spheres, all kinds of worlds, infinite worlds, worlds without boundaries, rotating worlds, sideways worlds, worlds facing upward and downward—in all worlds, such as these, they manifest a span of life and display various spiritual powers and demonstrations. There are enlightening beings there who by the power of resolution appear as Buddhas in all worlds for the sake of sentient beings who can be taught; with the knowledge of where all paths lead, they reveal everywhere the boundless freedom and spiritual power of the enlightened, the body of reality extending everywhere without distinction, equally entering all realms of phenomena and principles, the body of inherent buddhahood neither born nor perishing, yet by skillful expedients appearing throughout the world, because of realizing the true nature of things, transcending all, because of attainment of nonregressing power, because of birth among the people of vast power of unobstructed vision of the enlightened.'

"Great enlightening beings, by all the roots of goodness that they plant, vow to make offerings to all such Buddhas, with myriad beautiful flowers, myriad wonderful incenses, garlands, parasols, banners, pennants, clothing, lamps, and all other articles of adornment, and to do the same to effigies, tombs, and shrines of Buddhas. Their roots of goodness they dedicate in this way, with unconfused dedication, single-minded dedication, autonomous dedication, respectful dedication, unshakable dedication, nonobsessive dedication, independent dedication, dedication without the mentality of worldly people, dedication without haste or struggle, dedication with a tranquil mind.

"They also think, 'Throughout the space of the cosmos, in all ages, past, future, and present, the Buddhas, the World Honored Ones, attain omniscience and become enlightened; with innumerable different names, at various times, they manifest attainment of true awakening, all abiding for a span of life, throughout the future, each adorning themselves with the adornments of the realm of reality, their sites of enlightenment and congregations pervading the cosmos; in all lands they appear according to the time and perform the work of buddhahood. To all these Buddhas I dedicate roots of goodness; I vow to offer respectfully countless canopies of fragrance, banners of fragrance, pennants of fragrance, drapes of fragrance, nets of fragrance, statues of fragrance, lights of fragrance, flames of fragrance, clouds of fragrance, thrones of fragrance, parks of fragrance, shelters of fragrance, worlds of fragrance, mountains of fragrance, seas of fragrance, rivers of fragrance, trees of fragrance, robes of fragrance, lotus blossoms of fragrance, palaces of fragrance, flowers of fragrance; infinite canopies of flowers, and so on, up to infinite palaces of flowers; boundless canopies of garlands, and so on, up to boundless palaces of garlands; incomparably many canopies of powdered incense, and so on, up to incomparably many palaces of powdered incense; uncountable canopies of perfume, and so on, up to uncountable palaces of perfume; incalculable canopies of raiment, and so on, up to incalculable palaces of raiment; inconceivable numbers of canopies of jewels, and so on, up to inconceivable numbers of palaces of jewels; immeasurable numbers of canopies of lamps, and so on, up to immeasurable numbers of palaces of lamps; unspeakable numbers of canopies of ornaments, and so on, up to unspeakable numbers of palaces of ornaments; unspeakably unspeakable numbers of canopies, banners, pennants, drapes, nets, statues, lights, flames, clouds, seats, parks, shelters, lands, mountains, seas, rivers, trees, robes, lotus blossoms, and palaces, all made of jewel crystals, all unspeakably unspeakable in number: in each of these objects are countless balustrades, palaces, bowers, doors, crescents, defensive barriers, windows, pure jewels, and ornaments—all such offerings I present to those Buddhas, aspiring to cause all worlds to become purified and all sentient beings to attain emancipation, abide in the stage of the ten powers and attain unhindered understanding of truth; to cause all sentient beings to be fully endowed with bases of goodness, to gain complete self-mastery, to have minds as infinite as space, going to all fields without going anywhere, entering all lands, passing on good ways, always able to see Buddhas, planting roots of goodness, accomplishing the great vehicle, not clinging to anything, replete with virtue, establishing innumerable practices, entering into all the boundless realms of reality, developing the spiritual faculties of the Buddhas, and attaining the omniscient knowledge of the enlightened ones. Just as selflessness includes all things, so also may my roots of goodness include all the Buddhas by making offerings to them all; include all truths by understanding them without hindrance; include all enlightening beings by ultimately having the same roots of goodness; include all practices of enlightening beings by fulfillment through the power of my original vows; include all enlightening beings' understandings of things by comprehending all things without obstruction; include all the great spiritual powers of the Buddhas by perfecting innumerable roots of goodness; include all the powers and fearlessnesses of the Buddhas by developing immeasurable will and fulfilling them all; include all the enlightening beings' methods of meditation, powers of elucidation, and concentration formulae by being able to illumine and comprehend nonduality; include the Buddhas' skill in means by manifesting the great spiritual powers of the enlightened; include all the past, present, and future Buddhas' birth in the world, attainment of enlightenment, turning the wheel of true teaching, taming sentient beings, and entering final decease, by respectfully presenting offerings to all of them everywhere; include all worlds of the ten directions by adorning and purifying buddha-lands to the ultimate degree; include all ages by appearing therein and cultivating enlightening practice unceasingly; include all realms of being by appearing to be born therein; include all realms of sentient beings by fulfilling the practice of the Universally Good enlightening being; include all delusive habit energy by using appropriate means to clean it all away; include the innumerable differences in faculties of sentient beings by knowing them all; include the understandings and inclinations of all sentient beings by causing them to get rid of confusion and defilement and attain purity; include all activities that edify sentient beings by appearing in forms appropriate to their needs; include all ways of adaptively responding to sentient beings by entering into all realms of sentient beings; and include the essence of knowledge of all enlightened ones by preserving the teachings of the Buddhas.'

"When great enlightening beings dedicate roots of goodness in this way, they use the absence of object of attainment as a means: they do not distinguish consequences in actions, they do not distinguish actions in consequences; though they have no discrimination, they enter all realms of phenomena and principles; though they have no striving, yet they always abide in roots of goodness; though they initiate nothing, yet they diligently practice excellent principles. They do not believe in things, yet can enter deeply into them; they do not consider things as existent, yet they know and see them all. Creation and noncreation are both ungraspable. They know that by nature all things are never independent. Though they see all things, yet they are not seeing anything; they know everything without knowing anything.

"Thus do enlightening beings comprehend the objective world, knowing that all things are based on causes and conditions. They see the reality-body of all Buddhas and arrive at the untainted ultimate reality of all things. They understand all worlds are like magical apparitions. They clearly realize that sentient beings are only one phenomenon and do not have two natures. They do not give up the realm of action: with skill in expedient means they show the uncreated in the midst of the realm of compounded things, without destroying the characteristics of compounded things; they show compounded things in the midst of the realm of the uncompounded, without distinguishing marks of the uncompounded. Thus enlightening beings always observe all things as ultimately null and void. They develop all pure roots of goodness and arouse the will to save and protect sentient beings. Their knowledge clearly realizes the ocean of all truths. They always gladly cultivate practice to get rid of ignorance and folly. They have already fully accomplished transmundane virtues, and they no longer practice worldly ways. They have attained the pure eye of knowledge, stripped of the blinders of ignorance, and with skill in means they practice the path of dedication.

"Great enlightening beings, dedicating roots of goodness in this way, accord with the will of all the Buddhas, beautify and purify all buddha-lands, teach, edify, and mature all sentient beings, fully accept and maintain all principles of the Buddhas, become supreme fields of blessings for all sentient beings, become wise guides for all caravans, become pure suns for all worlds. Each of their roots of goodness fills the cosmos, able to rescue and safeguard all sentient beings and cause them to be filled with pure virtuous qualities.

"When the great enlightening beings practice dedication in this way, they are able to preserve the lineage of all Buddhas, to develop all sentient beings to maturity, to beautify and purify all lands, to avoid spoiling all works, to thoroughly understand all things, to impartially observe the nonduality of all things, to go to all lands in the ten directions, to comprehend the ultimate reality apart from desire, to achieve pure faith, and to have clear, sharp faculties.

"This is great enlightening beings' fourth dedication, dedication reaching all places. When great enlightening beings abide in this dedication, they achieve physical action reaching all places, being able to appear responsively in all worlds; they achieve verbal action reaching all places, expounding the truth in all places; they achieve mental action reaching all places, accepting and holding the truth explained by all Buddhas; they attain the power of psychic travel reaching everywhere, going in response to beings' minds; they attain recollective and explanatory powers reaching all places, able to please beings according to their mentalities; they gain entry into the realm of reality reaching all places, able to enter all worlds in a single pore; they attain entry into bodies reaching all places, able to enter the bodies of all beings in the body of one being; they attain universal perception of the ages reaching all places, in each age always seeing all the Buddhas; they attain instantaneous universal perception reaching all places, moment to moment seeing all the Buddhas appear before them. When great enlightening beings attain dedication reaching all places, they are able to dedicate roots of goodness in this way."

Then the enlightening being Diamond Banner, empowered by the Buddhas, looked over the ten directions and said,

> To all internal and external worlds
> Enlightening beings have no attachments at all,
> Yet do not abandon works beneficial to sentient beings:
> The great ones cultivate this kind of knowledge.

> In all lands in the ten directions
> They do not depend or dwell on anything;
> They do not grasp things, such as livelihood,
> And do not arbitrarily create distinctions.

> They deal with all sentient beings
> In all worlds in the ten directions;
> Observing their essential nature has no existence,
> They practice dedication reaching everywhere.

Dealing with all compounded and uncompounded things,
They do not entertain errant thoughts about them,
Or in regard to anything in the world:
The Lamps that Illumine the World are aware in this way.

The works carried out by enlightening beings
Are different in superior, middling, and lower grades;
In all of them they dedicate roots of goodness
To all the Buddhas of the ten directions.

Enlightening beings, by dedication, reach transcendence,
Accomplishing what they learn from the Buddhas;
They always think well based on subtle knowledge
And embody the best of human qualities.

Their pure roots of goodness they universally dedicate
To help the deluded, never abandoning them:
They enable all sentient beings to become
Unexcelled lamps that illumine the world.

They never conceptualize sentient beings
Nor think of things with false imagination;
Though in the world, they have no attachments,
Yet also do not abandon conscious creatures.

Enlightening beings always enjoy tranquil nullity
By following which they attain the realm of nirvana;
Yet they do not abandon the realm of sentient beings:
They have attained such subtle knowledge.

Enlightening beings do not conceptualize actions
And do not grasp their results:
All worlds are born from conditions—
Things cannot be seen apart from causality.

Deeply entering such realms,
They do not create vain discriminations therein:
The tamers of all sentient beings
Herein understand skilled dedication.

"What is great enlightening beings' dedication of inexhaustible treasuries of virtue? Here they dedicate the roots of goodness produced by repentance and removal of hindrances caused by past actions, the roots of goodness produced by paying respect to all Buddhas, the roots of goodness produced by requesting all Buddhas to teach, the roots of goodness produced by listening to Buddhas' teaching, diligently practic- ing it, and realizing the vast realm of the inconceivable, the roots of goodness produced by rejoicing at the virtues of all Buddhas and all sentient beings of the past, future, and present, the roots of goodness of all Buddhas, the roots of goodness achieved by the dilligent practice of infinite enlightening beings, the roots of goodness produced by enlight- ening beings knowing of and rejoicing in the Buddhas of all times attaining true enlightenment, teaching the truth, and taming sentient beings, the roots of goodness in rejoicing at the Buddhas of all times cultivating enlightening practice from their first inspiration, attaining supreme true awakening, finally appearing to enter ultimate extinction, and, after their extinction, the true teaching remaining in the world until passing away; thus enlightening beings think of the inexplicable realm of the Buddhas as well as their own realm and the unhindered realm of enlightenment—such tremendous, innumerable different roots of goodness, all they accumulate, all they believe in, all they rejoice in, all they fulfill, all they accomplish, all they practice, all they attain, all they are aware of, all they embody, all they develop, they dedicate to adorn all the buddha-lands, like the realm of action of all the Buddhas in all worlds in boundless eons of the past—that is, incalculable, innu- merable systems of buddha-worlds, known to the knowledge of Buddhas, perceived by enlightening beings, sensed by the great mind, issuing from and drawn forth by pure actions adorning buddha-fields, arising in response to sentient beings, created by the sublime practices of the enlightening being Universally Good, in which all the Buddhas become enlightened and manifest various autonomous spiritual powers—and like the purely adorned buddha-lands which will be attained upon enlightenment by the Buddhas throughout the future, pervading the cosmos, boundless, borderless, endless, infinite, all born of the knowl- edge of the Buddhas, adorned by innumerable beautiful treasures— ornaments of all fragrances, all flowers, all raiment, all treasuries of worthy qualities, all powers of Buddhas, and the embellishments of all buddha-lands; the capitals of the enlightened ones, inhabited by incon- ceivable pure communities of people with existing affinity through similar practices who will attain true enlightenment in the future, developed by all the Buddhas, imperceptible to the world, visible only to the pure eyes of enlightening beings. These enlightening beings have great powers and have planted roots of goodness in the past; knowing all things are like phantoms and illusions, they cultivate the pure deeds of enlightening beings, entering absorption in inconceivable freedom, and with skill in means can perform the work of Buddhas, emanate the light of Buddhas and illumine the world everywhere without limit. All the Buddhas of the present also adorn worlds in this way, with bound- less forms, lights, and colors, all made by virtues: innumerable fragrances, innumerable jewels, innumerable trees, innumerable ornaments, innu- merable palaces, innumerable sounds, associates in accord with affinities from the past, manifesting adornments of all worthy qualities, without end—adornments of all fragrances, garlands, powdered incenses, jewels, pennants, multicolored streamers of precious silk, balustrades of jewels, countless ornaments of gold nets, rivers, clouds and rain, and music, innumerable such embellishments adorning the buddha-lands in all worlds throughout space, created by various deeds, known to the Buddhas and told of by the Buddhas: that is, buddha-lands of adornments, buddha-lands of purity, buddha-lands of equanimity, buddha-lands of subtle refinements, buddha-lands of magnificent virtue, buddha-lands of immensity, buddha-lands of peace and bliss, buddha-lands of indestructibility, buddha-lands of inexhaustibility, buddha-lands of infinity, buddha-lands of imperturbability, buddha-lands of fearlessness, buddha-lands of light, buddha-lands free from opposition, buddha-lands of delight, buddha-lands of all-illumining brightness, buddha-lands of splendor, buddha-lands of refined beauty, buddha-lands of wonderful skill, preeminent, excellent, extraordinary, supreme, absolutely supreme, surpassing, unexcelled, peerless, incomparable, indescribable buddha-lands. To emulate these adornments of all the buddha-lands of past, future, and present, the great enlightening beings willingly dedicate their own roots of goodness to adorn a world in the same way, with the pure adornments of the lands of all Buddhas of past, future, and present, to produce, purify, gather, manifest, array, and maintain all adornments like those of the lands of all Buddhas, and to do the same for all worlds throughout the space of the cosmos, that they be replete with the various adornments of the lands of the Buddhas of all times.

"Great enlightening beings also dedicate roots of goodness in this way: 'May all the buddha-lands I cultivate be filled with great enlightening beings who are truly genuine, with comprehensive knowledge, able to distinguish all worlds and sentient beings, to enter deeply into the realm of reality as well as the realm of space, who cast off folly and perfect the recollection of the Buddhas, recollection of the truth of the teaching, recollection of the infinity of the community, omnipresent everywhere, and who also remember equanimity, their sun of truth full and round, their light of knowledge illumining everywhere, seeing without obstruction, born from nonacquisition, producing all aspects of Buddhahood, possessed of myriad supreme roots of goodness, engendering the determination of unexcelled enlightenment, abiding in the powers of Buddhas, heading for omniscience, destroying the works of demons, purifying the realm of sentient beings, entering deeply into the essential nature of things, forever getting rid of delusion, bringing all roots of goodness and great vows to fruition—may such enlightening beings fill those lands, born in such places, having such virtues, always performing the work of buddhahood, attaining the pure light of complete enlightenment, possessed of knowledge of the realm of reality, manifesting the power of spiritual faculties, filling all realms with one body, attaining great knowledge and wisdom, entering the sphere of omniscience, able to distinguish infinite, boundless expressions and meanings of realms of phenomena and principles, having no attachments in any land, yet able to appear in all buddha-lands, their minds like space, not relying on anything, yet able to distinguish all realms of phenomena and principles, able to enter and emerge from inconceivable profound concentrations, intent on omniscience, dwelling in the buddha-fields, attaining the power of buddhahood, expounding countless truths without fear, conforming to the roots of goodness of Buddhas of all times, totally illumining the cosmos of truth of all enlightened ones, able to accept and hold all Buddhas' teachings, knowing countless ways of speaking, able to enunciate inconceivably many different sounds, entering the unsurpassed stage of freedom of the Buddhas, traveling throughout all worlds in the ten directions without hindrance, practicing noncontention and nonreliance, not falsely discriminating anything, cultivating, practicing, and enlarging the determination for enlightenment, attaining knowledge of skill in means, of expression and meanings, able to explain and expound them step-by-step. I vow to cause such enlightening beings to adorn those lands, distributed throughout, living in peace and accord, well cultivated, extremely well cultivated, pure, extremely pure, calm and serene. May there be, in each and every region of one buddha-land infinitely many such great enlightening beings filling it, and may all buddha-lands throughout space, throughout the cosmos, all be filled with great enlightening beings in the same way.'

"Great enlightening beings expediently dedicate all roots of goodness to all buddha-lands, to all enlightening beings, to all Buddhas, to the enlightenment of all Buddhas, to all great vows, to all essential ways of emancipation, to purifying all realms of sentient beings, to always seeing the Buddhas appear in all worlds, to always seeing the life of the enlightened ones as infinite, and to always seeing the Buddhas pervading the cosmos turning the unimpeded, nonregressing wheel of teaching.

"When great enlightening beings dedicate roots of goodness in this way, because they enter all buddha-lands, all buddha-lands are purified; because they reach all realms of sentient beings, all enlightening beings are purified; because they will the appearance of Buddhas in all buddha-lands, in all buddha-lands in all universes the embodiments of the enlightened transcendentally manifest.

"By means of such peerless dedication great enlightening beings proceed toward omniscience, their minds broad and vast as space, without any limitations; entering inconceivability, they know all actions and the resulting consequences are null, so their minds are always equanimous. Having no bounds, they are able to enter all realms of reality.

"When great enlightening beings practice dedication in this way, they do not conceive of self or possessions, do not conceive of Buddha or

Buddha teaching, do not conceive of lands or adornment, do not conceive of sentient beings or civilization, do not conceive of action or results of action; they do not cling to thought or what is produced by thought, they do not deny cause and effect, they do not grasp things, they do not grasp principles, they do not say birth and death has mentation, they do not say nirvana is eternal tranquility, they do not say the enlightened realize buddhahood—there is not the slightest thing that coexists with reality.

"When great enlightening beings practice dedication in this way, they give all roots of goodness over to sentient beings, to assure their development of maturation, teaching and edifying them impartially, without mental images, without objectification, without assessment, without falsehood, avoiding all vain discrimination and conceptual clinging.

"Once great enlightening beings have made this dedication, they attain inexhaustible roots of goodness: that is, they attain inexhaustible roots of goodness because they keep all enlightening beings in mind; they attain inexhaustible roots of goodness because they purify the buddha-lands; they attain inexhaustible roots of goodness because they purify all realms of sentient beings; they attain inexhaustible roots of goodness because they delve deeply into the realm of reality; they attain inexhaustible roots of goodness because they cultivate immeasurable minds equal to the realm of space; they attain inexhaustible roots of goodness because they profoundly understand the realm of all Buddhas; they attain inexhaustible roots of goodness because they diligently cultivate the work of enlightening beings; they attain inexhaustible roots of goodness because they comprehend the past, present, and future.

"When great enlightening beings dedicate all roots of goodness in this way, they understand that all realms of sentient beings have no sentient beings; they understand that all things have no life; they know that all things have no creator; they realize all things have no personality; they comprehend that all things have no conflict; they see that all things come from conditions and have no abode; they know all things have no basis; they know all lands have no location; they observe that enlightening beings' practices also have no locus; they see that all objects have no existence.

"When great enlightening beings practice such dedication, their eyes ultimately never see impure buddha-lands, nor do they see sentient beings of differing characteristics; there is not the slightest thing entered by knowledge, nor the slightest knowledge entering things. They understand the body of the Enlightened is not like empty space, because it is perfected by all virtues and infinite sublime qualities, and because in all places it causes sentient beings to accumulate a sufficiency of roots of goodness.

"These great enlightening beings moment to moment attain unspeakably unspeakable numbers of stages of the ten powers, are filled with all virtues, fully develop pure roots of goodness, and are fields of blessings for all sentient beings. These great enlightening beings develop treasuries of virtues like wish-fulfilling jewels, obtaining all comforts as needed, able to adorn all lands wherever they go, purifying untold numbers of sentient beings wherever they go, because of embracing virtue, cultivating and mastering the practices.

"When great enlightening beings practice dedication in this way, they cultivate the practices of all enlightening beings, their virtues are extraordinary, their appearance is incomparable, their spiritual force and radiance surpass all worldlings, so that demons and demonic people cannot look upon them. Their roots of goodness are complete, their great vows are accomplished, their minds ever broadening, equal to the omniscient. In a single moment of attention they can pervade innumerable buddha-lands. The power of their knowledge is immeasurable, and they have arrived at the sphere of all Buddhas. They have profound faith in all Buddhas, and abide in boundless knowledge, the power of their will for enlightenment as vast as the cosmos, as ultimate as space.

"When great enlightening beings abide in this dedication, they attain ten inexhaustible treasuries: they attain an inexhaustible treasury of seeing Buddhas, because in a single pore they see countless Buddhas appearing in the world; they attain an inexhaustible treasury of entry into truth, because by the power of Buddha-knowledge they see all things in one truth; they attain an inexhaustible treasury of memory, because they retain the teachings expounded by all Buddhas without forgetting any; they attain an inexhaustible treasury of certain wisdom, because they know the secret techniques in the teachings expounded by all Buddhas; they attain an inexhaustible treasury of understanding meaning and intent, because they know the distinctions of principles of the teachings; they attain an inexhaustible treasury of boundless realization, because they comprehend all things of all times by means of spacelike knowledge; they attain an inexhaustible treasury of felicitous virtues, because they satisfy the wishes of all sentient beings without end; they attain an inexhaustible treasury of intrepid knowledge and awareness, because they are able to remove and destroy all sentient beings' blinders of ignorance and folly; they attain an inexhaustible treasury of definitive powers of elucidation, because they expound the impartial teaching of all Buddhas so that all sentient beings understand; they attain an inexhaustible treasury of the ten powers and four fearlessnesses, because they fulfill all practices of enlightening beings, wrap their heads in the turban of nondefilement, and arrive at an unobstructed omniscience. When great enlightening beings dedicate all roots of goodness, they attain these ten inexhaustible treasuries."

Then the enlightening being Diamond Banner looked over the ten directions and said in verse,

Enlightening beings perfect profound mental power,
Attaining mastery of all the teachings;
The blessings of their petitions and appreciation
They dedicate by unimpeded means.

The enlightened ones of past, present, and future
Beautify buddha-lands throughout the cosmos:
Enlightening beings, fulfilling all virtues,
Dedicate them to purify lands the same way.

The teachings of Buddhas of all times
Enlightening beings ponder carefully,
Taking them all into their minds,
Thereby adorning the buddha-lands.

Be the virtues of all buddha-lands extolled
Throughout all eons of past, present, and future,
The eons of all time may be exhausted
But the virtues of buddha-lands have no end.

All such buddha-lands
Do enlightening beings see:
Therewith is adorned one buddha-land
And all buddha-lands, this way.

There are Buddha-children whose minds are pure,
All born by transformation from the enlightening teaching,
With all virtues adorning their minds,
Who fill all buddha-lands.

Those enlightening beings all are endowed
With bodies adorned with infinite signs of greatness;
With powers of clarification their teaching fills the world,
Inexhaustible as the ocean.

Enlightening beings sojourn in many concentrations
And have fulfilled all necessary practices;
Their minds are pure beyond compare
And their light illumines all worlds.

Thus are all buddha-lands
Filled with such enlightening beings:
They've never thought of the listeners' vehicle
Or sought the individual illuminates' way.

Thus are enlightening beings pure of heart,
Dedicating virtues to all living beings,
Wanting to cause all to become truly enlightened
And fully know the Buddha's truths.

All demons and enemies in the ten directions
The enlightening beings' awesome power subdues;
Their intrepid knowledge and wisdom are invincible
As they practice with certainty the ultimate way.

Due to enlightening beings' great will power
Their dedications cannot be hindered;
They enter the inexhaustible treasury of virtue
Which is forever endless, throughout all time.

Enlightening beings observe all conditioned things
And understand their nature is not independent;
Thus knowing the nature of things is like this
They don't wrongly grasp acts or results.

There are no things with form, nor formless things;
Nor are there concepts of being or nonbeing;
Existence and nonexistence—neither exist;
They realize all are ungraspable.

All things are born of causes and conditions—
Their essential nature is neither existent or nonexistent;
And in causes and conditions, what they produce
They ultimately have no attachments at all.

Of what all sentient beings say
They ultimately don't grasp anything;
They know names and signs are all mentation
And clearly understand things are identityless.

As the nature of sentient beings is fundamentally null,
So do they know all things are null;
All things in past, present, and future,
Lands and deeds—all are equal.

Such knowledge do they dedicate,
Virtous action born according to their understanding:
The signs of these virtues too they understand thus,
That there's nothing to grasp therein.

Thus their mind of dedication's unsullied;
Never calculating the nature of things,
Comprehending their nature is not a nature,
They do not dwell in the world yet do not leave it.

The good works which they do
They dedicate to all living beings,
Not failing to realize their true nature,
Abandoning discrimination.

All the false views there are
They abandon entirely;
Free from inflaming afflictions, always cool,
They abide in the unobstructed state of liberation.

Enlightening beings do not destroy anything
Or annihilate the nature of things:
They understand all things are like echoes
And have no attachment to them at all.

They know all sentient beings of all times
Come from combinations of causes and conditions:
They also know their inclinations and habits
And never annihilate anything.

They realize the nature of actions is not action
And yet do not contradict the characteristics of things,
And they do not destroy the results of deeds,
But explain the nature of things as conditional.

They understand sentient beings have no birth
And there are no sentient beings to transmigrate:
There are no real sentient beings to speak to,
But according to conventional norms they provisionally teach.

"What is great enlightening beings' dedication causing all roots of goodness to endure? Here the enlightening beings may be rulers of great nations, their virtue extending to all, their fame shaking the world; their enemies all submit to them, and their commands are all based on correct principles. They hold a single canopy that gives shade to all quarters, and travel everywhere as leaders of the land, unobstructed wherever they turn, tying on the turban of nondefilement. They are sovereign masters of the law, and all who see them submit. They do not torture or punish people, yet all obey, moved by their virtue. They deal with sentient beings with liberality, kind words, beneficial actions, and cooperation; as universal rulers, they provide for everyone.

"Enlightening beings, abiding in such sovereign virtues, have a great retinue; they cannot be undermined, they are rid of all faults. No one ever tires of seeing them; adorned with felicitous virtues, their marks of greatness and embellishments are fully developed. Their bodies and limbs are well proportioned, and they have robust, healthy, ideal human bodies. Their great strength is consummate and they cannot be constrained or overcome by anyone. They attain pure action and are free from all barriers caused by actions.

"They fully practice all giving; sometimes they give food and drink, sometimes they give delicacies, sometimes they give conveyances, or clothing, or flower garlands, or incenses and perfumes, beds, seats, houses, lamps, medicines, precious vessels, jeweled carriages, trained elephants and horses, all magnificently adorned—they give all these gladly. If any come and ask for their throne, or canopies or parasols, banners, pennants, treasures, or other adornments, or the jeweled crowns on their heads, or the radiant jewels in their topknots, or even the rank of ruler itself, they begrudge nothing. If they see sentient beings in prison, they give up their treasures, their spouses, children, retinue, and even their own bodies, to rescue them and free them. If they see prisoners about to be executed, they give up their bodies in exchange for those prisoners' lives. Then again, if they see anyone come begging from them, begging for even their flesh or hair, they gladly give them ungrudgingly; their eyes, ears, noses, tongues, teeth, heads, hands, feet, blood, flesh, bones, marrow, internal organs, skin, fingers, toes, and nails, all they give with a joyful heart.

"In their quest for teachings they have never heard they would hurl themselves into pits of fire. In order to preserve the true teaching of the Buddhas they would endure all kinds of pain. In seeking the teaching, for even one word of it they can give up everything within the four seas. They continually civilize and guide sentient beings by means of right teaching, causing them to cultivate good practices and abandon evil. If they see sentient beings physically harming others, they kindly rescue them and cause them to give up wrongdoing.

"If they see Buddhas attain supreme enlightenment, they praise them, causing everyone to hear and know of them. They may donate land and provide for and attend to them. They may give their own bodies to those who ask, or they may give them to the Buddhas. Because of their quest for the truth they are extremely joyful; they provide service and support for sentient beings. They might give up their kingship, their cities, towns, villages, palaces, gardens and groves, spouses, children, and retinues, fulfilling all requests. Sometimes they give away all necessities of life to establish great assemblies of giving, from which none are prohibited, and provide for the needs of all the sentient beings who come—all kinds of fields of blessings—whether they come from afar or nearby, whether they are intelligent or stupid, no matter what they look like, whether they are male or female, whether human or nonhuman, their mental patterns different, their requirements each different; the enlightening give to all to satisfy everyone.

"When enlightening beings give in this way, they develop a mind of good control, with which they practice dedication: controlling the body well, controlling sensation, conception, action, and consciousness well, controlling sovereignty well, controlling followers well, controlling means of subsistence well, controlling generous giving well, they accordingly cause all roots of goodness to be firm and enduring.

"Whatever great enlightening beings give, their charity being boundless, they dedicate those roots of goodness in this way: when they give fine food to sentient beings, their minds are pure and have no covetousness or attachment to what they give, nor do they begrudge anything; they practice giving fully, praying that all sentient beings gain the food of knowledge and wisdom, their minds unobstructed, comprehending the nature of food and having no greed or attachment, only enjoying the food of truth and the food of emancipation, filled with knowledge and wisdom, firmly abiding by the truth, embodying roots of goodness, with the body of reality and the body of knowledge traveling in purity; taking pity on sentient beings, to be fields of blessing they appear to take solid food. This is great enlightening beings' dedication of good roots when they give food.

"When great enlightening beings give something to drink, they dedicate these roots of goodness in this way: they pray that all sentient beings drink of the water of the flavor of truth, diligently cultivate the whole way of enlightening beings, cut off thirst for the world, always seek enlightened knowledge, leave the realm of desire, attain the joy and bliss of truth, produce their bodies from the pure teaching, always tune and control their minds by means of concentration, enter the ocean of knowledge, produce great clouds of teaching, shower great rain of teaching. This is great enlightening beings' dedication of roots of goodness when they give things to drink.

"Great enlightening beings give various flavors—pungent, sour, salty, bland, as well as sweet, various flavors, rich, able to cause the body's elements to be settled and harmonious, the skin and body well developed, the energy strong, the heart clear and pure and always joyful; not causing vomiting when eaten, making the senses clear and sharp, the internal organs fully developed and impervious to poison and disease, without distress, forever attaining comfort. These roots of goodness they dedicate in this way: 'May all sentient beings gain the supreme flavor of ambrosia; may all sentient beings obtain the flavor of the knowledge of truth, and comprehend the function of all flavors; may all sentient beings obtain the flavor of infinite truths, know the realm of reality, and abide at peace in the great citadel of truth in ultimate reality; may all sentient beings produce great clouds of teachings throughout the cosmos, shower the rain of truth everywhere, teach, edify, and civilize all sentient beings; may all sentient beings gain the flavor of supreme knowledge, that the unexcelled joy of truth fill their minds and bodies; may all sentient beings obtain all the excellent flavors of nonattachment, and not be addicted to mundane tastes, but always diligently cultivate and practice all aspects of buddhahood; may all sentient beings gain the flavor of one truth and realize that all Buddha teachings are without difference; may all sentient beings gain the flavor of supreme victory and ride on omniscience, never turning back; may all sentient beings gain the flavor of entry into the truth of the nondifference of all Buddhas, and be able to distinguish all faculties; may all sentient beings attain increase of the savor of the teaching and always be able to fulfill the Buddhas' teaching of nonobstruction.' This is the great enlightening beings' dedication of roots of goodness when giving flavorings, to cause all sentient beings to cultivate virtue and all be fully endowed with the body of unobstructed knowledge.

"When great enlightening beings give conveyances, they dedicate the roots of goodness in this way: 'May all sentient beings gain the vehicle of complete omniscience, and ride in the Great Vehicle, the indestructible vehicle, the supreme vehicle, the highest vehicle, the swift vehicle, the vehicle of great power, the vehicle replete with virtue, the vehicle leaving mundanity, the vehicle that produces the innumerable enlightening beings.' This is the great enlightening beings' dedication of roots of goodness when giving conveyances.

"When great enlightening beings give clothing, they dedicate the roots of goodness in this way: 'May all sentient beings gain the raiment of shame and conscience wherewith to cover their bodies; may they give up the erroneous practice of heretics who expose their bodies; may their color be lustrous and their skin fine and soft; may they attain the foremost bliss of the Buddhas, and attain the most pure comprehensive knowledge of ways of liberation.' This is great enlightening beings' dedication of roots of goodness when giving clothing.

"Great enlightening beings are constantly giving out various fine flowers—flowers of subtle fragrance, flowers of various colors, innumerable extraordinary flowers, beautiful flowers, delightful flowers, flowers of all seasons, celestial flowers, flowers of the human world, highly prized flowers, extremely fragrant and delightful flowers—innumerable such fine flowers they offer to living Buddhas and to the shrines of extinct Buddhas, to those who expound the teaching, to mendicants, to all enlightening beings, to good teachers, to Buddhist disciples, to self-enlightened ones, to parents, relatives, even themselves, as well as to all the poor and destitute. When they give, they dedicate the roots of goodness in this way: 'May all sentient beings attain the flowers of concentration of the Buddhas, able to cause all the teachings to bloom; may all sentient beings become as pleasing and endlessly delightful to all they meet, as the Buddhas are; may all sentient beings be satisfied by what they see, and be free from disturbance and agitation; may all sentient beings fully carry out far-reaching pure works; may all sentient beings always remember good associates, their minds unchanging; may all sentient beings be like all-curing medicine, able to remove the toxins of all afflictions; may all sentient beings fulfill great vows and all get to be rulers of unexcelled knowledge; may all sentient beings, with the light of the sun of knowledge and wisdom, destroy the darkness of ignorance and folly; may all sentient beings' pure moon of enlightenment wax full; may all sentient beings enter the land of great treasures, meet true knowers, and fully develop all roots of goodness.' This is the great enlightening beings' dedication of roots of goodness when giving flowers, to cause sentient beings to all attain pure, unobstructed knowledge.

"When great enlightening beings give garlands, they dedicate the roots of goodness in this way: 'May all sentient beings be a pleasure for all people to behold, so that all who see them admire them, all who see them feel friendly toward them, all who see them like them, all who see them look up to them, all who see them are relieved of anxiety, all who see them become joyful, all who see them give up evil, all who see them may always approach the Buddhas, and all who see them are purified and attain omniscience.' This is the great enlightening beings' dedication of roots of goodness when giving garlands.

"When great enlightening beings give incense, they dedicate the roots of goodness in this way: 'May all sentient beings be filled with the fragrance of morality, and attain to the standards of not being heedless, not being impure, not being defiled, having nothing to regret, becoming free from bondage, being unfrenzied, nontransgression, nonextremism, emancipation from the world, and the transcendent ways of enlightening beings. May all sentient beings, by these precepts, all accomplish the body of morality of all Buddhas.' This is great enlightening beings' dedication of roots of goodness when giving incense, in order to cause sentient beings all to be able to complete the body of unobstructed morality.

"When great enlightening beings give perfumes, they dedicate the roots of goodness in this way: 'May all sentient beings be perfumed with the fragrance of generosity, able to give whatever they have. May all sentient beings be perfumed with the fragrance of morality, attaining the ultimately pure morality of the enlightened. May all sentient beings be perfumed with the fragrance of tolerance, giving up all harmful intentions. May all sentient beings be perfumed with the fragrance of energy, always wearing the armor of heroic effort of the great vehicle. May all sentient beings be perfumed with the fragrance of concentration, abiding peacefully in the concentration in which the Buddhas appear to them. May all sentient beings be perfumed with the fragrance of wisdom, in a single moment becoming sovereigns of unexcelled knowledge. May all sentient beings be perfumed with the fragrance of truth, attaining fearlessness in the highest teaching. May all sentient beings be perfumed with the fragrance of virtue, developing all knowledge of great merit and virtue. May all sentient beings be perfumed with the fragrance of enlightenment, attain the ten powers of buddhahood, and reach the other shore. May all sentient beings be perfumed with the sublime fragrance of pure ways and forever annihilate all bad qualities.' This is great enlightening beings' dedication of roots of goodness when giving perfumes.

"When great enlightening beings give couches, they dedicate the roots of goodness in this way: 'May all sentient beings obtain celestial couches and realize great knowledge and wisdom; may all sentient beings obtain the couch of sages, give up the mentality of ordinary men and abide in the aspiration for enlightenment; may all sentient beings obtain the couch of peace and happiness, forever parting from all the pains and afflictions of birth and death; may all sentient beings obtain the couch of the ultimate and get to see the autonomous spiritual powers of the Buddhas; may all sentient beings obtain the couch of equanimity, and always cultivate all good ways; may all sentient beings obtain the couch of supremacy and fulfill pure action which has no peer in the world; may all sentient beings obtain the couch of tranquility, realize the truth and reach ultimate reality; may all sentient beings obtain the couch of purity, and cultivate the Buddha's sphere of pure knowledge; may all sentient beings obtain the couch of security and have the constant protection of good teachers; may all sentient beings obtain the couch of lions and lie on their right sides the way Buddhas do.' This is the great enlightening beings' dedication of roots of goodness when giving couches.

"When great enlightening beings give rooms and shelters, they dedicate the roots of goodness in this way: 'May all sentient beings gain peaceful residence in pure buddha-lands and diligently cultivate all virtues, abide peacefully in the realm of profound concentration and give up all attachment to dwelling places, realize all dwelling places have no existence, detach from all worlds, abide in omniscience, take in the abodes of all Buddhas, live in the abode of peace and comfort of the ultimate path, always rest on supremely pure roots of goodness, and never leave the unexcelled abode of the Buddhas.' This is great enlightening beings' dedication of roots of goodness when giving shelters, because they wish to benefit all sentient beings and think of how to help them out according to their needs.

"When great enlightening beings give places to live, they dedicate the roots of goodness in this way: 'May all sentient beings obtain what is really good for them, that their minds be happy and at peace; may all sentient beings live according to the Buddha, according to great knowledge, according to good teachers, according to what is most worthy of respect, according to good actions, according to great kindness, according to great compassion, according to the six ways of transcendence, according to the great determination for enlightenment, and according to the path of all enlightening beings.' This is great enlightening beings' dedication of roots of goodness when giving places to live, because they want to cause everyone's virtue, ultimate state, knowledge, path, principles, morality, aspirations, faith, vows, and all qualities of spiritual faculties, to be pure.

"When great enlightening beings give lamps—butter lamps, oil lamps, jewel lamps, crystal lamps, lacquer lamps, fire lamps, aloe lamps, sandalwood lamps, lamps of all fragrances, lamps with lights of infinite colors—when they give innumerable such lamps, in order to benefit all sentient beings, to include all sentient beings, they dedicate the roots of goodness in this way: 'May all sentient beings attain infinite light and illumine the true teachings of all Buddhas; may all sentient beings attain pure light, and clearly perceive the most subtle and minute forms in the world; may all sentient beings attain unclouded light, and realize that the realms of sentient beings are empty, without existence; may all sentient beings attain boundless light, so their bodies emit subtle radiance illumining everything; may all sentient beings attain all-illuminating light, and their minds never retreat from the teachings of the Buddhas; may all sentient beings attain the pure light of Buddhas, appearing in all lands; may all sentient beings attain unobstructed light, one light illumining everything in the cosmos; may all sentient beings attain uninterrupted light, illuminating the buddha-lands, the light unbroken; may all sentient beings attain the light of the banner of knowledge, illumining the world; may all sentient beings attain light of infinite colors, shining on all fields and manifesting spiritual powers.' Thus enlightening beings, when they give lamps, wishing to benefit all sentient beings, to give peace and happiness to all sentient beings, follow all sentient beings by these roots of goodness, embrace all sentient beings by these roots of goodness, distribute to all sentient beings these roots of goodness, treat all sentient beings kindly by these roots of goodness, satisfy all sentient beings by these roots of goodness, take care of all sentient beings by these roots of goodness, rescue all sentient beings by these roots of goodness, focus their minds on sentient beings by these roots of goodness, equally benefit all sentient beings by these roots of goodness, and observe all sentient beings by these roots of goodness. This is great enlightening beings' dedication of roots of goodness when giving lamps. They dedicate thus without hindrance, causing sentient beings to dwell on roots of goodness.

"When enlightening beings give medicines, they dedicate the roots of goodness in this way: 'May all sentient beings attain ultimate emancipation from all shrouds and bonds; may all sentient beings forever be rid of the body of sickness and attain the body of the enlightened; may all sentient beings become great medicines themselves, annihilating the sickness of all that is not good; may all sentient beings perfect the medicine that relieves all illness and abide securely in the enlightening beings' stage of nonregression; may all sentient beings develop the medicines of enlightenment and be able to extract the poison arrows of all afflictions; may all sentient beings draw near to worthies and sages, annihilate afflictions, and cultivate pure practices; may all sentient beings become great physicians, forever eliminating all illnesses and not letting them recur; may all sentient beings be indestructible trees of medicine, able to cure all sentient beings; may all sentient beings attain the light of omniscience and remove the myriad arrows of sickness; may all sentient beings know how to formulate worldly medicines, to cure the illnesses there.' When great enlightening beings give medicines, they dedicate the roots of goodness in this way to cause all sentient beings to be forever free from sicknesses, to be ultimately at ease, to be ultimately pure, to be free from illusion like the Buddha, to remove the arrows of all sicknesses, to attain an inexhaustible, healthy body, to attain an indestructible body, to attain a strong body, to attain the complete comfort of Buddhahood, which cannot be taken away, and to attain the independent, strong body of all Buddhas.

"Great enlightening beings are able to generously give all kinds of vessels—gold vessels filled with jewels, silver vessels filled with jewels, lapis lazuli vessels filled with various precious substances, glass vessels filled with innumerable jewel ornaments, mother-of-pearl vessels filled with red pearls, agate vessels filled with coral, white jade vessels filled with myriad delicacies, sandalwood vessels filled with celestial raiment, diamond vessels filled with myriad sublime fragrances—countless precious vessels of all kinds, filled with innumerable various treasures; they give them to Buddhas, because they believe the Buddhas' field of blessings is inconceivable; they give to enlightening beings, because they know that wise teachers are hard to find; they give to holy mendicants, to cause the Buddha teachings to remain in the world; they give to disciples of Buddhas and to individual illuminates, because they have pure faith in the sages; they give to their parents, out of respect; they give to their teachers and predecessors, that they may always teach, to induce the cultivation of virtues in accord with the injunctions of the sages; they give to the lowly, poor, and destitute, because they regard all sentient beings equally with the loving eye of great benevolence and compassion; they give out of devotion to fulfillment of the transcendent generosity of all enlightening beings of past, present, and future; they give everything to everyone, because they never reject sentient beings. When they give in this way, they have no attachment to the gift or the receiver.

"When great enlightening beings give various precious vessels filled with innumerable precious things like this, they dedicate the roots of goodness in this way: 'May all sentient beings become vessels equal to the boundless receptacle of space, with vast recollective power able to absorb and retain all worldly and transmundane scriptures, without forgetting anything; may all sentient beings become vessels of purity, able to understand the extremely profound true teaching of the Buddhas; may all sentient beings become vessels of unexcelled jewels, able to receive and hold the teachings of Buddhas of all times; may all sentient beings become vast vessels of teaching of the enlightened, with indestructible faith taking in the methods of enlightenment of the Buddhas of all times; may all sentient beings become vessels adorned by supreme treasures, abiding in the most powerful will for enlightenment; may all sentient beings become vessels which are receptacles of virtue, developing pure faith in the infinite knowledge and wisdom of the enlightened; may all sentient beings become the vessel of approach and entry into omniscience and ultimately attain the unhindered liberation of the enlightened; may all sentient beings become vessels of enlightening practices throughout the future, able to cause sentient beings to all abide securely in the power of omniscience; may all sentient beings become vessels of the supreme qualities of the family of Buddhas of all times, able to receive and retain what is said by the Buddhas in their sublime voices; may all sentient beings become vessels containing the congregations and enlightenment scenes of all Buddhas of all worlds throughout the space of the cosmos, becoming great human beings, leaders in praising the Buddhas and requesting them to turn the wheel of true teaching.' This is great enlightening beings' dedication of roots of goodness when giving vessels, because they want to cause all sentient beings to be able to complete the vessel of the practice and vows of the Universally Good enlightening being.

"Great enlightening beings give various chariots, adorned with jewels, to the Buddhas, to enlightening beings, teachers, worthy companions, disciples of Buddhas and individual illuminates, and innumerable various such fields of blessings, including the poor and destitute. Of these people, some come from afar, some come from nearby; some come because they have heard of the enlightening beings, some come because of affinities with the enlightening beings, some come because they have heard of the vow of generosity which the enlightening beings made in the past, some come at the request of the enlightening beings themselves. At such a time, the enlightening beings may give jeweled chariots or gold chariots, all beautifully adorned, covered with nets of chimes, with precious streamers trailing; they may give chariots of the finest lapis lazuli, decorated with countless rareties; they may give silver chariots, covered with golden nets, drawn by swift horses; they may give chariots adorned with countless mixed jewels, covered with jewel nets, drawn by elephants; they may give sandalwood chariots, with wheels of sublime jewels, canopies of mixed jewels, with lion seats of jewels set out in fine arrays with a hundred thousand girls sitting in rows thereon, the carts driven by a hundred thousand strong men; or they may give chariots of clear crystal, decorated with mixtures of gems, filled with beautiful women, covered with jeweled curtains, with banners and pennants on the sides; they may give chariots of stores of agate, embellished with all precious substances, perfumed with various fragrances, adorned with all kinds of beautiful flowers, with a hundred thousand girls holding jewel ornaments, the carts pulled by steeds equally well-trained, able to travel over dangerous places with ease; or they may give chariots of solid perfume, with wheels of precious substances, with massive, beautiful adornments, covered with jeweled drapes, trailing jewelled nets, the insides spread with various precious robes, emitting fine, pure, pleasing fragrances, attended by countless celestials as they move along, providing all kinds of precious substances from time to time; they may present chariots of luminous jewels, the beautiful hues of the various jewels thoroughly translucent, covered with nets of many wonderful jewels, with ornaments of mixed jewels hanging down on all sides, sprinkled with powdered incense, fragrant and clean inside and out, with charming men and women riding on them.

"When great enlightening beings present such chariots of myriad beautiful gems to Buddhas, they dedicate the roots of goodness thus: 'May all sentient beings be able to make offerings to the highest field of blessings, give to Buddhas with deep faith, and attain infinite rewards; may all sentient beings turn their whole minds to the Buddha, and always meet infinite pure fields of blessings; may all sentient beings begrudge nothing to the Buddhas, and fully perfect the mind of great relinquishment; may all sentient beings practice giving to the Buddhas, give up the aspirations of the two lesser vehicles, and attain the unobstructed liberation and omniscient knowledge of the Buddhas; may all sentient beings practice endless giving to the Buddhas and enter the knowledge and wisdom of Buddhas, with infinite virtues; may all sentient beings enter the supreme knowledge of Buddhas and be able to become sovereigns of pure, unexcelled knowledge; may all sentient beings attain the Buddhas' spiritual faculty of reaching everywhere without obstruction, and go wherever they wish freely; may all sentient beings enter deeply into the Great Vehicle, attain immeasurable knowledge, and be stabilized therein, imperturbable; may all sentient beings be able to bring forth ways to omniscience and become supreme fields of blessings for humans and celestials; may all sentient beings have no antagonism toward the Buddhas, diligently plant roots of goodness, and happily seek enlightened knowledge; may all sentient beings spontaneously be able to go to all buddha-fields, going throughout the cosmos in a single instant, without tiring; may all sentient beings attain the free spiritual faculties of enlightening beings, distribute their bodies throughout space, approach and make offerings to all Buddhas; may all sentient beings attain the incomparable body, going everywhere in the ten directions, without wearying; may all sentient beings attain a vast body flying swiftly wherever they want to go, never flagging; may all sentient beings attain the ultimate power of freedom of all Buddhas, in a single instant manifesting the Buddhas' spiritual powers and mystic displays throughout space; may all sentient beings cultivate peaceful, blissful practice, following the path of all enlightening beings; may all sentient beings attain speed in action, and consummate the knowledge and spiritual abilities of the ten powers; may all sentient beings enter all lands in the cosmos, annulling the boundaries so they are equal and without distinction; may all sentient beings carry out the practice of universal goodness and wisdom, never retreating, reach the other shore, and attain omniscience; may all sentient beings climb into the vehicle of peerless knowledge and, following the nature of things, see the truth as it really is.' This is the great enlightening beings' dedication of roots of goodness when presenting precious chariots to all Buddhas of the present or to the memorial shrines of Buddhas after they have passed away; this is to cause sentient beings to gain the unobstructed vehicle of ultimate emancipation of the enlightened.

"When great enlightening beings give precious chariots to good teachers such as enlightening beings, they dedicate the roots of goodness in this way: 'May all sentient beings always remember the teachings of the wise and concentrate diligently on preserving them so they may not be lost; may all sentient beings share the same benefits as good teachers, all-inclusive, and have the same roots of goodness; may all sentient beings draw near to good teachers, respect and provide for them, giving up all they have to please them; may all sentient beings develop good aspirations and follow good associates, never leaving them; may all sentient beings always get to meet good teachers, wholeheartedly attend to them, and not oppose their instructions; may all sentient beings like good teachers and never reject them, so there is no alienation, no mixup, and no error; may all sentient beings be able to give themselves to good teachers, following their instructions without opposition; may all sentient beings be accepted by good teachers, cultivate great compassion, and depart from all evils; may all sentient beings follow good teachers and listen to the truths spoken by the Buddhas; may all sentient beings have the same roots of goodness as the teachers, with pure results of action, and practice the same vows as the enlightening beings, ultimately accomplishing the ten powers; may all sentient beings be able to accept and apply the methods of good teachers, and reach the realms of all concentrations, knowledge, wisdom, and spiritual powers; may all sentient beings be able to accept and hold all right teachings, put them into practice, and reach the other shore; may all sentient beings ride in the Great Vehicle, without any hindrance or obstruction, and ultimately complete the path of omniscience; may all sentient beings manage to climb into the vehicle of all knowledge and reach the abode of peace, without ever turning back; may all sentient beings know how to act according to reality, and attain the ultimate of all the Buddha-teachings they hear, never forgetting; may all sentient beings be accepted by the Buddhas and attain unhindered knowledge of ultimate truth; may all sentient beings attain autonomous spiritual powers which never fade away, and be able to go wherever they want to in a single thought; may all sentient beings come and go freely, widely teaching and guiding, causing others to abide in the Great Vehicle; may all sentient beings' acts be fruitful, borne by the vehicle of knowledge to the stage of the ultimate; may all sentient beings gain the vehicle of nonobstruction and reach all places by unimpeded knowledge.' This is great enlightening beings' dedication of roots of goodness when giving various chariots and cars to good teachers; it is to cause sentient beings to be filled with virtues equal to the Buddhas and enlightening beings.

"When great enlightening beings give precious chariots to mendicants, they engender the will to practice all giving, the will to comprehend thoroughly by knowledge, the will to purify virtuous qualities, the mind which accords with relinquishment, the thought that true Buddhist mendicants are hard to meet, a mind of deep faith in the religious community, and the will to uphold right teaching. They abide in supreme aspiration, to an unprecedented degree. They hold great assemblies of giving, producing immeasurably great merit, with profound faith in the Buddha's teaching which cannot be undermined. They dedicate the roots of goodness in this way: 'May all sentient beings enter comprehensively into the Buddha-teachings and keep them in mind; may all sentient beings leave the state of ordinary ignorant people and enter the realm of sages; may all sentient beings quickly enter the ranks of the sages and be able to use the Buddha-teachings to awaken and guide step-by-step; may all sentient beings be respected and trusted by all the world; may all sentient beings enter into the equality of all things and know that the inherent nature of things is nondual; may all sentient beings be born from the realm of enlightened knowledge and be surrounded by docile harmonious people; may all sentient beings abide by the methods for removing defilement, getting rid of the stains of all afflictions; may all sentient beings be able to form a supreme religious community, leave the state of ordinary people and enter the congregation of worthies and sages; may all sentient beings diligently practice good principles, attain unhindered knowledge, and be endowed with sagelike qualities; may all sentient beings attain wisdom, not be attached to the past, present, or future, and be free as kings among the masses; may all sentient beings ride the vehicle of knowledge and wisdom and turn the wheel of right teaching; may all sentient beings be endowed with spiritual faculties and be able to go to innumerable worlds in a single thought; may all sentient beings ride the body of space, their knowledge unobstructed in any world; may all sentient beings enter all congregations of Buddhas throughout cosmic space, and accomplish the foremost practices of transcendence; may all sentient beings attain physical lightness and comfort and extraordinary knowledge and wisdom, and be able to enter all buddha-fields; may all sentient beings attain unbounded skillful power of psychic travel, manifesting their bodies in all lands; may all sentient beings attain a body which relies on nothing at all, appearing everywhere like a reflection, by spiritual faculties; may all sentient beings attain inconceivable autonomous spiritual powers, whereby they appear before those who may be taught, to edify and civilize them; may all sentient beings attain unhindered means of entry into the reality realm, in a single thought traveling throughout all lands in the ten directions.' This is great enlightening beings' dedication of roots of goodness when giving precious chariots to mendicants; it is to cause sentient beings to all ride the vehicle of pure, unsurpassed knowledge, and in all worlds turn the unobstructed wheel of knowledge of truth.

"When great enlightening beings give precious chariots to Buddhist disciples and individual illuminates, they engender these frames of mind: consciousness of fields of blessings; honor and respect; consciousness of oceans of virtues; consciousness of ability to produce virtue and wisdom; consciousness of birth from the power of the virtues of the enlightened; consciousness of myriad eons of cultivation; consciousness of ability to cultivate enlightening practices over innumerable eons; consciousness of escape from the bondage of all delusion; consciousness of destruction of all demons; consciousness of the light of wisdom illumining the unexcelled truth. The roots of goodness in this giving of chariots they dedicate in this way: 'May all sentient beings be supreme fields of blessings, believed in by the world, fulfilling unexcelled transcendent generosity; may all sentient beings give up useless talk, always enjoy solitude, and have no second thoughts; may all sentient beings become most excellent pure fields of blessings, taking in all sentient beings and inducing them to cultivate acts which produce felicity; may all sentient beings become fonts of wisdom and be able to bestow on living beings immeasurable, innumerable rewards of roots of goodness; may all sentient beings persist in unhindered action, fully developing a pure, excellent field of blessings; may all sentient beings abide in noncontention, realizing that all things do nothing and have essencelessness for their essence; may all sentient beings always get to be near the supreme field of blessings, fully cultivating immeasurable virtues; may all sentient beings be able to manifest immeasurable spiritual powers and include all conscious beings in a pure field of blessings; may all sentient beings be endowed with a field of blessings of inexhaustible virtues, able to bestow on beings the ten powers of the enlightened, the fruit of the foremost vehicle; may all sentient beings become fruitful, genuine fields of blessings, and develop the inexhaustible collection of blessings of all knowledge; may all sentient beings attain the way to extinguish wrongdoing, and be able to receive and hold the expressions and meanings of Buddhas' teachings which they have never heard; may all sentient beings always diligently listen to and absorb all Buddha-teachings, and understand everything they hear, so that it is not in vain; may all sentient beings hear the principles of the Buddhas, comprehend their ultimate import, and be able to expound them according to what they have learned; may all sentient beings believe and practice the instructions of the enlightened, and forever give up all the false views of erroneous philosophies; may all sentient beings always see worthies and sages and develop all the most excellent foundations of goodness; may all sentient beings always trust people who act wisely, and associate with and respect the sages; may all sentient beings, hearing the names of Buddhas, not let it go to waste, but all get to see with their eyes those they have heard of; may all sentient beings analyze and know well the right doctrines of the Buddhas, and be able to protect those who hold the Buddha-teaching; may all sentient beings always enjoy listening to all Buddha-teachings, absorb and hold them, read and recite them, expound upon them, illumine them, and comprehend them; may all sentient beings believe and understand the true virtues of the Buddha's teachings, and give whatever they have in respectful offerings.' This is the dedication of roots of goodness of great enlightening beings when giving various chariots and cars to disciples of Buddhas or individual illuminates, to cause all sentient beings to attain fulfillment of pure, supreme knowledge and spiritual powers, to cultivate practice diligently, and attain omniscience, power, and fearlessness.

"When great enlightening beings give precious chariots to fields of blessings including the poor, the destitute, and the orphaned, they joyfully and tirelessly give whatever is needed, and even apologize to those people, 'I should have gone to offer you provisions, rather than trouble you to come so far and wear yourself out.' Then they bow and kneel before them, ask about their health, and give them whatever they need. Sometimes they give crystal chariots with the finest women in the land; sometimes they give gilded chariots with women prized in society; sometimes they give lapis lazuli chariots with dancing girls; sometimes they give chariots of various extraordinary jewels with maidens like goddesses; sometimes they give chariots adorned with innumerable jewels, with bejewelled women, gentle and bright, eloquent and intelligent; sometimes they give sandalwood chariots to ride; sometimes they give crystal chariots with bejewelled women in them, incomparably beautiful, dressed in sumptuous robes, a delight to all who see; sometimes they give agate chariots, with crown princes riding in them; sometimes they give chariots of aromatic resins with all their sons and daughters in them; sometimes they give chariots adorned with all precious substances, with their relatives and good friends, so hard to give up, riding in them.

"Great enlightening beings respectfully give innumerable such precious chariots when they are asked for, to satisfy all wishes and make people happy and content. They dedicate these roots of goodness in this way: 'May all sentient beings ride the universal vehicle, which rolls unimpeded and never turns back, to reach inconceivable trees of enlightenment; may all sentient beings ride the vehicle of knowledge of the great teaching, based on pure causes, and cultivate enlightening practice throughout the future, never turning back; may all sentient beings ride the vehicle of the nonexistence of all things, forever part from all conceptual clinging, and always practice the path of omniscience; may all sentient beings ride the vehicle of truthfulness and honesty, without flattery or deception, and go to all buddha-fields freely, without hindrance; may all sentient beings follow and abide by the vehicle of omniscience, pleasing each other with the principles of buddhahood; may all sentient beings all ride the vehicle of pure practices of enlightening beings and fulfill all the ways of emancipation and the bliss of concentration of enlightening beings; may all sentient beings ride a vehicle of four wheels—that is, living in a good land, staying with good people, building up excellent virtues, and making great vows—hereby fulfilling the pure religious practice of all enlightening beings; may all sentient beings obtain the vehicle of the light of truth illumining everywhere throughout the ten directions, and cultivate the power of knowledge of all enlightened ones; may all sentient beings ride the vehicle of Buddha-teaching, and arrive at the other shore of all things; may all sentient beings ride the vehicle of the inconceivable teaching of myriad felicitous virtues, and show the right path of peace and serenity throughout the ten directions; may all sentient beings ride the vehicle of great generosity, sloughing off the dirt of stinginess; may all sentient beings ride the vehicle of pure morality, maintaining pure precepts as boundless as the cosmos; may all sentient beings ride the vehicle of forbearance, and always be free of the pollution of anger toward sentient beings; may all sentient beings ride the nonregressing vehicle of great diligence, steadfastly cultivate excellent practices, and proceed on the path of enlightenment; may all sentient beings ride the vehicle of meditation concentration, quickly reach the site of enlightenment, and realize enlightened knowledge; may all sentient beings ride the vehicle of wisdom and skill in means, and emanate bodies filling the realms of the Buddhas in all universes; may all sentient beings ride the vehicle of mastery of the teaching, develop fearlessness, and constantly distribute to all people teachings of methods to attain omniscience; may all sentient beings ride the vehicle of knowledge without attachment and be able to enter everywhere in the ten directions into the real nature of things, and not be disturbed by anything; may all sentient beings ride the vehicle of the teachings of all Buddhas, appearing to be born in all lands throughout the ten directions, without losing the path of the Great Vehicle; may all sentient beings ride the vehicle of the supreme treasury of omniscience, and fulfill the practices and vows of the Universally Good enlightening being, without growing weary of it.' This is the great enlightening beings' dedication of roots of goodness when giving precious chariots to fields of blessings, including the poor and the orphaned, to cause sentient beings to have immeasurable knowledge, to be joyful and buoyant, and to all ultimately attain the vehicle of universal knowledge.

"Great enlightening beings give prize elephants, which are docile, physically complete and in their prime years, with six tusks, pure and clean, lotuslike mouths red in color, bodies pure white, like mountains of snow; they are ornamented with golden banners, covered with nets of jewels, with various exquisite gems adorning their trunks; all find endless delight in looking at them; they can walk thousands of miles without tiring. Also, enlightening beings give trained prize horses with all the characteristics of celestial steeds, with moonlike discs of exquisite jewels as luminous ornaments, covered with nets of gold bells, stepping evenly and straight so that the riders are comfortable, going wherever wished as fast as the wind, traveling freely and unimpeded throughout the four continents. Enlightening beings give these prize elephants and horses to their parents, teachers, and to poor, suffering beings; their hearts are broad and without regret or grudge, only increasing in joy and feeling more and more compassion and pity as they cultivate the virtues of enlightening beings and purify the enlightening mind. They dedicate these roots of goodness in this way: 'May all sentient beings abide in the vehicle of harmony and docility and increase in all the virtuous qualities characteristic of enlightening beings; may all sentient beings attain the vehicle of liberative skills and be able to produce all enlightening teachings as necessary; may all sentient beings obtain the vehicle of resolute faith, universally illumining the power of unhindered knowledge of the enlightened; may all sentient beings attain the vehicle of inspiration, and be able to conceive all great vows; may all sentient beings fulfill the impartial vehicle of the ways of transcendence, and completely fulfill all impartial roots of goodness; may all sentient beings perfect the vehicle of treasures, bearing the unexcelled treasure of knowledge of all verities of Buddhahood; may all sentient beings perfect the vehicle of adornment by the practices of enlightening beings, causing the flowers of the meditations of enlightening beings to bloom; may all sentient beings obtain the vehicle of unbounded swiftness, purifying the enlightening mind and earnestly contemplating for countless eons, comprehending all things; may all sentient beings perfect the great vehicle of supreme self-mastery, with skill in means fulfilling the stages of enlightening beings; may all sentient beings perfect the highest, broadest, sturdiest Great Vehicle, able to carry all sentient beings to the state of all-knowledge.' This is great enlightening beings' dedication of roots of goodness when giving elephants and horses, to cause sentient beings to all ride the vehicle of unobstructed knowledge, the vehicle to perfect completion and arrival at Buddhahood.

"When great enlightening beings give seats or lion thrones to sit on, those seats are high and wide and extremely beautiful, with lapis lazuli legs, spread with soft, supple raiment made of gold thread, arrayed with jeweled banners, perfumed with various delicate fragrances, decorated with ornaments of innumerable various jewels, covered overhead with golden nets and jewel chimes rustling in the breeze and producing exquisite sounds, magnificently embellished all around with adornments of myriad unusual designs, looked up to by all people, occupied only by crowned monarchs proclaiming the law respectfully followed by all states. Those monarchs are also adorned with beautiful jewels—luminous jewels, sapphires, giant sapphires, jewel crystals from the finest mines, bright and clear as the sun, pure and cool as the moon; surrounding in profusion, like myriad stars, are ornaments of supreme beauty, incomparable jewels of the sea, solid banner-like treasures of the sea, with extraordinary patterns and unusual appearances; their heads are crowned with turbans of finest gold and pure jewels, they receive the rank of coronation, reign over the continent Jambu, endowed with immeasurable charismatic power, making kindness principal, conquering all those who are hostile and inimical, obeyed wherever their commands reach. Great enlightening beings, becoming such monarchs, then give such jewel-adorned thrones to Buddhas, the foremost fields of blessings, and to enlightening beings, genuine teachers, wise and holy mendicants, preachers of the teaching, parents, relatives, Buddhist disciples and individual illuminates, as well as those setting out on the vehicle of enlightening beings, and also to monuments of Buddhas, and to all the poor and destitute, the orphaned and homeless—they give everything according to need. These roots of goodness they dedicate in this way: 'May all sentient beings sit on the seat of enlightenment and thoroughly awaken to the truth realized by all Buddhas; may all sentient beings sit on the seat of freedom and attain independence of things, which even diamond mountains could not break, and be able to smash and conquer all the hordes of delusions; may all sentient beings gain the Buddha's lion throne of freedom, looked up to by all beings; may all sentient beings obtain chairs adorned with unspeakably unspeakable numbers of various exquisite jewels, become masters of the teachings, and guide sentient beings; may all sentient beings attain the throne which is supreme in all worlds, adorned by extensive great foundations of goodness; may all sentient beings obtain seats which pervade unspeakably unspeakable numbers of worlds, such as could not be fully eulogized in immeasurable eons; may all sentient beings obtain the seat of profound mystic virtues, and their bodies fill all universes; may all sentient beings obtain seats of inconceivable numbers of all kinds of jewels, and extensively carry out the giving of teaching to whatever sentient beings are considered in their past vows; may all sentient beings obtain seats of refined subtlety and manifest the spiritual powers of untold Buddhas; may all sentient beings obtain seats of all jewels, of all incenses, of all flowers, of all robes, of all garlands, of all crystals, and so on—seats of inconceivably many various precious things, seats of innumerable worlds, pure seats of the adornments of all worlds, seats of all diamonds, and manifest the powers and freedom of Buddhas, and fulfill most perfect enlightenment.' This is great enlightening beings' dedication of roots of goodness when giving seats of precious things, to cause sentient beings to obtain the seat of great enlightenment beyond the world and spontaneously become aware of the truths realized by all Buddhas.

"Great enlightening beings give various precious canopies, these canopies extraordinary, used by nobles, adorned with various great jewels, most excellent among billions of fine canopies, with supports made of all precious substances, covered with fine meshes, with golden bells on jeweled strings hanging down all around and draped with crystal necklaces making elegant sounds in harmony with the stirring of the breeze, all decorated with treasuries of pearls and jades, filled with innumerable various rareties, scented with sandalwood and aloe, fully embellished with infinite precious substances like radiantly pure gold: such canopies they give with pure hearts to Buddhas, or to monuments of Buddhas after their extinction, or, for the sake of the teaching, they give them to enlightening beings, good teachers, famous ministers of the teaching; or they give them to parents, or to mendicants, or to all the Buddhist teachings, or to various sentient beings as fields of blessings, or to religious leaders or venerable adepts, or those who have just set their minds on enlightenment, and to all the poor, destitute, orphaned, and homeless—to all who seek, they give. These roots of goodness they dedicate in this way: 'May all sentient beings cultivate foundations of goodness whereby to cover their bodies, and always be protected by the Buddhas; may all sentient beings make virtue and wisdom their canopies and forever part from all the afflictions of the world; may all sentient beings shade themselves with virtues and get rid of the dust and dirt and searing afflictions of the world; may all sentient beings attain a treasury of knowledge and wisdom, causing everyone to always enjoy seeing them; may all sentient beings shade themselves with the pure way of dispassionate tranquility, and all attain the indestructible state of Buddhahood; may all sentient beings shield their bodies with good and ultimately attain the pure body of reality of the Buddhas; may all sentient beings become universal canopies and cover the whole world with the knowledge of the ten powers; may all sentient beings attain sublime wisdom, transcending the world, free from attachments; may all sentient beings gain the canopy of worthiness, become superlative fields of blessings, and receive all offerings; may all sentient beings obtain the supreme canopy, attain unsurpassed knowledge, and naturally realize enlightenment.' This is great enlightening beings' dedication of roots of goodness when giving canopies, umbrellas, and parasols, to cause all sentient beings to obtain the canopy of freedom and be able to uphold all good ways; to cause all sentient beings to be able to cover all fields and lands in all realms in space, and manifest the free spiritual powers of the Buddhas, without regressing; to cause all sentient beings to be able to adorn all worlds in the ten directions with one canopy, and offer it to the Buddha; to cause all sentient beings to offer beautiful banners, pennants, and jeweled canopies to all the enlightened ones; to cause all sentient beings to obtain a canopy of universal adornment and cover the lands of all the Buddhas; may all sentient beings obtain a vast canopy to cover sentient beings everywhere and cause them all to engender faith in the Buddha; to cause all sentient beings to offer innumerable canopies of wonderful precious adornments to one Buddha, and to do the same for innumerable Buddhas; to cause all sentient beings to attain the high, wide canopy of the enlightenment of Buddhas, covering all the enlightened ones; to cause all sentient beings to obtain canopies adorned with all jewels, canopies adorned with all jewelry, canopies adorned with all solid perfumes, canopies with pure adornments of various jewels, canopies with pure adornments of innumerable jewels, immense canopies with adornments of pure jewels, covered with jewel nets, hung with jewel bells waving in the breeze producing sublime sounds, covering the bodies of the Buddhas in all worlds in the space of the cosmos; to cause all sentient beings to obtain canopies adorned with unhindered, unimpeded knowledge, covering all the enlightened ones; also because they want to cause all sentient beings to attain the highest knowledge and wisdom; and because they want to cause all sentient beings to attain the adornment of the virtues of buddhahood; because they want to cause all sentient beings to attain the immeasurable, boundless treasures of the free mind; because they want to cause all sentient beings to be filled with the independent knowledge of all truths; because they want to cause all sentient beings to cover all with virtues; because they want to cause all sentient beings to perfect the canopy of supreme knowledge; because they want to cause all sentient beings to perfect the all-covering canopy of the ten powers; because they want to cause all sentient beings to be able to cover all buddha-fields in the cosmos; because they want to cause all sentient beings to be masters of all the enlightening teachings; because they want to cause all sentient beings to attain the free mind of great mystic power; because they want to cause all sentient beings to attain vast knowledge permanently; because they want to cause all sentient beings to attain immeasurable ultimate virtues, covering all; because they want to cause all sentient beings to cover their minds with virtuous qualities; because they want to cause all sentient beings to shield all living creatures with an impartial mind; because they want to cause all sentient beings to attain skillful means of dedication; because they want to cause all sentient beings to attain pure minds of supreme aspiration; because they want to cause all sentient beings to attain pure wills with good intentions; and because they want to cause all sentient beings to attain great dedication covering all living beings.

"Great enlightening beings may give various splendid banners and pennants, their poles made of various jewels, pennants made of precious silk, banners of various mixed colors and patterns, draped with jeweled nets, shining colors filling everywhere, jewel bells gently stirring, ringing in harmony, with rare jewels shaped like the half moon and gold more radiant than the sun placed atop each banner, decorated with various wonderful things caused to appear by results of actions in various worlds—such marvelous banners and pennants, uncountable millions of billions of them, their radiance joining and highlighting each other, the light pure, covering the ground, filling all buddha-lands in the realms in space in ten directions, the great enlightening beings, with pure-hearted faith give to Buddhas currently existing, or to their monuments after death, or to the treasury of the teaching, or to the religious community, or to enlightening beings, or to Buddhist disciples, or to self-enlightened beings, or to good teachers, or to Buddhist disciples, or to self-enlightened ones, or to the masses, or to particular people—to all who come seeking they give, and dedicate these roots of goodness in this way; 'May all sentient beings be able to set up banners of virtue on all foundations of goodness, so that they cannot be destroyed; may all sentient beings set up the banner of mastery of all the teachings, respecting, admiring, and diligently preserving them; may all sentient beings write down the true teachings on precious silk, preserving the treasury of teachings of Buddhas and enlightening beings; may all sentient beings set up high, outstanding banners, and light the lamp of wisdom, illuminating all the world; may all sentient beings set up the banner of steadfastness and be able to destroy all delusive actions and manias; may all sentient beings set up the banner of the power of knowledge, which no delusion can damage; may all sentient beings attain the banner of great knowledge and wisdom, destroying all the flags of worldly pride; may all sentient beings gain the banner of great light of the sun of knowledge, and illumine the whole realm of reality with the light of the sun of knowledge; may all sentient beings be endowed with banners adorned with innumerable jewels, filling all worlds in the ten directions, and offer them to the Buddhas; may all sentient beings obtain the banner of realization of thusness, and destroy all the erroneous views of misleading paths.' This is great enlightening beings' dedication of roots of goodness when giving banners and pennants, to cause all sentient beings to attain the pure paths of the banner of the extremely profound, lofty, and wide-ranging practices of enlightening beings, and the banner of the action of spiritual powers of enlightening beings.

"Great enlightening beings open up storehouses of myriad treasures and hundreds of billions of trillions of fine, rare jewels to all the countless sentient beings, giving whatever they wish unbegrudgingly. They dedicate the roots of goodness in this way: 'May all sentient beings always see the treasure of the Buddha, give up folly and cultivate right mindfulness; may all sentient beings be fully endowed with the light of the treasure of the Teaching and preserve the treasury of teachings of all Buddhas; may all sentient beings be able to support the entire treasure of the community, tirelessly providing for its needs; may all sentient beings attain the highest treasure of mind, omniscience, and may their pure aspiration for enlightenment never recede; may all sentient beings attain the treasure of knowledge, entering into all things without doubt or confusion; may all sentient beings be endowed with the treasure of virtuous qualities of enlightening beings, reveal and expound immeasurable knowledge; may all sentient beings attain a treasure of immeasurable sublime qualities, cultivate and attain the knowledge of the ten powers of true awareness; may all sentient beings attain the treasure of the sixteen knowledges of refined meditation, and ultimately fulfill broad, great knowledge and wisdom; may all sentient beings develop the treasure of the supreme field of blessings, and awaken to the unexcelled knowledge and wisdom of the enlightened; may all sentient beings become masters of the most excellent treasure, and expound all truths with inexhaustible discernment.' This is great enlightening beings' dedication of roots of goodness when giving treasures, to cause all sentient beings to obtain the jewel of complete, supreme knowledge, the treasure of the unobstructed pure eye of the enlightened.

"Great enlightening beings may give various beautiful decorations—decorations for all bodies, causing the body to be beautiful and pleasing to all. Great enlightening beings regard all creatures in the world equally, like an only child, and want to cause them all to have adornments purifying their bodies, to attain supreme peace and comfort, to attain the bliss of enlightened knowledge, abide by the Buddha-teachings and benefit living beings. With innumerable, various exquisite jewel ornaments such as these they diligently practice giving, and when they are giving they dedicate the roots of goodness in this way: 'May all sentient beings develop unexcelled, wonderful adornments and adorn humans and celestials with pure virtue and knowledge; may all sentient beings attain features of pure adornment, adorning themselves with pure felicitous virtues; may all sentient beings attain features of most sublime adornment, and array themselves with all marks of virtue; may all sentient beings attain features of unconfused adornments, adorning themselves with all marks of Buddhahood; may all sentient beings attain the features of adornment by good, pure speech, endowed with all kinds of unlimited intellectual powers; may all sentient beings attain the features of adornment by voices with all good qualities, their voices pure and clear, pleasing to all who hear; may all sentient beings attain the feature of adornment by the delightful speech of the Buddhas, causing living beings to hear the teaching, rejoice in it, and cultivate pure practice; may all sentient beings attain the features of adornment of mind, entering deep meditative concentration and seeing the Buddhas; may all sentient beings attain the features of adornment by total mental command, illumining the true teachings of all Buddhas; may all sentient beings attain the features of adornment by wisdom and knowledge, adorning their minds with the wisdom and knowledge of buddhahood.' This is great enlightening beings' dedication of roots of goodness when generously giving all kinds of ornaments, to cause sentient beings to be endowed with the adornments of the complete fulfillment of all the innumerable qualities of Buddhas, complete virtue and knowledge, and to forever shed all conceit and self-indulgence.

"Great enlightening beings give to all sentient beings the jeweled crowns and topknot jewels they received when crowned as independent kings, without regret in their hearts, always cultivating themselves diligently to be generous donors, learning the wisdom of giving, developing the faculty of relinquishment; with knowledge and skill in means, their minds broad and magnanimous, they give to all, and dedicate those roots of goodness in this way: 'May all sentient beings be crowned by the Buddha-teachings and achieve universal knowledge; may all sentient beings attain the foremost knowledge and reach the other shore; may all sentient beings save living beings with the treasure of sublime knowledge and cause them all to fulfill the summit of virtue; may all sentient beings attain completion of the precious crown of knowledge and wisdom and be worthy of the honor of the world; may all sentient beings' heads be graced with the crown of knowledge and become autonomous monarchs and masters of the law; may all sentient beings tie the clear jewel of knowledge to their heads, invisible to all worldlings; may all sentient beings be worthy of the obeisance of the world, perfect the peak of wisdom, and illumine the Buddha-teachings; may all sentient beings be crowned with the crown adorned by the ten powers, filled with the purity of the ocean of jewels of knowledge and wisdom; may all sentient beings reach the summit of the great stages of enlightenment, attain omniscience, fulfill the ten powers, and destroy the bands of maniacs at the peak of the realm of desire; may all sentient beings manage to attain the highest summit of sovereignty, and attain the peak of radiance of omniscience, which cannot be outshone.' This is great enlightening beings' dedication of roots of goodness when giving jeweled crowns, to cause sentient beings to attain the realm of utmost purity of supreme knowledge, and the crown of jewels of wisdom.

"When great enlightening beings see sentient beings in prisons or dungeons, dark and dim, shackled and chained, unable to rise or sit in comfort, assailed by myriad pains, without relatives or friends, without refuge or salvation, naked, hungry, emaciated, suffering unbearable torture, the enlightening beings, having seen this, give what they have, all their wealth, their spouses, children, and households, and even their own bodies, to rescue those creatures in prison, like the enlightening being Great Compassion and the enlightening being King of Wondrous Eyes did; and, having rescued them, they give them whatever they need, relieving their suffering, enabling them to gain peace and comfort—after that, they give them the supreme treasure of the teaching, cause them to give up indulgence, firmly establish roots of goodness, and not shrink away or withdraw from the Buddhist teaching. When great enlightening beings rescue sentient beings from prison, they dedicate the roots of goodness in this way: 'May all sentient beings be ultimately liberated from the bonds of covetousness and craving; may all sentient beings cut off the stream of birth and death and climb up onto the shore of wisdom; may all sentient beings do away with ignorance and folly, develop knowledge and wisdom, and shed the fetters of afflictions; may all sentient beings destroy the bonds of the worlds of desire, form, and formlessness, attain universal knowledge and be ultimately emancipated; may all sentient beings forever cut off all the bonds of afflictions and reach the other shore of knowledge and wisdom, the ground of nonobstruction, where there are no afflictions; may all sentient beings be free from stirring thoughts, musing, and vain discrimination, and enter the realm of equanimous, imperturbable knowledge; may all sentient beings shed the bonds of desires, forever leaving behind all mundane cravings, and have no attachments in the worlds of desire, form, or formlessness; may all sentient beings attain supreme aspiration and always have the Buddhas teach them; may all sentient beings attain liberated minds, with no attachments and no bondage, broad and vast as the cosmos, comprehensive as space; may all sentient beings attain the spiritual powers of enlightening beings, taming sentient beings in all worlds, causing them to detach from the mundane and abide in the Great Vehicle.' This is great enlightening beings' dedication of roots of goodness when saving sentient beings suffering in prison, to enable sentient beings to enter the realm of knowledge and wisdom of the enlightened.

"Great enlightening beings, seeing prisoners bound hand and foot, suffering all sorts of pain, beaten and oppressed by their jailers, on the brink of death, having given up all earthly comforts, forever parted from their relatives and friends, laid out on butchering blocks to be dismembered, or impaled on wooden stakes, or doused with oil and set afire, the enlightening beings, having seen them oppressed by such tortures, give up their own bodies to take their places, as did the enlightening beings Invincible, King of Most Excellent Action, and other great enlightening beings who gave up their own lives to spare others, bearing cruel suffering in their stead. At that time the enlightening beings say to the wardens, 'I wish to give up my body in exchange for their lives. You may apply those tortures to me. Just as you are doing to those people, you may do what you want, even more, to me—I will endure even incalculable times as much, so that they may be freed. If I see them about to be killed and do not give up my life to redeem them from their misery, then I cannot be said to be dwelling in the mind of an enlightening being. Why? Because I have made the determination for omniscient enlightenment for the purpose of saving all beings.'

"When great enlightening beings give up their own lives to save sentient beings, they dedicate the roots of goodness in this way: 'May all sentient beings attain endless, ultimate life and be forever free from disaster, oppression, and affliction; may all sentient beings stay with the Buddhas, receive universal knowledge, fulfill the ten powers, and receive the prediction of enlightenment; may all sentient beings rescue conscious beings everywhere, cause them to be free from fear and to forever leave the states of woe; may all sentient beings attain total life and enter the realm of undying knowledge; may all sentient beings be forever free from hostility and enmity, have no calamities, and always be in the care of Buddhas and good teachers; may all sentient beings abandon all weapons and instruments of evil and suffering, and practice all kinds of pure, good action; may all sentient beings be free from all fears and crush the armies of demons at the tree of enlightenment; may all sentient beings be free from terrors, their hearts pure and fearless in regard to the highest teaching, and be able to make the supreme lion's roar; may all sentient beings attain unobstructed lionic knowledge and wisdom and cultivate right action in all worlds; may all sentient beings reach the realm of fearlessness and always attend to the salvation and protection of suffering sentient beings.' This is great enlightening beings; dedication of roots of goodness when giving up their own lives to save prisoners about to be executed, to cause sentient beings to be free from the pains of birth and death and to attain the sublime bliss of the enlightened.

"Great enlightening beings give the knot of flesh on their heads to beggars as did the enlightening beings Jewel Topknot King, Supremely Wonderful Body, and countless others. At such a time, seeing a beggar come, the enlightening beings' hearts fill with joy and they say, 'If you need a flesh topknot, take it from me—mine is the best in the land.' And when they say this, their minds are undisturbed, they do not think of other actions; they relinquish the world and seek dispassionate serenity; ultimately pure, diligent, straightforward, they are bent on omniscience. They then take a sharp knife and cut off the topknot of flesh on their heads; with their right knee kneeling on the ground, they join their palms and give their topknots away with a concentrated mind, thinking of the practices of all Buddhas and enlightening beings of the past, present, and future, conceiving great joy, increasing in determination. Intellectually they skillfully analyze and understand phenomena, and do not grasp pain, knowing that the sense of pain has no signs and no origin, that all sensations occur relatively and none are permanent. Therefore they develop great blissful faith that they should practice great relinquishment like all enlightening beings of past, future, and present, seeking universal knowledge without retreating, without relying on others' teaching or the power of a teacher.

"When great enlightening beings carry out this giving, they dedicate the roots of goodness in this way: 'May all sentient beings attain the

invisible crown and develop the pagodalike topknot of enlightening
beings; may all sentient beings have hair like the Buddha, and be able to
extinguish all afflictions of sentient beings; may all sentient beings have
glossy hair, thick hair, hair which doesn't grow on the forehead; may
all sentient beings have hair like the Buddha and forever be free from all
afflictions and binding habits; may all sentient beings have radiant hair,
shining with light that illumines all worlds in the ten directions; may all
sentient beings have undisturbed hair, clean like the Buddha's; may all
sentient beings develop the pagodalike hair of the saint, so that for all
who see it it is like seeing the Buddha's hair; may all sentient beings
have hair like the Buddha, without stain, without attachment, forever
rid of all obscuring dust and dirt.' This is great enlightening beings'
dedication of roots of goodness when giving their flesh topknots, to
cause sentient beings to be dispassionate and serene of mind, fulfill all
concentration formulae, and consummate the enlightened one's knowledge of all ways of liberation and its ten powers.

"Great enlightening beings give their eyes to those who come and
ask for them, just as the enlightening beings Gladdening Practice,
Moonlight King, and countless others gave theirs. When great enlightening beings give their eyes, they arouse a pure mind to give eyes; they
arouse the mind of the eye of pure knowledge, arouse a mind resting on
the light of truth; arouse the mind witnessing the unexcelled Buddha
Way; awaken a mind dedicated to great knowledge; awaken a mind to
give with equanimity equal to the enlightening beings of past, present,
and future; awaken the unobstructed eye; arouse a mind of indestructible pure faith; arouse a mind of joyful acceptance in regard to those
who ask. To consummate all spiritual powers, to produce the enlightened eye, to increase and broaden the great determination for enlightenment, to cultivate great compassion, and to master the senses, they
set their minds on these things.

"When great enlightening beings give eyes, they conceive great love
for those who ask, and establish charity for them, increasing the power
of the teaching, giving up mundane emotional views and indulgence,
cutting off the bonds of desire, cultivating enlightenment, and oblig-
ingly satisfying their requests with unperturbed minds, always in accord with the practice of nondualistic equanimity. These roots of goodness
they dedicate thus: 'May all sentient beings attain the supreme eye and
guide everyone; may all sentient beings attain the unobstructed eye and
open up the treasury of universal knowledge; may all sentient beings
attain the pure physical eye, its light perceptively penetrating, impossible to block; may all sentient beings attain the pure celestial eye, seeing
the births and deaths and fruits of actions of all sentient beings; may all
sentient beings attain the pure objective eye and be able to enter the
realm of those who realize thusness; may all sentient beings attain the
eye of wisdom and abandon all conceptual grasping and attachment;
may all sentient beings be endowed with the Buddha-eye, capable of

total awareness and understanding of all things; may all sentient beings perfect the universal eye, comprehending all realms without hindrance; may all sentient beings attain the pure, unclouded eye, realizing the realm of sentient beings is empty and has no existence; may all sentient beings be fully endowed with the pure unobstructed eye and all be able to consummate the ten powers of the enlightened.' This is great enlightening beings' dedication of roots of goodness when giving eyes, to cause all sentient beings to attain the pure eye of universal knowledge.

"Great enlightening beings are able to give ears and noses to those who ask, as did King of Superlative Action, Invincible, and countless other enlightening beings. When they give, they hand them over personally to those who ask, single-mindedly cultivating the deeds of enlightening beings, endowed with the seed nature of buddhahood, born in the house of the enlightened. Recollecting the acts of giving practiced by the enlightening beings, they constantly strive to activate the pure faculties of enlightenment of Buddhas, their virtues and wisdom. Observing all realms of existence, they see that not one thing endures. They aspire to always be able to see the Buddhas and enlightening beings. They recollect all Buddha-teachings according to the situation. They know the body is illusory, empty, void of existence, with nothing to cling to. Thus when enlightening beings give away ears and noses, their minds are always dispassionate and peaceful; they have tamed their senses. They save sentient beings from the dangers of perversity and evil, develop all knowledge and virtues, enter the ocean of great generosity, comprehend the meanings of the teachings, fully cultivate the ways they point out, acting in accord with knowledge and wisdom, attaining mastery of truth, and substitute an indestructible body for the perishable body.

"When great enlightening beings give ears, they dedicate the roots of goodness in this way: 'May all sentient beings attain unobstructed ears and hear all sounds speaking the truth; may all sentient beings attain unblocked ears and be able to understand all sounds; may all sentient beings attain the ears of the enlightened and perceive all without hindrance; may all sentient beings attain pure ears, not producing false discriminations based on the medium of hearing; may all sentient beings attain ears without deafness, causing ignorant consciousness not to arise; may all sentient beings attain ears pervading the cosmos and know the voices of teachings of all Buddhas; may all sentient beings attain unobstructed ears and realize all ways of nonobstruction; may all sentient beings attain indestructible ears, that no one be able to break down the discourses of good teachers; may all sentient beings attain all-hearing ears, far-reaching and pure, supreme of all ears; may all sentient beings be endowed with the celestial ear and the enlightened ear.' This is great enlightening beings' dedication of roots of goodness when giving ears, to cause all sentient beings to attain pure ears.

"When great enlightening beings give noses, they dedicate the roots of goodness in this way: 'May all sentient beings attain high, straight noses, refined noses, well-formed noses, beautiful noses, pleasing noses, pure noses, docile noses, outstanding noses, enemy-conquering noses, the noses of the enlightened; may all sentient beings attain faces free from anger, faces of all truths, faces of nonobstruction, faces good to see, docile faces, pure clean faces, impeccable faces, round full faces like the Buddha, faces pervading all places, faces of immeasurable beauty.' This is great enlightening beings' dedication of roots of goodness when giving noses, to cause sentient beings to ultimately gain entry into the teachings of all Buddhas, to cause sentient beings to ultimately absorb the teachings of all Buddhas, to cause sentient beings to ultimately comprehend the teachings of the Buddhas, to cause sentient beings to ultimately abide by the teachings of the Buddhas, to cause sentient beings to ultimately always see the Buddha, to cause all sentient beings to attain realization of the principles of Buddha, to cause sentient beings to ultimately develop indestructible minds, to cause sentient beings to adorn all buddha-lands, to cause sentient beings to all attain the body of great power of the enlightened ones. This is the dedication of roots of goodness of enlightening beings when giving ears and noses.

"Great enlightening beings, abiding securely in the state of indestructible freedom, are able to give teeth to sentient beings, as did Flower Teeth King, Six Tusk Elephant King, and other enlightening beings of antiquity. When great enlightening beings give teeth, their minds are pure, to a degree rarely found: that is, they give with an inexhaustible mind, give with a mind of great faith, give with a mind at every step attaining immeasurable detachment, give with a mind in control of the senses, give with a mind relinquishing all, give with a mind aspiring to universal knowledge, give with a mind to comfort sentient beings, give with great generosity, ultimate generosity, superb generosity, supreme generosity, give with a mind to relinquish their own physical necessities without resentment.

"At this time, the enlightening beings dedicate the roots of goodness in this way: 'May all sentient beings have sharp, white teeth, becoming supreme reliquaries, receiving the offerings of humans and celestials; may all sentient beings have even teeth, like those of the Buddha, without any gaps; may all sentient beings have well-controlled minds and skillfully carry out the transcendental practices of enlightening beings; may the mouths of all sentient beings be pure and clean, their teeth bright white, showing clearly; may all sentient beings have teeth with memorable adornments, their mouths pure and clean, with no foul appearance; may all sentient beings have a full set of teeth, always producing various rare, exquisite fragrances; may all sentient beings have well-controlled intellects and their teeth be clean and bright, like white lotuses, forming gammadion patterns; may all sentient beings' mouths and lips be fresh and clean, their teeth clean and white, shining with innumerable lights illuminating everywhere; may all sentient beings' teeth be fine and sharp, so there are no whole grains left in their food when they eat and they have no attachment to taste and become excellent fields of blessings; may all sentient beings always radiate light from between their teeth, giving enlightening beings the foremost prediction of enlightenment.' This is great enlightening beings' dedication of roots of goodness when giving teeth, to cause sentient beings to be endowed with omniscience, their knowledge of all things clear and pure.

"If people come to great enlightening beings asking for their tongues, they compassionately speak kind and gentle words to them, as did Handsome King, Unregressing, and countless other enlightening beings of ancient times. When great enlightening beings are born in the various realms of existence, when countless sentient beings come to them asking for their tongues, they place those people on lion seats, and, with minds free from anger, malice, and resentment, with minds of great power, minds born of the essence of Buddhas, minds abiding in the abode of enlightening beings, minds never polluted or disturbed, minds abiding in great power, minds with no attachment to the body, and minds with no attachment to words, they kneel on the ground, open their mouths, show their tongue to the beggars, and say to them with kind and gentle words, 'This body of mine is all yours—you may take my tongue and use it as you will, to fulfill your wishes.'

"At that time, the enlightening beings dedicate the roots of goodness in this way: 'May all sentient beings attain the universal tongue and be able to expound all principles of speech and language; may all sentient beings attain tongues that can cover their faces, and may their speech be nondual and all true to reality; may all sentient beings attain a tongue that covers all buddha-lands, demonstrating the autonomous spiritual powers of Buddhas; may all sentient beings have soft, thin tongues, always tasting fine, pure flavors; may all sentient beings have eloquent tongues, able to cut through the net of doubts of all beings; may all sentient beings have luminous tongues, able to radiate countless billions of light beams; may all sentient beings attain tongues of definite certainty, inexhaustibly explaining all things with discernment; may all sentient beings attain masterful tongues, able to unlock all essential mysteries, causing all to accept and believe what they say; may all sentient beings attain tongues of universal fluency, able to enter into the ocean of all languages; may all sentient beings attain tongues capable of explaining all aspects of the teachings, thoroughly attaining ultimate perfection of knowledge of words and speech.' This is enlightening beings' dedication of roots of goodness when giving tongues, to cause sentient beings to all attain complete unobstructed knowledge.

"Enlightening beings give their heads to those who come ask for them, as did Supreme Knowledge, Great Light, and other great enlightening beings. The giving that the great enlightening beings practice is because they want to develop the head of supreme knowledge comprehending all truths, because they want to develop the head realizing great enlightenment and saving sentient beings, because they want to have the supreme head seeing all things, because they want to attain the head of pure knowledge which sees truly, because they want to develop the head of nonobstruction, free from hindrance, because they want to realize the head attaining the highest states, because they seek the head of knowledge supreme in the world, because they want to develop the head of pure wisdom, the crown of which cannot be seen by any in the realms of desire, form, or formlessness, because they want to attain the head of sovereignty of knowledge appearing throughout the ten directions, and because they want to fulfill the head of freedom which cannot be broken by anything at all.

"Great enlightening beings, abiding by this practice and diligently applying it, then, because they have already entered the family of the Buddhas, emulate the giving practiced by the Buddhas. Conceiving pure faith in the Buddhas, they develop and mature roots of goodness, and cause those in need to all be happily satisfied. Their own minds are pure and joyful beyond measure; with pure faith and understanding they clearly illumine the Buddha teachings, activate the will for enlightenment, and abide in equanimity and resignation. All their senses are blissful; their virtous qualities grow and develop and they give rise to good aspirations, and always like to practice magnanimous giving.

"At that time the enlightening beings dedicate the roots of goodness in this way: 'May all sentient beings attain the head of the enlightened, and attain the invisible crown, which none anywhere can surpass, the supreme head in all buddha-fields, hair curling to the right, radiant, clean, lustrous, adorned with gammadions, a wonder of the world; may they be endowed with the head of Buddhas, the head of consummate knowledge, the foremost head in the world, and be heads of completeness, of purity, and of comprehensive knowledge sitting on the site of enlightenment.' This is great enlightening beings' dedication of roots of goodness when giving their heads away, to enable sentient beings to attain the highest truth and achieve unexcelled great wisdom.

"Great enlightening beings give their hands and feet to sentient beings, like Always Diligent, Sorrowless King, and countless other enlightening beings and others gave their hands and feet in various places of birth in all realms of existence. Using faith for hands, they initiate beneficial works, coming and going, reaching everywhere, diligently practicing the true teaching, aspiring to attain jewel-producing hands, giving their hands, fulfilling the path of enlightening beings without doing anything in vain. They always extend their hands to obtain great wisdom, and walk peacefully as they go, bold and fearless. By the power of pure faith they fulfill diligent effort, to destroy unwholesome states and to perfect enlightenment.

"When great enlightening beings give in this way, they open the gate of pure teaching with hearts of immeasurable magnanimity, enter the ocean of Buddhahood, perfect the hand of giving, and provide for all in the ten directions. With the power of will they maintain the path of universal knowledge, and abide in the mind ultimately free of impurity, the body of reality, and the body of knowledge, endless and incorruptible. They cannot be shaken by any delusive influences; following good teachers, they make their minds firm and stable, and cultivate the practice of transcendence by giving, same as all enlightening beings.

"When great enlightening beings give their hands and feet, seeking omniscience for the sake of all sentient beings, they dedicate the roots of goodness in this way: 'May all sentient beings be endowed with spiritual powers, and all attain jewel-producing hands, and, having attained jewel-producing hands, respect each other as fields of blessings and give each other all kinds of jewels, and also give myriad jewels to Buddhas, producing clouds of wonderful jewels covering all buddha-lands.' They cause sentient beings to be kind to each other and not harm each other. They roam the buddha-fields, secure in fearlessness, naturally endowed with ultimate spiritual powers. They also cause all to attain hands producing jewels, hands producing flowers, hands producing clothing, hands producing canopies, hands producing garlands, hands producing incense, hands producing ornaments, boundless hands, immeasurable hands, universal hands, and, having attained these hands, to always diligently travel to all buddha-lands by means of spiritual power. They can touch all buddha-worlds with one hand, and hold all sentient beings with the hand of freedom. They attain hands of sublime features, emanating immeasurable light. They can cover all sentient beings with a single hand. They attain hands like the Buddha, with webbed fingers and copper fingernails. At this time the enlightening beings cover all sentient beings with the hand of great vows, praying that all sentient beings set their minds on always gladly seeking unexcelled enlightenment, producing the ocean of all virtues, rejoicing when they see people come begging, never tiring of them, entering the ocean of buddhahood, with the same roots of goodness as the Buddha. This is enlightening beings' dedication of roots of goodness when giving hands and feet.

"Great enlightening beings wound themselves and draw blood to give to sentient beings like Principled Action, Benevolent King, and countless other enlightening beings in various realms of existence. When they give blood, they arouse a mind to achieve omniscience, a mind of longing for great enlightenment, a mind of pleasure in cultivating the practices of enlightening beings, a mind not to grasp painful sensations, a mind of gladness to see beggars, a mind not averse to beggars, a mind directed toward the path of all enlightening beings, a mind to preserve the equanimity of all enlightening beings, a mind to increase and broaden the benevolent giving of enlightening beings, an unregressing mind, an unremitting mind, a mind free from self-love. The roots of goodness they dedicate in this way: 'May all sentient beings attain fulfillment of the body of reality and the body of knowledge; may all sentient beings attain an adamantine, indefatigable body; may all sentient beings attain an indestructible body that nothing can injure; may all sentient beings attain a phantom-like body, appearing throughout the world without limit; may all sentient beings attain a delightful body, clean, beautiful, strong and healthy; may all sentient beings attain a body born of the realm of reality, same as the enlightened, depending on nothing; may all sentient beings attain a body like the radiance of beautiful jewels, which no worldly people can outshine; may all sentient beings attain a body which is a treasury of knowledge, and realize freedom in the realm of immortality; may all sentient beings attain a body of an ocean of jewels, which is unfailingly beneficial to all who see it; may all sentient beings attain the body of space, which none of the troubles of the world can affect.' This is great enlightening beings' dedication of roots of goodness, with the mind of the Great Vehicle, a pure mind, a broad mind, a joyful mind, a happy mind, an enraptured mind, a mind in control, a peaceful mind, an unpolluted mind, when giving blood from their bodies.

"When great enlightening beings see people come and ask for their bodies' marrow and flesh, they are joyful and speak gently to them, telling them to take their bodies' marrow and flesh as they wish, just as Benefactor, All-Giving King, and innumerable other enlightening beings gave their marrow and flesh in various circumstances in various realms of being. When they give to those who ask, their joy is great, their generosity grows; they cultivate roots of goodness the same as all enlightening beings, depart from the dust and dirt of the world, and attain profound determination. They give their bodies to all, their minds inexhaustible; endowed with immeasurable great roots of goodness, they embody the treasures of all virtues. According with the principles of enlightening beings, they tirelessly put them into practice, their minds always delighting in the virtues of giving. They give all without regret, clearly observing that all things come from conditions and have no substance; they have no greed for the act of giving or for the rewards of giving, and give impartially to whomever they meet.

"When great enlightening beings give in this way, all the Buddhas appear to them, because they think of them as parents and receive their protection; all sentient beings appear to them, because they cause all to live in peace by the pure teaching; all worlds appear to them, because they adorn and purify all buddha-lands; all living beings appear to them, because they serve all with great compassion; all Buddha qualities appear to them, because they like to observe the ten powers of the enlightened ones; all enlightening beings of the past, present, and future appear to them, because they share the same complete roots of goodness; all fearlessnesses appear to them, because they are able to make the supreme lion roar; all the past, present, and future appear to them, because they have attained knowledge of equality observing all; all worlds appear to them, because they initiate great, far-reaching vows to cultivate enlightenment throughout the future; the tireless practices of enlightening beings all appear to them, because they develop infinite great aspirations.

"When great enlightening beings give marrow and flesh, they dedicate the roots of goodness in this way: 'May all sentient beings attain the indestructible body; may all sentient beings attain the enduring mystic body, which never diminishes; may all sentient beings attain mentally produced bodies, adorned and pure like the Buddha's body; may all sentient beings attain bodies adorned with all marks of merit and signs of greatness; may all sentient beings attain bodies beautifully adorned with all kinds of embellishments, endowed with the ten powers, indestructible; may all sentient beings attain the body of those who realize thusness, ultimately pure, impossible to delimit or measure; may all sentient beings attain the body of firmness and stability, which no demons or enemies can injure; may all sentient beings attain the body of oneness, and be one with the Buddhas of all times; may all sentient beings attain the unobstructed body, pervading space with the pure body of reality; may all sentient beings attain the body of the matrix of enlightenment, able to contain all worlds.' This is the dedication of roots of goodness of enlightening beings giving marrow and flesh, seeking universal knowledge, to cause all sentient beings to attain the ultimately pure infinite body of those who realize thusness.

"Great enlightening beings give their hearts to those who come and ask for them, as did No Regret, Unobstructed King, and countless other great enlightening beings. When they give their own hearts to beggars, they cultivate the mind of free giving, develop the mind of total giving, learn the mind of carrying out transcedent giving, perfect the mind of transcendent giving, cultivate the mind of giving of all enlightening beings, the inexhaustible mind relinquishing all, the mind accustomed to giving all, the mind taking on all enlightening beings' practice of giving, the mind correctly mindful of the manifestation of all Buddhas, the mind presenting gifts to all who come and ask, without end.

"When great enlightening beings give in this way, their minds are pure: in order to liberate all sentient beings, in order to attain the realm of enlightenment with the ten powers, in order to cultivate practice in accord with their great vows, because they want to abide in peace in the path of enlightening beings, because they want to develop omniscience, and because they do not give up their original vows, they dedicate the roots of goodness in this way: 'May all sentient beings attain diamond treasury hearts, which all diamond mountains cannot break; may all sentient beings attain diamond-realm hearts, adorned with the mystic gammadion; may they attain unshakable hearts, attain hearts that cannot be frightened; may they attain ever inexhaustible hearts benefiting the world; may they attain hearts that are treasuries of knowledge and wisdom, marked by great courage; may they attain hearts marked by firm strength; may they attain hearts as infinite as the ocean of living beings; may they attain hearts which nothing can spoil; may they attain hearts destroying all delusive activities and armies of demons; may they attain fearless hearts; may they attain hearts of great spiritual force; may they attain hearts of constant energy; may they attain hearts of great courage; may they attain hearts that cannot be shocked; may they attain hearts with indestructible armor; may they attain the supreme hearts of enlightening beings; may they attain hearts full of the light of enlightenment into the Buddha teachings; may they attain hearts sitting under the tree of enlightenment, abiding by the true teachings of all Buddhas, divorcing all illusions and attaining omniscience; may they attain hearts accomplished in the ten powers.' This is great enlightening beings' dedication of roots of goodness when giving their hearts, to cause all sentient beings to be unstained by the world and to be endowed with the ten-powered mind of the enlightened.

"If anyone comes to great enlightening beings asking for their internal organs, they give all, like Good Giver, Demon-Conquering Sovereign, and countless other great enlightening beings. When practicing this giving, they are glad to see people come begging and look upon them lovingly; in the quest for enlightenment they give as they are asked, without any regret in their hearts. They observe that this body has no permanence or stability, and reflect that they should give this body away and get an indestructible body. They also are mindful that this body will eventually decay, disgusting to all who see, and will be eaten by animals, that this body is impermanent, eventually to be abandoned and eaten by others, without awareness or cognition. When enlightening beings make these observations, they know that the body is transient and the height of impurity; understanding the teaching, they become very joyful. With a respectful mind, they see those who come ask of them as good friends who have come to protect them, and generously give them whatever they ask, substituting the enduring body for the unstable one.

"When great enlightening beings give in this way, they dedicate all the roots of goodness, that all sentient beings may attain the body of the treasury of knowledge, inwardly and outwardly pure; that all sentient beings may attain the body of the treasury of virtue, able to preserve the vow for omniscience; that all sentient beings may attain a supremely wonderful body, inwardly full of sublime fragrance, outwardly radiating light; that all sentient beings may attain a body without a protruding belly, upper and lower body straight, limbs and joints well coordinated; that all sentient beings may attain the body of knowledge and wisdom, filled with joy, enriched and nourished by the savor of the Buddha teaching; that all sentient beings attain an inexhaustible body and cultivate peaceful abiding in the most profound nature of truth; that all sentient beings may attain the body of the pure treasury of concentration spell formulae, and elucidate all truths with marvelous eloquence; that all sentient beings may attain the body of purity, body and mind both inwardly and outwardly clean; that all sentient beings may attain the body of practice of deep contemplation with knowledge of realization of thusness, filled with wisdom, showering the rain of truth; that all sentient beings may attain a body that is inwardly tranquil while outwardly being a supreme representation of knowledge for sentient beings, emanating great light universally illuminating everything. This is great enlightening beings' dedication of roots of goodness when giving internal organs, to cause sentient beings to be inwardly and outwardly pure and to all achieve stability in unobstructed knowledge.

"Great enlightening beings give those who ask for them their limbs, joints, and bones, like Treasury of Truth, King of Light, and innumerable other great enlightening beings. When they give their limbs, joints, and bones, upon seeing people come begging, they give rise to love, joy, pure faith, peace of mind, courage, kindness, an unobstructed mind, a pure mind, a mind to give whatever they are asked. When the great enlightening beings give their limbs and bones, they dedicate the roots of goodness in this way: 'May all sentient beings attain phantom-like bodies, and receive bone, flesh, and blood bodies no more; may all sentient beings attain indestructible, invincible bodies; may all sentient beings attain the body of reality, replete with all knowledge, born in the realm where there are no bounds, no attachments, no fetters; may all sentient beings attain the body of powers of knowledge, all faculties complete, fully developed, uninterrupted and incorruptible; may all sentient beings attain the body of the power of truth, with independent power of knowledge reaching the other shore; may all sentient beings attain a healthy, enduring body, upright and true, never decaying; may all sentient beings attain a body able to respond to needs, to teach and civilize all beings; may all sentient beings attain a body perfumed by wisdom, with the great strength of limb of the mighty; may all sentient beings attain a permanent, enduring body, forever free from all fatigue; may all sentient beings attain a stable body of great strength, able to fulfill the great power of energy and effort; may all sentient beings attain the equally omnipresent body of reality and abide in the realm of immeasurable supreme knowledge; may all sentient beings attain the body of the power of virtue, beneficial to all who see it, removed from all evil; may all sentient beings attain an independent body, which rests on nothing, and all be endowed with nonreliant, unattached knowledge; may all sentient beings attain a body under the protection of the Buddhas; may all sentient beings attain a body beneficial to all living beings, able to enter into all realms of existence; may all sentient beings attain a body of universal manifestation, able to reflect all the Buddha teachings; may all sentient beings attain a body endowed with vigor, concentrating on and diligently cultivating the practice of the knowledge of the Great Vehicle; may all sentient beings attain a pure body free from pride and conceit, their knowledge always stable and not shaken by anything; may all sentient beings attain a body of firm action, accomplishing the work of universal knowledge of the Great Vehicle; may all sentient beings attain a body of firm action, accomplishing the work of universal knowledge of the Great Vehicle; may all sentient beings attain a body in the house of Buddhas, forever leaving all mundane birth and death.' This is great enlightening beings' dedication of roots of goodness when giving limbs and bones, to cause all sentient beings to attain omniscience and be eternally pure.

"When great enlightening beings see people come to them with knives and ask for their skin, their hearts become joyful, their senses delighted, just like someone who has been done a great favor; they welcome them, invite them in, set out a seat for them, and bow to them respectfully, thinking, 'These seekers are most rare; they come seeking aid from me, working to fulfill my vow for omniscience.' Joyfully, with a mild countenance, they say to them, 'This body of mine I relinquish entirely—take as much of my skin as you need,' just like Treasury of Purity, Golden-sided Deer King, and countless other great enlightening beings of the past. At that time, the enlightening beings dedicate these roots of goodness in this way: 'May all sentient beings have fine skin, like that of the Buddha, its color pure and clear, so that people never tire of seeing it; may all sentient beings have unbreakable skin, like diamond, which nothing can break; may all sentient beings have golden skin, like the finest real gold, pure and clear; may all sentient beings have clear, lustrous skin, endowed with the softness and purity of the ascetic, characteristic of the Buddha; may all sentient beings attain skin of the finest color, inherently pure, its color and features incomparable; may all sentient beings develop the pure-colored skin of Buddha, adorned with the marks and embellishments of greatness; may all sentient beings have skin of exquisite color, radiating great light, illuminating everything; may all sentient beings have skin like luminous mesh, like the lofty banner of the world, radiating unspeakably many spheres of light; may all sentient beings have lustrous skin, its color and features all pure.' This is great enlightening beings' dedication of roots of goodness when giving their skin, to cause all sentient beings to reach all pure adorned buddha-fields and be endowed with the great virtues of Buddha.

"Great enlightening beings give their fingers and toes to those who ask for them, like Persevering, Sovereign King of Jambudvipa, and countless other great enlightening beings. At that time the countenance of the enlightening beings is peaceful and happy, their minds are stable and healthy, without any delusion. Riding the Great Vehicle, they do not seek satisfaction of sensual desires, nor do they prize name and fame; they only conceive the great determination of enlightening beings, getting rid of all defilements of greed and jealousy, turning wholeheartedly to the supremely wonderful teaching of the enlightened ones.

"When great enlightening beings give in this way, they concentrate the roots of goodness and dedicate them thus: 'May all sentient beings have slender, long fingers, no different from Buddha; may all sentient beings have fingers of even circumference, the upper and lower parts in proportion; may all sentient beings have fingers with ruddy copper nails, the nails rounded and shiny; may all sentient beings have the fingers of the omniscient supreme human, able to hold all truths; may all sentient beings have fingers with the refinements of Buddhas' fingers, and be adorned with the ten powers; may all sentient beings have the fingers of a great human, slender and even; may all sentient beings have fingers marked with lotus gammadions, adorned with marks and embellishments resulting from the working of the ten powers; may all sentient beings have fingers that are mines of light, radiating great light beams illumining unspeakably many buddha-worlds; may all sentient beings have well-proportioned fingers, adorned with the characteristics of Buddhas' fingers.' This is great enlightening beings' dedication of roots of goodness in giving fingers and toes, to cause all sentient beings to attain purity of mind.

"When great enlightening beings are seeking the teaching, if someone says, 'If you can give me your fingernails, I'll give you the teaching,' the enlightening beings reply, 'Just give me the teaching, and you may take and use my fingernails as you wish,' as did Sovereign King Seeking Truth, Inexhaustible, and countless other great enlightening beings. In their search for the true teaching, and because of their desire to expound the true teaching for the benefit of sentient beings, to cause all of them to be fulfilled, they give their fingernails away to those who ask for them. At that time the enlightening beings dedicate these roots of goodness in this way: 'May all sentient beings have the ruddy copper nails that are a mark of the Buddha; may all sentient beings have glossy nails, adorned with embellishments; may all sentient beings have shiny clean nails, clear as mirrors, finest of all; may all sentient beings have the nails of the omniscient, and be endowed with the marks of great human beings; may all sentient beings have peerless nails, not defiled by or attached to any world; may all sentient beings have nails with marvelous adornments, with light illumining all worlds; may all sentient beings have unbreakable nails, pure, clean, and complete; may all sentient beings have nails marked by entry into the techniques of all Buddha-teachings, vast knowledge and wisdom thoroughly pure; may all sentient beings have well-formed nails, the fruit of enlightening actions, all sublimely pure; may all sentient beings have the nails of the great omniscient guide, radiating treasuries of beautiful lights of infinite hues.' This is great enlightening beings' dedication of roots of goodness when giving their nails in their quest for the teaching, to cause sentient beings to be endowed with the unobstructed power of nails of omniscience of all Buddhas.

"Great enlightening beings seek the treasury of Buddha teachings with reverence and respect, considering it difficult to find. If someone who can expound it comes to them and says, 'If you can throw yourself into a pit of fire seventy feet deep I will give you the teaching,' the enlightening beings, hearing this, jump for joy and reflect, 'I would stay forever even in miserable places like uninterrupted hell and experience immeasurable suffering for the sake of the truth; how much the more readily would I jump into the fire of the human world to hear the teaching. How wonderful it is that the true teaching is so easy to obtain; without suffering the infinite tortures of hell one gets to hear it merely by entering a pit of fire. Just explain to me and I'll go into the pit of fire,' and like the enlightening beings King in Quest of the Good Teaching and Adamantine Meditation, they enter the pit of fire in quest of the teaching.

"At this time, the enlightening beings dedicate these roots of goodness in this way: 'May all sentient beings abide in the teaching of universal knowledge, the abode of Buddhas, and never regress or retreat from unexcelled enlightenment; may all sentient beings be free from all perils and experience the peace and ease of buddhahood; may all sentient beings attain fearless minds and be free from all terrors; may all sentient beings always gladly seek truth, full of joy and bliss, adorned by the teachings; may all sentient beings leave the courses of evil and extinguish the raging fires of the three poisons; may all sentient beings always be in peace and happiness, full of the supremely refined pleasures of the enlightened; may all sentient beings attain the mind of enlightening beings and forever part from the fires of craving, anger, and delusion; may all sentient beings attain the pleasures of concentration of enlightening beings and see the Buddhas everywhere, their minds full of joy; may all sentient beings skillfully explain the true teaching, ultimately never forgetting its principles; may all sentient beings have the sublime bliss of spiritual powers of enlightening beings and ultimately abide in knowledge of all ways of enlightenment.' This is great enlightening beings' dedication of roots of goodness when plunging into a pit of fire in quest of the true teaching, for the purpose of causing sentient beings to give up hindering actions and all attain the full endowment of the fire of wisdom.

"When great enlightening beings, in quest of the true teaching, analyze and expound the path of enlightening beings, point out the road of enlightenment, proceed toward highest knowledge, diligently cultivate the ten powers, extend the mind of universal knowledge, attain the state of unobstructed knowledge, purify sentient beings, abide in the sphere of action of enlightening beings, earnestly cultivate great knowledge, and preserve complete enlightenment, they experience immeasurable suffering and tribulation, as did Seeker of the Good Teaching, Brave King, and countless other great enlightening beings. To save even the most evil people, who repudiate the truth, are shrouded by evil deeds, are in the grip of delusion, the enlightening beings, for the sake of the truth, accept for those people all the torments they should suffer. These roots of goodness they dedicate in this way: 'May all sentient beings be forever freed from all suffering and oppression, and attain peace and happiness, freedom and spiritual power; may all sentient beings be forever free from all miseries, and attain all happiness; may all sentient beings annihilate the body of accumulated suffering, attain the body of illumination, and always experience ease and bliss; may all sentient beings escape from the prison of suffering and perfect wise action; may all sentient beings see the path of peace and depart from all evil courses; may all sentient beings attain the joy and bliss of truth and forever end all misery; may all sentient beings extirpate all suffering, love one another, and have no malevolence; may all sentient beings attain the bliss of the Buddhas and leave the pains of birth and death; may all sentient beings attain pure, peerless peace and ease, impervious to all pains and vexations; may all sentient beings attain all supreme bliss, ultimately filled with the unobstructed bliss of buddha-hood.' This is great enlightening beings' dedication of roots of goodness when accepting suffering for the sake of the truth, because they want to rescue all beings and bring them to safety, free them from peril and difficulty and cause them to live in the realm of omniscient, unhindered liberation.

"When great enlightening beings occupy the rank of ruler and seek true teaching, they consider even one sentence, one word, one phrase, one doctrine hard to obtain, and will give up everything within the seas, near or far—land, cities, towns, populace, storehouses, gardens, ponds, houses, forests, flowers, produce, including all rare and precious things, palaces, bowers, spouses, children, retinues, even rulership—they are able to give up all, seeking that which endures while in the midst of the transient; because they want to benefit all living beings, they earnestly seek the Buddhas' path of unhindered liberation and ultimately pure universal knowledge, as did Great Moral Force, King of Supreme Virtue, and countless other great enlightening beings. They diligently seek true teaching, even a little bit; for every one word they prostrate themselves on the ground. Properly meditating on the teachings of all Buddhas of past, present, and future, they devotedly practice them, never greedy for fame or fortune. They abandon the independent rulership of all worldly realms to seek autonomous mastery of truth. They have no attachment to worldly pleasures, and nourish their minds with transmundane teachings, forever leaving behind all idle speculations and inanities of the world, abiding in the truth of the Buddhas, which is free from inanity.

"At that time, enlightening beings dedicate the roots of goodness in this way: 'May all sentient beings always gladly give generously, relinquishing everything; may all sentient beings be able to give up whatever they have without regret; may all sentient beings always seek the truth without begrudging their lives or sustenance; may all sentient beings gain the benefit of the teaching and be able to stop everyone's doubts and confusion; may all sentient beings be able to give up their lives and sovereignty in quest of the Buddha teaching, cultivating highest enlightenment with great determination; may all sentient beings honor and respect the true teaching with ever profound aspiration, not begrudging their bodily lives; may all sentient beings preserve the most difficult-to-find Buddha teaching, always practicing it diligently; may all sentient beings attain the Buddhas' light of enlightenment, accomplishing the practice of enlightenment, awakening without relying on another for understanding; may all sentient beings always be able to analyze all Buddha teachings, pull out the arrow of doubt, and attain peace of mind.' This is great enlightening beings' dedication of roots of goodness when giving up their countries and cities in quest of the true teaching, in order to cause sentient beings' knowledge and insight to be complete, and always to be able to remain in the path of peace.

"Great enlightening beings, becoming monarchs of great countries, masters of the law, promulgate commands to eliminate work involving killing: in all cities, towns, and villages, all butchery and slaughtering is prohibited—to all creatures, legless, two-legged, four-legged, or many-legged, they give freedom from fear and aggression. Extensively cultivating the practices of all enlightening beings, they treat beings with humanity and kindness, not acting in aggressive or harmful ways. They conceive the wonderful, precious will to give peace to sentient beings, and establish profound determination for buddhahood; always abiding themselves by the three kinds of pure precepts, they also induce sentient beings to do the same.

"Great enlightening beings, causing sentient beings to abide by the five precepts and forever stop occupational killing, dedicate these roots of goodness in this way: 'May all sentient beings awaken the determination for enlightenment, be filled with knowledge and wisdom, and preserve everlasting life; may sentient beings live for immeasurable ages, make offerings to all Buddhas, with reverence and respect diligently cultivating to increase the lifespan even more; may all sentient beings fully practice the method of removing old age and death, so that calamities and poisons cannot threaten their lives; may all sentient beings fully develop bodies free from illness and affliction, so they may live as long as they wish; may all sentient beings attain inexhaustible life, and abide by the practice of enlightening forever and ever, teaching and taming all sentient beings; may all sentient beings be doors of life, wherein the good foundations of the ten powers grow; may all sentient beings be replete with roots of goodness, attain unlimited life, and fulfill great vows; may all sentient beings see all the Buddhas and serve them, and live indefinitely, cultivating and building up roots of goodness; may all sentient beings learn well what there is to learn from the enlightened, attain the joy of the way of sages and infinite life; may all sentient beings attain a permanent life-root, neither aging nor becoming ill, progress with vigor and courage to enter the knowledge and wisdom of buddhahood.' This is great enlightening beings' dedication of roots of goodness when abiding by the three bodies of pure precepts and forever stopping slaughter, to cause sentient beings to attain the complete ten-powered knowledge of Buddhas.

"When great enlightening beings see people cruelly castrating domestic animals, making their bodies incomplete and causing them pain, they are moved to compassion and save the animals out of pity, and order all the people in the land to stop this practice. The enlightening beings then say to those people, 'Why do you do such an evil thing? I have a treasury full of all kinds of conveniences which I will give to you according to your needs. What you are doing is wrong and I urge you not to do it. This occupation of yours is not right or reasonable—even if you gain something, what is the use? To harm others for your own profit after all isn't right. All bad actions like this are not praised by the enlightened.' And having spoken thus, they give them all their goods, and also explain the sublime teaching to them with fine words to gladden them: that is, they point out to them the way to peace and serenity, causing them to believe and accept, to do away with what is not good, to practice pure deeds, to be kind to one another and not to harm each other. Those people hearing this, forever give up evil.

"At that time, the enlightening beings dedicate these roots of goodness in this way: 'May all sentient beings be physically complete; may all sentient beings be courageous and cultivate pure religious practices; may all sentient beings have brave, bold strength, always be leaders, and abide in unobstructed knowledge, never retreating; may all sentient beings forever abandon craving and have no attachments; may all sentient beings develop rectitude and intelligence, and their knowledge increase, worthy of the praise of the Buddhas; may all sentient beings be endowed with the strength of great people and always be able to cultivate the roots of goodness of the ten powers; may all sentient beings never be emasculated, always cultivating rare qualities of virtue and knowledge; may all sentient beings have no attachment or ties to sensual desires, attain mental liberation, detach from the mundane and abide in enlightening practice; may all sentient beings become people of supreme knowledge and wisdom, trusted and obeyed by all; may all sentient beings fully possess the great knowledge and wisdom of enlightening beings, soon to become Buddhas.' This is enlightening beings' dedication of roots of goodness when prohibiting all castration, to cause sentient beings to have healthy bodies, and all be able to protect good human beings, to be born in the families of worthies and sages, full of intelligence, always cultivating healthy practices, with healthy capabilities, endowed with the healthy seed of enlightenment, the true teaching, courage, vigor, wisdom, and purity of genuine humans.

"If great enlightening beings see a Buddha appear in the world and expound the true teaching, they announce to all in a loud voice, 'A

Buddha has appeared in the world! A Buddha has appeared in the world!' This is to cause sentient beings to hear the name of Buddha and give up all pride and inanity. They also exhort and lead them to hasten to see the Buddha, to remember the Buddha, to resort to the Buddha, to concentrate on the Buddha, to contemplate the Buddha, to laud the Buddha; also they extensively explain to them how rare it is to meet a Buddha, who appears but once in a quadrillion eons. Due to this, sentient beings get to see the Buddha, give rise to pure faith, dance for joy, and respectfully attend the Buddha. Also, from the Buddha they hear the names of many Buddhas and go on to meet countless Buddhas, plant roots of goodness, cultivate and develop them.

"Then, countless quadrillions of sentient beings, because of seeing the Buddha, all attain purity and ultimate pacification. Those sentient beings think of the enlightening beings as most excellent friends and benefactors, as due to the enlightening beings they achieve enlightened qualities and distribute the roots of goodness they have planted over countless eons throughout the world, thus performing Buddha-work.

"When great enlightening beings teach sentient beings and induce them to see Buddha, they dedicate the roots of goodness in this way: 'May all sentient beings go to see Buddhas of their own accord, without being urged to do so, and may they serve, provide for, and gladden them all; may all sentient beings always enjoy seeing Buddhas, without any feeling of rejection; may all sentient beings always diligently cultivate vast knowledge, absorbing and retaining the treasury of all Buddha teachings; may all sentient beings understand all Buddha teachings they hear and cultivate enlightening practice for immeasurable eons; may all sentient beings abide in right mindfulness, and always see the Buddhas' emergence with the eye of knowledge; may all sentient beings not think of different occupations, but always think of seeing Buddha and diligently cultivate the ten powers; may all sentient beings always see Buddhas in all places, comprehending that the realization of thusness pervades the realm of space; may all sentient beings become equipped with the free body of buddhahood, realizing enlightenment and expounding the truth throughout the ten directions; may all sentient beings meet good teachers, always hear the Buddha teachings, and attain unbreakable faith in the Buddhas; may all sentient beings be able to eulogize the emergence of Buddhas, and cause those who see them to attain universal purity.' This is enlightening beings' dedication of the roots of goodness of praising Buddhas' appearance in the world, to cause sentient beings to see all Buddhas, provide for and serve them, and attain ultimate purity in the highest teaching.

"Great enlightening beings give away land—they may give it to Buddhas, building retreats, or they may give it to enlightening beings and teachers, to use as they wish, or they may give it to mendicant groups for a place of abode, or they may give it to their parents, or to other people, to Buddhist disciples, to individual illuminates, to various fields of blessings, including the poor, orphaned, homeless, and others. They give whatever is wished, to fulfill their needs. They may build Buddhas' mausoleums, and provide all necessary articles for such places, so they may be used as wished, without fear or hesitation.

"Whenever great enlightening beings give land, they dedicate the roots of goodness in this way: 'May all sentient beings fully realize the pure stage of universal knowledge and arrive at the consummation of the practices of Universal Good; may all sentient beings attain the stage of total mental command and receive and hold all Buddha teachings with right recollection; may all sentient beings attain sustaining power and be able to preserve all Buddha teachings; may all sentient beings attain a mind like the earth, with intentions ever pure and free from evil thoughts toward sentient beings; may all sentient beings maintain the lineage of Buddhas, accomplishing the processes of the stages of enlightening beings, without interruption; may all sentient beings become abodes of safety for all, causing all to be harmonized and pacified and to abide in the path of purity; may all sentient beings benefit the world the same as enlightened ones, causing all to diligently cultivate themselves and abide securely in the power of buddhahood; may all sentient beings be liked by all the world and cause everyone to abide in the highest happiness of Buddhahood; may all sentient beings attain skill in means of liberation and abide in the power and fearlessness of buddhahood; may all sentient beings attain knowledge like the earth and freely practice all Buddha teachings.' This is great enlightening beings' dedication of roots of goodness when giving land, to cause sentient beings to all attain ultimate consummation of the pure state of all enlightened ones.

"Great enlightening beings give servants as offerings to all Buddhas and enlightening beings, genuine teachers; or they may give them to the religious community, or to their parents, honorable fields of blessings, or again they may give them to sentient beings suffering from illness, to fulfill their needs and preserve their lives, or they may give them to the poor and helpless and all others without attendants, or they may give countless servants from time to time to look after the shrines and mausoleums of Buddhas or to transcribe the true teachings of the Buddhas. Those servants are all intelligent and highly skilled, naturally obedient, always diligent and never lazy, with honest minds, peaceful and happy minds, altruistic minds, humane and benevolent minds, respectful minds, minds free from resentment and hostility, able to adjust to the customs of those for whom they work, able to be of benefit to everyone. Also, from the influences of the enlightening beings' pure conduct, they have talent and artistry, and are masters of crafts and mathematics. They are skilled in service and able to please.

"At that time, the enlightening beings dedicate the roots of goodness in this way: 'May all sentient beings attain docile minds, cultivating roots of goodness with all Buddhas; may all sentient beings obediently provide offerings to all Buddhas and be able to hear and absorb what the Buddhas teach; may all sentient beings be accepted by the Buddhas, always observe the enlightened ones, without any other thought; may all sentient beings not spoil the seed of buddhahood, diligently cultivating all roots of goodness in accord with the Buddhas; may all sentient beings always diligently provide for all Buddhas, not wasting any time; may all sentient beings hold the sublime doctrines of the Buddhas, their words pure, traveling without fear; may all sentient beings always be happy to see Buddhas, never tiring, not begrudging their lives to the Buddhas; may all sentient beings get to see the Buddhas, their minds without indulgence or attachment, free from worldly dependence; may all sentient beings only take refuge in Buddha and forever leave all false resorts; may all sentient beings follow the Buddha-way, their minds always blissfully contemplating the supreme Buddha teaching.' This is great enlightening beings' dedication of roots of goodness when giving servants, to cause sentient beings to get rid of defilement, clear the ground of buddhahood, and be able to manifest the free body of the enlightened.

"Great enlightening beings give their bodies to those who come ask for them; when they give, they engender a humble mind, a mind like the earth, a mind enduring all suffering without changing or wavering, a mind to serve sentient beings tirelessly, a mind regarding all sentient beings like a benevolent mother, turning over all their virtues to them, a mind of forgiveness for the various impositions and aggressions of ignorant evil beings, and rest on the foundations of goodness, diligently performing service.

"At that time enlightening beings dedicate all the roots of goodness in this way: 'May all sentient beings never lack what they need, cultivate the practices of enlightening beings unremittingly, not give up the just rewards of all enlightening beings, remain on the path traveled by enlightening beings, comprehend the equal real nature of enlightening beings, get to be of the number of the family of Buddhas, abide by truthful speech, sustain enlightening practice, cause all worldlings to be able to clarify the Buddha-teaching, deeply believe in it, and realize the ultimate consummation of the teaching, and cause sentient beings to produce pure, excellent roots of goodness, abide in great virtue, and fulfill universal knowledge. Also with these roots of goodness I will cause all sentient beings to always get to attend all Buddhas, to understand all their teachings, to bear the teachings, reading and reciting them, never forgetting them or letting them be lost or scattered, their minds well subdued. Those who are not self-controlled I will tame, training them with the methods of stillness and serenity. I will cause sentient beings, in the presence of the Buddhas, to persevere in these things. Also, by these roots of goodness I will cause all sentient beings to be the foremost monument, worthy of receiving the various offerings of the world. I will cause all sentient beings to become supreme fields of blessings, attain Buddha knowledge, and enlighten everyone. I will cause all sentient beings to become the best of recipients, able to benefit all living beings. I will cause all sentient beings to become the best of benefactors, able to foster the endowment of all roots of goodness. I will cause all sentient beings to become the finest receivers of gifts, able to cause the givers to obtain infinite rewards. I will cause all sentient beings to attain emancipation from the realms of desire, form, and formlessness. I will cause all sentient beings to become the foremost of leaders, able to show the world the path that accords with truth. I will cause all sentient beings to attain marvelous total mental command, fully holding all the true teachings of the Buddhas. I will cause all sentient beings to attain realization of the infinite primary cosmos of reality, and fulfill the true path unobstructed as space.' This is great enlightening beings' dedication of roots of goodness when giving their own bodies, to cause all sentient beings to attain the body of infinite knowledge of the sanctified ones.

"Great enlightening beings are joyful when they hear the teaching; they conceive pure faith, and are able to offer their own bodies to the Buddha, raptly believing in the treasure of the unexcelled teaching. They think of the Buddhas as their parents, and read and recite, absorb and hold the teachings of the path of nonobstruction, entering into all the gates of countless teachings, jewels of wisdom, roots of goodness. Their minds always think of infinite Buddhas. They enter the sphere of buddhahood and attain to deep comprehension of its principles. They are able, with the subtle, mysterious pure voice of the enlightened, to produce clouds of Buddha teachings and shower rain of Buddha teachings. Bravely and freely they are able to analytically explain the supreme state of the omniscient. Fully consummating the vehicle of all-knowledge, they fulfill all potentials with immeasurable hundreds of thousands of millions of great teachings.

"When great enlightening beings hear such teachings from Buddhas, their joy knows no bounds; they abide firmly by the truth, cut off their own doubt and confusion, and also cause others' doubts to be removed as well. Their minds are always light and happy, full of virtuous qualities, replete with roots of goodness. Their attention is continuous, helping sentient beings without their minds ever being exhausted. They attain supreme knowledge and become treasuries of diamonds. They associate closely with Buddhas and purify buddha-fields, always diligently attend all the enlightened ones. At that time the enlightening beings dedicate the roots of goodness in this way: 'May all sentient beings attain a fully developed, most excellent body, in the care of all Buddhas; may all sentient beings always be near the Buddhas, abide with the Buddhas, and always gaze upon them, never leaving; may all sentient beings attain a pure indestructible body, endowed with all virtue and knowledge; may all sentient beings always diligently serve all Buddhas, and carry out the ultimate pure practice of nonassumption;

may all sentient beings attain the egoless body, divorced from self and possession; may all sentient beings be able to distribute their bodies throughout the lands of the ten directions, like reflections appearing, without coming or going; may all sentient beings attain the body of freedom, going everywhere in the ten directions without self or reception; may all sentient beings attain the buddha-body, born in the home of the unexcelled embodiment of the realization of thusness; may all sentient beings attain the great power of forbearance of the body of power of truth, which none can break down; may all sentient beings attain the incomparable body and realize the pure body of reality of the enlightened; may all sentient beings develop the body of transmundane virtues, born in the pure realm of reality where nothing is obtained.' This is the dedication of roots of goodness of enlightening beings when offering their bodies to Buddhas, to cause sentient beings to dwell forever in the house of the Buddhas of past, present, and future.

"Great enlightening beings give their bodies to all sentient beings, because they want to cause them to develop roots of goodness, and to remember and think of roots of goodness. Great enlightening beings wish their bodies to be great bright lamps able to illumine all sentient beings, to be means of life supporting all beings, to be treasuries of wonderful teaching able to sustain all living beings, to be pure light to awaken all sentient beings, to be lights of the world causing all sentient beings to always see, to be causes and conditions of roots of goodness causing sentient beings to always get the opportunity to meet them, to be genuine teachers causing all sentient beings to receive instruction and guidance, to be even paths on which all sentient beings may tread, to be unexcelled, complete comfort enabling all sentient beings to be freed from suffering and be purified, to be clear suns universally and impartially benefiting the world.

At that time enlightening beings dedicate the roots of goodness in this way: 'May all sentient beings always associate with the Buddhas and enter the realm of Buddha knowledge; may all sentient beings attain adaptable knowledge and abide in unexcelled awareness; may all sentient beings always be in the assemblies of Buddhas and their minds be well tuned; may all sentient beings always comport themselves with the dignity of Buddhas; may all sentient beings attain nirvana and profoundly understand the meaning of the teaching; may all sentient beings be complete in knowledge and conduct and be born in the house of the Buddhas; may all sentient beings give up ignorant craving and abide in the aspiration of buddhahood; may all sentient beings develop excellent roots of goodness and sit at the tree of enlightenment; may all sentient beings slay the brigands that are the afflictions and get rid of these enemies; may all sentient beings fully preserve all Buddha teachings.' This is great enlightening beings' dedication of roots of goodness when giving their bodies to all sentient beings, because they want to benefit all sentient beings and cause them to reach the realm of supreme peace.

"Great enlightening beings personally attend the Buddhas, wanting to requite their great benevolence, thinking of them as like parents. They have deep faith in the Buddhas, and preserve enlightenment, abiding by the principles of the Buddhas, detaching from mundane conceptions. Born in the house of the enlightened, they follow the Buddhas, leaving the realm of delusion. They arrive at the sphere of action of all Buddhas and become vessels of the teachings of all Buddhas. At that time the enlightening beings dedicate these roots of goodness in this way: 'May all sentient beings attain pure minds and adorn themselves with the jewel of universal knowledge; may all sentient beings abide in good self-control and avoid all bad actions; may all sentient beings gain indestructible, steadfast retinues, able to absorb the true teaching of the Buddhas; may all sentient beings become students of Buddhas and reach the enlightening beings' stage of coronation; may all sentient beings always be in the keeping of the Buddhas and forever give up whatever is not good; may all sentient beings follow the Buddhas and practice the supreme principle of enlightening beings; may all sentient beings enter the sphere of Buddhas and receive the prediction of omniscience; may all sentient beings be thoroughly equal to the Buddhas and master all the Buddha teachings; may all sentient beings be in the care of the Buddhas and always be able to practice acting without grasping or attachment; may all sentient beings become the foremost attendants of the Buddhas, and in the company of the Buddhas cultivate the practice of knowledge and wisdom.' This is great enlightening beings' dedication of roots of goodness when attending Buddhas, because they want to actually realize the enlightenment of the Buddhas, because they want to save all sentient beings, because they want to transcend all in the triple world, because they want to perfect nonmalevolence, because they want to attain immeasurably great enlightenment, because they want to develop knowledge illuminating the Buddha teachings, because they want to always receive acceptance by the Buddhas, because they want to gain the protection of the Buddhas, because they want to truly understand all Buddha teachings, because they want to develop roots of goodness equal to those of the Buddhas of all times, and because they want to fully develop an unembittered mind and realize the teachings of all Buddhas.

"Great enlightening beings give up their countries, able to relinquish all things, including kingship; their minds attain freedom from all worldly concerns, and they have no ties, no bonds, no obsessions or attachments. They avoid evil deeds and work for the benefit of sentient beings without attachment to the results of their deeds. They do not take pleasure in worldly things, and are no longer attached to or eager for any realm of existence. Though they live in the world, they do not set their hearts on it. They do not cling to material, mental, or sense phenomena, and their minds do not rest on anything internal or external. They never forget the practices of enlightening beings, and never abandon the wise; keeping the far-reaching practical commitments of enlightening beings, they always gladly serve all good companions.

"At such times, the enlightening beings dedicate these roots of goodness in this way: 'May all sentient beings become monarchs of truth, masters of truth, and reach the other shore; may all sentient beings become monarchs of the Buddha teaching and destroy their enemies, the afflictions; may all sentient beings dwell in the sovereignty of buddhahood, attain enlightened knowledge, and expound the Buddha teachings; may all sentient beings live in the realm of buddhahood and be able to turn the wheel of the teaching of unexcelled freedom; may all sentient beings be born in the house of the enlightened ones, master the teachings, and preserve the family of Buddhas forever; may all sentient beings reveal innumerable true teachings of the king of truth, perfecting boundless great enlightening beings; may all sentient beings abide in the pure realm of reality, become monarchs of the great truth, and manifest the emergence of Buddhas, continuing unbroken; may all sentient beings be monarchs of knowledge and wisdom in all worlds, edifying and guiding living beings without ever abandoning them; may all sentient beings be donors of truth to all sentient beings in all worlds throughout the space of the cosmos, enabling them all to abide in the Great Vehicle; may all sentient beings manage to become monarchs replete with myriad virtues, with roots of goodness equal to those of the Buddhas of past, present, and future.' This is great enlightening beings' dedication of roots of goodness when giving away kingship, because they want to cause all sentient beings to ultimately live in peace.

"When great enlightening beings see people come asking for the magnificent buildings of the royal capital as well as the revenues from customs duties collected at the borders, they give it all ungrudgingly, wholeheartedly turning toward enlightenment, making great vows, abiding in great benevolence, practicing great compassion, their minds joyfully intent on helping sentient beings. By great knowledge they understand the profound truth and abide in the equal real nature of Buddhas. They practice giving because they are determined to find omniscience, because they have profound longing for freedom, because they seek realization of independent knowledge, because they purify all virtues, because they abide in steadfast great knowledge, because they extensively gather all kinds of roots of goodness, because they carry out the undertakings of all the Buddha teachings, because they spontaneously awaken to the principle of great knowledge, because they abide in enlightenment without regressing, because they cultivate the practical vows of all enlightening beings, and because they thoroughly consummate knowledge of methods of enlightenment.

"These roots of goodness they dedicate in this way: 'May all sentient beings be able to purify infinite lands and present them to the Buddhas to live in; may all sentient beings always enjoy living in forests, silent, peaceful, undisturbed; may all sentient beings not dwell in capitals or cities, their hearts delighting in peace and quiet, forever attaining ultimate serenity; may all sentient beings be forever unattached to any world and always gladly avoid all mundane talk; may all sentient beings attain hearts free from covetousness, giving whatever they have without regret; may all sentient beings attain emancipated minds, giving up occupation with business; may all sentient beings be free from miserliness and always practice generous giving; may all sentient beings have unattached minds, transcending the events of home life; may all sentient beings attain freedom from suffering and eliminate all fear of calamity; may all sentient beings purify all worlds in the ten directions and present them to the Buddhas.' This is great enlightening beings' dedication of roots of goodness when giving away royal capitals, to cause sentient beings to all be able to purify the buddha-fields.

"Great enlightening beings' ladies-in-waiting are all beautiful and talented, witty and graceful, skilled in conversation, dancing, and singing, adorned with various clothes, flowers, and perfumes, endlessly delightful to all who see them: such precious women, countless numbers of them, are all born of the good deeds of enlightening beings, free to do as they will, yet impeccably respectful and agreeable—all of them the enlightening beings give to those who ask for them, without longing for them, without missing them, without obsession with them, without attachment to them, without clinging to them, without craving for them, without thinking about them, without pursuing them, without attachment to their appearance, without lust for them.

"At such a time the enlightening beings contemplate the roots of goodness and dedicate them to enabling all sentient beings to attain emancipation, to attain the joy of the Buddha teachings, to attain the enduring in the midst of the unenduring, to attain the incorruptible mind of adamantine knowledge, to enter the site of Buddha's enlightenment, to reach the other shore, to attain the supremely enlightened mind, to be able to comprehend all things, to produce all roots of goodness, to enter the house of the Buddhas of all times.

"Great enlightening beings, abiding by this principle, are born in the house of the enlightened, develop the pure, supreme causal basis of the Buddhas, produce the supreme path of universal knowledge, enter deeply into the far-reaching work of knowledge of enlightening beings, and get rid of all worldly defilements and afflictions. They are always able to provide offerings to the virtuous fields of blessings. They expound the wondrous teaching to sentient beings, skillfully arranging it, causing them to cultivate pure practices, always endeavoring to embody all roots of goodness.

"At such a time the enlightening beings dedicate the roots of goodness in this way: 'May all sentient beings always attain a retinue of innumerable concentrations, the supreme concentration of enlightening beings, continuing uninterrupted; may all sentient beings always delight in seeing Buddha and enter absorption in the adornments of Buddhas;

may all sentient beings accomplish the inconceivable concentration of enlightening beings, sporting freely in immeasurable spiritual powers; may all sentient beings enter concentration in accord with truth and attain incorruptible minds; may all sentient beings thoroughly attain the most profound concentration of enlightening beings, and realize freedom in all meditations and concentrations; may all sentient beings attain liberated minds and accomplish the group of all concentration states; may all sentient beings attain skill in all kinds of concentration, able to take in all aspects of concentration; may all sentient beings attain concentration of supreme knowledge, able to learn and practice the various methods of concentration; may all sentient beings attain unobstructed concentration and enter into deep meditation concentration, never regressing or losing it; may all sentient beings attain unattached concentration, their minds always sensing truly and not grasping duality.' This is great enlightening beings' dedication of roots of goodness when giving away their retinues, because they want to cause all sentient beings to gain indestructible pure retinues, because they want to cause all sentient beings to gain retinues of enlightening beings, because they want to cause all sentient beings to be able to fulfill the powers of omniscience, because they want to cause all sentient beings to realize supreme wisdom, because they want to cause all sentient beings to have amenable retinues, because they want to cause all sentient beings to attain the pure reality-body of the enlightened, because they want to cause all sentient beings to attain orderly, reasonable powers of elucidation and skillfully expound the inexhaustible treasury of the Buddha's teachings, because they want to cause all sentient beings to forever relinquish all conventional mundane virtues and equally cultivate pure transmundane virtues, because they want to cause all sentient beings' purifying work to be complete, and develop all pure qualities, and because they want to cause all Buddha teachings to be evident to all sentient beings, universally purified by the light of truth.

"Great enlightening beings can give away their beloved spouses and children, as did the Loving Prince, Adornment Manifesting King, and countless other great enlightening beings. At such a time, the enlightening beings mount the mind of all-knowledge, carry out total giving, and purely cultivate the path of giving of enlightening beings, their minds clear and without regret. They give up what they prize in quest of omniscience, to cause sentient beings to have profound, pure aspirations, accomplish the practice of enlightenment, observe the path of enlightening beings, reflect on the enlightenment of the Buddhas, and abide in the family of Buddhas.

"When great enlightening beings have developed such a giving mind, they determine to seek the body of buddhahood; they observe their own bodies to be bound to everything and unable to be independent. Still, they help all sentient beings with their own bodies, like continents of treasure, giving all, causing the unfulfilled to be fulfilled. Thus do enlightening beings care for sentient beings, wishing to cause their own bodies to be the best of monuments, to cause all to become joyful. They want to create an egalitarian, equanimous attitude in the world. They want to be reservoirs of pure coolness for sentient beings. They want to give all peace and happiness to sentient beings. They want to be great donors to sentient beings. They are capable of such magnificent commitments because their knowledge is free and they know the practices carried out by enlightening beings. Proceeding toward omniscience, they vow to become supremely wise fields of blessings. They care for all sentient beings and always follow and protect them, while being able to accomplish their own salvation. Their light of knowledge and wisdom illumines the whole world. They always conscientiously remember the generosity of enlightening beings and always raptly contemplate the sphere of realization of thusness.

"Great enlightening beings dedicate the roots of virtue collected by giving away spouses and children with unbound, unattached, liberated minds in this way: 'May all sentient beings, abiding in the enlightenment of Buddhahood, produce phantom bodies pervading the cosmos, turning the wheel of teaching that never turns back; may all sentient beings attain the body of nonattachment and go to all buddha-fields by the power of will; may all sentient beings give up the mind of love and hate and sever the knot of greed and anger; may all sentient beings be children of the Buddhas, following the course of the Buddhas; may all sentient beings steadfastly think of the Buddhas as themselves; may all sentient beings always be children of Buddha, born by transformation from the teaching; may all sentient beings reach the ultimate and accomplish the independent knowledge and wisdom of the enlightened; may all sentient beings realize the enlightenment of buddhahood and be forever free of afflictions; may all sentient beings be able to fully expound the way to enlightenment, always blissfully practicing the giving of the unsurpassed teaching; may all sentient beings attain a rightly concentrated mind, their concentration unbroken by any objects; may all sentient beings sit at the tree of enlightenment, attain supreme true awakening, and teach innumerable good men and women born by transformation from the teaching.' This is enlightening beings' dedication of roots of goodness when giving spouses and children, to cause sentient beings to all realize the unattached knowledge of unhindered liberation.

"Great enlightening beings give houses and furniture to any who ask for them, practicing the principle of generosity, having no attachments to home, leaving behind all thoughts of home life, fed up with family business, having no craving or taste for comforts and conveniences. Their minds are without ties or attachments; they know the household is fragile, and they disdain it, having no craving for it at all, only wanting to leave home and cultivate the practices of enlightening beings, adorning themselves with the enlightening teachings and qualities of buddhahood. They give up all without regret, always praised by the Buddhas, generously giving whatever they have—houses, goods— wherever they are, without attachment in their minds. When they see beggars come they are joyful, and the enlightening beings dedicate these roots of goodness in this way: 'May all sentient beings be liberated from the ties of householding, enter homelessness, and cultivate religious practice in Buddhism; may all sentient beings get rid of the taint of miserliness and gladly give all, their minds never shrinking back; may all sentient beings forever detach from householding, have few desires, be content, not storing anything; may all sentient beings leave the home of conventional society and live in the home of the enlightened; may all sentient beings be free from clinging to home and family, and though they live at home have no attachment in their minds; may all sentient beings be skillful teachers and guides, expounding enlightened wisdom without leaving lay life; may all sentient beings, while physically living at home, mentally always live in accord with Buddha-knowledge; may all sentient beings, while in the state of lay home life, dwell in the state of buddhahood and cause infinite sentient beings to develop joyful minds.' This is great enlightening beings' dedication of roots of goodness when giving houses, to cause sentient beings to accomplish the various practical vows and spiritual powers and knowledge of enlightening beings.

"Great enlightening beings give all kinds of gardens, groves, terraces, and pleasant parks, with this thought: 'I should make a fine grove for all sentient beings; I should show all sentient beings the pleasure of the teaching; I should give all sentient beings joy; I should show all sentient beings boundless enjoyment; I should open the gate of the teaching of purity for all sentient beings; I should cause all sentient beings' minds to swell with joy; I should cause all beings to attain complete enlightenment; I should cause all beings to fulfill the great vow; I should be like a benevolent father to all sentient beings; I should cause all sentient beings to observe with knowledge and wisdom; I should give all beings the necessities of life; I should be like a loving mother to all sentient beings, nurturing all roots of goodness and great aspirations.'

"When great enlightening beings cultivate roots of goodness like this, they do not detest evil sentient beings and do not make the mistake of thinking to reject them; even if all the beings in the world are ingrates, they never have any hatred or resentment, and never give a thought to revenge—they only want to annihilate their innumerable sufferings and afflictions. In all worlds their minds are like space, unaffected and unattached; everywhere they observe the true character of all things. They take the great vow to extinguish the suffering of sentient beings, never wearying of or abandoning the determination of the Great Vehicle. Annihilating all views, they cultivate the impartial practice and vows of enlightening beings.

"Great enlightening beings, having contemplated in this way, unify all their roots of goodness and dedicate them all in this way: 'May all sentient beings richly produce innumerable good qualities moment to moment, and develop minds like supreme gardens and groves; may all sentient beings attain imperturbability, see all Buddhas, and make them happy; may all sentient beings enjoy the garden of truth and attain to sublime enjoyment of the gardens of the buddha-lands; may all sentient beings attain pure minds and always see the garden of psychic powers of the enlightened ones; may all sentient beings attain the playful enjoyment of buddhahood, always sporting in the realm of wisdom; may all sentient beings attain the pleasure of carefree roaming, traveling to the assemblies at enlightenment sites in buddha-fields everywhere; may all sentient beings accomplish the liberated roaming of enlightening beings and carry out the practices of enlightening beings throughout the future without ever tiring of it; may all sentient beings see all Buddhas filling the cosmos, develop vastly broad minds, and abide in the groves of buddhahood; may all sentient beings be able to go to all buddha-fields and give offerings to the buddhas in each and every field; may all sentient beings attain hearts of good desires, purifying and adorning all buddha-fields.' This is great enlightening beings' dedication of roots of goodness when giving away all gardens, groves, and terraces.

"Great enlightening beings perform countless great charitable works, all pure, approved by the Buddhas, never injuring a single sentient being, causing all sentient beings to avoid all evils, to purify their action, speech, and thought, and to achieve wisdom. They clear countless spheres of purity and pile up therein countless fine things to support life; activating the most rarely attained spirit of enlightenment, they practice unlimited giving, causing sentient beings to abide in the path of purity, good in the beginning, the middle, and the end, and to engender pure faith. They gladden countless sentient beings according to their hearts' desires; with great benevolence and compassion they bring all to safety. They serve and provide for the Buddhas of the past, present, and future. Because they want to develop the seed of Buddhahood, they practice giving without regret in their hearts, increasing the development of the faculty of faith, fulfilling superlative conduct, moment to moment progressing to transcendence.

"At such times the enlightening beings dedicate the roots of goodness in this way: 'May all sentient beings develop the mind of the Great Vehicle and be able to accomplish the giving of the Great Vehicle; may all sentient beings be able to carry out giving to the masses, total giving, good giving, supreme giving, unexcelled giving, most unsurpassable giving, incomparable giving, giving transcending all worlds, giving praised by all the Buddhas; may all sentient beings become the best of donors, rescuing sentient beings from the various conditions of misery and enabling them to enter the path of unobstructed knowledge, cultivating impartial vows, roots of goodness in accord with truth, attaining nondiscrimination, realizing inherent knowledge; may all sentient beings abide securely in the dispassionate, serene knowledge of meditation concentrations, enter the undying path, consummate knowledge of all spiritual powers, persevere bravely to fulfill the enlightened qualities adorning all the stages and reach the other shore, never turning back; may all sentient beings set up great charities without ever wearying, providing for and helping sentient beings unceasingly, consummating the unexcelled knowledge of all means of liberation; may all sentient beings always diligently plant all roots of goodness, and reach the other shore of myriad virtues; may all sentient beings always be praised by the Buddhas and be great donors in the world, replete with virtues, filling the cosmos, illumining the ten directions, giving unexcelled happiness; may all sentient beings establish great charities, widely gathering roots of goodness, equally including all sentient beings, and arrive at the other shore; may all sentient beings accomplish supreme giving, causing sentient beings everywhere to abide in the foremost vehicle; may all sentient beings give at appropriate times, forever avoid improper timing, and consummate great giving; may all sentient beings accomplish good giving and reach the other shore of great giving of the Buddhas; may all sentient beings ultimately always carry on magnificent giving, considering all Buddhas their teachers, able to approach them all and make great offerings; may all sentient beings abide in pure giving, gathering infinite virtues, equal to the cosmos, and reach the other shore; may all sentient beings be great donors in all worlds, vowing to liberate all creatures and live in the realm of the enlightened.' This is great enlightening beings' dedication of roots of goodness when establishing great charities, to cause sentient beings to practice supreme giving, giving to consummate buddhahood, giving to perfect goodness, incorruptible giving, giving of offerings to Buddhas, giving without resentment, giving to save sentient beings, giving to attain omniscience, giving to always see the Buddhas, giving with great perseverence, great giving to perfect the virtues of all enlightening beings and the knowledge and wisdom of buddhahood.

"Great enlightening beings give all necessities of life unbegrudgingly, without seeking reward, without hoping for worldly prosperity or happiness. They rid the mind of errant thought, and meditate well on the truth, because they want to benefit all sentient beings and clearly perceive the true nature of all things. According to the various different needs of sentient beings, they prepare innumerable things to support life, the embellishments of which are all fine and beautiful. They carry out unbounded giving, total giving, and giving of everything internal and external. When they carry out this giving, they increase their power of determination, gain great virtue, perfect the jewel of mind, and are ever able to safeguard all sentient beings, causing them all to develop the most excellent aspirations, yet with never a thought of seeking reward. Their roots of goodness are equal to those of the Buddhas of past, present, and future, and by them they all fulfill the knowledge of all means of liberation.

"Great enlightening beings dedicate all the roots of goodness in this giving to sentient beings, that all sentient beings may be purified and master themselves; that all sentient beings may extinguish afflictions and purify all buddha-fields; that all sentient beings, with a pure mind, may pervade the cosmos in a single moment of thought; that all sentient beings may fill the cosmos of space with knowledge; that all sentient beings attain universal knowledge, enter everywhere in the three realms of desire, form, and formlessness, and tame sentient beings, at all times turning the irreversible wheel of the pure teaching; that all sentient beings may be endowed with omniscience and be able to manifest the techniques of spiritual powers to benefit sentient beings; that all sentient beings be able to awaken to complete enlightenment and forever ceaselessly expound the true teaching in all regions, causing all beings to get to hear and know of it; that all sentient beings may cultivate the practices of enlightening beings for countless eons and manage to fulfill them all; that all sentient beings may cultivate the practices of enlightening beings in all worlds that may be accounted or spoken of, be they defiled or pure worlds, small or large, gross or subtle, inverted or upright, uniformly or variously adorned, extending throughout them all; that all sentient beings may in every passing moment perform the work of Buddhas of past, present, and future, teaching and transforming sentient beings and turning them toward universal knowledge.

"Great enlightening beings provide sentient beings with everything they need, in order to cause the Buddha-teaching to continue unbroken. With great compassion they save all sentient beings. Abiding stably in great benevolence, they cultivate the practices of enlightening beings. They never violate the teachings of the Buddha; with skill in means, they practice whatever is good, not letting the lineage of Buddhas die out. They give whatever is required, without being troubled; they give all with never a regret, being always earnestly dedicated to the path of universal knowledge.

"At such times, the various forms and species of living creatures from the lands of the ten directions, various fields of blessings, all come and gather around the enlightening beings, making various requests of them: the enlightening beings, seeing them, receive them all, their hearts becoming joyful, like seeing good friends; with great compassion and mercy they want to satisfy their wishes. Their generosity increases unceasingly, and without weariness; they fulfill their requests, satisfying them according to their needs, freeing them from the miseries of destitution. Then the seekers are very happy and spread the voice of praise of the virtue of the enlightening beings, so that their good repute becomes widespread and everyone comes to them. The joy of the enlightening beings upon seeing them has no measure—even if one experienced the pleasures of Indra, king of gods, for a trillion quadrillion eons, experienced the pleasures of the Suyama heaven for countless eons, experienced the pleasures of the Tushita heaven for immeasurable eons, experienced the pleasures of the heaven of good emanations for boundless eons, experienced the pleasures of the heaven of free enjoyment of others' emanations for incomparable eons, experienced the pleasures of the Brahma kings for uncountable eons, experienced the three thousand royal pleasures of world monarchs for unaccountable eons, experienced the pleasures of the heaven of universal purity for unthinkable eons, and experienced the pleasures of the heaven of pure abodes for unspeakably many eons, none of it could equal the joy and delight of great enlightening beings upon seeing the needy come to them. They are happy and ebullient, their faith grows, their aspiration is pure, their faculties are harmoniously tuned, their resolution is fully developed, and they progress toward complete enlightenment.

"The great enlightening beings dedicate these roots of goodness to the welfare of all sentient beings, to the peace and happiness of all sentient beings, to the true benefit of all sentient beings, to the purification of all sentient beings, to induce all sentient beings to seek enlightenment, to cause all sentient beings to attain equality, to cause all sentient beings to attain intelligent, benevolent minds, to cause all sentient beings to enter the Great Vehicle, to cause all sentient beings to attain wisdom, and to cause all sentient beings to fulfill the practical undertakings of the Universally Good enlightening being, fulfill the vehicle of the ten powers, and actually realize true awakening.

"When great enlightening beings dedicate roots of goodness this way, they are liberated in word, thought, and deed; they have no attachments or bonds, no concept of sentient beings, no concept of a life, no concept of a personality, no concept of a person, no concept of a youth, no concept of one born, no concept of an agent, no concept of a receiver, no concept of existence, no concept of nonexistence, no concept of present life or afterlife, no concept of dying here and being born there, no concept of permanence, no concept of impermanence, no concept of the three realms of existence, no concept of the nonexistence of the three realms; they are not perceiving, nor are they not perceiving. Thus, they are not practicing dedication bound, not practicing dedication liberated from bonds, not practicing dedication by action, not practicing dedication by the results of action, not practicing dedication with discrimination, not practicing dedication indiscriminately, not practicing dedication thinking, not practicing dedication after thought, not practicing dedication with mind, not practicing dedication mindlessly.

"When great enlightening beings practice dedication in this way, they do not cling to inside or outside, subject or object, cause or effect, right or wrong, thought or nonthought, from the birth of form, the passing away of form, or to sensation, perception, patterning, or consciousness, or to the birth or passing away of sensation, perception, patterning, or consciousness. If great enlightening beings are able to not be bound by these things, then they are not bound by form or by the birth or passing away of form; they are not bound by sensation, perception, patterning, or consciousness, or by the birth or passing away of sensation, perception, patterning, or consciousness. If they are able to not be bound by these things, then they also are not released from these things. Why? Because there does not exist the slightest thing being born, already born, or to be born—there is nothing that can be apprehended, nothing that can be clung to. All things are inherently like this—they have no intrinsic nature of their own: they are intrinsically incompatible with any characterization, neither one nor two, not many and not infinite, not small or large, not narrow or broad, not deep or shallow, not nullity and not concepts, not so and not not so, not truth and not not truth, not substantial and not insubstantial, not existent and not nonexistent. Enlightening beings thus see things as not things, while in terms of speech they follow convention in defining what are not things as things: they do not cut off the paths of action and do not give up enlightening practices; they seek omniscience without ever turning back. They know that all conditions of action are like dreams, that sounds and voices are like echoes, that sentient beings are like shadows, that all things are like phantoms—yet they do not deny the power of the action of causes and conditions; they know that the function of actions is far-reaching. They understand that all things do nothing, and traverse the path of nondoing without ever giving it up.

"These great enlightening beings abide in universal knowledge, dedicating all, whether positive or negative, to omniscience—they practice dedication in all places without ever retreating. In what senses, by what meanings, is it called dedication? It is called dedication because of having crossed over the world forever and arrived at the other shore. It is called dedication because of crossing over the path of speech and arriving at the other shore. It is called dedication because of leaving behind all sorts of concepts and reaching the other shore. It is called dedication because of having forever ended the idea of corporeality and arrived at the other shore. It is called dedication because of having left dependency behind forever and reached the other shore. It is called dedication because of having ended contrivance forever and reached the other shore. It is called dedication because of having left all states of existence forever and arrived at the other shore. It is called dedication because of having abandoned all grasping forever and arrived at the other shore. It is called dedication because of having left all worldly things forever and arrived at the other shore.

"When great enlightening beings practice dedication in this way, then they are living in accord with the Buddha, in accord with the Truth, in accord with knowledge, in accord with enlightenment, in accord with its meaning, in accord with its sphere, in accord with its practice, in accord with reality, and in accord with purity. When great enlightening beings practice dedication in this way, then they comprehend all things; then they serve all Buddhas; there is not a single Buddha they do not attend, not a single thing they do not offer; there is not a single thing that can be destroyed, not a single thing that can be turned away from, not a single thing that can be clung to, not a single thing that can be avoided. They do not see anything at all, internal or external, that has any disintegration or violates causality. They are replete with the power of the teaching, and never cease.

"This is the sixth of the great enlightening beings' dedications, following up and making permanent all roots of goodness, causing them to endure. When great enlightening beings abide in this dedication, they are always in the care of the Buddhas; they firmly endure, unregressing, and enter the profound essence of things, cultivating universal knowledge. They accord with the meaning of the Teaching, accord with the nature of things, accord with all enduring roots of goodness, accord with all completely fulfilled great vows, and fully embody the truth which accords with perdurance, which cannot be broken by even the adamant. In the midst of all things they attain independence."

Then the enlightening being Diamond Banner, surveying the ten directions, looking over the assembled masses, and viewing the cosmos, entered into the most profound meaning of verbal expression, cultivated an immeasurably broad mind, covered the whole world with the mind of great compassion, developed the mind of the family of Buddhas of past, future, and present, entered into the virtues of all Buddhas, perfected the body of independent powers of the Buddhas, observed the mental inclinations of sentient beings, and, according to their roots of goodness that could be developed and matured, manifested physical bodies to them based on the body of the essence of things. Imbued with spiritual power from the Buddha, he said in verse,

> Enlightening beings appear physically as monarchs
> In the highest worldly ranks,
> Their virtues and glory surpassing all,
> Providing benefit for all living creatures.
>
> Their minds are pure, without attachment;
> They are masters of the world, respected by all.
> They promulgate true teaching to educate people,
> And cause sentient beings everywhere to attain peace.
>
> Manifesting birth among the noble, rising to monarchy,
> They always carry on the teaching according to the truth.
> Benevolent by nature, free from cruelty,
> All in the ten directions look up to them and obey them.

Their knowledge and discernment always clear,
Their capacities are fully complete.
As rulers and leaders they are followed by all;
They crush the armies of demons and annihilate them.

They hold fast to pure morality, without transgression;
With firm determination they forbear, unshakably.
They vow to forever clear away anger from the mind
And always gladly practice the teachings of Buddha.

Food and drink, perfumes and garlands, as well as clothes,
Vehicles, chairs, cushions, and lamps—
Enlightening beings give these to people to help them,
And give innumerable other kinds of things as well.

They practice giving to be of aid,
Causing them to open their hearts.
In regard to the Supreme as well as others
Their minds are pure and full of joy.

Enlightening beings provide for all,
Able to give up everything they have, internal and external,
Unfailingly causing their minds to be forever pure
And never to be narrow or mean.

They may give their heads or eyes
Or give their hands or feet,
Skin, flesh, bones, marrow, and so on—
All they give up unbegrudgingly.

Enlightening beings, on the throne of royalty,
Of the most noble of tribes,
Open their mouths and put forth their tongues to give living beings,
Their hearts joyful, without sorrow or attachment.

The virtues of giving their tongues
They dedicate to all sentient beings,
Praying that based on this excellent cause
All may attain the universal tongue of the enlightened.

They may give their spouses and children, or their royal rank,
Or give themselves to be servants;
Their minds are pure and always joyful,
Thus they have no remorse or regret.

They give whatever is required,
Aiding according to the time, unwearied;
All they have they can disburse
So that all seekers be satisfied.

They give their bodies to hear the teaching
And practice austerities seeking enlightenment;
And for the sake of the living they give up all,
Seeking unexcelled knowledge without turning back.

By the true teaching heard from the Buddhas
They give up their bodies to be servants,
Because they want to save all living beings;
They develop a mind of infinite joy.

They see the World-Honored Guide
Can bring widespread weal with kindness;
Then they dance with joy
And absorb the savor of the profound teaching of enlightenment.

Whatever roots of goodness enlightening beings have
They dedicate all to sentient beings;
They rescue all without exception,
Forever liberating them, so they're eternally at peace.

Enlightening beings' retinues
Are attractive, talented, eloquent and intelligent,
Adorned with all manner of embellishments—
Flower garlands, clothes, and perfumes:
These retinues, rare as they are,
Enlightening beings are able to give away,
Wholeheartedly seeking true enlightenment to liberate beings,
Never for a moment giving up this determination.

Enlightening beings thus think clearly
And fully carry out various great works,
Dedicating all to conscious beings
Without developing a grasping mind.

Enlightening beings give up their royal ranks
As well as their land and cities,
Palaces, bowers, gardens, and groves,
Servants and attendants, all ungrudgingly.

Over countless millions of eons
They travel everywhere giving,

Whereby they teach and lead living beings,
Causing them to ascend to the unexcelled shore.

Countless species, each different,
Come and gather from all worlds;
Seeing them, enlightening beings are joyful
And satisfy them according to need.

Like the dedication of the Buddhas of all times
Enlightening beings perform similar works;
The course of the Human Taming Lords
They emulate to reach the other shore.

Enlightening beings examine all things:
Who can comprehend these things?
What is comprehension, what is comprehended?
Thus their giving dwells nowhere.

The adaptive knowledge of enlightening beings' dedication,
The expedient methods of enlightening beings' dedication,
The true meaning of enlightening beings' dedication:
They have no attachment to those things.

Their minds do not conceptualize actions arbitrarily,
And they are not obsessed with results of action;
They know the nature of enlightenment comes from conditions,
And enter the profound realm of reality, without opposition.

They do not have action in their bodies,
Nor does it dwell in the mind.
By wisdom they realize there's no essence to action,
Yet due to causality action's not lost.

Their minds do not wrongly grasp things of the past,
Nor crave for things of the future,
Nor dwell on aught in the present:
They know the three times are all void.

Enlightening beings have already reached the other shore of form
And of sensation, perception, patternings, and consciousness;
They go beyond the flow of birth and death in the world,
Their minds humble and always pure.

They clearly analyze the five clusters, eighteen elements,
Twelve sense media, and their own bodies,

Looking for enlightenment in each:
Their essential nature cannot be grasped.

They do not cling to appearances of permanence in things,
Nor cling to the appearance of annihilation:
The nature of things is neither existent nor nonexistent,
While the process of the principle of action ultimately never
   ends.

They do not dwell on anything at all,
Do not see "sentient beings" or "enlightenment":
Throughout all lands in all times
They ultimately find they cannot be found.

If one can see things in this way,
One will accord with the understanding of the Buddhas;
Though one seek their essence, it cannot be found,
Yet enlightening beings' practices are not in vain.

Enlightening beings understand things exist due to conditions,
And they do not deviate from the paths they should travel.
They clarify and explain the marks of all actions,
Wanting to purify all sentient beings.

This is the path traversed by the wise,
Taught by all the enlightened ones;
Following it reflectively, entering the true meaning,
One will naturally awaken and become enlightened.

Phenomena have no birth or extinction,
And they have no coming or going;
Not dying here and reborn there—
Such people understand the Buddha teachings.

Comprehending the true nature of things,
Yet not conceptualizing the nature of things,
Knowing things have no essence and no discrimination—
Such people can enter the Buddha's knowledge.

The nature of things is in all places,
All sentient beings and all lands,
In all times, past, present, and future,
Yet has no apprehensible form.

That which the Buddhas all realize
Is all-inclusive, omitting naught.

Though they explain all things in all times,
All these things are not existent.

As the nature of things pervades everywhere,
So does the dedication of enlightening beings:
Thus dedicated to sentient beings,
They never retreat from the world.

"What is great enlightening beings' dedication equally adapting and according to all sentient beings? The enlightening beings accord with whatever roots of goodness they have accumulated—small roots of goodness, great roots of goodness, extensive roots of goodness, manifold roots of goodness, measureless roots of goodness, various roots of goodness, roots of goodness as numerous as atoms, incalculable roots of goodness, boundless roots of goodness, inconceivable roots of goodness, immeasurable roots of goodness, roots of goodness of the sphere of buddhahood, roots of goodness of the sphere of the teaching, roots of goodness of the sphere of the religious community, roots of goodness of the sphere of teachers, roots of goodness of the spheres of all sentient beings, roots of goodness of the sphere of skill in means, roots of goodness of the sphere of cultivation of good states of mind, internal roots of goodness, external roots of goodness, roots of goodness of the sphere of boundless aids to the fostering of enlightenment, roots of goodness of diligently cultivating universal relinquishment, roots of goodness of establishing supreme determination and ultimately keeping pure precepts, roots of goodness of equanimously enduring all, roots of goodness of constant, unregressing perseverence, roots of goodness of entering innumerable concentrations by great skill in means, roots of goodness of skillful analysis by knowledge and wisdom, roots of goodness of knowing the differences in mental patterns of all sentient beings, roots of goodness of universally protecting and nurturing all worlds.

"Great enlightening beings cultivate and live by these roots of goodness, entering into them, absorbing them, accumulating them, fully developing them; their awareness and understanding clear, they demonstrate and put them into action. Then they attain forbearance, close the doors of the courses of misery, skillfully embody roots of goodness, bear themselves with complete dignity, get rid of delusion, and fulfill correct action. They are capable of being vessels of the Buddha teaching, and can be fertile fields of blessings and virtue for sentient beings. In the care of the Buddhas, they develop the roots of goodness of buddhahood, live by the vows of Buddhas, and carry out the works of the Buddhas. Their minds attain freedom equal to the Buddhas of past, present, and future; they proceed to the site of Buddhas' enlightenment, plunge into the power of the Enlightened, and are endowed with the marks of

Buddhas. Transcending all worlds, they do not desire birth in a heaven, do not covet wealth and pleasure, and do not cling to activities. Dedicating all roots of goodness, they are mines of virtue for sentient beings. Abiding in the ultimate path, they envelop all. They remove sentient beings from the paths of delusion and cause them to live by all good principles. They reach all realms, uninterrupted and inexhaustible, opening the gates of omniscient enlightenment, setting up the banner of knowledge, clarifying the Great Path, able to show it to all worldlings, causing them to get rid of impurity. Their minds well trained, they are born in the house of the enlightened and purify their buddha-nature. Replete with virtuous qualities, they are great fields of blessings; a refuge for the world, they firmly stabilize sentient beings, purifying them all, diligently cultivating all roots of goodness.

"When great enlightening beings cultivate roots of goodness by the power of pure determination for enlightenment, they think in these terms: 'These roots of goodness are accumulated by the aspiration for enlightenment, thought of by the aspiration for enlightenment, initiated by the aspiration for enlightenment, willed by the aspiration for enlightenment, caused to grow by the aspiration for enlightenment: they are all due to pity for all sentient beings; they are for the quest for knowledge of all ways of liberation; they are all for the sake of accomplishing the ten powers of the enlightened.' While they thus reflect, their roots of goodness develop further, never regressing.

"Great enlightening beings also form this thought: 'May I practice the deeds of enlightening beings forever by these roots of goodness, giving them all to sentient beings, dedicating them all to all sentient beings, including all, excepting none. May they cause countless worlds to be filled with treasures, countless worlds to be filled with raiment, countless worlds to be filled with fine fragrances, countless worlds to be filled with adornments, countless worlds to be filled with infinite jewels, countless worlds to be filled with exquisite flowers, countless worlds to be filled with fine flavorings, countless worlds to be filled with goods, countless worlds to be filled with chairs covered with jeweled screens and spread with fine fabrics, countless worlds to be filled with jeweled crowns variously adorned—even if one person should be forever coming seeking, I would give these things unceasingly; and as for one, so would I do for all sentient beings.'

"When great enlightening beings give in this way, they have no mind of falsehood or artifice, no mind of seeking or expectation, no desire for name and fame, no regret, no irritating afflictions in their minds; they only develop a mind solely intent on the path of universal knowledge, a mind to give away everything, a mind of pity for sentient beings, a mind to teach and perfect, a mind to cause all to abide in the mind of omniscient knowledge. Great enlightening beings dedicate the roots of goodness in this way, forever carrying out generous giving.

"Great enlightening beings also form this thought: 'For the sake of even one sentient being I would like to cause countless worlds to be filled with prize tame elephants, with gold banners, covered with gold mesh, adorned with all kinds of jewels, to use as gifts; I would cause countless worlds to be filled with prize horses, adorned with all kinds of precious ornaments, to use as gifts; I would cause countless worlds to be filled with female musicians capable of playing all sorts of beautiful music, to use for giving; I would cause countless worlds to be filled with my own body, arousing the will for enlightenment, to use for giving; I would cause countless worlds to be filled with my own head, developing a nonindulgent mind, to use for giving; I would cause countless worlds to be filled with my own eyes to use for giving; I would cause countless worlds to be filled with my body's blood, flesh, bones and marrow, without feeling any attachment, to use for giving; I would cause countless worlds to be filled with the rank of sovereign to use for giving; I would cause countless worlds to be filled with servants, to use for giving.' Great enlightening beings give various such things to one sentient being, abiding in a magnanimous, totally generous state of mind; and as to one, so do they give to all sentient beings in the whole realm of sentient beings.

"Great enlightening beings perform the acts of enlightening beings throughout the future in one world, giving such things to one and all, satisfying everyone; and as they do in one world, so also do they do in all worlds in space throughout the cosmos. They cover all with great compassion, unremittingly, extending sympathy and mercy to all, providing them with what they need. They do not let conditions stop their practice of giving, and never grow weary of it, even for a moment.

"When great enlightening beings give in this way, they give rise to these frames of mind: an unattached mind, an unfettered mind, a liberated mind, a mind of great strength, an extremely profound mind, a well-concentrated mind, a nonclinging mind, a nonsubjective mind, a well-controlled mind, an undistracted mind, a mind without arbitrary conceptions, a mind endowed with all kinds of precious essences, a mind not seeking reward, a mind comprehending all things, a mind abiding in great dedication, a mind skillfully determining meanings, a mind to cause all sentient beings to abide in unexcelled knowledge, a mind producing the great light of truth, a mind entering omniscient knowledge.

"In every moment of thought great enlightening beings dedicate the roots of goodness they have gathered in this way: 'May all sentient beings have abundant wealth and lack nothing; may all sentient beings develop inexhaustible stores of great virtues; may all sentient beings fully experience all peace and happiness; may all sentient beings develop and extend the work of great enlightening beings; may all sentient beings fulfill infinite supreme qualities; may all sentient beings gain the vehicle of universal knowledge, which never rolls back; may all sentient beings see all the Buddhas of the ten directions; may all sentient beings be forever rid of the dust and dirt of confusions and delusions of the world; may all sentient beings attain pure, impartial minds; may all sentient beings be free from difficulties and attain omniscience.'

"When great enlightening beings practice dedication in this way, they are inspired with joy: it is to cause all sentient beings to gain well-being and peace; to cause all sentient beings to attain impartial minds; to cause all sentient beings to live with a mind capable of relinquishment; to cause all sentient beings to live with an all-giving mind; to cause all sentient beings to live with a joyfully giving mind; to cause all beings to live with a mind to give to bring eternal freedom from destitution; to cause all sentient beings to live with a mind to give all goods and treasures; to cause all sentient beings to live with a mind of universal giving, immeasurable giving, total giving; to cause all sentient beings to live with a mind to unending giving; to cause all sentient beings to live with a mind giving away all without regret or affliction; to cause all sentient beings to live with a mind to give away all things to support life; to cause all sentient beings to live with a mind to appropriate giving; to cause all sentient beings to live with a mind to inclusive giving; to cause all sentient beings to live with a mind of extensive, great giving; to cause all sentient beings to live with a mind to give away unlimited adornments as offerings; to cause all sentient beings to live with a mind of giving without attachment; to cause all sentient beings to live with a mind of equanimous, impartial giving; to cause all sentient beings to live with a mind of giving with extremely great adamantine strength; to cause all sentient beings to live with a mind giving like the light of the sun; to cause all sentient beings to live with a giving mind embracing the wisdom of the enlightened; to cause all sentient beings to be fully accompanied by roots of goodness; to cause all sentient beings to always be in the presence of roots of goodness, knowledge, and wisdom; to cause all sentient beings to attain the fullness of incorruptible pure minds; to cause all sentient beings to develop the most pure roots of goodness; to cause all sentient beings to wake up from the stupefaction of afflictions; to cause all sentient beings to annihilate all doubt and confusion; to cause all sentient beings to attain the pure virtues of equanimous knowledge; to cause all sentient beings' virtuous qualities to be fully developed and immune to deterioration or corruption; to cause all sentient beings to have pure, imperturbable concentration; to cause all sentient beings to abide in indestructible omniscience; to cause all sentient beings to fully accomplish the functions of innumerable enlightening beings' pure spiritual powers; to cause all sentient beings to accumulate roots of goodness free from attachment; to cause all sentient beings to think of all Buddhas of past, present, and future with pure minds; to cause all sentient beings to produce superlative pure roots of goodness; to cause all sentient beings to eliminate all hindrances to enlightenment produced by the action of demons; to cause all sentient beings to be fully endowed with unobstructed, pure, equal virtuous qualities; to cause all sentient beings to open wide the doors of all roots of goodness and be able to fully develop pure virtues; to cause all sentient beings to always recollect the Buddhas with a broad mind, never slacking or giving up; to cause all sentient beings to always approach the Buddhas and diligently attend them; to cause all sentient beings to have immeasurable minds, broad and great minds, most excellent minds, thoroughly pure; to cause all sentient beings to develop minds of pure impartial generosity; to cause all sentient beings to keep the Buddhas' precepts equally and purely; to cause all sentient beings to attain great transcendent forbearance; to cause all sentient beings to have transcendent energy, never becoming lazy; to cause all sentient beings to abide in immeasurable concentration and be able to awaken all kinds of spiritual knowledge; to cause all sentient beings to attain transcendent wisdom knowing all phenomena have no inherent nature; to cause all sentient beings to fulfill the infinite pure realm of truth; to cause all sentient beings to fully develop the pure roots of goodness of all mystic powers; to cause all sentient beings to abide in the practice of impartiality, build up good qualities, and perfect them all; to cause all sentient beings to be able to comprehensively enter the spheres of all Buddhas; to cause all sentient beings to be universally pure in thought, word, and deed; to cause the results of all sentient beings' good works to be universally pure; to cause all sentient beings' understanding of all things to be universally pure; to cause all sentient beings' realization of true meaning to be universally pure; to cause all sentient beings' cultivation of excellent practices to be universally pure; to cause all sentient beings to fulfill the great vows of all enlightening beings with universal purity; to cause all sentient beings to fulfill all roots of goodness based on unity of being and to dedicate them to the production of the vehicle of universal knowledge, perfecting them in every way; to cause all sentient beings to realize all virtues and knowledge with universal purity; to cause all sentient beings to fully develop vision of all Buddhas without attachment; to cause all sentient beings to be endowed with Buddhas' marks and embellishments, their adornments of virtue fully complete; to cause all sentient beings to fully develop clear speech, thoroughly trustworthy, adorned with a hundred thousand qualities, replete with the unhindered subtle voice of the Buddhas; to cause all sentient beings to attain unobstructed, equanimous minds adorned by the ten powers; to cause all sentient beings to attain the inexhaustible light of truth of all Buddhas, with all powers of elucidation fully developed; to cause all sentient beings to manage the Lion's Roar of the unexcelled fearless hero among humans; to cause all sentient beings to attain universal knowledge and turn the wheel of teaching which never rolls back; to cause all sentient beings to have full comprehension of all the teachings and to reveal and expound them; to cause all sentient beings to cultivate pure ways appropriate to the times, fully developing them; to cause all sentient beings to equally and purely perfect the unexcelled treasures of teachings of the Guide; to cause all sentient beings to fully perfect individual adornments, innumerable adornments, great adornments, the adornments of all Buddhas; to cause all sentient beings to equally penetrate all objects in all times, reaching them all; to cause all sentient beings to be able to go to all buddha-fields, listen to and absorb the true teachings; to cause all sentient beings' wisdom and altruism to be honored by the world, equal to the Buddhas'; to cause all sentient beings to know all things comprehensively by means of universal knowledge; to cause all sentient beings to carry out the practice of unshakability and realize the fruit of non-obstruction, consummating these in every way; to cause all sentient beings' roots of goodness to evolve into spiritual powers, able to know the faculties of all living beings; to cause all sentient beings to attain nondiscriminatory, impartial knowledge, universally pure in regard to unity; to cause all sentient beings not to deviate from truth and to be endowed with all roots of goodness; to cause all sentient beings to clearly comprehend all the autonomous spiritual powers of enlightening beings; to cause all sentient beings to attain the inexhaustible virtues of all Buddhas, completely equal whether in terms of virtue or knowledge; to cause all sentient beings to arouse the determination for enlightenment and to understand perfectly the equality and unity of all things; to cause all sentient beings to comprehend the truth and become the highest fields of blessings for the world; to cause all sentient beings to develop impartial pure compassion and be fields of great power for all donors; to cause all sentient beings to be foremost in steadfastness, so that nothing can break them down; to cause all sentient beings to be beneficial to all who see them, and to be invincible; to cause all sentient beings to be well able to comprehend all true principles and attain fearlessness; to cause all sentient beings to radiate a single light which illumines all worlds in the ten directions; to cause all sentient beings to cultivate all the enlightening beings' vigorous practices without shrinking back; to cause all sentient beings to fulfill all practical vows by means of one practical vow; to cause all sentient beings to make all hearers attain understanding by means of one sublime voice; to cause all sentient beings to be able to fully develop the pure mind of all enlightening beings; to cause all sentient beings to get the opportunity to meet good teachers and serve them all; to cause all sentient beings to unremittingly cultivate the practices of enlightening beings and harmonize and pacify living beings; to cause all sentient beings to teach according to potential, with inexhaustible powers of elucidation; to cause all sentient beings to be able to know all minds with one mind, and to impartially dedicate all roots of goodness; to cause all sentient beings to always gladly accumulate all sorts of goodness and establish sentient beings in pure knowledge; to cause all sentient beings to attain the pure body of virtue and knowledge of omniscience; to cause all sentient beings to know the roots of goodness of all living beings, to practice dedication perceptively and perfect them all; to cause all sentient beings to attain universal knowledge and realize true enlightenment, complete in every way; to cause all sentient beings to attain full knowledge of spiritual powers, appearing in all places when appearing in one place; to cause all sentient beings to attain knowledge of universal adornment, all communities being adorned and purified when they adorn and purify one community; to cause all sentient beings to see all buddha-lands in one buddha-land; to cause all sentient beings to adorn all buddha-lands throughout with all adornments—unspeakably many adornments, innumerable adornments, infinite adornments; to cause all sentient beings to be able to understand with certainty the most profound meaning of all things; to cause all sentient beings to attain the foremost autonomous spiritual powers of the enlightened ones; to cause all sentient beings to attain autonomous spiritual powers which are not one, not different, and replete with all virtuous qualities; to cause all sentient beings to fulfill all equal roots of goodness and be crowned by the Buddhas; to cause all sentient beings to fully realize the body of pure knowledge, supreme in all realms of existence.

"Thus do great enlightening beings compassionately aid and comfort all sentient beings, causing them all to be purified, to give up envy and jealousy, to experience the most wonderful bliss, to be endowed with great charisma, to develop great resolute faith, to forever abandon anger and other blinding pollutants, so their hearts are pure, straightforward, and gentle, without deception or deviousness, confusion or folly, so they carry out emancipating practices, consolidating an incorruptible mind of impartiality, never regressing, their power of pure conduct fully developed, without affliction or loss. They practice dedication skillfully, always cultivating right practices, civilizing sentient beings, destroying all bad actions, cultivating the roots of goodness of all austerities. They also induce sentient beings to cultivate themselves, accepting suffering for the sake of all conscious creatures. Observing roots of goodness with the eye of great knowledge, knowing they all have knowledge and wisdom as their essence, they expediently dedicate them to all sentient beings. This is to cause all sentient beings to be able to abide in the realm of all pure virtues; to cause all sentient beings to be able to embody all roots of goodness, to know the natures and meanings of virtues; to cause all sentient beings to purify all roots of goodness; to cause all sentient beings to plant good qualities in fields of blessings, and have no regrets in their hearts; to cause all sentient beings to be able to embrace all living beings and cause everyone to head for universal knowledge; to cause all sentient beings to take in all roots of goodness, all in accord with impartial dedication.

"Also, they dedicate these roots of goodness in this way: 'May all sentient beings attain ultimate peace; may all sentient beings attain ultimate understanding; may all sentient beings ultimately live in pure ways; may all sentient beings attain unhindered insight; may all sentient

beings tune their minds well; may all sentient beings be fully endowed
with the ten powers and tame living beings.'

"When great enlightening beings practice dedication in this way, they
do not become attached to actions, to consequences, to the body, to
objects, to lands, to places, to sentient beings, to the nonexistence of
sentient beings, to all things, or to the nonexistence of all things. When
great enlightening beings make dedication in this way, they distribute
these roots of goodness throughout the world, that all sentient beings
may fully develop buddha-knowledge, attain pure minds with clear,
comprehensive wisdom, their inner minds silent and serene, unmoved
by external objects, as they extend and develop the family of Buddhas
of past, present, and future.

"When great enlightening beings cultivate and practice such dedications they transcend all, so none can surpass them; all the words of
praise in the world would be insufficient to describe them. They cultivate all the practices of enlightening beings and are able to go to all
buddha-lands and see all the Buddhas without hindrance. Also they can
see the courses of action of the enlightening beings of all worlds. With
expert skill in means they analyze the most profound statements and
meanings of all the teachings; attaining total mental command, they
endlessly expound the wondrous teaching. For the sake of sentient
beings, from moment to moment they appear, like reflections, in
untold worlds, attending the Buddhas; in every instant they adorn
untold worlds, causing all to be completely adorned and purified
throughout. They cultivate the knowledge to adorn buddha-lands
tirelessly. Moment to moment they cause untold hundreds of thousands
of billions of sentient beings to attain purity and complete impartiality.
In those buddha-lands they diligently practice all ways of transcendence,
save sentient beings, accomplish pure action, and attain unobstructed
ears, hearing, absorbing, and retaining the teachings of each Buddha in
untold worlds, energetically practicing them without even a thought of
giving up. They abide in the spiritual powers of enlightening beings in
which there is no acquisition, no dependence, no fabrication, and no
attachment; in a single instant, in the time of a fingersnap, they can
project themselves to untold buddha-worlds. They have the same insight as all enlightening beings.

"When great enlightening beings cultivate the practice of enlightening beings in this way, they can fully develop infinite pure virtues,
which could never be exhaustively recounted or extolled, and accomplish unexcelled enlightenment, realizing the equality and purity of all
buddha-fields, equality and purity of all sentient beings, equality and
purity of all bodies, equality and purity of all faculties, equality and
purity of all fruits of action, equality and purity of all congregations and
sites of enlightenment, equality and purity of all completely fulfilled
practices, equality and purity of all knowledge of methods of the

teaching, equality and purity of the vows and dedications of all Buddhas, and equality and purity of the realms of spiritual powers of all Buddhas.

"When great enlightening beings practice dedication in this way, they attain the complete adornment of infinite virtues of gladdening teachings of which all qualities are pure. In this dedication, sentient beings are not at variance with all lands, lands are not at variance with all sentient beings; lands and sentient beings are not at variance with actions, actions are not at variance with lands and beings; thought is not at variance with mind, mind is not at variance with thought; thought and mind are not at variance with objects, objects are not at variance with thought and mind; actions are not at variance with consequences, consequences are not at variance with actions; practice is not at variance with the course of practice, the course of practice is not at variance with practice; the nature of things is not at variance with their characteristics, the characteristics of things are not at variance with their nature; the birth of things is not at variance with their nature, the nature of things is not at variance with their birth; the equality of lands is not at variance with the equality of living beings, the equality of living beings is not at variance with the equality of lands; the equality of all living beings is not at variance with the equality of all things; the equality of all things is not at variance with the equality of all living beings; the equality of the realm of dispassion is not at variance with the equality of stability of all living beings, the equality of stability of all living beings is not at variance with the equality of the realm of dispassion; the past is not at variance with the future, the future is not at variance with the past; the past and future are not at variance with the present, the present is not at variance with the past and future; the equality of worlds is not at variance with the equality of Buddhas, the equality of Buddhas is not at variance with the equality of worlds; the actions of enlightening beings are not at variance with universal knowledge, universal knowledge is not at variance with the actions of enlightening beings.

"When great enlightening beings dedicate in this way, they realize the equality of actions, the equality of consequences, the equality of bodies, the equality of expedients, the equality of vows, the equality of all sentient beings, the equality of all lands, the equality of all practices, the equality of all knowledge, the equality of the Buddhas of all times; they get to serve all Buddhas, attend and provide for all enlightening beings, and plant all roots of goodness; they are able to fulfill all great vows, teach and transform all sentient beings, and know all actions comprehensively; they get to serve and provide for all good teachers, and enter all enlightenment sites with pure congregations; they manage to comprehend and master all true teachings, and fully develop all pure qualities.

"This is the great enlightening beings' seventh dedication, dedication equally adapting to all sentient beings, dedication in accord with all sentient beings. When great enlightening beings accomplish this dedication, then they can crush all demons; pulling out the thorns of craving, they attain the bliss of emancipation. Abiding in nonduality, they have great mystic powers; they rescue sentient beings and protect them, being monarchs of virtue. Their power of psychic travel is unhindered, and they go to all lands. They enter the realm of extinction, yet may assume any form. They accomplish the deeds of enlightening beings, and their minds attain autonomy in all practices and vows. They analyze and comprehend all things. They are able to be born in all buddha-fields. They attain unobstructed ears and can hear all sounds and voices in all lands. They attain the pure eye of wisdom and always see all Buddhas. In all realms they develop roots of goodness, their minds without pride or obsequiousness. They attain nonacquisitiveness in regard to all things. Great enlightening beings dedicate all roots of goodness equally in accord with all sentient beings."

Then the enlightening being Diamond Banner, spiritually empowered by the Buddha, looked over the ten directions and said in verse,

> The virtues of what enlightening beings do
> Are subtle, great, and most profound;
> Their practice of even one moment
> They can dedicate without bounds.

> Enlightening beings' accoutrements,
> Various, abundant, in limitless numbers—
> Prize elephants and horses, drawing carts,
> Clothing, rare goods, all especially fine,
> Or their heads, eyes, hands, and feet,
> Or their bodies, flesh, bones, and marrow,
> They give to all in infinite worlds,
> Filling the ten directions.

> The virtues they've cultivated for countless eons
> They dedicate, all,
> Wishing to rescue sentient beings,
> Never retreating from this determination.

> Enlightening beings, to serve the living,
> Always practice supreme dedication,
> Causing all worlds to attain peace and happiness
> That everyone may attain the highest fruit.

> Enlightening beings universally make impartial vows,
> And whatever pure works they have accumulated
> They dedicate to all living beings,
> Never giving up this great commitment.

Enlightening beings' will power is unlimited and dauntless,
Taking in all worlds,
Thus dedicated to living beings
With never any discrimination.

They vow that sentient beings' knowledge be clear,
Their generosity and self-control all pure,
Diligent in cultivation, indefatigable:
This great commitment they never give up.

Enlightening beings' dedication reaches the other shore—
They open the gates of the pure, sublime teaching;
Their knowledge the same as the Buddha,
They analyze the true meaning and attain the ultimate.

Enlightening beings are masters of verbal expression
And various kinds of knowledge;
They explain the teaching according to truth, without hindrance,
And yet their minds are not attached to it.

They do not create duality in things,
Nor do they create nonduality;
They are free of duality and nonduality,
Realizing they are just manners of speaking.

They know all worlds are equal,
Being naught but the doings of mental talk;
And sentient beings are phantoms, without reality,
All results of conditions.

The various consequences in all worlds
Are each different—
All are made from the power of acts;
If action is stopped, all come to an end.

Enlightening beings observe all worlds,
Their words, deeds, and thoughts impartial;
And they induce sentient beings to be impartial
Like the peerless great sage.

Enlightening beings' good works they dedicate all
To the purification of beings;
They're fully endowed with virtue and skill in means,
Same as the Supreme Tamer.

Enlightening beings aid all living creatures,
Dedicating their whole ocean of virtues,

Vowing to cause their light to go beyond the world
And attain the body of intrepid power.

The virtues they cultivate
They pray will purify the world,
That the purity of sentient beings be like
The incomparable purity of Buddha.

Enlightening beings are skilled in interpretation,
And know the supreme teaching of the Buddhas;
They equally dedicate all good works,
Vowing to make all beings the same as Buddha.

Enlightening beings know all things are empty
And all worlds have no existence;
There is no creation and no creator,
Yet the consequences of beings' actions remain.

All things—null? not null?
They divorce this dualistic discriminating mind;
They know all notions are worldly views:
Entering the absolute state, conceptualization ends.

Thus are true children of Buddha
Born by transformation from the Enlightened One's teaching;
They can practice such dedication well
To remove all the world's confusion.

"What is great enlightening beings' dedication with the character of true thusness? Here enlightening beings' correct mindfulness is clear and perfect, their mind is firm and stable, they get beyond confusion, and cultivate practice single-mindedly, their profound mind unstirring, accomplishing indestructible works, proceeding toward omniscience without ever regressing. They are determined to seek the Great Vehicle, bold and fearless; planting roots of virtue, they bring peace to the world, producing excellent roots of goodness and cultivating pure qualities. Their great compassion grows, their mind-treasure develops; they always remember the Buddhas and preserve the true teaching. Their belief in the path of enlightening beings is firm and enduring, they perfect immeasurable pure roots of goodness, diligently cultivating all virtues and knowledge. As spiritual guides they produce myriad good principles, dedicating their knowledge and skill in liberative means to the salvation of others.

"At such a time enlightening beings examine all roots of goodness—immeasurable, boundless—with the eye of wisdom: those roots of goodness, in the course of being cultivated and gathered, involve seeking conditions, preparing instruments, purification, orientation and involvement, concentration and effort, initiation and execution, clarification and understanding, refined examination, and explanation; thus all have various facets, various spheres, various characteristics, various phenomena, various proportions, various acts, various names, various distinctions, various productions, various practices—all the roots of goodness therein are established by the mind directed toward the vehicle of the ten powers, and are all dedicated solely to the knowledge of all means and sciences of liberation.

"The roots of virtue they dedicate in this way: they vow to attain complete, unobstructed action to carry out enlightening practices; they vow to attain pure unobstructed speech, to carry out enlightening practices; they vow to attain fully developed unobstructed mental action and abide in the Great Vehicle; they vow to attain complete, unobstructed minds and purely cultivate all practices of enlightening beings; they vow to develop minds of infinitely magnanimous generosity and provide for all sentient beings; they vow to master all the teachings and spread the light of the great teaching, which nothing can veil; they vow to arrive at the realm of universal knowledge, illumining the world with the will for enlightenment; they vow to always correctly remember the Buddhas of past, present, and future, always clearly picturing the Enlightened present before them; they vow to live by fully developed powerful aspiration and get away from all demons and enemies; they vow to attain stabilization in the ten powers of knowledge of Buddhas and teach all sentient beings ceaselessly; they vow to attain concentration and travel through the worlds without being affected by or attached to the worlds; they vow to live in the world unwearied and always edify and influence sentient beings; they vow to activate innumerable liberative techniques of thought and wisdom and accomplish the inconceivable path of enlightening beings; they vow to attain knowledge never confused in any place, able to distinguish all worlds; they vow to attain the power of knowledge of autonomous spiritual capabilities, able to purify all lands in a single instant; they vow to penetrate the intrinsic nature of things and see all worlds as pure; they vow to develop knowledge of nondifferentiation, entering all fields in one field; they vow to reveal all the adornments of all fields to edify and influence infinite sentient beings; they vow to show the boundless cosmos in a single buddha-field, and to do likewise in all buddha-fields; they vow to attain free psychic powers and spiritual knowledge and be able to travel to all buddha-lands.

"By means of roots of goodness great enlightening beings vow to accomplish the adornment of all buddha-lands; they vow to be able to pervade all worlds; they vow to accomplish contemplative investigation by knowledge. As they thus dedicate roots of goodness for themselves in this way, so also do they do so for all sentient beings; that is, they vow that all sentient beings become forever free from hells, animality, and ghosthood; they vow that all sentient beings get rid of all hindering actions; they vow that all sentient beings attain universal minds with impartial knowledge and wisdom; they vow that all sentient beings deal with opponents and friends impartially, causing them all to be secure and happy, their knowledge and wisdom pure; they vow that all sentient beings' knowledge become fully complete, with pure light illuminating everywhere; they vow that all sentient beings' wisdom from reflection be fully developed and that they understand the real truth; they vow that all sentient beings seek enlightenment with pure aspiration and attain immeasurable knowledge; they vow that all sentient beings will be able to reveal the abode of peace.

"Great enlightening beings always dedicate their good will in this way, to cause all sentient beings to encounter the cloud of pure coolness showering the rain of truth, to cause all sentient beings to always encounter the excellent environment of fields of virtue, to cause all sentient beings to be able to enter the treasury of the spirit of enlightenment and preserve it themselves, to cause all sentient beings to shed all veils and live properly, to cause all sentient beings to attain knowledge of unhindered spiritual faculties, to cause all sentient beings to attain free bodies appearing everywhere, to cause all sentient beings to achieve supreme knowledge of all ways of liberation and bring about unfailing benefit, to cause all sentient beings to purify all creatures, to cause all sentient beings to be able to consummate universal knowledge, to cause all sentient beings to be unshakable and unobstructed in mind.

"Great enlightening beings, seeing delightful countries, gardens and groves, plants, trees, and fruits, distinguished scents and excellent clothing, rare jewels and goods, various decorations, or seeing delightful villages, towns, or hamlets, or seeing the majesty of sovereigns, or seeing abodes free from clamor, employ their knowledge of means and diligently cultivate innumerable sublime virtues, earnestly seeking good for the sake of sentient beings, never slacking off, widely gathering much good, vast as the ocean, and cover all with infinite good, being bases of myriad good things, expediently dedicating roots of goodness without discrimination, pointing out infinite various roots of goodness, always knowingly observing all sentient beings, their minds always remembering the realms of roots of goodness. They ceaselessly dedicate to sentient beings roots of goodness as impartial as true thusness. At such a time, they dedicate the roots of goodness in this way: 'May all sentient beings attain the delightful visions of the enlightened, see the true nature of things, equal and impartial, without any grasping or attachment, complete and pure; may all sentient beings see the most delightful, perfect offerings of the Enlightened Ones; may all sentient beings be reborn in all the most delightful pure buddha-lands, free of all afflictions; may all sentient beings manage to perceive the most delightful teaching of the Buddhas; may all sentient beings always happily preserve the pleasing practices of all enlightening beings; may all sentient beings acquire the enjoyable eyes of the wise and see without obstruction; may all sentient beings always see all pleasing things, nothing offensive; may all sentient beings realize all delightful truths and diligently preserve them; may all sentient beings attain pure illumination in the pleasing teachings of all Buddhas; may all sentient beings cultivate all the delightful attitudes of generosity of enlightening beings; may all sentient beings attain fearlessness and be able to expound all admirable teachings; may all sentient beings attain the enlightening beings' extremely delightful most profound concentration; may all sentient beings attain the enlightening beings' most pleasant methods of mnemonic spells; may all sentient beings attain enlightening beings' most admirable analytic knowledge; may all sentient beings be able to manifest enlightening beings' most delightful autonomous spiritual powers; may all sentient beings be able to expound the pleasing most profoundly wonderful teaching in the great congregations of the Buddhas; may all sentient beings be able to skillfully analyze and explain the most pleasing expressions of differentiation; may all sentient beings always be able to activate most pleasant impartial great compassion; may all sentient beings in every thought activate the most admirable aspiration for enlightenment, always causing their senses to be joyful and blissful; may all sentient beings be able to enter all the most pleasant houses of the enlightened ones; may all sentient beings achieve the admirable action whereby they are able to harmonize and pacify, taming sentient beings unceasingly; may all sentient beings attain the most pleasing inexhaustible eloquence of enlightening beings, expounding all truths; may all sentient beings abide for unspeakably many unspeakable numbers of eons in all pleasant worlds, teaching and transforming sentient beings without wearying; may all sentient beings, by means of innumerable techniques, be able to understand and enter into all the most delightful teachings of the Buddhas; may all sentient beings attain delightful unobstructed liberative techniques and know all things have no basis; may all sentient beings attain the delightful realm of freedom from greed and craving, know all things are ultimately nondual, and cut through all barriers; may all sentient beings develop the delightful way of enlightening beings which is free from inanity; may all sentient beings attain the diamond-mine mind of effort and accomplish the delightful path of universal knowledge; may all sentient beings be endowed with delightful unobstructed roots of goodness and destroy all afflictions; may all sentient beings find the delightful door of omniscience and realize true awakening throughout the world.' When great enlightening beings cultivate such roots of goodness, they gain the light of knowledge; they are taken into the care of good teachers; the sun of wisdom of the Buddhas illumines their minds, forever annihilating the darkness of ignorance. They diligently practice the true teaching, enter into works of knowledge, and learn the stages of knowledge. They spread roots of goodness, filling the cosmos, dedicating them wisely. They plumb the depths of the source of enlightening beings' roots of goodness; by means of knowledge they enter deeply into the ocean of liberative means and develop immeasurably great roots of goodness.

"Great enlightening beings dedicate these roots of goodness in this way: they do not cling to the world, they do not grasp sentient beings; their minds are pure, not relying on anything; they are correctly mindful of all things and dismiss discriminatory views; they do not give up the independent wisdom of all Buddhas; they accord with all impartial truths, and do not destroy the Buddha's true characteristics; they do not deviate from the correct way of dedication of all Buddhas; they look upon the triple world equally, without any image of sentient beings; they follow the path of Buddha well and explain its principles well, with profound understanding of their meaning; they enter the supreme stage and awaken to the real truth; their knowledge is complete, their faith is firm; though they practice correct actions well, they know the nature of action is empty; they understand all things are like phantoms, and know all things have no intrinsic essence of their own; they observe all meanings and all kinds of practices according to their conventional explanations and are not attached to them; they abolish all causes and conditions of grasping and clinging; they know the truth and see the nature of all things being null and void; they comprehend that all things have the same unique real character; they know the characteristics of things are not mutually opposed; they live with enlightening beings and practice their path; taking all sentient beings into their care, they enter the door of dedication of all enlightening beings of past, future, and present; their minds are not startled or frightened by the Buddha's teachings; with minds of boundless kindness, compassion, joy, and equanimity, they cause all sentient beings to attain purity; in the worlds of the ten directions, they do not develop selfish, possessive grasping and clinging; they do not conceive of anything in the world; they do not give rise to obsession with any objects; they diligently practice all ways to transcend the world and have no attachments to or reliance on any mundane realm; their insight into the profound, wonderful path is accurate and steady, and they are rid of all erroneous views; they understand the real truth.

"Just as true thusness permeates all places, without boundaries, so also does their dedication of roots of goodness pervade everywhere unbounded; just as true thusness has reality as its essence, so likewise does their dedication of roots of goodness have as its essence understanding of the reality of all things; just as true thusness always retains its original nature without change, so too does their dedication of roots of goodness preserve its original nature unchanging throughout; just as true thusness has as its nature the essencelessness of all things, so also does their dedication of roots of goodness have as its nature the understanding of the essencelessness of all things; just as the mark of true

thusness is signlessness, so too is the mark of their dedication of roots
of goodness the signlessness of all things; just as those who realize true
thusness never backslide, likewise those who attain this dedication of
roots of goodness never retreat from the Buddha teachings; just as true
thusness is the sphere of action of all Buddhas, so too is this dedication
of roots of goodness the sphere of action of all Buddhas; just as the
realm of true thusness is unconnected to any mark of boundary or
realm, so also is the dedication of roots of goodness free from any sign
of boundary or realm, yet it is the realm of all Buddhas of past, present,
and future; just as true thusness can have establishments, so too can the
dedication of roots of goodness establish all sentient beings; just as the
nature of true thusness always adapts, so also does the dedication of
roots of goodness forever adapt ceaselessly; just as true thusness cannot
be measured, likewise the dedication of roots of goodness is equal to
the realm of space and the minds of all sentient beings cannot measure
it; just as true thusness fills all, so also does the dedication of roots of
goodness pervade the cosmos in a single instant; just as true thusness is
eternal and inexhaustible, so also is the dedication of roots of goodness
ultimately inexhaustible; just as true thusness has no compare, likewise
the dedication of roots of goodness can fulfill all the Buddha teachings
without compare; just as the essence of true thusness is stable, so also is
the essence of dedication of roots of goodness stable, impervious to
delusions and afflictions; just as true thusness is indestructible, so too is
the dedication of roots of goodness stable, impervious to delusions and
afflictions; just as true thusness is indestructible, so too is the dedication
of roots of goodness, which no creatures can damage; just as the body
of true thusness is illumination, so also the nature of the dedication of
roots of goodness is universal illumination; just as true thusness is
omnipresent, likewise the dedication of roots of goodness is present in
all places; just as true thusness pervades all times, so also does the
dedication of roots of goodness pervade all times; just as the nature of
true thusness is eternally pure, likewise the dedication of roots of goodness
abides in the world yet is essentially pure; just as true thusness is
unhindered by things, so too the dedication of roots of goodness
extends everywhere unobstructed; just as true thusness is the eye of all
phenomena, likewise the dedication of roots of goodness is an eye for
all sentient beings; just as the nature of true thusness has no fatigue, so
also is the dedication of roots of goodness, cultivating all the practices
of enlightening beings with never any fatigue; just as the inherent
nature of true thusness is most profound, so too is the nature of
dedication of roots of goodness most profound; just as there is not a
single thing in true thusness, likewise there is not a single thing in the
essence of dedication of roots of goodness; just as the nature of true
thusness is not manifestation, similarly the substance of dedication of
roots of goodness is subtle and refined and hardly visible; just as true
thusness is apart from all defilements and obscurations, so too is dedica-

tion of roots of goodness, the eye of wisdom pure and unclouded by ignorance; just as the nature of true thusness has no equal, so also is the dedication of roots of goodness, accomplishing all practices of enlightening beings, peerlessly supreme; just as the essential nature of true thusness is absolutely quiescent, so also is dedication of roots of goodness well able to accord with the truth of quiescence; just as true thusness has no basis, likewise is dedication of roots of goodness able to penetrate all baseless phenomena; just as the inherent nature of true thusness is boundless, similarly dedication of roots of goodness purifies boundless numbers of sentient beings; just as the essential nature of true thusness has no attachments, likewise the dedication of roots of goodness is ultimately divorced from all attachments; just as true thusness has no obstructions, so also the dedication of roots of goodness eliminates all barriers in the world; just as true thusness is not a mundane sphere, so too the dedication of roots of goodness cannot be carried out by any worldling; just as the essential nature of the true thusness has no abode, so also is the dedication of roots of goodness not the dwelling place of any birth and death; just as true thusness by nature has no fabrication, so too does dedication of roots of goodness relinquish all fabrication; just as the essential nature of true thusness remains steady, so also does dedication of roots of goodness abide steadily in truth; just as true thusness corresponds with all things, so too does dedication of roots of goodness correspond with the learning and practice of the enlightening beings; just as true thusness is inherently always equal in all things, likewise does the dedication of roots of goodness practice impartiality in all worlds; just as true thusness is not apart from all phenomena, similarly dedication of roots of goodness never ever abandons the world; just as true thusness is ultimately inexhaustible in all things, so too is dedication of roots of goodness inexhaustibly directed toward sentient beings; just as true thusness is not at variance with all things, likewise dedication of roots of goodness is not at variance with the teachings of all Buddhas of past, present, and future; just as true thusness universally includes all things, so too does dedication of roots of goodness completely include the roots of goodness of all sentient beings; just as true thusness is of the same essential nature as all things, so is dedication of roots of goodness of the same essential nature of the Buddhas of all times; just as true thusness is not divorced from all things. likewise dedication of roots of goodness holds all mundane and transmundane things; just as true thusness cannot be obscured, similarly none in any world can obscure dedication of roots of goodness; just as true thusness cannot be stirred, in the same way dedication of roots of goodness cannot be disturbed by any demonic activity; just as the essence of true thusness has no pollution, so too is dedication of roots of goodness like this, cultivating the practices of enlightening beings without defilement; just as true thusness is without change, so also is dedication of roots of goodness, compassionately caring for sentient beings without change of mind; just as true thusness is inexhaustible, so is dedication of roots of goodness—it cannot be exhausted by mundane norms; just as the nature of true thusness is always aware, likewise dedication of roots of goodness is able to be aware of all truths; just as true thusness cannot be lost or destroyed, dedication of roots of goodness is also like this, arousing great commitment to sentient beings which is never lost or destroyed; just as true thusness is able to greatly illumine, in the same way dedication of roots of goodness illumines all worlds with the light of great knowledge; just as true thusness cannot be explained in words, likewise all words and speech cannot explain dedication of roots of goodness; just as true thusness holds all worlds, likewise dedication of roots of goodness holds all the practices of enlightening beings; just as true thusness goes along with conventional verbal expression, similarly dedication of roots of goodness goes along with all verbal expression of wisdom; just as true thusness pervades all phenomena, so does dedication of roots of goodness pervade all buddha-fields in the ten directions, manifesting great spiritual powers and fulfilling true enlightenment; just as true thusness has no discrimination, so too dedication of roots of goodness has no discrimination in regard to all beings in all worlds; just as true thusness is in all bodies, so also is dedication of roots of goodness in the infinite bodies of the lands of the ten directions; just as the essential nature of true thusness is birthless, so too is dedication of roots of goodness, expediently manifesting birth yet having no birth; just as true thusness is omnipresent, in the same way dedication of roots of goodness is omnipresent in the buddha-lands of all times and places, everywhere manifesting spiritual powers; just as true thusness permeates the night, so also dedication of roots of goodness emits great light in all nights, giving it to perform buddha-work; just as true thusness permeates the day, so does dedication of roots of goodness cause all sentient beings in the day to see Buddha's spiritual displays expounding the nonregressive teaching, free from defilement, pure, beneficial to all; just as true thusness is omnipresent in the fortnight and month, the dedication of roots of goodness requires skill in dealing with the succession of seasons in all worlds, knowing all times in a single moment; just as true thusness is present throughout the years, likewise does dedication of roots of goodness abide for measureless eons, clarifying and maturing all faculties, developing them to completion; just as true thusness is omnipresent in ages of becoming and decay, so also dedication of roots of goodness abides in all ages, pure and unaffected, educating beings and purifying them; just as true thusness extends throughout the future, dedication of roots of goodness cultivates the pure sublime practices of enlightening beings throughout the future, fulfilling their great vows, never retreating; just as true thusness pervades past, present, and future, dedication of roots of goodness causes sentient beings to see the Buddhas of past, present, and future in a single instant, never parting for a moment; just as true thusness is in all places, so too dedication of roots of goodness transcends the triple world and reaches everywhere in complete freedom; just as true thusness abides in existence and nonexistence, similarly dedication of roots of goodness comprehends all existent and nonexistent things, ultimately pure; just as the essential nature of true thusness is pure, dedication of roots of goodness is able to assemble aids to enlightenment by means of expedient techniques and purify the practices of enlightening beings; just as the essential nature of true thusness is immaculate, similarly dedication of roots of goodness causes enlightening beings to attain the immaculate mind of concentration; just as the essential nature of true thusness has no defilement, so too is dedication of roots of goodness beyond all defilements, fulfilling all pure intentions; just as true thusness has no self or possessions, dedication of roots of goodness fills all buddhalands in the ten directions with the selfless, nonpossessive pure mind; just as the essential nature of true thusness is impartial, likewise dedication of roots of goodness attains impartial universal knowledge, illumining all things, free from all clouds of ignorance; just as true thusness is beyond all calculations and measurements, likewise dedication of roots of goodness abides together with the treasury of powerful teaching of the vehicle of universal knowledge which is beyond all calculation and measurement, spreading vast clouds of teaching throughout all worlds in the ten directions; just as true thusness is poised in equality, so too is dedication of roots of goodness, initiating all enlightening practices, poised equanimously in the path of omniscience; just as true thusness subsists in all realms of sentient beings, similarly dedication of roots of goodness fulfills unhindered knowledge of all kinds of ways of liberation and appears in all realms of sentient beings; just as true thusness has no discrimination and universally abides in knowledge of all sounds, so too the dedication of roots of goodness has in it knowledge of all sounds of speech and can everywhere manifest all kinds of speech sounds to teach sentient beings; just as true thusness is forever detached from the world, so also does dedication of roots of goodness cause sentient beings to be forever detached from the world; just as the essential nature of true thusness is immensely vast, so too dedication of roots of goodness can retain the extensive Buddha teachings of past, future, and present, never forgetting, diligently cultivating all practices of enlightening beings; just as true thusness is uninterrupted, likewise dedication of roots of goodness, out of desire to place all sentient beings securely on the ground of great knowledge, cultivates enlightening practice unceasingly through all ages; just as the essential nature of true thusness is spacious and open, so too is the dedication of roots of goodness, with pure mindfulness unobstructed, containing all spacious open doors to truth; just as true thusness embraces all kinds of creatures, similarly dedication of roots of goodness realizes knowledge of innumerable types and species, and cultivates the genuine sublime practices of enlightening beings; just as true thusness has no grasping or attachment, dedication of roots of goodness too has no clinging to anything, destroying all mundane grasping and attachment, purifying all worldings; just as the essential nature of true thusness is unmoving, likewise dedication of roots of goodness abides steadily in the perfect complete practical commitments of Universal Good, ultimately unmoving; just as true thusness is the sphere of Buddhas, so too dedication of roots of goodness causes sentient beings to fulfill all spheres of great knowledge and annihilate the spheres of afflictions, causing them to be purified; just as true thusness cannot be ruled or conquered, so also dedication of roots of goodness is not ruled or conquered by any delusive actions or erroneous theories; just as true thusness is not something that can be cultivated yet not something that cannot be cultivated, similarly dedication of roots of goodness abandons all illusions and attachments and has no discrimination between cultivating and not cultivating; just as true thusness has no withdrawal, so also is dedication of roots of goodness like this, always seeing Buddhas, rousing the aspiration for enlightenment adorned with great vows, never withdrawing or giving up; just as true thusness universally contains the sounds of all speech of all beings, similarly dedication of roots of goodness potentiates acquisition of superknowledge of all different languages, producing all kinds of utterances; just as true thusness has no seeking in respect to anything, likewise dedication of roots of goodness causes sentient beings to ride the vehicle of Universal Good to emancipation, having no craving for anything; just as true thusness abides in all stages, so too dedication of roots of goodness causes all sentient beings to give up the stages of mundanity and abide in the stages of knowledge and wisdom, adorning themselves with the practice of Universal Good; just as true thusness has no end, dedication of roots of goodness is also like this, attaining fearlessness in all truths, expounding them everywhere according to the languages of the audience, without end; just as true thusness is free from all taints, so too dedication of roots of goodness causes all sentient beings to develop objective knowledge, comprehend the truth, and fulfill the untainted qualities of enlightenment; just as there is not the slightest thing that can damage or disturb true thusness and cause it to be even slightly unaware, likewise dedication of roots of goodness causes universal awareness of all truths with a boundless mind pervading the cosmos; just as true thusness has no beginning in the past, no end in the future, and no variation in the present, likewise dedication of roots of goodness continually renews the vow of the aspiration for enlightenment for all sentient beings, enabling them all to be purified and forever freed from birth and death; just as true thusness has no discrimination among past, present, and future, dedication of roots of goodness is also like this, the mind always aware in each instant of the present, and totally pure in past and future; just as true thusness develops all Buddhas and enlightening beings, likewise dedication of roots of goodness, initiating means of expediting all great vows, develops the great knowledge of the Buddhas; just as true thusness is ultimately pure and not concurrent with the afflictions, so too dedication of roots of goodness can extinguish all sentient beings' afflictions and fulfill all pure knowledge and wisdom.

"When great enlightening beings practice dedication in this way, they realize the equality of all buddha-fields, because they adorn and purify all worlds; they realize the equality of all sentient beings, because they turn the wheel of the teaching of nonobstruction for all of them; they realize the equality of enlightening beings, because they produce all knowledge and vows; they realize the equality of all Buddhas, because they observe the essence of the Buddhas is nondual; they realize the equality of all things, because they know the nature of things is invariable; they realize the equality of all worlds, because by means of knowledge of expedients they understand all manners of speaking; they realize the equality of all practices of enlightening beings, because they dedicate all roots of goodness as they plant them; they realize the equality of all times, because they diligently carry out buddha work at all times, never ceasing; they realize the equality of all fruits of action, because they have no obsession with or attachment to any mundane or transmundane roots of goodness, while consummating them all; they realize the equality of spiritual powers of Buddhas, because they manifest buddha work adapted to the world.

"This is great enlightening beings' eighth dedication, dedication with the character of true thusness. When great enlightening beings abide in this dedication, they attain realization of innumerable pure teachings, and are able to make the lion roar of the enlightened, free and without fear; with skill in means they teach and develop countless enlightening beings, never ceasing at any time; they attain the infinite complete body of Buddhahood, one body filling all worlds; they attain the infinite complete voice of Buddhahood, one utterance enlightening all beings; they attain the infinite complete power of Buddhahood, able to contain all lands in a single pore; they attain the infinite complete occult abilities of Buddhahood, placing sentient beings in a single atom; they attain the infinite complete liberation of Buddhahood, manifesting all spheres of buddhahood in the body of a single being, attaining true enlightenment; they attain the infinite complete concentration of Buddhahood, able to manifest all concentrations in one concentration; they attain the infinite complete powers of analysis and elucidation of Buddhahood, explaining a single statement of principle forever without exhausting it, removing the doubts and confusion of all sentient beings; they attain the infinite complete being of Buddhahood, endowed with the ten powers of Buddhahood, manifesting the attainment of true enlightenment throughout the realm of sentient beings. This is great enlightening beings' dedication of all roots of goodness in accord with the character of true thusness."

Then the enlightening being Diamond Banner, invested with the awesome power of Buddha, looked over the ten directions and spoke these verses:

> Enlightening beings' determination is stable,
> With true mindfulness steadfast, free from ignorance and confusion.
> Their minds are flexible, always cool;
> They build up boundless virtuous practices.

> Enlightening beings are humble and inoffensive;
> Their aspirations are all pure.
> They have attained the great light of wisdom,
> Able to illumine all acts.

> Enlightening beings' meditations and works are great,
> Variously different, extremely rare;
> They cultivate practice with determination, not retreating,
> Thereby to aid all living beings.

> Their acts are infinitely various;
> Enlightening beings practice them all diligently,
> Adapting to sentient beings, not opposing their wishes,
> Causing all minds to be pure and joyous.

> They have already ascended to the honored stage of the Human
>   Tamer,
> Freed from all burning afflictions, their minds unobstructed;
> They know the meanings of all the teachings
> And practice them ever more diligently for the benefit of the living.

> The good practices cultivated by enlightening beings
> Are measureless, countless, variously different;
> They know the particulars of all of them,
> And dedicate them to help living beings.

> With subtle knowledge they ever examine
> The ultimate, universal truth,
> Cutting off all hypostases,
> Dedicating in accord with true thusness.

> Just as true thusness pervades all,
> So do they embrace all worlds;
> This mind do enlightening beings dedicate
> To freeing sentient beings from attachment.

The power of enlightening beings' vows is all-pervasive,
Just as true thusness is omnipresent;
Their mindfulness comprehends the seen and unseen,
Whereby they dedicate virtues.

Subsisting in the night and the day,
In the fortnight and the month,
And in the year and the eon:
As is true thusness, so is their practice.

In all times and all lands,
All sentient beings and all phenomena—
Abiding therein yet without dwelling anywhere,
They dedicate practice like this.

Like the fundamental essence of true thusness,
Such a great mind do enlightening beings awake:
True thusness's whereabouts is everywhere—
Such practice do they dedicate.

As in the fundamental essence of true thusness
There has never been a single thing,
Ungraspable essence the true essence,
Such work do they dedicate.

As is the character of true thusness, so is their work;
As is the essence of true thusness, so is their work:
As the essence of true thusness is basically real,
So is their work the same as true thusness.

Just as true thusness has no limits,
So too is their work boundless—
And yet they have no ties therein,
Therefore this work is pure.

Thus are brilliant true children of Buddha,
Their will steadfast, unwavering;
By their power of knowledge they comprehend well
And enter the treasury of Buddhas' techniques.

Awakening to the true teaching of Buddha,
They are not obsessed or bound by it—
Thus their free mind is unobstructed—
They've never seen anything to originate.

The acts of the Buddhas' reality body,
The features of all worlds as they are,
The explanation of the signs of things as signless:
Knowing such characteristics is knowing the teachings.

Enlightening beings abide in the inconceivable,
In which thought is inexhaustible:
Entering this inconceivable realm,
Thought and nonthought are both silenced.

Thus do they contemplate the nature of things,
Comprehending all distinctions in acts;
Obliterating all attachment to self,
They abide in virtue, immovable.

The fruits of the acts of enlightening beings
Are all stamped by inexhaustible knowledge;
This infinity's inherently null,
Therefore inexhaustible expedients vanish.

Enlightening beings observe the mind is not outside
And also is not found within;
They know the nature of mind has no existence,
Detached from self and things, forever extinct.

Thus do those buddha-children know
The nature of all things is eternally void,
And there's not a single thing that can create—
They realize selflessness, same as the Buddhas'.

They know that all worlds
Are equal to the nature and characteristics of true thusness;
Seeing these inconceivable characteristics,
They can know the uncharacterized.

If any abide in this profound truth,
Always happily cultivating enlightening practices,
Desiring to aid all living beings,
Adorned with great vows, unregressing,
They then transcend the mundane,
Not creating erroneous concepts of birth and death,
Comprehending the mind is like a magical production,
Diligently cultivating practices to liberate sentient beings.

Enlightening beings observe the world with true awareness,
Seeing that all comes from active conditions;

They cultivate practices in order to liberate,
Including all in the triple world.

They know the various differences of sentient beings
Are discriminations of mental imagery and action:
This they observe with complete clarity,
Without destroying the nature of things.

The wise comprehend all Buddha teachings
And dedicate such practices,
Taking pity on all living beings,
Causing them to contemplate rightly the truth.

"What is great enlightening beings' unattached, unbound, liberated dedication? Here they honor and respect all roots of goodness: that is to say, they honor and respect emancipation from birth and death, embodiment of all roots of goodness, seeking all roots of goodness, repentance of past acts, moral support of roots of goodness, expression of respect for Buddhas, making prostrations before tombs and shrines, and exhorting Buddhas to expound the teaching—they honor and respect such various roots of goodness, recognizing and approving them all.

"When great enlightening beings honor, respect, recognize and approve these roots of goodness, they are extremely delighted, and affirm their faith, attaining peace and stability themselves and also enabling others to attain peace and stability. They diligently cultivate roots of goodness without attachment, freely building them up, developing supreme determination, abiding in the realm of the enlightened, their power growing, able to see and know all. They dedicate the roots of goodness in this way: with unattached, unbound, liberated mind to accomplish the deeds of Universal Good; with unattached, unbound, liberated mind to purify the speech of Universal Good; with unattached, unbound, liberated mind to perfect the mental action of Universal Good; with unattached, unbound, liberated mind to arouse the vast energy of Universal Good; with unattached, unbound, liberated mind to fulfill the methods of concentration formulae of unobstructed expression of Universal Good, their voices pervading the ten directions; with unattached, unbound, liberated mind to fulfill the method of concentration formulae for perception of all Buddhas of Universal Good, always seeing all Buddhas of the ten directions; with unattached, unbound, liberated mind to achieve and understand the method of concentration formulae of all sounds, the same as all sounds, expounding infinite principles; with unattached, unbound, liberated mind to accomplish Universal Good's method of concentration formulae abiding through all ages, cultivating enlightening practice everywhere in the ten directions; with unattached, unbound, liberated mind to accomplish the power of freedom of Universal Good, in the body of one being showing the cultivation of the practices of all enlightening beings, eternally throughout the future, ever unceasing, and as in the body of one being, so also in the bodies of all beings; with unattached, unbound, liberated mind to achieve the power of freedom of Universal Good to enter into the enlightenment sites of all congregations, appearing before all Buddhas, and cultivating the practices of enlightening beings; with unattached, unbound, liberated mind to accomplish the power of freedom of buddhahood of Universal Good, and appear to spend endless eons on various methods, causing all sentient beings to attain entry into enlightenment, appearing bodily before all Buddhas; with unattached, unbound, liberated mind to attain the power of freedom of Universal Good, and moment to moment enable untold beings to abide in the knowledge of the ten powers, without weariness of mind; with unattached, unbound, liberated mind to accomplish the power of freedom of Universal Good, in the bodies of all sentient beings manifesting all Buddhas' autonomous spiritual powers, causing all sentient beings to live by the practice of Universal Good; with unattached, unbound, liberated mind to develop the power of freedom of Universal Good, in the speech of one being producing the speech of all beings, causing each and every being to dwell in the stage of universal knowledge; with unattached, unbound, liberated minds to attain the power of freedom of Universal Good and contain the bodies of all beings in the body of each individual being, causing all to think they have attained the buddha-body; with unattached, unbound, liberated mind to achieve the power of freedom of Universal Good and be able to adorn all worlds of the ten directions with a single flower; with unattached, unbound, liberated minds to accomplish the power of freedom of Universal Good and produce a great voice pervading the cosmos, heard in all buddha-lands, pacifying all beings; with unattached, unbound, liberated mind to attain the power of freedom of Universal Good, able to enter, in each passing instant of the endless future, all worlds everywhere, adorning them as they wish by the spiritual power of Buddha; with unattached, unbound, liberated mind to achieve the power of freedom of Universal Good and through the ages of the future always be able to enter into all worlds and manifest attainment of Buddhahood in the world; with unattached, unbound, liberated mind to accomplish the practice of Universal Good, with one light illumining all worlds in the realm of space; with unattached, unbound, liberated mind to achieve the practice of Universal Good, attain immeasurable knowledge, be endowed with all spiritual powers, and explain all kinds of truths; with unattached, unbound, liberated mind to accomplish the practice of Universal Good, and enter the eternal immeasurable spiritual knowledge of the enlightened; with unattached, unbound, liberated mind to accomplish the practice of Universal Good, abide in the realm of the enlightened ones throughout the cosmos, and by the spiritual power of the enlightened cultivate the physical, verbal, and mental actions of the practices of enlightening beings, never flagging; with unattached, unbound, liberated mind to accomplish the practice of Universal Good, and be pure in speech, not deviating from the truth or corrupting the teaching, with inexhaustible eloquence teaching and pacifying all sentient beings so that they may attain the unexcelled enlightenment of all Buddhas; with unattached, unbound, liberated mind to cultivate the practice of Universal Good, and when entering into a single aspect of the teaching emit immeasurable light illuminating inconceivably many aspects the teaching, abide in the practices of enlightening beings, master of the teaching, arrive at the other shore adorned by Universal Good, and examine and gain understanding of every single object by means of universal knowledge, without universal knowledge being exhausted; with unattached, unbound, liberated mind to live by the practice of Universal Good from this life forever onward, never ceasing, attaining omniscience and realizing innumerable truths, to be ultimately free from confusion and delusion in regard to truth; with unattached, unbound, liberated mind to cultivate the work of Universal Good, with mastery of technique, attaining the light of truth and illumining the practices of enlightening beings without obstruction; with unattached, unbound, liberated mind to cultivate the practice of Universal Good and attain knowledge of all means of liberation—that is, innumerable means, inconceivable means, the means of enlightening beings, means of universal knowledge, all enlightening beings' means of training, means of activating innumerable cycles of teachings, means appropriate to unspeakably many times, means of explaining all kinds of methods, means of the boundless treasury of fearlessness, means of explaining all truths; with unattached, unbound, liberated mind to live by the practice of Universal Good, accomplish actions that cause all witnesses to rejoice and not give rise to slander or repudiation and to set their minds on enlightenment with ultimate purity, never regressing; with unattached, unbound, liberated mind to cultivate the practice of Universal Good and attain pure knowledge of the languages of all sentient beings, fully adorned by all verbal expression to respond to all sentient beings and gladden them; with unattached, unbound, liberated mind to abide by the practice of Universal Good and establish an extraordinary will, have a pure mind, attain great spiritual powers and vast knowledge and wisdom, and go to all vast worlds and vast lands, and to immense congregations of sentient beings expound unspeakably many far-reaching teachings of the Buddhas, their **treasuries full of vast adornments; with unattached, unbound, liberated** mind to fulfill the practice and vows of dedication of Universal Good and attain the pure body, pure mind, and pure understanding of all Buddhas, embody the virtues of buddhahood, abide in the realm of buddhahood, universally illumining with the seal of knowledge, revealing the pure deeds of enlightening beings, entering into the meanings of all different expressions, demonstrating the tremendous freedom of the Buddhas and enlightening beings, and for the sake of all sentient beings manifest the attainment of true enlightenment; with unattached, unbound, liberated mind to diligently cultivate the practical commitments of the faculties of Universal Good and attain clear, sharp faculties, well-tuned faculties, faculties free in all ways, inexhaustible faculties, faculties diligently cultivating all roots of goodness, equanimous faculties of the range of all Buddhas, faculties of great vigor giving all enlightening beings the prediction of nonregression, faculties knowing the realm of indestructibility of all Buddhas, faculties of adamantine flames of the illuminating light of knowledge of all Buddhas, faculties freely distinguishing all capacities, faculties for establishing all sentient beings in universal knowledge, boundlessly vast faculties, totally complete faculties, pure unhindered faculties; with unattached, unbound, liberated mind to cultivate the practice of Universal Good and attain all enlightening beings' spiritual powers—spiritual powers of boundlessly great strength, spiritual powers of immeasurable independent knowledge, spiritual power to appear in all buddha-fields without physically moving, spiritual power of unhindered, uninterrupted freedom, spiritual power to concentrate all buddha-fields in one place, spiritual power to pervade all buddha-fields with one body, spiritual power of unhindered, liberated roaming, spiritual power of instantaneous freedom without doing anything, spiritual power abiding in essencelessness and nonreliance, and spiritual power to progressively set up untold worlds in a single pore, traveling to all Buddhas' enlightenment sites throughout the cosmos to teach sentient beings and cause them all to enter the door of great knowledge; with unattached, unbound, liberated mind to enter the door of Universal Good, produce the practices of enlightening beings, and with independent knowledge enter into innumerable buddha-lands in a single instant, contain immeasurable buddha-lands in one body, attain knowledge of how to purify buddha-lands, and always observe boundless buddha-lands with knowledge and wisdom, never developing the mentality of individual salvation; with unattached, unbound, liberated mind to cultivate the practices of expedient means of Universal Good, enter the realm of wisdom, be born in the house of the enlightened, abide in the path of enlightening beings, fulfill infinite supreme aspirations, carry out infinite vows without ever ceasing, and know all realms of reality of all times; with unattached, unbound, liberated mind to accomplish the pure teaching of Universal Good, able to contain the innumerable worlds of the cosmos throughout all space in a spot as big as a hairtip, causing all to be clearly seen, with the same applying to every single point throughout the space of the cosmos; with unattached, unbound, liberated mind to accomplish the profound mental techniques of Universal Good, able in a single mental moment to manifest the states of mind of one sentient being over untold eons, and in the same way manifest the states of mind of all sentient beings over untold eons;

with unattached, unbound, liberated mind to enter the stage of employment of techniques of dedication of Universal Good, able to contain in
one body the unspeakably unspeakable numbers of bodies throughout
the cosmos, without there being any increase or decrease in the realm of
sentient beings, and as of one body, so also of all bodies throughout the
cosmos, so all contain all in the same way; with unattached, unbound,
liberated mind to accomplish the means of the vows of Universal
Good, abandon all delusions of thought, mind, and view, and enter the
sphere of all Buddhas and always see the pure Buddhas' reality-body,
equal to space, to be adorned with the marks and embellishments of
buddhahood, master spiritual powers, and always teach unimpededly
and uninterruptedly with a sublime voice, causing all who hear to
absorb and retain what they have been taught, and to realize the body
of enlightenment has no acquisition; with unattached, unbound, liberated mind to cultivate the practice of Universal Good and abide in the
stages of enlighenment, in a single moment entering all worlds—upright
worlds, inverted worlds, untold numbers of immense worlds in the ten
directions enmeshing all locations—and with the means of distinction of
the cosmic net of Indra, distinguish all reality-realms, having various
worlds enter one world, having untold infinities of worlds enter one
world, having the infinite worlds structured by all realms of phenomena
and principles enter one world, having the infinite worlds established in
all realms of space enter one world, yet without destroying the features
of their structures, causing all to be clearly seen; with unattached,
unbound, liberated mind to cultivate Universal Good's practical vows
of enlightening and be crowned by the Buddha, instantly entering the
stage of skill in means, fully developing the treasure of knowledge
steadfastly living by enlightening practices, capable of comprehensive
knowledge of all perceptions—perceptions of sentient beings, perceptions of phenomena, perceptions of fields, perceptions of locations,
perceptions of Buddha, perceptions of worlds, perceptions of action,
perceptions of practices, perceptions of realms, perceptions of understandings, perceptions of faculties, perceptions of time, perceptions of
continuity, perceptions of afflictions, perceptions of purity, perceptions
of maturation, perceptions of seeing Buddha, perceptions of turning the
wheel of teaching, perceptions of hearing the teaching and understanding,
perceptions of training, perceptions of infinity, perceptions of emancipation, perceptions of various stages, perceptions of innumerable stages,
perceptions of knowledge of enlightening beings, perceptions of training
of enlightening beings, perceptions of concentrations of enlightening
beings, perceptions of enlightening beings emerging from concentration,
perceptions of the becoming of enlightening beings, perceptions of
disintegration of enlightening beings, perceptions of the demise of
enlightening beings, perceptions of the birth of enlightening beings,
perceptions of the liberation of enlightening beings, perceptions of the
independence of enlightening beings, perceptions of the preservation of

enlightening beings, perceptions of the spheres of enlightening beings, perceptions of the formation and decay of ages, perceptions of light, perceptions of darkness, perceptions of day, perceptions of night, perceptions of changes of the fortnight, month, season, and year, perceptions of going, perceptions of coming, perceptions of standing still, perceptions of sitting, perceptions of sleeping, perceptions of waking—able to know all these perceptions in an instant of thought, while at the same time detached from all perceptions, without arbitrary discrimination, cutting through all barriers, without any attachments, the knowledge of all Buddhas filling their minds, all Buddha teachings developing their roots of goodness, having the same one body as all Buddhas, in the keeping of all Buddhas, free from defilement, thoroughly pure, cultivating all Buddha teachings as appropriate, reaching the other shore; with unattached, unbound, liberated mind to cultivate the practice of Universal Good for the sake of all sentient beings and produce the jewel of great knowledge, knowing infinite minds in each individual mind, seeing clearly their various fixations, notions, various natures, doings, functions, features, thoughts, and awareness; with unattached, unbound, liberated mind to perfect the jewel of knowledge of the great vows of Universal Good, knowing infinite places in one place, and likewise in all places; with unattached, unbound, liberated mind to cultivate the stage of knowledge of practice of Universal Good, and in one action be able to know all actions, clearly seeing the various conditions making up those actions, and as of one action, so of all actions; with unattached, unbound, liberated mind to cultivate and learn Universal Good's knowledge of all things, knowing infinite things in one thing, knowing one thing in all things, these things each different, without obstruction, without opposition or attachment; with unattached, unbound, liberated mind to live by the practice of enlightening beings and acquire the unobstructed ear faculty of Universal Good, in the sound of one utterance knowing the boundless differentiations in countless utterances, without clinging, and as of one utterance, so of all utterances; with unattached, unbound, liberated mind to cultivate the knowledge of Universal Good, initiate the practice of Universal Good, and abide in the state of Universal Good, in each individual principle expounding countless principles, those principles far-reaching, variously different, teaching, transforming, saving, in accord with inconceivable expedient means, at all times, in accord with the inclinations, understandings, and faculties of sentient beings, in accord with the time expounding the teaching for them with the voice of Buddha, with one marvelous voice gladdening innumerable sentient beings in the congregations at unspeakably many sites of enlightenment, so the innumerable enlightening beings with all Buddhas fill the cosmos, making extraordinary determinations, producing great insights, ultimately knowing all practices abiding in the state of Universal Good, according to the principles explained able to enter moment to moment into the space of a single instant and develop and increase a store of infinite great knowledge forever and ever—to teach this way, to cultivate in all fields great practices equal to space, fully perfecting them; with unattached, unbound, liberated mind to cultivate the methods of operation of the faculties of Universal Good, becoming masters of great action, in each and every faculty able to know innumerable faculties, innumerable mental inclinations, and the sublime practice born of the realm of inconceivability; with unattached, unbound, liberated mind to live by the heart of great dedication practice by Universal Good and attain the most subtle knowledge of form, the most subtle knowledge of bodies, the most subtle knowledge of lands, the most subtle knowledge of ages, the most subtle knowledge of worlds, the most subtle knowledge of places, the most subtle knowledge of times, the most subtle knowledge of numbers, the most subtle knowledge of consequences of actions, and the most subtle knowledge of purity, able to know all such subtleties instantly, without fear, confusion, distraction, cloudiness, or depression of mind, being single-minded, skilled in quiet concentration and discernment, the mind well stabilized; with unattached, unbound, liberated mind to abide in the knowledge of enlightening beings and cultivate the practice of Universal Good tirelessly, able to know the details of the tendencies of sentient beings, the details of the deaths of sentient beings, the details of the births of sentient beings, the details of the subsistence of sentient beings, the details of the locations of sentient beings, the details of the types of sentient beings, the details of the realms of sentient beings, the details of the acts of sentient beings, the details of the grasping of sentient beings, the details of sentient beings' clinging to objects, able to know all such details instantly; with unattached, unbound, liberated mind to establish profound determination, cultivate the practice of Universal Good, and be able to know the details of efforts of all enlightening beings for the sake of living creatures from their first inspiration—the details of cultivation of enlightening beings' practices, the details of enlightening beings' abodes, the details of enlightening beings' spiritual powers, the details of enlightening beings' travels to innumerable buddha-lands, the details of enlightening beings' pure eyes, the details of enlightening beings' development of transcendent mentality, the details of enlightening beings' visits to congregations at enlightenment sites of all Buddhas, the details of enlightening beings' knowledge of methods of concentration spells, the details of enlightening beings' expositions of the treasury of all skills of analysis and elucidation of the stage of infinite fearlessness, the details of the characteristics of innumerable concentrations of enlightening beings, the details of enlightening beings' knowledge of concentration on vision of all Buddhas, the details of enlightening beings' knowledge of extremely deep concentration, the details of enlightening beings' knowledge of concentration on great adornments, the details of enlightening beings' knowledge of concentration in great autonomous spiritual powers, the details of enlightening beings' knowledge of concentration on preservation of great practices throughout the future, the details of enlightening beings' knowledge of production of innumerable different concentrations, the details of enlightening beings' knowledge of concentration on being born in the presence of all Buddhas and diligent practice of service of the Buddhas, never leaving them, the details of enlightening beings' knowledge of cultivation of all profound, vast, unobstructed states of concentration, the details of enlightening beings' unobscured knowledge of concentration of the stage of consummation of universal knowledge, the stage of knowledge and practice of preservation, the stage of great spiritual powers, and the stage of certitude of meaning, able to know all such details completely; with unattached, unbound, liberated mind to cultivate the practice of Universal Good and know the details of all enlightening beings' knowledge of structures, the details of enlightening beings' stages, the details of enlightening beings' innumerable activities, the details of enlightening beings' production of dedication, the details of enlightening beings' attainment of the treasuries of all Buddhas, the details of enlightening beings' analytic knowledge, the details of enlightening beings' spiritual capabilities and will power, the subtleties of enlightening beings' explanations of concentration, the details of enlightening beings' versatile skill in means, the details of the gestures of enlightening beings, the details of enlightening beings' life on the threshold of buddhahood, the details of enlightening beings' birth in Tushita heaven, the details of enlightening beings' sojourn in the celestial palace, the details of enlightening beings' purification of a buddha-land, the details of enlightening beings' observation of the human world, the details of enlightening beings radiating great light, the details of the excellence of families of enlightening beings, the details of the congregations at the enlightenment sites of enlightening beings, the details of enlightening beings' birth throughout all worlds, the details of enlightening beings' manifestation of the end of a life of all bodies in one body, the details of enlightening beings entering their mothers' wombs, the details of enlightening beings' life in their mothers' wombs, the details of enlightening beings' free manifestation of the congregations at the sites of enlightenment in all realms while yet in their mothers' wombs, the details of enlightening beings' manifestation of the spiritual powers of all Buddhas while in their mothers' wombs, the details of enlightening beings' manifestation of birth, the details of the knowledge of enlightening beings walking seven steps like a lion, the details of enlightening beings' knowledge of skill in means, expediently appearing to abide in a royal palace, the details of enlightening beings leaving home and cultivating practices for self-mastery, the details of enlightening beings sitting under trees of enlightenment at sites of enlightenment, the details of enlightening beings conquering armies of demons and attaining unexcelled complete perfect enlightenment, the details of the realized ones sitting on the seat of enlightenment and emanating great light illumining the worlds of the ten directions, the details of the enlightened ones showing innumerable mystical trans- figurations, the details of the enlightened ones' lion roar and great extinction, the details of the enlightened ones taming all sentient beings without hindrance, the details of the enlightened ones' inconceivable autonomous powers like the adamantine mind of enlightenment, the details of the enlightened ones minding all worlds, the details of the enlightened ones doing buddha work in all worlds forever and ever without ceasing, the details of the enlightened ones' unobstructed spiri- tual powers pervading the cosmos, the details of the enlightened ones appearing in all worlds throughout space to fulfill buddhahood and tame sentient beings, the details of the enlightened ones manifesting innumerable buddha-bodies in one buddha-body, the details of the enlightened ones' knowledge of the freedom to be at the site of enlight- enment in the past, future, and present, completely knowing all such minute details with consummate clarity, able to manifest appearance in all worlds, moment to moment increasing in knowledge, perfecting nonregressive skill in liberative means, cultivating enlightening practice without ceasing, fulfilling the stage of dedication of Universal Good, attaining the virtues of all Buddhas, never tiring of or giving up what enlightening beings practice, producing the enlightening beings' state of presence, with innumerable means of enlightenment, all pure, wishing to pacify all sentient beings, cultivating the deeds of enlightening beings and accomplishing the enlightening beings' stage of great power, attain- ing the aspiration of the enlightening mind, reaching the gate of dedica- tion of Diamond Banner, producing the treasury of qualities of the realm of truth, always in the care of the Buddhas, entering the doors of the profound principles of enlightening beings, expounding all true meanings, flawlessly skilled in teaching, carrying out great vows, never abandoning sentient beings, thoroughly knowing the mine of conceiv- able and inconceivable realms, demonstrating the production of thought in the realm of inconceivability, detaching from verbal expression, abiding in knowledge, doing as all enlightening beings do, with the power of spiritual freedom demonstrating the path of attainment of Buddhahood forever and ever without cease, by spiritual power and the power of vows able to show all worlds, sentient beings, and ages, defined by illusory ideas and speech; with unattached, unbound, liber- ated mind to cultivate the practice of Universal Good and attain knowl- edge of the minute details of the realms of all sentient beings—knowledge of the details of distinctions of realms of sentient beings, knowledge of the details of the verbal expression of realms of sentient beings, knowl- edge of the details of the attachments in realms of sentient beings, knowledge of the details of the different species in the realms of sentient beings, knowledge of the details of similar species in the realms of sentient beings, knowledge of the details of the innumerable tendencies in the realms of sentient beings, knowledge of the details of the inconceivably many artifices of various conceptions in the realms of sentient beings, knowledge of the details of the immeasurable pollution in the realms of sentient beings, knowledge of the details of the immeasurable purity in the realms of sentient beings—able to instantly know such minute details as these of all realms of sentient beings, knowing them as they truly are, widely expounding the truth for sentient beings, showing them various kinds of pure teachings and practices to enable them to cultivate the vast knowledge and wisdom of enlightening beings, emanating countless bodies, gladdening to all who see, illumining enlightening beings' minds with the sun of knowledge, causing their understanding to open up and their wisdom to be freed; with unattached, unbound, liberated mind to cultivate the practices of Universal Good in all worlds for the sake of all beings, attaining detailed knowledge of all worlds in the cosmos of space—detailed knowledge of small worlds, detailed knowledge of large worlds, detailed knowledge of polluted worlds, detailed knowledge of pure worlds, detailed knowledge of incomparable worlds, detailed knowledge of various worlds, detailed knowledge of broad worlds, detailed knowledge of narrow worlds, detailed knowledge of worlds with unobstructed adornments, detailed knowledge of Buddhas' appearance throughout all worlds, detailed knowledge of explanation of truth throughout all worlds, detailed knowledge of bodily manifestation throughout all worlds, detailed knowledge of emanation of great light throughout all worlds, detailed knowledge of manifestation of the Buddhas' autonomous spiritual powers throughout all worlds, detailed knowledge of entry into the congregations at enlightenment sites of buddha-fields in all worlds, detailed knowledge of demonstration of all tones with one voice throughout all worlds, detailed knowledge of making all buddha-fields in the cosmos into one buddha-field, detailed knowledge of making one buddha-field into all buddha-fields in the cosmos, detailed knowledge of awareness that all worlds are like dreams, detailed knowledge of awareness that all worlds are like reflections, detailed knowledge of awareness that all worlds are like illusions—knowing all this thoroughly, producing the path of all enlightening beings, enter the knowledge and spiritual powers practiced by Universal Good, fulfill the meditation of Universal Good, cultivate enlightening practices unceasingly, attain the free mystic metamorphoses of all Buddhas, acquire unobstructed bodies, abide in nonreliant knowledge, be without grasping or attachment to anything, being nonacquisitive in all mental actions, developing detachment in all situations, thinking of enlightening practice as purification, having no thought of grasping or clinging to universal knowledge, adorning themselves with concentrations, their knowledge in accord with all realms of reality; with unattached, unbound, liberated mind to enter the door of practices of Universal Good and attain detailed knowledge of innumerable realms of reality, detailed knowledge of explanations of all realms of reality, detailed knowledge of entry into vast realms of reality, detailed knowledge of distinction of inconceivably many realms of reality, detailed knowledge of distinction of all realms of reality, detailed knowledge of one thought pervading all realms of reality, detailed knowledge of entry into all realms of reality, detailed knowledge of awareness that all realms of reality are ungraspable, detailed knowledge of observation of all realms of reality without obstruction, detailed knowledge of awareness that all realms of reality have no birth, detailed knowledge of manifestation of miracles in all realms of reality, with vast knowledge knowing such minute details of all realms of reality as they truly are, mastering the truth, demonstrating the practice of Universal Good, causing all sentient beings to be fully satisfied, not abandoning principle yet not clinging to doctrine, producing impartial, unobstructed knowledge, aware of the basis of nonobstruction, not dwelling on anything at all, not destroying the nature of things as it really is, pure and spacelike, while producing verbal explanation adapted to the world, opening up the true meaning, pointing out the silent, null essence, not relying or dwelling on any object, without vain discrimination, clearly seeing the universal structure of the realm of reality, comprehending that all worlds and all things are equal and nondual, divorcing all attachments; with unattached, unbound, liberated mind to cultivate the practices of Universal Good and develop detailed knowledge of all eons—detailed knowledge of making unspeakably many eons one moment, detailed knowledge of making one moment unspeakably many eons, detailed knowledge of fitting incalculable eons into one eon, detailed knowledge of one eon entering incalculable eons, detailed knowledge of long eons entering short eons, detailed knowledge of short eons entering long eons, detailed knowledge of entry into eons with Buddhas and eons without Buddhas, detailed knowledge of the number of all eons, detailed knowledge of how all eons are not eons, detailed knowledge of seeing all eons past, present, and future in a single moment—instantaneously knowing all such minute details of all eons as they truly are by means of enlightened knowledge, attaining to the mind mastering the completely fulfilled practices of enlightening beings, the mind entering the practice of Universal Good, the mind free from all inane speculation and erroneous conceptualization, the mind tirelessly making great vows, the mind perceiving the network of innumerable worlds filled with Buddhas, the mind able to learn and remember the roots of goodness of the Buddhas and the practices of the enlightening beings, the mind which, having heard, never forgets the great practices for comforting all sentient beings, the mind which can manifest the appearance of Buddha in the world in all ages, the mind which unceasingly practices unshakability and imperturbability in all worlds forever and ever, the mind which in all worlds fills the bodies of enlightening beings with the behavior of the enlightened; with unattached, unbound, liberated mind to cultivate the practice of Universal Good, accomplish nonregression, and attain extremely detailed knowledge of principles and phenomena—detailed knowledge of the principles and phenomena of mysticism, detailed knowledge of far-reaching principles and extensive phenomena, detailed knowledge of various principles and phenomena, detailed knowledge of principles and phenomena of adornment, detailed knowledge of the immeasurability of all principles and phenomena, detailed knowledge of all principles entering one principle, all phenomena entering one phenomenon, all principles entering one phenomenon, all phenomena entering one principle, detailed knowledge of one principle entering all principles, one phenomenon entering all phenomena, one principle entering all phenomena, one phenomenon entering all principles, detailed knowledge of all principles and phenomena entering what is not principle or phenomenon, detailed knowledge of defining all principles and phenomena where there are none, without contradiction, detailed knowledge penetrating the techniques of all Buddha-teachings—knowing as they truly are all such things as defined by all speech in all worlds, with extremely detailed and subtle knowledge equal to all of them, that knowledge unobstructed, attaining the mind which enters the boundless realm of reality, abiding steadfastly with a profound mind in each sphere of reality, perfecting unobstructed practice, filling all faculties with universal knowledge, entering the knowledge of buddhahood, properly mindful of expedient means, accomplishing the great qualities of Buddhas, filling the entire cosmos, realizing all the bodies of the enlightened, manifesting all the physical actions of enlightening beings, expounding the teaching in the terms of expression of all worlds, attaining the mental activity of knowledge spiritually empowered by all Buddhas, producing omniscient knowledge skillfully distinguishing all things; with unattached, unbound, liberated mind to cultivate the practice of Universal Good and produce detailed knowledge of all kinds—that is, detailed knowledge of all lands and fields, detailed knowledge of all sentient beings, detailed knowledge of the fruits of all practices, detailed knowledge of the minds of all sentient beings, detailed knowledge of the proper timing of all expositions of the teaching, detailed knowledge of all realms of reality, detailed knowledge of all past, present, and future worlds throughout space, detailed knowledge of all manners of verbal expression, detailed knowledge of all worldly activities, detailed knowledge of all transmundane activities, and detailed knowledge of the paths of all Buddhas, the paths of all enlightening beings, and the paths of all sentient beings—cultivating enlightening practices, living by the path of Universal Good, knowing all expressions and meanings truly, bearing knowledge that all are like reflections, like dreams, like illusions, like echoes, like phantoms, like space, bearing knowledge of nullity, bearing knowledge of all realms of reality, bearing independent knowledge, bearing knowledge of all principles of Buddhahood.

"Enlightening beings dedicate their unattached, unbound, liberated minds, without forming arbitrary notions of worlds or worldly things, of enlightenment or enlightening beings, of the practices of enlightening beings or the paths of emancipation, of Buddhas or Buddha teachings, of taming or not taming sentient beings, of roots of goodness or dedication, of self or others, of gifts or recipients, of practices of enlightening beings or true enlightenment, of truth or knowledge.

"Great enlightening beings dedicate those roots of goodness in this way: that minds be unattached, unbound, liberated; that bodies be unattached, unbound, liberated; that speech be unattached, unbound, liberated; that actions be unattached, unbound, liberated; that rewards be unattached, unbound, liberated; that worlds be free from attachment and bondage and be liberated; that buddha-lands be free from attachment and bondage and be liberated; that sentient beings be free from attachments and bondage and be liberated; that laws be free from attachment and bondage and be liberated; that knowledge be free from attachment and bondage and be liberated.

"When great enlightening beings practice dedication in this way, they do so as the Buddhas of past, present, and future during their enlightening: they study the dedication of Buddhas of the past, make the dedication of Buddhas of the future, and live by the dedication of Buddhas of the present; they remain on the path of dedication of the Buddhas of the past, do not give up the path of dedication of the Buddhas of the future, and follow the path of dedication of the Buddhas of the present; they diligently practice the teachings of the Buddhas of the past, accomplish the teachings of the Buddhas of the future, and know the teachings of the Buddhas of the present; they fulfill the equanimity of the Buddhas of the past, achieve the equanimity of the Buddhas of the future, and abide in the equanimity of the Buddhas of the present; they traverse the ranges of the Buddhas of the past, abide in the ranges of the Buddhas of the future, and equal the ranges of the Buddhas of the present; they attain the roots of goodness of the Buddhas of past, present, and future, are endowed with the essential nature of all Buddhas of past, present, and future, abide in the sphere of action of all Buddhas of past, present, and future, and accord with the realm of all Buddhas of past, present, and future.

"This is great enlightening beings' ninth dedication, dedication with unattached, unbound, liberated mind. When great enlightening beings live by this dedication, they cannot be broken down even by adamantine mountains; their physical characteristics are supreme among all sentient beings; they can destroy all the evildoing of demons; they appear in all worlds in the ten directions, cultivating the practices of enlightening beings; because they want to enlighten all sentient beings, they expound the Buddha-teachings to them in appropriate ways; attaining great knowledge and wisdom, they have no confusion in their minds about the teachings of the Buddhas; wherever they live, whether they go or stay, they always encounter incorruptible company; they are able to absorb and retain the teachings expounded by the Buddhas of all

times by means of pure mindfulness; they cultivate the practice of
enlightening beings forever and ever, never ceasing, developing and
fulfilling the practical vows of Universal Good, attaining universal
knowledge, disbursing it as buddha-work, perfecting the autonomous
spiritual powers of enlightening beings."

Then the enlightening being Diamond Banner, spiritually empowered by Buddha, looked over the ten directions and said in verse,

> The peerless honored ones of the ten directions
> Have never had a thought of pride;
> Whatever virtuous works they perform,
> They are still respectful and reverent.

> All the virtues they cultivate
> Are not for themselves or others;
> Always, with a mind of supreme resolve,
> They dedicate them to the benefit of all the living.

> They have never developed pride or conceit,
> Yet they are not self-demeaning;
> The actions of the enlightened ones
> They inquire into and earnestly practice.

> The various roots of goodness they cultivate
> Are all for the benefit of conscious creatures;
> They abide in profound will and broad understanding,
> Dedicated to the most honorable, virtuous human state.

> The various skills and marvels
> There are in the world, beyond measure,
> Crude and fine, broad and deep,
> They practice and master all.

> All the various bodies in the world
> They enter by equality of bodies;
> Cultivating this, they attain understanding
> And accomplish nonregression in the door of wisdom.

> The lands in the worlds, innumerable kinds,
> Minute, immense, with different orientations,
> Enlightening beings can, via the door of knowledge,
> See all in a single pore.

> Sentient beings' mental activities, without measure,
> They can cause to equally enter one mind:

Through the door of knowledge they understand all,
And do not regress in their practice.

Sentient beings' faculties and inclinations,
Superior, middling, and inferior, are each unlike;
All are profoundly hard to know:
But enlightening beings can comprehend them in accord with
their fundamental nature.

Sentient beings' various actions,
Superior, middling, and inferior, are each different:
Enlightening beings, deeply entering enlightened power,
Clearly see all through the door of knowledge.

Inconceivably innumerable eons
They can cause to equally enter one instant;
Thus having seen, throughout the ten directions
They cultivate all pure actions.

Past, future, and present—
They know their characteristics, each different,
Yet without deviating from the principle of equality—
This is the great mind's practice of clear comprehension.

The actions of the sentient beings of the world are not the same—
Sometimes apparent, sometimes hidden, there are innumerable kinds:
Enlightening beings know all their different forms,
And know too their forms are formless.

The autonomous spiritual power manifested
By all Buddhas in the worlds in the ten directions,
Vast, extensive, inconceivable,
Enlightening beings are able to distinctly know.

The naturally enlightened Human Lions
In the Tushita heavens of all worlds,
Their virtues great, pure, beyond compare,
All their features the enlightening can see.

Sometimes they manifest spiritual descent into the mother's womb,
Or innumerable autonomous miraculous displays—
Attaining Buddhahood, teaching, showing extinction,
Throughout the world, unceasingly.

When the Human Lions are first born,
All those of superior knowledge serve them:

The gods, such as Indra and Brahma,
All respectfully attend to them.

In the infinite, boundless realms
Throughout the ten directions,
Without beginning or end, far or near,
They manifest the powers of the enlightened.

After the Honored Human Leaders manifest birth,
They walk seven steps in each direction:
Wishing to enlighten the living by the wondrous truth,
The Buddhas therefore observe all.

They see sentient beings sunk in the sea of cravings,
Veiled by blindness and folly:
The Free Humans show a smile
And reflect that they should save beings from suffering.

The great Lion's Roar emits a wondrous voice:
"I am most honored in the world;
I should light the lamp of clear pure knowledge
And destroy the darkness of ignorance and folly in birth and
    death."

When the Human Lion Kings appear in the world
They radiate infinite great beams of light
Causing an end to the courses of misery
And extinguishing the sufferings of the world.

Sometimes they manifest life in a royal palace,
Sometimes they manifest leaving home and cultivating enlighten-
    ment;
Because they want to benefit sentient beings
They demonstrate such powers of freedom.

When the Buddhas first sit on the enlightenment site,
The whole earth trembles;
All worlds in the ten directions are bathed in light,
And beings in all states are relieved of pain.

Shaking the palaces of all demons,
Awakening the minds of all sentient beings,
Those who received the teaching and practiced it in the past
They cause to know the true meaning.

All the lands in the ten directions
Completely enter a pore;
The lands in all pores are boundless:
Therein they manifest spiritual powers.

Enlightening beings understand the innumerable methods
Expounded by all the Buddhas;
Even those the Buddhas have not explained
They understand and diligently practice.

All the demon armies create conflicts
Filling all worlds of the universe;
The infinite varied ills they create
Unhindered knowledge can all destroy.

The Enlightened may be in buddha-fields,
Or may appear to be in celestial palaces.
Sometimes they manifest their bodies in Brahma's palace—
Enlightening beings see all without obstruction.

Buddha manifests infinite, various bodies,
Turning the wheel of the pure teaching;
No bounds to this can ever be found,
Even throughout all times.

Jeweled thrones, high and wide, without compare,
Fill the infinite worlds of the ten directions,
Adorned with various wondrous forms:
Buddhas sit on them, inconceivable,
Surrounded by crowds of enlightening beings
Filling the whole of the cosmos,
Revealing infinite practices for enlightenment,
The paths followed by all the Buddhas.

The appropriate acts of the Buddhas
Are infinite, boundless as the cosmos;
The wise are able, by one technique,
To know them all entirely.

The Buddha's spiritual powers
Manifest all kinds of bodies:
They may show infinite lives in all states of being,
Or may appear surrounded by concubines,
Or else they may in countless worlds
Manifest leaving home and attaining buddhahood,

Add on the final demise,
Distribution of relics and setting up of shrines.

By these boundless varied actions
The guides explain the abode of buddhahood;
The great virtues of the World Honored
Enlightening beings vow to cultivate and achieve.

When they dedicate those roots of goodness
They abide in such expedient means,
Thus cultivating enlightening practice,
Their minds never wearied or lazy.

The great spiritual powers of the Buddhas
As well as their boundless supreme virtues
And also wise acts in the mundane world:
All they know exhaustively.

Thus all lordly humans
In whatever realms they may be
Understand all at once
Yet don't give up enlightenment practice.

The subtle, refined practices of the Buddhas
And the various laws of all fields,
They are able to know as they encounter them,
Ultimately dedicating them to transcendence.

Finite or infinite, all ages
Enlightening beings know are the same as one instant:
Herein they enter enlightenment practice,
Always cultivating it diligently, never regressing.

All the lands in the ten directions,
Some polluted, some pure,
And all the Buddhas there
Enlightening beings can distinguish and know.

In every moment they clearly see
Inconceivably many eons;
Thus, throughout all times,
They cultivate enlightening practice.

Into all minds they penetrate,
And penetrate all things equally too,

The same for all buddha-fields throughout space,
Comprehending all their excellent practices.

They produce all kinds of knowledge
Of sentient beings and phenomena
As well as spiritual powers of enlightening beings:
All of this inexhaustible.

Knowledge of all minute details, each distinct,
Enlightening beings thoroughly absorb:
Similar and different aspects they all know well,
Thus cultivating far-reaching practice.

Innumerable are the sentient beings in each
Of the innumerable buddha-lands in the ten directions:
Their conditions and types are variously different—
By the power of their practice enlightening beings can know them
    all.

All the guides there are
In past, present, and future worlds—
If one has knowledge and dedication like them,
One's practice is equal to those Buddhas.

If people can practice this dedication,
This is learning the path of the Buddhas:
They'll attain the virtues of all Buddhas,
And the knowledge and wisdom of Buddhas.
Invulnerable to all worldlings,
Accomplishing all that is to be learned,
They'll always be able to recollect all Buddhas
And see all the Lamps of the World.

Enlightening beings' excellent practices are immeasurable,
And so are their virtuous qualities:
Once living by the unexcelled practice of the Enlightened,
They know all the spiritual powers of the Buddhas.

"What is great enlightening beings' boundless dedication equal to the cosmos? Here they wrap their heads with the turban of nondefilement, dwell in the position of a teacher of truth, and extensively carry out the giving of teaching, with great kindness and compassion establishing sentient beings in the aspiration for enlightenment. Always practicing charity, by the determination for enlightenment they nurture roots of goodness. Being directors for sentient beings, they point out to them the path of universal knowledge. Being suns of truth for sentient beings, the light of their roots of goodness illumines all. Their minds are impartial toward all sentient beings. They practice good works without rest. Their hearts are pure, free from stain, and their knowledge and wisdom are free. They never give up good works, and, acting as wise caravan leaders for sentient beings, they bring them all into the right path of peace. Being leaders and guides for sentient beings, they have them cultivate the practices of all roots of goodness. Being incorruptible, steadfast, good friends to sentient beings, they cause their roots of goodness to develop and mature.

"These great enlightening beings make giving of teaching principal; developing all pure, good qualities, they embody the mind directed toward universal knowledge, their supreme will power ultimately enduring, developing, and growing. They are endowed with great powers and virtues. They trust good spiritual friends, their minds have no deceitfulness. They contemplate and examine the boundless realms of the way into universal knowledge.

"These roots of goodness they dedicate in this way: they vow to become able to cultivate, perfect, and increase all perspectives of universal nonobstruction; they vow to become able to absorb, retain, and expound whatever they hear of the true teaching of the Buddhas, even a single line or verse; they vow to become able to recollect all the Buddhas, past, future, and present, of all worlds, innumerable, boundless, equal to the cosmos, and, having remembered them, to cultivate enlightening practices; they also vow to cultivate enlightening practice for one being in one world forever by this root of goodness of remembrance of Buddhas, and as in one world, so in all worlds, throughout the space of the cosmos, and as for one being so for all sentient beings, in each case being eternally adorned with great vows for their sake, eradicating any thought of separation from the Buddhas and spiritual friends, always seeing the Buddhas before them, able to draw near to every Buddha that appears in the world. The pure religious practices extolled and expounded by all Buddhas and enlightening beings they vow to cultivate and completely fulfill—religious practice of unbroken morality, flawless morality, unalloyed morality, spotless morality, impeccable morality; religious practice that cannot be shrouded, religious practice lauded by Buddhas, religious practice of nonreliance, religious practice of nonacquisitveness, religious practice of increasing the purity of the enlightening being, religious practice as carried out by the Buddhas of all times, religious practice of nonobstruction, religious practice of nonattachment, religious practice of noncontention, religious practice without extinction, religious practice of stabilization of good will, religious practice of incomparable compassion, religious practice of immutable joy, religious practice of undisturbed equanimity, religious practice of freedom from anger.

"If great enlightening beings are able to cultivate such pure religious practices for their own sake, then they will be able to do so for the sake of all sentient beings, enabling all sentient beings to attain stability, enabling all sentient beings to attain open understanding, enabling all sentient beings to attain completion, enabling all sentient beings to attain purity, enabling all sentient beings to attain nondefilement, enabling all sentient beings to attain illumination, enabling all sentient beings to be unstained by sense objects, enabling all sentient beings to be free from blinding hindrances, enabling all sentient beings to be freed from inflaming afflictions, enabling all sentient beings to be freed from all bonds, enabling all sentient beings to forever depart from all evils, enabling all sentient beings to be harmless and ultimately pure. Why? If great enlightening beings cannot themselves be pure in religious practice, they cannot cause others to attain purity; if they themselves regress from religious practice, they cannot cause others not to regress; if they themselves are corrupt in religious practice, they cannot cause others to be free from corruption; if they themselves stray from religious practice, they cannot cause others not to stray; if they themselves are lazy in religious practice, they cannot cause others not to slack off; if they themselves have no faith in religious practice, they cannot cause others to have faith; if they themselves do not live steadily by religious practice, they cannot cause others to live steadily; if they themselves have no realization of religious practice, they cannot cause others' minds to attain realization; if they themselves give up religious practices, they cannot cause others to persevere; if they themselves waver in religious practice, they cannot cause others not to waver. Great enlightening beings act without delusion and teach doctrine that is free from delusion; what they say is truthful, and they practice what they preach. They purify their deeds, words, and thoughts, eliminating all dross and defilements. They abide in unobstructed action and annihilate all hindrances. Great enlightening beings themselves attain pure minds and explain to others ways to purify the mind; they themselves cultivate harmony and tolerance, taming their minds with roots of goodness, and cause others to be harmonious and tolerant, taming their minds with roots of goodness. They themselves get rid of doubt and regret, and also cause others to be forever rid of doubt and regret. They themselves attain pure faith and also cause others to attain indestructible pure faith. They themselves abide by the truth, and also cause others to live by the truth.

"Great enlightening beings also dedicate the roots of goodness arising from giving of teaching in this way: 'May I attain the infinite means of teaching of all Buddhas and analyze and explain them for all sentient beings, causing them all to rejoice and be satisfied in mind, shattering all false philosophies; may I be able to expound the ocean of teachings of the Buddhas of past, present, and future for all sentient beings, in terms of the upshot of each teaching, the meanings and principles of each teaching, the interpretation of each teaching, the revelation of each teaching, the ways of access to each teaching, the awakening to each teaching, the contemplation and investigation of each teaching, and the field and position of each teaching, attain infinite treasuries of truths, acquiring fearlessness, endowed with all powers of analysis and elucidation, extensively analyzing and explaining for sentient beings, throughout the future, inexhaustibly.' Because they want to enable all sentient beings to establish transcendent will and develop unhindered, impeccable discernment; because they want to cause all sentient beings to be joyful; because they want to enable all sentient beings to develop the light of all pure principles, unceasingly expounding them in expressions adapted to the type of audience; because they want to cause all sentient beings to be profoundly faithful and joyful, they abide in universal knowledge, discern and comprehend all things, and cause them to be without confusion, thinking in these terms: 'I should earnestly cultivate practice in all worlds for the sake of sentient beings, attain an infinite free body pervading the cosmos, attain an infinite great mind pervading the cosmos, become endowed with infinite pure speech equal to the realms of the cosmos, appear in sites of enlightenment of infinite congregations throughout the extent of the cosmos, cultivate enlightening practices as infinite as the cosmos, attain stations of enlightening beings as infinite as the cosmos, realize equanimity of enlightening beings as infinite as the cosmos, learn principles of enlightening beings as infinite as the cosmos, live by practices of enlightening beings as infinite as the cosmos, and enter into dedications of enlightening beings as infinite as the cosmos.' This is great enlightening beings' dedication of roots of goodness, to cause all sentient beings to be able to attain universal knowledge.

"Great enlightening beings also dedicate roots of goodness to their aspiration to see Buddhas infinite as the cosmos, to tame sentient beings infinite as the cosmos, to maintain buddha-lands infinite as the cosmos, to realize enlightening knowledge infinite as the cosmos, to attain fearlessness infinite as the cosmos, to attain enlightening beings' inconceivable abodes infinite as the cosmos, to be endowed with virtues infinite as the cosmos, and to fulfill roots of goodness beneficial to sentient beings as infinite as the cosmos. They also pray that by these roots of goodness they will be enabled to attain impartiality of virtue, impartiality of knowledge, impartiality of power, impartiality of fearlessness, impartiality of purity, impartiality of freedom, impartiality of true awakening, impartiality of teaching, impartiality of doctrine, impartiality of certitude, and impartiality of all spiritual powers, fully developing all these qualities and also vowing that all sentient beings should attain them just as they have.

"Great enlightening beings also dedicate roots of goodness in this way: that is, as the cosmos is infinite, so is the dedication of roots of goodness—the wisdom attained is ultimately infinite; as the cosmos is boundless, so is the dedication of roots of goodness, seeing all Buddhas without any bounds; as the cosmos is unlimited, so is the dedication of roots of goodness, going to buddha-fields without limit; as the cosmos has no boundaries, so also is the dedication of roots of goodness, cultivating enlightening practices in all worlds, without boundaries; as the cosmos has no end, so too is the dedication of roots of goodness, abiding in universal knowledge forever without end; as the cosmos is of one nature, so too is the dedication of roots of goodness of the same nature of knowledge as all beings; as the cosmos is inherently pure, so too is the dedication of roots of goodness, causing all sentient beings to ultimately be pure; as the cosmos is adaptive, so too is the dedication of roots of goodness, causing all sentient beings to accord with the practical vows of Universal Good; as the cosmos is adorned, so too is the dedication of roots of goodness, causing all sentient beings to be adorned with the practices of Universal Good; as the cosmos cannot be lost or destroyed, so too is the dedication of roots of goodness, causing all enlightening beings never to lose or destroy pure practices.

"Great enlightening beings also dedicate roots of goodness in this way: 'By these roots of goodness may we serve all Buddhas and enlightening beings and gladden them all; by these roots of goodness may we quickly attain entry into the essence of universal knowledge; by these roots of goodness may we cultivate omniscience in all places; by these roots of goodness may we cause all sentient beings to always get to go see all the Buddhas; by these roots of goodness may we cause all sentient beings to always see the Buddhas and be able to do buddha-work; by these roots of goodness may we enable all sentient beings to always see the Buddhas and never be lazy about buddha-work; by these roots of goodness may we enable all sentient beings to always see the Buddhas and be joyful and pure in mind and never regress; by these roots of goodness may we enable all sentient beings to always get to see the Buddhas and attain good understanding; by these roots of goodness may we cause all sentient beings to always see the Buddhas and not give rise to clinging attachments; by these roots of goodness may we cause all sentient beings to always see the Buddhas and comprehend without obstruction; by these roots of goodness may we enable sentient beings to always see the Buddhas and accomplish the practices of Universal Good; by these roots of goodness may we cause all sentient beings to always see the Buddhas appearing before them, never leaving them for moment; by these roots of goodness may we cause all sentient beings to always see the Buddhas and produce the infinite powers of enlightening beings; by these roots of goodness may we enable all sentient beings always to see the Buddhas and never forget their teachings.'

"Great enlightening beings also dedicate the roots of goodness in these ways: they dedicate them in conformity with the nonoriginated nature of the cosmos; they dedicate them in conformity with the fundamental nature of the cosmos; they dedicate them in conformity with the inherent essential nature of the cosmos; they dedicate them in conformity with the nonreliant nature of the cosmos; they dedicate them in conformity with the unforgetting nature of the cosmos; they dedicate them in conformity with the empty nature of the cosmos; they dedicate them in conformity with the placeless nature of the cosmos; they dedicate them in conformity with the tranquil nature of the cosmos; they dedicate them in conformity with the immutable nature of the cosmos; they dedicate them in conformity with the undifferentiated nature of the cosmos.

"Great enlightening beings also dedicate the revelations and enlightenment of the giving of teaching, as well as the roots of goodness arising therefrom, in this way: 'May all sentient beings become enlightening teachers, always in the care of the Buddhas; may all sentient beings become unsurpassed teachers, skillfully establishing all sentient beings in universal knowledge; may all sentient beings become indefatigable teachers, never stymied by challenging questions; may all sentient beings be unobstructed teachers, attaining the unobstructed light of all truths; may all sentient beings be teachers with a treasury of knowledge, able to skillfully explain all Buddha teachings; may all sentient beings become teachers with the freedom of the enlightened ones and be able to skillfully analyze the knowledge of the enlightened; may all sentient beings be teachers with the eye of thusness, explaining the truth without depending on the instruction of another; may all sentient beings become teachers who remember all the teachings of Buddhas, expounding them in accord with their principles, not deviating from the meaning of their expressions; may all sentient beings become teachers practicing the signless path, adorning themselves with subtle characteristics, emanating immeasurable light, skillfully entering into all truths; may all sentient beings become great-bodied teachers, their bodies pervading all lands, creating great clouds of teaching, showering the Buddha-teachings; may all sentient beings become teachers preserving the treasury of the teachings, setting up the banner of invincibility, preserving the Buddha-teachings, causing the ocean of true teaching not to diminish; may all sentient beings become teachers who are suns of all truths, attain the powers of analysis and elucidation of Buddhas, and skillfully explain all truths; may all sentient beings become teachers with skill in means of vocal expression, skillfully explaining the boundless treasury of the realm of truth; may all sentient beings become teachers who have arrived at the other shore of the doctrine, opening up the treasury of teaching with the spiritual powers of knowledge; may all sentient beings become teachers stably abiding by the true teaching, and expound the ultimate knowledge of the enlightened; may all sentient beings become teachers who have thoroughly comprehended all the teachings, able to explain infinite, inexhaustible virtues; may all sentient beings become teachers who don't deceive the world, able with skill in means to enter reality; may all sentient beings become teachers destroying the throngs of demons, able to be well aware of all workings of demons; may all sentient beings become teachers accepted by the Buddhas and get rid of the mind taken in by ego and possessiveness; may all sentient beings become teachers pacifying all worlds, accomplishing the will power of teaching of truth of enlightening beings.'

"Great enlightening beings also dedicate roots of goodness in this way: they do not dedicate them because of attachment to deeds, they do not dedicate them because of attachment to rewards, they do not dedicate them because of attachment to mind, they do not dedicate them because of attachment to things, they do not dedicate them because of attachment to events, they do not dedicate them because of attachment to cause, they do not dedicate them because of attachment to words and speech, they do not dedicate them because of attachment to names, phrases, and statements, they do not dedicate them because of attachment to dedication, they do not dedicate them because of attachment to benefiting sentient beings.

"Great enlightening beings also dedicate roots of goodness in this way: they do not dedicate them because of involvement in forms, they do not dedicate them because of involvement in sounds, smells, tastes, feelings, or things, they do not dedicate them to seek birth in heaven, they do not dedicate them to seek pleasure, they do not dedicate them because of attachment to objects of desire, they do not dedicate them in hopes of getting followers, they do not dedicate them in quest of rulership, they do not dedicate them for the sake of mundane happiness, they do not dedicate them because of attachment to life, they do not dedicate them because of enjoyment of existences, they do not dedicate them in search of the pleasures of union, they do not dedicate them because of seeking that which one may be fondly attached to, they do not dedicate them because of maliciousness, they do not dedicate them for that which would destroy roots of goodness, they do not dedicate them because of dependence on the world, they do not dedicate them because of attachment to stages of meditation, liberation, or concentration, they do not dedicate them because of dwelling in the vehicles of Buddhas' disciples and self-enlightened people—they only dedicate them to edify and pacify all sentient beings, to fulfill all-knowledge, to attain unobstructed knowledge, to attain unhindered pure roots of goodness, to cause all sentient beings to transcend birth and death and realize great knowledge, to cause the great determination for enlightenment to be adamant and unbreakable, to accomplish the method of ultimate immortality, to adorn the lineage of Buddhas with infinite adornments, to reveal the freedom of universal knowledge, to seek enlightening beings' great spiritual superknowledge clarifying all things, to carry out the practice of Universal Good in all buddha-fields throughout the space of the cosmos, completely fulfilling it without regressing, don the strong, durable armor of great vows and cause all sentient beings to abide in the realm of Universal Good, to liberate sentient beings throughout the future without resting, and show the unobstructed light of the stage of universal knowledge, forever uninterrupted.

"When great enlightening beings dedicate these roots of goodness, they dedicate them in these frames of mind: they dedicate roots of goodness with mindfulness of the equality of fundamental nature, with mindfulness of the equality of the essence of things, with mindfulness of the equality of the infinity of all sentient beings, with mindfulness of the equality of noncontradiction, with mindfulness of the equality of nonproduction of inherent nature, with a mind knowing all things without disturbance, with a mind entering into the equality of past, present, and future, with a mind producing the seed nature of Buddhas of all times, with a mind that has attained undiminishing spiritual powers, with a mind producing and maturing practical applications of universal knowledge.

"Also, they dedicate the roots of goodness to cause all sentient beings to forever leave behind all hells, to cause all sentient beings not to enter into animalistic dispositions, to cause sentient beings not to go to the realm of ghosts, to cause all sentient beings to get rid of all factors hindering enlightenment, to cause all sentient beings to fulfill all roots of goodness, to cause all sentient beings to be able to expound the teaching in accord with the time and bring joy to all, to cause all sentient beings to enter the sphere of the ten powers, to cause all sentient beings to fulfill the boundless pure ways and vows of enlightening beings, to cause all sentient beings to follow the instructions of all good spiritual teachers so the vessel of the determination for enlightenment may be fulfilled, to cause all sentient beings to absorb, retain, and apply the most profound Buddha teachings and attain the light of knowledge of all Buddhas, to cause all sentient beings to cultivate the unobstructed practices of enlightening beings and always be in their presence, to cause all sentient beings to always see the Buddhas appearing before them, to cause all sentient beings to always be in the presence of the pure light of the truth, to cause the fearless great determination for enlightenment to always be present in all sentient beings, to cause the inconceivable knowledge of enlightening beings to always occur to all sentient beings, to cause all sentient beings to everywhere rescue and safeguard living beings and cause the pure mind of great compassion to always be present, to cause all sentient beings to adorn all buddha-fields with unspeakably many superb ornaments to cause all sentient beings to obliterate all ensnaring doings of conflict provoked by all demons, to cause all sentient beings to cultivate enlightening practices in all buddha-fields without relying on anything, to cause all sentient beings to develop knowledge of all means of liberation and enter the wide doors of all Buddha teachings.

"Great enlightening beings also dedicate these roots of goodness with purity of right mindfulness; with certainty of knowledge; knowing all the methods and expedients of the Buddhas' teachings; in order to accomplish immeasurable unobstructed knowledge; desiring to fulfill pure transcendent aspirations; by virtue of abiding kindness toward all sentient beings; by virtue of abiding compassion for all sentient beings; by virtue of abiding joy for all sentient beings; by virtue of abiding equanimity toward all sentient beings; in order to forever abandon attachment to duality and to live by supreme roots of goodness; in order to ponder, investigate, distinguish, and explain all aspects of interdependent origination; in order to establish the mind marked by great courage; in order to establish the treasury of invincibility; in order to demolish the hordes of demons; in order to attain unobstructed mindfulness of the purity of all things; in order to cultivate all enlightening practices without regressing; in order to attain the mind that happily seeks the supreme truth; in order to attain the free pure omniscient mind happily seeking all virtuous qualities; in order to fulfill all wishes and remove all conflict, attain free, pure, unobstructed buddhahood and expound the nonregressive teaching for all sentient beings; in order to become adorned by the hundreds of thousands of light beams of the sun of knowledge of the supreme truth of the enlightened ones and illumine the sentient beings of all realms; in order to tame all sentient beings, always satisfying them according to their pleasures, not giving up their original vows throughout all time, listening to the true teaching, cultivating its great practice, attaining the undefiled light of pure wisdom, getting rid of all conceit, dissolving all afflictions, breaking the net of craving, destroying the darkness of delusion, and fulfilling the undefiled unobstructed teaching; in order to always cultivate the practice of universal knowledge through incalculable eons for the sake of all beings, without regressing, causing each to attain unobstructed wisdom, and manifest the autonomous spiritual powers of the Buddhas without cease.

"When great enlightening beings dedicate roots of goodness in this way, they should not greedily cling to objects of desire. Why? Great enlightening beings should dedicate roots of goodness free from greed, should dedicate roots of goodness free from anger, should dedicate roots of goodness free from delusion, should dedicate roots of goodness free from malevolence, should dedicate roots of goodness free from pride, should dedicate roots of goodness free from deceitfulness, should dedicate roots of goodness of honesty, should dedicate roots of goodness of diligence, should dedicate roots of goodness of cultivation and practice.

"When great enlightening beings practice dedication in this way, they attain minds of pure faith, joyfully accepting the practices of enlightening beings, cultivating the pure great path of enlightening beings, endowed with the essence of buddhahood, attaining enlightened knowledge and wisdom, abandoning all evil, getting rid of all manias, associating with good spiritual friends, and, fulfilling their own great vows. they invite all sentient beings to partake of their charity.

"Great enlightening beings also dedicate the roots of goodness produced by this giving of teaching in this way: they cause all sentient beings to acquire clear beautiful voices, gentle voices, voices like celestial drums, voices capable of articulating innumerable sounds, pleasant voices, pure voices, voices pervading all buddha-fields, voices adorned by countless qualities, far-ranging voices, sonorous voices eliminating all distraction, voices filling the cosmos, voices able to pick up the languages of all sentient beings; and to acquire knowledge of the boundless sounds of all sentient beings, knowledge of all pure sounds of speech, knowledge of infinite sounds of speech, knowledge of the supremely free sound that enters all sounds; and to acquire all pure adorning speech tones, tones which all beings never tire of hearing, speech ultimately not bound to any world, joyful tones, pure tones of the speech of Buddhas, tones of speech expressing all Buddha teachings, unmuffled by delusion, famed everywhere, tones that cause all sentient beings to acquire the adornment of concentration formulations of all the teachings, tones of speech expressing innumerable kinds of teachings, sounds of speech reaching the infinite congregations at enlightenment sites throughout the cosmos, tones of speech containing indestructible expressions of inconceivable truths, speech revealing all facts, speech able to expound the treasury of knowledge of differences in unspeakably many words and phrases, speech that explains all things without attachment or interruption, speech shining with the light of all truths, speech able to cause all worldlings to be purified and ultimately reach universal knowledge, speech that contains the expressions and meanings of all the teachings, free uninhibited speech maintained by spiritual powers, speech of the knowledge which reaches the other shore of all worlds.

"Also by these roots of goodness, they enable all sentient beings to acquire nongroveling speech, fearless speech, unobsessed speech, speech gladdening all congregations at sites of enlightenment, harmonious, beautiful speech, speech able to explain all the principles of buddhahood, speech cutting off the doubts of all sentient beings and causing them to awaken, speech endowed with all powers of analysis and elucidation, speech awakening all sentient beings from their slumber in the long night of ignorance.

"Great enlightening beings also dedicate the roots of goodness in this way: 'May all sentient beings attain the pure reality body free from all faults and ills; may all sentient beings attain pure sublime virtues free from all faults and ills; may all sentient beings attain pure sublime characteristics free from all faults and ills; may all sentient beings attain the pure results of action free from all faults and ills; may all sentient beings attain the pure mind of universal knowledge free from all faults and ills; may all sentient beings attain the infinite pure will for enlightenment free from all faults and ills; may all sentient beings attain impeccable skill in means of comprehending all faculties; may all sentient beings attain impeccable pure faith, may all sentient beings attain impeccable pure diligence in carrying out commitments unimpeded; may all sentient beings attain impeccable pure right mindfulness, knowledge, and powers of analysis and elucidation.'

"Great enlightening beings also dedicate roots of goodness for the sake of all sentient beings to the attainment of various pure subtle bodies—the body of light, the body of freedom from pollution, the body of nonobsession, the body of purity, the body of extreme purity, the body of detachment from objects of sense, the body of ultimate detachment from objects of sense, the body of freedom from defilement, the body of beauty, the body of nonobstruction—manifesting images of action in all worlds, manifesting images of speech in all worlds, manifesting images of construction in all abodes, like a clear mirror in which all kinds of images of forms spontaneously appear, showing sentient beings the practices of enlightenment, showing sentient beings the most profound truths, showing sentient beings all kinds of virtuous qualities, showing sentient beings the path of practice, showing sentient beings developmental practices, showing sentient beings the undertakings of enlightening beings, showing sentient beings in all worlds the appearance in the world of the Buddhas of all worlds, showing sentient beings the spiritual powers and mystical transfigurations of all Buddhas, showing sentient beings the awesome power of the inconceivable liberation of all enlightening beings, showing sentient beings the essence of omniscience fulfilling the practical vows of the enlightening being Universally Good. Great enlightening beings skillfully take care of all sentient beings with such subtle pure bodies and enable them to attain the body of all-knowledge with pure qualities.

"Great enlightening beings also dedicate the roots of goodness generated by giving of the teaching to the aspiration to live in all worlds cultivating enlightening practices, so that sentient beings who see them do not do so in vain, but develop the determination for enlightenment without ever regressing, follow the truth unshakably, and in all worlds, throughout all time, live undefatigably by the path of enlightening beings, with great compassion, impartial and universal, as vast as the cosmos, knowing the faculties of sentient beings and ever explaining the truth to them according to the time, always rightly mindful of spiritual friends, never forgetting for an instant, all the Buddhas always appearing before them, their minds always truly aware, never flagging, cultivating roots of goodness without any falsehood, placing all sentient beings in universal knowledge, causing them not to regress, imbued with the light of all the Buddha teachings, holding the clouds of the great teaching, receiving the rain of the great teaching, cultivating the practices of enlightening beings, entering in among all sentient beings, entering all buddha-fields, penetrating all phenomena and principles, penetrating all times, penetrating the knowledge of consequences of all sentient beings, penetrating the knowledge of skillful methods of all enlightening beings, penetrating the knowledge of production of all enlightening beings, penetrating the knowledge of the pure realm of all sentient beings, penetrating the autonomous spiritual powers of all Buddhas, penetrating all the boundless realms of reality, and herein cultivating enlightening practice.

"Great enlightening beings also dedicate the roots of goodness cultivated by giving of teaching to the aspiration to purify all buddha-lands and adorn them with inexpressibly many embellishments, each buddha-land as vast as the cosmos, purely good, without obstructions, with pure light, the Buddhas manifesting the attainment of true awakening therein, the pure realms in one buddha-land able to reveal all buddha-lands, and as of one buddha-land, so of all buddha-lands, each of those lands adorned with arrays of pure exquisite treasures, as measureless as the cosmos—countless thrones of pure jewels spread with precious robes, countless jeweled curtains and jeweled nets draping, countless precious canopies with all kinds of jewels reflecting each other, countless jewel clouds raining jewels, countless jewel flowers all around, completely pure, countless pure arrays of balustrades made of jewels, countless jewel chimes always emitting the subtle tones of the Buddhas circulating throughout the cosmos, countless jewel lotuses of various jewel colors blooming with glorious radiance, countless jewel trees arrayed in rows all around, with flowers and fruits of innumerable jewels, countless jewel palaces with innumerable enlightening beings living in them, countless jewel mansions, spacious, magnificent, long and wide, far and near, countless jewel ramparts with exquisite jewel ornaments, countless jewel gates hung all around with strings of beautiful jewels, countless jewel windows with pure arrays of inconceivable numbers of jewels, and countless jewel palms, shaped like crescent moons, made of clusters of jewels—all of these embellished with myriad jewels, spotlessly pure, inconceivable, all produced by the roots of goodness of the enlightened, replete with adornments of countless treasuries of jewels. There are also countless jewel rivers from which flow all pure good principles; countless jewel seas filled with the water of the teaching; countless jewel lotuses always emitting the sound of the lotus of the sublime teaching; countless jewel polar mountains, monarchs of the mountains of wisdom, standing out completely pure; countless eight-faced jewels, strung on precious threads, incomparably beautiful and clear; countless jewels of pure light always emanating the unimpeded light of great knowledge illumining the entire cosmos; countless jewel chimes striking one another and producing wonderful tones; countless pure jewels filled with jewels of enlightening beings; countless jeweled streamers of many colors hung all around, with radiant, clear colors; countless jeweled banners adorned with jewel crescents; countless jeweled pennants, each one able to shower innumerable jeweled pennants; countless jeweled sashes hanging in the sky, beautifully adorned; countless precious mats able to produce various kinds of subtle pleasant feelings; countless jewel wreaths showing the enlightening beings' eye of universal knowledge; countless jewel garlands, each garland the superb adornment of a hundred thousand enlightening beings; countless jewel palaces, absolutely peerless; countless jewel ornaments embellished with diamonds; countless ornaments of all kinds of jewels always displaying all pure wonderful colors; countless jewels with different shapes and colors, their lights reflecting with thorough clarity; countless jewel mountains surrounding like a fence all around, with unhindered purity; countless precious scents perfuming all worlds; countless precious magical events, each one pervading the cosmos; countless jewel light beams, each beam manifesting all lights; there are also countless jewel lights, the lights of pure knowledge, comprehensively illumining all things, and countless unimpeded jewel lights, each pervading the cosmos; there are countless jewel places where there are all kinds of precious substances, and countless jewel treasuries revealing all the treasuries of the true teaching; countless jewel banners emblematic of the enlightened standing out on high; countless precious saints, images of saints of great knowledge, thoroughly pure; countless gardens of jewels producing the bliss of meditation of enlightening beings; countless precious sounds, the wondrous voice of the enlightened teaching all the world; countless jewel forms, each one emanating countless lights of sublime doctrines; countless precious marks, each one transcending common characteristics; countless precious modes of bearing, all who see which develop the joy and rapture of enlightening beings; countless collections of jewels, all who see which develop a collection of jewels of wisdom; countless precious peaceful abodes, all who see which develop a precious well-stabilized mind; countless precious garments, those who wear which develop the peerless concentration of enlightening beings; countless precious vestments, those who wear which attain the spell of good vision as soon as they wish; countless jewel practices, those who see which know that all 'jewels' are results of action, definitively pure; countless precious unhindered insights, those who perceive which can realize all pure objective vision; countless treasuries of jewel lights, those who see which immediately can attain the treasury of great knowledge; countless jewel thrones with Buddhas sitting on them like great lions roaring; countless jewel lamps always radiating the light of pure knowledge; countless jewel trees arrayed in rows, wound with jewel ropes, their adornments thoroughly pure, also having countless jewel trunks, standing high, straight, round, and clean, countless jewel boughs, thick with adornments, with inconceivable numbers of birds flying around and gathering there, always warbling beautiful songs expressing the true teachings, countless jewel leaves emitting the light of great knowledge pervading everywhere, countless jewel flowers, with innumerable enlightening beings sitting on each blossom, traveling throughout the cosmos, and countless jewel fruits, those who see which will attain the fruit of nonregression from all-knowledge; also there are countless jewel villages, those who see which give up the ways of worldly habitats; countless jewel cities filled with free beings, countless palaces with monarchs in them who are endowed with the godlike body of enlightening beings, courageous and steadfast, wearing the armor of the truth, their minds unshrinking; countless jewel houses, those who enter which can eliminate the mind of attachment to house and home; countless jewel garments, those who wear which can foster the understanding of nonattachment; countless jewel palaces filled with enlightening beings who have left home; countless jewel curios which bring immeasurable joy to those who see them; countless jewel wheels emanating inconceivable lights of knowledge, turning the wheel that never turns back; countless jewel trees adorned with Indra nets, all pure; countless jeweled grounds, inlaid with inconceivably many jewels; countless jewel pipes, their clear sounds filling the cosmos; countless jewel drums, their wondrous sounds beating in harmony unbroken throughout the eons; countless jewel sentient beings, all able to bear the jewel of the unexcelled teaching, with countless jewel bodies replete with innumerable jewels of virtuous qualities, countless jewel mouths always uttering the voice of the jewels of all the sublime teachings, countless jewel minds endowed with the jewel of pure intention set on great knowledge, jewel mindfulness cutting off all folly and ultimately solidifying the jewel of universal knowledge, jewel superknowledges reciting and retaining the jewels of all Buddha teachings, jewel intellects understanding with certainty the treasure of all Buddha teachings, jewel knowledges attaining the jewel of great complete omniscience, jewel eyes mirroring the treasure of the ten powers without obstruction, jewel ears hearing the infinite sounds of the whole realm of reality clearly and without obstruction, jewel noses always smelling the pure jewel fragrance of harmony, jewel tongues able to enunciate countless rules of speech, jewel bodies traveling unhindered throughout the ten directions, jewel minds always diligently cultivating the practical vows of Universal Good, jewel voices, clear and beautiful, pervading the worlds in the ten directions, jewel acts guided by knowledge, jewel speech always explaining the cultivation of the jewel of unobstructed knowledge, and jewel thought attaining the treasure of unimpeded great knowledge, which is ultimately complete.

"The great enlightening beings vow that in all those buddha-lands, in each direction of each buddha-land, in each and every place, even so minute as a hairtip, there be incalculable, boundless, unspeakable numbers of great enlightening beings, all accomplished in pure clear knowledge, filling everywhere, in every point of space in every place in every direction of every buddha-land throughout the cosmos. This is great enlightening beings' dedication of roots of goodness vowing that all the buddha-lands should be replete with all kinds of precious adornments, as extensively told of the jewel ornaments, that they should have such adornments of fragrances, flowers, garlands, perfumes, incenses, aromatic powders, robes, parasols and canopies, banners, pennants, crystals, and so on, a hundredfold more, all like the 'jewel' ornaments.

"Great enlightening beings dedicate the roots of goodness amassed by such practices as the giving of teaching to nurturing all roots of goodness; to purifying all buddha-lands; to fully developing all sentient beings; to causing all sentient beings' minds to be pure and imperturbable; to causing all sentient beings to enter the most profound Buddha teaching; to causing all sentient beings to attain unsurpassable pure qualities; to causing all sentient beings to attain indestructible power of pure virtue; to causing all sentient beings to attain inexhaustible power of knowledge, liberate all living beings, and enable them to enter buddhahood; to causing all sentient beings to attain impartial, inexhaustible, pure speech; to causing all sentient beings to attain the equanimous unobstructed eye and achieve knowledge equal to the entire cosmos throughout space; to causing sentient beings to attain pure recollection and know all worlds of past ages; to causing all sentient beings to attain unobstructed great knowledge and be able to comprehend with certainty all treasuries of truths; to causing all sentient beings to attain unlimited, immeasurable great enlightenment, pervading the cosmos without any hindrance; to causing all sentient beings to attain impartial, nondiscriminatory, homogeneous roots of goodness; to causing all sentient beings to attain pure physical, verbal, and mental action adorned with all virtues; to causing all sentient beings to accomplish action the same as Universally Good; to causing all sentient beings to be able to enter all homogeneously pure buddha-fields; to causing all sentient beings to examine universal knowledge, penetrate it, and fulfill it; to causing all sentient beings to be able to avoid partial roots of goodness; to causing all sentient beings to attain equanimous, unvarying will, gradually fulfilling all-knowledge; to causing all sentient beings to be able to live steadily by all good principles; to causing all sentient beings to instantly realize universal knowledge and reach the ultimate; to causing all sentient beings to be able to fulfill the pure path of omniscience—this is wherein they dedicate their roots of goodness.

"Once great enlightening beings have dedicated their roots of goodness in this way for the sake of all living beings, they also dedicate these roots of goodness because they want to fulfill and expound the power of all pure practical methods; because they want to achieve the spiritual power of pure practice and comprehend unspeakably many oceans of truths; because they want to be imbued with infinite lights of pure knowledge, equal to the cosmos, in each ocean of truths; because they want to analyze and explain the different expressions and meanings of all teachings; because they want to accomplish the boundless vast concentration of the lights of all teachings; because they want to follow the powers of elucidation of the Buddhas of past, present, and future; because they want to develop the free body of all Buddhas of past, present, and future; because they respect the admirable unhindered state of all Buddhas; in order to fulfill the heart of great compassion and rescue all sentient beings without ever retreating; because they want to achieve the mind of unobstructed knowledge of infinite differentiations, untainted purity of senses, and enter all congregations in all sites of enlightenment; because they want to always turn the wheel of the impartial, nonregressive teaching in all buddha-lands, whether inverted or upright, coarse or subtle, broad or narrow, small or large, tainted or pure; because they want to attain fearlessness in every moment, without end, all kinds of analytic and expository skills, and the light of the sublime teaching, to reveal and explain the truth; in order to happily seek all goodness, to learn and practice with determination, all faculties growing better, to attain the great spiritual knowledge of all truths; because they want to draw near to and provide offerings at all congregations' enlightenment sites, and expound the teachings to all sentient beings to make them joyful.

"Great enlightening beings also dedicate these roots of goodness in this way: they dedicate them by abiding in abodes infinite as the cosmos, by abiding in physical action infinite as the cosmos, by abiding in verbal action infinite as the cosmos, by abiding in mental action infinite as the cosmos, by abiding in the equality of matter infinite as the cosmos, by abiding in the equality of sensation, perception, patterning, and consciousness infinite as the cosmos, by abiding in the equality of aggregates infinite as the cosmos, by abiding in the equality of elements infinite as the cosmos, by abiding in the equality of sense media infinite as the cosmos, by abiding in internal equality infinite as the cosmos, by abiding in external equality infinite as the cosmos, by abiding in the equality of impulses infinite as the cosmos, by abiding in the equality of wills infinite as the cosmos, by abiding in the equality of means of liberation infinite as the cosmos, by abiding in equality of inclinations infinite as the cosmos, by abiding in the equality of faculties infinite as the cosmos, by abiding in equality of beginnings, middles, and ends infinite as the cosmos, by abiding in the equality of acts and consequences infinite as the cosmos, by abiding in the equality of defilement and purity infinite as the cosmos, by abiding in the equality of living beings infinite as the cosmos, by abiding in the equality of buddha-fields infinite as the cosmos, by abiding in the equality of phenomena infinite as the cosmos, by abiding in the equality of mundane lights infinite as the cosmos, by abiding in the equality of Buddhas and enlightening beings infinite as the cosmos, by abiding in the equality of practices and vows infinite as the cosmos, by abiding in the equality of emancipations of enlightening beings infinite as the cosmos, by abiding in the equality of teaching and training of enlightening beings infinite as the cosmos, by abiding in the equality of nonduality of realms of reality infinite as the cosmos, by abiding in the equality of sites of enlightenment and congregations of Buddhas, infinite as the cosmos.

"When great enlightening beings practice dedication in this way, they abide in equal pure embodiments infinite as the cosmos, they abide in equal pure speech infinite as the cosmos, they abide in equal pure minds infinite as the cosmos, they abide in equal pure commitments of enlightening beings infinite as the cosmos, they abide in equal pure sites of enlightenment of congregations infinite as the cosmos, they abide in pure knowledge infinite as the cosmos equally explaining things for all enlightening beings, they abide in bodies infinite as the cosmos equally able to enter into all worlds in the cosmos, they abide in equal pure fearlessness of the light of all truths able to cut away the nets of doubts of all sentient beings with one voice, gladdening them in accord with their faculties and inclinations, abiding in the ways of emancipation, the great virtues and spiritual powers and fearlessness of knowledge of all sciences of liberation. This is great enlightening beings' tenth dedication, dedication as infinite as the cosmos.

"When great enlightening beings dedicate all roots of goodness, such as giving of teaching, in this way, they fulfill the infinite, boundless commitment of Universal Good, are able to purify all buddha-fields throughout the cosmos, equal to space, and cause all sentient beings to also attain such fully developed boundless knowledge, understand all truths, in every moment see all Buddhas appearing in the world, and in every moment see all Buddhas' infinite boundless powers—vast powers, powers of nonattachment, powers of unimpeded freedom, powers to purify all sentient beings, powers to structure all worlds, powers to manifest all languages, powers to appear appropriately in accord with the time, powers dwelling in irreversible spiritual knowledge, powers to explain all realms of reality exhaustively, powers producing the boundless eye of the enlightening being Universally Good, powers of hearing the true teachings of infinite Buddhas with unobstructed ear consciousness, powers to pervade the infinite cosmos with one body while sitting still without crowding the sentient beings, powers of penetration of all the infinite phenomena of past, present, and future by means of complete knowledge. They also realize infinite purities—purity of all sentient beings; purity of all buddha-fields; purity of all things; purity of comprehensive knowledge of all realms; purity of boundless knowledge pervading the realm of space; purity of knowledge of all different vocal sounds, using various kinds of verbal expression adapted to all sentient beings; purity of radiance of infinite spheres of light illuminating all the boundless worlds; purity of knowledge producing the practices of all enlightening beings of past, present, and future; purity of knowledge instantly entering the sites of enlightenment of congregations of all Buddhas of past, present, and future; purity of entering into all worlds, boundless though they be, and causing all sentient beings to do what they should do—in all these they attain fulfillment, completion, accomplishment, equanimity, actualization, direct knowledge, and true realization, having seen into all of them, attained purity in all respects, and reached the other shore."

At that point, by the spiritual power of the Buddha, in each of the ten directions as many worlds as atoms in a million buddha-lands quaked in six ways—trembling, trembling all over, trembling equally all over; rising, rising all over, rising equally all over; surging, surging all over, surging equally all over; shaking, shaking all over, shaking equally all over; roaring, roaring all over, roaring equally all over; crashing, crashing all over, crashing equally all over. Because of the Buddha's spiritual power, and by natural law, it rained celestial flowers, celestial garlands, celestial incense powders, celestial mixed perfumes, celestial raiment, celestial gems, celestial ornaments, celestial crystals, celestial aloe wood, celestial sandalwood incense, celestial parasols of surpassing beauty, all kinds of celestial banners, multicolored celestial pennants, countless celestial bodies, innumerable billions of unspeakable numbers of celestial sounds of the wonderful teaching, inconceivably many celestial voices praising Buddha, countless celestial sounds of joyful eulogy. Innumerable celestials bowed in respect, countless celestial children constantly remembranced the Buddhas and the immeasurable rare virtues of the Enlightened Ones, countless celestial children made music and sang hymns of praise to offer the Enlightened, countless billions of celestials emanated great lights illuminating all buddhafields in the entire cosmos throughout space, revealing countless realms of Buddhas and disguised bodies of the Enlightened, surpassing all celestial beings.

As such a teaching was expounded in the palace of the Tushita heaven of happiness and satisfaction in this world, so it was in the celestial palaces of the Tushita heavens in all worlds throughout the ten directions.

Then, again by the spiritual power of Buddha, there assembled as many enlightening beings as atoms in a million buddha-fields from beyond as many worlds as atoms in a million buddha-fields in each of the ten directions, filling all quarters, all saying "Good, good! Child of Buddha, you have ably explained these great dedications. We all have the same name—Diamond Banner—and all have come here from the presence of Diamond Banner Buddhas in worlds in Diamond Light. In those worlds we expound this teaching by the spiritual power of Buddha, and the congregations, the followings, the expressions and doctrines are all like this, no more and no less: we have all come from those lands, empowered by the Buddhas, to stand as witnesses for you. And we have come to this assembly to be your witnesses, so also do the hosts of enlightening beings come to all the jewel-adorned halls of the palaces of the Tushita heavens in all worlds in the ten directions to be witnesses in the same way."

Then the enlightening being Diamond Banner, spiritually empowered by Buddha, looked over all the congregations in the ten directions, reaching throughout the cosmos; knowing expression and meaning well, he expanded his great mind, with great compassion covering all beings, fixing his mind on the lineage of the Buddhas of past, present, and future and dwelling steadily thereon, he entered into the ways to the qualities of all Buddhas, and attained the body of freedom of the Buddhas. He observed the inclinations of the minds of sentient beings as well as all the roots of goodness they had planted, knowing them all distinctly, and in accord with the body of reality he manifested for them bodies of pure sublime forms. Then at this time he uttered verses saying,

Enlightening beings accomplish knowledge of truth,
Understanding boundless ways of right teaching:
Becoming teachers with the light of truth,
They know the unobstructed genuine verity.

Enlightening beings are great guides to truth;
They reveal the most profound teaching, hard to attain:
Leading the measureless masses of the ten directions,
They cause them to abide securely in truth.

Enlightening beings have drunk the ocean of Buddha teachings;
Their clouds of truth shower the worlds of the ten directions.
The sun of truth appears in the world,
Revealing the sublime teaching for the benefit of the living.

They are always rarely-met donors of teaching,
Understand convenient means to enter truth.
The light of truth, pure, illumines their minds,
And they teach in the world without fear.

They have cultivated a mind in command of the teachings,
Able to understand all aspects thereof;
Developing the deep deep ocean of wondrous teaching,
They beat the drum of truth for all sentient beings.

They proclaim the most profound, rare teaching,
With which are nurtured all virtues;
Endowed with the mind of pure joy in truth,
They show the world the treasury of Buddhahood.

Anointed and crowned by the Buddhas, kings of truth,
Having developed the body of knowledge of the nature of things,
They are able to understand the true character of all things,
And abide by all good ways.

Enlightening beings practice the foremost giving
Praised by all the enlightened ones—

All their acts are approved by Buddhas,
Thereby they perfect the most honorable humans.

Enlightening beings have attained the subtle truth body
Personally born by transformation of the Buddha teachings.
To benefit the living they are lamps of truth,
Expounding countless supreme principles.

According to the giving of the wonderful teaching they practice,
They also examine their roots of goodness;
The good deeds they do for sentient beings
They dedicate all with knowledge.

The virtuous ways to attain buddhahood
They pass on to living beings,
Wishing that all may be pure
And reach the Buddhas' magnificent other shore.

The buddha-lands of the ten directions are infinite,
And all have infinite great adornments:
Such adornments, inconceivable,
Are all used to adorn one land.

The pure knowledge of the enlightened
They vow to enable all beings to have,
Like Universally Good, the true offspring of Buddha,
Adorning themselves with all virtues.

Accomplishing vast spiritual power,
They travel throughout all worlds,
Causing all beings without exception
To practice the enlightening path.

The countless sentient beings of the ten directions
Awakened by the Buddhas
They cause to be like Universally Good,
Fully carrying out the highest practice.

The various different virtues
Achieved by the Buddhas and enlightening beings
They vow to have everyone fulfill,
Boundless though they be.

Enlightening beings are endowed with the power of freedom
And go to study wherever they should learn;

Manifesting all great psychic powers,
They go to the infinite lands of the ten directions.

Enlightening beings are able in one instant
To see countless Buddhas, many as beings,
And also in a single hairtip
Concentrate all things, seeing all clearly.

The sentient beings of the worlds, without measure,
Enlightening beings can distinguish and know.
The Buddhas are as infinite as living beings;
They generously present offerings to them all.

All kinds of wonderfully scented flowers,
Jewels, clothes, pennants, and parasols,
They distribute throughout the cosmos,
Determined to offer them to all Buddhas.

In a single pore they clearly see
All the inconceivably many Buddhas—
And so it is in every pore:
They bow to all the lamps of the worlds.

With their whole bodies they successively bow
In respect for those boundless Victors;
They also praise them with their words
Forever and ever more.

Their offerings to one Buddha
Are as numberless as sentient beings;
Thus do they make offerings to one Buddha
And to all Buddhas in the same way.

They provide for and laud the Buddhas
Throughout all ages of the world;
The ages of the world may come to an end,
But enlightening beings' offerings never cease.

In the various ages of all worlds
They cultivate practices there,
Honoring and attending one Buddha
Tirelessly throughout all ages.

As they provide for one Buddha for immeasurable eons,
So do they also for all Buddhas;

Yet they do not think of the number of eons,
Or ever tire of making offerings.

The cosmos is boundlessly vast:
Enlightening beings observe it with clear comprehension,
Spreading great lotus blossoms throughout
As presents to Buddhas infinite as beings.

Jewel flowers of perfect color and scent,
Pure ornaments, most delicate,
Beyond compare in any world,
They bring to offer the most noble of humans.

Infinite lands, many as sentient beings,
They fill with precious canopies,
Which they offer to one Buddha
And do the same for all Buddhas.

Perfumes, incomparable, most excellent,
Never before found in any world,
They offer to the Guide of humans and divines
Throughout eons as many as beings.

Powder and burning incense, exquisite flowers,
Jewels, raiment, and ornaments,
They present to the Supreme Victors
Joyfully serving them tirelessly.

World-Illumining Lamps, as many as beings,
Attain great enlightenment every moment,
And boundless verses of eulogy and exposition
They present to the Human Tamers.

To Buddhas numerous as living beings
They make most excellent offerings;
For eons countless as living beings,
They praise them without end.

When they make offerings to the Buddhas this way,
By Buddhas' spiritual power they extend everywhere,
Seeing all the infinite Buddhas of the ten directions,
Abiding in the practice of the Universally Good enlightening
   being.

All the roots of goodness
Of past, future, and present,

Enable us to always carry out Universal Good practice
And quickly gain the station of the realm of Universal Good.

May the infinite sentient beings of the worlds
Seen by all the Buddhas
Become like Universally Good,
Praised by the intelligent.

This is the practice of dedication
Cultivated in common by all great beings;
All the Buddhas explain for us
This unexcelled practice of dedication,
To enable all living beings
In all worlds in the ten directions
To attain awakening and enlightenment
And to always act as Universally Good does.

Practicing giving in accord with their dedication
And also strictly maintaining the precepts,
Persevering over the long run, unshrinking,
Tolerant, gentle, minds unstirred,
In meditation keeping the mind on one point,
By wisdom comprehending objects, same as concentration,
Penetrating past, future, and present,
To which none in the world can find any bounds—
Enlightening beings' physical, verbal, and mental actions,
Like this practice, are all pure;
All they cultivate, omitting none,
All on a par with the enlightening being Universally Good.

Like the cosmos, free from false discrimination,
The stain of inanity is forever gone;
And as nirvana has no obstructions,
Their minds likewise are free from all grasping.

The principles of dedication of the wise
The Buddhas have revealed;
All kinds of roots of goodness they dedicate,
Therefore they can accomplish the enlightening path.

Offspring of Buddha learn this dedication well,
Fulfilling innumerable undertakings,
Taking in the cosmos comprehensively;
Therefore they can attain the power of the Blissful Ones.

If you want to accomplish, as the Buddha explains,
The great, superlative practices of enlightening beings,
You should live by this dedication—
Such offspring of Buddha are called Universally Good.

All living beings may be counted,
And the experience of past, present, and future minds may be
    known,
But the virtues of such Universally Good
Offspring of Buddha cannot be measured.

The bounds of space may be measured with a hair,
The number of atoms in all lands may be known,
But the practical vows by which these sages live
Cannot be measured by anyone.

BOOK TWENTY-SIX

The Ten Stages

THUS HAVE I HEARD. Once the Blessed One was sojourning in the heaven of control of others' emanations. Not long after his perfect enlightenment—the second week—he was in the palace of the king of that heaven, a shining, radiantly pure treasury of jewels, together with a large group of enlightening beings, all of them beyond regression and bound to become perfectly enlightened in one lifetime, who had come from different worlds. Those enlightening beings were abiding in the sphere of knowledge of all enlightening beings; their sphere of action was that of ceaseless penetration into the entries of the realm of knowledge of all enlightened ones; they were skilled in showing all feats of power appropriately timed for the development and liberating guidance of all sentient beings; in order to fulfill all the great vows of enlightening beings, in all worlds and times, all ages, and all lands they diligently cultivated practices unceasingly; they had fulfilled the inexhaustible stores of virtue, knowledge, and occult powers of all enlightening beings, for the benefit of all worldly beings; having attained the highest ultimate reaches of transcendental knowledge and expedient liberative means of enlightening beings, they showed entries into mundane existence and nirvana, while not interrupting the application of means of practices of enlightening beings; sporting freely in the meditations, liberations, concentrations, attainments, and mystic knowledges of enlightening beings, they were skilled in the demonstration of all feats of mystic knowledge; having attained the occult powers and command of enlightening beings, going without effort in a single mental instant to the circles of all buddhas, they acted as leading interlocutors; holding the wheels of teachings of all buddhas, they had gone to make offerings to and wait on many buddhas; they had realized the manifestation of bodies in all worlds engaged in the undertaking of the deeds of all enlightening beings; their voices sounded in all realms without obstruction, and the sphere of knowledge of the mind unobstructed in all places and times was revealed to them; they had thoroughly fulfilled the attainments of qualities of all enlightening beings, and their qualities could never be exhaustively explained even in untold eons. Their names were Diamond Matrix, Jewel Matrix, Lotus Matrix, Matrix of Glory, Matrix of Lotuslike Splendor, Solar Matrix, Sun Matrix, Earth Matrix, Matrix of Lunar Purity, Matrix of Manifestation of All Arrays of Adornments, Matrix of Illumination of Knowledge, Matrix of Radiance, Matrix of Blossoming Glory, Matrix of Blue Lotus Splendor, Matrix of Celestial Qualities, Matrix of Splendor of Virtue, Matrix of Purity of Unobstructed Knowledge, Matrix of Godlike Majesty, Matrix of Purity, Matrix of Nondefilement, Matrix of Adornment of Varied Eloquence, Matrix of Radiance of Great Webs of Light Beams, Matrix of Radiance of Power of Splendor of Undefiled Light, Matrix of Pure Radiance of Accumulated Gold, Matrix of Pure Splendor Adorned by All Characteristics of Enlightening Beings, Matrix of Glorious Adornments of Diamond Flames, Matrix of Beauty of Flames of Light, Matrix of Light of Majesty of the Stars, Matrix of Unhindered Knowledge of the Treasury of the Sky, Matrix of Sweet Sounds with Unobstructed Spheres of Resonance, Matrix of Spells Supporting the Aspirations of All Beings, Matrix of Adornments of the Ocean, Matrix of Majesty of the Polar Mountain, Matrix of Purity of All Qualities, Matrix of Splendor of Those Who Realize Thusness, Matrix of Majesty of the Enlightened, and Moon of Liberation. The Buddha was with innumerable enlightening beings assembled from various buddha-lands, led by Diamond Matrix, these being the main ones.

At that time Diamond Matrix, by the power of Buddha, entered the concentration called Light of the Great Vehicle, and as soon as he had done so there appeared to him as many buddhas as atoms in ten billion buddha-lands from beyond as many worlds as atoms in ten buddha-lands in each of the ten directions, all of whom were alike named Diamond Matrix. Those buddhas said, "It is good that you have entered this concentration of enlightening beings' Light of the Great Vehicle. In this you are supported by the Buddhas numerous as atoms in ten billion buddha-lands beyond worlds as numerous as atoms in ten billion buddha-lands in the ten directions, and by the power of the ancient vow of Vairocana Buddha, and it is also due to the excellence of your virtue and knowledge, so that all enlightening beings may enter the stages of knowledge of the illuminating power of the inconceivable Buddha teachings, to attain all roots of goodness, for skill in analyzing all Buddha teachings, for breadth of knowledge of things, for the exposition of well-constructed teachings, for the purification of holistic knowledge, so as to be unstained by worldly things, for the purification of supramundane roots of goodness, for the discovery of particulars of the sphere of inconceivable knowledge, and for the realization of the sphere of omniscient knowledge: that is to say, it is for the sake of the undertaking and attainment of the ten stages of enlightening beings, for the sake of correct explanation of skill in setting up the stages of enlightening beings, for the sake of proper focusing onthe teachings of the buddhas, to distinguish undefiled phenomena, for skill with the light of great wisdom with knowing discernment, for entry into complete definitive adaptive knowledge, for the light of eloquence to explain without hesitation or obstruction in accord with differences in capability and station, to fulfill the stage of great discursive knowledge, to never forget the determination for enlightenment, to develop all beings to perfection, and to attain skill in discernment in all situations. Furthermore, you should explain this teaching, skill in differentiation of means of revealing truth, by the power of the Buddha, by the aid of the light of knowledge of the Buddha, for the perfect purification of your own roots of goodness, for the thorough purification of the cosmos, for the protection of sentient beings, for the body of knowledge of the body of reality, to receive the anointment of all buddhas, for the manifestation of the most exalted being in all worlds, to completely transcend all worldly paths, to purify the path to the supramundane, to fulfill omniscience."

Then those buddhas gave the enlightening being Diamond Matrix physical invincibility, the ability to teach with unhindered presence of mind, pure knowledge of differentiation, the power of unfailing recollection, skill with certain intellect, unfailing understanding in all situations, the invincible power of the perfectly enlightened, indomitability of power and expertise of a buddha, attainment of discernment and teaching by the discursive knowledge of the omniscient, and gave him the well-arrayed physical, verbal, and mental adornments of all buddhas. Why? Because of his attainment of the reality of this concentration in accord with its name; because of the upshot of his past vows; because of his thoroughly pure determination; because of his purification of his sphere of knowledge; because of his having stored well the provisions for the Path; because of his having accomplished well what he had to do; because of his being an immeasurable vessel of remembrance; because of his having purified clear faith; because of his having mastered the method of concentration spells without corruption; because of his being perfectly stamped with the seal of self-knowledge; and because of his being perfectly stamped with the seal of knowledge of the realm of reality.

Then those buddhas, by their occult power, extended their right hands from where they were and rubbed the head of Diamond Matrix, at which point the enlightening being arose from that concentration and said to the other enlightening beings, "Perfectly sure, O blessed offspring of the Victorious, is the vow of enlightening beings, unadulterated, impossible to see in its entirety, vast as the cosmos, including all space, eternal, rescuing all beings, wherein alone the blessed enlightening beings enter the stage of knowledge of the past buddhas, enter the stage of knowledge of the future buddhas, and enter the stage of knowledge of the present buddhas. There are ten stages of enlightening beings that enter into the stage of knowledge of the buddhas. And what are these ten stages of enlightening beings that have been, will be, and are being explained by the buddhas of the past, future, and present? Having meditated on them, I will now tell you. They are the enlightening beings' stage called Extreme Joy, that called Purity, that called Refulgence, that called

Blazing, that called Difficult to Conquer, that called Presence, that called Far-Going, that called Immovable, that called Good Mind, and the stage of enlightening beings called Cloud of Teaching. These are the ten stages of enlightening beings that have been, will be, and are expounded by the buddhas of the past, future, and present. I have never seen any buddha-land where the buddhas do not elucidate these ten stages of enlightening beings. Why? This is the supreme light of teaching method to purify the path of enlightening being—that is the definition of the specifics of the ten stages. Inconceivable is this realm of knowledge of the ten stages."

Then Diamond Matrix, having mentioned the names of these ten stages, fell silent and gave no further definitions.

Thereupon the assembly of enlightening beings became anxious, having heard only the names of the stages, their definition not having been explained. They wondered why Diamond Matrix remained silent after mentioning only the names of the ten stages and did not analyze them further.

At that time there was among the assembly of enlightening beings an enlightening being named Moon of Liberation who knew what was on the minds of the assembly of enlightening beings and who asked Diamond Matrix in verse,

> O ye of pure intent, mindfulness, knowledge, and virtue,
> Having mentioned the supreme stages, why do you not explain them?
>
> All these honored enlightening beings are sure in mind;
> Why, having mentioned the stages, do you not define them?
>
> These experienced offspring of buddhas want to hear—
> Please explain the meanings and ways of the correct stages.
>
> This assembly is quiet, free from sloth, pure;
> Purified, steadfast, full of virtue and knowledge.
>
> All stand there gazing respectfully,
> Desirous, as bees for honey, for the ultimate ambrosia.

Having heard this, the wise, experienced Diamond Matrix spoke to please the assembly:

> Difficult, supreme is this, rare, the revelation of enlightening beings' practice.
> Supreme is the discernment of the practices of the stages whence buddhahood is attained.
>
> Subtle, hard to see, beyond thought, beyond the ground of mind, hard to approach,

It is the realm of the wise with untainted minds, hearing which confuses the worldly.

Keeping the mind as stable as diamond, believe in the supremacy of buddha-knowledge:
Knowing the mind-ground is selfless, then one can hear this subtle knowledge.

Like colors painted in the sky, like the wind in space—
So is this undefiled knowledge of Buddha hard to see, though it be defined.

Such is my understanding of that—it's hard to find anyone in the world who knows it,
Or even believes in it—thus I cannot explain this ultimate.

This having been said, the enlightening being Moon of Liberation said to Diamond Matrix, "Pure is this assembly that has gathered, enlightening beings with thoroughly purified aspiration, thoroughly purified will, who have done their work well, who have attended hundreds of thousands of billions of buddhas, who have thoroughly gathered the provisions for the Path, who have attained immeasurable knowledge and virtue, who are free from folly and confusion, free from affliction, impurity, and attachment, who are firm in determination and faith, whose undivided attention is on these buddhas' teachings. Speak, therefore, for the enlightening beings directly witness this realm."

Diamond Matrix said, "What though this assembly of enlightening beings is pure, with thoroughly purified aspirations and will, having done their work well, having well attended countless buddhas, having attained immeasurable virtue and knowledge, free from folly and delusion, undefiled, with well-established determination and zeal, with undivided attention on these teachings of buddhas, yet because of the lack of benefit and the suffering in the long night of ignorance for those others who would give rise to dissent and doubt upon hearing of such inconceivable states, it is out of compassion for them that I want to remain silent."

Then Moon of Liberation again asked Diamond Matrix for this doctrine: "Very well, explain by the power of the Enlightened—these inconceivable stations will be well protected and believed in. Why? Because that naturally occurs when these stages are being explained: this is what all buddhas keep in mind, and all enlightening beings are intent on the protection of this knowledge. Why? This is the fundamental practice, and this is the fulfillment of the Buddha teachings. It is like the instruction of combinations of letters—it begins and ends with the basic characters; there is nothing expressed by combinations of letters without indication of the basic characters. In the same way all the Buddha teachings are based on the stages and their practices are fulfilled thereby. The

consummations of the stages lead to the attainment of the knowledge of
the independent. Therefore speak; the realized ones, the saints, the perfectly enlightened ones will protect and support you.''

At this point those enlightening beings uttered verses in one voice
asking Diamond Matrix for this teaching:

> O ye of supreme wisdom and boundless eloquence,
> Speak the finest words, in accord with ultimate truth.

> With recollection, steadfastness, pure knowledge, pure resolve to
>   attain the ten powers,
> And discerning intellect, explain these ten supreme stages.

> Tranquil, disciplined, with accumulated goodwill, free from
>   afflictions, delusion, pride, and views,
> Free from doubt, this assembly hopes for your explanation.

> As the thirsty desire cool water, the hungry food, the sick
>   medicine,
> And bees honey, so does this assembly desire your words.

> Therefore, ye of pure knowledge, speak of the exalted stages, free
>   from taint,
> Joined to the ten powers, unobstructed, producing all good states.

At that time a radiance called "light of power of enlightening beings"
emanated from the circle of hair between the eyebrows of Shakyamuni
Buddha, accompanied by innumerable rays of light, illuminating all
worlds in all ten directions, stopping all evils and suffering, eclipsing
all realms of demons, illuminating the circles of innumerable buddhas,
revealing the features, occult powers, and mystic transfigurations in
the inconceivable realm of the buddhas, illuminating the enlightening
beings empowered to teach in the circles of all buddhas in all worlds in
the ten directions; having shown the inconceivable mystical power of
the Buddha, it formed a great tower of networks of clouds of light up
in the sky and remained there.

In the same way, lights called "light of power of enlightening beings"
emanated from the circle of hair between the eyebrows of the other
buddhas, accompanied by innumerable beams of light, illuminating all
worlds in the ten directions, stopping all evils and suffering, eclipsing all
realms of demons, illuminating the circles of innumerable buddhas,
revealing the features, occult powers, and mystic transfigurations in the
inconceivable realm of buddhas, illuminating the enlightening beings
empowered to teach in the circles of all buddhas in all worlds in the ten
directions; having revealed this inconceivable mystic power of buddhas,
and having illuminated the circle of Shakyamuni Buddha and the body

of the enlightening being Diamond Matrix, in the same way the beams formed a great tower of webs of clouds of light up in the sky and remained there.

Thus by means of the light beams emanated from the circle of hair between the eyebrows of Shakyamuni Buddha, those worlds and those circles of buddhas and the bodies and sitting places of their enlightening beings were clearly illumined. By the lights emanated by those other buddhas, this world system, the circle of Shakyamuni Buddha, and the body and sitting place of Diamond Matrix were seen clearly illumined.

Then, from the great tower of webs of clouds of light, by the power of the Buddha, this sound emerged:

> By those with the ten powers, peerless, equal to space, with
> boundless virtues,
> By the teachings of Shakyamuni, by those beyond all men and
> gods, is this miraculous display made.

> By the power of the buddhas, open the storehouse of the Kings of
> Truth
> And reveal the supreme practice and stages of knowledge
> distinctly.

> Those who hear this supreme teaching will also be
> Empowered and supported by the buddhas and enlightening
> beings,
> Who will cause them to attain buddhahood once they attain the
> ten powers,
> After having gradually fulfilled the undefiled ten stages.

> Even sunk in the ocean or thrown into the holocaust,
> They will be able to hear this teaching, without doubt.

> But those stuck to folly, suspicious and unreceptive,
> Will never get to hear it.

> The path of knowledge of the stages, supreme, from entry,
> station, and attainment,
> Please explain in order, including the practice and sphere of
> action.

Then Diamond Matrix, looking over the ten directions, in order to increase the purity of this assembly, at this juncture spoke these verses:

> Subtle and hard to know is the path of the great sages,
> Nonconceptual, beyond conception, most difficult to contact.
> It is pure, known only to the wise,

Its nature is quiescent, without extinction or origination.
Inherently empty, utterly tranquil, nondual, inexhaustible,
Liberated from all states, impartially reaching nirvana,
Without extremes or mean, not expressed by words,
Outside of time, like the sky,
Quiescent, ultimately silent, realized by the enlightened,
Most difficult to express by any manner of speaking:
Such are the stages and their practice—
Most difficult to speak of, more difficult to hear.

Beyond thought and the path of mind,
Elicited by knowledge, realized by the highest sages,
Not revealed by the elements of matter and sense,
Unattainable by mind, intellectually inconceivable:
Just as the tracks of a bird in the sky
Cannot be described or seen even by the enlightened,
In the same way all the stages
Cannot be told of, much less heard.

I will tell just the beginning, then,
Out of kindness, compassion, commitment:
I will tell of them in order; yet not by spheres of thought
But by knowledge are they to be fulfilled as one wishes.

Such a realm is hard to see, impossible to tell of—
It just rests in one's own mind;
But I will speak out by the power of Buddha—
It should be heard with concentration and respect.

This entry of knowledge, being as such,
Cannot be explained even in eons:
I will now give a summary,
According to the meaning of the teaching as it is.

Attend respectfully, blessed ones;
I will speak by the power of Buddha.
I will utter the voice of the highest teaching,
In appropriate words, with examples.

Though it is difficult to express in speech,
Yet mine is the power to do so,
By the immeasurable power of Buddha and the power of the
    body of light
That have entered into me.

"Now then, in beings who have well-developed roots of goodness,
who have done their tasks well, who have accumulated provisions for

the Path, who have attended buddhas in the world, who have consolidated pure practices, who are in the care of spiritual friends, who have thoroughly purified their intentions, who have great determination, who are endowed with supreme zeal, and who actualize pity and compassion, the aspiration for enlightenment is aroused, for the quest of enlightened knowledge, for the attainment of the ten powers, for the atttainment of great expertise, for the attainment of the enlightened quality of impartiality, for the salvation of all beings, for the purification of great mercy and compassion, for the attainment of knowledge of all in the ten directions, for the unobstructed purification of all buddha-lands, for awareness of past, present, and future in a single instant, and for expertise in turning the wheel of the great Teaching.

"This intention of enlightening beings, furthermore, is aroused and guided by great compassion, controlled by wisdom and knowledge, sustained by skill in means, stabilized by will and determination, immeasurable as the power of buddhas, clearly distinguishing the power of sentient beings and the power of Buddha, focused on unfragmented knowledge, in accord with spontaneous knowledge, completely receptive to the guidance of wisdom and knowledge of all Buddha teachings; it is as ultimate as the cosmos, as enduring as space, abiding forever.

"With this arousing of the mind the enlightening being is beyond the stage of mundane beings, has entered the rank of enlightening beings, is born in the family of the enlightened, cannot be slandered by any racial slur, has left all mundane paths and has entered the transmundane Path, is stationed in the reality of enlightened beings, is properly established in the abode of enlightening beings, has attained equanimity, is established in the lineage of buddhas of past, present, and future, certain to become perfectly enlightened. Established in these things, the enlightening being is established in the first stage of enlightening beings, that of Extreme Joy, by attainment of imperturbability.

"Here, standing on the stage of Extreme Joy of enlightening beings, one is filled with extreme joy, filled with calm, filled with happiness, filled with ebullience, filled with exaltation, filled with delight, greatly invigorated, most uncontentious, most harmless, and free from anger.

"Thus is the enlightening being extremely joyful when stationed in the enlightening beings' stage of joy; one becomes extremely joyful thinking of the buddhas, of the Buddha teachings, of the enlightening beings, of the practices of enlightening beings, of the purification of the transcendent ways, of the eminence of the stages of enlightening beings, of the indestructibility of enlightening beings, of the teachings of the buddhas, and of the ability to benefit beings; and, thinking of the means of entry into the knowledge of all buddhas, the enlightening being is imbued with extreme joy. 'Detached am I from all mundane objects; I have entered the vicinity of buddhahood; I have left behind the stage of infantile ignorance and drawn near to the stage of knowledge; I am cut off from all evil and states of misery; I am a refuge for all beings; I am near to the vision of all buddhas; I am born in the realm of all buddhas;

I have reached equality to all enlightening beings; gone from me are all fears and terrors'—thus thinking, the enlightening being gives rise to extreme joy. Why? Because that is what happens to all fears with the enlightening being's attainment of the stage of joy—fears such as fear of not surviving, fear of ill repute, fear of death, fear of states of misery fear of intimidation by groups—all these fears leave. Why is that? Inasmuch as the very concept of self is gone, there is no self-love, much less any love for material things; therefore there is no fear of not surviving. One does not seek any honor from anyone, but rather thinks one should provide others with sufficient means of subsistence, therefore there is no fear of ill repute. And because one has no view of self, one has no concept of self and therefore no fear of dying. Thinking that when one is dead, one will certainly not be separated from the buddhas and enlightening beings, one therefore has no fear of states of misery. Thinking that there is no aspiration in any world equal to, much less greater than, one's own aspiration for enlightenment, there is no fear of intimidation by groups. Thus all fears and terrors are removed.

"Furthermore, the enlightening being, due to having made great compassion foremost, strives all the more with an indestructible, extraordinary will, for the fulfillment of all roots of goodness, by mastery of perfect faith, by purity of intention, by wealth of true understanding, by having developed mercy and compassion, by having attained great kindness, by indefatigability of mind, by adornment with conscience, by attainment of joy in tolerance, by honor and respect for the teachings of the completely enlightened, by tireless collection of roots of goodness night and day, by service to good spiritual friends, by enjoyment of true teaching, by insatiable search for learning, by correct contemplation of the teachings as they are heard, by mental nonattachment, by absence of craving for gain, honor, or fame, by absence of desire for goods, by tireless production of a jewel-like mind, by seeking the stage of omniscience, by concentration on the powers, expertise, and unique buddha-qualities of all enlightened ones, by unattached seeking of the transcendent ways, by abandonment of all deception and dishonesty, by acting in accord with one's words, by constant preservation of truthful speech, by not allowing the family of the enlightened to die out, by not abandoning the teachings of enlightening beings, by mountainlike imperturbability of mind, by discerning knowledge of all mundane doings, by attainment of the transmundane path of relinquishment, by constant seeking of the supreme ultimate.

"Imbued with these ways of purifying the stages, enlightening beings are well established in the stage of Extreme Joy. Once established in this stage, enlightening beings undertake great vows, great resolutions, great undertakings such as the following: They undertake a first great vow to make offerings to each and every buddha, in the best of forms, with the highest purity of faith, as extensively as the cosmos, to the furthest reaches of space, throughout all time. They undertake a second great vow to maintain the eye of the teachings spoken by all buddhas, to associate with all buddhas and enlightening beings, to preserve the teachings of all complete buddhas, to take in all truths, to the extent of the cosmos, to the furthest reaches of space, throughout all time, without ceasing, in all eons for as many buddhas as appear in the world. They undertake a third great vow to go to all places in all worlds where buddhas appear— from their existence in the heaven of satisfaction, descending into the human world, entry into the womb, abiding in the womb, birth, youthful enjoyments, married life, renunciation, practice of austerities, conquering demons, enlightenment, being requested to teach, setting the wheel of the great teaching in motion, and entry into great absolute nirvana—to go to all places at once, taking the lead in making offerings, receiving the teaching, and applying it in practice, to the extent of the cosmos, to the farthest reaches of space, throughout all time, without ceasing in all eons for as many buddhas as appear in the world, until the attainment of great absolute nirvana. They undertake a fourth vow to bring forth the determination to disseminate instruction in the accomplishment of means of purification of the ways of transcendence, accurate explanation of the path of the stages, the practices of all enlightening beings, bringing forth their total and particular aspects, with consideration of their common and distinctive features, as they are formed and dissolved, the many extensive immeasurable holistic practices of all buddhas and enlightening beings contained in the ways of transcendence, purifying all the stages of enlightening beings, vowing to call forth this aspiration to the extent of the cosmos, to the furthest reaches of space, throughout all time. They undertake a fifth great vow to fully develop all beings, corporeal or immaterial, thinking, nonthinking, or neither, born of eggs, wombs, moisture, or spontaneously, in all realms contained in the worlds of desire, forms, and formlessness, bound to the six paths of mundane existence in all places of birth, caught up in names and forms—to develop them to lead them into the Buddha teaching, to free them from all mundane groupings, to establish them in omniscience, to develop and mature all beings forever, to the extent of the cosmos, throughout the reaches of space, for all time, for as many eons and beings as there be. They undertake a sixth great vow for direct knowledge of the innumerable distinctions in all the worlds of the ten directions, variously reflecting one another, subtle and gross, upside-down, inverted, and upright, their appearance and consolidation—they vow to comprehend the distinctions of worlds, to the extent of the cosmos, throughout the reaches of space, for all time. They undertake a seventh great vow, to show all beings the purification of all lands in one land and one land in all lands, the adornment of innumerable buddha-lands with arrays of light, entering into the supreme realm of buddhas from which all afflictions are removed, completely purified and filled with wise beings, showing this to all beings to please them in accord with their mentalities, vowing to thoroughly purify all buddha-lands, to the extent of the cosmos, to the farthest reaches of space, throughout all time, unceasing for as many eons and buddha-lands as there may be. They undertake an eighth great vow, to work with the same one determination as all enlightening beings, to build up roots of goodness without opposition, to be equally focused on the same one object as all enlightening beings, to be in concert with all enlightening beings, to manifest appearances of Buddha as desired, to attain the knowledge of the powers of the Enlightened at will, to attain ever-present mystic knowledge, to travel to all worlds, to appear in the circles of all buddhas, to adapt to all situations, to attain realization of the inconceivable great vehicle, to continue to carry out the practices of enlightening beings, vowing to enter the great vehicle, to the extent of the cosmos, to the furthest reaches of space, throughout all time, unceasing for as many eons and practices as there may be. They undertake a ninth great vow to carry out the practice of enlightening beings, riding on the wheel that never rolls backward, by means of fruitful words, thoughts, and deeds, so that those who see them will surely realize buddhahood, those who hear what they say will attain knowledge, and so that those who have pure faith will be freed from afflictions—they vow to attain a state like a master physician, to attain embodiment of magical fulfillment of aspirations, to carry out the practices of enlightening beings as extensively as the cosmos, to the farthest reaches of space, throughout all time, unceasing for as many eons and as many practices as there be, that their deeds not be in vain. They undertake a tenth great vow, to awaken completely to unexcelled perfect enlightenment in all worlds, to show at every point—without leaving one place—birth, leaving home, transfiguration, austere practice, conquering demons, sitting at the pinnacle of enlightenment, turning the wheel of the teaching, and final absolute nirvana, to attain the knowledge of power of the vast realm of buddhahood and in each instant show all sentient beings the emergence of a buddha in accordance with their mentalities so that they may attain enlightenment and perfect peace, to universally realize the nirvana of all phenomena by one pefect enlightenment, to please all beings according to their mentalities with a single utterance, to show great ultimate nirvana without cutting off the power of practice, to show the construction of all teachings of the stages of great knowledge, to pervade all worlds by the mystic power of the knowledge of truth and the mystic knowledge of illusoriness, vowing to bring forth great knowledge to the extent of the cosmos, to the farthest reaches of space, throughout all time, never ceasing for all eons, for all true enlightenments.

"Thus, having brought to the fore such great aspirations, great purposes, great undertakings, through ten great vows, enlightening beings stationed in the stage of Extreme Joy undertake countless consummate vows, which they undertake in ten ultimate terms: that is, to the ultimate extent of living beings, to the ultimate extent of worlds, to the ultimate extent of space, to the ultimate extent of the cosmos, to the ultimate extent of the realm of nirvana, to the ultimate extent of the emergence of buddhas, to the ultimate extent of enlightened knowledge, to the ultimate extent of realms of mental objects, to the ultimate extent of entries of knowledge into the sphere of buddhas, to the ultimate extent of the courses of worlds, the courses of teachings, and the courses of knowledge. Enlightening beings vow that their undertakings shall be coterminous with living beings, worlds, space, the cosmos, nirvana, the emergence of buddhas, enlightened knowledge, mental objects, entries of knowledge into the sphere of buddhas, the courses of worlds, the courses of teachings, and the courses of knowledge; and that just as all of these are endless, so shall the enlightening beings' roots of goodness be endless.

"In those who have taken such vows upon themselves, the workable mind and the gentle mind are incorruptibly pure. The enlightening beings have faith in the perfectly enlightened buddhas' attainments of past practices, their realization of the transcendent ways, their consummate attainment of the stages, their consummate attainment of the powers, their complete fulfillment of expertise, the indestructibility of unique qualities of buddhahood, the inconceivability of buddhahood, the attainment of the sphere of buddhas, which is infinitely various, the attainment of immeasurable knowledge, the complete entry into the realm of those who arrive at Thusness. Enlightening beings believe in the consummation of the fruits; in sum, they believe in the practice of enlightening beings, including all that upon which is based the teaching of the stage of knowledge of enlightened ones.

"Furthermore, it occurs to the enlightening beings that these qualities of buddhahood are so profound, so detached, so peaceful, so empty, so signless, so desireless, so undefiled, so vast, so immeasurable, so supreme, so hard to approach.

"What is more, enlightening beings reflect, ignorant creatures, because of continually slipping into erroneous views, because of minds shrouded by the darkness of ignorance, because of being puffed up with pride, because of conceptions, because of mental fixations of desires caught in the net of craving, because of hopes pursued by actions in the tangle of deceit and falsehood, because of deeds connected with envy and jealousy producing mundane states, because of accumulation of actions rife with passion, hatred, and folly, because of the flames of mind ignited by anger and resentment, because of undertakings of actions bound up with delusion, because of seeds in the mind, intellect, and consciousness bound to the flows of lust, existence, and ignorance, therefore produce sprouts of subsequent life in the world. That is to say, name and form are born together, inseparable; and by the development of name and form, the assembly of six sense mediums takes place; once the mediums are formed, from their mutual contact sensation comes to be; and that sensation being enjoyed and sought more and more, the operation of craving grows; craving being developed, existence comes to be;

once there is existence, birth, death, sorrow, lamentation, suffering, sadness, and anxiety appear. Thus does the mass of suffering of sentient beings arise. Seeing these beings' inability to escape from this mass of suffering—not realizing it is without self or anything pertaining to self, that it is unreal, insubstantial, void, inert, ineffective, insensate as wood and stone, like a reflection—the enlightening beings develop great compassion to rescue them and free them from their miseries, and develop great kindness to bring them to endless bliss and nirvana.

"Thus, abiding in the first stage, by sympathy and kindness and by supreme will the enlightening beings, relinquishing all things with an equanimous mind, cultivate great relinquishments in a spirit of most urgent quest for enlightened knowledge. These relinquishments are: relinquishment of goods, food, stores, houses, gold, jewels, all kinds of treasure and money, jewelry and adornments, animals and vehicles, pleasant ponds, parks, forest retreats and monasteries, servants and employees, spouses and children, home, city, town, society, homeland, metropolis, and all parts of the body. Thus, having become indifferent to these, the intellect most ardently seeking enlightened knowledge relinquishes all things. Thus does the great relinquishment of those in the first stage of enlightening beings come to be.

"Thus, based on compassion, kindness, and relinquishment, the enlightening beings, for the sake of the salvation and liberation of all beings, more and more seek mundane and transcendental benefits for them, and while seeking arouse an unwearying mind. Thus do the enlightening beings become indefatigable and, being indefatigable, become expert in all learning. Thus in possession of learning, by intelligent consideration of what should and should not be done, the enlightening beings arrive at what is variously appropriate for inferior, mediocre, and superior beings, according to their power and endowments, thus attaining knowledge of the world and humanity. And the enlightening beings, knowing the world, acting in accord with time and measure, adorned with constant modesty and conscience, strive for the benefit of self and others. Thus the enlightening beings become modest and conscientious. And in those efforts the enlightening beings become uninterested in mundane satisfactions and attain nonreceding, undiminishing power; hence the arising of enlightening beings' stable support of power. Thus stably empowered, the enlightening beings work on service to buddhas and receive their instructions. Hence arise in the enlightening beings the elements that purify the ten stages—faith, compassion, kindness, relinquishment, indefatigability, knowledge of the teachings, knowledge of the world and humanity, modesty and conscience, stable power, and attendance on buddhas.

"Enlightening beings in this stage of Joy get to see many buddhas, by broad vision and by the power of vows seeing many hundreds of buddhas, many thousands of buddhas, many hundreds of thousands of buddhas, many millions, many billions, many trillions of buddhas. Having seen those buddhas, those saints, those completely enlightened ones, by broad vision and the power of vows, the enlightening beings honor and serve them with supreme zeal, presenting them with the necessities of life, such as food, clothing, drink, vessels, bedding, and medicines, and they also bring comforts for enlightening beings, and they also respect and support the religious community. These supreme roots of goodness the enlightening beings dedicate to consummate enlightenment.

"From this service of buddhas arise means of development of beings, and the enlightening beings develop sentient beings to maturity by giving and by kind speech, the other two means of salvation helping out by the power of faith, though as yet without complete knowledge and attainment. Of the ten transcendent ways, the transcendent way of giving is foremost; not that the others are not cultivated, but they are practiced according to the enlightening beings' power and endowment. And as the enlightening beings serve the buddhas and work for the development of sentient beings, practicing to accumulate these elements that purify the stages, thus do the enlightening beings' roots of goodness, dedicated to universal knowledge, become more and more purified and capable of application as desired. Just as when gold is plunged into fire over and over by a skilled smith, it becomes more and more purified and workable and can be made into various ornaments as desired, in the same way as the enlightening beings attend buddhas and work for the perfection of sentient beings and cultivate the factors that purify the stages, so do their roots of goodness become more and more purified and useful.

"Then the enlightening beings in this stage should ask buddhas, enlightening beings, and spiritual friends about the characteristics and attainments of this first stage and should be tireless in seeking fulfillment of the components of this stage. In the same way, in order to fulfill the components of the stages of enlightening beings up to the tenth, the enlightening beings should become versed in the problems and solutions of the stages, in the formation and dissolution of the stages, in the forms and actions of the stages, in the attainments and cultivation of the stages, in the purification of the elements of the stages, in the progression from stage to stage, in the attainment of each stage without regression, in the purification of all stages of enlightenment, and in the accession to the stage of enlightened knowledge.

"There is no cease in the ascent of the enlightening beings who are skilled in fostering the forms of practice of the stages up to accession to the tenth stage; by unceasing progress on the Path and by the light of knowledge of the stages, the enlightening beings attain the light of buddha-knowledge. It is like a skilled caravan leader who, wanting to lead a large caravan to a great city, first finds out about the qualities of the road to be traveled, the defects of the road, the best places to stop along the way, the places not to stop, and what is to be done about provisions for the trip, thus knowing well how to get to the great city, from the beginning to the end of the journey. Thus, by fully preparing for the way by this intelligent consideration, the caravan leader finally reaches the great city along with the caravan, without the caravan or himself being beset by difficulties in desolate places. In the same way the enlightening beings, as clever caravan leaders, when established in the first stage of enlightening beings, become familiar with the issues and solutions of the stages, the formation and dissolution of the stages, the practical aspects of the stages, the attainments and cultivation of the stages, the purification of the elements of the stages, the progression from one stage to another, the consolidation of each stage, the special knowledge of each stage, attainment of each stage without regression, and accession to the stage of buddha-knowledge by means of the quality of purification of all the stages of enlightening beings. Then the enlightening beings, having gotten together provisions of great virtue and knowledge, and having well established a store of knowledge, wishing to lead the great caravan of sentient beings to the city of omniscience, first inquire into and find out the qualities of the path of the stages, deviations from the path of the stages, errors on the path of the stages, the best of stations along the path of the stages, and what is to be done about the provisions of virtue and knowledge for the path of the stages, asking buddhas, enlightening beings, and spiritual friends about this to become versed in how to reach the great city of omniscience. Thus, by intelligent consideration of the way before proceeding and by thus fully preparing provisions of virtue and knowledge, the enlightening beings lead the great caravan of sentient beings according to their maturity across the wasteland of the mundane whirl to the great city of omniscience, without either the caravan or the enlightening beings being beset by the ills of the wasteland. Thus enlightening beings should work tirelessly on the cultivation of stages.

"This is a brief explanation of enlightening beings' entry into the first stage of Extreme Joy. Enlightening beings in this stage are mostly monarchs of a continent, having attained great power and sovereignty, guardians of right, wise and capable, taking good care of beings with great generosity, undertaking unlimited acts of charity to rid beings of the taint of envy and discontent. And whatever acts the enlightening beings undertake, whether by giving, or by kind speech, or by beneficial action, or by cooperation, those acts are never apart from thoughts of Buddha, of the Teaching, of the Community, of enlightening being, of the practices of enlightening beings, of the transcendent ways, of the stages, of the expertise and unique qualities of buddhas, of omniscience complete in all respects. To what purpose? To become the best of beings, unexcelled leaders and guides, and ultimately omniscient refuges.

"Those who seek to be thus undertake the appropriate effort, by which they give up all comforts and go forth in conformity with the teaching of Buddha. Having gone forth, enlightening beings instantly attain a hundred concentrations and see a hundred buddhas and acknowledge their power; they stir a hundred worlds, go to a hundred lands, illumine a hundred worlds, mature a hundred beings, live for a hundred eons, penetrate a hundred eons past and future, contemplate a hundred teachings, and manifest a hundred bodies, each body manifesting a company of a hundred enlightening beings. Then enlightening beings with superior power of commitment, by the quality of excellence of vows, transform their bodies, auras, mystic powers, vision, spheres of operation, voices, conduct, adornments, power, resolutions, and performances in countless ways."

Then Diamond Matrix spoke these verses explaining the meaning of this stage:

Having accumulated pure qualities and attained virtues,
Done service, following enlightened kindness and compassion,
Embodying supreme faith and pure goodwill,
They produce an incomparable mind for enlightened knowledge.

Intent on the power, purification, and energy of the all-knowing
    buddhas,
To attain the state of the Victorious and save the world,
The supreme will arises to develop great compassion,
Turn the wheel of the teaching, and purify the buddha-lands.

To know all times in an instant without discriminating thought,
To clarify good timing in the world in its variety,
Seeking, in short, all the qualities of the Guides,
This noble mind, immeasurable as space, is born.

Commanded by wisdom, led by compassion, endowed with skill
    in means,
Pure in resolution and intent, measureless in power,
Unobstructed, direct, not relying on another's guidance,
Knowledge of the supreme mind equal to the enlightened,
With the birth of this mind-jewel of enlightening beings
One transcends the sphere of the ignorant and reaches the sphere
    of buddhas,
Is born in the family of the enlightened, impeccable,
Gone to equality with buddhas, certain of highest enlightenment.

Once one produces this mind, one attains this stage,
The will immovable as a mountain,
Joyful and happy, serene, resolute, and forceful,
With a buoyant mind,
Nonviolent, harmless, free from anger,
Modest and respectful, with superior honesty, self-controlled;
One remembers the immeasurable knowledge that saves the
    world
And becomes joyful in anticipation of that state.

712 The Flower Ornament Scripture

When one attains this stage, five fears depart—
Not being able to make a living, dying, reputation, misery, fear
    of groups—
Thus fear is gone: why?
Because there is no attachment to self.

Those free from fear and full of compassion and kindness,
With faith, respect, and modesty, rich in virtues,
Practicing good day and night, seek the teaching for the sake of
    truth
And not for enjoyment of mundane desires.

Considering well the teachings they have heard with unattached
    minds,
Their will for enlightenment directed without desire for gain,
Seeking knowledge and power, the purifying teachings of
    buddhas,
They work on the ways of transcendence, free from delusion and
    conceit.

Acting in accord with their words, steadfast in truthful speech,
They do not sully the family of buddhas, carrying out the study
    of enlightenment;
Detached from mundane doings, wishing benefit for the world,
Tireless in good works, they climb ever higher.

Thus seeking the truth, intent on the quest for virtue,
They undertake the vow to behold the buddhas;
To preserve the true teaching and approach the seers,
They undertake the vows of those whose acts are supreme.

To develop beings and purify the buddha-land,
To populate their land with enlightening beings,
With unity of purpose, not in vain,
They seek enlightenment everywhere.

They undertake many such vows, which are infinitely extensive,
Enduring as space, beings, time, the nature of things, nirvana,
The world, the emergence of buddhas,
And the ground of knowledge.

They will their vows to last as long as there are mental objects
And access to knowledge, endless in the world as long as it
    operates:
"When these end, may my undertakings end too—
May I attain practice enduring as these."

Thus thoroughly dedicated, with harmonious, flexible minds,
They put faith in the virtues of buddhas and observe sentient
    beings:
Knowing beings are conditioned, out of compassion they feel
They should rescue suffering beings from afflictions.

For that purpose they undertake various kinds of giving—
Of kingship, all kinds of treasures, horses and elephants,
Their heads, hands, feet, eyes, even their blood and flesh—
All they give away, without becoming distressed in mind.

They seek out various teachings, indefatigable;
Learned, they accord with the ways of the world.
Knowing the world, modest and steadfast,
They serve innumerable buddhas with reverence and respect.

Thus they practice constantly, day and night,
Their virtue refined as gold in fire;
Thus having made the preparations for the ten stages,
They attain freedom from hindrance, having destroyed the
    obstacles.

Just as a caravan leader, for the benefit of the great caravan,
Asks about the features of the road and then goes safely,
So do enlightening beings in the first stage setting out
Reach enlightenment unhindered, by way of the ten stages.

Stationed here, they become virtuous sovereigns,
Guiding aright, nonviolent and benevolent;
Leaders of the whole continent, they bring all people
To relinquishment and the highest buddha-knowledge.

Having boldly abandoned rulership in search of truth,
They betake themselves to Buddha's teaching and begin to
    practice it;
Attaining a hundred concentrations and seeing a hundred
    buddhas,
They shake a hundred lands and travel as illuminators.

They purify a hundred beings, seek out a hundred doors of truth,
And penetrate a hundred eons, manifesting a hundred bodies;
They manifest a hundred enlightening beings, or even more,
The power of their supreme vows immeasurable.

"This is an explanation of the excellent first stage of enlightening
beings seeking benefit for all worlds. Such is the first stage of enlightening beings, which is called Extreme Joy."

Having heard about the supreme felicitous realm of this stage, the enlightening beings were delighted, their minds and thoughts pure: getting up from their seats and rising into the air, they scattered flowers all around, uttering words of praise:

> Excellent, Diamond Matrix, replete with great wisdom and
>   expertise;
> You have explained well this stage practiced by enlightening
>   beings.

> The assembly pure in mind, Moon of Liberation asks
> To hear about the next highest, second stage.

> How should the mind be directed to see the second stage?
> Speak forth, O wise one—the enlightening beings desire to hear.

The enlightening being Diamond Matrix said, "The enlightening beings who have successfully accomplished the requirements of the first stage and seek the second stage should activate ten mental dispositions: honesty, gentleness, capability, docility, tranquillity, goodness, non-defilement, nonattachment, broad-mindedness, and magnanimity. When these ten dispositions are operative, one is established in the second stage of enlightening beings, the stage of Purity.

"Enlightening beings in the stage of Purity naturally become imbued with ten virtuous ways of acting: they avoid taking life, they abandon weapons and hostility, they have conscience and sympathy and are compassionate and kind to all living beings, wishing for their welfare. They do not harm living beings even in their fantasies, much less injure other beings by gross physical harm with the conception of beings as such.

"The enlightening beings also abandon taking what is not given. They are satisfied with what they have and do not desire others' possessions. Thinking of things that belong to others as belonging to others, they do not give rise to any intention to steal and do not take even so much as a blade of grass or a leaf that is not given to them, much less take the necessities of life from others.

"The enlightening beings also abandon sexual misconduct. They are satisfied with their own spouses and do not desire the spouses of others. They do not give rise to desire for others' spouses, much less have sexual intercourse with them.

"The enlightening beings also abandon false speech, speaking truthfully, according to what is so, in a manner appropriate to the time, and acting accordingly. Even in dreams they do not speak falsehood with the intention to deceive by concealing what they see, believe, wish, intend, or desire; they do not tell lies even in dreams, much less consciously.

"The enlightening beings also abandon malicious talk and are not divisive or annoying to sentient beings. They do not gossip or tell tales here and there to cause division; they do not break up those who are together or increase the division of those already split. They do not enjoy disunion, do not delight in separation, and do not speak words that cause division, whether they are true or not.

"The enlightening beings also abandon coarse speech and give up speech that is out of place, crude, dirty, harsh to others, openly or covertly annoying to others, vulgar, worldly or impure, unpleasant to hear, provocative, irritating, outrageous, displeasing, disagreeable, unpleasant, destructive to self or others. Having given up such speech, the enlightening beings speak words that are unabrasive and gentle, agreeable, sweet, causing pleasure, delightful, beneficial, pure, pleasant to the ears, congenial, likable, elegant and clear, understandable, worth hearing, not mixed up, desirable to many people, liked by many people, pleasing to many people, agreeable to many people, enlightening, beneficial and pleasurable to all beings, mentally uplifting, purifying self and others.

"The enlightening beings also abandon useless speech; they speak prudently, in accord with time, truthfully, meaningfully, rightly, logically, instructively. They speak words with content, carefully considering and guarding their speech, in accord with the occasion, in well-regulated order, reflecting even before telling a joke, and never, of course, chattering at random.

"The enlightening beings also become free from covetousness, not even conceiving any craving for others' wealth, pleasures, enjoyments, goods, and possessions, much less desiring to possess what belongs to others; they do not seek or hope for or desire gain.

"The enlightening beings also become free from malevolence and anger; they are kind to all beings, desirous of their welfare, sympathetic, solicitous, loving, protective of all, attentive to what is good for them. Giving up everything of the nature of the blemish of anger, resentment, and unfriendliness, opposition, and attack inflamed by ill will and hostility, the enlightening beings are to reflect on what is beneficial, considering what is called for by kindness for the welfare and happiness of all beings.

"The enlightening beings also come to have right insight and follow the right Path. They give up divination and various misguided views, see rightly, do not practice deception, and set their minds on the Buddha, Teaching, and Community.

"As the enlightening beings constantly preserve these ten virtuous ways, they evoke this intent: 'Whatever ills, states of woe, and pitfalls beset sentient beings, all are caused by practicing nonvirtuous action, so I myself will abide in right action and also lead others to right action. Why? It is impossible to get others to abide in right action as long as one does not abide in right action oneself.'

"They also think thus: the realms of hells, animality, and ghosthood are established by the practice of bad ways of action, and the states from humanity up to the highest realm of existence are established by the practice of good ways of action. The ten ways of good action on a higher level practiced by wisdom, due to narrowness, fear of the world, lack of great compassion, and following the speech of another, develop the vehicle of hearers. Purified on a yet higher level, because of not being led by another, because of self-realization without following anyone, because of self-enlightenment without seeking from another, because of lack of great compassion and skill in means, and because of profound understanding of conditionality, they develop the vehicle of individual illuminates. Purified on an even higher level, by immeasurable broad-mindedness, sympathy and compassion, absorption of skill in means, undertaking of great vows, not abandoning sentient beings, and focus on the vast knowledge of buddhahood, they make for the breadth of practice to purify the stages of enlightening beings and the ways of transcendence. Purified on a yet higher level, they are conducive to the perfection of all characteristics of enlightenment, up to endowment with the ten powers and the full realization of all qualities of buddhahood. Therefore, by means of these ways of good action, having undertaken them all equally, effort should be made to accomplish the complete purification of all of their aspects.

"They also realize this: bad actions at their worst, when developed and done a lot, are the cause of hell; at a middling degree, they are the cause of animality; at their least they are the cause of the underworld. Taking life leads to hell, to animality, to the underworld, but if one is born human, it brings about two consequences: a short life and much sickness. Stealing leads to hell, to animality, to the underworld, but if one is born human, it brings about two consequences: material poverty and common possession of property. Sexual misconduct leads to hell, to animality, to the underworld, but if one is born human, it brings about two consequences: an unruly society and an unfaithful spouse. Lying leads to hell, to animality, to the underworld, but if one is born human it brings on two consequences: much slander and unreliability. Divisive talk leads to hell, to animality, to the underworld, but if one is born human it brings about two consequences: a broken home and a wretched family. Harsh talk leads to hell, to animality, to the underworld, but if one is born human it brings about two consequences: hearing what is displeasing, and argumentativeness. Confused, senseless talk leads to hell, to animality, to the underworld, but if one is born human it brings about two consequences: one's words will not be believed and one's speech will be unclear. Covetousness leads to hell, to animality, to the underworld, but then if one is born human it brings about two consequences: dissatisfaction and ambitiousness. Anger leads to hell, to animality, to the underworld, but then if one is born human it brings on two consequences: falling into bad views and becoming tricky and deceitful. Thus these ten bad ways of action tend to the formation of an immeasurably great mass of misery—so let us leave behind these ten bad ways of action and enjoy the delights of the garden of righteousness.

"Having abandoned these ten bad ways of action, they live by the ten good ways of action and also lead others to them. Even more do the enlightening beings arouse toward all sentient beings desire for their welfare and happiness, with kindness, sympathy, compassion, and desire to care for them and protect them, thinking of all beings as equal to themselves, thinking of them as examples and teachers.

"This is what the enlightening beings think: 'Alas, these beings have fallen into wrong views; their thinking and disposition of mind is wrong: traveling on erroneous paths, in the midst of entanglements, they should be set by us on the true way, the road of right insight, in accord with reality. Alas, these beings are at odds, argumentative, involved in disputes, always burning with anger and hatred—we should establish them in the exercise of unexcelled great kindness. Alas, these beings are insatiable, coveting others' goods, following bad ways of making a living— we should establish them in pure deed, word, thought, and livelihood. Unfortunately, these beings follow the motivations of lust, hatred, and delusion, are burned by the flames of various afflictions, and do not seek a means of final escape from them—we should lead them to nirvana, where all afflictions cease and there are no ills. Regrettably, these beings are veiled by the darkness and obscurity of delusion and covered by the darkness of ignorance; they have entered a vast tangle of darkness, have become far estranged from the realm of wisdom and fallen into a great darkness, entered a wilderness of erroneous views—we should clarify their eye of unobstructed wisdom, so they will know all things as they really are without being directed by another. Alas, these beings are traveling in the desert of routine existence; they are in trouble, uneasy, fallen into a great pitfall, facing a fall into the realms of hells, animality, or the underworld; they are ensnared in the dangerous net of false views, entangled in delusion; they have gone off on the wrong road, are blind, lack a guide, and think what is not salvation is salvation; bound by the rope of demons, they are taken in by the thieving sense objects, are without a good guide, and have entered a thicket of demonic dispositions, becoming far estranged from the enlightened mentality: we should save them from such hardships of the wasteland of the mundane whirl and should settle them in the city of fearlessness, the city of all knowledge, where there is no affliction or pain. These beings, unfortunately, are sunk in the waves of great torrents, plunged into the flows of desire, existence, ignorance, and views, swept along by the current of the mundane whirl, fallen into the river of craving, into a great rapids, unable to see objectively, going along the creepers of thoughts of lust, malice, and viciousness, caught by the demon of the view of real existence of the body, plunged into the swirling abyss of desire, into the midst of passion for enjoyment, cast up on the land of self-conceit, rotten inside with misconduct and bad behavior, unable to escape the danger of the village of the six senses, without anyone to rescue them, without a savior or protector, without a refuge: we should bring forth great compassion, virtue, and power, and set them on the jewel island of omniscience, free from troubles, free from passion, peaceful, happy, free from danger, beyond all fears. These beings are unfortunately locked up in much suffering, sadness, and irritation, in bonds of love and hate, like and dislike, in sadness and grief, in the fetters of craving, in the tangles of illusion, deceit, and ignorance, in the prison of the triple world: we should lead them to nirvana, detached from the triple world, the city of fearlessness, where all suffering ceases, free from obstruction. Alas, these beings are attached to self and possessions, unable to get out of clinging to the elements of body and mind, acting according to delusions, dwelling in the desolate village of the senses, attacked by the vipers of physical constituents, besieged by the murderous bandits of the body-mind clusters, experiencing immeasurable pain: we should bring them to supreme bliss, free from all attachments—that is, to nirvana void of all obstructions. It is a pity that the aspirations of these beings are base and narrow and they lack the will for highest omniscience; even if they want to escape, they think of the vehicles of those aiming for individual enlightenment and liberation alone—we should set them in the unexcelled Great Vehicle of universal salvation in accord with focus on the great resolution for supreme buddhahood and the perspicacity of omniscience.'

"Thus many buddhas come within the range of perception of the enlightening beings who are in accord with the sustaining power of morality, who have skillfully activated sympathy, compassion, and kindness, who are unsolicited good friends to all beings, who have not abandoned sentient beings, who skillfully accomplish what is to be done, who are stationed in the enlightening beings' stage of purity, by the enlightening beings' great vision and willpower: the enlightening beings perceive enormously many buddhas, many hundreds, thousands, millions, billions, trillions of buddhas, by their tremendous vision and the power of their vows. Having seen those buddhas, they honor and pay respect and homage to them with lofty intent, and provide them with the necessities—clothing, food and drink, bedding, and medicine; they also provide comforts for enlightening beings and pay respect to the religious community. They dedicate these roots of goodness to unexcelled perfect enlightenment. Also they attend those buddhas and respectfully learn from them the ten ways of virtuous action and never forget them as they have learned them; over countless eons rid of the defilements of envy and bad behavior, they therefore attain purity of generosity and morality.

"Just as gold becomes more and more free from all impurities when put in vitriol, so do enlightening beings in this stage of Purity, by virtue of riddance of the impurities of envy and bad behavior, accomplish purity of generosity and morality. Among the four means of salvation, kind speech is paramount in them; among the ten transcendent ways, morality is paramount. This does not mean they do not practice the rest—they do so as best they can, as is appropriate.

"This is a brief explanation of the second stage of enlightening beings, the stage of Purity. Many of the enlightening beings in this stage are sovereigns, lords of four continents and masters of the law, competent, powerful, able to rid beings of the impurities of bad behavior, to set them on the ten paths of virtuous conduct. Whatever acts the enlightening beings undertake, whether by way of giving, or kind speech, or beneficial action, or cooperation, all of it is done with no other thoughts in mind but thoughts of the Buddha, the Teaching, the Community, enlightening beings, the practices of enlightening beings, the ways of transcendence, the stages, the powers, the expertises, the unique qualities of buddhas, and all aspects of omniscience. Why? To become the best of beings, unexcelled leaders and guides, and ultimately omniscient refuges.

"Those who seek to be thus undertake the appropriate effort, by which they give up all comforts and go forth into the teaching of Buddha. Having gone forth, in a single instant they suddenly attain a thousand concentrations, see a thousand buddhas and recognize their power, shake a thousand worlds, go to a thousand fields, illumine a thousand worlds, mature a thousand beings, live for a thousand eons, penetrate a thousand eons past and future, contemplate a thousand teachings, and manifest a thousand bodies, each body manifesting a company of a thousand enlightening beings. Then enlightening beings with superior power of commitment, by the quality of excellence of vows, transform their bodies, auras, mystic powers, vision, spheres of operation, voices, conduct, adornments, power, resolutions, and performances in countless ways."

Then Diamond Matrix spoke these verses explaining the meaning of this stage:

> They are gentle, honest, mild, capable,
> Of goodwill, docile, unalloyed, unattached, of lofty awareness;
> With breadth of mind they enter the second stage.
>
> Here, they are bearers of virtue, imbued with good.
> Avoiding the taking of life, their minds are free from viciousness.
>
> They do not take what is not given or take others' spouses.
> They are truthful, do not slander, are not harsh in speech.
> They have no desire for others' possessions, are kind-hearted,
> Follow the right Path, and have no deceitful mind.
> With phantom bodies, beautifully adorned,
> They honor the Teacher and are always diligent.
>
> The pains of hells and animal realms,
> Punishment in the underworld, eternal burning and hunger,
> All are produced by evil doings;
> Rejecting them, let us arrive at truth.

From birth in the human realm as desired,
Up to the peak of existence, free from strife, with the bliss of
    meditation,
The vehicle of solitary illuminates, the vehicles of disciples and
    buddhas,
All come to exist from the ten paths of virtue.

Knowing this, enlightening beings are always diligent,
Firmly abiding by ethics and also inducing others to do so.
Furthermore, imbued with compassion,
Knowing beings are suffering, they give rise to sympathy.

"Fallen into wrong views are these ignorant ones,
With minds quick to anger, hate, and argue,
Always unsatisfied, seeking objects ever more—
These beings motivated by desire, hatred, and delusion should be
    liberated.

"They are covered by a great darkness, plunged into delusion,
On a bad road in a wilderness, in a great net of views;
In the cage of mundane life, enemies attack them—
We should liberate those in the cage of the devil.

"Taken by the waves of afflictions, sunk in the torrents,
They are tormented by a hundred miseries in the triple world,
Wrapped up in the clusters, thinking of them as self—
For their sake we strive, to release them from pain.

"Having given up this supreme vehicle of buddhahood,
Though they aim for escape, their aspiration is low;
We will establish them in the undefiled knowledge of the
    enlightened."
Thus enlightening beings arouse incomparable vigor in the cause
    of enlightenment.

In this stage the great sages, having gathered hundreds of virtues,
See many buddhas and honor them with offerings.
Their virtue is burnished the more for countless eons,
Like gold plunged into vitriol.

Here enlightening beings become monarchs,
Leading sentient beings by the ten virtues:
By all the virtue they have amassed,
They will to become saviors of the world, rich in the ten powers.

Willfully giving up the pleasures of kingship,
Gone forth into the supreme Teaching, steadfast,
Full of vigor, they attain supreme concentration
And instantly see a thousand buddhas.

The enlightening beings in this stage also display
Many spiritual powers, of such worthy intentions;
Beyond this, imbued with the power of vows and knowledge,
They guide beings with many kinds of miracles.

"Thus has been explained the second stage, exalted, of enlightening beings, who work for the weal of all worlds."

Having thus heard of the supreme stages of practice in the sphere of enlightening beings, inconceivable, the enlightening beings in the audience, delighted, scattered multitudes of flowers from the sky, saying, "Excellent! Well have you explained, out of compassion for all beings, the body of conduct of the wise, the sphere of the second of the highest stages. Truthfully, without falsehood or change, have you explained the delightful practice of enlightening beings, with supreme clarity, for the welfare and happiness of all beings. Go on to speak of the third of the most excellent stages—let this superlative realm be told of as it is, linked with true knowledge and action. Tell of the path of the conduct of the Victorious, the practice of charity and morality of the sages, patience, energy, tranquillity, wisdom, skillfulness, supreme kindness, and compassion—tell all, omitting naught."

Moon of Liberation said, "O Diamond Matrix, tell of the disposition of those who approach the third stage."

Diamond Matrix said, "The enlightening beings who have thoroughly purified the mind in the second stage come to the third stage. One enters the third stage by ten conscious focusings of the mind: purity, stability, disillusion, dispassion, nonregression, steadfastness, ardor, tirelessness, high-mindedness, and magnanimity. By consciously focusing the mind on these ten things, one enters the third stage.

"Furthermore, the enlightening beings in this third stage examine the impermanence of all that is conditioned, as it truly is; and they examine the painfulness, impurity, unreliability, destructibility, instability, instantaneous arising and passing away, not-coming-to-be-previously, not-reaching-the-past, and nonperdurance in the present of all that is conditioned. Seeing all conditioned things in this way, the enlightening beings, seeing themselves without refuge, without protection, in grief, sadness, distress, bound by likes and dislikes, with much suffering, dejection, and turmoil, without resources, burned by the fires of lust, hatred, and delusion, filled with many diseases, cause their minds to be more and more liberated from all conditioned things and direct their minds toward enlightened knowledge. The enlightening beings also recognize the inconceivability of enlightened knowledge and recognize its incomparability, its immeasurability, its difficulty of access, its independence, its freedom from afflictions, its freedom from distress, and how it arrives at the city of fearlessness and never comes back from it, and how it saves many people.

"Thus observing the immeasurability of enlightened knowledge, and observing how full of ills all conditioned states are, the enlightening beings further develop ten feelings toward sentient beings: the feeling that they are without a leader or a refuge; the feeling that they are always destitute; the feeling that they are burned by the fire of passion, hostility, and folly; the feeling that they are locked in the prison of existence; the feeling that they are always veiled in sleep in the thickets of afflictions; the feeling that they are incapable of viewing things objectively; the feeling that they have abandoned the desire for good; the feeling that they have lost the way to enlightenment; the feeling that they go along with the flow of the mundane whirl; the feeling that they have lost the means to liberation.

"Seeing the world of sentient beings so full of afflictions, the enlightening beings arouse their energy, thinking, 'I should rescue and liberate these beings; I should purify and emancipate them; I should lead them, direct them, make them happy, develop them, and cause them to reach perfect peace.'

"Thus disillusioned with all conditioned things, considerate toward all sentient beings, seeing the benefit in omniscience, taking refuge in enlightened knowledge, dedicated to the salvation of all beings, the enlightening beings reflect thus: 'By what means can these beings, fallen as they are into so much misery, be lifted out of it and established in the ultimate bliss of nirvana and be caused to attain freedom from doubt about all things?' It occurs to these enlightening beings, 'The means to do this is nowhere else but in the realm of knowledge of unobstructed liberation; and the knowledge of unobstructed liberation is nowhere else but in awareness of all things as they are; and awareness of all things as they are is nowhere else but in transcendent knowledge of the unconditioned and unproduced; and that light of knowledge is nowhere else but in contemplation by the analytic intellect skilled in meditation; and that contemplation by the analytic intellect skilled in meditation is nowhere else but in skill in learning.'

"The enlightening beings thus apply this contemplative knowledge to the quest of the Buddha Way, day and night intent on hearing the Teaching, desirous of the Teaching, enjoying the Teaching, delighted in the Teaching, relying on the Teaching, devoted to the Teaching, concentrated on the Teaching, intent on the Teaching, taking refuge in the Teaching, dwelling on the Teaching, saved by the Teaching, acting in accord with the Teaching.

"While the enlightening beings are thus focused on the quest for the Buddha Way, there is nothing they do not give up—goods, supplies, dwelling, precious things, even their own bodies—and because of their desire for truth they do not consider this difficult to do; they only consider it difficult to find a person who utters the truth, who teaches even a single phrase of truth. For the sake of the Buddha Teaching there is no external thing whatsoever that they are attached to that they do not give up, and there is nothing whatsoever within themselves that they do not give up. There is no service to teachers they do not take on; there is no pride or conceit they do not abandon and no humility of action they do not accept; there is no physical suffering they do not bear. They are more glad to hear a single verse of the Teaching that they have not heard than they would be to get a galaxy full of jewels; they are more glad to hear a well-spoken verse than they would be to gain kingship; they are more glad to hear a new phrase of teaching spoken by a complete buddha purifying enlightening practice than they would be to attain godhood for many hundreds of thousands of eons. If someone should declare to the enlightening beings, 'I too have a phrase of teaching spoken by a perfectly enlightened buddha that purifies the practice of enlightening beings, which I will tell you if you throw yourself in a great blazing pit of fire and endure the agony,' the enlightening beings think, 'For the sake of even a single phrase of teaching spoken by a completely enlightened buddha I could even bear to hurl myself from the heavens into a whole galaxy of fire, to say nothing of an ordinary pit of fire. Indeed, we should seek the Buddha Teaching even through all the afflictions and pains of hells, to say nothing of the pains of life in the human world.' They seek the teachings with such heroic vigor as this; and they contemplate the teachings truthfully as they hear them. Furthermore, having heard these teachings, with profound meditation in their own minds, alone in solitary places, they think, 'It is by realization and practice of the Teaching through appropriate methods that these doctrines of Buddha are to be followed—they cannot be clarified just by talk.'

"Enlightening beings in this stage of Refulgence leave desires and evil and unwholesome things for the sake of realization of the Teaching and its practical application: with thought and reflection, becoming aloof, joyful and blissful, they attain the first stage of meditation and abide there. By cessation of thought and reflection, inner purity, and mastery of single-mindedness, free from thought and cogitation, concentrated, joyful and blissful, they attain and abide in the second stage of meditation. By freedom from desire for joy they abide in equanimity; with mindfulness and precise knowledge, they experience physical bliss: as the sages say, those who are dispassionate, mindful, blissful, and detached from joy attain to and abide in the third stage of meditation. By the abandonment of pleasure and pain, and by the disappearance of former joy and dejection, free from both pleasure and pain, equanimous, with pure mindfulness, they attain to and abide in the fourth stage of meditation.

"By transcendence of all perceptions of form, by disappearance of all perceptions of objects, by not placing the attention on various perceptions, they attain to and abide in the realm of infinity of space, aware of infinite space. Totally transcending the realm of infinity of space, they attain to and abide in the realm of infinity of consciousness, aware of boundless consciousness. By totally transcending the realm of infinity of consciousness, they attain to and abide in the realm of nothingness, aware of the absence of anything at all. Totally transcending the realm of nothingness, they attain to and abide in the realm of neither perception nor nonperception. This is done on a basis not of enjoyment, but only for the purpose of accomplishment of practical application of the Teaching.

"With minds imbued with kindness, broad-minded, magnanimous, nondualistic, immeasurable, free from hostility and enmity, unobstructed, unafflicted, extending everywhere, they travel to the farthest reaches of the cosmos, reaching all worlds throughout space. In the same way, with minds imbued with compassion, joy, and equanimity, broad-minded, magnanimous, nondualistic, without hostility or enmity, without obstruction or affliction, reaching everywhere, they roam throughout the cosmos, to all worlds in space. They experience many kinds of miraculous actions, even shaking the earth; being one, they become multiple, and having become multiple, they become one; they are able to appear and disappear; they go through walls and even through mountains, just as through space; they travel sitting through the sky like birds; they emerge from and sink into the earth unhindered as though in water, and walk on water as on earth; they produce smoke and flames like a great bonfire and emit water from their bodies like great clouds, by which torrents this world system, set ablaze, is annihilated; even the sun and moon here, powerful and mighty, they take in hand, and extend their power even up to the heaven of Brahma; by the divine ear, purified, beyond humans, they hear both celestial and human voices, whether soft or loud, far or near, hearing even the sounds of insects; they know the minds of other beings, other persons, as they really are—they know if they are covetous or desireless, if they are hateful or not, if they are deluded or not, if they are afflicted or not, if they are small-minded or broad-minded, if they are magnanimous, if they are beyond measure, if they are confused or not, if they are concentrated or not, if they are liberated or not, if they are defiled or not, if their minds are crude or not—all this they know as it really is; in this way they know the minds of other people as they really are. They remember many former abodes: they remember one lifetime, two, three, four, five, ten, one hundred, two hundred, three hundred, four hundred, five hundred—they remember hundreds of lifetimes, many hundreds of lifetimes, many thousands of lifetimes, many hundreds of thousands of lifetimes, many hundreds of thousands of billions of trillions of lifetimes; they remember the age of becoming, the age of disintegration, the age of becoming and disintegration, and remember many ages of becoming and disintegration, hundreds of ages, thousands of ages, hundreds of thousands of ages, hundreds of millions of ages, hundreds of billions of ages, up to hundreds of billions of trillions of ages—they know, 'I was in such and such a place named such and such, of such and such a family, of such and such a caste, with such and such a diet, with such and such a life span, abiding so long, experiencing such and such pleasures and pains; I died there and was born here, died here and was born there'—they know many kinds of former abodes, including their characteristics, appearances, and speech there. With the divine eye, purified, beyond that of humans, they see beings, dying, being born, of good character, of bad character, in good states, in bad states, inferior, superior, following the force of their deeds; they know beings as they truly are: 'These beings are badly behaved in thought, word, and eed, they slander the sages, they entertain false views; owing to the pursuit of actions based on false views, by that cause, that condition, after the disintegration of the body and death they fall into states of woe and are born in hells. These other beings are virtuous in thought, word, and deed, they do not slander the sages, they see rightly; because of their deeds and undertaking of duty based on right views, after they die they are born in blissful states in heavens.' Thus, by the divine eye, purified, beyond that of humans, they see beings, their characteristics, appearances, and speech, dying, being born, of good and bad appearance and character, in good or bad states, inferior and superior, according to their deeds—they know them as they truly are. They enter and arise from these meditations, liberations, concentrations, and attainments, without being born by their force. If they see somewhere where the elements of enlightenment may be fulfilled, they are purposely born there by willpower because such is the mental consistency of enlightening beings, having accomplished skill in means.

"The enlightening beings in this stage of Refulgence see many buddhas, by great vision and the power of will—they see many hundreds of buddhas, many hundreds of thousands, millions, billions, trillions of buddhas, by great vision and willpower. Having seen those buddhas, those completely enlightened ones, they honor and make offerings to them with great earnestness, providing them with food, clothing, medicines, and seats and beds. They also provide comforts for enlightening beings and honor the religious community. They dedicate these roots of goodness to consummate enlightenment. They also attend those buddhas, respectfully listen to their teachings, take up and maintain the teachings, cause them to be repeated, and apply and practice them according to their ability. They observe the absence of process and nonextinction and conditionality of all things; all their bonds of desire become weaker, all their bonds to form, all their bonds to existence, all their bonds of ignorance become weaker, and their bonds caused by views have already been removed. Wrong desires are gone from the enlightening beings in the stage of Refulgence because of countless eons of nonaccumulation, and so are wrong hatred and misguided delusions, because they do not produce or accumulate them. Their roots of goodness become clarified, purified, and useful. Just as gold in the hands of a skillful smith remains the same weight, in the same way the wrong desire, hatred, and delusion are gone from the enlightening beings in the stage of Refulgence, not being accumulated for countless ages, while their roots of goodness become clarified and purified and useful.

"Furthermore, their patience and gentleness are purified, as well as their friendliness, freedom from anger, imperturbability, calmness, freedom from pride and self-abasement, freedom from desire to be honored, freedom from desire for reward for what they do, honesty, and nonentanglement— all these are purified. For them, among the four means of salvation, beneficial action is paramount, and among the ten transcendent ways, transcendent tolerance is paramount, while they practice the others according to their power.

"This is a summary of the third stage of enlightening beings, the stage of Refulgence. The majority of the enlightening beings in this stage are Indras, chiefs of the celestial beings of the thirty-three heavens, capable, powerful, providing means of detaching beings from lust and desire, skilled in extricating beings from the mud of desire. Whatever the enlightening beings do—whether by charity, kind speech, beneficial action, or cooperation—their thoughts are always fixed on Buddha, the Teaching, the Community, enlightening beings, the practices of enlightening beings, the transcendent ways, the stages, the expertises and unique qualities of buddhas, including complete omniscience. To what purpose? To become the best of beings, unexcelled leaders and guides, and ultimately omniscient refuges.

"Those who seek to be thus undertake the appropriate effort, by which they instantly attain a hundred thousand concentrations, see a hundred thousand buddhas and recognize their power, shake a hundred thousand worlds, go to a hundred thousand lands, illumine a hundred thousand worlds, mature a hundred thousand beings, live for a hundred thousand eons, penetrate a hundred thousand eons past and future, contemplate a hundred thousand teachings, and manifest a hundred thousand bodies, each body accompanied by a hundred thousand enlightening beings. Then enlightening beings with the power of vows perform, by the excellence of their vows, countless transformations of their bodies, auras, mystic powers, vision, spheres of operation, voices, conduct, adornments, power, resolutions, and performances."

Then Diamond Matrix spoke these verses explaining the meaning of this stage:

With pure minds, full of virtue, keen of mind,
Dispassionate and unregressing,
Steadfast, ardent, firm, energetic, magnanimous,
They enter the third stage.

In the third stage, Refulgence, they contemplate
The principle of suffering, impermanence, impurity,
Dissolution, evanescence, momentariness, inefficiency,
And absence of coming and going, of all that is conditioned.

They see the conditioned as sickness, accompanied by grief and
    lament,
Affliction, bound by attraction and aversion,
An abode of suffering and unhappiness, like blazing fire,
All this endlessly arising together.

Disillusioned with all states of being, unattached,
Single-mindedly seeking enlightened knowledge,
They see the knowledge of buddhas as inconceivable,
Unthinkable, incomparable, free from affliction.

Seeing buddha-knowledge free from all ills,
They pity those who are helpless, forever destitute,
Burned by the fires of passion and folly,
Minds bound by a hundred miseries in hellish existences.

They undertake steadfast effort to save those veiled in afflictions,
Those who are without insight, who have little will,
Who are deprived of the jewel of the way of enlightenment,
Following the flow of the mundane whirl, afraid of liberation.

Seeking knowledge, unattached, acting for the sake of the world,
They consider how the liberation of the world may be caused—
It is nowhere but in the unobstructed knowledge of the
    enlightened,
And the endless knowledge of Buddhas is born of wisdom.

Reflecting that wisdom comes from learning,
Enlightening beings strive diligently as learners;
Day and night, in the cause of learning, doing nothing else,
They seek the truth as the ultimate goal.

Collections of jewels and pearls, beloved relatives,
Sovereignty, endless kinds of cities and fine abodes,
Spouses and children, agreeable companions—
All they relinquish without attachment for the sake of truth.

Head, hands, feet, eyes, flesh, tongue, teeth, ears,
Heart, blood, bones, marrow,
They gladly give away, not considering it hard,
Only considering it hard to get to hear the truth.

If someone should tell them
He would give a jewel of the Buddha's teaching
To anyone who would jump into a blazing fire,
They would jump in without anxiety.

For a single phrase of the Teaching they would leap
From the heavens into a galaxy of fire:
How hard is this supreme enlightenment of buddhas to attain,
That is gained by such human suffering?

They would endure the unremitting pains of hell
For as long as it takes to attain the knowledge of the seers,
To say nothing of the mass of pain of the human world—
They will accept pain for the sake of the supreme Teaching.

And having heard the Teaching, they think about it reasonably
And accomplish the four meditations, immeasurable minds,
Formless trances, and five supreme mystic knowledges,
But, having mastered them, are not born under their sway.

Here the bearers of virtue pay honor to myriad buddhas
And with doubt-free minds listen to the Teaching;
In this stage they become free from error, purified,
Like gold freed from dross, undiminished.

Here the virtuous ones undertake celestial lordship,
Powerful, free from lust,
Making manifold groups of people virtuous and dispassionate,
Intent on seeking the qualities of buddhahood.

Here enlightening beings undertake vigorous effort;
Having attained a full hundred thousand concentrations,
They see buddhas' bodies' various eminent characteristics,
And infinitely more qualities, by superlative will.

"This has been an explanation of the third stage of enlightening beings, who seek benefit for all people."

Thus having heard of this far-reaching practice, this lofty, eminent stage, the enlightening beings were delighted and showered the Buddha with flowers. When this teaching was spoken, the oceans and earth trembled; beautiful devoted goddesses reveled in the Teaching in song, while the gods, overjoyed, showered heavenly jewels on the Buddha and said, "A victor who speaks beneficially has arisen, having reached the ultimate weal and virtue. We have now heard of the superlative way, the supreme conduct of enlightening beings, the stage of the wise, which is hard to get to hear of even in a hundred eons. Speak further, O sage, for the benefit of heaven and earth, of the excellent practice of enlightening beings. This crowd of celestials wants to hear the definitive, exhaustive truth."

Moon of Liberation said to Diamond Matrix, "Heroic speaker, tell the enlightening beings of the exalted state of those who enter the fourth stage."

Diamond Matrix said, "Whoever has thoroughly purified vision in the third stage enters the fourth stage. One attains this stage by ten entries into the light of the Teaching: by entry into the light through contemplation of the realms of beings; by entry into the light through contemplation of the realms of the world; by entry into the light through contemplation of the realms of phenomena and principles; by entry into the light through contemplation of the realm of space; by entry into the light through contemplation of the realm of consciousness; by entry into the light through contemplation of the realm of desire; by entry into the light through contemplation of the realm of form; by entry into the light through contemplation of the realm of formlessness; by entry into the light through contemplation of the realm of high-minded devotion; and by entry into the light through contemplation of the realm of inclinations of the magnanimous mind.

"Here, in this fourth stage, called Blazing, simultaneous with the attainment of this stage the enlightening beings are born in the family of buddhas, so as to attain the qualities proper to it by means of ten things that develop and mature knowledge: by nonregressing will; by ultimate unbreakable faith in the three treasures; by contemplation of the origination and extinction of conditioned things; by contemplation of the non-origination of inherent nature; by contemplation of the formation and disintegration of worlds; by contemplation of coming into existence due to actions; by contemplation of the mundane whirl and nirvana; by contemplation of actions of beings and lands; by contemplation of past and future; and by contemplation of nonbeing and nonannihilation. Having embodied these ten things that mature knowledge, enlightening beings are born in the family of buddhas by attainment of the principles that are proper to it.

"Furthermore, the enlightening beings in this Blazing stage carry on examination of the inner body vigorously, with precise awareness and mindfulness, getting rid of worldly desire and dejection. They carry on examination of the external body vigorously, with precise awareness and mindfulness, getting rid of worldly desire and dejection. They do the same to internal sensation, external sensation, and internal and external sensation, to the internal mind, the external mind, and the internal and external mind. They carry on examination of internal phenomena, precisely aware and mindful, getting rid of worldly desire and dejection. They carry on examination of external phenomena, precisely aware and mindful, getting rid of worldly desire and dejection. They carry on examination of internal and external phenomena, precisely aware and mindful, getting rid of worldly desire and dejection.

"The enlightening beings will and strive for the nonarising of bad and unwholesome states that have not yet arisen; they initiate vigorous effort, commanding the mind and directing it properly. They will and strive for the destruction of bad and unwholesome states that have arisen, initiating vigorous effort, commanding the mind and directing it properly. They will and strive for the arising of good states that have not yet arisen, initiating vigorous effort, commanding the mind and directing it properly. They will and strive for the stabilization, prevention of loss, augmentation, increased production and cultivation, and complete fulfillment of good states that have already arisen, initiating vigorous effort, commanding the mind and directing it properly.

"They develop the basis of mystical power of will combined with concentration and exertion, based on detachment, based on dispassion, based on extinction, given to relinquishment. They develop the basis of mystical power of energy combined with concentration and exertion, based on detachment, based on dispassion, based on extinction, given to relinquishment. They develop the basis of mystical power of attention combined with concentration and exertion, based on detachment, based on dispassion, based on extinction, given to relinquishment. They develop the basis of mystical power of contemplation combined with concentration and exertion, based on detachment, based on dispassion, based on extinction, given to relinquishment.

"They develop the faculty of faith, based on detachment, based on dispassion, based on extinction, given to relinquishment. They develop the faculty of energy, based on detachment, based on dispassion, based on extinction, given to relinquishment. They develop the faculty of recollection, based on detachment, based on dispassion, based on extinction, given to relinquishment. They develop the faculty of concentration, based on detachment, based on dispassion, based on extinction, given to relinquishment. They develop the faculty of wisdom, based on detachment, based on dispassion, based on extinction, given to relinquishment.

"They develop the power of faith, based on detachment, based on dispassion, based on extinction, given to relinquishment. They develop the power of energy, based on detachment, based on dispassion, based on extinction, given to relinquishment. They develop the power of recollection, based on detachment, based on dispassion, based on extinction, given to relinquishment. They develop the power of concentration, based on detachment, based on dispassion, based on extinction, given to relinquishment. They develop the power of wisdom, based on detachment, based on dispassion, based on extinction, given to relinquishment.

"They develop the branch of enlightenment of mindfulness, based on detachment, based on dispassion, based on extinction, given to relinquishment. They develop the branch of enlightenment of investigation of things, based on detachment, based on dispassion, based on extinction, given to relinquishment. They develop the branch of enlightenment of energy, based on detachment, based on dispassion, based on extinction, given to relinquishment. They develop the branch of enlightenment of joy, based on detachment, based on dispassion, based on extinction, given to relinquishment. They develop the branch of enlightenment of tranquillity, based on detachment, based on dispassion, based on extinction, given to relinquishment. They develop the branch of enlightenment of concentration, based on detachment, based on dispassion, based on extinction, given to relinquishment. They develop the limb of enlightenment of equanimity, based on detachment, based on dispassion, based on extinction, given to relinquishment.

"They develop right thought, based on detachment, based on dispassion, based on extinction, given to relinquishment. They develop right seeing, based on detachment, based on dispassion, based on extinction, given to relinquishment. They develop right speech, based on detachment, based on dispassion, based on extinction, given to relinquishment. They develop right action, based on detachment, based on dispassion, based on extinction, given to relinquishment. They develop right livelihood, based on detachment, based on dispassion, based on extinction, given to relinquishment. They develop right effort, based on detachment, based on dispassion, based on extinction, given to relinquishment. They develop right mindfulness, based on detachment, based on dispassion, based on extinction, given to relinquishment. They develop right concentration, based on detachment, based on dispassion, based on extinction, given to relinquishment.

"Furthermore, all this is due to concern for all beings, due to the support of carrying out past vows, due to being led by great compassion, due to realization of great kindness, due to being principally focused on omniscience, due to being engaged in the full accomplishment of the powers, expertise, unique qualities, marks, embellishments, and voice of all enlightened ones, due to being in quest of the final supreme truth, due to following what is learned of the liberation of the profound teaching of buddhas, and due to reflection on the great power of skill in liberative means.

"Moreover, the enlightening beings in the stage of Blazing are freed from all points of attachment—to what is considered wealth, what is considered one's own possessions, what is guarded and kept, what is thought of, what is ruminated on, what is conceived of, appearing and disappearing, aroused by attachment to the ideas of a real body, self, being, life, growth, person, personality, mental and physical clusters, elements, and sense mediums. Whatever acts should not be done, are disapproved by perfect buddhas, and provoke affliction, the enlightening beings get rid of; whatever acts should be done, are approved by perfect buddhas, and are appropriate for provisions for the Path of enlightenment, these the enlightening beings take on.

"As the enlightening beings increasingly develop the elements of the Path accomplished by skill in means and wisdom for the attainment of the Path, their minds accordingly become gentle, mild, workable, and altruistic, unafflicted, seeking the final ultimate excellence, seeking higher knowledge, liberating all beings, obeying and respecting their teachers, practicing the teachings as they have learned. They also become grateful and appreciative of what has been done for them, and they become extremely courageous, easy to live with, honest, gentle, uncomplicated, undeluded, free from conceit, easy to talk to, skillfull in grasping the speaker's meaning. Thus the enlightening beings attain patience, self-control, and tranquillity.

"Thus patient, controlled, and calm, they contemplate the elements of the Path to purify the higher stages with unremitting vigor, unafflicted vigor, unregressing vigor, immense vigor, endless vigor, blazing vigor, unequaled vigor, invincible vigor, vigor in developing all beings to maturity, vigor in discerning what is instructive and what is not. And their mentality becomes more and more purified, their prevailing will doesn't die out, and their element of zeal blazes; great roots of goodness are produced, and they accomplish destruction of worldly defilements. All their doubts and uncertainties are cut off, and they accomplish presence of mind free from doubt. They also attain joy and serenity. They come into the presence of the power of the enlightened and attain immeasurable will.

"To the enlightening beings in this stage of Blazing, many buddhas become visible, by great vision and willpower: many hundreds of buddhas, many thousands of buddhas, many hundreds of thousands of buddhas, many millions of buddhas, many hundreds of millions of buddhas, many billions of buddhas, many trillions of buddhas become visible to the enlightening beings by great vision and willpower. Having seen those enlightened ones, they honor and make offerings to them with great zeal, providing useful items such as clothing, food and drink, bedding, seat cushions, and medicines; they also provide comforts for enlightening beings and pay honor to the religious community. These roots of goodness they dedicate to unexcelled complete perfect enlightenment.

"Also they attend those buddhas and respectfully listen to their teachings, taking them up, remembering them, and putting them into practice to the best of their ability. In many cases the enlightening beings go forth from home into the tutelage of those buddhas. Their will, purpose, devotion, and equanimity are further purified. In this stage of blazing the enlightening beings abide in purity of will, purpose, devotion, and equanimity for many eons, many hundreds and thousands and millions and billions and trillions of eons, and their roots of goodness become radiant with extreme clarity. Just as gold fashioned by a skilled goldsmith into ornaments cannot be outshone by gold that has not been worked, in the same way the roots of goodness of enlightening beings in the stage of Blazing cannot be outshone by the roots of goodness in the lower stages.

And just as the light produced from a jewel, light emanating from a sphere of completely pure radiance, cannot be outshone by other pure lights produced from jewels, and the light cannot be destroyed by any wind, water, or rain, in the same way the enlightening beings in this stage of Blazing cannot be outshone by enlightening beings in the lower stages, and their knowledge cannot be destroyed by the actions of any demons or afflictions.

"Of the four means of salvation, cooperation is predominant in these enlightening beings, and among the ten transcendent ways, energy is predominant—nonetheless they do practice the others as best they can.

"This is a summary of the fourth stage of enlightening beings, the stage called Blazing. Most of the enlightening beings in this stage are celestial sovereigns of the heaven of timely portion, powerful, able to remove beings' view of a really existent body and establish them in right insight. Whatever actions the enlightening beings in this stage undertake, whether by giving, by kind speech, by beneficial action, or by cooperation, it is never apart from thoughts of Buddha, the Teaching, the Community, enlightening beings, the practices of enlightening beings, the ways of transcendence, the powers, expertise, and unique qualities of buddhas, up to omniscience consummate in all respects. Why? To become the best of beings, unexcelled leaders and guides, and ultimately omniscient refuges.

"Those who seek to be thus undertake the appropriate effort, by which they instantly attain a billion concentrations, see a billion buddhas and recognize their power, shake a billion worlds, go to a billion lands, illumine a billion worlds, mature a billion beings, abide for a billion eons, penetrate a billion eons past and future, contemplate a billion teachings, and manifest a billion bodies, each surrounded by a billion enlightening beings. Then enlightening beings with the power of vows, by the excellence of their vows, perform countless transformations of the body, aura, mystic powers, sphere of operation, voice, conduct, adornment, power, resolution, and performances."

Then Diamond Matrix spoke these verses describing the meaning of this stage:

Those who have accomplished the third stage, Refulgence,
Contemplating the deeds of beings, the world, and phenomena,
With purity of resolution and will, they enter
The realm of space, the realm of mind, and the triple realm.

As soon as those of great power attain the stage of Blazing,
They are born in the family of the Teacher, never to regress,
Inseparable from the Buddha, the Teaching, and the Community,
Viewing the inertness of the continuum of birth and death.

Reflecting on the coming into existence of action that causes the
world to develop,

On cyclic existence, nirvana, lands, and beings,
As well as phenomena, past and future, nonextinction and
    nonorigination,
They grow in the family of the Teacher, acting in accord.

Having realized these principles, kind and compassionate,
They contemplate the phenomena of their bodies and minds;
They contemplate the inner, outer, and both,
Reflecting on the four points of mindfulness, free from
    attachment.

From the destruction of evil, having developed good qualities,
They actualize the four right efforts:
They develop the four bases of mystic powers, the powers and
    faculties,
The light of the jewels of the limbs of enlightenment, and thus
    the supreme Path.

They develop these for the benefit of beings, focusing their minds
    on this,
Their vow supporting them, with compassion foremost,
Seeking omniscient knowledge, the field of buddhas,
Thinking of supreme power and the highest path.

Steadfast in seeking also the unshakable state of wisdom
And the supreme buddha-voice of the Teacher,
The jewel of the profound path and the abode of liberation,
They develop great means.

Free from the view of a real body and from all erroneous views,.
Free from ego and possession, from living and gaining,
In this fourth stage the defilement of attachment
To the clusters, sense mediums, and elements is removed.

Whatever actions are condemned by buddhas
As being conducive to affliction and not beneficial
These enlightening beings abandon and with purified intent
Undertake good deeds for the benefit of the world.

They become gentle in mind,
Careful, mild, genial, honest, kind, easy to live with;
Unafflicted, they seek the highest path in quest of supreme
    knowledge,
Acting for the benefit of the world.

Respectfully approaching the worthy, wishing to learn,
They are grateful, easy to teach, not hypocritical.
Free from pride and guile, equanimous and courageous,
They arouse nonregressing vigor in cultivation.

Those established in the splendor of this stage
Have their minds set on pure truth;
Their zeal blazes, they increase good qualities—
All defilement, impurity, heedlessness, and doubt vanish.

The enlightening beings here, the best of people,
Pay respect to billions of buddhas, hear their teaching,
And detach from the world to enter it,
Impossible to spoil, like ornaments of gold.

The virtuous state of mind, knowledge, expedient practice,
And the path of purification of the sages in this stage
Cannot be turned back even by billions of demons,
Just as the radiance of jewels cannot be leached away by rainwater.

Those in this stage, worthy of human and celestial respect,
Become lords of the heaven of timely portion, carrying out
    celestial justice;
They withdraw beings from the tangle of views and accumulate
    good
For the sake of enlightened knowledge.

Full of vigor, they see a billion buddhas,
Due to concentration, single-minded:
After that for many eons they carry out beneficial actions,
Supreme undertakings characterized by knowledge.

"Children of Buddha, I have explained this fourth stage of enlightening beings, called Blazing, which is pure and involves the immaculate conduct of those with virtue and knowledge."

Having thus heard the practice of this excellent stage of the wise, the enlightening beings were pleased, delighted by the teaching. Uplifted, they showered a rain of flowers in the sky, saying, "Well have you spoken, great enlightening one!" The king of gods, with a group of celestials, stood in the sky to honor the Buddha, their minds elevated: delighted, happy, they made clouds of various glows for the Buddha, with pleasing lights. Goddesses in concert sang and played music to offer to the Teacher; manifesting such power of enlightening beings, they spoke these words:

At long last is the will of the Sage fulfilled;
At long last has the Victor attained the emancipation of
    enlightenment.
At long last is Shakyamuni seen in the celestial city,
Having accomplished human and divine weal.

At long last are the waters of the ocean stirred,
At long last is the pure light of the Victor released;

At long last do suffering beings become happy,
At long last is the Teaching of the Compassionate One heard.

At long last is the great Sage met
Who has attained the consummation of all virtues,
Having destroyed the darkness of conceit and heedlessness,
The great mendicant, worthy, respected.

Those who have honored him are gone to heaven,
Enjoying many kinds of happiness;
Those who have honored him put an end to all suffering
And gain supreme knowledge.

The Victor is pure as space,
Undefiled by the world, like a lotus in water,
Like the polar mountain rising from the sea—
So honor the Buddha glad in mind.

Then the wise one Moon of Liberation said to Diamond Matrix, "Please tell us the characteristics of the fifth stage."

Diamond Matrix said, "Whoever has fulfilled the path of the fourth stage enters the fifth stage; one enters the fifth stage by tenfold impartiality with purity as the focus of the mind: by impartiality of focus on the purity of the teachings of past buddhas, by impartiality of focus on the purity of the teachings of future buddhas, by impartiality of focus on the purity of the teachings of present buddhas, by impartiality of focus on purity of conduct, by impartiality of focus on purity of mind, by impartiality of focus on purity of removal of views and doubt and uncertainty and perplexity, by impartiality of focus on purity of knowledge of right and wrong paths, by impartiality of focus on purity of knowledge of application and relinquishment, by impartiality of focus on purity of the final ultimate discernment and realization of all the elements of enlightenment, and by impartiality of focus on purity of perfecting all beings.

"Furthermore, the enlightening beings who have reached the fifth stage, from having cultivated these elements of enlightenment and branches of the path, and from having thoroughly purified their intent—practicing what is needed for the quest for a higher path in the future, being supported by the power of vows, compassionately and kindly not abandoning beings, accumulating provisions of virtue and knowledge, never ceasing, putting skill in means into operation, seeing the light of the later stages, seeking the power of the Buddha, being supported by the power of intellect and action and awareness and recollection—attain unwavering attention; and doing so, they accurately know as it really is what the truth of suffering recognized by sages is, what the truth of the cause of suffering is, what the extinction of suffering is, and what the truth of its attainment is. They become well versed in conventional truth, in ultimate truth, in the truth of characteristics, the truth of distinctions, the truth of structure, the truth of substance, the truth of becoming, the truth of knowledge of extinction and nonorigination, the truth of entry into knowledge of the path; and by having accomplished the continuity of accession to the stages of enlightening beings, they become well versed in the truth of the accumulation of the knowledge of the enlightened.

"They know the conventional truth from satisfying other beings according to their inclinations. They know the ultimate truth by comprehending all in one principle. They know the truth of characteristics from awareness of individual and common characteristics. They know the truth of differentiation from learning the definitions of differentiations in the Teaching. They know the truth of structure from learning the definitions of the clusters, elements, and sense mediums. They know the truth of substance from realizing the pressure of the body and mind. They know the truth of becoming from the continuity of realms of existence. They know the truth of knowledge of extinction and nonorigination from the ultimate extinction of all burning torments. They know the truth of entry into the knowledge of the path from the accomplishment of nonduality. By accomplishment of continuity of accession to the stages of enlightening beings from perfect awareness of all their features, ultimately they know the truth of accumulation of the knowledge of the enlightened. This is, however, on the basis of the power of knowledge in the process of application, not by ultimate exhaustive knowledge.

"By means of the awareness effected by this knowledge of truths, they know in truth that all that is conditional is void, unreal, delusive, deceptive, fooling the ignorant. They become all the more compassionate toward beings, and the light of great goodwill shines forth. Supported by the power of knowledge, with concern for all beings, seeking enlightened knowledge, they examine all conditioned activities, past and future. They know for a fact how the mass of suffering of beings, sprung from ignorance and craving for existence from the past, borne along in the stream of cyclic existence, never having gotten free from the dwelling of the physical and mental clusters, increases, and that it has no self, no being, no life, no soul, no personality, no self or personal possessions. They also know in truth whether or not there is an end, limit, or escape from their deluded wishing for the nonexistent future.

"It occurs to the enlightening beings, 'How strange and pitiful these ignorant, deluded creatures, whose countless bodies have perished, will perish, and are perishing, yet even while they are passing away they do not give rise to disaffection with the body; they increase the fetters of suffering, flowing along in the stream of the mundane whirl, not turning back from great danger and trouble, not letting go of the dwelling of the body-mind clusters; they do not reject the vipers of the elements, they are unaware of the prison of greed for happiness; they do not pull out the arrows of pride and views, they do not extinguish the flames of desire, hatred, and delusion; they do not disperse the darkness of ignorance; they do not evaporate the flood of craving; they do not seek an enlightened guide; going along with maniacs, they swim around in the sea of the mundane whirl, in the confusion of grasping of various bad thoughts. Being without refuge, they fall into intense distress and individually experience many pains, such as birth, old age, sickness, death, grief, lament, dejection, mental disturbance. For the sake of these beings, who are suffering distress, without a leader, without a savior, without a refuge, without a reliance, without an island of safety, without direction, in the dark, wrapped up in the shell of ignorance, overcome by darkness, we alone will gather such stores of virtue and knowledge as will enable these beings to be ultimately purified, and finally that they may arrive at the state of unimpeded knowledge of those with the ten powers.'

"Whatever goodness the enlightening beings undertake with this mind which has realized well-considered knowledge, they undertake it all for the salvation of all beings, for the benefit of all beings, for the happiness of all beings, out of compassion for all beings, so that all beings will be free from trouble, for the liberation of all beings, to take care of all beings, for the purification of all beings, to lead all beings to freedom, for the ultimate nirvana of all beings.

"The enlightening beings in this fifth stage, the stage Difficult to Conquer, become all the more mindful, by not forgetting the nature of things; they become wise, by certain knowledge; they become wayfarers, by realizing the hidden meanings intended by the scriptures; they become conscientious because of protecting self and others; they become steadfast, by maintaining disciplined behavior; they become awake because of careful consideration of what is true and what is not; they become followers of knowledge because of not being led by others; they become followers of wisdom because of skill in expression distinguishing the meaningful and meaningless; they become skilled in maturing beings because of skill in effecting higher knowledge; they become accomplished in mystic knowledge because of skill in accomplishing meditation; they become skilled in expedients because of adaptation to the world; they become tireless because of accumulation of virtues; they become ceaselessly energetic because of seeking knowledge; they become unflagging in determination because of having accumulated great kindness and compassion; they become devoted to tireless seeking because of being in quest of the ten powers, infallible expertise, and unique qualities of buddhas; they become imbued with well-accomplished attention because of having accomplished buddha-land adornment; they become engaged in various good works because of having accumulated the distinctive marks and embellishments of buddhahood; they become constantly engaged in right effort because of seeking the physical, verbal, and mental adornments of the enlightened; they become most respectful in conduct because of listening to all enlightening beings and expounders of truth; they become unhindered in mind because of continually traveling through the world by the great skill in means of enlightening beings; they become undistracted at all times because of application of effort to the full development of all beings.

"Thus engaged, the enlightening beings develop people by means of charity, kind speech, beneficial action, and cooperation; they develop people by showing forms, by revelation of enlightening action, by making clear the greatness of the enlightened, by showing the ills of the mundane whirl, by lauding the knowledge of buddhas, and by production of great spiritual manifestations and application to various practices and works.

"The enlightening beings, thus engaged in the development of sentient beings, with minds continually following buddha-knowledge, engaged in unregressing goodness, intent on the search for supreme truth, practice whatever in the world would benefit sentient beings, such as writing, teaching, mathematics, sciences of various realms or elements; medical sciences; prevention of consumption, epilepsy, and possession; warding off poison, zombies, and witchcraft; song and dance, drama, music, storytelling, and entertainment; the construction of villages, cities, parks, canals, reservoirs, ponds abounding in lotuses, groves producing flowers, fruits, and medicines; the discovery of gold, jewels, and other precious substances; methods of pointing out the signs of the sun, moon, planets, stars, constellations, movements of the earth, omens, dreams, and the characteristics of coordination of general and specific actions and forms of limbs and parts of the body; points of cultivation of discipline, meditation, mystic knowledge, the immeasurables and formless states—and whatever else is not harmful or injurious, that which is conducive to the benefit and well-being of all creatures, that the enlightening beings undertake, guided by compassion, to establish them in the way of buddhas.

"To the enlightening beings in this stage, Difficult to Conquer, there appear many buddhas, by great vision and willpower—many hundreds of buddhas, many thousands, many hundreds of thousands, many millions, many billions, many trillions of buddhas. Having seen those buddhas, the enlightening beings honor and serve them with great resolution, providing the necessities of life, also providing comforts for enlightening beings and honoring the religious community, and dedicate these roots of goodness to unexcelled, complete, perfect enlightenment. The enlightening beings also attend those buddhas and with greatest respect and reverence listen to, take up, and remember their teachings and, having heard them, apply them as much as possible.

"Many enlightening beings go forth from society into the tutelage of those buddhas and, having gone forth, become holders of learning and preachers of the Teaching. Moreover, they become preachers who have attained command of the practices they have learned, because of not forgetting what they have learned from billions of buddhas over billions of eons.

"The roots of goodness of many eons of the enlightening beings in this stage are refined, purified thoroughly, and become more radiant, over hundreds and thousands and millions and billions of eons, just as gold adorned with jewels becomes brighter, purer, and more radiant. Because of accomplishment of the virtues of application of knowledge, they also become impeccable in conduct. Just as the light of the sun, moon, planets, and stars cannot be diverted by the winds and is not of a class with the winds, in the same way the roots of goodness of the enlightening beings in the Difficult to Conquer stage, in accord with the thought of the skillful, wise, knowing mind, cannot be surpassed by any who learn or attain individual liberation, and are not of the same class as the worldly.

"For enlightening beings in this stage the transcendent way of meditation is paramount, while they practice the rest as best they can. This is the stage of enlightening beings called Difficult to Conquer. Most of the enlightening beings in this stage become celestial sovereigns of the heaven of complete satisfaction, capable, powerful, able to detach beings from all false teachers and to establish them in the truth. Whatever acts they undertake, whether by giving, kind speech, beneficial action, or cooperation, it is all never apart from thoughts of Buddha, the Teaching, the Community, enlightening beings, the conduct of enlightening beings, the ways of transcendence, the stages, the powers, expertise, and unique qualities of buddhas, including omniscience complete in all respects. Why? Because they want to be the best of beings, unexcelled leaders and guides, and ultimately omniscient refuges.

"Those who seek to be thus undertake the appropriate effort, by the energy of which they instantly attain a trillion concentrations, see a trillion buddhas and perceive their power, shake a trillion worlds, go to a trillion lands, illumine a trillion realms, mature a trillion beings, abide for a trillion eons, penetrate a trillion eons past and future, contemplate a trillion doctrines, and manifest a trillion bodies, each appearing surrounded by a trillion enlightening beings.

"Beyond that, enlightening beings with the power of vows, by the excellence of their vows, perform countless transformations of body, aura, mystic powers, vision, sphere of operation, voice, conduct, adornments, power, resolution, and performances."

Then Diamond Matrix spoke these verses describing this stage:

Thus purified in the excellent practices of the fourth stage,
They contemplate the equality of the buddhas of past, present,
    and future—
In conduct, mental attainment, purity of the Path,
And freedom from doubt—and enter the fifth stage.

Their bow is recollection, their arrows the spiritual faculties,
  undeflected;
Their horses the right efforts, the bases of mystic power their
  chariot,
The five powers their armor, which no bandits can break
  through;
Heroic, never retreating, they enter the fifth stage.

Clothed in conscience and modesty, wise, with the fragrance of
  pure conduct,
With the garland of the elements of enlightenment, the unguent
  of high meditation,
With excellent methods adorned by wisdom and reflection,
Entering the garden of mental command, they come to this fifth
  stage.

The four bases of mystic power their feet, pure mindfulness their
  necks,
Noblest kindness and compassion their eyes, lofty wisdom their
  teeth,
The roar of selflessness overcoming the thieving afflictions,
The human lions, equanimous, wise, enter this fifth stage.

Having attained this excellent fifth stage,
They further cultivate the luster of the pure path:
With a pure intent, to attain buddhahood,
They think of compassion and kindness, without distress.

By gathering stores of virtue and higher knowledge,
By many means they observe the range of the stages.
Mindful of the power of the Buddha, imbued with intelligence
  and reason,
They contemplate the four truths completely.

They delve into the ultimate truth, the conventional truth,
The truth of characteristics, of distinctions, and structure,
The truth of substance, of the tainted and annihilation,
The truth of the Path, up to the truth of the unobstructed.

Yet though their subtle discernment seeks the truth
They do not attain highest unobstructed liberation;
Still, by great knowledge and application they surpass
All virtues of which worldlings are capable.

Thus having developed veritable discernment of truth,
They know the conditioned is unreal by nature and valueless.

They gain the light of compassion and kindness of buddhas yet
    more,
Seeking enlightened knowledge for the benefit of sentient beings.

They observe the past and future of the conditioned,
Those shrouded in the darkness of delusion, caught up in
    suffering,
And rescue worldlings bound to this mass of suffering,
Though they are without self or soul and equal to grass and trees.

"Because of two simultaneous afflictions are you reborn,
Past, present, and future; you find no end to suffering."
They see these people are lost, not turning back
From the mundane whirl, though it has no being of its own.

Dwelling in the clusters, with the serpents of the senses,
Infested with errant views, hearts burning with fire, shrouded in
    darkness,
Sunk in a flood of craving through lack of insight,
Without the guidance of Buddha, they are stranded in the sea of
    suffering.

Knowing this, enlightening beings strive yet more diligently,
Undertaking the liberation of all sentient beings:
They become mindful, discerning, intent, steadfast;
They become conscientious, hence awake and full of wisdom.

They do not cease their accumulation of virtue and higher
    knowledge;
Without weariness or laxity seeking power,
They develop lands, features, and voices of buddhas
Unceasing, all their deeds being for the weal of the living.

In order to mature people, they establish arts and skills—
Writing, printing, mathematics, medical sciences,
Exorcism, antidotes, curing,
Establishing excellent education, compassionate, kind, intelligent.

Witty in the finest song and dance, they build delightful places—
Canals, parks with flowers and fruits, places to sit,
Doing many things for the pleasure of beings,
Even revealing many kinds of treasure troves.

Mastering observation of the movements of celestial bodies and
    earth

As well as physiognomy,
They accomplish formless meditations, mystic knowledges, and
    the immeasurables,
Desiring well-being and happiness for the world.

Arriving in the Difficult to Conquer stage, practitioners of higher
    wisdom
Serve billions of buddhas and hear their teaching:
Their goodness and heart become more radiant,
Like gold sprinkled with jewels.

As the jewel palaces of the constellations
Are not swept away by the wind, so are enlightening beings
Unaffected while working in the world for beings' sake,
Like lotuses to which water does not cling.

In this stage, those experienced lords of contentment
Destroy the actions of false teachers, the abodes of manifold
    views.
All the good they do is in the cause of enlightened knowledge,
Wishing to become saviors of beings, rich in the ten powers.

Arousing superior energy, unflagging,
They serve a trillion buddhas;
Having attained concentration, they shake a trillion worlds,
Bearing the undertakings of the virtuous.

"Thus have enlightening beings, excellent guardians of the living,
told of the fifth stage, called Difficult to Conquer, in myriad different
ways."

Having heard of the superior practice of this exalted stage of the wise,
the host of enlightening beings, delighted, showered flowers and sprinkled
the Buddha with sublime jewels radiating pure light, uttering praise. A
hundred thousand celestial beings in the sky, pleased, scattered exquisite
varicolored celestial jewel dust on the Buddha, presenting incense, garlands, perfumes, parasols, decorative banners and pennants, and ornamental crescents. The commanding lord of the celestials, along with all
heavenly hosts, hovering in the empyrean, well pleased and serene,
showered clouds of jewels in offering to the Victor, urging the enlightening beings to speak. A thousand goddesses in the sky sang pleasantly
and played music, singing as with one voice in praise of the Buddha,
destroyer of the fire of afflictions:

Empty nature quiescent, all things are signless,
Equal to space, beyond discriminating thought, totally pure;

Beyond motion or stillness, beyond philosophy, all equal in
  suchness,
By their suchness, the essence of things is beyond thought.

Those who understand all things thus
Are unmoved by existence or nonexistence:
With compassion for the world, striving for liberation,
They are offspring of Buddha, born from the Teaching.

They practice generosity without concern for appearances,
With well-disciplined minds, fundamentally tranquil, extremely
  calm:
They tolerate what is made in the world, knowing the imperishable truth;
They are endowed with vigor and strength, detached from all
  things.

Having fully entered into meditation, exhausted afflictions, they
  are purified;
Knowing all things, they are centered in primordial emptiness.
Rich in knowledge and practical power, they are always devoted
  to the welfare of the world,
For they are great beings, offspring of Buddha, having extinguished all evil.

Having uttered a thousand such songs, those beautiful goddesses hovered
in the sky silently gazing at the Buddha, serene, enraptured with admiration for the Teaching. Moon of Liberation said, continuing, to Diamond
Matrix, "What are the characteristices of attainment of the next stage
after this fifth one?"

The enlightening being Diamond Matrix said, "Those who have
thoroughly fulfilled the path of the fifth stage of enlightening beings
enter into the sixth stage. They enter by way of ten equalities of things:
by the equality of signlessness of all things; by the equality of nonorigination of all things; by the equality of absence of characteristic marks of
all things; by the equality of nonbirth of all things; by the equality of
detachment of all things; by the equality of primordial purity of all
things; by the equality of nonconceptuality of all things; by the equality
of all things in neither coming nor going; by the equality of all things in
being like illusions, dreams, reflections, echoes, the moon's image in the
water, or apparitions; and by the equality of nonduality of existence and
nonexistence of all things. Thus observing all things in terms of their
intrinsic nature and according with it without opposition, they attain the
sixth stage of enlightening beings, the stage of Presence. But this is only
by penetrating conformative tolerance; they have not yet attained the
tolerance of the nonorigination of things.

"Thus understanding all things in their intrinsic nature, enlightening beings, all the more guided by compassion, commanded by great compassion, in order to completely fulfill great compassion, observe the formation and disintegration of the world. While observing the formation and disintegration of the world, it occurs to them, 'The origins of worldly ways are all due to attachment to self. In those who have no attachment to self the development of worldly ways does not take place.'

"It also occurs to them, 'These beings, intellectually infantile, attached to their selves, covered by the blinders of nescience, seeking existence and nonexistence, thinking illogically, gone on a wrong path, acting perversely, accumulate conditioned states of good, bad, and immobility. The mental seed conceived and planted by those conditioned states, imbued with taint and grasping, leads to future birth, old age, and death, coming into being as a result of renewed existence. In the field of action, in the darkness of ignorance, with the moisture of craving and the flow of egotism, the net of views grown, the sprouts of name and form appear. Having appeared, they grow, and, name and form having developed, the five senses become operative. From the intercourse of the operative senses comes contact. From the intercourse of contacts comes sensation. After sensation there is desire; thence craving and grasping grow. Once grasping is developed, becoming comes into existence. Once becoming has come into existence, the five clusters emerge. The five clusters having emerged, they progressively deteriorate in the five courses of existence. Having deteriorated, they disintegrate. From deterioration and disintegration there is anguish. Caused by anguish, all troubles of sadness, lament, pain, and dejection arise together. And yet there is no one who collects these. Of their own nature, spontaneously they disintegrate; there is no one who disintegrates them.'

"In this way enlightening beings examine interdependent origination in order of progression. They think: 'Not knowing the truth in the highest sense is called ignorance. The fruit of action fashioned by ignorance is conditioning. The initial mentation based on conditioning is consciousness. The four grasping clusters arising together with consciousness are name and form. The development of name and form is the six sense mediums. The conjunction of the sense faculties, objects, and consciousnesses is tainted contact. Born together with contact is sensation. Clinging to sensation is craving. Craving develops into grasping. Tainted action issuing from grasping is becoming. The outcome of action is birth, the emergence of the clusters. The development of the clusters is old age. The disintegration of the aged clusters is death. The mental anguish of the dying, the disintegrating, who are deluded and attached, is grief; crying out in grief is lament; in the five senses it is pain; in the vision of the mind it is dejection. The coming into being of much pain and dejection is torment. Thus this whole mass of suffering, this tree of suffering, grows, without any agent or knower.'

"They also think, 'From attachment to an agent, actions are cognized—

where there is no doer, doing cannot, in the ultimate sense, be found either.' They also think, 'All that is in the world is only mind. These twelve elements of becoming analyzed and explained by the Buddha are also all based on one mind. Why? Whenever the mind is aroused with desire for a thing, that is consciousness, and the "thing" is conditioning. The delusion of conditionings is ignorance. Name and form are born together with the ignorant mind. The development of name and form is the six sense mediums. Connected with the six mediums is contact. Born together with contact is sensation. Obsession with sensation is craving. The unrelenting seizing of what is picked up by craving is grasping. The conjunction of these elements of existence is becoming. The emergence of becoming is birth. The full development of birth is old age. The end of old age is death.'

"The ignorance there tends to produce two kinds of effects: as an object, it confuses beings, and it provides a cause for the development of conditioning. Conditionings also tend to produce two kinds of effects: they manifest future development and provide a cause for the emergence of consciousness. Consciousness also tends to produce two kinds of effects: it makes the continuity of existence and also provides cause for the development of name and form. Name and form also tend to produce two kinds of effects: they make mutual support and also provide cause for the development of the six sense mediums. The six sense mediums also tend to produce two kinds of effects: they show the differentiation of their own spheres and provide cause for the emergence of contact. Contact also tends to produce two kinds of effects: it contacts objects and provides cause for the emergence of sensation. Sensation also occasions two kinds of effects: it effects reception of the desired, of that which is not desired, and of that which is neither, and it also provides cause for the emergence of craving. Craving also occasions two kinds of effects: it creates intense desire for desirable things and provides cause for the emergence of grasping. Grasping also occasions two kinds of effects: it creates bondage by afflictions and provides cause for the emergence of becoming. Becoming also occasions two effects: it creates a tendency toward other courses of existence and provides cause for the emergence of birth. Birth also occasions two effects: it produces the emergence of the clusters and provides cause for old age. Old age also occasions two effects: it produces changes in the faculties and provides the cause for meeting in death. Death also occasions two effects: it destroys the compounded and causes continuation through lack of perfect knowledge.

"Therein, 'conditionings grounded on ignorance' means the continuation and support of conditionings by ignorance as a cooperating cause. 'Consciousness grounded on conditionings' means the continuation and support of consciousness by conditioning as a cooperating cause. 'Name and form grounded on consciousness' means the continuation and support of name and form by consciousness as a cooperating cause. 'The six sense mediums grounded on name and form' means the continuation and support of the six sense mediums by name and form as a cooperating cause. 'Contact grounded on the six sense mediums' means the continuation and support of contact by the six sense mediums as a cooperating cause. 'Sensation grounded on contact' means the continuation and support of sensation by contact as a cooperating cause. 'Craving grounded on sensation' means the continuation and support of craving by sensation as a cooperating cause. 'Grasping grounded on craving' means the continuation and support of grasping by craving as a cooperating cause. 'Becoming grounded on grasping' means the continuation and support of becoming by grasping as a cooperating cause. 'Birth grounded on becoming' means the continuation and support of birth by becoming as a cooperating cause. 'Old age and death grounded on birth' means the continuation and support of old age and death by birth as a cooperating cause.

"The extinction of conditionings due to the extinction of ignorance means the stilling and nonestablishment of conditionings due to the nonexistence of ignorance as a cooperating cause. The extinction of consciousness due to the extinction of conditionings means that without conditionings as a cooperating cause, consciousness is stilled, unsupported. The extinction of name and form due to the extinction of consciousness means that without consciousness as a cooperating cause, name and form are stilled, unsupported. The extinction of the six sense mediums due to the extinction of name and form means that without name and form as a cooperating cause, the six sense mediums are stilled, unsupported. The extinction of contact due to the extinction of the six sense mediums means that without the six sense mediums as a cooperating cause, contact is stilled, unsupported. The extinction of sensation due to the extinction of contact means that without contact as a cooperating cause, sensation is stilled, unsupported. The extinction of craving due to the extinction of sensation means that without sensation as a cooperating cause, craving is stilled, unsupported. The extinction of grasping due to the extinction of craving means that without craving as a cooperating cause, grasping is stilled, unsupported. The extinction of becoming due to the extinction of grasping means that without grasping as a cooperating cause, becoming is stilled, unsupported. The extinction of birth due to the extinction of becoming means that without the cooperating cause of becoming, birth is stilled, unsupported. The extinction of old age and death due to the extinction of birth means that without the cooperating cause of birth, old age and death are stilled, unsupported.

"Ignorance, craving, and grasping are the continuation of the course of affliction. Conditioning and becoming are the continuation of the course of action. The rest are the continuation of the course of suffering. The preceding and the succeeding annihilated by analysis, these courses are cut off. Thus these three courses—affliction, action, and suffering—have no self and have nothing to do with anything pertaining to self; becoming and decaying, it is all in essence like a hollow reed.

"Also, what are called conditionings grounded on ignorance are connected to the past; consciousness up to sensation are connected to the present; craving up to becoming are connected to the future. Henceforth there is continuation of this. The extinction of conditionings due to the extinction of ignorance is the cutting off of their connection—the same is true of the rest.

"Furthermore, the state of triplex suffering is due to these twelve elements of becoming. Therein, ignorance, conditioning, up to the six sense mediums are the suffering that is due to conditionality; contact and sensation are the suffering that is due to pain; the rest of the elements of becoming are the suffering that is due to disintegration. The extinction of conditionings due to the extinction of ignorance is the cutting off of the triplex suffering. The same is so of the rest. 'Conditionings grounded on ignorance' means the nature of conditioning being produced by causal relations; the same is so of the rest. The extinction of conditioning due to the extinction of ignorance means the nonexistence of conditioning; this is so of the rest too. 'Conditionings grounded on ignorance' means attachment to origination; 'the extinction of conditioning due to the extinction of ignorance' means attachment to annihilation. This is so of the rest too. 'Conditionings grounded on ignorance' is viewing it according to existence, and this is so of the rest too. The 'extinction of conditionings due to the extinction of ignorance' is viewing it according to annihilation, and this is so of the rest too.

"Enlightening beings contemplate interdependent origination in these ten patterns, forward and backward: that is, in terms of the interconnection of the elements of becoming, in terms of being all together in one mind, in terms of differentiation of one's own action, in terms of inseparability, in terms of the procession of the three courses of affliction, action, and suffering, in terms of the connection of past, present, and future, in terms of accumulation of the three kinds of suffering, in terms of production by causes, in terms of attachment to origination and annihilation, and in terms of contemplation of becoming and annihilation.

"Enlightening beings thus contemplate interdependent origination in ten patterns; because of contemplating it in terms of being without self, without being, without soul, without person, inherently empty, without doer or subject, the door of emptiness and liberation becomes manifest to them. Because of the nullity of own-being of these elements of becoming, being in the presence of ultimate liberation, no sign of any thing occurs to them. In those who have thus entered into emptiness and signlessness, no desire whatsoever arises, except, led by great compassion, for the full development of sentient beings: thus the door of liberation of wishlessness becomes manifest to them. Causing these three doors of liberation to become manifest, they leave behind the ideas of self and other, of agent and perceiver, of being and nonbeing. All the more, filled with compassion, they work to perfectly attain the elements of enlightenment which they have not yet attained.

"The enlightening beings think, 'That which is fabricated goes on because of linkage—without linkage it does not proceed; the fabricated goes on because of assemblage—without assemblage it does not go on. Having recognized the many ills and bad effects of the fabricated states of conditioning, we should cut off this linkage, this assemblage. But we should not go to the ultimate cessation of the created, for the sake of the full development of sentient beings.' This abode of transcendent wisdom, encountered by enlightening beings examining the many ills of fabricated conditioned states, by nature without inherent existence, unborn and not annihilated, is called the presence of unattached knowledge; it is realized by undertaking great compassion and not abandoning duty to living beings, by merging with its light. Endowed with such knowledge, illumined by transcendent wisdom, they bring together the cooperating causes conducive to the elements of enlightenment, but they do not abide in the created state. They also observe the essential nullity of conditioned states, but they do not settle down in that, because they have not yet completely fulfilled the elements of enlightenment.

"The enlightening beings in this stage, the stage of Presence, realize the concentration of enlightening beings called 'entry into emptiness.' They attain absorption in emptiness of inherent nature, emptiness of ultimate reality, supreme emptiness, great emptiness, emptiness of union, emptiness of production, nonconceptual emptiness according to reality, emptiness of concern, emptiness of disconnection and nondisconnection. With these ten doors of concentration on emptiness in the forefront, a hundred thousand doors of concentration on emptiness become manifest to them, and so do a hundred thousand doors of concentration on signlessness and a hundred thousand doors of concentration on wishlessness.

"Furthermore, the enlightening beings in this stage of Presence fully develop unbreakable intent, certain intent, good intent, profound intent, unretreating intent, unrelenting intent, pure intent, endless intent, intent to seek knowledge, intent to perfectly unite means and wisdom. These ten intents of enlightening beings lead to the enlightenment of buddhas; the enlightening beings become courageous and do not retreat before verbal opposition; they enter the stage of knowledge; they give up the stages of listeners and individual illuminates, being wholly directed toward buddha-knowledge. They also become immune to the doings of demons and afflictions, and become firmly established in the light of enlightening beings. They also become fully imbued with the practices of the principles of emptiness, signlessness, and wishlessness, and they become one with the contemplations of means and wisdom, and they become filled with the elements of enlightenment.

"In the enlightening beings in this stage of Presence, the abode of transcendent wisdom becomes paramount, and they attain the third acceptance of these principles, that of keen accord, by following them without opposition.

"To the enlightening beings in this stage many buddhas become visible, by great vision and willpower—many hundreds of buddhas, many thousands, hundreds of thousands, millions, billions, trillions of buddhas. Having seen these buddhas, with great zeal they pay honor and respect to them, providing them with offerings of food, clothing, bedding, medicines, and other furnishings, and also bring comforts for enlightening beings, and also honor the religious community. They dedicate all these roots of goodness to perfect enlightenment. They also attend those buddhas and listen to their teachings in person with great respect and appreciation of their rarity, taking up the teachings and remembering them. Having heard the teachings, they practice them by means of true application, wisdom, knowledge, and illumination, and effectively preserve them in action. They reach further into the store of teachings of the enlightened.

"The roots of goodness of the enlightening beings in this stage of Presence become more and more radiant over many eons, over hundreds, thousands, millions, billions, trillions of eons. Just as gold covered with jewels becomes even more radiant, so do the roots of goodness of enlightening beings in this stage, cultivated by expedient means and wisdom, become all the more radiant. They also become more and more tranquil and imperturbable. Just as moonlight refreshes and delights people and cannot be diverted by the four winds, in the same way those roots of goodness of enlightening beings in the stage of Presence quench the fires of afflictions of countless beings and make them refreshed and happy, and those roots of goodness cannot be diverted by the four demons.

"Among the ten transcendent ways, transcendent wisdom is paramount in these enlightening beings, but they also practice the others as best they can. This is a brief summary of the sixth stage of enlightening beings, called the stage of Presence, most of the enlightening beings in which are masters of emanation, expert and powerful in stopping people's conceit, skilled in drawing people away from the conditions of pride and arrogance. They cannot be distracted by the interrogations of all listeners. They are skilled in introducing beings into interdependent origination. Whatever actions they undertake, whether by giving, or by kind speech, or by beneficial action, or by cooperation, all of it is never apart from thoughts of Buddha, the Teaching, the Community, enlightening beings, the practice of enlightening beings, the transcendent ways, the stages, the powers, expertise, and unique qualities of buddhas, including omniscience complete in all respects. Why? To become the best of beings, unexcelled leaders and guides, and ultimately omniscient refuges.

"Those who seek to be thus undertake the appropriate effort, by which exertion they instantly attain a hundred trillion concentrations, see a hundred trillion buddhas and recognize their power, shake a hundred trillion worlds, go to a hundred trillion lands, illumine a hundred trillion worlds, mature a hundred trillion beings, remain for a hundred trillion eons, penetrate a hundred trillion eons past and future, contemplate a hundred trillion doctrines, manifest a hundred trillion bodies, each body manifesting a company of a hundred trillion enlightening beings. Beyond that, enlightening beings with the power of vows perform, by the excellence of their vows, countless transfigurations of body, aura, mystic powers, vision, sphere of operation, voice, conduct, adornment, power, resolution, and performance."

Then the great enlightening being Diamond Matrix uttered these verses describing this stage:

Having fulfilled the practice of the path of the fifth stage,
Realizing knowledge of the signlessness, formlessness, and
    birthlessness of things,
Knowledge of their nonorigination, primordial purity, and
    inexpressibility,
Thus enlightening beings enter the sixth stage.

The objective eye tracing phenomena consistently
Without rejection or attachment, without false ideas,
Knowing them to be of the nature of illusion, apart from being
    and nonbeing,
Enlightening beings enter the higher sixth stage.

Stable in keen accord, full of knowledge and power,
They observe becoming and decay in all worlds.
The becoming of the world is in essence the becoming of the dark
    of delusion;
When that delusion is destroyed, becoming is nonexistent.

They contemplate conditional creation, ultimately empty,
Without contradicting the causal relations of action or the
    function of names;
Knowing in truth action has no agent,
They look upon the fabricated as like dense clouds, without will.

Not knowing the truth in the highest sense is ignorance;
Action and consciousness are the results thereof;
Then, born together based on consciousness are name and form;
Thus all come into being, the whole mass of suffering.

They realize the three realms are only mind—
And the twelve elements of becoming are in one mind,
Born of desire and produced by the mind;
Thus extinction and becoming, too, are distinctions of the mind.

The function of ignorance is dual; it creates delusion,
And in delusion also provides a cause for sensations;
And so on, up to old age, degeneration, and death—
The production of all suffering from this has no end.

It cannot be cut off under conditions of ignorance,
But having stopped this continuous production, all ceases
     completely—
Delusion, craving, and grasping are the courses of affliction;
Action and becoming are conditionings, the rest are suffering.

From delusion to the sense mediums is suffering due to
     conditionality,
Contact and the development of sensation are suffering due to
     painfulness,
The rest of the elements are suffering due to degeneration;
If their development is stopped, that suffering has no self.

The forerunners are ignorance and conditioning;
Consciousness and sensation operate in the present;
Craving, becoming, and suffering take place in the future:
Those who observe unattached cut off their inception and
     progress.

The condition of delusion creates bondage;
The end of bondage is the extinction of conditions.
The production of result by cause does not happen without cause:
Enlightened knowledge sees it as void of inherent existence.

Following delusion is the cause and force of becoming;
Opposing it, all becoming is cut off by the annulment of the
     cause.
Those with unattached minds observe in ten ways
The profound interrelation of one thing and another.

Intention, the elements of becoming, and the locus of action
Are inseparable in the forefront of the three courses:
Unoriginated and unperishing is the procession of conditions,
The cause and destruction of the three forms of suffering, origin
     and extinction.

Thus do enlightening beings comprehend interdependent
     origination—
Like illusion, unreal, without knowing or doing,
Like a dream, like a reflection, void of intrinsic being,
Like the mirage of the ignorant and deluded.

Whoever meditates thus rests in the emptiness of the wise;
They realize this signlessness of conditions:
Knowing they're completely unreal, they have no wishes,
But they go on living out of compassion for beings.

Thus having accomplished this door of liberation, the great beings
Are even more compassionate in mind and seek the qualities of
 buddhahood.
Observing the fabricated is a matter of conjunction,
They become more diligent, replete with many virtues.

Having fulfilled myriad concentrations in emptiness,
As well as signless and wishless liberation,
Their wisdom and conformative acceptance increase,
And their freedom and knowledge mature.

They also serve many buddhas resolutely
And practice the Way in the buddhas' tutelage.
Attaining the treasury of Buddha teachings, they propagate roots
 of goodness
Like gold encrusted with jewels.

As moonlight refreshes the minds of people in the world
Undeflected by the four winds,
The light of enlightening beings, overcoming the path of demons,
Quenches the burning of afflictions of those suffering from pain.

Having reached this stage, they become celestial monarchs,
Adept at emanation, destroyers of conceit.
Whatever they do on the path of knowledge
Is insuperable, steadfast, beyond the path of listeners.

Seeking, the enlightening beings, imbued with vigor,
Having attained a hundred trillion consummate concentrations,
See in an instant the buddhas in the ten directions
Blazing like the sun in the midsummer sky.

"Here I have told of the sixth stage of great beings, the stage of Presence,
which is profound, hard to see, hard for listeners and self-conquerors to
know."

Now the crowd of celestials, exhilarated, showered clouds of various
lights and uttered sweet words full of supreme pure joy, praising the
supremely acute mind, master of knowledge, imbued with a hundred
virtues, excellent in conduct, blissful, benefactor of the world, one of
the lotuses of humanity. The great gods traversing the sky showered
sublime immeasurable light on the best of humans, and clouds of fra-

grance of supreme beauty, to destroy afflictions. The host of celestials spoke in sweet, pleasing, beautiful voices of how they had gained supreme benefit on hearing the explanation of this stage. The goddesses, delighted, playing sweet music, spoke in praise of this eminent practice, by the power of Buddha:

> Best in conduct among the wise,
> Tamers of the tamed, benefactors of the world,
> Having transcended the world,
> They act in the world, showing the subtle.

> They manifest various bodies,
> All the bodies one with the essence of things;
> Peaceful, uncontentious,
> They speak without the idea of having said even a syllable.

> They go to a hundred lands and pay respect to the Guides,
> Those who are most worthy of honor,
> Having given up their concept of a land,
> Being masters of knowledge.

> They fully develop beings,
> Yet have no concept of self or other,
> They accumulate highest goodness,
> Yet have no attachment to accumulation of good.

> Having seen the world burning
> With desire, hatred, and delusion,
> They get rid of all concepts
> And out of compassion undertake higher efforts.

The gods and goddesses, having offered their splendid song, became silent, enraptured, all gazing at Buddha. "This assembly is calm," they said to the enlightening being; "tell us the features of the seventh stage, abode of virtues."

The enlightening being Diamond Matrix said, "Any enlightening beings who have thoroughly fulfilled the course of the sixth stage come to the seventh stage. They gain access to the seventh stage by means of ten kinds of special undertaking in the Path which are accomplished by skill in means, transcendent wisdom, and knowledge. What are these ten? They develop a mind well trained in focus on emptiness, signlessness, and wishlessness, yet they collect great provisions of virtue and knowledge. They enter into the selflessness, absence of being, absence of soul, absence of individuality, and absence of personality in all things, yet they do not give up the production of the four immeasurables—immeasurable kindness, compassion, joy, and equanimity. They perform transcendent practices to increase virtuous ways, yet they do not cling to anything. They become detached from everything in the world, yet they produce arrays of adornments for the world. They become ultimately calm and tranquil due to removal from the fires of afflictions, yet they undertake to accomplish the extinction of the flames of afflictions of lust, hatred, and delusion of all beings. They realize the nonduality of essence of being and nonbeing, all things being like illusions, mirages, dreams, reflections, echoes, apparitions, yet they put into effect resolution in innumerable different deeds and works. They have cultivated the perception that all lands and paths are equal to space, yet they undertake the adornment of buddha-lands. They arrive at the nature of all buddhas as being fundamentally and essentially the reality-body, yet they undertake the production of the adornments of the marks of distinction and embellishments of the physical body of a buddha. They grant that the voice of the buddha is unutterable, free from sound, and by nature ultimately silent, yet they undertake the production of pure arrays of all different tones to communicate with all beings. In a single instant they enter buddhas' awareness of past, present, and future, yet they enter into distinctions of various appearances, ages, and reckonings by discernment of beings' minds. By these ten kinds of special undertaking on the Path, accomplished by skill in means, wisdom, and knowledge, enlightening beings enter the seventh stage; and they are said to be in this stage by virtue of the manifestation of the practice of these undertakings.

"Enlightening beings in this seventh stage penetrate infinite realms of beings, unlimited acts of guidance by which buddhas develop beings, infinite networks of worlds, infinite purification of buddha-lands by the enlightened ones, the infinite variety of phenomena, the infinite realization of knowledge of buddhas, the unlimited methods of calculating ages, the buddhas' immeasurable awareness of past, present, and future, the infinite differences in beings' interests, the infinite variety of manifestations of the material body of buddhas, the infinite variety of mental dispositions and faculties of beings, the infinite gladdening of the stream of beings by the utterances of the buddhas, the infinite variety of mental actions of beings, the buddhas' infinite following of the progress of knowledge, the infinite variety of application to the way of emancipation of the vehicle of listeners, the infinite manifestations of teachings of the Path of the buddhas, the infinite consummation of the attainment of the vehicle of individual illuminates, the infinite teachings of ways of ingress into the profound knowledge of the buddhas, the infinite application of enlightening beings to the conduct of enlightening beings, and the buddhas' infinite teachings of entry into the assembly of the Great Vehicle.

"It occurs to the enlightening beings that the spheres of the buddhas, those who have realized Thusness, the perfectly enlightened ones, are infinite and could not be counted even in hundreds of millions of billions of trillions of eons, and that they themselves should develop these spheres of buddhas and fulfill them, effortlessly, without vain thought, without false discrimination.

"Thus with perspicacious mystic knowledge, continuous application, replete with skill in means and wisdom, they become well established in these special undertakings on the Path, by unshakable application. While undertaking the accomplishment of the Path, they do not leave it for a moment; even while walking, standing, sitting, reclining, and even sleeping they are devoted to the accomplishment of knowledge. They are free from all obstruction, they maintain proper conduct, and they keep in mind such thoughts, by the inspiration of which they collectively fulfill the ten transcendent ways of enlightening beings. How so? In that way do the enlightening beings dedicate each thought, led by great compassion, to the fulfillment of buddhahood and enlightened knowledge.

"The giving to beings of their own roots of goodness by those attending to living beings compassionately while seeking enlightened knowledge is their transcendent generosity. The extinguishing of the burning of all afflictions is their transcendent discipline. Tolerance toward all beings out of kindness and compassion is their transcendent forbearance. Strength in tireless undertaking of ultimately good practices is their transcendent vigor. Proceeding toward omniscient knowledge without distraction is transcendent meditation. Tolerance in face of the essential nonorigination of all things is their transcendent wisdom. The accomplishment of unlimited knowledge is their transcendent skill in means. The realization of the penetration of knowledge of the ultimate undertaking is their transcendent vowing. Not suffering their path to be cut off by any opponents or gangs of demons is their transcendent power. The accomplishment of knowledge of all things as they are is their transcendent knowledge. Thus are the ten transcendent ways of enlightening beings fulfilled in every instant in this stage, which is called Far-Going. In the same way the four means of salvation, the four powers, the thirty-seven elements of enlightenment, the three doors of liberation—in sum, all aspects of enlightenment—are fulfilled moment to moment."

When Diamond Matrix had said this, the enlightening being Moon of Liberation said to him, "Are all the elements of enlightenment fulfilled moment to moment only by enlightening beings in the seventh stage, or in all ten stages?"

Diamond Matrix said, "All the elements of enlightenment are fulfilled moment to moment by enlightening beings in all ten stages, but especially in this seventh stage. Why? This stage of enlightening beings fulfills practice that involves appropriate efforts and accedes to the practice of knowledge and mystic knowledge. Now in the first stage of enlightening beings the elements of enlightenment are fulfilled in the enlightening beings moment to moment by focus on all vows; in the second, by removal of mental defilements; in the third, by increase in commitment and attainment of the illumination of the Teaching; in the fourth, by entry into the Path; in the fifth, by going along with worldly occupations; in the sixth, by entry into the door of the teaching of profundity; and in this seventh stage all elements of enlightenment are fulfilled moment to moment by the establishment of all qualities of buddhahood. What is the reason for this? All the elements of effort to evoke knowledge that are accomplished by enlightening beings in the first through seventh stages are accomplished without effort beginning in the eighth stage, and on until the final end.

"It is as if there are two worlds, one defiled and impure, and one thoroughly pure; it is difficult to cross over the gap between these two worlds, except by the great power of higher knowledge: in the same way it is hard to cross over the gap between alloyed and pure practice of enlightening beings, and it is impossible to do so except by the empowerment of great vows, skill in means, and higher mystic knowledge."

Moon of Liberation said, "Then is the practice of enlightening beings in this seventh stage to be considered alloyed with afflictions, or pure?"

Diamond Matrix said, "From the first stage of enlightening, all enlightening beings' practices should be considered free from the blemishes of afflictions, due to the dominance of dedication to enlightenment, but because of being even with the path that accords to their station, up to the seventh stage it cannot be called practice which has completely transcended afflictions. It is like a king riding around on an elephant, recognizing people's afflictions of suffering and poverty without himself being affected thereby—yet he has not thus far totally gone beyond the human condition. Then if he is born in the Brahma heaven, having relinquished the human body, and ascends to the Brahma palace, with little effort he goes around looking at the universe and shows the radiance of Brahma, he then cannot be called human. In the same way, from the first stage enlightening beings, mounted on the vehicle of the transcendent ways, course through all worlds, recognizing the ills of afflictions, but are not affected by them because of being on the right Path, but thus far cannot be said to have completely gone beyond the ills afflicting all beings. Having given up the practices of the seventh stage, they enter the eighth, and then, mounted on the completely pure vehicle of enlightening beings, traveling around all worlds, they recognize the ills afflicting all worldly beings, but they are not affected by those ills, having totally transcended worldly actions.

"Yet the enlightening beings in this seventh stage have mostly transcended the mass of all afflictions, beginning with greed; enlightening beings practicing this seventh stage, Far-Going, cannot be said either to be defiled with affliction or to be free of affliction. Why? Because they do not act out any afflictions, they cannot be said to be afflicted; because they are seeking buddha-knowledge and have not yet completely fulfilled their aspiration, they cannot be said to be without affliction.

"Enlightening beings in this seventh stage become endowed with physical, verbal, and mental action that is pure in intent; and they get beyond all bad courses of action that are disapproved of by the enlightened, and continually act in accord with the virtuous paths of conduct recognized by the enlightened. Also, whatever worldly arts and crafts and businesses they do in the fifth stage all operate without effort in the seventh stage. They become universally accepted as teachers, except of perfect buddhas and enlightening beings from the eighth stage on, who have no peer, whether in terms of will or practice. All their meditations, concentrations, attainments, mystic knowledges, and liberations become present to them, in terms of cultivation, but not as yet as mature accomplishments, just as in the eighth stage the power of cultivation of wisdom and means in every thought by enlightening beings in the seventh stage is fulfilled. They attain all the elements of enlightenment to an even greater degree than before.

"In this seventh stage enlightening beings attain an enlightening concentration called perfect conscious ascertainment, one called careful consideration of meaning, one called preeminent intellect, one called store of differentiation of meanings, one called ascertainment of all meanings, one called ascertainment of meanings of things as they are, one called firmly established root, one called door of knowledge and mystic power, one called purification and adornment of the phenomenal realm, one called praise of the enlightened, and a concentration called door of existence and nirvana concealing various meanings. In this way, beginning with these, fulfilling the ways of ingress into great mystic knowledge, they attain a hundred thousand sets of ten concentrations that purify the stages. By attainment of these concentrations in which means and wisdom are purified, and by the power of great compassion, they go beyond the stages of listeners and individual illuminates, and encounter the stage of contemplation with wisdom and knowledge. The unlimited actions of enlightening beings in the seventh stage are carried on without specific marks, as are their unlimited speech and thought. Thoroughly purified is the manifestation of acceptance of the nonorigination of all things."

Moon of Liberation said, "Are not the unlimited physical, verbal, and mental actions of enlightening beings in the first stage beyond the practice of listeners and individual illuminates?"

Diamond Matrix said, "They are, but that is because of the magnitude of their intense focus on the Buddha Way, not by their own conscious contemplation. But in this seventh stage of enlightening beings they become insuperable because of realization through contemplation in their own sphere of awareness. It is like a prince born of a king and queen, who has the marks of kingship and as soon as he is born is superior to the ministers—that is because of the lordship of the king, not due to thought by his own intellectual power. Then when he grows up, he goes beyond the works of all the ministers because of his own intellectual power. In the same way, enlightening beings excel all listeners and individual illuminates as soon as they are inspired, because of the greatness

of their determination, not because of contemplation by their own intelligence. But enlightening beings in this seventh stage go beyond all
listeners and individual illuminates by establishment in greatness and
preeminence of their own experiential knowledge. Furthermore, enlightening beings in this seventh stage attain profound, unattached, in-
conspicuous physical, verbal, and mental action, yet they do not give up
intense effort seeking greater excellence, by which questing effort they
reach extinction but do not make it their final realization."

Moon of Liberation said, "From what stage do enlightening beings
arrive at extinction?"

Diamond Matrix said, "They arrive at extinction from the sixth stage.
In the seventh stage they enter and emerge from extinction in each
mental instant, but they may not be said to actually experience extinction. Because of that they are said to have inconceivable physical, verbal,
and mental action. It is a marvel how enlightening beings abide in ultimate reality without actually experiencing extinction. Just as a person
with good knowledge of the characteristics of the waters of the ocean,
educated, wise, and intelligent, with consideration relevant to every
point, when on board a ship in the ocean becomes familiar with the
winds and the currents and is unscathed by the ocean waters, in the same
way enlightening beings in the seventh stage, having entered the ocean
of omniscience of the great vehicle on board the vessel of the transcendent ways, abide in the sphere of ultimate reality, the limit of existence,
yet do not experience extinction, and are not affected by the ills of
thoughts of complete ultimate extinction of the compounded.

"Having attained this power and support of knowledge, by means of
great awareness in which concentration, knowledge, and power are developed, by the power of skill in means and wisdom, they also show the
face of mundane existence, while their minds are gone to nirvana. They
are also surrounded by a great company, yet they have attained to constant detachment of mind. They undertake birth in the world by willpower for the sake of development of beings, but they are not stained by
the ills of the world. They also become tranquil, extremely calm and
serene, yet by expedient means they 'burn,' without, however, being
burned by burning. They are born in the knowledge of buddhas and
leave the stages of listeners and individual illuminates. While they come
to reach the storehouse of the realm of buddha-knowledge, yet they
appear to have entered the realm of demons. Though they have completely transcended the paths of the four demons, yet they show the
sphere of operation of the demons. They appear to practice the ways of
non-Buddhists, yet their minds have not abandoned Buddhism. They
appear to follow all worldly occupations, yet they attain the way to
transcendence of the world. They acquire adornments surpassing those
of all creatures, human, celestial, or fabulous, but they do not take their
attention off delight in the way of the enlightened.

"To the enlightening beings in this seventh stage of Far-Going, many buddhas become visible, by great vision and willpower—many hundreds of buddhas, many thousands, many hundreds of thousands, many hundreds of thousands of millions, many hundreds of thousands of billions, many hundreds of thousands of trillions of buddhas. Having seen those buddhas, they honor and serve them with great zeal, providing them with food and drink, clothing, bedding, medicines, and furnishings, and also providing comforts for enlightening beings and paying respect to the religious community. Those roots of goodness they dedicate to perfect enlightenment. They attend those buddhas and listen to their teachings, take them up and remember them. Having heard the teachings, they put them into practice by means of the light of true attainment, wisdom, and knowledge, and protect them by accomplishing them, and become preservers of the teachings of the buddhas, unfazed by the intelligent questions of all listeners and individual illuminates. Their acceptance of the profound teaching, for the salvation of beings, becomes yet more purified.

"The roots of goodness of enlightening beings in this stage of Far-Going are forged over many eons, are purified, and become workable; they become immaculately pure over hundreds of thousands of millions of billions of trillions of eons. Just as gold studded with all kinds of jewels becomes yet more radiant, more luminous, and all the more outclasses all other ornaments, in the same way the roots of goodness of enlightening beings in this seventh stage of Far-Going, produced by skill in means, wisdom, and knowledge, become all the more radiant, luminous, and immaculate, and cannot be outshone by listeners and individual illuminates. Just as the light of the sun cannot be outshone by the lights of the stars and moon, and dries up most of the swamps and ripens the crops, in the same way those roots of goodness of enlightening beings in this stage of Far-Going cannot be outshone by listeners and individual illuminates, and mostly dry up delusions and their swamps of afflictions, and cause bodies defiled by afflictions to become wholesome.

"For these enlightening beings, among the ten transcendent ways, transcendent skill in means becomes paramount, while they practice the rest as best they can.

"This is a summary exposition of the seventh stage of enlightening beings, called Far-Going, most of the enlightening beings in which become celestial sovereigns with command of others' emanations, competent and powerful, inexhaustible in evoking clear understanding in beings, and in answering the questions of listeners and individual illuminates, skilled at leading beings into certainty. Whatever acts they undertake, whether by giving, or kind speech, or beneficial action, or cooperation, all of it is never apart from thoughts of Buddha, the Teaching, the Community, enlightening beings, the practice of enlightening beings, the transcendent ways, the stages, the powers, expertise, and unique qualities of buddhas, including omniscience complete in all

respects. Why? Because they want to become the best of beings, unexcelled leaders and guides, and ultimately omniscient refuges.

"Wishing to be thus, they undertake appropriate effort, by whose
energy they instantly attain a quadrillion concentrations, see a quadrillion buddhas and recognize their power, shake a quadrillion worlds, go
to a quadrillion lands, illumine a quadrillion worlds, develop a quadrillion beings to maturity, live for a quadrillion eons, penetrate a quadrillion eons past and future, contemplate a quadrillion means of teaching,
manifest a quadrillion bodies, manifesting each body with a company of
a quadrillion enlightening beings. Beyond that, enlightening beings with
the power of vows can, by the excellence of their vows, perform countless transformations, of body, aura, mystic powers, vision, sphere of
action, voice, conduct, adornment, empowerment, resolution, and performances."

Then Diamond Matrix spoke these verses describing this stage:

With profound knowledge following the trail of ultimate truth,
Mind stabilized in the sixth stage, perfectly concentrated,
Accomplishing the union of wisdom and means,
They enter the seventh stage of superior practice.

Empty, signless, wishless, yet with compassion and kindness,
Gone to the state of felicity, yet honoring the buddhas,
Tireless in virtue and power, while knowing them to be empty,
They enter the realm of the seventh stage.

In the world, with great forbearance, they've acquired
    detachment,
Extinguished the flames of afflictions and stilled worldly cravings,
Coursing in the nonduality of things as like reflections, illusions,
    dreams,
Yet they show compassion, and enter the seventh stage.

They purify the land, while their own minds, equanimous, are
    without discriminatory thought;
They're endowed with the marks of a buddha, while immovable
    in the essence of truth.
They speak for the benefit of the world, while detached from
    sound;
And in an instant enter the mind of knowledge of buddhas.

Illumined, they contemplate these teachings.
Entering the higher stage desiring to benefit the world.
In this stage they do endless works for living beings,
Doing the deeds of buddhas, immeasurable.

They understand lands, their various orders and ages,
Inclinations, intentions, various states of mind,
And teach without end, faithfully,
To develop all to maturity.

Those who have reached the supreme Path by this mind of
    knowledge,
Combining wisdom and means in all their actions,
Having attained in each moment of thought herein the virtues of
    the Path,
Fulfill the ten transcendent states.

The seeking of good for all beings is giving;
Discipline is the cessation of afflictions, tolerance is noninjury;
Energy is ever-greater vigor in their undertakings;
Imperturbability on the Path is the meditation of the virtuous.

Acceptance of nonorigination, dispassionate, is supreme wisdom;
Dedication is skill in means, vowing is seeking greater success;
Indestructibility hence is power, knowledge is joy in guidance:
Thus they attain the qualities of enlightenment moment to
    moment.

In the first stage virtues are fulfilled by focus of mind on them;
In the second, removal of defilement; in the third, cutting of
    bonds;
In the fourth, the Path; in the fifth, impartial action;
In the sixth, knowledge of nonorigination operates.

Hence, as soon as they reach the seventh stage,
They commence virtuous undertakings of many kinds;
Why? The knowledge and deeds they achieve hence
Purify all that develops into the eighth stage.

Far-Going is hard to cross; by many developmental practices
They cross, as one would cross a path between two lands.
Coursing in the seventh stage, they are undefiled, like kings;
While established in the Path, yet they have not definitely
    transcended all.

When they reach the eighth stage of knowledge, further,
They transcend mental objects, established in the action of
    knowledge.
Just as a god does not look on the world as a human does,
So do they act, like lotuses unstained.

In this stage they get beyond various afflictions—
Their afflictions are neither active nor completely destroyed.
Being on the Path, they do not act on afflictions,
Yet, filled with zeal for supreme knowledge, their affliction is not
    yet ended.

They know various worldly arts and crafts, the use of medicines
    and spells,
And are well versed and grounded in all sciences.
They attain meditation, mystic knowledge, and powers, by
    cultivation,
And further accomplish various concentrations.

Having transcended the practices of listeners and the self-
    awakened,
They are established in the infinite practice of enlightening beings,
Before by determination, from now on by knowledge;
They are like children of kings, full of power when grown.

Having reached profundity, they proceed yet further;
Reaching extinction of mind, still they do not make it their
    experience,
Like having gone into the ocean on a steady-faring ship,
Seeing all the water before them yet not being destroyed by it.

Further endowed with the best of means, wisdom, and power,
Rich in virtues of knowledge and action, hard for the world to
    know,
They serve millions of buddhas, becoming more pure,
Like gold adorned with jewels.

The light of the eminent wisdom of the sages in this stage
Evaporates the wetness of craving, like the light of the sun.
Having attained this stage, they become commanders,
Capable, skilled in teaching the fruit of knowledge.

Seeking, imbued with stability, vigor, and strength,
They see a quadrillion buddhas
In all directions, by concentration,
And even more, those of immeasurable, superior will.

"This is the seventh stage, called Far-Going, purifying means and wisdom, hard for all worldlings and those who practice only for themselves
to know."
    Having heard about this excellent practice of the wise, the gods and

celestial hosts were joyful and made offerings to the Buddha and the multitude of enlightening beings, benefactors of the world—they gave flower garlands, banners and pennants, aromatic powders, precious cloth, many splendid parasols studded with jewels, and exquisite clouds of pearl necklaces. The goddesses produced many kinds of music, with pleasing, sweet sounds and superb rhythm, in offering to the Buddha and enlightening beings, sages of eminent character; they said,

> All-seer, mighty, foremost and best, who shows the realm of
>   buddhas for the benefit of the world,
> It is you who evoke this music, with the strumming of various
>   instruments.
>
> On a hairtip more buddhas than grains of sand in trillions of
>   Ganges rivers
> Peaceful, peerless, teach the pure doctrine, preeminent, supreme.
>
> In a single pore are infinite lands, each with four continents and
>   seas,
> As well as polar and peripheral mountains, all seen therein,
>   uncrowded.
>
> On a point the size of a hairtip are all realms of being—
> Ghosts, beasts, fiends, humans and gods, goblins and serpents,
>   experiencing the various realms of action.
>
> In all the spheres of the lands the supreme wheel of the Purifiers is
>   turned,
> As the buddhas teach while adapting to the minds and thoughts of
>   beings.
>
> In the body of each being are various lands, in the lands, beings;
> Those of higher development are humans and celestials—
> Knowing them in their variety, the Buddha teaches them.
>
> A great land comes to seem to be minute, a mote of dust comes
>   to seem huge—
> These and more are the spiritual powers of Buddha, of which all
>   beings could not exhaustively tell.

When such words of grandeur had been spoken, the assembly, silent, gazed happily at the Best of Speakers. Seing the assembly had grown silent, Moon of Liberation spoke again: "Please tell us the way into the practice of the eighth stage."

Diamond Matrix said, "Those who have well accomplished investigation of the seventh stage of enlightening beings, who have purified the path by wisdom and skill in means, have accumulated ample provisions of virtue and knowledge, have thoroughly committed themselves to the great vow, are surely supported by the empowerment of the Buddha, have acquired the support of the power of their own roots of goodness, have their attention on the powers, expertise, and unique qualities of buddhas, have purified their intent and thought, have attained the power of virtue and knowledge, strive compassionately and follow the Path of infinite knowledge, realize the primordial nonorigination of all things as it really is, and also realize the nonbirth, signlessness, absence of becoming or annihilation, nonconsummation, nonprogression, nonregression, essential nonexistence, equality of beginning, middle, and end, and nonconceptuality of all things, accessible to nonconceptual universal knowledge, equal to thusness—they realize these qualities of all things as they really are. They are wholly detached from mind, intellect, consciousness, thought, and ideation. Unattached, not grasping, equal to space, having entered into the nature of openness—this is called having attained acceptance of the nonorigination of things.

"Then, imbued with this acceptance, as soon as enlightening beings attain the eighth stage, Immovability, they attain the profound abode of enlightening beings, which is hard to know, unadulterated, ungraspable by any notion, unoriginated, measureless, unconquerable by any listeners or individual illuminates, aloof, facing total detachment. Just as when a monk with spiritual powers and ultimate control of mind has, through successive stages, reached the ninth level of attainment, extinction, he becomes free of all stirring cogitation and flowing thoughts, in the same way enlightening beings, as soon as they attain the eighth stage, Immovability, become freed from all efforts and attain the state of effortlessness, freed from physical, verbal, and mental striving, freed from stirring cogitation and flowing thoughts, and become stabilized in a natural state of development.

"It is as if a person in a dream saw himself in a great torrent, he then would make great effort, eagerly striving to get out, and because of that great effort and striving he would wake up, and as soon as he woke up he would be freed from all that effort and striving. In the same way the enlightening beings, seeing the mortal being in the four torrents, desiring to come to the rescue, exert great efforts and striving for awakening of all-knowledge, acting with great vigor; as soon as they reach the stage of Immovability, they become free from all efforts.

"In these enlightening beings no actions based on views, passions, or intentions are manifest. Just as in the Brahma heaven no afflictions of the realm of desire are acted on, in the same way enlightening beings in this stage of Immovability do not carry on action of mind, intellect, or consciousness. They do not even carry on the conduct of Buddhas, of enlightenment, of enlightening beings, of nirvana, or of learners and self-illuminates—how much less would they carry on the conduct of worldlings.

"Furthermore, to the enlightening beings who have reached this stage of Immovability, who are stabilized by the supporting power of their past vows, the buddhas, in the course of that means of access to the Teaching, miraculously effect the bestowal of knowledge of reality and say, 'Good, good! This is acceptance of the ultimate truth, in accord with the teaching of buddhas. However, you do not yet have our ten powers, expertise, and unique qualities of buddhahood fully developed. Therefore, work vigorously in quest of the full development of buddhahood. Do not let this acceptance go; nevertheless, though you have attained this abode of peace and liberation, you should care for these restless, agitated ignorant beings acting on various afflictions and ravaged by various thoughts. Also, always remember your past vows, the benefit of beings, and the inconceivability of the source of knowledge. Furthermore, the essence of all phenomena remains the same whether or not buddhas emerge; the realm of reality of the essence is permanent, for it is the emptiness and ungraspability of all things. It is not only by this that buddhas are revealed as such—even listeners to the Buddhist teaching and individual illuminates also attain this nonconceptual essence. Yet you should observe the infinity of the body of us buddhas, the infinity of our knowledge, the infinity of the lands of buddhas, the infinity of accomplishments of knowledge, the infinity of spheres of light, and the infinity of purity of voice, and strive to achieve the same. Furthermore, you have only this one illumination, which is the illumination of absence of false ideas about things. But such illuminations of buddhas are endless in extent, endless in action, endless in manifestation, their number being incalculable and immeasurable; you should strive to attain them. Also, observe the infinity of lands in the ten directions, the infinity of beings, and the infinite differentiations of phenomena, and undertake to comprehend them as they actually are.' Thus do the buddhas present to the enlightening beings immeasurable, incalculable ways of accomplishing knowledge, beginning with these. By these ways of accomplishing knowledge, the enlightening beings, by infinite differentiations of knowledge, cause works productive of knowledge to be consummated.

"I tell you, if the buddhas did not introduce the enlightening beings this way into ways of effecting omniscient knowledge, the enlightening beings would become completely extinct in parinirvana and would cease all work for sentient beings. Therefore, the buddhas give the enlightening beings such infinite tasks to develop knowledge, the knowledge-producing deeds effected in a single instant of which are immeasurably, incalculably greater than all former undertakings from the first inspiration up to the attainment of stability in the seventh stage. Why? Because previously it was practice undertaken with one body, whereas having climbed to this stage the power of practice of enlightening beings is realized by infinite different bodies, by production of infinite voices, by accomplishment of infinite knowledge, by accomplishment of infinite manifestations, by purification of infinite lands, by development of infinite beings, by service of infinite buddhas, by realization of infinite principles of buddhahood, by accomplishment of infinite powers of mystic knowledge, by realization of infinite differences of circles of assemblies; by infinite accomplishments of physical, verbal, and mental actions, the power of enlightening beings' practice is fully realized by immovable application.

"It is like a boat going to the ocean—before it reaches the ocean, it is dragged with much effort, but once it reaches the ocean it is propelled without effort by the wind. The distance it travels on the ocean in one day is farther than it could be dragged by force in even a hundred years. In the same way, enlightening beings, having stored provisions of roots of goodness and boarded the ship of the Great Vehicle, reaching the great ocean of practice of enlightening beings, arrive at omniscience in a moment by effortless knowledge, which could not be reached even in countless eons by their former practices involving effort.

"Then when enlightening beings have attained the eighth stage, by the effortless awareness produced by skill in means and knowledge, they contemplate the sphere of omniscience, contemplate the becoming and dissolution of the world. As the world forms, they know it, and as the world disintegrates they know it. They know by what accumulation of actions the world forms, and they know by what ending of actions the world disintegrates. They know how long the world forms and they know how long the world disintegrates. They know how long the world subsists once it has formed, and they know how long the world remains disintegrated. Everywhere, without exception, they know the limitation of the earth element, they know its extensiveness, its infinity, and its differentiation. They know the limitation of the water element, they know the extensiveness, infinity, and differentiation of the water element. They know the limitation, the extensiveness, infinity, and differentiation of the fire element. They know the limitation, extensiveness, infinity, and differentiation of the wind element. They know the minuteness of atomic particles, they know their grossness, their measurelessness, and differentiation. They also know the skill of differentiation of measureless atomic particles. They know how many atomic particles of each element there are in this world; they know how many varieties of precious substances there are and how many atomic particles of precious substances there are. They know how many atomic particles of beings' bodies there are. They know the total number of particles of land masses. They know the grossness of beings' bodies, the fineness of their bodies, and the differentiation of their bodies. They know how many particles are formed into bodies of beings in hell, how many into bodies of animals, of ghosts, of titans, of celestial beings, and of human beings.

"Having penetrated this knowledge of differentiation of atomic particles, they know the formation of the realm of desire as it really is; they know the formation of the realm of form as it really is, and they know the formation of the formless realm as it really is. They know truly the dissolution of the realm of desire, the dissolution of the realm of form, and the dissolution of the formless realm. They know truly the limitation, the extension, the infinity, and the differentiation of the realm of desire, of the realm of form, and of the formless realm. They know truly what is of these three realms. Furthermore, illumined by well-developed knowledge, versed in knowledge of varieties of bodies of beings, versed in knowledge of differences in bodies of beings, and versed in knowledge of differentiations of land masses, they apply their intelligence to the production of mediums of manifestation as beings; in whatever form beings are born and attain their desires, enlightening beings adopt these forms themselves for the purpose of developing beings to maturity.

"Permeating a billion-world universe, enlightening beings undertake manifestation according to the form of the beings there, according to their various different inclinations, doing so by following knowledge of how to appear as reflections, according to how beings may become ripe for perfect enlightenment and liberation. In the same way they pervade two, three, four, five, ten, twenty, thirty, forty, fifty, up to an unspeakable number of universes and undertake manifestations in the forms of the beings there according to their various inclinations, by means of knowledge of how to appear as a reflection.

"Imbued with such knowledge, well established in this stage, while not moving from one buddha-land, they appear as reflections in the circles of buddhas in untold buddha-lands. According to the differences in beings' physical characteristics, their colors, appearances, statuses, physical sizes, inclinations, and dispositions, in various circles in various buddha-lands, in each the enlightening beings manifest the appropriate forms. In circles of mendicants they appear as mendicants; in circles of priests they appear as priests; in circles of warriors and administrators they appear as warriors and administrators; in circles of peasants they appear as peasants; in circles of servants they appear as servants; in circles of householders they appear as householders; in circles of various classes of celestial beings they appear as those particular types of celestial beings; and in circles of demons they appear as demons. To beings who should be taught by Buddhist followers, they appear as Buddhist followers. To those who should be taught by individual illuminates, they appear as individual illuminates. To those who should be taught by enlightening beings, they appear as enlightening beings. To those who should be taught by buddhas, they appear as buddhas. Thus, to the extent of the realms of beings' forms of existence, senses, and inclinations, in the realms of untold buddha-lands, enlightening beings appear differently in accord with each of them. They are free from all discriminatory conceptions of bodies and have realized the equality of bodies; their manifestation of bodies, endless and not in vain, is for the development and education of all.

"They know the body of sentient beings, they know the body of lands, they know the body of fruition of action, they know the body of Buddhist followers, they know the body of individual illuminates, they know the body of enlightening beings, the body of buddhas, the body of knowledge, the body of reality, and the body of space. Knowing the wishes of beings, according to time, development, education, progress, and desire, the enlightening beings make the body of beings into their own body. In the same way they make the body of lands, the body of fruition of action, the body of Buddhist followers, the body of individual illuminates, the body of enlightening beings, the body of buddhas, the body of knowledge, the body of reality, and the body of space into their own body. Knowing the heart's desire of beings, according to their desire, the enlightening beings make their own body into the body of sentient beings. In the same way they make the body of beings into the body of lands, the body of fruition of the Teaching, the body of fruition of action, the body of Buddhist followers, the body of individual illuminates, the body of enlightening beings, the body of buddhas, the body of knowledge, the body of reality, the body of space. Knowing the inclination of sentient beings, the enlightening beings put their own bodies into whatever body they wish.

"The enlightening beings know the embodiments of the bodies of beings as a mass of action, as a mass of consequences, as a mass of afflictions, as a mass of form, and they know formless embodiment. They know the smallness and greatness of bodies of lands, their measurelessness, their defilement and purity, their confusion, their inversion, their evenness, their interaction, and their differentiation of place and time. They know conventional distinctions of bodies of fruition of action; in the same way they know the conventions of distinctions of realization of bodies of Buddhist followers, individual illuminates, and enlightening beings. They know the bodies of buddhas as the embodiment of perfect enlightenment, as the embodiment of vows, as the emanation body, as the embodiment of empowerment, as the body arrayed with marks and embellishments of greatness, as the body of light, as the mentally produced body, as the embodiment of virtue, as the body of reality, and as the body of knowledge. They know the well-considered nature of the bodies of knowledge, their derivation from truth, their inclusion in fruition and effort, their division into mundane and supramundane, their establishment of the Three Vehicles, their generality and uniqueness, their liberative or nonliberative qualities, whether they are proper to those undergoing training or to those beyond it. They know the equality of reality bodies, their indestructibility, their conventional definitions according to situation and agreed usage, their definition in terms of animate and inanimate, and their definition in terms of the realities of Buddha and the realities of the holy community. They know the infinity of bodies of space, their all-pervasiveness, their incorporality, their absence of falsity, and their revelation of bodies of form.

"Having realized such knowledge of bodies, the enlightening beings become powerful; they acquire control over life span among all beings, by virtue of the power to live endlessly, for untold eons. They acquire control of mind, by virtue of immersion in knowledge of measureless, countless concentrations and contemplations. They acquire control over implements, in terms of demonstration of the creation of many magnificently adorned sites in all worlds. They acquire control over action, in terms of showing the power of fruition of deeds according to the time. They acquire power over birth, in terms of manifesting birth in all worlds. They acquire control over inclination, in terms of showing all worlds filled with buddhas. They acquire control over vows, in terms of manifesting perfect enlightenment in any buddha-land in any time desired. They acquire control over mystic powers, in terms of showing miracles by mystic powers in all buddha-lands. They acquire control of the Teaching, in terms of showing the light of the Teaching in its infinite aspects. They acquire control of knowledge, in terms of showing the power, expertise, unique qualities, special marks and embellishments, and actualization of perfect enlightenment of buddhas. With the attainment of these ten controlling powers of enlightening beings, they are imbued with inconceivable knowledge, incomparable knowledge, immeasurable knowledge, vast knowledge, insuperable knowledge.

"In the enlightening beings who have attained this stage and are imbued with such knowledge, ultimately impeccable conduct of physical, verbal, and mental action operates, led by knowledge, following knowledge, ruled by the ten transcendent ways, with great compassion in the forefront, skill in means well articulated, determination well developed, completely stabilized by the empowerment of Buddha, ceaselessly working for knowledge to benefit beings, aware of the endless distinction in realms of worlds. In sum, the physical, verbal, and mental actions of the enlightening beings who have attained this stage of Immovability operate for the concerted development of all aspects of buddhahood.

"Thus having attained this stage of Immovability, the enlightening beings become well established in willpower, through freedom from the activity of all afflictions; they become firmly established in the power of determination, never deviating from the Path; they become well established in the power of great compassion, not giving up the benefit of sentient beings; they become well established in the power of great kindness, being saviors of sentient beings; they become well established in the power of mnemonic control, not forgetting the teachings; they become well established in the power of elocution, through skill in examination of the distinctions of all the Buddha teachings; they become well established in the power of mystic knowledge, through familiarity with the actions in endless worldly realms; they become well established in the power of vows, never giving up all enlightening practices; they become well established in the power of the transcendent ways, through concerted cultivation of all the Buddha teachings; they become well established in the power of the support of buddhas, confronting omniscient knowledge in all its aspects. Having attained the support of these powers of knowledge, they show all activities, impeccable and undefiled in all acts.

"This eighth stage of enlightening beings is called Immovable because the enlightening beings cannot be deflected from their course; it is called the stage of nonregression because of the nonregression of knowledge; it is called the stage difficult to reach because of being difficult for any worldlings to know; it is called the stage of youth, because of innocence; it is called the stage of birth, because of power to effect whatever is wished; it is called the stage of perfection, there being nothing further to do; it is called the stage of completion because of having thoroughly accomplished ascertainment by knowledge; it is called the stage of nirvana because of having thoroughly accomplished vows; it is called the stage of empowerment because of being invulnerable to others; it is called the stage of effortlessness because of having been effected by what went before.

"Furthermore, having developed such knowledge, the enlightening beings enter the family of buddhas, are illumined by the light of the virtues of buddhas, accord with the conduct of buddhas, come face to face with the realm of buddhahood, and are constantly sustained by the power of buddhas. They are welcomed by Indra, Brahma, and the world guardians, constantly attended by the thunderbolt bearers; they are never without the power of concentration, able to produce infinite different embodiments, imbued with the power of action in all bodies, consummate in development of great mystic knowledge, in control of endless concentration, receivers of infinite indications of enlightenment, and demonstrators of attainment of perfect enlightenment according to the maturity of sentient beings.

"Having attained such knowledge of this stage and entered the circle of the Great Vehicle, with well-considered wisdom and mystic knowledge, constantly emanating the light of wisdom, having entered the unobstructed path of the realm of reality, able to distinguish many paths in the world, showing all aspects of virtue, in control of their own resolutions, with perspicacious knowledge of past and future, endowed with the knowledge to turn back all demons, having entered the realm and sphere of all enlightened ones, they carry out the conduct of enlightening beings in endless places in the realms of the world, with nonregressing application; thus are they said to have attained the eighth stage of enlightening beings, Immovable.

"Then, having attained the Immovable stage of enlightening beings, they are never without the constant vision of endless buddhas, because of accomplishment of the power of concentration. Yet they never give up extensive meeting and attendance on buddhas: in every age, in every world, they honor, respect, serve, and provide in all ways for many buddhas, many hundreds, thousands, millions, billions, trillions, quadrillions of buddhas; they attend those buddhas and receive from them pro-

visions of illumination through their teachings, beginning with light on
the differentiations of worldly realms. They further acquire the treasury
of teachings of the buddhas, and become invincible in answering questions in the world.

"Those roots of goodness of theirs, forged and purified over many
eons, become more radiant; over many hundreds, thousands, millions,
billions, trillions, quadrillions of eons their roots of goodness are further
forged, purified, and become more radiant. Just as well-refined gold
made by a good goldsmith into an ornament and fastened on the neck
or head of an emperor cannot be outshone by the ornaments of all the
people in the realm, in the same way the roots of goodness of enlightening beings in this Immovable stage cannot be outshone by all listeners,
individual illuminates, and enlightening beings up to the seventh stage.

"The light of wisdom and knowledge of enlightening beings who
have reached this stage annihilates the darkness of afflictions of sentient
beings, through accomplishment of accurate discernment of the means
of knowledge. Just as a great Brahma god of a thousand worlds, pervading the thousand worlds with benevolence, illumines them with light, in
the same way enlightening beings in this Immovable stage, pervading up
to as many worlds as atoms in a million buddha-lands with the light of
goodwill, progressively extinguish the fires of beings' afflictions and cool
them off.

"Among the ten transcendent ways, transcendent vowing becomes
predominant in these enlightening beings, while they practice the others
as best they can.

"This is a summary of the eighth stage of enlightening beings, called
Immovable, the details of which would take forever to explain. Most of
the enlightening beings in this stage become great Brahmas, lords of a
thousand worlds, supreme, invincible, seeing what is beneficial, imbued
with controlling power, capable, mighty, skilled in the presentation of
explanation of the transcendent ways of all listeners, individual illuminates, and enlightening beings, insuperable in answering questions
about the differentiations of worldly realms. Whatever they do, whether
by way of giving, or kind speech, or beneficial action, or cooperation, is
never apart from thoughts of Buddha, the Teaching, the Community,
enlightening beings, the practices of enlightening beings, the ways of
transcendence, the stages, the powers, expertise, and unique qualities of
buddhas, and ultimately of omniscience in all its aspects. Why? That
they may become the best of beings, unexcelled leaders and guides, and
ultimately all-knowing refuges.

"Accordingly, they bring forth such energy, by which they instantly
attain as many concentrations as atoms in a million billion-world systems, see as many buddhas as atoms in a million billion-world systems
and acknowledge their power, shake as many lands as atoms in a million
billion-world systems, illumine as many worlds as atoms in a million

billion-world systems, mature as many beings as atoms in a million billion-world systems, abide for as many eons as atoms in a million billion-world systems, penetrate as many eons past and future as atoms in a million billion-world systems, ascertain as many ways into the Teaching as atoms in a million billion-world systems, and manifest as many bodies as atoms in a million billion-world systems, manifesting each body with a company of as many enlightening beings as atoms in a million billion-world systems; beyond that, enlightening beings with the power of vowing produce, by the excellence of their vows, countless transformations of the body, aura, light, mystic powers, vision, sphere of action, voice, activity, adornment, power, resolution, or performances."

Then Diamond Matrix spoke these verses describing this stage:

Having purified wisdom and means in the seventh stage,
Well provided for the Way, committed to great vows,
Firmly established, the best of humans, imbued with goodness,
Seeking knowledge, they enter the eighth stage.

With virtue and knowledge, compassion and benevolence,
Going on infinite paths of knowledge, with awareness like space,
With the power of certain understanding of the teachings they
    hear,
The great sages attain acceptance of nonorigination, tranquil and
    subtle.

Primordially unborn, unoriginated, signless, all is
Imperishable, not having become, unproduced,
Void of essence of being, *thus,* beyond conception;
So they are freed from thought and mentation, just like space.

Accepting all things as such, free from idle fancy,
Profoundly immovable, they arrive at peace of mind.
It can hardly be known by worldlings, by their analytic
    reasoning,
Because it is beyond concepts grasping mental images.

Thus stabilized, there is no thinking in their minds,
Like a monk who has reached extinction and attained
    nonthought,
Like one dreaming of being in a river freed from concern on
    awakening,
Like being in pure heaven, aloof of attachment to pleasure.

On the basis of their previous resolution, the buddhas further
    exhort them:

"This tolerance is higher than coronation by the buddhas,
But our vast knowledge and supreme buddhahood
Is not yet yours, so begin heroic effort.

"Though you have extinguished the burning of the fire of
    affliction,
Having seen the world still afflicted, remember your past vows;
Having thought of the welfare of the world, work in quest
Of the cause of knowledge, for the liberation of the world.

"The real essence of things is permanent, *suchness*, beyond
    thought,
In all buddhas, buddhas' disciples, and individual illuminates—
It is not by this that the buddhas appear in the world with ten
    powers,
But only by vast knowledge, unattached to past, present, or
    future."

Thus do the incomparable ones, worthy of the honor of humans
    and gods,
Provoke in the enlightening beings thoughts of many aspects of
    knowledge,
Endless entry into consummation of the Buddha teachings,
Of which past enlightening practice was not even a fraction.

Having thereby reached this stage of knowledge, these majestic
    people
Pervade everywhere in an instant, having gained entry into
    knowledge
And having reached higher mystic knowledge,
Like a ship on the ocean being borne along by the wind.

Free from mental effort, established in the work of knowledge,
They discern the becoming, decay, and subsistence of lands
And penetrate the differentiations of the elements,
Their fineness, grossness, and distinctions.

They go into every atom in the billion-world system,
The differentiation of the elements and bodies of beings,
The distinctions and particles of precious substances in the realms
    of bliss:
Knowing these, by their range of knowledge they calculate them
    all.

Their minds developed in knowledge, they bring all bodies
Into their own body, for the benefit of the beings;

Pervading the billion worlds with various forms,
They manifest various bodies in endless worlds.

Just as the sun and moon, while in the sky,
Appear as reflections in water,
Remaining in the highest knowledge of the unmoving essence of
    Thusness,
Enlightening beings appear, as reflections, intending to purify the
    world.

According to beings' dispositions, and the differences in their
    forms,
Enlightening beings appear in all groups, in all worlds:
They appear as disciples, as self-enlightened, as enlightening
    beings,
And in the glorified form of buddhas.

Beings, lands, as well as bodies of fruition of deeds,
The various bodies—of reality, of knowledge—the bodies of
    sages,
The body of space, majestic, all equal,
They manifest, with various mystic powers, to satisfy the world.

With tenfold control and reflection based on pure knowledge,
Acting in accord with knowledge, following kindness and
    compassion,
Doing whatever produces the qualities of all buddhas,
Physically, verbally, mentally, they are stable as a mountain.

All the ten powers of enlightening beings, unshakable,
They attain to, invulnerable to all demons.
Empowered by buddhas, they are honored by the gods
And always attended by thunderbolt-bearers.

The virtues of those who have attained this stage are endless
And could not be exhausted in a billion eons.
Furthermore, they associate with millions of buddhas
And become radiant as regal crowns.

The enlightening beings who have attained this stage
Become great Brahmas, lords of a thousand worlds, rich in virtue.
Able to expound the three vehicles inexhaustibly,
Their pure light of benevolence destroys the afflictions of the
    world.

In a single instant they attain concentrations
Numerous as atoms in a million world systems, steadfast,

And see that many abodes of beings in the ten directions;
And those with superior will go even beyond this.

"This has been a summary of the eighth stage of enlightening beings,
the details of which would take forever to tell."
When this stage had been explained, the Buddha's power shook millions of lands, incalculable, unthinkable. Shining light emanated from
the body of the All-Seer; the lands illumined by the light, the beings
therein were enraptured. A thousand enlightening beings hovering in
the sky presented the Buddha with gifts surpassing those of the gods.
The gods of the higher heavens, ecstatic, honored the Ocean of Virtue
with a variety of offerings. Then a thousand goddesses, thrilled, their
senses all delighted, honored the Teacher with celestial song:

These enlightening beings are all free from defects and defilement,
Impeccably practicing whatever stage they are in;
Considering the weal of the world, they go to all regions,
Showing the way of the Victor, their minds equal to space.

In the realms of humans, celestials, and dragon kings,
The adornments in the ten directions are stamped with higher
    blessings;
Greater still, incomparable, is what the enlightening beings
    show—
They produce the jewels of the path of knowledge.

In one land unmoving, detached in all lands,
Reaching all worlds like the cool light of the moon,
Their minds have ceased all thought of sound;
Their utterances are like echoes from the mountains.

To those who are weak-minded and prone to dejection
They teach the practice of listeners.
Those of keen mind inclined to analyze conditions
They show the knowledge of the way of individual illuminates.

Those who incline to benevolence, for the good of all,
They show the practice of enlightening beings.
To those of foremost wisdom
They show the peerless body of Buddha.

Like magicians performing magic, they show millions of different
    bodies
For the benefit of sentient beings, all of them without real
    existence.
Thus do enlightening beings, involved in the magic of knowledge,
Show all practices, all without real existence.

Having uttered these sweet words of what they'd heard, the goddesses, seeing the Buddha, became silent.

"This assembly is calm and clear," said Moon of Liberation; "speak of the practice beyond the eighth stage, of the kings of the true teaching."

Diamond Matrix said, "Enlightening beings who, by means of the mind which has thus reflected on the infinite possibilities of knowledge, are intent upon yet higher tranquillities and liberations, thinking of consummate attainment of yet higher enlightened knowledge, entering into the secret of the buddhas, ascertaining the greatness of inconceivable knowledge, purifying the ascertainment of spell-concentration, extending mystic knowledge, acting in accord with the differences in worlds, cultivating the insuperability of the powers, expertise, and unique qualities of buddhas, following the might of the turning of the wheel of Teaching of buddhas, not abandoning the attainment of empowerment of great compassion, thus come to the ninth stage of enlightening beings.

"Enlightening beings in this stage of the Good Mind accurately know the performance of good, bad, and neutral things, the performance of mundane and transmundane things, the performance of conceivable and inconceivable things, the performance of tainted and untainted things, the performance of regular and irregular things, the performance of things listeners and individual illuminates do, the performance of things enlightening beings do, the performance of things pertaining to buddhahood, and the performance of fabricated and unfabricated things—all these they know as they really are.

"By means of this knowing awareness, they know accurately how all beings get into entanglement of mind, how they get into entanglement in afflictions, entanglement in acts, entanglement in senses, entanglement in resolutions, entanglement in dispositions, entanglement in inclinations and propensities, entanglement in birth, entanglement in the continuation of habit energies, and how they get into entanglement in the definition of what is beneficial, what is not beneficial, and what is neither beneficial nor unbeneficial—all this they know as it really is.

"They also know the compartmentalization of mind of sentient beings—they accurately know their complexity of mind, the dissolution and nondissolution in instantaneous action of mind, the incorporeality of mind, the endless, ubiquitous all-pervasiveness of mind, the luminosity of mind, the defilement or nondefilement of mind, the bondage or liberation of mind, the creation by illusion of mind, the manifestation of mind according to the state of being; they accurately know hundreds of thousands of differences of mind.

"They also know accurately how far-reaching afflictions are, the endlessness of their applications, their inseparable simultaneity, their being the sole cause of the appearance of propensities, their interconnection and disconnection with the mind, their appearance according to the state of being in the continuity of births, their distinction of being in the realm of desire, form, or formlessness, the great blameworthiness of pride stuck with craving ignorance and views, the continuity of the causality of physical, verbal, and mental actions; in sum, they accurately know the pervasiveness of activities of up to eighty-four thousand afflictions.

"They also accurately know the goodness, badness, or neutrality of actions; whether they are evident or not; their inextricable coexistence with mind; their continuity of fruition through accumulation in spite of their own essence instantly disintegrating; whether or not they have developments; the variety of differences in rewards of pure, impure, and mixed actions; the infinity of the field of action; the difference in holiness and mundanity; how what is produced in the present state is experienced another time around; whether or not actions are a means of release; and whether or not they are sure—in sum, they accurately know as many as eighty-four thousand different aspects of action, as well as how to skillfully ascertain their differences.

"They also know accurately the weakness, mediocrity, and strength of faculties; their disjunction or continuity past to future; their superiority, mediocrity, and inferiority; their inextricable coexistence with afflictions; whether or not they are vehicles of liberation, sure or unsure; their suitability for guidance, according to maturity or immaturity; their nature as grasping of appearances in the rapid disintegration repeated in the net of faculties; the invincibility of the overlordship of faculties; the difference in regressing and nonregressing faculties; their various differences of extent and concurrence—in sum, they accurately know as many as eighty-four thousand different aspects of faculties.

"They also know the weakness, mediocrity, and strength of intentions; their disjunction or continuity past to future; their superiority, mediocrity, and inferiority; their coexistence with afflictions; whether they are vehicles of liberation, sure or not; their nature as grasping of appearances in the rapid disintegration repeated in the net of intentions; the invincibility of the overlordship of intent; the difference in regressing and nonregressing intent; differences in extent and concurrence—in sum, they know as many as eighty-four thousand various aspects of intent.

"They also accurately know the weakness, mediocrity, or strength of dispositions; their disjunction or continuity past and future; their superiority, mediocrity, or inferiority; their concurrence with afflictions; their qualities of being vehicles of liberation or not, sure or not; the certainty or uncertainty of their maturation; their nature of being grasping of appearances in the swift dissolution repeated in the net of dispositions; the invincibility of overlordship of disposition; their persistence and differentiation; differences in extent and concurrence—in sum, they know accurately as many as eighty-four thousand different aspects of inclinations and thousands of various aspects of dispositions.

"They also accurately know the weakness, mediocrity, or strength of wills; their disjunction or continuity past to future; their superiority, mediocrity, or inferiority; their concurrence with afflictions; their quality of being vehicles of liberation or not, sure or not; their certainty or uncertainty of maturity; their being grasping of appearances in the swift dissolution repeated in the net of wills; the invincibility of the overlord-ship of will; their persistence and variety; their extent and concurrence—they accurately know as many as eighty-four thousand different aspects of will as well as thousands of ways of thinking.

"They know accurately how propensities are born together with in-tent and mind; their connection with mind; their disconnection, division, and extent; their never having been uprooted and cast out since begin-ningless time; their being incompatible with all meditations, liberations, concentrations, trances, and mystic knowledges; their binding of the continuity of existence in the world; their activity of binding the mind since beginningless time; their nature of manifestation of accretions in the realms of sense; their being something to be quelled; their presence or absence in the states of the stages of enlightening; their being extracted only by the path of sages—all this enlightening beings know accurately.

"They also accurately know the variety of births; birth according to actions; the differentiation of hells, animal, ghost, and titan realms, humans and celestials; birth in the realms of form and formlessness; birth in realms with thought and without thought; the sprouting of future be-coming from the field of action, the moisture of craving, the darkness of ignorance, and the seeds of consciousness; the concurrence of name and form; continuity due to ignorant craving for becoming; the beginning-lessness and endlessness of desire for enjoyment, desire for existence, and the likes of sentient beings; and how birth is brought forth by grasping for things of the world—all this they know as it really is.

"They also know whether or not habit energies are active; infusion by impressions according to involvements; habituation according to activi-ties of beings; habituation according to acts, afflictions, and customs; habituation to good, bad, and neutral customs; habituation dominating future courses of existence; habituation gradually becoming dominant; habituation in which there persist aberrations producing long-lasting affliction; substantial and insubstantial habituation; and permeation by impressions of seeing and hearing Buddhist practitioners, individual illu-minates, enlightening beings, and buddhas—all these they know as they are.

"They also know accurately the correct stabilization, incorrect stabi-lization, and correct and incorrect stabilization of groups of people; their correct stabilization by correct views, their incorrect stabilization by incorrect views, their nonstabilization without either, their incorrect stabilization by one of the five hellish deeds that bring immediate con-sequence, their correct stabilization by the five religious faculties, their lack of stability without either, their incorrect stabilization in the eight deviations, their correct stabilization in the eightfold right path, their lack of further involvement with either, their indeterminacy without either, their incorrect stabilization on unrelenting envy, jealousy, and lack of sympathy, their stabilization in correctness of practice of the supreme Path of sages, and the indeterminacy of groups apart from both of these—they know all these as they really are. Enlightening beings who have attained such knowledge are said to be established in the ninth stage, Good Mind.

"Enlightening beings in this stage of Good Mind, knowing the differences in sentient beings' conduct, undertake to effect their liberation accordingly. They truly know the maturity of sentient beings as well as their discipline; they truly know the teachings of the vehicle of listeners, the teachings of the vehicle of individual illuminates, the teachings of the vehicle of enlightening beings, and the teachings of the stage of buddhahood.

"Knowing all this, they expound teachings to beings so they may realize Thusness. They expound teachings according to differences in mental dispositions, according to differences in propensities, according to differences in faculties, according to differences in inclinations, through approaching knowledge according to differences in spheres of action, through proceeding according to knowledge of all spheres of action, through proceeding according to tendencies toward entanglement according to disposition, through adaptation to the afflictions, actions, and habits of the various states of being, through going along with the structures of groups, according to the application of whatever means by which liberation may be attained, by appearing in endless forms, by appearing in all worlds in ways congenial to the beings there, by knowing how to say everything, and by skill in ascertainment of all specific knowledge necessary for elucidation of the teachings.

"Enlightening beings established in the stage of Good Mind act as preachers of the Teaching and preserve the treasury of teaching of the Enlightened. In these enlightening beings the unadulterated four special knowledges of enlightening beings are always operative. What are the four? They are the special knowledge of principles, of meanings, of expression, and of elocution. By the knowledge of principles they know the specific characteristics of principles; by knowledge of meanings they know the differentiations of principles; by knowledge of expression they know the unconfused teaching of principles; by knowledge of elocution they know the interrelated continuity of principles.

"Also, by specific knowledge of principles they know the nonexistent body of things. By specific knowledge of meanings, they know the beginning and end of things. By specific knowledge of expression they expound the Teaching by means of interconnected representations of all things. By specific knowledge of elocution they can expound the Teaching boundlessly without destroying representations as they are.

"Also, by specific knowledge of principles they know the present differentiation of things. By specific knowledge of meanings they know the past and future differentiation of things. By specific knowledge of expression they expound the Teaching without mixup of past, future, and present. By specific knowledge of elocution they expound the Teaching in each of the past, future, and present by the beginningless and endless light of truth.

"Also, by specific knowledge of principles they know the variety of phenomena and principles. By specific knowledge of meanings they know the variety of meanings. By specific knowledge of expression they expound the Teaching according to the local language. By specific knowledge of elocution they expound the Teaching according to mental dispositions and knowledge.

"Also, by specific knowledge of principles they know the skill of differentiation of direct knowledge of things without mixup. By specific knowledge of meanings they know the arrangement of suchness by inductive knowledge. By specific knowledge of expression they teach by demonstration of conventional knowledge without mixup. By knowledge of elocution they expound the Teaching by familiarity with knowledge of ultimate truth.

"Also, by specific knowledge of principles, they know one indestructible principle in all things. By specific knowledge of meanings, they enter into realization of familiarity with the interdependent origination of matter and mind, senses, sense data, and sense consciousnesses, and the truths. By specific knowledge of expression they teach in words pleasing and easy to understand for all beings. By specific knowledge of elocution they teach by more and more endless illumination of the Teaching.

"Also, by specific knowledge of principles they know the variety of entries into the One Vehicle. By specific knowledge of meanings they know the distinctions of different vehicles. By the specific knowledge of expression they teach without confusing all vehicles. By specific knowledge of elocution they teach each vehicle with endless illumination of principles.

"Also, by the specific knowledge of principles they enter into action in accord with all practices of enlightening beings, practice of knowledge and practice of principles. By the specific knowledge of meanings they comprehend the differentiations of the teaching of the arrangement of the ten stages. By the specific knowledge of expressions they teach by presenting the path without confusion according to the stage. By specific knowledge of elocution they teach each stage in terms of its endless aspects.

"Also, by the specific knowledge of principles they comprehend all buddhas' attaining enlightenment in an instant. By specific knowledge of meaning they know accord with various differences in times, phenomena, and characteristics. By knowledge of expression they teach by different utterances according to attainment of correct enlightenment. By knowledge of elocution they expound each phrase of the Teaching continuously for endless eons.

"Also, by knowledge of principle they know action in accord with all buddhas' speech, powers, expertises, qualities of buddhahood, great compassion, analytic knowledge, application, teaching, and omniscient knowledge. By knowledge of meaning they know the eighty-four thousand utterances of buddhas according to sentient beings' mental dispositions, faculties, and different inclinations. By knowledge of expression they teach the buddhas' sayings according to the differences in actions of all beings. By knowledge of elocution they expound the Teaching by focus on the sphere of practice reflecting the knowledge of the enlightened.

"The enlightening beings who are thus skillful in effectuation of the science of these specific analytic knowledges, having reached the ninth stage, having attained the treasury of teachings of the enlightened, acting as great preachers of the Teaching, come to attain the concentration spell containing meanings, the concentration spell containing principles, the concentration spell containing evocation of knowledge, the concentration spell containing illumination, the concentration spell of good intellect, the concentration spell containing treasures, the concentration spell containing vital energy, the concentration spell leading into nonattachment and nonobstruction, the concentration spell of infinity, and the concentration spell containing a store of various meanings. They attain countless millions of kinds of concentration spells filled by such spell formulae as these. They expound the Teaching by countless millions of skillfully adapted utterances and unlimited adaptive means of eloquent analysis. By means of these countless millions of concentration spells as doors of access, they listen to the Teaching directly from innumerable buddhas of the ten directions and, having heard the Teaching, do not forget it, and also expound it, with innumerable differentiations, as they have heard it. They completely learn teachings from one buddha through the mediums of countless millions of concentration spells, and as from one, so too from endless buddhas, by measure of their will, to a yet greater extent do they receive the light of the means of access to the Teaching, such as cannot be attained by the retentive power of greatly learned disciples who take up and hold what they learn, even in a hundred thousand eons.

"Thus having attained mental command through concentration spells, having attained eloquence, sitting on the seat of teaching, they pervade a billion worlds and expound the Teaching to beings according to the differences in the mentalities of the beings. As they sit on the seat of teaching, their seat of teaching has immeasurably greater splendor than any except those of the buddhas and the enlightening beings who have reached the stage of coronation. Sitting on the seat of teaching, at will they make one utterance causing all congregations to perceive it as various different utterances. At will they convey knowledge by various different utterances and nuances. At will they draw forth ways of entry into the Teaching by emanating beams of light. At will they emit voices from all their pores. At will they bring forth voices of teaching from all forms manifest in the universe. At will they convey knowledge of all phenomena by means of one utterance. At will they make all sounds into the sound of the Teaching. At will they bring forth the voice of the Teaching from the song and music of all worldly realms. At will they draw forth all the different expressions of the Teaching from a single syllable. At will they draw forth untold ways of entry into the Teaching from each and every atom in the clusters of elements of earth, water, fire, and wind in untold worlds.

"Even if the beings of a billion worlds were to come up, all at the same moment, and ask questions, each of them asking questions with countless nuances, each one asking a different question, the enlightening beings would take in every tone and nuance, and with a single utterance would satisfy all those beings' minds. Even if the beings of untold worlds all came up in the same moment and asked questions, each with innumerable nuances, each different, the enlightening beings would take them all on instantly and edify them all with a single utterance. Pervading untold worlds, they expound the Teaching according to beings' dispositions, faculties, and inclinations. Sitting in discourse on the Teaching, receiving the empowerment of the buddhas, they simultaneously face all beings, doing the work of buddhahood.

"All the more do they undertake the absorption of the light of knowledge in this way: 'Even if on a single point there be buddhas as numerous as atoms in untold worlds teaching in the same immeasurable number of assemblies, each buddha teaching according to the differences of all those innumerable beings, presenting to each being's disposition of mind an equally immeasurable number of teachings, and as one buddha does in one assembly, so also all buddhas, and as in one point so in all universes, there we should produce a memory of such enormous extent and receive the revelation of the Teaching at once from all the buddhas without missing a single word. We should purify the ability to express with certainty such revelation of wisdom as will instantly satisfy all the beings in the aforementioned assemblies, with their various groups, ways, and tendencies, as well as the beings in so many worlds.'

"Enlightening beings who have reached this stage of Good Mind, becoming all the more single-minded in their focus of attention, day and night, entering the sphere of buddhas, joining the company of buddhas, reach the profound liberation of enlightening beings. Enlightening beings acting in accord with such knowledge never stop the vision of buddhas in concentration—in each age seeing countless buddhas, they honor, respect, and venerate them. With immense vision of buddhas they ceaselessly attend them respectfully and ask the buddhas questions. They attain mental command of the Teaching and can expound it.

"Those purified roots of goodness of enlightening beings become all the more beyond compare. Just as gold fashioned into ornaments, perfected by a skilled goldsmith and put on the head or neck of a universal monarch, cannot be outshone by the adornments of all minor kings and people of the four continents, in the same way the roots of goodness of enlightening beings in the stage of Good Mind, well arrayed by the light of great knowledge, are so purified that they cannot be outshone by all listeners, individual illuminates, and enlightening beings in lower stages. The light of their roots of goodness, shining on the mental tangles of afflictions of sentient beings, put an end to them. Just as great Brahmas of million-world systems illumine the thickets and lowlands in all worlds of the million-world system, in the same way does the light of roots of goodness of enlightening beings in this stage of Good Mind shine on the mental thickets of afflictions of sentient beings and put an end to them. Of the ten transcendent ways, transcendent power is predominant in these enlightening beings, while they practice the others as best they can.

"This is a summary explanation of the ninth stage of enlightening beings, called Good Mind, the full details of which would take forever to tell. Most of the enlightening beings in this stage become great Brahmas of enormous power, lords of a million worlds, eminent, unsurpassed, seers of what is beneficial, masterful, able and strong in the exposition of the ways of transcendence of all listeners, individual illuminates, and enlightening beings, invincible in answering questions according to beings' dispositions. Whatever actions they undertake, whether by giving, kind speech, beneficial action, or cooperation, it is never apart from thoughts of Buddha, the Teaching, the Community, enlightening beings, the practices of enlightening beings, the ways of transcendence, the stages, the powers, expertises, and unique qualities of Buddhas, and ultimately omniscience in all its aspects. Why? Because they want to become the best of beings, unexcelled leaders and guides, and ultimately omniscient refuges.

"With this desire they exert their energy, by which exertion of energy they attain in one instant as many concentrations as atoms in countless millions of buddha-lands, see as many buddhas as atoms in countless millions of buddha-lands and become aware of their power, shake as many worlds as atoms in countless millions of buddha-lands, go to as many buddha-lands as atoms in countless millions of buddha-lands, illumine as many lands as atoms in countless millions of buddha-lands, mature as many beings as atoms in countless millions of buddha-lands, abide for as many eons as atoms in countless millions of buddha-lands, penetrate as many eons past and future as atoms in countless millions of buddha-lands, ascertain as many ways of entry into the Teaching as atoms in countless millions of buddha-lands, and manifest as many bodies as atoms in countless millions of buddha-lands, manifesting each body accompanied by as many enlightening beings as atoms in countless millions of buddha-lands. Beyond that, enlightening beings with the power of vows perform, by the excellence of their vows, countless transformations, of the body, aura, mystic powers, vision, sphere of action, voice, conduct, adornment, power, resolution, and performances."

Then Diamond Matrix spoke these verses describing this stage:

> Contemplating with immeasurably powerful intellect,
> With very subtle knowledge, atom-splitting knowledge,
> Thus entering into the abode of the secret of buddhas,
> They reach the ninth stage, benefactors of the world.

Their mental command and concentration are great,
Their far-reaching mystic knowledge enters all lands.
With certainty of knowledge and power, this is the abode of
    steadfastness of the conquerers—
The wise with commitment and compassion enter this ninth
    stage.

Those who have reached this stage, holders of buddhas' treasury,
Know what is good, what is bad, and what is neutral,
What is tainted and worldly, and what is transcendent,
What is conceivable and what is inconceivable.

They examine what is certain and what is uncertain,
And foster the practices accomplishing the Three Vehicles.
Teachings of the stages, according to inclinations and conduct,
They prepare and enter the world accordingly.

With superior subtle intellect following such knowledge,
They search out the mental tangles of sentient beings:
They search out the various tangles of mind
And comprehend who can be taught, what the end and the
    beginning are.

They comprehend beginningless afflictions, in their
    interrelatedness of application,
As well as the continuity of their courses through compulsive
    propensities,
And in terms of the various differences in process of action,
And the vanishing of effect with extinction of cause.

They comprehend which faculties are weak, middling, and
    strong,
And continuity between past and future:
Inclinations of various kinds, and whether or not they are pure,
They comprehend, all, eighty-four thousand.

Worldly beings are developed into different dispositions,
Gone into the tangles of afflictions and views, beginningless,
    endless, never cut off,
Continually bound up with the mind
Born together with and stuck to inclinations and propensities.

Those inclinations and propensities are not real things,
They have no location and are not apart from mind;
Hard to know, unconquerable by the states of meditation,
They can be cut off only by the diamond thunderbolt of the Path.

Entering the variety of six courses of migration of life,
Craving being the moisture, ignorance the shade, action the field,
Consciousness the seeds, name and form the simultaneous
   sprouts—
Thus do they see beings in the world, beginningless and endless.

Those beings' minds are full of the action of afflictions, according
   to patterns of habit—
Apart from this they have no desire for further continuation of
   transmigration.
The enlightening beings know who are stabilized in truth, in
   error, and indeterminate,
Who are those sunk in views, and who are those with knowledge.

With these reflections, stationed in this stage,
Enlightening beings reveal the Teaching in different ways
According to people's dispositions, faculties, and inclinations,
Versed in analytic knowledge, meanings, elocution, and
   expression.

They are in the position of preachers of the Teaching,
Like lions, like bulls, like majestic mountains;
They shower the sweet rain of the elixir of immortality,
Just as the water spirits fill the sea.

Skilled in seeking out meanings, as well as the essence of things,
Comprehending all expressions, they have mastered elocution;
Having attained countless millions of decades of concentration
   spells,
They hold the Teachings as the ocean holds the rain.

Thus having attained concentration by purification through spells,
They see thousands of buddhas in one instant;
And having gained the treasure of the Teaching, they expound it,
Reaching each and every sphere with its purifying sound.

They set the various beings of the billion worlds
Free by means of the three treasures,
Satisfying all according to their faculties and dispositions,
Like water spirits filling the ocean.

With even greater virtue they exert their energy
And think how there are, in a minute point,
Unthinkable numbers of buddhas teaching, and various beings;
Hearing the teachings, they hold them as the earth holds seeds.

As many beings as there are in the ten directions,
All sit in a single circle of assembly:
Appearing to them all in a single instant, enlightening beings
Will satisfy them all with a single utterance.

Stationed here, masters of the Teaching, highest of humans and
    gods,
They become children of buddhas, moving by the teachings:
Day and night they are in the company of the buddhas,
Established in profound tranquillity, firm in knowledge and
    liberation.

They attend millions of buddhas
And become purified, like the adornments of a monarch;
Their light overcomes the obscurities of afflictions
Like the light of Brahma illumining a million worlds.

In this stage they become Brahma gods, imbued with virtue,
And satisfy beings with the teachings of the Three Vehicles.
What they undertake is for the benefit of all beings;
Following enlightened knowledge, they attain virtue and
    knowledge.

In a single instant they attain as many concentrations
As atoms in immeasurable lands, steadfast:
Seeing the buddhas of the ten directions, they hear the Teaching,
And beyond that, by willpower, they work innumerable
    miracles.

"Thus has been told the ninth stage of those contemplating great
knowledge, profound, hard to see, subtle, the ninth stage of enlightening
beings, called Good Mind."

Thus having heard of unsurpassed practice, millions of celestials of the
Pure Abodes were delighted; they stood in the sky, their senses enraptured, and paid honor to the Buddha. Endless millions of enlightening
beings hovering in the sky were gladdened; they burnt clouds of incense,
incomparably delightful, destroying the afflictions of the world. The
king of the heaven of power, pleased, was in the sky with a retinue of
trillions, all respectfully showering vestments, beautiful, excellent, by the
hundreds. Many goddesses, their senses delighted, honored the Buddha
respectfully, playing trillions of musical instruments, uttering such words
as these:

The Buddha, sitting in one land,
Appears reflected in all lands;

Bodies of millions of varieties, pleasing,
Pervade the reaches of the cosmos.

From one hair of the Buddha light beams
Emerge, annihilating the afflictions of the world;
The elemental particles of the land may be counted,
But the number of those light beams cannot be known.

Sometimes they show buddhas imbued with supreme
       characteristics
Turning the wheel of the highest teaching;
Sometimes there appears the lord of humans, pure and calm,
With his most excellent, unsurpassed conduct, in other lands.

The Guide is seen in the abode of happiness,
Dying there and so coming to earth,
In the womb, thus in millions of lands,
Or seen being born there in the land.

The Guide, going forth for the sake of the world
And becoming supremely enlightened,
So turning the wheel of the Teaching,
Is seen in millions of lands.

Just as a magician versed in the arts of magic
Shows many objects for people,
So does the Teacher, versed in supreme knowledge,
Show all bodies to people.

Empty, quiescent, essentially signless,
The nature of things is equal to space—
The enlightened Teacher, by ultimate truth,
Shows the exalted sphere of buddhas.

As is the essence of the buddhas,
So is that of sentient beings—found in the nature of things.
Signs and signlessness are equal in that way—
All things are ultimately signless.

Those who seek enlightened knowledge
Abandon assumptions, notions, imaginations;
Aware that being and nonbeing are the same in essence,
They will quickly become supreme human leaders.

Having spoken thousands of such sweet words, the goddesses, looking at
the Buddha, became silent and remained quiet. Knowing the assembly

was settled, the fearless Moon of Liberation asked Diamond Matrix, the dauntless enlightening being, "Tell us, in order, all the characteristics, qualities, and sphere of those who come to the tenth stage, as well as their marks and miracles."

Diamond Matrix said, "Those enlightening beings who, having wisely reflected on the possibilities of knowledge up to the ninth stage, have made a thorough and discerning investigation, have thoroughly fulfilled pure practices, have gathered inexhaustible provisions, have acquired great stores of virtue and knowledge, have attained great, far-reaching compassion, are familiar with the distinctions and differentiations of worldly realms, have gone into the thickets of the realms of sentient beings, focus their perception and attention on approaching entry into the sphere of buddhas, and are intent on the powers, expertises, and other qualities of buddhahood, are said to have reached the stage of coronation with omniscience in all its aspects.

"Furthermore, enlightening beings who accord with this knowledge and have reached the stage of coronation realize a concentration called undefiled, one called entry into the analysis of differentiations of the cosmos, one called array of adornments of the pinnacle of enlightenment, one called flower of lights of all appearances, one called oceanic container, one called oceanic plenitude, one called vast as space, once called ascertainment of the intrinsic essence of all things, one called adjusting to the mental behavior of all beings, and one called appearing in the presence of all buddhas. Beginning with these, they realize incalculable millions of concentrations.

"They enter and emerge from all these concentrations, and, having attained skill in concentration, they experience all the effects of concentration. At the end of the incalculable millions of concentrations, one realizes a concentration of enlightening beings called bearing coronation by the special property of omniscient knowledge. At the moment one realizes this concentration, there appears an immeasurable lotus made of the finest jewels, as large as ten billion-world universes, inlaid with all kinds of jewels, beyond the range of all worlds, arisen from transmundane roots of goodness, existing in the realm of the essence of illusoriness, appearing based on the cosmos, beyond the range of the heavens, with a jewel stem, a pericarp of incomparable sandalwood, a fringe of huge emeralds, leaves of shining gold, its body flowering with innumerable rays of light, its interior filled with all the finest jewels, covered with a boundlessly vast net of jewels, surrounded by as many great jewel lotuses as atoms in ten billion-world universes.

"The enlightening being, in a corresponding form, stands by and, immediately upon attainment of the concentration bearing coronation with the special qualities of omniscience, appears seated on the great jewel lotus. As soon as the enlightening being is seated on this great jewel lotus, as many enlightening beings as there are surrounding jewel lotuses come from the ten directions, circle that enlightening being, and sit on those great surrounding jewel lotuses, and each of them enter a million concentrations, while gazing on the central enlightening being. Immediately upon everyone's entry into concentration, all worlds quake, all ills cease, all universes are pervaded with revealing light, all worlds are purified, the names of all buddha-lands are voiced, all enlightening beings of the same practice gather, all celestial and human music and song sound forth, all beings become blissful, the inconceivable honoring and attendance of all the perfectly enlightened ones commence, and the circles of all the buddhas are made known.

"What is the reason for that? As soon as the enlightening being sits on this great jewel lotus, from the soles of the enlightening being's feet emerge countless millions of light rays, which illumine the uninterrupted great hells in the ten directions and extinguish the torments of the beings in the hells. From the circles on the knees of the enlightening being emerge countless millions of light rays which illumine all the animal realms in the ten directions and extinguish the sufferings of all the animals. From the sphere of the navel emerge countless millions of rays of light which illumine all the ghost realms in the ten directions and extinguish all the pains of all the beings in the ghost realms. From the left and right sides of the enlightening being emerge countless millions of rays of light which illumine the humans in the ten directions and extinguish human sufferings. From both hands emerge countless millions of light rays which illumine the abodes of celestials and titans, extinguishing their pains. From the shoulders emerge countless millions of rays of light which illumine all those in the vehicle of listeners, followers of the elementary teachings in the ten directions, and present to them a way of entry into the light of the Teaching. From the back of the neck emerge countless millions of rays of light which illumine all the individually awakened ones in the ten directions and present to them a method for quiescent concentration. From the face emerge countless millions of light rays which illumine all the enlightening beings in the ten directions, from those who have just been inspired for the first time up to those who have reached the ninth stage, and present to them the principle of wisdom and skill in means. From the circle of hair between the brows of the enlightening being emerge countless millions of rays of light which shine on the abodes of demons in the ten directions and eclipse them, and then illumine the enlightening beings who have reached the stage of coronation and disappear into their bodies. From the top of the head emerge as many rays of light as atoms in countless millions of billion-world universes, illumining the sites of congregation of all buddhas throughout the reaches of the space of the cosmos, then circling the world to the right in ten ways, then stopping in the sky and forming a great circular network of lights, and then proceeding to make a great offering called 'blazing light' to all buddhas. That offering is such that the offerings of all enlightening beings from the first inspiration up to the ninth stage cannot compare even to the smallest fraction of it.

"Furthermore, from that great circular network of lights there rain, in all universes in the ten directions, manifestations of flowers, incenses, garlands, perfumes, aromatic powders, robes, parasols, banners, pennants, clothing, ornaments, jewels, and more, all beyond the scope of all worlds, produced by the influence of stores of transmundane roots of goodness, complete in all their features and qualities, sustained by the inconceivable power of nirvana—rains of various arrays of great riches pour as from a great cloud on the places of assembly of each and every buddha. And whoever perceives those offerings becomes assured of perfect enlightenment.

"Then the lights, having made these offerings, again illumine the circles of assembly of all buddhas, then circle the world to the right in ten ways, and disappear into the soles of the feet of those buddhas. Thence it is known to those buddhas and those enlightening beings that in this world, this realm, this place, the enlightening being following such a practice has reached the time of coronation. Then, from incalculable lands in the ten directions, enlightening beings up to the ninth stage come to that enlightening being, encircle the enlightening being, make great offerings, and, while gazing on that enlightening being, enter a million concentrations.

"From the gloriously adorned thunderbolt symbols of well-being on the bodies of enlightening beings who have attained the stage of coronation emerges a great light ray called demon-conqueror, each ray accompanied by countless millions of light rays; having illumined the ten directions and shown countless miracles, the light rays again disappear into the enlightening beings' thunderbolt symbols of well-being. As soon as those light rays of a hundred thousand higher qualities disappear, there appears an increase in the power and strength of the enlightening being.

"Then there emerges from the circle of hair between the eyebrows of the buddhas beams of light called possessors of omniscient superknowledge, accompanied by countless light beams; illumining all worlds in the ten directions, circling the worlds in ten ways to the right, inspiring many hundreds of quadrillions of enlightening beings, causing all buddha-lands to quake in six ways, stopping all death and rebirth in bad conditions, eclipsing all abodes of demons, showing the settings of enlightenment of all buddhas, and illuminating all worlds throughout the cosmos to the furthest reaches of space, then returning again, circling all assemblies of enlightening beings to the right and manifesting an immense array, those beams of light disappear into the top of the enlightening being's head. The accompanying light beams in the same way enter into the heads of the enlightening beings assembled around that enlightening being who has reached the tenth stage, whereupon they attain a million concentrations that they have never attained before.

"At the same time as those light beams enter the enlightening being's head, the enlightening being is said to be coronated; in the realm of perfectly completely enlightened ones, having fulfilled the ten powers, the enlightening being enters the ranks of the perfect buddhas. It is like the son of a universal ruler, the crown prince, borne by the principal wife, becoming imbued with the characteristics of a universal ruler: the universal ruler seats him on a magnificent golden elephant throne and, bringing water from the four seas, setting over the palace great arrays of flowers, incenses, lamps, garlands, perfumes, aromatic powders, cloths, parasols, banners, pennants, music and song, he takes the golden pitcher containing water from the four oceans and anoints the head of his son with the water, whereupon the son joins the ranks of the consecrated rulers. Then, when he has fulfilled the tenfold path of good action, he gains the name of universal ruler, the one who turns the wheel of the law. In the same way, as soon as the enlightening being is coronated by those blessed buddhas, the enlightening being is said to be anointed with great knowledge. And having fulfilled the ten powers by the anointment of complete buddhas, the enlightening being enters the ranks of the truly consummately enlightened ones. This is the enlightening being's anointment, or coronation, with great knowledge, in quest of which the enlightening being undertakes many hundreds of thousands of difficult practices. Thus coronated, matured in immeasurable virtue and knowledge, the enlightening being is said to be established in the tenth stage, which is called Cloud of Teaching.

"Enlightening beings in this stage have accurate knowledge of the totality of the realm of reality, the realm of desire, the realm of form, the formless realm, the realm of worlds, the realm of all beings, the realm of consciousness, the realms of the created and the uncreated, the realm of space, and the teaching of being and nonbeing; they have accurate knowledge of the totality of the realm of nirvana, and of afflictions created by views; they have accurate knowledge of the totality of the becoming and decay of worlds, of the practice of followers of the elementary Buddhist teachings, of the practice of individual illuminates, of the practice of enlightening beings, of the buddhas' powers, expertises, unique qualities of buddhahood, and material and spiritual bodies, of omniscience in all its aspects, of demonstration of attainment of enlightenment and turning the wheel of teaching—in sum, they have accurate knowledge of accomplishment of all the different ways of access to truth. They also have accurate knowledge of the projection of the world, the projection of the cosmos, the projection of Buddhist followers, the projection of individual illuminates, the projection of enlightening beings, the projection of buddhas, and the feasibility or unfeasibility of all projections.

"They also know the basis of all buddhas as it really is; they know, too, the basis of the Teaching, the basis of the Community, the basis of action, the basis of affliction, the basis of time, the basis of commitment, the basis of reverence, the basis of conduct, the basis of ages, and the basis of knowledge, all as they truly are.

"Also, all knowledge of the buddhas entering into subtleties—

knowledge of details of practice, of death in heaven and rebirth on earth, of birth, of leaving home, of attaining enlightenment, of miracles, of setting the wheel of the Teaching in motion, of preaching the truth, of the full details of the Teaching, of the support of the life span, of the manifestation of the body of glorified form, of the orderly guidance of all beings, of manifestation in all worlds, of observing the mental behavior of all beings, of observing past, present, and future in a single instant, of the entire past and future, of the totality of mental actions of beings in all their variety, of the inconceivable powers, expertises, and special qualities of the enlightened, of the ultimate nirvana of the buddhas, of the lasting of the true Teaching based on instruction—beginning with these, they accurately know all the incalculable knowledges of buddhas entering into subtleties.

"They know all the secret matters of the buddhas, such as the secret of the body, the secret of speech, the secret of mind, the secret of consideration of right and wrong timing, the secret of giving enlightening beings predictions of enlightenment, the secret of taking care of sentient beings, the secret of encouragement and censure as means of guidance, the secret of impartiality in timely admonition and instruction, the secret of establishing a variety of vehicles of liberation, the secret of distinction of beings' conduct and faculties, the secret of penetrating beings' acts and deeds, the secret of distinction of enlightening beings' practices and faculties, the secret of enlightenment through practice and realization of inherent power, the secret of the basis of realization of intrinsic essence, the secret of manifestation and liberation, the secret of attraction and expulsion, the secret of showing the attitudes of standing, walking, sitting, and reclining, the secret of provision of food and physical necessities, the secret of showing speech, silence, meditation, liberation, concentration, and attainment; they know all such secret matters of the buddhas as they really are.

"They also accurately realize all the buddhas' knowledges of the interpenetration of ages, such as one age as containing incalculable ages, incalculable ages as containing one age, calculable ages as containing incalculable ages, incalculable ages as containing calculable ages, a moment of thought as containing ages, ages as containing moments of thought, ages as containing nonages, nonages as containing ages, ages with buddhas as containing ages without buddhas, ages without buddhas as containing ages with buddhas, past ages as containing future and present ages, present ages as containing past and future ages, future ages as containing past and present ages, long ages as containing short ages, short ages as containing long ages, the containment of what is made of perceptions in all ages, the containment of ages in all that is made of perceptions.

"They also accurately know all the complete buddhas' penetrating knowledges, such as knowledge penetrating a point the size of a hairtip, knowledge penetrating atomic particles, knowledge penetrating realization of enlightenment in the body and land of a buddha, knowledge penetrating realization of enlightenment with the body and mind of a sentient being, knowledge penetrating the realization of enlightenment in all places, knowledge penetrating demonstration of preposterous actions, knowledge penetrating demonstration of conformist behavior, knowledge penetrating demonstration of unconventional behavior, knowledge penetrating demonstration of conceivable and inconceivable acts, acts that can be recognized by the world and acts that cannot be recognized, knowledge penetrating demonstration of acts that can be understood by buddhas' disciples, acts that can be understood by self-enlightened people, acts that can be understood by enlightening beings, and acts that can be understood by buddhas. Just as such vast extent of knowledge of the buddhas is immeasurable, so also the penetrating knowledge of enlightening beings in this stage is infinite.

"Furthermore, the enlightening beings following this stage attain the liberation of enlightening beings that is called inconceivable, and the liberations called unobstructed, pure discernment, all-sided illumination, treasury of realization of thusness, following the unhindered wheel, comprehending past, present, and future, matrix of the cosmos, radiance of the circle of liberation, and attainment of the realm of totality. Beginning with these, enlightening beings in the tenth stage attain countless hundreds of thousands of doors of liberation, and in the same way they attain hundreds of thousands of concentrations, mental controls, super-knowledges, and spiritual powers; they attain hundreds of thousands of lights of knowledge, mystical transformations, accomplishments of analytic knowledge, masteries of means and wisdom, floods of great compassion, and entries into the controlling powers of enlightening beings.

"By means of intellect in accord with such knowledge, they become imbued with infinite ability to recollect anything. They are able to receive, take in, and hold infinite great revelations, clarifications, and clouds of teachings from the buddhas of the ten directions in a single instant. Just as no place on earth except the ocean can bear, can receive, can take in, can hold the great mass of water showered by the clouds of the oceanic water spirit, in the same way the entries into the mysteries of the buddhas—great revelations, great clarifications, great clouds of teachings—cannot be born, received, taken in, or held by all sentient beings, listeners, or self-enlightened ones, or even by enlightening beings from the first to the ninth stages. It is the enlightening beings in the tenth stage, cloud of teaching, who bear, receive, take in, and hold it all. It is as the ocean bears, receives, takes in, and holds the great clouds of one water spirit, or two, or three, up to the innumerable great clouds of innumerable water spirits in a single moment, because of the immeasurable vast breadth of the ocean. In the same way, enlightening beings in this tenth stage, Cloud of Teaching, bear, receive, take in, and hold, in a single instant, immeasurable great revelations, clarifications, and clouds of great teachings from two, three, up to infinitely many buddhas. Thus this stage is called Cloud of Teaching."

The enlightening being Moon of Liberation said, "Is it possible to count how many buddhas the enlightening beings receive and hold the great revelations, clarifications, and clouds of teachings from in a single instant?"

Diamond Matrix said, "It is not possible to give a numerical account of how many buddhas enlightening beings receive teachings from in a single instant. I will, however, make a simile. Suppose that in each of the ten directions, in worlds as numerous as atoms in untold quintillions of buddha-lands, and all the realms of beings found therein, there were one being with the mental command to retain whatever he heard, an attendant of buddhas, a great disciple, foremost of the holders of learning, and that being were endowed with such power of skill in learning. Now suppose all the beings in all those worlds were similarly endowed, and what was learned by each one was not learned by another. What do you think—would the learning ability of all those beings be immeasurable?" Moon of Liberation said, "Great, immeasurable would be the learning ability of those beings." Diamond Matrix said, "I tell you, in an instant the enlightening beings in this stage of Cloud of Teaching bear, receive, take in, and hold from a buddha a great cloud of lights of revelation of teaching called 'treasury of past, present, and future of the cosmos'—the aforementioned ability in learning cannot compare to the minutest fraction of this ability to hold the cloud of light of revelation of the teaching. And just as they receive this from one buddha, so also do they receive and hold the cloud of lights of revelation of great teaching called 'treasury of the past, present, and future of the cosmos' from as many buddhas as atoms in all the worlds of the ten directions, and from yet more, from infinite buddhas, all in a single instant. Hence this stage is called Cloud of Teaching.

"Furthermore, enlightening beings in this stage, by the power of their own vows, cause great clouds of compassion to arise, manifesting the thunder of the great Teaching, flashing the lightning of mystic knowledge, science, and expertise, whipping up a great wind of radiance, covering all with a dense cloud of virtue and knowledge, showing a dense swirl of various bodies, uttering the proclamation of the great Teaching, routing the horde of demons; and, in one instant, throughout as many quadrillions of worlds as atoms in the worlds in the ten directions mentioned above, and throughout yet more worlds, incalculable hundreds of quadrillions of worlds, they show great rains of goodness-bearing elixir of immortality and settle and extinguish all the dust and flames of afflictions of beings produced by ignorance. Hence this stage is called Cloud of Teaching.

"Furthermore, the enlightening beings in this stage of Cloud of Teaching manifest all the works of buddhas in one world, beginning with abiding in the heaven of satisfaction, then descending to earth, abiding in the womb, birth, leaving home, attaining enlightenment, being requested to teach, setting in motion the wheel of the Teaching, and the stage of great ultimate nirvana, manifesting these to beings according to their dispositions and capacities for being guided. As they do this in one world, so also do they do the same in two worlds, up to unspeakable, untold numbers of worlds. Having attained such control of knowledge, with absolutely certain great knowledge and mystic knowledge, at will they show a defiled world as pure, show a pure world as defiled, show a narrow world as broad, show a broad world as narrow; in this way, by mystic power, they show magical transformations of all worlds—vast, measureless, minute, erroneous, deranged, inverted, upright, and so on. If they want they can put a whole world, including its peripheral mountains and seas, into a single atom, yet without expanding the atom or shrinking the world, displaying all functions therein. They put two, three, four, five, up to untold numbers of worlds into one atom, yet without expanding the atom, and still displaying all the functions in the worlds. At will they show in one world the arrays of two worlds or, as they wish, show the arrays of up to an untold number of worlds. As they wish, they show the array of one world in two worlds, or in up to an unspeakable number of worlds. As they wish they show in one world the beings in up to an unspeakable number of worlds yet without injuring or troubling those beings. As they wish they show the beings of one world in an unspeakable number of worlds, without injuring or disturbing the beings. As they wish they show the full array of a buddha-realm in a point the size of a hairtip; if they wish they show the full arrays of untold buddha-realms in one point. As they wish they instantly emanate as many bodies as atoms in untold worlds, manifest that many hands on each individual body, and make offerings to the buddhas of the ten directions with those hands; with each hand they sprinkle as many baskets of flowers on those buddhas as there are grains of sand in the Ganges River, and do likewise with fragrances, garlands, perfumes, aromatic powders, robes, parasols, banners, and pennants. They also manifest that many heads on each body, and manifest that many tongues in each head, telling of the glory of the buddhas.

"In the arising of a thought they go throughout the ten directions, in each moment of thought causing the appearance of infinite sets of the process of attainment of enlightenment up to great ultimate nirvana. They also manifest infinite embodiments in all times, and also cause to appear in their own bodies the immeasurable arrays of qualities of lands of infinite buddhas. They also cause the appearance of all worlds becoming and disintegrating in their own bodies. They also emit all whirlwinds from a single pore, yet without hurting or troubling sentient beings. And, if they wish, they can make endless worlds a single body of water and set a great lotus thereon; the array of lights of that great lotus pervades endless worlds, showing therein the branches of the trees of enlightenment and all aspects of omniscience.

"In their own bodies they manifest the lights of the ten directions, including the lusters of jewels, lightning, the lights of the sun and moon, and the lights of all deities of light. With each breath they shake endless worlds, yet without frightening the sentient beings therein. They also manifest the destruction by gales, fires, and floods in the ten directions. Also they cause the appearance of physical adornments according to the wishes of beings: they manifest the body of Buddha in their own body; they manifest their own body in the body of Buddha; they manifest their own buddha-land in the body of Buddha; they manifest the body of Buddha in their own buddha-land.

"Thus do enlightening beings in this stage of Cloud of Teaching show these and infinitely more magical transformations."

At that point it occurred to the enlightening beings in the assembly, as well as to the spirits, goblins, nymphs, titans, and various gods, "If the range of performances of mystical powers of enlightening beings is thus measureless, what must that of the buddhas be like?"

Then Moon of Liberation, knowing what was going on in the minds of the congregation, said to Diamond Matrix, "This assembly is in doubt; show something of the miracles of enlightening beings to stop their doubts."

Then Diamond Matrix entered the concentration of enlightening beings called "revelation of the essence of the body of all buddha-lands," whereupon all the beings in the assembly perceived themselves being within the body of the enlightening being Diamond Matrix, and there they perceived the formation of a buddha-land, the array of features within which could not be all told of in millions of eons. There the tree of enlightenment was as broad as a million billion-world universes, the lofty tops of its innumerable branches wide enough to fill ten million billion-world universes. On the terrace of enlightenment there was a broad lion seat, with characteristics corresponding to the tree, on which was seen a buddha named King with a Mind Endowed with All Mystic Knowledges, on the supreme place of enlightenment. Thus they saw such magnificent arrays of adornments as could not be all told in a million eons. Then, having displayed this great miracle, Diamond Matrix put all the enlightening beings, gods, dragons, goblins, nymphs, titans, fairies, and other creatures back in their respective places. At that point they all fell silent in unprecedented wonder and stood there looking at Diamond Matrix.

Then Moon of Liberation said to Diamond Matrix, "The range of production of magnificent arrays of this well-nigh inconceivable concentration is most extraordinary—what is the name of this concentration?"

Diamond Matrix said, "It is called 'revelation of the essence of the body of all buddha-lands.'"

Moon of Liberation said, "What is the arrangement of the sphere of action of this concentration?"

Diamond Matrix said, "By successful cultivation of this concentration, enlightening beings can, at will, show in their own bodies as many buddha-lands as atoms in as many worlds as grains of sand in the Ganges River, and even more. You know, enlightening beings in the stage of

Cloud of Teaching attain many hundreds of thousands of enlightening concentrations like this. Because of this, enlightening beings who have reached even the stage of 'crown prince of the teaching' and are established in the ninth stage, Good Mind, cannot know the body or physical action of enlightening beings in the tenth stage, cannot know their speech or verbal action, cannot know their mind or mental action, cannot know their spiritual powers, cannot know their observation of past, present, and future, cannot know their entry into the state of concentration, cannot know their sphere of knowledge, cannot know their liberation and freedom, cannot know their acts of emanation, mystical power, and radiance, cannot even know, to sum up, even the raising and lowering of their feet as they walk. This is how infinite the enlightening beings' stage of Cloud of Teaching is. This is a brief summary explanation; the full details could never be all told.''

Moon of Liberation said, "What is the entrance into the range of the sphere of buddhas like, if the realm and power of the practice of enlightening beings is so infinite?"

Diamond Matrix said, "Your question seems to me like that of a man who picks up a few pebbles and says, 'Which is bigger, the endless realms of the earth or these pebbles?' How can you compare the state of enlightening beings to that of the buddhas, the completely enlightened, who have measureless knowledge? That which can be picked up off the ground by hand is small, while the rest of the earth is immeasurable: in the same way, even this Cloud of Teaching stage of enlightening beings would only be told to a small extent even if it were explained for countless eons—how much the more so of the stage of buddhahood!

"I will now tell you about buddhahood, so you will know; and the buddhas stand before me to bear me witness. Suppose in each of the ten directions as many buddha-lands as atoms in infinite worlds were filled with enlightening beings who had reached this stage: the accomplishments of those enlightening beings effected over endless eons do not amount to the minutest fraction, do not compare at all, to the scope of one moment of knowledge of Buddha. Following this knowledge, enlightening beings, with body, speech, and mind not other than those of Buddha, do not abandon the power of concentration of enlightening beings, yet they visit and attend buddhas, and pay each one honor in all kinds of undertakings for endless eons. Because of their extensive service they receive from the buddhas the illumination of empowerment, and become all the more unfazed in answering questions as variegated as the cosmos, for millions and millions of eons.

"Just as a great ornament, inlaid with great jewels, fashioned by a celestial craftsman, fastened on the head or neck of the king of the gods of controlling power, cannot be outshone by the ornaments of other gods or humans, in the same way the ornament of knowledge gained by enlightening beings in this tenth stage of Cloud of Teaching cannot be outshone by all sentient beings, Buddhist followers, solitary illuminates, or enlightening beings from the first to the ninth stages. The light of knowledge of the enlightening beings in this stage is conducive to the introduction of sentient beings into omniscience, and cannot be outshone by other lights of knowledge. Just as the light of the great lord god is beyond all realms of birth and delights the bodies of living beings, in the same way the light of enlightening beings in the stage of Cloud of Teaching cannot be eclipsed by all followers, solitary illuminates, and enlightening beings from the first to the ninth stages, and even ultimately leads beings to the state of omniscience.

"Furthermore, enlightening beings following this knowledge are told by the buddhas knowledge of past, present, and future, knowledge of the differentiations of the cosmos, knowledge of pervasion of all worlds, knowledge of the power of the illumination of all worlds, thorough knowledge of all beings, lands, and phenomena, knowledge of the mental behaviors of all beings, knowledge of how to develop all beings to maturity according to the time, with impeccable discipline and skill in analytic knowledge of all things; in sum they are told infinite revelations of omniscient knowledge. In these enlightening beings the transcendent way of knowledge is paramount, while they practice the other transcendent ways according to their power and their lot.

"This is a summary of the tenth stage of enlightening beings, called Cloud of Teaching; it would take forever to tell the full details. Most of the enlightening beings in this stage are great lord gods, capable, mighty in teaching beings the ways of transcendence of disciples, solitary illuminates, and enlightening beings, unfazed in answering questions on the differentiations of the cosmos. Whatever acts they undertake, whether through giving, or kind speech, or beneficial action, or cooperation, it is all never apart from thoughts of Buddha, the Teaching, the Community, enlightening beings, the practice of enlightening beings, the transcendent ways, the stages, the powers, expertises, and unique qualities of buddhahood, and ultimately of omniscience in all its aspects. Why? Because they would become the best of beings, unexcelled leaders and guides, and ultimately omniscient refuges.

Accordingly, they initiate such effort, by which burst of energy they instantly attain as many concentrations as atoms in ten quintillion unspeakable numbers of buddha-lands, see that many buddhas and realize their power, shake that many worlds, go to that many buddha-lands, illumine that many worlds, mature that many beings, abide for that many eons, penetrate that many eons past and future, ascertain that many ways of access to truth, and show that many bodies, each body surrounded by that many enlightening beings. Beyond that, enlightening beings with the power of vows perform, by the excellence of their vows, countless transformations of their bodies, auras, mystic powers, vision, spheres of action, voices, conduct, adornments, powers, resolutions, and performances."

Bequest

These, in sum, are the stages of enlightening beings, the details of which
would take forever to tell. These are the stages which have been, will be,
and are expounded by the buddhas of past, future, and present.

Furthermore, these ten stages of enlightening beings are to be seen
in accord with omniscience in all its aspects, as it gradually becomes
manifest.

It is like the water flowing from the lake Heatless; by four great river
currents it suffices the continent, inexhaustible, ever increasing, benefiting
infinite beings, and finally pours into the great ocean: that water from
the very beginning is headed for the ocean. In the same way, the water of
roots of goodness flowing from the great lake of the will for enlightenment, by the currents of four great vows and integrative methods of
salvation, suffices all realms of beings, inexhaustible, ever increasing,
benefiting infinite beings, and finally pours into the great ocean of complete omniscience: that water of roots of goodness from the very beginning is headed for the ocean of omniscience.

Furthermore, those ten stages of enlightening beings are manifested
based on enlightened knowledge. It is as the ten great mountains are
manifested based on the earth. They are like the Snowy Mountains,
Intoxicating with Fragrance Mountain, Crystal Mountain, Wizard
Mountain, Yoke-Bearing Mountain, Horse Ear Mountain, Fish-Holding
Mountain, the Circular Enclosure Mountains, Endowed with Brightness
Mountain, and the polar mountain Wonderfully High. Just as the
Snowy Mountains are mines of all kinds of medicinal plants, which may
be collected without exhausting them, in the same way an enlightening
being in the stage of Joy becomes a mine of all worldly poetry, writing,
and the science of magic spells, which may be applied endlessly. Just as
the mountain Intoxicating with Fragrance is a mine of all kinds of
fragrances, whence all kinds of fragrances may be collected inexhaustibly,
an enlightening being in the stage of Purity becomes a mine of the
fragrance of all the ethical conduct of enlightening beings, whence the
fragrance of all ethical conduct of enlightening beings may be collected
inexhaustibly. Just as Crystal Mountain is a mine composed of pure
jewels, from which all kinds of jewels may be taken inexhaustibly, in the
same way an enlightening being in the stage of Refulgence becomes a
mine of all worldly meditations, mystic knowledges, liberations, concentrations, and attainments, inexhaustible in answering questions about
all meditations, mystic knowledges, liberations, concentrations, and
attainments in the world. Just as Wizard Mountain is a pure jewel abode
of wizards with five mystic knowledges, where there are countless such
wizards, in the same way an enlightening being in the stage of Blazing
becomes a mine of higher knowledges of penetration and explanation of
all paths to liberation and paths that do not lead to liberation, inexhaustible in answering questions with higher knowledge of the disparity

between liberative paths and nonliberative paths. Just as Yoke-Bearing Mountain is a pure jewel abode of spirits of great magical powers, where there are countless such spirits, in the same way an enlightening being in the stage Difficult to Conquer becomes a mine of mystic knowledges, spiritual powers, occult transformations, and miraculous effects, able to answer questions about these phenomena inexhaustibly. Just as Horse Ear Mountain is a pure jewel mine of all kinds of fruits, from which all kinds of fruits may be gathered inexhaustibly, an enlightening being in the stage of Presence becomes a mine of penetration and explanation of interdependent origination, inexhaustible in answering questions about realization of the fruits of Buddhist discipleship. Just as Fish-Holding Mountain is a pure jewel abode of all water spirits of great magical powers, where there are countless water spirits, similarly an enlightening being in the stage of Far-Going becomes a mine of teaching of means and wisdom, inexhaustible in answering questions about the realization of the fruits of individual illumination. Just as the Circular Enclosure Mountains are a pure jewel abode of those imbued with power, where there are countless powerful beings, similarly an enlightening being in the stage of Immovability becomes a mine of effects of powers of enlightening beings, inexhaustible in answering questions about the differentiations of worlds. Just as the mountain Endowed with Brightness is a pure jewel home of titans with great magical powers, where there are countless titans, similarly an enlightening being in the stage of Good Mind becomes a mine of application of knowledge of the becoming and passing away of all beings, inexhaustible in answering questions about the formation and disintegration of all worlds. Just as the mountain Wonderfully High is the pure jewel home of divinities of great power, where the divinities are countless, similarly an enlightening being in the stage of Cloud of Teaching becomes a mine of the powers, expertises, and unique qualities of buddhas, inexhaustible in answering questions about the manifestation of the works of buddhas. Just as these ten great mountains exist in the ocean and appear from the ocean, in the same way these ten stages of enlightening beings exist in omniscience and appear from omniscience.

Just as an ocean undeniably counts as an ocean because of ten characteristics—that is, because of progressively becoming deeper, because of not lodging a corpse, because other waters lose their identity in the ocean, because of uniform flavor, because of containing many valuables, because its depths are hard to reach, because it is immeasurably vast, because it is the abode of giant creatures, because the tides do not exceed their bounds, and because it receives all the rains of the clouds without being filled—in the same way the practice of enlightening beings is undeniably counted as such because of ten characteristics: because of gradual deepening of accomplishment of vows, in the stage of Joy; because of not lodging the corpse of bad conduct, in the stage of Purity; because of relinquishment of worldly designations, in the stage of Refulgence; because of the uniform flavor of unbreakable pure faith in Buddha, in the stage of Blazing; because of innumerably many valuable accomplishments of works in the world by higher knowledge and expedient means, in the stage Difficult to Conquer; because of the hard-to-fathom profundity of examination of interdependent origination, in the stage of Presence; because of immeasurable vastness of skill in discernment, in the stage of Far-Going; because of being the abode of colossal displays of production of supernal manifestations, in the stage of Immovability; because of accurate comprehension of profound liberation and worldly actions without going over the boundary, in the stage of Good Mind; because of receiving the water of the great clouds of revelations of teachings of all buddhas without being sated, in the stage of Cloud of Teaching.

When a great jewel, surpassing the ten classes of jewels, is picked up, fired by a skillful craftsman, well rounded, purified, well polished, skillfully pierced, strung on a precious thread, mounted above a banner on a jewel pole, emanates all kinds of light and becomes recognized by a king, then it serves as a basis for the gathering of all precious things by all beings. In the same way, when enlightening beings' determination for omniscience, surpassing the ten religious groups, is aroused, fired by austerity, frugality, discipline, and training, well rounded by meditation and concentration and absorption, purified by the practices of the Path, polished by expedient means and higher knowledge, pierced by interdependent origination, strung on the variegated precious thread of means and wisdom, mounted atop a banner on a great jewel pole of spiritual power, emanates the light of knowledge of observation of the conduct of living beings, and arrives at coronation with enlightened knowledge by the Buddha; then it becomes a basis for all beings' collection of the jewels of all Buddha works.

Furthermore, this book on the way into the teaching of assembly of the practices of enlightening beings and accumulation of the qualities of omniscience cannot be heard by those who have not planted roots of goodness.

The enlightening being Moon of Liberation said, "With how much virtue do they become imbued who hear the book on the way into the teaching of accumulation of the qualities of omniscience?"

The enlightening being Diamond Matrix said, "As much as derives from omniscience, that much would the quantity of virtue be, owing to the objective embraced by the determination for omniscience. As much virtue as accrues from the objective embraced by determination for omniscience, that much virtue would be attained by turning to this teaching. Why? None but enlightening beings can hear this book on the way into the teaching of accumulation of the qualities of omniscience, or devote themselves to it, or take to it, or take it up, or hold it, or preserve it, much less cultivate it, act on it, apply it, foster it, or attain it. Thus it is those who follow the way to omniscience that can preserve it, those who hear this book on the way to accumulate the qualities of omniscience, and, having heard it, devote themselves to it, preserve it, and apply it in practice."

Then, by the spiritual power of Buddha, and as a result of the natural order, the worlds of the ten directions, as many worlds as atoms in a hundred million buddha-lands, quaked in six ways, with eighteen characteristics—they trembled, trembled intensely, trembled everywhere intensely, shook, shook intensely, shook everywhere intensely, quaked, quaked intensely, quaked everywhere intensely, resounded, resounded intensely, resounded everywhere intensely, stirred, stirred intensely, stirred everywhere intensely, roared, roared intensely, roared everywhere intensely. By the power of Buddha, and by the natural order, celestial clouds of flowers and garlands, robes, parasols, jewels, ornaments, banners, and pennants showered. Also magnificent high celestial clouds of solar orb jewels rained, and magnificent high clouds of musical jewels and clouds of pure gold orbs showered, and celestial music and singing was heard. Also clouds of songs of praise of the stage of omniscience, surpassing the celestials, were heard.

As in this world, in the heaven of control of others' emanations, in the palace of the chief god, on the jewel mine seat this teaching was spoken, so it was also throughout all worlds in the ten directions. By the power of Buddha, and by the natural order, from the ten directions, from beyond as many worlds as atoms in a hundred million buddha-lands, there came and assembled as many enlightening beings as atoms in a hundred million buddha-lands; having arrived, pervading the ten directions, they said, "It is very good, Offspring of Buddha, how well you express the true nature of enlightening beings. We also have the same name, Diamond Matrix, and have come here from worlds called Diamond Splendor, from the presence of buddhas called Diamond Banner; in all of those worlds this teaching is also carried on, by the empowerment of the buddhas, in assemblies like this, with the same phrasing and expression driving at the same meaning, with no decrease or increase. We have come here as your witnesses by the power of the buddhas. Just as we have arrived in this world, so have we arrived at the jewel mine throne in the palace of the god king in the heaven of control of others' emanations in the four continents of each and every world in the ten directions."

Then the enlightening being Diamond Matrix, having looked over the ten directions and the congregations everywhere, observing the cosmos, by way of praising the determination for omniscience, revealing the sphere of enlightening beings, purifying the power of practice, expounding the absorption of omniscience, removing all the defilements of the world, presenting omniscient knowledge, showing the crest of inconceivable knowledge, and revealing the qualities of enlightening beings, spoke these verses by the power of Buddha, describing the meaning of the stages:

Listen to the excellent practices of enlightening beings,
Who practice calmness and self-control, are tranquil and peaceful
    in mind,
Who are like the sky, similar to space,
Who have shed all defilement and abide in knowledge of the
    Way.

Having cultivated good for countless eons
And served hundreds of thousands of buddhas
And honored many self-conquerors and saints,
The will for enlightenment is born for the good of the world.

Born is the will for enlightenment, equal to the Enlightened,
In those refined by discipline and austerity, who have reached
    ultimate patience,
Who act with modesty and dignity, born of virtue and
    knowledge,
Who are broad-minded and intent on enlightened knowledge.

To honor all the buddhas of past, present, and future,
Purify all lands throughout space,
Truly comprehend all truths and liberate beings,
The will for enlightenment is born.

To do good for all is the will for enlightenment born
In the joyful and benevolent who practice giving,
Who are always determined to benefit all beings,
Who apply the virtues of buddhas and pledge to protect the
    living.

Born is the will for enlightenment, for the weal of all beings,
In those divorced from evil, whose conduct is pure,
Who practice self-control, whose senses are calm and cool,
Who have taken refuge in Buddha, intent on enlightening
    practice.

Born is the will for enlightenment, for the benefit of all,
In those who practice good, vessels of patience and coolness,
Who know the flavor of virtue, have abandoned arrogance and
    insolence,
With minds detached and pure, calm and cool.

Initiating pure action, enduring with firmness and vigor,
Human lions striving for the welfare of all people,
Having conquered afflictions by persistence in virtue,
In this state of mind the will for enlightenment is born.

With well-concentrated minds, the darkness of delusion dissolved,
Arrogance gone, they have abandoned defiled paths;
Enjoying the bliss of peace, they have given up attachments to
   routine life—
In this state of mind the will for enlightenment is born.

With minds clear as the sky, with knowledge, abstract and
   applied,
Having killed the demons, dropped afflictions and conceit,
Abiding in the refuge of Buddha, finding the truth, their desire,
In this state of mind their will for enlightenment is born.

Firm in means and intelligence to achieve liberation from the
   realms of being,
Endowed with technique, science, and spiritual power to escape
   the force of evil,
Seeking the qualities of buddhas, desirous of virtue,
In this state of mind their will for enlightenment is born.

Wishing all beings well, having fulfilled the provisions for
   enlightenment,
With determined minds, they do even what may be difficult,
Enlightening beings never giving up their intent to do good;
In this state of mind their will for enlightenment is born.

Thus they should carry out enlightenment practices of multifold
   virtues;
Vowing to follow Buddha's footsteps, they should attain truth
   and spiritual power;
Having purified the three realms of being, they should attain the
   will for enlightenment;
Having purified the three refuges, they should become
   enlightening beings.

This will be reiterated in sum, so listen;
When the will for enlightenment is attained, those who practice
   giving
Then, having reached Extreme Joy, will become lords of the land.

There, protecting beings by providing what they require,
Having established their own giving, they can get others to do so.

Having settled all in enlightenment, they will have perfected
   giving;
By following this principle they will arrive at discipline.

Having achieved right conduct, they will become well behaved;
Thence having reached Purity, they will become lords of four
    continents.

Stationed there, protecting beings by stopping evil,
Abiding in their own moral conduct, they can get others to do so
    too.

Having settled all in enlightenment, they will have perfected
    morality;
By maturation of this practice, they will come to the practice of
    forbearance.

Maintaining the practice of right forbearance, they will become
    good bearers of patience;
Thence having reached Refulgence, they will become lords of the
    thirty-three heavens.

There, protecting beings by stopping the courses of afflictions,
Abiding in their own practice of forbearance, they can get others
    to do so too.

Having settled all in enlightenment, they will have perfected
    patience;
By maturation of this virtue, they will come to the practice of
    vigor.

Having concentrated right energy, they will become good at
    maintaining vigor;
Thence having reached Blazing, they will become lords of the
    heaven of timely portion.

There protecting beings by stopping wrong views,
They will establish right insight and foster enlightenment by
effort.

Stable in their own practice of vigor, they can exhort others as
    well;
Having settled all in enlightenment, they will have perfected
    vigor.

By the results of this virtue they will come to the practice of
    meditation;
Having conquered all afflictions they will become stabilized in
    concentration.

Having concentrated on right meditation, they will become
  skilled in concentration;
Thence having reached the Difficult to Conquer, they will
  become lords of the heaven of the satisfied,

There protecting beings by stopping wrong paths,
Having established right teaching and fostered enlightenment by
  effort.

Abiding in their own practice of meditation, they can urge others
  to do so too;
Having established all in enlightenment, they will have perfected
  meditation.

By the results of this virtue they will come to the practice of
  wisdom;
Having conquered all demons, they will possess wisdom, higher
  knowledge, and spiritual power.

Having accomplished true wisdom, they will become skilled in
  mystic knowledge;
Having thence attained Presence, they will become lords of the
  heaven of pleasant emanations,

There protecting beings by stopping conceit,
Having settled them in emptiness and fostered enlightenment
  diligently.

Abiding in their own practice of wisdom, they can induce others
  to do so too;
Having settled all in enlightenment, they will have perfected
  wisdom.

By the results of this virtue they will practice right means;
Having conquered all views, they will be skilled in right teaching.

By the exercise of right means they will lead beings into
  enlightenment;
Thence having reached Far-Going, they will become lords of the
  heaven of control,

There protecting beings by awakening realization,
Enlightening them after having set them in the way of
  enlightening beings.

Abiding in their own skill in means, they will also exhort others;
Having settled all in enlightenment, they will have perfected
   means.

By the powers of this virtue they will come to good vows;
Having conquered false views, they will be wise, having attained
   right insight.

Settled in true enlightenment by a rightly resolved mind,
Thence having attained Immovability, they will become Brahma
   lords of a thousand worlds,

There protecting beings by teaching the Three Vehicles,
Enlightening them by establishing them in comprehension of the
   world.

Abiding by their own vows, they can also induce others;
Having settled all in enlightenment, they will have perfected
   commitment.

By the power of this virtue, they will come to the practice of
   power,
Certain of perfect enlightenment, once all views are conquered.

By the combined exertions of right power, they will overcome all
   those in error;
Thence having attained Good Mind, they will become Great
   Brahmas, powerful.

There they will protect beings by teaching the Buddha Vehicle,
Enlightening them by establishing them in the knowledge of
   beings' minds.

Steadfast in their own power, they can also induce others;
Having settled all in enlightenment, they will have perfected
   power.

By the results of this virtue they will come to the practice of
   knowledge,
Enlightening beings, mines of virtue, having conquered the four
   demons.

Having attained right knowledge, they will be skilled in true
   teaching;
Having thence reached Cloud of Teaching, they will become
   great lords, adept.

There they will protect beings by enlightening them in all ways,
Enlightening them by establishing them in highest omniscience.

Stable in their own knowledge, they will also guide others;
When they have settled all in enlightenment, they will have
    perfected knowledge.

By the powers of this virtue, they will be victors, lords of the ten
    powers,
Imbued with all virtues, omniscient, in the course of nature.

Having contemplated this, the noble should practice with
    concentrated minds,
To attain the state of perfect enlightenment, having fulfilled the
    ten ways of transcendence.

Thus having attained enlightenment and liberation, and
    conquered the four demons,
Having settled all in enlightenment, you will attain perfect peace.

Having heard this and thoroughly known the means and
    accomplishment of enlightening beings,
You will attain unobstructed enlightenment, the state of the
    Felicitous.

"This has been a summary exposition of the ten stages of enlightening
beings, to be seen in accord with omniscience complete in all aspects."
    At that point the billion-world universe quaked in six ways, all kinds
of flowers rained steadily, celestial and human music played, and the
intoxicating sound was heard to the very summit of existence.
    Then the Buddha said, addressing Moon of Liberation and all the
other enlightening beings, "Good people, this complete perfect enlightenment, developed over countless eons, I commend to you, entrusting it
to you, with the ultimate charge that you will yourselves hold this teaching and also fully elucidate it for others. To put it succinctly, if the Buddha were to remain alive for an eon expounding the glories of this teaching day and night, neither would the glory of this teaching be ended nor
would the eloquence of the Buddha be exhausted. Just as the Buddha's
conduct, concentration, wisdom, liberation, knowledge, and vision are
measureless and endless, likewise is the case of those who will take up
this teaching, preserve it, recite it, write it down, cause it to be written
down, master it, put it into action, and fully expound it in the community, who will tell it to people faithfully and respectfully with consideration of how these people might attain the lofty teaching, and get
them to reflect on it reasonably, who will write it down in a book and
have it kept, respected, taken seriously, and honored in the home, who

will tell the glories of this teaching without envy and speak it so it may be written, told, recited, honored, and revealed: their virtue also has no end."

Then the Buddha, to again make the bequest of this teaching, spoke these verses:

> If the beings I see by my enlightened vision
> Were saints equal to Shariputra,
> And one should honor them for millions of ages,
> As many as the sands of the Ganges River;
> And if someone honored an individual illuminate
> Day and night, cheerful,
> With the finest garlands and such,
> And thereby created excellent virtue;
> And if all were individual illuminates,
> If one honored them diligently
> With flowers and incense, food and drink,
> For many eons,
> Still if one made even one bow to one buddha
> And with a pure mind declared obeisance,
> The virtue would be greater than all that.

> If all beings were to become buddhas,
> And someone would honor them as mentioned before,
> With celestial and human flowers of many kinds for many eons,
> One who, at the time of the extinction of the true teaching,
> Having relinquished body and life, would give this scripture, day
>   and night,
> Would be superior in virtue.

> Whoever wants to honor the buddhas,
> Or individual illuminates or Buddhist disciples,
> Should rouse firm determination for enlightenment
> And always give this lofty scripture.

> For this is the king of all good messages;
> It has emerged from all the buddhas.
> The Buddha is in the house
> Where this scripture-jewel is placed.

> Who passes on even one line from this scripture
> Will attain pure and endless light;
> One who gives this scripture to others
> Will not be deprived of a syllable, of a meaning.

Supreme is that one among guides of humanity;
No being can be found like this one;
Having heard and accomplished this teaching,
One will be inexhaustible as the ocean.

When the Buddha said this, Moon of Liberation and all the enlightening beings, the celestials, the disciples and other people, and the whole assembly were all transported with joy at the Buddha approving what Diamond Matrix said.

BOOK TWENTY-SEVEN

The Ten Concentrations

AT THAT TIME the World Honored One was at the site of enlightenment in a forest in the country of Magadha, having just attained perfect enlightenment; in the hall of universal light he entered the buddhas' concentration on the absolute instant, and by the inherent spiritual power of universal knowledge manifested the body of a realized buddha, pure and untrammeled, not relying on anything, with no clinging to objects, abiding in the ultimate tranquillity of cessation, endowed with great power, without any attachments, able to cause all beholders to gain awakening, appearing as appropriate, in accord with the time, always abiding in one form, which is no form.

He was with as many great enlightening beings as atoms in ten buddha-lands, all of whom were of the rank of coronation, had fulfilled enlightening practices as measureless and boundless as the cosmos, and had attained the enlightening beings' concentration state of universal vision. With great compassion they brought peace and calm to all sentient beings. Their powers and mastery were the same as those of buddhas. By their wisdom they profoundly penetrated and expounded the truth and were endowed with universal knowledge. They had conquered all demons, and though they entered into the world their minds were always calm; they dwelled in the nondwelling liberation of enlightening beings. Their names were Indestructible Knowedge, Peerless Knowledge, Knowledge of Meanings and Expressions, Supreme Knowledge, Eternally Equanimous Knowledge, Dragon Knowledge, Consummate Knowledge, Well-Tuned Knowledge, Immensely Powerful Knowledge, Inconceivable Knowledge, Unhindered Knowledge, Masterful Knowledge, Knowledge of Universal Service, Rational Knowledge, Adaptable Knowledge, Knowledge Mastering All Teachings, Knowledge of Truth, Dispassionate Knowledge, Spacelike Knowledge, Knowledge of Unity, Good Knowledge, Knowledge of Illusoriness, Vast Knowledge, Forceful Knowledge, Worldly Knowledge, Knowledge of Buddhahood, True Knowledge, Holy Knowledge, Illuminate Knowledge, Boundless Knowledge, Adorned with Mindfulness, Arrived at the Limit of Space, Natural Adornments, Most Profound

Realm, Comprehending What Is So and What Is Not, Great Light, Eternal Light, Understanding the Seed of Buddhahood, Mind King, One Practice, Always Manifesting Spiritual Powers, Sprouts of Wisdom, Abode of Virtues, Lamp of Truth, Illumining the World, Sustaining the World, Most Serene, Supreme, Unexcelled, Incomparable, Peerless, Unhindered Action, Flames of Light, Moonlight, One Atom, Steadfast Practice, Showering the Rain of True Teaching, Supreme Banner, Universal Adornment, Eye of Wisdom, Objective Eye, Cloud of Wisdom, Spellbinding King, Nondwelling Vows, Mine of Knowledge, Mind King, Inner Awareness, Abiding in Enlightened Knowledge, Forceful Power of Spells, Earth-Sustaining Power, Beautiful Moon, Peak of the Polar Mountain, Jewel Summit, Universal Illumination, Charismatic King, Wheel of Knowledge, Great Power, Dragonlike, Straightforward Action, Nonregressive, Holding the Banner of the Teaching, Unforgetting, Caring for All Beings, Inconceivable Certain Knowledge, Freely Unbounded Knowledge, Inexhaustible Treasury of Wonderful Teachings, Sun of Knowledge, Sun of Truth, Treasury of Knowledge, Luster of Knowledge, Universal Vision, True Vision, Diamond Insight, Diamond Knowledge, Diamond Flame, Diamond Wisdom, Universal Eye, Sun of Buddhahood, Holding the Indestructible Secret Meaning of the Buddha, Adornments of Knowledge of the Sphere of the Universal Eye, and so on; there were as many such enlightening beings as atoms in ten buddha-lands, who had all cultivated the same practices of roots of goodness of enlightening beings with Vairocana Buddha in the past.

Then the great enlightening being Universal Eye, imbued with the spiritual power of the Buddha, rose from his seat, bared his right shoulder, knelt with his right knee on the ground, joined his palms in respect, and said to the Buddha, "World Honored One, I want to ask the Completely Enlightened One about something—please permit me to do so." The Buddha said, "You may ask whatever you want; I will explain for you and gladden you." Universal Eye said, "How many concentrations and liberations have the enlightening being Universally Good and the enlightening beings who live by the vows and practices of Universal Good attained, that they may enter and exit and abide at rest in the great concentrations of enlightening beings and, by skillfully entering and emerging from the inconceivable vast state of concentration of enlightening beings, are able to command all concentrations, with ceaseless mystical powers?"

The Buddha said, "Very good, Universal Eye; you are asking this for the benefit of the enlightening beings of past, future, and present. The enlightening being Universally Good is now here, already capable of freely accomplishing inconceivable spiritual effects, beyond those of all enlightening beings, rarely encountered, born of immeasurable enlightening practices. He has purified the great vows of enlightening beings and is unregressing in all the practices he carries out; he has already attained innumerable aspects of transcendence, unhindered access to memory, and inexhaustible powers of elucidation, thoroughly pure and uninhibited. He compassionately aids all beings, through the power of his fundamental vows, forever unwearying. You should ask him—he will explain to you those concentrations, powers, and liberations."

Then the enlightening beings in the assembly, hearing the name of Universally Good, immediately attained inconceivably infinite concentration, their minds unobstructed, silent, and unstirring; their knowledge became immeasurably vast, their realm of experience most profound, without compare. They saw countless buddhas before them, attained the power of the enlightened, and, of the same nature as the enlightened, they clearly perceived all the past, future, and present. Their blessings and virtues were inexhaustible, and they were endowed with all spiritual powers. Those enlightening beings conceived respect for Universally Good and urgently wished to behold him—they looked all over the assembled masses but ultimately did not see him, nor did they see the seat on which he sat. This was because of the support of the awesome power of the Enlightened, and also Universally Good's command of mystic power caused it to be so.

Then the enlightening being Universal Eye said to the Buddha, "Where is the enlightening being Universally Good now?" The Buddha replied, "The enlightening being Universally Good is in the Assembly at this enlightenment site, near me—he has never moved." At that Universal Eye and the enlightening beings again searched throughout the assembly, and then said to the Buddha, "We still cannot find Universally Good." The Buddha said, "That is so. Why can you not see him? Because the dwelling place of the enlightening being Universally Good is most profound and inexplicable. Universally Good has attained boundless aspects of knowledge, entered the 'lion emergence' concentration, attained unexcelled freedom of action, entered pure nonobstruction, and developed the ten powers of the enlightened: his body is the matrix of the cosmos, on which all enlightened ones concentrate together. In an instant he can thoroughly realize and enter the unfragmented knowledge of the buddhas of all times. This is why you cannot see him."

Then Universal Eye, hearing the Buddha speak of the pure qualities of Universally Good, attained ten thousand infinities of concentrations. With the power of concentration he again looked all over, eager to see Universally Good, but still could not see him. The other enlightening beings could not see him either. Then Universal Eye rose from concentration and said to the Buddha, "I have entered ten thousand infinities of concentrations and sought to behold Universal Good but after all have not succeeded. I do not see his body or physical actions, his speech or conversation, his mind or mental activity, his seat or his place—none of them is visible."

The Buddha said, "So it is, so it is. Know that this is all because of the enlightening being Universally Good's power of abiding in inconceivable liberation. Universal Eye, what do you think—can anyone explain the dwelling place of various illusory forms in magical writings?"

Universal Eye said, "No."

The Buddha said, "Universal Eye, if illusory forms in illusions cannot be explained, how much less can one enter or see the esoteric physical realm, the esoteric verbal realm, or the esoteric mental realm of the enlightening being Universally Good. Why? Because the realm of Universally Good is extremely profound, inconceivable, without measure, beyond measure. To sum it up, the enlightening being Universally Good, by means of adamantine wisdom, pervades the cosmos of realities, yet does not course in any world or dwell anywhere—he knows that the bodies of all beings are not bodies, and have no coming or going. He has attained inexhaustible, undivided, free spiritual powers, independent, uncontrived, inactive, reaching the ultimate bounds of the cosmos. If any can get to see the enlightening being Universally Good, or get to attend him, or get to hear his name, or think about him, or remember him, or believe in him, or strive to observe him, or orient themselves toward him, or properly seek him, or initiate vows, continuing uninterrupted, all will gain benefit—none of this is in vain."

Then Universal Eye and all the other enlightening beings, their hearts conceiving longing to behold the enlightening being Universally Good, spoke these words: "Honor to all the buddhas; honor to the enlightening being Universally Good." Saying this three times, they bowed in respect. At that point the Buddha said to the enlightening being Universal Eye and the others in the assembly, "Offspring of the buddhas, you should bow to Universally Good again and earnestly entreat him; and you should look upon the ten directions with utmost single-mindedness and visualize the body of Universally Good before you. Thinking thus, that Universally Good is omnipresent throughout the cosmos, believe deeply, detach from everything, vow to practice the same undertaking as Universally Good, and enter nondual true reality; the body of Universally Good appears everywhere in all worlds, with comprehensive knowledge of the differences in faculties of all beings, assembling the path of Universally Good in all places. If you can initiate such a great vow, then you will be able to see the enlightening being Universally Good." Now Universal Eye and the other enlightening beings, hearing the Buddha say this, bowed their heads to the ground and sought to get to see the great being Universally Good.

Then the enlightening being Universally Good, by the power of liberated spiritual faculties, manifested physical bodies in accord with their needs, causing all those enlightening beings to see Universally Good near the Buddha, sitting on a lotus seat in the midst of this assembly of all the enlightening beings; they also saw him with all the buddhas in all other worlds, continuously coming from there; they also saw him with all those buddhas, expounding all practices of enlightening beings, revealing the path of omniscience, explaining all enlightening beings' spiritual powers, distinguishing all enlightening beings' charismatic virtues, and showing the buddhas of past, present, and future.

At this point, Universal Eye and all the other enlightening beings, witnessing this miracle, were overjoyed and all bowed to the enlightening being Universally Good with respect, as if they were seeing all the buddhas of the ten directions.

Then, by the great spiritual power of the Buddha as well as the power of faith of the enlightening beings and the power of the original vow of Universally Good, there spontaneously rained ten thousand kinds of clouds, such as clouds of various flowers, clouds of various garlands, clouds of various fragrances, clouds of various aromatic powders, clouds of various canopies, clouds of various robes, clouds of various ornaments, clouds of various jewels, clouds of various burning incenses, and clouds of various streamers; unspeakably many worlds quaked, celestial music played and was heard afar throughout unspeakably many worlds, great light radiated and illuminated unspeakably many worlds, causing the states of misery to become extinct, adorning unspeakably many worlds, causing unspeakably many enlightening beings to enter into the practice of Universally Good, and causing unspeakably many enlightening beings to thoroughly fulfill the vows of practice of universal good and attain unexcelled complete perfect enlightenment.

Then the enlightening being Universal Eye said to the Buddha, "World Honored One, the enlightening being Universally Good is one who abides in great power, in incomparability, in unsurpassability, in nonregression, in equanimity, in indestructibility, in all differentiated things, in all undifferentiated things, in the abode of the skillful mind of all beings, in absorption in liberation, free in all things."

The Buddha said, "It is so; it is as you say. The enlightening being Universally Good has innumerable pure qualities—the qualities of peerless adornment, the qualities of innumerable jewels, the qualities of inconceivable oceans, the qualities of infinite forms, the qualities of boundless clouds, infinite incomparable qualities, the qualities of inexhaustible truths, untold qualities, the qualities of all buddhas, qualities that cannot ever be exhaustively extolled."

Then the Buddha said to the enlightening being Universally Good, "You should explain the ten concentrations for Universal Eye and the enlightening beings in this assembly, so that they may be able to enter them and fulfill the practical vows of universal good. Because the great enlightening beings expound these ten concentrations, they enable the enlightening beings of the past, present, and future to attain emancipation. What are the ten concentrations? One, the great concentration of universal light; two, the great concentration of subtle light; three, the great concentration of successive journeying to the buddha-lands; four, the great concentration of the action of the pure profound mind; five, the great concentration of knowledge of the stores of adornments of the past; six, the great concentration of the treasury of light of knowledge; seven, the great concentration of knowledge of the adornments of the buddhas of all worlds; eight, the great concentration of the differentiated bodies of sentient beings; nine, the great concentration of freedom in the elemental cosmos; ten, the great concentration of the unimpeded wheel.

"These ten great concentrations the great enlightening beings can skillfully enter; all the buddhas of past, future, and present have expounded, will expound, and are expounding them. If enlightening beings gladly and respectfully cultivate and practice them without slacking, they will be able to accomplish them; such people are called buddhas, they are called those who have arrived at Thusness, and they are called people who have attained the ten powers, and they are called guides, and they are called great leaders, and they are called omniscient, and they are called all-seers, and they are called those who abide in non-obstruction, and they are called those who have comprehended all objects, and they are called masters of all spiritual truths. These enlightening beings enter into all worlds without being attached to anything in any world; they enter the realms of all beings without grasping beings; they enter all bodies without being hindered by bodies; they enter all elemental realms and know the cosmos is boundless. They draw near all the buddhas of all times and clearly see all the buddhas' teachings; they skillfully explain all words and comprehend all provisional names. They accomplish the pure path of all enlightening beings and are firm in all the different practices of enlightening beings. In a single instant they attain all knowledge of past, present, and future, and know all things in all times. They expound all the buddhas' teachings and turn all the irreversible wheels. In each age, past, future, and present, they realize all paths to enlightenment, and in each enlightenment comprehend what all the buddhas say. These are the gates of the characteristics of the principles of enlightening beings; these are the gates of the knowledge and awareness of enlightening beings; these are the gates of the invincible knowledge of all means of liberation; these are the gates of the practices vowed by the Universally Good enlightening being; these are the gates of the undertakings of penetrating spiritual powers; these are the gates of all mnemonic command and powers of elucidation; these are the gates to the differentiations of all things of past, present, and future; these are the gates of manifestations of all buddhas; these are the gates to stabilizing all beings by universal knowledge; these are the gates to beautifying and purifying all worlds by means of spiritual powers of buddhas.

"If enlightening beings enter these concentrations, they attain cosmic power that has no end; they are enabled to travel through space without hindrance; they attain the rank of spiritual sovereignty, with immeasurable independence and command, like being coronated and enthroned in the world; they attain boundless knowledge comprehending all; they attain vast powers, ten kinds perfectly fulfilled; they develop noncontentious hearts and enter dispassionate tranquillity; they are compassionate and fearless as lions; they are heroes of knowledge and wisdom and light the bright lamp of truth. All their merits and virtues cannot be fully told of—no hearers of self-enlightened ones can conceive of them. They attain knowledge of the realm of reality and abide in infinity, yet are able to discourse in various ways according to worldly conventions; they abide in formlessness, yet can easily penetrate the characteristics of things. They attain the treasury of inherent purity and are born in the pure house of the enlightened. They skillfully open up various different gates of teaching, yet by means of wisdom they know that nothing exists. They are expert at knowing proper timing and always carry out the giving of teaching to enlighten everyone. They care for all beings and purify them all. By knowledge of expedient means they demonstrate the attainment of buddhahood, yet they always carry out the practices of enlightening beings without end. Entering the realm of means of universal knowledge, they manifest various great spiritual powers. Therefore, Universally Good, you should now analyze and expound the ten great concentrations of all enlightening beings. All in this assembly want to hear about this."

Then the enlightening being Universally Good, receiving the directive of the Enlightened One, looked at Universal Eye and the other enlightening beings and said to them, "Offspring of Buddha, what is the great enlightening beings' concentration of universal light? Here the enlightening beings have ten kinds of inexhaustible qualities: inexhaustible knowledge of the buddhas' emergence in the world; inexhaustible knowledge of the metamorphoses of beings; inexhaustible knowledge of the world's being like a reflection; inexhaustible knowledge penetrating deeply into the realm of reality; inexhaustible knowledge skillfully dealing with enlightening beings; inexhaustible knowledge of the nonregression of enlightening beings; inexhaustible knowledge observing the meanings of all principles; inexhaustible knowledge of skillful maintenance of mental power; inexhaustible knowledge abiding in the vast spirit of enlightenment; inexhaustible knowledge abiding by all enlightened teachings and the willpower of omniscience. These are called the ten inexhaustible qualities of great enlightening beings.

"These great enlightening beings awaken ten kinds of boundless will: they awaken the boundless will to liberate all sentient beings, the boundless will to attend all buddhas, the boundless will to provide for all buddhas, the boundless will to see all buddhas, the boundless will to receive and hold all Buddha teachings without forgetting any, the boundless will to manifest the infinite spiritual metamorphoses of all buddhas, the boundless will not to abandon any enlightening practices to attain enlightened power, the boundless will to enter into the subtle realm of all-knowledge and explain all Buddha teachings, the boundless will to enter into the inconceivable vast realm of buddhahood, the boundless will to develop profound aspiration for the buddhas' powers of elucidation and receive all Buddha teachings, the boundless will to manifest all kinds of free bodies and enter the circles of all enlightened ones.

"These enlightening beings have ten kinds of knowledge of differentiation of entry into concentration: entering into concentration in the east and emerging in the west, entering in the west and emerging in the east, entering in the south and emerging in the north, entering in the north and emerging in the south, entering in the northeast and emerging in the southwest, entering in the southwest and emerging in the northwest, entering in the southwest and emerging in the northeast, entering in the northwest and emerging in the southeast, entering in the southeast and emerging in the northwest, entering in the nadir and emerging in the zenith, entering in the zenith and emerging in the nadir.

"These enlightening beings have ten kinds of knowledge of skills in entry into great concentration: they make a billion-world universe a single lotus blossom and appear sitting cross-legged on this lotus blossom, covering it entirely, and in the body manifest another billion-world universe, wherein there are ten billion quadruplex earths, in each of which they manifest ten billion bodies, each body entering into one hundred sextillion billion-world universes, in each of the quadruplex worlds of which they manifest one hundred sextillion enlightening beings engaged in practice, the practice of each enlightening being producing one hundred sextillion certain understandings, each certain understanding causing one hundred sextillion potentials to be fulfilled, each potential developing into the nonregressive work of one hundred sextillion enlightening ways: yet the physical manifestations are neither one nor many, and not mixed up in entry into concentration or emergence from concentration. It is like the case of the titan king Rahula, whose original body is seven hundred leagues tall, while his transformed body is 168,000 leagues tall; the half of his body emerging from the ocean is just level with the polar mountain Sumeru. Though that titan king transforms his body into a colossus, that does not destroy his original form—all the psychophysical elements are the same, his mind is not disturbed, he does not think of his transformed body as other or of his original body as not himself. The body he was born with is always blissful, and his transformed body is always manifesting all kinds of miraculous powers. The titan king has greed, ill-will, and delusion, and is full of pride and conceit, and yet is able to transform his body in this way—how much the more so the enlightening beings who profoundly realize that mental states are like illusions, that all beings are like dreams, that the appearance in the world of all buddhas is like reflected images, that all worlds are like magical productions, that all speech is like echoes: they see reality as is and have reality as their body, knowing all things are inherently pure, realizing that the body and mind have no real substance; their bodies are omnipresent in infinite realms and by the great light of buddha-knowledge purify and practice all the deeds of enlightening beings.

"Enlightening beings in this concentration transcend the world and are detached from the world; nothing can disturb them or overpower them. Just as when a monk contemplates inside the body and dwells in the view of impurity, seeing the body as impure, so do enlightening beings in this concentration observe the reality body, seeing all worlds enter the body, therein seeing all mundane realms and phenomena without any attachment to them. This is called the great enlightening beings' practical knowledge of the first great concentration, of universal light.

"What is the great enlightening beings' concentration of subtle light? Here enlightening beings can enter as many billion-world universes as there are atoms in a billion-world universe, and in each world manifest as many bodies as atoms in a billion-world universe, each body emitting as many lights as atoms in a billion-world universe, each light revealing as many colors as atoms in a billion-world universe, each color lighting as many worlds as atoms in a billion-world universe, in each world pacifying as many beings as atoms in a billion-world universe. The enlightening beings know all the various dissimilarities of these worlds: that is, the clutter and pollution of worlds, the purity and cleanness of worlds, the causes of worlds, the structures of worlds, the concomitants of worlds, the colors of lights of worlds, the comings and goings of worlds—the enlightening beings know all these and enter all these, and these worlds also enter the bodies of the enlightening beings, yet the worlds have no mixup or confusion and the various phenomena do not disintegrate or vanish either.

"It is like when the sun comes out and circles the polar mountain, illumining the mountains made of seven precious substances: on those mountains of seven precious substances and in the valleys in between them are light beams clearly shining—the sunbeams on the jewel mountains all appear in the lights of the valleys, and the sunbeams in the valleys all appear in the lights of the mountains: in this way they mutually reflect back and forth. Sometimes it is said that the sunbeams emerge from the mountains of seven precious substances, sometimes it is said that the sunbeams emerge from the valleys between the mountains; sometimes it is said that the sunlight enters the mountains, sometimes it is said that the sunlight enters the valleys—but the sunbeams reflect back and forth boundlessly; their nature is not existent, not nonexistent, not abiding in the mountains, not apart from the mountains, not dwelling in the water, not apart from the water. So it is also with enlightening beings in this vast concentration of subtle light: they do not dissolve the features of the structure of the world, do not annihilate the natures of the phenomena of the world, do not dwell within the world or outside the world; they do not discriminate anything in any world, yet do not destroy the features of worlds, they see all things as one form which is formless, and yet do not destroy the identities of things—they abide in real Thusness, never leaving it.

"It is like a magician, expert in magical arts, standing at a crossroads performing magic tricks: in one day, in the space of a moment, he may manifest a day or a night, or he may make it appear to be seven days and nights, or a fortnight, a month, a year, a century; according to desire, he can manifest the appearance of cities, towns, villages, springs, streams, rivers, seas, sun, moon, clouds, rain, palaces, mansions, houses, all of this complete. Yet he does not destroy the original one day or one hour by making it appear that years have passed, and the brevity of the actual time does not destroy the appearance of the passage of days, months, or years. The illusory appearances clearly show, yet the actual time is not extinguished. In the same way great enlightening beings, entering this vast concentration of subtle light, manifest countless worlds entering into one world, each of those countless worlds having earth, water, fire, and air, oceans and mountains, cities and towns, groves and houses, abodes of various kinds of beings complete with all kinds of adornments; they have realms of desire, of form, and of formlessness, solar systems and galaxies, acts and consequences, death in one place and rebirth in another, all the times and seasons of all worlds—moments, days, nights, fortnights, months, years, centuries, eons of becoming and eons of decay, polluted lands, clean lands, big lands, small lands, buddhas appearing therein, in buddha-lands that are pure, with circles of enlightening beings and autonomous spiritual powers teaching sentient beings; every place in those lands is filled with countless people and various beings of different forms and conditions, immeasurable, boundless, inconceivable, past, future, and present, the power of pure deeds producing infinite jewels of supreme refinement. They show all such things in one world, wherein the enlightening beings all see clearly, entering into all, observing all, contemplating all, comprehending all, knowing all truly by means of inexhaustible knowledge. The multiplicity of the worlds does not destroy this one world, and the singleness of this world does not destroy the multiplicity of those worlds. Why? Because enlightening beings know all phenomena are selfless, they are said to have penetrated the principle of lifelessness and noncreation. Because enlightening beings diligently cultivate noncontention in all worlds, they are said to abide in the principle of selflessness. Because enlightening beings see all bodies as they really are, all deriving from conditions, they are said to abide in the principle of nonexistence of beings. Because enlightening beings know that everything which is born and passes away comes from causes, they are said to abide in the principle of nonexistence of persons. Because enlightening beings know the fundamental nature of all things is equal, they are said to abide in the principle of nonexistence of mental productions or the human being. Because enlightening beings know the fundamental nature of all things is still, they are said to abide in the principle of stillness. Because enlightening beings know that all things are uniform, they are said to abide in the principle of nondiscrimination. Because enlightening beings know the realm of reality does not have various differentiated phenomena, they are said to abide in the principle of inconceivability. Because enlightening beings diligently cultivate all liberative means and skillfully pacify beings, they are said to abide in the principle of great compassion.

"In this way enlightening beings can put countless worlds into one world, know the various differences of countless beings, see the individual procedures of countless enlightening beings, and observe countless buddhas appearing here and there, able to absorb the teachings expounded by those buddhas, also seeing themselves there practicing them; without leaving here, they appear to be there, and without leaving there, they appear to be here, this body and that body being undifferentiable, because they are in the realm of reality. They always practice contemplation earnestly, unceasingly, never abandoning wisdom, because they do not regress.

"It is like a magician in a given place practicing the arts of illusion: he does not destroy his actual place by the illusory place, and does not destroy the actual day by the illusory day. In the same way, enlightening beings manifest the existence of a land where there is no land, and manifest the nonexistence of a land where there is a land; where there are sentient beings they manifest nonexistence of sentient beings, and where there are no sentient beings they manifest the existence of sentient beings; where there is no form they manifest form, and where there is form they manifest formlessness—the beginning does not disarray the aftermath, and the aftermath does not disarray the beginning. The enlightening beings know that all the things of the world are like this, the same as illusions: knowing phenomena are illusory, they know knowledge is illusory; because they know knowledge is illusory, they know action is illusory. Once they know that knowledge is illusion and action is illusion, they develop illusion knowledge, observing all actions. Just as the illusions of the world do not manifest their illusions outside of their place, and do not have a place outside of illusion, in the same way great enlightening beings do not enter the world outside of emptiness and also do not enter emptiness outside of the world. Why? Because emptiness and the world have no difference. Living in the world is also living in emptiness. Great enlightening beings are able to perceive and cultivate the various different adorning activities of all worlds within emptiness. In a single instant they are able to know countless worlds, becoming or decaying, and also know the continuity and succession of all ages. They are able to manifest countless ages in a single instant without enlarging the instant.

"Great enlightening beings attain the illusion knowledge of inconceivable liberation, arrive at the other shore, abide in the realm of illusion, and enter the illusions of the world. They think of all things as like illusions, do not oppose the illusory world, have perfect knowledge of illusion, comprehend that past, present, and future are not apart from illusion, and definitively realize the boundlessness of mind. Like the enlightened ones, they abide in knowledge of illusoriness, their minds equanimous; they know all worlds are like illusions, and they have no attachments anywhere, having no self or possessions. Just as the magician creates illusory phenomena, though he does not live with those illusory phenomena, yet has no confusion about illusory phenomena, in the same way the great enlightening beings know all things reach the other shore, and in their minds they do not imagine that they are able to enter into things, and they have no confusion about things. This is the knowledge of the skill of the enlightening beings' second great concentration, of subtle light.

"What is great enlightening beings' concentration of spiritual power successively journeying to the buddha-lands? Here the great enlightening beings pass countless worlds to the east, and also pass as many worlds as atoms in that many worlds: in those worlds they enter this concentration, maybe entering for an instant, or for a moment, or entering continuously, or entering in the morning, or at midday, or in the afternoon, or in the evening, or at night, or after midnight, or entering for one day, or for five days, or for a fortnight, or for a month, or for a year, or for a century, or for a millennium, or for a hundred millennia, or for a hundred million years, or for ten trillion years, or for an octillion years, or for one eon, or for a hundred eons, or for a hundred thousand eons, or for an octillion eons, or for countless eons, or for measureless eons, or for boundless eons, or for incomparable eons, or for innumerable eons, or for unaccountable eons, or for unthinkable eons, or for immeasurable eons, or for unspeakable eons, or for untold eons. As for the various dissimilarities—of far and near, of phenomena or time, and so on—the enlightening beings do not create discriminations in regard to them; their minds are not obsessed with them; they do not take them to be dual or nondual, universal or particular. Though they are aloof from these discriminations, yet by expedient techniques of spiritual powers, when they arise from concentration they remember everything and reach the ultimate end. It is like, for example, the sun going around giving light, never stopping day or night; the emergence of the sun is called day and the disappearance of the sun is called night—it is not born with the day and does not perish at night. In the same way the great enlightening being enters concentration of spiritual power in countless worlds, and having entered concentration, clearly sees those countless worlds. This is called the technical knowledge of the third great concentration of great enlightening being, the great concentration of spiritual power successively traveling to buddha-lands.

"What is great enlightening beings' concentration of action of the pure profound mind? Here the enlightening beings know that embodiments of Buddha are as numerous as all beings, and see innumerable buddhas, more than the number of atoms in countless worlds. To all those buddhas they offer all kinds of fine fragrances, all kinds of beautiful flowers, all kinds of canopies, vast as countless buddha-lands, all kinds of exquisite adornments surpassing those of all worlds, all kinds of precious substances, parks arrayed with all kinds of embellishments, treasuries of countless jewels, food and drink produced by enlightened spiritual power, surpassing that of all the heavens in flavor, and all the various superb offerings in all buddha-lands, which they are able to gather by spiritual power. To each of those buddhas they pay utmost respect and honor, prostrating themselves on the ground and asking for the Buddha's teaching, praising the impartiality of Buddha, extolling the magnificent virtues of the buddhas. They enter the great compassion that all buddhas enter, attain the unhindered power that is equal in all buddhas, and in a single instant seek the wondrous teaching from all buddhas. Yet they do not apprehend, in regard to those buddhas, such signs as appearance in the world or entry into ultimate nirvana. Just as the scattered, stirring mind, distinguishing objects, does not know what the conditions of mind's arousal and quiescence are, in the same way, these great enlightening beings do not discriminate the characteristics of the appearance and nirvana of buddhas.

"It is like a mirage in the daytime—it does not come from clouds or lakes, it does not rest on land or water, neither exists nor does not exist, is not good or bad, not pure or polluted, it cannot be drunk, cannot be polluted, it neither has nor does not have substance, neither has nor does not have taste. Through causes and conditions it manifests the appearance of water, as perceived by the consciousness. When one looks at it from afar it resembles water, and so one imagines there is water, but when one approaches there is none, so the image of water naturally disappears. Similarly the great enlightening beings do not apprehend forms of the buddhas emerging in the world or entering nirvana: the characteristics of existence or nonexistence of buddhas are discriminations of the conceiving mind.

"This concentration is called the action of pure, profound mind. The great enlightening being, after having entered this concentration, emerges without forgetting, like someone awakening from sleep remembering what he has dreamed—even though when one is awake the dream scenes are not there, still one can remember them. In the same way the great enlightening beings enter this concentration, see buddhas and hear teachings, then arise from concentration, yet remember it all and use these teachings to enlighten all communities at enlightenment sites, and adorn all buddha-lands; they clearly comprehend all the immeasurable meanings and intentions, and all the means of teaching are also purified. They light the torch of great wisdom and perpetuate the seed of buddhahood. Their freedom from hesitation is complete, and their powers of elucidation are inexhaustible; they reveal and expound the treasury of the most profound Teaching. This is the technical knowledge of the fourth great concentration of great enlightening beings, the concentration of action of the pure, profound mind.

"What is great enlightening beings' concentration of knowledge of the stores of adornments of the past? Here great enlightening beings are able to know the manifestations of the buddhas of the past. That is, within the order of eons, the order of lands; within the order of lands, the order of eons; within the order of eons, the order of buddhas' appearances; within the order of buddhas' appearances, the order of teaching; within the order of teaching, the order of inclinations; within the order of inclinations, the order of faculties; within the order of faculties, the order of training; within the order of training, the order of life spans of Buddhas; within the order of life spans, they know the order of numbers of trillions of years.

"Because these great enlightening beings gain such boundless knowledge of order, they therefore know the past buddhas, therefore know past lands, therefore know past teachings, therefore know past ages, therefore know past phenomena, therefore know past minds, therefore know past understandings, therefore know past beings, therefore know past afflictions, therefore know past manners, therefore know past purities.

"This concentration is called the pure treasury of the past; in a single moment it can enter a hundred eons, a thousand eons, a hundred thousand eons, an octillion eons, countless eons, measureless eons, boundless eons, incomparable eons, uncountable eons, unaccountable eons, unthinkable eons, immeasurable eons, unspeakable eons, untold, inexpressible eons. When those great enlightening beings enter this concentration, they do not annihilate the present or focus on the past.

"When those great enlightening beings emerge from this concentration, they receive ten kinds of inconceivable anointment from the Enlightened, and also attain, purify, consummate, enter, realize, fulfill, and hold them, comprehending them equally, the three spheres pure. What are the ten? One, explanation not violating meaning; two, inexhaustibility of teaching; three, impeccable expression; four, endless eloquence; five, freedom from hesitation; six, truthfulness of speech; seven, the trust of the community; eight, liberating those in the triple world; nine, supreme excellence of roots of goodness; ten, command of the wondrous Teaching. These are the ten anointments. When enlightening beings enter this concentration and emerge from it, immediately they become like a spirit when it enters the womb, the consciousness instantly being born therein—in the same way, when the great enlightening beings emerge from this concentration, in the presence of the Enlightened they instantly attain these ten qualities. This is called the technical knowledge of the great enlightening beings' fifth great concentration, the concentration of knowledge of the stores of adornments of the past.

"What is great enlightening beings' concentration of the treasury of light of knowledge? The great enlightening beings in this concentration know the various different names of all buddhas in all ages in all worlds in the future, whether they have been spoken of yet or not, whether they have been given the prediction of buddhahood yet or not. That is, they know countless names, untold names of buddhas, and that they will appear in the world, will benefit beings, will be spiritual sovereigns, will perform the tasks of buddha, will explain what is beneficial, will praise

goodness, will explain what is pure, will clear away all evils, will abide
in virtue, will reveal the ultimate truth, will enter the rank of coronation, will attain omniscience. Those buddhas' cultivation of complete
action, undertaking of complete vows, entry into complete knowledge,
leadership of a complete circle, fulfillment of complete adornments,
accumulation of complete virtues, realization of complete truth, attainment of complete fruition, endowment with complete qualities, and fulfillment of complete enlightenment, as well as those buddhas' names,
their methods and skills, their spiritual powers and miracles, their development of beings, and their entry into final nirvana—all this the
enlightening beings here thoroughly know.

"These enlightening beings can in a single instant enter one eon, a
hundred eons, a thousand eons, a hundred thousand eons, a hundred
thousand billion eons; they enter into as many eons as atoms in a continent, as many eons as atoms in four continents, as many eons as atoms
in a solar system, as many eons as atoms in a galaxy, as many eons as
atoms in a universe, as many eons as atoms in a buddha-land, as many
eons as atoms in a hundred thousand buddha-lands, as many eons as
atoms in a hundred thousand billion buddha-lands, as many eons as
atoms in countless buddha-lands, as many eons as atoms in untold,
inexpressible numbers of buddha-lands—by their wisdom they are able
to know the numbers of eons in all future worlds. And because they
know them, their minds also enter the doors of ten kinds of preservation:
because they enter the presence of the buddhas, they gain the protection
of buddhas as numerous as atoms in untold buddha-lands; because they
enter the presence of the Teaching, they attain inexhaustible intellectual
powers illumined by ten kinds of total mental command; because they
enter the presence of practice, they produce perfectly rounded, outstanding vows; because they enter the presence of power, no one can
dominate or overpower them; because they enter the presence of knowledge, the Buddha teachings they practice are free from obstruction;
because they enter the presence of great compassion, they turn the wheel
of the pure teaching, which never turns back; because they enter the
presence of expression of skillful handling of distinctions, they turn the
wheel of all letters and clean the ground of all teachings; because they
enter the presence of the state of the lion being born, they open the lock
of the Teaching and leave the mind of desire; because they enter the
presence of the power of knowledge, they cultivate enlightening practice
unceasingly; because they enter the presence of the power of good companionship, they cause boundless beings to become purified; because
they enter the presence of the power of nondwelling, they enter unspeakable, untold numbers of vast eons; because they enter the presence
of the power of the Teaching, by uninhibited knowledge of means, they
know all things are inherently pure.

"Once great enlightening beings are in this concentration, they skillfully live in untold numbers of ages and lands; they skillfully know

untold numbers of various sentient beings; they skillfully know untold numbers of different characteristics of sentient beings; they skillfully know untold numbers of similar and different consequences of action; they skillfully know untold numbers of practices differentiated by vigor, faculties, habit energies, and continuity; they skillfully know untold numbers of various tainted and pure contemplations; they skillfully know untold numbers of various meanings of teachings and innumerable written and verbal expressions; they skillfully know untold numbers of various buddhas' appearances, families, times, manifestations, teachings, actions, buddha-works, and entries into ultimate final nirvana; they skillfully know untold numbers of boundless doors of wisdom and knowledge; they skillfully know untold numbers of the boundless different manifestations of all spiritual powers.

"It is as when the sun comes out, all the villages and towns, mansions and houses, mountains, marshes, birds and beasts, trees, forests, flowers and fruits, and so on, can be clearly seen by all people with vision; the light of the sun is impartial and has no discrimination, yet can cause the eye to see all kinds of forms. This concentration is also like this: it is in essence impartial, without any discrimination, yet can cause enlightening beings to know countless numbers of different characteristics.

"When the great enlightening beings realize such knowledge, they cause beings to attain ten kinds of fruitfulness: one, fruitful seeing, because of causing sentient beings to develop roots of goodness; two, fruitful hearing, causing sentient beings to gain maturity; three, fruitful association, causing sentient beings' minds to be pacified; four, fruitful aspiration, causing sentient beings to do as they say and master the meanings of all the teachings; five, fruitful action, causing boundless worlds to be purified; six, fruitful companionship, cutting off countless beings' doubts in the presence of the buddhas of countless worlds; seven, fruitful vows, causing whatever sentient beings are thought of to make excellent offerings and accomplish undertakings; eight, fruitful skillful methods, causing all to be able to abide in pure knowledge of unobstructed liberation; nine, fruitful showering of the rain of Teaching, expediently revealing the practice of universal knowledge to countless beings of various faculties and causing them to abide in the path of buddhahood; ten, fruitful appearance, manifesting boundless forms, causing all sentient beings to be bathed in illumination.

"When great enlightening beings abide in this concentration and attain ten kinds of fruitfulness, the kings of the heavens all come and bow to them; the dragon kings produce great fragrant clouds; the yaksha kings bow to their feet; the titan kings honor them with offerings; the garuda kings circle them in respect; the kings of the Brahma heavens come and propitiate them; the kinnara kings draw near them; human kings serve and support them. This is the technical knowledge of the sixth great concentration of great enlightening beings, the concentration of the treasury of light of knowledge.

"What is great enlightening beings' concentration of knowledge of the adornments of buddhas of all worlds? Why is this concentration called knowing the adornments of buddhas of all worlds? Great enlightening beings in this concentration can successively enter the worlds of the east, can successively enter the worlds of the south, west, north, southeast, northeast, southwest, northwest, zenith, and nadir. They can successively enter all these worlds and see the buddhas emerging in the world, and also see all the spiritual powers of those buddhas, and can also see all the feats of those buddhas, and can also see the immense charisma of those buddhas, and also see the supreme freedom of those buddhas, and also see the great lion roar of those buddhas, and also see the practices cultivated by the buddhas, and also see the various adornments of the buddhas, and also see the psychic projections of the buddhas, and also see the vast congregation of those buddhas, the unity of the congregations, the multiplicity of congregations, the locations of the congregations, the abodes of the congregations, the development of the congregations, the training of the congregations, the dignity of the congregations—all this they clearly see. They also see the size of the congregations equal to a continent, and also see the congregations equal to four continents, those equal to a solar system, those equal to a galaxy, those equal to a universe, those filling ten sextillion buddha-lands, those filling countless buddha-lands; they see congregations filling as many buddha-lands as there are atoms in a hundred buddha-lands, filling as many buddha-lands as atoms in a thousand buddha-lands, filling as many buddha-lands as atoms in ten sextillion buddha-lands, filling as many buddha-lands as atoms in countless buddha-lands, measureless buddha-lands, boundless buddha-lands, incomparable buddha-lands, innumerable buddha-lands, unreckonable buddha-lands, unthinkable buddha-lands, untold, inexpressible numbers of buddha-lands. They also see the buddhas amid those congregations displaying various forms, various times, various lands, various transfigurations, various spiritual powers, various adornments, various masteries, various physical sizes, and various actions. The great enlightening beings also see themselves in those congregations, and see themselves preaching there, and see themselves receiving the words of the buddhas, and see themselves comprehending interdependent origination, and see themselves poised in the air, and see themselves in the reality-body, and see themselves not producing attachments, and see themselves not dwelling on discrimination, and see themselves being indefatigable, and see themselves entering into all knowledge, and see themselves knowing all meanings, and see themselves entering all stages, and see themselves entering all states of being, and see themselves knowing all expedient means of liberation, and see themselves in the presence of the buddhas, and see themselves entering all the powers of enlightenment, and see themselves entering True Thusness, and see themselves entering noncontention, and see themselves entering all truths. When they see in this way, they do not discriminate lands, beings, buddhas, or phenomena; they do not cling to the body, to physical actions, to the mind, or to the intellect. Just as things do not discriminate their essence and do not discriminate sound, yet their essence is not abandoned and names do not pass away, in the same way great enlightening beings do not abandon actions, according with the doings of the world, yet have no attachments to them.

"Great enlightening beings see infinite lights and colors, forms and features of buddhas, perfectly developed, equal and pure, each one appearing clearly to their senses. Sometimes they see the various lights of the buddhas' bodies; sometimes they see buddhas' auras to a depth of one fathom; sometimes they see buddhas' bodies like blazing suns; sometimes they see subtle hues of light of buddhas' bodies; sometimes they see buddhas' bodies as clear, or they may see buddhas' bodies as golden, or as diamond-colored, or as violet, or as of infinite colors, or as sapphire; they may see buddhas' bodies seven cubits tall, or ten cubits tall, or twenty cubits tall, or thirty cubits tall, or up to a hundred cubits tall, or half a league tall, or ten leagues tall, or a hundred leagues tall, or a thousand leagues tall, or a hundred thousand leagues tall; or they may see buddhas' bodies the size of a continent, or the size of four continents, or the size of a solar system, or the size of a galaxy, or the size of a universe, or the size of a hundred universes, or the size of a thousand universes, or the size of a hundred thousand universes, or the size of ten quintillion universes, or the size of incalculable numbers of universes.

"In this way enlightening beings see the buddhas' infinite colors, infinite physical forms, infinite manifestations, infinite lights, and infinite webs of light; the measure of those lights is equal to the cosmos, illumining all things therein, causing all to develop unexcelled knowledge. They also see the buddhas' embodiments without attachment, without obstruction, supremely pure.

"Enlightening beings see the embodiment of Buddha in these ways, yet the body of the Enlightened does not increase or decrease. It is like space: in a worm hole in a seed it is not diminished, and in countless worlds it is not expanded. So it is with the bodies of the buddhas: when they are seen as large, still there is no increase, and when they are seen as small, there is no decrease. Just as the moon is seen as small by people on earth, yet is not diminished, and is seen as large by beings on the moon, yet does not expand, so also do enlightening beings in this concentration see various transfigurations of the buddhas' bodies, according to their inclinations, receiving and retaining their verbal teachings, there being all the while no increase or decrease in the body of the Enlightened.

"Just as after beings' lives end and they are about to be reborn, they are not apart from mind and what they see is pure, so also is what enlightening beings see, while in this profound concentration, utterly pure.

"Great enlightening beings in this concentration develop ten kinds of rapidity: rapid growth in practices and fulfillment of great vows; rapid illumination of the world with the light of the teaching; rapid liberation of sentient beings by appropriate projection of the teachings; rapid manifestation of buddhas' pure lands according to the actions of beings; rapid entry into the ten powers by impartial knowledge; rapid joining of the Enlightened Ones in their abode; rapid destruction of the armies of demons by the power of great compassion; rapid removal of beings' doubts, producing joy in them; rapid manifestation of spiritual displays in accord with dominant inclinations; rapid purification of worldly realms by means of various sublime expressions of truth.

"These enlightening beings also attain ten kinds of truth seal, which stamp all things: one, having the same roots of goodness equal in all buddhas of past, future, and present; two, attaining the reality body with boundless knowledge, same as all buddhas; three, abiding in nonduality, same as the buddhas; four, seeing the infinite objects of all times as all equal, same as the buddhas do; five, gaining comprehension of the unobstructed realm of the cosmos of reality, same as that of the buddhas; six, achieving the ten powers, same as the buddhas, being unhindered in function; seven, having forever cut off opinions and passions, dwelling in the state of freedom from conflict, same as the buddhas; eight, ceaselessly teaching sentient beings, same as the buddhas do; nine, having ability to observe adaptive skill in knowledge and meaning, same as the buddhas; ten, being equal to all buddhas, same as all enlightened ones.

"If great enlightening beings accomplish the techniques of this great concentration of knowledge of adornments of buddhas of all worlds, they are teacherless because they can enter all principles and qualities of buddhas by themselves, without depending on another's instruction. They are people of power because they can enlighten all sentient beings. They are pure because they know that the nature of mind is fundamentally pure. They are foremost because they can liberate all worldlings. They are comforters because they can awaken all sentient beings. They are stabilizers because they can establish in the family of buddhas those who are not yet so established. They are true knowers because they enter the door of universal knowledge. They are without varying conceptions because what they say is nondual. They abide in the treasury of truth because they vow to know all Buddha teachings. They are able to shower the rain of the Teaching, because they satisfy all beings in accord with their inclinations.

"It is like the god-king Indra placing a jewel in his topknot; by the power of the jewel his majestic light becomes all the more effulgent. When the god-king first obtained this jewel, he gained ten things surpassing all the gods of the thirty-three-fold heaven: one, color; two, physical form; three, manifestation; four, retinue; five, appurtenances; six, voice; seven, magical powers; eight, control; nine, intellectual understanding; ten, cognitive function. In these ten ways he surpasses all the other gods of the thirty-three-fold heaven. In the same way, when enlightening beings first attain this concentration, they gain ten kinds of treasuries of great knowledge: one, knowledge illumining all buddha-lands; two, knowledge of the births of all beings; three, knowledge of how to make magical displays of past, future, and present; four, knowledge of all buddha-bodies; five, knowledge comprehending all Buddha teachings; six, knowledge embracing all pure phenomena; seven, knowledge of how to cause all beings to enter the reality-body; eight, pure knowledge of the universal directly perceiving all things; nine, knowledge of total freedom reaching the other shore; ten, knowledge establishing all universal principles.

"Enlightening beings in this concentration also gain ten kinds of extremely pure bodies of power: one, emitting unspeakably unspeakable numbers of light spheres to illumine unspeakably unspeakable numbers of worlds; two, emitting unspeakably unspeakable numbers of spheres of light of infinite colors to purify all worlds; three, emitting unspeakably unspeakable numbers of light spheres to pacify living beings; four, emanating unspeakably unspeakable numbers of bodies to be near to all the buddhas; five, raining unspeakably unspeakable numbers of clouds of flowers of various wonderful scents to present to all buddhas; six, magically producing unspeakably unspeakable numbers of various kinds of infinitely free miraculous effects to develop and mature sentient beings; eight, crossing unspeakably unspeakable numbers of worlds in a single step in order to ask to hear the Teaching from all the variously named buddhas of the ten directions; nine, showing a body of immeasurably various forms, the crown of which none can see, so that all who see or hear of it will not have done so in vain; ten, uttering unspeakably unspeakable numbers of words to reveal countless secret truths to sentient beings.

"Once enlightening beings gain these ten kinds of extremely pure body of power, they can cause sentient beings to attain ten kinds of fulfillment: one, they can enable sentient beings to see Buddha; two, they can induce sentient beings to deeply believe in Buddha; three, they can induce sentient beings to listen to the Teaching; four, they can cause sentient beings to know there is a world of buddhahood; five, they can cause sentient beings to perceive the miracles of Buddha; six, they can cause sentient beings to recollect accumulated deeds; seven, they can cause sentient beings to perfect concentration; eight, they can introduce sentient beings into the purity of buddhahood; nine, they can induce sentient beings to aspire to enlightenment; ten, they can enable sentient beings to fulfill enlightened knowledge.

"When great enlightening beings have caused sentient beings to attain these ten kinds of fulfillment, they also perform ten kinds of buddha-work for sentient beings: they perform verbal buddha-work, to develop and mature beings; they perform physical buddha-work, to train sentient beings; they perform mental buddha-work to purify sentient beings; they shake the world as buddha-work to make sentient beings give up bad tendencies; they perform buddha-work by expedient awakening, to cause sentient beings not to lose mindfulness; they perform buddha-work by manifesting forms in dreams, to cause sentient beings to be constant in right mindfulness; they perform buddha-work by radiating great light to embrace all beings; they perform buddha-work by cultivating the practices of enlightening beings, to cause sentient beings to live by superior aspirations; they perform buddha-work by attaining perfect enlightenment to cause sentient beings to know illusion; they perform buddha-work by turning the wheel of the sublime teaching, to teach sentient beings in accord with the time; they perform buddha-work by appearing to live for a certain span, in order to tame sentient beings; they perform buddha-work by manifesting nirvana, because they know sentient beings will become weary.

"This is the technical knowledge of the great enlightening beings' seventh great concentration, the concentration of knowledge of adornments of buddhas of all worlds.

"What is great enlightening beings' concentration of the differentiated bodies of all sentient beings? Great enlightening beings in this concentration attain ten kinds of nonattachment: nonattachment in all lands; nonattachment in all places; nonattachment in all times; nonattachment in respect to all beings; nonattachment in respect to all phenomena; nonattachment in respect to all enlightening beings; nonattachment in respect to all enlightening beings' vows; nonattachment in respect to all concentrations; nonattachment in respect to all buddhas; nonattachment in respect to all the stages of enlightenment.

"How do great enlightening beings enter into and emerge from this concentration? They enter this concentration internally and emerge externally; entering externally, they emerge internally; entering in the same body, they emerge in a different body; entering in a different body, they emerge in the same body; entering in a human body, they emerge in a yaksha body; entering in a yaksha body, they emerge in a human body; entering in a dragon body, they emerge in a titan body; entering in a titan body, they emerge in a celestial body; entering in a celestial body, they emerge in a Brahma-king body; entering in a Brahma-king body, they emerge in a desire-realm body; entering in a heaven, they emerge in a hell; entering in a hell, they emerge in the human world; entering in the human world, they emerge in other realms of being; they enter in a thousand bodies and emerge in one body; entering in one body, they emerge in a thousand bodies; entering in a hundred billion bodies, they emerge in one body; entering in one body, they emerge in a hundred billion bodies; entering among people of the south, they emerge among people of the west; entering among people of the west, they emerge among people of the north; entering among people of the north, they emerge among people of the east; entering among people of the east, they emerge among people of three continents; entering among people of three continents, they emerge among people of four continents; entering among people of four continents, they emerge among the different creatures of all seas; entering among different creatures of all seas, they emerge among the spirits of all seas; entering among the spirits of all seas, they emerge in the water element of all seas; entering in the water element of all seas, they emerge in the earth element of all seas; entering in the earth element of all seas, they emerge in the fire element of all seas; entering in the fire element of all seas, they emerge in the air element of all seas; entering in the air element of all seas, they emerge in all four gross elements; entering in all four gross elements, they emerge in the truth of nonorigination; entering in the truth of nonorigination, they emerge on the polar mountain; entering on the polar mountain, they emerge on the mountain of seven precious substances; entering on the mountain of seven precious substances, they emerge on the black mountain of various crops and forests of all soils; entering on the black mountain of various crops and forests of all soils, they emerge in precious arrays of all flowers of sublime fragrances; entering in precious arrays of all flowers of sublime fragrances, they emerge in the incarnations of all beings of the four quarters, the zenith and nadir; entering in the incarnations of all beings of the four quarters, the zenith and nadir, they emerge in the beings of the solar system; entering in the beings of the solar system, they emerge in beings of the galaxy; entering in the beings of the galaxy, they emerge in the beings of the universe; entering in the beings of the universe, they emerge in the beings of a hundred thousand hundred billion universes; entering in the beings of a hundred thousand hundred billion universes, they emerge in the beings of countless worlds; entering in the beings of countless worlds, they emerge in the beings of measureless worlds; entering in the beings of measureless worlds, they emerge in the beings of boundless buddha-lands; entering in the beings of boundless buddha-lands, they emerge in the beings of incomparable buddha-lands; entering in the beings of incomparable buddha-lands, they emerge in the beings of innumerable worlds; entering in the beings of innumerable worlds, they emerge in the beings of incalculable worlds; entering in the beings of incalculable worlds, they emerge in the beings of unthinkable worlds; entering in the beings of unthinkable worlds, they emerge in the beings of immeasurable worlds; entering in the beings of immeasurable worlds, they emerge in the beings of unspeakable worlds; entering in the beings of unspeakable worlds, they emerge in the beings of unspeakably unspeakable numbers of worlds; entering in the beings of unspeakably unspeakable numbers of worlds, they emerge in impure beings; entering in impure beings, they emerge in pure beings; entering in pure beings, they emerge in impure beings; entering in the eye, they emerge in the ear; entering in the ear, they emerge in the eye; entering in the nose, they emerge in the tongue; entering in the tongue, they emerge in the nose; entering in the body, they emerge in the mind; entering in the mind, they emerge in the body; entering in their own senses, they emerge in others' senses; entering in others' senses, they emerge in their own senses; entering in a single atom, they emerge in the atoms of countless worlds; entering in the atoms of countless worlds, they emerge in one atom; entering in hearers of Buddha's voice, they emerge in self-enlightened ones; entering in self-enlightened ones, they emerge in hearers; entering in their own bodies, they emerge in the body of Buddha; entering in the body of Buddha, they emerge in their own bodies; entering in a single instant, they emerge in a hundred million eons; entering in a hundred million eons, they emerge in an instant; entering in the same instant, they emerge in different times; entering in different times, they emerge in the same instant; entering in the past, they emerge in the future; entering in the future, they emerge in the past; entering in past, present, and future, they emerge in a moment; entering in a moment, they emerge in past, present, and future; entering in True Thusness, they emerge in verbalization; entering in verbalization, they emerge in True Thusness.

"It is as when a man is possessed by a demon, his body trembles and he cannot relax—the demon does not show its body; it causes the body of another to be that way. In the same way, great enlightening beings in this concentration enter concentration in their own bodies and emerge in others' bodies, enter concentration in others' bodies and emerge in their own bodies.

"It is like a corpse able to get up and act effectively through the power of a magic spell; though the corpse and the spell are distinct, yet they can join together and accomplish things. In the same way, a great enlightening being in this concentration enters concentration in the same object and emerges in a different object, enters concentration in a different object and emerges in the same object.

"It is as a monk who has attained freedom of mind may make many bodies of one body or one body of many bodies, yet it is not that one body vanishes and many bodies are born, or that many bodies vanish and one body is born. In the same way, a great enlightening being in this concentration enters concentration in one body and emerges in many bodies, enters concentration in many bodies and emerges in one body.

"Just as the flavor of soil is one while the flavors of the crops it produces are variously different, the flavors having difference even though the soil has no difference, in the same way a great enlightening being in this concentration, though free from discrimination, may enter concentration in one element and emerge in many elements, or enter concentration in many elements and emerge in one.

"Great enlightening beings in this concentration are lauded for ten praise-worthy qualities: they enter into True Thusness, and so are called Tathagata, those who have arrived at Thusness; they are aware of all truths, and so are called buddha, enlightened; they are praised by all worlds, and so are called teachers of truth; they know all things, and so are called omniscient; they are resorted to by all worlds, and so are called refuge; they have mastered all teaching methods, and so are called guides; they lead all beings into universal knowledge, and so are called great leaders; they are lamps for all worlds, and so are called light; their aspirations are fulfilled, they have accomplished salvation, they have done their tasks, they abide in unobstructed knowledge and individually know all things, so they are called adepts of the ten powers; they thoroughly comprehend all cycles of the Teaching, so they are called all-seers.

"Great enlightening beings in this concentration also acquire ten kinds of illumination: they acquire the light of all buddhas because they are equal to them; they acquire the light of all worlds because they can beautify them all; they acquire the light of all beings because they go to pacify them all; they acquire the light of immeasurable expertise because they preach on the stage of the cosmos of realities; they acquire undifferentiated light because they know that phenomena have no differentiation in essence; they acquire the light of expedient means because they have realized freedom from desire for anything; they acquire the light of truth because their minds are equanimous in the realm of desirelessness; they acquire the light of mystic transfigurations pervading all worlds because they are ceaselessly empowered by the Buddha; they acquire the light of proper meditation because they reach the other shore of freedom of all buddhas; they acquire the light of True Thusness of all things because they can explain everything in a single point.

"Great enlightening beings in this concentration also attain ten kinds of nondoing: the nondoing of physical acts; the nondoing of verbal acts; the nondoing of mental acts; the nondoing of spiritual powers; the nondoing of comprehension of the essencelessness of phenomena; the nondoing of knowledge of the nondissolution of the force of actions; the nondoing of nondiscriminatory knowledge; the nondoing of knowledge of nonorigination; the nondoing of knowing things have no destruction; the nondoing of following the letter without destroying the meaning.

"When great enlightening beings are in this concentration, the innumerable realms are variously different—entering in one, arising in many, entering in many, arising in one, entering in the same one, arising in different ones, entering in different ones, arising in the same one, entering in the subtle, arising in the gross, entering in the gross, arising in the subtle, entering in the great, arising in the small, entering in the small, arising in the great, entering in the congenial, arising in the adverse, entering in the adverse, arising in the congenial, entering incorporeally, arising corporeally, entering corporeally, arising incorporeally, entering in the formless, arising in forms, entering in forms, arising in the formless, entering in arising, arising in entering—these are all realms of freedom of this concentration.

"It is as when a magician keeps repeating a spell, he can become able to cause various different forms to appear—the spell and the illusions are distinct, yet the spell can create illusions; though the spell is just a sound, yet it can produce various illusory perceptions, various forms perceived by the eye-consciousness, various sounds perceived by the ear-consciousness, various smells perceived by the nose-consciousness, various tastes perceived by the tongue-consciousness, various feelings perceived by the body-consciousness, various objects perceived by the mind-consciousness. In the same way, the enlightening being in this concentration also enters concentration in sameness and arises from concentration in difference, enters concentration in difference and arises from concentration in sameness.

"It is as when the gods of the thirty-three-fold heaven battled with the titans and the gods prevailed and the titans retreated in defeat. The king of titans was seven hundred leagues tall and was accompanied by several tens of millions of cohorts, yet by magic he led his army all at once into a hole in a lotus root. In the same way, the great enlightening being has already achieved the stage of knowledge of illusions: knowledge of illusion is the enlightening being, the enlightening being is knowledge of illusion—therefore the enlightening being can enter concentration in the undifferentiated and emerge in the differentiated, can enter concentration in the differentiated and emerge in the undifferentiated.

"Just as when a farmer plants seeds in the fields, the seeds are below yet the fruits grow above, so also does an enlightening being in this concentration enter concentration in one and emerge in many, enter concentration in many and emerge in one.

"It is as when the sperm and ovum unite and there is a living being conceived, at which time it is called an embryo; after this it lives in the womb for nine months, and by the power of proper actions all its limbs and organs achieve completion and its consciousness is clear. That life energy and the organs and physical form are distinct, yet by the power of action that energy can make them gradually develop and experience various consequences of similar and different types. In the same way, the great enlightening being in this concentration, from the stage of emyonic omniscience, gradually grows in faith, understanding, resolution, and power, the mind broad, effortlessly and freely entering concentration in nonbeing and emerging in being, entering concentration in being and emerging in nonbeing.

"It is like the case of the palaces of water spirits, built on the earth and not in the sky; the water spirits also live in the palaces and not in the sky, yet they can create clouds spreading through the sky. The palaces that people may see when they look up you may be sure are mirages, not water-spirit palaces. Though water spirits dwell below, the clouds are spread above—in the same way, the great enlightening being in this concentration enters in formlessness and emerges amid forms, enters in forms and emerges in formlessness.

"It is like the case of the palace where the great Brahma-king-god of subtle light lives; called 'pure treasury supreme of all worlds,' in this great palace can be seen all the abodes of all the various creatures in all lands in the galaxy, as well as the natural and man-made features of those lands—even down to minute particles of dust floating in the air, all can be seen reflected in this brahma palace, like seeing one's face in a mirror. The great enlightening beings in this great concentration of the different bodies of all sentient beings know all kinds of lands, see all kinds of buddhas, liberate all kinds of beings, realize all kinds of truths, accomplish all kinds of spiritual practices, fulfill all kinds of understandings, enter all kinds of trances, produce all kinds of psychic powers, attain all kinds of knowledge, and live through all kinds of moments.

"Such great enlightening beings reach ten kinds of other shores of spiritual powers: they reach the other shore of spiritual powers of the buddha that extend throughout space and are present everywhere in the cosmos; they reach the other shore of enlightening beings' ultimately nondiscriminatory free spiritual powers; they reach the other shore of spiritual powers of buddha-work able to initiate the far-reaching practical commitments of enlightening beings and enter the gate of realization of Thusness; they reach the other shore of spiritual powers able to shake all objects in all worlds and purify them all; they reach the other shore of spiritual powers able to freely know that the inconceivable results of actions of all sentient beings are all like illusory productions; they reach the other shore of spiritual powers able to freely know the different characteristics—crude and subtle, those in entry and emergence—of all concentrations; they reach the other shore of spiritual powers able to boldly enter the realm of the enlightened and therein produce great vows; they reach the other shore of spiritual powers able to cause buddhas to appear and teach, taming beings, causing them to be born in the family of buddhas, causing them to enter the vehicle of buddhahood and swiftly attain fulfillment; they reach the other shore of spiritual powers able to comprehend all the countless esoteric statements and teach in such a way as to clarify countless aspects of truth; they reach the other shore of spiritual powers able to cause the past, present, and future to appear in a single instant without depending on the numbers of days, nights, months, years, or epochs.

"This is called the technical knowledge of the great enlightening beings' eighth great concentration, the concentration of the differentiated bodies of all beings.

"What is great enlightening beings' great concentration of freedom in the elemental cosmos? Here the great enlightening beings enter concentration in the medium of their own eyes, in the mediums of their other senses, including the medium of their own minds—this is called freedom in the elemental cosmos.

"Enlightening beings enter this concentration in each pore of their bodies. They are spontaneously able to know all worldly beings, all worldly phenomena, and all worlds; they know ten quintillion worlds, they know incalculable numbers of worlds, they know as many worlds as atoms in untold buddha-lands. They see in all worlds when buddhas emerge, congregations of enlightening beings filling them all, their radiant light clear, purely good, unalloyed, with great arrays of all kinds of treasures adorning them. Therein the enlightening beings ceaselessly cultivate enlightening practices, for an eon or a hundred eons, or a thousand eons, or a million eons, or a billion eons, or countless eons, or untold eons, or for as many eons as atoms in untold numbers of buddha-lands.

"Also, they remain in this concentration through these immeasurable eons, also entering, also emerging, also perfecting worlds, also pacifying beings, also comprehending the elemental cosmos, also knowing all times, also expounding all truths, also manifesting all kinds of techniques of great spiritual powers, without attachment or obstruction.

"Because they have attained freedom in the elemental cosmos, they ably analyze the eye, ear, nose, tongue, body, and intellect—they ably analyze all manner of such distinctions, to their furthest extent.

"Once enlightening beings ably know and see in this way, they are able to produce illumination of principles in a trillion concentration formulae, accomplish a trillion purifying practices, acquire a trillion eyes, fulfill a trillion mystic powers, enter a trillion trances, perfect a trillion psychic forces, nurture a trillion powers, fulfill a trillion aspirations, operate a trillion empowerments, demonstrate a trillion mystic metamorphoses, acquire a trillion freedoms of enlightening beings, fulfill a trillion aids to the path of enlightening beings, accumulate a trillion treasuries of enlightening beings, illumine a trillion methods of enlightening beings, expound a trillion doctrines, accomplish a trillion vows, produce a trillion dedications, purify a trillion proper states of enlightening beings, comprehend a trillion teachings, reveal a trillion explanations, and cultivate a trillion purities of enlightening beings.

"These great enlightening beings also have innumerable virtues, measureless virtues, boundless virtues, incomparable virtues, uncountable virtues, incalculable virtues, unthinkable virtues, immeasurable virtues, unspeakable virtues, inexhaustible virtues. These enlightening beings have already prepared these virtues, accumulated them, arrayed them, purified them, clarified them, embodied them—they can produce them all, all are worthy of praise; they can make them endure, they have perfected them all.

"When great enlightening beings dwell in this concentration, they are under the care of buddhas of the east, whose names are as numerous as atoms in ten thousand incalculable numbers of buddha-lands, each name also applying to as many other buddhas as there are atoms in ten thousand incalculable numbers of buddha-lands, each different—and the same is true of the buddhas of the south, west, north, the four intermediate directions, and the zenith and nadir. Those buddhas all appear before the enlightening beings and show them the pure lands of the buddhas, tell them about the infinite bodies of the buddhas, about the inconceivable eye of the buddhas, the infinite ear of the buddhas, the pure nose of the buddhas, the pure tongue of the buddhas, the nondwelling mind of the buddhas, and the unsurpassed spiritual powers of the buddhas, causing them to cultivate the unexcelled enlightenment of buddhas, to acquire the pure, clear voice of buddhas; they reveal the nonregressive teaching of the buddhas and the boundless congregations of the buddhas, causing them to enter the infinite mystery of the buddhas; they laud all the bases of goodness of the buddhas and cause them to realize the equality of all buddhas; they explain the lineage of buddhas of past, present, and future, display the boundless forms of buddhas, preach the teaching guarded by the buddhas, utter the buddhas' subtle voice of truth, clearly discern the worlds of all buddhas, extol the meditation of all the buddhas, show the order of the assemblies of the buddhas' audiences, preserve the buddhas' inconceivable teaching, explain that all things are like magical productions, elucidate the inertness of the essence of all phenomena, teach the highest principles, praise the infinite virtues of the enlightened, and cause the enlightening beings to enter the clouds of all concentrations and know their minds are like illusions, like emanations, boundless and inexhaustible.

"When great enlightening beings abide in this concentration of cosmic freedom, those buddhas by names as numerous as atoms in ten thousand incalculable numbers of buddha-lands from each of the ten directions, with as many buddhas as atoms in ten thousand incalculable numbers of buddha-lands in each name, simultaneously watch over the enlightening beings and enable them to acquire boundless bodies, enable them to attain unobstructed minds, enable them to attain unfailing recollection of all truths, enable them to attain certain comprehension of all truths, enable them to increase in intelligence and absorb all truths, enable them to clearly understand all truths, enable them to attain skill in spiritual capacities, with power and keenness of all faculties, cause their sphere to be boundless, extending through the cosmos unceasingly, enable them to attain unhindered knowledge, ultimately pure, and enable them to manifest attainment of buddhahood in all worlds by mystical power.

"Enlightening beings in this concentration attain ten kinds of ocean: they attain the ocean of buddhas because they see them all; they attain the ocean of sentient beings because they pacify them all; they attain the ocean of truths because they can comprehend them all by wisdom; they attain the ocean of lands because they go to them all by psychic realization of essenceless, uncreated spiritual powers; they attain the ocean of virtues because they cultivate them all to perfection; they attain the ocean of spiritual powers because they are able to manifest them extensively to awaken enlightenment; they attain the ocean of faculties because they know all their various differences; they attain the ocean of minds because they know the infinite various different minds of sentient beings; they attain the ocean of practices because they can fulfill them all by willpower; they attain the ocean of vows because they cause them all to be fulfilled, eternally pure.

"Once great enlightening beings have attained to these ten oceans, they also attain ten kinds of excellence: they are foremost among all sentient beings; they are supremely outstanding among celestials; they are most powerful among Brahma-kings; they have no attachments in any world; no one in any world can overshadow them; no demons can disturb them; they can enter any state of being without hindrance; wherever they may be born, they know it is not permanent; they attain mastery of all Buddha teachings; they can manifest all spiritual powers.

"Once great enlightening beings have attained these ten kinds of excellence, they also attain ten kinds of power, cultivating practices in the realm of sentient beings: first is the power of courageous strength, because they tame worldlings; second is the power of energy, because they never backslide; third is the power of nonattachment, because they get rid of defiling obsessions; fourth is the power of silent calm, because they have no disputes about anything; fifth is the power to oppose or conform, because they are free in the midst of all things; sixth is the power of the nature of things, because they attain mastery of all truths; seventh is the power of nonobstruction, because their knowledge and wisdom is immensely vast; eighth is the power of fearlessness, because they can explain all truths; ninth is the power of intellect, because they can hold all truths; tenth is the power of revelation, because their knowledge and wisdom is boundless.

"These ten kinds of power are immense powers, supreme powers, invincible powers, immeasurable powers, well-developed powers, immovable powers, enduring powers, powers of knowledge, powers of accomplishment, powers of supreme concentration, pure powers, extremely pure powers, powers of the body of reality, powers of the light of truth, powers of the lamp of the Teaching, powers of the methods of the Teaching, indestructible powers, powers of extreme strength, powers of great people, powers cultivated by good people, powers of attainment of true awareness, powers of roots of goodness accumulated in the past, powers stabilizing immeasurable roots of goodness, powers stabilizing the realization of Thusness, powers of meditation, powers enhancing the joy of enlightening beings, powers producing the pure faith of enlightening beings, powers increasing the heroism of enlightening beings, powers born of the aspiration for enlightenment, powers of enlightening beings' pure resolve, powers of the enlightening beings' supreme determination, powers of development of the roots of goodness of enlightening beings, powers of finding out the ultimate truth about all things, powers of the unobstructed body, powers of entry into the principles of skill in means of enlightenment, powers of the pure subtle truth, powers of stable force that cannot be upset, powers that all beings cannot overshadow.

"These great enlightening beings can produce these virtuous qualities, can perfect them, fulfill them, illumine them, fully embody them, embody them everywhere, expand them, solidify them, enhance them, purify them, and purify them in all ways.

"No one can tell the bounds of these enlightening beings' virtues, knowledge, practice, teaching, freedom, austerities, accomplishments, purity, emancipation, or mastery of the Teaching. Even in unspeakably many eons no one could fully explain all the teachings that these enlightening beings have attained, have accomplished, have entered into, have actualized, have experienced, have contemplated, have realized, have purified, have comprehended, and have set up.

"Great enlightening beings in this concentration are able to thoroughly know all the infinite concentrations there are, and the sphere of each concentration, immeasurably vast, in each sphere clearly seeing entry, emergence, and abiding, with their characteristics, manifestations, realms of action, concurrent experiences, inherent natures, extinctions, and emancipations.

"They are like the palace of the great water spirit that negates the tormenting heat, from which flow four rivers that are free from turbidity and pollution and are clear as space itself. The lake there has on each of its four sides a mouth, from each of which flows a river. From the Elephant mouth flows the Ganges River; from the Lion mouth flows the Sita River; from the Ox mouth flows the Sindhu River; and from the Horse mouth flows the Vakshu River. When the four great rivers flow forth, from the mouth of the Ganges River flows silver sand; from the mouth of the Sita River flows diamond sand; from the mouth of the Sindhu River flows gold sand, and from the mouth of the Vakshu River flows lapis lazuli sand. The Ganges River mouth is silver color, the Sita River mouth is diamond color, the Sindhu River mouth is golden, and the Vakshu River mouth is the color of lapis lazuli. Each river mouth is a league wide. After emerging, each river circles the great lake seven times and then flows off in its own direction, racing like quicksilver flowing into the ocean. Between each turn of the rivers are red, blue, and white lotuses made of celestial jewels, of extraordinary fragrance and pure color, their petals, leaves, and calyxes all made of gems, spontaneously shining and reflecting each other and the Heatless Lake, fifty leagues around, its floor covered with beautiful jewel sands, adorned with all kinds of crystals, with innumerable exquisite jewels adorning its shores. The wonderful fragrance of sandalwood is everywhere; lotuses and other fine flowers fill the lake, and when the breeze stirs them, the breath of fragrance is carried afar, pervading everywhere. Flowery forests of jewel trees circle the lake, and when the sun comes out, they reflect everything in and outside the lake, joining the reflections and radiance into a network of light. Myriad things are like this—far and near, high and low, broad and narrow, coarse and fine, even down to the tiniest grain of sand and mote of dust, all being beautiful jewels, clearly mirroring lights, all reflected in the orb of the sun, and all reflecting and rereflecting each other; these reflections, neither increasing nor decreasing, neither merged nor separated, are clearly visible as though they were the original substance itself.

"Just as the great lake Heatless pours forth four rivers from four mouths into the ocean, so also do great enlightening beings pour forth various practices from the four powers of understanding, ultimately to enter the ocean of omniscience. Just as the great river Ganges streams silver sand from the silver Elephant mouth, so do great enlightening beings, by means of the power of understanding meanings, explain all the doctrines expounded by all the buddhas, producing all pure virtuous qualities, ultimately entering into the ocean of unobstructed knowledge. Just as the great river Sita streams diamond sands from the diamond-colored Lion mouth, so do great enlightening beings, by means of the power of understanding doctrines, explain for all beings the adamantine sayings of the Buddha and elicit adamantine knowledge, ultimately flowing into the ocean of unobstructed knowledge. Just as the great river Sindhu streams forth gold sand from the golden Ox mouth, so do great enlightening beings, by means of the power of understanding of expressions, open up the understanding of beings by conditionally produced techniques in accord with the world, causing all to rejoice, taming and maturing them, to ultimately enter the ocean of conditionally originated means. Just as the great river Vakshu streams forth lapis lazuli sands from the blue Horse mouth, so do great enlightening beings, by the power of understanding facilitating inexhaustible eloquence, shower countless teachings to refresh and enliven those who hear, ultimately to enter the ocean of the principles of buddhahood.

"Just as the four great rivers enter the oceans in four directions after having circled Heatless Lake, so do great enlightening beings, accomplishing harmonious deeds, words, and thoughts, and accomplishing deeds, words, and thoughts guided by knowledge, flow in the four directions and ultimately enter the ocean of omniscience. What is meant by the 'four directions' of enlightening beings? They are: seeing all buddhas and attaining enlightenment; hearing all enlightening teachings and absorbing and retaining them; fulfilling all the practices of the ways of transcendence; expounding the Teaching compassionately, satisfying sentient beings. Just as the four great rivers circle the great lake and therein blue, red, and white lotuses fill everywhere, in the same way great enlightening beings, in their determination for enlightenment, do not abandon sentient beings, but teach them in order to pacify them and enable them to fulfill incalculable concentrations and see the purity of arrays of the buddha-lands.

"Just as the great lake Heatless is circled by jewel trees, so also do great enlightening beings cause the rings of adornments of the buddha-lands to appear, inspiring sentient beings to seek enlightenment.

"Just as the great lake Heatless is fifty leagues in length and breadth and is clear and free from turbidity, so also is great enlightening beings' determination for enlightenment infinite, boundless, filled with virtues, pure, clean, and without turbidity.

"Just as the shores of the great lake Heatless are arrayed with countless treasures and sandalwood incense is scattered everywhere, so also are the shores of great vows of the determination for enlightenment of great enlightening beings adorned with countless treasures of the tenfold knowledge and sprinkled with the wonderful fragrance of all virtues.

"Just as the floor of the great lake Heatless is spread with gold sand and arrayed with all kinds of pearls, similarly great enlightening beings' subtle knowledge observing everywhere is arrayed with all kinds of metaphysical treasures of the inconceivable liberation of enlightening beings, attaining unobstructed illumination of all truths, abiding in the abode of all buddhas, entering into all the most profound liberative techniques of enlightening.

"Just as the chief water spirit Heatless is forever free from the torments of heat among the water spirits, in the same way great enlightening beings are forever free from the anxieties and vexations of all worlds—though they be born therein, they are not affected or attached.

"Just as the four great rivers water the whole continent and then enter the ocean, likewise do great enlightening beings refresh celestial and human beings, ascetics and priests, with four rivers of knowledge, causing them to enter the great ocean of knowledge of unexcelled complete perfect enlightenment, adorned with four kinds of power. What are the four? First is the river of the knowledge of vows, rescuing and pacifying all sentient beings, never ceasing; second is the river of knowledge of transcendent ways, cultivating enlightening practices for the benefit of sentient beings, continuing past, future, and present, without end, ultimately entering the ocean of knowledge of the buddhas; third is the river of knowledge of concentrations of enlightening beings, arrayed with countless concentrations, perceiving all buddhas, entering the ocean of buddhas; fourth is the river of knowledge of great compassion, with great universal compassion, autonomous, saving sentient beings everywhere, caring for them by appropriate means, ceaselessly, cultivating the way of esoteric virtues, ultimately entering the ocean of the ten powers.

"Just as the four great rivers emerge from the lake Heatless, and having streamed forth are ultimately inexhaustible and enter the ocean, similarly great enlightening beings cultivate enlightening practice by the power of great vows, their independent knowledge and insight inexhaustible, ultimately entering the ocean of omniscience.

"Just as nothing can prevent the four great rivers from entering the ocean, similarly great enlightening beings always diligently carry out the practical vows of universal good, perfect the light of all knowledge and wisdom, abide in the way of enlightenment of all buddhas, and enter the knowledge of those who realize Thusness, without any hindrance.

"Just as the four great rivers rush into the ocean, never tiring eon after eon, similarly enlightening beings carry out the deeds of enlightening beings forever by the practical vows of universal good, entering the ocean of realization of Thusness, never giving rise to weariness.

"Just as when the sun comes out, the golden, silver, diamond, and lapis lazuli sands in Heatless Lake, as well as all the other jewels and treasures, are imbued with sunlight and reflect the golden sands and other treasures, each reflection also containing reflections of all the others, everything mutually reflecting and rereflecting ad infinitum without obstruction, so is the experience of enlightening beings in this concentration: in each pore of their own bodies they see as many buddhas as atoms in untold buddha-lands, and also see those buddhas' lands, enlightenment sites, and audiences; they listen to the teaching of each buddha, absorb and retain it, believe and understand it, and pay honor for untold billions of eons each, without any notion of length or brevity of time; also, those audiences are not cramped therein. Why? Because with a subtle mind they enter into boundless realms of the cosmos, because they enter into peerless fruits of distinct actions, because they enter the sphere of inconceivable concentration, because they enter the sphere of inconceivable meditation, because they enter the sphere of fluidity of all buddhas, because they gain the protection of all buddhas, because they have acquired the great miraculous capacities of all buddhas, because they have attained the ten powers of enlightened ones, which are difficult to attain and difficult to know, because they have entered the realm of fulfillment of the practical undertakings of universally good enlightening beings, and because they have attained the indefatigable spiritual power of all buddhas.

"Though great enlightening beings can enter and leave concentration instantly, still they don't give it up; even though remaining in concentration for a long time, they still have no attachment. Though they do not dwell on any object, yet they do not abandon all points of attention. Though they can enter into the realm of a single instant, yet to benefit all beings they manifest enlightening spiritual powers tirelessly. Though they enter equally into all phenomenal realms, they do not apprehend their boundaries; though they have no abode and no location, yet they are always proceeding into the path of all-knowledge. By the power of mystical projection they enter everywhere into countless groups of beings and fully adorn all worlds. Though they are free from the erroneous conceptions of the world and are beyond the realm of all discriminations, yet they do not abandon forms in all their variety. Though they are capable of fully equipping themselves with expedient skills, yet they are ultimately pure. Though they do not distinguish the various stages of enlightenment, yet they have already entered them all.

"Just as space, though containing all things, is apart from existence and nonexistence, in the same way, great enlightening beings, though entering all worldly realms, are free from conceptions of the world. Though they strive to liberate all beings, yet they are free from conceptions of beings. Though they have profound knowledge of all phenomena, yet they are free from conceptions of phenomena. Though they enjoy seeing all buddhas, yet they are free from conceptions of buddhas. Though they skillfully enter various concentrations, yet they know all things are inherently *thus*, and have no attachment. Though they expound inexhaustible statements of the Teaching with boundless intelligence, yet their minds always dwell on the truth beyond words. Though they enjoy contemplating the wordless teaching, yet they always manifest pure voices. Though they abide in the realm of all things beyond words, yet they always manifest various forms. Though they teach beings, yet they know all things are ultimately inherently empty. Though they diligently cultivate universal compassion and liberate beings, they know the realm of sentient beings is inexhaustible and has no dissolution. Though they realize the realm of reality is everlasting and invariable, yet they ceaselessly guide beings by reading their minds and giving them appropriate instruction. Though they always rest in the abode of the enlightened, yet they always ceaselessly turn the wheel of the Teaching, analytically expounding all kinds of truths with purity of knowledge and unhesitating expertise.

"This is the technical knowledge of the great enlightening beings' ninth great concentration, the concentration of freedom in the elemental cosmos.

"What is the great enlightening beings' unimpeded wheel concentration? When great enlightening beings enter this concentration, they abide in unobstructed physical, verbal, and mental action, live in buddha-lands free from obstruction, attain unobstructed knowledge of how to develop and perfect beings, acquire unobstructed knowledge of how to tame beings, radiate unobstructed light, cause networks of unobstructed light beams to appear, demonstrate unobstructed miracles on a vast scale, turn the unobstructed wheel of the pure Teaching, and attain the unobstructed freedom of enlightening beings. They enter into the powers of buddhas, abide in the knowledges of buddhas, perform the deeds of buddhas, purify what buddhas purify, manifest the spiritual powers of buddhas, gladden the buddhas, carry out actions of buddhas, abide in the path of buddhas, associate with innumerable buddhas, perform the works of buddhas, and succeed to the lineage of buddhas.

"Once great enlightening beings are in this concentration, they investigate omniscience, contemplating it in general and in particulars; they accord with omniscience, reveal omniscience, concentrate on omniscience, see omniscience, see omniscience as a whole, and see omniscience in particulars. They forever advance and constantly continue the great vow, great will, great practice, great aim, great experience, great light, great manifestation, great care, great miracle, and great path of the Universally Good enlightening being, without interruption, without retreating, without stopping, without changing, without wearying, without giving up, without distraction, without confusion. Why? These great enlightening beings, in the midst of all things, accomplish great undertakings, activate the Great Vehicle of universal enlightenment, and enter into the ocean of enlightening techniques of the Buddha teaching; by means of extraordinary willpower they illumine the practices carried out by enlightening beings with their knowledge and wisdom, and achieve skill in all of them; they fully accomplish enlightening beings' spiritual powers and miracles; they are able care for and guard living beings, as do all the buddhas of past, future, and present; they always arouse great compassion for all living beings, and they attain the unchanging truth of the realization of Thusness.

"Just as when someone puts a clear crystal on a colored robe, the crystal assumes the color of the robe without losing its own nature, in the same way great enlightening beings, perfecting knowledge and wisdom as the jewel of the mind, observe all-knowledge and all appears clearly, yet they do not abandon the practices of enlightening beings. Why? Great enlightening beings undertake great vows to benefit all beings, to liberate all beings, to serve all buddhas, to purify all worlds, to comfort all beings; they enter deeply into the ocean of truth, and to purify the realm of sentient beings they manifest great mastery, provide for sentient beings, illumine the world, and enter the boundless gate of teaching by phanton emanations, without backsliding or growing wearied.

"Just as space holds myriad worlds, be they in the process of becoming or subsisting, without aversion or weariness, without wearing out or perishing, without dissolving or breaking down, without changing or varying, without differentiation, not giving up its own nature, because the inherent nature of space is to be thus, in the same way, great enlightening beings establish infinite great vows to liberate all sentient beings, without their minds wearying.

"Just as infinite beings past, future, and present pass away into nirvana without its ever rejecting or wearying, because the essential purity of all phenomena is called *nirvana*, in the same way, great enlightening beings appear in the world because they want to liberate all beings and enable them to be emancipated—how could they become wearied in mind?

"Just as universal knowledge, omniscience, can enable all enlightening beings of all times to be born in the family of buddhas, and eventually enable them to attain supreme enlightenment, without ever tiring, because omniscience is none other than the cosmos of realities and is not attached to anything at all, in the same way, great enlightening beings' minds abide equanimously in universal knowledge—how could they have any weariness of mind?

"These great enlightening beings have a lotus blossom that is as vast as the whole extent of the ten directions, adorned with untold numbers of petals, jewels, and fragrances. Those untold numbers of jewels each also reflect all kinds of jewels, pure, exquisite, extremely fine, resting on the blossom, emanating light beams of many colors, illumining all worlds of the ten directions without obstruction. Webs of pure gold cover it, while jewel chimes gently swaying produce subtle tones that bespeak the elements of omniscience. This great lotus blossom incorporates the pure adornments of those who realize Thusness, produced by all foundations of goodness, with an auspicious sign as its emblem, manifested by spiritual power, with myriad infinities of pure qualities, perfected by the wondrous path of enlightening beings, flowing forth from the omniscient mind; the reflections of the buddhas of the ten directions appear in it, and the worlds gaze on it as on a monument of Buddha, and all beings who see it bow in respect. It is born of the true teaching of ability to comprehend illusion and is actually beyond any worldly comparison.

"When an enlightening being sits on this blossom, the size of the enlightening being's body corresponds to the blossom. The miraculous empowerment of all buddhas causes each pore of the enlightening being's body to emanate rays of light as numerous as atoms in untold billions of buddha-lands, each ray of light revealing jewels as numerous as atoms in untold billions of buddha-lands. Those jewels are all called treasuries of universal light and are adorned with various colors and characteristics, made of infinite virtues. Nets of jewels and flowers cover them above, scattering billions of superb fragrances. The arrays of innumerable various colors and forms also manifest ornamental canopies of inconceivable arrays of jewels. Each jewel reflects pavilions as numerous as atoms in untold billions of buddha-lands, and each pavilion reveals as many lion thrones, each lion throne manifesting as many light beams, each light beam showing as many colors, each color showing as many orbs of light, each orb of light showing as many radiant jewel flowers, each flower showing as many pedestals, on each pedestal there appearing as many buddhas, each buddha displaying as many miracles, each miracle purifying as many congregations, with as many freedoms of buddhahood appearing in each congregation, each freedom showing as many Buddha teachings, each Buddha teaching having as many scriptures, each scripture expounding as many doctrines, each doctrine having as many spheres of truth penetrated by adamantine knowledge, different words each explaining each sphere of truth, maturing as many realms of sentient beings as atoms in untold billions of buddha-lands, each realm having as many beings as atoms in untold billions of buddha-lands achieving peace in the Buddha teaching.

"Great enlightening beings in this concentration, causing infinite emanations of such miraculous scenes to appear, know they are all like mirages and are not obsessed by them or attached to them. They abide in the unimpeded realm of extremelessness, the unspeakable reality, inherent purity, the realm of reality, the true form, the nature of realization of thusness, which has no coming or going, which is not before or after, is infinitely profound, is realized by direct experience and spontaneously entered by knowledge and not understood from another. Their minds are free from confusion and discriminatory conceptualization; they are lauded by all buddhas; they flow forth from the power of the buddhas and enter into the realm of all buddhas; they directly witness essential nature as it really is with pure eyes, and see everywhere with the eye of wisdom; they develop the enlightened eye and become bright lamps for the world; they course in the realm known to the eye of knowledge and are able to widely expound subtle truths. They develop the will for enlightenment and head for the highest humanity. They are not obstructed by any objects. They enter the seed nature of knowledge and produce all kinds of knowledge. They are detached from worldly things, yet they appear to live in the world, transforming beings through spiritual powers and taming them by appropriate means. They are skilled in all such matters. Their virtues, understanding, and will are all thoroughly pure, extremely refined and thoroughly developed. Their knowledge and wisdom are vast as space, and they are adept at observing the realms of the sages. Their faith, practice, and willpower are firm and steadfast, immovable. Their virtues are inexhaustible, admired by the world. In the ocean of omniscience, the place of great enlightenment, the treasury watched by all buddhas, they collect myriad sublime jewels and become great sages. Just like lotus blossoms, they are inherently pure and clean, a delight and benefit to all who see them. The light of their knowledge illumines everywhere, and they see infinite buddhas and clarify all truths. Their actions are dispassionate and calm, and they are ultimately without impediment in realization of the teaching of buddhas. By means of appropriate techniques they always live by the virtuous action of enlightenment, in which they are born. They embody the knowledge of enlightening beings and are leaders of enlightening beings, protected by all the buddhas together. They attain the spiritual force of buddhas and develop the spiritual body of buddhas. Their mental powers are inconceivable; they are one-pointed on the objective realm, yet objectless. Their activity is far-reaching, signless, unimpeded, infinite as the cosmos. The enlightenment they realize is like space, boundless, without binding attachment. They work for the universal weal of all in the world, flowing from the foundations of goodness of the ocean of omniscience. They are able to comprehend infinite objective realms. They have perfected the practice of pure generosity, live by the heart of enlightening, purify the seed of enlightening beings, and are able accordingly to give birth to the enlightenment of the buddhas. They are well versed in all the Buddha teachings and can employ them skillfully; they embody their subtle practices and achieve stable, enduring power.

"The autonomous spiritual powers of all buddhas, which sentient beings can hardly hear of, the enlightening beings know entirely; they enter the gate of nonduality, abide in the formless truth, and though they have forever relinquished all forms, they are able to explain extensively all kinds of things according to the mentalities, inclinations, and understandings of sentient beings, pacifying and satisfying them. The cosmos is their body; they are free from discriminatory thinking; the sphere of their knowledge is inexhaustible. Their will is always powerful; their mind is always equanimous. They see the extent of the virtues of all buddhas. They know the differences and order of all ages.

"They expose all truths, live peacefully in all lands, beautify all buddha-lands, manifest the light of all true principles, and expound the teachings of all buddhas of past, future, and present. They point out the dwelling places of the enlightening beings, serve as lamps illumining the world, produce all roots of goodness, eternally detach from the world, and are forever born where the buddhas are. They acquire the knowledge and wisdom of buddhas, which is supreme: they are in the care of all the buddhas and have already entered the ranks of buddhas of the future. They grow from association with good companions, and whatever they set their wills on bears fruit. They have great power and abide in lofty determination and are able to explain whatever they hear.

"Also, to show the roots of goodness of hearing the Teaching, they abide in the sphere of reality, their minds unobstructed in the midst of all things; they do not abandon their practices, but divorce discriminatory thought. Their minds have no stirring thoughts in the midst of all things; they acquire the illumination of knowledge and wisdom, and destroy the darkness of ignorance. They are able to clearly reflect all Buddha teachings. Not destroying the various realms of existence, they are born therein, and comprehend that all realms of existence fundamentally are inert. Their physical, verbal, and mental activities are all without extremes.

"Though they say all kinds of things by way of explanation in accord with local usage, they never destroy the truth which is beyond words. They enter deeply into the ocean of the enlightened, know that all things only have names, and have no bonds or attachments to objects. They understand that all things are empty, without existence; the practices they cultivate are born from the realm of reality. Like space, they are signless and formless; entering deeply into the realm of reality, they explain everything, producing universal knowledge through a single object.

"They contemplate the stage of the ten powers and cultivate it by knowledge. Knowledge is their bridge to omniscience; by the eye of knowledge they see things without obstruction and ably enter the various stages of enlightenment. They know all kinds of principles, attain clear understanding of each and every facet of doctrine, and accomplish all their great undertakings.

"By this, great enlightening beings reveal the undifferentiated essence of all enlightened ones. This is the gate of unimpeded skill in means. This can produce all groups of enlightening beings. This state is only in the realm of concentration. This is able to plunge into omniscience, this is able to reveal all ways of access to concentration, this can enter unimpeded into all lands, this can tame all sentient beings, this can abide in the realm of no beings, this can show all Buddha teachings, this does not apprehend any objects.

"Though they teach and explain at all times they are always free from arbitrary conceptions and discriminatory thought; though they know all things are inert, yet they are able to demonstrate all actions; though they know the buddhas have no duality, yet they are able to reveal the buddhas; though they know there are no forms, yet they explain all forms;

though they know there is no sensation, yet they explain all sensations; though they know there is no perception, yet they explain all perceptions; though they know there is no disposition, yet they explain all dispositions; though they know there is no consciousness, yet they explain all consciousnesses; they always reveal everything by means of the wheel of the Teaching. Though they know phenomena have no difference, yet they explain their aspects of differentiation; though they know phenomena have no origin or annihilation, yet they explain all characteristics of origination and annihilation; though they know phenomena have no coarseness or subtlety, yet they explain the coarse and subtle aspects of phenomena; though they know all phenomena have no superiority, mediocrity, or inferiority, yet they can explain what is best; though they know phenomena cannot be explained in words, yet they can speak pure words; though they know phenomena have no inside or outside, yet they explain all internal and external phenomena; though they know phenomena cannot be comprehensively cognized, yet they explain various kinds of knowledge and contemplation; though they know phenomena have no true reality, yet they expound a real path of emancipation; though they know phenomena are ultimately inexhaustible, yet they can expound the exhausting of all taints; though they know phenomena have no differences and no contradiction, yet they do not deny the differences among one another; though they know things ultimately have no teacher, yet they always respect all teachers and those of experience; though they know true understanding of things does not come from another, yet they always respect skillful guides; though they know things are inoperative, yet they turn the wheel of the Teaching; though they know things have no origination, yet they point out causes and conditions; though they know things have no precedent, yet they extensively explain the past; though they know things have no aftermath, yet they extensively explain the future; though they know things have no duration, yet they extensively explain the present; though they know things have no creator, yet they explain the acts that form them; though they know things have no causality, yet they explain the conglomerated causes; though they know things have no comparison, yet they explain the ways of equality and inequality; though they know things have no verbal explanation, yet they definitively explain the things of past, present, and future; though they know things have no basis of support, yet they expound attainment of emancipation based on what is good; though they know things have no body, yet they extensively explain the body of reality; though they know the buddhas of past, present, and future are boundless, yet they can explain how there is only one Buddha; though they know things have no form, yet they can manifest various forms; though they know things have no vision, yet they can expound many views; though they know things have no specific marks, yet they can explain all kinds of specific marks; though they know things have no objective sphere, yet they can extensively expound the spheres of knowledge; though they know things have no differentiation, yet they explain the various differences in fruits of action; though they know things have no escape, yet they explain pure practices for emancipation; though they know things are fundamentally permanent, yet they explain all things in flux; though they know things have no illumination, yet they always extensively explain means of illumination.

"When great enlightening beings enter the circle of knowledge of this immensely powerful concentration, they are then able to witness the truth of all Buddha teachings, able to proceed into the Buddha teachings, able to accomplish them, able to fulfill them, able to build them up, able to clarify them, able to live by them, able to comprehend them, in harmony with the inherent nature of all things. And yet these great enlightening beings do not entertain the idea that there are so many enlightening beings, so many principles of enlightening beings, so many ultimate ends of enlightening beings, so many illusory ultimate ends, so many fabricated ultimate ends, so many attainments of spiritual powers, so many attainments of knowledge, so many meditations, so many realizations, so many aims, so many realms. Why? Because the concentration of enlightening beings is thus in essence, is thus without bounds, is thus transcendent.

"This concentration has various spheres, various powers, various deep entries. That is to say, it enters untold gates of knowledge, it enters arrangements beyond discriminatory thought, it enters boundless excellent ways of transcendence, it enters countless meditation states, it enters untold hundreds of thousands of millions of far-reaching cognitions, it enters vision of boundless exalted treasuries of buddhas, it enters objective worlds ceaselessly, it enters into pure application of the aids to the path of enlightenment, it enters into great psychic powers of strong and keen faculties, it enters into objective worlds without hindrance to the mind, it enters into the eye that sees the equality of all buddhas, it enters into the development of the high-minded practices of Universal Good, it enters into the state of the celestial body of subtle knowledge, it enters into explanation of the knowledge and wisdom of the enlightened, it enters into production of incalculable mystical projections, it enters into production of ways into the inexhaustible knowledge of all buddhas, it enters into clarification of the autonomous knowledge of the Universally Good enlightening being, it enters into revelation of incomparable all-sided knowledge, it enters into universal awareness of all subtle realms in the cosmos, it enters into the light of all higher knowledge, it enters into universal revelation of all subtle realms in the cosmos, it enters into the reaches of all magical powers, it enters into the sphere of teachings of all intellectual powers, it enters into the body of knowledge omnipresent throughout the cosmos, it enters into accomplishment of the path of action extending everywhere, it enters into ability to remain in all different concentrations, and it enters into knowledge of the mind of all buddhas.

"These great enlightening beings abide in the practice of Universal Good and enter untold billions of concentrations in every successive instant, yet they do not see anything prior to the concentration of Universal Good and the adornments of the realm of buddhahood. Why? Because they know all things are ultimately inexhaustible, because they know all buddha-lands are boundless, because they know all realms of sentient beings are inconceivable, because they know the past has no beginning, because they know the future has no end, because they know the present is boundless, comprehending all space and the whole cosmos, because they know the realm of all buddhas is inconceivable, because they know the practices of enlightening beings are countless, because they know the realms explained by the intellectual powers of all buddhas are unspeakably boundless, and because they know illusory mental objects are infinite.

"Just as a wishing jewel grants all wishes, satisfying endless seekers without losing its power, in the same way a great enlightening being, entering this concentration, knows the mind is like an illusion and produces all objects everywhere inexhaustibly. Why? The great enlightening being accomplishes the knowledge of unimpeded action of Universal Good and observes infinite extensive illusory realms, seeing them as like reflected images, without increase or decrease.

"Just as ordinary people individually give rise to mental states, past, present, and future, without bound, without cease, without end, the continuous flow and change of their mental states going on unbroken, inconceivably, in the same way, great enlightening beings entering this concentration of access to universal illusion have no bounds and are unfathomable. Why? Because of the infinite phenomena in the Universally Good enlightening being's door of access to universal illusion.

"Just as when the water spirits shower rain, the raindrops are like wheel hubs, without bound, the clouds are not exhausted, though they shower so much rain, this being the realm of nonstriving of the water spirits, in the same way great enlightening beings in this concentration enter the Universally Good enlightening being's door of concentration, door of knowledge, door of teaching, door of perception of Buddha, door of traveling everywhere, door of mental freedom, door of empowerment, door of mystical projection, door of spiritual powers, door of phantom emanations, door of the illusory quality of all things, door filled with untold numbers of enlightening beings, door of approach to buddhas as numerous as atoms in untold buddha-lands, door of entry into the unspeakably vast network of illusions, door of knowledge of untold numbers of immense different buddha-lands, door of knowledge of untold numbers of worlds with substantial nature and without substantial nature, door of knowledge of the thoughts of untold numbers of sentient beings, door of knowledge of untold numbers of distinctions in time, door of knowledge of the becoming and disintegration of untold numbers of worlds, and door of knowledge of untold numbers of inverted and upright buddha-lands. They know all these as they really are in a single instant. When they enter in this way there are no bounds, there is no end; they are not tired, not wearied, they do not stop, do not rest, do not withdraw, do not slip. In all things they do not dwell on untruth; constantly meditating rightly, they do not become either oblivious or excited.

"They seek omniscience without ever retreating or giving up. They become lamps to light up the world in all buddha-lands. They operate untold numbers of cycles of the Teaching. With sublime intelligence they question the enlightened, never reaching a point of exhaustion. They demonstrate the attainment of the Buddha Way without bound. They pacify sentient beings, never giving up. They always diligently practice the undertakings of Universal Good, never ceasing. They manifest bodies of infinite forms, without end. Why? Just as fire burns unceasingly whenever the appropriate conditions are present, in the same way, great enlightening beings see the realms of sentient beings, the realms of reality, and the realms of worlds as boundless as space—in a single instant they are able to go visit as many buddhas as atoms in untold buddha-lands, in the company of each buddha enter untold different aspects of omniscience, cause untold beings to give up attachments for the sake of the Way and cultivate virtue and be ultimately purified, cause untold enlightening beings who have not yet attained certainty about the practice of the vows of Universal Good to attain certainty and to abide securely in the way of knowledge of Universal Good, by innumerable means enter untold different ages—becoming, subsisting, disintegrating—of past, present, and future, and in the different realms of those untold eons of becoming, subsistence, and disintegration, produce as many great vows of great compassion and pacify all sentient beings. What is the reason? These great enlightening beings, for the purpose of liberating all sentient beings, cultivate the practice of Universal Good, develop the knowledge of Universal Good, and fulfill the undertakings of Universal Good.

"Therefore, enlightening beings should diligently cultivate practice in such types of action, such perspectives, such powers, such greatness, such infinity, such inconceivability, such all-sided illumination, such presence with all buddhas, such protection by all buddhas, such consummation of past roots of goodness, such imperturbable concentration wherein the mind is unimpeded, getting rid of all burning afflictions, without wearying or backsliding, with steadfast will and courage, following the realm of concentration into the stage of inconceivable knowledge, not depending on words, not clinging to the world, not grasping phenomena, not producing discriminatory thoughts, not becoming attached to worldly things, not thinking about objects.

"In terms of knowledge of the teachings, they should just abide by them and not try to measure them. This refers to associating with the omniscient and understanding the enlightenment of the buddhas, attaining the light of truth and shedding it on the foundations of goodness of all sentient beings, pulling sentient beings out of the realm of demons and enabling them to enter the realm of the Buddha teachings, causing them not to give up great aspirations, to earnestly examine the Path of emancipation, to expand the sphere of purity, to accomplish the means of transcendence, to develop profound faith in all buddhas. They should always look into the nature of all things without quitting even for a moment; they should know that their own bodies and the nature of things are universally equal; they should clearly understand the doings of the world and point out wisdom and means that accord with truth; they should always be energetic, without lapsing; they should observe the paucity of roots of goodness in themselves and should strive to increase roots of goodness in others; they should themselves cultivate the Path of universal knowledge; they should strive to expand the sphere of enlightening beings; they should gladly approach expert teachers; they should associate with fellow practitioners; they should not discriminate among buddhas; they should not give up detachment from thought; they should always abide in the impartial realm of reality; they should know all states of mind and consciousness are illusory; they should know all events in the world are like dreams; they should know the appearance of the willpower of the buddhas is like reflected images; they should know all great actions are like emanations; they should observe all phenomena as like magic tricks; they should know all things that are born and perish are like echoes; they should know all the buddha-lands they go to have no substantial nature; they should never tire of asking buddhas for teaching; they should diligently carry on education to enlighten all beings, never abandoning them; they should unremittingly expound the teachings in a timely fashion in order to pacify all sentient beings.

"Great enlightening beings thus practice the deeds of Universal Good, thus fulfill the sphere of action of enlightening beings, thus master the way of emancipation, thus absorb and hold the teachings of the buddhas of past, present, and future, thus investigate all aspects of knowledge, thus reflect on the unchanging truth, thus purify powerful determination, thus believe in all enlightened ones, thus know the immense power of buddhas, thus make certain the unimpeded mind, thus take care of all living beings.

"When great enlightening beings enter this concentration of great knowledge and wisdom, wherein the Universally Good enlightening being abides, there appear before them as many buddhas as atoms in untold buddha-lands from untold numbers of lands in the ten directions, each buddha having as many names as atoms in untold lands, each name also including untold numbers of buddhas: these buddhas give the enlightening beings the memory power of the enlightened, so they do not forget the realm of buddhahood; they give them ultimate knowledge of all things, so they may enter omniscience; they give them definitive wisdom cognizant of the various meanings of all teachings, enabling them to absorb and hold all Buddha teachings and enter into them without impediment; they give them unexcelled enlightenment, so they can enter universal knowledge and open up their awareness of the cosmos of reality; they give them the ultimate wisdom of enlightening beings, enabling them to attain the light of all truths, to be free from darkness; they give them nonreceding knowledge, so that they know appropriate and inappropriate timing and guide sentient beings with skill in means; they give them the unobstructed intellectual powers of enlightening beings, enabling them to understand boundless truths and explain them inexhaustibly; they give them the power of spiritual capacities and production of mystical projections, enabling them to manifest untold numbers of different bodies, with boundless forms and appearances, all variously different, to awaken sentient beings; they give them universal speech, enabling them to manifest untold numbers of different sounds and various languages to enlighten sentient beings; they give them power that is not wasted, to enable all sentient beings who see them or hear their teaching to achieve development and not waste the experience.

"Because great enlightening beings fulfill Universally Good practice in this way, they acquire the power of the enlightened, purify the path of emancipation, are imbued with universal knowledge, and by means of unimpeded intellectual powers, spiritual faculties, and mystical emanations, ultimately harmonize and pacify all sentient beings. Full of the spiritual force of enlightenment, they purify Universally Good practice, abide in the path of Universal Good, and operate the subtle cycles of teaching of all buddhas for ever and ever, to pacify all living beings.

"Why? When these great enlightening beings accomplish the practices of enlightening beings guided by such lofty, great vows, they become teachers of all worlds, sums of truth for all worlds, moons of knowledge for all worlds; they become lofty polar mountains for all worlds, majestically standing out high, steadfast, immutable; they become shoreless oceans of knowledge for all worlds, they become bright lamps of right teaching for all worlds, illumining everywhere, boundlessly, continuously, uninterrupted; they reveal boundless pure virtues for all sentient beings, inducing them to live steadily based on virtuous qualities and foundations of goodness; they act in accord with universal knowledge, and their great vows are impartial; they cultivate the far-reaching practice of Universal Good and are always able to inspire countless beings; persisting in untold numbers of concentrations of great efficacy, they manifest great freedom.

"These enlightening beings attain such knowledge, verify such principles, thoroughly abide by and clearly see such truths, acquire such spiritual powers, sojourn in such realms, manifest such mystical projections, produce such spiritual communications, always abide in great compassion, always help sentient beings, show sentient beings the true path of peace and serenity, set up the great banner of light of virtue and knowledge, experience inconceivable liberation, abide in the liberation of universal knowledge, reach the other shore of liberation of buddhas, have learned and mastered the aspects of expedient means of inconceivable liberation, enter the doors of differentiation of the cosmos without confusion, freely roam in the untold numbers of concentrations of Universal Good, and abide in rapidly expanding knowledge, their minds and intellects unimpeded.

"Their minds always abide in ten great metaphysical treasuries: remembering all buddhas; remembering all Buddha teachings; great compassion to pacify all beings; knowledge to reveal inconceivable pure lands; certain understanding entering deeply into the realm of buddhahood; enlightenment equal in all features in all buddhas, past, present, and future; nonimpediment and nonattachment; the signlessness of all things; the equal roots of goodness of all buddhas, past, present, and future; the guiding knowledge of the cosmic, nondiscriminatory physical, verbal, and mental action of all buddhas of past, present, and future; contemplation of all buddhas of all times being born, leaving home, going to the site of enlightenment, attaining true awakening, turning the wheel of the Teaching, and finally passing utterly away, all in the space of an instant. These ten great metaphysical treasuries are immensely vast, without measure, incalculable, unthinkable, inexplicable; they are inexhaustible, difficult to bear, impossible for any and all worldly knowledge to expound.

"These great enlightening beings have already reached the transcendental consummation of the practices of Universal Good and have witnessed the pure truth. Their willpower is immense. They teach sentient beings innumerable roots of goodness and increase all the powers of enlightening beings. In every succeeding moment they fulfill all the virtues of enlightening beings, accomplish all practices of enlightening beings, attain the methods of mental command of all buddhas, and absorb and hold the teachings of all buddhas. Though they always abide in the reality of True Thusness, yet they adapt to all conventional terms to show the ways to pacify and harmonize all sentient beings. Why? Because when great enlightening beings are in this concentration, they are naturally like this.

"By means of this concentration great enlightening beings acquire the vast knowledge of all buddhas; they gain the free intellectual powers to skillfully explain all great teachings; they attain the unhesitating expertise that is most excellent and pure in the world; they gain entry into knowledge of all concentrations; they master all enlightening beings' skillful techniques; they find the door of illumination of all truths; they reach the final consummation of the way to comfort all worldly beings; they know what is timely and what is not for all sentient beings; they illumine everywhere in the worlds of the ten directions; they enable all living beings to attain higher knowledge; they are unexcelled teachers of all worlds; they persist in all virtues; they reveal pure concentration to all sentient beings and enable them to enter supreme knowledge.

"Why? When great enlightening beings cultivate practice in this way, they benefit living beings, so they increase great compassion, so they draw near to worthy associates, so they see all buddhas, so they comprehend all truths, so they go to all lands, so they enter all regions, so they enter all worlds, so they realize the equality of all things, so they know the equality of the buddhas, so they abide in the equanimity of universal knowledge.

"In this practice they carry out this kind of action, no other: they abide in the mind that is not complacent; they abide in the mind that is not distracted or confused; they abide in the mind that can concentrate on one point; they abide in the mind that diligently cultivates enlightenment; they abide in the certain mind; they abide in the nonchanging mind. In this manner do they think, act, and reach the ultimate end.

"Great enlightening beings have no different speech or action—they speak and act thus. Why? Just as, for example, adamant is unbreakable and gets its name from that, never being apart from unbreakability, in the same way, great enlightening beings get their name from their various practical principles and are never apart from them.

"Just as gold gets its name from its beautiful color and is never apart from its beautiful color, so do great enlightening beings get their name from their virtuous acts and are never apart from good deeds.

"Just as the sun gets its name from its orb of light and is never apart from the orb of light, so do great enlightening beings get their name from the light of wisdom and are never apart from the light of wisdom.

"Just as the polar mountain Wonderfully High gets its name from its four jewel peaks rising high over the ocean, never leaving its four peaks, in the same way, great enlightening beings get their name from their roots of goodness standing out loftily in the world, never giving up roots of goodness.

"Just as the ground gets its name from sustaining everything, never giving up its supportive ability, so do great enlightening beings get their name from liberating all, never leaving great compassion.

"Just as the ocean gets its name from taking in myriad waters, never rejecting water, so do great enlightening beings get their name from their great vows, never for a moment giving up the vow to liberate sentient beings.

"Just as a military leader gets his name from ability to learn and practice methods of battle, never abandoning this ability, so do great enlightening beings get their name from being able to learn and practice such concentration, until they accomplish omniscience, never abandoning this practice.

"Just as a world ruler commands the continents, always diligently protecting all living beings so they will always be happy and will not suffer unnatural death, so do great enlightening beings, entering such great concentrations, always strive to transform and liberate all sentient beings, until they effect their ultimate purification.

"Just as seeds planted in the ground can eventually grow stalks and leaves, so great enlightening beings cultivating the practice of Universal Good can cause all sentient beings' good qualities to grow.

"Just as great clouds shower rain during the hot months of summer and cause all seeds to grow, similarly great enlightening beings, entering such great concentrations, cultivating enlightening practice, shower the rain of the great Teaching, which can cause all sentient beings to be ultimately purified, ultimately serene, ultimately peaceful, ultimately transcendent, ultimately happy, ultimately free from doubt. They are the ultimate field of blessings for sentient beings, enabling their actions to become purified, enabling them all to abide in the path of nonregression, enabling them alike to attain omniscience, enabling them to attain emancipation from the world, enabling them all to attain ultimate knowledge, enabling them all to attain the ultimate truth of the enlightened ones, placing all sentient beings in the realm of universal knowledge.

"Why? When enlightening beings accomplish this teaching, their knowledge and wisdom are clear and comprehensive; they enter the door to the cosmos of reality and are able to purify the inconceivably infinite practices of enlightening beings. That is to say, they are able to purify all knowledge because they seek omniscience; they are able to purify sentient beings because they cause them to be pacified; they are able to purify lands because of constant dedication; they are able to purify things because of perfect knowledge; they are able to purify fearlessness because they have no timidity; they are able to purify unhindered intellect because they teach skillfully; they are able to purify mental command because they have mastered all the teachings; they are able to purify the practice of association because they see all buddhas appearing in the world.

"Great enlightening beings in this concentration attain untold myriads of such pure qualities because they gain mastery of such realms of concentration, because they are empowered by all buddhas, because they are borne along by the power of their own roots of goodness, because they enter the great magnificent force of the stage of knowledge and wisdom, because of the strength of guidance of worthy associates, because of crushing the power of all demons, because of the pure power of roots of goodness in proportion, because of the power of great vows, because of the power of the full development of the roots of goodness they have planted, and because of the unopposed power of inexhaustible virtue transcending all worlds.

"Great enlightening beings in this concentration attain ten things that are the same as in all buddhas, past, future, and present; they acquire the same variegated arrays of marks and refinements as all buddhas; they are able to emanate networks of pure light, the same as all buddhas; they perform miracles and displays of spiritual power to attune and pacify sentient beings, the same as all buddhas; their boundless physical bodies and universal voices are the same as those of all buddhas; they manifest pure buddha-lands according to the actions of sentient beings, the same as all buddhas; they are able to remember the speech of all sentient beings, the same as all buddhas; with inexhaustible intellectual powers they teach in accord with the mentalities of sentient beings, developing wisdom in them, the same as all buddhas; their lion's roar is fearless as they enlighten living beings by innumerable teachings, the same as all buddhas; by great spiritual power they enter past, present, and future in a single instant, the same as all buddhas; they are able to show all sentient beings the adornments of the buddhas, the powers of the buddhas, and the states of the buddhas, the same as all buddhas."

Then the enlightening being Universal Eye said to the enlightening being Universally Good, "If great enlightening beings attain such things the same as the buddhas, why are they not called Buddha? Why are they not called Ten-Powered? Why are they not called Omniscient? Why are they not called Those Enlightened in All Things? Why can they not be called Universal Eye? Why are they not called Unhindered Seers in All Realms? Why are they not called Aware of All Things? Why are they not called Those Who Abide in the State of Nonduality with the Buddhas of Past, Present, and Future? Why are they not called Those Who Dwell in Absolute Reality? Why do they still carry out the practical undertakings of Universal Good without rest? Why can they not find the ultimate end of the cosmos and give up the path of enlightening beings?"

Universally Good said to Universal Eye, "Very good, offspring of Buddha! As you say, if these great enlightening beings are the same as all buddhas, why are they not called Buddha and so on, and why can they not give up the path of enlightening beings?

"These great enlightening beings, having already ably practiced the various activities and undertakings of all enlightening beings of past, future, and present worlds, and entered the realm of knowledge, are then called Buddha; unceasingly cultivating the enlightening practices cultivated by the buddhas, they are called enlightening beings. Having completely entered the powers of the enlightened, they are called Ten-Powered; ceaselessly carrying out the activities of Universal Good after having attained the ten powers, they are called enlightening beings. Knowing all truths and being able to explain them, they are called Omniscient; though able to expound all truths, yet never ceasing to think about each truth with versatility, they are called enlightening beings. Knowing all things are nondual, they are called Enlightened in All Things; skillfully examining the path of differentiation of all things, dual and nondual, ceaselessly developing further and further, they are called enlightening beings. Able to clearly see the realm of the Universal Eye, they are called Universal Eye; though able to witness the realm of the Universal Eye, ceaselessly developing in every moment, they are called enlightening beings. Able to clearly perceive all things without any obscurity or barrier, they are called Unimpeded Seers; always diligently remembering the unimpeded seers, they are called enlightening beings. Having attained the eye of knowledge of all buddhas, they are called Aware of All Things; observing the buddhas' correctly awakened eye of knowledge without slacking, they are called enlightening beings. Abiding in the abode of buddhas, not other than buddhas, they are called Those Who Abide in a State of Nonduality with the Buddhas; cultivating various knowledges in the care of the buddhas, they are called enlightening beings. Always observing the limit of reality of all worlds, they are called Those Who Dwell in Absolute Reality; though always observing absolute reality of all things, yet neither entering it experientially by extinction nor abandoning it, they are called enlightening beings. Not coming, not going, without sameness or difference, all such distinctions having ceased forever—such are called Those Who Have Set Their Undertakings to Rest; extensively cultivating fulfillment without turning back, they are called Those Who Have Not Ceased the Undertakings of Universal Good. Perfectly knowing the cosmos has no bounds and all things are one form, which is formless, this is called reaching the ultimate end of the cosmos and giving up the way of enlightening beings; though knowing the cosmos has no bounds, yet knowing all various different forms, evolving a mind of great compassion and liberating beings for ever and ever without wearying, this is called the Universally Good enlightening being.

"It is like the case of the king of elephants, who lives in a jewel cave in a gold mountain; the cave has jewel railings all around, jewel trees in rows, gold nets covering above. The elephant's body is pure white, like jade or snow, and sports gold banners; it is ornamented with gold, and a jewel net covers its trunk, with jewel bells hanging down. Its limbs are fully developed, and it has six tusks; it is dignified and handsome, pleasing to all who see it. It is well trained and docile. If the emperor of gods wants to go somewhere, the elephant immediately knows his intention and disappears from the jewel cave to appear in heaven before the emperor of gods. By magical powers it transforms its appearance in various ways, causing its body to have thirty-three heads, magically producing seven tusks on each head, magically producing seven lakes on each tusk, with seven lotus blossoms in each lake, with seven nymphs on each blossom, simultaneously playing a hundred thousand celestial melodies. At this point the emperor of gods mounts this bejeweled elephant and proceeds from the unsurpassable palace to the flower garden, which is filled with white lotuses. When the emperor of gods gets to the flower garden, he dismounts from the elephant and enters a palace arrayed with all jewels. Attended by countless nymphs, he enjoys their singing and playing. At that point the elephant king again magically conceals his elephant form and appears as a god, having a good time in the lotus garden along with the other gods and the nymphs, his physical features, aura, clothing, comportment, speech, and looks being just like the other gods', indistinguishable from them, so that it is impossible to tell whether it is the elephant or a god, so similar are they.

"That elephant king, in its jewel cave in the gold mountain, without any transformation, goes to heaven to make offerings to the emperor of gods, produces various enjoyable things, and experiences celestial pleasures no different from the gods. Similarly, for great enlightening beings, cultivation of the practice of the vows and concentrations of the Universally Good enlightening being are their ornaments of jewels; the seven limbs of enlightenment are the enlightening beings' bodies; the lights they emanate are nets; they set up the banner of the great Teaching, ring the bells of the great Teaching. Great compassion is their cave, steadfast great vows are their tusks. Knowing and wise, fearless as lions, their heads are wrapped with the turban of truth. They reveal mysteries and reach the other shore of the practice of vows of enlightening beings. Wanting to sit on the seat of enlightenment, achieve universal knowledge, and attain perfect enlightenment, they develop and expand the great undertakings of Universal Good without retreating, without resting, without stopping, without giving up great compassion, energetically liberating suffering sentient beings for ever and ever, not giving up the path of Universal Good, actualizing perfect enlightenment. They manifest untold numbers of doors to attainment of true awareness, reveal untold cycles of teaching, manifest untold doors of profound determination, and in untold vast lands show the door of manifestation of nirvana. They appear to live in untold different worlds cultivating the practice of Universal Good; they manifest untold buddhas attaining perfect enlightenment under enlightenment trees in untold lands, with untold congregations of enlightening beings drawing near and encircling them, sometimes attaining true enlightenment after cultivating Universally Good practice for an instant, or for a moment, or for an hour, or for a day, or for a fortnight, or for a month, or for a year, or for countless years, or for an eon, and so on, up to attaining true enlightenment after untold eons of cultivating Universally Good practice. Also they are leaders in all buddha-lands, approaching the buddhas, paying respects to them and presenting offerings to them and soliciting teaching. They examine the realm of illusion and purify enlightening beings' infinite practices, infinite knowledges, various miracles, various powers, various kinds of wisdom, various states, various psychic faculties, various freedoms, various liberations, various understandings, and various methods of teaching and training.

"The great enlightening beings' original bodies do not perish or vanish, but by the power of action and will they appear transfigured in these ways. Why? Because they want to pacify all sentient beings by the free spiritual powers of universal good; to enable untold numbers of sentient beings to attain purity; to cause them to forever cut off the cycle of birth and death; to purify and magnify the worlds; always to see all buddhas; to enter deeply into the stream of all Buddha teachings; to remember the lineage of buddhas of past, present, and future; to remember the teachings and the reality of all buddhas of the ten directions; to cultivate all practices of enlightening beings to fulfillment; to enter the stream of Universal Good and be able to realize omniscience independently.

"You should observe these great enlightening beings not giving up the practice of Universal Good, not stopping the path of enlightening beings, seeing all buddhas, realizing all knowledge, freely employing the elements of omniscience. Just as the elephant king goes to heaven without leaving its elephant body, is ridden by a god, experiences celestial bliss, romps in celestial play, serves the lord of the gods, and sports with the celestial nymphs the same as the gods, no different, in the same way, great enlightening beings, not giving up the practices of the Great Vehicle of Universal Goodness, not retreating from their vows, attain the freedom of Buddha, one imbued with universal knowledge, experience the liberation of buddhas, achieve thorough purity without hindrance or obstruction, have no attachments to any worlds, have no discriminatory concepts about the Buddha teaching; though they know all things are equal and nondual, yet they always clearly see all buddha-lands; though they are already equal to the buddhas of past, present, and future, yet they continue to cultivate the conduct of enlightening beings.

"Great enlightening beings live by this great principle of the undertaking of Universal Good: know that these people's minds are pure.

"This is the great knowledge of the superior mind of the great concentration of the unimpeded wheel, the tenth concentration of great enlightening beings.

"These are the ten great spheres of concentration practiced by the Universally Good enlightening being, in which great enlightening beings abide."

BOOK TWENTY-EIGHT

The Ten Superknowledges

THEN THE GREAT ENLIGHTENING BEING Universally Good said to the enlightening beings, "Offspring of Buddha, great enlightening beings have ten kinds of superknowledge. What are the ten? By means of knowledge of others' minds, great enlightening beings know the differences of the minds of living beings in a world system: good minds, bad minds, broad minds, narrow minds, big minds, small minds, minds that go along with birth and death, minds that turn away from birth and death, minds of learners, minds of self-enlightened ones, minds of enlightening beings, celestial minds, water-spirit minds, yaksha minds, titan minds, garuda minds, kinnara minds, mahoraga minds, human minds, nonhuman minds, hellish minds, bestial minds, netherworld minds, hungry-ghost minds, minds of beings in difficult situations. They know distinctly such countless different sentient beings: as in one world, so in a hundred worlds, a thousand worlds, a hundred thousand worlds, a billion worlds, as many worlds as atoms in untold buddha-lands—they know distinctly the minds of all beings therein. This is called great enlightening beings' first superknowledge, the spiritual power of accurate knowledge of others' minds.

"By means of the superknowledge of the unobstructed pure celestial eye great enlightening beings see sentient beings in worlds as many as atoms in untold buddha-lands, dying in one place, being born in another, their good and bad tendencies and courses of action, their virtuous and sinful characteristics, whether they are beautiful or ugly, defiled or pure: they see innumerable sentient beings of such kinds—celestial beings, water spirits, demons, hobgoblins, titans, demigods, serpents, humans, nonhumans, microscopic creatures, gigantic creatures, small groups, and large groups. They clearly see various sentient beings with unobstructed eyes, unerringly seeing whatever deeds they have accumulated, whatever suffering and happiness they experience, whatever mentalities, thoughts, and views they have, whatever languages they speak, whatever their motives and acts, whatever their concerns and productions. This is called great enlightening beings' superknowledge of the celestial eye.

"By means of the superknowledge of instant recall of past lives, great enlightening beings are able to know the events of past lives of themselves as well as of the beings in countless worlds over countless eons—where they were born, their names, their castes, their races, their diets, their pains and pleasures. The beginningless development of continuous cycles in the various states of existence through causes and conditions, various classes, various lands, various forms of life, various physical characteristics, various activities, various bonds and compulsions, various mentalities and thoughts, various differences in circumstances of birth—they know all such things as these.

"Also they remember the names, manner of emergence, congregations, parents, attendants, disciples, and foremost two disciples of as many buddhas as atoms in so many buddha-lands in worlds as many as atoms in so many buddha-lands, as many eons ago as atoms in so many buddha-lands, and the cities where they lived, how they left home, the enlightenment trees under which they attained true awakening, where they sat, what scriptures they preached, how they benefited so many beings, how long they lived, what buddha-works they performed, how they passed away into the realm of ultimate nirvana without residue, how long their teachings lasted after their demise—all this they can recall.

"Also they remember as many buddha-names as atoms in untold numbers of buddha-lands, there being to each name as many buddhas as atoms in untold buddha-lands, from their first determination establishing their vows, cultivating practices, honoring buddhas, taming sentient beings, their congregations, their teachings, their life spans, their spiritual powers and miracles, and so on, including their entry into nirvana without residue, how long their teaching lasted after their complete nirvana, the setting up of monuments to them, their various adornments, causing sentient beings to plant roots of goodness—all these they are able to know.

"This is called great enlightening beings' third superknowledge, the spiritual faculty of knowing past lives.

"Great enlightening beings, by superknowledge of the eons of the entire future, know the ages in worlds as numerous as atoms in untold buddha-lands, the deaths and births of all the beings in each age, the continuity of existences, their actions, the results and consequences of their deeds—whether good or not, whether emancipated or not, whether certain or not, whether wrongly focused or rightly focused, whether their basic virtues are together with compulsions or not, whether they have fully embodied basic virtues or not, whether they absorb basic virtues or not, whether they accumulate basic virtues or not, whether they accumulate criminal qualities or not. All of these the enlightening beings are able to know.

"Also they know the whole future of worlds as numerous as atoms in untold buddha-lands, with as many eons, each eon with as many buddha-names, each name with as many buddhas; they are able to know all such things as the first inspiration and determination of each buddha, their practices, their service to buddhas, their education of beings, their congregations, their teachings, their life spans, their spiritual powers and miracles, and so on, up to their entry into nirvana without remainder, how long their teachings remain in the world after their ultimate nirvana, and the building of their monuments, with various adornments, causing sentient beings to plant roots of goodness.

"This is called great enlightening beings' fourth superknowledge, the power of knowing the ages of the entire future.

"Great enlightening beings develop the unobstructed celestial ear, fully matured, far-reaching, penetratingly sensitive, free from blockage, perceiving without hindrance, thoroughly developed, able to hear or not hear all sounds at will.

"In the east there are as many buddhas as atoms in untold buddhalands; the great enlightening beings are able to receive and hold the pure teachings explained, revealed, exposed, expounded, set up, taught, tuned, recollected, and analyzed by those buddhas, deep and vast, with various differences, their infinite means and skills. Also they are able to remember the meanings and expressions therein, addressed to one person or to many, according to their language, according to their wisdom, according to what they comprehend, according to what is shown, according to what is to be subdued, according to their realms, according to their bases, according to their paths of emancipation; the enlightening beings remember all this without forgetting, without halting, without retreating, without delusion, without confusion, explaining it to others to enable them to attain understanding, ultimately never missing a single point. As in the east, the same is also true of the south, west, and north, the four intermediate directions, and the zenith and nadir.

"This is called great enlightening beings' fifth superknowledge, that of the unobstructed pure celestial ear.

"Great enlightening beings abide in superknowledge of insubstantiality, effortless superknowledge, superknowledge of equality, far-reaching superknowledge, measureless superknowledge, independent superknowledge, superknowledge manifesting forms at will, creative superknowledge, superknowledge of nonorigination, undiminishing superknowledge, uninterrupted superknowledge, indestructible superknowledge, enriching superknowledge, superknowledge going anywhere.

"These great enlightening beings, hearing the names of buddhas in all worlds extremely distant—names of buddhas in countless worlds, measureless worlds, worlds as many as atoms in unspeakably many buddhalands—immediately see themselves where those buddhas are. Some of those worlds are upright, some inverted; they have various forms, locations, differentiations, boundless, unobstructed, various lands, times, eons, infinite qualities, in different arrays; those buddhas appear therein, manifest miracles, and make known their names, infinitely countless, each different: as soon as the enlightening beings hear those buddhas' names, without moving from where they are they see themselves where those buddhas are, paying respects to and attending those buddhas, asking about the principles of enlightening, entering buddha-knowledge; they are able to apprehend the buddhas' lands, enlightenment sites, congregations, and teachings, up to the ultimate end, without any attachment.

"In this way they pass as many eons as atoms in untold buddha-lands, reaching everywhere in the ten directions without going anywhere, yet traveling to the lands, seeing the buddhas, hearing the teachings, inquiring after the Way, without stopping or giving up, without rest, without weariness, cultivating the practice of enlightening beings, accomplishing their great undertakings, causing them all to be fulfilled, without regressing, to cause the immense family of buddhas not to come to an end.

"This is called great enlightening beings' sixth superknowledge, that of going to all buddha-lands while dwelling in insubstantiality, without motion or action.

"By the superknowledge that skillfully understands the speech of all living beings, the great enlightening beings know the various verbal expressions of beings in as many worlds as atoms in untold numbers of buddha-lands: the words of sages, the words of those who are not sages, celestial words, the words of water spirits, goblins, cherubim, titans, birds, hobgoblins, serpents, humans, nonhumans, and untold numbers of beings—all their words and speech, their individual expressions and various distinctions, the great enlightening beings can know completely.

"Whatever world these enlightening beings enter, they are able to know the natures and inclinations of all the beings therein, and speak to them in accord with their natures and inclinations so that they can understand completely without doubt or confusion. Just as the sunlight when it appears illumines all forms so that all with eyes can see them clearly, in the same way do great enlightening beings with knowledge understanding all speech enter into the masses of all verbal expressions and cause the intelligent to gain thorough understanding of all verbalization.

"This is called great enlightening beings' seventh superknowledge, the power of understanding all language.

"Great enlightening beings, by the superknowledge of production of arrays of infinite physical forms, know that all phenomena are apart from physical forms, have no signs of distinction, have no signs of variety, have no signs of infinity, have no signs of discrimination, have no signs of color. Enlightening beings thus entering the realm of reality can manifest their bodies in various forms: that is, for example, boundless forms, infinite forms, pure forms, adorned forms, all-pervasive forms, incomparable forms, all-illumining forms, predominating forms, nonantagonistic forms, forms with various characteristics, forms free from all that is bad, majestic forms, honorable forms, inexhaustible forms, forms with myriad interwoven subtleties, extremely beautiful forms, immeasurable forms, well-guarded forms, forms able to bring about maturation, forms changing according to those who are taught, uninhibited forms, very clear forms, unsullied forms, extremely pure forms,

forms of great strength, forms with inconceivable skills, incorruptible forms, flawless forms, unclouded forms, well-settled forms, superbly arrayed forms, forms with handsome features, forms with various minor refinements, forms of great nobility, forms of marvelous realms, well-polished forms, forms with pure determination, forms of blazing refulgence, forms of supreme grandeur, uninterrupted forms, independent forms, peerless forms, forms filling unspeakably many buddha-lands, increasing forms, steadfast, receptive forms, forms of supreme qualities, forms that accord with inclinations, forms of pure understanding, forms of accumulated splendors, forms of skillful ascertainment, forms without solidity, forms of spacious clarity, pure delightful forms, untainted forms, incalculable forms, forms wondrous to behold, forms seen everywhere, forms appearing according to the time, tranquil forms, dispassionate forms, forms of fields of blessings, forms able to create peace, forms removing all fear, forms free from foolish actions, forms of wisdom and courage, forms with physical characteristics free from resistance, forms traveling everywhere, forms with minds not relying on anything, forms created by great kindness, forms manifested by great compassion, impartially emancipating forms, forms replete with blessed qualities, forms according to thoughts in the mind, forms of boundless jewels, forms of the lights within jewels, forms trusted by sentient beings, forms in which omniscience appears, forms with happy eyes, forms of the foremost arrays of jewels, forms without location, forms freely manifested at will, forms of various spiritual powers, forms of those born in the family of buddhas, forms beyond all comparisons or metaphors, forms pervading the cosmos, forms to which the masses flock, various forms, forms of perfection, forms of emancipation, forms adapted to those to be taught, forms of dignified conduct, forms that one never tires of seeing, varied clear, pure forms, forms able to emanate countless webs of light, forms of untold various differentiations of light, forms of inconceivable fragrances and light beyond the world, forms of radiance of light of innumerable suns, forms showing incomparable lunar bodies, forms of clouds of innumerable pleasant flowers, forms producing arrays of clouds of garlands of all kinds of lotus blossoms, forms of fragrant flames beyond all worlds perfuming everywhere, forms producing all embryos of enlightenment, forms with untold voices revealing and expounding all truths, forms fulfilling all the practices of Universal Good.

"Great enlightening beings entering deeply into this formless cosmos of reality are able to manifest such various form bodies, to cause those to be taught to see, to cause those to be taught to remember, to operate the cycles of the Teaching for those to be taught in accord with proper timing for those to be taught, in accord with the characteristics of those to be taught, to cause those to be taught to draw near, to cause those to be taught to awaken, producing various miracles for those to be taught, manifesting various powers for those to be taught, doing whatever they can for those to be taught.

"This is called great enlightening beings' eighth superknowledge, of countless form bodies, diligently cultivated and perfected for the purpose of liberating all living beings.

"By superknowledge of phenomena, enlightening beings know all phenomena are nameless, without essence, neither come nor go, are neither different nor not different, neither various nor not various, neither dual nor nondual, have no identity, have no compare, are not born, do not perish, do not shift, do not disintegrate, have no reality, have no falsehood, are of one form which is formless, are not nonexistent, are not existent, are not phenomenal, are not nonphenomenal, are not in conformity with conventions, are not not in conformity with conventions, are not actions, are not not actions, are not consequences, are not not consequences, are not compounded, are not uncompounded, are not absolute, are not nonabsolute, are not the path of enlightenment, are not not the path of enlightenment, are not emancipation, are not not emancipation, are not a certain measure, are not measureless, are not mundane, are not not mundane, are not born from cause, are not not born from causes, are not definite, are not indefinite, are not complete, are not incomplete, are not emerging, are not not emerging, are not distinguished, are not indistinguishable, are not logical, are not illogical.

"These great enlightening beings do not grasp conventional truth, do not dwell in absolute truth, do not discriminate phenomena, do not set up words; they accord with the essence of extinction, yet they do not give up their undertakings. Seeing what is true and knowing the principles thereof, they spread clouds of teaching and shower rains of teaching. Though they know the character of reality cannot be verbally expressed, yet by expedient means and endless intellectual power they teach in an orderly fashion according to principles and according to meanings. Because they have mastered the skills of verbal explanation of phenomena and principles, their great kindness and compassion purified, they produce words for all things that are actually beyond words, according to their principles and meanings, without contradiction, explaining that all things arise from conditions. Though they do use words to explain, yet they are not attached to them at all. They explain all things, with endless intellectual power, analyzing, defining, revealing, guiding, causing the nature of all things to be fully revealed, cutting through the web of doubts, causing all to be clarified. Even while they take care of sentient beings, they do not abandon true reality. They do not regress from nonduality, and they are always able to expound the reality of nonobstruction. By means of myriad subtle nuances they adapt to the minds of sentient beings, showering the rain of truth on all according to proper timing.

"This is called great enlightening beings' ninth superknowledge, knowledge of all phenomena.

"By the superknowledge of concentration on the extinction of all things, great enlightening beings enter into concentration on the extinction of all things in every moment; yet they do not retire from the Path of enlightening beings, they do not give up the tasks of enlightening beings, they do not abandon the heart of great kindness and compassion. They cultivate the transcendent ways unceasingly and investigate all buddha-lands tirelessly. They do not give up the vow to liberate sentient beings, do not stop the work of turning the wheel of the Teaching, do not abandon the activity of civilizing sentient beings, do not give up the practice of honoring and serving the buddhas, do not abandon the door of mastery of all teachings, do not give up seeing all buddhas, do not abandon always listening to all their teachings. They know all things are equal and do not hinder one another. They freely accomplish all Buddha teachings, and attain fulfillment of all their excellent vows. They know the differentiations of all lands. They enter the family of buddhas and reach the other shore. They are able to study all things in each world and comprehend that all things are signless; they know all things come from conditions and have no intrinsic being of their own, nevertheless they explain them expediently according to conventional usage. Though their minds do not dwell on anything, yet in accord with sentient beings' faculties and dispositions they expediently explain all kinds of things.

"When these enlightening beings are in concentration, they may remain in concentration for an eon, a hundred eons, a thousand eons, a million eons, a billion eons, a trillion eons, or any number of eons, if they wish. When the enlightening beings enter this concentration on the extinction of all things, no matter how many eons they pass in this concentration, their bodies do not disintegrate, waste away, or change. They are neither visible nor invisible. They do not pass away, decay, or tire out—it is inexhaustible. Though they do nothing at all in respect to existence or nonexistence, yet they are able to accomplish the tasks of enlightening beings: that is to say, they never abandon sentient beings, teaching and harmonizing them according to proper timing, causing them to increase in all enlightened qualities; they attain fulfillment of all practices of enlightening beings, and for the sake of aiding and benefiting all sentient beings they ceaselessly work miracles. Like rays of light, they appear everywhere while remaining silent and unmoving in concentration.

"This is called great enlightening beings' tenth superknowledge, of concentration on the extinction of all things.

"Great enlightening beings abiding in these ten kinds of superknowledge are inconceivable to any celestial or human beings, to any sentient beings, to any Buddhist disciples, individual illuminates, or even to other enlightening beings. The physical, verbal, and mental actions of these great enlightening beings are inconceivable; their freedom in concentration and the realms of their knowledge, too, are inconceivable. Only the buddhas and the enlightening beings who also have attained these superknowledges are able to tell of the virtues and sing the praises of these people.

"These are the ten superknowledges of great enlightening beings. If great enlightening beings abide in these superknowledges, they will completely attain superknowledge unhindered in all times."

BOOK TWENTY-NINE

The Ten Acceptances

THEN THE GREAT ENLIGHTENING BEING Universally Good said to the enlightening beings, "Offspring of Buddha, great enlightening beings have ten kinds of acceptance. If you acquire these acceptances, you will manage to arrive at the stage of unhindered acceptance. What are the ten? They are acceptance of the voice of the Teaching; conformative acceptance; acceptance of the nonorigination of all things; acceptance of illusoriness; acceptance of being miragelike; acceptance of being dreamlike; acceptance of being echolike; acceptance of being like a reflection; acceptance of being phantomlike; acceptance of being spacelike. These ten acceptances have been expounded, are being expounded, and will be expounded by the buddhas of past, present, and future.

"What is great enlightening beings' acceptance of the voice of the Teaching? It means when they hear the teachings expounded by the buddhas, they are not startled or frightened or overawed; they believe deeply, understand, appreciate, aim for, concentrate on, remember, practice, and abide by them. This is called great enlightening beings' acceptance of the voice of the Teaching.

"What is great enlightening beings' conformative acceptance? It means they contemplate the Teaching, investigate it, impartially conform to it without opposition, comprehend it, purify their minds, live correctly by the Teaching, apply it, enter into it, and fulfill it. This is called great enlightening beings' second acceptance, that of conforming to the Teaching.

"What is great enlightening beings' acceptance of the nonorigination of things? These great enlightening beings do not see that there is anything at all that originates and do not see that there is anything at all that perishes. Why? If there is no origination, there is no perishing; if there is no perishing, there is no extinction; if there is no extinction, they are free from defilements; if they are free from defilements, there is no differentiation; if there is no differentiation, there is no location; if there is no location, there is quiescence; if there is quiescence, there is detachment from desire; if there is detachment from desire, there is no doing; if there is no doing, there is no wish; if there is no wish, there is no dwelling; if there is no dwelling, there is no coming and no going. This is called great enlightening beings' acceptance of the nonorigination of things.

"What is great enlightening beings' acceptance of illusoriness? These great enlightening beings know all things are like illusions and arise from causes and conditions. In one thing they understand many things, and in many things they understand one thing. These enlightening beings, knowing the illusoriness of things, comprehend lands, comprehend sentient beings, comprehend the cosmos, comprehend the equality of worlds, comprehend the equality of appearances of buddhas, comprehend the equality of past, present, and future, and accomplish various spiritual powers and mystic transformations.

"Just as illusions are not elephants, not horses, not chariots, not walking, not men, not women, not boys, not girls, not trees, not leaves, not flowers, not fruits, not earth, not water, not fire, not wind, not day, not night, not a day, not a month, not a fortnight, not a year, not a hundred years, not an eon, not many eons, not stable, not confused, not pure, not alloyed, not one, not variegated, not broad, not narrow, not many, not few, not finite, not infinite, not gross, not subtle, not any things at all—variety is not illusion, illusion is not various, yet by illusion are manifested all kinds of different things—in the same way do great enlightening beings look upon all worlds as illusory; that is, the worlds of action, the worlds of affliction, the worlds of lands, the worlds of phenomena, the worlds of time, the worlds of dispositions, the worlds of becoming, the worlds of decay, the worlds of movement, the worlds of creativity. When great enlightening beings see all worlds as like illusions, they do not see beings born or dying, they do not see countries born or perishing, they do not see phenomena born or perishing, they do not see a past that can be differentiated, they do not see a future that has a beginning, they do not see a present that remains for even a moment; they do not examine enlightenment, do not discriminate enlightenment, do not see buddhas emerging, do not see buddhas passing away into nirvana, do not see abiding by great vows, do not see entry into the absolute, do not go out of the essence of equality.

"Though these enlightening beings develop buddha-lands, they know lands have no differentiation; though they develop sentient beings, they know sentient beings have no differentiation; though they examine the cosmos, yet they abide peacefully in the essence of reality, silent and unmoving; though they realize past, present, and future are equal, yet they do not oppose the distinction of past, present, and future phenomena; though they are fully complete in physical, mental, and sense elements, they do not rely on anything; though they liberate sentient beings, yet they know the cosmos is impartial and makes no distinctions; though they know all things are beyond words and cannot be verbally explained, yet they always explain things with inexhaustible powers of analysis; though they are not attached to the work of teaching beings, yet they do not give up great compassion, turning the wheel of Teaching to liberate all; though they reveal to them past causes and conditions, yet they know that conditionality has no movement. This is called great enlightening beings' acceptance of illusoriness.

"What is great enlightening beings' acceptance of being miragelike? These great enlightening beings know that all worlds are like mirages. Just as mirages have no location, are not inside or outside, not existent or nonexistent, not finite or eternal, not uniform or multiform or formless, but just expressed in conventional terms, in the same way do enlightening beings truly see and know all things, actually realizing this of all things, attaining complete acceptance. This is called enlightening beings' acceptance of being miragelike.

"What is great enlightening beings' acceptance of being dreamlike? Here great enlightening beings know all worlds are like dreams. Just as dreams are neither of the world nor apart from the world, not of the realm of desire, not of the realm of form, not of the formless realm, not arising, not disappearing, not defiled, not pure, and yet obviously manifest, in the same way do enlightening beings know all worlds to be like dreams, unchanging, because of being free like dreams, because of clinging like dreams, because of being inherently unconnected like dreams, because of being like the basic nature of dreams, because of being like visions in dreams, because of being undifferentiated like dreams, because of being like thoughts in dreams, because of being as when awakening from a dream. This is called great enlightening beings' acceptance of being dreamlike.

"What is great enlightening beings' acceptance of being echolike? Here the great enlightening beings, hearing buddhas explain the truth, seeing into the nature of things, applying this practically, achieving realization and reaching the other shore, know that all sounds are the same as echoes, with no coming or going, appearing in this way. The great enlightening beings observe the voice of the buddhas as emerging without emerging from inside or outside or both. Though they understand that this voice does not emerge from inside, outside, or both, yet it is possible to produce skillful expressions to accomplish explanation. Like echoes in a valley, it is produced by conditions and is not at variance with the nature of things. It enables sentient beings each to understand according to kind and to be able to practice this learning.

"Just as the wife of the emperor of gods can produce a thousand tones in one sound without consciously trying to do so, so also do great enlightening beings enter the realm of nondiscrimination, develop a voice that skillfully adapts to different types, and forever turn the wheel of the Teaching in boundless worlds. These enlightening beings skillfully observe all beings and preach to them with a universal tongue, their voices pervading all lands in the ten directions unhindered, causing all to hear the Teaching differently according to their needs. Though they know sound has no origin, they manifest the sound of their voice everywhere; though they know there is nothing to say, they extensively explain all things. Their wondrous voice is impartial, all understand it according to species and type, while the enlightening beings comprehend this all by means of their knowledge. This is called great enlightening beings' acceptance of being echolike.

"What is great enlightening beings' acceptance of being like a reflection? These great enlightening beings are not born in the world, do not die in the world; they are not in the world, not outside the world; they do not act in the world, yet are not inactive in the world; they are not the same as the world, yet are not different from the world; they do not go to the world, nor do they not go to it; they do not dwell in the world, nor do they not dwell in the world; they are not worldly or unworldly. They are not cultivating the practices of enlightening beings, yet they do not give up their great vow; they are neither real nor unreal. Though they always carry out all Buddha teachings, yet they are able to manage all mundane affairs; they do not follow the mundane stream, nor dwell in the religious stream.

"Just as the sun, moon, men, women, houses, mountains, rivers, springs, and so on, are reflected in anything clear—in oil, water, a jewel, a mirror, and so on—and the reflections are neither one with nor different from the oil, water, jewel, or mirror, are neither separated nor united, not flowing along in river currents, not sinking in lakes or wells, appearing therein without being affected, and people know that such and such a reflection is in such and such a place and not elsewhere, and, though things far and near cast their reflections, there is no corresponding distance of the images from one another, similarly great enlightening beings know their own bodies and others' bodies are all spheres of cognition and do not understand them dualistically as self and others, and simultaneously appear in their own lands and other lands. Just as there are no roots, sprouts, stalks, nodes, branches, or leaves in a seed, yet it can produce these things, so also do great enlightening beings distinguish duality in that which is nondual, their skill in means completely fluid and all-encompassing, without blockage. This is called great enlightening beings' acceptance of being like a reflection.

"When great enlightening beings achieve this acceptance, though they do not travel to the lands of the ten directions, yet they can appear in all buddha-lands, neither leaving here nor going there. They are like reflections appearing everywhere, unhindered wherever they go, causing sentient beings to see different bodies with the same appearance of solidity as the world. However, these differentiations are not differentiation—difference and nondifference do not obstruct one another. These great enlightening beings are born from the lineage of the buddhas—their bodies, speech, and minds are pure and unimpeded, so they are able to acquire pure bodies of boundless forms.

"What is great enlightening beings' acceptance of being phantomlike? These great enlightening beings know all worlds are like phantoms—that is, all sentient beings are phantoms of mentalization, being created by consciousness and thought; all worldly realms are phantoms of acts and conditioning, being created by discrimination; all pain and pleasure are phantoms of delusion, being produced by arbitrary clinging; all worlds are phantoms of unreal phenomena, being made apparent by verbalization; all afflictions are phantoms of discrimination, being created by thoughts. There is also the phantom of pure pacification, being manifested by nondiscrimination; the phantom of not changing through time, because of the equality of the uncreate; the phantom of enlightening beings' willpower, because of their extensive practices; the phantom of buddhas' great compassion, based on expedient demonstrations; the phantoms of means of teaching, being expounded by wisdom, expertise, and intellectual powers.

"Thus do enlightening beings know mundane and transmundane phantoms; they know them by direct experience, with extensive knowledge, boundless knowledge, factual knowledge, independent knowledge, true knowledge, incapable of being overturned by false views, going along with the events of the world without loss or corruption.

"Just as a phantom does not arise from the mind or from mental states, does not arise from action, does not experience consequences, is not born in the world, does not die in the world, cannot be pursued, cannot be grasped or touched, is not long-lasting, is not momentary, is not acting in the world, is not apart from the world, is not bound to one location, is not ubiquitous, is not finite, is not infinite, does not weary or rest, is not unwearying or unceasing, not ordinary, not holy, not defiled, not pure, not born, not dead, not wise, not foolish, not seen, not unseen, not based in the world, not entering the reality realm, not clever, not dull, not grasping, not nongrasping, not birth and death, not nirvana, not existent, not nonexistent, in the same way do enlightening beings course through the world by skill in means, cultivating the path of enlightening beings, knowing worldly phenomena, multiplying their bodies for phantomlike travel, not clinging to the world, not attached to their own bodies, not conceptualizing anything in the world or themselves, not dwelling in the world, not leaving the world, not dwelling on things, not aloof from things. Because of their fundamental vow they do not abandon a single sentient being, they do not guide only a few sentient beings, they do not discriminate things yet are not indiscriminate. They know the nature of things has no coming or going, and though they have no existence, they fulfill the Buddha teachings, knowing everything is like a phantom, neither existent nor nonexistent.

"When great enlightening beings thus abide in acceptance of being phantomlike, they are able to fulfill the path of enlightenment of all buddhas and benefit living beings. This is called enlightening beings' acceptance of being phantomlike: when great enlightening beings achieve this acceptance, like magicians, everything they do is phantomlike. They do not dwell on anything in any buddha-land, do not cling to the world, tirelessly proceed toward enlightenment without producing false ideas about the Buddha teachings, cultivate the practices of enlightening beings, and get rid of delusion. Though they have no body, yet they manifest all bodies; though they have no abode, yet they abide in myriad buddha-lands; though they have no form, yet they manifest myriad forms; though they do not cling to ultimate truth, yet they clearly perceive the essential nature of things, impartially and completely.

"These great enlightening beings, not relying on anything, are called liberated; having shed all errors, they are called disciplined; entering the congregations of all buddhas everywhere without moving, they are called masters of spiritual power; well versed in the truth of nonorigination, they are called unregressing; imbued with all powers, which even mountains cannot impede, they are called unobstructed.

"What is great enlightening beings' acceptance of being spacelike? These great enlightening beings understand that all phenomena are like space because they are signless; all worlds are like space because they have no origin; all things are like space because they are nondual; all actions of sentient beings are like space because they have no course; all buddhas are like space because they have no discrimination; all buddhas' powers are like space because they have no distinctions; all meditation concentrations are like space because of equality of past, present, and future; all the principles the buddhas teach are like space because they cannot be explained in words; all buddha-bodies are like space because they have no attachment and no obstruction. In this way enlightening beings, by means of the device of being spacelike, comprehend that all things have no existence.

"When great enlightening beings comprehend all things by the knowledge that recognizes and accepts their spacelike nature, they acquire spacelike bodies, spacelike physical action, spacelike speech, spacelike minds, and spacelike mental action. Just as space, the harbor of all things, is not born and does not perish, so also are all the bodies of realities of great enlightening beings unborn and imperishable. Just as space is indestructible, similarly are the powers of knowledge of great enlightening beings indestructible; just as all worlds rest in space while space rests on nothing, similarly all true teachings rest on great enlightening beings while they rest on nothing. Just as space, without any origin or destruction, can hold the origin and destruction of all worlds, similarly great enlightening beings, without aim or attainment, can show aim and attainment, causing all worldlings to cultivate purity. Just as space, without direction or angles, can manifest innumerable directions and angles, similarly great enlightening beings, without actions or consequences, are able to show all kinds of actions and consequences. Just as space is not walking or standing yet can reveal all kinds of postures and movements, similarly great enlightening beings are not walking or standing yet can differentiate all movements. Just as space is not form and not not form, yet can reveal all kinds of forms, similarly great enlightening beings are not mundane corporeality or transmundane corporeality, yet can manifest all forms. Just as space is not old or new, yet can perdure, revealing all things, similarly great enlightening beings are not ancient or recent, but can perdure, revealing the practices carried out by enlightening beings. Just as space is not clean or dirty, yet is not apart from cleanness and pollution, similarly great enlightening beings are not obstructed or unobstructed, yet are not apart from obstruction and nonobstruction. Just as all worlds appear to space while space does not appear to all worlds, similarly all things appear to great enlightening beings while great enlightening beings do not appear to all things. Just as space penetrates everywhere, without boundaries, similarly great enlightening beings penetrate all things, yet their minds have no boundaries.

"Why is this? Because enlightening beings' doings are like space. That is to say, all their practices, all their purifications, and all their accomplishments are all impartial, of one substance, one flavor, one essence, of the same measure as space, pure and all-pervasive. Thus do they witness and know all things without fabricated notions of things, purify all buddha-lands, perfect all supporting bodies, comprehend all realms without confusion, embody all powers, which are indestructible, fulfill all virtues, which are boundless, arrive at the realm of all profound truths, master the paths of all ways of transcendence, sit on all adamantine seats of enlightenment everywhere, utter all voices adapting to all species, and operate the cycles of the Teaching for all worlds according to proper timing. This is called great enlightening beings' acceptance of being spacelike.

"When great enlightening beings attain these acceptances, they acquire a body that does not come from anywhere because it does not go anywhere; they acquire a birthless body, having no extinction; they acquire a motionless body, having no disintegration; they acquire an insubstantial body, being beyond falsehood; they acquire a uniform body, being formless; they acquire an infinite body, the power of buddhahood being infinite; they acquire an impartial body, being the same characteristic of Thusness; they acquire an undifferentiated body, seeing past, present, and future as equal; they acquire a body that reaches everywhere, their pure eye perceiving equally, without obstruction; they acquire a body free from the realm of desire, knowing that all phenomena neither form nor dissolve; they acquire a body as boundless as space, their store of virtue being as inexhaustible as space; they acquire a body of endless knowledge of the equality of the nature of things, knowing the forms of all things are one form and their nature is natureless, like space; they acquire a body of infinite, unobstructed sound, being unopposed and unobstructed like space; they acquire a body of pure action of enlightening beings endowed with all skills, being unhindered in all places, like space; they acquire a body of continuity of succession of the oceans of all Buddha teachings, because like space they cannot be brought to an end; they acquire a body manifesting infinite buddha-lands within all buddha-lands, being free from greed and attachment, unbounded as space; they acquire a body ceaselessly manifesting all aspects of miraculous power, being boundless as the sky and ocean; they acquire a body of indestructible durable strength, sustaining all worlds like space; they acquire a body with all senses clear and sharp, indestructible as adamant, because like space they cannot be burned by the fires that end an eon; they acquire a body of power to hold all worlds, their power of knowledge being like space.

"These are called the ten acceptances of enlightening beings."

Then the great enlightening being Universally Good, in order to restate this teaching, spoke these verses:

Just as people of the world
Hearing of a mine of jewels
Become glad at heart
Because they can obtain them,
So enlightening beings,
Endowed with great wisdom,
Hearing the buddhas' teaching,
The most profound character of nullity,
Become calm at heart
When they hear this teaching.

They are not startled or frightened,
Nor are they overawed;
Great beings seeking enlightenment,
Hearing this grandiose message,
Minds pure, able to accept,
Have no doubt about it.

Thinking to themselves that by hearing this
Exceedingly profound and subtle teaching
They will become omniscient
Guides of heaven and earth,
Enlightening beings, hearing this message,
Are very glad at heart.

Producing steadfast determination,
Vowing to seek the buddhas' truths,
Because they incline to enlightenment
Their minds are gradually tamed.

It causes their faith to grow,
Not repudiating truth—
Therefore, hearing this message,
Their minds are able to accept it.

Immutable, stable,
They cultivate enlightening practice;
In their quest for enlightenment,
They proceed wholeheartedly toward that path.

Diligent, vigorous, never turning back,
They do not cast off the yoke of virtues.

Because they seek enlightenment,
Their minds are without fear;
Hearing the truth, they become yet braver
And serve the buddhas, gaining rapport with them.

As someone of great fortune
Who has found a treasure of gold
Makes whatever ornaments
Are suitable to wear,
So do enlightening beings,
Hearing this most profound doctrine,
Think and increase the ocean of knowledge,
Thereby cultivating conformity to the teaching.

The existence of things they know accordingly,
The nonexistence of things they also know accordingly;
As the truth of the teaching is thus,
Thus do they know all things.

Achieving a pure mind,
Thoroughly clear, full of joy,
They know things arise from conditions
And vigorously cultivate practice;
They see all things impartially
And comprehend their inherent nature.

Not straying from the Buddha's teaching,
They are aware of all things;
Their determination is always firm
As they purify enlightenment.

Immovable as mountains,
Single-mindedly seeking true awakening,
With a mind inspired to effort
They also cultivate the path of concentration,
Practicing diligently for countless eons,
With never any regression or digression.

The principles enlightening beings enter
Are the sphere of action of buddhas;
Able to know them thoroughly,
Their minds without aversion or sloth,
As the Peerless One teaches,
They look upon things impartially.

Without impartial acceptance
None can attain equanimous knowledge;

Following the Buddha's teaching,
They accomplish this facet of acceptance;
They know things as they are
Yet have no notion of things.

All the gods
Of the thirty-three heavens
Eat from the same vessel
Yet their food is not the same:
The various foods they eat
Do not come from the ten directions—
They spontaneously appear in the vessel
According to the actions of the gods.

In the same way do enlightening beings
Observe all phenomena
As arising from conditions—
Having no origin, they have no destruction;
Having no destruction, they have no extinction;
If there is no extinction, there is no defilement.

In the changing things of the world
They know there is no change;
There being no change, there is no location,
And no location means nullity.

Their minds without attachment,
They vow to liberate all the living,
Thinking only of the Buddha Way,
Never distracted or perturbed,
Ever with compassionate will
Acting expediently in the world.

Diligently seeking the ten powers,
They are in the world without lingering;
Without coming or going,
They expediently teach the truth.

These acceptances are supreme,
Comprehending truth without end,
Entering the cosmos of reality,
Yet actually without entering anywhere.

Enlightening beings abiding in these acceptances
See the buddhas everywhere
Simultaneously giving them directions—
This is called getting the joy of buddhahood.

They comprehend the nullity and purity
Of all things of all times,
Yet can influence sentient beings
Into the path of virtue.

The various things of the world
Are all illusory;
If one can know this is so,
One's mind will be unshakable.

All acts are born from mind,
Therefore it is said mind is like magic:
If one gets rid of this false imagination,
One extinguishes all paths of existence.

Just as a skillful magician
Causes forms to appear,
Causing the masses to crave them in vain,
While they ultimately get nothing,
So also is the world—
All in it is illusion,
Without essence or origin,
Yet appearing variously.

Liberating living beings,
Letting them know things are illusory,
Living beings, too, are not other than illusion—
On comprehending illusion, there are no "living beings."

Living beings and lands,
All things there are in all times,
In the same way, without exception,
Are all illusory.

Making illusory forms of men and women,
Elephants, horses, cattle, and sheep,
Houses, ponds, springs, and such,
Gardens, groves, flowers, and fruits,
Illusory things have no awareness
And also have no abode;
Ultimately of the character of nullity,
They only appear according to imagination.

Enlightening beings are able to see
Things of the world this way—
All things, existent and nonexistent,

They realize are illusions;
Living beings and lands
Are made by various acts.

Entering the realm of illusion,
They have no attachment therein;
Thus attaining skillfulness,
They are tranquil, free from folly.

In the state of nonobstruction
Manifesting great power everywhere,
The courageous offspring of Buddha
Accordingly enter the sublime Teaching,
Accurately perceiving all conceptions
As wrapping up the world in their mesh,
The conceptions like mirages
Causing beings to misunderstand.

Enlightening beings, knowing conceptions well,
Get rid of all delusions.
Living beings, each different,
Are not the same in form and type;
Enlightening beings understand these are all conceptions,
All without true reality.

All beings in the ten directions
Are shrouded by conceptions;
If they would give up erroneous views,
They would end their conceptions of the world.

The world is like a mirage,
Differentiated because of conceptions;
Knowing the world is an ideation,
One is freed from delusion of thought, view, and mind.

Just as a mirage in the heat
People think is water,
Yet the water does not exist
And the wise should not seek it,
The same is true of sentient beings:
Worldly states are all nonexistent,
Like mirages, existing in the perception—
This is the realm of the unobstructed mind.

If one detaches from conceptions
One will get rid of false descriptions,

Liberating all the ignorant
Who are attached to ideas.

Avoiding pride and conceit,
Eliminating conceptions of the world,
Dwelling on the point of extinction and infinity,
This is enlightening beings' method.

Enlightening beings realize things of the world
Are all like dreams,
Neither having nor lacking location,
Eternally null in essence.

All things have no discrimination;
Like dreams, they are not different from mind—
The worlds of past, present, and future
Are all like this.

The substance of dreams has no birth or destruction
And also has no location.
The three worlds are all like this—
Those who see this are freed in mind.

Dreams are not in the world,
Nor are they unworldly:
Not discriminating these two,
One enters the stage of acceptance.

Just like seeing in dreams
Various different forms,
So also is the world
No different from a dream.

Those in dream-concentration
Realize all in the world is like a dream,
Not the same and not different,
Not one and not various.

The acts of beings and lands,
Polluted and pure,
They understand all
Are equal to dreams.

The practices of enlightening beings
As well as their great vows
They understand are all like dreams,
No different from the world.

Realizing the world is empty,
They do not destroy the things of the world,
Like long, short, and such forms,
As seen in a dream.

This is called acceptance of the dreamlike;
Understanding things of the world by this,
One swiftly attains unhindered wisdom
To liberate sentient beings.

Cultivating such practice
Produces broad understanding,
Knowing well the nature of things,
Without mental attachment to things.

All the various sounds and voices
Of all realms of the world
Are not internal or external:
Realizing all are like echoes,
Like hearing all kinds of echoes,
The mind doesn't discriminate.

When enlightening beings hear sounds
Their minds are also like this;
Looking to the buddhas
And listening to the sound of their teachings,
Their discourses without number,
Though they hear, they are not attached.

As echoes come from nowhere,
So do the voices they hear;
Yet they can distinguish the principles
And not violate or mistake them.

They understand utterances
While not discriminating among voices;
Knowing all voices are empty and null,
They broadcast pure, clear sounds.

Understanding truth is not in words,
They enter the wordless realm,
Yet can explain in words,
Like echoes filling the world.

They know the ways of speech
And are vocally well equipped;

884 The Flower Ornament Scripture

While knowing the nature of sound is null,
They speak the language of the world.

According to the voice of the world
They show the same differentiations,
Their voice pervading everywhere
Awakening living beings.

Enlightening beings, attaining this acceptance,
Influence the world with a pure message,
Skillfully explaining past, present, and future,
Without attachment to the world.

Because they want to help the world,
They single-mindedly seek enlightenment,
While always entering the nature of things
Without discriminatory thought therein.

They see all worlds
To be null, devoid of intrinsic nature,
Yet always cultivate practice intently
In order to benefit beings.

Not dwelling in the world,
Not leaving the world,
They do not rely on anything in the world—
Reliance cannot be found.

They know the nature of the world
And are not attached to that nature;
While they do not rely on beings,
They teach beings to transcend.

They know the inherent nature
Of everything in the world;
Understanding things are not dual,
They still have no attachment to nonduality.

Their minds are not apart from the world,
Nor do they dwell on the world;
It is not outside the world
That they cultivate all-knowledge.

Just as reflections in water
Are not inside or outside,
Enlightening beings seeking enlightenment

Know the world is not the world:
They do not dwell in or leave the world,
Because the world is inexplicable;
And they are not inside or outside,
Appearing in the world like reflections.

Entering this profound truth,
They are thoroughly purified;
Not giving up their original vow,
They are radiant lamps of wisdom.

Worlds without bound
Their knowledge enters, all equally;
Edifying beings everywhere,
They cause them to give up attachments.

Contemplating the most profound truth,
Aiding living beings,
Henceforth they enter into knowledge
And cultivate all its ways.

Enlightening beings examine all things,
Clearly realize all are like phantoms,
And carry out phantomlike practice,
Never giving it up.

Conforming to phantomlike nature,
They practice the way of enlightenment;
All things are like phantoms,
And so is enlightening beings' practice.

All worldly realms
And infinite acts
Are equally phantomlike,
Ultimately resting in nullity.

The buddhas of all times
Are all like phantoms too;
Originally vowing to perform certain deeds,
They metamorphose into buddhas.

Buddhas liberate phantom beings
By great kindness and compassion;
The liberation is also phantomlike;
By phantom power they teach them.

Knowing the world is all phantomlike,
They do not discriminate worldly realms;
Phantom phenomena, various, different,
All come from differences of action.

Cultivating enlightening practices,
Adorning phantom treasuries,
With arrays of infinite goodness
They make the world according to deeds.

Phantomlike things are beyond conception,
And they do not conceptualize things;
Both things and concepts are null and void—
Such is enlightening beings' practice.

The sea of phantoms understood by knowledge,
The phantom nature stamps the world;
Phantoms are not things born and perishing—
The same is true of knowledge.

The tenth acceptance clearly sees
Sentient beings and phenomena
Are null and void in essence,
Like space, with no location.

Attaining this spacelike knowledge,
One is forever free from grasping and clinging:
Like space, it has no variation
And is unobstructed in the world.

Achievement of acceptance of being like space
Is, like space, inexhaustible:
Objects are like space,
Yet one does not think of them as space.

Space has no intrinsic nature,
And yet it is not nothingness,
But has no variation—
The power of knowledge is also like this.

Space has no beginning,
No middle, and no end;
Its measure cannot be found—
Enlightening beings' knowledge is also thus.

Thus observing the nature of things,
All like space,

With no origin or destruction,
Is the attainment of enlightening beings:
Themselves abiding in the principle of being spacelike,
They also explain it to others,
Conquering all demons—
This is the method of the acceptances.

The distinctions of features of the world
Are empty, without any marks;
Entering into signlessness,
All signs are equal.

By one single means
They enter all worlds:
That is knowing that all things in all times
Are in essence equal to space.

Knowledge and voice
And the enlightening beings' body
Are in essence like space—
All are quiescent and void.

These ten acceptances
Are cultivated by offspring of buddhas;
Their minds rest at peace,
And they explain them to others.

Learning them well,
They develop great power;
The powers of truth and knowledge
Become means to enlightenment.

Arriving at these acceptances,
They achieve unobstructed knowledge
Transcending the masses
And turn the unexcelled wheel of the Teaching.

The great practices they carry out
Are beyond measure—
Only the ocean of knowledge of the Tamer
Can know them in detail.

Giving up their egos to cultivate practice,
They plunge into the profound nature of reality;
Their minds always dwelling on pure truths,
These they give to others.

The number of living beings
And atoms in lands may be known,
But no limit can be ascertained
To the virtues of enlightening beings.

Enlightening beings are able to accomplish
These ten acceptances;
Their wisdom and their conduct
No sentient beings can fathom.

BOOK THIRTY

The Incalculable

AT THAT TIME the enlightening being Mind King said to the Buddha, "World Honored One, the buddhas speak of incalculable, measureless, boundless, incomparable, innumerable, unaccountable, unthinkable, immeasurable, unspeakable, untold numbers—what are these?"

The Buddha said, "It is good that you ask the Buddha, the Truly Enlightened One, in order to have the beings of the world penetrate the meaning of the numbers known to the Buddha. Listen carefully and think well about this; I will explain for you." Then the enlightening being Mind King willingly received the teaching. The Buddha said, "Ten to the tenth power times ten to the tenth power equals ten to the twentieth power; ten to the twentieth power times ten to the twentieth power equals ten to the fortieth power; ten to the fortieth power times ten to the fortieth power equals ten to the eightieth power; ten to the eightieth power times ten to the eightieth power equals ten to the power of 160; ten to the power of 160 squared equals ten to the power of 320; ten to the power of 320 squared equals ten to the power of 640; ten to the power of 640 squared equals ten to the power of 1,280; ten to the power of 1,280 squared equals ten to the power of 2,560; that squared equals ten to the power of 5,120; that squared equals ten to the power of 10,240; that squared equals ten to the power of 20,480; that squared is ten to the power of 40,960; that squared is ten to the power of 81,920; that squared is ten to the power of 163,840; that squared is ten to the power of 327,680; that squared is ten to the power of 655,360; that squared is ten to the power of 1,311,720; that squared is ten to the power of 2,623,540; that squared is ten to the power of 5,247,080; that squared is ten to the power of 10,494,160; that squared is ten to the power of 20,988,320; that squared is ten to the power of 41,976,640; that squared is ten to the power of 83,953,280; that squared is ten to the power of 167,906,560; that squared is ten to the power of 335,813,120; that squared is ten to the power of 671,626,240; that squared is ten to the power of 1,343,252,480; that squared is ten to the power of 2,686,504,960; that squared is ten to the power of 5,373,009,920; that squared is ten to the power of 10,746,019,840; that squared is ten to the power of 21,492,039,680;

that squared is ten to the power of 42,984,079,360; that squared is ten to the power of 85,968,158,720; that squared is ten to the power of 171,936,317,440; that squared is ten to the power of 343,872,634,880; that squared is ten to the power of 687,745,269,760; that squared is ten to the power of 1,375,490,539,520; that squared is ten to the power of 2,750,981,079,040; that squared is ten to the power of 5,501,962,158,080; that squared is ten to the power of 11,003,924,316,160; that squared is ten to the power of 22,007,848,632,320; that squared is ten to the power of 44,015,697,264,640; that squared is ten to the power of 88,031,394,529,280; that squared is ten to the power of 176,062,789,058,560; that squared is ten to the power of 352,125,578,117,120; that squared is ten to the power of 704,251,156,234,240; that squared is ten to the power of 1,408,502,302,468,480; that squared is ten to the power of 2,817,004,604,936,960; that squared is ten to the power of 5,634,009,209,893,920; that squared is ten to the power of 11,268,018,419,747,840; that squared is ten to the power of 22,536,036,839,495,680; that squared is ten to the power of 45,072,073,678,991,360; that squared is ten to the power of 90,144,147,357,982,720; that squared is ten to the power of 180,288,294,715,965,440; that squared is ten to the power of 360,576,589,431,930,880; that squared is ten to the power of 721,153,178,863,861,760; that squared is ten to the power of 1,442,306,357,727,723,520; that squared is ten to the power of 2,884,612,715,455,447,040; that squared is ten to the power of 5,769,225,430,910,894,080; that squared is ten to the power of 11,538,450,861,821,788,160; that squared is ten to the power of 23,076,901,773,643,576,320; that squared is ten to the power of 46,153,803,447,287,152,640; that squared is ten to the power of 92,307,606,894,574,305,280; that squared is ten to the power of 184,615,213,789,148,610,560; that squared is ten to the power of 369,230,427,578,297,221,120; that squared is ten to the power of 738,460,895,156,594,442,240; that squared is ten to the power of 1,476,921,790,313,188,884,480; that squared is ten to the power of 2,953,843,580,626,377,768,960; that squared is ten to the power of 5,907,687,161,252,755,537,920; that squared is ten to the power of 11,815,374,322,505,511,065,840; that squared is ten to the power of 23,630,748,645,011,022,131,680; that squared is ten to the power of 42,261,497,290,022,044,263,360; that squared is ten to the power of 94,522,994,580,044,088,526,720; that squared is ten to the power of 189,045,989,160,088,177,053,520; that squared is ten to the power of 378,091,978,320,176,354,107,040; that squared is ten to the power of 756,183,956,640,352,708,214,080; that squared is ten to the power of 1,512,367,913,280,705,416,428,160; that squared is ten to the power of 3,024,735,826,561,410,832,856,220; that squared is ten to the power of 6,049,71,653,122,821,665,712,640; that squared is ten to the power of 12,98,943,306,245,643,331,425,280; that squared is ten to the power of 24,197,886,612,491,286,462,850,560; that squared is ten to the power of 48,395,773,224,982,672,925,701,120; that squared is ten to the power of 96,791,546,449,965,145,831,402,340; that squared is ten to the power of 193,583,092,899,930,291,662,804,480; that squared is ten to the power of 387,166,185,799,860,583,325,608,960; that squared is ten to the power of 774,332,371,599,721,166,651,217,920; that squared is ten to the power of 1,548,664,743,199,442,333,302,635,840; that squared is ten to the power of 3,097,329,486,398,884,666,605,271,680; that squared is ten to the power of 6,194,658,972,797,769,333,210,543,360; that squared is ten to the power of 12,389,317,945,595,538,666,421, 086,720; that squared is ten to the power of 24,778,635,891,191,077, 332,842,173,440; that squared is ten to the power of 49,557,271,782, 382,154,665,686,346,880; that squared is ten of the power of 99,114, 543,564,764,309,331,372,693,760; that squared is ten to the power of 198,229,087,129,528,618,662,745,387,520; that squared is ten to the power of 396,458,174,259,057,237,325,490,775,040; that squared is ten to the power of 792,916,348,518,114,474,650,981,550,080; that squared is ten to the power of 1,585,832,697,036,228,949,301,963,100,160; that squared is ten to the power of 3,171,665,394,072,457,898,603,926,200, 320; that squared is ten to the power of 6,343,330,788,144,915,797, 207,852,400,640; that squared is ten to the power of 12,686,661,576, 289,831,594,415,704,801,280; that squared is ten to the power of 25, 373,323,152,579,663,188,831,409,602,560; that squared is ten to the power of 50,746,646,305,159,326,377,662,819,205,120; that squared is ten to the power of 101,493,292,610,318,652,755,325,638,410,240; that squared is an incalculable; an incalculable to the fourth power is a measureless; a measureless to the fourth power is a boundless; a boundless to the fourth power is an incomparable; an incomparable to the fourth power is an innumerable; an innumerable to the fourth power is an unaccountable; an unaccountable to the fourth power is an unthinkable; an unthinkable to the fourth power is an immeasurable; an immeasurable to the fourth power is an unspeakable; an unspeakable to the fourth power is an untold, which is unspeakably unspeakable; an untold multiplied by itself is a square untold."

Then the Buddha spoke these verses to the enlightening being Mind King:

Untold unspeakables
Fill all unspeakables;
In unspeakable eons
Explanation of the unspeakable cannot be finished.

If untold buddha-lands are reduced to atoms,
In one atom are untold lands,
And as in one,
So in each.

The atoms to which these buddha-lands are reduced in an instant
    are unspeakable,
And so are the atoms of continuous reduction moment to
    moment
Going on for untold eons;
These atoms contain lands unspeakably many,
And the atoms in these lands are even harder to tell of.

Counting this way for unspeakable eons,
Using unspeakable numbers,
Counting eons by these atoms,
One atom standing for ten myriad unspeakable numbers of eons,
If you praise a single Universally Good for that many eons,
It would still be impossible to exhaust the amount of virtue of
    Universal Good.

On a point the size of the tip of a single fine hair
Are unspeakably many Universally Goods;
The same is true of all points
All throughout the cosmos.

The lands on a point the size of a hairtip
Are measureless, unspeakable;
So are the lands on every single point
Throughout the whole of space.

The lands on those points
Have innumerable different kinds of abode;
There are untold lands of different kinds,
Untold lands of the same kind.

On untold points of hairtip size
Are untold pure lands,
Their various arrays unspeakable,
Their various wonders unspeakable:
On each point in them
Are recited untold buddha-names,
There being to each and every name
Untold numbers of buddhas.

On the body of each buddha
Appear unspeakably many pores;
In each of these pores
They manifest unspeakably many forms.

The unspeakably many pores
Each radiate unspeakably many beams of light;

In each of those beams of light
Appear unspeakably many lotuses;
In each of those lotuses
Are unspeakably many petals;
In each of those petals
Appear unspeakably many forms;
In those untold forms
Also appear untold petals;
In the petals are untold light rays,
In the light rays untold forms;
In each of those untold forms
Appear untold lights;
In the lights appear untold moons,
And the moons also manifest untold moons;
In each of those untold moons
Appear untold beams of light;
In each of those light beams
Also appear untold suns;
In each of those untold suns
Are manifest untold forms;
And in each of those forms again
Are manifest untold rays of light;
In each of those rays of light
Appear untold lion thrones,
Each with untold ornaments,
Each with untold lights,
With untold beautiful forms in the lights,
With untold pure lights in the forms;
In each of those pure lights
Also appear various subtle lights;
These lights also radiate various lights,
Untold, unspeakably many.
In each of these various lights
Appear wondrous jewels like mountains;
The jewels appearing in each light
Are unspeakably many, untold.

One of those mountainlike jewels
Manifests untold lands;
All of the mountainlike jewels
Manifest lands like this.

Reducing one land to atoms,
The forms in each atom are untold;
All of the lands atomized, each atom's forms
Are unspeakably many, untold.

These various forms in atoms
All produce untold lights;
In each light appear untold buddhas.
Untold are each buddha's discourses,
In each discourse are untold sublime verses;
Untold are those who gain understanding on hearing them.
Untold understandings in each mental instant
Reveal unspeakably many truths.

They reveal all future buddhas,
Externally expounding their teachings,
Each buddha's teachings unspeakably many,
With untold purities of all sorts.

Uttering unspeakably many subtle voices,
Turning untold cycles of true teaching,
In each cycle of teaching
Expounding unspeakably many scriptures,
In each scripture
Defining unspeakably many doctrines,
In each of those doctrines
Explaining unspeakably many principles,
With each of those principles
Taming untold sentient beings.

Then again, on a single point
Buddhas may dwell for untold eons,
And as on one point, so on all points,
For the same number of eons,
The nonobstruction of their minds unspeakable,
Emanating unspeakably many buddhas,
Each emanation buddha
Also manifesting untold emanations.

The reality bodies of those buddhas are unspeakably many,
The emanated bodies of those buddhas are unspeakably many,
Their adornments are unspeakably measureless.
They travel infinitely through the ten directions,
Coursing through untold lands,
Observing untold sentient beings,
Purifying untold sentient beings,
Taming untold sentient beings.

Their embellishments are unspeakable,
Their masteries are unspeakable,
Their mystic transformations are unspeakable,

Their spiritual powers are unspeakable,
Their spheres are unspeakable,
Their empowerments are unspeakable,
The worlds they live in are unspeakable,
Their pure characteristics of reality are unspeakable.

They deliver untold discourses,
In each and every discourse
Expounding untold doctrines,
In each and every doctrine
Explaining untold principles,
Each and every principle
Containing untold definitions,
Each and every definition
Conquering untold beings.

Unspeakable homogeneous principles, unspeakable homogeneous
    minds,
Unspeakable heterogeneous principles, unspeakable heterogeneous
    minds,
Unspeakable heterogeneous faculties,
Unspeakable heterogeneous languages—
In every mental moment, wherever they go,
They tame unspeakable numbers of beings.

Their occult projections are unspeakable,
Their miraculous displays are unspeakable;
The times and ages therein are unspeakable,
The differentiations therein are unspeakable.

Enlightening beings can explain them in particular,
While mathematicians cannot comprehend them;
The great and small lands on a point,
Polluted, pure, gross, and subtle,
All of them unspeakably many,
Enlightening beings comprehend and can distinguish.

Reducing a land to atoms,
Those atoms are measureless, untold;
Boundless lands, as many as these atoms,
Are gathered on a single hairtip.

These lands, unspeakable,
Are together on a hairtip without crowding;
Without causing the hairtip to expand,
Those lands all gather there.

The lands therein
Retain their original form, without mixup;
Just as one land does not disorder the others,
The same is true of all lands.

The realms in space, without bound,
All are arrayed on a hairtip;
These lands on a hairtip
Enlightening beings can tell of in an instant.

Into a minute pore
Untold lands enter in succession;
The pore can admit those lands,
But those lands cannot fill the pore.

The number of eons of their entry is unspeakable,
The number of eons of their admission is unspeakable;
The durations of their procession, array, and abiding
Are all unspeakable eons.

Thus having taken in and settled these lands,
Enlightening beings' spheres are unspeakable;
Their devices during entry are unspeakable,
Their deeds after entry are unspeakable.

The clear comprehensions of their cognitive faculties are
    unspeakable,
Their journeys in all directions are unspeakable,
Their vigorous endeavors are unspeakable,
Their autonomous mystic transfigurations are unspeakable.

Their meditations are unspeakable.
Their great vows are unspeakable,
Their spheres of action are unspeakable,
All their attainments are unspeakable.

The purities of their physical actions are unspeakable,
The purities of their verbal actions are unspeakable,
The purities of their mental actions are unspeakable,
The purities of their resolutions are unspeakable.

The purities of their subtle knowledge are unspeakable,
The purities of their sublime wisdom are unspeakable,
Their perceptions of reality are unspeakable,
Their cessations of doubts are unspeakable.

Their escapes from birth and death are unspeakable,
Their ascents to the absolute state are unspeakable,
Their deep concentrations are unspeakable,
Their total comprehensions are unspeakable.

All sentient beings are unspeakable,
All buddha-lands are unspeakable,
Knowledge of sentient beings' forms is unspeakable,
Knowledge of their dispositions is unspeakable,
Knowledge of their deeds and the results is unspeakable,
Knowledge of their intellects is unspeakable,
Knowledge of their embodiments is unspeakable,
Knowledge of their types is unspeakable,
Knowledge of their species is unspeakable,
Knowledge of their birthplaces is unspeakable,
Knowledge of when they are born is unspeakable,
Knowledge of their having been born is unspeakable,
Knowledge of their understandings is unspeakable,
Knowledge of their tendencies is unspeakable,
Knowledge of their languages is unspeakable,
Knowledge of their works is unspeakable,

Enlightening beings with great compassion
Benefit all worldly beings,
Manifesting untold bodies everywhere,
Entering untold buddha-lands,
Seeing untold enlightening beings,
Developing untold knowledges,
Seeking untold teachings,
Broadcasting untold lessons of buddhas.

They manifest untold various bodies,
Traveling to untold lands,
Showing untold spiritual powers,
Pervading untold regions,
Emanating untold bodies in each place,
Approaching untold buddhas,
Making untold offerings
Of untold infinite varieties,
Untold pure clear jewels,
Untold beautiful lotus blossoms,
Untold garlands of the finest scent,
Offering them to untold enlightened ones,
Their pure faith untold,
Supreme resolution untold,

Powerful aspiration untold,
Honoring untold buddhas.

They practice untold generosity.
Their minds in the untold past
Giving to all who seek, untold,
Giving all, untold times.

The purities of their self-control are untold;
The purities of their minds are untold;
They eulogize untold buddhas,
Delight in untold truths.

They accomplish untold forbearances,
Their acceptance of nonorigination untold;
They embody untold tranquillities,
Dwelling in untold states of peace.

They exude untold energy,
Their past determinations untold,
Their irreversible aspiration untold,
Their immutable wills untold.

Their treasuries of all concentrations are untold;
They examine untold phenomena and principles,
Stilled in untold concentrations,
Mastering untold meditations.

Their attainments of wisdom are untold,
Their freedoms in concentration are untold,
Their comprehensions of things are untold,
Their clear visions of buddhas are untold.

They cultivate measureless, untold practices,
Undertake untold far-reaching vows;
Their profound spheres are untold,
Their pure means of teaching are untold.

The power of enlightening beings' ways is unspeakable,
The stations of enlightening beings' ways are unspeakable,
Their right recollection is unspeakable,
Their realms of principle and fact are unspeakable.

They cultivate unspeakably many means of enlightenment,
They study unspeakably many profound sciences;

Their immeasurable wisdom is unspeakable,
Their ultimate wisdom is unspeakable.

Their knowledge of things is unspeakable,
Their pure cycles of teaching are unspeakable,
Their great clouds of teachings are unspeakable,
Their great rain of teaching is unspeakable.

Their spiritual powers are unspeakably many,
Their techniques are unspeakably many,
Their knowledge of empty quiescence is unspeakable,
The continuity of mental instants is unspeakable.

Their measureless practices are unspeakable,
Their constancy instant to instant is unspeakable;
The oceans of buddha-lands are untold,
They can go to them all, unspeakably.

The differences in the lands are untold,
Their various purities are untold,
Their different adornments are untold,
Their boundless forms are untold.

Their various arrays are untold,
Their various refinements are untold;
Pure buddha-lands are unspeakably many,
Polluted buddha-lands are unspeakably many.

Knowing sentient beings is unspeakable,
Knowing their natures is unspeakable,
Knowing their deeds and rewards is unspeakable,
Knowing their mentalities is unspeakable.

Knowing beings' characters is unspeakable,
Knowing their understandings and inclinations is unspeakable;
Their defilement and purity are unspeakable,
Observing and civilizing them are unspeakable.

Transforming powers are unspeakable;
Manifesting various bodies, untold,
Cultivating untold energy,
Enlightening beings liberate untold sentient beings.

They manifest untold mystic transfigurations,
Emanate untold great beams of light,

With untold various forms,
And purify untold sentient beings.

Each of their pores, untold,
Radiate webs of light, untold,
The webs of light manifesting untold hues,
Illumining untold buddha-lands.

Their courage and fearlessness are untold,
Their technical skills are untold,
Taming untold sentient beings,
Emancipating them from birth and death.

Their pure deeds are untold,
Their pure words are untold,
Their boundless thoughts are untold,
Their sublime practices are untold.

They develop untold jewels of knowledge,
And enter untold realms of reality.
Enlightening beings' mnemonic powers are unutterable,
They are able to learn inexplicably.

The voices of the wise are untold,
The purity of their voices is unspeakable;
Their accurate awareness of reality is untold,
Their awakening of sentient beings is untold.

They embody untold dignified bearing;
Their pure actions are untold.
They achieve untold expertise
And educate untold worldlings.

The offspring of buddhas are unspeakably many
And so are their pure, excellent acts.
They eulogize untold buddhas,
Their praises inexhaustible, beyond telling.

The guides of the world are unspeakably many;
So are their expositions and descriptions.
Those enlightening beings are unspeakably many,
Their pure virtues untold.

Their spheres are unutterable,
They can remain there indefinitely,

Their knowledge therein untold;
They live through all ages, which none can ever tell.

They are gladdened by untold buddhas,
Their wisdom and equanimity are beyond speech;
They penetrate untold truths,
With untold freedom from obstruction amid phenomena.

Past, present, and future being like space, unspeakable,
Their knowledge of all times is untold;
Their comprehension of past, present, and future unutterable,
They dwell in knowledge beyond speech.

Their superlative actions are untold,
Their measureless vows are untold,
Their pure great vows are untold,
They accomplish ineffable enlightenment.

The enlightenment of the buddhas is inexpressible;
They develop untold knowledge,
Discern untold principles,
Know all laws,
Beautify untold buddha-lands,
And cultivate untold powers.

They cultivate practice for an unutterably long time,
And are ineffably enlightened in a single instant.
The buddhas' freedoms are unspeakable,
Their extensive explanations of truth cannot be recounted.

Their various spiritual powers are inexplicable,
They appear in untold worlds;
Their cycles of pure teaching are ineffable,
Their courageous ability to teach unspeakable,
Their various expositions unutterable,
Their compassion for the world cannot be told.

Through all eons, unspeakably many,
They praise untold merits and virtues;
While unspeakable eons may end,
Those untold virtues cannot be exhausted.

Untold enlightened ones
With untold tongues
Praise the untold virtues of buddhas,
Impossible to exhaust in untold eons.

The living beings in the ten directions
All attain enlightenment at once;
Therein one buddha can manifest to all
Untold embodiments,
Each of these untold bodies
Manifesting untold heads,
Each of these untold heads
Manifesting untold tongues,
Each of the untold tongues
Manifesting untold voices,
Each of the untold voices
Remaining for untold eons.

As is one, so are all buddhas;
As one body, so all bodies;
As one head, so all heads;
As one tongue, so all tongues;
As one voice, so all voices,
Ever praising the enlightened for untold eons;
The untold eons may end,
But praise of enlightened virtues cannot be exhausted.

In a single atom there can be
Untold lotus worlds;
In each lotus world
Are untold Chief of Goodness Buddhas,
Pervading the entire cosmos
And every atom therein.

Worlds, becoming, subsisting, and decaying,
Are measureless, unspeakable in number;
The point of a single atom is boundless,
Containing measureless lands therein.

The differentiations of the ten directions are unutterable,
The arrays of the oceans of worlds cannot be all told of;
In each land are buddhas
With life spans of unspeakable eons.

Those buddhas' deeds cannot be recounted,
Their profound teachings are unutterable,
Their great spiritual powers are ineffable,
Their unimpeded knowledge is inexpressible.

They enter into a point,
The events at that point untold;

They achieve the ten powers, unspeakable,
And awaken to ineffable enlightenment.

Entering untold realms of pure principle,
They gain untold treasuries of deep knowledge:
Various numerical measurements, untold,
They comprehend, all, as they are;
Various physical measurements, untold,
They completely master;
Various concentrations, untold,
They can pass eons in, each one.

In the presence of untold buddhas,
The purifications they practice are untold;
They attain unutterable mental freedoms
And journey in all directions, beyond the power of speech.

The manifestations of their spiritual powers are untold,
Their spheres of action are boundless, ineffable;
They go to untold lands
And understand untold buddhas.

Their vigor and courage are unspeakable,
Their knowledge and comprehension unutterable.
They do not act on rules, nor do they not act on them,
Their penetration of realms of objects is infinite.

For unreckonable vast eons
They travel constantly through the ten directions, infinitely.
Their knowledge of enlightening means is infinite,
Their knowledge of truth is infinite,
Their knowledge of spiritual powers is infinite,
Their miracles in each mental instant are infinite.

They comprehend infinitely each one
Of the infinite buddhas' teachings;
They can realize enlightenment at once
Or can enter realization at various times.

The buddha-lands on a hairtip are infinite,
The buddha-lands in an atom are infinite;
They can go to all these buddha-lands
And see the infinite buddhas.

They realize one truth infinitely,
And enter the infinite line of buddhas.

The buddhas' lands are infinite—
They can travel to all and attain enlightenment.

The lands, beings, and buddhas
Have infinite distinctions in individuality;
As such, past, present, and future worlds are boundless:
Enlightening beings can see them all.

BOOK THIRTY-ONE

Life Span

THEN THE ENLIGHTENING BEING Mind King, in the congregation, said to all the enlightening beings, "Offspring of Buddha, one eon in this world Endurance, the field of Shakyamuni Buddha, is a day and a night in the world Bliss, the field of Amitabha Buddha; one eon in the world of Bliss is a day and night in the world Vestment Banner, the field of the Buddha Adamant; one eon in the world Vestment Banner is a day and night in the world Wheel of Speech Which Does Not Roll Back, the field of the Buddha Lotus Blossoms of Sublime Light Blooming; one eon in the world Wheel of Speech Which Does Not Roll Back is a day and night in the world Free from Defilement, the field of the Buddha Banner of Truth; an eon in the world Free from Defilement is a day and night in the world Good Lamp, the field of the Buddha Lion; an eon in the world Good Lamp is a day and night in the world Subtle Light, the field of the Buddha Treasury of Light; an eon in the world Subtle Light is a day and night in the world Hard to Surpass, the field of the Buddha Blooming Lotus of Light of Truth; an eon in the world Hard to Surpass is a day and night in the world Adorning Wisdom, the field of the Buddha Light of All Spiritual Powers; an eon in the world Adorning Wisdom is a day and night in the world Mirror Light, the field of the Buddha Moon Knowledge: this succession goes on past a million zillion worlds; an eon in the last of these worlds is a day and a night in the world Supreme Lotus, the field of the Buddha Supreme in Goodness, which is filled by the enlightening being Universally Good and the great enlightening beings engaged in the same practice."

BOOK THIRTY-TWO

Dwelling Places of Enlightening Beings

THEN THE GREAT ENLIGHTENING BEING Mind King said to the enlightening beings, "In the east there is a place called Wizard Mountain where enlightening beings have lived since ancient times. At present there is an enlightening being named Best of Diamonds there with a group of followers, three hundred enlightening beings, always there expounding the Teaching. In the south there is a place called Outstanding Peak, where enlightening beings have dwelled since ancient times. Now there is an enlightening being named Spiritual Wisdom there with a group of followers, five hundred enlightening beings, always there expounding the Teaching. In the west there is a place called Diamond Flame Mountain, where enlightening beings have lived since ancient times. Now there is an enlightening being named Vigorous Fearless Action there with a following of three hundred enlightening beings, always expounding the Teaching. In the north there is a place called Mass of Fragrance Mountain, where enlightening beings have lived since ancient times; now there is an enlightening being named Musky Elephant there with a following of three thousand enlightening beings, always expounding the Teaching. In the northeast there is a place called Clear, Cool Mountain, where enlightening beings have lived since ancient times; now there is an enlightening being there named Manjushri, with a following of ten thousand enlightening beings, always expounding the Teaching. In the ocean there is a place called Diamond Mountain, where enlightening beings have lived since ancient times; now there is an enlightening being named Born of Truth there with a following of twelve hundred enlightening beings, always expounding the Teaching. In the southeast there is a place called Monument Mountain, where enlightening beings have lived since ancient times; now there is an enlightening being named Celestial Crown there with a following of a thousand enlightening beings, always expounding the Teaching. In the southwest there is a place called Mountain of Light, where enlightening beings have lived since ancient times; now there is an enlightening being named Best of Sages there with a following of three thousand enlightening beings, always expounding the Teaching. In the northwest there is a place called Fragrant Breeze Mountain, where enlightening beings have lived since ancient times; now there is an enlightening being named Fragrant Light there with a following of five thousand enlightening beings, always expounding the Teaching.

"In the ocean there is also a dwelling place called Cave of Adornments, where enlightening beings have lived since ancient times. South of Vaishali there is a dwelling place called Stable Roots, where enlightening beings have stayed since ancient times. In the city of Mathura there is a dwelling place called Cave of Satisfaction, where enlightening beings have lived since ancient times. In the city of Kuchana there is a dwelling place called Seat of the Law, where enlightening beings have lived since ancient times. In the city Pure Other Shore there is a dwelling place called Mucilinda, where enlightening beings have lived since ancient times. In the state of Maratha there is a dwelling place called Built by the Uninhibited Dragon King, where enlightening beings have lived since ancient times. In Afghanistan there is a dwelling place called Producing Compassion, where enlightening beings have lived since ancient times. In China there is a dwelling place called Cave of Original Man, where enlightening beings have lived since ancient times. In Kashgar there is a dwelling place called Oxhead Mountain, where enlightening beings have lived since ancient times. In Kashmir there is a dwelling place called Process, where enlightening beings have lived since ancient times. In the city of Increasing Joy there is a dwelling place called Seeing a Hundred Million Treasuries of Light, where enlightening beings have lived since ancient times. In the state of Gandhara there is a place called Shangrila Cavern, where enlightening beings have lived since ancient times."

BOOK THIRTY-THREE

Inconceivable Qualities of Buddhas

AT THAT TIME there were in the assembly enlightening beings who were thinking, "How are the buddhas' lands inconceivable? How are the buddhas' original vows inconceivable? How are the families of buddhas inconceivable? How are the manifestations of buddhas inconceivable? How are the bodies of buddhas inconceivable? How are the voices of buddhas inconceivable? How are the knowledge and wisdom of buddhas inconceivable? How are the freedoms of buddhas inconceivable? How is the nonobstruction of buddhas inconceivable? How is the liberation of buddhas inconceivable?"

The Buddha, knowing what the enlightening beings were thinking, used the support of spiritual power, the embrace of knowledge, the radiance of light, and the fulfillment of occult force to cause the enlightening being Blue Lotus Blossom Trove to abide in the nonhesitation of buddhas, enter the reality realm of buddhas, acquire the mystic power and psychic freedom of buddhas, attain the unimpeded, immensely broad insight of buddhas, know the succession of all lineages of buddhas, and abide by the untold means of buddhas' teachings. Thereupon that enlightening being was able to commune with the unobstructed realm of reality, thus was able calmly to sustain profound practice free from impediments, thus was able to fulfill the great vow of universal good, thus was able to know and perceive all aspects of buddhahood. With great compassion he observed sentient beings, wishing to cause them to be pure and diligent in self-cultivation, to accept and apply all the principles of enlightening beings. In a single mental instant he produced enlightened knowledge and understood all the inexhaustible means of knowledge, his mnemonic command and intellectual powers complete.

By the power of Buddha he said to the enlightening being Lotus Blossom Calyx, "The buddhas, World Honored Ones, have innumerable abodes—the abode of eternity, the abode of great compassion, the abode of various bodies performing buddha-work, the abode of equanimously turning the wheel of the pure Teaching, the abode of explaining innumerable principles by means of analytic knowledge, the abode of the inconceivable qualities of all buddhas, the abode of the sound of purity pervading infinite lands, the abode of the inexpressibly profound realm of reality, the abode of manifesting all supreme spiritual powers—and are able to reveal the ultimate truth that has no barrier.

"The buddhas have ten things that pervade the infinite cosmos. What are these ten? All buddhas have unbounded bodies, with pure forms, entering into all states of being without defilement or attachment. All buddhas have unbounded, unobstructed eyes that can clearly see all things. All buddhas have unbounded, unobstructed ears that can understand all sounds and utterances. All buddhas have unbounded, unobstructed noses that can reach the other shore of freedom of the buddhas. All buddhas have universal tongues that utter sublime sounds pervading the cosmos. All buddhas have unbounded bodies that appear to sentient beings in accord with their minds. All buddhas have unbounded minds that dwell on the unobstructed impartial body of reality. All buddhas have unbounded, unobstructed liberation, manifesting inexhaustible great spiritual powers. All buddhas have unbounded pure worlds, manifesting buddha-lands according to the pleasures of sentient beings, replete with infinite adornments, yet without giving rise to any obsession or attachment to them. All buddhas have unbounded practical undertakings of enlightening beings, having complete knowledge, spiritual freedom, and ability to master all elements of buddhahood. These are the ten phenomena of buddhahood that pervade the cosmos without bound, which are in the perfectly enlightened ones.

"The buddhas have ten kinds of instantly creative knowledge. What are these ten? All buddhas can, in a single instant, appear to descend from heaven in infinite worlds. All buddhas can, in a single instant, manifest birth as enlightening beings in infinite worlds. All buddhas can, in a single instant, manifest renunciation of the mundane and study of the way to liberation in infinite worlds. All buddhas can, in a single instant, manifest attainment of true enlightenment under enlightenment trees in infinite worlds. All buddhas can, in a single instant, manifest turning the wheel of the Teaching in infinite worlds. All buddhas can, in a single instant, manifest education of sentient beings and service of the enlightened in infinite worlds. All buddhas can, in a single instant, manifest untold variety of buddha-bodies in infinite worlds. All buddhas can, in a single instant, manifest all kinds of adornments in infinite worlds, innumerable adornments, the freedoms of the enlightened, and the treasury of omniscience. All buddhas can, in a single instant, manifest countless pure beings in infinite worlds. All buddhas can, in a single instant, manifest the buddhas of past, present, and future in infinite worlds, with various faculties and characters, various energies, and various practical understandings, attaining true enlightenment in the past, present, and future.

"The buddhas have ten kinds of proper timing. What are these ten?

All buddhas develop and mature those with affinity at the appropriate time. All buddhas give enlightening beings instructions for the future at the proper time. All buddhas show spiritual powers in accord with sentient beings' minds at the proper time. All buddhas show buddha-bodies in accord with sentient beings' understandings at the proper time. All buddhas persist in great relinquishment at the proper time. All buddhas go into inhabited places at the appropriate time. All buddhas receive the pure and faithful at the proper time. All buddhas tame evil sentient beings at the appropriate time. All buddhas reveal the inconceivable occult powers of the enlightened at the proper time.

"The buddhas have ten peerless inconceivable realms. What are they? All buddhas, once sitting, pervade infinite worlds in the ten directions. All buddhas, uttering one logical statement, can express all Buddha teachings. All buddhas, emanating one light, can illumine all worlds. All buddhas, in one body, can manifest all bodies. All buddhas can show all worlds in one place. All buddhas can ascertain all things within one knowledge without any impediment. All buddhas can travel to all worlds in the ten directions in a single moment of thought. All buddhas can manifest the infinite spiritual powers of the enlightened in a single instant. All buddhas can focus on all the buddhas and sentient beings of past, present, and future in a single instant without confusion of mind. All buddhas are in one instant essentially the same as all buddhas of past, future, and present.

"The buddhas can produce ten kinds of knowledge. What are they? All buddhas know all things have no aim, yet they can produce knowledge of dedicated undertaking. All buddhas know all things have no body, yet they can produce knowledge of pure bodies. All buddhas know all things are fundamentally nondual, yet they can produce knowledge capable of awareness and understanding. All buddhas know all things have no self and no being, yet they can produce knowledge to civilize beings. All buddhas know all things fundamentally have no marks, yet they can produce knowledge of all marks. All buddhas know all worlds have no becoming or decay, yet they can produce knowledge of becoming and decay. All buddhas know all things have no creation, yet they can produce knowledge of the effects of action. All buddhas know all things have no verbal explanation, yet they can produce knowledge of verbal explanation. All buddhas know all things have no defilement or purity, yet they can produce knowledge of defilement and purity. All buddhas know all things have no birth or extinction, yet they can produce knowledge of birth and extinction.

"The buddhas have ten kinds of ways of entry into universality. What are they? All buddhas have immaculate bodies that penetrate past, present, and future. All buddhas are endowed with three kinds of mastery—of diagnosis, prescription, and occult powers—by which they edify beings everywhere. All buddhas are endowed with mnemonic powers able to receive and hold all Buddha teachings. All buddhas are endowed with four special knowledges—of principles, meanings, expressions, and elocution—and operate all cycles of pure teaching everywhere. All buddhas have impartial great compassion and never abandon all sentient beings. All buddhas have profound meditation concentration and always observe all sentient beings everywhere. All buddhas have roots of goodness beneficial to others, and civilize sentient beings unceasingly. All buddhas have unobstructed minds, able to abide calmly in all universes. All buddhas have unimpeded spiritual powers and are able to manifest the buddhas of past, present, and future in one instant. All buddhas have unobstructed intellect, in a single instant defining sets of ages of past, present, and future.

"Buddhas have ten great qualities that are hard to believe in. What are they? All buddhas can destroy all demons. All buddhas can overcome all false teachers. All buddhas can tame all sentient beings and make them all happy. All buddhas can go to all worlds and guide the myriad types of beings there. All buddhas can knowingly experience the most profound realm of reality. All buddhas can, by means of a nondual body, manifest various bodies, filling the world. All buddhas can, with pure voices, produce the special knowledges of principle, meaning, expression, and elocution, and expound truths endlessly, to the unfailing benefit of those who accept. All buddhas can manifest buddhas as numerous as atoms in all worlds in a single pore, without end. All buddhas can manifest in a single atom as many lands as atoms in all worlds, replete with all kinds of fine adornments, and continuously turn the wheel of the sublime Teaching therein for the edification of sentient beings—yet the atom is not enlarged and the worlds are not small; they always abide in the realm of reality by realizational knowledge. All buddhas arrive at the pure realm of reality, shatter the darkness of ignorance of the world by means of the light of knowledge, cause all to gain understanding of the Buddha teachings, follow the enlightened, and dwell in the ten powers.

"The buddhas have ten kinds of great virtue that are impeccably pure. What are they? All buddhas are endowed with great spiritual power, impeccably pure. All buddhas are born in the families of the enlightened ones of past, present, and future, of people harmonious and good, impeccably pure. All buddhas' minds are free from obsession forever, impeccably pure. All buddhas are free from attachment to anything in the past, present, or future, impeccably pure. All buddhas know all kinds of natures are one nature, coming from nowhere, impeccably pure. All buddhas' virtues, past, present, and future, are inexhaustible, equal to the cosmos, impeccably pure. All buddhas' boundless physical forms pervade all lands of the ten directions, teaching all sentient beings at the appropriate times, with impeccable purity. All buddhas acquire the fourfold fearlessness, are freed from all fears, and roar the great lion's roar among the masses, clearly discerning all things, impeccably pure. All the buddhas enter final nirvana in untold ages, and when sentient beings hear their names they gain immeasurable benefit, same as if the buddhas were presently existing, impeccably pure. All buddhas, though in untold distant worlds, can be seen by sentient beings who correctly meditate on them single-mindedly, impeccably pure.

"The buddhas have ten kinds of ultimate purity. What are they? All buddhas' past great vows are ultimately pure. The religious conduct maintained by all buddhas is ultimately pure. All buddhas' separation from the confusions of worldly beings is ultimately pure. All buddhas' adorned lands are ultimately pure. All buddhas' followings are ultimately pure. All buddhas' families are ultimately pure. All buddhas' physical characteristics and refinements are ultimately pure. The non-defilement of the reality-body of all buddhas is ultimately pure. All buddhas' omniscient knowledge, without obstruction, is ultimately pure. All buddhas' liberation, freedom, accomplishment of their tasks, and arrival at completion are ultimately pure.

"Buddhas have ten kinds of buddha-work in all worlds in all times. What are they? If there are sentient beings who think of them single-mindedly, the buddhas appear before them. If there are sentient beings whose minds are unruly, they explain the Teaching to them. If there are sentient beings able to develop pure faith, they will surely cause them to acquire immeasurable roots of goodness. If there are sentient beings able to enter the ranks of truth, they will appear to testify to it, so that they know all. They teach and influence sentient beings tirelessly. They travel to all buddha-lands, coming and going without impediment. With great compassion they do not abandon sentient beings. They manifest transfigured emanation bodies, continuing forever. Their exercise of spiritual powers is ceaseless. They abide in the cosmos of reality, able to observe everywhere.

"Buddhas have ten kinds of virtues of inexhaustible oceans of knowledge. What are they? The virtue of the inexhaustible ocean of knowledge of the boundless body of reality of all buddhas; the virtue of the inexhaustible ocean of knowledge of the infinite buddha-works of all buddhas; the virtue of the inexhaustible ocean of knowledge of the sphere of the enlightened eye of all buddhas; the virtue of the inexhaustible ocean of knowledge of the infinite, inconceivable roots of goodness of all buddhas; the virtue of the inexhaustible ocean of knowledge of all buddhas showering all liberating teachings everywhere; the virtue of the inexhaustible ocean of knowledge of all buddhas extolling the qualities of enlightenment; the virtue of the inexhaustible ocean of knowledge of the various undertakings and practices carried out by all buddhas in the past; the virtue of the inexhaustible ocean of knowledge of the eternal performance of buddha-work by all buddhas; the virtue of the inexhaustible ocean of knowledge of all buddhas comprehending the mental patterns of all sentient beings; the virtue of the inexhaustible ocean of knowledge of the unsurpassable adornments of virtue and knowledge of all buddhas.

"Buddhas have ten kinds of eternal law. What are they? All buddhas always carry out all the transcendent ways. All buddhas are always free from confusion in regard to all things. All buddhas always have universal compassion. All buddhas always have the ten powers. All buddhas always turn the wheel of the Teaching. All buddhas always demonstrate the accomplishment of true awakening for the benefit of sentient beings. All buddhas always gladly lead all sentient beings. All buddhas always correctly remember the truth of nonduality. All buddhas, after having taught sentient beings, always show entry into nirvana without remainder, because the realm of the buddhas has no bounds.

"Buddhas have ten kinds of exposition of the innumerable facets of the Teaching of the buddhas. What are they? All buddhas expound innumerable facets of the realms of sentient beings. All buddhas expound innumerable facets of the activities of sentient beings. All buddhas expound innumerable facets of effects of acts of sentient beings. All buddhas expound innumerable facets of teaching sentient beings. All buddhas expound innumerable facets of purifying sentient beings. All buddhas expound innumerable facets of vows of enlightening beings. All buddhas expound innumerable facets of practices of enlightening beings. All buddhas expound innumerable facets of the ages of becoming and decay of all worlds. All buddhas expound innumerable facets of enlightening beings devotedly purifying buddha-lands. All buddhas expound innumerable facets of the successive emergence in each age of the past, present, and future buddhas in innumerable worlds. All buddhas expound the ways of knowledge of all buddhas.

"Buddhas have ten kinds of performance of buddha-work for sentient beings. What are they? All buddhas manifest physical forms to do buddha-work for sentient beings. All buddhas make subtle utterances to do buddha-work for sentient beings. All buddhas accept things to do buddha-work for sentient beings. All buddhas accept nothing to do buddha-work for sentient beings. All buddhas do buddha-work for sentient beings by means of earth, water, fire, and air. All buddhas magically show all realms of objects to do buddha-work for sentient beings. All buddhas do buddha-work for sentient beings by various names and epithets. All buddhas do buddha-work for sentient beings by means of the realms of objects of buddha-lands. All buddhas adorn and purify buddha-lands to do buddha-work for sentient beings. All buddhas do buddha-work for sentient beings silently, without words.

"Buddhas have ten kinds of supreme qualities. What are they? All buddhas' great vows are firm and steadfast and cannot be broken; they do what they say without fail, and there is no duplicity in their words. All buddhas tirelessly practice the deeds of enlightening beings throughout all future ages, in order to perfect and fulfill all virtues. All buddhas will go to untold worlds in order to guide a single sentient being, and do the same for all sentient beings, endlessly. All buddhas universally regard both faithful and scornful beings with great compassion, impartially, without any discrimination. All buddhas, from their initial aspiration to their attainment of buddhahood, never lose the determination for perfect enlightenment. All buddhas accumulate immeasurable virtues and dedicate them all to omniscience, with never any attachment to the world or its creatures. All buddhas learn physical, verbal, and mental practices from buddhas, only carrying out buddha-practice, not the practice of the vehicles of individual liberation, all to be dedicated to omniscience, to attain unexcelled true enlightenment. All buddhas emanate great light, that light impartially illumining all places, and illuminating all the buddhas' teachings, enabling enlightening beings' minds to become purified and to fulfill universal knowledge. All buddhas give up worldly pleasures, without craving or attachment, and wish that all worldlings would be free from suffering and attain bliss, and have no false ideas. All buddhas, out of compassion for sentient beings, undergo all kinds of hardship, preserving the seed of buddhahood, course in the sphere of buddhahood, leave birth and death, and arrive at the stage of the ten powers.

"Buddhas remain unhindered in ten ways. What are they? All buddhas can travel to all worlds, remaining unhindered. All buddhas can walk, stand, sit, and recline in all worlds, remaining unhindered. All buddhas can abide in all worlds, remaining unhindered. All buddhas can expound the truth in all worlds, remaining unhindered. All buddhas can abide in the heaven of contentment in all worlds, remaining unhindered. All buddhas are able to enter all the pasts, presents, and futures of the cosmos, remaining unhindered. All buddhas are able to sit at all enlightenment sites in the cosmos, remaining unhindered. All buddhas are able to observe the mental patterns of all sentient beings in each moment of thought, and use their powers of diagnosis, prescription, and occult effects to teach and tune them, remaining unhindered. All buddhas are able to sojourn at the places of innumerable buddhas with one body, and in all places, benefiting living beings, remaining unhindered. All buddhas are able to expound true teachings spoken by infinite buddhas, remaining unhindered.

"Buddhas have ten kinds of supreme adornment. What are they? All buddhas have all the marks and refinements of greatness—this is the first, buddhas' supreme physical adornment. All buddhas have sixty kinds of vocal sound, each with five hundred elements, each element with countless hundreds of thousands of pure, clear tones adorning it, and they are able, in the midst of all groups in the cosmos, without any qualms or fears, to roar the great lion's roar, expounding the meaning of the extremely profound teaching of the enlightened, so that all who hear are delighted and are edified according to their faculties and inclinations—this is the second, buddhas' supreme adornment of speech. All buddhas are endowed with the ten powers, the great concentrations, and the eighteen unique qualities, adorning their mental activity; in their sphere of operation, they comprehend and master all enlightening principles without obstruction, and all attain the adornments of the all-inclusive cosmos of reality as their adornment; they are able to clearly perceive in a single instant the mental patterns, past, present, and future, each different, of the beings of the cosmos—this is the third, the supreme mental adornment of buddhas. All buddhas are able to emanate countless beams of light, each beam of light accompanied by untold webs of light, illumining all buddha-lands, destroying the darkness in all worlds, revealing the emergence of innumerable buddhas, their bodies equal, all pure, their buddha-works all effective, able to cause sentient beings to reach nonregression—this is the fourth, buddhas' supreme adornment of light. When the buddhas smile, zillions of rays of light radiate from their faces, each light having innumerable, inconceivably many hues of all kinds, lighting up all the worlds in the ten directions; among the masses they utter truthful words, giving innumerable, countless, inconceivably many sentient beings directions for supreme complete perfect enlightenment—this is the fifth, buddhas' supreme adornment of a smile, free from the delusion and confusion of the world. All buddhas have the reality-body, pure, unobstructed, with ultimate comprehension of all truths, abiding in the cosmos of reality, without bounds, though being in the world, not getting mixed up in the world, understanding the true nature of the world, acting on transmundane principles, beyond the power of speech, transcending the realms of matter and sense—this is the sixth, the buddhas' supreme adornment of the reality-body. All buddhas have infinite constant subtle lights with untold colors of all kinds adorning them, forming a treasury of light producing infinite orbs of light illuminating the ten directions without obstruction—this is the seventh, buddhas' supreme adornment of constant subtle light. All buddhas have boundless sublime forms, delightful sublime forms, pure sublime forms, sublime forms that appear in accordance with the mind, forms that outshine all in the realms of desire, form, and formlessness, unexcelled sublime forms arriving at the other shore—this is the eighth, buddhas' supreme adornment of sublime forms. All buddhas are born in the family of the buddhas of past, present, and future, accumulate myriad treasures of virtue, ultimately pure, without fault, impeccable, being adorned by the most pure, refined acts among all things, fully accomplishing total knowledge and character beyond reproach—this is the ninth, buddhas' supreme adornment of human character. All buddhas array themselves with the power of great compassion, ultimately pure, without any cravings, their physical actions forever at rest, their minds well liberated, so that none tire of seeing them, saving all worldly beings, the foremost fields of blessing, the most worthy recipients, mercifully helping all sentient beings to develop stores of unlimited virtue and knowledge—this is the tenth, buddhas' supreme adornment of the qualities of great kindness and compassion.

"Buddhas have ten kinds of mastery. What are they? All buddhas have command of all the teachings, clearly comprehend all kinds of bodies of expression and nuance, and explain all things with unhindered intellect—this is the first mastery of buddhas. All buddhas teach sentient beings without ever missing the appropriate timing, endlessly explaining the right teaching to them in accord with their states of mind, causing them all to become receptive to truth—this is the second mastery of buddhas. All buddhas are able to cause all worlds throughout space, arrayed in countless different ways, to quake in six ways, causing those worlds to rise or fall, to expand or contract, to combine or dissolve, without ever harming a single living being, the creatures in those worlds being unaware, not cognizant of this happening, not even suspecting it—this is the third mastery of buddhas. All buddhas are able to beautify and purify all worlds by means of spiritual powers, in the space of an instant manifesting the adornments of all worlds, these adornments beyond recounting even in countless eons, all free from defilement, incomparably pure; all the adornments and purities of all buddha-fields they cause to equally enter one field—this is the fourth mastery of buddhas. All buddhas, seeing a single sentient being capable of being taught, extend their lives indefinitely for that being, sitting without fatigue of body or mind, concentrating single-mindedly on that being, without ever becoming heedless or forgetful, guiding that being by appropriate means, with appropriate timing, and also do the same for all living beings as they do for one—this is the fifth mastery of buddhas. All buddhas can go to all worlds, to the realms of action of all enlightened ones, without ever leaving behind any phenomenal realms, the ten directions each different, there being in each direction incalculable oceans of worlds, there being in each ocean of worlds incalculable world systems; by spiritual powers buddhas reach all of them in a single instant, and turn the wheel of the unobstructed pure Teaching—this is the sixth mastery of buddhas. All buddhas, in order to civilize all sentient beings, attain unexcelled complete perfect enlightenment in each mental instant, yet in regard to all elements of buddhahood, they have not already cognized them, do not cognize them, and are not yet to cognize them, and also do not dwell in the stage of learning, yet they know them all, see them all, mastering them without hindrance; with immeasurable knowledge and freedom they teach and tame all sentient beings—this is buddhas' seventh mastery. All buddhas can do the buddha-work of the ears with their eyes, can do the buddha-work of the nose with the ears, can do the buddha-work of the tongue with the nose, can do the buddha-work of the body with the tongue, can do the buddha-work of the mind with the body, and with the mind can sojourn in all kinds of realms, mundane and transcendental, in all worlds, able to perform immeasurable great buddha-works in each realm—this is buddhas' eighth mastery. All buddhas can contain all sentient beings in each pore of their bodies, each sentient being's body equal to untold buddha-lands, yet there is no crowding; each sentient being can pass countless worlds with every step and go on for countless eons, seeing all the buddhas emerging in the world and edifying beings, turning the wheel of the pure Teaching, showing untold phenomena of past, future, and present, the embodiments of sentient beings in various realms of existence throughout space, their comings and goings and deportment, their needs all fully supplied, yet without any obstruction therein—this is buddhas' ninth mastery. All buddhas, in the space of an instant, manifest as many buddhas as atoms in all worlds, each buddha attaining enlightenment in all universes, sitting on a lotus lion throne in a world of vast arrays of exquisite lotus blossoms, showing the miraculous powers of buddhas, and as in the world of vast arrays of exquisite lotus blossoms, so in untold worlds in all universes, variously arrayed, with various realms of objects, various shapes and forms, various manifestations, various numbers of ages, and as in one instant so in each instant of immeasurable, boundless, incalculable eons, all appearing in one instant, with infinite abodes in one instant, yet without using the slightest power of expedient means—this is buddhas' tenth mastery.

"Buddhas have ten kinds of measureless, inconceivable ways of fulfillment of buddhahood. What are they? The pure features of all buddhas each contain a hundred blessings. All buddhas accomplish all Buddha teachings. All buddhas perfect all roots of goodness. All buddhas perfect all virtuous qualities. All buddhas can teach all sentient beings. All buddhas can be leaders of sentient beings. All buddhas perfect pure buddha-lands. All buddhas achieve omniscient knowledge. All buddhas develop the physical marks and refinements of greatness; all who see them benefit, this effort is not in vain. All buddhas are imbued with the impartial reality of enlightened ones. All buddhas, after having done their buddha-work, manifest entry into nirvana.

"Buddhas have ten kinds of skill in means. What are they? All buddhas know all things are beyond idle philosophizing, yet can demonstrate the roots of goodness of all buddhas. All buddhas know all things have no vision and are unknown to each other, have no bondage or release, no reception or assembly, and no consummation, and independently ultimately reach the other shore; meanwhile they know the true reality of all things is unvarying, not different, and they attain freedom, selflessly, without grasping, not destroying ultimate truth; having already reached the state of great freedom, they always observe all realms of reality. All buddhas are forever aloof from all appearances; their minds do not dwell on anything, yet they know all appearances without confusion or error; while they know all appearances have no intrinsic nature of their own, yet they are able to perceive them all in accord with their essence and also manifest the infinite appearances of the various adornments of innumerable physical bodies and pure buddha-lands, gather lamps of knowledge and wisdom, and destroy the delusions of sentient beings. All buddhas abide in the realm of reality; they do not dwell in the past, future, or present, because in Thusness as such there are no marks of the three time frames of past, future, or present; yet they can speak about the emergence in the world of the innumerable buddhas of past, future, and present, causing those who hear to see the realms of all the buddhas.

All buddhas, in their physical, verbal, and mental actions, do not create anything, have no coming or going, and no abiding; beyond all categories, they reach the other shore of all things, yet are treasuries of all truths, imbued with immeasurable knowledge, comprehending all kinds of mundane and transmundane things, their knowledge and wisdom unhindered, manifesting immeasurable autonomous spiritual powers, edifying the sentient beings of all realms. All buddhas know that all things cannot be seen, are neither one nor different, are neither finite nor infinite, are not coming or going, all being without inherent nature of their own, yet they do not contravene the phenomena of the world; the all-knowers see all things in the midst of nonexistence of own-being or inherent nature; being independent of things, they extensively explain things while always abiding steadily in the real nature of True Thusness. All buddhas know all times in one time; endowed with pure virtues, they enter the absolute state, yet without any attachment to it; in regard to time frames such as day, month, year, eon, becoming, and decomposition, they neither remain within them nor abandon them, yet they are able to show day or night, beginning, middle, and end, one day, one week, a fortnight, a month, a year, a century, an eon, many eons, inconceivable eons, inexpressible eons, as far as all the eons throughout the future, always turning the wheel of the sublime Teaching for the sake of sentient beings, without interruption, without retreating, without pause. All buddhas always remain in the realm of reality, develop the infinite fearlessness of the buddhas, as well as their countless, measureless, inexhaustible, ceaseless, boundless, unique, endless, and true intellectual powers, appropriately demonstrating explanation of all expressions and explanation of all principles, delivering untold millions of discourses using various doctrines adapted to faculties and natures, inclinations and understandings, all ultimately good in the beginning, the middle, and the end. All buddhas, abiding in the pure realm of reality, know all things originally have no names, there being no name of past, present, or future, no name of sentient beings, no name of inanimate beings, no name of country or land, no name of noncountry, no name of law or nonlaw, no name of virtue or nonvirtue, no name of enlightening being, no name of Buddha, no names of sets, no names of nonsets, no name of birth, no name of extinction, no name of existence, no name of nonexistence, no name of unity, no name of variety, because the essential nature of things is inexpressible—all things are without location or position, cannot be explained as assembling or dispersing, as one or as many, no verbalization can reach them, all words fail; though the buddhas speak in various ways according to conventional usage, they do not cling to anything as mental objects, do not make anything up, and avoid all false conceptual attachments: in this way they ultimately reach the other shore. All buddhas know the fundamental nature of all things is null: because it has no birth, it is not form; because it has no manifestation it is not sensation; because it has no names or categories it is not conception;

because it has no action it is not conditioning; because it has no grasping it is not consciousness; because it has no access it is not sense mediums; because it apprehends nothing it is not sense elements—yet it does not destroy things, because the original nature has no origination, is like space. All phenomena are empty and quiescent; there is no action or effect, no cultivation, no accomplishment, no production. They are not in sets, yet not out of order; not existent or nonexistent; not born or annihilated, not defiled or pure; not entering or existing; not abiding, not transitory; not edifying, not unedifying; not beings, not not beings; not living, not lifeless; not caused, not causeless. While knowing this, the buddhas know all sentient beings, whether they are rightly stabilized, wrongly stabilized, or not stabilized, and teach them the subtle truth to enable them to reach the other shore, attain the ten powers and four fearlessnesses, be able to roar the lion's roar, be imbued with universal knowledge, and abide in the realm of buddhahood. These are the ten kinds of skill in means achieved by buddhas.

"Buddhas have ten kinds of great buddha-work, immeasurable, boundless, inconceivable, unknowable to all celestial and human worldlings, unknowable even to the past, future, and present Buddhist disciples and self-enlightened ones, except by the spiritual power of the buddhas. What are they? All buddhas appear to be born in the heavens of contentment in all worlds throughout the cosmos, carry out enlightening practices, and perform great buddha-works in the spheres of operation of infinite forms, infinite powers, infinite lights, infinite sounds, infinite verbal expressions, infinite concentrations, and infinite knowledge, taking in all humans, celestials, demons, monks, priests, titans, and so on, their great kindness uninhibited, their great compassion ultimate, impartially aiding and benefiting all living beings, enabling them to be born in heaven or in the human realm, or purifying their senses, or tuning their minds, sometimes explaining three different vehicles of salvation for them, sometimes explaining the complete, full unitary vehicle for them, saving and liberating all, enabling them to get out of birth and death—this is the first great buddha-work.

"All buddhas descend spiritually from the heaven of contentment into the mother's womb; by means of ultimate concentration they observe the phenomenon of taking on life as like an illusion, like a phantom, like a reflection, like space, like a mirage, and they take on life however they wish, without bound, without hindrance. Entering the state of noncontention, they develop knowledge without attachment; free from desire, clear and pure, they develop a vast treasury of wondrous adornments, take on their final embodiment, live in a great jewel-adorned mansion and perform buddha-work. They may do buddha-work by spiritual powers, or by right recollection, or by showing miracles, or by manifesting the sun of knowledge, or by revealing the enormous spheres of buddhahood, or by showing the immeasurable lights of the buddhas, or by entering countless great concentrations, or by manifesting emergence from concentration. The buddhas, at that time, in the mother's womb, wishing to benefit all worldlings, show all kinds of appearances to do buddha-work. They may appear to be born, or appear as children, or appear as princes, or appear as leaving home, or they may show the appearance of atttaining true enlightenment, or show the appearance of turning the wheel of the Teaching, or show the appearance of entering final extinction. In this way all of them, by various means, perform buddha-work in all regions, all networks, all circles, all systems, in all worlds. This is the second great buddha-work.

"All good works of all buddhas are already pure, and their knowledge of all life is clear and immaculate: so by birth they lead and guide the deluded, causing them to open up in understanding and practice all that is good. For the sake of sentient beings they appear to be born in a royal palace. All buddhas have already abandoned all materialistic desires for palaces and pleasure; they have no craving or obsession, and always reflect upon the emptiness and essencelessness of all existents, that all comforts and delights are not truly real. Keeping the pure precepts of buddhas, ultimately fulfilling them, observing the palace ladies and attendants, they develop great compassion; observing that all sentient beings are unreal, they develop great kindness; observing that there is nothing enjoyable in the world, they develop great joy; their minds gaining freedom in the midst of all things, they develop great relinquishment. Imbued with the qualities of buddhahood, they manifest birth in the phenomenal realm, their physical features perfect, their associates pure, yet they have no attachment to anything. With voices adapting to types, they explain the truth to the masses, causing them to become disillusioned with worldly things; they point out to them the results of what they are doing. Also they use expedient means to teach in accord with needs, causing the immature to develop maturity, causing the mature to attain liberation, doing buddha-work for them to cause them not to regress. Also, by virtue of a heart of universal love and compassion they continually explain all kinds of principles to sentient beings and also manifest the powers of diagnosis, prescription, and occult influence for them, to enable them to awaken and attain purity of mind. Though the buddhas be in the inner palace, seen by all the people, yet they are performing buddha-work in all worlds. By means of great knowledge and great energy they manifest the various spiritual powers of buddhas, unhindered, inexhaustible. They always continue three kinds of skillfull, expedient action—that is, their physical activity is ultimately pure, their verbal activity is always carried out in accord with knowledge, and their mental activity is exceedingly profound and has no blockage or inhibition; by these means they benefit living beings. This is the third great buddha-work.

"All buddhas show analytic examination and disenchantment while living in a palace of all kinds of adornments, thereupon giving it up and leaving home, wishing to let sentient beings realize that things of the world are all illusions, impermanent, and perishable, and become deeply disillusioned, avoid creating attachments, forever cut off the affliction of worldly craving, cultivate purifying practices, and benefit living beings. When the buddhas leave home, they give up conventional manners, abide in noncontention, and fulfill the immeasurable virtues of their fundamental vow. By the light of great knowledge they destroy the darkness of delusion of the world and become unexcelled fields of blessings for all beings. They always extol the virtues of buddhas for the benefit of sentient beings, causing them to plant roots of goodness with the buddhas. They see truth with the eye of wisdom. They also extol renunciation for the benefit of sentient beings, its purity and blamelessness. They are eternally emancipated and are forever lofty paragons of wisdom for the world. This is the fourth great buddha-work.

"All buddhas have omniscience and already know and see infinite realities. Attaining perfect true enlightenment under the tree of enlightenment, vanquishing all demons, their majesty supreme, their bodies fill all worlds. Their deeds of spiritual power are boundless and inexhaustible. They attain mastery of all meanings in the sphere of omniscience. They have cultivated virtues to consummation. Their seats of enlightenment are fully adorned and pervade all worlds in the ten directions; the buddhas sit on them and turn the wheel of the sublime Teaching, explaining all the undertakings of enlightening beings, revealing the infinite realms of the buddhas, causing the enlightening beings to awaken to and enter into them. They carry out all kinds of pure practices and are able to direct and guide all living beings, cause them to plant roots of goodness, be born in the ground of equality of the enlightened, continue in the boundless good practices of enlightening beings, and develop all the most excellent qualities. The buddhas know perfectly all worlds, all beings, all buddha-lands, all phenomena, all enlightening beings, all teachings, all pasts, presents, and futures, all disciplines, all mystic transformations, and the inclinations of all sentient beings' minds, and based on this knowledge perform buddha-work. This is the fifth great buddha-work.

"All buddhas turn the irreversible wheel of the Teaching, to cause the enlightening beings not to backslide; they turn the immeasurable wheel of the Teaching, to cause all worldlings to know; they turn the wheel of Teaching, awakening all, because they can fearlessly roar the lion's roar; they turn the wheel of Teaching, which is a treasury of knowledge of all truths, to open the door of the treasury of truth and remove the obstacle of obscurity; they turn the unobstructed wheel of the Teaching, being equal to space; they turn the wheel of Teaching of nonattachment, because they see that all things are neither existent nor nonexistent; they turn the world-illuminating wheel of Teaching, to cause all sentient beings to purify their vision of reality; they turn the wheel of Teaching revealing all knowledge, pervading all things in all times; they turn the wheel of Teaching, which is the same one of all buddhas, because all

Buddha teachings are not mutually opposed or contradictory. All buddhas, by means of measureless, countless hundreds of thousands of millions of billions of such wheels of Teaching, perform buddha-work inconceivably according to the differences in mental patterns of sentient beings. This is the sixth great buddha-work.

"All buddhas enter into all capital cities and perform buddha-work for the beings. That is, they enter human capitals, celestial capitals, capitals of water spirits, monsters, cherubim, titans, birds, hobgoblins, serpents, goblins, demons, and so on. When they enter the gates of the city, the earth trembles, light shines everywhere, the blind gain vision, the deaf are able to hear, the insane regain their sanity, the naked are clothed, the troubled and suffering all gain peace and happiness; all musical instruments spontaneously play, all adornments, used or not, emit marvelous sounds that delight all hearers. The buddhas' physical forms are pure and clean, fully endowed with the marks and refinements of greatness, so that none ever tire of seeing them. They are able to do buddha-work for the benefit of sentient beings—whether looking, examining, moving, stretching, walking or standing still, sitting or reclining, silent or speaking, whether manifesting occult powers, or explaining principles, or giving instructions—in all these they are performing buddha-work for the benefit of sentient beings. All buddhas, in all the countless worlds, in the midst of the oceans of mental inclinations of all kinds of sentient beings, urge them to remembrance the buddhas, always diligently considering and planting roots of goodness, cultivating the practices of enlightening beings, lauding the subtlety and supremacy of the buddhas' appearance, which is hard for any living being to get to meet; if beings see buddhas and are inspired with faith, then they produce all the immeasurable good qualities and amass the virtues of buddhas, all pure. Thus, having extolled the virtues of buddhas, they multiply their bodies to go to all worlds in the ten directions to let the sentient beings behold them, meditate on them and contemplate them, attend and serve them, plant roots of goodness, gain the good graces of the buddhas, and increase the family of buddhas, all being certain to attain buddhahood. By these actions they perform buddha-work, sometimes manifesting physical bodies for sentient beings, sometimes making sublime utterances, sometimes just smiling, causing them to believe, honor, praise, and behave courteously. All buddhas, by means of innumerable, untold, inconceivable such buddha-works of all kinds, in all worlds, according to the inclinations of sentient beings' minds, teach them expediently, by the power of their original vows, the power of great love and compassion, and the power of omniscience, causing them all to be civilized. This is the seventh great buddha-work.

"All buddhas may do buddha-work while dwelling in forest retreats, or in quiet places, or in desolate places, or in buddhas' dwelling places; or they may do buddha-work while in trance, or while alone in a grove, or while concealing themselves from view, or while abiding in knowledge of the ultimate profundity, or while dwelling in the incomparable realm of the buddhas; or they may do buddha-work while carrying on various imperceptible physical actions, adapting to sentient beings' mentalities, predilections, and understandings to teach them as is expedient, without cease. Or they may do buddha-work seeking omniscience in the form of celestial beings, or they may do buddha-work seeking omniscience in the form of water spirits, goblins, cherubim, titans, birds, serpents, humans, subhumans, and so on. They may also do buddha-work by seeking omniscience in the form of listeners, solitary illuminates, or enlightening beings. Sometimes they preach, sometimes they are silent in doing buddha-work. Sometimes they do buddha-work saying there is one Buddha, sometimes saying there are many buddhas. Sometimes they do buddha-work saying all practices and all vows of enlightening beings are one practice and vow; sometimes they do buddha-work saying one practice and one vow of enlightening beings are infinite practices and vows. Sometimes they do buddha-work saying the realm of buddhahood is the world, sometimes they do buddha-work saying the world is the realm of buddhahood. Sometimes they do buddha-work saying the realm of buddhahood is not the world. Sometimes they remain for a day, or a night, or a fortnight, or a month, or a year, up to untold eons, to do buddha-work for the benefit of sentient beings. This is the eighth great buddha-work.

"All buddhas are mines that produce pure roots of goodness, causing sentient beings to engender pure faith and resolution in the buddha-teachings, so their faculties are tamed and they forever detach from the world. They cause enlightening beings to be full of knowledge, wisdom, and clarity in regard to the way of enlightenment and not depend on another for understanding. Sometimes they do buddha-work manifesting nirvana, sometimes they do buddha-work showing the evanescence of all in the world, sometimes they do buddha-work explaining the buddha-bodies, sometimes they do buddha-work explaining the accomplishment of all that is to be done, sometimes they do buddha-work explaining the flawless fulfillment of virtuous qualities, sometimes they do buddha-work explaining the extirpation of the root of all existences. Sometimes they do buddha-work causing sentient beings to turn away from the world to follow the buddha-mind; sometimes they do buddha-work explaining the inevitable ending of life; sometimes they do buddha-work explaining that there is nothing enjoyable in the world. Sometimes they do buddha-work preaching the eternal service of buddhas; sometimes they do buddha-work explaining the buddhas' turning of the wheel of pure Teaching, causing the hearers to become very joyful. Sometimes they do buddha-work expounding the sphere of buddhahood, inspiring people to cultivate spiritual practices. Sometimes they do buddha-work expounding concentration on remembrance of Buddha, inspiring people to always delight in visions of Buddha. Sometimes they do buddha-work expounding the purification of the senses, diligent search for the Buddha Way with unflagging spirit. Sometimes they do buddha-work visiting all buddha-lands and observing the various causes and conditions of their environments. Sometimes they do buddha-work uniting all bodies of living beings into a buddha-body, causing all lazy and self-indulgent sentient beings to abide by the pure precepts of the enlightened. This is the ninth great buddha-work.

"When buddhas enter extinction, countless sentient beings mourn and weep; looking at each other in great grief and distress, they say, 'The buddha had great sympathy and compassion, mercifully aiding all worldly beings, a savior and a refuge for all living creatures. The emergence of a buddha is difficult to encounter, an unexcelled field of blessings, and now the buddha has passed away forever.' Thus they use this to cause sentient beings to mourn and miss the buddha, thereby doing buddha-work. Also, in order to transform and liberate all celestials, humans, spirits, goblins, titans, cherubim, and so on, according to their desires, they pulverize their own bodies to make countless relics, to cause sentient beings to develop faith, honor, respect, and joyfully reverence them, and cultivate virtues to complete fulfillment. They also build monuments, variously adorned, in the abodes of all kinds of creatures, for religious services; their teeth, nails, and hair are all used to make monuments, to cause those who see them to remember the Buddha, the Teaching, and the Community, to believe with unswerving faith, sincerely respect and honor them, and make offerings to them wherever they are, and cultivate virtues, so that by this merit they may be born in heaven or among humans, of noble and prosperous families with ample property and pure retinues, not enter into evil ways, always get to see buddhas, fulfill pure ways, quickly attain emancipation from the three realms of existence, each attain the fruit of their own vehicle according to their aspiration, recognize and requite their debt to buddhas, and forever be a reliance for the world. Though the buddhas be extinct, they are still inconceivable pure fields of blessings for living beings, with inexhaustible virtues, supreme fields of blessings, causing sentient beings' roots of goodness to be complete and their virtue to be fully developed. This is the tenth great buddha-work.

"These buddha-works are immeasurably great, inconceivable: no beings of the world, celestials or humans, and none of the listeners or individual illuminates of past, future, or present can know them, unless they are empowered by Buddha.

"Buddhas have ten kinds of mastery of nondual action. What are they? All buddhas can speak words of prediction of enlightenment, definitively, without duality. All buddhas can satisfy sentient beings according to their wishes, definitely, without duality. All buddhas can manifestly be awake to all truths and expound their meanings, definitively, without duality. All buddhas have all the wisdom and knowledge of the buddhas of past, future, and present, definitive, without duality. All buddhas know that all instants, past, future, and present, are one instant, definitely, without duality. All buddhas know that all past, future, and present buddha-lands inhere in one buddha-land, definitely, without duality. All buddhas know the words of all buddhas of all times are the words of one buddha, definitely, without duality. All buddhas know that all buddhas of all times and all the beings they teach are essentially equal, definitely, without duality. All buddhas know that worldly phenomena and Buddhist principles are essentially not different, definitely, without duality. All buddhas know that the roots of goodness of all buddhas of all times are the same one root of goodness, definitely, without duality. These are the ten.

"Buddhas have ten kinds of abode, abiding therein in all things. What are they? All buddhas abide in awareness of all realms of reality. All buddhas abide in compassionate speech. All buddhas abide in the fundamental great vow. All buddhas abide in persistence in civilizing sentient beings. All buddhas abide in the principle of absence of selfhood. All buddhas abide in impartial salvation. All buddhas abide in recollection of truth. All buddhas abide in the unobstructed mind. All buddhas abide in the constantly rightly concentrated mind. All buddhas abide in equal comprehension of all things without violating the character of ultimate reality.

"All buddhas have ten exhaustive knowledges. What are they? They know all things of the past exhaustively. They know all things of the future exhaustively. They know all things of the present exhaustively. They know all principles of language exhaustively. The know all sentient beings' minds exhaustively. They know all the various ranks, high, middling, and low, of the roots of goodness of enlightening beings. They know all buddhas' complete knowledge and virtues do not increase or decrease. They know all phenomena come from interdependent origination. They know all world systems exhaustively. They know all the different phenomena in all worlds, interrelated in Indra's net.

"Buddhas have ten kinds of might with enormous power, supreme power, measureless power, grandiose, awesome power, power difficult to acquire, undiminishing power, stable power, indestructible power, power inconceivable to any worldlings, power that all living beings cannot shake. What are they? All buddhas have indestructible bodies and life that cannot be cut off—no worldly poisons can affect them; the floods, fires, and gales of all worlds cannot harm the buddhas' body. Even if all demons, gods, sprites, goblins, angels, titans, and sundry other creatures were to rain thunderbolts as big as mountains with all their strength, hurling them down all at once throughout the universe, they could not cause the buddhas' mind to be startled or frightened and could not even move a single hair of the buddhas. Walking, standing still, sitting, or reclining, the buddhas never change. That rain cannot fall where the buddhas are unless they let it, and even if they do not prevent it, and let it rain, it does not harm them. If there are any beings sustained by the buddhas or in the service of the buddhas, that rain of thunderbolts cannot even harm them, much less the buddhas. This is the buddhas' first mighty quality.

"All buddhas put the mountains, oceans, forests, and buildings in all worlds in all universes into a single pore for all future ages, yet the sentient beings are not aware, do not know, unless they are empowered by the Buddha. Then the buddhas, holding all those worlds in a pore throughout the ages to come, whether walking, standing still, sitting, or reclining, do not conceive a single thought of fatigue. Just as space holds all the worlds in the cosmos without fatigue, so do all buddhas hold all worlds in a single pore. This is buddhas' second mighty quality.

"All buddhas can take as many steps as atoms in untold worlds in a single moment, passing as many lands as atoms in untold buddha-lands with each step, and travel thus for as many eons as atoms in all worlds: if there were a great adamantine mountain equal in measure to all those buddha-lands, the buddhas could place as many such mountains as atoms in untold buddha-lands in a single pore; the pores on a buddha's body being equal in number to all beings in the cosmos, they place the same number of great adamantine mountains in each pore, and, holding all those mountains, walk in the ten directions, entering all worlds in space, from the past throughout the future, through all ages, without resting— yet the buddhas' bodies are not injured and they do not get tired; their minds are always in concentration, without distraction. This is the buddhas' third mighty quality.

"Buddhas, after a meal, sit in the lotus posture through the untold eons of past and future, and enter the inconceivable bliss experienced by buddhas; their bodies remain stable, still and unmoving, yet they do not abandon the work of teaching sentient beings. Suppose someone measured each world throughout space one after another with a hairtip; the buddhas are able to sit cross-legged forever on a point the size of the hairtip, and likewise on all points. Suppose the size and weight of each being in all worlds in the ten directions were equal to those of worlds as numerous as atoms in untold buddha-lands; the buddhas could put all those beings on a fingertip forever and could do the same with all their fingertips, and enter each world in all of space carrying all those beings, exhausting the whole cosmos, yet the buddhas would never be weary in body or mind. This is buddhas' fourth mighty quality.

"Buddhas can cause to appear on one body as many heads as atoms in untold buddha-lands, manifesting as many tongues in each head as atoms in untold buddha-lands, each tongue producing as many different voices as atoms in untold buddha-lands, which all beings in the cosmos hear, each voice delivering as many troves of discourses as atoms in untold buddha-lands, each trove of discourses expounding as many principles as atoms in untold buddha-lands, each principle having as many terms, statements, and meanings as atoms in untold buddha-lands. They preach this way for as many eons as atoms in untold buddha-lands, and when they finish these eons, they again preach for as many eons as atoms in untold buddha-lands, going on like this successively until they exhaust eons as numerous as atoms in all worlds, as numerous as the thoughts of all living beings. The eons of the future may be exhausted, but the cycles of teaching operated by the emanated bodies of buddhas have no end. This means the cycle of teaching expounded by knowledge, the cycle of teaching cutting off doubts, the cycle of teaching illumining all things, the cycle of teaching opening the treasury of nonobstruction, the cycle of teaching causing sentient beings to be joyful and docile, the cycle of teaching revealing all the practices of enlightening beings, the cycle of teaching of the high-rising, perfectly round sun of knowledge, the cycle of teaching of the bright lamp of wisdom illumining all the world, the cycle of teaching of various adornments of intellectual powers and confidence: just as one buddha-body, by spiritual power, operates different cycles of teaching such as these, to which no comparison in the world may be drawn, in the same way throughout space, in every single point, there are as many worlds as atoms in untold buddha-lands, and in each world the buddhas manifest in each mental instant as many emanation bodies as atoms in untold buddha-lands, each emanation body also producing voices and teachings like these, each filling all realms, so all beings therein can understand—yet the voice of the buddhas does not change or die out; it is inexhaustible. This is the fifth mighty quality of buddhas.

"All buddhas adorn their chests with the sign of virtue, indestructible as adamant, and sit at the foot of a tree of enlightenment: hordes of demons, boundless in number, with various forms so terrifying that all sentient beings who see them become crazed with fear, or even drop dead—such hordes of demons fill the sky, but when the buddhas see them, they are not frightened, they do not pale, not even one hair stands on end, they are not moved or disturbed, they do not think of anything— aloof from emotions, they are tranquil and clear, abiding in the abode of buddhas, imbued with the power of love and compassion, their senses under control, their hearts without fear, impossible for the hordes of demons to upset. In fact, it is they who can subdue the demons, cause them to change their minds and take refuge in the buddhas, after which the buddhas teach them by means of correct diagnosis, prescription, and mystic influence, so that all now develop the aspiration for unexcelled, complete perfect enlightenment, never to regress. This is the sixth mighty quality of buddhas.

"All buddhas have unobstructed voices that pervade all worlds in the ten directions, and all sentient beings who hear them spontaneously become docile. The sounds of the voices of the buddhas cannot be blocked by any mountains, any habitations of any creatures, or any sounds of any world, no matter how loud. According to the ways in which they need to be influenced, all sentient beings hear articulated statements and doctrines and all attain understanding. This is the seventh mighty quality of buddhas.

"All buddhas' minds are unobstructed, eternally pure; all buddhas of past, future, and present are of the same one essence, unpolluted, un-blinkered, without egoism or possessiveness, either internally or exter-nally; they realize objects are void, they do not conceive arbitrary ideas, do not depend on anything, do not fabricate anything, do not dwell on appearances, forever end false imaginings, give up all thoughts clinging to objects, are pure in their fundamental nature, are forever free from conflict while in the midst of all things, abiding in ultimate reality, free from desire, thoroughly pure; entering the cosmos of reality, their teach-ing is inexhaustible, beyond all illusory ideas of assessment and wrong assessment, totally beyond all talk of the compounded and the uncom-pounded. Having comprehended untold, boundless realms of objects, with unimpeded, inexhaustible knowledge and method they accomplish the ten powers, and their embellishments of all virtues are thoroughly pure. They expound innumerable various principles, all without contra-dicting the character of reality, impartial with respect to the phenomena of past, present, and future of the cosmos, without variance, ultimately free, entering into the supreme treasury of all truths, correctly remem-bering all facets of truth without confusion, abiding unperturbed in the fields of all buddhas in the ten directions. Attaining unbroken knowl-edge, they know all things ultimately, without exception; putting an end to contamination, their minds are liberated and their intellects are liber-ated. Abiding in ultimate reality, their perceptivity is unimpeded, and their minds are always correctly stabilized. In a single thought they comprehend the things of past, present, and future as well as the mental activities of all sentient beings, without any hindrance. This is the eighth mighty quality of buddhas.

"All buddhas have the same one reality-body, a body of infinite range, a body of boundless qualities, a body with no limit in the world, a body undefiled by the realms of desire, form, or formlessness, a body manifested at will, an impartial, pure body that is neither real nor unreal, an indestructible body with no coming or going, no compounding, a body of the inherent essence of phenomena, of one form which is formless, an omnipresent body without position or location, a body of boundless forms produced by free psychic transformations, a body of all kinds of manifestations entering universally into everything, a body of skillful employment of subtle truth, a body of a treasury of knowledge illumining everywhere, a body showing the equality of phenomena, a body pervading the cosmos, a body of eternal purity without movement or discrimination, neither existent nor nonexistent, a body manifest in accord with the various interests and understandings of all beings capable of being edified, which is not an expedient yet not inexpedient, neither perishes nor does not perish, a body born of the treasury of all virtues, a body of True Thusness, containing all the teachings of the buddhas, a body free from obstruction, its fundamental nature absolutely still, a body in which all qualities of nonobstruction are developed, a body omnipresent in all realms of pure principle, a body omnipresent in all worlds in multiple forms, a body of universal comprehension, free from clinging to objects, free from regression, forever liberated, imbued with omniscience. This is the ninth mighty quality of buddhas.

"All buddhas equally understand all the teachings of buddhas and equally cultivate all the practices of enlightening beings; whether undertakings or knowledge, they are purely impartial, like the great ocean, all reaching fulfillment. Their power of action is supreme, and they never shrink back. Abiding in the measureless realms of the various concentrations, they show all paths, encourage good, and warn against evil. Their power of knowledge is foremost; they expound the truth without fear and are able to answer any question well. Their knowledge, wisdom, and teaching are equally pure; their physical, verbal, and mental actions are all unalloyed. They abide in the abode of buddhahood, the family of buddhas, doing buddha-work by means of enlightened knowledge and wisdom. Abiding in omniscience, they explain innumerable things as having no basis and no boundaries. Their psychic powers and knowledge are inconceivable, incomprehensible to any worldlings. Their knowledge profoundly penetrating, they see all things. The subtle, far-reaching, measureless, boundless gates of truth of past, present, and future, they thoroughly comprehend. In all worlds they are able to awaken understanding by means of transmundane knowledge. In all worlds they perform untold buddha-works of all kinds, attain unregressing knowledge, and enter the ranks of the buddhas. Though they have already realized untold truths that are beyond verbal expression, yet they can explain all verbal expressions. By means of Universally Good knowledge, they accumulate good qualities. Achieving instantaneous subtle knowledge, they comprehend all things and give out teachings to beings in accord with whatever courses of action are appropriate for them as individuals. All things, all worlds, all sentient beings, all times in the cosmos, the range of these phenomena unlimited, they are able to know and see by means of unobstructed knowledge. All buddhas appear in the world in the time of a single thought, according to the possibilities for enlightening, abide in a pure land, attain true awakening, manifest spiritual powers, and open up and enlighten the mind, intellect, and consciousness of all sentient beings of past, present, and future, according to appropriate timing. Sentient beings are boundless, worlds are boundless, realms of natural law are boundless, past, present, and future are boundless, and the supremacy of the buddhas is also boundless; they appear in the midst of them all, attain true awareness, and skillfully enlighten them by means of buddha-knowledge, never ceasing. All buddhas manifest the most wondrous incarnation by means of spiritual power, abide in boundlessness, with great compassion and skill in means, their minds without obstruction, at all times explaining the wondrous teaching for the benefit of all living beings. This is the tenth mighty quality of buddhas. These mighty qualities of all buddhas are infinite, boundless, inconceivable, incomprehensible to any sentient beings or followers of individual liberation in any time, unless spiritually empowered by Buddha.

"All buddhas have ten definite principles. What are they? All buddhas definitely come down from the heaven of happiness to be born on earth. All buddhas definitely appear to be born, spending ten lunar months in the womb. All buddhas definitely tire of social convention and gladly seek to leave the world. All buddhas definitely sit at the foot of the tree of enlightenment, achieve true awakening, and realize all elements of enlightenment. All buddhas definitely realize all truths instantly and manifest spiritual power in all worlds. All buddhas definitely can teach in accord with the time. All buddhas definitely can teach people at the appropriate times in accordance with the bases of goodness they have developed, and give them directions for enlightenment. All buddhas definitely can do buddha-work in accord with the time. All buddhas definitely predict the enlightenment of all fully developed enlightening beings. All buddhas definitely can answer all sentient beings' questions in a single instant.

"All buddhas have ten kinds of speed. What are they? Any who see any buddha are speedily able to avoid bad dispositions. Any who see any buddha are speedily able to fulfill superior virtues. Any who see any buddha are speedily able to develop extensive bases of goodness. Any who see any buddha speedily attain rebirth in an immaculate heaven. Any who see any buddha can speedily get rid of all doubts and confusion. Any who have already aroused the aspiration for enlightenment who see any buddha can soon develop immense resolve, never to turn back, and can be able to teach people according to their needs; if they have not yet aroused the aspiration for enlightenment, they will quickly be able to arouse the determination for unexcelled, complete perfect enlighten-ment. Any who see any buddha before having entered the absolute state will speedily enter the absolute state. Any who see any buddha will speedily be able to purify all roots of goodness, mundane and supra-mundane. Any who see any buddha will speedily manage to destroy all obstruction. Any who see any buddha will speedily be able to acquire fearless intellectual powers.

"All buddhas have ten kinds of pure things that should always be remembered. What are they? All buddhas' past events should be always remembered by enlightening beings. All buddhas' pure superior actions should be always remembered by enlightening beings. All buddhas' ful-fillment of the ways of transcendence should be always remembered by enlightening beings. All buddhas' accomplishment of great undertakings should always be remembered by enlightening beings. All buddhas' accumulation of virtues should always be remembered by enlightening beings. All buddhas' embodiment of spiritual practice should always be remembered by enlightening beings. All buddhas' actualization of true enlightenment should always be remembered by enlightening beings. The infinity of all buddhas' physical forms should always be remembered by enlightening beings. The infinity of all buddhas' spiritual powers should always be remembered by enlightening beings. All buddhas' ten powers and confidences should always be remembered by enlightening beings.

"All buddhas have ten stations of omniscience. What are they? All buddhas instantly know the minds and mental patterns of all sentient beings of past, present, and future. All buddhas instantly know the acts and the resulting consequences of those acts amassed by all sentient beings in past, present, and future. All buddhas instantly know the needs of all sentient beings and teach and civilize them by means of correct diagnosis, prescription, and occult influence. All buddhas instantly know the mental characteristics of all sentient beings in the cosmos, manifest the emergence of Buddha in all places, and take those beings into their care by expedient means. All buddhas instantly manifest expositions of teaching according to the mental inclinations, desires, and understandings of all sentient beings in the cosmos, causing them to become civilized. All buddhas instantly know the inclinations of the minds of all sentient beings in the cosmos and manifest spiritual powers for them. All buddhas instantly manifest appearance in all places according to all the sentient beings who may be taught, and explain to them that the embodiment of Buddha is not graspable. All buddhas instantly reach all places in the cosmos, all sentient beings, and their particular paths. All buddhas instantly go in response to any beings who think of them, wherever they may be. All buddhas instantly know the understandings and desires of all sentient beings and manifest immeasurable physical forms for their benefit.

"All buddhas have ten kinds of immeasurable inconceivable buddha-concentrations. What are they? All buddhas, while always in correct concentration, instantly reach all places to expound the sublime Teaching for sentient beings everywhere. All buddhas, while always in correct concentration, instantly reach all places to teach all sentient beings ultimate selflessness. All buddhas, while always in correct concentration, instantly enter the past, present, and future in all places. All buddhas, while always in correct concentration, instantly enter the immense buddha-lands in the ten directions, pervading all places. All buddhas, while always in correct concentration, instantly manifest innumerable various buddha-bodies in all places. All buddhas, while always in correct concentration, instantly in all places manifest body, speech, and mind in accord with the various understandings of sentient beings. All buddhas, while always in correct concentration, instantly, in all places, explain the ultimate reality of all things, beyond desire. All buddhas, while always in correct concentration, instantly, in all places, expound the inherent nature of interdependent origination of everything. All buddhas, while always in correct concentration, instantly, in all places, manifest immeasurable worldly and transcendental great adornments, causing sentient beings always to get to see Buddha. All buddhas, while always in correct concentration, instantly, in all places, enable sentient beings to master all enlightened teachings, attain infinite liberation, and ultimately reach unsurpassed transcendence.

"Buddhas have ten kinds of unimpeded liberation. What are they? All buddhas can cause the emergence in the world of untold buddhas in a single atom. All buddhas can cause untold buddhas actively teaching to appear in a single atom. All buddhas can cause untold sentient beings being taught and guided to appear in a single atom. All buddhas can cause untold buddha-lands to appear in a single atom. All buddhas can cause untold enlightening beings receiving predictions of buddhahood to appear in a single atom. All buddhas can cause all buddhas of past, future, and present to appear in a single atom. All buddhas can cause all past, present, and future miracles to appear in a single atom. All buddhas can cause all sentient beings of past, present, and future to appear in a single atom. All buddhas can cause all past, present, and future buddha-works to appear in a single atom."

BOOK THIRTY-FOUR

The Ocean of Physical Marks of the Ten Bodies of Buddha

THEN THE GREAT ENLIGHTENING BEING Universally Good said to the enlightening beings, "I now will tell you about the ocean of marks of the Buddha. On top of the Buddha's head there are thirty-two marks of great people, adorned with jewels. Among them is a mark of greatness called light illumining all regions, radiating immeasurable webs of great beams of light. It is adorned by all exquisite jewels, covered with jewel hair, soft, dense, and fine, each hair radiating jewel lights filling all the boundless worlds, manifesting embodiments of Buddha in all, complete with all the marks of buddhahood. This is the first.

"Next there is a mark of greatness called clouds of light of the Buddha-eye. It is variously arrayed with the finest gems, producing a golden light like the light emanating from the curl of hair between Buddha's eyebrows. That light illuminates all worlds. This is the second.

"Next there is a mark of greatness called clouds filling the cosmos. It is arrayed with discs of the finest jewels and radiates the light of the lamp of virtue and knowledge of the enlightened, illumining the oceans of worlds in all universes, making all buddhas and enlightening beings visible. This is the third.

"Next there is a mark of greatness called clouds manifesting universal illumination, variously adorned with gold and jewels. Those exquisite jewels all radiate light, illuminating inconceivable numbers of buddha-lands, with all the buddhas appearing therein. This is the fourth.

"Next there is a mark of greatness called radiating clusters of jewel lights, with pure arrays of diamonds and flowers of lapis lazuli, their light shining on all worlds in the ten directions, therein manifesting all kinds of mystical projections extolling the past practices, wisdom, and virtues of the enlightened. This is the fifth.

"Next there is a mark of greatness called manifestation of clusters of great powers of Buddha pervading the cosmos, crowned by crystals of flames of jewels in the configurations of mystical projections of enlightening beings, ringed with wheels of light of flames of jewels containing the power of the Buddha enlightening all, those lights illuminating the worlds of the ten directions, making manifest therein all buddhas sitting on the site of enlightenment, clouds of all knowledge filling infinite worlds throughout space. This is the sixth.

"Next there is a mark of greatness called multitudes of universal lamps of the enlightened, adorned by a sea of jewels of great power that can shake all lands in the cosmos, emanating pure light filling the cosmos, showing therein the oceans of virtues of the enlightening beings of the ten directions and the oceans of standards of knowledge of the buddhas of past, present, and future. This is the seventh.

"Next there is a mark of greatness called immense cloud reflecting all buddhas, adorned with sapphires, wish-fulfilling jewels, and pearls, always radiating light of enlightening beings' flaming lamps, illumining all worlds in the ten directions, therein revealing all buddhas' ocean of physical forms, ocean of vocal sounds, and ocean of pure powers. This is the eighth.

"Next there is a mark of greatness called cloud of light spheres, adorned by flowers of all kinds of jewels, with great webs of flames unfolding from all the jewels and filling all worlds in the ten directions, where all sentient beings see the Buddha sitting before them, praising the qualities of the reality-body of buddhas and enlightening beings, introducing them into the pure realm of the enlightened. This is the ninth.

"Next there is a mark of greatness called clouds of light illumining the treasury of practices of all enlightening beings, adorned by exquisite flowers made of all kinds of jewels, the lights of the jewels illumining innumerable worlds, the blaze of the jewels covering all lands, reaching all universes in the ten directions without impediment, causing the voice of Buddha to vibrate, telling the ocean of truths. This is the tenth.

"Next there is a mark of greatness called clouds of radiant light shining, adorned with lapis lazuli, sapphires, and diamonds, the colors of the jewel clusters clear, illuminating all oceans of worlds, producing wondrous sounds filling the cosmos, all emanating from the ocean of great virtues of knowledge of the Buddha. This is the eleventh.

"Next there is a mark of greatness called cloud of true awakening, adorned with flowers of mixed jewels, the jewel flowers all emitting light beams in all of which there are buddhas sitting on the site of enlightenment, filling boundless worlds, causing the worlds to be purified, putting an end to all deluded thoughts. This is the twelfth.

"Next there is a mark of greatness called clouds of radiance of light, adorned by crystallizations of the sovereign faculty of mind from the oceanic treasury of jewel flames, radiating great beams of light in which appear countless enlightening beings and the deeds they carry out, the body of knowledge, the body of realities, and the ocean of physical forms of all buddhas, filling the cosmos. This is the thirteenth.

"Next there is a mark of greatness called clouds of adornments shining in all directions, arrayed with diamond flowers and lapis lazuli, radiating great beams of light in which there are great jewel lotus blossom thrones, fully adorned, covering the cosmos, spontaneously expounding the practices of enlightening beings, the sound pervading the ocean of all universes. This is the fourteenth.

"Next there is a mark of greatness called manifestation of the clusters of practices of the ocean of concentration of buddhas, instantly revealing the infinite adornments of Buddha, adorning the inconceivable oceans of worlds in all universes. This is the fifteenth.

"Next there is a mark of greatness called clouds of universal illumination of the ocean of mystic projections, adorned by mountainous lotus blossoms of exquisite jewels, the light of the jewels born from the vows of the Buddha, manifesting mystical projections without end. This is the sixteenth.

"Next there is a mark of greatness called cloud of liberations of all buddhas, adorned by pure fine jewels, emanating great lights, adorning all buddhas' lion thrones, showing images of forms of all buddhas, as well as the infinite Buddha teachings and the ocean of buddha-lands. This is the seventeenth.

"Next there is a mark of greatness called cloud of illumination of independent means, adorned by lapis lazuli flowers, gold lotus blossoms, crystal lamps, and multitudes of flames of sublime teachings, emanating pure light from dense clouds of jewel flames of all buddhas, filling the cosmos, showing therein all the fine items of adornment. This is the eighteenth.

"Next there is a mark of greatness called cloud of awareness of the lineage of buddhas, adorned by infinite jewel lights with a thousand spheres, thoroughly pure within and without, born of roots of goodness of the past, those lights illuminating the worlds of the ten directions, kindling the sun of knowledge, spreading the ocean of truths. This is the nineteenth.

"Next there is a mark of greatness called cloud of manifestation of all buddhas' freedom of form, adorned by necklaces of all jewels and lapis lazuli flowers, unfolding great jewel flames, filling the cosmos, manifesting therein the measureless buddhas of past, future, and present, as many as atoms in all buddha-lands, bold and fearless as majestic lions, replete with all the marks and knowledge of buddhahood. This is the twentieth.

"Next there is a mark of greatness called cloud illuminating the entire cosmos, adorned by the purity of the precious characteristics of the enlightened, radiating great lights illuminating the cosmos, revealing the sublime treasury of knowledge of all the infinite buddhas and enlightening beings. This is the twenty-first.

"Next there is a mark of greatness called cluster of features of Vairocana Buddha, adorned by flowers of the finest jewels as well as pure moons of jewels, all radiating countless trillions of crystal lights, filling all space and the cosmos, therein manifesting countless buddha-lands with buddhas sitting in them. This is the twenty-second.

"Next there is a mark of greatness called cloud of light revealing all buddhas, adorned with beautiful lamps of myriad jewels, emitting pure light illumining all worlds in the ten directions, showing all the buddhas teaching. This is the twenty-third.

"Next there is a mark of greatness called cloud of manifestation of all adornments, embellished by all kinds of jewel flames, radiating pure light filling the cosmos, in every successive instant constantly manifesting all the untold, unspeakable numbers of buddhas and enlightening beings sitting at sites of enlightenment. This is the twenty-fourth.

"Next there is a mark of greatness called cloud producing the sounds of all universes, adorned with oceans of jewels and finest sandalwood, emitting great webs of flames filling the cosmos, producing therein subtle sounds pointing out the ocean of all actions of sentient beings. This is the twenty-fifth.

"Next there is a mark of greatness called cloud reflecting the spheres of mystical projections of all buddhas, adorned by the pure eyes of the enlightened, illuminating all worlds with light, in which appear all the adornments of the buddhas of past, future, and present, and producing sublime sounds expounding the inconceivably vast ocean of truth. This is the twenty-sixth.

"Next there is a mark of greatness called cloud of light illumining the ocean of buddhas, that light illuminating all worlds in the cosmos without obstruction, with a buddha sitting in each. This is the twenty-seventh.

"Next there is a mark of greatness called cluster of jewel lamps, emitting the far-reaching light of the enlightened, illuminating all universes in the ten directions, showing therein all buddhas, enlightening beings, and the ocean of inconceivable numbers of various beings. This is the twenty-eighth.

"Next there is a mark of greatness called cloud of nondifferentiation of the realm of reality, radiating the light of great knowledge of the enlightened, illuminating all the buddha-lands of the ten directions, all the enlightening beings, the congregations at the sites of enlightenment, and the infinite ocean of teachings, manifesting therein all kinds of miraculous powers, and also emitting sublime voices explaining the undertakings of Universally Good enlightening beings according to the inclinations of sentient beings, causing them to dedicate themselves to Universal Good. This is the twenty-ninth.

"Next there is a mark of greatness called clouds of radiant illumination abiding in the oceans of all worlds, emanating jewel lights filling all universes in space, revealing therein immaculate sites of enlightenment as well as the physical forms of buddhas and enlightening beings, causing those who see to attain objectless vision. This is the thirtieth.

"Next there is a mark of greatness called cloud of flames of pure light of all jewels, emitting the pure light of the exquisite jewels of the infinite buddhas and enlightening beings, illuminating all universes in the ten directions, revealing all the oceans of enlightening beings therein, all imbued with the spiritual power of the enlightened, forever traveling through the network of all lands in space. This is the thirty-first.

"Next there is a mark of greatness called cloud of illumination of the arrays of all universes; it is right in the middle, at the crest of a gradual rise, adorned with a pure gold cosmic net, emanating clouds of pure light filling the cosmos, instant after instant constantly showing the buddhas, enlightening beings, and congregations at the sites of enlightenment in all worlds. This is the thirty-second.

"The top of Buddha's head is embellished with these thirty-two marks of great people. Between the Buddha's eyebrows is a mark of great people called cloud of light permeating the cosmos, adorned with jewel flowers, emanating great beams of light containing the hues of all jewels, clear and pure as the light of the sun and moon, that light illumining the lands of the ten directions, revealing the bodies of all buddhas therein, and also emitting sublime sounds expressing the ocean of truths. This is the thirty-third mark.

"Buddha's eyes have a mark of greatness called cloud of independent universal vision, adorned by many beautiful jewels, their crystalline light pure and clear, seeing all without any obstruction. This is the thirty-fourth.

"Buddha's nose has a mark of greatness called cloud of knowledge of all spiritual powers, adorned by pure jewels, covered with lights the colors of all jewels, wherein appear infinite phantom buddhas sitting on jewel lotus blossoms, going to all worlds, expounding to all enlightening beings and all sentient beings the inconceivable ocean of all aspects of buddhahood. This is the thirty-fifth.

"Buddha's tongue has a mark of greatness called cloud manifesting reflected images of sound, adorned by beautiful jewels of all colors, produced by the roots of goodness of former times; his tongue's length and breadth covers all oceans of worlds; whenever the Buddha smiles, he emits lights of all jewels that illumine all the universes in the ten directions, causing all minds to become clear and cool; all the buddhas of past, future, and present appear clearly in the lights, all uttering far-reaching, subtle sounds pervading all lands and remaining for infinite eons. This is the thirty-sixth.

"The buddha's tongue has another mark of greatness called cloud of reality realms. It is perfectly flat, adorned with jewels, radiating exquisite jewel lights complete with colors and characteristics like the lights emanating from the hair between the Buddha's eyebrows. Those lights illumine all buddha-lands, showing them to be only made of atoms, having no intrinsic essence. In the lights there also appear countless buddhas, all uttering subtle messages explaining all truths. This is the thirty-seventh.

"The tip of Buddha's tongue has a mark of greatness called cloud of light illuminating the cosmos, adorned with wish-fulfilling jewels, always spontaneously producing golden flames wherein appear reflections of the ocean of all buddhas. It also causes subtle sounds to resonate, filling all the boundless worlds, each sound containing all sounds, and explaining the sublime truth, to the joy of the hearers, who appreciate for measureless eons without forgetting. This is the thirty-eighth.

"The tip of Buddha's tongue has another mark of greatness, called cloud lighting up the cosmos, adorned with diamonds, emanating subtle lights of myriad colors, filling infinite lands of the ten directions throughout the cosmos, all pure, all containing infinite buddhas and enlightening beings, such uttering all kinds of sublime messages, received in person by all enlightening beings. This is the thirty-ninth.

"The Buddha's gums have a mark of greatness called cloud showing the inconceivable realm of reality, adorned with sapphires and lapis lazuli, emanating clouds of pure light from flames of fragrant lamps, filling the cosmos, showing all kinds of means of mystic powers, expounding the profound, inconceivable truth everywhere in all oceans of worlds. This is the fortieth.

"The Buddha's lower right teeth have a mark of greatness called cluster of teeth of Buddha, adorned with jewels set in gammadion patterns, radiating great beams of light illuminating the cosmos, with all buddha-bodies appearing therein, circulating throughout the ten directions, enlightening sentient beings. This is the forty-first.

"The Buddha's upper right teeth have a mark of greatness called clouds of high banks of jewel flames, adorned with treasuries of jewels, emitting pure light of indestructible fragrant flames, each light ray filling the cosmos, showing the spiritual powers of all buddhas, and also showing the pure sites of enlightenment in all worlds in the ten directions. This is the forty-second.

"The Buddha's lower left teeth have a mark of greatness called clouds of radiant illumination from jewel lamps, adorned with all kinds of beautiful jewels emitting flowers and scents, emanating pure light from clouds of lamp flames, filling all oceans of worlds, revealing therein all buddhas sitting on lotus blossoms surrounded by enlightening beings. This is the forty-third.

"The Buddha's upper left teeth have a mark of greatness called cloud reflecting the enlightened ones, adorned with gold of pure brilliance, nets and flowers of jewels, emanating great spheres of flames filling the cosmos, revealing therein all the buddhas using their spiritual powers in space to distribute the milk of the Teaching, the lamps of the Teaching, the treasure of the Teaching, to educate all groups of enlightening beings. This is the forty-fourth.

"The Buddha's front teeth have a mark of greatness called cloud of omnipresent light; between each tooth are arrays of oceans of marks that all radiate light when the Buddha smiles, with crystal flames of the colors of all jewels, swirling to the right, circulating throughout the cosmos, uttering the voice of Buddha, explaining the practice of Universal Good. This is the forty-fifth.

"The Buddha's lips have a mark of greatness called cloud reflecting lights of all jewels, radiating immense beams of light the color of rose gold, of lotuses, and the colors of all jewels, illumining the cosmos and completely purifying it. This is the forty-sixth.

"The Buddha's neck has a mark of greatness called cloud shining on all worlds, adorned by diamonds. His neck is supple, soft, slender, and moist, and gives off radiant pure light filling all worlds in the ten directions, revealing all buddhas therein. This is the forty-seventh.

"The Buddha's right shoulder has a mark of greatness called Buddha's immense cloud of all jewels, emanating lights of the colors of all jewels, gold, and lotus blossoms, forming a network of crystal flames, illuminating the cosmos, revealing all enlightening beings therein. This is the forty-eighth. The Buddha's right shoulder has another mark of greatness, called cloud of supreme jewels shining radiantly, pure as gold in color, emanating crystal light filling the cosmos, revealing all enlightening beings therein. This is the forty-ninth.

"The Buddha's left shoulder has a mark of greatness called cloud of supreme light illuminating the cosmos, variously adorned like the marks on his crown and between his eyebrows, emitting golden, lotus-colored, and jewel-colored lights forming great networks of flames filling the cosmos, showing therein all occult powers. This is the fiftieth. The Buddha's left shoulder has another mark of greatness, called cloud of light shining everywhere, whirling to the right, adorned with gold and diamonds, radiating lights of fragrant flames of flowers of jewels, filling the cosmos, showing all buddhas and all purified lands therein. This is the fifty-first. The Buddha's left shoulder has another mark of greatness, called cloud of universal radiance, whirling to the right, with subtle mysterious adornments, emitting pure light from clouds of flames of buddhas' lamps, filling the cosmos, revealing the various adornments of all enlightening beings therein, all superbly beautiful. This is the fifty-second.

"The Buddha's chest has a mark of greatness shaped like a gammadion called oceanic cluster of auspicious signs, adorned with crystal jewel flowers emitting all kinds of orbs of light flames of the colors of all jewels, filling the cosmos, making it all pure, and also producing marvelous sounds expressing the ocean of the teachings. This is the fifty-third.

"To the right of the mark of auspicious signs is a mark of greatness called cloud of revelation of light, adorned by the cosmic net of Indra, radiating a vast circle of light filling the cosmos, revealing therein infinite buddhas. This is the fifty-fourth.

"There is another mark of greatness to the right of the mark of auspicious signs, called cloud manifesting the Buddha everywhere, adorned by the jewel crowns of enlightening beings, emanating great lights shining on all worlds in the ten directions. Purifying them all, showing therein the buddhas of past, future, and present sitting on the sites of enlightenment, manifesting spiritual powers, and widely expounding the ocean of teachings. This is the fifty-fifth.

"There is another mark of greatness to the right of the mark of auspicious signs, called cloud of blooming flowers, adorned by crystal jewel flowers, radiating pure light rays from precious lamps of fragrant flames, shaped like lotus blossoms, filling the world. This is the fifty-sixth.

"There is another mark of greatness to the right of the mark of auspicious signs, called cloud of pleasant golden color, adorned by diamonds from the Mind King treasury of all jewels, emanating pure light illuminating the cosmos, revealing therein immensely radiant jewel treasuries like the eyes of Buddha. This is the fifty-seventh.

"There is another mark of greatness to the right of the mark of auspicious signs, called cluster of oceans of buddhas, adorned by gems, fragrant lamps, and flower garlands, emanating the pure light of great flames of fragrant lamps of diamond, filling space, pervading all lands, showing the assemblies at the sites of enlightenment there. This is the fifty-eighth.

"To the left of the mark of auspicious signs there is a mark of greatness called clouds of light of revelation, adorned with countless enlightening beings sitting on jewel lotus blossoms, emanating jewel-flame light beams, studded with diamonds, purifying all oceans of universes, revealing therein infinite buddhas and their sublime voices expounding all truths. This is the fifty-ninth.

"There is another mark of greatness to the left of the mark of auspicious signs, called cloud of light appearing throughout the cosmos, adorned by an ocean of jewels, emitting great light pervading all worlds, showing the enlightening beings therein. This is the sixtieth.

"There is another mark of greatness to the left of the mark of auspicious signs, called cloud of universal eminence, adorned with garlands of jewel orbs made of diamonds that shine like the sun, emanating great flames of light filling all oceans of worlds in the cosmos, showing therein all worlds, all buddhas, and all sentient beings. This is the sixty-first.

"There is another mark of greatness to the left of the mark of auspicious signs, called cloud of the sublime sound of the turning of the wheel of the Teaching, adorned by lamps of all truths and flowers of pure fragrance, emitting great beams of light filling the cosmos, revealing therein the ocean of marks and ocean of mind of all the buddhas. This is the sixty-second.

"There is another mark of greatness to the left of the mark of auspicious signs, called cloud of adornments, adorned by the ocean of all buddhas of past, future, and present, radiating immaculate light purifying all buddha-lands, showing therein all the buddhas and enlightening beings as well as the deeds they carry out. This is the sixty-third.

"The Buddha's right hand has a mark of greatness called cloud of oceanic illumination, adorned by myriad jewels, constantly emitting pure light like the aura of the moon, filling all worlds in space, emanating thunderous voices extolling all the practices of enlightening beings. This is the sixty-fourth.

"Buddha's right hand has another mark of greatness, called cloud of reflected radiance, adorned with flowers of lapis lazuli and sapphires, shedding great light illuminating all the worlds in the ten directions where enlightening beings abide, their troves of lotus blossoms, jewels and so on, therein showing the infinite buddhas sitting at the enlightenment tree with the pure body of reality, causing all the lands of the ten directions to quake. This is the sixty-fifth.

"Buddha's right hand has another mark of greatness, called cloud of lamp flame garlands adorning everywhere, arrayed with radiant jewels, emitting great beams of light forming networks of miraculous displays of mystical emanations, showing therein hosts of enlightening beings, all wearing jeweled crowns, expounding the ocean of enlightening practices. This is the sixty-sixth.

"Buddha's right hand has another mark of greatness, called cloud revealing all jewels, adorned with lamps with lotuslike flames, emitting oceanic treasuries of light pervading the cosmos, showing therein infinite buddhas sitting on lotus thrones. This is the sixty-seventh.

"Buddha's right hand has another mark of greatness, called cloud of light, adorned with oceans of crystal flames, emitting flames of all jewels and flames of flowers of fragrant fire, their pure light filling all networks of worlds, showing all buddhas' sites of enlightenment therein. This is the sixty-eighth.

"Buddha's left hand has a mark of greatness called cloud of lamps of jewel-like purity, adorned with the colors of precious elements, radiating light of the golden hue of the Buddha, moment to moment constantly causing all the finest adornments to appear. This is the sixty-ninth.

"Buddha's left hand has another mark of greatness, called cloud of voices of the lamp of knowledge of all lands, adorned with diamond flowers in a cosmic net, radiating pure golden light illumining all worlds in the ten directions. This is the seventieth.

"Buddha's left hand has another mark of greatness, called cloud of light resting on a precious lotus, adorned with exquisite flowers of all precious substances, emanating great light, like a mountainous lamp, lighting all the worlds of the ten directions. This is the seventy-first.

"Buddha's left hand has another mark of greatness, called cloud of universal illumination of the cosmos, adorned with a cosmic net of jewel garlands, jewel discs, and jewel vases, as well as myriad sublime appearances, emitting great light illumining all lands in the ten directions, showing therein all buddhas of all oceans of worlds in all universes, sitting on lotus blossoms. This is the seventy-second.

"Buddha's right fingers have a mark of greatness called cloud showing the whirlpool of lands of all ages, adorned with flowers of all the finest jewels from treasuries of the glow of the moon reflected in the water, emanating great beams of light filling the cosmos, constantly producing therein subtle sound filling the lands of the ten directions. This is the seventy-third.

"Buddha's left fingers have a mark of greatness called cloud resting on all jewels, adorned with sapphires and diamonds, radiating the lights of all jewels, filling the cosmos, showing therein all buddhas and enlightening beings. This is the seventy-fourth.

"Buddha's right palm has a mark of greatness called cloud of radiance, adorned with a thousand-spoked diamond wheel, emanating jewel light whirling to the right filling the cosmos, showing therein all buddhas, each buddhas' body blazing with flames of light, teaching the truth and liberating people, purifying worlds. This is the seventy-fifth.

"Buddha's left palm has a mark of greatness called cloud of flaming wheels, expanding and magically causing all the sites of enlightenment in the cosmos to appear, adorned with a thousand-spoked wheel of sunlike jewels, radiating great beams of light filling all oceans of worlds, revealing therein all enlightening beings, expounding the ocean of practices of Universal Good, entering into all buddhas' lands, each enlightening innumerable sentient beings. This is the seventy-sixth.

"Buddha's genital organ has a mark of greatness called cloud emanating the voice of Buddha, adorned with all kinds of fine jewels, emitting flowery flame light from crystal lamps, the light refulgent, containing the colors of all jewels, illuminating all universes in space, showing therein all buddhas traveling, coming and going, reaching everywhere. This is the seventy-seventh.

"Buddha's right buttock has a mark of greatness called cloud of radiant garlands of jewel lamps, adorned with jewels, emitting inconceivable jewel flame rays of light spreading throughout all universes in the ten directions, being of the same one appearance as the cosmos of space, yet able to produce all appearances, manifesting in each appearance the autonomous mystical projections of the buddhas. This is the seventy-eighth.

"Buddha's left buttock has a mark of greatness called cloud of light covering the sky showing all oceans of universes like lotuses, adorned with pure jewels, emanating networks of light rays illumining all universes in the ten directions, revealing there clouds of all kinds of forms. This is the seventy-ninth.

"Buddha's right thigh has a mark of greatness called cloud of ubiquitous manifestation, adorned with crystals of many colors. The thigh is proportionate to the calf; it radiates lights of the true Teaching, like jewel flames, able to instantly reveal the ocean of forms of the striding of the king of all treasures. This is the eightieth.

"Buddha's left thigh has a mark of greatness called cloud showing the infinite oceans of features of all buddhas, adorned with an ocean of all jewels resting on each one, traveling vast distances, emanating pure light shining on all sentient beings, causing them all to seek the supreme state of buddhahood. This is the eighty-first.

"Buddha's deerlike right calf has a mark of greatness called cloud of all universes in space, adorned with sublime jewels of light. The calf is round and straight and walks well; it emanates pure golden light illuminating all buddhas' worlds and emits great sounds causing them all to quake. It also shows all buddha-lands stationed in space, arrayed with jewel-like flames, from which countless enlightening beings magically appear. This is the eighty-second.

"Buddha's deerlike left calf has a mark of greatness called cloud of oceans of adornments. Golden-hued, it can walk through all buddha-lands, emitting the pure light of all jewels, filling the cosmos, given to perform buddha-works. This is the eighty-third.

"The jewel hair on the Buddha's lower legs has a mark of greatness called cloud of manifestations of reflected images of the cosmos. The hair curls to the right, and each hairtip radiates jewel light filling all universes in the ten directions, showing all buddhas' spiritual powers. The hair pores all emit lights in which appear all buddha-lands. This is the eighty-fourth.

"The soles of Buddha's feet have a mark of greatness called cloud of arrangements of the ocean of all enlightening beings, diamond-colored, with pure lotus blossoms of gold, radiating jewel-like light illumining all oceans of worlds in the ten directions, with clouds of jewel-like fragrant flames reaching everywhere. When he lifts his foot to take a step, a fragrant air circulates, replete with the colors of all jewels, filling the cosmos. This is the eighty-fifth.

"On Buddha's right instep is a mark of greatness called cloud of light shining on everything, adorned with all kinds of jewels, radiating great lights filling the cosmos, showing all buddhas and enlightening beings. This is the eighty-sixth.

"On Buddha's left instep is a mark of greatness called cloud of manifestations of all buddhas, adorned with jewels, emanating jewel light moment to moment showing the miraculous displays of all buddhas, as well as their oceans of teachings, and the enlightenment sites they sit at, this continuing unbroken forever. This is the eighty-seventh.

"Between Buddha's right toes is a mark of greatness called cloud of light illuminating all oceans of universes, variously adorned with diamonds like mountainous lamps and thousand-spoked wheels of flames, radiating great beams of light filling the oceans of worlds in all universes in the ten directions, showing therein the various forms of precious adornments of all buddhas. This is the eighty-eighth.

"Between Buddha's left toes is a mark of greatness called cloud showing the ocean of all buddhas, adorned with jewel flowers, garlands of fragrant flaming lamps, and discs of all jewels, constantly emitting pure lights from an ocean of jewels, filling space, reaching all worlds in the ten directions, showing therein such features of all buddhas and enlightening beings as their universal voices and their mystic gammadion signs of felicity, benefiting all the infinite sentient beings. This is the eighty-ninth.

"Buddha's right heel has a mark of greatness called cloud of independent radiance, adorned with powdered sapphires, always emanating the exquisite jewel light of the buddhas, the splendor of that light filling the cosmos, all the same one appearance, without any differences, therein showing all buddhas sitting at the site of enlightenment and expounding the sublime teaching. This is the ninetieth.

"Buddha's left heel has a mark of greatness called cloud manifesting sublime voices expounding the ocean of truths, adorned with jewels from the ocean of mystic projections, jewels from flowers of a polar mountain in an ocean of fragrant flames, as well as cat's-eye gems, all radiating great beams of light filling the cosmos, showing therein the spiritual powers of the buddhas. This is the ninety-first.

"Buddha's right ankle has a mark of greatness called cloud shining with the light of all adornments, with extremely fine adornments made of all kinds of precious substances, radiating pure golden light, illumining all universes in the ten directions, the light appearing as an enormous cloud covering the sites of enlightenment of all buddhas. This is the ninety-second.

"Buddha's left ankle has a mark of greatness called cloud showing all colors, adorned with radiant jewels and sapphires containing the glow of all moons, moment to moment traveling through the ocean of universes, radiating crystal lamps' fragrant flames' light, that light pervading all universes. This is the ninety-third.

"The circumference of Buddha's right foot has a mark of greatness called universal treasury cloud, adorned with emeralds and diamonds, emanating jewel light filling space, therein showing all buddhas sitting on crystal lion thrones at the sites of enlightenment. This is the ninety-fourth.

"The circumference of Buddha's left foot has a mark of greatness called cloud of light illumining the whole cosmos, adorned with jewel flowers, radiating great lights filling the cosmos, all equal and uniform, therein showing the mystic power of all the buddhas and enlightening beings, with great wondrous voices expounding the endless ways of entry into truth there are in the cosmos. This is the ninety-fifth.

"The tips of Buddha's right toes have a mark of greatness called cloud showing adornments, arrayed with very pleasing pure gold, emanating great rays of light filling all universes in the ten directions, showing therein the boundless ocean of teachings, various virtues, and spiritual powers of all buddhas and enlightening beings. This is the ninety-sixth.

"The tips of Buddha's left toes have a mark of greatness called cloud showing the mystic transformations of all buddhas, adorned with inconceivable buddhas' halos, moon glow, pervasive perfume, and wheels of jewel flames, emanating pure lights of the colors of all jewels, filling all oceans of worlds, showing therein all buddhas and enlightening beings expounding the ocean of all Buddha teachings. This is the ninety-seventh.

"Vairocana Buddha has as many such marks of greatness as atoms in ten Flower Treasury oceans of worlds, each limb adorned with sublime marks of myriad jewels."

BOOK THIRTY-FIVE

The Qualities of the Buddha's Embellishments and Lights

THEN THE WORLD HONORED ONE said to the enlightening being Jewel Hand, "Offspring of Buddha, the perfectly enlightened one has an embellishment called the foremost sphere, from which emanates a great light called effulgence, with seven million infinities of light rays. When I was an enlightening being in the palace of Tushita heaven, I emanated a great light called lightbanner king, illuminating as many worlds as atoms in ten buddha-lands; the sentient beings in the hells of those worlds who were touched by this light gained respite from their torments, and they obtained ten kinds of pure eyes, ears, noses, tongues, bodies, and minds, and all danced for joy. When their lives ended they were reborn in Tushita heaven. In Tushita heaven is a drum called most delightful; when they had been born in heaven, this drum sounded, declaring to them, 'O godlings, because your minds were not indulgent and you planted roots of goodness in the presence of buddhas, and because in the past you associated with the wise, and by the great spiritual power of Vairocana, you have been born in this heaven after the end of your life elsewhere.'

"The thousand-spoked wheels on the soles of my feet as an enlightening being were called king of universal light. They had an embellishment, called the foremost sphere, always emanating forty kinds of light, among them a light called pure virtue, illumining as many worlds as atoms in a hundred trillion buddha-lands, causing all sentient beings to develop maturity according to their various actions and inclinations. Sentient beings in excruciating pain in uninterrupted hell, encountering this light, were born in Tushita heaven after their lives ended. When they were born in heaven, they heard the sound of the celestial drum declare to them, 'Very good! Godlings, the enlightening being Vairocana has entered undefiled concentration; you should pay respects.' Then the godlings, hearing this exhortation from the sound of the celestial drum, thought, 'How wonderful—what is the cause of this subtle sound?' Then the drum answered, 'The sound I make is produced by the power of roots of goodness. Godlings, just as I speak of myself without

946

attachment to self or to what is mine, so too do the buddhas say they are buddhas, yet have no attachment to "I" or "mine." Just as my sound does not come from the east or from the west, the south, the north, or the intermediate directions or the zenith or nadir, in the same way the achievement of buddhahood as a consequence of actions does not come from any of the ten directions. It is as when you were in hell before: the hell and your bodies did not come from any of the ten directions; it was only due to your deluded evil deeds and bondage by folly that you were incarnated in hell—this has no basis, it does not come from anywhere. The enlightening being Vairocana, by spiritual power, emanated great light, yet this light did not come from any of the ten directions; in the same way, my sound does not come from any of the ten directions—it is just the power of good roots of concentration and by the spiritual power of transcendent wisdom that produces this pure sound and manifests these various abilities. Just as Sumeru, the polar mountain, has thirty-three celestial palaces of exalted splendor, with various appurtenances that do not come from any of the ten directions, likewise my sound does not come from any of the ten directions. Just as I teach as many sentient beings as there are atoms in a trillion worlds, each in accord with their inclinations, causing them great joy, yet do not get tired of them or shrink from them, and I do not become proud or heedless, so also does the enlightening being Vairocana do the same, while abiding in un-defiled concentration. From one embellishment on his right palm he emanates one ray of light that manifests innumerable magical powers such as even individually liberated ones cannot know, much less sentient beings. You should go to that enlightening being and attend and serve him. Do not indulge in the pleasures of the senses anymore—attachment to sensual desires obstructs roots of goodness. Just as the world-ending holocaust completely burns away the polar mountain, so also does crav-ing bind up the mind and prevent it from developing the will to remem-ber Buddha. You should be grateful for your blessings and requite the favor you have received. Many ingrates meet untimely deaths and are reborn in hell. You were formerly in hell, when your bodies were illu-mined with light and you left there and were reborn here. You should now quickly rededicate and increase your roots of goodness. Just as I, the heavenly drum, am not male or female, yet can produce measureless, boundless, inconceivable things, so too you gods and goddesses are not male or female yet are able to enjoy all kinds of sublime palaces and groves. Just as my heavenly drum is not born and does not perish, the same is true of material form, sensation, perception, action, and con-sciousness. If you can understand this, know that you will then enter the concentration defined by independence.'

"The godlings, having heard this message, realized unprecedented wonder. Then they all magically produced myriad clouds of flowers, fragrances, music, banners, parasols, and eulogies, and went together to the palace where the enlightening being Vairocana was staying. Joining their palms in respect, they stood to one side and wished to behold him, but they could not see him. The godlings then said, 'The enlightening being Vairocana has already passed away from here and been born in the human world, in the house of King Shuddhodana. He has mounted the sandalwood bower and is in the womb of Lady Maya.' Then the godlings, by means of the celestial eye, saw the body of the enlightening being in the family of the king Shuddhodana in the human realm, being attended by gods of the Brahma heavens and heavens of desire. The godlings then thought, 'If we do not go to the enlightening being and pay our respects, and should give rise to even a single thought of attachment to these celestial palaces, that would not be right.'

"Then each of the godlings, with a retinue of a hundred million, was going to go down to earth. At that point the celestial drum produced a voice telling them, 'The great enlightening being has not ended his life here and been reborn there: it is just that he has, by spiritual power, caused sentient beings to perceive him according to their psychological needs. Just as I now am not visible to the eye, yet can produce a voice, so also the great enlighening being, in undefiled concentration, is not visible to the eye, yet can appear to be born anywhere, without vain discrimination, free from conceit, without attachments. You should arouse the determination for unexcelled, complete perfect enlightenment, purify your minds, lead well-behaved lives, and repent of and get rid of all obstructions due to past actions, obstructions due to afflictions, obstructions due to retribution, and obstructions due to views; with bodies as many as beings in the cosmos, with tongues as many as beings in the cosmos, with good deeds of body, speech, and mind as many as beings in the cosmos, repent of and get rid of all obstructions and faults.'

"The godlings, hearing this, attained unprecedented wonder and were very joyful. They asked, 'How does the great enlightening being repent of and get rid of all faults?' The celestial drum, by the power of roots of goodness of concentration of the enlightening being, said, 'The enlightening being knows that conditioning acts do not come from any particular location, yet they accumulate and dwell in the mind. They come only from delusion and have no abode. The enlightening being clearly sees this with certainty and has no doubt or confusion. Just as I, the celestial drum, speak of actions and consequences, of practice and discipline, of joy and peace, and of various concentrations, so do buddhas and enlightening beings speak of "I" and "mine," speak of sentient beings, of covetousness, wrath, and delusion and their various actions, yet there really is no self or possession—all actions performed, the resulting consequences of the six paths of transmigration, cannot be found wherever you may seek. Just as my voice is not born and does not perish, while the celestials who do evil do not hear my voice but the voice waking them up by means of hell, so also are all actions neither born nor perishing, while according to their practice and accumulation their consequences are experienced. My drum sound is eternally inexhaustible and uninterrupted, and neither coming nor going can be apprehended in it; if there were coming or going, there would be extinction and permanence—the buddhas never say there is extinction or permanence, except as an expedient to develop sentient beings. Just as my sound makes itself available to beings in infinite worlds according to their mentalities, so do all buddhas make themselves visible according to the mentalities of beings. Suppose there is a glass mirror called "reflector," clearly reflecting, equal in size to ten worlds, with the images of all the mountains and rivers, and all the sentient beings, including in the hells, the animals and ghosts, all reflected therein—what do you think, can you say those images enter and exit the mirror?' The godlings answered, 'No.' 'All actions are also like this; though they can produce resulting consequences, there is no place they come or go. Just as a magician deceives people's eyes by illusion, so do actions also do the same. If you know this, this is true repentance of all evils so that all are cleared.'

"When this teaching was spoken, the Tushita godlings in worlds as numerous as atoms in ten quintillion buddha-lands attained acceptance of the nonorigination of all things; immeasurable, inconceivable infinities of godlings of the six heavens of the realm of desire were inspired to seek unexcelled, complete perfect enlightenment; all the goddesses of the heavens of the desire realm relinquished the female body and became determined to attain supreme enlightenment. Then the godlings, because of attaining the ten stages on hearing the tremendous dedication of Universal Good told, because of attaining concentration adorned by various powers, and because of repenting of and clearing away all serious hindrances by means of pure physical, verbal, and mental actions equal in number to living beings, thereupon saw lotus blossoms made of all precious substances, as many blossoms as atoms in ten quintillion buddha-lands, with an enlightening being sitting on each blossom emanating great beams of light; in those beams of light were as many buddhas as there are living beings, sitting in the lotus posture expounding the teaching in accordance with the mentalities of sentient beings—yet still not even a little of the power of undefiled concentration was as yet manifested.

"Then the godlings, by means of the flowers and other things they had produced before, again magically produced in each pore of their bodies as many clouds of fine flowers and so on as there are living beings, to offer to the realized one Vairocana, and took them and scattered them on the Buddha; all of them hovered over the Buddha's body while the fragrant clouds rained over worlds as many as atoms in countless buddha-lands. Any sentient beings who were enveloped in that fragrance became physically peaceful and blissful, like a mendicant who has entered the fourth stage of meditation, in whom all obstructions due to past actions vanish. Sentient beings have five hundred internal afflictions and five hundred external afflictions relating to form, sound, smell, flavor, and tactile feeling; those rife with covetousness have 21,000, those rife with anger have 21,000, those rife with delusion have 21,000, and those equally habituated to all three also have 21,000—but if they smell this fragrance, they realize that all these are unreal. Once they realize this, they develop pure roots of goodness with the light of mystic power, like clouds of fragrant banners.

"Those who see the canopies produced by the enlightening beings plant the innumerable roots of goodness of universal monarchs of the pure gold net of the tenth stage of enlightening. When enlightening beings are in this status of universal monarch, they edify beings in worlds as numerous as atoms in ten quintillion buddha-lands. In the case of the buddha called Knowledge Like the Moon, of the world called Clear Mirror, there are always monks, nuns, laymen, laywomen, and others from countless worlds who project their bodies to come listen to the Teaching; that buddha, without a moment's pause, relates to them the events of former lives. Any sentient beings who hear the name of the buddha will surely be reborn in the land of the Buddha. That case of enlighening beings in the rank of universal monarch with the pure golden net is also like this: any who encounter their light will surely attain the tenth stage of enlightening beings, because of the power of roots of goodness previously cultivated. When one has attained the first meditation, though one's life has not yet ended, one can see the palaces in the Brahma heaven and can experience the bliss of the Brahma world; likewise those who attain the other stages of meditation. The great enlightening beings in the rank of universal monarch with the pure golden net radiate pure light such that any beings who are touched by it all gain the tenth stage of enlightening and attain immeasurable light of knowledge, acquire ten kinds of pure eyes, ten kinds of pure ears, noses, tongues, bodies, and ten kinds of pure intellects; they accomplish immeasurable profound concentrations and achieve such a pure physical eye.

"Suppose someone took ten trillion buddha-lands and reduced them to atoms, and then reduced to atoms as many buddha-lands as those atoms, then put all those atoms in his left hand and carried them past an equal number of worlds to the east, and then put down one atom, and continued this way to the east until all the atoms were exhausted, and did the same in the other nine directions: if all the worlds in the ten directions, both those in which he had deposited an atom and those in which he had not, were all assembled to form a single buddha-land, do you think that the immeasurable vastness of this buddha-land would be conceivable or not?"

Jewel Hand said, "It would not be conceivable. The enormous size of such a land would be immeasurable, extraordinary, inconceivable. If any sentient beings heard this comparison and believed and understood it, that would be even more extraordinary."

The Buddha said, "This is so, Jewel Hand. It is as you say. If any good man or woman should hear this example and believe in it, I would give them the prediction that they will certainly attain unexcelled, complete perfect enlightenment and will acquire the unsurpassed knowledge of buddhas.

"Suppose again, Jewel Hand, that someone reduced to atoms as many enormous buddha-lands of the magnitude described above as atoms in a hundred billion buddha-lands, and deposited each of these atoms, as in the foregoing example, and all of these worlds, those on which an atom was deposited as well as those in between, were united in a single buddha-land. Then again suppose this buddha-land were reduced to atoms, and so on, repeating this process eighty times: the enlightening being's pure physical eye, a consequence of action, can clearly see in a single instant every particle in all those immense buddha-lands, and also see buddhas as numerous as atoms in ten billion immense buddha-lands, just as the pure light of the crystal mirror reflects as many worlds as atoms in ten buddha-lands. Jewel Hand, all this is accomplished by the virtues of the most profound concentration of the universal monarch of the pure gold net."

BOOK THIRTY-SIX

The Practice
of Universal Good

AT THAT TIME the great enlightening being Universal Good also said to the great congregation of enlightening beings, "Offspring of Buddha, what has been expounded up till now is just a brief exposition of a little bit of the realm of buddhas, adapted so as to be appropriate to the faculties and capacities of sentient beings. Why? The buddhas emerge in the world because sentient beings are ignorant and do what is bad, they conceive of self and possessions, they cling to the body, they are deluded and confused, they discriminate on the basis of false views and are always in bondage, following the flow of birth and death away from the path of enlightenment.

"I do not see anything that is a bigger mistake than for enlightening beings to become angry at other enlightening beings. Why? Because if enlightening beings become angry at other enlightening beings, that creates a million obstacles. What are those million obstacles? They are the obstacle of not seeing enlightenment, the obstacle of not hearing the true Teaching, the obstacle of being born in an impure world, the obstacle of being born in miserable states, the obstacle of being born in places where it is difficult to become enlightened, the obstacle of sickliness, the obstacle of being the object of much slander, the obstacle of being born stupid, the obstacle of loss of right mindfulness and recollection, the obstacle of lack of intelligence, obstacles of eye, ear, nose, tongue, body, and mind, the obstacle of bad advisers, the obstacle of bad companions, the obstacle of inclination toward practice of individualistic liberation, the obstacle of inclination toward associating with the vulgar, the obstacle of not believing in people of great spiritual power, the obstacle of living with people who have strayed from correct perception, the obstacle of being born in a family of heretics, the obstacle of dwelling in the realm of demons, the obstacle of being estranged from the right Teaching of Buddha, the obstacle of not seeing good companions, the obstacle of blockage of roots of goodness, the obstacle of increase of bad conditions, the obstacle of meanness, the obstacle of being born in a remote area, the obstacle of being born in a family of evil people, the obstacle of being born among evil spirits, evil ghosts, hobgoblins, demons, titans, vipers, and so on, the obstacle of not caring for the Buddha teachings, the obstacle of habituation to infantile behavior, the obstacle of clinging to the small vehicle of individual salvation, the obstacle of not liking the Great Vehicle of universal salvation, the obstacle of fearfulness, the obstacle of anxiety, the obstacle of clinging to mundane routines, the obstacle of not concentrating on the way to enlightenment, the obstacle of not liking to see or hear of the spiritual powers of Buddha, the obstacle of not acquiring the faculties of enlightening beings, the obstacle of not applying the purifying practices of enlightening beings, the obstacle of shrinking from the determination of enlightening beings, the obstacle of not making the great vow of enlightening beings, the obstacle of not developing the determination for omniscience, the obstacle of slacking off from the practice of enlightening beings, the obstacle of not being able to purify acts, the obstacle of not being able to incorporate great virtues, the obstacle of the power of knowledge not being clear and keen, the obstacle of shutting off great wisdom and knowledge, the obstacle of not preserving the practices of enlightening beings, the obstacle of inclination to repudiate all words of wisdom, the obstacle of estrangement from the enlightenment of the buddhas, the obstacle of inclination to abide in the realms of demons, the obstacle of not concentrating on cultivating the realm of buddhahood, the obstacle of not definitively making the universal commitment of enlightening beings, the obstacle of not liking to live with enlightening beings, the obstacle of not seeking the roots of goodness of enlightening beings, the obstacle of being opinionated and suspicious, the obstacle of the continual befuddlement of the mind, the obstacle of being unwilling to give because of inability to practice the impartial generosity of enlightening beings, the obstacle of transgression of precepts by being unable to maintain the precepts of the Buddha, the obstacle of foolish malevolence and anger due to inability to achieve tolerance and forbearance, the obstacle of the defilement of laziness due to inability to act with the great vigor of enlightening beings, the obstacle of distraction and confusion due to inability to attain concentration, the obstacle of misused intellect due to failure to cultivate transcendent wisdom, the obstacle of lack of familiarity with what is so and what is not so, the obstacle of having no means to liberate beings, the obstacle of inability to contemplate the knowlege of enlightening beings, the obstacle of not knowing enlightening beings' means of emancipation, the obstacle of failure to develop the ten great eyes of enlightening beings and therefore being as if blind, the obstacle of being dumb as an animal due to not hearing the teaching of nonobstruction, the obstacle of destruction of the nose due to not having the marks and embellishments of buddhahood, the obstacle of inability to understand speech and the consequent inability to speak, the obstacle of physical problems due to demeaning sentient beings, the obstacle of mental problems due to lack of control of mind, the obstacle of physical actions due to not keeping the precepts, the obstacle of verbal actions due to continually committing faults of speech, the obstacle of mental actions due to conceiving much covetousness, anger, and erroneous views, the obstacle of seeking the teaching with a thieving mind, the obstacle of cutting off the perspective of enlightening beings, the obstacle of shrinking from the effort of enlightening beings, the obstacle of laziness of mind on the enlightening beings' way to emancipation, the obstacle of the mind stopping at the entry of the light of knowledge of enlightening beings, the obstacle of becoming weak-minded and incapable of the recollective power of enlightening beings, the obstacle of being unable to retain the teachings of the buddhas, the obstacle of being unable to approach enlightening beings' path of detachment from birth, the obstacle of inability to cultivate the incorruptible path of enlightening beings, the obstacle of following the absolute state of one-sided detachment, the obstacle of estrangement from the family of the buddhas and enlightening beings of all times.

"If an enlightening being conceives a single feeling of anger toward enlightening beings, that produces a million obstacles such as these. Why? I do not see anything that is as big a mistake as for enlightening beings to become angry at other enlightening beings. Therefore, if great enlightening beings want to quickly fulfill the practices of enlightening beings, they should diligently practice ten principles: in their minds they should not abandon sentient beings; they should think of enlightening beings as buddhas; they should never slander any teachings of the buddhas, they should know that there is no end to different lands; they should be profoundly devoted to enlightening practices; they should not give up the cosmic, spacelike, impartial mind of enlightenment; they should contemplate enlightenment and enter the power of buddhas; they should cultivate unobstructed intellectual and expository powers; they should teach and enlighten beings tirelessly; they should live in all worlds without attachment in their minds.

"When great enlightening beings are living by these ten principles, they are able to embody ten kinds of purity. What are these ten? Purity of comprehension of the most profound truth; purity of association with good associates; purity of preserving the Buddha teachings; purity of comprehension of the realm of space; purity of profound penetration of the realm of reality; purity of observation of infinite minds; purity of having the same roots of goodness as all enlightening beings; purity of nonattachment to the various ages; purity of observation of past, present, and future; purity of practice of all enlightening teachings.

"When great enlightening beings persist in these ten things, they become imbued with ten kinds of broad knowledge: that is, knowledge of all sentient beings' mental behavior; knowledge of the consequences of actions of all sentient beings; knowledge of all Buddha teachings; knowledge of the profound, occult import of all Buddha teachings;

knowledge of all methods of concentration spells; knowledge of interpretation of all writings; knowledge of the language and speech of all sentient beings; knowledge of manifestation of their bodies in all worlds; knowledge of manifestation of their reflections in all assemblies; knowledge of embodying omniscience in all realms of being.

"Once great enlightening beings are established in this knowledge, they realize ten kinds of universal entry: all worlds enter one point, one point enters all worlds; all beings' bodies enter one body, one body enters all beings' bodies; untold eons enter one instant, one instant enters untold eons; all Buddhist principles enter one principle, one principle enters all Buddhist principles; untold places enter one place, one place enters all places; untold faculties enter one faculty, one faculty enters untold faculties; all faculties enter nonfaculty, nonfaculty enters all faculties; all perceptions enter one perception, one perception enters all perceptions; one utterance enters all utterances, all utterances enter one utterance; all pasts, presents, and futures enter one time frame, one time frame enters all pasts, presents, and futures.

"Once great enlightening beings have contemplated in this way, they abide in ten kinds of sublime mind: the sublime mind in which none of the perceptions and thoughts of sentient beings can abide; the sublime mind of the ultimate realm of space; the sublime mind of the boundless cosmos; the sublime mind of all the profound esoteric principles of buddhahood; the sublime mind of the extremely profound state of nondifferentiation; the sublime mind annihilating all doubt and confusion; the sublime mind of the nondifferentiated equality of all worlds; the sublime mind of the equality of all buddhas of past, present, and future; the sublime mind of the infinity of the power of all buddhas.

"Once great enlightening beings abide in these ten kinds of sublime mind, they acquire ten kinds of technical knowlege of the Buddha teachings: technical knowledge comprehending the most profound Buddha teaching; technical knowledge of the production of far-reaching Buddha teachings; technical knowledge of exposition of all kinds of Buddha teachings; technical knowledge of realizing the Buddha teaching of equality; technical knowledge of understanding the Buddha teaching of differentiation; technical knowledge of understanding the Buddha teaching of nondifferentiation; technical knowledge of profound penetration of the Buddha teaching of adornment; technical knowledge of penetrating the Buddha teachings by one means; technical knowledge of penetrating the Buddha teachings by innumerable means; technical knowledge of nondifference of the boundless Buddha teachings; technical knowledge of nonregression in the Buddha teachings by one's own mind and one's own power.

"When great enlightening beings have heard this teaching, they should all be inspired and respectfully accept and hold it. Why? Great enlightening beings who hold this teaching quickly attain unexcelled, complete perfect enlightenment with a minimum of effort, and all are enabled to embody all qualities of buddhahood, equal to the qualities of the buddhas of all times.''

Then, by the spiritual power of the Buddha as well as by natural law, in each of the ten directions as many worlds as atoms in ten unspeakable numbers of tens of quintillions of buddha-lands all quaked in six ways and rained showers from clouds of all flowers surpassing those of the heavens, as well as clouds of perfumes, incenses, robes, canopies, banners, pennants, jewels, and all kinds of decorations; there rained clouds of music, clouds of enlightening beings, clouds of physical forms of untold buddhas, clouds of infinite praises of the buddhas, clouds of voices of buddhas filling all universes, untold clouds of magically arrayed worlds, untold clouds developing enlightenment, untold clouds of light shining, and untold clouds of mystic manifestations expounding the Teaching.

As in this world, at the site of enlightenment, under the tree of enlightenment, in the palace of the enlightening being, the Buddha, the Completely Enlightened One, was seen expounding this teaching, so it was in all worlds in the ten directions.

Then, owing to the spiritual power of the Buddha as well as by natural law, there came to this land as many great enlightening beings as atoms in ten buddha-lands from each of the ten directions, from beyond as many worlds as atoms in ten infinities of buddha-lands. Filling the ten directions, they spoke these words to Universal Good: "It is very good, Offspring of Buddha, that you can explain this profound teaching of the giving of the prophecy of enlightenment, the greatest promise of the buddhas. We are all named Universal Good, the same as you, and each have come to this land from a world called Universal Excellence, from the company of buddhas called Freedom Representative of Universality. All, by the spiritual power of Buddha, expound this teaching, with such assemblies and such utterances, all equal, with neither increase nor decrease. We have all come to this enlightenment site by the Buddha's spiritual power to be witnesses for you. As we innumerable enlightening beings serve as witnesses at this site of enlightenment, the same is so in all worlds in the ten directions."

Then the great enlightening being Universal Good, by the spiritual power of the Buddha and by the power of his own roots of goodness, looked over the ten directions, throughout the cosmos; wishing to elucidate the practice of enlightening beings, to tell of the realm of enlightenment of the buddhas, to explain the realm of great vows, to explain the reckoning of ages of all worlds, to clarify the timely appearance of the buddhas, to explain how the buddhas develop beings according to their faculties, appearing to let them attend them, to make it clear that the effort of the buddhas' appearance in the world is not wasted, to make it clear that roots of goodness that are planted will surely bear fruit, and to clarify how enlightening beings of great spiritual power manifest forms for all sentient beings to teach and enlighten them, spoke these verses:

You should rejoice,
Get rid of all veils,
And single-mindedly listen with respect
To the vows and acts of enlightening beings.

The enlightening beings of the past
Were supreme lions of humanity;
The practices they carried out
I shall tell in order.

I will also tell the numbers of ages
The worlds and acts
And the peerless honored ones
Who emerged therein.

As for those past buddhas
Who appeared in the world by their vows,
How did they destroy afflictions
For all sentient beings?

All the lions of philosophy
Continue practice to fulfillment,
Attaining the state of equality of buddhas,
The realm of omniscience.

Seeing all the human lions
Of past ages
Emanating great networks of lights
Illumining the worlds of the ten directions,
They reflected and made their vows:
"I should be a lamp for the world
Replete with the virtues of buddhahood,
Their ten powers, their omniscience.
All sentient beings
Burn with greed, anger, and folly;
I should save and free them,
Have them extinguish the pains of the states of woe."

They make such vows,
Steadfast, unregressing,
To cultivate all enlightening practices
And gain the unimpeded ten powers.

Having made such vows,
They cultivate practice without shrinking back.

None of their actions are in vain,
Thus they are called lions of philosophy.

In one eon of virtue
A thousand buddhas emerged in the world:
Their universal eyes
I will explain in order.

As in one eon of virtue
So too in measureless eons;
Those future buddhas' practices
I will explain distinctly.

As in one type of buddha-land,
So in numberless lands;
The practices of future buddhas
I will now explain.

Buddhas' successive emergence in the world,
What were their vows, what their names,
What were the prophecies they received,
What were their life spans,
What were the true principles they practiced
Solely seeking the unobstructed path,
Who were the beings they taught,
How long their right teaching remained in the world,
What were the buddha-lands they purified,
The sentient beings there and the cycles of teaching,
Their explanation of proper and improper timing,
Progressively purifying beings,
What were the actions of the beings,
Their patterns and inclinations,
High, middling, low, not the same,
How they influenced them to practice—
Penetrating such knowledge,
The future buddhas cultivated the supreme practice,
Always doing the work of Universal Good,
Widely freeing the living.

Physical actions unimpeded,
Verbal actions all pure,
Mental actions also thus,
Always like this at all times—
Enlightening beings acting thus
Consummate the path of Universal Good,

Producing the sun of pure knowledge
Illuminating the cosmos.

The lands of future eons
Are unspeakably many in number;
They know them all in an instant
Without discrimination among them.

Those who practice can enter into
Such a supreme state:
Of these principles of enlightening beings
I shall tell a little.

Knowledge and wisdom boundless,
They realize the scope of buddhahood;
Entering completely therein,
Their practice does not regress.

Replete with Universally Good wisdom,
They fulfill Universally Good vows
And enter the peerless knowledge;
I shall tell of their practice.

In a single atom
They see all worlds;
If sentient beings should hear of this,
They'd go mad in confusion.

As in one atom,
So in all atoms;
All worlds enter therein—
So inconceivable is it.

In every single atom
Are all things of all places and times;
The states and lands, innumerable,
The enlightening discern and know.

In every single atom
Are countless kinds of buddha-lands,
And each kind is also countless;
They know all in one.

All the various different features
That there are in the cosmos,

The types of beings, each different,
They can discern and know.

Deeply entering subtle knowledge,
They distinguish the worlds;
The becoming and decay of all ages
They can clearly explain.

They know the length and brevity of all ages,
And that past, present, and future are one moment:
The sameness and difference of myriad practices
They all distinctly know.

They penetrate all worlds,
Vast and small,
One body countless lands,
One land, countless bodies.

The innumerable features
Of the worlds of different species
In the ten directions
They know entirely.

Those of most profound knowledge
Comprehend the becoming and decay
Of the numberless lands
Of past, present, and future.

Of the worlds in the ten directions,
Some are forming, some decaying:
Infinite though they be,
The virtuous comprehend them all.

There are some lands
With variously adorned ground,
And the beings are also adorned—
This is due to purity of action.

Then again some lands
Have countless kinds of pollution;
This is due to beings experiencing everything
According to their acts.

Infinite, boundless worlds,
The enlightening know are one land;

Thus do they enter all lands,
Whose number cannot be known.

All worlds
Enter one land:
The worlds do not become one,
Yet there is no mixup.

Worlds are inverted and upright,
Some high, some low—
All are the perceptions of beings:
The enlightening discern them all.

The wide worlds
Are infinite, boundless;
They know all kinds are one
And know that one is various.

The Universally Good offspring of Buddha
Can, by Universally Good knowledge,
Know the number of lands,
Though the number is boundless.

They know the projections of worlds,
The projections of lands and beings,
The projections of teachings and buddhas—
All to the ultimate point.

All worlds,
Micro- and macrocosmic,
Various different arrays—
All arise from action.

Infinite enlightening beings
Learn to enter the reality realm;
Their spiritual powers free,
They reach everywhere in the ten directions.

If the names of those worlds were spoken
For eons as many as beings,
They still could not be all told—
Only Buddha can reveal them.

The various names
Of the worlds and buddhas

Could not be fully told
Even in countless eons.

The most excellent wisdom,
The teachings of buddhas of all times,
Are born from the realm of reality
And fill the state of enlightenment.

With pure, unobstructed mindfulness,
Boundless, unimpeded wisdom,
They analyze the reality realm
To reach the other shore.

The worlds of the past,
Great and small,
The arrangements they have developed,
Buddhas know in an instant.

The human lions therein
Cultivate the various practices of buddhas,
Attain to true awakening,
And manifest their freedoms.

Enlightening beings know all
Such buddhas of the future,
The most noble of humans
In boundless ages to come,
All their undertakings,
All their various states,
How they strive in practice,
And therein attain enlightenment.

They know their congregations,
Their life spans, and the beings they teach,
By what means they teach,
Turning the wheel of truth for the masses.

Knowing this, enlightening beings
Abide in the stage of Universally Good practice,
Their knowledge and wisdom, thoroughly clear,
Giving birth to all the buddhas.

They enter deeply
Into all the buddha-lands
There are in the present
And arrive at the reality realm.

All the present buddhas
In all those worlds
Are masters of teaching,
Unhindered in discourse.

They also know their congregations,
Pure lands, and adaptive powers;
For countless million eons
They always ponder these things.

The awesome psychic powers
And endless stores of knowledge
Of the noble Tamers of the World,
The enlightening beings know all.

Producing unobstructed eyes,
Unobstructed ears, noses, bodies,
And unobstructed universal tongues,
They can gladden sentient beings.

Their supreme, unobstructed minds
Are broad and totally pure;
Their knowledge pervading all,
They know all things of all times.

They study all projections,
Projections of lands and beings,
Of worlds and civilizations,
And finally reach the other shore of projections.

The various distinctions of all worlds
All are there due to perceptions and thoughts;
Entering buddhas' knowledge of means,
They clearly understand all this.

For each of untold groups
They manifest embodiment
Causing all to see the Buddha,
And liberating boundless beings.

The profound knowledge of buddhas
Is like the sun coming out in the world,
Ever appearing everywhere
In all lands.

They realize all worlds
Are provisional names, without reality;

Sentient beings and worlds
Are like dreams, like shadows.

They do not produce false discriminatory views
About the things of the world:
Those free from false discrimination
Do not even see false discriminations.

Measureless, countless eons
They understand are one moment;
And they know a moment has no moment—
Thus do they see the world.

Innumerable lands
They cross over in an instant,
Yet through measureless eons
They don't move from their original place.

Untold eons
Are the space of a moment;
Not seeing long or short,
They find ultimate instantaneousness.

Mind is in the world,
World is in the mind—
About this they do not wrongly create
Discriminations of duality and nonduality.

Beings, worlds, ages,
Buddhas and Buddha teachings—
All are like illusory projections:
In the reality realm all is equal.

Throughout the lands of the ten directions
They manifest infinite bodies;
Knowing bodies arise from conditions,
They have no attachments at all.

Based on nondual knowledge
They manifest the buddhas,
Without attachment to nonduality,
Knowing there is no duality or nonduality.

They realize that all worlds
Are like flames, like lights,

Like echoes, like dreams,
Like illusions, like emanations.

Thus they accordingly enter
The sphere of action of the buddhas
And achieve Universally Good knowledge
Illumining all the profound realm of truth.

Attachments to beings and lands
They completely give up,
Yet rouse minds of great compassion
And purify all worlds.

Enlightening beings always rightly remember
The marvelous teachings of the buddhas,
Pure and clear as space,
Yet producing great expedient means.

Seeing the world always deluded,
They determine to save and liberate all:
Their undertakings are all pure,
Extending throughout all universes.

Buddhas and enlightening beings,
Buddhist principles and things of the world—
If you see their reality,
All are no different from one another.

Buddhas' reality-body matrix
Is in all worlds,
Yet while being in the world
Has no attachment to the world.

Just as in clear water
Reflections have no coming or going,
The reality-body's being in the world
Is also like this.

Thus freed from attachment,
Body and world are both pure:
Clear and still as space,
There is no birth at all.

Knowing the body has no end,
No birth and no destruction,

Being neither eternal nor impermanent,
They show it in all worlds.

Destroying false views,
They point out correct insight:
The essence of things has no coming or going,
Is uninvolved with self or possession.

As when a skilled magician
Causes various things to appear,
Their coming is from nowhere
And they go nowhere,
The nature of illusions is not finite
Nor is it infinite,
But in the midst of the crowd
He manifests the finite and infinite,
Similarly by the mind in silent concentration
Cultivating roots of goodness
Produces all buddhas,
Neither finite nor infinite:
Finiteness and infinity
Are deluded notions—
Comprehending all states of being,
The enlightening do not cling to finiteness or infinity.

The buddhas' most profound truth
Is vast, deep, ultimate quiescence;
Their profound, measureless knowledge
Knows the deepest states.

Enlightening beings are freed from delusion,
Their purity of mind is continuous;
By means of spiritual powers
They skillfully liberate numberless beings.

To those not at rest they bring rest,
To those at peace they show the site of enlightenment.
Thus do they go throughout the cosmos,
Their minds without attachment.

Not dwelling on ultimate reality
And not entering nirvana,
Thus they go throughout the worlds
Enlightening living beings.

The classes of phenomena and beings
They know without being attached;

Everywhere showering the rain of truth,
They fill and enrich all worlds.

In all worlds
They realize true awakening moment to moment
Yet cultivate the practice of enlightening beings
Without ever retreating.

The various bodies in the world
They know all completely;
Thus knowing physical phenomena
They realize the body of buddhas.

They know all sentient beings,
All ages and lands,
Throughout the ten directions, boundless,
Entering fully into the ocean of knowledge.

Beings' forms are infinite;
For each the buddhas manifest a body.
The buddhas' bodies are boundless—
The wise observe them all.

What they know in one moment
Manifests the buddhas,
Impossible to fully tell
Even in measureless eons.

The buddhas can manifest their bodies
Passing finally away in any place;
In an instant innumerable relics
Are individually divided.

Thus those of certain knowledge
Know the infinite will for enlightenment
Of the seekers of buddhahood
In the ages to come.

Ability to know in this way
All the enlightened ones
Of past, present, and future
Is called maintaining the practice of Universal Good.

Thus distinctly knowing
Countless stages of practice,
Entering the abode of wisdom,
The cycle never rolls back.

Subtle, extensive knowledge
Entering deeply into the sphere of buddhahood
And having entered, not regressing
Is called Universally Good wisdom.

All the supremely noble ones
Enter the realm of buddhahood;
Their practice never regressing,
They attain unexcelled enlightenment.

The different individual actions
Of infinitely many minds
All come from accumulations of conceptions:
The equanimous know them all.

Defiled or undefiled,
Learners' minds, nonlearners' minds—
Untold numbers of minds
They know at every moment.

They know they are not one or two,
Not defiled and not pure,
And also without mixture—
All arise from one's own notions.

Thus they clearly see
All living beings
With minds and thoughts each different
Creating various worlds.

By such means
Cultivating supreme practice
And being reborn from the Teaching
They can be called Universally Good.

Sentient beings all wrongly produce
The conceptions of the good and bad states;
Because of this they may be born in heaven
Or then again fall into hell.

Enlightening beings see the worlds
As produced by the action of false ideas;
Because false ideas are boundless
Infinite too are the worlds.

All lands are manifestations
Of the network of conceptions;
By the means of the net of illusion
One can instantly enter them all.

Eye, ear, nose, tongue, body,
And the intellect too are thus—
Conceptions of the world are different;
All can be equally contained therein.

In each object of the eye
There are infinite eyes immanent,
Their various natures different,
Measureless, unspeakable.

What is seen has no difference
And also no mixup;
Everyone, according to his own acts,
Experiences the resulting consequences.

The power of Universal Good is infinite,
Knowing them all completely;
In all objects of eyes
There is great knowledge immanent.

Thus enlightening beings know distinctly
Every worldly realm
And cultivate all enlightening practices
Without ever turning back.

Buddhas teach, beings teach,
And lands teach too:
Everything in all times teaches thus—
The enlightening ones know every particular.

The future is the past,
The present is the future,
The three times look to each other;
The enlightening understand each.

Thus in infinite ways
They awaken the worlds:
No boundaries can be found
To the means of total knowledge.

BOOK THIRTY-SEVEN

Manifestation of Buddha

THEN, from the circle of white hair between his brows, the Buddha emitted a great beam of light called manifestation of the realizer of Thusness, accompanied by countless trillions of light beams. That light illumined all the worlds in the whole cosmos, circling ten times to the right, revealing the immeasurable powers of the enlightened, awakening countless enlightening beings, shaking all worlds, extinguishing the suffering of all states of misery, eclipsing the abodes of all demons, and showing all buddhas sitting on the seat of enlightenment attaining perfect awakening, as well as all the assemblies at the sites of enlightenment. Having done all this, the light returned and circled the assembly of enlightening beings, then entered the head of the enlightening being Wondrous Qualities of Natural Origination of Buddha.

Now the masses at this enlightenment site were elated, ecstatic; they thought, "How extraordinary! Now that the Buddha has radiated great light, surely he will expound a most profound great teaching." Then the enlightening being Wondrous Qualities of Natural Origination of Buddha, on a lotus blossom seat, bared his right shoulder, knelt on his right knee, joined his palms, turned toward the Buddha with total attention, and spoke these verses:

> The Truly Awake, the Virtuous, the Great Sage, emerges,
> Comprehending all objects, reaching the Other Shore,
> Equal to the buddhas of past, present, and future;
> Therefore I now pay reverent obeisance.
>
> Having risen to the shore of the signless realm
> And appeared in a body magnificently arrayed with wondrous
>   marks,
> He radiates thousands of undefiled beams of light
> And destroys the hordes of demons entirely.
>
> All the worlds in the ten directions
> He causes to quake without exception,

Yet without frightening a single sentient being—
Such is the spiritual power of the Felicitous One.

Equal in essence to space and the cosmos,
He can remain as stable as they.
All the living, without count or measure,
He has destroyed evil and removed defilements.

Working hard at austere practices for countless ages,
He fully attained the highest enlightenment,
His knowledge unhindered in the midst of all objects,
Of the same nature as all the buddhas.

The Guide radiates these great beams of light,
Shaking the worlds in the ten directions;
Displaying measureless mystic powers,
They have returned and entered my body.

Well able to learn the definitive teaching,
Countless enlightening beings have assembled here
And inspired me to ask about the Teaching,
Wherefore I now petition the Sovereign Teacher.

This assembly is now clear and serene,
Able to liberate all in the world,
Their wisdom boundless, without attachments—
Such eminent sages have all gathered here.

The benefactor of the world, the noble guide,
With wisdom and energy beyond measure
Now illumines the crowd with great light
Causing me to ask about the unexcelled Teaching.

Who can truly expound in full
The profound realm of the great wizard?
Who is the inheritor of the Buddha doctrine?
Noble Guide of the World, please show us.

Then the Buddha emitted a great beam of light, called unimpeded confidence, from his mouth, accompanied by countless trillions of light beams, illumining all worlds in the cosmos, circling ten times to the right, showing the various controlling powers of the Buddha, awakening innumerable enlightening beings, shaking all the worlds of the ten directions, extinguishing the pains of all states of misery, eclipsing all abodes of demons, and showing all the buddhas on the seat of enlightenment attaining true awakening, as well as the assemblies at all those sites of enlightenment. Having done all this, the lights came back, circled the assembly of enlightening beings, and entered the mouth of the enlightening being Universally Good, after which the body and lion throne of Universally Good surpassed their former condition, and that of the other enlightening beings a hundredfold, surpassing all except the lion throne of the Buddha.

Then the enlightening being Wondrous Qualities of Natural Origination of Buddha asked the great enlightening being Universally Good, "This vast miraculous display manifested by the Buddha, causing all the enlightening beings joy, is inconceivable, incomprehensible to the world—what is this auspicious sign?" Universally Good replied, "In the past when I saw buddhas show such tremendous mystic displays, they expounded the teaching of the manifestation of Buddha. I think that now since he has displayed this sign, he is going to expound this teaching. When this teaching is expounded, the whole earth quakes and immeasurable lights asking about the teaching are produced."

Then the enlightening being Wondrous Qualities of Natural Origination of Buddha asked the enlightening being Universally Good, "How should great enlightening beings know the principle of the manifestation of the buddhas, those who realize Thusness, those who are truly awake? Please tell us; these countless trillions of enlightening beings have all cultivated purifying practice for a long time, their recollection and precise awareness is fully developed, they embody the dignity of all buddhas, they have reached the consummation of ultimate great adornment, they correctly remember all buddhas without forgetting, they observe all sentient beings with great compassion, they know with certainty the spheres of spiritual powers of great enlightening beings, they have already received the support of the spiritual power of buddhas, they are able to receive the sublime teachings of all buddhas: imbued with immeasurable such virtues, they have all come and gathered here. You have already attended and served countless quintillions of buddhas, accomplished the supreme practice of enlightening beings, have attained mastery of all modes of concentration, have penetrated the esoteric secrets of all buddhas, know all ways of enlightenment, have put an end to all doubt, are supported by the spiritual power of the buddhas, know the faculties of sentient beings and explain ways of genuine liberation to them according to their inclinations, follow the knowledge of Buddha, expound the Buddha teachings, and have reached the Other Shore. You have infinite such virtues, worthy of praise. Please explain the phenomena of the manifestation of the buddhas, those who realize Thusness, the truly awake—their physical forms, utterances, states of mind, practices, enlightenment, and preaching, until their manifestation of entry into ultimate extinction, and the roots of goodness generated by seeing, hearing, and associating with them. Please tell us about all these things."

Then the enlightening being Wondrous Qualities of Natural Origin of Buddha, desiring to reiterate his point, spoke these verses to the enlightening being Universally Good:

Excellent sage of unimpeded wisdom,
You are well aware of the boundless realm of equality.
Please explain the practices of infinite buddhas;
The enlightening beings will be happy to hear them.

How can enlightening beings follow and comprehend
The buddhas' emergence in the world?
What are their spheres of body, speech, and mind?
Tell us this, and their spheres of action too.

How do buddhas attain true enlightenment?
How do buddhas turn the wheel of the Teaching?
How do the Blissful Ones pass away?
The masses will be happy to hear.

Of those who see the buddhas, great spiritual sovereigns,
Attend them and develop roots of goodness,
Please tell us the stores of virtue
And what the beings who see them attain.

If any hear of buddhas' names,
Whether present in the world or extinct,
And deeply believe in their treasury of merit,
Tell us how they will benefit.

These enlightening beings, all in an attitude of respect,
Are gazing at the Buddha, and at you and me;
Please tell them of the ocean of virtues
Which purifies living beings.

Please explain the meanings in the wondrous teaching
With stories and examples;
When beings hear, they will be greatly inspired,
Their doubts will end and their knowledge will be clear as space.

Like the glorified bodies manifested
By buddhas throughout all lands,
By marvelous speech, stories, and examples
Please show the enlightenment of buddhas like them.

In millions of buddha-lands in the ten directions,
In countless billions of eons,
It is hard to see such enlightening beings
As have gathered here now.

These enlightening beings are all reverent,
Eager for the subtle doctrine;

Please expound with pure mind
The great phenomena of Buddha's manifestation.

Then the enlightening being Universally Good said to the great congregation of enlightening beings, "This matter is inconceivable. The Buddha, the one who realizes Thusness, the worthy, the truly awake, becomes manifest by means of infinite phenomena. Why? It is not by one condition, by one phenomenon, that the manifestation of Buddha can be accomplished. It is accomplished by ten infinities of things. What are the ten? It is accomplished by the mind of enlightenment that took care of infinite sentient beings in the past. It is accomplished by the infinite supreme aspirations of the past. It is accomplished by great benevolence and compassion, which infinitely saved all sentient beings in the past. It is accomplished by infinite continuous commitments of the past. It is accomplished by infinite cultivation of virtues and knowledge tirelessly in the past. It is accomplished by infinite service of buddhas and education of sentient beings in the past. It is accomplished by infinite pure paths of wisdom and means in the past. It is accomplished by infinite pure virtues of the past. It is accomplished by infinite ways of adornment in the past. It is accomplished by infinite comprehensions of principles and meanings in the past. When these infinite, incalculable aspects of the Teaching are fulfilled, one becomes a buddha.

"It is as a billion-world universe is not formed just by one condition, not by one phenomenon—it can be formed only by innumerable conditions, innumerable things. That is to say, the rising and spreading of great clouds and showering of great rain produce four kinds of atmosphere, continuously making a basis. What are those four? One is called the holder, because it can hold the great waters. Second is called the evaporator, because it can evaporate the great waters. Third is called structure, because it sets up all places. Fourth is called arrangement, because the arrangement and distribution are all functional. These are all produced by the joint actions of sentient beings and by the roots of goodness of enlightening beings, enabling all sentient beings to get the use of what they need. Innumerable such causes and conditions form the universe. It is such by the nature of things—there is no producer or maker, no knower or creator, yet the worlds come to be.

"The manifestation of Buddha is also like this—it does not come about through just one condition or thing, but by innumerable causes and conditions, innumerable phenomena. That is, having heard, received, and held the clouds and rain of the great Teaching from past buddhas, by this can be produced the four kinds of atmosphere of great knowledge of the enlightened. What are these four? One is the atmosphere of great knowledge of mental command able to retain memory without forgetting, being able to hold the great clouds and rain of teachings of all buddhas. Second is the atmosphere of great knowledge producing tranquillity and insight, being able to evaporate all afflictions.

Third is the atmosphere of great knowledge of skillful dedication, being able to perfect all roots of goodness. Fourth is the atmosphere of great knowledge producing undefiled, variegated, magnificent arrays of adornments, causing the roots of goodness of all beings taught in the past to be purified, and consummating the power of the untainted roots of goodness of the enlightened. The buddhas' attainment of enlightenment in this way is thus by the nature of things—without production or creation, it nevertheless takes place. This is the first characteristic of the manifestation of the completely enlightened, the truly awake. Great enlightening beings should know it as such.

"Furthermore, just as when a billion-world universe is about to form, the rain falling from the great clouds, called 'the deluge,' cannot be absorbed or held by any place except the universe when it is about to form, in the same way when the Buddha rouses the clouds of the great Teaching and showers the rain of the great Teaching, those of the two lesser vehicles, whose minds and wills are narrow and weak, cannot absorb or hold it—this is possible only for the great enlightening beings with the power of mental continuity. This is the second characteristic of the manifestation of Buddha—great enlightening beings should know it as such.

"Furthermore, just as sentient beings, by the force of their acts, shower rain from great clouds, which do not come from anywhere or go anywhere, in the same way great enlightening beings, by the power of their roots of goodness, rouse the clouds of the great Teaching and shower the rain of the great Teaching, yet it comes from nowhere and goes nowhere. This is the third characteristic of the manifestation of Buddha—great enlightening beings should know it as such.

"Furthermore, just as no beings in the universe can count the drops of rain pouring from great clouds, and would go crazy if they tried, for only the overlord god of the universe, by the power of roots of goodness cultivated in the past, is aware of every single drop, in the same way the Buddha produces great clouds of teachings and showers great rain of teachings that all sentient beings, seekers of personal salvation, and self-enlightened ones cannot know, and they would surely go mad if they tried to assess them in thought; only the great enlightening beings, lords of all worlds, by the power of awareness and intellect cultivated in the past, comprehend every single expression and phrase, and how they enter beings' minds. This is the fourth characteristic of the manifestation of Buddha—great enlightening beings should know it as such.

"Furthermore, it is as when great clouds shower rain, there is a great cloud raining called the extinguisher, because it can extinguish fires; there is a great cloud raining called producer, because it can produce floods; there is a great cloud raining called stopper, because it can stop floods; there is a great cloud raining called maker, because it can make all kinds of jewels; there is a great cloud raining called distinguisher, because it can distinguish the billion worlds of the universe. The Buddha manifesting is also like this, producing great clouds of teaching, showering great rains of teaching: there is a great rain of teaching called extinguisher because it can extinguish all sentient beings' afflictions; there is a great rain of teaching called producer because it can produce all sentient beings' roots of goodness; there is a great rain of teaching called stopper because it can stop all sentient beings' delusions of views; there is a great rain of teaching called maker because it can make all jewels of wisdom; there is a great rain of teaching called distinguisher because it distinguishes the inclinations of all sentient beings. This is the fifth characteristic of the manifestation of Buddha—great enlightening beings should know it as such.

"Furthermore, just as the great clouds rain water of one flavor, yet there are innumerable differences according to where it rains, in the same way Buddha appearing in the world rains water of teaching of one flavor of great compassion, yet his sermons according to the needs of the situation are infinitely variegated. This is the sixth characteristic of the manifestation of Buddha—great enlightening beings should know it as such.

"Furthermore, as when a billion-world universe first forms, the abodes of the heavens in the realm of form are made first, then the abodes of the heavens in the realm of desire, and then the abodes of human and other beings, similarly Buddha appearing in the world first produces the knowledge of practices of enlightening beings, then the knowledge of practices of individual illuminates, then the knowledge of practices of listeners, then the knowledge of practices of the conditional roots of goodness of other sentient beings. Just as the great clouds rain water of one flavor while the abodes created are variously dissimilar according to the differences in roots of goodness of the sentient beings, Buddha's spiritual rain of the one flavor of compassion has differences according to the vessels, or capacities of sentient beings. This is the seventh characteristic of the manifestation of Buddha—great enlightening beings should know it as such.

"Furthermore, when the worlds are beginning, there is a great flood filling the billion-world universe, producing enormous lotus flowers, called array of jewels of virtues of the manifestation of Buddha, which cover the surface of the waters, their radiance illumining all worlds in the ten directions. Then the overlord god, the gods of the pure abodes, and so on, seeing these flowers, know for certain that in this eon there will be that many buddhas appearing in the world. At that time there arises an atmosphere called highly purified light which makes the mansions of the heavens of the realm of form. There arises an atmosphere called array of pure lights which makes the mansions of the heavens of the world of desire. There arises an atmosphere called firm, dense, and indestructible, which makes the great and small peripheral mountains and the iron mountains. There arises an atmosphere called supremely high which makes the polar mountains. There arises an atmosphere called immovable which makes the ten great mountains. There arises an atmo-

sphere called stabilization which makes the earth. There arises an atmosphere called adornment which makes the palaces of the earth and sky,
of the water and sound spirits. There arises an atmosphere called inexhaustible treasury which makes all the oceans of the billion worlds.
There arises an atmosphere called treasury of universal light which
makes all the jewels of the billion worlds. There arises an atmosphere
called steadfast root which makes all the wish-fulfilling trees of the billion worlds. The one-flavored water rained by the great clouds has no
distinctions, but because the roots of goodness of sentient beings are not
the same, the atmospheres are not the same, and because of the differences of the atmospheres, the worlds are different. The manifestation of
Buddha is also like this, replete with the virtues of all roots of goodness,
emitting the light of unexcelled great knowledge, called inconceivable
knowledge perpetuating the lineage of buddhas, illumining all worlds in
the ten directions, giving the enlightening beings the prediction that they
will be coronated by all buddhas, attain true enlightenment, and appear
in the world. The Buddha manifesting has another light of unexcelled
great knowledge, called pure and undefiled, which makes the untainted
inexhaustible knowledge of the enlightened. There is another light of
unexcelled great knowledge, called universal illumination, which makes
the Buddha's inconceivable knowledge universally penetrate the realm
of reality. There is another light of unexcelled great knowledge, called
sustaining the nature of buddhahood, which makes the insuperable
power of Buddha. There is another light of unexcelled great knowledge,
called outstanding and incorruptible, which makes Buddha's fearless and
incorruptible knowledge. There is another light of unexcelled great
knowledge, called all spiritual powers, which makes Buddha's unique
qualities and omniscience. There is another light of unexcelled great
knowledge, called producing mystic transformation, which makes Buddha's knowledge of how to cause the roots of goodness produced by
seeing, hearing, and attending Buddha to not be lost or decay. There is
another light of unexcelled great knowledge, called universal accord,
which makes Buddha's body of endless virtue and knowledge, doing
what is beneficial for all beings. There is another light of unexcelled
great knowledge, called inexhaustible, which makes Buddha's extremely
profound, subtle knowledge causing the lineage of the three treasures not
to die out, according to those who are enlightened by it. There is another
light of unexcelled great knowledge, called various adornments, which
makes the glorified body of Buddha, gladdening all sentient beings.
There is another light of unexcelled great knowledge, called indestructible, which makes the inexhaustible, supreme life span of Buddha equal
to the cosmos and the realm of space. Buddha's water of the one flavor
of compassion has no distinction, but because sentient beings' inclinations are not the same and their faculties and characters are different, it
produces various atmospheres of great knowledge, enabling the sentient
beings to accomplish the actual manifestation of buddhahood. All bud-

dhas are one and the same in essence; from the sphere of great knowledge they produce various kinds of lights of knowledge. You should know that Buddha, from the single flavor of liberation, produces infinite, inconceivable qualities of various kinds, which sentient beings think are products of the Buddha's supernormal powers, but which actually are not created by the supernormal powers of Buddha. There is not a single enlightening being who can ever attain even a little bit of the knowledge and wisdom of buddhas without having planted roots of goodness in the company of buddhas. It is just that by the spiritual power of the buddhas sentient beings are enabled to embody the qualities of buddhahood; yet the buddhas have no discrimination. There is no creation, no destruction, no creator, and nothing created. This is the eighth characteristic of the manifestation of Buddha—great enlightening beings should know it as such.

"Furthermore, it is like the arising of four atmospheres in space that can sustain the sphere of water. Of these four, one is called stability, the second permanence, the third ultimacy, and the fourth firmness. These four atmospheres can sustain the sphere of water; the sphere of water can sustain the earth and prevent it from falling apart—therefore it is said that the sphere of earth rests on the sphere of water, the sphere of water rests on the atmosphere, the atmosphere rests on space, and space does not rest on anything; but though space does not rest on anything, it enables the universe to abide. The manifestation of Buddha is also like this, producing Buddha's four kinds of atmosphere of great knowledge based on the unimpeded light of wisdom, able to sustain the roots of goodness of all sentient beings. What are those four? The atmosphere of great knowledge taking care of all sentient beings and inspiring joy in them; the atmosphere of great knowledge setting up right teaching and causing sentient beings to take to it; the atmosphere of great knowledge preserving all sentient beings' roots of goodness; the atmosphere of great knowledge containing all appropriate means, arriving at the realm where there are no taints or contaminations. The buddhas benevolently rescue all living beings, compassionately liberate all living beings, their great benevolence and compassion universally aiding all: however, great benevolence and great compassion rest on great skill in means; great skill in means rests on the manifestation of Buddha; the manifestation of Buddha rests on the light of unimpeded wisdom; the light of unimpeded wisdom does not rest on anything. This is the ninth characteristic of the manifestation of Buddha—great enlightening beings should know it as such.

"Furthermore, once the billion-world universe has formed, it benefits countless various sentient beings—the water creatures receive the benefits of the water, the land creatures receive the benefit of the land, the sky creatures receive the benefit of the sky. In the same way the manifestation of Buddha variously benefits all kinds of beings—those who become joyful on seeing Buddha gain the benefit of joy, those who abide by the pure precepts gain the benefit of pure conduct, those who abide in the meditations, concentrations, and immeasurable minds gain the benefit of transmundane spiritual powers of saints, those who abide in the lights of the ways of entry into the Teaching gain the benefit of the nondissolution of cause and effect, those who abide in the light of nonexistence gain the benefit of nondissolution of all truths. Therefore we say the manifestation of Buddha benefits all sentient beings. This is the tenth characteristic of the manifestation of Buddha—great enlightening beings should know it as such.

"When great enlightening beings know the manifestation of Buddha, they know it is infinite because they know it consummates infinite practices; then they know it is immensely vast because they know it pervades the ten directions; then they know it has no coming or going because they know it is apart from birth, subsistence, and extinction; then they know it has no action and nothing acted upon because they know it is beyond mind, intellect, and consciousness; then they know it is impartial because they know all sentient beings have no self; then they know it is endless because they know it pervades all lands without end; then they know it is unreceding because they know it will never be stopped in the future; then they know it has no decay because the Buddha's knowledge has no counterpart; then they know it is nondual because they know Buddha equally observes the conditional and the unconditional; then they know all sentient beings gain benefit because the dedication of Buddha's original vows are freely fulfilled."

Then the great enlightening being Universally Good, wishing to restate his point, spoke these verses:

The Ten-Powered Great Hero is supreme,
Incomparable as space,
With a sphere so vast it cannot be measured,
Virtues most eminent, beyond the world.

The virtues of the ten powers are boundless,
Unreachable by thought:
A single teaching of the human lion
No sentient beings can know in a hundred million eons.

If the lands of the ten directions were reduced to dust,
Those motes of dust might be counted,
But the virtues in a single hair of Buddha
Could not be told in a trillion eons.

If someone took a ruler to measure space
And someone followed to keep the account,
The bounds of space could not be found—
So it is with the realm of Buddha.

If someone could know in an instant
The minds of the beings of all times,
Even over eons as many as beings,
Such a one could know the essence of one thought of Buddha.

Just as the reality realm pervades all
Yet cannot be perceived as being all,
So also is the realm of the Ten-Powered:
It pervades all yet is not all.

True Thusness, free of falsehood, is ever silent;
Birthless, deathless, it is all-pervasive.
The realm of the buddhas is also thus;
Essentially equal, not increasing or decreasing.

Just as ultimate reality has no limit.
Is in all times yet is not therein,
So is the realm of the Guide,
Pervading all times without obstruction.

The nature of things is uncreate, unchanging,
Fundamentally pure, like space:
So also is the purity of nature of buddhas—
Their fundamental nature is not a nature, is beyond being and
    nonbeing.

The nature of things is not in discussion,
It is speechless, beyond speech, eternally quiescent.
The nature of the realm of the Ten-Powered is also thus;
No words can explain it.

Buddha knows the nature of things is null,
Like birds flying through the sky without a trace;
By the power of past vows he manifests a body,
Showing the great spiritual transfiguration of Buddha.

Any who wish to know the realm of Buddha
Should make their minds clean as space,
Getting rid of false notions and graspings,
Making the mind unhindered wherever it turns.

Therefore offspring of Buddha should listen well
As I illustrate the realm of Buddha with a few examples;
The virtues of the Ten-Powered cannot be measured,
But to enlighten all beings I summarize them.

The vistas exposed by the Guide
In acts of body, speech, and mind,
Their teaching and final extinction,
All roots of goodness I now will tell.

Just as the establishment of worlds
Cannot be achieved by one cause or condition,
And countless appropriate causes and conditions
Form this billion-world universe,
The manifestation of Buddha is also like this,
Only accomplished through infinite virtues;
The atoms of lands and thoughts of minds may be known,
But the productive causes of the Ten-Powered none can measure.

Just as clouds pour rain at the start of one eon
And create four great atmospheres,
And the roots of goodness of sentient beings and the power of
    enlightening beings
Establish the billion worlds securely,
So do the clouds of teaching of the Ten-Powered
Produce atmospheres of knowledge, pure minds,
Guiding beings to which they were previously dedicated
To fulfillment of the highest reward.

Just as there is a great deluge
Which no place can contain
Except the great wind force in pure space
At the beginning of the universe,
So also is the Buddha's manifestation,
Showering rain of truths filling the cosmos
Which the weak-minded cannot bear,
Only those of pure and broad minds.

Just as the downpour of rain in the sky
Comes from nowhere and goes nowhere,
With no producer or receiver,
Naturally filling all with moisture thus,
The rain of teaching of Buddha is also thus,
Without coming or going, uncreate;
Based on past practice, with the power of enlightening beings,
All the great-minded hear and accept it.

As the clouds in the sky shower rain,
And no one can count the drops,
Except the lord of the universe

Whose power is able to comprehend them,
So also·is the rain of teaching of the Felicitous;
No sentient beings can measure it,
Except people who are free in the world,
Who see it as clearly as a jewel in the hand.

Just as the rain pouring from the clouds in the sky
Can extinguish, can produce, and can stop,
Can make all jewels
And distinguish all in the universe,
The rain of Buddha's teaching is also thus,
Extinguishing delusion, producing good, stopping views,
Making all jewels of knowledge,
Distinguishing beings' inclinations.

The one flavor of the rain in the sky
Is different according to the places it rains—
It is not that the rain has any distinction,
But it is naturally thus according to the differences in things.
The rain of teaching of Buddha is not one or varied:
Impartial, quiescent, it is free from discrimination,
Yet according to the various differences of those taught
It naturally has unlimited aspects.

When the world is first formed,
First are formed the palaces of the form-realm heavens,
Then the desire heavens, then human abodes,
And last the gandharva palaces;
The manifestation of Buddha is also like this,
First producing boundless enlightening beings' practices,
Then teaching those aware of conditioning, who like tranquillity,
Then the listeners, then finally sentient beings.

When the gods first see the lotus blossom open
They know buddhas will appear and are glad;
Water, based on the power of wind, produces the world,
Dwellings, mountains, and rivers are all set up.
The great light of the developed goodness of Buddha
Skillfully distinguishes enlightening beings and gives them
    predictions;
The spheres of knowledge, all pure,
Can each reveal the ways to buddhahood.

The forest exists dependent on the earth,
The earth remains solid based on water,
Water depends on wind, wind on space,

While space does not depend on anything.
All Buddha teachings depend on compassion,
And compassion is established depending on means;
Means depend on knowledge, knowledge on wisdom,
While the body of unimpeded wisdom does not depend on
    anything.

Once the world comes to be,
All beings receive its benefits—
Living on the earth, in the water, in the sky,
Two-legged, four-legged, all receive benefit.
The manifestation of the spiritual sovereign is also thus—
All beings gain its benefits;
If any see, hear, or associate with Buddha,
It will cause all confusions and afflictions to be removed.

The elements of Buddha's manifestation are boundless;
The deluded of the world cannot know them.
Out of desire to enlighten all conscious beings
Similes are told where there is no comparison.

"How should great enlightening beings see the body of Buddha?
They should see the body of Buddha in infinite places. Why? They
should not see Buddha in just one thing, one phenomenon, one body,
one land, one being—they should see Buddha everywhere. Just as space
is omnipresent, in all places, material or immaterial, yet without either
arriving or not arriving there, because space is incorporeal, in the same
way Buddha is omnipresent, in all places, in all beings, in all things, in all
lands, yet neither arriving nor not arriving there, because Buddha's body
is incorporeal, manifesting a body for the sake of sentient beings. This is
the first characteristic of the body of Buddha; great enlightening beings
should see it thus.

"Furthermore, just as space is wide open, is not a form yet can reveal
all forms, yet space is without discrimination or false description, so also
is the body of Buddha like this, causing all beings' mundane and transmundane good works to be accomplished by illumining all with the
light of knowledge, yet without discrimination or false descriptions,
having originally terminated all attachments and false descriptions. This
is the second characteristic of the body of Buddha—great enlightening
beings should see it this way.

"When the sun comes out, infinite living beings all receive its benefits
—it disperses the darkness and gives light, dries up moisture, causes
plants and trees to grow, matures crops, permeates the sky, causes lotuses
to bloom, allows travelers to see the road, allows people to do their work
—because the orb of the sun radiates infinite beams of light everywhere.
The sun of knowledge of Buddha is also like this, benefiting sentient

beings everywhere by infinite works—destroying evil and producing good, breaking down ignorance and creating knowledge, benevolently saving, compassionately liberating, causing growth of faculties, powers, and elements of enlightenment, causing beings to develop profound faith, enabling them to see inevitable cause and effect, fostering in them the celestial eye to see where beings die and are born, causing their minds to be unimpeded and not destroy roots of goodness, causing them to cultivate illumination by knowledge and open the flower of awakening, causing them to determine to fulfill their fundamental task. Why? Because Buddha's immense sun-body of knowledge and wisdom radiates infinite light, illumining everywhere. This is the third characteristic of the body of Buddha; great enlightening beings should see it thus.

"When the sun rises, first it lights up the highest mountains, then the lower mountains, then the high plateaus, and finally the whole land; but the sun does not think, 'First I will illumine here, afterward I will illumine there'—it is just because of difference in height of the mountains and land that there is a succession in illumination. The Buddha, similarly, having developed the boundless orb of knowledge of the realm of reality, always radiating the light of unimpeded knowledge, first of all illumines the high mountains, which are the great enlightening beings, then illumines those who are awakened by understanding of conditioning, then illumines those who listen to the message, then illumines sentient beings whose foundations of goodness are sure and stable, revealing vast knowledge according to beings' mental capacities, finally illumining all sentient beings, even reaching those who are fixated on error, to be a beneficial cause for the future, that they may develop to maturity. But the light of the sun of great knowledge of Buddha does not think, 'I will first illumine the great deeds of enlightening beings and at the very last shine on the sentient beings who are fixated on error'—it just radiates the light, shining equally on all, without obstruction or impediment, without discrimination. Just as the sun and moon appear in their time and impersonally shine on the mountains and valleys, so also does the knowledge of Buddha shine on all without discrimination, while the light of knowledge has various differences according to the differences in faculties and inclinations of sentient beings. This is the fourth characteristic of the body of Buddha; great enlightening beings should see it thus.

"When the sun comes out, those born blind cannot see it, because they have no faculty of vision; yet even though they do not see it, they are benefited by the light of the sun. Why? By this it is possible to know the times of day and night and to have access to food and clothing to comfort the body and free it from distress. The sun of knowledge of Buddha is also like this; the blind without faith or understanding, immoral and heedless, sustaining themselves by wrong means of livelihood, do not see the orb of the sun of knowledge of the Buddhas because they have no eye of faith, but even though they do not see it, they are still benefited by the sun of knowledge. Why? Because by the power of Buddha it makes the causes of future suffering of those beings—physical pains and psychological afflictions—all vanish.

"Buddha has a light called accumulating all virtues, a light called total universal illumination, a light called pure, free illumination, a light called producing great wondrous sound, a light called understanding all languages and gladdening others, a light called the realm of freedom showing the eternal cancellation of all doubts, a light called independent universal illumination of nondwelling knowledge, a light called free knowledge forever terminating all false descriptions, a light called producing marvelous sayings according to need, a light called producing free utterances adorning lands and maturing sentient beings. Each pore of the Buddha emits a thousand kinds of light like these: five hundred lights beam downward, five hundred lights beam upward, illumining the congregations of enlightening beings at the various places of the buddhas in the various lands; when the enlightening beings see these lights, all at once they realize the realm of buddhahood, with ten heads, ten eyes, ten ears, ten noses, ten tongues, ten bodies, ten hands, ten feet, ten stages, and ten knowledges, all thoroughly pure. The states and stages previously accomplished by those enlightening beings become more pure upon seeing these lights; their roots of goodness mature, and they proceed toward omniscience. Those in the two lesser vehicles have all their defilements removed. Some other beings, who are blind, their bodies blissful, also become purified in mind, gentle and docile, able to cultivate mindfulness and knowledge. The sentient beings in the realms of hells, hungry ghosts, and animals all become blissful and are freed from pains, and when their lives end are reborn in heaven or the human world. Those sentient beings are not aware, do not know by what cause, by what spiritual power, they came to be born there. Those blind ones think, 'We are Brahma gods, we are emanations of Brahma.' Then Buddha, in the concentration of universal freedom, says to them, 'You are not Brahma gods, not emanations of Brahma, nor were you created by the king-god Indra or the world-guardian gods: all this is the spiritual power of Buddha.' Having heard this, those sentient beings, by the spiritual power of Buddha, all know their past life and become very happy. Because their hearts are joyful, they naturally produce clouds of udumbara flowers, clouds of fragrances, music, cloth, parasols, banners, pennants, aromatic powders, jewels, towers adorned with lion banners and crescents, clouds of songs of praise, clouds of all kinds of adornments, and respectfully offer them to the Buddha. Why? Because these sentient beings have gained clear eyes, and therefore the Buddha gives them the prophecy of unexcelled, complete perfect enlightenment. In this way Buddha's sun of knowledge benefits sentient beings born blind, fostering the full development of basic goodness. This is the fifth characteristic of the body of Buddha; great enlightening beings should see it this way.

"Furthermore, it is like the moon, with four special extraordinary qualities: first, it outshines all the stars; second, as time passes it shows waning and waxing; third, its reflection appears in all clear waters; fourth, all who see it see it right before them, yet the moon has no discrimination and no arbitrary conceptions. The moon of the body of Buddha similarly has four special extraordinary qualities: it outshines all hearers and individual illuminates, whether they are in the stage of learning or beyond learning; according to the needs of the situation, it manifests different life spans, yet without increase or decrease in the Buddha-body; its reflection appears in all vessels of enlightenment, sentient beings with pure minds, in all worlds; all sentient beings who behold it think the Buddha is in their presence alone. According to their inclinations, Buddha teaches them, liberating them according to their states, causing them to perceive the Buddha-body according to their needs and potentials for edification, yet the Buddha-body has no discrimination, no arbitrary conceptions; all benefits it renders reach the ultimate end. This is the sixth characteristic of the body of Buddha; great enlightening beings should see it thus.

"Furthermore, just as the supreme Brahma god of a billion-world universe simply manifests its body in the billion worlds, and all beings see Brahma before them, yet Brahma does not divide its body and does not have multiple bodies, in the same way the buddhas have no discrimination, no false representations, and do not divide their bodies or have multiple bodies, yet they manifest their bodies in accord with the inclinations of all sentient beings, without thinking that they manifest so many bodies. This is the seventh characteristic of the body of Buddha; great enlightening beings should see it this way.

"A master physician is well versed in all medications and the science of hypnosis, fully uses all the medicines in the land, and, also because of the power of the physician's past roots of goodness, and because of using hypnotic spells as an expedient, all those who see the physician recover from illness. That master physician, sensing impending death, thinks, 'After I die, sentient beings will have no one to rely on; I should manifest an expedient for them.' Then the master physician compounds drugs, which he smears on his body, and supports his body by spell power, so that it will not decay or shrivel after death, so its bearing, seeing, and hearing will be no different from before, and all cures will be effected. The Buddha, the Truly Enlightened One, the unexcelled master physician, is also like this, having developed and perfected the medicines of the Teaching over countless eons, having cultivated and learned all skills in application of means and fully consummated the power of illuminating spells, is able to quell all sentient beings' afflictions. Buddha's life spans measureless eons, the body pure, without any cogitation, without activity, never ceasing the works of buddhas; the afflictions of all sentient beings who see Buddha dissolve away. This is the eighth characteristic of the body of Buddha; great enlightening beings should see it in this way.

"In the ocean there is a great jewel called radiant repository, in which are assembled all lights: if any sentient beings touch its light, they become assimilated to its color; if any see it, their eyes are purified; whenever the light shines it rains jewels called felicity that soothe and comfort beings. The body of Buddha is also like this, being a treasury of knowledge in which are collected all virtues: if any sentient beings come in contact with the light of precious knowledge of the body of Buddha, they become the same as Buddha in appearance; if any see it their eye of reality is purified; wherever that light shines, it frees sentient beings from the miseries of poverty and ultimately imbues them with the bliss of enlightenment. The body of Buddha has no discrimination and no false conceptions, but can perform great buddha-works for all sentient beings. This is the ninth characteristic of the body of Buddha; great enlightening beings should see it in this way.

"In the ocean is a great wish-fulfilling jewel called treasury of adornments of all worlds, fully endowed with a million qualities, eliminating calamities and fulfilling wishes of beings wherever it is. However, this jewel cannot be seen by beings of little merit. The supreme wish-fulfilling jewel of the body of Buddha is also like this; called able to gladden all beings, if any sentient beings see the body of Buddha, hear the name, and praise the virtues, they will all be enabled to escape forever the pains and ills of birth and death. Even if all beings in all worlds focus their minds all at once on the desire to see Buddha, they will all be enabled to see and their wish will be fulfilled. The Buddha-body cannot be seen by sentient beings of little merit unless they can be tamed by the spiritual power of Buddha; if sentient beings, because of seeing the body of Buddha, plant roots of goodness and develop them, they are enabled to see the body of Buddha for their development. This is the tenth characteristic of the body of Buddha; great enlightening beings should see it thus, because their minds are measureless, pervading the ten directions, because their actions are as unhindered as space, because they penetrate everywhere in the realm of reality, because they abide in absolute truth, because they have no birth or death, because they remain equal throughout past, present, and future, because they are forever rid of all false discriminations, because they continue their eternal vows, because they purify all worlds, because they adorn each buddha-body."

Then the great enlightening being Universally Good, in order to again clarify what he meant, said in verse,

> Just as space pervades the ten directions,
> Like form but not a form, existent but not existent,
> Omnipresent, without bounds,
> In beings' bodies and lands, in all times,
> So does the true body of buddhas
> Pervade all phenomena,
> Invisible, ungraspable,
> Yet manifesting bodies to teach beings.

Just as space cannot be grasped
Yet lets all beings do their work
Without thinking what it does,
How it does it, or for whom,
The physical action of buddhas is also thus,
Causing beings to practice good ways,
Yet the buddha never has any notion
Of acting on them variously.

When the sun comes up over the land
It completely removes the darkness.
Mountains, trees, lakes, flowers, earth, and all beings,
All the various species receive benefit.
The sun of Buddha emerging too is thus,
Causing human and celestial good actions to grow,
Obliterating the darkness of ignorance so they gain the light of
   knowledge
And always experience all glorious bliss.

When the sun first comes up
It shines first on the high mountains, then the others,
Then shines on the high plains, then the whole land,
Yet the sun never has any discrimination.
The light of Buddha is also thus,
First illumining the enlightening beings, then the self-enlightened,
Then last the listeners and all sentient beings,
Yet the Buddha basically has no stirring thoughts.

Just as the blind cannot see the sun,
Yet sunlight still benefits them,
Enabling them to know time and season and receive food and
   drink,
To be freed from troubles and gain physical ease,
In the same way faithless beings do not see Buddha,
Yet Buddha benefits them as well;
By hearing Buddha's name or being touched by Buddha's light
They can even reach enlightenment.

Just as the moon in the sky
Outshines the stars and appears to wax and wane,
Shows its reflection in all waters,
And appears face to face with those who behold it,
The clear moon of Buddha is also thus,
Outshining other vehicles, showing length and brevity,
Appearing in the clear mind-water of humans and gods,
Seeming to be present to everyone.

Just as the god Brahma, while in its own palace,
Appears in all the Brahma abodes in the universe
So all humans and celestials can see it,
Yet does not actually divide its body to go to them,
Likewise does the Buddha's manifestation of bodies
Pervade everywhere in the ten directions,
Those bodies countless, incalculable in number,
Yet without dividing bodies, without discrimination.

Like a physician skilled in his arts,
Seeing whom all are cured,
And though his life is ended he embalms his body
So that it will work as before,
So also does the Supreme Healer
Have all knowledge of techniques,
Manifesting embodiment as Buddha by excellent practices of
     yore,
So the afflictions of all who see are destroyed.

In the ocean is a superb jewel
Which radiates countless beams of light;
Those who come in contact with it become the same color,
And the eyes of those who see it are purified:
The Supreme Jewel is also thus;
Those whom its light touches become the same in appearance,
In those who get to see it the five eyes open;
They break through the darkness of the senses and dwell in
     buddhahood.

The wish-fulfilling jewel
Satisfies all desires;
Those of little virtue cannot see it,
Though this is not by the jewel's discrimination:
The jewel of Buddha is also thus,
Fulfilling all desires;
Faithless beings cannot see it,
But not because Buddha abandons them.

"How should great enlightening beings know the voice of Buddha? They should know Buddha's voice is omnipresent, because it pervades all sounds. They should know Buddha's voice pleases all according to their mentalities, because its explanation of truth is clear and comprehensive. They should know Buddha's voice gladdens all according to their resolve, because their minds gain clarity and coolness. They should know Buddha's voice teaches without error in timing, because all who need and are able to hear it do. They should know Buddha's voice has no birth or death, because it is like the echo of a call. They should know Buddha's voice has no owner, because it is produced by cultivation of all appropriate practices. They should know Buddha's voice is extremely profound, because it cannot be measured. They should know Buddha's voice has no falsehood or deviousness, because it is born of the realm of truth. They should know Buddha's voice has no end, because it permeates the cosmos. They should know Buddha's voice has no change, because it reaches the ultimate.

"Great enlightening beings should know that Buddha's voice is neither quantified nor unquantified, neither has a master nor lacks a master, neither communicates nor does not communicate. Why? It is as when the world is about to disintegrate, there is no master, no maker, yet it spontaneously emits four voices. One says, 'You all should know that the well-being of the first meditation stage, free from the ills of desire, surpasses the realm of desire.' The sentient beings hearing this are naturally able to accomplish the first meditation stage, relinquish the body of the realm of desire and be born in Brahma heaven. The second voice says, 'You should know that the well-being of the second meditation stage, without reflection and rumination, surpasses the Brahma heaven.' The sentient beings hearing this naturally manage to accomplish the second meditation stage, relinquish the body of Brahma heaven, and are born in the light-sound heaven. The third voice says, 'You should know that the well-being of the third meditation stage has no flaws and surpasses the light-sound heaven.' Hearing this, the sentient beings are naturally able to achieve the third meditation stage, relinquish the body of the light-sound heaven, and are born in the heaven of universal purity. The fourth voice says, 'You should know that the tranquillity of the fourth meditation stage surpasses the heaven of universal purity.' Hearing this, the sentient beings are naturally able to achieve the fourth meditation stage, relinquish the body of the heaven of universal purity, and are born in the heaven of vast results. These voices have no master or maker—they are just produced by the power of good practices of sentient beings.

"The voice of Buddha is also like this, without master or maker, without discrimination, not entering, not emerging, yet producing four great voices from the power of the virtuous qualities of Buddha. One voice says, 'You all should know that all conditioned states are miserable. There is the misery of hells, the misery of animality, the misery of hungry ghosthood, the misery of lack of virtue, the misery of clinging to self and possessions, the misery of evildoing. If you want to be born human or divine, you should plant roots of goodness. Born in the human world or in a heaven, you will leave all situations in which enlightenment is difficult.' Sentient beings, having heard this, give up error and perversity, practice good actions, leave all difficulties behind, and are born in the human world or in heaven. The second voice says, 'You should know that the myriad pains of all conditioned states are as searing as balls of hot iron. Conditioned states are impermanent and pass away. Nirvana is tranquil, unfabricated well-being, beyond all burning, extinguishing all inflaming afflictions.' Having heard this, sentient beings diligently practice good principles, and in the vehicle of listeners to Buddha's voice attain the tolerance of conformity to the message. The third voice says, 'You should know that those in the vehicle of listeners follow the words of another to understand; their knowledge and wisdom is narrow and inferior. There is a higher vehicle called the vehicle of the individually awakened, whose enlightenment does not depend on a teacher. You should learn it.' Those inclined to a superior path, having heard this voice, give up the path of listeners and cultivate the vehicle of the individually awakened. The fourth voice says, 'You should know that there is an even higher path beyond the ranks of these two vehicles, which is called the great vehicle, practiced by enlightening beings, following the six transcendent ways, not stopping enlightening practice, not relinquishing the determination for enlightenment, being in the midst of infinite birth and death without getting sick of it. Going beyond the two vehicles of individual liberation, it is called the Great Vehicle, the foremost vehicle, the preeminent vehicle, the supreme vehicle, the highest vehicle, the unexcelled vehicle, the vehicle of benefiting all sentient beings.' If there are any sentient beings whose resolve is very great, whose faculties are strong and keen, who have planted roots of goodness in the past, who are spiritually empowered by the buddhas, who have superior inclinations and seek buddhahood, once they have heard this voice they arouse the determination for enlightenment. Buddha's voice does not come from the body or from the mind, yet it can benefit infinite sentient beings. This is the first characteristic of Buddha's voice; great enlightening beings should know it thus.

"Furthermore, just as an echo arises due to mountains, valley, and sound, and has no form, cannot be seen, and though it has no discrimination can follow all words, so also is the voice of Buddha—it has no form, cannot be seen, has no direction or location yet is not without direction and location; it just emerges according to the conditions of sentient beings' inclinations and understandings. Its nature ultimately has no words, no information, and cannot be explained. This is the second characteristic of the voice of Buddha; great enlightening beings should know it thus.

"Furthermore, it is like the heavens' great drum of law, called awakener: when the celestials act without restraint, the drum produces a voice in the sky saying, 'You should know that all pleasures are impermanent, unreal, illusory, changing and disintegrating in a moment. They only fool the ignorant, causing attachment. Don't be indulgent, for the unrestrained fall into bad ways, and it is of no use to regret afterward.' The indulgent celestials, having heard this voice, are greatly distressed and frightened; they leave the pleasures in their own abodes, go to the king of gods, seek the truth and practice the way. The sound of that drum has no master, no maker, no origin, no destruction, yet it can benefit infinite sentient beings. Know that Buddha likewise utters the voice of infinite sublime truths in order to awaken indulgent beings: the voice of non-attachment, the voice of nonindulgence, the voice of impermanence, the voice of suffering, the voice of selflessness, the voice of impurity, the voice of annulment, the voice of nirvana, the voice of measureless spontaneous knowledge, the voice of incorruptible enlightening practices, the voice of all-pervasive effortless knowledge of buddhas. These voices pervade the cosmos, awakening the beings therein; countless sentient beings, having heard them, all become joyful and diligently cultivate good ways, each seeking emancipation by their respective vehicles of emancipation—that is, some practice the vehicle of listeners, some practice the vehicle of individual awakening, and some practice the unsurpassed Great Vehicle of enlightening beings. Yet the voice of Buddha does not remain in any place; it has no speech. This is the third characteristic of the voice of Buddha; great enlightening beings should know it thus.

"Again, it is like the case of the celestial concubine of the great lord god, named Beautiful Mouth, whose voice corresponds to a hundred thousand kinds of music, within each of which are also a hundred thousand different tones. Just as that goddess Beautiful Mouth produces countless sounds in one utterance, in the same way Buddha produces innumerable voices in one utterance, according to the differences in mentalities of sentient beings, reaching them all and enabling them to gain understanding. This is the fourth characteristic of the voice of Buddha; great enlightening beings should know it thus.

"Also it is like the case of the great god Brahma, abiding in the Brahma palace, uttering the voice of Brahma, which all the Brahma masses hear, while the sound of the voice does not go outside that group; the Brahma divinities all think Brahma is speaking to them alone. The sublime voice of Buddha is also like this; all in the congregation at the site of enlightenment hear it, while the sound does not go outside that group. Why? Because those whose faculties are not yet mature cannot hear it. Those who hear the voice each think Buddha is talking to them alone. The voice of Buddha neither emerges nor remains, yet can accomplish all works. This is the fifth characteristic of the voice of Buddha; great enlightening beings should know it thus.

"Also, just as waters are all of one flavor, but according to the difference of the vessel water has distinctions, yet the water has no thought or discrimination, similarly the speech of Buddha is of one flavor only, the flavor of liberation, but has innumerable distinctions according to the differences in mental vessels of sentient beings, yet without thought or discrimination. This is the sixth characteristic of the voice of Buddha; great enlightening beings should know it thus.

"Also, it is like the case of the water spirit Heatless producing great dense clouds covering the continent, showering sweet rain all over, so all the crops can grow and all the rivers, streams, springs, and lakes are full;

this great rainwater does not come from the water spirit's body or mind, yet can benefit sentient beings in various ways. Similarly, Buddha produces the cloud of great compassion covering all worlds in the ten directions, showering the rain of immortal truth, causing all sentient beings to become joyful, increase in goodness, and fulfill all vehicles of liberation. The voice of Buddha does not come from without and does not emerge from within, yet can benefit all sentient beings. This is the seventh characteristic of the voice of Buddha; great enlightening beings should know it thus.

"Also it is like when the water spirit Thoughtful is going to shower rain, it does not do so immediately but first produces great clouds covering the sky, remaining still for seven days waiting for people to finish their work, because that water spirit is benevolent and compassionate and does not want to trouble them; after seven days it showers a fine rain, moistening the earth. Similarly, when Buddha is going to shower the rain of truth, he does not do so at once, but first produces great clouds of teaching in order to mature sentient beings so they will not be startled or frightened; after they are mature he showers on all the rain of immortal truth, expounding the most profound, subtle good teaching, gradually filling them with the flavor of the unexcelled teaching of omniscience of buddhas. This is the eighth characteristic of the voice of Buddha; great enlightening beings should know it thus.

"In the ocean is a great water spirit called Magnificent Array; when it showers rain on the ocean, it may shower rain in ten kinds of arrays, or a hundred, or a thousand, or rain in a hundred thousand kinds of arrays. The water has no discrimination; it is just the inconceivable power of the water spirit that causes its arrays to be infinitely different. Similarly, when Buddha teaches truth, it may be expressed in ten different tones, or a hundred, or a thousand, or a hundred thousand, or eighty-four thousand tones explaining eighty-four thousand practices, up to countless hundreds of thousands of millions of tones, each explaining the truth in particular ways to gladden all who hear. The voice of Buddha makes no discrimination; it is just that buddhas, complete and pure in the profound realm of truth, are able to make various utterances in accord with the needs of sentient beings, making them happy. This is the ninth characteristic of the voice of Buddha; great enlightening beings should know it thus.

"When the water spirit Ocean wants to manifest the controlling power of the water spirit for the benefit of sentient beings to make them happy, it raises a great network of clouds from the earth to the heaven of control of others' emanations, covering all over: those clouds are of infinite different colors—some are the color of golden light, some are the color of lapis lazuli light, some are the color of silver light, some are the color of crystal light, some are the color of emerald light, some are the color of agate light, some are the color of red pearl light, some are the color of light of infinite fragrances, some are the color of light of spotless cloth, some are the color of light of pure water, some are the color of light of various ornaments. This network of clouds, having spread all over, emits lightning of various colors: the golden clouds emit lapis lazuli lightning; the lapis lazuli clouds emit golden lightning; the silver clouds emit crystal lightning; the crystal clouds emit silver lightning; the emerald clouds emit agate lightning; the agate clouds emit emerald lightning; the infinite-fragrance-colored clouds emit spotless-cloth-colored lightning; the spotless-cloth-colored clouds emit infinite-fragrance-colored lightning; the pure-water-colored clouds emit various-ornament-colored lightning; the various-ornament-colored clouds emit pure-water-colored lightning; multicolored clouds emit one-colored lightning; one-colored clouds emit multicolored lightning. There also issue from the clouds various sounds of thunder, according to the minds of sentient beings, making them all happy—sounds like goddesses singing, like celestial musicians playing, like water nymphs singing, like gandharva girls singing, like kinnara girls singing, like earthquakes, like the waves and tide of the ocean, like the king of beasts howling, like beautiful birds calling, as well as innumerable other kinds of sounds. When the thunder has sounded, there arises a cool breeze, delighting the mind of sentient beings. Finally it rains, various kinds of rain, benefiting and comforting infinite beings. In all places from the heavens to earth the rain is different: on the ocean it rains clear, cool water called endless; in the heaven of control of others' emanations it rains various music such as pipes and flutes, named beautiful; in the heaven of enjoyment of emanation it rains jewels called radiating great light; in the heaven of happiness it rains great ornaments, called hanging crests; in the heaven of timely portion it rains large, beautiful flowers, called various adornments; in the thirty-three-fold heaven it rains many sublime fragrances, called pleasing; in the heaven of the four world guardians it rains precious celestial robes, called covering; in the palace of water spirits it rains red pearls, called flowing light; in the palace of the titans it rains weapons, called conquering enemies; in the northern region of earth it rains various flowers, called blooming; in the other regions of earth it also rains differently according to the place. Though the mind of the water spirit is impartial, without discrimination, simply because the roots of goodness of sentient beings are different, the rain has distinctions. Similarly, when Buddha, the truly enlightened, the supreme spiritual sovereign, wants to edify sentient beings with right teaching, first he spreads clouds of embodiments over the cosmos, appearing differently according to inclinations of beings. For some beings he manifests clouds of mortal bodies; for some, clouds of emanated bodies; for some, clouds of power-bodies; for some, clouds of form-bodies; for some, clouds of glorified bodies; for some, clouds of virtue-bodies; for some, clouds of knowledge-bodies; for some, clouds of bodies whose powers do not deteriorate; for some, clouds of bodies of fearlessness; for some, clouds of cosmic bodies. Buddha covers all worlds with infinite such body-clouds and manifests various kinds of lightning in accord with the individual differences in inclinations of sentient beings: for some beings he manifests lightning called reaching every-where; for some, lightning called boundless light; for some, lightning called penetrating the secret teaching of Buddha; for some, lightning called reflected light; for some, lightning called illumination; for some, lightning called entering the door of endless mental command; for some, lightning called right mindfulness undisturbed; for some, lightning called ultimately incorruptible; for some, lightning called adaptively entering all states of being; for some, lightning called fulfilling all wishes and making everyone happy. Having manifested lightnings of infinite such lights, Buddha then produces infinite thunders of concentration, accord-ing to the inclinations of sentient beings: the thunder of the concentra-tion of well-aware knowledge; the thunder of the concentration of the refulgent, undefiled ocean; the thunder of the concentration of mastery of all the teachings; the thunder of the adamantine wheel concentration; the thunder of the concentration symbolized by the polar mountain; the thunder of the ocean-seal concentration; the thunder of the solar lamp concentration; the thunder of the inexhaustible treasury concentration; the thunder of the concentration of the indestructible power of libera-tion. After the thunder of infinite different concentrations such as these have emerged from the clouds of embodiments of Buddha, when about to shower the rain of truth, first he manifests an auspicious sign to awaken sentient beings: from the mind of unhindered compassion he manifests the atmosphere of great knowledge of Buddha, called able to cause all sentient beings to develop inconceivable happiness and well-being. Once this sign has appeared, the bodies and minds of all enlightening beings and sentient beings become clear and cool. After that, from the cloud of the great reality-body of Buddha, the cloud of great compassion, the cloud of great inconceivability, showers the inconceivable, far-flung rain of teaching, causing all beings' bodies and minds to be pure: for enlight-ening beings sitting at the site of enlightenment there showers a great rain of teaching called nondifferentiation of the realm of reality; for en-lightening beings in their final embodiment there showers a great rain of teaching called enlightening beings' easy mastery of the esoteric teaching of Buddha; for enlightening beings to become fully enlightened in the next life there showers a great rain of teaching called pure universal light; for coronated enlightening beings there showers a great rain of teaching called adornment by the embellishments of buddhahood; for enlighten-ing beings who have attained tolerance there showers a great rain of teaching called flowers of knowledge with jewels of virtue blooming, not ceasing the compassionate practices of enlightening beings; for en-lightening beings in progress there showers a great rain of teaching called entering the profound method of manifestation of occult transforma-tions and carrying on enlightening practice without stopping or weary-ing; for newly inspired enlightening beings there showers a great rain of teaching called producing the practice of great love and compassion of buddhas to save sentient beings; for those who seek the vehicle of individual enlightenment there showers a great rain of teaching called deeply knowing the principles of conditional origination, avoiding extremes, and attaining the nondecaying fruit of liberation; for those who seek the vehicle of listeners there showers a great rain of teaching called cutting down all obstructing afflictions with the sword of great knowledge and wisdom; for stabilized and unstabilized sentient beings who accumulate roots of goodness there showers a great rain of teaching called facilitating the accomplishment of various ways into the teaching, producing great happiness. The Buddha showers great rains of teaching like these in accordance with the mentalities of sentient beings, filling all worlds. A buddha, perfectly enlightened, is impartial in mind and does not begrudge the teaching; simply because the faculties and inclinations of sentient beings are not the same, the rains of teaching appear differently. This is the tenth characteristic of the voice of Buddha; great enlightening beings should know it thus.

"The voice of Buddha has ten kinds of infinity: it is as infinite as the realm of space because it extends to all places; it is as infinite as the cosmos because it pervades everywhere; it is as infinite as the realm of sentient beings because it gladdens all hearts; it is as infinite as all acts because it explains their results and consequences; it is as infinite as afflictions because it removes them all; it is as infinite as the speech of sentient beings because it enables them to hear according to their understanding; it is as infinite as the inclinations and understandings of sentient beings because it observes them all to rescue and liberate them; it is as infinite as past, present, and future because it has no boundaries; it is as infinite as knowledge because it distinguishes everything; it is as infinite as the realm of buddhahood because it enters the cosmos of reality of buddhahood. The voice of Buddha, the completely enlightened, comprises incalculable infinities such as these; great enlightening beings should know it thus."

Then the enlightening being Universally Good, to again clarify what he meant, spoke these verses:

> When a billion-world universe is about to dissolve,
> The power of beings' virtue announces that
> The four meditations are peaceful and painless,
> Causing them to leave desire when they have heard.
> Ten-Powered Buddha, also like this,
> Produces a sublime voice pervading the cosmos,
> Explaining that conditioned states are painful and impermanent,
> So beings may cross for good the sea of birth and death.
>
> Just as a canyon deep in the mountains
> Echoes any sound,
> And though it accords with others' voices

The echo has no discrimination,
So also is the speech of Buddha
Revealed according to the maturity of faculties,
Causing them to be controlled and happy,
Yet without self-consciousness of preaching.

As the celestial drum called awakener
Vibrates with the sound of the law in the sky,
Admonishing the self-indulgent celestials,
Causing them to give up attachments when they hear,
So too is the drum of Buddha's teaching like this,
Producing various wonderful sounds,
Awakening all living beings
So they all realize enlightenment.

The lord god has a precious concubine
Who voices all kinds of music
Producing a hundred thousand sounds in one voice
With a hundred thousand tones in each sound.
The voice of Buddha is also like this,
Producing all tones in one voice,
Different according to beings' characters and inclinations,
Causing each to end afflictions when they hear.

Just as king Brahma utters a sound
Which makes all Brahmas happy,
The voice reaching only Brahmas, no one else,
Each thinking he alone hears it,
So also does the Buddha utter a word
Which fills the cosmos,
Yet only reaches the faithful
Because the faithless cannot receive it.

Just as all waters are of one and the same essence,
With no difference in flavor,
But the land they are on and the vessels they are in are not the
    same,
So that causes them to be variously different,
The voice of Omniscience is similar to this;
The essence of truth has one flavor, undifferentiated,
Yet according to beings' actions, which are not the same,
It causes them to hear in various different ways.

When the water spirit Heatless
Showers rain to moisten the land
Causing plants and trees to grow,

The rain does not come from its body or mind.
Likewise the wondrous voice of buddhas
Rains throughout the cosmos, filling all,
Fostering good and extinguishing evil,
But not coming from inside or outside.

Just as the water spirit Thoughtful
Raises clouds for seven days before raining,
Waiting for all people to finish their work
And then showering rain for their benefit,
The teaching of Buddha is likewise,
First civilizing beings and developing them,
And afterward expounding the profound truth,
So the hearers will not be frightened.

The water spirit Great Adornment in the ocean
Showers ten arrays of rain,
Or a hundred, a thousand, a hundred thousand;
Though the water is one flavor, the arrays are different.
The ultimate teacher likewise
Explains ten or twenty teachings,
Or a hundred, a thousand, up to infinity,
Without any notion of difference.

The supreme water spirit Ocean
Covers the earth with clouds;
The rain in each place is different,
But the spirit has no thought of distinction.
Likewise Buddha, sovereign of truth,
Extends clouds of great compassion in all directions,
Raining differently for each practitioner,
Yet without discriminating among them.

"How should great enlightening beings know the mind of Buddha, the truly awake? The mind, intellect, and consciousness of Buddha are ungraspable. One can know the mind of Buddha only in terms of the infinity of knowledge. Just as space is the resting place of all things, while space has no resting place, so also is the knowledge of Buddha the resting place of all mundane and transcendental knowledge, while the knowledge of Buddha has no resting place. This is the first characteristic of the mind of Buddha; great enlightening beings should know it thus.

"Just as the realm of truth always produces the liberations of Buddhist followers, individual illuminates, and enlightening beings, while the realm of truth has no increase or decrease, in the same way the knowledge of Buddha always produces all kinds of worldly and transmundane knowledge without itself increasing or decreasing. This is the second characteristic of the mind of Buddha; great enlightening beings should know it thus.

"Just as the ocean water flows under the continents and islands, so that all who drill for water find it, yet the ocean does not form any notion of itself giving out water, in the same way the water of the ocean of knowledge of Buddha flows into the minds of all sentient beings, so that if they examine things and practice ways of entering truth they will find knowledge, pure and clear, with lucid understanding—yet the knowledge of Buddha is equal, nondual, without discrimination; but according to the differences in sentient beings' mental patterns, the knowledge they obtain is not the same. This is the third characteristic of the mind of Buddha; great enlightening beings should know it thus.

"In the ocean there are four jewels imbued with infinite qualities that produce all the precious jewels in the ocean; if these jewels were not in the ocean, it would be impossible to find even one jewel. What are these four? One is called accumulation of treasures; another is called inexhaustible treasury; another is called removal of burning heat; the other is called replete with adornments. These jewels cannot be seen by any ordinary people or sea creatures. Why? The king water spirit Ocean, because the jewels are magnificent with perfect lines and proportions, keeps them in a deeply hidden place within the palace.

"The great ocean of knowledge of Buddha similarly has four great jewels of knowledge, with infinite qualities of knowledge and virtue, whereby are produced all the jewels of knowledge of the stages of learning and beyond learning of ordinary people, Buddhist followers, and individual illuminates, and of enlightening beings. What are the four? They are the jewel of great knowledge of unattached skill in means; the jewel of great knowledge of skillfully distinguishing the conditioned and the unconditioned; the jewel of great knowledge analytically explaining countless things without violating the essential nature of things; and the jewel of great knowledge knowing appropriate and inappropriate timing without ever a miss. If these four jewels were not in the Buddha's ocean of knowledge, not a single being would ever be able to enter the Great Vehicle of liberation. These four jewels of knowledge cannot be seen by unworthy beings. Why? Because they are kept in the deeply secret treasury of Buddha. These four jewels of knowledge are even, symmetrical, straight and true, immaculately beautiful, and able to universally benefit all enlightening beings, enabling them to attain the light of knowledge. This is the fourth characteristic of the mind of Buddha; great enlightening beings should know it thus.

"Also, the ocean has four jewels of blazing light spread on its floor, which by nature are extremely, fiercely hot; they are able to drink up and shrink the immeasurable quantities of water poured in by all the rivers, so that the ocean neither increases nor decreases. What are these four? One is called solar matrix; the second is called removing moisture; the third is called flame light; the fourth is called thorough exhaustion. If these four jewels were not in the ocean, the whole world, up to the highest heaven of material existence, would all be flooded. The light of this great jewel solar matrix, when it shines on seawater, turns it to milk; the light of the great jewel removing moisture, when it shines on the milk, turns it to cream; the light of the great jewel flame light, when it shines on the cream, turns it to butter; the light of the great jewel thorough exhaustion, when it shines on the butter, turns it to ghee, blazing like fire, consuming it without remainder.

"Buddha's ocean of great knowledge similarly has four kinds of jewels of great knowledge, with light of immeasurable power; when the light of these jewels of knowledge touches enlightening beings, it ultimately causes them to attain the great knowledge of Buddha. What are the four? They are the jewel of great knowledge stopping all the waves of scattered goodness; the jewel of great knowledge eliminating all emotional attachment to the teachings; the jewel of great knowledge of the universal illumination of the light of intelligence; the jewel of great knowledge of boundless effortlessness equal to Buddha.

"When enlightening beings practice the methods of fostering enlightenment, they rouse innumerable waves of scattered goodness, which all worldly beings, celestials, humans, or titans cannot destroy; when Buddha touches those enlightening beings with the light of the jewel of great knowledge of stopping all the waves of scattered good, it causes them to leave behind the waves of scattered good, keep their minds on one point, and dwell in concentration. Then, touching the enlightening beings with the light of the jewel of great knowledge, removing all emotional attachment to the teachings, causes them to give up clinging to the taste of concentration and awaken great spiritual powers. Then, touching the enlightening beings with the light of the jewel of great knowledge of the universal intelligence causes them to relinquish the occult powers they exercise and to engage in the active employment of great science. Then, touching the enlightening beings with the light of the jewel of great knowledge of boundless effortlessness equal to Buddha causes them to relinquish the active exercise of great science they have been engaged in so that they finally reach the equanimity of Buddhas and cease all effort completely. Without the contact of the great light of these four jewels of knowledge of Buddha it would be impossible for a single enlightening being to attain buddhahood. This is the fifth characteristic of the mind of Buddha; great enlightening beings should know it thus.

"The million lands from the sphere of water up to the heaven of neither perception nor nonperception, the abodes of sentient beings in the realm of desire, the realm of form, and the formless realm, all arise from space and rest in space. Why? Because space is everywhere. But though space contains all the realms of desire, form, and formlessness, yet it has no discrimination. The knowledge of Buddha is also like this: the knowledge of listeners, the knowledge of individual illuminates, the knowledge of enlightening beings, the knowledge of formulated practices, and the knowledge of unformulated practices, all arise from the knowledge of Buddha and rest in the knowledge of Buddha, because the knowledge of Buddha pervades all; though it contains innumerable knowledges, it has no discrimination. This is the sixth characteristic of the knowledge of Buddha; great enlightening beings should know it thus.

"Atop the Snowy mountains there is an excellent medicinal tree called inexhaustible roots; the roots of that medicinal tree grow from 168,000 leagues, all the way down to the adamantine ground and the sphere of water. When that medicinal tree grows roots, it causes the roots of all trees on the continent to grow; when the medicinal tree grows a stem, it causes the stems of all trees on the continent to grow. The same is true of the branches, leaves, flowers, and fruits. The roots of the medicinal tree can grow stems, and the stems can grow roots—the roots are inexhaustible, so it is called inexhaustible roots. That medicinal tree can foster growth everywhere, except for two places where it cannot perform the beneficial action of promotion of growth—that is, in the pits of hells and in the sphere of water; yet it has no aversion to them. The great tree of the supreme medicine of the knowledge of Buddha, likewise, by past development, fully perfects all good qualities of knowledge, shades all realms of sentient beings, and destroys all the miseries of bad states. Universal compassion and commitment form its roots; it is born from the seed of true knowledge of all buddhas. It is steadfast and immovable; skill in means is its trunk, the transcendent perfections of cosmic knowledge are its branches; meditations, liberations, and the great concentrations are its leaves; mental command, intellectual skills, and the elements of enlightenment are its flowers, and the ultimate unchanging liberation of buddhas is its fruit. Why may the medicinal tree of knowledge of Buddha be called 'inexhaustible roots'? Because of ultimately never ceasing, because of not stopping enlightening activity. The practice of enlightening beings is the nature of Buddha, the nature of Buddha is the practice of enlightening beings. Therefore it can be called inexhaustible roots. When the roots of the medicinal tree of buddha-knowledge grow, it causes enlightening beings to grow the root of great love and compassion, which does not abandon sentient beings. When its trunk grows, it causes all sentient beings to grow the trunk of profound determination with steadfast vigor. When its branches grow, it causes all enlightening beings to grow the branches of all transcendent ways. When its leaves grow, it causes enlightening beings to grow the leaves of pure conduct, austerity, virtue, paucity of desire, and contentment. When its flowers grow, it causes all enlightening beings to be replete with the flowers of magnificent arrays of the marks and embellishments of virtues. When its fruit grows, it causes all enlightening beings to gain the fruits of acceptance of nonorigination up to acceptance of coronation by all buddhas. The supreme medicine tree of knowledge of Buddha cannot perform its beneficial growth-fostering function in two places only: in those in the two vehicles of individual salvation who have fallen into the abyss of nondoing, and in unsuitable sentient beings with rotten roots of goodness who are sunk in the floodwaters of erroneous views and craving—yet Buddha never has rejected these people. The knowledge of Buddha has no increase or decrease, because its roots are stable and grow ceaselessly. This is the seventh characteristic of the mind of Buddha; great enlightening beings should know it thus.

"When the eonic holocaust starts in the universe, it burns up all the plants and trees, and even the mountains, consuming all without leaving anything. Suppose someone picked up some dry straw and threw it in that fire—do you think it could do aught but burn?"

"No."

"It is more possible for that straw not to burn than for Buddha's knowledge, analyzing all sentient beings, all lands, all ages, and all phenomena of all times, not to know something. Why? Because that knowledge impartially comprehends all clearly. This is the eighth characteristic of the mind of Buddha; great enlightening beings should know it thus.

"When a gale destroys the worlds, a great wind called destruction arises, able to pulverize the billion worlds of the universe, their iron mountains and so on, to smithereens. There is another wind, called blocker, circling the billion-world universe, blocking the gale of destruction so that it cannot reach the worlds in other places. Without this blocking wind, all the worlds in the ten directions would be completely destroyed. Buddha similarly has a great wind of knowledge, called extinguisher, which can extinguish the afflictions and habit energies of all great enlightening beings; and a great wind of knowledge called skillful sustaining, which skillfully sustains the enlightening beings whose faculties are not yet mature, not letting the extinguishing whirlwind totally eliminate all their afflictions and habit energies. Without Buddha's skillfully sustaining wind of knowledge, countless enlightening beings would fall into the states of those content with individual salvation. By this knowledge enlightening beings are enabled to transcend the stages of the two lesser vehicles of individual salvation and abide in the ultimate rank of Buddha. This is the ninth characteristic of the mind of Buddha; great enlightening beings should know it thus.

"There is nowhere the knowledge of Buddha does not reach. Why? There is not a single sentient being who is not fully endowed with the knowledge of Buddha; it is just that because of deluded notions, erroneous thinking, and attachments, they are unable to realize it. If they would get rid of deluded notions, then universal knowledge, spontaneous knowledge, and unobstructed knowledge would become manifest. It is as if there were a great scripture, equal in extent to a billion-world universe, in which are written all the things of the universe—there are written the things of the iron peripheral mountains, to an extent equal to those mountains; there are written the things on the land, to an extent equal to the land; there are written the things in the million-world galaxies, to an extent equal to the galaxies; there are written the things in the thousand-world systems, to an extent equal to the systems; there are written the things in the continents, to an extent equal to the continents; and so on; the things of the oceans, the polar mountains, the abodes of earth and sky, the celestial abodes in the sky of the desire realm, the abodes in the form realm, the abodes in the formless realm, are each written down to an equivalent extent. Though this scripture is equal in measure to a billion-world universe, yet it entirely rests in a single atom; and as this is so of one atom, it is also true of all atoms. Then suppose someone with clear and comprehensive knowledge, who has fully developed the celestial eye, sees these scriptures inside atoms, not benefiting sentient beings in the least, and, with this thought—'I should, by energetic power, break open those atoms and release those scriptures so that they can benefit all sentient beings'—then employs appropriate means to break open the atoms and release the great scriptures, to enable all sentient beings to benefit greatly. Similarly, the knowledge of Buddha, infinite and unobstructed, universally able to benefit all, is fully inherent in the bodies of sentient beings; but the ignorant, because of clinging to deluded notions, do not know of it, are not aware of it, and so do not benefit from it. Then the Buddha, with the unimpeded, pure, clear eye of knowledge, observes all sentient beings in the cosmos and says, 'How strange—how is it that these sentient beings have the knowledge of Buddha but in their folly and confusion do not know it or perceive it? I should teach them the way of sages and cause them forever to shed deluded notions and attachments, so they can see in their own bodies the vast knowledge of buddhas, no different from the buddhas.' Then Buddha teaches them to practice the way of sages, so they get rid of deluded notions, after which they realize the infinite knowledge of Buddha and aid and comfort all living beings. This is the tenth characteristic of the mind of Buddha; great enlightening beings should know it thus.

"Great enlightening beings should know the mind of Buddha, who has realized Thusness and is completely awake, in terms of such infinite, unimpeded, inconceivably great characteristics."

Then the great enlightening being Universally Good, in order to explain again what he meant, spoke in verse:

If you want to know the mind of buddhas,
Observe the buddhas' knowledge.
Buddhas' knowledge has no resting place,
Just as space rests on nothing.

Sentient beings' various inclinations,
And knowledge of expedients,
All rest on buddhas knowledge,
While buddha's knowledge rests on nothing.

The liberations of buddhas,
Disciples, and the self-enlightened,
All depend on the reality realm,
While reality has no increase or decrease.
Buddha's knowledge, similarly,
Produces all knowledges,
Without increase or decrease,
Without beginning or end.

Just as water flows under the ground
So those who seek it find it,
Without thought, without end,
Its effective power all-pervasive,
Buddha knowledge is also like this,
Being in all creatures' minds;
If any work on it with diligence,
They will soon find the light of knowledge.

Just as the water spirit has four jewels
Which produce all gems,
Hidden in a secret place
Where ordinary people cannot see,
So too do Buddha's four knowledges
Produce all knowledge,
While no one can see them
Except great enlightening beings.

As in the ocean are four jewels
Which can drink up all waters
So that the ocean does not overflow
And does not increase or decrease,
Likewise does Buddha's knowledge
Stop waves and remove attachment to teachings;
Boundlessly great and vast,
It produces enlightening beings and buddhas.

From the nadir to the summit of being,
The desire, form, and formless realms,
All rest in space,
While space does not discriminate:
The knowledge of enlightening beings,
Of disciples and the self-enlightened,
All rest in the knowledge of Buddha,
While buddha-knowledge has no discrimination.

On the Snowy mountains is a medicine
Called inexhaustible roots

Which can make all trees grow—
Their roots, trunks, leaves, flowers, and fruits.
Buddha's knowledge too is like this,
Grown from the seed of enlightenment;
Once enlightenment is attained,
It also produces the practices of enlightening beings.

If someone puts a handful of straw
In the eonic fire,
Where even diamond blazes,
The straw could not but be burned:
The ages and lands of all times
And the sentient beings therein
Buddha completely knows
More surely than the burning of that straw.

There is a wind called destruction
Which can pulverize a universe;
If not stopped by another wind,
Destruction would reach infinite worlds.
The great wind of knowledge is also like this,
Extinguishing the delusions of enlightening beings;
There is another wind of skillfulness,
Enabling them to live, in the land of buddhahood.

It is as there is a great scripture
Equal in extent to a universe
Existing inside one atom,
And in all atoms as well;
Someone with intelligence and wisdom
Sees all clearly with pure eyes
And breaks the atoms, releasing the scriptures
For the benefit of all beings.
Buddha-knowledge, likewise,
Is in all beings' minds;
Wrapped up in deluded thoughts,
They are unaware, unknowing;
The buddhas' great compassion
Causes them to get rid of deluded ideas
So knowledge can appear
And benefit enlightening beings.

"How should great enlightening beings know the sphere of Buddha, who has realized Thusness and is completely awake? Knowing the spheres of all worlds by means of unobstructed, unimpeded knowledge is the sphere of Buddha. Knowing the spheres of all times, all lands, all things, and all beings, the undifferentiated sphere of True Thusness, the unobstructed sphere of the reality realm, the boundless sphere of absolute truth, the unquantified sphere of space, and the objectless sphere, is the sphere of Buddha. Just as the spheres of all times, and so on, up to the objectless sphere, are all infinite, so is the sphere of Buddha infinite. Just as the objectless sphere has no existence in all places, so also does the sphere of Buddha have no existence in all places.

"Great enlightening beings should know the sphere of mind is the sphere of Buddha; just as the sphere of mind is measureless and boundless, without bondage or liberation, so too is the sphere of Buddha measureless and boundless, without bondage or liberation. Why? Because by such and such thoughts there are infinite such and such manifestations. It is like when the great water spirit showers rain according to will, the rain does not come from inside or outside; the sphere of Buddha is also like this—according to such and such thoughts, there are infinite such and such manifestations, yet they do not come from anywhere in the ten directions. Just as the water of the ocean all comes from the mental power of the king water spirit, so too does the water of the ocean of omniscience of all buddhas all come from the buddhas' past vows.

"The ocean of omniscience is infinite, boundless, inconceivable, and inexpressible, but I will tell something of it by way of simile, so please listen carefully. The southern continent has 2,500 rivers, which flow into the ocean; the western continent has 5,000 rivers, which flow into the ocean; the eastern continent has 7,500 rivers, which flow into the ocean; the northern continent has 10,000 rivers, which flow into the ocean. These four continents thus have 25,000 rivers, which continuously flow into the ocean. What do you think—is that a lot of water?"

"Yes indeed."

"There is also a water spirit Ten Light Beams, which rains even more water than that into the ocean; the water spirit Hundred Light Beams rains even more water than that into the ocean; the water spirits Magnificent Arrays, Thoughtful, Thundering, Joy, Infinite Light, Continuous Shower, Great Victory, Great Surge, and eight billion more such water spirits each rain more and more into the ocean; the son of the water spirit Ocean, named Rose Apple Banner, rains even more than that. The water in the abode of the water spirit Ten Light Beams flows into the ocean, even more than the aforementioned; the water in the palace of the water spirit Hundred Light Beams flows into the ocean, even more; the water of the palaces of each of the water spirits, each with more and more water, flows into the ocean, and the water in the palace of the water spirit Rose Apple Banner, son of the water spirit Ocean, which is yet more, also flows into the ocean. The water in the palace of the water spirit Ocean, which is even more, surges forth into the ocean; the water it produces is violet, and it surges forth at regular times, so the tide of the ocean is regular. Thus the ocean's water is infinite, its treasures are infinite, its creatures are infinite, and the earth it rests on is infinite too. Do you think that the ocean is infinite or not?"

"It is truly infinite, incomparably so."

"The infinity of this ocean does not come up to the smallest fraction of the infinity of the ocean of buddha-knowledge. Similes are made for beings according to their mentalities, but the sphere of Buddha is beyond similitude. Great enlightening beings should know that the ocean of knowledge of Buddha is infinite, because of ceaseless cultivation of all enlightening practices from the very first determination for enlightenment. They should know that the collection of treasures therein is infinite, because all elements of enlightenment, the seeds of the three treasures, continue unending. They should know the sentient beings in which it dwells are infinite, because it is used by all listeners and self-illuminates, those still learning and those beyond learning. They should know the ground it rests on is infinite, because it is the abode of all enlightening beings, from the first stage of Joy to the ultimate stage of Nonobstruction. Great enlightening beings, in order to enter infinite knowledge and benefit all sentient beings, should know the sphere of Buddha in this way."

Then Universally Good uttered these verses to again explain his meaning:

As the sphere of mind is infinite,
So is the sphere of buddhas.
As the sphere of mind is born from intellect,
So should the sphere of Buddha be seen.

The water spirits, without leaving their places,
Shower rain by the power of mind;
Though the rain does not come from or go anywhere,
Yet it falls everywhere according to the minds of the spirits:
The Ten-Powered Sage, in like manner,
Does not come from anywhere or go anywhere,
To those with pure minds appearing physically,
Vast as the cosmos, yet fitting in a pore.

The treasures of the ocean are infinite,
So are its creatures and ground;
The nature of the water is one flavor, equal, without distinction,
While those born therein each receive benefit.
The ocean of buddha-knowledge is also thus;
All it contains is infinite;
Those in the stages of learning and no learning
All gain benefit therein.

"How should great enlightening beings know the conduct of Buddha? Great enlightening beings should know unobstructed action is the conduct of Buddha; they should know the conduct of true thusness is the conduct of Buddha. Just as True Thusness is not born in the past, does not move into the future, and does not arise in the present, likewise the conduct of Buddha is not born, does not move, and does not arise. Just as the realm of reality is not quantified or unquantified, because it has no form, likewise the conduct of Buddha is not quantified or unquantified, because it has no form. It is as if a bird flew through the sky for a hundred years, the places it passed and those it had not passed would both be immeasurable, because the realm of space has no boundaries: in the same way, if someone spent trillions of eons expounding the particulars of the conduct of Buddha, what was explained and what was not yet explained would both be immeasurable, because the action of Buddha has no bounds.

"Buddha, completely enlightened, engaged in unobstructed action, has no dwelling place, yet can show what he does to all beings and enables them to go beyond all obstructed paths once they have seen this. It is as when the golden-winged king of birds flies in the sky, it circles and hovers, observing the dragon palaces in the ocean with its clear eyes; exerting its forceful strength, it churns the ocean waters with its wings, causing the waters to part, and snatches dragons, male or female, whose life it knows is about to end. The 'golden-winged bird king' Buddha, in like manner, engaged in unimpeded action, observes all sentient beings in all abodes in the cosmos with the clear Buddha-eye; if any have planted roots of goodness that have developed to maturity, the Buddha exerts the forceful ten powers and with the two wings of tranquillity and insight churns the waters of emotion of the ocean of birth and death, causing the water to part, then snatches those beings, places them in the Buddha teaching, and causes them to stop all deluded notions and false descriptions and abide in the nondiscriminatory unobstructed action of the enlightened.

"Just as the sun and moon travel alone through the sky conferring benefit on sentient beings, with no notion of where they come from or where they are going, likewise the buddhas, by nature fundamentally silent and extinct, without discrimination, appear to course all universes, performing buddha-work to benefit sentient beings without cease, yet not producing false notions of coming from somewhere or going somewhere. Great enlightening beings should see and know the actions conducted by Buddha in terms of infinite such means, infinite natures and characteristics."

Then Universally Good, to recapitulate, uttered these verses:

Just as True Thusness is not born, does not perish,
Has no location, and cannot be seen,
Likewise the action of the Great Benefactor
Transcends in the triple world and cannot be measured.

The reality realm is not the reality realm, yet not not the reality
   realm;
It is not quantified and not unquantified.
The action of the Great Worthy is also thus,
Neither quantified nor unquantified, because there is no body.

If a bird flies for billions of years,
The sky behind and ahead are equal, no different;
When Buddha's conduct is expounded for eons,
The told and the untold cannot be measured.

The golden bird in the sky watches the sea,
Parts the waters and snatches dragons;
The Ten-Powered can pull out virtuous people,
Remove them from the sea of existence, and rid them of delusion.

Like sun and moon traversing the sky
Shining on all without distinction,
The World-Honored traverses the cosmos
Teaching beings without stirring a thought.

"How should great enlightening beings know the attainment of enlightenment of Buddha? They should know that Buddha's attainment of
enlightenment has no view of any phenomena, is impartial toward
things, has no doubts, no duality, no signs, no activity, no cessation, no
measure, no boundaries; avoiding extremes, abiding in the middle way,
it is beyond all verbal explanation. Buddha knows the thoughts and
mental patterns of all sentient beings, their faculties, dispositions, inclinations, afflictions, obsessions, and habits; in sum, Buddha instantly
knows all things in all times.

"It is as the ocean can reflect the physical forms of all sentient beings
on earth, and therefore is called the ocean: the enlightenment of the
buddhas is also like this, reflecting the thoughts, faculties, dispositions,
and inclinations of all sentient beings, yet without reflecting anything—
therefore it is called the enlightenment of the buddhas.

"The enlightenment of buddhas cannot be expressed in writing, cannot be reached by any verbal expression, cannot be explained in any
language; but it is expediently elucidated according to need.

"When buddhas attain true awakening, they acquire a body equal in
extent to all sentient beings, a body equal in extent to all phenomena, a
body equal in extent to all lands, a body equal in extent to all times, a
body equal in extent to all buddhas, a body equal in extent to all
languages, a body equal in extent to True Thusness, a body equal in
extent to the cosmos, a body equal in extent to space, a body equal in
extent to the realm where there is no obstruction, a body equal in extent
to all vows, a body equal in extent to all practices, and a body equal in
extent to the ultimately calm realm of nirvana. As are the bodies they

acquire, so is their speech and mind; they attain measureless, countless such pure spheres of body, speech, and mind.

"Upon attaining true awakening, buddhas see within their body all sentient beings attaining true awakening, and see all sentient beings enter nirvana, all of the same nature, which is no nature. No nature of what kind? That is, no nature of appearances, no nature of exhaustion, no nature of birth, no nature of destruction, no nature of self, no nature of nonself, no nature of living being, no nature of nonliving being, no nature of enlightenment, no nature of the cosmos, no nature of space, and also no nature of attaining true awakening. By knowing all things are natureless, a buddha attains omniscience, and by great compassion continues to save sentient beings.

"Just as space never increases or decreases whether all worlds become or disintegrate, because space has no birth, similarly the enlightenment of buddhas has no increase or decrease whether there is attainment of enlightenment or not, because enlightenment has no signs or counter-signs, no unity and no variety.

"Suppose someone were able magically to produce as many minds as grains of sand in the Ganges River, and each mind also produced as many buddhas as grains of sand in the Ganges River, all featureless, formless, and signless, and continued to do so incessantly throughout as many eons as there are grains of sand in the Ganges River—how many buddhas do you think would be magically produced by that person's magically produced minds?"

The enlightening being Wondrous Qualities of Natural Origination of Buddha said, "As I understand your meaning, magical production and nonproduction are equal and have no distinction—how can you ask how many there would be?"

The enlightening being Universally Good said, "Very good—it is as you say. Even if all sentient beings were to instantly attain enlighten-ment, that would be equal to not attaining enlightenment, no different. Why? Because enlightenment is signless. If it has no signs, it has no increase or decrease.

"Great enlightening beings should thus know that attainment of true awakening, the same as enlightenment, is uniformly formless. A buddha, attaining true awakening, by the means of unity, enters the concentra-tion of thoroughly aware knowledge and, having entered it, manifests, in one vast body attaining true awakening, as many bodies as there are sentient beings dwelling in that body. As this is so of one vast body attaining true awakening, so it is of all vast bodies attaining true awakening.

"Buddha has infinite such doors of attainment of true awakening; therefore you should know that the bodies Buddha manifests are infinite, and because they are infinite we say the body of Buddha is infinite realms, equal to the realms of living beings.

"Great enlightening beings should know that in one pore of Buddha's body are buddha-bodies as numerous as all sentient beings. Why? Because the body of the Buddha's attainment of true awakening ultimately has no birth or destruction. And as this is so of one pore, so is it of every point in the entire cosmos. Know that there is not a bit of space where there is no buddha-body. Why? Because Buddha's attainment of true awakening reaches everywhere. According to capability and power, on the lion seat under the enlightenment tree at the site of enlightenment, with various bodies, Buddha attains true awakening.

"Great enlightening beings should know that in each moment of thought of their own minds there are always buddhas attaining true awakening. Why? Because the buddhas do not attain true awakening apart from this mind. As this is true of one's own mind, so is it also true of the minds of all sentient beings—in all are buddhas attaining true awakening, all-pervasive, existing everywhere, without separation or annihilation, without cease, entering the inconceivable doors or means of enlightenment. Great enlightening beings should know Buddha's attainment of enlightenment this way."

Then, to recapitulate, the enlightening being Universally Good spoke these verses:

> The truly awake know all things
> Are nondual, beyond duality, all equal,
> Inherently pure as space,
> Not distinguishing self and nonself.

> As the ocean reflects beings' bodies
> And is therefore called the ocean,
> Enlightenment reflects all mental patterns
> And hence is called true awareness.

> Just as worlds have formation and decay
> While space does not increase or diminish,
> While all buddhas appear in the world,
> The one form of enlightenment is ever formless.

> When someone emanates minds emanating buddhas,
> Emanation and nonemanation are no different in essence;
> Though all sentient beings attain enlightenment,
> There is no increase or decrease, enlightenment or no.

> Buddha has a concentration called well aware;
> Entering this concentration under the enlightenment tree,
> Buddha emits light beams as many as beings,
> Awakening all kinds, like lotuses blooming.

As many thoughts, faculties, and desires
As are in beings in lands of all times,
That many bodies appear—
Hence true awareness is called infinite.

"How should great enlightening beings know Buddha's turning of
the wheel of teaching? They should know it thus: Buddha, by the free
power of mind, turns the wheel of teaching without arising or turning,
because of knowing that all things forever have no arising. Buddha turns
the wheel of teaching by three kinds of turning, the cycles of the path of
insight, the path of practice, and the path beyond learning, and stops
what should be stopped, because of knowing that all things are apart
from extremes of annihilation and eternity. Buddha turns the wheel of
teaching apart from the realm of desire and the realm of negation,
because of penetrating the spacelike limit of all things. Buddha turns the
wheel of teaching without verbal explanation, because of knowing that
all things are inexpressible. Buddha turns the wheel of teaching ultimately quiescently, because of knowing that all things are of the essence
of nirvana. Buddha turns the wheel of teaching with all means of literature and language, because the voice of Buddha reaches everywhere.
Buddha turns the wheel of teaching knowing that the voice is like an
echo, because of comprehending the true nature of all things. Buddha
turns the wheel of teaching producing all messages in one message,
because there is ultimately no center. Buddha turns the wheel of teaching
without omission or exhaustion, because of absence of clinging inside
or outside.

"Just as all writing and speech cannot be exhaustively told of, the
same is true of Buddha's turning the wheel of teaching—all letters are
arranged to express it, without cease, without ever exhausting it. The
wheel of teaching of Buddha enters into all speech and writing, yet has
no dwelling place. Just as writing enters into all business, all words, all
calculations, all mundane and transmundane subjects, yet dwells nowhere, so also does the voice of Buddha enter into all points, all beings,
all phenomena and principles, all works, and all consequences, yet does
not dwell anywhere. All the various languages of all sentient beings are
not apart from the wheel of teaching of Buddha, because the real aspect
of speech and sound is identical to the wheel of teaching. Great enlightening beings should know the turning of the wheel of teaching of
Buddha thus.

"Also, if great enlightening beings want to know the wheel of teaching that Buddha turns, they should know where Buddha's wheel of
teaching comes from. What is the provenance of the Buddha's wheel
of teaching? Buddha makes so many utterances, turning the wheel of
teaching according to the innumerable differences in mental patterns
and inclinations of all sentient beings. Buddhas, truly awake, have a concentration called ultimately unimpeded and fearless; having entered this

concentration, with each mouth of each body of attainment of true enlightenment they produce as many utterances as there are sentient beings, each utterance containing all sounds, each different, turning the wheel of teaching, to make all sentient beings happy. Those who know the turning of the wheel of teaching thus are considered to be following all Buddha teachings. Those who do not know this are not following them. Great enlightening beings should know Buddha's turning the wheel of teaching thus, because it universally enters the infinite realms of living beings.''

Then, to recapitulate, Universally Good said in verse,

> Buddhas' wheel of teaching has no turning;
> It has no arising and no attainment at any time.
> Just as writing is never exhausted,
> So is the teaching-wheel of the Ten-Powered.

> Just as writing enters everywhere, yet with no arrival,
> Such is the teaching-wheel of the Enlightened,
> Entering all speech without entering aught,
> Able to make all beings rejoice.

> Buddhas have a concentration called ultimate;
> They preach after entering this concentration,
> Speaking to enlighten all beings,
> Boundless though they be.

> In each utterance they also utter
> Countless sayings, each different,
> Free in the world, without discrimination,
> Causing all to hear according to inclination.

> Words do not come from inside or outside,
> Are neither lost nor accumulate;
> Yet for sentient beings buddhas turn the teaching-wheel—
> This freedom is most extraordinary.

"How should great enlightening beings know Buddha's ultimate nirvana? If great enlightening beings want to know the greate nirvana of buddhas, they should know its fundamental essence. As is the nirvana of ultimate reality, so is the nirvana of Buddha; as is the nirvana of space, so is the nirvana of Buddha; as is the nirvana of the nature of things, so is the nirvana of Buddha; as is the nirvana of detachment from desire, so is the nirvana of Buddha; as is the nirvana of formlessness, so is the nirvana of Buddha; as is the nirvana of selfhood, so is the nirvana of Buddha; as is the nirvana of the ultimate essence of all things, so is the nirvana of Buddha; as is the nirvana of ultimate True Thusness, so is the nirvana of

Buddha. Why? Because nirvana has no birth and no emergence; if something has no birth and no emergence, then it has no extinction.

"Buddha does not tell enlightening beings about the ultimate nirvana of buddhas and does not show it to them. Why? Because Buddha wants to cause them to see all buddhas always present before them, to see in one moment all the buddhas of past and future, in their full splendor, just as if they were actually present, yet without entertaining any notions of duality or nonduality. Why? Because great enlightening beings permanently abandon all conceptual clinging.

"Buddhas appear in the world in order to provoke inspiration in sentient beings and manifest nirvana in order to provoke longing in sentient beings: in reality the buddhas have no appearance in the world and no nirvana either. Why? Buddha always abides in the pure realm of reality, manifesting nirvana according to the minds of sentient beings.

"For example, when the sun comes out and illumines the world, its image is reflected in all clean vessels of water, being in all places without coming or going. If one vessel breaks, then the reflection of the sun does not appear in it. Do you think it is the fault of the sun that its reflection does not appear there?"

"No—it is just because the vessel is broken; it's no fault of the sun."

"The knowledge of realization of Thusness, buddha-knowledge, is also like this, appearing throughout the cosmos, without before or after: Buddha appears in the clean mind-vessels of all sentient beings. If the mind-vessel is always clean, the embodiment of Buddha is always seen; if the mind is polluted, the vessel breaks and the Buddha cannot be seen.

"If there are any sentient beings who can be liberated by nirvana, Buddha then manifests nirvana for them; but really Buddha has no birth, no death, no crossing over into extinction.

"It is like, for example, the element fire, which can make fires in all worlds. Sometimes in one place the fire will go out, but do you think the fire in all worlds is extinguished?"

"No."

"Similarly Buddha performs the tasks of buddhahood in all worlds; if what can be done in one world is finished, a buddha manifests entry into nirvana, but the buddhas in all worlds do not all pass away into extinction. Great enlightening beings should know the great nirvana of the truly enlightened thus.

"Again, suppose, for example, a magician well versed in magical arts, by the power of the techniques of illusion, manifests phantom bodies in all cities, towns, and villages in all lands in a billion-world universe, and sustains them there by magical power for an eon, while in other places, the magic performance being finished, the bodies disappear. Do you think that when that great magician disappears in one place, he disappears in all places?"

"No."

"In a similar way Buddha, the Truly Enlightened, knowing the various magical arts of infinite wisdom and means, manifests in all universes, sustaining that permanently, throughout the future. If in one place, according to the minds of beings, what is to be done is finished, Buddha manifests nirvana; but can you say because Buddha has appeared to enter nirvana in one place that Buddha becomes extinct everywhere? Great enlightening beings should know the great ultimate nirvana of Buddha in this way.

"Furthermore, Buddha, when manifesting nirvana, enters immovable concentration, and having entered this concentration, emanates from each body infinite trillions of great light beams, each light beam producing countless lotus blossoms, each lotus blossom having untold petals of exquisite jewels, with a lion throne on each petal and a buddha sitting cross-legged on each throne. The number of those buddhas is exactly equal to the number of sentient beings; all are fully adorned with the most sublime virtues, produced by the power of past vows. If there are any sentient beings with mature roots of goodness who see the buddha-incarnations, they will all receive the teaching; those buddha-bodies remain forever, teaching and liberating sentient beings according to the situation, without losing an opportunity. The bodies of buddhas have no locus, are not real or unreal; only by the power of the past vows of the buddhas, and the capacity of sentient beings to be liberated, do they appear. Great enlightening beings should know the great nirvana of Buddha in this way. Buddha abides in the infinite, unobstructed, ultimate realm of reality, in the realm of space, in the essence of True Thusness, without birth or death, and in ultimate truth, appearing to sentient beings according to the time, sustained by past vows, without ever ceasing, not abandoning all beings, all lands, all phenomena."

Then, to recapitulate, Universally Good said in verse,

> While the sun sheds light illumining the world,
> When a vessel breaks and water leaks out, the reflection
>   disappears;
> So it is with the sun of supreme knowledge;
> Those without faith see it as extinct.
>
> Fire makes fires in the world,
> While in one city it goes out sometime:
> Likewise the Buddha pervades the cosmos
> And appears to pass away where the work of teaching is done.
>
> A magician makes bodies appear in all lands,
> Which disappear when their function is done:
> So does Buddha disappear when the teaching is done,
> While always seen in other lands.

Buddha has a concentration, called unmoving,
Which is entered after teaching beings:
Instantly Buddha's body emanates infinite lights,
The lights produce lotuses, on which are buddhas:
The buddha-bodies are countless as phenomena,
Visible to those with virtue;
Each of these countless bodies
Has a full span of life and array of adornments.

Like birthlessness is the emergence of Buddha,
Like deathlessness the nirvana of Buddha:
All words and similes end—
All purposes are achieved, beyond compare.

"How should great enlightening beings know the roots of goodness planted by seeing, hearing, and attending Buddha? They should know these roots of goodness are not fruitless, because they produce endless awareness, because they remove all obstacles, because they certainly reach the ultimate end, because they are free from falsehood, because all vows are fulfilled, because they do not end creative action while according with knowledge of the uncreate, because they generate the knowledge of buddhas, because they go on throughout the future, because they accomplish all kinds of excellent practices, and because they reach the stage of effortless knowledge.

"For example, if a man eats a little bit of diamond, it will never be digested, but must pass through the body. Why? Because diamond is incompatible with the impurities of the physical body. In the same way, planting a little bit of roots of goodness with Buddha must pass through the body of afflictions of all conditioning and reach the abode of unconditioned ultimate knowledge. Why? Because this little bit of root of goodness is incompatible with the afflictions of conditioning.

"Even if one piled up dry straw as high as a mountain, if one tossed an ember of fire the size of a seed into it, it would all burn up for sure. Why? Because fire burns straw. Like this, planting a little bit of roots of goodness with Buddha surely can burn up all afflictions and ultimately enable one to attain nirvana without remainder, because the essence of this little bit of root of goodness is ultimate.

"For example, in the Snowy mountains there is a tree of the finest medicine called good sight: if any see it, their eyes are purified; if any hear of it, their ears are purified; if any smell it, their noses are purified; if any taste it, their tongues are purified; if any touch it, their bodies are purified; if any take the earth it grows in, that can also perform the beneficial function of removing disease. The supreme medicine of Buddha similarly can perform all benefits for sentient beings. If any see the physical body of Buddha, their eyes are purified; if any hear the name of Buddha, their ears are purified; if any smell the fragrance of the morality of Buddha, their noses are purified; if any taste the flavor of the teaching of Buddha, their tongues are purified, they gain the universal tongue and understand the principles of language; if any come in contact with the light of Buddha, their bodies are purified and they ultimately attain the supreme body of reality; if any think of Buddha, they attain purity of Buddha-remembrance concentration. If any sentient beings honor the ground Buddha has crossed, or a tomb or shrine, they too will be endowed with roots of goodness, annihilate all afflictions, and attain the felicity of sages. I tell you, even if there are sentient beings who see and hear Buddha, but because of being veiled by obstructions due to their deeds do not become believers, if they still plant roots of goodness, none will be in vain—they will reach the ultimate end and enter nirvana. Great enlightening beings should thus know that the roots of goodness planted by seeing, hearing, and attending Buddha are free from all evil and imbued with good.

"Buddha uses all kinds of similes to explain all kinds of things, but there is no simile that can explain this principle. Why? Because the road of intellectual knowledge ends, because it is inconceivable. The buddhas and enlightening beings just tell sentient beings similes according to their mentalities in order to gladden them, but this is not the ultimate. This gate of the teaching is called the secret point of the buddhas; it is called that which cannot be known by any worldlings; it is called entry into the seal of Buddha; it is called opening the door of great knowledge; it is called revealing the essence of Buddha; it is called perfecting all enlightening beings; it is called that which all worldlings cannot destroy; it is called wholly conforming to the realm of buddhas; it is called able to purify all realms of sentient beings; it is called expounding the ultimate inconceivable teaching of the real nature of Buddha. Buddha does not expound this teaching to anyone but enlightening beings intent on the Great Vehicle, only expounding it to enlightening beings riding the inconceivable vehicle of enlightenment. This gate of teaching does not come into the hands of anyone but great enlightening beings.

"It is like, for example, the seven treasures of a universal ruler, by which universal rulership is shown; these treasures do not come into the hands of anyone but the crown prince born of the first wife who has developed the characteristics of a sage ruler. If the universal ruler does not have a son with many virtues, after the ruler's life ends the treasures will disperse and perish in seven days. The treasure of this scripture is also like this: it does not come into the hands of anyone but the true offspring of the sovereign Buddha, born in the house of Buddha, who plant the roots of goodness characteristic of buddhas. If there are no true offspring of Buddha, this teaching will perish before long. Why? Because those in the two lesser vehicles of individual salvation do not hear this scripture, much less absorb and hold it, read, recite, or copy it, or analyze and explain it—only the great enlightening beings can do these things.

"Therefore, great enlightening beings, hearing this teaching, shall rejoice and receive it with respect. Why? Because great enlightening beings appreciating this scripture will quickly attain unexcelled, complete perfect enlightenment. Even if enlightening beings spend countless eons practicing the six ways of transcendence and cultivating the various elements of enlightenment, as long as they have not heard this teaching of the inconceivable great power of Buddha, or if they have heard it and do not believe or understand it, do not follow it, enter it, or attain it, they cannot be called true enlightening beings, because they cannot be born in the house of Buddha. If they get to hear this teaching of the immeasurable, inconceivable, unobstructed, unhindered knowledge of Buddha, and having heard it, take it to heart, follow it, and awaken to it, these people will be born in the house of Buddha, accord with the sphere of all buddhas, be endowed with all qualities of enlightening beings, detach from all mundane things, develop the conduct of all buddhas, realize the true nature of all enlightening beings, have no doubts about the power of Buddha, abide in the teacherless truth, and plunge deeply into the unimpeded realm of buddhahood.

"After great enlightening beings have heard this teaching, then they can know infinite things by knowledge of equality; then they can part with arbitrary discriminations by means of a straightforward, honest mind; then they can see the buddhas before them by means of supreme devotion; then they can enter the impartial realm of space by means of the power of attention; then they can travel the boundless cosmos by means of free thought; then they can acquire all virtues by means of the power of knowledge and wisdom; then they can shed all worldly defilements by means of spontaneous knowledge; then they can enter the network of all ten directions by means of the will for enlightenment; then they can know the buddhas of all times are of one and the same essence, by means of great observation; then they can enter this teaching by the knowledge of dedication of roots of goodness, entering without entering, not clinging to a single thing, always observing things through one universal principle. Great enlightening beings, perfecting these accomplishments, attain teacherless, spontaneous knowledge with a minimum of effort."

Then Universally Good, to recapitulate, spoke these verses:

Immeasurable are the virtues attained
By seeing, hearing, and honoring buddhas;
Ultimately endless in action,
Needed to destroy afflictions and remove misery.

As when a man ingests a little diamond
It is not digested but must pass through,
The virtues of honoring buddhas
Destroy illusion and lead to adamantine knowledge.

Just as straw piled high as a mountain
A tiny ember of fire will burn up,
The small virtue of honoring buddhas
Will end affliction and lead to nirvana.

In the Snowy mountains is an herb called good to see
Which relieves all sickness when seen, heard of, smelled, or
    touched;
If any see or hear of buddhas,
They will gain excellent virtues and reach buddha-knowledge.

Then, by the spiritual power of Buddha, and by natural law, untold hundreds of quintillions of worlds in each of the ten directions quaked in six ways: surging up in the east, sinking in the west; surging up in the west, sinking in the east; surging up in the south, sinking in the north; surging up in the north, sinking in the south; surging up on the periphery, sinking in the middle; surging up in the middle, sinking on the periphery—moving in eighteen ways: trembling, trembling all over, trembling equally all over; rising, rising all over, rising equally all over; surging, surging all over, surging equally all over; quaking, quaking all over, quaking equally all over; roaring, roaring all over, roaring equally all over; crashing, crashing all over, crashing equally all over. There rained clouds of all kinds of flowers, parasols, banners, pennants, fragrances, garlands, perfumes, ornaments, and radiant jewels, all surpassing those of the heavens, as well as clouds of enlightening beings singing eulogies, clouds of different bodies of untold enlightening beings, clouds of true awakening, clouds of purifying inconceivable worlds, clouds raining the sounds of the words of the buddhas, filling boundless universes. As on this earth the power of Buddha manifested in this way, causing all enlightening beings to rejoice greatly, so did this transpire in all worlds throughout the ten directions.

At that time, in each of the ten directions, past as many worlds as atoms in eighty unspeakable numbers of hundreds of septillions of buddha-lands, there were eighty unspeakable numbers of hundreds of septillions of buddhas, alike named Universally Good, who all appeared to the enlightening beings and said, "Bravo, Offspring of Buddha! You are able, imbued with the power of the enlightened, conforming to the nature of reality, to expound the teaching of the manifestation of Buddha. We buddhas of the same name, eighty unspeakable numbers of hundreds of septillions of us in each of the ten directions, all expound this teaching. And what we expound, so do all Buddhas in all worlds in the ten directions. In this assembly as many great enlightening beings as atoms in a hundred thousand buddha-lands have attained the concentration of spiritual powers of all enlightening beings; we give them the prediction that they will attain unexcelled, complete perfect enlightenment in one lifetime. As many sentient beings as atoms in a buddha-land have roused the determination for unexcelled, complete perfect enlightenment; we also give them a prediction, that in the future, after as many eons as atoms in unspeakable buddha-lands, they will all become buddhas, all with the same name, Supreme Realm of the Enlightened. In order to enable the enlightening beings of the future to hear this teaching, we all preserve it together. As the sentient beings are liberated in this world, so are the sentient beings liberated in all worlds in the cosmos."

Then, owing to the spiritual power of the buddhas of the ten directions, owing to the power of the original vows of Vairocana, because the natural order is so, because of the power of roots of goodness, because the buddhas activate knowledge in an instant, because buddhas respond to conditions without missing the time, because they awaken enlightening beings at appropriate times, because their past deeds have no loss or decay, because they foster the attainment of the great practice of Universal Good, and because they manifest the mastery of omniscience, in each of the ten directions, past as many worlds as atoms in ten unspeakable numbers of tens of quadrillions of buddha-lands, there were as many enlightening beings as atoms in ten unspeakable numbers of tens of quadrillions of buddha-lands who came here, filling all universes in the ten directions, showing the vast magnificent adornments of enlightening beings, emitting networks of great beams of light, shaking all worlds in the ten directions, demolishing the palaces of all demons, extinguishing the pains of the states of ill, revealing the power of all enlightened ones, singing praises of the infinite different virtuous qualities of the enlightened, showering all kinds of rains, manifesting infinite different bodies, receiving the teachings of infinite buddhas. By the spiritual power of Buddha, they each said, "Bravo, offspring of Buddha: you are able to explain this indestructible teaching of buddhas. We are all named Universally Good, and we each have come here from the presence of a buddha called Freedom Marked by Universality, from worlds called Universal Light. In those worlds we also expound this teaching, with the same expressions, the same principles, the same explanations, the same certitude, without increase or decrease. We have all come here, by the spiritual power of Buddha, and by having attained the Buddhas' teaching, to be witnesses for you. And as we come here, the same is true of all worlds in the whole cosmos, throughout space, in all ten directions."

Then the enlightening being Universally Good—with the spiritual power of Buddha, looking over all the great congregations of enlightening beings, wishing to recapitulate the immense power of the manifestation of Buddha, the indestructibility of the true teaching of the enlightened, how infinite roots of goodness are not in vain, how the emergence of buddhas in the world always comprises all supreme qualities, the ability to observe skillfully the minds of all sentient beings and teach them the truth according to their needs, without missing the right time, producing the infinite light of truth of enlightening beings; the adornments of freedom of all buddhas, and how all enlightened ones are one body, no different, produced by great practices of the past—said in verse:

> The actions of all buddhas
> Are beyond mundane similitudes;
> In order to enlighten sentient beings,
> They make similes of nonsimiles for illustration.

> This subtle, mysterious, profound teaching
> Is hard to get to hear in a billion ages;
> Those with vigor, wisdom, and self-control
> Can get to hear this mystery.

> Any who hear this teaching and rejoice
> Have served countless buddhas;
> Being absorbed into the power of Buddha,
> Gods and humans honor and praise them.

> This is the foremost wealth transcending the world:
> This can liberate all living beings,
> This can produce the pure Path—
> You should keep it attentively.

BOOK THIRTY-EIGHT

Detachment from the World

AT THAT TIME the World-Honored One was in the country of Magadha, in the forest, in the shrine of universal light at the site of enlightenment, sitting on a lotus lion seat; he had completely fulfilled ineffable enlightenment, put an end to afflictions and views, and arrived at formless truth. Abiding in the abode of buddhas, he had attained the equanimity of buddhas and arrived at nonobstruction in the state of imperturbability. All his actions were unimpeded. He stood in the inconceivable and saw through all time. His body continually pervaded all lands; his knowledge always comprehended all things. He understood all activities. He exhausted all doubts. His knowledge was that sought by all enlightening beings. He had arrived at the nondual ultimate perfection of buddhahood and fully attained the equal liberation of the enlightened. He had realized the stage of impartiality of buddhas, which is without extremes or middle, extending throughout the cosmos, equal to space.

He was with as many great enlightening beings as atoms in untold quadrillions of buddha-lands, all of whom were to attain unexcelled, complete perfect enlightenment in one lifetime, and had come from various lands in other regions. All of them were endowed with the means and wisdom of enlightening beings: that is, they skillfully observed sentient beings and civilized them by the power of appropriate means so that they would live by the way of enlightening beings; they skillfully observed all worlds and went to them by the power of appropriate means; they skillfully examined the realm of nirvana and meditated on it and assessed it; they did away with all false conceptions and cultivated sublime practices without interruption; they were well able to take care of all sentient beings; they skillfully penetrated the principles of infinite liberative means; they knew sentient beings are empty and have no existence, yet they did not deny the fruits of action; they knew the various differences in the compulsions, faculties, spheres, and means of sentient beings' minds; they were able to absorb and hold the teachings of buddhas of past, present, and future, to understand them themselves, and also explain them to others; they were well versed in all mundane and transmundane things and knew their true reality; they examined all compounded and uncompounded things and knew them to be nondual; in a single moment of thought they were able to acquire all the knowledge and wisdom of the buddhas of all times; they were able to show attainment of true awakening moment to moment, to cause sentient beings to become inspired and attain the Way; they knew the spheres of all sentient beings in the mental objects of one sentient being; though they entered the stage of the enlightened, they did not give up the works carried out by enlightening beings; their deeds, knowledge, and means did not fabricate anything; they stayed in the world for countless ages for each and every sentient being, yet they were hard to meet even in incalculable eons; they turned the wheel of the true Teaching, pacifying sentient beings without fail; they had already fulfilled the pure practical commitments of the buddhas of past, present, and future. They had perfected infinite such virtues, so that even if all the buddhas spoke for boundless eons they could not tell of them all. Their names were Universally Good, Universal Eye, Universal Emanation, Universal Wisdom, Universal Vision, Universal Light, Universal Contemplation, Universal Illumination, Universal Symbol, Universal Awareness, and so on. There were as many such enlightening beings as atoms in untold quadrillions of buddha-lands: all of them had accomplished the vow of practice of Universal Good; their profound determination and great vows were already fulfilled; they traveled to all places where buddhas were appearing in the world, requested them to turn the wheel of teaching, and were well able to receive and hold the eye of truth of the buddhas, perpetuating the lineage of buddhas; they knew the order of all buddhas' appearance in the world and giving instructions, their names, countries, attainment of enlightenment, and turning the wheel of teaching; in worlds where there were no buddhas, they appeared and became buddhas, able to purify defiled sentient beings, able to destroy the action obstructions of enlightening beings, and enter the unimpeded pure realm of reality.

Then the great enlightening being Universally Good entered a vast concentration called Buddha flower array. When he entered this concentration, all worlds quaked in six ways, moving in eighteen ways, producing a tremendous sound that none did not hear. After that he rose from concentration. At that point the enlightening being Universal Wisdom, knowing the congregation had assembled, asked the enlightening being Universally Good, "Please tell us—what are the reliances of great enlightening beings? What are their extraordinary thoughts? What are their practices? What are their spiritual friends? What are their exertions of energy? What are their attainments of peace of mind? What are their ways of developing sentient beings? What are their precepts? How do they receive the prediction of enlightenment? How do they enter into the state of enlightening beings? What are their entries into enlightenment? What are their penetrations of the activities of sentient beings? What are their entries into worlds? What are their entries into ages?

What are their explanations of past, present, and future? What are their entries into past, present, and future? What are their developments of a tireless mind? What are their knowledges of differentiation? What are their mental masteries? What are their explanations of Buddha? What are their developments of the Universally Good mind? What are their principles of Universally Good practice? For what reasons do they generate great compassion? What are the causes of their development of the will for enlightenment? What are their expressions of respect to spiritual friends? What are their purities? What are their transcendent ways? What are their conscious knowledges? What are their realizational knowledges? What are their powers? What are their impartialities? What are their expressions of the true meaning of the Buddha teaching? What are their teachings? What do they preserve? What are their intellectual powers? What are their masteries? What are their qualities of nonattachment? What are their equanimities? What are their generations of knowledge? What are their magical displays? What are their supports of powers? What are their attainments of great joy and solace? What are their profound penetrations of the Buddha teaching? What are their bases? What are their developments of fearlessness? What are their developments of minds free from doubt? What are their inconceivabilities? What are their skillful esoteric sayings? What are their skillful analytic knowledges? What are their entries into concentration? What are their universal entries? What are their doors of liberation? What are their spiritual powers? What are their insights? What are their liberations? What are their groves? What are their palaces? What are their enjoyments? What are their adornments? What are their developments of an unshakable mind? What are their profound, great determinations they don't give up? What are their contemplations? What are their explanations of things? What are their purities? What are their definitive marks? What are their illuminations of knowledge? What are their peerless states? What are their indomitable attitudes? What are their outstanding minds? What are their oceanic knowledges entering unexcelled enlightenment? What are their jewel-like states? What are their adamantine commitments to universal enlightenment? What are their great undertakings? What are their ultimate great tasks? What are their indestructible faiths? What are their ways of receiving the prediction of enlightenment? What are their dedications of roots of goodness? What are their attainments of wisdom? What are their developments of a boundlessly broad mind? What are their hidden treasures? What are their rules of behavior? What are their controls? What are their unimpeded functions? What are their unimpeded functions in respect to sentient beings? What are their unimpeded functions in respect to lands? What are their unimpeded functions in respect to phenomena and principles? What are their unimpeded functions in respect to bodies? What are their unimpeded functions in respect to vows? What are their unimpeded functions in respect to realms? What are their unimpeded functions of knowledge?

What are their unimpeded functions of spiritual capacities? What are their unimpeded functions of miraculous abilities? What are their unimpeded functions of power? What are their versatilities? What are their spheres? What are their powers? What are their fearlessnesses? What are their unique qualities? What are their activities? What are their bodies? What are their physical actions? What is their speech? What is their purification of speech? What are the protections they receive? What are their accomplishments of great works? What are their minds? What are their determinations? What are their comprehensive minds? What are their profound minds? What do they strive to practice? What are their certain understandings? What are their certain understandings of worlds? What are their certain understandings of beings? What are their habit energies? What are their graspings? What do they cultivate? What are their accomplishments of the Buddha teachings? What makes them regress from the way of the Buddha teachings? What are their paths of emancipation? What are their qualities of certainty? What are their ways of generating the qualities of buddhahood? What are their appellations of greatness? What are their paths? What are their infinite paths? What are their aids to enlightenment? What are their ways of cultivation? What are their ways of adornment? What are their feet? What are their hands? What are their guts? What are their internal organs? What are their hearts? What is their armor? What are their weapons? What are their heads? What are their eyes? What are their ears? What are their noses? What are their tongues? What are their bodies? What are their minds? What is their action? What is their abiding? What is their sitting? What is their reclining? What are their dwelling places? What are their spheres of action? What are their observations? What are their universal observations? What is their springing? What is their lion's roar? What is their pure giving? What is their pure discipline? What is their pure tolerance? What is their pure energy? What is their pure concentration? What is their pure wisdom? What is their pure benevolence? What is their pure compassion? What is their pure joy? What is their pure equanimity? What are their principles? What are their pure laws? What are their virtues used to foster enlightenment? What are their knowledges used to foster enlightenment? What are their sufficiencies of insight? What are their quests for truth? What are their understandings of truth? What are their norms of practice? What are demons? What are demons' actions? How are the actions of demons gotten rid of? What are visions of Buddha? What are actions of Buddha? What are actions of conceit? What are actions of knowledge? What is possession by demons? What is being supported by Buddha? What is being supported by truth? What do enlightening beings do while living in the heaven of satisfaction? Why do they die in that heaven? Why do they appear to abide in the womb? Why do they manifest subtle processes? Why do they manifest birth? Why do they manifest a smile? Why do they show the act of walking seven steps? Why do they appear as children? Why do they appear to live in a palace? Why do they appear to leave home? Why do they demonstrate austerities? How do they go to the site of enlightenment? How do they sit on the site of enlightenment? What are the extraordinary signs when they sit on the site of enlightenment? Why do they demonstrate the conquering of demons? What are the attainments of the power of the enlightened? How do they turn the wheel of teaching? How are good and pure ways acquired due to the turning of the wheel of teaching? Why do the enlightened ones manifest extinction in final nirvana? Please explain these things to us."

Then the great enlightening being Universally Good said to Universal Wisdom and the others, "Offspring of Buddha, great enlightening beings have ten kinds of reliance. They take the determination for enlightenment as a reliance, as they never forget it. They take spiritual friends as a reliance, harmonizing as one. They take roots of goodness as a reliance, cultivating, gathering, and increasing them. They take the transcendent ways as a reliance, fully practicing them. They take all truths as a reliance, as they ultimately end in emancipation. They take great vows as a reliance, as they enhance enlightenment. They take practices as a reliance, consummating them all. They take all enlightening beings as a reliance because they have the same one wisdom. They take honoring the buddhas as a reliance because their faith is purified. They take all buddhas as a reliance because they teach ceaselessly like benevolent parents. These are the ten: if enlightening beings rest in these principles, they can become abodes of the unexcelled great knowledge of buddhas.

"Great enlightening beings have ten kinds of extraordinary thought. What are they? They think of all roots of goodness as their own roots of goodness. They think of all roots of goodness as seeds of enlightenment. They think of all sentient beings as vessels of enlightenment. They think of all vows as their own vows. They think of all truths as emancipation. They think of all practices as their own practices. They think of all things as teachings of Buddha. They think of all modes of language as the path of verbal expression. They think of all buddhas as benevolent parents. They think of all buddhas as one. These are the ten: if great enlightening beings rest on these principles, they will attain unexcelled skillful thought.

"Great enlightening beings have ten kinds of practice. What are they? Practice dealing with all sentient beings, to develop them all to maturity; practice seeking all truths, to learn them all; practice of all roots of goodness, to cause them all to grow; practice of all concentrations, to be single-minded, without distraction; practice of all knowledge, to know everything; practice of all cultivations, to be able to cultivate them all; practice dealing with all buddha-lands, to adorn them all; practice dealing with all good companions, respecting and supporting them; practice dealing with all buddhas, honoring and serving them. These are the ten: if great enlightening beings rest on these principles, they will attain the practice of the unexcelled knowledge and wisdom of buddhas.

"Great enlightening beings have ten kinds of spiritual friends. What are they? Spiritual friends who cause them to persist in the determination for enlightenment; spiritual friends who cause them to generate roots of goodness; spiritual friends who cause them to practice the ways of transcendence; spiritual friends who enable them to analyze and explain all truths; spiritual friends who enable them to develop all sentient beings; spiritual friends who enable them to attain definitive analytic and expository powers; spiritual friends who cause them not to be attached to any world; spiritual friends who cause them to cultivate practice tirelessly in all ages; spiritual friends who establish them in the practice of Universal Good; spiritual friends who introduce them to the reaches of knowledge of all buddhas. These are the ten.

"Great enlightening beings have ten kinds of exertion of energy: exertion of energy to educate all sentient beings, to enter deeply into all Buddha teachings, to purify all worlds, to practice all sciences of enlightening beings, to eliminate all evils of sentient beings, to stop the miseries of all vicious cycles, to destroy all demons, to become pure, clear eyes for all sentient beings, to honor all buddhas, and to please all buddhas. These are the ten: if great enlightening beings abide by these things, they will be able to fully achieve the unexcelled transcendent energy of the buddhas.

"Great enlightening beings have ten kinds of attainment of peace of mind. What are they? Abiding themselves in the will for enlightenment, they should also induce others to abide in the will for enlightenment, to attain peace of mind. Ultimately free from anger and strife themselves, they should also free others from anger and strife, to attain peace of mind. Free from the state of ordinary ignorance themselves, they also free others from the state of ordinary ignorance, and attain peace of mind. Diligently cultivating roots of goodness themselves, they also induce others to cultivate roots of goodness, and attain peace of mind. Persisting in the path of the transcendent ways themselves, they also induce others to abide in the path of the transcendent ways, and attain peace of mind. Being born themselves in the house of Buddha, they should also enable others to be born in the house of Buddha, to attain peace of mind. Deeply penetrating the real truth of absence of intrinsic nature, they also introduce others into the real truth of absence of inherent nature, and attain peace of mind. Not repudiating any of the buddhas' teachings, they also cause others not to repudiate any of the buddhas' teachings, and attain peace of mind. Fulfilling the vow of all-knowing enlightenment, they also enable others to fulfill the vow of all-knowing enlightenment, and attain peace of mind. Entering deeply into the inexhaustible treasury of knowledge of all buddhas, they also lead others into the inexhaustible treasury of knowledge of all buddhas, and attain peace of mind. These are the ten; if great enlightening beings abide by these principles, they will attain the peace of the supreme knowledge of the buddhas.

"Great enlightening ‚beings have ten ways of developing sentient beings: by giving, by their physical bodies, by teaching, by cooperation, by nonattachment, by showing the practices of enlightening beings, by clearly showing all worlds, by showing the great magnificent qualities of the Buddha teachings, by various manifestations of spiritual powers, and by various subtle skillful means. These are ten ways in which enlightening beings develop and perfect the realm of sentient beings.

"Great enlightening beings have ten kinds of precepts: not giving up the determination for enlightenment, leaving behind the stages of individual salvation, observing and benefiting all sentient beings, inducing all sentient beings to live by the teachings of Buddha, cultivating all the sciences of enlightening beings, not being acquisitive in respect to anything, dedicating all roots of goodness to enlightenment, not being attached to any of the incarnations of buddhas, reflecting on all things and getting rid of grasping and clinging, and regulating all their faculties. These are the ten; if great enlightening beings abide by these principles, they will attain the unexcelled great transcendent discipline of the buddhas.

"Great enlightening beings have ten ways of receiving the prediction of buddhahood, by which they know inwardly they will receive the prediction: arousing the determination for enlightenment with extraordinary will; never giving up the practices of enlightening beings; continuing to carry out the practices of enlightening beings in all ages; practicing all Buddha teachings; having complete faith in the guidance of all buddhas; cultivating all roots of goodness and bringing them to fulfillment; placing all sentient beings in the enlightenment of buddhas; harmonizing and unifying with all spiritual friends; thinking of all spiritual friends as buddhas; perpetually preserving the fundamental aspiration for enlightenment with diligence.

"Great enlightening beings have ten ways of entry into the state of enlightening beings: they enter into fundamental vows, practices, precepts, ways of transcendence, attainment, different undertakings, various understandings, adornment of buddha-lands, command of spiritual powers, and manifestation of incarnation. By these they enter into the states of enlightening beings of all times.

"Great enlightening beings have ten ways of entering enlightenment: they enter boundless realization of true awareness, boundless turning of the wheel of teaching, boundless means of liberation, boundless different explanations, boundless taming of sentient beings, boundless command of spiritual powers, boundless different embodiments, boundless concentrations, boundless powers and fearlessnesses, and boundless revelation of nirvana. By these great enlightening beings enter among all the enlightened ones of all times.

"Great enlightening beings have ten kinds of penetrations of actions of sentient beings: they penetrate all sentient beings' past actions, future actions, present actions, good actions, bad actions, mental actions, actions of senses, actions of understanding, actions of afflictions and habit energies, timely and untimely actions of teaching and training. By these enlightening beings penetrate the actions of all beings.

"Great enlightening beings have ten kinds of entry into worlds: they enter defiled worlds, pure worlds, small worlds, large worlds, worlds within atoms, subtle worlds, inverted worlds, upright worlds, worlds where there are buddhas, and worlds where there are no buddhas. Thereby enlightening beings enter all worlds in the ten directions.

"Great enlightening beings have ten kinds of entry into ages: they enter into past ages, future ages, present ages, countable ages, uncountable ages, countable ages as uncountable ages, uncountable ages as countable ages, all ages as not ages, nonages as all ages, and all ages as one instant. Thereby they enter into all ages.

"Great enlightening beings have ten kinds of explanation of past, present, and future: they speak of the past of the past, the future of the past, and the present of the past; they speak of the past of the future, the present of the future, and the endlessness of the future; they speak of the past of the present, the future of the present, and the equality of the present; they speak of past, present, and future being the one instant of the present. These are the ten ways by which enlightening beings explain all pasts, presents, and futures.

"Great enlightening beings have ten ways of knowing the worlds of past, present, and future: they know their definitions, their speech, their deliberations, their rules, their appellations, their orders, their provisional names, their endlessness, their quiescence, and their total emptiness. Thus do enlightening beings know all things in all times.

"Great enlightening beings develop ten kinds of tireless mind: honoring and serving all buddhas tirelessly; attending all spiritual teachers tirelessly; seeking all truths tirelessly; listening to true teaching tirelessly; expounding true teaching tirelessly; educating and civilizing all sentient beings tirelessly; placing all sentient beings in the enlightenment of the buddhas tirelessly; spending untold eons in each and every world carrying out enlightening practices tirelessly; traveling in all worlds tirelessly; examining and pondering all Buddha teachings tirelessly. These are the ten; if enlightening beings abide by these principles they will attain the tireless supreme knowledge of buddhas.

"Great enlightening beings have ten kinds of knowledge of differentiation: knowledge of differentiations of sentient beings, differentiations of faculties, differentiations of consequences of action, differentiations of forms of birth, differentiations of worlds, differentiations of spheres of reality, differentiations of buddhas, differentiations of phenomena, differentiations of times, and differentiations of all ways of speaking. If great enlightening beings rest on these principles, they will attain the buddhas' unexcelled, far-reaching knowledge of differentiation.

"Great enlightening beings have ten kinds of mental command:

mental command of retaining what they hear, as they retain all teachings without forgetting; mental command of practice, as they skillfully observe all things as they really are; mental command of reflection, as they comprehend the nature of all things; mental command of the light of the teachings, as they illumine the inconceivable attributes of buddhahood; mental command of concentration, as their minds are not distracted as they hear the teachings of all buddhas of the present; mental command of universal sound, as they understand inconceivable numbers of utterances; mental command of all times, as they expound the inconceivable Buddha teachings of all times; mental command of various intellectual powers, as they expound boundless Buddha teachings; mental command of producing unobstructed ears, as they hear all the teachings of untold buddhas; mental command of all qualities of buddhahood, as they are firmly established in the powers and fearlessnesses of the enlightened. If enlightening beings want to attain these things, they should study and practice diligently.

"Great enlightening beings speak of ten kinds of Buddha: the Buddha of attainment of true enlightenment, the Buddha of vows, the Buddha of rewards of action, the Buddha of preservation of true teaching, the Buddha of nirvana, the Buddha of the cosmos, the Buddha of mind, the Buddha of concentration, the Buddha of fundamental nature, the Buddha adapting to mentalities.

"Great enlightening beings develop ten kinds of Universally Good mind: they develop a mind of great benevolence, to save all beings; they develop a mind of great compassion, to bear suffering in place of all beings; they develop a mind of total giving, relinquishing all they have; they develop a mind that thinks of omniscience above all, gladly seeking all Buddha teachings; they develop a mind adorned with virtues, learning all practices of enlightening beings; they develop an adamantine mind, so as not to become heedless wherever they may live; they develop an oceanic mind, as all pure qualities flow in; they develop a mind like a mountain, enduring all harsh words; they develop a peaceful mind, giving to all sentient beings without fear; they develop a mind with ultimate transcendent wisdom, skillfully observing that all things have no existence. If enlightening beings establish these minds, they will soon be able to achieve the skillful knowledge of the enlightening being Universally Good.

"Great enlightening beings have ten principles of Universally Good practice: vowing to live through all future ages; vowing to serve and honor all buddhas of the future; vowing to settle all sentient beings in the practice of Universally Good enlightening beings; vowing to accumulate all roots of goodness; vowing to enter all ways of transcendence; vowing to fulfill all practices of enlightening beings; vowing to adorn all worlds; vowing to be born in all buddha-lands; vowing to carefully examine all things; vowing to attain supreme enlightenment in all buddha-lands. If enlightening beings practice these principles diligently, they will soon be able to fulfill the practical undertakings of Universal Good.

"Great enlightening beings arouse great compassion by ten kinds of observations of sentient beings: they see sentient beings have nothing to rely on for support; they see sentient beings are unruly; they see sentient beings lack virtues; they see sentient beings are asleep in ignorance; they see sentient beings do bad things; they see sentient beings are bound by desires; they see sentient beings are sunk in the sea of birth and death; they see sentient beings chronically suffer from illness; they see sentient beings have no desire for goodness; they see sentient beings have lost the way to enlightenment. Enlightening beings always observe sentient beings with these awarenesses.

"There are ten kinds of causes of enlightening beings' development of the will for enlightenment: they become determined to reach enlightenment to educate and civilize all sentient beings, to remove the mass of suffering of all sentient beings, to bring complete peace and happiness to all sentient beings, to eliminate the delusion of all sentient beings, to bestow enlightened knowledge on all sentient beings, to honor and respect all buddhas, to follow the guidance of the buddhas and please them, to see the marks and embellishments of the physical embodiments of all buddhas, to comprehend the vast knowledge and wisdom of all buddhas, and to manifest the powers and fearlessnesses of the buddhas.

"When enlightening beings develop the will for supreme enlightenment and attend and serve spiritual teachers in order to awaken to omniscient knowledge, they should generate ten kinds of spirit: a spirit of service, a spirit of joy, a spirit of noncontention, a spirit of docility, a spirit of not seeking anything else, a spirit of wholehearted devotion, a spirit of having the same virtues, a spirit of having the same vows, a spirit of being in the presence of enlightenment, a spirit of cooperation in perfection of action.

"If great enlightening beings arouse such spirits, they will attain ten kinds of purity: purity of profound determination, reaching the ultimate end without corruption; purity of physical embodiment, appearing according to need; purity of voice, comprehending all speech; purity of intellectual powers, skillfully explaining boundless Buddha teachings; purity of wisdom, getting rid of the darkness of all delusion; purity of taking on birth, being imbued with the power of freedom of enlightening beings; purity of company, having fully developed the roots of goodness of sentient beings they worked with in the past; purity of rewards, having removed all obstructions caused by past actions; purity of great vows, being one in essence with all enlightening beings; purity of practices, riding the vehicle of Universal Good to emancipation.

"Great enlightening beings have ten transcendent ways: transcendent giving, relinquishing all they have; transcendent discipline, keeping the precepts of buddhas pure; transcendent tolerance, abiding in the tolerance and forbearance characteristic of the enlightened; transcendent vigor, not regressing in whatever they do; transcendent meditation, focusing their minds on one point; transcendent wisdom, observing all things as they truly are; transcendent knowledge, entering into the powers of buddhas; transcendent vowing, fulfilling the great vows of Universal Good; transcendent spiritual powers, demonstrating all autonomous actions; transcendent teaching, penetrating all buddhas' teachings. If enlightening beings abide by these principles, they will attain the supreme transcendent knowledge of the buddhas.

"Great enlightening beings have ten kinds of conscious knowledge: conscious knowledge of the infinite differentiations of all worlds; conscious knowledge of the inconceivability of all realms of sentient beings; conscious knowledge of all things, each individual being immanent in the variegated manifold, and the variegated manifold being immanent in each individual unit; conscious knowledge of the vastness of all spheres of reality; conscious knowledge of the ultimacy of all realms of space; conscious knowledge of all worlds entering the past; conscious knowledge of all worlds entering the future; conscious knowledge of all worlds entering the present; conscious knowledge of the infinite undertakings and vows of all buddhas reaching fulfillment in one knowledge; conscious knowledge that the buddhas of past, present, and future all attain emancipation by one and the same practice. By these, enlightening beings can attain the illumination of mastery of all truths; their vows will all be fulfilled, and they will be instantly able to understand all buddhas' techniques and attain true enlightenment.

"Great enlightening beings have ten kinds of realizational knowledge: they know the unity of all things; they know the infinity of all things; they know the presence of all things in a single instant; they know the interpenetration of mental activities of all sentient beings; they know the equality of faculties of all sentient beings; they know the impassioned habitual activities of all sentient beings; they know the mental compulsions of all sentient beings; they know the good and bad acts of all sentient beings; they know all enlightening beings' vows and practices, masteries, preservation of the Teaching, and mystical transfigurations; they know all buddhas' fulfillment of the ten powers and attainment of true enlightenment. By these, enlightening beings can attain skillful use of all the teachings.

"Great enlightening beings have ten kinds of power: the power to comprehend the inherent essence of all things; the power to comprehend that all things are like phantoms; the power to comprehend that all things are like illusions; the power to comprehend that all things are Buddha's teachings; the power to have no attachments to anything at all; the power to clearly understand all things; the power of the respectful mind never abandoning spiritual teachers; the power to cause all roots of goodness to reach supreme knowledge; the power of deep faith in all buddhas' teachings without rejection; the power of skill in preventing the will for omniscience from backsliding. Based on these powers, enlightening beings can acquire the supreme powers of buddhas.

"Great enlightening beings have ten kinds of impartiality: impartiality toward all sentient beings, all things, all lands, all determinations, all roots of goodness, all enlightening beings, all vows, all ways of transcendence, all practices, and all buddhas. If enlightening beings abide by these principles, they will attain the supreme impartiality of buddhas.

"Great enlightening beings have ten kinds of expression of the true meaning of the Buddhas' Teaching: that is, all things only have names; all things are like illusions; all things are like reflections; all things only originate conditionally; all things are pure in action; all things are just made by words; all things are the ultimate reality; all things are signless; all things are the highest truth; all things are the realm of reality.

"Great enlightening beings expound ten kinds of teaching: the teaching of profundity; the teaching of enormity; the teaching of variegation; the teaching of omniscience; the teaching of following the ways of transcendence; the teaching of generating the powers of the enlightened; the teaching of the interrelation of past, present, and future; the teaching of causing enlightening beings not to regress; the teaching of praising the virtues of buddhas; the teaching of the sciences of all enlightening beings; the equality of all buddhas, and the interrelation of all spheres of enlightenment. Based on these principles, enlightening beings can accomplish the supremely skillful preaching of the buddhas.

"Great enlightening beings preserve ten things: they preserve all the virtues they have accumulated, all the teachings spoken by all buddhas, all similes, all means of access to true principles, all means of generating mental command, all means of removing doubt and confusion, means of perfecting all enlightening beings, the equal doors of concentration explained by all buddhas, the ways of ingress into the illumination of all truths, and the free exercise of spiritual powers of all buddhas. Based on these principles, enlightening beings can attain the power of preservation of supreme knowledge of buddhas.

"Great enlightening beings have ten kinds of intellectual power: the intellectual power of not arbitrarily discriminating among things; the intellectual power of not fabricating anything; the intellectual power of not being attached to anything; the intellectual power of realizing emptiness; the intellectual power of freedom from the darkness of doubt; the intellectual power of receiving support from Buddha in all things; the intellectual power of spontaneous awareness of all truths; the intellectual power of skill in differentiation of expressions of all truths; the intellectual power of truthfully explaining all things; the intellectual power of gladdening all sentient beings according to their mentalities. Based on these principles, enlightening beings can attain the supremely skillful intellectual powers of buddhas.

"Great enlightening beings have ten kinds of mastery: mastery of educating and civilizing all sentient beings; mastery of illumining all truths; mastery of cultivating all virtuous practices; mastery of extensive knowledge; mastery of the discipline of nonreliance; mastery of directing all roots of goodness to enlightenment; mastery of undiminishing energy; mastery of wisdom crushing all demons; mastery of inducing the determination for enlightenment according to inclinations; mastery of manifesting attainment of true enlightenment according to the needs of those to be taught. Based on these principles, enlightening beings can attain the mastery of the supreme knowledge of buddhas.

"Great enlightening beings have ten kinds of nonattachment: non-attachment to all worlds, all sentient beings, all phenomena, all actions, all roots of goodness, all places of birth, all vows, all practices, all enlightening beings, and all buddhas. Based on these principles, enlightening beings can quickly overturn all concepts and attain supreme pure wisdom.

"Great enlightening beings have ten kinds of equanimity: equanimity in accumulating all virtues; equanimity in undertaking all different vows; equanimity in regard to all living beings; equanimity in regard to the consequences of actions of all living beings; equanimity in regard to all phenomena; equanimity in regard to all pure and defiled lands; equanimity in regard to all phenomena; equanimity in regard to the understandings of all sentient beings; equanimity in regard to nonconceptualization of all practices; equanimity in regard to the nondifference of all buddhas' powers; equanimity in regard to the wisdom of all buddhas. If enlightening beings rest in these, they will attain the supreme great equanimity of buddhas.

"Great enlightening beings have ten ways of generating knowledge: they generate knowledge by knowing the understandings of all sentient beings; knowing the various distinctions of all buddha-lands; knowing the domains of the network of the ten directions; knowing all worlds, inverted, upright, and so on; knowing the unity, variety, and universality of all things; knowing all the various physical forms; knowing the misconceptions and delusions of all worldlings without clinging to them; knowing that all truths ultimately lead to emancipation by one path; knowing the spiritual power of the enlightened can enter all universes; knowing that the seed of enlightenment in all sentient beings, past, present, and future, does not die out. Based on these principles, enlightening beings can comprehend all things.

"Great enlightening beings have ten kinds of magical displays: magical display of all sentient beings, all bodies, all lands, all gifts, all voices, all practical undertakings, all education and civilization of sentient beings, all attainments of true enlightenment, all explanations of truth, and all empowerments. Based on these phenomena, enlightening beings can acquire all means of supreme magical displays.

"Great enlightening beings have ten kinds of support of power: support by the power of buddhas, support by the power of truth, support by the power of sentient beings, support by the power of acts, support by the power of practices, support by the power of vows, support by the power of the environment, support by the power of time, support by the power of good, and support by the power of knowledge. Based on these, enlightening beings can gain the support of the power of supreme mastery of all truths.

"Great enlightening beings have ten kinds of great joy and solace. Enlightening beings determine to follow, serve, and please all buddhas that emerge in the world throughout the future; thinking of this, they become very happy. They also determine to honor those buddhas with the best of offerings; thinking of this, they become very happy. They also think, 'When I make offerings to those buddhas, they will surely teach me, and I will faithfully listen with respect and practice according to the Teaching, and will surely always be born in the state of enlightening beings,' and thinking this they become very happy. They also think, 'I shall carry out the practices of enlightening beings for untold eons and always be with the enlightening beings and buddhas,' and they become very happy at this thought. They also think, 'The fears I had in the past before I set my heart on supreme enlightenment—fear of not being able to live, fear of a bad reputation, fear of death, fear of falling into miserable conditions, fear of the authority of the crowd—have all gone since I set my mind on enlightenment, so that I no longer fear, am not afraid, cannot be intimidated, and cannot be hurt by any demons or cultists.' With these thoughts they become very happy. They also think, 'I shall enable all sentient beings to attain supreme enlightenment; after they attain enlightenment, I shall cultivate the practices of enlightening beings in the company of those buddhas for as long as they live, faithfully provide them with offerings appropriate to buddhas, and, after they pass away, set up innumerable monuments to each of them, honor their relics, and preserve the teachings they leave.' With these thoughts they become very happy. They also think, 'I shall array all worlds with the finest adornments, filling them with all kinds of marvels, equally pure. I shall also cause all kinds of spiritual powers, sustaining forces, tremors, and shining lights to pervade them all.' With these thoughts they become very happy. They also think, 'I shall put an end to the doubts and confusions of all sentient beings, purify all sentient beings' desires, open up all sentient beings' minds, annihilate all sentient beings' afflictions, close the doors of the states of misery for all sentient beings, open the doors of states of felicity for all sentient beings, break through the darkness of all sentient beings, give light to all sentient beings, cause all sentient beings to get free from the action of demons, and cause all sentient beings to reach the abode of peace.' With these thoughts they become very happy. Great enlightening beings also think, 'The buddhas are as rare and difficult to meet with as the udumbara flower, which one can hardly get to see once in countless ages. In the future, when I want to see a buddha, I will immediately be able to do so; the buddhas will never abandon me, but will always be with me, allow me to see them, and constantly expound the Teaching to me. After I have heard the Teaching, my mind will be purified, free from deviousness, straightforward, and free from falsehood, and I will always see the buddhas in each moment of thought.' With these thoughts they become very happy. They also think, 'In the future I shall attain buddhahood, and by the spiritual power of the enlightened will show the attainment of enlightenment individually to all sentient beings in all worlds, pure and fearless, roaring the great lion's roar, pervading the cosmos with my original universal undertaking, beating the drum of truth, showering the rain of truth, performing the giving of true teaching, perpetually expounding the truth, with physical, verbal, and mental action, sustained by great compassion, untiring.' With these thoughts they become very happy. Based on these ten kinds of great joy and solace, enlightening beings can attain the unexcelled great joy and solace of the knowledge and wisdom of true enlightenment.

"Great enlightening beings have ten kinds of profound penetration of the buddhas' teachings: they penetrate all worlds of the past; they penetrate all worlds of the future; they penetrate the numbers, patterns, explanations, and purities of worlds of the present; they penetrate the variety of all worlds; they penetrate the various actions and consequences of all sentient beings; they penetrate the various practices of all enlightening beings; they know the order of appearance of all buddhas of the past; they know the order of appearance of all buddhas of the future; they know the lands and congregations of all buddhas present in the cosmos, their teaching and training; they know principles of the world, principles of Buddhist disciples, principles of individual illuminates, principles of enlightening beings, and principles of buddhas, but though they know all these principles, they have no discrimination, and yet expound various principles. They thoroughly penetrate the realm of reality because there is nothing to penetrate. According to these principles they penetrate the most profound essence of the great knowledge and wisdom of unexcelled, complete perfect enlightenment.

"Great enlightening beings have ten kinds of basis on which they carry out their practices: they carry out the practices of enlightening beings based on honoring all buddhas, taming all sentient beings, associating with all good companions, accumulating all roots of goodness, purifying all buddha-lands, entering deeply into all transcendent ways, fulfilling all vows of enlightening beings, and on infinite will for enlightenment and the enlightenment of all buddhas. Based on these, enlightening beings carry out their practices.

"Great enlightening beings have ten kinds of development of fearlessness: they develop fearlessness annihilating all obstructing actions, preserving the true teaching after the extinction of buddhas, conquering all demons, not begrudging their bodies and lives, smashing all the false arguments of heretics, gladdening all sentient beings, causing all congregations to rejoice, taming all spirits, goblins, titans, sprites, and serpents, leaving the states of the two lesser vehicles of individual salvation and entering the most profound teaching, and carrying out enlightening practices tirelessly for untold eons. Based on these enlightening beings can attain the supreme fearlessness of great knowledge of buddhas.

"Great enlightening beings have ten ways of developing a mind free from doubt. They make this determination: 'I shall take care of all sentient beings by giving; I shall take care of all sentient beings by ethical conduct, tolerance, vigor, meditation, wisdom, benevolence, compassion, joy, and equanimity.' When they make this determination, they are definitely free from doubt—no doubt can arise in their minds. This is their first way of developing a mind free from doubt. Great enlightening beings also think, 'When the future buddhas appear in the world, I shall serve and honor them in all ways.' When they make this determination, they are definitely free from doubt—no doubt can arise in their minds. This is their second development of a mind free from doubt. Great enlightening beings also think, 'I shall adorn all worlds with various marvelous webs of light.' When they make this determination, they are definitely free from doubt—no doubt can arise in their minds. This is the third development of a mind free from doubt. Great enlightening beings also think, 'I shall cultivate the practices of enlightening beings throughout all future ages and fully develop countless sentient beings throughout the entire cosmos by means of the supreme methods of teaching and taming.' When they make this determination, they are definitely free from doubt—no doubt can arise in their minds. This is the fourth development of a mind free from doubt. Great enlightening beings also think, 'I shall cultivate the practices of enlightening beings, fulfill the great vows, acquire omniscience, and abide therein.' When they make this determination, they are definitely free from doubt—no doubt can arise in their minds. This is the fifth development of a mind free from doubt. Great enlightening beings also think, 'I shall carry out the practices of enlightening beings for the sake of all beings in the world, become a pure light of all truths, and illumine all the teachings of buddhas.' When they make this determination, they are definitely free from doubt—no doubt can arise in their minds. This is the sixth development of a mind free from doubt. Great enlightening beings also think, 'I should know all things are Buddha teachings and explain them to sentient beings according to their mentalities to enlighten them all.' When they make this determination, they are definitely free from doubt—no doubt can arise in their minds. This is the seventh development of a mind free from doubt. Great enlightening beings also think, 'I shall attain the way to nonobstruction in the midst of all things, by knowing that all obstructions are ungraspable.' Thus their minds are free from doubt and they abide in the essence of truth, finally to attain supreme complete perfect enlightenment. When they make this determination they are definitely free from doubt—no doubt can arise in their minds. This is the eighth development of a mind free from doubt. Great enlightening beings also think, 'I should know that all things are transmundane things, get rid of all false notions and delusions, and adorn myself with the adornment of unity, there being nothing to adorn.' Here they understand by themselves and not through another. When they make this determination they are definitely free from doubt—no doubt can arise in their minds. This is the ninth development of a mind free from doubt. Great enlightening beings also think, 'I should realize supreme enlightenment in regard to all things, by getting rid of all false notions and delusions, by attaining instantaneous knowledge, because unity and difference cannot be grasped, by transcending all categories, by ultimate nonfabrication of false descriptions, by detachment from all words, and by dwelling in the realm of ineffability.' When they make this determination, they are definitely free from doubt—no doubt can arise in their minds. This is the tenth development of a mind free from doubt. Based on these, enlightening beings can be free from all doubt and confusion regarding all Buddha teachings.

"Great enlightening beings have ten kinds of inconceivability. All their roots of goodness are inconceivable. All their vows are inconceivable. Their knowledge that all things are like illusions is inconceivable. Their arousal of aspiration for enlightenment and cultivation of enlightening practice without losing roots of goodness and without arbitrary notions is inconceivable. Their not grasping extinction and liberation in spite of having profoundly penetrated all things, because all their vows are not fulfilled, is inconceivable. They cultivate the path of enlightening beings and manifest the appearances of incarnation, birth, leaving home, austere practices, going to the site of enlightenment, conquering demons, achieving supreme enlightenment, teaching, and passing away, their spiritual transformations free, unceasing, not abandoning their vow of compassion, saving and protecting sentient beings—all of this is inconceivable. Though they are able to manifest the ten powers of buddhas and their freedom of mystical projection, yet they do not give up the mind equal to the cosmos, and teach sentient beings—this is inconceivable. They know that in all things signlessness is their sign, their signs are signless, nondiscrimination is discrimination, discrimination is nondiscrimination, nonexistence is existence, existence is nonexistence, inaction is action, action is inaction, nonexplanation is explanation, explanation is nonexplanation—this is inconceivable. They know mind is equal to enlightenment, they know enlightenment is equal to mind, they know mind and enlightenment are equal to sentient beings, yet they do not give rise to confusion of mind, confusion of thoughts, or confusion of views—this is inconceivable. From moment to moment they enter absorption in extinction and exhaust all contamination, yet they do not experience ultimate reality and do not end roots of goodness with contamination: though they know all things are free from contamination, yet they know the end and extinction of contaminations; though they know the principles of buddhas are identical to the things of the world and the things of the world are identical to the principles of buddhas, yet they do not form notions of worldly things within the principles of buddhas, and do not form notions of principles of buddhas in the things of the world—all things enter the realm of reality because there is nothing entered; they know all things are nondual because there is no change: this is the tenth inconceivable. These are the ten inconceivabilities of enlightening beings; if enlightening beings abide in them, they will attain the supreme inconceivable qualities of all buddhas.

"Great enlightening beings have ten kinds of skillful esoteric sayings: the skillful esoteric sayings in all the discourses of buddhas; skillful esoteric sayings about all places of birth; skillful esoteric sayings about all enlightening beings' spiritual manifestations and attainment of enlightenment; skillful esoteric sayings about the consequences of actions of all sentient beings; skillful esoteric sayings about the defilement and purity produced by all sentient beings; skillful esoteric sayings about how to be ultimately unobstructed in the midst of all things; skillful esoteric sayings about how in every place in space are worlds, some becoming, some decaying, without any gaps in between; skillful esoteric sayings about how everywhere in all places in all universes, in all phenomena, even in microscopic points, there are buddhas manifesting birth, attainment of buddhahood, and entry into final nirvana, filling the cosmos, each distinctly seen; skillful esoteric sayings about seeing all sentient beings as equally nirvanic, being unchanging, yet not giving up great aspirations, causing them to be fulfilled by the vow for omniscience; skillful esoteric sayings about not abandoning teachers in spite of knowing that truths are not realized through the agency of another, honoring the enlightened even more, becoming one with spiritual friends in cultivating, dedicating, and living by virtues, with the same actions, the same essence, the same emancipation, the same fulfillment. Based on these, enlightening beings can master the unexcelled skillful esoteric speech of the buddhas.

"Great enlightening beings have ten kinds of skillful analytic knowledge: skillful analytic knowledge penetrating all lands; skillful analytic knowledge penetrating all abodes of sentient beings; skillful analytic knowledge penetrating the mental activities of all sentient beings; skillful analytic knowledge penetrating the faculties of all sentient beings; skillful analytic knowledge penetrating the consequences of actions of all sentient beings; skillful analytic knowledge penetrating the practices of all Buddhist disciples; skillful analytic knowledge penetrating the practices of all individual illuminates; skillful analytic knowledge penetrating the practices of all enlightening beings; skillful analytic knowledge penetrating all mundane things; skillful analytic knowledge penetrating all principles and attributes of buddhahood. Based on these, enlightening beings can attain the supreme knowledge of buddhas that skillfully distinguishes all things.

"Great enlightening beings have ten kinds of entry into concentration: entry into concentration in all worlds; entry into concentration in the bodies of all sentient beings; entry into concentration in all phenomena; entry into concentration seeing all buddhas; entry into concentration and remaining for all ages; entry into concentration and manifesting inconceivable bodies on emerging; entry into concentration in all buddha-bodies; entry into concentration realizing the equality of all sentient beings; entry into concentration instantly comprehending all enlightening beings' knowledge of concentration; entry into concentration accomplishing all the deeds and vows of enlightening beings in one instant and never ceasing. If enlightening beings abide in these, they will attain the buddhas' supremely skillful methods of concentration.

"Great enlightening beings have ten kinds of universal entry: universal entry among sentient beings, into lands, into the various features of worlds, into fires, into floods, into buddhahood, into arrays of adornments, into the embodiments of boundless virtues of buddhas, and into all kinds of explanations of truth. Based on these, enlightening beings can attain the buddhas' means of penetrating everything by great knowledge.

"Great enlightening beings have ten kinds of doors of liberation: pervading all worlds with one body, showing infinite various forms in all worlds, putting all worlds in one buddha-field, universally supporting all realms of sentient beings, filling all worlds with the adornment bodies of all buddhas, seeing all worlds in one's own body, showing the emergence of all buddhas in one world, filling all worlds with one body, and showing the free play of spiritual powers of all buddhas in a single instant. Through these, enlightening beings can attain the supreme door of liberation of buddhas.

"Great enlightening beings have ten kinds of spiritual power: the power of knowledge of means of remembering past lives; the power of knowledge of means of unhindered clairaudience; the power of knowledge of means of knowing the inconceivably many mental actions of sentient beings; the power of knowledge of means of unobstructed clairvoyant vision; the power of knowledge of means of manifesting inconceivable great mystic powers according to the minds of sentient beings; the power of knowledge of means of appearing in infinite worlds with one body; the power of knowledge of means of entering innumerable worlds in a moment of thought; the power of knowledge of means of producing infinite adornments and adorning inconceivable worlds; the power of knowledge of means of displaying innumerable emanated bodies; the power of knowledge of means of manifesting unexcelled complete perfect enlightenment in untold worlds, in accord with the minds of innumerable sentient beings. Through these, enlightening beings can attain the supreme skillful spiritual power of buddhas, displaying them variously to all sentient beings to make them learn.

"Great enlightening beings have ten kinds of insight: the insight of practical knowledge of the consequences of actions of all sentient beings; the insight of practical knowledge of the quiescence, purity, and nonconceptuality of all realms of sentient beings; the insight of practical knowledge that the mental objects of all sentient beings are of but one character, totally ungraspable, and that all things are indestructible; the insight of practical knowledge of ability to cause infinite subtle utterances to be heard in all worlds; the insight of practical knowledge of how to universally destroy the obsessions of all minds; the insight of practical knowledge of how to appear to be born or not to be born by expedient means; the insight of practical knowledge of abandoning all objects of perception and sensation; the insight of practical knowledge that all things are neither forms nor formless, are of one nature, which is no nature, not discriminating anything yet able to comprehend all kinds of truths and explain them analytically for measureless ages, abiding in the realm of reality and realizing unexcelled, complete perfect enlightenment.

"Great enlightening beings know that the birth of all sentient beings is fundamentally birthless because they comprehend that birth cannot be grasped: yet they know causes, know conditions, know events, know objects, know actions, know birth, know extinction, know speech, know confusion, know freedom from confusion, know delusion, know freedom from delusion, know defilement, know purity, know birth and death, know nirvana, know graspability, know ungraspability, know attachment, know nonattachment, know rest, know movement, know departure, know return, know origination, know nonorigination, know dissolution, know emancipation, know maturity, know faculties, know how to civilize—they teach beings according to needs, never forgetting the deeds of all enlightening beings. Why? Because enlightening beings set their minds on complete perfect enlightenment for the sole purpose of helping sentient beings. Therefore, enlightening beings always edify sentient beings without tiring, in harmony with what is to be done in all worlds. This is called the insight of practical knowledge of interdependent origination.

"Great enlightening beings have no attachment to Buddha and do not develop attachments; they have no attachment to the teachings and do not develop attachments; they have no attachment to lands and do not develop attachments; they have no attachments to sentient beings and do not develop attachments. They do not see that there are sentient beings, yet they carry on educational activity, civilizing and teaching ways of liberation; they do not give up the practices of enlightening beings, with great compassion and great commitment. Seeing buddhas and hearing their teachings, they act accordingly; trusting the buddhas, they plant roots of goodness, ceaselessly honoring and serving them. They are able to shake infinite worlds in the ten directions by spiritual powers; their minds are broad, being equal to the cosmos. They know various explanations of truth, they know how many sentient beings there are, they know the differences among sentient beings, they know the birth of suffering, they know the extinction of suffering; while knowing all acts are like reflected images, they carry out the deeds of enlightening beings. They sever the root of all subjection to birth. They carry out the practices of enlightening beings for the sole purpose of saving all sentient beings and yet do not practice anything. Conforming to the essential nature of all buddhas, they develop a mind like an immense mountain. They know all falsehood and delusion, and enter the door of omniscience. Their knowledge and wisdom are broad and vast and unshakable, due to attain true enlightenment. This is the insight of practical knowledge of equally saving all sentient beings in the ocean of birth and death.

"These are the ten insights; based on these, enlightening beings can attain the supreme insight of practical knowledge of buddhas.

"Great enlightening beings have ten kinds of liberation: liberation from afflictions; liberation from false views; liberation from all grasping; liberation from mental and physical elements; liberation transcending the two lesser vehicles of individual emancipation; liberation by accepting the nonorigination of things; liberation by freedom from attachment to all worlds, all lands, all beings, and all things; liberation in infinite abodes, liberation rising from the practices of enlightening beings into the stage of nondiscrimination of buddhas; liberation able to know all pasts, presents, and futures in a single moment. Based on these, enlightening beings can perform the supreme deeds of buddhas and teach and develop all sentient beings.

"Great enlightening beings have ten kinds of grove. Birth-and-death is a grove for enlightening beings because they do not reject it. Teaching sentient beings is a grove for enlightening beings because they do not tire of it. Living in all ages is a grove for enlightening beings because they embrace all great deeds. Purifying the world is a grove for enlightening beings because it is where they themselves sojourn. All abodes of demons are a grove for enlightening beings because they conquer them all. Thinking about the teachings they hear is a grove for enlightening beings because they examine them truthfully. The six ways of transcendence, four means of integration, and thirty-seven aids to enlightenment are a grove for enlightening beings because they succeed to the domain of the Buddha. The ten powers, four fearlessnesses, eighteen unique qualities, and all other aspects of buddhahood are a grove for enlightening beings because they do not think of anything else. Manifesting the autonomous spiritual capacities of all enlightening beings is a grove for enlightening beings because they use great spiritual powers to turn the wheel of teaching unceasingly and civilize sentient beings. Instantly showing all sentient beings the attainment of true enlightenment in all places is a grove of enlightening beings because the body of reality pervades all worlds in space. Based on these, enlightening beings can achieve the buddhas' unexcelled peaceful, happy action, free from sorrow and affliction.

"Great enlightening beings have ten kinds of palace. The determination for enlightenment is a palace of enlightening beings because they never forget it. The blessing and wisdom of virtuous conduct are a palace of enlightening beings because they civilize sentient beings in the realm of desire. The meditative concentrations of pure benevolence, compassion, joy, and equanimity are a palace of enlightening beings because they teach the sentient beings in the realm of form. Birth in the heaven of pure abodes is a palace of enlightening beings because no afflictions can affect them. Birth in the formless realm is a palace of enlightening beings because they enable sentient beings to escape difficult situations. Birth in the world of defilement is a palace of enlightening beings because they enable all sentient beings to cut off afflictions. Appearing to abide in a mansion with spouse, children, and retinue, is a palace of enlightening beings, because they develop their past associates.

Appearing to dwell in the rank of ruler, celestial world guardian, Indra, or Brahma is a palace of enlightening beings, in order to tame beings with the mentality of controllers. Persisting in all practices of enlightening beings, freely exercising spiritual powers and attaining mastery of them all, is a palace of enlightening beings because they autonomously and skillfuly exercise the knowledge of meditations, liberations, and concentrations. The guarantee that all buddhas receive of coronation as a monarch of all knowledge, supremely independent, is a palace of enlightening beings because they abide among the adornments of the ten powers and perform the autonomous deeds of all monarchs of truth. Based on these ten, enlightening beings can attain coronation by truth and freedom of spiritual powers in all worlds.

"Great enlightening beings have ten kinds of enjoyment. They enjoy right mindfulness because their minds are not distracted. They enjoy knowledge, distinguishing all things. They enjoy visiting all buddhas, listening to the teachings tirelessly. They like the buddhas because they fill the ten directions without bound. They like enlightening beings because they freely appear in infinite ways for the benefit of sentient beings. They enjoy the doors of concentration because in one door of concentration they enter all doors of concentration. They enjoy mental command of mnemonic formulae because they hold all the doctrines without forgetting and hand them on to others. They enjoy unhindered powers of analysis and elucidation, expounding a single saying inexhaustibly. They enjoy attaining true enlightenment, manifesting bodies in infinite ways, attaining true enlightenment for the sake of sentient beings. They enjoy turning the wheel of true teaching, destroying all misleading doctrines. Based on these, enlightening beings can attain the supreme enjoyment of truth of all buddhas.

"Great enlightening beings have ten kinds of adornment: the adornment of power, being indestructible; the adornment of fearlessness, being invincible; the adornment of meaning, explaining untold meanings inexhaustibly; the adornment of doctrines, contemplating and expounding the collection of eighty-four thousand doctrines without forgetting them; the adornment of vows, the universal vows undertaken by all enlightening beings never regressing; the adornment of deeds, cultivating the deeds of Universal Good and gaining emancipation; the adornment of lands, making all lands one land; the adornment of the universal voice, showering the rain of truth throughout all buddha-worlds; the adornment of empowerment, carrying out innumerable deeds in all ages without cease; the adornment of mystic manifestations, showing in the body of one being as many bodies as there are sentient beings, causing all sentient beings to perceive them and seek all-knowledge without regressing. Based on these, enlightening beings can attain the adornment of all supreme attributes of buddhas.

"Great enlightening beings develop ten kinds of unshakable mind: an unshakable mind able to give up all possessions; an unshakable mind pondering and examining all teachings of Buddha; an unshakable mind recollecting and honoring all buddhas; an unshakable mind pledging not to harm living beings; an unshakable mind caring for all sentient beings without choosing between enemies and friends; an unshakable mind ceaselessly seeking all attributes of buddhahood; an unshakable mind carrying out the practice of enlightening beings for untold ages without wearying or regressing; an unshakable mind perfecting well-rooted faith, clear faith, unpolluted faith, pure faith, extremely pure faith, undefiled faith, faith respecting and honoring all buddhas, unregressing faith, inexhaustible faith, indestructible faith, and ecstatic faith; an unshakable mind believing, accepting, and not repudiating the methods of practice of enlightening beings. Based on these, enlightening beings can attain the supreme unshakable mind of omniscience.

"There are ten kinds of profound great determinations that enlightening beings do not abandon: they do not abandon the profound great determination to fulfill the enlightenment that all buddhas realize, to edify and civilize all sentient beings, to perpetuate the lineage of buddhas, to associate with all good spiritual friends, to honor all buddhas, to wholeheartedly seek all the virtuous qualities of the Great Vehicle of universal salvation, to cultivate religious practice in the company of all buddhas and maintain pure conduct, to associate with all enlightening beings, to seek the means of applying and preserving all Buddha teachings, and to fulfill all practices and vows of enlightening beings and develop all qualities of buddhahood. Based on these, enlightening beings will be able not to abandon all principles of buddhahood.

"Great enlightening beings have ten kinds of contemplation of knowledge: contemplation of knowledge of skillfully analyzing and explaining all things, knowing all roots of goodness of past, present, and future, knowing the practices of all enlightening beings, being able to transform freely, knowing the meanings of all doctrines, knowing the powers of all buddhas, knowing all methods of concentration formulae, expounding truth in all worlds, entering all universes, knowing all spaces are inconceivable, and knowing the light of knowledge of all Buddha teachings is unobstructed. Based on these, enlightening beings can attain the contemplation of supreme knowledge of buddhas.

"Great enlightening beings have ten kinds of explanation of things: they say all things arise from conditions; all things are like magical illusions; all things are free from contradiction; all things are boundless; all things are baseless; all things are indestructible; all things are *thus*; all things are quiescent; all things are emancipation; all things are one, inherently complete. Based on these, enlightening beings can skillfully explain all things.

"Great enlightening beings have ten kinds of purity: purity of determination; purity of cutting through doubts; purity of detachment from views; purity of perspective; purity of the quest for omniscience; purity of intellectual powers; purity of fearlessness; purity of living by the knowledge of all enlightening beings; purity of accepting all the guidelines of behavior of enlightening beings; purity of full development of the felicitous characteristics, pure qualities, and all fundamental virtues of unexcelled enlightenment. Based on these, enlightening beings can attain the supreme purity of buddhas.

"Great enlightening beings have ten kinds of definitive mark. Great enlightening beings, knowing the suffering of pain, the suffering of disintegration, and the suffering of transitoriness, single-mindedly seek the way of enlightenment; without becoming lazy, they carry out the practices of enlightening beings, unwearied, without fear or apprehension or anxiety; not giving up this great undertaking, seeking omniscience steadfastly, not retreating, ultimately attaining unexcelled, complete perfect enlightenment: this is their first definitive mark.

"Great enlightening beings, seeing that there are sentient beings who are foolish and deluded to the point of madness, reviling, attacking, and injuring one another by words and weapons, do not abandon the attitude of an enlightening being because of these scenes; they just forbear with tolerance and gentility, concentrate on cultivating the way of enlightenment, abide in the supreme Path, and enter the state of detachment. This is their second definitive mark.

"When great enlightening beings hear explanation of the most profound teaching of buddhas relating to omniscience, they are able by their own knowledge to deeply believe and accept it, to understand and enter into it. This is their third definitive mark.

"Great enlightening beings also think, 'Having made the profound determination to seek omniscience, I shall become a buddha and attain supreme, complete perfect enlightenment. All sentient beings are flowing in the whirl of mundane conditions, suffering immeasurable pains—I should also get them to set their minds on enlightenment, to believe and delight in it, and to cultivate it diligently and steadfastly without regressing. This is their fourth definitive mark.

"Great enlightening beings know the knowledge of buddhas is boundless and do not try to assess it in limited terms. Enlightening beings, having heard of the boundlessness of buddhas' knowledge from innumerable buddhas, are able not to make limited assessments. Everything written or said in all worlds has limitations and cannot comprehend the knowledge of buddhas. This is the fifth definitive mark.

"In regard to unexcelled, complete perfect enlightenment, great enlightening beings have supreme desire, profound desire, vast desire, great desire, complex desire, insuperable desire, unsurpassed desire, steadfast desire, desire that cannot be destroyed by any demons or false teachers or their cohorts, unyielding desire to seek omniscience. Enlightening beings, dwelling in such desire, ultimately never turn back from supreme enlightenment. This is their sixth definitive mark.

"Great enlightening beings carry out enlightening actions without concern for their own bodies or lives. No one can discourage or frustrate them, because they proceed with determination toward all-knowledge, because the essence of omniscience is always apparent to them, and because they have the light of knowledge of all buddhas. They never give up on the enlightenment of buddhas and never abandon the wise. This is their seventh definitive mark.

"When great enlightening beings see good men and women aiming for the Great Vehicle of universal enlightenment, they foster the growth of their determination to seek buddhahood, cause them to stabilize all foundations of goodness, to internalize the determination for omniscience, and never to turn back from the quest for supreme enlightenment. This is their eighth definitive mark.

"Great enlightening beings cause all sentient beings to achieve an impartial mind, and induce them to cultivate the path of universal knowledge. They explain the truth to sentient beings compassionately and cause them never to turn back on the Path of enlightenment. This is their ninth definitive mark.

"Great enlightening beings have the same foundations of goodness as all buddhas; they perpetuate the seed of buddhahood and ultimately reach omniscient knowledge. This is their tenth definitive mark.

"These are the ten definitive marks of enlightening beings; by these they can quickly achieve supreme perfect enlightenment and become endowed with the mark of buddhas' unexcelled knowledge of all truths.

"Great enlightening beings have ten illuminations of knowledge: the illumination of knowledge of certain attainment of supreme perfect enlightenment; the illumination of knowledge seeing all buddhas; the illumination of knowledge seeing all sentient beings dying in one place and being born in another; the illumination of knowledge understanding the doctrines of all scriptures; the illumination of knowledge developing the determination for enlightenment through association with the wise and accumulation of roots of goodness; the illumination of knowledge showing all buddhas; the illumination of knowledge teaching all sentient beings so they may abide in the state of enlightenment; the illumination of knowledge expounding inconceivable great means of access to truth; the illumination of knowledge skillfully comprehending the spiritual powers of all buddhas; the illumination of knowledge fulfilling all transcendent ways. Based on these, enlightening beings can attain the illumination of supreme knowledge of all buddhas.

"Great enlightening beings have ten peerless states, which no listeners or individual illuminates can equal. Though great enlightening beings see absolute truth, they do not grasp it as their realization, because all their vows are not yet fulfilled; this is their first peerless state. Great enlightening beings plant all roots of goodness, equal to all realities, yet do not have the slightest attachment to them; this is their second peerless state. Great enlightening beings, cultivating the practices of enlightening beings, know they are like phantoms because all things are still and void, yet they have no doubt about the way of buddhahood; this is their third peerless state. Great enlightening beings, though free from the false ideas of the world, still are able to focus their attention and carry out the deeds of enlightening beings for innumerable eons, fulfill their great undertakings, and never give rise to a feeling of weariness therein; this is their fourth peerless state. Great enlightening beings do not grasp anything, because the essence of all things is void, yet they do not experience nirvana, because the path of omniscience is not yet fulfilled; this is their fifth peerless state. Great enlightening beings know that all periods of time are not really periods of time, yet they enumerate periods of time; this is their sixth peerless state. Great enlightening beings know nothing creates anything, yet they do not give up making the way in search of buddhahood; this is their seventh peerless state. Great enlightening beings know that the realms of desire, form, and formlessness are only mind and that past, present, and future are only mind, yet they know perfectly well that mind has no measure and no bounds; this is their eighth peerless state. Great enlightening beings carry out enlightening actions for untold eons for sentient beings one and all, wishing to settle them in the state of omniscience, and yet they never tire or get fed up; this is their ninth peerless state. Great enlightening beings, though their cultivation of practice is completely fulfilled, still do not realize enlightenment, because they reflect, 'What I do is basically for sentient beings, so I should remain in birth-and-death and help them by expedient means, to settle them on the supreme path of enlightenment.' This is their tenth peerless state. Based on these ten peerless states, enlightening beings can attain the peerless state of supremely great knowledge and all qualities of buddhahood.

"Great enlightening beings have ten kinds of indomitable attitude. They think, 'I should conquer all celestial demons and their cohorts.' This is their first indomitable attitude. They also think, 'I should destroy all false teachings.' This is their second indomitable attitude. They also think, 'I should open sentient beings' minds and edify them with good words, making them all happy.' This is their third indomitable attitude. They also think, 'I should fulfill all transcendent practices throughout the cosmos.' This is their fourth indomitable attitude. They also think, 'I should amass all virtues.' This is their fifth indomitable attitude. They also think, 'Supreme enlightenment is vast and hard to accomplish; I should cultivate practice to bring it to complete consummation.' This is their sixth indomitable attitude. They also think, 'I should teach and tame sentient beings with the supreme teaching and the supreme training.' This is their seventh indomitable attitude. They also think, 'All worlds are variously different—I should attain enlightenment there in infinite bodies.' This is their eighth indomitable attitude. They also think, 'While I am cultivating the conduct of enlightening beings, if sentient beings should come and ask me for my hands, feet, ears, nose, blood, flesh, bones, marrow, spouse, children, elephant, horse, or royal status, I should be able to give them all up without a single thought of sorrow or regret, doing so only to benefit all sentient beings, not seeking resulting rewards, beginning with great compassion and ending with great kindness.' This is their ninth indomitable attitude. They also think, 'All in past, present, and future—all buddhas, all Buddha teachings, all sentient beings, all lands, all worlds, all times, all realms of space, all realms of phenomena, all realms of verbal usage, all realms of tranquil nirvana—all these various things I should, by means of instantaneous discernment, know, be aware of, see, realize, cultivate, and detach from, and have no conceptions of them, being detached from conceptions, not having various notions, having no attributes, no object. They are neither existent nor nonexistent, not one, not dual. I should know all duality by knowledge of nonduality, know all forms by formless knowledge, know all discriminations by nondiscriminatory knowledge, know all differences by knowledge of nondifference, know all distinctions by nondifferentiating knowledge, know all worlds by nonworldly knowledge, know all times by timeless knowledge, know all sentient beings by knowledge of nonexistence of sentient beings, know all attachments by unattached knowledge, know all abodes by nonabiding knowledge, know all defilements by undefiled knowledge, know all ends by endless knowledge, appear physically in all worlds by ultimate knowledge of the realm of reality, make untold statements by speechless knowledge, enter absence of intrinsic nature by knowledge of one intrinsic nature, manifest various realms by knowledge of one realm, know all things are inexplicable yet manifest free speech, realize the stage of omniscience, and manifest great spiritual powers and displays in all worlds in order to teach and tame all sentient beings.' This is their tenth indomitable attitude. Based on these ten indomitable attitudes, enlightening beings can attain the supreme quality of indomitability of buddhas.

"Great enlightening beings have ten kinds of mind outstanding like a mountain. They attentively cultivate the means of omniscience; this is the first. They always observe that the fundamental nature of all things is empty and ungraspable; this is the second. They vow to carry out the acts of enlightening beings over measureless eons and cultivate all pure qualities, and by living according to all good and pure principles, see and know the boundless wisdom of the buddhas; this is the third. In quest of all aspects of buddhahood, they serve all wise teachers impartially, without seeking anything else, with no ambition to steal the Teaching; with nothing but respect, they are never willful; they are able to give up everything they have, this is the fourth. If anyone reviles and slanders them, beats or wounds them, or even kills them, they can accept it all and do not become disturbed or hostile, and do not give up their universal vow of great compassion—indeed, they continually make it grow even more because they are truly emancipated from all things, have perfected relinquishment, realize the truth of all buddhas, and have mastered forbearance and gentility; this is the fifth. Great enlightening beings develop overmastering great virtues—virtue overmastering celestials, virtue overmastering humans, virtue overmastering form, virtue overmastering power, virtue overmastering dependents, virtue overmastering desire, virtue overmastering kingship, virtue overmastering sovereignty, virtue overmastering felicity, virtue overmastering intelligence—yet though they perfect such virtues, they are never attached to them: that is, they do not cling to enjoyment, desire, wealth, or followers; they only profoundly delight in truth, go according to truth, live according to truth, start out according to truth, end up according to truth, take truth for their reliance, take truth for their salvation, take truth for their refuge, take truth for their home. They guard the truth, love the truth, seek the truth, and ponder the truth. While great enlightening beings experience all kinds of delights of truth, they always avoid all manias, because in the past they determined to enable all sentient beings to get rid of all manias forever and abide in the realm of buddhas. This is their sixth outstanding mind. Great enlightening beings have already practiced the way of enlightening beings diligently for immeasurable eons in quest of unexcelled, complete perfect enlightenment, yet they still think of themselves as just having set their hearts on enlightenment and carry out the acts of enlightening beings, without fright or fear. Though they are able to attain unexcelled complete perfect enlightenment in an instant, yet for the sake of sentient beings they carry out enlightening practices ceaselessly for measureless eons. This is their seventh outstanding mind. Great enlightening beings know all sentient beings are by nature not harmonious or good and are difficult to harmonize, difficult to liberate, are heedless and ungrateful; therefore, enlightening beings make great vows for their sake, wishing to enable them to attain mental and intellectual freedom and autonomy, to be unhindered in their actions, to give up evil thoughts, and not to afflict others. This is their eighth outstanding mind. Great enlightening beings also think, 'Nobody makes me aspire to enlightenment, and I do not wait for others to help me cultivate practice. I aspire to enlightenment of my own accord, accumulate the qualities of enlightenment, and am determined to work on my own, traveling the path of enlightening beings forever, and accomplish unexcelled, complete perfect enlightenment. For this reason I now cultivate the practice of enlightening beings; I should purify my own mind and also purify others' minds, I should know my own sphere and also know the spheres of others; I should be equal in perspective to the buddhas of all times.' This is their ninth outstanding mind. Great enlightening beings perform this contemplation: 'There is not a single thing that cultivates the practice of enlightening beings, not a single thing that fulfills the practice of enlightening beings, not a single thing that teaches and tames all sentient beings, not a single thing that honors all buddhas, not a single thing that has been or will be or is ever attained or explained in complete enlightenment.' The teacher and the teaching are both ungraspable, yet they do not abandon unexcelled, complete perfect enlightenment. Why? Because enlightening beings search out all things and find they cannot be grasped—this is how

they develop supreme perfect enlightenment. Therefore, although they
do not obtain anything, yet they diligently cultivate dominant good
actions and pure curative measures, so that their knowledge and wisdom
develop fully, growing moment by moment to total repletion. They are
not frightened by emptiness and do not think, 'If all things are null, what
is the sense of seeking the Path of supreme enlightenment?' This is their
tenth outstanding mind. These are enlightening beings' ten mountainlike
outstanding minds directed toward unexcelled, complete perfect enlightenment, based on which enlightening beings can attain the mountainlike outstanding mind of supremely great knowledge of buddhas.

"Great enlightening beings have ten kinds of oceanic knowledge entering into unexcelled, complete perfect enlightenment. They penetrate
all realms of sentient beings—this is their first oceanic knowledge. They
penetrate all worlds without giving rise to arbitrary discriminations—
this is their second oceanic knowledge. They know all realms of space
are measureless and immaterial, and enter the network of all different
worlds in the ten directions—this is their third oceanic knowledge.
Great enlightening beings skillfully penetrate phenomena—they penetrate their fluidity, nonannihilation, noneternity, infinity, nonbirth, non-
destruction, and totality, because they know them all—this is their fourth
oceanic knowledge. Great enlightening beings know the roots of goodness accumulated by the buddhas, enlightening beings, listeners, individual illuminates, and all ordinary people, of the past, present, and
future, the roots of goodness they have accumulated, do accumulate, and
will accumulate, the roots of goodness already accomplished, now being
accomplished, and to be accomplished by the buddhas of all times in
perfect enlightenment, and the roots of goodness in the teaching and
civilizing of all sentient beings by the buddhas of all times—knowing all
these, they believe in them, approve of them, aspire to them, and cultivate them tirelessly; this is their fifth oceanic knowledge. Moment to
moment great enlightening beings enter untold eons of the past and
know how many buddhas appeared in each eon, no matter how unspeakably many they were, and know their congregations, their teaching
and training methods, the life spans of all the sentient beings, and how
long their doctrine lasted—all this they see clearly, in each and every
eon. They also know if there were sentient beings who planted roots of
goodness for enlightenment in ages when there were no buddhas. They
also know if there are any sentient beings who will get to see buddhas in
the future when their roots of goodness ripen. In this way they tirelessly
examine untold eons of the past. This is their sixth oceanic knowledge.
Great enlightening beings penetrate the ages of the future, examine and
distinguish all ages, measureless, boundless, and know what ages will
have buddhas and what ages will not, how many buddhas will appear in
what ages, what the names of each buddha will be, what worlds they
will live in, what the names of those worlds will be, how many sentient
beings they will liberate, and how long they will live—they observe in

this way throughout the future, knowing all endlessly, tirelessly; this is their seventh oceanic knowledge. Great enlightening beings enter the present, observe and reflect, and moment after moment see boundless kinds of worlds in the ten directions, each having buddhas who have attained, are attaining, and will attain supreme enlightenment, as they go to the site of enlightenment, sit under the tree of enlightenment, conquer the demons, attain unexcelled, complete perfect enlightenment, get up and go into the city, ascend to the heavens, expound the subtle truth, turn the great wheel of teaching, manifest spiritual powers, tame sentient beings, and finally hand on the teaching of complete enlightenment, give up their lives, and enter final nirvana; after they have entered nirvana, their teachings are collected to preserve them in the world; the buddhas' monuments are adorned and honored in various ways. The enlightening beings also see the sentient beings in those worlds encounter the buddhas' teachings, accept and preserve and repeat them, remember and ponder them, and increase in wisdom and understanding. They extend such observations throughout the ten directions and have no misunderstandings about the buddhas' teachings. Why? Because great enlightening beings know the buddhas are all like dreams, yet they go to all buddhas and honor them. At such times enlightening beings do not cling to their own bodies, they do not cling to the buddhas, they do not cling to the world, they do not cling to the congregation, they do not cling to the preaching, they do not cling to the age; yet they see the buddhas and hear the teachings, observe the world and enter into all ages tirelessly. This is their eighth oceanic knowledge. Great enlightening beings honor countless buddhas in each age, for untold eons, appearing to die in one place and be born in another; they honor the buddhas, as well as the enlightening beings and disciples in their congregations, with all kinds of transmundane offerings. After the buddhas pass away, they honor their relics with unsurpassed offerings and also extensively practice charity, satisfying sentient beings. With an inconceivable mind, a mind not seeking reward, with ultimate determination, determination to provide benefit, great enlightening beings, for the sake of supreme complete perfect enlightenment, honor the buddhas, benefit sentient beings, preserve the true teaching, and reveal and expound it, for untold eons. This is their ninth oceanic knowledge. Great enlightening beings wholeheartedly seek, from all buddhas, from all enlightening beings, from all teachers of truth, the principles expounded by enlightening beings, the principles studied by enlightening beings, the principles taught by enlightening beings, the principles practiced by enlightening beings, the methods of purification of enlightening beings, the methods of development of enlightening beings, the methods of training of enlightening beings, the methods of equanimity of enlightening beings, the methods of emancipation of enlightening beings, and enlightening beings' methods of total mental command. Having obtained these teachings, they absorb and retain them, read and repeat them, analyze and explain them, never tiring of this, causing countless sentient beings to develop an awareness of the Buddha teachings that corresponds to omniscience, to penetrate the characteristics of reality, and to attain nonregression in respect to unexcelled, complete perfect enlightenment. Enlightening beings continue this way tirelessly for untold eons; this is their tenth oceanic knowledge. These are the ten oceanic knowledges by which great enlightening beings enter unexcelled, complete perfect enlightenment; based on these, enlightening beings can attain the ocean of supreme knowledge of buddhas.

"Great enlightening beings have ten kinds of jewel-like state in unexcelled complete perfect enlightenment. They go to the buddhas in countless worlds, behold them, pay obeisance to them, serve them and honor them with offerings; this is their first jewel-like state. They listen to true teaching from inconceivably many buddhas, absorb it and remember it, analyze and ponder it, increasing in awareness and wisdom, carrying this out everywhere; this is their second jewel-like state.

"They disappear from this land and appear to be born elsewhere, yet have no confusion about the Buddha teaching; this is their third jewel-like state. They know how to elicit all principles from one principle and are able to analyze and explain each of them, because the various meanings of all principles are ultimately all one meaning; this is their fourth jewel-like state.

"They know how to reject afflictions, how to stop afflictions, how to prevent afflictions, and how to extirpate afflictions; they cultivate the practices of enlightening beings, do not experience absolute truth but ultimately arrive at the further shore of ultimate truth; with expedient skill they learn well what is to be learned and cause their past vows to reach fulfillment, without physical fatigue. This is their fifth jewel-like state.

"They know that all the objects of mental discriminations of enlightening beings have no location, yet they still say there are various locations; though they have no discrimination and do not create anything, yet because they want to tame all sentient beings they do cultivate practices and do act. This is their sixth jewel-like state. They know all things are of one and the same essence, which is no essence, no variety, no infinity, no calculability, no measurability, no form, no characteristics—whether one or many, all are ungraspable: yet they know for certain what the norms of buddhas, enlightening beings, individual illuminates, hearers, and ordinary people are, what things are good and what are not good, what is mundane and what is supramundane, what is in error and what is without error, what is contaminated and what is uncontaminated, what is compounded and what is uncompounded. This is their seventh jewel-like state.

"Great enlightening beings find that 'Buddha' cannot be grasped, 'enlightening beings' cannot be grasped, 'phenomena' cannot be grasped, and 'sentient beings' cannot be grasped; yet they do not give up the vow to tame sentient beings and enable them to attain true enlightenment.

Why? Great enlightening beings are skillful observers, and know the mentalities of all sentient beings, and know the perspectives of all sentient beings, and guide them accordingly, so that they can attain nirvana; they practice the deeds of enlightening beings zealously in order to fulfill their vow to enlighten sentient beings. This is their eighth jewel-like state.

"Great enlightening beings know that tactful instruction, manifestation of nirvana, and all means of liberating sentient beings are construed by mind and thought, and are not aberrant or false. Why? Enlightening beings realize that all things are equal in all times; they do not move from Thusness, yet do not abide in ultimate truth; they do not see that there are any sentient beings who ever have received, will receive, or do receive teaching, and they know in themselves they have nothing to practice, there being nothing at all born or perishing that can be grasped; yet they cause their vows not to be in vain by means of all things. This is their ninth jewel-like state.

"Great enlightening beings hear from countless buddhas predictions of future buddhas, each with different names, living in different ages; they listen to this for untold eons and, having heard, cultivate practice, not startled or frightened, not lost or confused, because they know the knowledge of buddhas is inconceivable, because the predictions of the buddhas have no ambiguity in their words, because of the extraordinary power of their own active commitment, and because they foster perfect enlightenment in all who are capable of being taught, fulfilling all their vows, equal in extent to the cosmos. This is their tenth jewel-like state. Based on these ten jewel-like states in unexcelled, complete perfect enlightenment, enlightening beings attain the jewel of supreme great knowledge and wisdom of buddhas.

"Great enlightening beings generate ten kinds of adamantine mind of commitment to universal enlightenment. They think, 'All truths are boundless, inexhaustible; I should realize them thoroughly by means of knowledge comprehending past, present, and future.' This is their first adamantine commitment to universal enlightenment.

"They also think, 'There are infinite sentient beings even on a point the size of a hairtip, to say nothing of in all universes—I should calm them and liberate them by means of unexcelled nirvana.' This is their second adamantine commitment to universal enlightenment.

"They also think, 'The worlds of the ten directions are measureless, boundless, limitless, inexhaustible: I should adorn them all with the finest adornments of the buddha-lands, with all the adornments being truly real.' This is their third adamantine commitment to universal enlightenment.

"They also think, 'Sentient beings are measureless, boundless, limitless, inexhaustible: I should dedicate all roots of goodness to them and illumine them with the light of unexcelled knowledge.' This is their fourth adamantine commitment to universal enlightenment.

"They also think, 'The buddhas are infinite, boundless, unlimited, inexhaustible: I should dedicate the roots of goodness I plant to offer to them, causing those roots of goodness to reach everywhere, with no lack; after that I will attain unexcelled complete perfect enlightenment.' This is their fifth adamantine commitment to universal enlightenment.

"Seeing all buddhas and hearing their teachings, great enlightening beings become very joyful: not attached to their own bodies or to the bodies of buddhas, they understand the body of a buddha is not real or unreal, not existent or nonexistent, not of a particular nature, not without nature, not material, not immaterial, not form, not formless, not born, not extinct, really without existence yet not destroying existence. Why? Because it cannot be grasped through any nature or characteristic at all. This is their sixth adamantine commitment to universal enlightenment.

"If anyone should revile or beat enlightening beings, cut off their hands or feet, gouge out their eyes, or even cut off their heads, they are able to bear it all and never become angry or vicious as a result of this. They cultivate the practices of enlightening beings for countless eons, taking care of sentient beings, never abandoning them. Why? Because enlightening beings have already observed all things to be nondual, and their minds are undisturbed. They can give up their own bodies and endure those pains. This is their seventh adamantine commitment to universal enlightenment.

"Great enlightening beings also think, 'The ages of the future are infinite, boundless, limitless, inexhaustible: I should travel the path of enlightening beings throughout those ages in one world, teaching sentient beings, and do the same in all worlds in the space of the cosmos, without fright or fear. Why? Because this is the way the path of enlightening beings should be in principle, cultivated for the sake of all sentient beings.' This is their eighth adamantine commitment to universal enlightenment.

"Great enlightening beings also think, 'Unexcelled, complete perfect enlightenment is based on the mind—if the mind is pure and clear, one can fulfill all roots of goodness and will surely attain freedom in enlightenment. If I wish to attain supreme consummate enlightenment, I can do so at will; if I wish to annihilate all grasping of objects, I can do that too—yet I do not annihilate, because I want to reach the ultimate end of the enlightenment of the buddhas. And I also do not immediately realize supreme enlightenment, in order to fulfill my original vow to carry out the practice of enlightening beings through all worlds and enlighten sentient beings.' This is their ninth adamantine commitment to universal enlightenment.

"Great enlightening beings know Buddha is ungraspable, enlightenment is ungraspable, enlightening beings are ungraspable, all things are ungraspable, sentient beings are ungraspable, the mind is ungraspable, action is ungraspable, the past is ungraspable, the future is ungraspable, the present is ungraspable, all worlds are ungraspable, and the created and uncreated are ungraspable: thus enlightening beings dwell in quiescence, profundity, silent extinction, noncontention, speechlessness, nonduality, incomparability, essence, truth, liberation, nirvana, and ultimate reality, yet do not give up any of their great vows, do not give up the will for omniscience, do not give up the deeds of enlightening beings, do not give up teaching sentient beings, do not give up the transcendent ways, do not give up taming sentient beings, do not give up serving buddhas, do not give up explaining truths, do not give up adorning the world. Why? Because great enlightening beings have made great vows. Though they comprehend the characteristics of all things, their great kindness and compassion increase, and they cultivate measureless virtues. Their minds do not abandon sentient beings, because while things have no absolute existence, the ignorant do not realize this, so enlightening beings are committed to enlightening them so that they clearly comprehend the nature of things. Why? All buddhas rest peacefully in quiescence, yet by great compassion they teach in the world ceaselessly—reflecting on this, enlightening beings do not abandon sentient beings. Also, they will not abandon great compassion because they have already developed great commitment and have vowed to certainly benefit all sentient beings, to accumulate all roots of goodness, to persist in appropriate dedication, to develop profound wisdom, to accommodate all sentient beings, to be impartial toward all sentient beings; they speak truthfully, without falsehood, vow to give all sentient beings the supremely great teaching, and vow to perpetuate the lineage of buddhas—as long as all sentient beings are not yet liberated, are not yet enlightened, and have not yet realized buddhahood, the enlightening beings' great undertaking is not completed and they will not give up great compassion. This is their tenth adamantine commitment to universal enlightenment.

"These are the ten adamantine commitments of enlightening beings to universal enlightenment: based on these they can attain the indestructible supreme spiritual knowledge of buddhas.

"Great enlightening beings have ten great undertakings. They think, 'I should serve and honor all buddhas.' This is their first great undertaking. They also think, 'After the final extinction of all buddhas, I should adorn monuments of the buddhas, offering all kinds of flowers, garlands, incenses, perfumes, aromatic powders, cloths, parasols, pennants, and banners, and take up and preserve the true teachings of the buddhas.' This is their third great undertaking. They also think, 'I should teach and tame all sentient beings so that they may realize supreme perfect enlightenment.' This is their fourth great undertaking. They also think, 'I should adorn all worlds with the supreme adornments of the buddha-lands.' This is their fifth great undertaking. They also think, 'I should develop great compassion and tirelessly carry out the acts of enlightening beings forever in all worlds for the sake of sentient beings, one and all, so that they may all attain the unsurpassed enlightenment of buddhas.' This is their sixth great undertaking. They also think, 'The buddhas are infinite: I should spend inconceivable eons with each and every buddha, honoring them and making offerings.' This is their seventh great undertaking. They also think, 'After the passing away of the buddhas, I should set up a precious monument for the relics of each one, those monuments to be as high and wide as untold worlds; I should also make effigies of buddhas in the same way, and present all kinds of precious banners and pennants, canopies, fragrances, flowers, and robes for inconceivable eons without a thought of weariness, in order to fulfill the teachings of buddhas, in order to honor the buddhas, in order to edify sentient beings, in order to preserve the true teaching, and in order to reveal and expound the teaching.' This is their eighth great undertaking. Great enlightening beings also think, 'By these roots of goodness I should accomplish unexcelled enlightenment, gain entry into the state of all buddhas, and be equal in essence to all buddhas.' This is their ninth great undertaking. Great enlightening beings also think, 'Once I have attained true awakening, I should expound the truth in all worlds for untold eons, and show inconceivable autonomous spiritual powers, without weariness of body, speech, or mind, and without deviating from the truth, because of being supported by the power of Buddha, because of diligently carrying out great vows for the sake of all sentient beings, because of great benevolence being foremost, because of great compassion being ultimate, because of having arrived at the formless truth, because of abiding by true speech, because of realizing that all things are silent and void, because of realizing that all sentient beings are ungraspable and yet not contradicting the doings of action, because of being the same one substance as the buddhas of past, present, and future, because of pervading the cosmos and space, because of realizing that all things are signless, because of attaining birthlessness and deathlessness, because of embodying all qualities of buddhahood, ceaselessly taming sentient beings and carrying out buddha-work by the power of great vows.' This is their tenth great undertaking. Based on these ten great undertakings, enlightening beings persist in the acts of enlightening beings and are imbued with the supremely great knowledge of buddhas.

"Great enlightening beings have ten ultimate great tasks: to honor and provide for all buddhas; to be able to save all the sentient beings they think of; to single-mindedly seek all facets of buddhahood; to accumulate all roots of goodness; to contemplate all Buddha teachings; to fulfill all vows; to accomplish all enlightening practices; to serve all genuine teachers; to visit the buddhas in all worlds; and to hear and remember the true teachings of all buddhas. Based on these, enlightening beings can accomplish the ultimate great task of the knowledge of unexcelled complete perfect enlightenment.

"Great enlightening beings have ten kinds of indestructible faith: they have indestructible faith in all buddhas, in all buddhas' teachings, in all wise and holy mendicants, in all enlightening beings, in all genuine teachers, in all sentient beings, in all great vows of enlightening beings, in all practices of enlightening beings, in honoring and serving all buddhas, in the skillful mystic techniques of enlightening beings, and in teaching and taming all sentient beings. Based on these, enlightening beings can attain the supreme indestructible faith of great knowledge of buddhas.

"Great enlightening beings have ten ways of receiving the predictions of enlightenment: having extremely profound inner understanding; being able to develop the roots of goodness of enlightening beings as appropriate; cultivating extensive great practices; open receiving of the prediction; occult receiving of the prediction; realizing enlightenment by their own minds; accomplishing tolerance; teaching and taming sentient beings; comprehending the number of all ages; and mastery of all practices of enlightening beings. By these, enlightening beings can receive the prediction of enlightenment from all buddhas.

"Great enlightening beings have ten kinds of dedication of roots of goodness, by which they can dedicate all roots of goodness. They dedicate their roots of goodness to be the same as the enlightened guides in terms of vows, mind, action, faculties, impartiality, mindfulness, purity, state, fulfillment, and incorruptibility; they dedicate their roots of goodness to develop in this way and none other. Based on this, they attain supreme dedication of roots of goodness.

"Great enlightening beings have ten kinds of attainment of wisdom: giving freely; deeply understanding all Buddha teachings; entering the boundless knowledge of buddhas; being able to cut off doubts in all dialogues; penetrating the doctrines of the wise; deeply understanding the skillful use of words by the buddhas in all their teachings; deeply understanding how planting a few roots of goodness in the company of buddhas will enable one to fulfill all pure qualities and attain the infinite knowledge of buddhas; accomplishing the inconceivable states of enlightening beings; being able to visit untold buddha-lands in one moment of thought; and awakening to the enlightenment of all buddhas, entering all realms of reality, hearing and holding the teachings expounded by all buddhas, and deeply penetrating the variously arrayed sayings of all buddhas. Based on these, enlightening beings can attain the supreme realizational knowledge of all buddhas.

"Great enlightening beings have ten kinds of development of a boundlessly vast mind: development in the company of all buddhas; observing the realms of all sentient beings; observing all lands, all worlds, all phenomena; observing all things as being like space; observing the extensive great practices of all enlightening beings; correctly remembering all buddhas of past, present, and future; observing the results of innumerable actions; purifying all buddha-lands; entering the great congregations of all buddhas; investigating the subtle pronouncements of all buddhas. Based on these, enlightening beings can attain the boundlessly vast ocean of knowledge of all Buddha teachings.

"Great enlightening beings have ten kinds of hidden treasury: they know all things are a treasury producing virtuous practices; they know all things are a treasury of right thought; they know all things are a treasury of illumination of mental control; they know all things are a treasury of intellectual powers and exposition; they know all things are a treasury of inexpressible accurate awareness of truth; they know all buddhas' autonomous spiritual powers are a treasury of observation of revelations; they know all things are a treasury of skillfully developing impartiality; they know all things are a treasury of constant vision of all buddhas; they know all inconceivable eons are a mine of realization that all exist like illusions; they know all buddhas and enlightening beings are treasuries producing joy and pure faith. Based on these, enlightening beings can attain the treasury of truth of supreme knowledge of buddhas, and can tame all sentient beings.

"Great enlightening beings have ten kinds of rules of behavior: they should not slander any enlightening teachings; their faith in the buddhas should be indestructible; they should honor and respect all enlightening beings; they should never give up their friendship with wise people; they should not think of those who seek individual salvation; they should avoid all regression on the Path of enlightening beings; they should not give rise to any malice toward sentient beings; they should cultivate all roots of goodness to perfection; they should be able to conquer all demons; they should fulfill all the ways of transcendence. Based on these, enlightening beings can attain the supreme discipline of great knowledge.

"Great enlightening beings have ten kinds of control: control of life, being able to remain alive for untold eons; control of mind, their intellect being able to enter countless concentrations; control of facilities, being able to array all worlds with infinite embellishments; control of action, being able to experience consequences at any time; control of birth, being able to manifest birth in all worlds; control of understanding, being able to see Buddha filling all worlds; control of will, being able to achieve true awakening in any lands whenever desired; control of spiritual powers, showing all kinds of great mystical displays; control of doctrine, revealing boundless gateways to truth; control of knowledge, in each moment of thought manifesting the ten powers and fearlessnesses of buddhas, attaining true enlightenment. Based on these ten controls, enlightening beings can attain mastery of enlightenment, fulfilling the transcendence, knowledge, and spiritual power of all buddhas.

"Great enlightening beings have ten kinds of unimpeded functions: unimpeded functions relating to sentient beings, lands, phenomena and principles, bodies, vows, realms, knowledge, spiritual capacities, miracles, and powers. What are their unimpeded functions relating to sentient beings and so on?

"Great enlightening beings have ten kinds of unimpeded functions relating to sentient beings: knowing that all sentient beings are void of being; knowing that all sentient beings are only upheld by thought; explaining the truth to all sentient beings in a manner appropriate to the time; magically producing the appearance of all realms of sentient beings;

placing all sentient beings inside a pore without crowding; showing all sentient beings other worlds; manifesting the bodies of the celestial beings Indra, Brahma, and the world guardians for all sentient beings; manifesting the calm behavior of buddhas' disciples and individual illuminates for all sentient beings; manifesting the deeds of enlightening beings for all sentient beings; manifesting the buddhas' physical embellishments, powers of omniscience, and attainment of enlightenment for all beings.

"Great enlightening beings have ten kinds of unimpeded function relating to lands: making all lands one land; fitting all lands in a pore; knowing that the totality of lands is inexhaustible; filling all lands with one body sitting; showing all lands in one body; shaking all lands without frightening the beings there; arraying one land with the adornments of all lands; pervading all lands with one buddha and one congregation, showing sentient beings; showing all sentient beings the infinite differentiations of the network of lands filling the ten directions—all small lands, middle-sized lands, large lands, broad lands, deep lands, upright lands, inverted lands, sideways lands, straight lands.

"Great enlightening beings have ten kinds of unimpeded function relating to phenomena and principles: they know that all phenomena are in one phenomenon and one phenomenon is in all phenomena, yet they do not contravene the understanding of sentient beings; they elicit all principles from transcendent wisdom, explain them to others, and enlighten them all; they know all things are beyond words, yet they enable all sentient beings to understand them; they know all things are of one characteristic, yet they can expound infinite characteristics of things; they know all truths are beyond explanation, yet they explain boundless ways of access to truth; they can skillfully operate a pregnant symbol representing all truths, accommodating all things in one principle without contradiction, expounding it for untold eons without exhausting it; including all things in the teaching of enlightenment, they enable all sentient beings to gain understanding; they know all things have no boundaries; they know the ultimate nonobstruction of all things, like a network of illusions, with infinite differentiations, explaining this to sentient beings for infinite eons without exhausting it.

"Great enlightening beings have ten kinds of unimpeded function relating to bodies: encompassing the bodies of all sentient beings in one's own body; merging one's own body into the bodies of all sentient beings; all buddha-bodies entering one buddha-body; one buddha-body entering all buddha-bodies; encompassing all lands in one's own body; pervading all things of all times with one body, showing sentient beings; showing boundless bodies in one body entering concentration; in one body showing as many bodies as sentient beings attaining enlightenment; showing the body of one being in the bodies of all beings, showing the bodies of all beings in the body of one being; showing the body of reality in the bodies of all beings, showing the bodies of all beings in the body of reality.

"Great enlightening beings have ten kinds of unimpeded function re-

lating to vows: they make the vows of all enlightening beings their own
vows; they manifest themselves attaining enlightenment by the power of
the vow of attainment of enlightenment of all buddhas; they themselves
attain supreme perfect enlightenment in accordance with the sentient
beings they are teaching; they never end their great vows, throughout all
eons, without bounds; detaching from the body of discriminating consciousness and not clinging to the body of knowledge, they manifest all
bodies by free will; they give up their own bodies to fulfill the aspirations of others; they edify all sentient beings without giving up their
great vows; they cultivate the deeds of enlightening beings in all ages,
yet their great vows never end; they manifest the attainment of true
enlightenment in a minute point, pervade all buddha-lands by the power
of vowing, and show this to each and every sentient being in untold
worlds; they explain a phrase of teaching, throughout all universes,
raising great clouds of true teaching, flashing the lightning of liberation,
booming the thunder of truth, showering the rain of elixir of immortality, fulfilling all sentient beings by the power of great vows.

"Great enlightening beings have ten kinds of unimpeded functions
relating to realms: they abide in the realm of reality without abandoning
the realm of sentient beings; they abide in the realm of buddhas without
abandoning the realm of demons; they abide in the realm of nirvana
without abandoning the realm of birth and death; they enter the realm
of omniscience without putting an end to the realm of the nature of
enlightening beings; they abide in the realm of tranquillity and calm
without abandoning the realm of distraction; they abide in the spacelike
realm where there is no coming or going, no conceptualization, no
form, no essence, and no verbalization, yet they do not abandon the
realm of all sentient beings, conceptual representations; they dwell in the
realm of occult powers and liberation, yet without abandoning the realm
of specific locations; they enter the realm of ultimate nonexistence of
sentient beings, yet do not give up teaching all sentient beings; they
dwell in the realm of meditation, liberation, spiritual powers, and higher
knowledges, quiet and peaceful, yet they manifest birth in all worlds;
they dwell in the realm of realization of true enlightenment adorned by
all the deeds of buddhas, yet they manifest the composed, tranquil comportment of the personally liberated and individually illuminated.

"Great enlightening beings have ten kinds of unimpeded function
relating to knowledge: inexhaustible analytic powers; retention of all
mnemonic concentration formulae; ability to know and explain with
certainty the faculties of all sentient beings; instantly knowing, by unhindered knowledge, the actions of the minds of all sentient beings;
knowing all sentient beings' inclinations, propensities, habits, and afflictions, and giving them remedies in accordance with their ailments; in a
single moment they are able to enter into the ten powers of buddhas; by
unimpeded knowledge they are able to know all ages of past, present,
and future and the sentient beings therein; moment to moment they

manifest the attainment of enlightenment, showing it to sentient beings endlessly; they know the actions of all sentient beings in the thoughts of one sentient being, understand the language of all sentient beings in the words of one sentient being.

"Great enlightening beings have ten kinds of unimpeded function relating to spiritual capacities: they show the bodies of all worlds in one body; in the audience of one buddha they hear the teachings spoken in the assemblies of all buddhas; in the mind and thoughts of one sentient being they accomplish inexpressible, unsurpassed enlightenment and open the minds of all sentient beings; with one voice they manifest the different sounds of speech of all worlds and enable sentient beings each to attain understanding; in a single moment they show the various differences in results of actions of all ages of the entire past, causing sentient beings all to know and see; they cause all worlds to be fully adorned; they penetrate all pasts, presents, and futures; they emanate the great light of truth and show the enlightenment of all buddhas and the acts and aspirations of sentient beings; they protect all living beings, saints, individual illuminates, enlightening beings, the ten powers of enlightenment they have, and the roots of goodness of enlightening beings. If enlightening beings attain these ten unimpeded functions, they can penetrate all Buddha teachings.

"Great enlightening beings have ten kinds of unimpeded functions of miraculous abilities: they place untold worlds in one atom; they manifest all buddha-lands, equal to the cosmos, in a single atom; they place the water of all oceans in one pore and travel throughout the universe, without the sentient beings therein being disturbed; they contain untold worlds within their own bodies and manifest all spiritual powers; they tie up innumerable mountain chains with a single hair and carry them through all worlds, without frightening sentient beings; they make untold ages one age and make one age untold ages, showing therein the differences of formation and disintegration, without scaring sentient beings; in all worlds they show various changes and devastations by floods, conflagrations, and gales, without troubling sentient beings; when such disasters arise, they can safeguard the necessities of life of all sentient beings in all worlds, not letting them be damaged or lost; they can hold inconceivably many worlds in one hand and toss them beyond untold worlds, without exciting fear in the sentient beings; they explain how all lands are the same as space, causing sentient beings all to gain understanding.

"Great enlightening beings have ten kinds of unimpeded function of power: unimpeded function of power relating to sentient beings, teaching and taming them without abandoning them; of power relating to lands, manifesting untold adornments and arraying them; of power relating to phenomena, causing all bodies to enter the bodiless; of power relating to eons, cultivating practices unceasingly; of the power of enlightenment, awakening those who are asleep; of the power of action, including all practices of enlightening beings; of the power of buddhas, liberating all sentient beings; teacherless power, spontaneously awakening to all truths; of the power of omniscience, attaining true enlightenment by omniscience; of the power of great compassion, not abandoning sentient beings.

"These are called the ten unimpeded functions of enlightening beings; for those who attain them, being on the verge of attaining supreme perfect enlightenment or not attaining it is up to them and makes no difference—though they attain enlightenment, they still do not stop carrying out the deeds of enlightening beings. Why? Because great enlightening beings vow to enter infinite doors of unimpeded function and manifest them skillfully, as is appropriate.

"Great enlightening beings have ten kinds of versatility: they make the body of sentient beings the body of lands, without destroying the body of sentient beings; they make the body of lands the body of sentient beings, without destroying the body of lands; in the body of Buddha they show the body of disciples and self-illumined ones, without diminishing the body of Buddha; in the body of disciples and self-illumined ones they show the body of Buddha, without augmenting the body of disciples and self-illumined ones; in the body of practices of enlightening beings they show the body of attainment of enlightenment, without cutting off the body of practices of enlightening beings; in the body of attainment of enlightenment they manifest cultivation of the body of practices of enlightening beings, without diminishing the body of attainment of enlightenment; they show the body of birth and death in the realm of nirvana, without clinging to birth and death; they show nirvana in the realm of birth and death, yet without finally entering nirvana; they enter into concentration, yet manifest all ordinary action, without relinquishing the correct reception of concentration; in the presence of one buddha they hear and absorb the teaching, not moving physically yet by the power of concentration appearing physically in the audiences of untold buddhas, neither dividing their bodies nor rising from concentration, continuously hearing and absorbing the teachings, in this way moment to moment producing untold concentration-bodies in each concentration-body, going on this way, so that the ages of time may be exhausted but the concentration-bodies of enlightening beings are inexhaustible. Based on these ten kinds of versatility, enlightening beings can attain the versatility of great knowledge of buddhas.

"Great enlightening beings have ten spheres: showing infinite ways of access to the realm of reality so that sentient beings can enter; showing the infinite wonderful arrays of all worlds, so that sentient beings can enter; traveling by projection to the realms of all sentient beings to enlighten them all by appropriate means; producing embodiments of enlightening beings from the body of Buddha, producing embodiment of Buddha from the body of an enlightening being; manifesting the world in the realm of space, manifesting the realm of space in the world;

manifesting the realm of nirvana in the realm of birth and death, manifesting the realm of birth and death in the realm of nirvana; producing verbalizations of all Buddha teachings in the language of one sentient being; showing all bodies as one body, one body as all different bodies; filling all universes with one body; in one instant causing all sentient beings to rouse the will for enlightenment, each manifesting infinite bodies attaining enlightenment. These are the ten spheres of enlightening beings; if they abide in them, they will attain the supreme sphere of great knowledge of buddhas.

"Great enlightening beings have ten kinds of power: the power of the profound mind, not getting mixed up in worldly feelings; the power of the overmastering profound mind, not giving up the ways of enlightenment; the power of means, consummating whatever they do; the power of knowledge, comprehending the activities of all minds; the power of vows, fulfilling all aspirations; the power of practice, continuing forever; the power of vehicles of liberation, able to produce all vehicles of liberation without abandoning the great universal vehicle; the power of miraculous transformations, showing all pure worlds and all buddhas appearing in the worlds in each pore; the power of enlightenment, inspiring all sentient beings to seek enlightenment and become buddhas, without end; the power of turning the wheel of the teaching, explaining one expression of truth in accord with the faculties, temperaments, and inclinations of all sentient beings. Based on these ten powers, enlightening beings can attain the buddhas' ten powers of omniscience.

"Great enlightening beings have ten kinds of fearlessness. They can remember all verbal explanations, and think that even if infinite people should come from all over and ask them about a hundred thousand great principles, they would see nothing difficult to answer about those questions. Because of this their minds become fearless and they ultimately reach the Other Shore of great fearlessness, able to answer any question and resolve doubts, without any timidity. This is enlightening beings' first fearlessness.

"Great enlightening beings attain the unimpeded intellectual powers bestowed by Buddha and arrive at the furthest reaches of revelation of the secrets intimated by all speech and writing. They think that even if infinite people should come from the ten directions and ask them about infinite doctrines, they would not see anything difficult to answer about those questions. Because of this their minds become fearless and they ultimately reach the Other Shore of great fearlessness. They are able to answer any question and resolve doubts, without any timidity. This is enlightening beings' second fearlessness.

"Great enlightening beings know all things are empty and are without self or anything pertaining to self, without creation or creator, without knower, without life, without soul, without personality, detached from mind, body, sense, and sense experience—they forever leave all views and their minds are like space. They reflect that they do not see sentient beings in any way harmful to them, in terms of physical, verbal, or mental action, because they do not see anything as having any essence at all. Therefore their minds become fearless and they ultimately reach the Other Shore of great fearlessness. They are firm, stable, and brave, impossible to discourage or break down. This is enlightening beings' third fearlessness.

"Great enlightening beings are protected and sustained by the power of Buddha, they live according to the conduct of buddhas, their action is truthful and never degenerates. They reflect that they do not see any conduct in themselves that would provoke the criticism of others. Therefore their minds become fearless and they teach calmly among the masses. This is enlightening beings' fourth fearlessness.

"The physical, verbal, and mental actions of great enlightening beings are all pure, immaculate, harmonious, free from all evils. They reflect that they do not see any physical, verbal, or mental action in them that is blameworthy. Therefore their minds become fearless, and they are able to cause sentient beings to live by the teachings of Buddha. This is enlightening beings' fifth fearlessness.

"Great enlightening beings are always accompanied and guarded by powerful thunderbolt-bearers, celestial rain spirits, demigods, celestial musicians, titans, Indra, Brahma, the world-guardian gods, and so on; and all buddhas watch over them heedfully. They reflect that they do not see that there are any demons, false teachers, or people with set views that can hinder their practice of the path of enlightening beings in any way. Therefore their minds become fearless and they ultimately reach the Other Shore of great fearlessness. They become very joyful and carry out the deeds of enlightening beings. This is enlightening beings' sixth fearlessness.

"Great enlightening beings have developed the faculty of recollection and are free from forgetfulness, as approved by buddhas. They reflect that they do not see any sign of forgetfulness of the ways of expressing the path of attainment of enlightenment as explained by the buddhas. Therefore they become fearless in mind, absorb and hold all buddhas' true teachings, and carry out the practices of enlightening beings. This is enlightening beings' seventh fearlessness.

"Great enlightening beings have already attained knowledge and skill in means, and have consummated the powers of enlightening beings. They always strive to edify all sentient beings. Their aspiration is always focused on perfect enlightenment, yet because of compassion for sentient beings, to perfect sentient beings, they appear to be born in the polluted world of afflictions, noble, with a full retinue, able to satisfy all their desires at will, leading a pleasant and happy life. Yet they reflect that although they are together with their family and associates, they do not see anything to be attached to to the extent of giving up their cultivation of the ways of enlightening beings, such as meditation, liberations, concentrations, mnemonic spells, and analytic and expository powers. Why?

Because great enlightening beings are already free in the midst of all things and have reached the Other Shore. They cultivate the practices of enlightening beings and vow never to stop. They do not see any object in the world that can disturb the path of the enlightening being. Because of this their minds become fearless, and they ultimately reach the Other Shore of great fearlessness. By the power of great vows they manifest birth in all worlds. This is enlightening beings' eighth fearlessness.

"Great enlightening beings never forget the determination for omniscience. Riding the Great Vehicle, they carry on the practices of enlightening beings. By the power of the great determination for omniscience, they demonstrate the tranquil comportment of all saints and individual illuminates. They reflect that they do not see in themselves any sign of needing to gain emancipation by means of the lesser vehicles of individual salvation. Because of this their minds become fearless and they ultimately reach the other shore of great fearlessness. While able to demonstrate to all the paths of all vehicles of liberation, they ultimately fulfill the impartial Great Vehicle of universal liberation. This is enlightening beings' ninth fearlessness.

"Great enlightening beings perfect all good and pure qualities, are imbued with virtue, fully develop spiritual powers, ultimately abide in the enlightenment of all buddhas, fulfill all practices of enlightening beings, receive from the buddhas the prediction of coronation with omniscience, and still always teach sentient beings, carrying on the path of enlightening beings. They reflect that they do not see any sign of even a single sentient being who can be developed to maturity to whom they cannot show the masteries of buddhas in order to develop them. Because of this, their minds become fearless and they ultimately reach the Other Shore of great fearlessness. They do not stop the practices of enlightening beings, do not give up the vows of enlightening beings, and show the sphere of buddhahood to any sentient beings who can learn, in order to teach and liberate them. This is enlightening beings' tenth fearlessness.

"These are the ten fearlessnesses of enlightening beings; based on these, enlightening beings can attain the supreme great fearlessness of buddhas without giving up the fearlessness of enlightening beings.

"Great enlightening beings have ten unique qualities. Without depending on the teaching of another, they spontaneously practice the six transcendent ways: they always gladly give generously and are not mean; they always keep pure precepts, without transgression; they are full of patience and forbearance, their minds imperturbable; they have great energy, never backsliding; they skillfully enter the various meditations, never distracted; they skillfully cultivate wisdom, getting rid of all wrong views. This is their first unique quality, practicing the six transcendent ways according to the path of transcendence without being taught by another.

"Great enlightening beings are well able to take care of all sentient beings: that is to say, they practice charity, giving material goods as well as teaching; they are rightly heedful at all times; they are mild of countenance and friendly in speech; their hearts are joyful as they point out what is true; they foster understanding of the enlightenment of buddhas; without aversion they impartially benefit all. This is enlightening beings' second unique quality, striving to unite sentient beings according to the four integrative methods, without being taught by another.

"Great enlightening beings skillfully practice dedication—dedication without seeking resulting rewards, dedication in conformity with enlightenment, dedication unattached to any worldly meditations or trances; dedication to benefiting all sentient beings, dedication to perpetuating the knowledge and wisdom of buddhas. This is enlightening beings' third unique quality, developing roots of goodness and seeking enlightened knowledge and wisdom without relying on the teaching of another.

"Great enlightening beings arrive at consummate skill in means; they are always concerned with the welfare of all sentient beings, they do not reject the realm of common ignorance, do not seek individual escape, do not cling to their own happiness. They only strive to edify and liberate others; they are able to enter and exit meditations and liberations, and have attained mastery of all concentrations. They come and go in birth and death as though roaming through a park, never getting sick of it. They may live in the palace of demons or may be celestial beings—they manifest their bodies in all realms of life. They may become mendicants in non-Buddhistic groups, yet they always avoid all false views. They display all secular literature, incantational arts, writing and mathematics, and even entertaining song and dance, being highly skilled in all of these. They may appear as beautiful women, intelligent and talented, foremost in the world. They are able to ask about and to answer about all mundane and transmundane principles, able to ultimately resolve all doubts. They also comprehend all mundane and transmundane phenomena to the ultimate degree. All sentient beings look up to them. Though they manifest the behavior of mendicants and individual illuminates, still they do not lose the mind of the Great Vehicle. Though they show attainment of true enlightenment moment to moment, still they do not stop the practice of enlightening beings. This is their fourth unique quality, the ultimate consummation of skill in means without relying on the teaching of another.

"Great enlightening beings know well the path of simultaneous practice of the provisional and the true; their intellect is free, and they reach the other shore. That is to say, they abide in nirvana, yet give the appearance of birth and death; they know there are no sentient beings, yet they diligently carry out teaching activities; they are ultimately calm and dispassionate, yet they appear to have afflictions; they abide in the one indestructible mystic reality-body of wisdom, yet they manifest infinite bodies of sentient beings everywhere; they always enter meditative concentration, yet they give the appearance of experiencing sensual pleasure; they are always aloof from the triple world, yet they do not abandon sentient beings; they always enjoy the pleasures of spirituality, yet they appear to have concubines who sing and play; though their bodies are arrayed with a multitude of marks and embellishments of greatness, yet they appear as ugly derelicts; they always accumulate virtues and are free from faults, yet they manifest birth in hells or as animals and hungry ghosts; though they have arrived at the furthest reaches of buddha-knowledge, they do not abandon the body of knowledge of enlightening beings. Even saints and solitary illuminates cannot know such infinite knowledge and wisdom developed by great enlightening beings—how much less can infantile sentient beings. This is enlightening beings' fifth unique quality, the simultaneous practice of the provisional and the true without being taught by another.

"Great enlightening beings' physical, verbal, and mental actions are carried out in accord with knowledge and wisdom and are all pure. That is to say, they are imbued with great compassion and forever abandon malice; they are imbued with true understanding and have no false views. This is enlightening beings' sixth unique quality, of physical, verbal, and mental action in accord with knowledge and wisdom, without depending on the teaching of another.

"Great enlightening beings are full of great compassion and do not abandon sentient beings; they accept suffering in place of all sentient beings—the sufferings of hell, the sufferings of animals, the sufferings of hungry ghosts. They do this in order to help, and do not become weary—they are only devoted to liberating all sentient beings. They never become addicted to objects of desire. They always diligently work to extirpate suffering for sentient beings. This is enlightening beings' seventh unique quality, always exercising great compassion without depending on the instruction of another.

"All beings like to see enlightening beings and never tire of seeing them, because great enlightening beings have for ages been pure in deed, without fault. This is enlightening beings' eighth unique quality, being a welcome sight to all sentient beings, without depending on the instruction of another.

"Great enlightening beings' determination, the adornment of the great commitment to omniscience, is unbending; though they be in dangerous, difficult places, among ordinary people, Buddhist disciples, or self-enlightened people, they never lose the clear, pure, wonderful jewel of the determination for omniscience. Just as there is a jewel called pure adornment whose luster does not change when it is put in mire, and which can clarify muddy water, in the same way, great enlightening beings, even though they be in places of confusion and pollution, among fools, they never lose or spoil the pure jewel mind seeking omniscience— they can even cause those evil sentient beings to get rid of erroneous views, afflictions, and defilements, and gain the pure mind-jewel seeking omniscience. This is enlightening beings' ninth unique quality, not losing the precious will for omniscience even though in difficult situations, even without the instruction of another.

"Great enlightening beings achieve the knowledge of the realm of self-awakening and become enlightened spontaneously without a teacher. Ultimately free, they arrive at the other shore. The turban of the state of freedom from defilement crowns their heads. Still they do not give up association with the wise and always gladly honor the buddhas. This is enlightening beings' tenth unique quality, attaining the supreme state without abandoning the wise or giving up honoring buddhas, without depending on the teaching of another.

"These are the ten unique qualities of enlightening beings, based on which they can attain the buddhas' supreme, grandiose unique qualities.

"Great enlightening beings have ten kinds of activity: activity related to all worlds, able to purify them all; activity related to all buddhas, able to provide offerings to them all; activity related to all enlightening beings, planting the same roots of goodness; activity relating to all sentient beings, able to teach and transform them all; activity relating to the future, able to take in the whole future; activity of all spiritual powers, able to reach all worlds without leaving one world; activity of all light, emanating lights of infinite colors, with an enlightening being sitting on a lotus seat appearing in each light beam; activity perpetuating the lineage of the three treasures, preserving and sustaining the buddhas' teachings after the demise of the buddhas; activity of all miraculous transformations, expounding the truth and teaching the sentient beings in all worlds; activity of all empowerments, instantly appearing to sentient beings according to their mental inclinations, causing all aspirations to be fulfilled. Based on these ten kinds of activity enlightening beings can achieve the supremely great activity of buddhas.

"Great enlightening beings have ten kinds of body: the noncoming body, not being born in any world; the nongoing body, impossible to find in any world; the nonreal body, realizing all worlds as they really are; the nonfalse body, showing the world the truth; the inexhaustible body, never being annihilated; the stable body, impossible for demons to destroy; the imperturbable body, impossible for demons and false teachers to disturb; the formal body, manifesting pure marks of virtue; the formless body, the forms of all things being ultimately formless; the omnipresent body, being the same one body as all buddhas of all times.

"Great enlightening beings have ten kinds of physical action: filling all worlds with one body; ability to appear before all sentient beings; ability to undertake birth in all states of being; traveling in all worlds; going to the assemblies of all buddhas; ability to cover all worlds with one hand; ability to grind the iron surrounding mountains of all worlds to dust with one hand; manifesting the formation and disintegration of all buddha-lands in one's own body to show sentient beings; admitting all realms of sentient beings into one body; in one's own body manifesting all pure buddha-lands, with all sentient beings attaining enlighten-ment therein. Based on these ten, enlightening beings can attain the supreme action of buddhas and be able to enlighten all sentient beings.

"Great enlightening beings also have ten more kinds of body: the body of transcendent ways, due to correctly practicing them all; the body of the four integrative methods, due to not abandoning sentient beings; the body of great compassion, due to accepting immeasurable suffering in place of all sentient beings without wearying; the body of great benevolence, due to saving all sentient beings; the body of blessings and virtue, due to benefiting all sentient beings; the body of wisdom, being of the same one nature as the bodies of all buddhas; the body of reality, being forever free from undergoing birth in conditioned states; the body of expedient means, appearing in all places; the body of spiritual powers, manifesting all mystic transformations; the body of enlighten-ment, achieving true awareness at any time, as desired. Based on these, enlightening beings attain the supreme body of wisdom of buddhas.

"Great enlightening beings have ten kinds of speech: gentle speech, causing all sentient beings to be calm; sweet elixir speech, causing all sentient beings to be clear and cool; nondeceptive speech, everything they say being true; truthful speech, not lying even in dreams; great speech, being honored by all the gods; profound speech, revealing the essence of things; steadfast speech, expounding truth inexhaustibly; straightforward speech, their statements being easy to understand; vari-ous speech, being spoken according to the occasion; speech enlightening all sentient beings, enabling them to understand according to their in-clinations. Based on these, enlightening beings attain the supreme subtle speech of buddhas.

"Great enlightening beings have ten ways of purifying speech: joyfully listening to the voice of Buddhas; joyfully listening to explanations of the virtues of enlightening beings; not saying anything unpleasant to sentient beings; truly avoiding all faults of speech; joyfully praising the enlightened; singing the praises of buddhas aloud at the monuments of deceased buddhas; giving teachings to sentient beings with a profound, pure mind; praising Buddha with music and song; listening to the true Teaching without worrying about one's body or life; giving oneself up to serve all enlightening beings and teachers of truth, and receiving the sublime teaching from them.

"Based on these ten things which purify speech, great enlightening beings gain ten kinds of protection: they are protected by all celestial beings, by all nagas, all yakshas, all gandharvas, all titans, all garudas, all kinnaras, all maharagas, all Brahmas, and all teachers of truth, beginning with the buddhas.

"Having received this protection, great enlightening beings are able to accomplish ten great works: gladdening all sentient beings; going to all worlds; knowing all faculties; purifying all devotions; exterminating all afflictions; getting rid of all habit energy; purifying all inclinations; increasing all profound determinations; causing all to pervade all universes; causing all nirvanas to be clearly seen.

"Great enlightening beings have ten kinds of mind: a mind like the earth, able to hold the roots of goodness of all sentient beings and make them grow; a mind like the ocean, with the water of truth of infinite great knowledge of all buddhas all flowing into it; a mind like the polar mountain, placing all sentient beings on the supreme transmundane foundations of goodness; a mind like the finest jewel, their desires being pure and unpolluted; a mind like diamond, deeply penetrating all truths with certainty; a mind like the adamantine world-surrounding mountains, being invulnerable to disturbance by any demons or false teachers; a mind like a lotus blossom, which worldly things cannot affect; a mind like an udumbara flower, difficult to encounter through all time; a mind like the clear sun, destroying the darkness; a mind like space, being immeasurable. Based on these, enlightening beings can attain the supreme pure mind of buddhas.

"Great enlightening beings have ten determinations: to liberate all beings; to cause all beings to get rid of their afflictions; to cause all sentient beings to extinguish their habit energies; to eliminate all doubts; to remove all sentient beings's miseries; to extirpate the difficulties of the states of woe; to respectfully follow all buddhas; to study what all enlightening beings should learn; to show the enlightenment of all buddhas at each point in all worlds; to beat the drum of the highest teaching in all worlds, to cause all sentient beings to gain understanding in accord with their faculties and inclinations. Based on these, enlightening beings can attain buddhas' mind of great determination and competence.

"Great enlightening beings have ten kinds of comprehensive mind: a mind comprehending all spaces, their intentions far-reaching; a mind comprehending all realms of reality, deeply penetrating infinity; a mind comprehending all past, present, and future, knowing them all in a single thought; a mind comprehending the manifestation of all buddhas, clearly understanding their entry into the womb, birth, leaving home, attainment of enlightenment, teaching activity, and ultimate nirvana; a mind comprehending all sentient beings, knowing their faculties, inclinations, and habit energies; a mind comprehending all knowledge, knowing the realms of reality everywhere; a mind comprehending all infinities, knowing the differentiations of the networks of illusions; a mind comprehending all nonorigination, not apprehending any intrinsic nature in any thing; a mind comprehending all nonobstruction, not dwelling on the mind of self or the mind of other; a mind comprehending all freedoms, manifesting realization of buddhahood everywhere in a single instant. Based on these, enlightening beings can attain the comprehensive adornments of supreme buddhahood.

"Great enlightening beings have ten kinds of faculties: joyful faculties, seeing all buddhas, with faith indestructible; hopeful faculties, understanding whatever Buddha teachings they hear; nonregressing faculties, consummating all their tasks; steadfast faculties, not stopping the practices of enlightening beings; subtle faculties, entering the subtle principle of transcendent wisdom; unceasing faculties, consummating the tasks of all sentient beings; adamantine faculties, realizing the nature of all things; indestructible glowing faculties, illumining all spheres of buddhahood; undifferentiated faculties, being the same one body as all buddhas; unobstructed faculties, deeply penetrating the ten powers of the enlightened. Based on these, enlightening beings can attain the supreme faculties of fulfillment of great knowledge of buddhas.

"Great enlightening beings have ten kinds of profound mind: a profound mind not stained by any worldly things; a profound mind not alloyed with the ways of the lesser vehicles of individual salvation; a profound mind comprehending the enlightenment of all buddhas of past, present, and future; a profound mind following the path of omniscience; a profound mind unmoved by any demons or heretics; a profound mind clarifying the comprehensive knowledge of all enlightened ones; a profound mind accepting and holding all truths heard; a profound mind not clinging to any state of life; a profound mind imbued with all subtle knowledge; a profound mind cultivating all qualities of buddhahood. Based on these, enlightening beings can attain the supreme, pure, profound mind of omniscience.

"Great enlightening beings have ten kinds of intense profound mind: an intense profound mind not backsliding, because they accumulate all roots of goodness; an intense, profound mind removing doubt, because they understand the esoteric sayings of all buddhas; an intense profound mind holding truth, being born by great vows and great deeds; a supremely intense profound mind, deeply penetrating all Buddha teachings; a masterful intense profound mind, mastering all Buddha teachings; a vast intense profound mind, entering into various ways of access to truth; a leading intense profound mind, accomplishing all tasks; a free intense profound mind, adorned by all concentrations, spiritual powers, and mystical transformations; an abiding intense profound mind, embracing their past vows; an unceasing intense profound mind, developing all sentient beings to maturity. Based on these, enlightening beings can attain the supremely pure intense profound mind of all buddhas.

"Great enlightening beings have ten kinds of diligent practice: diligent practice of giving, relinquishing all without seeking reward; diligent practice of self-control, practicing austerities, having few desires, and being content; diligent practice of forbearance, detaching from notions of self and other, tolerating all evils without anger or malice; diligent practice of vigor, their thoughts, words, and deeds never confused, not regressing in what they do, reaching the ultimate end; diligent practice of meditations, liberations, and concentrations, discovering spiritual powers, leaving behind all desires, afflictions, contention, and their congeners; diligent practice of wisdom, tirelessly cultivating and accumulating virtues; diligent practice of great benevolence, knowing that all sentient beings have no nature of their own; diligent practice of great compassion, knowing that all things are empty, accepting suffering in place of all sentient beings without wearying; diligent practice to awaken the ten powers of enlightenment, realizing them without obstruction, manifesting them for sentient beings; diligent practice of the nonreceding wheel of teaching, proceeding to reach all sentient beings. Based on these ten, enlightening beings can attain the supreme practice of great knowledge and wisdom of buddhas.

"Great enlightening beings have ten kinds of certain understanding: certain understanding of the supreme, planting roots of goodness of respect; certain understanding of adornment, producing various adornments; certain understanding of breadth and magnanimity, their minds never narrow or mean; certain understanding of quiescence, able to penetrate the most profound essence of things; certain understanding of universality, their determination for enlightenment extending everywhere; certain understanding of capacity, able to receive the support of the power of Buddha; certain understanding of strength, able to crush all demon activities; certain understanding of clear decision, knowing the consequences of all actions; certain understanding of presence, able to manifest spiritual powers at will; certain understanding of succession, receiving the prediction of buddhahood from all buddhas; certain understanding of freedom, attaining buddhahood at will at any time. Based on these, enlightening beings can attain the supreme certain understanding of buddhas.

"Great enlightening beings have ten kinds of definitive understanding of worlds: they know all worlds penetrate one world; they know one world penetrates all worlds; they know the body and lotus throne of one buddha pervades all worlds; they know all worlds are like space; they know all worlds are endowed with the adornments of buddhas; they know all worlds are filled with enlightening beings; they know all worlds enter one pore; they know all worlds enter the body of a single sentient being; they know the enlightenment tree and site of enlightenment of one buddha pervade all worlds; they know all worlds are pervaded by one message that allows sentient beings to hear it differently, to their delight. Based on these, enlightening beings can attain buddhas' supreme great understanding of buddha-lands.

"Great enlightening beings have ten kinds of certain understanding of the realm of sentient beings: they know that all realms of sentient beings essentially have no reality; they know that all realms of sentient beings enter the body of one sentient being; they know that all realms of sentient beings enter the body of an enlightening being; they know that all realms of sentient beings enter the matrix of enlightenment; they know the body of one sentient being enters all realms of sentient beings; they know that all realms of sentient beings can be vessels of the buddhas' teachings; they know all realms of sentient beings and manifest the bodies of celestial beings for them according to their desires; they know all realms of sentient beings and manifest the tranquil, composed behavior of saints and individual illuminates for them, according to their inclinations; they know all realms of sentient beings and manifest to them the bodies of enlightening beings adorned with virtues; they know all realms of sentient beings and show them the marks and embellishments and the tranquil comportment of buddhas, and enlighten sentient beings. Based on these ten, enlightening beings can attain the supremely powerful certain understanding of buddhas.

"Great enlightening beings have ten kinds of habit energy: the habit energy of determination for enlightenment; the habit energy of roots of goodness; the habit energy of edifying sentient beings; the habit energy of seeing Buddha; the habit energy of undertaking birth in pure worlds; the habit energy of enlightening practice; the habit energy of vows; the habit energy of transcendence; the habit energy of meditation on equality; the habit energy of various differentiations of state. Based on these, enlightening beings can forever get rid of all afflictive habit energies and attain buddhas' habit energy of great knowledge, the knowledge that is not energized by habit.

"Great enlightening beings have ten kinds of grasping, by which they perpetuate the practices of enlightening beings: they grasp all realms of sentient beings, to ultimately enlighten them; they grasp all worlds, to ultimately purify them; they grasp Buddha, cultivating the practices of enlightening beings as offerings; they grasp roots of goodness, accumulating the virtues that mark and embellish the buddhas; they grasp great compassion, to extinguish the pains of all sentient beings; they grasp great benevolence, to bestow on all beings the happiness of omniscience; they grasp the transcendent ways, to accumulate the adornments of enlightening beings; they grasp skill in means, to demonstrate them everywhere; they grasp enlightenment, to attain unobstructed knowledge; in sum, enlightening beings grasp all things, to comprehend them everywhere with clear knowledge. Based on these, enlightening beings can perpetuate the practices of enlightening beings and attain the buddhas' supreme state of not grasping anything.

"Great enlightening beings have ten kinds of cultivation: they cultivate the ways of transcendence, learning, wisdom, purpose, righteousness, emancipation, manifestation, diligence, accomplishment of true awakening, and operation of right teaching. Based on these, enlightening beings achieve supreme cultivation and practice all truths.

"Great enlightening beings have ten ways of fulfillment of the Buddha teachings: not leaving wise associates; deeply believing in the words of buddhas; not repudiating truth; dedicating unlimited roots of goodness; focusing on the infinity of the sphere of Buddha; knowing the realms of all worlds; not abandoning the realm of cosmic reality; avoiding all

realms of demons; correctly recollecting the realm of all buddhas; seeking
the realm of the ten powers of buddhas. Based on these, enlightening
beings can achieve the supreme great wisdom of buddhas.

"There are ten things that cause enlightening beings to regress from
the Buddha teachings, which they should avoid: slighting the wise;
fearing the pains of birth and death; getting tired of practicing the acts of
enlightening beings; not caring to remain in the world; addiction to
concentration; clinging to roots of goodness; liking the ways of individual liberation; having aversion to enlightening beings. If enlightening
beings avoid these ten things, they will enter the enlightening beings'
paths of emancipation.

"Great enlightening beings have ten paths of emancipation: evoking
transcendent wisdom, yet always observing all sentient beings; detaching
from all views, yet liberating all sentient beings bound by views; not
minding any appearances, yet not abandoning sentient beings attached
to appearances; transcending the triple world, yet always being in all
worlds; forever leaving afflictions, yet living together with all sentient
beings; attaining desirelessness, yet always most compassionately pitying
all sentient beings attached to desires; always enjoying tranquillity and
serenity, yet always appearing to be in company; being free from birth
in the world, yet dying in one place and being reborn in another,
carrying on the activities of enlightening beings; not being affected by
any worldly things, yet not stopping work in the world; actually realizing
full enlightenment, yet not abandoning the vows and practices of enlightening beings. These are enlightening beings' ten ways of emancipation, which are not common to worldlings, and also are not alloyed with
the practices of the two vehicles of individual liberation; if enlightening
beings live by these principles, they will attain the qualities of certainty
of enlightening beings.

"Great enlightening beings have ten qualities of certainty: they are
certainly born in the family of buddhas; they certainly live in the realm
of buddhas; they certainly know the tasks of enlightening beings; they
certainly persist in the transcendent ways; they certainly get to join the
assemblies of buddhas; they certainly can reveal the nature of buddhahood; they certainly abide in the powers of the enlightened; they certainly
enter the enlightenment of buddhas; they certainly are one and the same
body as all buddhas; their abode is certainly none other than that of all
buddhas.

"Great enlightening beings have ten ways of generating the qualities
of buddhahood: following good friends is a way of generating qualities
of buddhahood, because they plant roots of goodness together; profound
devotion is a way of generating qualities of buddhahood, because they
know the masteries of buddhas; making great vows is a way of generating
qualities of buddhahood, because their minds become broad; recognizing
their own roots of goodness is a way of generating qualities of buddhahood, because they know their action is not wrong; tirelessly cultivating

practice in all ages is a way of generating qualities of buddhahood, because it comprehends the future; appearing in countless worlds is a way of generating qualities of buddhahood, by maturing sentient beings; not stopping the practices of enlightening beings is a way of generating qualities of buddhahood, by increasing great compassion; infinite aware-ness is a way of generating qualities of buddhahood, by pervading all of space in a single moment of thought; excellent action is a way of generating qualities of buddhahood, because what has been put into practice is not lost; the potential of enlightenment is a way of generating qualities of buddhahood, causing all sentient beings to gladly set their minds on enlightenment and sustain this will by all virtues. Based on these, enlightening beings gain ten appellations of greatness.

"Great enlightening beings have ten appellations of greatness: they are called beings of enlightenment because they are born of knowledge of enlightenment; they are called great beings because they dwell in the Great Vehicle; they are called foremost beings because they realize the foremost truth; they are called superior beings because they are aware of higher laws; they are called supreme beings because their knowledge is supreme; they are called exalted beings because they reveal the unexcelled teaching; they are called beings of power because they have extensive knowledge of the ten powers; they are called incomparable beings be-cause they have no peer in the world; they are called inconceivable beings because they become buddhas in an instant. If enlightening beings win these appellations, they accomplish the paths of enlightening beings.

"Great enlightening beings have ten kinds of path. One path is a path of enlightening beings because they do not give up the sole determina-tion for enlightenment. Two paths are a path of enlightening beings because they develop wisdom and skill in means. Three paths are a path of enlightening beings because they practice emptiness, signlessness, and wishlessness, and are not attached to the three worlds. Four practices are a path of enlightening beings: ceaselessly removing the barriers of wrongdoing by repentance, rejoicing in virtue, honoring the enlightened and requesting them to teach, and skillfully practicing dedication. The five faculties are a path of enlightening beings: they rest on pure faith, steadfast and imperturbable; they generate great energy, finishing their tasks; they are single-minded in right recollection, without wandering attention; they know the techniques for entering and emerging from concentration; they are able to distinguish spheres of knowledge. The six psychic powers are a path of enlightening beings: with the celestial eye they see all forms in all worlds and know where sentient beings die and are born; with the celestial ear they hear all buddhas teaching, absorb and remember their teachings, and expound them widely to sentient beings according to their faculties; with telepathic knowledge they are able to know the minds of others freely, without interference; with recollection of past life they are able to remember all ages of the past and increase roots of goodness; with the power of psychic travel they are able to appear variously to beings capable of being enlightened, to induce them to delight in truth; with knowledge of extinction of contamination they actually realize the ultimate truth, while carrying out the deeds of enlightening beings without cease. Seven remembrances are a path of enlightening beings: they remember buddhas because they see infinite buddhas in a single pore opening the minds of all sentient beings; they remember the Teaching because they do not leave the assemblies of all buddhas—they personally receive the sublime Teaching in the assemblies of all buddhas and expound it to sentient beings according to their faculties, temperaments, and inclinations, to enlighten them; they remember the harmonious Community because they continually see enlightening beings in all worlds; they remember relinquishment because they know all enlightening beings' practices of relinquishment increase magnanimous generosity; they remember the precepts because they do not give up the aspiration for enlightenment, and dedicate all roots of goodness to sentient beings; they remember heaven because they always keep in mind the enlightening beings in the heaven of happiness who are to become buddhas in the next lifetime; they remember sentient beings because they teach and tame them with wisdom and skill in means, reaching them all, without interruption. Following the holy Eightfold Path to enlightenment is a path of enlightening beings: they travel the path of right insight, getting rid of all false views; they exercise right thought, abandoning arbitrary conceptions, their mind always following universal knowledge; they always practice right speech, getting rid of faults of speech and following the words of sages; they always cultivate right action, teaching sentient beings to make them peaceful and harmonious; they abide by right livelihood, being frugal and content, careful and correct in behavior, eating, dressing, sleeping, eliminating evil, and practicing good, all in accord with enlightenment, forever getting rid of all faults; they arouse right energy, diligently cultivating all the difficult practices of enlightening beings, entering the ten powers of buddhas without hindrance; their minds always recollect correctly, able to remember all messages, eliminating all mundane distraction; their minds are always correctly concentrated, they enter the door of inconceivable liberation of enlightening beings, and in one concentration they produce all concentrations. Entering the nine successive concentrations is a path of enlightening beings: they detach from craving and ill-will, and expound the truth without inhibition in all they say; they extinguish thought and reflection, yet teach sentient beings with the thought and reflection of omniscience; they give up joy and emotion, yet they are most joyful when they see all buddhas; they give up worldly enjoyments and follow the transcendent enjoyment of the Path of enlightening beings; henceforth they are unshakable and enter formless concentration, yet without abandoning life in the realms of desire and form; though they abide in concentration in which all perception and sensation are extinguished, they do not stop the activity of enlightening beings. Learning the ten powers is a path of enlightening beings: knowledge of what is so and what is not so; knowledge of the causes and effects, deeds and consequences, past, future, and present, of all sentient beings; knowledge of the differences in faculties of all sentient beings and explaining the truth to them as is appropriate; knowledge of the infinite different natures of sentient beings; knowledge of the differences in weak, middling, and superior understanding of all sentient beings, and means of introducing them to truth; knowledge of manifesting the appearance and conduct of Buddha throughout all worlds, all lands, all times, all ages, without abandoning the practices of enlightening beings; knowledge of all meditations, liberations, and concentrations, whether defiled or pure, timely or not, expediently producing doors of liberation for enlightening beings; knowledge of distinctions in all sentient beings' death in one place and birth in another in the various states of existence; instantaneous knowledge of all ages in past, present, and future; knowledge of extinction of all sentient beings' desires, compulsions, delusions, and habits, without abandoning the practices of enlightening beings. Based on these ten paths, enlightening beings can attain the path of unexcelled skill in means of all buddhas.

"Great enlightening beings have infinite paths, infinite aids to enlightenment, infinite ways of cultivation, and infinite ways of adornment.

"Great enlightening beings have ten kinds of infinite path: because space is infinite, so are the paths of enlightening beings; because the cosmos is infinite, so are the paths of enlightening beings; because the realms of sentient beings are infinite, so are the paths of enlightening beings; because the worlds are infinite, so are the paths of enlightening beings; because time is infinite, so are the paths of enlightening beings; because the languages of all sentient beings are infinite, so are the paths of enlightening beings; because the embodiments of Buddha are infinite, so are the paths of enlightening beings; because the utterances of Buddha are infinite, so are the paths of enlightening beings; because the power of Buddha is infinite, so are the paths of enlightening beings; because omniscience is infinite, so are the paths of enlightening beings.

"Great enlightening beings have ten kinds of infinite aids to enlightenment: as space is infinite, so is enlightening beings' development of aids to enlightenment; as the cosmos is infinite, so is enlightening beings' development of aids to enlightenment; as the realms of sentient beings are infinite, so is enlightening beings' development of aids to enlightenment; as worlds are infinite, so is enlightening beings' development of aids to enlightenment; as the number of eons can never be fully told, so too all worldlings cannot fully tell of enlightening beings' development of aids to enlightenment; as the languages of sentient beings are infinite, so is enlightening beings' development of aids to enlightenment, producing knowledge to comprehend ways of speaking; as the embodiment of Buddha is infinite, so is enlightening beings' development of aids to enlightenment, extending to all sentient beings, all lands, all worlds, and all times; as the utterances of Buddha are infinite, enlightening beings utter one word pervading the cosmos, heard by all sentient beings, so the aids to enlightenment they develop also are infinite; as the power of Buddha is infinite, the aids to enlightenment accumulated by enlightening beings through the power of Buddha are infinite too. Based on these factors, enlightening beings can attain the infinite knowledge of buddhas.

"Great enlightening beings have ten kinds of infinite ways of cultivation: cultivation without coming or going, because their physical, verbal, and mental doings have no action; neither existent nor nonexistent cultivation, there being no inherent nature; cultivation without increase or decrease, being in accord with fundamental essence; cultivation like an illusion, a dream, a shadow, an echo, an image in a mirror, a mirage in the heat, the moon's image in the water, being free from all clinging; empty, signless, wishless, nondoing cultivation, clearly seeing the triple world yet ceaselessly accumulating virtues; inexplicable, inexpressible cultivation beyond speech, apart from all definitions and constructions; cultivation of the indestructible realm of reality, directly knowing all phenomena; cultivation of the ultimate reality of True Thusness, entering the space of ultimate reality of True Thusness; cultivation of vast wisdom, the power of their deeds being inexhaustible; equal cultivation of the ten powers, four fearlessnesses, and omniscience of buddhas, directly seeing all things without doubt or confusion. Based on these ten elements, enlightening beings can accomplish the supremely skillful cultivation of omniscience of buddhas.

"Great enlightening beings have ten kinds of way of adornment. Without leaving the realm of desire, they enter the meditations, liberations, and trances of the realm of form and formlessness, yet they are not thereby born in those realms. This is their first way of adornment. Their knowledge appears to enter the path of personally liberated saints, yet they do not take emancipation by this route; this is their second way of adornment. Their knowledge appears to enter the path of individual illumination, yet they do not cease to generate great compassion; this is their third way of adornment. Though they have human and celestial retinues surrounding them, hundreds and thousands of concubines and troupes of singers and dancers, they never for a moment leave meditation, liberation, and concentration; this is their fourth way of adornment. They take part in amusements and experience pleasure and happiness with all sentient beings, but they never for a moment leave the concentration of equanimity of enlightening beings; this is their fifth way of adornment. They have already transcended all worlds and have no attachments to anything, yet they do not abandon efforts to liberate sentient beings; this is their sixth way of adornment. They live by the right path, right knowledge, and right insight, yet they can appear to enter false paths, without taking them to be true or pure, to cause the sentient beings involved in them to abandon false principles; this is their seventh way of adornment. They always maintain the Buddha's pure precepts, and their thoughts, words, and deeds are faultless, but because they want to edify immoral sentient beings, they appear to perform the acts of ordinary ignorant people; though they are already filled with pure virtues and abide in the course of enlightening beings, yet they appear to live in such realms as hells, animality, ghosthood, and in difficulty and poverty, in order to enable the beings therein to gain liberation—really the enlightening beings are not born in those states; this is their eighth way of adornment. Without being taught by another, they attain unhindered intellect and the light of knowledge, are able to illumine and understand all Buddha teachings, are sustained by the spiritual power of all buddhas, are one and the same body of reality with all buddhas, accomplish all incorruptible mystic states of clarity and purity of great people, abide in all equal vehicles of liberation, are aware of all spheres of buddhahood, are endowed with the light of all worldly knowledge, and clearly see all realms of sentient beings; they are able to be truth-knowing teachers for sentient beings, yet they make the appearance of ceaseless search for truth; though they actually are unexcelled teachers of sentient beings, they show respect to preceptors and religious mentors, because great enlightening beings, by skillful expedients, abide in the path of enlightening beings yet manifest whatever is necessary; this is their ninth way of adornment. Their roots of goodness are sufficient, their practices are completed; they are coronated by all buddhas together and reach the furthest extent of mastery of all the teachings, their heads crowned with the turban of the state of nonobstruction. Their bodies reach all worlds and everywhere they show the body of Buddha that has no resistance. Masters of the teachings, they attain supreme fulfillment and turn the unimpeded pure wheel of teaching. They have already accomplished all manner of freedom of enlightening beings, but for the sake of sentient beings they appear to be born in all lands. They are in the same realm as all buddhas, yet they do not abandon the practices of enlightening beings, do not give up the principles of enlightening beings, do not neglect the works of enlightening beings, do not leave the path of enlightening beings, do not slacken the conduct of enlightening beings, do not cut off the graspings of enlightening beings, do not cease the skillful methods of enlightening beings, do not stop doing the tasks of enlightening beings, do not tire of the developmental activities of enlightening beings, do not put an end to the sustaining power of enlightening beings. Why? Because enlightening beings want to quickly realize unexcelled, complete perfect enlightenment, so they examine the ways of access to omniscience and cultivate the practices of enlightening beings unceasingly. This is their tenth way of adornment. Based on these principles enlightening beings can attain the supreme way of great adornment of buddhas.

"Great enlightening beings have ten kinds of feet: the feet of discipline, fulfilling all higher aspirations; the feet of energy, assembling all elements of enlightenment without regressing; the feet of spiritual knowledge, gladdening all sentient beings according to their desires; the feet of psychic powers, going to all buddha-lands without leaving one buddha-land; the feet of determination, seeking all higher laws; the feet of resolute commitment, fulfilling all their tasks; the feet of accord, not opposing the teachings of all the honorable; the feet of delight in truth, tirelessly hearing and holding all teachings spoken by buddhas; the feet of rain of teaching, lecturing to the masses without timidity; the feet of cultivation, getting rid of all evils. Based on these, enlightening beings can attain the supreme feet of buddhas, which can reach all worlds in one step.

"Great enlightening beings have ten kinds of hands: hands of deep faith, wholeheartedly accepting and ultimately taking up the teaching of buddhas; hands of giving, satisfying all those who seek, according to their desires; hands of initiating greetings, extending their right palm to welcome and lead; hands of honoring buddhas, tirelessly gathering blessings and virtues; hands of learning and skillfulness, cutting off the doubts of all sentient beings; hands of fostering transcendence of the triple world, extending them to sentient beings and extricating them from the mire of craving; hands of settlement on the Other Shore, saving drowning sentient beings from the four torrents; hands of generosity with right teaching, revealing all sublime principles; hands of skillful use of philosophies, quelling diseases of body and mind with the medicine of knowledge and wisdom; hands always holding jewels of knowledge, unfolding the light of truth to obliterate the darkness of afflictions. These are the ten: based on these, enlightening beings can acquire the supreme hands of buddhas covering all worlds in the ten directions.

"Great enlightening beings have ten kinds of guts: guts free from deception, their hearts being pure; guts free from falsehood, being honest by nature; nonprevaricating guts, having no crookedness; nonswindling guts, having no greed for anything; guts cutting off afflictions, being full of wisdom; pure-minded guts, being free from all evils; guts examining food and drink, remembering reality; guts observing noncreation, being aware of interdependent origination; guts aware of all ways of emancipation, fully developing the will; guts rid of the defilement of all extreme views, enabling all sentient beings to enter into the guts of Buddha. These are the ten; based on these, enlightening beings can acquire the supreme, vast guts of buddhas, able to contain all sentient beings.

"Great enlightening beings have ten kinds of internal organs. Perpetuating the seed of buddhas is an organ of enlightening beings, manifesting the immeasurable spiritual power of the Buddha teaching. Causing the seed of the Teaching to grow is an organ of enlightening beings, generating the immense light of knowledge. Preserving the seed of the spiritual community is an organ of enlightening beings, enabling them to gain access to the irreversible wheel of teaching. Awakening those who are rightly stabilized is an organ of enlightening beings, instantly adapting to the time. Fully developing unstable sentient beings is an organ of enlightening beings, producing continuity of causal basis. Conceiving compassion for wrongly stabilized sentient beings is an organ of enlightening beings, causing thorough development of causal basis for the future. Fulfilling the indestructible bases of the ten powers of buddhas is an organ of enlightening beings, with unopposable roots of goodness that conquer the armies of demons. The supremely fearless lion's roar is an organ of enlightening beings, gladdening all sentient beings. Attaining the eighteen unique qualities of buddhas is an organ of enlightening beings, with knowledge penetrating everywhere. Knowing all sentient beings, all lands, all things, and all buddhas is an organ of enlightening beings, clearly seeing all in a single instant. These are the ten; based on these, enlightening beings can attain the indestructible internal organs of great knowledge with supreme virtues of buddhas.

"Great enlightening beings have ten kinds of heart: a heart of diligence, fulfilling all tasks; a heart of perseverance, accumulating embellishing virtuous practices; a heart of great courage and strength, crushing all armies of demons; a heart acting according to truth, extinguishing all afflictions; a heart of nonregression, never ceasing until enlightenment is reached; a heart of inherent purity, knowing the mind is immovable, not having any attachments; a heart of knowledge of sentient beings, adapting to their understandings and inclinations to emancipate them; a heart of great kindness, compassion, joy, and equanimity, leading into the way of enlightenment, knowing the various understandings and inclinations of sentient beings, and saving them without using separate paths; a heart of emptiness, signlessness, wishlessness, and nonfabrication, seeing the characteristics of the triple world without grasping them; a heart adorned with an indestructible supreme treasury of marks of felicity, thoroughly invulnerable to all demons. Based on these ten, enlightening beings can attain the supreme heart of the treasury of light of great knowledge of buddhas.

"Great enlightening beings have ten kinds of armor: they wear the armor of great benevolence, rescuing all sentient beings; they wear the armor of great compassion, enduring all suffering; they wear the armor of great commitment, fulfilling all their tasks; they wear the armor of dedication, constructing the adornments of all buddhas; they wear the armor of virtue, benefiting all sentient beings; they wear the armor of the ways of transcendence, liberating all conscious beings; they wear the armor of wisdom, destroying the darkness of affliction of all sentient beings; they wear the armor of skill in means, generating universal roots of goodness; they wear the armor of the firm stability and freedom from distraction of the mind of universal knowledge, not enjoying other vehicles; they wear the armor of single-minded certainty, free from doubts and confusion in regard to all things. Based on these ten, enlightening beings can wear the supreme armor of buddhas and crush all demon armies.

"Great enlightening beings have ten kinds of weapon: giving is a weapon of enlightening beings, destroying all stinginess; self-control is a weapon of enlightening beings, getting rid of all crime; impartiality is a weapon of enlightening beings, removing all discrimination; wisdom is a weapon of enlightening beings, dissolving all afflictions; right livelihood is a weapon of enlightening beings, leading away from all wrong livelihood; skill in means is a weapon of enlightening beings, manifesting in all places; in general, all afflictions such as desire, wrath, and folly are weapons of enlightening beings because they liberate sentient beings through afflictions; birth-and-death is a weapon of enlightening beings because they continue enlightening practices and teach sentient beings; teaching the truth is a weapon of enlightening beings, able to break up all clinging; all knowledge is a weapon of enlightening beings because they do not give up the avenues of practice of enlightening beings. Based on these ten, enlightening beings can annihilate the afflictions, bondage, and compulsions accumulated by all sentient beings in the long night of ignorance.

"Great enlightening beings have ten kinds of head: the head of nirvana, as no one can see the top; the head of honor, respected by all humans and celestials; the head of universal higher understanding, being supreme in the universe; the head of foremost roots of goodness, honored by the sentient beings of the three worlds; the head bearing sentient beings, developing an indestructible crown; the head of not despising others, in all places always respectful; the head of transcendent wisdom, nurturing all virtuous qualities; the head of union of knowledge and skill in means, everywhere appearing in compatible forms; the head of teaching all sentient beings, taking all sentient beings as disciples; the head of preservation of the eye of reality of buddhas, able to perpetuate the seeds of the three treasures. Based on these ten, enlightening beings can attain the supreme head of knowledge and wisdom of buddhas.

"Great enlightening beings have ten kinds of eye: the flesh eye, seeing all forms; the celestial eye, seeing the minds of all sentient beings; the wisdom-eye, seeing the ranges of the faculties of all sentient beings; the reality-eye, seeing the true character of all things; the buddha-eye, seeing the ten powers of the enlightened; the eye of knowledge, knowing and seeing all things; the eye of light, seeing the light of Buddha; the eye of leaving birth and death, seeing nirvana; the unobstructed eye, its vision without hindrance; the eye of omniscience, seeing the realm of reality in its universal aspect. Based on these ten, enlightening beings attain the eye of supreme knowledge of buddhas.

"Great enlightening beings have ten kinds of ear: hearing the voice of praise, they eliminate craving; hearing the voice of criticism, they eliminate anger; hearing explanation of the two lesser vehicles of individual salvation, they do not cling to or seek them; hearing of the Path of enlightening beings, they rejoice greatly; hearing of places of pain and trouble, such as the hells, they arouse great compassion and make vows of universal salvation; hearing tell of the wonderful things of the human and celestial worlds, they know they are impermanent phenomena; hearing praise of the virtues of buddhas, they work diligently to quickly fulfill them; hearing tell of such practices as the six ways of transcendence and four means of integration, they determine to practice them and reach their ultimate end; hearing all sounds of the world, they know they are all like echoes, and penetrate untold profound meanings; great enlightening beings, from their first determination until they reach the site of enlightenment, always hear the true Teaching yet do not give up the work of transforming sentient beings. These are the ten; if enlightening beings accomplish these things, they will attain the supreme ear of great wisdom of buddhas.

"Great enlightening beings have ten kinds of nose: when they smell foul things, they do not consider them foul; when they smell fragrances, they do not consider them fragrant; when they smell both fragrance and foulness, their minds are equanimous, abiding in relinquishment; if they smell the fragrance and foulness of people's clothes, bedding, or bodies, they can discern their conditions of greed, anger, and delusion; if they smell the scents of hidden repositories, plants and trees and so on, they can discern them as if they were right before their eyes; if they smell scents from the hells below to the heavens above, they know the past deeds of the beings there; if they smell the fragrance of generosity, morality, learning, and wisdom of buddhas' disciples, they remain steady in the will for omniscience and do not let it be distracted; if they smell the fragrances of all enlightening practices, they enter the state of buddhahood by impartial wisdom; if they smell the fragrance of the sphere of knowledge of all buddhas, they still do not give up the practices of enlightening beings. If enlightening beings accomplish these things, they will acquire the infinite, boundless nose of buddhas.

"Great enlightening beings have ten kinds of tongue: a tongue that reveals and explains the acts of infinite sentient beings; a tongue that reveals and explains infinite doors to truth; a tongue that sings the praises of the infinite virtues of buddhas; a tongue of infinite eloquence; a tongue that expounds aids to the Path of the Great Vehicle; a tongue that covers all space; a tongue that illumines all buddha-fields; a tongue that awakens the understanding of all sentient beings; a tongue that causes all to praise the buddhas; a tongue that defeats all demons and false teachers, destroys all afflictions of birth and death, and fosters arrival at nirvana. If enlightening beings accomplish these things, they will acquire the supreme tongue of buddhas, which covers all buddhalands.

"Great enlightening beings have ten kinds of bodies: human bodies to teach humans; nonhuman bodies to teach denizens of hells, animals, and hungry ghosts; celestial bodies to teach the beings of the realms of desire, form, and formlessness; learners' bodies to demonstrate the stage of learning; nonlearners' bodies to demonstrate the stage of sainthood; individual illuminates' bodies to teach the way to enter the stage of individual enlightenment; enlightening beings' bodies to foster the accomplishment of the Great Vehicle; buddhas' bodies, anointed by the water of knowledge; mentally produced bodies, generated by adaptive skills; the uncontaminated reality-body, effortlessly manifesting the bodies of all sentient beings. If they accomplish these, they attain the supreme body of buddhas.

"Great enlightening beings have ten kinds of mind: a mind of leadership, generating all roots of goodness; a stable mind, with profound faith steadfast and unwavering; a mind of profound penetration, understanding in accord with the teachings of buddhas; a mind of insight, knowing the mentalities of all sentient beings; an undisturbed mind, not adulterated with any afflictions; a clear, clean mind, which externals cannot stain or adhere to; a mind observing sentient beings well, not missing proper timing in dealing with them; a mind choosing well what to do, never making a mistake anywhere; a mind closely guarding the senses, taming them and not letting them run wild; a mind skilled in entering concentration, entering deeply into the concentrations of buddhas, without egoism or selfishness. Based on these ten, enlightening beings can attain the supreme mind of all buddhas.

"Great enlightening beings have ten kinds of action: hearing the Teaching, out of fondness for truth; expounding the Teaching, to benefit sentient beings; getting rid of covetousness, anger, delusion, and fear, by taming their own minds; action in the realm of desire, to teach beings in that realm; concentrations in the realms of form and formlessness, to foster quick return to noncontamination; aiming for the meaning of the Teaching, to quickly attain wisdom; action in all realms of life, to freely edify sentient beings; action in all buddha-lands, honoring all buddhas; nirvanic action, not cutting off the continuity of birth and death; fulfilling all qualities of buddhahood, without giving up application of the principles of enlightening beings. Based on these ten, enlightening beings can achieve the action of buddhas that has no coming or going.

"Great enlightening beings have ten kinds of abiding: abiding in the will for enlightenment, never forgetting it; abiding in the transcendent ways, not tiring of fostering enlightenment; abiding in the teaching of truth, increasing wisdom; abiding in dispassion, realizing great meditational concentration; abiding in conformity to universal knowledge, austerity, contentment, moderation in food, clothing, and dwelling, and getting rid of evil, because few desires means few concerns; abiding in deep faith, bearing the true Teaching; abiding in the company of the enlightened, to learn the conduct of buddhas; abiding in generation of spiritual powers, to fulfill great knowledge; abiding in attainment of acceptance, fulfilling the forecast of enlightenment; abiding in the site of enlightenment, fulfilling power, fearlessness, and all aspects of buddhahood. Based on these ten, enlightening beings can reach the buddhas' supreme abiding in omniscience.

"Great enlightening beings have ten kinds of sitting: the sitting of universal monarchs, promoting all virtuous behavior; the sitting of guardian deities, independently establishing the Buddha teaching in all worlds; the sitting of Indra, king of gods, being superior lords of all sentient beings; the sitting of Brahma, being in control of their own and others' minds; the sitting of lions, being able to expound the truth; the sitting of right teaching, holding forth by means of mental command and intellectual powers; steadfast sitting, vowing to reach the ultimate end; the sitting of great benevolence, bringing happiness to all evil sentient beings; the sitting of great compassion, tirelessly enduring all pains; adamantine sitting, conquering demons and false teachers. Based on these, enlightening beings can attain the buddhas' supreme sitting of true awareness.

"Great enlightening beings have ten kinds of reclining: the reclining of silent tranquillity, because of practicing in accord with principle; the reclining of concentration, because of body and mind being supple; the reclining of Brahma, because of not disturbing self or others; the reclining of good works, because of having no regrets afterward; the reclining of true faith, because of being unshakable; the reclining of the right Path, because of awakening by good companions; the reclining of sublime aspirations, because of skillful dedication; the reclining of completion of all tasks, because of having accomplished all that is to be done; the reclining of relinquishment of all effort, because of thorough training. Based on these enlightening beings can attain the supreme reclining of the great teaching of buddhas and be able to awaken all sentient beings.

"Great enlightening beings have ten kinds of abode: the abode of great goodwill, being impartial toward all sentient beings; the abode of great compassion, not slighting the uncultivated; the abode of great joy, aloof from all vexations; the abode of great equanimity, regarding the created and uncreated equally; the abode of all transcendent ways, being led by the aspiration for enlightenment; the abode of universal emptiness, by virtue of skillful analysis; the abode of signlessness, not leaving the absolute state; the abode of wishlessness, examining the experience of taking on life; the abode of recollection and awareness, by virtue of full development of recognition of truth; the abode of equality of all things, by virtue of having gained the prediction of buddhahood. Based on these ten, enlightening beings can reach the supreme abode of buddhas where there is no obstruction.

"Great enlightening beings have ten kinds of sphere of action: they take right mindfulness as their sphere of action, as they fulfill the points of mindfulness; they take all realms of being as their sphere of action, as they become truly aware of the implications of the Teaching; they take wisdom as their sphere of action, gaining the joy of buddhas; they take the transcendent ways as their sphere of action, as they fulfill omniscience; they take the four integrative practices as their sphere of action, as they educate sentient beings; they take birth and death as their sphere of action, as they accumulate roots of goodness; they take bantering with all sentient beings as their sphere of action, as they teach them according to their needs and cause them to become free; they take spiritual powers as their sphere of action, as they know the realms of the senses of all sentient beings; they take skill in means as their sphere of action, uniting them with transcendent wisdom; they take the site of enlightenment as their sphere of action, as they attain universal knowledge, without stopping the practices of enlightening beings. Based on these ten, enlightening beings can reach the supreme sphere of action of great wisdom of buddhas.

"Great enlightening beings have ten kinds of observation: observation knowing all acts, seeing all details; observation knowing various tendencies, not grasping sentient beings; observation knowing faculties, comprehending the nonexistence of faculties; observation knowing phenomena, not violating the realm of reality; observation seeing the verities of buddhahood, cultivating the enlightened eye; observation attaining wisdom, explaining things as they really are; observation accepting the nonorigination of things, definitely comprehending the teaching of Buddha; observation in the state of nonregression, destroying all afflictions and transcending the three worlds and the stages of the lesser vehicles; observation in the stage of coronation, by virtue of unshakable mastery of all Buddha teachings; observation in concentration with hyperconscious knowledge, practicing charity everywhere as Buddhist service. Based on these ten, enlightening beings can attain the supremely great observational knowledge of buddhas.

"Great enlightening beings have ten kinds of universal observation: they observe all who come seeking of them, satisfying them without aversion; they observe all immoral sentient beings and establish them in the pure precepts of buddhas; they observe all malicious sentient beings and settle them in the power of enlightened tolerance; they observe all lazy sentient beings and urge them to be diligent and not give up bearing the burden of the Great Vehicle; they observe all confused sentient beings and get them to abide in the state of universal knowledge of buddhas, where there is no distraction; they observe all deluded sentient beings and clear away their doubts and break down reification; they observe all impartial good friends and follow their instructions to live by the Buddha teachings; they observe all principles they hear and quickly attain realizational insight into the supreme meaning; they observe the infinite sentient beings, never abandoning the power of great compassion; they observe the teachings of all buddhas and quickly manage to accomplish universal knowledge. Based on these ten, enlightening beings can attain the universal observation of supreme wisdom of buddhas.

"Great enlightening beings have ten kinds of springing: the springing of a majestic bull, overshadowing all dragons, yakshas, kinnaras, gandharvas, and other creatures; the springing of a majestic elephant, their minds well tamed and gentle, carrying all sentient beings; the springing of a great water spirit, producing dense clouds of the great Teaching, flashing the lightning of liberation, reverberating with the thunder of truth, and showering the sweet rain of the spiritual faculties and powers, the elements of enlightenment, meditations, liberations, and concentrations; the springing of the great golden-winged bird, evaporating the water of covetousness, breaking the shell of delusion, catching the evil poisonous dragons of affliction, and lifting beings out of the ocean of suffering of birth and death; the springing of a great majestic lion, resting secure in fearless, impartial great knowledge and, using that as a weapon, crushing demons and false teachers; the springing of courage and strength, able to destroy the enemy, afflictions, on the great battlefront of birth and death; the springing of great knowledge, knowing the elements of body, mind, and sense experience, as well as all other interdependent productions, and freely explaining all things; the springing of mental command, retaining teachings by the power of recollection and awareness, and expounding them according to the faculties of sentient beings; the springing of intellectual powers, uninhibited and swift, analyzing everything and causing everyone to receive benefit and be happy; the springing of realization of Thusness, fulfilling all aids to the way to omniscience, and with instantaneous wisdom attaining all that can be attained, understanding all that can be understood, sitting on a lion throne, conquering hostile demons, and realizing unexcelled, complete perfect enlightenment. Based on these ten, enlightening beings can achieve the supreme springing of buddhas in the midst of all things.

"Great enlightening beings have ten kinds of lion's roar. They declare, 'I will surely attain true enlightenment'—this is the great lion's roar of the determination for enlightenment. 'I will enable those who have not yet transcended the world to transcend, liberate those who are not yet liberated, pacify those who are not yet at peace, and enable those who have not attained nirvana to attain it'—this is the great lion's roar of great compassion. 'I will perpetuate the seeds of the Buddha, the Teaching, and the harmonious Community'—this is the great lion's roar of requiting the benevolence of the Buddha. 'I will purify all buddha-lands'—this is the great lion's roar of ultimately firm commitment. 'I will get rid of all evil ways and difficult situations'—this is the lion's roar of personally maintaining pure conduct. 'I will fully attain the adorning features of body, speech, and mind of all buddhas'—this is the great lion's roar of tirelessly seeking virtue. 'I will fully accomplish the knowledge of all buddhas'—this is the great lion's roar of tirelessly seeking knowledge. 'I will annihilate all demons and all the works of demons'—this is the great lion's roar of cultivating right practice to stop afflictions. 'I will realize that all things are selfless, without being, without life, without personality, empty, signless, wishless, and pure as space'—this is the great lion's roar of the acceptance of the nonorigination of all things. Enlightening beings in their last life shake all buddha-lands and make them all pure: thereupon all the Indras, Brahmas, and guardian deities come and praise them and entreat them, 'Please, enlightening being, with the truth of birthlessness, appear to be born.' The enlightening beings then observe all sentient beings in the world by the unobstructed eye of wisdom and see that there are none who compare to themselves—so they appear to be born in royal palaces, walk seven steps by themselves, and declare in a great lion's roar, 'I am supreme in the world—I will forever end the realm of birth and death.' This is the great lion's roar of doing what one says. Based on these ten, enlightening beings can attain the supremely great lion's roar of buddhas.

"Great enlightening beings have ten kinds of pure giving: impartial giving, not discriminating among sentient beings; giving according to wishes, satisfying others; unconfused giving, causing benefit to be gained; giving appropriately, knowing superior, mediocre, and inferior; giving without dwelling, not seeking reward; open giving, without clinging attachment; total giving, being ultimately pure; giving dedicated to enlightenment, transcending the created and the uncreated; giving to teach sentient beings, never abandoning them, even to the site of enlightenment; giving with its three spheres pure, observing the giver, receiver, and gift with right awareness, as being like space. Based on these ten principles, enlightening beings can accomplish the supreme, pure, magnanimous giving of buddhas.

"Great enlightening beings have ten kinds of pure discipline: pure discipline of body, guarding themselves from evil deeds; pure discipline of speech, getting rid of faults of speech; pure discipline of mind, forever getting rid of greed, hatred, and false views; the pure discipline of not destroying any subjects of study, being honorable leaders among people; the pure discipline of preserving the aspiration for enlightenment, not liking the lesser vehicles of individual salvation; the pure discipline of preserving the regulations of the Buddha, greatly fearing even minor offenses; the pure discipline of secret protection, skillfully drawing out undisciplined sentient beings; the pure discipline of not doing any evil, vowing to practice all virtuous principles; the pure discipline of detachment from all views of existence, having no attachment to precepts; the pure discipline of protecting all sentient beings, activating great compassion. Based on these ten principles, enlightening beings can attain the supreme flawless pure discipline of buddhas.

"Great enlightening beings have ten kinds of pure tolerance: pure tolerance calmly enduring slander and vilification, to protect sentient beings; pure tolerance calmly enduring weapons, to protect self and others; pure tolerance not arousing anger and viciousness, the mind being unshakable; pure tolerance not attacking the low, being magnanimous when above; pure tolerance saving all who come for refuge, giving up one's own life; pure tolerance free from conceit, not slighting the uncultivated; pure tolerance not becoming angered at injury, because of observation of illusoriness; pure tolerance not revenging offenses, because of not seeing self and other; pure tolerance not following afflictions, being detached from all objects; pure tolerance knowing all things have no origin, in accord with the true knowledge of enlightening beings, entering the realm of universal knowledge without depending on the instruction of another. Based on these ten, enlightening beings can attain all buddhas' supreme tolerance of truth, understanding without depending on another.

"Great enlightening beings have ten kinds of pure energy: pure physical energy, to attend buddhas, enlightening beings, teachers, and elders, honoring fields of blessings, never retreating; pure verbal energy, extensively explaining to others whatever teachings they learn and praising the virtues of buddhahood, without wearying; pure mental energy, able to enter and exit kindness, compassion, joy, equanimity, meditations, liberations, and concentrations, without cease; pure energy of honesty, being free from deceptiveness, flattery, deviousness, and dishonesty, not regressing in any of their efforts; pure energy of determination on increasing progress, always intent on seeking higher and higher knowledge, aspiring to embody all good and pure qualities; unwasteful pure energy, embodying charity, morality, tolerance, learning, and diligence, continuing unceasingly until enlightenment; pure energy conquering all demons, able to extirpate greed, hatred, delusion, false views, and all other bonds and veils of affliction; pure energy fully developing the light of knowledge, being carefully observant in all actions, consummating them all, preventing later regret, and attaining all the unique qualities of buddhahood; pure energy without coming or going, attaining true knowledge, entering the door of the realm of reality, body, speech, and mind all impartial, understanding forms are formless and having no attachments; pure energy developing the light of the Teaching, transcending all stages and attaining the coronation of buddhas, and with an uncontaminated body manifesting the appearances of death and birth, of leaving home and attaining enlightenment, of teaching and passing away, fulfilling such tasks of Universal Good. Based on these ten, enlightening beings can attain the supreme great energy of buddhas.

"Great enlightening beings have ten kinds of pure meditation: pure meditation always gladly leaving home, giving up all possessions; pure meditation finding genuine good companions, to teach the right way; pure meditation living in the forest enduring wind and rain and so on, being detached from self and possessions; pure meditation leaving clamorous sentient beings, always enjoying tranquil silence; pure meditation with harmonious mental activity, guarding the senses; pure meditation with mind and cognition silent, impervious to all sounds and nettles of meditational concentration; pure meditation aware of the methods of the Path of enlightenment, contemplating them all and actually realizing them; pure meditation detached from clinging to its experiences, neither grasping nor rejecting the realm of desire; pure meditation awakening psychic knowledge, knowing the faculties and natures of all sentient beings; pure meditation with freedom of action, entering into the concentration of buddhas and knowing there is no self. Based on these ten, enlightening beings can attain the supreme pure meditation of buddhas.

"Great enlightening beings have ten kinds of pure wisdom: pure wisdom knowing all causes, not denying consequences; pure wisdom knowing all conditions, not ignoring combination; pure wisdom knowing nonannihilation and nonpermanence, comprehending interdependent origination truly; pure wisdom extracting all views, neither grasping nor rejecting characteristics of sentient beings; pure wisdom observing the mental activities of all sentient beings, knowing they are illusory; pure wisdom with vast intellectual power, distinguishing all truths and being unhindered in dialogue; pure wisdom unknowable to demons, false teachers, or followers of the vehicles of individual salvation, deeply penetrating the knowledge of all buddhas; pure wisdom seeing the subtle reality body of all buddhas, seeing the essential purity of all sentient beings, seeing that all phenomena are quiescent, and seeing that all lands are the same as space, knowing all characteristics without impediment; pure wisdom with all powers of mental command, analytic abilities, liberative means, and ways of transcendence, fostering the attainment of all supreme knowledge; pure wisdom instantly uniting with adamantine knowledge comprehending the equality of all things, attaining the most honorable knowledge of all things. Based on these ten, enlightening beings can attain the unobstructed great wisdom of buddhas.

"Great enlightening beings have ten kinds of pure benevolence: impartial pure benevolence, caring for all sentient beings without discrimination; helpful pure benevolence, bringing happiness by whatever they do; pure benevolence taking care of people in the same way as oneself, ultimately bringing about emancipation from birth and death; pure benevolence not abandoning the world, the mind always focused on accumulating roots of goodness; pure benevolence able to bring liberation, causing all sentient beings to annihilate all afflictions; pure benevolence generating enlightenment, inspiring all sentient beings to seek omniscience; pure benevolence unobstructed by the world, radiating great light illuminating everywhere equally; pure benevolence filling space, reaching everywhere to save sentient beings; pure benevolence focused on truth, realizing the truth of Thusness; pure benevolence without object, entering enlightening beings' detachment from life. Based on these ten, enlightening beings can attain the supreme, vast, pure benevolence of buddhas.

"Great enlightening beings have ten kinds of pure compassion: pure compassion without companion, as they make their determination independently; tireless pure compassion, not considering it troublesome to endure pain on behalf of all sentient beings; pure compassion taking on birth in difficult situations, for the purpose of liberating sentient beings; pure compassion taking on birth in pleasant conditions, to show impermanence; pure compassion for the sake of wrongly fixated sentient beings, never giving up their vow of universal liberation; pure compassion not clinging to personal pleasure, giving happiness to all sentient beings; pure compassion not seeking reward, purifying their minds; pure compassion able to remove delusion by explaining the truth. Great enlightening beings know all things are in essence pure and have no clinging or irritation, but suffering is experienced because of afflictions of adventitious defilements: knowing this, they conceive great compassion for sentient beings. This is called essential purity, as they explain to them the principle of undefiled pure light. Great enlightening beings know that all phenomena are like the tracks of birds in the sky, but that sentient beings' eyes are clouded by delusion and they cannot clearly realize this; observing them, enlightening beings conceive great compassion. This is called true knowledge, as they teach them the principle of nirvana. These are ten kinds of pure compassion, based on which enlightening beings attain the supremely great compassion of buddhas.

"Great enlightening beings have ten kinds of pure joy: the pure joy of aspiring to enlightenment; the pure joy of relinquishing all possessions; the pure joy of not rejecting undisciplined sentient beings but teaching them and maturing them; the pure joy of being able to tolerate evildoing sentient beings and vowing to save and liberate them; the pure joy of giving one's life in search of truth, without regret; the pure joy of giving up sensual pleasures and always taking pleasure in truth; the pure joy of inducing sentient beings to give up material pleasures and always take pleasure in truth; the pure joy of cosmic equanimity tirelessly honoring and serving all buddhas they see; the pure joy of teaching all sentient beings to enjoy meditations, liberations, and concentrations, and to freely enter and emerge from them; the pure joy of gladly carrying out all austere practices that accord with the way of enlightening beings and realizing the tranquil, imperturbable supreme calmness and wisdom of the sage. Based on these ten, enlightening beings can attain the supremely great pure joy of buddhas.

"Great enlightening beings have ten kinds of pure equanimity: the pure equanimity of not becoming emotionally attached to sentient beings who honor and support them; the pure equanimity of not being angered at sentient beings who slight and revile them; the pure equanimity of always being in the world but not being affected by the vicissitudes of worldly things; the pure equanimity of instructing sentient beings who are fit for the Teaching at the appropriate times, while not conceiving aversion for sentient beings who are not fit for the Teaching; the pure equanimity of not seeking the states of learning or nonlearning of the two lesser vehicles; the pure equanimity of the mind always being aloof from all desires that are conducive to affliction; the pure equanimity of not praising the two lesser vehicles' aversion to birth and death; the pure equanimity of avoiding worldly talk, talk that is not of nirvana, talk that is not dispassionate, talk that is not according to truth, talk that disturbs others, talk of individual salvation, and in general all talk that obstructs the Path of enlightening beings; the pure equanimity of waiting for the appropriate times to teach sentient beings whose faculties are mature and have developed mindfulness and precise awareness but do not yet know the supreme truth; the pure equanimity of waiting for the appropriate times to teach sentient beings whom the enlightening being has already instructed in the past but who cannot be tamed until the enlightening being reaches buddhahood; the pure equanimity of not considering people as higher or lower, being free from grasping and rejection, being aloof from all kinds of discriminatory notions, always being rightly concentrated, penetrating truth and attaining tolerance. Based on these ten, enlightening beings can attain the supremely pure equanimity of buddhas.

"Great enlightening beings have ten kinds of principle: the principle of great learning, steadfastly putting it into practice; the principle of truth, skillfully thinking about it and discerning it; the principle of emptiness, the ultimate truth being emptiness; the principle of silence and calm, being detached from the clamor and confusion of sentient beings; the principle of inexpressibility, not clinging to words; the principle of according with truth, realizing that past, present, and future are equal; the principle of the realm of reality, all things being one in essence; the principle of True Thusness, as all who realize Thusness enter it; the principle of the limit of reality, realizing ultimate truth; the principle of great ultimate nirvana, extinguishing all suffering yet carrying out the practices of enlightening beings. Based on these ten, enlightening beings can attain the supreme principle of omniscience.

"Great enlightening beings have ten kinds of law: the law of truth, practicing what they teach; the law of detachment from clinging, detaching from both the clinger and that which is clung to; the law of noncontention, being free from all confusing conflicts; the law of silent extinction, extinguishing all irritations; the law of dispassion, all covetousness being ended; the law of freedom from false notions, all arbitrary conceptualization clinging to objects permanently ceasing; the law of birthlessness, being immovable as space; the law of the uncreated, being detached from appearances of origin, subsistence, and annihilation; the law of basic essence, being inherently pure; the law of abandoning all nirvana in which there is still suffering, to be able to generate all practices of enlightening beings and carry them out uninterruptedly. Based on these ten, enlightening beings can attain the supremely great law of buddhas.

"Great enlightening beings have ten kinds of virtues instrumental in fostering enlightenment: urging sentient beings to generate the aspiration for enlightenment is one of enlightening beings' virtues instrumental in fostering enlightenment, because it perpetuates the three treasures; following the ten kinds of dedication is one of enlightening beings' virtues instrumental in fostering enlightenment, because it stops all that is not good and accumulates all that is good; wisely guiding and teaching is one of enlightening beings' virtues instrumental in fostering enlightenment, because it transcends the virtues of the worlds of desire, form, and formlessness; indefatigability of mind is one of enlightening beings' virtues instrumental in fostering enlightenment, because thereby they finally liberate all sentient beings; relinquishing all internal and external possessions is one of enlightening beings' virtues instrumental in fostering enlightenment, because of having no attachments to anything at all; working unflaggingly to fully develop spiritual refinements is one of enlightening beings' virtues instrumental in fostering enlightenment, by opening the gate of great charity, without limit; dedicating all roots of goodness, superior, middling, or lesser, to supreme enlightenment without slighting any is one of enlightening beings' virtues instrumental in fostering enlightenment, being consonant with skill in means; generating great compassion for bad sentient beings who are mean and fixed on error, not despising them, is one of enlightening beings' virtues instrumental in fostering enlightenment, by virtue of always activating the heart of universal commitment of great people; honoring and serving all buddhas, thinking of all enlightening beings as buddhas, and bringing joy to all sentient beings, is one of enlightening beings' virtues instrumental in fostering enlightenment, as they keep their original will most firm and steadfast. Great enlightening beings accumulate roots of goodness over measureless eons, wishing to attain realization of supreme enlightenment themselves, as though it were in their palm; yet they give away all their roots of goodness to all sentient beings without any grief or regret, their minds being as broad as space—this is a virtue of enlightening beings instrumental in fostering enlightenment, as they develop great wisdom and realize great truth. Based on these ten, enlightening beings can embody the supremely great mass of virtues of buddhas.

"Great enlightening beings have ten kinds of knowledge instrumental in fostering enlightenment. They associate with learned, genuine teachers, and respectfully attend them, obeying them in every way, not deviating from their instructions; this is one, being totally honest, without falsehood. They give up conceit forever, they are always humble and respectful, their thoughts, words, and deeds are free from coarseness, they are harmonious and agreeable, and do not prevaricate; this is the second, as their beings become capable of bearing the Buddha teaching. They are mentally collected, aware, always alert, never distracted or confused; conscientious and agreeable, their minds are calm and imperturbable; they always remember the six thoughts, always practice the sixfold respect, and always abide by the six principles of steadfastness; this is the third, being a way to develop tenfold knowledge. They take pleasure in truth and principle, always enjoying listening to teaching of truth, abandoning worldly philosophies and theses, always concentrating on listening to transcendental talk, leaving the lesser vehicles of individual salvation behind and entering the wisdom of the Great Vehicle of universal salvation; this is the fourth, singlemindedly recollecting without distraction. They bear the six ways of transcendence in mind wholeheartedly, have already

perfected the practice of the four immeasurable minds, follow the methods of illumination and skillfully put them into practice; they earnestly
question intelligent people of knowledge, avoid bad tendencies, and aim
for good ways; their minds always like contemplation with right recollection; they subdue their own feelings and protect the minds of others:
this is the fifth, firmly executing true practice. They always appreciate
emancipation and do not cling to the world; they are always aware of
their own minds and never have any evil thoughts; they have done away
with greed, anger, and malevolence, and their thoughts, words, and deeds
are all good; they have certain knowledge of the inherent nature of mind:
this is the sixth, able to purify one's own and others' minds. They observe
the five clusters as being like illusory phenomena, the elements like poisonous snakes, the sense mediums like desolate villages, all things as like
illusions, flames, reflections, dreams, shadows, echoes, images, like paintings in the sky, like a turning wheel of fire, like the colors of the rainbow,
like sunlight and moonlight, signless and formless, neither permanent
nor ending, not coming or going, and not abiding either—contemplating
in this way, they know all things have no origin and no destruction: this
is the seventh, knowing that the essential nature of all things is empty
and quiescent. When great enlightening beings hear that phenomena
have no self, no being, no soul, no person, no mind, no object, no greed,
no anger, no delusion, no body, no thing, no master, no sustenance, no
attachment, and no action, all of these having no existence, being ultimately nil—having heard this, they deeply believe it, without doubt or
repudiation: this is the eighth, being able to perfect complete understanding.
Great enlightening beings tame their faculties well, and they cultivate action according to truth; they always abide in tranquillity and insight, and
their minds are silent and calm, with no disturbing thoughts arising; they
have no self, no person, no fabrication, no conditioning, no idea of self,
no idea of self doing anything, no excess or lack, and no sense of attainment of this either; their physical, verbal, and mental actions have no
coming or going, no energy, no vigor; they see all things and all beings
impartially and do not dwell on anything; they are neither of this world
nor beyond it, notions of 'here' and 'there' being inherently irrelevant;
they come from nowhere and go nowhere—they always meditate in
this way by means of knowledge and wisdom: this is the ninth, reaching
transcendence of forms of discriminations. Because great enlightening
beings see the principle of interdependent origination, they see the purity
of phenomena; because they see the purity of phenomena, they see the
purity of lands; because they see the purity of lands, they see the purity of
space; because they see the purity of space, they see the purity of the
realm of reality; because they see the purity of the realm of reality, they
see the purity of knowledge; this is the tenth, cultivating and accumulating all-knowledge. These are enlightening beings' ten kinds of knowledge
instrumental in fostering enlightenment, based on which they can attain
the buddhas' store of un-impeded, pure, subtle knowledge of all truths.

"Great enlightening beings have ten kinds of sufficiency of insight: skillfully analyzing all things; not grasping or clinging to anything; divorcing all deluded views; illumining all senses with the light of knowledge; skillfully generating rightly directed energy; being able to deeply penetrate knowledge of absolute truth; extinguishing the actions of afflictions and developing the knowledge of extinction and knowledge of birthlessness; observing everywhere with the knowledge of the celestial eye; knowing the purity of the past by the recollection of past states; annihilating the contaminations of sentient beings by the spiritual knowledge of ending contamination. Based on these ten, enlightening beings can attain the supreme illumination of all teachings of the buddhas.

"Great enlightening beings have ten kinds of quest for truth: quest for truth with a straightforward mind, being free from dishonesty; diligent quest for truth, being free from laziness; wholly devoted quest for truth, not begrudging their lives; quest for truth to destroy all sentient beings' afflictions, not doing it for fame, profit, or respect; quest for truth to benefit self and others, all sentient beings, not just helping themselves; quest for truth to enter knowledge and wisdom, not taking pleasure in literature; quest for truth to leave birth and death, not craving worldly pleasures; quest for truth to liberate sentient beings, engendering the determination for enlightenment; quest for truth to resolve the doubts of all sentient beings, to free them from vacillation; quest for truth to fulfill buddhahood, not being inclined to lesser aims. Based on these ten, enlightening beings can attain great knowledge of all elements of buddhahood without being instructed by another.

"Great enlightening beings have ten kinds of understanding of truth: generating and developing roots of goodness in accord with the conventional world is the way of understanding of truth of unenlightened ordinary people; attaining indestructible faith, aware of the essence of things, is the way of understanding truth of people acting according to faith; leaving behind erroneous ways and turning to the eightfold right path is the way people aiming for stream-entering understand truth; getting rid of bonds, putting an end to the contaminations of birth and death, and seeing reality is the stream-enterer's understanding of truth; seeing tasting as affliction and knowing no coming or going is the once-returner's understanding of truth; not taking pleasure in the world, seeking to end contamination, not having so much as a single thought of attachment to life, is the nonreturner's understanding of truth; attaining the six spiritual powers, eight liberations, nine concentration states, and four special knowledges, all fully developed, is the saint's understanding of truth; naturally being inclined to contemplate uniform interdependent origination, the mind always tranquil and content, having few concerns, understanding causality, awakening on one's own without depending on another, accomplishing various kinds of spiritual knowledge, is the individual illuminate's understanding of truth; having vast knowledge, all faculties clear and sharp, always inclined to liberate all sentient beings, diligently cultivating virtue and knowledge to foster enlightenment, fully developing buddhas' ten powers, fearlessnesses, and other attributes, is the enlightening being's understanding of truth. Based on these ten, enlightening beings can attain the understanding of truth of the supreme great knowledge of buddhas.

"Great enlightening beings have ten norms of practice: honoring the wise; always being alerted by the celestial spirits; always having shame and conscience before the buddhas; having pity for sentient beings and not abandoning birth and death; carrying tasks through to consummation without change of mind; single-mindedly following the enlightening beings who aspire to universal enlightenment and diligently learning; getting rid of wrong views and earnestly seeking the right Path; destroying demons and the actions of afflictions; knowing the different faculties and temperaments of sentient beings and teaching them to enable them to live in the state of buddhahood; abiding in the infinitely vast cosmos of reality, removing afflictions and purifying the body. Based on these ten, enlightening beings can attain the buddhas' supreme method of practice.

"For great enlightening beings there are ten kinds of demons: the demon of the clusters of mental and material elements, giving rise to attachments; the demon of afflictions, perpetually confusing and defiling; the demon of actions, able to obstruct and inhibit; the demon of mind, which gives rise to pride; the demon of death, which abandons life; the demon of heaven, being self-indulgent; the demon of roots of goodness, because of perpetual clinging; the demon of concentration, because of long indulgence in the experience; the demon of spiritual teachers, because of giving rise to feelings of attachment; the demon of the phenomenon of enlightenment, because of not wanting to relinquish it. Great enlightening beings should apply appropriate means to quickly escape these demons.

"For great enlightening beings there are ten kinds of demons' actions: cultivating roots of goodness while forgetting the aspiration for enlightenment; giving with ill-will, keeping precepts with hatred, rejecting people of bad character, rejecting the slothful, slighting the confused, and despising the ignorant; being jealous and stingy with the profound teaching, not explaining it to those who are capable of being enlightened, insisting on explaining it to people without the capacity for it as long as wealth and honor are thereby available; not liking to hear about the ways of transcendence, not practicing them even when hearing about them, tending to negligence even when practicing them, becoming narrow and mean in spirit because of laziness, and not seeking supreme great enlightenment; avoiding good companions, associating with bad companions, craving personal release, not wanting to accept life, wishing for the desirelessness and tranquillity of nirvana; arousing hatred and anger toward enlightening beings, looking at them with malevolent eyes, looking for faults in them, talking of their faults, cutting off their support; repudiating true teaching and being averse to hearing it, immediately criticizing it when hearing it, having no respect for those who expound it, claiming oneself to be right and others all wrong; indulging in the study of secular literature, expounding the vehicles of individual salvation while obscuring the profound Teaching, or giving subtle doctrines to unsuitable people, straying from enlightenment and persisting in false paths; always liking to associate with those who are already liberated and at peace, and giving them offerings, while not being willing to approach or edify those who have not yet attained liberation or peace; developing conceit, having no respect, often troubling or hurting sentient beings, not seeking genuine knowledge of truth, being mean and difficult to awaken. These are the ten kinds of demons' actions, which enlightening beings should quickly get away from to seek enlightened action.

"Great enlightening beings have ten ways of getting rid of demons' actions: associating with the wise and honoring and serving them; not elevating themselves or praising themselves; believing in the profound Teaching of Buddha without repudiating it; never ever forgetting the determination for omniscience; diligently cultivating refined practices, never being lax; always seeking all the teachings for enlightening beings; always expounding the truth tirelessly; taking refuge with all the buddhas of the ten directions, thinking of them as saviors and protectors; faithfully accepting and remembering the support of the spiritual power of the buddhas; equally planting the same roots of goodness with all enlightening beings. Based on these ten, enlightening beings can escape all demonic ways.

"Great enlightening beings have ten ways of seeing buddhas: the buddha of abiding in the world attaining true enlightenment they see by nonattachment; they see the buddha of vows by production; they see the buddha of rewards of action by deep faith; they see the buddha of preservation by following the Teaching; they see the buddha of nirvana by deeply entering it; they see the cosmic buddha everywhere; they see the buddha of mind by peaceful stability; they see the buddha of concentration by infinite independence; they see the buddha of fundamental essence by clear comprehension; they see the buddha of adaptation by universal awareness. By these they always see the supreme Buddha.

"Great enlightening beings have ten kinds of buddha-action. Guiding at appropriate times is buddha-action because it fosters correct cultivation of practice. Causing dream visions is buddha-action because it awakens awareness of past roots of goodness. Expounding to others scriptures they have not yet heard is buddha-action because it causes growth of knowledge and resolution of doubts. Teaching the way to emancipation to those bound up in regrets is buddha-action because it frees them from a doubting mind. Manifesting the glorified body of Buddha for the sake of sentient beings with stingy minds, ignorant minds, minds interested in personal salvation, malevolent minds, doubting minds, scattered minds, or conceited minds, is buddha-action because it nurtures past roots of goodness. Widely expounding the true Teaching in times when true Teaching is difficult to come across, causing those who hear it to attain concentrated knowledge and knowledge of spiritual powers, to be able to benefit innumerable sentient beings, is buddha-action because the resolution is pure. If anything demonic occurs, being able to manifest a voice equal to space explaining the principle of not harming others, in order to quell it, causing the awakening of understanding and causing the majesty of demons who hear to vanish, is buddha-action because the will is extraordinary and the power great. The mind having no lapse, being constantly alert, not permitting experiential entry into the absolute state of individual liberation, and never speaking of the realm of liberation to those whose faculties and characters are not yet mature, is buddha-action because it is the performance of the original vow. Shedding all the bonds and contaminations of birth and death, cultivating the practices of enlightening beings continuously, taking care of sentient beings with great compassion, causing them to undertake such practice and eventually be liberated, is buddha-action because it does not stop the practice of the deeds of enlightening beings. Enlightening beings realize that their own bodies as well as sentient beings are fundamentally quiescent and null, yet, not being surprised or afraid, they still tirelessly cultivate virtue and knowledge; though they know all things have no creation, yet they do not ignore the individual characteristics of things; though they are forever aloof of craving for objects, yet they always gladly behold the form bodies of buddhas; though they know one is enlightened into the truth without depending on another, yet they seek omniscience through many kinds of methods; though they know all lands are like space, they always enjoy adorning all buddha-lands; though they always observe that there is no real person or self, yet they tirelessly teach and enlighten sentient beings; though fundamentally unmoving in the cosmos of reality, yet they manifest a multitude of transformations by spiritual powers; though they have already accomplished omniscience, yet they practice the acts of enlightening beings without ceasing; though they know all things are inexplicable, yet they turn the wheel of the pure Teaching and gladden the hearts of all beings; though they are able to manifest the spiritual powers of buddhas, yet they do not reject embodiment as enlightening beings; though they appear to enter ultimate final extinction, they manifest birth in all places—being able to perform these practices, simultaneously carrying out the provisional and the true, is buddha-action. Based on these ten, enlightening beings can achieve supreme teacherless great action without relying on the instruction of another.

"For great enlightening beings there are ten kinds of conceited action. Not respecting teachers, parents, mendicants, people on the right Path, people aiming for the right Path, or honorable fields of blessings, is conceited action. If there are teachers who have attained to supreme truth, who ride the Great Vehicle of universal enlightenment, who know the way to emancipation, who have attained mental command and expound the great principles of the scriptures, to be haughty toward them or their teachings and to be disrespectful is conceited action. When in an audience hearing the sublime Teaching expounded, to be unwilling to laud its excellence and cause others to believe and accept it, is conceited action. Habitually conceiving the illusion of superiority, elevating oneself and looking down on others, not seeing one's own faults, not knowing one's own shortcomings, is conceited action. Habitually imagining that one is better than those who are better than oneself, not praising virtuous people who are praiseworthy, and not being happy when others praise them, is conceited action. When seeing someone preach, in spite of knowing it is the norm, the rule, the truth, the word of Buddha, to despise the teaching because of disliking the person, to slander it and incite others to slander it, is conceited action. Seeking a high seat for oneself, declaring oneself to be a teacher worthy of receiving offerings and not supposed to work, failing to rise to greet old people who have cultivated spiritual practice for a long time, being unwilling to serve them, is conceited action. Frowning unhappily on seeing people with virtue, speaking to them harshly and looking for faults in them, is conceited action. When seeing intelligent people who know the truth, not being willing to approach and attend them, respect and honor them, being unwilling to ask them what is good and what is not good, what should be done and what should not be done, what acts result in various benefits and comforts in the long night, being foolish and deluded, stubborn and contentious, swallowed by self-importance, never able to see the way to emancipation, is conceited action. There are also sentient beings with minds shrouded by conceit, who when buddhas appear in the world are unable to approach, respect, and honor them; in them no new good arises, and goodness from the past evaporates and vanishes; they say what they should not, they contend where they should not; in the future they will surely fall into a deep pit of danger and will not even encounter Buddha, much less hear the Teaching, for hundreds of thousands of eons, though because of having once conceived the aspiration for enlightenment they will in the end wake up on their own—this is conceited action. If enlightening beings get rid of these ten kinds of conceited action, they will attain ten kinds of actions of knowledge.

"The ten kinds of action of knowledge are believing in consequences of action and not denying causality; not giving up the determination for enlightenment, always remembering the buddhas; attending the wise, respecting and providing for them, honoring them tirelessly; enjoying the teachings and their meanings, never tiring of them, getting rid of wrong awareness and cultivating true awareness; getting rid of haughtiness toward all sentient beings, thinking of enlightening beings as buddhas, valuing the true Teaching as much as one's own being, honoring the enlightened as though protecting one's own life, thinking of practitioners as buddhas; being free from all that is not good in thought, word,

and deed, praising the excellences of sages and saints, and according with
enlightenment; not denying interdependent origination, getting rid of
false views, destroying darkness and attaining light, illumining all things;
acting in accord with the ten kinds of dedication, thinking of the ways of
transcendence as one's mother, thinking of skillful means as one's father,
and entering the house of enlightenment with a profound, pure mind;
diligently accumulating all practices that foster enlightenment, such as
charity, morality, learning, cessation and contemplation, virtue and wisdom; indefatigably cultivating any practice that is praised by the buddhas, that can break through the afflictions and conflicts of demons, that
can remove all obstructions, veils, shrouds, and bonds, that can teach
and tame all sentient beings, that can embrace the truth in accord with
knowledge and wisdom, that can purify a buddha-land, that can generate spiritual capacities and insights. Based on these ten actions of knowledge, enlightening beings can attain the supreme action of great knowledge of buddhas, including all skillful means of liberation.

"For great enlightening beings there are ten kinds of possession by
demons: laziness; narrowness and meanness of aspiration; satisfaction
with a little practice; exclusivity; not making great vows; liking to be
in tranquil extinction and annihilating afflictions; permanently annihilating birth and death; giving up the practices of enlightening beings;
not edifying sentient beings; doubting and repudiating the truth. If enlightening beings can get rid of these possessions by demons, they can
gain ten kinds of support by Buddha: they are supported by Buddha in
first being able to aspire to enlightenment; in preserving the will for enlightenment life after life without letting it be forgotten; in being aware
of manias and being able to avoid them; in learning the ways of transcendence and practicing them as taught; in knowing the pains of birth
and death yet not rejecting them; in contemplating the most profound
truth and gaining immeasurable reward; in expounding the principles of
the two lesser vehicles of salvation for the benefit of sentient beings without actually grasping the liberation of those vehicles; in happily contemplating the uncreated without dwelling therein, and not thinking of
the created and the uncreated as dual; in reaching the realm of birthlessness yet manifesting birth; in realizing universal knowledge yet carrying
out the practices of enlightening beings and perpetuating the seed of enlightening beings. Based on these ten, enlightening beings can attain the
supreme supportive power of buddhas.

"Great enlightening beings have ten kinds of support by truth: knowing all conditioned states are impermanent; knowing all conditioned
states are painful; knowing all conditioned states are identityless; knowing all phenomena are quiescent nirvana; knowing all phenomena arise
from conditions and do not come to be without conditions; knowing
that ignorance comes from wrong thought, and finally old age and death
come from ignorance, so if wrong thought is extinguished, ignorance is
extinguished, and finally old age and death are extinguished; knowing

the three doors of liberation and generating the vehicle of hearers, realizing the state of noncontention and generating the vehicle of individual illuminates; knowing the six transcendent ways and the four means of integration, generating the Great Vehicle; knowing that all lands, all phenomena, all sentient beings, and all times are spheres of knowledge of buddhas; knowing how to cut off all thoughts, abandon all grasping, detach from before and after, and accord with nirvana. Based on these ten, enlightening beings can attain the supreme support of truth of all buddhas.

"Great enlightening beings have ten kinds of activities in the heaven of satisfaction. First, they tell the celestials in the heavens of desire the principle of detachment, saying, 'All dominion is impermanent, all pleasures must fade and vanish,' and they urge the celestials to aspire to enlightenment. Second, to the celestials of the heavens in the realm of form they explain how to enter and emerge from the meditative and liberative concentrations, and if there are any who become attached to them and therefore regenerate views of the body, erroneous views, nescience, and so on, the enlightening beings explain true wisdom to them; if any conceive a deluded idea of purity of material or immaterial things, they explain that they are not pure and are all impermanent, and thus urge them to aspire to enlightenment. Third, in the heaven of satisfaction, great enlightening beings enter a concentration called magnificent array of light, and their bodies radiate light illumining the entire universe; according to the mentalities of sentient beings, they preach to them in various voices, so that the sentient beings, having heard, have pure faith and are reborn in the heaven of satisfaction after death, where the enlightening beings urge them to aspire to enlightenment. Fourth, the great enlightening beings in the heaven of satisfaction, with their unobstructed eyes, see all the enlightening beings in all the heavens of satisfaction in the ten directions, so that all the enlightening beings see each other; having seen each other, they discuss the marvelous Teaching— that is, descending spiritually into the mother's womb, being born, leaving home, going to the site of enlightenment, being imbued with magnificent adornments, and also showing the deeds they have been carrying out since ancient times, by which they attained this great knowledge and its virtues, being able to manifest these things without leaving their original places. Fifth, when a great enlightening being is in the heaven of satisfaction, the enlightening beings in the palaces of all the heavens of satisfaction in the ten directions come and gather around respectfully, and then the great enlightening being, wishing to enable those enlightening beings to fulfill their vows, and to gladden them, expounds teachings according to the states those enlightening beings should abide in, according to what they are to do and what they are to stop, what they are to practice and what they are to realize; having heard this, the enlightening beings are very happy and freshly inspired, and return to the places where they live in their own lands. Sixth, when great enlightening beings are in the heaven of satisfaction, the celestial devil, lord of the realm of desire, in order to spoil and disrupt the work of the enlightening beings, comes to the enlightening beings with a retinue of demons; then the enlightening beings, in order to crush the army of demons, abide in the gate of knowledge of skill in means of transcendent wisdom which is included in the adamantine path, and expound the truth to them in both gentle and harsh words, causing the demons to be unable to get the upper hand; and when the demons see the sovereign power of the enlightening beings, they all become inspired to seek supreme enlightenment. Seventh, great enlightening beings in the heaven of satisfaction know that the celestials in the realm of desire do not like to hear the truth; then the enlightening beings announce in a loud voice, 'Today an enlightening being is going to manifest wonders —those who wish to see should come at once.' Then the celestials, having heard this, gather in droves. The enlightening beings, seeing that the celestials have gathered, show them wonders in the palace that the celestials have never seen or heard of; having seen these, the celestials are totally enraptured. Then the enlightening beings also produce voices in music saying, 'Benevolent ones, all conditioned states are impermanent and painful, all things are void of identity; nirvana is tranquil extinction.' They also say, 'You all should cultivate the practices of enlightening beings and should fulfill omniscience.' When the celestials hear this voice of teaching, they grieve and lament and give rise to revulsion and are all inspired to seek enlightenment. Eighth, great enlightening beings living in the palace of the heaven of satisfaction are able, without leaving their original place, to go to the abodes of all the innumerable buddhas in the ten directions, see the buddhas, approach them and pay respects to them, and reverently listen to their teaching. At that time the buddhas, in order to enable enlightening beings to attain the supreme state of coronation, explain to them a stage of enlightening beings called 'all spiritual capacities,' in which all supreme virtues are attained by instantaneous realizational wisdom, and they enter the stage of all knowledge. Ninth, great enlightening beings living in the palace of the heaven of satisfaction, wishing to honor the buddhas, use great spiritual powers to produce various offerings called 'extraordinarily pleasing,' filling all worlds throughout the space of the cosmos, and present them to the buddhas—when the sentient beings of those worlds see those offerings, all are inspired to seek supreme enlightenment. Tenth, great enlightening beings in the heaven of satisfaction set forth infinite teachings like illusions, like reflections, pervading all worlds in the ten directions, manifesting various forms, various characteristics, various bodies, various modes of conduct, various activities, various methods, various metaphors, various explanations, gladdening all sentient beings according to their mentalities. These are the ten kinds of activities of enlightening beings in the heaven of satisfaction: if they accomplish these things, they can subsequently be born in the human world.

"When great enlightening beings in the heaven of satisfaction are about to descend to be born in the human world, they manifest ten things. First, they radiate a tremendous light from their feet, called adornment of peace and happiness, which illumines all the miserable states in the universe; all sentient beings who come in contact with this light attain peace and happiness free from suffering, and, having realized peace and happiness, they realize that an extraordinarily great person is going to come forth into the world. Second, they emit a tremendous light, called awakening, from the curl of white hair between their brows, illumining the whole universe, shining on all the enlightening beings they worked with in the past; those enlightening beings, bathed in this light, know that an enlightening being is about to be born down on earth, and each produce innumerable offerings and bring them to present to the enlightening being. Third, they emanate from their right palms a great light, called realm of purity, which can purify all universes: if there are any individual illuminates therein who have attained noncontamination and become aware of this light, they give up their lives; if they do not become aware of this light, they are moved to other worlds by the power of the light; all demons, false teachers, and sentient beings with opinions are also removed to other worlds, except sentient beings who are sustained by the spiritual power of buddhas and are fit to be taught. Fourth, they emit great lights from their knees, called pure adornments, which illumine all the palaces of all the heavens; all the celestial beings in those heavens realize that enlightening beings in the heaven of satisfaction are about to descend to be born in the human world, and they feel bereaved and saddened, and each brings various flower garlands, clothing, perfumes, aromatic powders, banners, canopies, and music to the enlightening beings and respectfully present them, and then follow the enlightening beings in their descent to birth and on till their extinction. Fifth, from their gammadion thunderbolt–adorned heart enlightening beings radiate tremendous light, called symbol of invincibility, which shines on the thunderbolt-bearers of power in all worlds; thereupon a hundred billion thunderbolt-bearers all gather and follow and guard the enlightening beings from their birth till their extinction. Sixth, from each pore of their bodies they radiate great lights, called distinguishing sentient beings, which illumine all universes and touch the bodies of all enlightening beings and also touch the bodies of all celestials and humans; the enlightening beings and others all think they should stay there and honor the buddhas and edify sentient beings. Seventh, from the great jewel palaces they radiate immense light, called continuous observation, which illumines the places where these enlightening beings are going to be born; thereafter other enlightening beings follow them down to earth and take on birth in the same houses, the same villages, or the same cities, in order to teach sentient beings. Eighth, from the celestial palace halls and from the ornaments of the magnificent balconies, they radiate a great light, called pure adornments of all palaces, which shines on the abdomens of the mothers by whom they will be born and causes the mothers to be calm and comfortable and replete with all virtues; in the bellies of the mothers there are naturally immense mansions adorned with great treasures in which to rest the bodies of the enlightening beings. Ninth, they emanate from their feet vast light, called skillfully abiding; celestials about to die who are bathed in this light all have their lives prolonged and provide for the enlightening beings from their birth till their extinction. Tenth, from their minor embellishments they radiate great light, called array of eyes which shows the enlightening beings' various deeds; at that time humans and celestials may see the enlightening beings in the heaven of satisfaction, or in the womb, or newborn, or leaving home, or attaining enlightenment, or conquering demons, or teaching, or entering extinction. Great enlightening beings emanate countless such lights from their bodies, their thrones, their palaces, their towers, all showing various works of enlightening beings; and, having shown these works, because they are replete with all virtues, they descend from the heaven of satisfaction to be born in the human world.

"There are ten phenomena involved in the great enlightening beings' manifestation of being in the womb. First, great enlightening beings want to develop sentient beings who are small-minded and low in understanding, and not let them get the idea that the enlightening beings are spontaneously born by transformation and that their knowledge and virtues do not derive from cultivation—for this reason enlightening beings appear in the womb. Second, because they want to ripen the roots of goodness of their parents, families, and those who did the same practices as they did in the past, they appear in the womb because the roots of goodness of those people will be developed by seeing the enlightening beings in the womb. Third, when the enlightening beings enter the womb, they are in a state of right mindfulness and right knowledge, without any confusion; and once they are in the womb they remain correctly mindful, without distraction. Fourth, while great enlightening beings are in the womb, they always expound the truth; the enlightening beings and major deities of all worlds gather around them and all are caused to attain boundless spiritual capacities and knowledge—the enlightening beings in the womb have developed such higher faculties of intellectual powers. Fifth, while the great enlightening beings are in the womb, they gather great congregations, and by the power of their past vows edify all the hosts of enlightening beings. Sixth, great enlightening beings achieve buddhahood among humans, so they should receive the best of births, as humans; therefore they appear in the mother's womb. Seventh, when the great enlightening beings are in the mother's womb, all the sentient beings in the universe see them, as if seeing their own faces in a mirror. At that time the great-hearted among the various beings all come to the enlightening beings and respectfully present offerings to them. Eighth, when great enlightening beings are in the mother's womb, all the enlightening beings from other worlds who are in their final lives come and assemble and recite a great collection of teachings called vast treasury of knowledge. Ninth, when great enlightening beings are in the mother's womb, they enter the concentration that is the treasury of purification and by the power of concentration manifest within the mother's womb all kinds of adornments of a great palace, all wonderfully fine, to which even the palace of the heaven of satisfaction cannot compare, and cause the mother's body to be comfortable and free from pain. Tenth, when great enlightening beings are in the mother's womb, by their enormous spiritual power they produce offerings called opening the pure treasury of virtue and offer them to all buddhas in all worlds; the buddhas all explain to them the infinite matrix of enlightening beings' abode in the cosmos of reality. These are the ten phenomena involved in great enlightening beings' appearance in the womb; if they master these, they can reveal extremely subtle processes.

"Great enlightening beings have ten extremely subtle processes: while in the mother's womb, showing the first inspiration for enlightenment up to the stage of coronation; while in the mother's womb, showing life in the palace of the heaven of satisfaction; while in the mother's womb, showing birth; while in the mother's womb, showing childhood; while in the mother's womb, showing life in a royal palace; while in the mother's womb, showing departure from householding life; while in the mother's womb, showing the practice of austerities, going to the site of enlightenment, and attaining true awakening; while in the mother's womb, showing the turning of the wheel of teaching; while in the mother's womb, showing ultimate extinction; while in the mother's womb, showing a great subtlety called infinite different aspects of the practices of all enlightening beings and the autonomous spiritual powers of all buddhas. Based on these, enlightening beings can attain buddhas' supreme subtle process of great knowledge.

"Great enlightening beings have ten kinds of birth: birth with right awareness and right knowledge, free from folly and delusion; birth radiating great networks of light beams illuminating the whole universe; birth in the final existence, never to be reincarnated; unborn, unoriginated birth; birth knowing the triple world to be like an illusion; birth appearing corporeally everywhere in all worlds in the ten directions; birth in a body realizing omniscience; birth in a body emanating the lights of all buddhas and awakening all sentient beings; birth in a body entering contemplative concentration with great knowledge. When great enlightening beings are born, they shake all buddha-lands, liberate all sentient beings, annihilate all states of misery, and eclipse all demons; innumerable enlightening beings come and gather around them. These are the ten kinds of birth of enlightening beings, which they manifest in order to pacify sentient beings.

"There are ten reasons why great enlightening beings smile and make a promise in their hearts. They think, 'All worldlings are sunk in the mire of craving, and no one but I can rescue them.' They also think, 'All worldlings are blinded by passions and afflictions, and only I now have wisdom.' They also think, 'Based on this so-called body I will attain the supreme reality-body of buddhas, which fills all times.' Then the enlightening beings, with unobstructed eyes, look over all the Brahma heavens and all the controlling heavens, and think, 'These sentient beings all think they have the power of great knowledge.' Then the enlightening beings observe sentient beings who have long planted roots of goodness and who now are regressing and sinking. The enlightening beings observe that though the seeds sown in the world be few, the fruits reaped are many. The enlightening beings see that all sentient beings who receive the teaching of Buddha will surely gain benefit. The enlightening beings see that enlightening beings who were their colleagues in past ages have become obsessed with other things and cannot attain the great virtues of the Buddha teaching. The enlightening beings see that the celestials and humans who were in the same communities with them in the past still are in mundane states, unable to detach from them, and not tiring of them either. Then enlightening beings are bathed in the lights of all buddhas and are even more joyful. These are the ten reasons great enlightening being smile and make a promise in their hearts; great enlightening beings appear in this way to pacify sentient beings.

"There are ten reasons great enlightening beings show the act of walking seven steps; to manifest the power of enlightening beings; to manifest the giving of the seven kinds of wealth; to satisfy the wishes of the spirits of the earth; to manifest the appearance of transcending the three worlds; to manifest the supreme walk of the enlightening being, beyond the walk of the elephant, the bull, or the lion; to manifest the characteristics of adamantine ground; to manifest the desire to give sentient beings courageous strength; to manifest the practice of the seven jewels of awakening; to show that the truth they have realized does not come from the instruction of another; to manifest supreme peerlessness in the world. These are the ten reasons they show the act of walking seven steps after birth; they manifest this to pacify sentient beings.

"Great enlightening beings appear as children for ten reasons: to manifest the learning of all worldly arts and sciences; to manifest the learning of riding and military art and various worldly occupations; to manifest the learning of all kinds of worldly things such as literature, conversation, games, and amusements; to manifest the shedding of errors and faults of word, thought, and deed; to manifest entering concentration, staying in the door of nirvana, and pervading infinite worlds in the ten directions; to show that their power goes beyond all creatures, celestial, human, and nonhuman; to show that the appearance and majesty of enlightening beings goes beyond all deities; to cause sentient beings addicted to sensual pleasures to joyfully take pleasure in truth; to show the reception of empowerment of buddhas and being bathed in the light of truth.

"Having appeared as children, great enlightening beings appear to live in a royal palace for ten reasons: to cause the roots of goodness of their colleagues of the past to develop to maturity; to show the power of roots of goodness of enlightening beings; to show the comforts of great spiritual power of enlightening beings to humans and celestials who are obsessed with comforts; to adapt to the minds of sentient beings in the polluted world; to manifest the spiritual power of enlightening beings, able to enter concentration in the heart of the palace; to enable those who had the same aspirations in the past to fulfill their aims; to enable their parents, family, and relatives to fulfill their wishes; to use music to produce the sounds of the sublime teaching to offer to all buddhas; to dwell in subtle concentration while in the palace and show everything from the attainment of buddhahood to final extinction; and to accord with and preserve the teachings of the buddhas.

"After enlightening beings in their final embodiment have appeared in a royal palace, they leave home. Great enlightening beings demonstrate leaving home for ten reasons: to reject living at home; to cause sentient beings attached to their homes to give up their attachment; to follow and appreciate the path of saints; to publicize and praise the virtues of leaving home; to demonstrate eternal detachment from extreme views; to cause sentient beings to detach from sensual and selfish pleasures; to show the appearance of transcending the world; to show independence, not being subject to another; to show that they are going to attain the ten powers and fearlessnesses of buddhas; and because it is natural that enlightening beings in their final life should do so. Enlightening beings use this manifestation of leaving home to pacify sentient beings.

"Great enlightening beings demonstrate the practice of austerities for ten reasons: to develop sentient beings with low understanding; to remove false views from sentient beings; to show the consequences of action to sentient beings who do not believe in consequences of action; because it is natural to do so in accordance with the adulterated and polluted world; to show the ability to endure toil and diligently work on the Way; to cause sentient beings to want to seek the truth; for the sake of sentient beings who are attached to sensual pleasures and selfish pleasure; in order to show that enlightening beings' effort is supreme, continuing to the very last life; to induce sentient beings to enjoy the state of calm and tranquillity and increase roots of goodness; to wait until the time is ripe to develop people's immature faculties. Enlightening beings use these expedient means to pacify all sentient beings.

"Ten things occur when great enlightening beings go to the site of enlightenment: they illumine all worlds; they cause all worlds to quake; they manifest their bodies in all worlds; they awaken all enlightening beings and all their colleagues of the past; they manifest all the adornments of the site of enlightenment; they manifest various kinds of deportment and all the adornments of the tree of enlightenment, showing them according to the inclinations of the minds of sentient beings; they see all the buddhas of the ten directions; they continually enter concentration with every step and become buddhas moment to moment, without interruption; the leaders of all creatures, unaware of each other, produce all kinds of wonderful offerings; with unobstructed knowledge they observe all the buddhas carrying out the deeds of enlightening beings in all worlds and fulfilling true enlightenment. By these ten things enlightening beings teach and influence sentient beings.

"Ten things occur when great enlightening beings sit on the site of enlightenment: they cause all worlds to quake in various ways; they equally illuminate all worlds; they remove all the sufferings of miserable states; they cause all worlds to be adamantine; they gaze on the lion thrones of all the buddhas; their minds are like space, without conceptualization; they manifest comportment as appropriate; they rest in adamantine concentration; they receive the pure, sublime place sustained by the spiritual power of all buddhas; they can strengthen all sentient beings with the power of their own roots of goodness.

"When great enlightening beings sit on the site of enlightenment, ten extraordinary, unprecedented events occur: all the buddhas of the worlds of the ten directions appear before them, raise their right hands, and praise them as unexcelled guides; all buddhas watch over them and give them power; the enlightening beings who were their colleagues in the past come and surround them and respectfully present various adornments; the plants and trees and all insentient things bend toward the site of enlightenment; the great enlightening beings enter a concentration called observing the cosmos, whose power can cause all enlightening practices to be fulfilled; they attain a spell called oceanic treasury of supreme pure light, and are able to receive the rain from the great clouds of teaching of all buddhas; by spiritual powers they produce superb offerings throughout all worlds which they present to the buddhas; they rest in highest knowledge and actually know the faculties and mental patterns of all sentient beings; they enter a concentration called 'well aware,' whose power enables their bodies to fill all worlds in all spaces in all times; they attain pure illumination and unobstructed great knowledge, enabling their physical actions to penetrate past, present, and future. These are the ten extraordinary things that happen when great enlightening beings sit on the site of enlightenment.

"When great enlightening beings are sitting on the site of enlightenment, they manifest the conquering of demons because of observing ten kinds of purpose: because the sentient beings in times of confusion are bellicose, enlightening beings want to show the spiritual power of enlightening beings; to cut off the doubts of people in celestial and mundane states who have doubts; to civilize and tame the armies of demons; to cause people who like the military to come and observe demon quelling, so their minds will be subdued; to show that no one in the world can oppose the powers of enlightening beings; to arouse the courage and strength of all sentient beings; out of pity for the sentient beings of degenerate times; to show that even up to the site of enlightenment there are still hordes of demons who come to create disturbance, and only after this does one finally manage to get beyond the reach of demons; to show that the force of afflictions is weak and inferior compared with the mighty power of great compassion and virtue; and to do what must be done in a polluted, evil world. These are the ten reasons why great enlightening beings manifest demon-conquering.

"Great enlightening beings have ten kinds of attainment of powers of the enlightened: they attain the powers of the enlightened because they transcend the afflictive activities of all demons; because they fulfill all enlightening practices and master all concentrations of enlightening beings; because they fully accomplish all the far-reaching meditations of enlightening beings; because they fulfill all the pure means of fostering enlightenment; because they attain illumination of knowledge of all things and can think and analyze well; because their bodies pervade all worlds; because they can support all by spiritual power; because their utterances are equal to the minds of all sentient beings; because they are physically, verbally, and mentally equal to the buddhas of all times, and can comprehend the things of all times in a single thought; because they attain concentration of precisely aware knowledge and are imbued with the ten powers of the enlightened, from knowledge of what is so and what is not so up to knowledge of extinction of contaminations. If enlightening beings acquire these ten powers, they are called buddhas, truly awake.

"There are ten aspects of the turning of the great wheel of teaching by truly awakened buddhas: they are imbued with the knowledge of the four pure fearlessnesses; they produce utterances consonant with the four intellectual powers; they are able to expound the characteristics of the four truths; they accord with the unobstructed liberation of all buddhas; they are able to provoke pure faith in the minds of all sentient beings; whatever they say is not in vain, being able to extract the poison arrows of suffering from sentient beings; they are supported by the power of great compassionate commitment; their utterances pervade all worlds; they teach endlessly for incalculable eons; the teachings they utter are all able to produce spiritual faculties and powers, ways of awakening, meditations, liberations, concentrations, and such phenomena. When buddhas teach, it involves infinite such phenomena.

"When truly awakened buddhas turn the wheel of teaching, by virtue of ten things they plant pure elements in the minds of sentient beings, which are not in vain: because of the power of their past vows; because of being sustained by great compassion; because of not abandoning sentient beings; because of freedom of knowledge able to teach according to the inclinations of sentient beings; because of unerring timing; because of according with suitability and not preaching arbitrarily; because of knowledge of past, present, and future; because buddhas are most excellent, without peer; because their sayings are free and unfathomable; because their knowledge is free and whatever they say is enlightening.

"When buddhas have done their buddha-work, they manifest final extinction because of ten considerations: to show that all activities are really impermanent; to show that all created things are unstable; to show that ultimate nirvana is the abode of peace, without fear; to show those attached to the physical body that the physical body is impermanent, so that they will aspire to dwell in the pure body of reality; to show that the power of impermanence cannot be overturned; to show that all created things do not remain as one wishes and are not under one's control; to show that all existents are like magical productions and are not hard and fast; to show that the nature of nirvana is ultimately stable and indestructible; to show that all things have no birth or origin, yet have the appearance of assemblage and dissolution. Once the buddhas have finished their buddha-work, have fulfilled their vows, have turned the wheel of teaching, have enlightened and liberated those who could be enlightened and liberated, and have made the predictions of buddhahood of the enlightening beings who become honored ones, as a matter of course they enter unchanging, great, ultimate nirvana. These are the ten points of consideration because of which they manifest ultimate extinction in nirvana.

"This teaching is called the far-reaching pure practice of enlightening beings. It is expounded by all the infinite buddhas. It can enable the wise to comprehend innumerable matters and to all become joyful. It enables the great undertakings and deeds of all enlightening beings to continue. If any sentient beings hear this teaching, believe it, understand it, and put it into practice, they will surely be able to attain supreme complete perfect enlightenment quickly. Why? Because they apply the teachings in practice. If enlightening beings do not practice in accord with the teaching, they will be forever estranged from the enlightenment of buddhas. Therefore, enlightening beings should practice the teaching.

"This flower of definitive meaning of the points of virtuous practices of all enlightening beings enters into all the teachings, produces all knowledge, transcends all worlds, is beyond the paths of the two lesser vehicles, is not common to all sentient beings, can illumine all ways of entry into truth, and develops transcendental roots of goodness in sentient beings. This book of the teaching of detachment from the world should be honored, listened to and absorbed, recited and remembered, contemplated, appreciated, and put into practice. People who can do this will soon attain unexcelled complete perfect enlightenment."

When this book was spoken, by the spiritual power of Buddha and by the nature of the teaching, infinite worlds in the ten directions quaked and great light shone everywhere. At that point, buddhas of the ten directions all appeared before the enlightening being Universally Good and said in praise, "It is very good, offspring of Buddha, how you can expound this book of transmundane principles of the flower of definitive meaning of points of virtuous practice of enlightening beings of the highest ranks, which enters into all Buddha teachings. You have learned this teaching well and expound this teaching well; you preserve this teaching by spiritual power. We buddhas all rejoice in this, and as we rejoice for you, so do all buddhas. We buddhas, all of the same mind, preserve this scripture, so that the enlightening beings of present and future who have not heard it may all get to hear it."

Then the great enlightening being Universally Good, by the power of Buddha, looked over all the masses in the ten directions, throughout the cosmos, and said in verse:

Cultivating difficult practices for measureless eons,
Born of the true teachings of infinite buddhas,
Causing countless beings to dwell in enlightenment—
Listen as I tell of the peerless deeds of enlightening beings.

Serving infinite buddhas, abandoning attachment,
Widely liberating sentient beings, without forming such concepts,
Seeking enlightened virtue, minds independent,
Their sublime practices I now tell.

Free from afflicting actions of demons of the three worlds,
Imbued with higher conduct with holy virtues,
Destroying delusions, minds at peace—
I now tell the path they travel.

Forever free of the deceptive illusions of the world,
Showing sentient beings various transformations;
Mind arising, abiding, passing away—they manifest myriad
    phenomena:
I tell of their abilities to gladden all.

Seeing sentient beings born, aging, and dying,
Bound and oppressed by afflictions and troubles,
They want to liberate them, and so inspire them—
Listen to their virtuous practices.

Generosity, ethics, tolerance, vigor, meditation, wisdom,
Skill in means, benevolence, compassion, equanimity, and so
    on—
They practice these for billions of eons:
Hear the virtues of those people.

Seeking enlightenment for billions of eons,
They never begrudge their lives,
Vowing to benefit sentient beings, not doing it for themselves—
I now tell of their compassionate deeds.

To expound their virtues for countless eons
Would hardly amount to a drop in the sea;
Their virtues are peerless, incomparable—
By the power of Buddha I now summarize them.

In their minds, no high or low—
They tirelessly seek the Path,
As they go, causing sentient beings
To live in good, purifying ways.

Their wisdom benefits all
Like trees, rivers, and springs,
And also like the earth
Upon which everything rests.

Enlightening beings are like lotus flowers,
With roots of kindness, stems of peace,
Petals of wisdom,
Fragance of conduct.

Buddha emanates the light of truth,
Causing them to bloom;
The water of the created not sticking to them,
All who see them are delighted.

The tree of sublime ways of enlightening beings
Grows in the ground of the straightforward mind;
Faith is its seed, compassion its roots,
Wisdom its trunk;
Skillful means are its boughs,
Five transcendent ways its branches,
Concentration its leaves, spiritual powers its flowers,
And omniscience its fruit;
Supreme powers are like birds perched in it
As it gives shade to the triple world.

The lion of enlightening beings
Has pure good ways for a body,
The four truths are its legs,
Right mindfulness is its neck,
Benevolence its eyes, wisdom its head,
Wearing the turban of liberation;
In the valley of emptiness of ultimate reality
It roars this teaching and scares all demons.

Enlightening beings are caravan leaders;
They see living beings everywhere
In the wasteland of birth and death,
Afflicted, in dangerous places,
Caught by the bandits of manias,
Ignorant, blind, straying from the right road:
Enlightening beings direct them to the right, straight road
So they may enter the city of fearlessness.

Enlightening beings see sentient beings
Afflicted by the three poisons,
Suffering all kinds of pains,
Feverish, oppressed through the long night;
Arousing great compassion for them,
They explain many ways of curing,
Eighty-four thousand kinds,
To eliminate all afflictions.

Enlightening beings are spiritual sovereigns,
Civilizing beings by the right way,
Causing them to avoid evil and cultivate good,
And wholeheartedly seek enlightened virtue.

Crowned and given predictions of supreme enlightenment
By all buddhas,
They distribute the wealth of sagacity of people,
The jewels of the elements of enlightenment.

Enlightening beings turn the wheel of teaching
Just like what the buddhas turn;
Conduct is its hub, concentration the spokes;
Knowledge is their adornment, wisdom is their sword.
Having defeated the bandit afflictions
And slaughtered the enemy demons,
They put false teachers to flight
Whenever they see them.

Enlightening beings' ocean of knowledge and wisdom
Is boundlessly deep and wide,
Suffused with the flavor of truth,
Filled with jewels of attributes of enlightenment.
A great mind is its boundless shore,
Omniscience is its tide:
No sentient beings can measure it,
It can never be fully explained.

Enlightening beings' polar mountain
Goes beyond the world:
Concentration of spiritual capacity its peak,
The great mind rests immovable.
Any who approach it
Are imbued with its color of wisdom.
It is far beyond all realms of objects;
There is no one who does not see it.

Enlightening beings are like diamond,
Determined to find omniscience,
Their faith and austere practice
Steadfast and unshakable.
Their minds without fear,
They aid living beings
And thoroughly annihilate
All demons and afflictions.

Enlightening beings' great benevolence and compassion
Are like layers of dense clouds;
Three superknowledges flash lightning,
Paranormal powers thunder,
And with the four intellectual powers
They rain water of eight qualities
Moistening all to relieve
The fever of afflictions.

The citadel of truth of enlightening beings
Has transcendent wisdom for walls,
Conscience for a deep moat,
Knowledge as its battlements.
Opening wide the gate of liberation,
Right mindfulness always guards it.
The four truths are the level royal road,
The six spiritual powers are the arsenal.
The banners of the great Teaching
Are hoisted all around;
The demons of the three worlds
Cannot enter at all.

The condor of enlightening beings
Has magic for its steady feet,
Skillful means for its mighty wings,
Kindness and compassion its clear eyes;
Perched on the tree of all knowledge,
It watches the ocean of existence,

Snatches human and celestial dragons
And places them on the shore of nirvana.

Enlightening beings' sun of truth
Rises in the world,
Its full orb of conduct
Running swiftly by psychic travel,
Shining with the light of wisdom,
Maturing the herbs of faculties and powers,
Destroying the darkness of afflictions,
Evaporating the ocean of craving.

The moon of the light of knowledge of enlightening beings
Has the realm of reality for its sphere,
Coursing through ultimate emptiness,
Seen by all the world.
In the minds of consciousness of the three worlds,
It waxes and wanes through time.
Among the stars of the Two Vehicles,
It has no peers at all.

The bodies arrayed with virtues
Of enlightening beings, spiritual sovereigns,
Are replete with all embellishments and marks of greatness,
Looked up to by all humans and celestials.
Pure eyes of skillful means,
A diamond scepter of wisdom,
They have mastery of spiritual law
And civilize beings with truth.

Enlightening beings, as great Brahma lords,
Independently transcend the three worlds;
They have ended all confusion by actions
And are imbued with benevolence and equanimity.
Everywhere they manifest their bodies
And enlighten with the voice of truth.
In the three worlds
They uproot erroneous views.

Enlightening beings, as controlling celestials,
Are beyond the realm of birth and death;
Their sphere is always pure,
Their wisdom never recedes.
Ending the path of lesser vehicles,
They receive the spiritual coronation.

Full of virtue and knowledge,
Their fame is heard everywhere.

Enlightening beings' knowing mind
Is clear and pure as space:
There is no essence, no reliance—
All is ungraspable.

They have great autonomous power,
Able to accomplish tasks in the world.
Themselves embodying pure conduct,
They induce others to do likewise.

Enlightening beings' earth of skills
Benefits sentient beings;
Enlightening beings' water of compassion
Drowns afflictions;
Enlightening beings' fire of wisdom
Burns the brush of delusive conditioning;
Enlightening beings' wind of nonabiding
Goes through the void of existence;
Enlightening beings are like precious jewels,
Able to save the poor;
Enlightening beings are like thunderbolts,
Able to smash perverted views;
Enlightening beings are like ornaments,
Adorning the body of existence;
Enlightening beings are like wishing jewels,
Enhancing all actions.

Enlightening beings' virtues are like flowers,
Always producing the branches of enlightenment;
Enlightening beings' vows are like garlands,
Always hung on the necks of sentient beings;
The fragrance of enlightening beings' pure conduct
Is sustained, without neglect or offense;
The perfume of enlightening beings' knowledge
Scents the three worlds;
Enlightening beings' powers are like screens
Able to block the dust of afflictions;
Enlightening beings' knowledge is like a standard,
Able to defeat the enemy pride;
Their sublime action is colored silk
Adorning their knowledge;
Conscience is clothing
Covering all living beings;

Enlightening beings' unobstructed vehicle
They ride out of the three worlds.

Enlightening beings' elephant of power
Is tame at heart;
Enlightening beings' horse of psychic travel
Bounds over all existences;
Enlightening beings, dragons of teaching,
Shower on the minds of all beings;
Enlightening beings, udumbara flowers,
Are rarely met in the world;
Enlightening beings, courageous generals,
Subdue all demons;
Enlightening beings' wheel of teaching
Is like what the buddhas turn;
Enlightening beings' lamp disperses darkness
So people can see the right road;
Enlightening beings' river of virtue
Always follows the course of truth.

Enlightening beings' bridge of effort
Liberates all kinds of beings;
Their great knowledge and universal vows
Together make a sturdy ship,
Bringing in sentient beings
And settling them safely on the shore of enlightenment.
Enlightening beings' garden of freedom
Truly delights sentient beings;
Enlightening beings' flowers of liberation
Adorn the palace of knowledge;
Enlightening beings are like wonderful medicines
Destroying the diseases of afflictions;
Enlightening beings are like the snowy mountains,
Producing the herb of wisdom;
Enlightening beings are equal to buddhas,
Awakening sentient beings.

In buddhas' mind is nothing else
But true awakening and awakening others;
Whence buddhas come forth,
Thence come enlightening beings;
And like the omniscient,
They enter universality by knowledge.

Enlightening beings skillfully lead
All living beings;

Enlightening beings naturally awaken
To the sphere of omniscience;
Enlightening beings' measureless power
Cannot be destroyed by the world;
Enlightening beings' fearless knowledge
Knows sentient beings and phenomena:
All worlds,
Forms and characteristics different,
Their languages and terms,
They can all distinguish.

Though detached from name and form,
They manifest various appearances;
No sentient beings can fathom their path:
Such virtues have enlightening beings accomplished.

Realizing natures are all natureless,
They have no clinging to existence or nonexistence;
This universal knowledge
Has no end and no dependence:
I now will explain
In order to gladden sentient beings.

Though knowing the appearances of things
Are like illusions, all empty and null,
Yet with compassion and commitment
And the spiritual power of buddhas
Enlightening beings, by mystical projection,
Show innumerable various things.
Such qualities as this
You all should hear about.

With one body they can manifest
Unlimited different bodies;
Without mind or object,
They respond to all beings.

In one voice
They can utter all words;
The languages of all beings
They can produce according to type.

Forever free of an afflicted body,
They manifest an autonomous body;
They know things cannot be explained,
Yet make various explanations.

Their minds are always silent and cool,
Clear and pure as space,
Yet they adorn lands everywhere,
Showing all beings.

They have no attachment to the body
Yet are able to manifest bodies
In all worlds,
Taking on birth according to need.

Though born in all places,
They do not dwell on birth;
They know bodies are like space,
Variously appearing, according to mind.

The body of enlightening beings is boundless,
Appearing in all places,
Always honoring and serving
The most worthy of people.

Perfumes, flowers, music,
Banners, pennants, and jeweled canopies,
They present to the buddhas,
Always with a pure mind.

Without leaving the assembly of one buddha
They are present in all buddhas' places;
In those great congregations
They ask about problems and listen to the Teaching.

Hearing the Teaching, they enter concentration
On each of numberless points,
And likewise emerge from concentration
With endless manifestations.

With knowledge and skill in means
They realize the world is all illusory,
Yet are able to manifest boundless
Illusory things of the world.

They manifest various forms,
As well as minds and languages;
They enter the net of ideas,
Yet without ever clinging.

Sometimes they manifest initial determination
To benefit the world;

Sometimes they manifest long-time practice,
Boundlessly extensive.

Charity, morality, tolerance, energy,
Meditation, and wisdom,
The four boundless minds, four integrative practices,
And all such higher principles
They may show carried to fulfillment,
Accepting them without false notions.

Sometimes they manifest immanent buddhahood,
Anointed and crowned by the enlightened;
Sometimes they appear like listeners,
Or like the self-awakened.
Everywhere in ultimate nirvana,
Still they do not give up enlightenment practice.

They may appear as Indras,
Or as Brahma kings,
Sometimes surrounded by goddesses,
Sometimes alone and silent.

Sometimes they appear as monks
Quietly taming their minds;
Sometimes they appear as monarchs,
Ordering the laws of society.

Sometimes they appear as artful women,
Sometimes as ascetics;
They may appear to enjoy sensual pleasures
Or to enter meditations.

Sometimes they appear newborn,
Sometimes young, old, or dying;
Any who tried to conceive of this
Would be doubtful and go mad.

Sometimes they appear in celestial palaces,
Sometimes they manifest spiritual descent;
Sometimes they enter or abide in the womb,
Sometimes they are buddhas preaching.

Sometimes born, sometimes extinct,
Sometimes they appear to enter halls of learning;
They may be with consorts,
Or apart from society practicing meditation.

Sometimes they sit on the site of enlightenment
And naturally realize true awakening;
Sometimes they manifest active teaching,
Or they may appear as beginning seekers of truth.

They may appear as embodiments of Buddha,
Sitting at peace in infinite lands;
Or they may be cultivating the nonregressive path,
Accumulating means of enlightenment.

They penetrate countless ages
And reach the Other Shore of them all,
Infinite ages a single moment of thought,
A single moment of thought, infinite ages.

All ages are not ages,
But they show them as ages to the world;
There is no advent and no accumulation,
Yet they accomplish the tasks of the ages.

In a single atom
They see all buddhas
In all places everywhere,
There being nowhere there is no buddha.

Lands, beings, phenomena—
They see them all, in order,
Through incalculable ages,
Ultimately inexhaustible.

Enlightening beings know the number of living beings
Is vast beyond bound:
All those creatures' bodies
Arise from measureless causal relations;
As they know one is infinite,
So indeed are all.

According to their competence,
They teach the uninstructed;
They know the faculties of sentient beings,
Superior, middling, inferior, are not the same.

They also know faculties change,
And which can be taught and which cannot,
And that one faculty and all faculties
Are mutually interrelated,

And their subtle individual differences,
And their precise order.

They also know the mental behavior
Of beings past, present, and future,
Their inclinations and understandings,
All their vexing habits.
They realize all actions
Have no coming or going.

Once they know people's behavior,
They tell them the unexcelled Teaching.
They know thoroughly all kinds
Of defiled and pure conduct;
In an instant becoming enlightened,
They accomplish omniscience.

Dwelling in buddhas' inconceivable
Mind of ultimate knowledge,
Instantly they are able to know
The actions of all beings.

Having mastered the functional power
Of enlightening beings' spiritual knowledge,
They can in a single moment
Travel to boundless lands.

Going swiftly like this
Throughout endless ages,
There is nowhere they do not reach,
Yet without stirring a hair.

Just as a skilled magician
Makes all kinds of forms appear
Yet one finds in those illusions
Neither form nor nonform,
Likewise do enlightening beings
Use the magic of knowledge of means
To manifest various forms
Throughout the world.

As the clear sun and moon,
Bright mirrors in the sky,
Reflect in myriad waters
Without being mixed up by the waters,
Likewise, you should know,

Enlightening beings' wheel of truth
Appears in the water of minds in the world
Without being mixed up by the world.

Just as a man in a dream
Makes all kinds of things
And may go on for millennia
Without one night ending,
Enlightening beings dwelling in the essence of reality
Reveal all phenomena,
And while countless eons may end,
Their instantaneous knowledge is endless.

As in mountain canyons
And in palatial halls
All sounds are echoed
Without discrimination,
Enlightening beings dwelling in the essence of reality
Can, with autonomous knowledge,
Widely utter words adapted to types,
Also without discrimination.

As one seeing a mirage
And thinking it is water
Chases it but finds no drink
And becomes even thirstier,
So too is the case
Of sentient beings' afflicted minds;
Enlightening beings take pity on them,
Rescue them and free them.

Seeing form as like clustered foam,
Sensations as like bubbles on water,
Conceptions as like heat waves,
Dispositions as like the pith of a plantain tree,
And consciousness as like magic
Manifesting various things,
Thus knowing the clusters as such,
The wise have no attachments.

The mediums of sense are all empty and silent,
Yet turn like the cogs of a machine;
The elements are in essence unconnected,
Yet fabricate the appearance of the world.
Enlightening beings abide in real truth,
The supreme truth of voidness;

They teach widely in many ways,
Yet their minds do not dwell on anything.

There is no coming and no going,
And also no remaining,
Yet afflictive actions, the cause of suffering,
Continue to flow and develop.

That which is interdependently originated
Is neither existent nor nonexistent, not real or false:
Thus do enlightening beings enter the middle way
And teach it without attachment.

They are able in an instant
To manifest the minds of past, present, and future,
And all the various phenomena
Of the realms of desire, form, and formlessness.

Following the three modes of conduct,
They expound the three liberations,
Define the paths of the Three Vehicles,
And accomplish omniscience.

They comprehend what is so and what is not,
All actions and all faculties,
Realms, understandings, meditations,
Where all paths lead,
Recollection of past lives, clairvoyance,
And annihilating all delusion.

They know the ten powers of buddhas,
But cannot yet fully achieve them;
They realize all things are void,
Yet always seek the sublime Teaching;
They are not mixed up in afflictions,
Yet still do not annihilate contamination.

With extensive knowledge of ways of emancipation
They liberate sentient beings;
In this they attain fearlessness
And do not give up cultivating their practices.

Unerring, not deviating from the Path,
They do not lose right mindfulness.
Their vigor, determination, concentration,
And meditative wisdom are undiminishing.

Pure in conduct, meditation, and altruism,
They clearly understand all times;
With great compassion for sentient beings,
They are totally unimpeded.

By entering these gates of truth
They accomplish such practices:
I now tell a little
Of the sense of their arrays of virtue.

Even if one told of their practices for countless eons
One would never exhaust them;
Now I tell a little bit,
Like a mote of dust of the earth.

Resting on buddha-knowledge,
They generate extraordinary thoughts,
Cultivate the best of actions,
And embody great benevolence and compassion.

Heroically striving, inwardly at peace,
They teach and enlighten conscious beings;
Abiding by pure precepts,
They fulfill practices leading to enlightenment.

Able to comprehend buddhas' virtues,
Sentient beings, actions, and lands,
They also know all ages
With never a thought of weariness.

With total command of differentiating knowledge,
They arrive at the meaning of truth;
They contemplate and explain the incomparable,
Peaceful, and calm true awareness.

They generate the mind of Universal Good
And cultivate the actions and vows;
With the causal power of compassion,
They proceed on the Path pure in mind.

Practicing the transcendent ways,
They perfect conscious knowledge;
Realizing power and freedom,
They attain unexcelled enlightenment.

Achieving impartial knowledge,
They expound the supreme truth;

Able to preserve it, endowed with sublime intelligence,
They arrive at the position of the supreme teacher.

Avoiding all attachments,
They expound impartiality of mind;
Generating knowledge and wisdom,
They produce miracles and attain enlightenment.

Preserving the truth through all ages,
The knowers are most joyful;
Deeply penetrating it and relying on it,
They have no fear or confusion.

They realize the inconceivable,
Unravel artful mysteries;
They skillfully enter concentrations
And see all spheres of knowledge.

Consummating the liberations,
They exercise spiritual insights;
Forever free from veils and bonds,
They roam freely in gardens and groves.

Virtuous ways are their mansions,
All their deeds are admirable;
They cause boundless adornments to appear,
Their minds unmoved by the world.

Observing well, profoundly intent,
They can elucidate with wonderful eloquence
The pure marks of enlightenment,
The light of knowledge illumining all.

Their dwelling place is peerless,
Their minds are indomitable;
Their will is like a high mountain,
Their virtues like a deep ocean.

They rest in truth like treasure,
Wear the armor of vows,
Undertake great works,
Ultimately invulnerable.

They gain the destiny of enlightenment,
And are steadily broad-minded;
Their hidden resources are inexhaustible,
They awaken to all truths.

Masters of worldly knowledge,
They function subtly, without obstruction:
Sentient beings, all lands,
And all kinds of phenomena,
Embodiments, vows, and realms,
Knowledge, spiritual capacities, and so on,
They manifest in the world,
Countless hundreds of billions.

Their spiritual powers and states
Are free—none can inhibit them;
They are adorned with all works
Of powers, fearlessnesses, and unique buddha-qualities.

Their bodies and physical deeds,
Their words and purified speech,
Are under protection,
So they can accomplish ten things.

When enlightening beings are first inspired
And when their minds pervade all,
Their senses are undistracted
And they attain higher faculties.

With profound minds, overmastering minds,
They get away from deception;
With various sure understandings,
They thoroughly penetrate the world.

Abandoning afflictive habits,
They take to the supreme Path;
Skillfully practicing it, they fulfill it
And arrive at omniscience.

Avoiding regression, they enter the absolute
And certainly realize silent extinction;
Generating the Path of enlightening teaching,
They embody epithets of virtue.

The paths, the paths of infinity,
Up to the paths of adornment—
Successively they go by these
Without attachment to any.

Hands, feet, and guts,
With hearts of adamant,
Wearing the armor of sympathy,

Equipped with many weapons,
Heads of knowledge, eyes of understanding,
Deeds of enlightenment their ears,
Pure conduct their noses,
They destroy darkness, unhindered.

Intelligence is their tongue,
Their bodies are omnipresent;
Higher knowledge is their mind,
They cultivate their practices in action and repose.

They walk on the site of enlightenment,
Sit on the lion throne,
Recline in universal goodwill, compassion, joy, and equanimity,
And rest in emptiness.

Their spheres of action and contemplation
Illumine the realm of enlightenment;
Observing the acts of sentient beings,
They spring forth and roar.

Free from greed, they practice pure giving;
Abandoning conceit, they preserve pure conduct.
Never angered, always tolerant,
Not lazy, always vigorous,
Mastering meditation,
Wisdom uncontrived,
Kindly saving, tirelessly compassionate,
They take joy in truth and abandon afflictions.

In all realms
They know meanings and principles;
Their virtues are fully developed,
Their wisdom is like a sharp sword.

Fully aware, they delight in learning
And clearly understand how to proceed;
They know demons and their ways
And vow to get rid of them all.

Seeing buddhas and buddha-works,
They determine to embody them all;
Free from pride, they cultivate knowledge,
Not taken in by the power of demons;
They are supported by the buddhas
And also sustained by truth.

They appear to live in the happy heaven
And also appear to die there;
They appear to abide in the mother's womb
And also show subtle processes.

They appear to be born and smile,
And appear to walk seven steps;
They demonstrate study of arts
And learning in the palace.

They leave home and practice austerities,
Go to the site of enlightenment,
Sit straight and radiate light,
Alerting living beings.

Conquering demons, they attain true enlightenment
And turn the wheel of the unexcelled teaching;
When their manifestations are done,
They enter great extinction.

Those practices of enlightening beings
Are cultivated over measureless eons;
They are boundlessly extensive,
And I now tell but a little.

Though they enable numberless beings
To become established in enlightened virtues,
They ultimately grasp nothing
Of sentient beings and religious principles.

Imbued with such conduct,
They freely exercise spiritual capacities:
They place myriad lands on a hairtip
And for trillions of eons,
Holding innumerable lands in their palms,
Go everywhere, without fatigue,
Then return and place them in their former locations,
Unbeknownst to the beings therein.

Enlightening beings place all lands,
Variously arrayed,
In a single pore
And show them as they really are.

Also in one pore
They contain all oceans

Without increase or decrease in the oceans
And without injuring sentient beings.

Numberless iron mountains
They pick up and crush to dust,
Place each mote in one land,
Using up every particle,
Then take that number of lands
And reduce them to particles too:
The number of these particles might be known,
But the knowledge of enlightening beings cannot be measured.

Through one pore
They radiate infinite light beams;
The lights of sun, moon, and stars,
Of jewels and fire,
And the lights of the gods
Are all eclipsed thereby.

Annihilating the pains of miserable states,
They teach beings there the unexcelled Way.
The various different kinds of speech
Of all worldly creatures
Enlightening beings can utter
In one language:
They can explain distinctly with certainty
All the Buddha teachings,
Causing the living who hear it
To all be very joyful.

All the ages of the past
They place in future and present;
The ages of future and present
They place far in the past.

They show infinite lands
Burning, becoming, and subsisting,
All the various worlds
Being in a single pore.

All buddhas of the ten directions,
Past, future, and present,
They clearly reveal
In their own bodies.

They know the methods of transfiguration
And skillfully adapt to beings' minds;

They manifest various bodies
Without attachment to any of them.

They may manifest the bodies of all sentient beings
In the six states of existence;
Or the bodies of Brahma, Indra, or world guardians,
Or the bodies of all other celestial beings,
The bodies of listeners or individual illuminates,
Or the bodies of realized buddhas;
Or they may appear as enlightening beings
Cultivating omniscience.

They skillfully penetrate the web of beings' thoughts,
Weak, middling, and superior;
And show the attainment of enlightenment,
And the lands of buddhas.

They comprehend the web of thoughts
And gain mastery of thought;
They show all the expedients
Of enlightening practices.

Far-ranging spiritual displays
Such as these they show;
Such realms of experience
No worldlings can know.

Though they produce manifestations,
Nothing is manifested; ultimately this is supreme.
They adapt to beings' minds
To get them to travel the way of truth.

Their bodies, speech, and minds
Are equanimous as space;
Pure conduct is their perfume,
Myriad practices are their clothes.

With the turban of truth, the topknot of purity,
The jewel of omniscience,
Their virtues are all-pervasive,
And they are crowned as sovereigns.

The transcendent ways are their weapons,
Spiritual capacities their elephants,
Psychic travel their horses,
Wisdom their bright jewels.

Sublime deeds are their consorts,
The four means of integration their treasures;
Skill in means are their generals,
Enlightening beings are the rulers.

Concentration is their citadel,
Empty silence is their palace.
With the armor of benevolence, the sword of wisdom,
The bow of mindfulness, the arrows of insight,
They spread the canopy of spiritual power on high
And raise the banner of knowledge.

Their forbearance immutable,
They break right through the devil's troops.

Mental command is the level ground,
Spiritual practices are the rivers,
Pure knowledge the wellsprings,
Sublime wisdom the forests,
Emptiness the clear lakes,
The branches of enlightenment lotus blossoms.

They adorn themselves with spiritual powers,
Always enjoying concentration.
Meditation is their consort,
Nirvana is their food, the taste of liberation their drink.

They freely employ the Three Vehicles;
These practices of enlightening beings
Subtly develop further as they cultivate them
Tirelessly over measureless ages.

They honor all buddhas,
Purify all lands,
And cause all sentient beings
To abide in omniscience.

Even if the number of atoms in all lands
Could be known,
And all realms of space
Could be measured with a grain of sand,
And every thought in the minds
Of all sentient beings could be counted,
Still the virtues of enlightening beings
Could not be fully told.

If you want to be endowed with these virtues
And higher subtle qualities,
And wish to enable living beings
To be free from suffering and always peaceful and happy,
And wish to make body, speech, and mind
All equal to those of the buddhas,
You should make an adamant resolution
To learn these virtuous qualities.

BOOK THIRTY-NINE

Entry into the Realm of Reality

THUS HAVE I HEARD. At one time the Blessed One was in Sravasti, in a magnificent pavilion in the garden of Anathapindada in the Jeta grove, together with five thousand enlightening beings, led by Samantabhadra, the universally good enlightening being, and Manjushri. The names were Endowed with Perspicacious Knowledge, Endowed with Essential Knowledge, Endowed with Unattached Knowledge, Endowed with Blossoming Knowledge, Endowed with Sunlike Knowledge, Endowed with Moonlike Knowledge, Endowed with Undefiled Knowledge, Endowed with Adamantine Knowledge, Endowed with Unemotional Knowledge, Endowed with Radiant Knowledge, Starlike, Mountainlike, Jewellike, Unattached, Flowerlike, Undefiled, Sunlike, Resplendent, Dispassionate, Radiant, Jewel Energy, Great Energy, Knowledge Thunderbolt Energy, Undefiled Energy, Energy of the Sun of Truth, Virtue Mountain Energy, Energy of the Light of Knowledge, Universal Glorious Energy, Universal Light Energy, Earth Matrix, Sky Matrix, Lotus Calyx, Jewel Matrix, Sun Matrix, Matrix of Virtues, Matrix of the Ocean of Truths, Matrix of Radiance, Matrix of Origination, Matrix of Lotus Splendor, Good Eye, Pure Eye, Undefiled Eye, Unobstructed Eye, All-Seeing Eye, Perceptive Eye, Observant Eye, Lotus Eye, Adamantine Eye, Jewel Eye, Space Eye, Universal Eye, Celestial Crown, Crown of Jewels Which Give Birth to All Buddhas, Crown Beyond All Worlds, All-Illumining Crown, Invincible Crown, Crown of Jewels Illuminating All Things in the Cosmos, Crown of the Essence of Enlightenment, Radiant Crown, Crown of Jewels Inset with the Lion Thrones of All Buddhas, Crown Illuminating the Space of the Whole Cosmos, Crest of Lord Brahma, Crest of the Lord of Dragons, Crest of Lights Emanated by All Buddhas, Crest of the Essence of Enlightenment, Crest of Most Excellent Jewels of the Sound of the Ocean of All Vows, Crest of a Spew of Jewels Emanating the Halos of All Buddhas, Crest Adorned with Jewels Showing the Nondifferentiation of All Surfaces of Space, Crest Covered with a Net of the Finest Jewels Representing the Lights Magically Produced by All Buddhas, Crest of Sounds of the Wheel of Teaching of All Buddhas, Crest Uttering the Names of Everything in Past, Present, and Future, Great Light, Undefiled Light, Light of Undefiled Energy, Jewel Light, Dispassionate

Light, Star Light, Light of Truth, Light of Peace, Sun Light, Magical Light, Celestial Light, Torch of Virtue, Torch of Knowledge, Torch of Truth, Torch of Superknowledge, Torch of Light, Flower Torch, Torch of Enlightenment, Torch of Brahma, Torch of Universal Illumination, Jewel Torch, Brahma Sound, Ocean Sound, Earth Roaring Sound, Voice of a World Leader, Sound of Mountains Colliding, Voice Pervading All Universes, Sound Emitted by the Ocean of All Universes, Sound of Crushing All Armies of Demons, Sound Emitted by All Didactic Devices of Great Compassion, Sound of Stopping the Sufferings of All Worlds and Giving Comfort, Born of Truth, Born of Excellence, Born of Knowledge, Born of a Polar Mountain of Virtue, Born of Radiance of Virtues, Born of Splendor, Born of Universal Illumination, Born of Great Kindness, Born of a Store of Knowledge, Born of the Family of Buddhas, Glowing Splendor, Preeminent Splendor, Exalted Splendor, Radiant Splendor, Splendor of Truth, Splendor of the Moon, Splendor of the Sky, Jewel Splendor, Splendor of Brilliance, Splendor of Knowledge, Mountain Lord, Lord of Truth, Lord of the World, Lord Brahma, Lord of the Masses, Lord of Gods, Lord of Peace, Immutable Lord, Mighty Lord, Eminent Lord, Supremely Tranquil Voice, Unobstructed Voice, Voice of Earth, Voice of the Ocean, Voice of Thunder, Voice of the Light of Truth, Voice of Space, Voice of the Roots of Goodness of All Beings, Voice of Encouragement of All Past Vows, Jewel Awareness, Knowing Awareness, Spacelike Awareness, Unattached Awareness, Undefiled Awareness, Purified Awareness, Awareness of All Times, Powerful Awareness, All-Observing Awareness, Awareness of Ways to the Reality Realm.

Beginning with these, there were five thousand great enlightening beings, all of whom had undertaken the acts and vows of universally good enlightening beings and were unhindered in their sphere of action, pervading all buddha-lands. They manifested boundless bodies, going to all buddhas. The sphere of their unobstructed eye was pure, seeing the miracles of all buddhas. They had attained to infinity in revelations, ceaselessly approaching the entries into enlightenment of all buddhas. Their illumination was measureless, having attained the light of knowledge of principles and didactic devices of the ocean of teachings of all buddhas. They could explain virtues forever, through purity of intellectual powers. They were unfettered in the purity of the realm of knowledge vaster than space, being able to appear in the world in any physical form they wished. They were clear-sighted, knowing the realm of beings to be void of beings or souls. They had spacelike knowledge, pervading all universes with a net of lights.

There were also five hundred hearers with great spiritual powers, all of them perfectly aware of the essence of true reason and the principles of truth. They had arrived at direct witness of the limit of reality, had penetrated the nature of phenomena, had gotten out of the ocean of existence and into the realm of space of those who have arrived at suchness, had stopped their propensities and habits and were beyond regression, dwelled in the abode of nonattachment and nonobstruction, were in a state as tranquil as space, had cut off all doubt in Buddha, and had entered the path intent on the ocean of buddha-knowledge.

There were also world rulers, who had served past buddhas, who had accomplished the welfare and happiness of all beings, who were unsolicited benefactors, who had accomplished the protection of others, who had entered into the bliss of the highest knowledge in the world, who were never indifferent toward sentient beings, who issued from the realm of the buddha-teaching, who had accomplished the preservation of the buddha-teaching, who vowed to sustain the lineage of buddhas, who were oriented toward birth in the family of buddhas, who sought omniscient knowledge.

At that time it occurred to those enlightening beings and their companions, to those hearers of great spiritual powers, and to those world rulers and their companions, "It is not possible for celestials or humans to understand or enter into or focus on or know or cognize or think about or perceive clearly or distinguish or elucidate or establish in the body and mind of other beings the sphere of the enlightened, the realm of knowledge of the enlightened, the basis, the power, the fearlessness, the concentration, the state, the mastery, the body, or the knowledge of the enlightened, except by the support, the magic, the empowerment, and the past vows of the enlightened, by having the qualities of roots of goodness perfected by past buddhas, by being in the charge of spiritual benefactors, by purification of faith, liberative means, and knowledge, by attainment of illumination of higher devotion, by purification of the higher will of enlightening beings, and by the proceeding of the higher will on the undertaking of realizing omniscience. May the Buddha show us, enlightening beings and sentient beings—according to our dispositions, different mental capacities, different orientations, different perceptions, different languages, different attainments, different masteries, different stages, different purity of faculties, different mental efforts, different realms of thought, focus on different qualities of buddhahood, and orientation toward various teachings—his past procedure toward omniscience, and show us his past undertaking of the vows of enlightening beings, his past purification of the spheres of the transcendent ways of enlightening beings, the wonder of his past accession to the stages of enlightening beings, his past fulfillment of the undertakings of the spheres of practices of enlightening beings, the appearance of his past accomplishment of the vehicle of enlightening beings, his past purification of the embellishment of the path of enlightening beings, the arrays of his past accomplishments of the ocean of ways of emancipation of enlightening beings, the splendors of the ocean of spiritual transformations he experienced in the past as an enlightening being, the oceans of his past efforts as an enlightening being, the oceans of his spiritual transformations on the threshold of perfect enlightenment, the power of his spiritual manifestations in turning the wheel of truth as a buddha, the oceans of spiritual transformations involved in buddha-land purification, the Buddha's methods of guiding sentient beings to liberation, the Buddha's lordship of the city of principles of omniscience, the Buddha's revelations of the paths of all sentient beings, the Buddha's transfigurations entering into the states of all beings, the Buddha's receiving of gifts from beings, the Buddha's presentations of teachings on right giving to all sentient beings, the Buddha's projection of the image of Buddha into the mental states of all beings, the Buddha's displays of miracles to sentient beings, the Buddha's miracles of teaching and admonishing sentient beings, and the Buddha's inconceivable manifestations of the realms of concentration of Buddha to all beings—may the Buddha show us these things."

Then the Buddha, knowing what the enlightening beings were thinking, entered the concentration known as "the coming forth of the lion," a world-illumining manifestation, of which the body is great compassion, the entryway is great compassion, the guide is great compassion, the means of access to the sky of truth is great compassion. As soon as the Buddha had entered this concentration, the magnificent pavilion became boundlessly vast: the surface of the earth appeared to be made of indestructible diamond, the surface of the ground covered with a net of all the finest jewels, strewn with flowers of many jewels, with enormous gems strewn all over; it was adorned with sapphire pillars, with well-proportioned decorations of world-illumining pearls of the finest water, with all kinds of gems, combined in pairs, adorned with heaps of gold and jewels, with a dazzling array of turrets, arches, chambers, windows, and balconies, made of all kinds of precious stones, arrayed with jewels in the forms of all world rulers, and embellished with oceans of worlds of jewels, covered with all kinds of jewels, with flags, banners, and pennants flying in front of all the portals, the adornments pervading the cosmos with a network of light. Outside the grounds where the inexpressibly vast circle of the assembly was, there was a magnificent array of balustrades, and in each direction was a stairway consisting of a mass of jewels, adorned superbly in a well-ordered fashion.

Also the Jeta grove and buddha-fields as numerous as atoms in untold buddha-fields all became coextensive, vastly expanded, by the power of Buddha. There appeared varied arrays of all kinds of jewels, plains variously set with untold jewels, fences of uncountable jewels set around, and palm trees of various jewels arrayed in rows. Also in those lands were innumerable rivers of fragrant water, winding endlessly, filled with perfumed water, with turbulent rapids of flowers of all jewels, whirling to the right, producing the sounds of the sayings of all buddhas. There were also inconceivable rows of jewel white lotuses, trees adorned with arrays of lotus blossoms made of jewels, as well as inconceivable numbers of rows of towers of various gems, enveloped in nets of all kinds of jewels, arrays of countless jewels radiating webs of light, countless arrays of all kinds of jewels, of celestial chariots of jewels, and arrays of chests of all kinds of incense releasing banks of all fragrances. There also stood innumerable emblems of jewels, emblems of cloth, emblems surfaced with jewels, emblems of flowers, emblems of ornaments, emblems of garlands, emblems of nets of small bells made of all kinds of jewels, emblems of parasols of the finest gems, emblems of jewels pervading everywhere with their radiance, emblems of the finest jewels resounding with the names of all buddhas, emblems of the finest jewels of leonine splendor, emblems of the finest jewels bespeaking the past efforts of all buddhas, emblems of reflections of all objects, arrays of emblems of the finest jewels, well-distributed arrays of ornaments of all kinds of emblems, standing in all quarters.

The entire sky of the Jeta grove was also adorned with inconceivable celestial cloud-palaces, countless clouds of trees of all fragrances, untold mountains of all kinds of magnificent arrays, untold sweet sounds of clouds of music and songs of praise of all buddhas, untold clouds of jewel lotuses, untold jewel lion thrones spread with celestial jeweled cloth with enlightening beings sitting on them singing beautiful eulogies of buddhas, individual pearly clouds in the forms of celestial lords facing the earth, untold clouds of webs of brilliant white pearls, untold clouds of towers of ruddy pearls, and untold clouds of diamond-raining ornaments.

What was the reason for that? So inconceivable is the virtue of the Buddha, the mass of pure qualities of Buddha, the mighty power of Buddha, the miracle of Buddha's pervasion of all worlds with one body, the display by all buddhas of the array of all buddha-lands in one body, the buddhas' display of the reflections of all phenomena in a single atom, the buddhas' display of the succession of all buddhas of past ages in one pore, the buddhas' illumination of the stream of atoms in all worlds with a single beam of light, the buddhas' pervasion of all buddha-lands with clouds as numerous as atoms in all worlds emitted from one pore, and the buddhas' display of the ages of becoming and decay of all worlds in a single pore: as the Jeta grove was in this way purified as a buddha-field, so were all worlds in the ten directions, throughout the space of the cosmos, likewise purified, appearing adorned, decorated, with the body of the Buddha clearly manifest therein, all together in the Jeta grove, filled with enlightening beings, with the ocean of Buddha's audience standing in orderly ranks, clouds raining all kinds of adornments, lights of energy of all jewels, decorations raining from clouds of all jewels, decorations covered with clouds of arrays of all lands, ornaments raining from clouds of all celestial bodies, ornaments raining from clouds of all flowers, flowery ornaments pervading space, clouds of all kinds of cloth raining robes of various colors, ornaments continuously showering densely from clouds of all kinds of garlands and wreaths, ornaments showering in the forms of all beings from clouds of various incenses hovering everywhere, ornaments of fine powders, dense webs of jewels, raining from clouds of webs of flowers made of all jewels, ornaments of clouds of all kinds of precious banners and pennants held by celestial maidens and carried around the sky, ornaments of lotuses of all jewels with circles of leaves of various gems set atop poles with filaments hanging down, their rustling producing sweet sounds, and ornaments of garlands of various jewels on the body of Buddha, a network of images of all jewels—all of these appeared there.

As soon as the Buddha had entered this "coming forth of the lion" concentration of buddhas, from the buddha-land of a buddha named King of Splendorous Illuminating Radiance, in the world Golden Cloud Lamp

Emblem, which was to the east, beyond as many oceans of worlds as atoms in untold buddha-lands, a great enlightening being named Light from the Origin of the Vows of the Illuminator, given leave by that buddha, left that vast assembly and came to this world Endurance along with as many enlightening beings as atoms in untold buddha-lands, adorning the sky with clouds of various magnificent arrays, showering a rain of clouds of celestial flowers, celestial perfumes, celestial jewel lotuses, celestial garlands, celestial gems, celestial ornaments, celestial jewel parasols, and fine celestial robes of various colors, setting up clouds of celestial jewel banners and pennants in the sky, filling the sky with beautiful arrays of clouds of all jewels; having come to the buddha with these, the great enlightening being and the company of enlightening beings paid respects to the Buddha, then, going to the east, magically produced towers covered with nets of jewels arranged all around, and lion thrones inside of lotuses made of the finest radiant gems, and sat on them, after having covered their bodies with ornamental webs of wish-fulfilling jewels.

From the south, beyond as many oceans of worlds as atoms in untold buddha-lands, from the land of the buddha King of the Treasury of All-Illumining Radiance, in the world of Diamond Ocean Womb, a great enlightening being named King of Invincible Energy, together with a company of as many enlightening beings as atoms in untold buddha-lands, given leave by that buddha and having disappeared from that assembly, came to this world Endurance, causing all oceans of worlds to appear decked with webs of all fragrances, causing every place in all buddha-lands to appear decked with webs of garlands of all jewels, causing all groups of lands to appear decked with webs of garlands of all flowers, causing the locations of all buddha-lands to appear decked with webs of braids of all kinds of garlands, causing the congregations in all buddha-lands to be supported by a diamond ground, causing the structures of all buddha-lands to be joined with webs of all kinds of jewels, causing all worlds to appear swathed in all kinds of cloth, conjuring up images of all buddha-lands decked with webs of bundles of garlands bearing images of all jewels, causing all lands to appear decked with webs of strings of the finest radiant jewels illumining all their adornments, and causing all worlds to appear held by a foundation of webs of strings of the most excellent jewels. The great enlightening being and company came and presented all this to the Buddha, then went to the south, magically produced towers of world-illumining jewels with lion thrones inside radiant jewel lotuses, and sat thereon, covering the enlightening beings' bodies with ornamental webs of flowers made of all kinds of jewels.

From the west, beyond as many oceans of worlds as atoms in untold buddha-lands, from the land of the buddha Lamp of Knowledge of the Realms of the World and the Realm of Reality, in the world Lamp Representing the Radiance of a Polar Mountain of Jewels, a great enlightening being named King of Fiery Energy of Universal Splendor, together with a company of as many enlightening beings as atoms in untold oceans of worlds, given leave by that buddha and having disappeared from that assembly, came to this world Endurance, filling all universes with clouds of mountains of fragrant banners of various colors, as many as atoms in untold buddha-lands, filling all universes with clouds of flowers of various scents, mountainous clouds of aromatic smoke of many kinds of incense, clouds of fragrances of various kinds, mountainous clouds of the finest jewels formed by lights from every hair in the shapes of all utensils, mountainous clouds of jewels like stars adorned with various spheres of light, mountainous clouds of spheres of various arrays of diamonds, mountainous clouds of jewels illumining all worlds, mountainous clouds of the finest jewels reflecting the elements of all mountains covering the sky, mountainous clouds of the finest jewels reflecting the appearances of all buddhas, mountainous clouds of jewels resounding with the practices of enlightening beings showing the images of the past efforts of all buddhas, and mountainous clouds of the finest jewels reflecting the summits of enlightenment of all buddhas, all these clouds as numerous as atoms in untold buddha-lands, filling all universes. These the great enlightening being and company brought and presented to the Buddha; they then went to the west and magically produced towers of the finest fragrances covered with nets of pearls, and lion thrones in lotuses made of jewels presenting the appearances of the lord of gods, and sat thereon, having covered their bodies with gold and jewels and put on crowns of wish-fulfilling gems.

From the north, beyond as many oceans of worlds as atoms in untold buddha-lands, from the land of the buddha Glorious Illuminator of the Space of the Cosmos, in the world Luminous Banner of Jewel Cloth, a great enlightening being named King of Unobstructed Splendor, together with a company of as many enlightening beings as atoms in untold oceans of worlds, given leave by that buddha and having disappeared from that assembly, came to this world Endurance, producing in the sky ornamental clouds of diadems of all jewels, ornamental clouds of jeweled robes of yellow color, with a yellow glow, ornamental showers from clouds of jeweled robes emitting various fragrances, ornamental clouds of robes of the finest sunlike jewels, ornamental clouds of robes of jewels blazing with golden splendor, ornamental clouds of robes of fiery jewels, ornamental clouds of robes of various jewels reflecting all the stars, clouds of robes of jewels of pale radiance bursting into view everywhere, clouds of robes of the finest jewels blazing with radiant splendor bursting into view everywhere, and clouds of robes of the finest jewels illumining everywhere with a radiant glow bursting into view everywhere, causing the sky to appear veiled in clouds of robes of jewels in oceanic arrays. These the great enlightening being and company offered to the Buddha; they then went to the north and magically produced towers made of the finest pearls from the sea, as well as lion thrones inside jewel lotuses, and sat thereon, having covered their bodies with nets of majestic jewels and tied starlike pearls in their topknots.

From the northeast, beyond as many oceans of worlds as atoms in untold buddha-lands, from the land of the buddha Independent Eye, in the world Emanating Webs of Light Beams from All the Finest Jewels of the Earth, a great enlightening being named Supreme Moon of Vows Emanated through the Cosmos, together with a company of as many enlightening beings as atoms in untold oceans of worlds, given leave by that buddha and having disappeared from that assembly, came to this world Endurance, causing all worlds to be completely covered with clouds of sandalwood towers, clouds of flower towers, clouds of pearl towers, clouds of diamond towers, clouds of gold towers, clouds of towers of robes, and clouds of lotus towers. The great enlightening being and company presented these to the Buddha, then went to the northeast and magically produced towers of enormous jewels, with turrets with doors looking on all things, and lion thrones in jewel lotuses of incomparable fragrance, and sat thereon, having covered their bodies with nets of the finest flowers and put on crowns of various interlaced jewels.

From the southeast, beyond as many oceans of worlds as atoms in untold buddha-lands, from the land of the buddha Dragon King, in the world Banner of Arrays of Clouds of Fragrance, an enlightening being named King of Fiery Energy of Truth, together with as many enlightening beings as atoms in untold oceans of worlds, given leave by that buddha and having disappeared from that assembly, came to this world Endurance, covering the whole sky with clouds of spheres of golden light, clouds of spheres of light of jewels of infinite colors, clouds of spheres of light the color of the curl of hair between the Buddha's eyebrows, clouds of spheres of light of various jewel colors, clouds of spheres of light the color of the inside of lotuses, clouds of spheres of light the color of superb jewels like circles of branches of jewel trees, clouds of spheres of light like the knot on the head of Buddha, clouds of spheres of light the color of fine gold, clouds of spheres of light the color of the sun, and clouds of forms of the discs of the sun and moon and stars. The great enlightening being and company brought and presented these to the Buddha, then went to the southeast and magically produced towers of flowers of coolly shining pearly radiance, and lion thrones in lotuses of excellent diamonds, and sat there, having covered their bodies with the finest pearls blazing with jewel light.

From the southwest, beyond as many oceans of worlds as atoms in untold buddha-lands, from the land of the buddha King of Universal Light of Knowledge of the Moon of Truth, in the world Filled with Jewel Sunlight, a great enlightening being named Standard of Knowledge Scattering All Bands of Demons, together with a company of as many enlightening beings as atoms in untold oceans of worlds, given leave by that buddha and having disappeared from that world, came to this world Endurance, from every pore issuing, to the farthest reaches of space, shining clouds of flowers, shining clouds of all kinds of music, shining clouds of jewels, shining clouds of precious robes emitting aromatic vapors of various scents, shining clouds of lightning produced by water spirits, shining clouds of radiant jewels, shining clouds of blazing gold jewels, shining clouds of the blaze of diamonds from splendorous mines, and shining clouds of eye-jewels illumining the seeds of events of past, present, and future, like the ocean of memory of the enlightened. The great enlightening being and company presented these to the Buddha, then withdrew to the southwest and magically produced towers of great jewels illumining the cosmos, particles of a web of light beams radiating in all directions, and lion thrones in lotuses of shining jewels like fragrant lamps, whereon they sat, having covered their bodies with nets of the finest jewels from pure mines and put on crowns of the finest jewels reverberating with the sounds of the abodes of all beings.

From the northwest, beyond as many oceans of worlds as atoms in untold buddha-lands, from the land of the buddha Majestic King of Radiant Splendor, in the world Containing Vows of Illumination, a great enlightening being named Flame of Knowledge of Vows of Illumination, together with a company of as many enlightening beings as atoms in untold oceans of worlds, given leave by that buddha and having disappeared from that assembly, came to this world Endurance, emanating from every physical characteristic, every pore, every part of the body, clouds of physical images of the buddhas of past, present, and future, clouds of physical images of the enlightening beings of past, present, and future, clouds of physical images of the audiences of the buddhas of past, present, and future, clouds of images of the spheres of emanations of the buddhas of past, present, and future, clouds of embodiments of images of the past efforts of the buddhas of past, present, and future, clouds of physical images of all hearers and individual illuminates of past, present, and future, clouds of images of the bodies of the buddhas of all times and the forms of the trees at their sites of enlightenment, clouds of embodiments of images of the miracles of the buddhas of past, present, and future, clouds of physical images of the rulers of the worlds of past, present, and future, and clouds of all the purified buddha-lands of past, present, and future, these all pervading space from moment to moment. The great enlightening being and company came to the Buddha, presented these, then withdrew to the northwest and magically produced towers containing the finest jewels illumining all quarters and lion thrones in lotuses made of jewels illuminating the world, and sat thereon, having covered their bodies with nets emanating unstoppable light and put on crowns of jewels whose radiance illumined everywhere.

From the nadir, beyond as many oceans of worlds as atoms in untold buddha-lands, from the land of the buddha King of the Banner of the Torch of Unobstructed Knowledge, in the world Radiance of the Halos of All Buddhas, a great enlightening being named Valiant One with Knowledge to Dissolve All Barriers, together with a company of as many enlightening beings as atoms in untold oceans of worlds, given leave by that buddha and having disappeared from that assembly, came to this world Endurance, emitting from every pore the sounds of utterances of the ocean of all incantations in the world, the sounds of the clouds of the oceans of instruction of the enlightening beings of past, present, and future, sounds of the ocean of vows, undertakings, and methods of all enlightening beings, sounds of the ocean of enlightening beings' means of pervading all lands with their spheres of action, sounds of the clouds of the oceans of all enlightening beings' means of purification and fulfillment of the ways of transcendence, sounds of the ocean of means of the accomplishments and spiritual effects of all enlightening beings, oceans of expressions of the spiritual transformations by means of which all buddhas go to the summit of enlightenment, disperse the opposition of demons, and realize enlightenment, clouds of sounds of the ocean of words used by all buddhas in turning the wheel of the teaching, expressions of the expedient means of teaching and training used to guide all people at the appropriate times, sounds of the ocean of means of teaching using methods appropriate to the aspiration, excellence of roots of goodness, and time, in order to lead to all-knowledge. Emanating these sounds, the great enlightening being and company came to the Buddha and offered them in respect, then withdrew to the nadir, magically produced towers of various mines of all kinds of jewels from the matrix of light of the palaces of all buddhas, as well as lion thrones in spaces held by lotuses inset with all jewels, upon which they sat, having put on crests of jewel emblems reflecting images of all sites of enlightenment and covered their bodies with nets of the finest jewels illumining all lands.

From the zenith, beyond as many oceans of worlds as atoms in untold buddha-lands, from the land of the buddha Voice Revealing the Sphere of Universal Knowledge, in the world Description of the Inexhaustible Lineage of Buddhas, a great enlightening being named Revealing the Base of Cosmic Aspiration, together with a company of as many enlightening beings as atoms in untold oceans of worlds, given leave by that buddha and having disappeared from that assembly, came to this world Endurance, from every physical feature, every pore, every part of the body, every limb and joint, every utterance, every article of clothing and adornment, showing images of the oceans of past efforts of all buddhas past, present, and future connected with transcendent giving which took place in all lands of the ten directions, as well as images of the receivers and the gifts, reflected in every mark and embellishment, every pore, every part of the body, every limb and joint, every utterance, every article of clothing and adornment of the company of enlightening beings as well as the buddha Vairocana; showing reflections of the oceans of their past efforts involved in transcendent morality, in transcendent tolerance—even involving showing amputation of limbs, in the transcendent energy of all enlightening beings, surging boldly forward, in the seeking and attainment of the ocean of meditations of all buddhas, in the seeking of the ultimate truth to which the wheel of teaching of all buddhas leads, in the manifestation of the embodiment of great determination which relinquishes all there is, in the joy of the vision of all buddhas, the path of all enlightening beings, and pleasing all beings, in the arrangements of purification of means of accomplishment of the ocean of vows of all enlightening beings, in the purification of the strength of the attainment of transcendent power of all enlightening beings; and showing images of the oceans of past efforts involved in the sphere of knowledge of all enlightening beings—all these reflected images bursting into plain view by clouds of all kinds of miraculous displays throughout the cosmos. The great enlightening being and company offered these to the Buddha, then went to the zenith, magically produced towers of various arrays of diamonds as well as lion thrones of the universally good enlightening being inside emerald lotuses, and sat thereon, having covered their bodies with nets of fiery jewels and put on crowns of jewels with crests of trailing strings of diamonds vibrating with the names of the buddhas of past, present, and future.

All those enlightening beings, with their retinues, were born of the practices and vows of the Universally Good enlightening being; they had the pure eye of knowledge to see all buddhas face to face; they were endowed with the acute ears to hear the ocean of teachings of all buddhas; they had reached the ultimate transcendent attainment of the masteries of all enlightening beings; from moment to moment they issued manifestations of going to all buddhas; they were in the range of pervading all worlds with one body; they had luminous bodies appearing in the circles of the congregations of all buddhas; they were in the realm of showing the reflections of all worlds and one world contained in each other in a single atom; they had the power to guide and develop all people with appropriate timing; they were in the realm of emitting clouds of teachings of all buddhas from every pore; they had attained the knowledge that all realms of beings are like illusions; they had realized that all buddhas are like reflections; they knew that all existence, states of beings, and births are like dreams; they had pure knowledge that all developments of actions are like images in a mirror; they were intensely aware that all becoming is like a mirage; they perceived that all worlds are like emanations; they had attained the illumination of the knowledges of the ten powers of buddhas; they were fearless and mighty, able to roar the lion's roar; they had entered the inexhaustible ocean of analytic knowledge; they had attained knowledge of expressions of principles of the ocean of instruments of thought of all people; they coursed in the knowledge of the unobstructed space of the reality realm; they had attained unimpeded knowledge of all things; they had purified the spheres of superknowledges of all enlightening beings; they had the rigor to roust out all bands of demons; they stood firm in the power of knowledge of past, present, and future; they had attained unobstructed omniscience; they coursed in the space of independence; they were powerful in the space of the effortless stage of omniscience; they coursed in knowledge of the ungraspability of all existence; they had exposed the knowledge of the ocean of principles of all realms of reality; they had entered the door of nondiscriminatory knowledge of all worlds; they demonstrated the mutual interpenetration of all worlds; they manifested incarnation in all realms of being; they knew the various forms of all worlds, subtle and gross, broad and narrow; they had attained knowledge of the interpenetration of minute objects and immense lands; they could reach all buddhas in a single moment of thought; they had the body of knowledge of all buddhas; they had attained unconfused knowledge of all regions; they could pervade the ocean of all locations in a single moment of thought by mystic metamorphosis.

The whole Jeta grove became filled with enlightening beings of such immeasurable attainments, by the power of the buddhas.

The great disciples, however—Shariputra, Maudgalyayana, Mahkashyapa, Revata, Subhuti, Aniruddha, Nandika, Kapphina, Katyayana, Purnamaitrayaniputra, and so so—did not see the transfiguration of the Buddha in the Jeta grove, the adornments of the Buddha, the majesty of the Buddha, the freedom of the Buddha, the magic of the Buddha, the mastery of the Buddha, the miracle performed by the Buddha, the light of the Buddha, the power of the Buddha, or the Buddha's purification of the land; nor did they see the inconceivable sphere of the enlightening beings, the descent of the enlightening beings, the gathering of the enlightening beings, the descent of the enlightening beings, the approach of the enlightening beings, the miracle of the enlightening beings, the magic of the enlightening beings, the circles of the enlightening beings, the locations of the enlightening beings, the array of lion thrones of the enlightening beings, the mansions of the enlightening beings, the deportment of the enlightening beings, the enlightening beings' mastery of concentration, the enlightening beings' observation, the enlightening beings' emergence, the enlightening beings' vigor, the enlightening beings' offerings to the Buddha, the enlightening beings' bequest of enlightenment, the enlightening beings' development, the enlightening beings' strength, the enlightening beings' clarification of the reality-body, the enlightening beings' fulfillment of the body of knowledge, the enlightening beings' manifestation of the body of vows, the enlightening beings' perfection of the physical body, the enlightening beings' purification of excellence of attributes, the enlightening beings' array of spheres of light of eternal power, the enlightening beings' radiation of networks of light beams, the enlightening beings' emission of clouds of emanations, the enlightening beings' pervasion of the network of all regions, or the transfiguration of the sphere of actions of enlightening beings.

Why didn't the disciples see any of this? Because of lack of corresponding roots of goodness. For they had not accumulated the roots of goodness conducive to vision of the transfiguration of all buddhas, and they had not had the purifications of the arrays of qualities of all buddha-lands in the ten directions described to them, and they had not had the various wonders of all buddhas described to them by the buddhas, and they had not established beings in supreme perfect enlightenment while they were involved in the world, and they had not instilled in others' minds the determination for enlightenment, and they were not capable of perpetuating the lineage of buddhas, and they were not engaged in the salvation of all beings, and they had not exhorted enlightening beings to practice transcendent ways, and while they were involved in the world they had not focused their minds on the stage of knowledge superior to all worldlings, and they had not developed the foundations of goodness conducive to omniscience, and they had not perfected the transmundane roots of goodness of buddhas, and they had not realized the miraculous superknowledge to purify all buddha-lands, and they did not know the source of the great vow of enlightening beings, which is the good root of concentration on unique world-transcending enlightenment that represents the range of vision of enlightening beings, and they were not born of the magical essence emanating from the power of the enlightened, and because hearers and individual illuminates do not share in the knowledge of enlightening beings' control over holding various perceptions as in dreams, the growth of the current of joy of enlightening beings, and the manifestations of the range of the eye of knowledge of the universally good enlightening being.

Because of that, those great disciples, who were the best of the best, did not see the miracle of the Buddha, did not hear it, know it, realize it, penetrate it, did not fix their minds on it, did not notice it, did not focus their attention on it, did not observe it, did not examine it, did not reflect on it, did not contemplate it. Why? Because that is the sphere of buddhas, not the sphere of disciples.

Therefore even though the disciples were in the very same Jeta grove, they did not see those miracles of the Buddha. For indeed they did not have the corresponding roots of goodness, they did not have that purity of the eye of knowledge, whereby they could have seen the miracles of Buddha. They did not know the concentration whose minute point of focus would have given them access to those vast magical manifestations. They did not know that liberation or that spiritual capacity or that might or that power or that mastery or that state or that perception or that power of vision whereby they might recognize or see or penetrate or approach or discover or head for or observe or experience or reveal to others or explain or show or describe or make visible or arrive at or produce or lead beings into the cultivation and realization of the realities of the miracles of Buddha. That knowledge did not belong to them.

Why? Because they were emancipated by the vehicle of hearers, they had realized the path of hearers, they had fulfilled the sphere of practices of hearers, they were fixed in the fruit of hearers; they rested on the knowledge of the light of truth, they were fixed at the limit of reality, they had gone to the state of eternal peace, they had no thought of great compassion and had no pity for the beings of the world; they had accomplished what they had to do for themselves.

They had gathered in the Jeta grove and were sitting there, in front of, behind, and to the left and right of the Buddha, in his presence, yet they did not see the miracles of the Buddha in the Jeta grove. Why? It is not possible for those who have not developed omniscient knowledge, have not accomplished omniscient knowledge, have not set out for omniscient knowledge, have not resolved on omniscient knowledge, have not undertaken omniscient knowledge, have not penetrated omniscient knowledge, have not purified omniscient knowledge, to understand or become aware of or see or discover the miraculous manifestation of the concentration of the Buddha. Why? Because that is discernible only to the range of the vision of developed enlightening beings, not to the range of the vision of hearers. That is why the great disciples, the great hearers, though in the Jeta grove, did not see the transfiguration of the Buddha, the magical appearances of the Buddha, the purifications of the buddha-land, the gathering of the enlightening beings.

The situation was like that of hundreds of thousands of ghosts gathered on the bank of the great river Ganges, hungry and thirsty, naked, without shelter, emaciated, dehydrated by the wind and heat, attacked by flocks of crows, terrorized by wolves and jackals—they do not see the Ganges River, or they may see it as dry, without water, or full of ashes, because they are shrouded by actions that blind them. In the same way the old great disciples there in the Jeta grove did not see or penetrate the transfigurations of the Buddha, because they rejected omniscience and their eyes were veiled by ignorance.

It was like the case of a man who has dozed off in the daytime in the midst of a large group of people and while asleep sees a celestial city with beautiful mansions appearing there in his dream, and sees the whole summit of the polar mountain, with groves and gardens, with innumerable nymphs all around, innumerable godlings living there, and various celestial flowers scattered about, and sees wish-fulfilling trees providing various celestial garments, jewel ornaments, and flower garlands, and sees musical trees producing all kinds of sweet celestial sounds, and many kinds of forms of pleasure and diversion, and hears the sweet sounds of the music and singing of the heavenly nymphs, and perceives himself as being there, seeing the adornment of the celestial arrays all over the place. The group of people who are there in the same place do not see this, are not aware of it, do not observe it, because it is the vision of the man in his dream, not the vision of the group of people in the same place. In the same way the enlightening beings and the world rulers on the verge of enlightenment, by virtue of the tremendous power of the Buddha, by the attainment of their own roots of goodness, by their own undertaking of the vow for omniscience, by development of the qualities of all buddhas, by stabilization in the magnificent path of enlightening beings, by accomplishment of the outgrowths of the teachings of all aspects of omniscient knowledge, by fulfillment and purification of the higher aspirations of the acts of the Universally Good enlightening being, by entering the spheres of knowledge of all the stages of enlightening beings, by mastery of all the states of concentration of enlightening beings, and by unhindered contemplation of all the spheres of knowledge of enlightening beings, saw the inconceivable power and mastery of the Buddha, understood and comprehended, whereas the great disciples, the best of the best, did not see or understand, because they did not have the eye of enlightening beings.

On the snowy king of mountains are many medicinal herbs, which someone who is expert in secret lore and medicine, knowing all the principles of herbal medicine, may go and pick, while herders and hunters on the same mountain, ignorant of herbal medicine, do not know the essence, energy, results, efficacy, or method of application of the herbs. In the same way, those enlightening beings who had entered the sphere of knowledge of buddhas and produced the transformed perceptions of enlightening beings were aware of the transfigured perceptions of the concentration of Buddha, while the great disciples, even though they were there in the same Jeta grove, being satisfied with their own task and having no desire to work for others, being indifferent, dwelt in the feeling of bliss because they were in a condition of bliss in their present state and so were not aware of the perceptions of the concentration and miraculous transfiguration of Buddha.

This earth is abundantly endowed with mines of jewels of all kinds, with hundreds of thousands of deposits, filled with endless supplies of various jewels. Someone who has acquired knowledge of precious substances, sees where the deposits are, has thoroughly studied the appropriate science and technology, and is supported by immense virtue and strength, then can take jewels and enjoy himself as he wishes, properly honor his parents, support his wife and children, and also distribute them evenly to the old, the poor, the destitute, the unfortunate, those without food and clothing. On the other hand, those who do not know about the deposits of jewels, who have not done good works, and have not clarified the eye of knowledge of the precious, do not discover the jewel mines in spite of the fact that they are walking on them—they do not take the jewels and do not do what can be done with jewels. Similarly, the enlightening beings in the Jeta grove who had clarified the eye of knowledge of the inconceivable sphere of Buddha and who had entered the sphere of the inconceivable knowledge of Buddha saw the miraculous transfigurations of Buddha, entered the oceans of principles of the Buddha teachings, attained oceans of concentrations, engaged in the service of the buddhas, took to embracing all truths, took all beings into their care with the four means of integration. The great disciples, however, did not see or notice the transfigurations of the Buddha or the great assembly of the enlightening beings.

It was, again, as if a man came to a land of jewels with his eyes blindfolded by a rag: he might walk around, stand, sit, and lie there, but he would not see the masses of jewels, he would not see the jewel trees, jewel clothes, jewel fragrances, or any of the other jewels. Furthermore, he would not know the use, value, or enjoyment of those jewels. He would not take the jewels and would not know what to do with the jewels. Someone whose eyes were uncovered, however, would see and distinguish them all. In the same way, those enlightening beings, having come to the land of jewels of truth, where the unsurpassed jewel of the enlightened, adornment of all worlds, was right before them, standing in the Jeta grove, saw the Buddha displaying inconceivable miraculous transfigurations. The great disciples, however, were standing at the Buddha's feet and gazing at the Buddha, but they did not see the miraculous occurrence emanating from the sphere of the Buddha's concentration, and did not see the great treasury of jewels which was the great assembly of enlightening beings. Why? They were inimical to omniscience, their eyes covered with the rag of ignorance, and they had not clarified the eye of unobstructed knowledge of enlightening beings, and they did not realize that all things interpenetrate, which is how they could have seen the miracle produced by the inconceivable power of the Buddha's concentration.

Again, it is as if there is an eye-purifier called "possessed of undefiled brilliance," which is incompatible with any darkness or obscurity: suppose someone obtained it and with that eye-clarifier "possessed of undefiled brilliance" went in the dark of night among a huge crowd of people in various postures unable to see in the darkness, and walked around, stood there, sat down, and so on—those people would not see this person or distinguish what he was doing. On the other hand, this person would see the crowd of people, their various postures, positions, locations, appearances, and dress. In the same way, the Buddha, together with his company of enlightening beings, having the pure unobstructed eye of knowledge, discerns and sees all beings. Buddha shows the miracle emanated from the great concentration of Buddha, but the great disciples did not see the miracle emanated from the concentration of great knowledge of Buddha, or the great company of the assembly of enlightening beings.

Also, it is as if a monk in the midst of a large group of people attained the concentration of total absorption in earth or water or fire or wind, or total absorption in blue, yellow, red, or white, or total absorption in heaven, or in the bodies of various beings, or in all sounds, or in all objects, that group of people would not see the body of water, would not see the realm of fire, would not see the various bodies or totality of objects in which the monk's mind was absorbed, except for those who had themselves attained those states of concentration. In the same way, the great disciples did not see the Buddha's revelation of the inconceivable wonder of the sphere of the concentration of Buddha, while the enlightening beings who had attained the path of the Buddha entered into the sphere of the Buddha.

Again, it is as if there were an ointment, which simply by being applied to one's eyes makes one invisible to others while one is able to see others. In the same way Buddha, beyond the world, beyond the spheres of all beings, having entered the sphere of omniscience, can be discerned by the eye of knowledge of enlightening beings, and sees all beings in the world, but the great disciples could not see those miracles of the Buddha.

It is also like the case of the celestial spirit born together with a person and always associated with the person—the spirit sees the person, but the person does not see the spirit. In the same way, the Buddha, in the sphere of omniscience, manifested great miraculous transfigurations of Buddha in the midst of the great assembly of enlightening beings, but the great disciples did not see, did not notice, the miracle of the transfiguration of the Buddha or the magical manifestation of the circle of enlightening beings.

Again, it is like the case of a monk who has attained perfect control of mind and has reached extinction of perception and sensation: he neither perceives nor cognizes and does nothing with his six sense organs, but still is not totally extinct. All the ordinary events of the world are going on there where he is, but he does not perceive or cognize them, because of the overmastery of the power of his concentration. In the same way, the great disciples were in the Jeta grove and had the six sense faculties, but they did not see, penetrate, perceive, or discern the miracle of the power emanated from the concentration of the Buddha, nor did they gain access to, see, or cognize the great gathering of the enlightening beings, the miracle of the enlightening beings, the transfiguration of the enlightening beings. Why? The sphere of Buddha is indeed profound, vast, immeasurable, difficult to see, difficult to realize, difficult to plunge into, completely beyond all worldlings: for all disciples and individual illuminates, the sphere of Buddha is unthinkable and ungraspable. Therefore, the great disciples, even though they were there in the Jeta grove at the feet of the Buddha, did not see the transfigurations of the Buddha, and they did not see or apprehend the great gathering of enlightening beings or their concentration of the arrays of qualities of enlightening beings or their concentration of the arrays of qualities of inconceivable, innumerable purified worlds in the Jeta grove, because they did not have the capacity to do so.

At that time the enlightening being Light from the Origin of the Vows of the Illumination, by the power of Buddha, looked over the ten directions and then spoke these verses:

> See how inconceivable is the enlightenment of Buddha, the best of beings:
> In the Jeta grove he shows the Victor's transfiguration of the enlightened.

> He exercises incalculable independent power,
> Whereat the world is confused, not knowing Buddha's qualities.

> Profound is the miracle worked by the Spiritual Sovereign,
> Infinite, inconceivable, beyond the range of the world.

> The buddhas are adorned with infinite attributes,
> But the truths revealed by the buddhas are signless.

> The Victor shows transfigurations in the Jeta grove,
> Boundlessly deep, most hard to put into words.

> The enlightening beings do not look at the assembly of saints,
> Having come from innumerable lands to see the Buddha.

> They have attained the sphere of unobstructed, unattached action
> By their determination; no one in the world can know their will.

> All those enlightened on their own and the disciples all around
> Do not know their doings or their state of mind.

> The enlightening beings, great in wisdom, are invulnerable, invincible,
> Paragons of heroism, undefiled, certain of the stage of knowledge;

Beyond measure, of great fame, they have attained concentration
And display a miracle extending throughout the cosmos.

Then the enlightening being King of Invincible Energy, by the power of
Buddha, looked over the ten directions and spoke these verses:

Full of virtue and great knowledge, gone to the goal of enlighten-
ing practice,
Givers of security to all worlds—behold these, the offspring of Buddha,
Intelligent, with boundless wisdom and well-concentrated minds,
In the realm of boundlessly deep and broad knowledge.

The great grove called Jeta, where the perfect Buddha sojourns,
Is adorned with magnificent arrays and filled with enlightening beings.

See the Great Oceans, nonreliant, independent,
Sitting on lotus thrones, having come from the ten directions:
Not resting on anything, not grasping, free from falsehood, with-
out abode,
With unattached minds, dispassionate, set on the reality realm.

Exemplars of knowledge, great heroes, with unshakable adamant minds,
In the midst of unperishing truths, they make a show of nirvana.

They have come together from countless worlds in the ten directions,
Come to the Buddha, without any notions of duality.

They see the miraculous transfiguration of the autonomous Buddha,
By the power of which these enlightening beings have come.

They are nondiscriminatory in regard to Buddha teachings and the
plane of realities;
The offspring of Buddha have thoroughly realized that distinctions
are merely mundane conventions.

The buddhas stand in the undifferentiated ultimate limit of the reality realm,
Yet show the differentiation of things by inexhaustible sayings.

Then the enlightening being King of Fiery Energy of Universal Splendor, by the power of Buddha, looked over the ten directions and spoke
these verses:

See the immense sphere of knowledge of the best of beings;
Knowing when is the right time and when not, he teaches the truth
to people.

Destroying the various arguments marshaled by heretics,
He shows beings' spiritual transfigurations according to their
   dispositions.

Buddha is not finite or infinite:
The great sage has transcended finitude and infinity.

Like the sun coursing through the sky giving light every day,
So does the sagacious guide appear, independent of past, present,
   and future.

As the sphere of the full moon shines at night,
So does one see the guide, full of pure qualities.

As the globe of the sun courses through space without stopping,
Such is the transfiguration of the Buddha.

Just as space is independent of all land,
So is the Buddha transfiguration of the Lamp of the World to be known.

As the earth is the support of all corporeal beings in the world,
In the same way is the wheel of teaching of the Lamp of the World
   steadfast.

As the wind blows swiftly through the sky, not sticking to anything,
In the same way does the nature of Buddha operate in the world.

Just as all lands are founded on a mass of water,
So are the buddhas of all times founded on a mass of knowledge.

Then the enlightening being King of Unobstructed Splendor, by the
power of Buddha, looked over the ten directions and spoke these verses:

Like a lofty mountain made of diamond
Does Buddha emerge in the world, savior of all beings.

Like the water of the ocean, immeasurable, pure,
Does the sight of Buddha stop the thirst of the world.

Just as the polar mountain emerges from the ocean water,
So does the Light of the World emerge from the ocean of truth.

Like an ocean filled with deposits of jewels
Is the Independent One's instant awareness of endless knowledge.

Profound is the Guide's knowledge, incalculable, infinite,

By which he shows infinite inconceivable Buddha
  transfigurations.

As an expert magician shows illusory forms,
Buddha, master of knowledge, displays transfigurations.

As a pure wish-fulfilling jewel grants what is desired,
The Victor fulfills the aspirations of those whose intentions are pure.

Like a luminous jewel shining,
Omniscience, pure, illumines beings' minds.

Like an octagonal jewel facing all directions,
The Unobstructed Lamp illumines the cosmos.

Like a water-clarifying light purifying water,
Vision of Buddha purifies people's senses.

Then the enlightening being Supreme Moon of Vows Emanated
throughout the Cosmos, by the power of Buddha, looked over the ten directions and spoke these verses:

As everywhere is made one hue by an emerald,
Vision of Buddha makes beings the hue of enlightenment.

In each atom Buddha shows transformation of various kinds,
Beyond measure, purifying the enlightening beings.

That is extremely profound, unlimited, hard to approach,
In the realm of knowledge of the wise, inaccessible to worldlings.

The full arrays of adornments purified by the works of Buddha
Are perceived by enlightening beings entering the reality realm.

The inconceivable buddha-lands where the Victor appears
Are filled with buddhas surrounded by the wise, everywhere.

The Teacher, master of all truths, the Hero of the Shakyas, has
  come forth:
It is his immeasurable miracle that has appeared.

You see the variety of the infinite deeds of the resolute:
The one of infinite splendor shows endless transformations.

The Leader of the World teaches the offspring of Buddha about the
  reality realm;

And they develop the range of knowledge unattached in all things.

Buddha's wheel of teaching turns by spiritual power,
Filled with hundreds of miracles, purifying all worlds.

In the realm of the Best of Beings, their sphere of knowledge purified,
The Great Dragons, rich in wisdom, liberate all beings.

Then the enlightening being King of Fiery Energy of Truth, by the power of Buddha, looked over the ten directions and spoke these verses:

The disciples trained in past, present, and future, foremost sages,
Do not even know a footstep of a perfect buddha.

Even all individual illuminates
Do not know a footstep of the Protector.

How much less could ordinary beings know the Guide,
As they are bound in chains and wrapped in the dark of ignorance.

Unquantifiable, the Victor cannot be known by any scales;
Endowed with unobstructed knowledge, Buddha transcends the path
    of words.

Radiant as the full moon, steady, adorned with a multitude of qualities,
He passes infinite eons creating transformations.

Thinking of the Buddha in every way with perfect concentration,
Even after untold billions of eons Buddha would still be inconceivable.

One cannot understand the limit of even a single attribute of the
    Independent,
Even while gazing on Buddha, for the qualities of Buddha are
    inconceivable.

Those who are intent on this, and whose minds delight therein,
Will attain these realms, which are so hard to see.

Valiant ones of great resources, intelligent, pure-minded, stable,
Enter into this teaching, made of endless virtue and knowledge.

Great is their aspiration, great their discipline of mind;
They will attain great enlightenment, having arrived at the sphere of
    the Victor.

Then the enlightening being Standard of Knowledge Scattering All

Bands of Demons, by the power of Buddha, looked over the ten directions and spoke these verses:

> Being the body of unobstructed knowledge, the Independent is incorporeal;
> In the realm of inconceivable knowledge, that cannot be conceived.

> The buddha-body is realized by inconceivable pure deeds;
> Undefiled by the triple world, it shines with distinctive embellishments.

> Universal light of the world, having clarified the reality realm,
> It is also the door of enlightenment, the mine of all knowledge.

> Dispassionate, free from falsehood, having shed all hindrances,
> As the sun of the world Buddha radiates lights of knowledge.

> That which removes the fears of existence and purifies those in the triple world,
> The development of enlightening beings is thus the mine of buddhas' enlightenment.

> Buddha shows infinite forms without sticking to any form,
> And shows those inconceivable forms through all living creatures.

> No one can reach the end of the knowledge of Buddha,
> By which inconceivable enlightenment is instantly clarified.

> Inexhaustible exposition of knowledge, wherein are the buddhas of all times,
> Is produced in a single instant, without any change in essence.

> The wise seeker of enlightenment, engaged in endless action, should always think—
> Although it be thought, no thought is born in this thought.

> The inconceivable elements of buddhahood realized by the perfectly enlightened
> Are profound beyond all telling, beyond the scope of words.

Then the enlightening being Flames of Knowledge of Vows of the Illuminator, by the power of Buddha, looked over the ten directions and spoke these verses:

> Those of unerring recollection, pure, born of truth, of certain mind

And inconceivable wisdom, are inexhaustible oceans of
enlightenment.

This is the sphere of action of those whose minds are resolved hereon;
Their knowledge is unshakable, they have ended doubt.

They do not become depressed or dejected;
Their minds are on the way to buddhahood.

Filled with good qualities realized over countless eons,
The peerless seekers of knowledge dedicate them all.

They think about the course of life but do not take refuge in it—
They take refuge in the Buddha teachings, sporting in the realm of
Buddha.

Whatever mundane fortune takes place in the world of sentient beings,
The resolute relinquish it all, for they are set on the attainment of
buddhahood.

Vainly clinging, the world is always fettered—
There, those of unobstructed action are always set on the welfare
of beings.

Unequaled in their action, inconceivable to all beings,
They consider the happiness of the world, whereby suffering is repelled.

They have purified knowledge of enlightenment and are sympathetic
to all beings,
As lights of the world, emancipating all beings.

Then the enlightening being Valiant One with Knowledge to Disperse
All Barriers, by the power of Buddha, looked over the ten directions and
spoke these verses:

The name of Buddha is hard to come by even in a billion eons—
How much more so the sight of Buddha, supreme, which ends all desires.

Buddha appears as the light of the world, gone to the goal of all truth,
Worthy of the offerings of the three worlds, purifier of all beings.

Those who regard the physical form of the impeccable best of beings
Never tire of it even in countless eons.

Offspring of the Victor looking at the form body of the Lord of Humans,

Unattached, dedicate themselves purely to enlightenment, seeking
the highest goal.

This is the door to enlightenment, the corporeal embodiment of the
Great Sage,
Whence issue unhindered, inexhaustible analytic intellectual powers.

Having illumined infinite beings, the Great Sage foretells their supreme
Enlightenment, having led them into the Great Vehicle.

The great field of blessings, a sphere of knowledge, has emerged
And illuminates infinite beings, increasing the mass of virtue.

There is no fear of evil ways for those who associate now with Buddha,
The one who cuts through the net of misery and purifies the mass
of knowledge.

A great mind is born in those who see the Buddha,
Immeasurable wisdom and power is born, radiant as the moon.

They will be sure of enlightenment, having seen the Buddha,
And will be certain that they will become buddhas themselves.

Then the enlightening being King of Superknowledge Discerning the
Differentiations of the Plane of the Cosmos, by the power of Buddha,
looked over the ten directions and spoke these verses:

Having seen the Sage endowed with infinite virtues,
The minds of those dedicated to the Great Vehicle are purified.

The buddhas appear for the welfare of all beings,
Universally compassionate, steadfast, turning the wheel of the teaching.

How can all creatures requite the buddhas'
Countless eons of dedication to their welfare?

It is better to burn in the fearsome three evils for eons
Than not to see the Teacher, who quells all attachments.

All the mass of suffering that takes place in all realms of being
Is tolerable, but not deprivation of the sight of Buddha.

It is better to live long in every miserable way in the world
Than not to hear the buddhas.

Each eon spent even in hell is better

Then elsewhere apart from Buddha, distant from enlightenment.

What is the reason for wanting to live long amid calamities?
It is to see the Buddha and increase in Knowledge.

All miseries are ended once the Buddha has been seen,
And entry into knowledge takes place, into the sphere of the enlightened.

All obstructions are removed when Buddha is seen,
Increasing measureless virtue, whereby enlightenment is attained.

Sight of Buddha severs all doubts of sentient beings
And fulfills all purposes, mundane and transcendental.

Then the great enlightening being Universally Good, having looked over the host of enlightening beings everywhere, to further analyze, discuss in detail, explain, reveal, elucidate, bring to light, illumine, and point out, by means of the cosmos of truths, equal to the realm of space, equal to past, present, and future, equal to the realm of realities, equal to the realm of beings, equal to the realm of all worlds, equal to all sets of actions, equal to the dispositions of beings, equal to the interests of beings, equal to the specific illustrations of truth, equal to the appropriate times for the maturation of beings, and equal to the faculties of all beings, elucidated this "lion emergence" concentration of Buddha by means of ten indications: indication of the succession of all buddhas and the succession of lands in the atoms of the buddha-lands throughout all universes; indication of the seeking and following of virtues of the buddhas in all buddha-lands in space throughout the future; indication of buddhas emerging in all buddha-lands and showing the ocean of infinitely various doors of enlightenment; indication of the hosts of enlightening beings in the circles of the buddhas in the buddha-lands throughout space facing the terrace of enlightenment; indication of pervading the cosmos in a moment of thought with emanations in the forms of the buddhas of past, present, and future, emitted from every pore; indication of the light of magical pervasion of all multitudes of lands in all the oceans in all directions equally with one body; indication of revelation of the power of concentration of all pasts, presents, and futures of the transfigurations of the state of buddhahood in the surfaces of all objects; indication of manifestation of the oceans of eons of various successive transfigurations of Buddha in the lands of past, present, and future, equal to the atoms in all lands; indication of the birth of enlightening beings from the endless power emanating from every pore by the ocean of vows of all buddhas of past, present, and future; indication of endless manifestation of varied expositions of truth amid equal adornments of sites of enlightenment with circles of enlightening beings around lion thrones equal in extent to the cosmos: "These ten, O offspring of the Victor," said Samantabhadra, the Universally Good enlightening being, "are the first ten of as many expressions of the 'lion emergence' concentration as atoms in untold buddha-lands, which I follow. However, these are the sphere of knowledge of those who arrive at Thusness."

Then the enlightening being Universally Good, illuminating the expression of the meaning of the "lion emergence" concentration of Buddha, by the empowerment of Buddha, while gazing on the face of Buddha, observing the ocean of assemblies everywhere, observing the infinitely various transfigurations of the concentration of Buddha in the inconceivable sphere of the enlightened, observing the magical nature of inconceivable knowledge, and observing all teachings expressed in an inconceivably infinite variety of manners of speaking, then uttered these verses:

> Like the atoms of all lands are the oceanic buddha-lands on a single hairtip:
> Surrounded by a circle of enlightening beings, there Buddha rests on the throne of the enlightened.

> In the ocean of buddha-lands on a single hair, on a lotus throne at the site of enlightenment
> Extended throughout the cosmos, the Guide is seen at the trees of enlightenment.

> Like the atoms in all lands are the buddhas assembled on a single hair:
> Surrounded by a host of enlightening beings, they expound all good actions.

> Buddha sits in one land pervading all lands;
> Endless hosts of enlightening beings go there from everywhere.

> Like atoms in countless lands, enlightening beings, radiant seas of virtue,
> Should appear in the audiences of the Teachers, throughout the cosmos.

> Appearing like reflections in all lands, oceans of knowledge of buddhas,
> Established in good practices, they arrive in the assemblies of all buddhas.

> Assembled everywhere in all lands, in the realm of the joy of enlightening practice,
> Delighted in hearing the myriad teachings, they pass millions of eons in each land.

> Enlightening beings carry out their practices coursing in the ocean of truth, emanating light;
> They enter the oceans of vows, established in the sphere of buddhahood.

> Born of the teachings of the buddhas, acting with universal good in mind,
> They enter the oceans of qualities of buddhas, in vast transfigurations.

Pervading the refuge of the reality realm, they constantly emanate a
  cloud of bodies,
Many as atoms in all lands, with the rain of truth, for enlightenment.

Then the blessed Buddha, wanting to establish those enlightening beings
in this lion emergence concentration of buddhas, went on to emanate from
the circle of hair between his brows a light called "illumining past, present,
and future, showing all ways into the reality realm," accompanied by as
many beams of light as atoms in untold buddha-lands, with which he illumined all lands in all oceans of worlds in the ten directions.

Then the enlightening beings who had gathered at the Jeta grove saw, in
every buddha-land in all universes throughout the farthest reaches of space,
in groups of buddha-lands within atoms of buddha-lands as numerous as
atoms in all buddha-lands, in buddha-lands of various powers, various purities, various locations, and various conditions, an enlightening being at the
summit of enlightenment sitting on a lion throne, attended by all world rulers, surrounded by a multitude of enlightening beings, attaining unexcelled
supreme perfect enlightenment, here teaching in circles as vast as untold
buddha-lands with a sphere of sound pervading the cosmos, there gone to
the various realms of existence, or in the cities, towns, communities, and
nations of the human world, teaching the truth by means of various miracles, various modes of conduct, various embodiments, various indications of
ways of concentration, various superknowledges from concentration,
appearing in various castes and races, with various auras of light, radiating
various webs of light beams, with various spheres of sound, in various congregations, setting up various interlocutors, setting up various instructions,
in various words and expressions.

And, as those enlightening beings saw the transfigurations of the profound concentration of the Buddha in all those assemblies, they saw
transfigurations of Buddha throughout the cosmos, in all worlds throughout space, in the arrays of the ten directions, in the sets of cycles in all places,
in the confluence of all spaces, in the media of principles in the various
regions, in the various realms of conception, in the conjunctions of the various regions, in the specific spaces of the various regions, in the oceans of all
regions—that is, in the north, south, east, west, northeast, southeast, southwest, northwest, nadir, and zenith—in the places of the body of lands, in the
places of the body of beings, in the places that are in the conceptions of
beings, in the regions of past ages, in the regions of the present in the ten
directions, in every point in all realms of space, in the locus of each and every
atom of all lands, in the points of entry of all spaces, in the locations of
occurrence of performance of various actions, in the conceptual locations of
infinite surfaces of space in a point the size of a hairtip, those transfigurations reflected in the minds of all living beings, using their languages, in the
perceptions of all living beings, without discrimination among beings,
equal in past, present, and future, coming forth equally everywhere as a
whole, with physical forms coming to all assemblies, descending into the

presence of all bodies of beings, with the same knowledge in all ages, appearing to all beings according to their mentalities, equally, everywhere in all lands, elucidating the teachings of buddhas and guiding sentient beings ceaselessly.

All of them were united by the blessed Vairocana Buddha, by the four integrative methods, by equality of past virtuous actions; they were fully developed by seeing, hearing, and remembering; they had already set their minds on supreme enlightenment; going to the buddhas here and there, they were united by fundamental virtues: in accord with the sameness of their roots of goodness and adoption of means of developing omniscience, the enlightening beings gained access to the projections of the concentration of the blessed Vairocana, which extended throughout the cosmos, to the farthest reaches of space. Some comprehended the reality-body, some the form-body, some the past attainment of Vairocana as an enlightening being, some the fulfillment of the ways of transcendence, some the pure adornment of the sphere of action, some the mystic projection of the stages of enlightening, some the mystical projection of perfect enlightenment, some the unconfused mystical projection of the concentrations in which buddhas sojourn, some the powers and fearlessnesses of buddhas, and some comprehended the ocean of analytic powers of buddhas—they entered into as many such oceans of mystical projections of Buddha as there are atoms in ten inexpressible numbers of buddha-lands. They entered those oceans of mystical projections of Buddha by way of various devotions, various paths, various doors, various entries, various penetrations, various methods, various approaches, various directions, various capacities, various places, various worlds, various attainments, various provisions, various transformations, various means, and various concentrations. Those enlightening beings gained access to the mystical projections, the miraculous transfigurations, of the blessed Buddha Vairocana by means of such enlightening beings; concentrations as these—adornment of the entire cosmos, illumination of the realm of unobstructed knowledge of all times, light of knowledge of the continuity of the planes of the cosmos, entry into the plane of the sphere of those who realize Thusness, illumination of the plane of space, free access to the ten powers of buddhas, bold emergence adorned by the fearlessness of the enlightened, whirlpool of the principles of the reality realm, moon pervading all universes with unhindered sound, and light of principles of universal order.

Those enlightening beings also entered the oceans of mystical projections of buddhahood of the blessed Vairocana by way of such enlightening concentrations as those known as emblem of the king of truth crowned by nonattachment, seeing oceans of buddhas in all objects, emblem of reflection of the different bodies of all realms of being, entry into the unalloyed sphere of the body of those who arrive at Thusness, container of compassion going along with the whirl of all worlds, founded on the power based on all truths, sphere of revelation of ultimately quiescent indifferent equality, universally projected reflection emanated purely without attachment, occult manifestation of the unity of all lands, effectuation of the manifestation of attainment of enlightenment in all buddha-lands, comprehension of embodiment of all oceanic virtues, endless spiritual power to effect the mystical transfiguration of all objects, entry into the ocean of past practices of all buddhas, basis of eternal preservation of the lineage of buddhas, power of devotion to purification of the ocean of all lands in the ten directions of the present, illumination of the states of all buddhas in a single moment of thought, entry into ultimate freedom from attachment to all objects, causing all worlds to appear in one buddha-field, production of emanations of all embodiments of buddhas, adamantine knowledge of the ocean of all faculties, causing all buddhas to appear within a single body, instantaneous state of discovering the principle of all things in the point of a moment of thought, spiritual power of manifesting nirvana in all realms in the cosmos, power to roam on the highest plane, magical manifestation of the differentiation of the bodies of beings in all buddha-lands, entry into the presence of the whirl of all knowledge, complete knowledge and differentation of past, present, and future in a single instant, containing the body of principles of the cosmos in every moment of thought, lion following the lineage of all buddhas, sphere of the eye of wisdom seeing the cosmos in all objects, vigorous undertaking of approach to the ten powers, sphere of the eye of universal vision of all objects, illumination of beings in all spheres of form, space of an unmoving whirl, showing all things in one thing, verbal analysis of truth.

Those enlightening beings also entered the oceans of mystic projections of Buddha made by Vairocana by way of such enlightening beings' concentrations as exposition of truth setting up the standard of all buddhas, illumination unattached to the borders of past, present, and future, continuous knowledge of all ages, entry into the ten powers by subtle means, accomplishment of unbreakable practice of the essence of enlightenment through all ages, clouds swiftly appearing everywhere, creation of magical appearances of attainment of enlightenment, characterized by all pleasures of feeling, adornment of space with all kinds of magnificent arrays, moment to moment producing clouds of crested images like beings of the world, light of the moon of realization of Thusness pure as space, spacelike base of all who realize Thusness, radiance of all spiritual faculties, lamp revealing the meanings of all things, illumination of the sphere of the ten powers, characterized by the brilliance of the buddhas of all times, the unique source of all buddhas, accomplishing undertakings in every passing moment, source of inexhaustible blessing, illumination of guidance of endless vision of Buddha, supreme adamantine basis of all truths, production of universal manifestations of the emanations of all buddhas, consummating the course of the sun of all buddhas, instantly illuminating past, present, and future, sound of the voice emitting universal light illumining the natural quiescence of all things, march to the boundary of vision of all buddhas, aware of all things like a collection of lotuses, observation of phenomena as baseless like the sky, whirlpool of concentration of the ocean of all spaces in one space, entering directly into the ground of all phenomena, oceanic source of all things, tranquil body shining light on all beings, accomplishment of the will for all higher knowledge in a single moment of thought, eternal manifestation of the attainment of enlightenment equally everywhere, entering into all universes by comprehending them as one single array, illumination of the body of recollection of all buddhas, intuition of vast higher knowledge of all worlds, merging one's being with the infinite cosmic principle in a single mental instant, illumination of the homologous order of all things in homologous universes, mystical manifestation of the fiery energy of the spheres of all Buddha teachings, basis of the determination and action taking all realms of beings into the net of Indra, continuity of the ground of all worlds, traveling everywhere by mystic projections of lotuslike splendor, intuitive knowledge of the cycles of the bodies of all beings, magical materialization in the presence of all beings, superknowledge of the means of analyzing mundane speech in the ocean of utterances of all beings, superknowledge of the distinctions of the seeds of all worlds, unalloyed incorruptible matrix of great compassion, entry of all buddhas into the goal of realization of Thusness, and lionlike emergence to behold the abode of liberation of all buddhas.

By entry into as many of the concentrations of enlightening beings as atoms in untold buddha-lands, beginning with these, those enlightening beings entered into the ocean of the blessed Vairocana's mystical projections of buddhahood, and they accordingly remembered equivalent transformations carried out in the past. Furthermore, by the mental-moment-to-mental-moment entry, pervading the whole cosmos, of those enlightening beings, who were in the presence of Buddha in the Jeta grove, sitting on lion thrones in lotuses of various jewels as vast as worlds as numerous as atoms in ten buddha-lands, born of the occult transformation of great knowledge and insight, having attained the stage of penetrating knowledge and insight, contemplating with universal knowledge, born of the source of wisdom, on the brink of omniscience, having unclouded eyes of knowledge, having arrived at the state of leaders of beings, having approached equality with all buddhas, always carrying out the principle of nondiscrimination, with specific knowledge of all objects, relating to all things as naturally calm, in the ultimate asylum of the quiescence and nirvana of all worlds yet upholding the variety of all worlds, going to all lands without attachment, in the midst of all things without reliance on anything, effortlessly establishing the measures of all teachings, knowing how to develop and guide all people, showing all beings the state of peace and serenity, risen to the realm of the abode of knowledge and liberation, embodying knowledge gone to the limit of dispassion, having emerged from the ocean of all existences, observing the limit of reality of all worlds, in the sphere of light of knowledge of the ocean of truths, with great compassionate minds perfectly unified by oceanic concentration, thoroughly aware of the principle of the illusoriness of phenomena, having comprehended that all worlds are like dreams, knowing the vision of all buddhas are like reflections, aware that all utterances are like echoes, knowing that the effects of all things are like magic productions, determined to reach the sphere of fulfillment, following skillful methods of purification of the sphere of universal knowledge, with ultimately peaceful and calm minds, with knowledge of all families of mystic spells, with fearless, even force of the the power of concentration, with the eye reaching the limit of the cosmos, in the stage of ungraspability of all things, contemplating the infinite ocean of wisdom, gone to the farther shore of transcendence by knowledge, having attained the sustaining power of transcendent wisdom, gone beyond all worlds by consummation of transcendent spiritual powers, masters of transcendent concentration, with correct knowledge of all buddhas' skillfullness in respect to meanings, with knowledge of the means of skillful elucidation of truth, with extraordinary knowledge of expression, being clouds of teaching with inexhaustible power of eloquence, roaring the fearless, mighty lion's roar, enjoying the unequaled bliss of nonreliance, having unclouded eyes seeing into all things, moons of knowledge of the state of intellect of all beings, beams of light of designations of principles of all truths from the sphere of wisdom, mountains of virtue with diamonds of knowledge, beyond all comparison, sprouting the knowledge of all spiritual faculties, heroic conquerors of all demons, full of the energy of the sphere of endless knowledge, physically beyond all worldlings, with unhindered insight into all things, aware of the bounds of finiteness and infinity, standing on the limit of reality, tallying with the universal limit, having the eye of knowledge observing signlessness, skilled in the causes of accomplishment of all practices of enlightening beings, coursing in nondualistic knowledge, observing all worldly trends, appearing in all buddha-lands without dwelling, free from obscurity in regard to all things, having reached the sphere of knowledge without darkness, engaged in the illumination of truth everywhere, excellent fields of blessings for all beings, moons of fulfillment of the wishes of all who see or hear of them, mountains of virtue rising above all worlds, bravely subduing all challengers, making their voices heard in all buddha-lands, tirelessly watching all the buddhas, able to control reflections of the bodies of all buddhas, adopting appropriate forms to guide all beings, pervading all lands with one body, having purified their spheres of accomplishment, having the capacity for the vehicle of great knowledge unobstructed as space, reflecting the bodies of all things in their sphere of knowledge, suns of knowledge appearing in all worlds, having the power to adapt to all worlds at will, having specific knowledge of the various dispositions and faculties of all beings, having arrived at all truths with unobstructed perspective, apprised of the inherent nature of all things being birthlessness, mature in the knowledge of the mutual interpenetration of the subtle and gross, resolved on the goal of the profound state of buddhahood, knowing the verbal designations of profound meaning, eloquently telling the meanings of endless words and expressions, expounding entry into the ocean of all scriptures by one word, supporting the vast body of knowledge of mystic formulae, having the power to hold them forever, knowing specifically their abodes over untold ages in a single moment of thought, having occult knowledge of all worlds, knowing past, present, and future in a single moment of thought, reflecting the infinite ocean of buddha-teachings in mystic formulae holding all principles, tirelessly turning the wheel of teaching leading all beings to knowledge, illumined with the knowledge of the sphere of buddhas, always in the concentration of good vision, having the superknowledge that discerns the differences among all things while being ultimately unattached, master of knowledge of the sphere of liberation, the highest of all states, causing all objects to appear in pure arrays, entering into the universes of the ten directions wherever they are, entering into the different universes in all directions, conscious of enlightenment in atomic particles subtle and gross, showing all colors beautiful in nature, concentrating the totality in one space, treasuries of knowledge and virtue mature in the knowledge of infinite qualities of one form, praised by all buddhas, having qualities that can never be fully told—those enlightening beings who had gathered at the Jeta grove and were sitting there immersed in the ocean of qualities of Buddha, illumined by rays of light from the buddhas, as they were in a state of great ecstasy, having attained the light of the inconceivable state of enlightening beings, from their ecstasy emanated great arrays of mystical projections pervading all universes, issuing from all of their bodies, their towers, their paraphernalia and their thrones, from everywhere in the Jeta grove: in each successive mental moment they emanated vast clouds of webs of light beams, pleasing to all worlds, suffusing the ten directions; they filled the ten directions with clouds of bells of all jewels ringing with sounds bespeaking the virtues and qualities of the buddhas of past, present, and future; they filled the ten directions with clouds of voices of all beings, issuing from all objects, making sweet sounds telling of the fruits of all beings' actions; they filled the ten directions with clouds of forms showing the vows of all enlightening beings and the various practices of enlightening beings, emanating voices telling of the undertakings of all enlightening beings; they emanated clouds of beatified embodiments of enlightening beings filling the ten directions telling of the succession of buddhas in all lands; they emanated clouds of sites of enlightenment like those of all buddhas of past, present, and future, filling the ten directions, showing magnificent displays of the transcendent enlightenment and emancipation of all buddhas; from all objects they emanated clouds of bodies of ruling water spirits, showering rain of all fragrances throughout the ten directions; they emanated clouds of bodies like the rulers of all worlds, pervading the ten directions, telling of the conduct of the enlightening being Universally Good; from all objects they sent forth clouds of reflections of all perfectly pure buddha-lands, made of all jewels, filling the ten directions, showing the turnings of the wheels of teachings of all buddhas. They emanated as many such clouds of magical displays of great magnificent arrays as atoms in untold buddha-lands, by the mystic power of those enlightening beings, and by virtue of their state of attainment of illumination of the inconceivable ocean of truths.

Then the enlightening being Manjushri, empowered by Buddha, observing all those mystical apparitions appearing throughout the ten directions, uttered these verses:

> Observe the infinite, vast power of Buddha arisen in the Jeta grove,
> Having emanated clouds of bodies as sense objects that pervade all
>> directions.

> The vast, pure arrays of offspring of Buddha, various, of infinite forms,
> Are all seen reflected from the thrones, which contain the objects
>> of sense.

> Clouds of jewel radiance, in various arrays, pervade the land, pour-
>> ing forth
> From the pores of the offspring of Buddha, emitting the sounds of
>> Buddha.

> Forms like Brahma and Indra, with pure bodies and tranquil deportment,
> Emerging from the trees and flowers, go forth telling of meditation.

> Enlightening beings like Universally Good, adorned with embellish-
>> ing marks,
> Inconceivable, countless, are produced from the Buddha's pores.

> Those clouds of adornments of the Oceans of Virtue bespeak the qualities
> Of the enlightening beings of all times, gathered in the Jeta grove.

> All the varied oceans of deeds of groups of beings in all directions
> Are heard, radiating from within the trees in the Jeta grove.

> Transfigurations of all buddhas of past, present, and future in
>> every land
> Appear from the ground, in every single object, numerous as atoms.

> At each and every point various oceanic clouds of buddhas
> Continuously reveal the abodes of the Victors and the masses of bud-
>> dhas there.

> As many as beings, pervading everywhere, as they develop beings by
>> expedient means,
> From their auras emerge oceanic clouds of fragrant flames and masses
>> of flowers.

> Precious mansions, measureless as the sky, adorned with all realities,
> Fill the lands in all directions, and all sites of enlightenment.

All the lands of the offspring of Buddha in past, present, and future, great healers,
Purified by means of the practice of universal good,

Their various arrays, purified over oceans of eons, infinite as beings,
Are all seen by reflection in the sky of the Jeta grove.

At that point, each of those enlightening beings, illuminated by the light of the concentration of Buddha, entered as many gates of great compassion as atoms in untold buddha-lands, and attained even greater capability to treat all beings beneficially. Thus concentrated, from each of their pores came forth as many rays of light as atoms in untold buddha-lands; from each ray of light came forth as many multitudes of phantom enlightening beings, bodies like those of all world rulers, bodies appearing to all beings, bodies adapted to the development of all beings. Having pervaded the cosmos with their emanations, they enlightened, developed, and guided sentient beings, by means of showing descent from heaven; by means of showing birth in all worlds; by means of showing the sphere of practice of enlightening beings; by means of dreams bearing messages to the mind; by means of release through the vows of all enlightening beings; by means of perfect knowledge of the world; by means of showing the practice of transcendent giving; by means of the positive and negative spheres of the virtues of all buddhas, what they cultivate and what they efface; by means of showing transcendental forbearance, even if dismembered; by means of transcendent energy of the great spiritual metamorphosis of enlightening beings; by means of shining light of the sphere of the path of buddha-knowledge by the meditations, liberations, concentrations, and attainments of all enlightening beings; by means of showing the relinquishment of countless bodies in quest of the meaning of each phase of the teachings in order to find out all buddha-teachings; by means of approaching all buddhas and asking about all the teachings; by means of communicating the light of the ocean of methods and principles of approaching and guiding beings according to the right timing and according to their mentalities, fulfilling omniscience; by means of showing the light of power of the stores of knowledge and virtue of all enlightening beings, which are invulnerable to demons and disputers; by means of showing the stage of knowledge which includes knowledge of all practical arts and mystic knowledge; by means of showing the stage of knowledge which includes knowledge and mystic knowledge of the differences among all beings; by means of showing the stage of knowledge which includes knowledge and mystic knowledge of the differences in the mentalities of all beings; by means of showing the stage of knowledge which includes knowledge and mystic knowledge of the faculties, procedures, and practices of all beings and the destruction of their various afflictions and habits; by showing the stage of knowledge which includes knowledge and mystic knowledge of the various results of deeds of all beings—with as many such means of developing and guiding beings as atoms in untold buddha-lands, those enlightening beings were seen to have come to the abodes of all sentient beings in all states of existence; with nondiscriminatory great compassion, with nondiscriminatory commitment, with nondiscriminatory knowledge, with nondiscriminatory effort to save all beings, for the purpose of fully developing beings according to their mentalities, beings who could be guided by seeing them, by hearing them, by their halos, by the sound of their names, by their auras, by radiating nets of light beams, the enlightening beings in the Jeta grove were seen by various arrays of projections pervading all realms of beings in all oceans of worlds, yet without leaving the presence of the Buddha: some appeared pervading the ten directions, their bodies on their thrones in their towers surrounded by their associates, yet without becoming absent from the presence of Buddha; some appeared emanating clouds of apparitions to develop beings, yet without becoming absent from the assembly around the Buddha; some appeared in the form of mendicants, some in the form of priests, some in bodies adorned head to foot with particular emblematic signs, some in the forms of scholars, scientists, doctors, some in the form of merchants, some in the form of ascetics, some in the form of entertainers, some in the form of pietists, some in the form of bearers of all kinds of arts and crafts—they were seen to have come, in their various forms, to all villages, cities, towns, communities, districts, and nations. With mastery of proper timing, proceeding according to the time, by modification of adapted forms and appearances, modifications of tone, language, deportment, situation, carrying out the practices of enlightening beings, which are like the cosmic network of all worlds, illumine the spheres of all practical arts, are lamps shedding light on the knowledge of all beings, are arrays of mystical displays of all realities, radiate the light of all truths, purify the establishment of vehicles of liberation of all places, and light up the spheres of all truths, they were seen to have come to all villages, towns, cities, districts, and nations for the purpose of leading sentient beings to perfection.

At that time Manjushri, in the form of a youth, was in his tower together with enlightening beings of equivalent practice, perpetually attendant thunderbolt bearers, physical deities who had undertaken the making of power for all worlds and were willingly committed to attendance on all buddhas, footstep-following deities committed to past vows, earth deities intent on hearing the Teaching, greatly compassionate deities of springs, lakes pools, reservoirs, and rivers, deities of fire shining with the radiance of the power of the light of wisdom, crowned deities of wind, area deities with knowledge illumining all regions, night deities involved in dispelling the darkness of ignorance, day deities involved in bringing forth the day of those who arrive at Thusness, sky deities engaged in the adornment of the space of all elements of reality, ocean deities involved in rescuing all beings from the ocean of existence, mountain deities involved in gathering the store of all knowledge with a mind based on transcendentally lofty virtue, river deities engaged in adorning the bodies of all beings with the vow to cause all the qualities of buddhas to appear, city deities engaged in protecting the city of the mind of all beings, and with dragon chiefs devoted to the city of all truths, spirit chiefs able to protect all beings, celestial musician chiefs engaged in increasing the bliss of all beings, demon chiefs engaged in repulsing all ghostlike tendencies, bird chiefs committed to taking all beings up out of the ocean of existence, titans resolved to perfect the power of the body of those who arrive at Thusness, which is beyond all worlds, serpent chiefs with bowed bodies who had attained the joy of the vision of Buddha, celestial chiefs appalled by the whirl of birth and death who looked to what is higher, and most respectful Brahma chiefs in attitudes of reverence; with a parade of such enlightening beings, the enlightening being Manjushri came forth from his place, circled the Buddha hundreds of times to his right, made many offerings to Buddha, then left the presence of the Buddha and went south on a journey in the human realm.

Then the venerable Shariputra, by the power of Buddha, seeing the young Manjushri with this transfigured array of enlightening beings having left the Jeta grove and going south, conceived the desire to go on the journey to the human world with Manjushri. With a group of sixty monks he went forth from where he was and approached the Buddha. Going up to the Buddha, he bowed his head to the Buddha's feet, then gazed at the Buddha; given permission by the Buddha, he circled the Buddha three times to his right, and went to Manjushri, accompanied by those sixty monks, who were staying with him and who were novices, having but recently left home. Among those sixty monks were Sagarabuddhi, Mahasudatta, Punyaprabha, Mahavatsa, Vibhudatta, Vishuddhacarin, Devashri, Indramati, Brahmottama, Prashantamati, and others. All those monks had served past buddhas, had planted roots of goodness, had far-reaching zeal, had thoroughly purified faith and reason, were great in understanding and action, were capable of viewing the realm of Buddha and comprehended the inherent nature of things, were intent on the welfare and development of others, and sought the qualities of those who arrive at Thusness. They were guided by the teaching of Manjushri.

At that point the venerable Shariputra, on the way, looked at all the monks and said to Sagarabuddhi, "See the inconceivable purity of form of Manjushri, along with the celestial and earthly beings, his variety of marks and embellishments, the purity of his sphere of radiance, his web of light beams developing countless beings, extinguishing all miseries, his wealth of followers, embraced by past virtues, arraying the path, which is eight steps wide. See the magnificent arrays of the procession on the path, facing the realms in all directions as they go, with overflowing great treasuries, auspicious and fair arrays, on the left and right; magnificent arrays of adornments emerge from within all the trees growing out of the roots of goodness of attendance on past buddhas; all the world chiefs are showering clouds of offerings in respect; from the curl of hair between the eyebrows of all buddhas from the ten directions, spheres of networks of light beams emanate, uttering all teachings of buddhas, and enter Manjushri's head."

Beginning with these, Shariputra revealed and described to the monks measureless arrays of qualities of the procession of Manjushri, and as Shariputra spoke of the qualities of Manjushri, the minds of the monks were purified, calmed, and delighted; they were thrilled, their mental states became suitable for religious practice, their senses became clear and tranquil, their gladness increased and their depression vanished, all obstructions disappeared, they came face to face with the vision of Buddha, they dedicated their minds to the buddha-teachings, their enlightening faculties were clarified, the power of faith of enlightening beings rose in them, great compassion developed in them, they entered the sphere of the transcendences, they conceived great vows and came to perceive the oceans of buddhas in the ten directions: with this supreme power of faith in omniscience, they said to Shariputra, "Teacher, lead us to the presence of that wise person." Then Shariputra went together with the monks to Manjushri and said, "O Manjushri, these monks want to see you." Then Manjushri, who was together with a great host of transfigured enlightening beings, turned with the gaze of an elephant and looked at the monks. The monks then bowed their heads to the feet of Manjushri, saluted him, and said, "By this root of goodness, witnessed by the blessed Shakyamuni Buddha—by the root of goodness may we become like you, may we attain bodies, voices, embellishments, and spiritual transfigurations like you."

To this Manjushri replied, "A man or woman setting out on the Great Vehicle imbued with ten indefatigable determinations will enter the stage of realization of Thusness, to say nothing of the stage of enlightening beings. What are the ten? The indefatigable resolution to see, attend, and serve all buddhas; to build up all roots of goodness without retreating; to seek all truths; to practice all the transcendent ways of enlightening beings; to fully accomplish all concentrations of enlightening beings; to enter successively into all ages; to thoroughly purify all oceans of buddha-lands in the ten directions; to lead all realms of sentient beings to perfect development; to carry out the practices of enlightening beings in all lands and ages; to fully attain each power of buddhas by maturing all beings through the process of practicing as many transcendent ways as atoms in all buddha-lands to mature each being. Men or women with faith who are imbued with these ten indefatigable determinations grow in all roots of goodness, leave all compulsive, routine mundane tendencies, drop out of all social castes, go beyond all stages of individual emancipation, are born in the family of all buddhas, fulfill the vows of enlightening beings, become pure with the attainment of all qualities of the enlightened, become clarified in all the practices of enlightening beings, develop all the powers of buddhas, overcome all demons and challengers, progress through all the stages of enlightening beings, and reach buddhahood."

Then the monks, having heard this teaching, attained a concentration called sphere of the unobstructed eye of vision of all buddhas, by the experience of which they saw the circles of assemblies of the buddhas in all worlds throughout the ten directions. They also saw all the beings in those worlds, and they also saw the various differentiations in those worlds. They also knew how many atoms were in these worlds. They also saw all the dwellings and furniture of those beings, made of various precious substances. They also heard the oceans of the qualities of the voice and the buddhas in those worlds, and understood the various statements, allusions, expressions, mystic formulae, terminology, and concepts of their teachings. They also discerned the minds, faculties, and dispositions of the beings in those worlds, and called to mind the events of ten lives past and future. They also comprehended the utterance of ten cycles of teaching of those buddhas. They also comprehended ten states produced by mystical powers, ten productions of guiding principles, and ten productions of instructive statements. They also comprehended ten accomplishments of analytic knowledge of those buddhas.

When they attained this concentration, they developed ten thousand qualities of the determination of enlightenment, entered ten thousand concentrations and purified ten thousand aspects of transcendence; having attained great illumination, being illumined by the sphere of great wisdom, they attained ten mystic knowledges of enlightening beings.

Manjushri exhorted and led them, now with soft and delicate sprouts of mystic knowledge and firm determination for enlightenment, into the practice of the universally good enlightening being. Based on the practice of the universally good enlightening being, they entered into the oceans of great vows and began to carry them out. By undertaking the oceans of great vows, and by purification of mind, they attained purity of body; by physical purity they gained physical lightness, by which physical purity and lightness they opened wide the doors to mystic knowledge and attained undiminishing mystic knowledge. By this attainment of mystic knowledge they appeared in multitudes of bodies to all the buddhas in the ten directions for the sake of accomplishing all Buddha teachings, yet without leaving the presence of Manjushri.

Then Manjushri, having set those monks on the foundation of unexcelled true enlightenment, continued his journey to the human realm and came to a great city in the south named Dhanyakara. There he stayed with his retinue in a forest called Array of Various Standards of Strength, to the east of the city, at a shrine where past buddhas had dwelt, established by buddhas for the sake of perfecting sentient beings, the repute of which resounded in infinite lands, a place where the Buddha, in the past, carrying out the practice of an enlightening being, relinquished many things that are difficult to relinquish, a place where gods, dragons, goblins, nymphs, titans, birds, centaurs, serpents, humans, and nonhumans always presented offerings to the earth. There Manjushri expounded a scripture called Illumination of the Principles of the Cosmos, whence flowed ten hundred thousand trillion scriptures. As he was expounding the scripture, many tens of hundreds of thousands of trillions of dragons came to him from the ocean; having heard this teaching, disdaining the condition of dragons and desiring the qualities of buddhahood, they left the state of dragons and gained birth as celestial or human beings. There ten thousand dragons became irreversible in their progress toward supreme perfect enlightenment. And during his exposition of the teaching, innumerable beings were edified through the Three Vehicles.

Now the people of the city heard that Manjushri had come and was staying at the shrine in the forest. Having heard this, pious men and women, boys and girls, each a company of five hundred, led by Mahaprajna, the foremost of the pious men, went from the city to where Manjushri was. Then the pious man Mahaprajna, with a company of five hundred pious men such as Sudatta, Vasudatta, Punyaprabha, Yashodeva, Somashri, Somanandi, Sumati, Mahamati, Rahulabhadra, and Bhadrashri, went to Manjushri, bowed their heads to his feet, circled him three times, and then sat to one side.

Then a pious woman named Mahaprajna, with a company of five hundred pious women including Suprabha, Sugatra, Subhadra, Bhadrashri, Candraprabhasa, Ketuprabha, Shribhadra, and Sulocana, went to Manjushri, bowed to him and circled him, and then sat to one side.

Then Sudhana, an outstanding boy, together with a company of five hundred outstanding boys including Suvrata, Sushila, Svacara, Suvikrami, Sucinti, Sumati, Subuddhi, Sunetra, Subahu, and Suprabha, went to Manjushri, bowed to him and circled him, and then sat to one side.

Then the girl Subhadra, daughter of the householder Mahaprajna, together with a group of five hundred girls including Bhadra, Abhiramavarta, Drdhamati, Brahmadatta, Shribhadra, Shriprabha, and Suprabha, went to Manjushri, bowed to him and circled him, and then sat to one side.

Then Manjushri, seeing that the women, men, boys and girls from the city had gathered and were seated, according to their dispositions overwhelmed them with his power over appearance, soothed them with his power of great benevolence, undertook to teach them with his power of great compassion, considered their mentalities with his power of knowledge, and, imbued with great analytic intelligence, wishing to expound the truth, he observed the outstanding boy Sudhana: "Why is Sudhana called Sudhana, which means 'Good Wealth'? When Sudhana was conceived in his mother's womb, there appeared in the house sprouts of seven precious substances, evenly distributed throughout the house. Beneath those precious sprouts were seven great treasuries, from which those sprouts emerged, splitting the surface of the earth as they grew, treasuries of gold, silver, sapphire, crystal, ruby, emerald, and coral. When his limbs were perfectly formed and he was born after ten months, those treasuries, which were seven spans high, wide, and long, rose to the surface of the earth, opened, glittered, and shone. Five hundred vessels made of precious substances also appeared in the house—vessels of clarified butter, sesame oil, honey, and fresh butter, each equipped with all the necessary utensils; there also appeared diamond vessels filled with all kinds of perfumes, fragrant vessels filled with various cloths, crystal vessels filled with various foods and drinks, pearl vessels filled with various jewels, gold vessels filled with silver powder, silver vessels filled with gold powder, gold and silver vessels filled with agates, crystal vessels filled with sapphires, sapphire vessels filled with crystal jewels, emerald vessels filled with rubies, ruby vessels filled with emeralds, star sapphire vessels filled with water-clarifying jewels, water-clarifying jewel vessels filled with star sapphires. Five hundred such precious vessels appeared in the storerooms of the house simultaneously with the birth of Sudhana, raining money, grain, gold, and various other valuables. Because of this great prosperity that appeared in the house by his mere birth, the fortune-tellers and priests and his parents and kin called him Sudhana, 'Good Wealth.'"

Sudhana, furthermore, having served past buddhas and planted roots of goodness, imbued with great zeal and devotion, intent on following spiritual benefactors, impeccable in word, thought, and deed, engaged in clarification of the path of enlightening beings, heading for omniscience, having become a vessel of the Buddha teachings, his course of mind purified, had achieved an unhindered, unattached determination for enlightenment.

At that point Manjushri, having regarded Sudhana, greeted him in a friendly manner and expounded the Teaching to him, dealing with all elements of buddhahood, the cultivation and attainment of all elements of buddhahood, the infinity of all buddhas, the successive appearance of all buddhas in the world, the purification of the congregations surrounding all buddhas, the achievement of the reality-body of all buddhas, the magnificent arrays of wisdom and eloquence of all buddhas, the purification of the array of spheres of light of all buddhas, and the equality of all buddhas.

Then Manjushri, having edified, inspired, sharpened, and delighted Sudhana and the great crowd of people with his talk on the Teaching, having caused them to set their minds on perfect enlightenment and made them remember their past roots of goodness, stopped his teaching there, given as it was to the people in accord with their mentalities, and left.

Then Sudhana, having heard from Manjushri of such magnificence of the qualities of Buddha, with the quest for supreme perfect enlightenment uppermost in his mind, uttered these verses as he watched Manjushri going:

> By your power, Great Sage, I am set on enlightenment for the good of all beings,
> Resolved on this, with an endless vista; hear what is on my mind.

> Moats filled with the water of delight, with high walls of conceit and pride,
> Its doors the conditions of all beings—that is how the great city of existence is.

> Shrouded in the great darkness of ignorance, burnt by the fire of lust and hate,

Ever under the sway of the lord of demons, the abode of the unenlightened.

Completely bound by the ropes and chains of craving, made desolate by the wastelands of deceit,
Blinded by doubt and confusion, standing on the ground of falsehood.

Bound up in envy and jealousy, becoming ghosts, animals, and fiends,
Oppressed by birth, sickness, age, and death, they wander lost in the wheel of transmigration.

May the pure orb of your compassion for them, a sun radiating the light of knowledge,
Risen to evaporate the sea of afflictions, shine on me like the sun.

Orb full of the power of love, radiating moonbeams of virtue, grant happiness;
You give light like the full moon appearing in the abodes of all beings.

Endowed with all virtues and powers, your mind is in the sky of the reality realm;
Instruct me, O King, with the jewel of the wheel of the teaching.

Boldly advancing, resolute, on the vehicle of enlightenment, having developed great virtue and knowledge,
O Caravan Leader arising to benefit all beings, protect me.

Girt with the armor of forbearance, strength, and firmness, wielding the sword of knowledge in the hand of compassion,
Facing the band of demons in battle, lead me to safety, O Hero.

Dwelling on the peak of the polar mountain of truth, surrounded by the archangels of concentration,
Destroyer of the titans of affliction, look upon me, O Mighty One.

In the city of existences, the abode of the unaware, your guidance out of afflictive action is definitive;
Amid the confusion of the cycle of transmigration on the ground of cause, as a lamp reveal to me the Way.

Turning away from the paths of woe, purifying the paths of bliss,
Transcender of all worldly states, lead me to the door of liberation.

I am stuck to the notions of permanence, self, and pleasure, blocked by falsehood and grasping—
With the sharp eye of truth, knowledge, and power, quickly open the door of liberation for me.

Knower of the paths of truth and falsehood, fearless in the varied
   knowledge of the Way,
Certain of the guidance of all paths, show me the Way to enlightenment.

Tree of right insight standing firm on the ground, nourished by the
   water of the virtues of all buddhas,
Showing flowers of virtues of buddha-teaching, show me the Way
   to enlightenment.

O teacher of the Way, show me the buddhas of the past, future,
   and present,
Makers of light, best of beings, gone to bliss.

Familiar with the various mechanics of action, expert in the mechanics
   of the vehicle of religion,
Sure of the various vehicles of knowledge, show me the vehicle of
   enlightenment.

Put me on the vehicle of enlightenment, driven by faith, studded with
   jewels of virtue,
A globe with wheels of prayer and vows, steeled by forbearance, resting on the axle of compassion.

Orb of all memory, purified, with a roof of kindness, well adorned,
And a beautiful bell-garland of analytic powers—put me in this
   supreme vehicle.

Adorned with a couch of pure conduct, filled with millions of
   concentration-ladies,
With the drum of truth resounding—bring me to this royal vehicle.

With an infinite chamber of the four integrative methods, adorned
   with jewels of knowledge and pearls of virtue,
Harnessed with the finest rope of modesty—show me the chief of
   vehicles.

It has the radiance of the pure sphere of light of relinquishment, the
   sandalwood of morality, the perfume of compassion,
With the lance of forbearance, and is held together by firmness—
   place me on the supreme vehicle.

It guides all beings, never turning back; its frame of meditation is set
   up on concentration,
It is drawn by the team of wisdom and means—place me on that eminent vehicle of truth.

Vows set the course and alignment of its wheels; it holds the truth
   steadfastly, having great power;

It is well made by the dynamics of knowledge, expertly—lift me onto
the vehicle of truth.

It is refined by Universally Good action, proceeding slowly with concern for beings:
Bring me to that vehicle of knowledge, of valor in pure conduct
everywhere.

Put me on that vehicle which cuts through all obstructions,
Steady and firm as the finest steel, adorned with garlands of knowledge.

It is spacious, clean, impartial toward people, a refuge for all beings,
bringing happiness:
Put me on that vehicle of enlightenment, which sheds light throughout the cosmos.

Its advance cuts through the mass of suffering, clears the sphere of dust
of afflictions of action,
And subdues all demons and challengers—put me on that vehicle
of truth.

Its scope is universal knowledge, it arrays the sky of the reality realm;
Bring me to that vehicle of truth, which fulfills the aspiration of
all beings.

Put me on that spiritual vehicle, pure and infinite as space,
Unstained by the ignorance and obscurity of views, serving all sentient beings.

Put me on that spiritual vehicle, swift as the wind,
Sustaining the world by the wind-power of vows, establishing the
ground of all citadels of peace.

Put me on the supreme vehicle, unshakable as the earth, carrying
its cargo
By the intense power of compassion, full of knowledge, beneficial to
the world.

It is like the sun, giving life to the world, a concentrated orb of
great lights,
Radiant with supreme purity of mental command; show me the sun
of knowledge.

Give me that mighty thunderbolt of knowledge, O Noble One,
which is learned over many eons,

> Knows the reasons and grounds of all causes, and smashes the fortress of conditioning.

> As you have learned a vast ocean of knowledge, an unequaled ocean of awareness,
> Imbued with all qualities of buddhas, tell me what it is like.

> As you have highly developed vision and are graced with the crown of the king of knowledge,
> Your head wrapped in the turban of truth, look into the city of the spiritual sovereign.

Then Manjushri, gazing like an elephant, said to Sudhana, "It is good that you follow spiritual benefactors, having set your mind on supreme enlightenment, that you think you should inquire into the practice of enlightening beings, wishing to fulfill the path of enlightening beings. Attending and serving spiritual friends is the beginning, the logical course, for the accomplishment of omniscience. Therefore you should tirelessly attend spiritual benefactors."

Sudhana said, "Noble One, please give me a full explanation of how an enlightening being is to study the practice of enlightening beings, how an enlightening being is to accomplish it. How is an enlightening being to initiate the practice of enlightening beings? How is an enlightening being to carry out the practice of enlightening beings? How is an enlightening being to fulfill the practice of enlightening beings? How is an enlightening being to purify the practice of enlightening beings? How is an enlightening being to comprehend the practice of enlightening beings? How is an enlightening being to effect the practice of enlightening beings? How is an enlightening being to follow the practice of enlightening beings? How is an enlightening being to keep to the practice of enlightening beings? How is an enlightening being to expand the practice of enlightening beings? How can an enlightening being fulfill the sphere of the universally good practice?"

Then Manjushri spoke to Sudhana in verse:

> Bravo, ocean of pure virtues, who has come to me;
> With a mind of vast compassion, you seek supreme enlightenment.

> You are committed to the peerless course of conduct for the sake of the liberation of all beings;
> You will become a savior of the world—this is the principle of enlightening beings' practice.

> Enlightening beings who are steadfast and indefatigable work within the mundane—
> They attain universal good, invincible and unobstructed.

Light of virtue, star of virtue, mine of virtue, ocean of virtue, pure—
You are committed to universal good in practice, for the welfare of
the world.

You will see infinite buddhas, in the worlds of the ten directions:
And you will hold their clouds of teachings by the power of memory.

As you see the buddhas in the buddha-lands of the ten directions,
You will clarify their ocean of vows in enlightenment practice.

Those who enter this ocean of principles and stand on the ground
of buddhahood
Will become all-seers, learning from the Guides of the world.

Having practiced the conduct of universal good throughout all lands,
for as many eons as there are atoms in the lands,
You will reach enlightenment, the abode of peace and bliss.

You should practice for boundless oceans of eons in all lands
And fulfill this undertaking of the conduct of universal higher good.

Behold the millions of beings who are happy to hear your vow,
Who seek enlightenment by the knowledge of universal good.

Then Manjushri, having uttered these verses, said to Sudhana, "It is good
that you think, having set your heart on supreme enlightenment, that you
should find out the practice of enlightening beings. It is hard to find beings
who set their hearts on supreme enlightenment. It is even harder to find
beings who, once they have set their minds on enlightenment, seek the practice of enlightening beings. An enlightening being is to attain certainty
through true spiritual friends, spiritual benefactors, for the realization of
omniscience. One should indefatigably seek spiritual benefactors and be
tireless in seeing spiritual benefactors. One should respectfully follow the
appropriate instructions of spiritual benefactors and should carry out the
techniques skillfully devised by spiritual benefactors, without interruption.
South of here is a country called Ramavaranta; there is a mountain there
called Sugriva, where a monk named Meghashri lives. Go to him and ask
how an enlightening being should learn the conduct of enlightening
beings, and how to apply it; how one is to fulfill, purify, enter into, carry out,
follow, keep to, and expand the practice of enlightening beings, and how an
enlightening being is to fulfill the sphere of universally good action. That
spiritual friend will tell you about the sphere of universally good conduct."

Then Sudhana, pleased, enraptured, transported with joy, delighted,
happy, and cheerful, laid his head at the feet of Manjushri in respect, circled
Manjushri hundreds and thousands of times, and looked at him hundreds
and thousands of times, with a mind full of love for the spiritual friend,

unable to bear not seeing the spiritual friend, with tears streaming down his face as he wept, and left Manjushri.

Meghashri

Then Sudhana proceeded by stages to the country of Ramavaranta. Having reached Ramavaranta, reflecting on and tasting the mentally pleasing enjoyments based on higher action born of past roots of goodness, he went to Mount Sugriva, climbed the mountain, and looked in every direction for the monk Meghashri. Finally, after seven days, he saw the monk walking on the plateau of another peak. He went to Meghashri, paid his respects, and said, "O noble one, I have determined to seek supreme enlightenment, but I do not know how an enlightening being should learn the conduct of enlightening beings, or how one should accomplish it, or how to begin the practice of enlightening beings, how to carry it out, fulfill it, purify it, comprehend it, realize it, follow it, keep to it, and expand it, or how an enlightening being is to fulfill the sphere of universally good action. I hear that you give instruction for enlightening beings, so please tell me how enlightening beings proceed to supreme perfect enlightenment."

The monk Meghashri replied to Sudhana, "It is good that you ask about the practice of enlightening beings, having set your mind on supreme perfect enlightenment. It is difficult, most difficult, to seek the practice of enlightening beings, to seek the sphere of enlightening beings, to seek the purification of emancipation of enlightening beings, to seek the purification of the path of enlightening beings, to seek the far-ranging purification of the conduct of enlightening beings, to seek the purification of the accomplishment of mystic knowledge of enlightening beings, to show the liberation of enlightening beings, to show enlightening beings' exercise of compassion for the world, to oblige people according to their mentalities in the manner of enlightening beings, to show enlightening beings' mundane and transcendental faces, to seek the thought and action of enlightening beings undefiled by the ills and fears of the created and the uncreated. Son, by virtue of mastery of the power of devotion, purity of the eye of perceptive faith, illumination of the light of knowledge without aversion, purity of the universal eye looking in all directions with unobstructed universal perspective and unobstructed vision skillfully observing, skillfulness in obeisance, bowing in all directions in a state of physical purity, and the power of memory command perfectly holding the masses of teachings of all buddhas, I see the buddhas in all the lands of the ten directions. That is, in the east I see one buddha, two buddhas, three buddhas, a hundred buddhas, a thousand buddhas, a hundred thousand buddhas, a million buddhas, a hundred million buddhas, a billion buddhas, a hundred billion buddhas, a quintillion buddhas—I see incalculable, immeasurable, uncountable, inconceivable, incomparable, incomprehensible, unlimited, ungraspable, inestimable, unutterable numbers of buddhas. I see as many buddhas as atoms in this continent; I see as many buddhas as atoms in the land masses of the four continents; I see as many buddhas as atoms in thousand-world, million-world, and billion-world buddha-lands; I see as many buddhas as atoms in ten buddha-lands; I see as many buddhas as atoms in a hundred buddha-lands; I see as many buddhas as atoms in a thousand buddha-lands; I see as many buddhas as atoms in a hundred thousand buddha-lands; I see as many buddhas as atoms in a million buddha-lands; I see as many buddhas as atoms in a hundred million buddha-lands; I see as many buddhas as atoms in a billion buddha-lands; I see as many buddhas as atoms in a hundred billion buddha-lands; I see as many buddhas as atoms in a quintillion buddha-lands; I see as many buddhas as atoms in untold numbers of buddha-lands. As in the east, in the same way I see untold buddhas in all the other directions as well; looking in each direction, I see buddhas with various appearances, I see buddhas with various forms, various transfigurations, various exercises of power, various congregations, radiating light in networks of rays of many colors, with various arrays of states of purity in their buddha-lands, various life spans, showing magical projections of various ways of purification of enlightenment to beings according to their mentalities, roaring the mighty lion roar of buddhas.

"Son, from this universal light in which is concentrated the information of all sense objects, I have attained mindfulness of the buddhas: but how can I know the practice, or tell of the virtues, of the enlightening beings who have purified the sphere of endless knowledge, who have attained the means of mindfulness of buddhas in the sphere of universal illumination, by seeing right before their eyes the pure arrays of abodes in all buddha-lands in the spheres of all buddhas; who have attained the means of mindfulness of buddhas in which the ten powers are developed, by following the infinite ten powers of the enlightened; who have attained the means of mindfulness of buddhas in which the truth is displayed, by observation of the clouds of bodies of all buddhas as sources from which the truth is heard; who have attained the means of mindfulness of buddhas which is the seed of illumination of all realms, by plunging into the undivided ocean of buddhas in all oceans of realms; who have attained the means of mindfulness of buddhas throughout the ten directions, by comprehending the majesty of projections of all buddhas in all microcosms; who have attained the means of mindfulness of buddhas in all ages, by communication of the inseparable vision of Buddha in all ages; who have attained the means of mindfulness of buddhas in all times, by seeing buddhas according to the time in all times and living with them inseparably; who have attained the means of mindfulness of buddhas in all fields, by communication of the vision of the transcendent, unsurpassed body of buddhas in all buddha-fields; who have attained the means of mindfulness of buddhas in all sense objects, by communication of vision of successive emergence of buddhas in all objects; who have attained the means of mindfulness of buddhas by which peace is developed, through revelation of the ultimate extinction of all buddhas in all worlds in a single instant; who have attained the means of mindfulness of buddhas by which detachment is developed, by revelation of all buddhas going forth from all abodes in one day; who have attained the means of mindfulness of buddhas in the past, by revelation of the bodies of buddhas, each buddha sitting cross-legged filling the cosmos; who have attained the means of mindfulness of buddhas in the minute, by entering into the service of untold buddhas appearing in a single point; who have attained the means of mindfulness of buddhas in supernal manifestations, by communication of visions of mystical displays of attainment of enlightenment in all worlds in one instant; who have attained the means of mindfulness of buddhas in religious actions, by attainment of the illumination of knowledge of the miracle of all buddhas coming forth and teaching; who have attained the means of projected mindfulness of buddhas, by apprehending appearances of all buddhas seen as they wish; who have attained the means of mindfulness of buddhas in deeds, by showing reflected images according to the deeds that all beings have done; who have attained the means of mindfulness of buddhas in mystic projections, by means of the ubiquitous manifestation of visions of tremendous projections of buddhas on lotus blossoms blooming in all phenomenal and noumenal realms; who have attained the means of mindfulness of buddhas in space, by vision of the space of the cosmos adorned by clouds of images of buddhas?

"Go, son—south of here is a place called Sagaramukha, where there lives a monk named Sagaramegha. Go to him and ask him how an enlightening being is to learn and accomplish the conduct of enlightening beings. He will reveal to you a spiritual benefactor; he will introduce you into the cause of accumulation of roots of goodness; he will get you to develop the vast ground of provisions for enlightenment; he will tell you of the immense, intense power of roots of goodness; he will inform you of the great cause of preparation of the determination for enlightenment; he will establish in you the great cause of the illumination of the vehicle of universal salvation; he will cause you to develop the great power of the set of transcendent ways; he will get you to purify extensive means of entry into the ocean of religious practice; he will get you to purify the vast sphere of vows; he will get you to develop extensive systems of all-sided emancipation; he will get you to develop the immense power of compassion."

Then Sudhana paid his respects to the monk Meghashri and left.

Sagaramegha

Then Sudhana, reflecting on the instructions of that spiritual benefactor, pondering that enlightening liberation, polishing that enlightening method of concentration, peering into that conductor into the ocean of the essence of enlightenment, intent upon the sphere of buddhahood, seeking that direction to the vision of Buddha, thinking about that ocean of buddhas, remembering the succession of buddhas, following that approach to the means of enlightenment, looking throughout that sky of the enlightened, went gradually to the monk Sagaramegha in the region of Sagaramukha. When he got there, he paid his respects to Sagaramegha and said, "O noble one, I have set out for supreme perfect enlightenment and want to enter the supreme ocean of knowledge; but I do not know how enlightening beings get out of the host of worldlings and into the host of the enlightened, emerge from the ocean of the mundane whirl and enter the ocean of omniscience, die away from the state of ignorant sentient beings and are born in the family of buddhas, withdraw from the stream of the mundane whirl and follow the stream of enlightening practice, escape from the wheel of transmigration in the mundane whirl and turn to the wheel of practice and vows of enlightening beings, destroy the gang of all demons and make manifest the light of the host of all buddhas, evaporate the ocean of craving and increase the water of great compassion, close all doors of decadence and miserable states and evils which are inopportune for enlightenment and open the door of heaven and nirvana, break through the door of the city of the mundane and enter the door of the city of omniscience, give up craving for all luxuries and give rise to the determination to care for all being."

To this Sagaramegha replied, "It is good that you have set your mind on supreme perfect enlightenment. The will for enlightenment is not developed by people who have not planted roots of goodness; the will for enlightenment is produced by those who have attained the illumination of all-sided roots of goodness, who are illumined by the light of knowledge of concentration on the path containing the means of enlightenment, who have accumulated a vast ocean of virtue as provisions for the path to enlightenment, who ceaselessly practice all that is pure and good, who tirelessly apply the methods set up by all spiritual benefactors, who are not worried about their physical subsistence, who are free from clinging to material things, whose minds are equanimous as the earth, without high or low, who are by nature compassionate and friendly, who face up to all states of being, who seek the sphere of those who realize Thusness. In such people arises the mind of enlightenment—the mind of great compassion, for the salvation of all beings; the mind of great kindness, for unity with all beings; the mind of happiness, to stop the mass of misery of all beings; the altruistic mind, to repulse all that is not good; the mind of mercy, to protect from all fears; the unobstructed mind, to get rid of all obstacles; the broad mind, to pervade all universes; the infinite mind, to pervade all spaces; the undefiled mind, to manifest the vision of all buddhas; the purified mind, to penetrate all knowledge of past, present, and future; the mind of knowledge, to remove all obstructive knowledge and enter the ocean of all-knowing knowledge.

"Son, I have been living here in Sagaramukha ('Ocean-Door') for twelve years, having focused my mind on the ocean and kept it present in my awareness, reflecting on the measureless vastness of the great ocean, its pure clarity, its unfathomable depth, its gradual deepening, its variety of deposits of precious substances, the measurelessness of its body of water, its infinity, its being the dwelling place of various immense creatures, its being covered by great clouds, and how it neither increases nor decreases. I think: is there anything else in the world as vast as the great ocean, as broad, as measureless, as deep, as various? While I was engaged in these thoughts, an enormous lotus from the bottom of the ocean appeared before me. Its stem was of unsurpassed jewels, sapphires, and diamonds, with a wreath of agate; its broad leaves of pure gold, with an array of buds of yellow sandalwood and filaments of emerald, as measureless in breadth as the ocean; its calyx was on a stem held by a million titan chiefs, it was covered by a net of a million various jewels, sprinkled by rain from clouds of fragrant water by a million chief water spirits, with a million bird chiefs trailing silks and strings of jewels over it, a million centaur chiefs gazing at it benevolently, a million serpent chiefs bowing to it in respect, a million goblin chiefs honoring it with bowed bodies, a million celestial musician chiefs celebrating it with music and song, a million celestial leaders raining on it clouds of heavenly flowers, fragrances, garlands, incenses, perfumes, aromatic powders, cloths, parasols, banners, and pennants, a million Brahma chiefs bowing their heads in respect, a million celestial beings of the pure abodes paying respect with joined palms, a million human rulers making offerings of precious substances, a million ocean deities emerging to pay respect; it was illumined by arrays of light beams from a million luminous jewels, adorned with a million pure jewels in orderly arrays, containing a million radiant jewels, blazing with the great splendor of a million dazzling jewels, shining endlessly with a million jewels from various sources, adorned with a million jewels symbolic of earth arrayed all around, incomparably arrayed with a million of the finest diamonds, brilliantly covered with a million sun-containing jewels, decorated with a million beautiful jewels in various colors, blazing with the light of an endless array of a million wish-fulfilling jewels. That great lotus is born from the transcendental roots of goodness of the enlightened; it appears everywhere, directed to the will of enlightening beings; it comes forth from the principle of illusoriness; it is produced by pure deeds; it is adorned by the principle of the state of noncontention; it is a presentation of the nature of being equal to a dream; it is marked by the principle of nonfabrication; it accords with the principle of nonattachment; it pervades all universes everywhere; it is in the realm of illumination by the light of the sphere of Buddha. It would be impossible to reach the end of the array of characteristics, qualities, forms, and appearances of that lotus even in countless hundreds of thousands of eons. Also I saw an embodiment of Buddha clearly manifest sitting cross-legged on that great lotus, completely filling it; I saw that embodiment of Buddha reaching from here to the very summit of being. I also saw the inconceivable adornments of the Buddha's throne, the inconceivable adornments of the Buddha's congregation, the inconceivable adornments of his aura of light, his inconceivable marks of greatness, various embellishments, and inconceivable majesty, the inconceivable projection of Buddha, the inconceivable purity of appearance of the Buddha; I heard the Buddha's inconceivable eloquence and drew near to the inconceivable infinity of Buddha's power, the inconceivable purity of his adornments of expertise, and his inconceivable accomplishment of the power of analytic knowledge; I recalled his past consummation of practices as an enlightening being, I saw the inconceivable transformation of the attainment of enlightenment, I heard of the inconceivable array of senses conveying universal insight and saw the inconceivable infinite division of his body into left and right and his consummate attainment of physical being beneficial to all creatures.

"Then the Buddha extended his right hand, rubbed my head, and revealed to me a teaching called universal eye, which is the sphere of all buddhas, revealing the practice of enlightening beings, showing the differentiation of the planes of all universes, showing the spheres of all truths together, the light purifying all lands, dispersing all challengers, crushing all demons and devils, making all beings happy, illumining the hidden recesses of all beings' minds, communicating to all beings in accord with their mentalities, illuminating the turning of the wheels of the senses of all beings. And I have taken up that teaching of the universal eye, keep it in mind, apply it, and contemplate it, taking it in this way—even if it were being written by a collection of pens the size of the polar mountains with as much ink as water in the oceans, it could never be finished; it would be impossible to finish even a part of a single line of a single formula of a single principle of a single doctrine of a single chapter of the teaching—it cannot be even partially exhausted, let alone fully exhausted or comprehended.

"So, son, having taken up this teaching of the universal eye for a full twelve years—taking it up in this way: in one day I master countless chapters by the light of mental command to retain what is heard; I penetrate countless chapters by the light of mental command that is a way of access to tranquillity; I plunge into countless chapters by the light of mental command that progresses endlessly; I contemplate and investigate countless chapters by the light of mental command that is imbued with fiery energy; I put countless chapters into practice by the light of mental command adorned with lotuses; I elucidate countless chapters by the light of mental command that is beyond words; I analyze countless chapters by the light of mental command that is a mass of brightness; I arrange countless chapters in order by the light of mental command containing the ocean—whatever beings come to me from the ten directions, I direct and introduce them all into this teaching of the universal eye, the manifestation of the practice of enlightened and enlightening beings; to all of them I elucidate, represent, illumine, describe, show, analyze, expound upon, open up, explain, unlock, and clarify the teaching of the universal eye.

"I know this teaching, son, but how can I know the practice or tell of the virtues of the enlightening beings who have entered into the ocean of all enlightening beings' practices in accord with pure vows; who have entered into the ocean of all vows, to remain in the world through all ages; who have entered into the mundane whirl of all beings, to act appropriately according to their mentalities; who have entered the ocean of minds of all beings, to communicate knowledge; who have entered the ocean of all virtues, to produce the vision of the knowledge of the ten powers without obstruction; who have entered the ocean of all beings' faculties, to guide them to maturity and perfection with appropriate timing; who have entered the ocean of all lands, by carrying out the vow to purify all lands; who have entered the ocean of all buddhas, by the power of the vow to honor and attend all enlightened ones; who have entered the ocean of all truths, for the communication of knowledge; who have entered the ocean of all virtues by pursuing their realization; who have entered the ocean of languages of all beings, to carry out the turning of the wheel of the teaching in all languages?

"Go, son, to a place called Sagaratira, in the region of Sri Lanka, sixty leagues south of here. A monk named Supratishthita lives there; go to him and ask how a great enlightening being is to purify enlightening practice."

Then Sudhana, paying his respects, departed from the presence of Sagaramegha.

Supratishthita

Then Sudhana, remembering that spiritual benefactor's teaching of the universal eye, reflecting on that projection of buddhahood, keeping in mind those multitudes of statements of the Teaching, entering into those oceans of entries into the Teaching, pondering that method of teaching, plunging into the principles of that whirlpool of teaching, entering fully into the space of that teaching, clarifying that sphere of teaching, and contemplating that treasure island of teaching, gradually made his way to Sagaratira in Lanka, where he looked in all directions, desiring to see the monk Supratishthita. He saw Supratishthita walking in the sky, surrounded by countless hundreds of thousands of celestial beings. He also saw the sky covered with clouds of celestial flowers, with the sound of countless clouds of heavenly music and countless streamers and banners offered by the chief celestials to the monk Supratishthita as tokens of respect. He also saw inconceivable clouds of black aloe-scented water thundering in the sky, raised on high by the chief water spirits. He also heard countless sounds of pleasing celestial music and song coming from the sky with words of reverence and hymns of praise, performed by supernatural beings; he also saw inconceivable clouds of fine cloths spread out in the sky by joyous serpent chiefs out of respect for Supratishthita. He also saw inconceivable clouds of jewels set in the sky by the chief titans, with the light of the magnificent array of their inconceivable qualities. He also saw inconceivable hosts of bird girls, standing in the sky with their hands joined in gestures of respect, with noninjury uppermost in their minds. He also saw inconceivable hundreds of thousands of goblin chiefs in the sky with their retinues, their bodies transfigured, directed there by goodwill toward the monk Supratishthita. He also saw inconceivable numbers of demigod chiefs with their retinues circling in the sky to protect Supratishthita. He also saw inconceivable hundreds of thousands of Brahma chiefs in the sky making salutations, uttering pleasant words of respect and songs of praise. He also saw inconceivable hundreds of thousands of celestial beings of the pure abodes in their palaces in the sky, paying their respects to the monk Supratishthita.

Then Sudhana, seeing the monk Supratishthita walking in the sky, was pleased, enraptured, transported, overjoyed, happy; he saluted and greeted Supratishthita and said to him, "Noble one, I have set my mind on supreme enlightenment, but I do not know how an enlightening being is to seek the qualities of buddhas, how an enlightening being is to acquire the qualities of buddhas, how an enlightening being is to accumulate the qualities of buddhas, how an enlightening being is to cultivate the qualities of buddhas, how an enlightening being is to actualize the qualities of buddhas, how an enlightening being is to act in accord with the qualities of buddhas, how an enlightening being is to assemble the qualities of buddhas, how an enlightening being is to contemplate the qualities of buddhas, how an enlightening being is to clarify the qualities of buddhas in order to accomplish all the tasks of enlightening beings, how an enlightening being is to approach and follow the qualities of buddhas. Noble one, I hear that you give instructions to enlightening beings: please tell me how an enlightening being is to set to work on the Buddha teachings, not to lose sight of Buddha whatever one is doing, not to lose sight of enlightening beings so as to be always in contact with reality, always to be involved with the Buddha teachings so as to be at one with the roots of goodness of all enlightening beings, always to be involved with the vows of enlightening beings so as to accord with knowledge, always to be involved in the practices of enlightening beings so as to accomplish the task of all enlightening beings, always to be pervading all buddha-fields so as to live continuously through all ages, to remain in the conditional for the manifestation of the projections of all buddhas, always to be hearing the Teaching in order to visit in one's own body the places of death and birth of all buddhas by the emanationlike action of enlightening beings, and to always be in contact with the light of knowledge so as to receive the teachings of all buddhas and accord with knowledge of past, present, and future."

To this, Supratishthita replied, "It is good that you have set your mind on supreme perfect enlightenment and ask about the qualities of buddhahood, the qualities of omniscience, the qualities of independence. I have attained the enlightening liberation 'unobstructed door.' Going in and out of this 'unobstructed door' liberation, practicing it, analyzing it, examining it, investigating it, and clarifying it, I have attained a light of knowledge called 'ultimate nonobstruction,' whereby I am free from obstruction in awareness of the mental actions of all sentient beings, knowing where all sentient beings die and are born, entries into the channels to memory of past states, associations with all beings in future ages, communications to all sentient beings of the present time, knowledge of the conventions of languages of all sentient beings, cutting off the doubts of all sentient beings, comprehending the differences in the faculties of all sentient beings, approaching all sentient beings at appropriate times to guide them to full development, comprehension of time divisions as being conceptual, and in noncorporeal pervasion of the buddha-fields in the ten directions, all by the attainment of nonbeing, nonabiding, and nondoing. By the realization of this mystic power of nondoing I walk, stand, sit, and lie down in the sky, disappear and appear, produce smoke and flame. Being one, I become many; being many, I become one. I become now visible, now invisible. I go through walls unhindered, as through empty space. While sitting cross-legged I travel in space, like a bird on the wing. I go in and out of the earth as if in water. I walk on water unhindered as on the earth. I smoke and flame like a great conflagration. I cause even the earth to quake. With my hand I polish even the sun and moon, those bodies of great potency, power, and light. I envelop even up to the Brahma world in my body. Covering the world with clouds of lights the colors of all jewels, I emit clouds in the forms of all beings. Emanating clouds of webs of light of infinite colors, I go forth in all directions: in each moment of thought I pass one world to the east, I pass two worlds, three worlds, a hundred worlds, a thousand worlds, a hundred thousand worlds, a million worlds, a hundred millions worlds, a billion worlds, a hundred billion worlds, a quintillion worlds, countless, measureless, endless, incomparable, inconceivable, incalculable, untold, unspeakably unspeakable numbers of worlds; and in those worlds are buddhas living, in each of those oceans of worlds, in each of those streams of worlds, in each region of those worlds, in each age of those worlds, in each set of those worlds, in each occurrence of those worlds, in each expression of those worlds, in each medium of those worlds, in each particular of those worlds, in each sacred place in those worlds, in each site of enlightenment in those worlds, in each assembly in those worlds—I go to each of the buddhas teaching in those worlds with as many bodies as atoms in endless buddha-lands, each body raining as many clouds of offerings as atoms in endless buddha-lands. Going to the buddhas, I ceaselessly make offerings of all kinds of flowers, fragrances, garlands, unguents, robes, banners, pennants, canopies, nets, and ornaments. Those buddhas explain, reveal, and elucidate, and I acknowledge and take up all that they teach. I also remember the purity of the buddha-lands of those buddhas. As in the east, so also in all directions do I go to innumerable worlds, see the buddhas teaching there, make offerings to them, acknowledge and take up what they say, and remember the purity of their buddha-lands. Also, all the beings who see me, to whom I come, are assured of supreme perfect enlightenment. Also, whatever beings I see, small or large, underdeveloped or well developed, happy or unhappy, I adopt a corresponding physical form, in order to guide them to maturity and perfection in the appropriate time. And all beings who come to me I establish in this enlightening liberation, which is everywhere at once and which is the consummation of unerring power.

"Son, I know this enlightening liberation 'unobstructed door,' which is everywhere at once engaged in the service of the buddhas, appropriate to the development of all beings. How can I know the practice, or tell the virtues, of the great enlightening beings who act on great compassion, who act in accord with the practice of the Great Vehicle, whose conduct never deviates from the path of enlightening beings, whose conduct is free from attachment, whose conduct always embodies the will of enlightening beings, who always act with the thought of enlightenment, whose action is focused on the way of the enlightened, who always act with the thought of omniscience, whose way of action is like the sky, whose conduct is independent of all mundane realms, whose conduct is flawless, whose conduct is uncorrupted, whose conduct is consistent, whose conduct is faultless, whose conduct is pure, whose conduct is unblemished, whose conduct is free from evil, whose conduct is honest, whose conduct is dispassionate, whose conduct is undefiled?

"Go south, son, to the Dravidian city Vajrapura. There lives a grammarian named Megha. Go to him and ask him how an enlightening being is to learn and practice the conduct of enlightening beings."

Then Sudhana again paid his respects to the monk Supratishthita and left.

Megha

Then Sudhana, mindful of the light of the Teaching, steeped in intensity of faith in the Teaching, his attention focused on thoughts of Buddha, intent on perpetuating the lineage of the three treasures, remembering spiritual friends, his mind having illumined the worlds of past, present, and future, thinking of great vows, striving for the salvation of all beings, his mind unattached to enjoyment of any created things, praising the tradition of dispassion, intent upon contemplation of the instrinsic essence of all things, firm in the commitment to purify all worlds, sojourning without attachment in the congregations of all buddhas, gradually approached the Dravidian city Vajrapura, looking for the grammarian Megha.

He saw Megha at a crossroads in the middle of the city, sitting on a lion seat to talk about the Teaching, elucidating a scripture called *Manifestation of Turning of the Wheel of Letters*. Sudhana went up to him, paid his respects, and said, "Noble one, I have set my mind on supreme perfect enlightenment, but I do not know how an enlightening being is to learn and carry out the practice of enlightening beings. How is an enlightening being to preserve the determination for enlightenment? How does one develop a will that is firm in all states of existence and is indefatigable? How does one purify one's intent, in accord with invincibility? How is the power of great compassion produced so that it never flags? How does one acquire mental command that is totally purified? How is the light of wisdom produced, light free from obscurity in regard to meaning, principle, expression, and presence of mind? How does one acquire the power of recollection, keeping in mind the teachings of all buddhas without confusion? How is the power of migration purified, illumining all states of existence with the truth? How is an enlightening being's power of concentration perfected, intent on the ascertainment and discernment of the meanings of all principles?"

Now Megha, out of respect for an enlightening being, got off his seat and prostrated himself before Sudhana, then showered Sudhana with golden flowers, precious jewels, and the finest sandalwood powders, covered him with hundreds of thousands of robes dyed in various colors, showered him with beautiful flowers of many various colors with pleasant scents, and honored him with various other offerings, then said to him, "It is good that you have set your mind on supreme perfect enlightenment; one who arouses the determination for supreme perfect enlightenment becomes engaged in the perpetuation of the lineage of buddhas, intent on correctly communicating the tradition of dispassion, engaged in purifying the family of all lands, directed toward guiding the family of all sentient beings to perfection, engaged in properly accomplishing all the teachings and transcending all things, intent on harmony of all actions, engaged in the fulfillment of all practices of enlightening beings, directed toward preserving the continuity of all religious vows, engaged in following knowledge of all times, active in making devotion steadfast, the focus of attention of all buddhas, near to equality with all buddhas, appreciated by all enlightening beings, praised by all sages, honored by all the chief Brahmas, protected by all the chief gods, respected, welcomed, and praised by the chiefs of the various supernatural beings, sought out by all world rulers; one becomes very well suited for putting an end to the three kinds of bad conditions in all worlds, getting rid of all difficult conditions inopportune for attaining enlightenment, getting beyond all states of destitution, attaining birth in celestial or human states, always seeing spiritual benefactors, consistently listening to the lofty buddha-teaching, purifying the will for enlightenment, cultivating the cause of the thought of enlightenment, gaining the illumination of the path of enlightening beings, following the knowledge of enlightening beings, and dwelling in the stages of enlightening beings.

"This is what I think of such a one: enlightening beings do what is difficult to do; it is hard to get to actually see them; they are comforts to the world; enlightening beings are the mothers and fathers of all sentient beings; enlightening beings are an adornment to the world with its gods; enlightening beings are a refuge for those oppressed by suffering; enlightening beings are a place of rest for the protection of all sentient beings; enlightening beings are the breath of life to those suffering all kinds of terrors and calamities; enlightening beings are a wind protecting all sentient beings from the heat of the three evils; enlightening beings are earth, causing the roots of goodness of all sentient beings to grow; enlightening beings are an ocean, a repository of endless treasures of virtue; enlightening beings are a sun, producing the light of knowledge; enlightening beings are the polar mountain, by virtue of the height of their roots of goodness; enlightening beings are a moon, the moon of knowledge of the essence of enlightenment having risen in them; enlightening beings are warriors crushing the armies of all demons; enlightening beings are heroic, having reached the city of the state of independence; enlightening beings are fire, annihilating the self-love of all sentient beings; enlightening beings are clouds, causing vast clouds of true teaching to shower; enlightening beings are rain, causing the sprouts of faculties such as faith to grow; enlightening beings are navigators, showing the way on the ocean of truth; enlightening beings are bridges conveying all sentient beings across the sea of mundane life; enlightening beings are a pathway to the holy for all sentient beings."

Thus praising enlightening beings to Sudhana in such terms, Megha applauded Sudhana. While he was saying these words pleasing to enlightening beings, there issued from his mouth a mass of flames that made a thousand worlds clearly visible; and all the sentient beings who perceived that light came to Megha, illumined by the light; to them, their attention commanded by Megha, their hands held forth in respectful supplication, their bodies and minds cooled, enraptured, inspired with reverence, divested of conceit, freed from deception, senses tranquil, Megha expounded and conveyed the teaching of the manifestation of the turning of the wheel of letters, upon hearing which they became irreversible in their progress toward supreme perfect enlightenment.

Megha sat back down on the seat of teaching and said to Sudhana, "I have attained the light of the spell of eloquence: I know the speech of all kinds of beings in a billion-world universe; I know the variety of speech of each kind of being; I know the unity of speech of each kind of being; I know the mixture of speech of each kind of being; I know the terms, speech, and concepts of all creatures; I know the ideas of all sages; I know the ideas of all ignoble people; I know the speech of enlightening beings, expressed according to the mentalities and languages of sentient beings; I enter into and focus on the oceans of utterances addressed to all sentient beings by the buddhas of past, present, and future. As in this billion-world universe in each moment of thought I enter into the oceans of all terms, expressions, speech, and concepts of sentient beings, I do the same in untold worlds in each of the ten directions.

"I know this light of the spell of eloquence of enlightening beings, but how can I know the practice or tell the virtues of the enlightening beings who have entered the ocean of what is in various conceptions, who have entered the ocean of the various conceptions and languages of all people, who have entered the ocean of the various conventions of verbal designation used by all people, who have entered the ocean of logical connections of all statements, who have entered the ocean of literalism, who have entered the ocean of designation of all objects of past, present, and future in one object, who have entered the ocean of teaching which is beyond verbal expression, who have entered the ocean of the teaching of the Buddha, who have entered the ocean of explanations of distinct types of statements, who have entered the ocean of explanation guiding the analysis of statements of all truths, who have entered the ocean of speech of all beings, who have gone into the pure arrays of all spheres of sound, who are conversant with the ultimate distinctions of the wheel of phonemes?

"Go, son—there is a country south of here called Vanavasin, where there lives a distinguished man named Muktaka. Go ask him how an enlightening being is to undertake the practice of enlightening beings and become familiar with it, and how the mind is to be observed."

Then Sudhana, having bowed to Megha and paid respect to the teaching, describing the faith rooted in him, observing that all-knowledge comes from following good spiritual benefactors, reluctantly took his leave and went on.

Muktaka

Then Sudhana, reflecting on that array of light of the spell of eloquence of enlightening beings, plunging into that enlightening beings' ocean of principles of speech, remembering that enlightening beings' mental purification, undertaking that enlightening beings' production of inclination to goodness, clarifying that enlightening beings' method of perfecting sentient beings, purifying that enlightening beings' knowledge of how to take care of sentient beings, making firm that enlightening beings' purity of willpower, establishing that enlightening beings' power of supreme resolve, clarifying that body of interest of enlightening beings, producing that goodness of intent and thought of enlightening beings, evoking that effort of enlightening beings, equipped with a mind of firm commitment and tireless consistency, with unrelenting energy and determination, imbued with unshakable power of faith, with an indestructible mind, follower of the instructions of all spiritual benefactors, with the perspective of sane knowledge, on the verge of all-sided purity, coursing in the purity of unobstructed knowledge, imbued with the light of the principle of the universal eye, illumined by the mystic formulations of all stages of enlightenment, his mind directed to the differentiations of the planes of the cosmos, aware of the pure essence of forms unfixed anywhere, intent on the sphere of absolute unity with no attachment, having purified the medium of powerful knowledge of all ideas, having broken through the boundaries of all spaces, progressively distinguishing the realms of worldly planes, progressively distinguishing the realms of planes of reality, intent on the manifestation of the vision of the varieties of abodes of Buddha, knowing about the distinctions of realms of time, his intellect bearing the radiant wheel of the teaching, his mind illumined by the light of the treasury of concentration of universally radiant knowledge, mentally and physically according with the stage of universal perspective, his mind illumined by the lightning of knowledge of those who realize Thusness, realizing the exaltation of faith in omniscience, never without the exaltation of faith in the buddha-teaching, filled with the exaltation of the empowerment of Buddha, illumined by the inherent mental light of all buddhas, hearing the vow to penetrate all networks of worlds with his own body, intent on putting all universes at once into his own body, made his way gradually to the country Vanavasin, arriving there after twelve years.

He looked for the noble Muktaka, saw him, paid his respects, and said, "Noble one, I have made gains, having met the spiritual benefactor Megha. Why do I say this? Spiritual benefactors are hard to get to see, hard to get to encounter, hard to visit, hard to attend, hard to approach, hard to stay with, hard to be perfected by, hard to associate with. But I have met the spiritual benefactor Megha. Noble one, I have set my mind on supreme perfect enlightenment, to attend all buddhas, to be on good terms with all buddhas, to see all buddhas, to know all buddhas, to approach equality with all buddhas, to follow the vows of all buddhas, to fulfill the vows of all buddhas, to view the knowledge attained by all buddhas, to produce all buddhas in my own body, to accomplish the realization of all buddhas in my own practice, to directly know the mystical transformations of all buddhas, to purify the powers and confidences of all buddhas, to hear all true teachings tirelessly, to listen to and take up the teachings of all buddhas, to hold the teachings of all buddhas, to distinguish the teachings of all buddhas, to preserve the instructions of all buddhas, to be one being with all buddhas, to be equal to all enlightening beings, to purify the practice of all enlightening beings, to fulfill the transcendent ways of enlightening beings, to purify the accomplishment of the vows of all enlightening beings, to attain all enlightening beings' store of mystical power of buddhas, to be illumined by the endless knowledge of the treasury of truths of all enlightening beings, to approach the treasury of enlightening beings, to produce the infinite treasury of enlightening beings, to realize the ultimate consummation of guidance of sentient beings with the treasury of great compassion of all enlightening beings, to know the treasury of spiritual transformations of all enlightening beings, to command in my own body the treasury of powers of all enlightening beings, to be fully arrayed with the treasury of purities of all enlightening beings.

"Noble one, I have come in such a spirit, with such desires, such wishes, such intentions, such thoughts uppermost in my mind, aiming for such a realm, determined to follow such principles, intent on such purity, seeking such adornments, with such a humble mind, applied to such good, my faculties oriented in this way. Noble one, I hear you give instructions to enlightening beings, explain principle and clarify procedure, explain the Path, take them across the bridge, open the door of the Teaching, cut off doubts, dispel craving, pull out the arrow of confusion, clear away the grime of uncertainty, light up the obscurity in the mind, remove defilement from the mind, calm the mental flow, remove deviousness from the mind, cool the fever of the mind, foster nonattachment, turn back the mind revolving in the mundane whirl, turn enlightening beings away from evil, separate them from hells, free them from attachments, direct them toward omniscience, lead them into the city of truth, establish them in great compassion, settle them in great kindness, introduce them into the practice of enlightening beings, cause them to enter into the development of ways of concentration, establish them in means of realization, fill them with contemplation of inherent nature, and explain mind according to power for the sake of attainment of equanimity toward all beings. Noble one, please tell me how an enlightening being is to learn, commence, and carry out the practice of enlightening beings, and how one so engaged can quickly purify the sphere of practice of enlightening beings."

At that juncture Muktaka entered an enlightening concentration medium called "collection of all buddha-fields," led by a mystic formula of endless progression, accomplishing entry into this concentration by the power of his past roots of goodness, by the empowerment of the Buddha, and by Manjushri's attention and gift of the light of knowledge. As soon as Muktaka had entered that state, his body became pure, and by that purity of body as many buddhas in the ten directions as atoms in ten buddha-lands were visible within his body, along with the adornments of their pure lands, their congregations, their pure lights, their past actions and abodes, their mystical projections, their vows, their pure arrays of liberative practices, their manifestations of attainment of perfect enlightenment, their turnings of the wheel of teaching, their developments of sentient beings, and the ultimate consummation of their teaching. All these were visible within Muktaka's body without mutual confusion, without mutual obstruction, clearly distinct, showing the various individual ages accurately defined, the various arrays of the buddha-lands, the various adornments of the congregations of enlightening beings, and the various miracles of the buddhas. Some buddhas were seen to be in the heaven of happiness in a world setting forth various means of liberation and illumining various undertakings; some were seen descending from the heaven of happiness doing the duty of buddhas; some were seen in the womb of the mother displaying various miracles; some were seen being born and showing a child's play; some were seen at home, some leaving home, some gone to the summit of enlightenment defeating the army of demons; some were seen surrounded by deities, spirits, and cherubim, being asked by Brahma and Indra to turn the wheel of the teaching; some were seen turning the wheel of teaching; some were seen in the abodes of all beings; some were seen passing away; in some cases the division of the relics of deceased buddhas in a world was seen, and in some cases people and celestial beings in a buddha-land were seen adorning a buddha's shrine. And what those buddhas said, in various groups of beings, in various beings' worlds, in various realms of existence, in various assemblies of beings, in various situations according to beings' virtues, states, inclinations, beliefs, and faculties, in various periods of time, amid various kinds of beings' activities, in various manifestations of worlds of beings carrying out various intentions, in the midst of beings with various degrees of purity of senses and various afflictions, habits, and propensities, teaching by various manifestations of buddhas' transfigurations and projections, by various expressions, various utterances, various enunciations of doctrine, various mystical mnemonic formulae, various intellectual analyses of principles, various stirrings of the ocean of names of truth, various roarings of the mighty lion's roar of buddhas, various manifestations of magical performances teaching beings bases of goodness, mystic projections showing various facets of memory, various lion roars foretelling the buddhahood of enlightening beings, various manifestations of the wheel of teaching of the enlightened, in infinite assemblies of infinite varieties, all interdependent, in groups variously purified, in large groups contained in small groups, in groups a league deep, ten leagues deep, up to groups the size of as many worlds as atoms in untold buddha-fields—all that those buddhas taught, Sudhana heard, took in, remembered, undertook, and contemplated. He also saw the mystic projection and the inconceivable power of concentration of the enlightening being.

Then Muktaka, mindful, perfectly cognizant, arose from that concentration and said to Sudhana, "I go in and out of a liberation of buddhas which is called 'unobstructed manifestation.' As I go in and out of the 'unobstructed mainfestation' liberation of buddhas, to the east I see in the world Golden Light a buddha named Supreme Savior, along with the whole group of enlightening beings there, led by the enlightening being Child of Radiance. To the south I see in the world Possessed of All Powers a buddha named Universal Spread of Fragrance, with the whole group of enlightening beings there, led by King of Thought. To the west I see in the World Possessed of All Fragrances and Beauties a buddha named Supreme Lamp, with the whole group of enlightening beings there, led by Unobstructed Mind. To the north I see in the world Vestment Banner a buddha named Diamond Crusher, with the whole group of enlightening beings there, led by Boldly Advancing on Indestructible Feet. To the northeast I see in the world Beauty of All Jewels a buddha named Radiance of the Independent Eye, with the whole group of enlightening beings there, led by Independent Emanation. To the southeast I see in the world Glow of Fragrant Flames a buddha named Fragrant Lamp, with the whole group of enlightening beings there, led by Supreme Intellect Differentiating the Planes of All Realms of Reality. To the southwest I see in a world Sunny Golden Shining a buddha named Illuminating Voice of Universal Knowledge, with the whole group of enlightening beings there, led by Hanging Crest of Radiant Flowery Flames. To the northwest I see in the land Brilliant Shining Treasury with Fragrant Adornments a buddha named Light of a Measureless Ocean of Virtue, with the whole group of enlightening beings there, led by Mind Blazing with Light in a Body Free from Attachments. In the nadir I see in the world Blaze of Lights from Jewel Lions a buddha named Beam of Light Illumining the Cosmos, with the whole group of enlightening beings there, led by Mind Born of the Light of the Cosmos. In the zenith I see in the world Radiant with Splendor of Appearance a buddha named Light of Liberation of Indestructible Virtue and Glory, with the whole group of enlightening beings there, led by Mind of Energy of Unobstructed Power. Beginning with these, I see as many buddhas in the ten directions as atoms in ten buddha-lands: and yet those buddhas do not come here and I do not go there. Also, whenever I want to see the buddha Infinite Light in the world Blissful, I see the buddha Diamond Light in the world Like Sandalwood, I see the buddha Jewel Light in the world Fragrant, I see the buddha Jewel Lotus Light in the world Lotuslike, I see the buddha Silent Light in the world Golden, I see the buddha Imperturbable in the world Joy, I see the buddha Lion in the world Standing Well, I see the buddha Moonlike Awareness in the world Mirror Globe Light, I see the buddha Luminous in the world Pure Clarity of Jewellike Splendor. In this way I see whatever buddha I wish in whatever world in whichever direction. I see whatever buddha I wish to see in whatever time in whatever abode involved in whatever past practice, whatever buddha I wish to see in whatever miraculous performances, in whatever teaching activity: and yet the buddhas do not come here, nor do I go there. Without discerning any coming from anywhere on the part of the buddhas, without discerning any going on the part of my own body, knowing the buddhas as like a dream, knowing my own mind as dreamlike thought, knowing the buddhas as like a reflection, knowing my own mind as like a vessel of clear water, knowing the buddhas as like magically produced forms, knowing my mind as like magic, knowing the nature of voices of the buddhas as the reverberation of the sound of echoes in the mountains, knowing my own mind as like an echo, I realize, I am mindful, that all enlightenment principles of enlightening beings are based on one's own mind, that all their purification of buddha-lands, all enlightening practices, all development and guidance of sentient beings, all undertaking of the vows of enlightening beings, all attainment to the ocean of omniscience, roaming in the inconceivable liberation of enlightening beings, attainment of the enlightenment of buddhas, spiritual communion with the cosmos, and knowledge of subtle communion with all ages, all are based on one's own mind.

"In this connection, I think that one's own mind should be supported by roots of goodness, moistened by the clouds of the Teaching, purified by principles that should be focused on, made firm by vigor, made calm by forbearance, guided by following knowledge, clarified by wisdom, developed in spiritual powers, expanded to equality with the buddhas, illumined by the ten powers of the enlightened.

"I know this buddha-liberation of unobstructed manifestation, and go in and out of it; how can I know the practice or tell of the virtues of enlightening beings whose minds are unobstructed, whose sphere is a state free from obstruction, who have attained concentration focused on the teachings of all buddhas of the present, who have attained concentration leading into enlightenment that does not become ultimately extinct, who have realized the equality of past, present, and future, who know the science of the sphere of concentration on the continuity of all planes, who distribute their bodies throughout all buddha-lands, who abide in the unfragmented state of buddhas, whose perspective faces in all directions, who observe the sphere of all-inclusive knowledge, who know the becoming and disintegration of all worlds in their own bodies, without any dualistic notions regarding their bodies or the worlds.

"Go south, to Milaspharana, on the tip of the continent. A monk named Saradhvaja lives there. Go to him and ask how an enlightening being is to learn and undertake the practice of enlightening beings."

Then Sudhana, paying his respects to Muktaka, eulogizing, contemplating, desiring, and dwelling on Muktaka's countless virtues, with love for spiritual benefactors, taking refuge in spiritual benefactors, seeking to please spiritual benefactors, not contesting the knowledge of spiritual benefactors, seeing omniscience as realized by following spiritual benefactors, obedient to spiritual benefactors, to be spiritually healed by the techniques of spiritual benefactors, his thoughts following the direction of spiritual benefactors, thinking of spiritual benefactors as a mother because they get rid of all that is not beneficial, thinking of spiritual benefactors as a father because they produce all good qualities, Sudhana left Muktaka.

Saradhvaja

Then Sudhana, reflecting on the instruction of the eminent Muktaka, following Muktaka's direction, remembering the inconceivable liberation of enlightening beings, remembering the inconceivable light of knowledge of enlightening beings, following the inconceivable entrance into the realm of reality, entering into the inconceivable principle of the communion of enlightening beings, observing the inconceivable transformation of those who realize Thusness, intent on the inconceivable communion of buddha-fields, clarifying the inconceivable manifestation of the magical power of buddhas, contemplating the magnificence of the inconceivable order of the concentrations and liberations of enlightening beings, following the steadfast determination to perform the inconceivable work of enlightening beings, conforming to the stream of undertaking of the inconceivable deeds of enlightening beings, gradually proceeded to Milaspharana on the tip of the continent, where he looked all over for the monk Saradhvaja.

He saw Saradhvaja by the side of a place for walking at a retreat, sitting in concentration, following his breath, not stirring, not thinking, his body straight, his mindfulness on the immediate present, by the inconceivable power of concentration producing to the left, right, and above an inconceivable infinite body in each successive mental moment manifesting an infinite variety of bodies. Sudhana saw an inconceivable miraculous display of the liberation of enlightening beings coming forth from every pore of the ecstatic body of Saradhvaja, who had attained such profound tranquility, silence, and objectlessness. With this miraculous display of the medium of liberation, Saradhvaja filled the cosmos moment to moment with endless varieties of mystic projections, to perfect all beings, to honor all buddhas, to purify all buddha-fields, to do away with the mass of suffering of all sentient beings, to cut off the courses of all bad conditions, to open the door to good conditions for all beings, to extinguish the burning of afflictions of all beings, to dissolve all beings' obstructions to knowledge, and to introduce all beings into omniscience.

Sudhana saw emanating from the soles of Saradhvaja's feet masses of grandees as numerous as atoms in countless buddha-lands, their forms like those of the grandees in all worldly realms, wearing gorgeous clothing, variously adorned, wearing variously crested jewel crowns, surrounded by images of sons. He also saw priests and householders going throughout the ten directions caring for the poor with all kinds of food and drink, services, supplies, clothing, flowers, garlands, fragrances, ointments, acts of love, jewels, dwellings, vessels, and implements, restoring life to the miserable world, satisfying sentient beings, purifying sentient beings' minds, developing sentient beings for enlightenment.

Sudhana saw forms of warrior sages, priestly sages, worldly sages, scholars versed in various crafts, humanistic scholars, scholars expert in knowledge of the sciences of mundane and transmundane activities, sages considered teachers of the world, emanate from the circles on Saradhvaja's knees and go throughout the ten directions in many forms and guises, speaking pleasant words, cheering up dejected sentient beings, taking care of spiritually and materially poor beings, comforting beings in distress, uplifting the fallen, reviving the shipwrecked, rescuing the imperiled, causing the voice of goodness to be heard, preaching rejection of evil, exhorting beings to virtuous practices, directing beings to beneficial actions, producing joy, uttering kind words, and showing the world the nature of cooperation.

Sudhana saw various forms of wizards, as many as there are living beings, emanating from Saradhvaja's navel and going throughout the ten directions, wearing leather, rags, and bark, carrying staffs and pitchers, their deportment extremely calm, up on the sky extolling the qualities of buddhas, causing the voice of the Teaching to be heard, speaking the voice of Buddhas, showing the community of enlightening beings, praising religious conduct, directing sentient beings to guard their senses, describing the meaning of the voidness of intrinsic essence, introducing sentient beings into the meaning of knowledge, teaching worldly science, showing the science of the Path to omniscience and emancipation, guiding beings in gradual practice.

Sudhana saw as many water spirit girls as all worldly events, in inconceivably many forms, emerging from Saradhvaja's sides, pervading all universes moment to moment, showing the miracle of water spirits, adorning the sky with inconceivable fragrant clouds, adorning the whole sky with inconceivable clouds of flowers, arraying the whole realm of space with inconceivable adornments of clouds of garlands, covering all universes with inconceivable adornment of bejeweled parasols, adorning the sky with inconceivable clouds of jeweled banners, inconceivable clouds of jeweled pennants, rain from inconceivable endless clouds of great jewels, rain from inconceivable clouds of jewel necklaces and various flowers, inconceivable clouds of jewel seats with enlightening beings sitting on them teaching the ways of enlightenment, inconceivable clouds of troves of celestial jewels, rain of clouds of sounds of goddesses singing praises of the Teaching, inconceivable raining clouds of jewel lotuses adorned with nets of pearls crowned with diamonds, inconceivable clouds of jewel crowns and rain of clouds of endless lights adorned by all jewels, inconceivable clouds of celestial beings graced with flowers, garlands, parasols, and banners, inconceivable clouds of goddesses, adornments of rain produced by clouds of songs of praise of buddhas' qualities sung by the goddesses on high standing with joined palms or scattering golden flowers, also covering all buddhas' assemblies with clouds of heaps of fragrances the colors of all jewels and clouds of smoke of the finest incense, adorning all worlds, delighting all beings, honoring all buddhas.

Sudhana saw as many titan kings as atoms in countless buddha-fields emerging from the auspicious mark on Saradhvaja's chest and pervading the cosmos moment to moment, displaying the inconceivable magic transformations of titans, agitating the oceans, causing hundreds of thousands of worlds to quake, causing all the highest mountains to crash together, shaking up all celestial abodes, eclipsing all hordes of demons, crushing all armies of demons, causing all people to destroy intoxication, conceit, and arrogance, restraining and purifying corrupt minds, restraining malicious minds, extinguishing being's bad qualities, shattering the mountains of afflictions, quieting grasping for pleasure, frightening sentient beings by exercises of titanic magical powers and scaring them away from evil, making them wary of the mundane whirl, getting them to leave all states of conditioned existence and enter into nondwelling, leading sentient beings to the thought of enlightenment, getting them to purify the conduct of enlightening beings, establishing enlightening beings in the transcendent way, causing them to enter the stages of enlightening beings, causing them to produce enlightening beings' light of the way to buddhahood, defining various principles and methods.

Sudhana saw as many bodies of Buddhist disciples and individual illuminates as atoms in countless buddha-fields emerge from Saradhvaja's spine and pervade the cosmos, telling sentient beings attached to self and suited to guidance by disciples or individual illuminates about selflessness and the voidness of the being, clarifying the impermanence of all conditioned states to those attached to eternity, telling the lustful about the contemplation of impurity, telling the hostile about love, telling the deluded about causality and interdependent origination, illumining principles connected with the sphere of knowledge to those who are equally lustful, hostile, and deluded, telling those attached to objects about nondwelling, causing those inclined to stick to tranquillity to like the superiority of undertaking vows, showing actions beneficial to beings, in all places, in the beginning of all turnings of the ocean of ways to truth.

Sudhana saw as many demigods and supernatural beings as atoms in countless buddha-fields emerging from Saradhvaja's shoulders and pervading the cosmos, with various physical forms, colors, and sizes, in various attitudes, riding various vehicles, surrounded by various retinues, striving to protect sentient beings, showing various powers, uttering various sounds, going everywhere employing various different means to guard the good actions of all sentient beings, to guard all circles of sages, to assist all enlightening beings, to protect those who are rightly oriented, to attend and honor all buddhas with the work of thunderbolt bearers, to remove all fallen sentient beings from evil ways, striving to annihilate all worldly calamities and perils such as disease, anxious to preserve the light of actions beneficial to beings, filling the stores of knowledge and virtue, causing the wheel of the teaching to roll along, restraining controversy.

Sudhana saw as many centaur chiefs as atoms in countless buddha-fields surrounded by countless hundreds of thousands of centaur princesses, and as many celestial musician kings as atoms in countless buddha-fields surrounded by countless hundreds of thousands of celestial musician princesses emerge from Saradhvaja's abdomen and pervade the cosmos, performing music and songs in praise of Buddha dealing with the essence of things, illumining the thought of enlightenment, describing the conduct of enlightening beings, eulogizing all ways to attainment of enlightenment, fostering understanding of all ways of presenting the Teaching, causing attraction to all ways of spiritual transformation, illumining all ways into ultimate release, publicizing all buddhas' teachings, gladdening all beings, purifying all buddha-fields, illuminating all ways to truth, removing all obstructions, begetting all roots of goodness.

Sudhana saw as many emperors as atoms in countless buddha-fields, each surrounded by seven treasures and four armies, emerge from Saradhvaja's face, pervading the cosmos, radiating arrays of light beams of great relinquishment, spewing forth masses of all kinds of jewels, distributing multitudes of all kinds of jewels, enriching the poor, causing people to desist from killing, fostering kindness in sentient beings, causing them to give up stealing, giving them countless beautifully adorned maidens, causing them to give up sexual misconduct, establishing them in chastity, causing them to desist from lying, enjoining on them supreme honesty, causing them to desist from slander, causing them to speak words of ultimate kindness and consideration, causing them to desist from harsh words and speak pleasantly, causing people to desist from all meaningless statements, statements connected with what is not beneficial and what is not right, urging them to certainty of distinction of statements of profound meaning, causing people to desist from all evils of speech and speak compassionately, removing mental defilements from people, enjoining the excellent state of having few desires and being content, causing people to desist from malice and urging them to be peaceful in their relations with others, extracting people from the web of all views, causing them to break up all kinds of uncertainties, throwing off all masses of doubts, taking away the darkness of all confusion and hesitation, definitively analyzing the truth for people, telling them about causality and interdependent origination, directing them to the principle of the truth about inherent existence, dispelling all obstacles, leading into the way of nonobstruction, illuminating the meaning of enlightenment.

Sudhana saw as many hundreds of thousands of suns as atoms in countless buddha-fields emanate from Saradhvaja's eyes, lighting up all the great hells, dispersing the great darkness in the world, removing the darkness of sentient beings' delusions, relieving the beings in the frigid hells from the pains of cold, shining clear light in lands made of lotus fibers, shining lapis-lazuli-colored light in gold lands, shining golden light in lands of lapis lazuli, shining golden light in silver worlds, shining crystal light in gold lands, shining golden light in crystal lands, shining coral light in gold lands, shining golden light in coral lands, shining golden light in ruby lands, shining ruby light in gold lands, shining golden light in emerald lands, shining emerald light in gold lands, shining light the color of sun-filled jewels in sapphire lands, shining sapphire light in lands made of sun-filled jewels, shining light the color of jewels containing networks of moonbeams in red pearl lands, shining light the color of red pearls in lands made of jewels containing networks of moonbeams, shining light the colors of various jewels in lands made of one jewel, shining light the color of one jewel in lands made of various jewels, thus involved in the infinite tasks of sentient beings, in the assemblies of all enlightening beings, pervading the universes of all beings.

From the circle of hair between Saradhvaja's eyebrows Sudhana saw as many moons as atoms in countless buddha-fields emerge, outshining all the celestial chiefs, turning all worldlings away from lust to enjoyment of the vision of Buddha, pervading the cosmos engaged in the guidance of infinite beings.

From Saradhvaja's forehead Sudhana saw as many great Brahmas as atoms in countless buddha-fields emerge, their deportment extremely tranquil, murmuring prayers, asking all buddhas for instruction, praising all buddhas, gladdening all enlightening beings, pervading all universes in the ten directions, involved in the infinite tasks of sentient beings.

From Saradhvaja's head Sudhana saw emerge as many enlightening beings as atoms in countless buddha-fields, manifesting bodies of various appearances, forms, adornments, and embellishments, emanating infinite spheres of light, taking up the past enlightening practices of all buddhas and projecting from every pore multitudes of forms practicing charity without attachment to giver, receiver, or gift, showing oceans of past efforts involved in the various ways of transcendence, commending the act of giving to the world, getting rid of the filth of envy, directing beings to give up all grasping, causing the world to appear adorned with all kinds of jewels, establishing sentient beings in the practice of transcendent giving and in command over material things, praising all virtues, and teaching the cause of the characteristics of buddhas.

He also saw as many enlightening beings as atoms in countless buddha-fields emerge praising transcendent morality, manifesting from every pore oceans of past efforts of all buddhas involved in transcendent morality, turning all beings away from the spheres of all mundane states and turning them toward the sphere of the enlightened, disdaining the world of desire, dispersing the veil of error from the world, stopping untrue thoughts and enjoining the way of life of enlightening beings, commending the ethic of great compassion and leading beings into the conduct of the practice of the path of buddhas to attain the conduct of the enlightened, showing sentient beings that the state of existence is like a dream and guiding them into power over afflictions caused by grasping sense objects so that they may fully enter into the way of acting as in a dream.

He also saw as many enlightening beings as atoms in countless buddha-fields emerge, lighting up the world with golden light, guiding beings to a state of mind without hatred or malice, free from all corruption and defect, emanating from every pore multitudes of past efforts of buddhas involved in transcendent tolerance in order to cut off all brutal tendencies, leading sentient beings into the power of tolerance, showing sentient beings mastery over phenomena.

He also saw as many enlightening beings as atoms in countless buddha-fields emerge, engaged in miraculous displays showing the endless power of energy of enlightening beings, commending tireless quest for the ocean of learning by the power of nonregression in progress toward omniscience, guiding beings to honor and attend all buddhas, leading beings to arouse great energy to get rid of the mass of all suffering, emanating from all their bodies multitudes of past efforts involved in enlightening beings' perfection of transcendent energy, shattering sentient beings' mountains of sloth, leading sentient beings into transcendent energy, guiding sentient beings to mastery over action.

He also saw as many enlightening beings as atoms in countless buddha-fields emerge guiding sentient beings into the path of mindfulness, dissolving the darkness of all obstructions, causing sentient beings to desist from all intoxication and leading them into sobriety, taking down the flags of pretentiousness, arrogance, and pride, telling of the ocean of branches of meditation of buddhas, describing transcendent meditation to people, emanating from every pore multitudes of past efforts involved in perfection of transcendent meditation, guiding sentient beings to mastery of mind, pervading the cosmos moment to moment.

He also saw as many enlightening beings as atoms in countless buddha-fields emerge and pervade the cosmos in every moment of thought emanating from every pore multitudes of past efforts involved in the search of buddhahood, uttering multitudes of perfections of transcendent wisdom by oceans of words, emanating the lightning of right insight, expressing the inherent nature of phenomena, shattering the mountainous masses of sentient beings' notion of self, extracting all arrows of views, dispersing the darkness of desire, heedlessness, and doubt, commending control of inclination.

He also saw as many enlightening beings as atoms in countless buddha-fields emerge and pervade the cosmos in a mental impulse, showing the sphere of methods of all buddhas' skill in liberative means, emanating from every pore multitudes of past efforts involved in skill in means, spreading the practice of skill in means in the world, illuminating the way of universal emancipation, describing the sphere of all buddhas, describing and showing the practice of enlightening beings which unites the mundane and the transcendental, guiding sentient beings to enlightening beings' perfection of skill in means, demonstrating in the world all enlightening beings' mastery of regeneration.

He also saw as many enlightening beings as atoms in countless buddha-fields emerge and pervade the cosmos in each moment of thought by various projections of will, emanating from every pore multitudes of oceans of names of all buddhas, radiating from every pore multitudes of past efforts involved in purification of transcendent vows of all enlightening beings, commending transcendent commitment, guiding sentient beings into the masteries of all enlightening beings, powering through the world the eternally rolling chariot wheel of great vows which follows all truths and gets rid of all afflictions and shatters the mountains of nescience.

He also saw as many enlightening beings as atoms in countless buddha-fields emerge and ceaselessly fill the cosmos in each moment of thought, manifesting the power of enlightening beings' consummation of power, emanating from every pore multitudes of past efforts producing the consummation of transcendental power, showing power which cannot be overcome by any demons or challengers, nurturing such power that all the adamantine mountains surrounding the earth would shatter upon contact with their bodies, showing power such that their bodies do not even blaze up in the ocean of fire that burns the universe at the end of each eon, showing the power to hold all worlds in their hands while hovering in space, guiding beings to control of magical powers.

He also saw as many enlightening beings as atoms in countless buddha-fields emerge and fill the cosmos in every thought illuminating the sphere of knowledge of sentient beings, emanating from every pore multitudes of past efforts involved in purification of consummate knowledge, manifesting in the world the stage of knowledge characterized by mystic knowledge of all buddhas' virtues and knowledges, showing the stage of knowledge characterized by mystic knowledge of all buddhas' perceptions, illuminating the stage of knowledge characterized by mystic knowledge of the undertaking of all vows, revealing the stage of knowledge characterized by mystic knowledge of the undertaking of the vow to save all sentient beings, revealing the stage of knowledge characterized by mystic knowledge penetrating the lack of self or independent existence in all beings, illumining the stage of knowledge characterized by mystic knowledge observing the ocean of minds of all sentient beings, analyzing the stage of knowledge characterized by mystic knowledge discerning the faculties of all sentient beings, describing the stage of knowledge characterized by mystic knowledge observing the inclinations and interests of all sentient beings, disclosing the stage of knowledge characterized by mystic knowledge comprehending the ocean of actions of all beings, showing the stage of knowledge characterized by mystic knowledge penetrating the ocean of commitments of all sentient beings, guiding sentient beings into the perfection of knowledge.

From Saradhvaja's topknot of flesh Sudhana saw emerge as many embodiments of buddhas as atoms in countless buddha-fields, adorned with the finest characteristics and embellishments, appearing like mountains of gold, with immeasurable auras of blazing light illumining everything in the ten directions and voices pervading the cosmos, suffusing all universes, showing endless miraculous transformations of Buddha, showering rain from clouds of teaching on all without discrimination—showering rain from a cloud of teaching called knowledge confronting the distinction of all planes of the cosmos on enlightening beings on the verge of enlightenment, showering rain from a cloud of teaching called the ground of universality on coronated enlightening beings, showering rain from a cloud of teaching called entry into the ground of universality on enlightening beings ordained as princes of the great teaching, showering rain from a cloud of teaching called universal arrangement on enlightening beings of youthful nature, showering rain from a cloud of teaching called steadfast head of great compassion on nonregressing enlightening beings, showering rain from a cloud of teaching called diamond of knowledge distinguishing the intrinsic essence of all phenomena on enlightening beings of purified intent, showering rain from a cloud of teaching called arrangement taking in all beings on enlightening beings accomplished in preparatory practices, showering rain from a cloud of teaching called cloud of communication with the assemblies of all buddhas of past, present, and future on regenerated enlightening beings, showering rain from a cloud of teaching called voice of the ground of intrinsic essence of all phenomena on enlightening beings engaged in concerted practice, showering rain from a cloud of teaching called source of clouds containing the ways and means of great compassion on enlightening beings engaged in primary practices, showering rain from a cloud of teaching called store of kindness on enlightening beings newly determined to see enlightenment, showering rain from a cloud of teaching called inexhaustible treasury of kindness of the buddhas' commitment to liberation on enlightening beings of great zeal, showering rain from a cloud of teaching called inexhaustible treasury of the universal ground on beings in the world of form, showering rain from a cloud of teaching called sound produced by the measureless ocean of principles on Brahma body deities, showering rain from a cloud of teaching called inexhaustible treasury of power producing spiritual methods on controlling deities, showering rain from a cloud of teaching called sound cleaning variously represented provisions for omniscience on demon-body deities, showering rain from a cloud of teaching called varied cargo of jewels of knowledge on the deities who enjoy emanations, showering rain from a cloud called varied representation of the vows of enlightening beings on deities in the heavens of happiness, showering rain from a cloud of teaching called treasury of recollection of all buddhas on deities in the heavens of timely portion, showering rain from a cloud of teaching called source of the rapture of the vision of Buddha on the abodes of the chief deities, showering rain from a cloud of teaching called multitude of transformations of Buddha pervading the space of the cosmos on the abodes of the chief demigods, showering rain from a cloud of teaching called sound of eulogies of the qualities of all enlightened ones on the abodes of the chief celestial musicians, showering rain from a cloud of teaching called indestructible sphere of ways to knowledge on the abodes of the chief titans, showering rain from a cloud of teaching called multitude of means of development of all enlightened ones on the abodes of the chief birds, showering rain from a cloud of teaching called source of the magical utterances of enlightening beings traveling swiftly through the states of existence on the abodes of the chief dragons, showering rain from a cloud of teaching called speed of increase of the ocean of joy on the abodes of the chief serpents, showering rain from a cloud of teaching called sphere of the highest knowledge of all beings on the realms of humans, showering rain from a cloud of teaching called ornament bearing the words of the holy path bespeaking the extinction of all the pains of mundane existence on the hells, showering rain from a cloud of teaching called round body of clouds of remembrance of buddhas bespeaking the practice of impeccable action on the realms of animals, showering rain from a cloud of teaching called declaration of the transcendence of all buddhas producing a mind of nonattachment in all sentient beings on the ghost realms, showering rain from a cloud of teaching called comforting sound effecting the cessation of all pains on beings in distress.

He also saw as many orbs of webs of light beams as atoms in countless buddha-fields emerge from every pore, countless whirling arrays of phantom forms of power, manifestations of countless various works, pervading the entire cosmos. From some orbs of webs of light beams he saw scenes of the practice of pure giving, relinquishing everything; from some orbs of webs of light beams he saw scenes of the procedures of all past, present and future enlightening beings' investiture with ethical precepts; from some orbs of webs of light beams he saw scenes of all enlightening beings of past, present, and future practicing forbearance, enduring dismemberment, beatings, having their hearts and eyes gouged out, and he saw magically produced images of the practices of forbearance of all enlightening beings by the oppressed enlightening beings of past, present, and future with bodies sundered in the search of omniscience, enduring, forgiving, and overlooking all physical and mental harassment, out of great compassion; from some orbs of webs of light beams he saw scenes of different forms of the immensity of the practice of vigor of all enlightening beings, scenes of the great prowess of enlightening beings shaking the world, agitating the seas, startling sentient beings, scaring all heretics; from some orbs of webs of light beams he saw embodiments of all deeds of enlightening beings, the forms taken on, the perfections of physical bodies to be born in good families, the acceptance of instructions of spiritual benefactors, the states of practice of the teachings of spiritual benefactors, the abandonments of home, country, and city for suitable abodes to accomplish the branches of meditation of the enlightened, the seers, the meditation adepts, the kings, the recluses, the manners of disciplined conduct; from some orbs of webs of light beams he saw embodiments involved in seeking all truths in the station of practice of transcendent wisdom; from the orbs of webs of light beams from each and every pore Sudhana saw the bodies by which each statement of the Teaching was sought from the midst of all beings by relinquishing all that exists, sought from all spiritual benefactors through attendance and service, sought from buddhas with all the strength generated by faith and respect, and all the statements of the Teaching related to transcendent wisdom similarly sought by bodies manifested in the forms of all sentient beings; from some orbs of webs of light beams he saw all enlightening beings entering the ocean of states of being with means of development, endeavoring to save all sentient beings; from orbs of webs of light beams from every pore he saw enlightening beings saving sentient beings, engaged in the practice of skill in means taken on by their original bodies, approaching each and every being in a form resembling those beings; from some orbs of webs of light beams he saw the conduct of the Buddha's undertaking of vows in all past ages, the conduct of the undertaking of the vow to perfect all beings, the conduct of the undertaking of the vow to purify all lands, the spheres of accomplishment of all vows effected by each buddha by the specific cures for each of the ills of the mundane whirl. Sudhana saw all this from orbs of lights from each pore; from some orbs of webs of light beams he saw oceans of past efforts involved in the practice of transcendent power; from some orbs of webs of light beams he saw oceans of past efforts involved in the con-templations of the practice of omniscience and the awakening of sentient beings asleep in the slumber of ignorance.

Then, observing the monk Saradhvaja thus concentrated in meditation, mindful of that sphere of concentration and liberation, contemplating the inconceivable power of concentration of enlightening beings, entering into that inconceivable ocean of ways of benefiting sentient beings, remember-ing that inconceivable medium of the performance of supernal manifesta-tions confronting all the senses, strongly focusing his attention on it, entering that door of knowledge of purity of arrangement of the cosmos, aspiring to that enlightened power, expanding in knowledge, recognizing that controlling power of enlightening beings, stabilizing the power of vows of enlightening beings, extending the power of practice of enlighten-ing beings, Sudhana stood before Saradhavja for a day and a night, for two days and nights, seven days and nights, a fortnight, a month, six months, and then six more days and nights.

After six months and six days and nights, the monk Saradhvaja rose from concentration. Sudhana said, "It is marvelous, noble one, how profound this concentration is, how vast, how measureless its scope, how inconceivable its arrays of projections, how incomparable its light, how innumerable its man-ifestations, how unsurpassable its range, how pure its sphere, how it illumines everywhere equally, how it works for the benefit of infinite beings, in that it is directed to the extinction of the measureless mass of suf-fering of all sentient beings, to extinguish the sufferings of the destitute, to end hellish states, to rescue beings from brutish states, to close the door on all conditions inopportune for enlightenment, to lead the way to heavenly states, to produce human and celestial pleasure and happiness, to foster expe-rience of the pleasure of meditation, to increase happiness in the conditioned world, to show the way out of the mundane. It is set forth to illumine the cause of production of the aspiration of enlightenment, to develop the cause of production of provisions of virtue and knowledge, to increase the inten-sity of vast great compassion, to generate the power of great vows, for the attainment of the light of the path of enlightening beings, for the arrangement of the great vehicle of the transcendent ways, for the accomplishment of the supreme attainment of the Great Vehicle, for the vision of the knowledge of universally good action, for the attainment of the light of the knowledge of the stages of enlightening beings, for accomplishment of the purification of the array of means of emancipation in the practice of the vows of all enlightening beings, for the empowerment of accession to the sphere of omniscience. Noble one, what is the name of this concentration?"

Saradhvaja said, "There is a perfection of wisdom called equanimity of the universal eye, and this concentration is its light, called manifestation of universal purification. By the perfect accomplishment of the concentration of manifestation of universal purification, which springs from the light of the perfection of wisdom of equanimity of the universal eye, countless tens of hundreds of thousands of complete concentrations, beginning with the manifestation of universal purification, are born."

Sudhana said, "Is this the greatest range of this concentration?"

Saradhvaja said, "One who has fully accomplished this concentration has the power to discern worlds, to enter worlds, to travel freely in worlds, to adorn worlds, to purify worlds, to beautify worlds, to see buddhas, to observe the grandeur of buddhas, to know the emanations of buddhas, to enter the powers of buddhas, to plunge into the ocean of virtues of buddhas, to receive the teachings of buddhas, to follow the knowledge of the unity of all buddhas' teachings, to enter the ocean of congregations of buddhas, to go anywhere in the ten directions, to observe the teaching activity of the buddhas, to see the realms of the buddhas, to embrace all with great compassion, to pervade everywhere with love, to plunge tirelessly into the vision of buddhas everywhere, to enter into the ocean of all beings, to know the ocean of faculties of all beings, to know the distinction of faculties of all beings.

"I know this state of perfection of wisdom; but how can I know the practice, tell of the virtues, show the realm, reveal the sphere, describe the power of great vows, illumine the way of emancipation, elucidate the attainment, shed light on the path, follow the stream of concentration, know the range of mind, or reach equality with the knowledge, of the enlightening beings who have entered the ocean of states of perfection of wisdom, who have clarified the cosmic perspective, who know where all teachings lead, who pervade an infinite sphere with vast awareness, who command the light of great mental control, who have purified the light of all spheres of concentration, who issue from the magical power of mystic knowledge, who have entered the inexhaustible ocean of intelligence, who speak pleasantly of the stages of enlightenment, who are refuges for all beings?

"Go south, to a place called Samudravetadin, where there is a park called Samantavyuha, in front of the city Mahaprabha, where a lay woman named Asha, wife of king Suprabha, dwells; go to her and ask her how an enlightening being is to learn and apply the practice of enlightening beings."

Then Sudhana, pleased, uplifted, transported, overjoyed, joyful and happy, invigorated and sustained by Saradhvaja, having entered the realm of concentration, having attained illumined knowledge, having attained the light of concentration, his consciousness illumined by the light of the principles of teaching pursuant to purifications of interest, seeing the way to purity, with knowledge emanating light in all directions, paid his respects to Saradhvaja and left, looking at him again and again, bowing to him, thinking and meditating on him, praising him, recalling his virtues and keeping them firmly in mind, joining in with his vow, seeking his vision, remembering his words, recalling his appearance, contemplating the excellence of his knowledge, plunging into his sphere of concentration, fixing his mind on his sphere of undertaking, reflecting on the scope of his experience, illumined by his knowledge.

Asha

Then Sudhana, uplifted by the virtues of the spiritual benefactor, sent forth by the spiritual benefactor, having gained access to the vision of the spiritual benefactor, putting the instructions of the spiritual benefactor into practice, remembering the words of the spiritual benefactor, kindly disposed toward spiritual benefactors, seeing spiritual benefactors as mines of the vision of buddhas, seeing spiritual benefactors as those who show the teachings of buddhas, seeing spiritual benefactors as teachers of the elements of omniscience, seeing spiritual benefactors as eyes to see the sky of buddhahood, gradually made his way to Samantavyuha Park in Samudravetadin.

He saw the park surrounded by fences made of all kinds of jewels, in the midst of rows of all kinds of jewel trees, adorned throughout with beautiful delicate flowers like sets of all kinds of jewels releasing pollen, adorned by all kinds of jewel trees, strewn with the various blossoms of the flowers of all kinds of jewel trees, with rows of trees of all kinds of fragrances giving off their scents in all directions, trees of garlands of all jewels with their flower buds bursting forth streaming a rain of garlands of various jewels, the ground beautifully spread with various decorations made of jewels from trees of all kinds of diamonds, the area well distributed with cloths of various colors hanging down from trees of flowers of various forms, with trees of all kinds of musical instruments making beautiful sounds surpassing the heavens when stirred by the wind, the ground level throughout, neither high nor low, adorned with various trailing streamers of ornaments welling forth from the flower buds of trees of all ornaments. In the park, furthermore, were ten hundred thousand arrays of turrets adorned with all kinds of precious jewels, extremely pure; ten hundred thousand towers covered with gold, ten hundred thousand mansions adorned with radiant jewels, ten hundred thousand lotus ponds made of all kinds of jewels, inlaid with jewel bricks, with varied stairways made of seven precious substances, surrounded by benches made of various gems, fragrant as pools of water scented with celestial sandalwood, the bottoms covered with golden sand, spread with ten layers of pure gold and jewels, stairways set on four sides, filled with water of eight qualities, vibrant with the beautiful sounds of the calls of various birds, surrounded by rows of jewel palms, covered by nets of gold bells chiming sweetly when stirred by the wind, with canopies of great jewels above, surrounded by enclosures of trees of various jewels, with banners and streamers flying from jewel nets. There were also ten hundred thousand pools, lined with sandalwood clay, covered with lotuses of various colors made of all kinds of jewels, with pure water shining with lotuses of huge gems.

In the middle of the park was a large mansion called Multicolored Banner standing on a ground of jewels, adorned with pillars of sapphire, roofed with gold, surfaced with arrays of world-illumining jewels, its base blazing with webs of countless jewels, graced by the scent of unsurpassed jewels of fragrance, perfumed by jewels of compounded fragrances, filled with jewels of awakening fragrance extinguishing the heat of the senses.

In that mansion were arranged infinite seats—the calyxes of lotuses, luminous jewel lotuses, radiant jewel lotuses, world-illumining jewel lotuses, lotuses of various treasures, lotuses of pure jewels, lotuses inlaid with jewels, lotuses of omnifaceted jewels, lotuses of jewels with auras of light, lotuses of jewels shining with the radiant lights of arrays of pure jewels of the ocean, jewel lotuses covered with diamond lions.

The many turrets of the mansion were made of inconceivably many jewels, arrayed with varicolored jewels, their forms resplendent with light of inconceivably many colors.

The park was also covered above by ten hundred thousand canopies, such as canopies of cloth, canopies of plant tendrils, canopies of flowers, canopies of garlands, canopies of fragrances, canopies of jewels, golden canopies, canopies of jewels glittering like diamonds, canopies of nymphs magically produced by the chief of the water spirits, canopies of jewels prized by the king of gods.

It was also covered by ten hundred thousand precious nets such as nets of bells with jewels inside, nets of jeweled streamers, nets of jewel figures, nets of pearls, nets of sapphires, nets of moonlike jewels, nets emanating fragrance, nets of jeweled crowns.

It was also illumined by ten hundred thousand great lights, such as starlight-jewel light, sun-filled-jewel light, moonlike-jewel light, scenting-flame-jewel light, luster-filled-jewel light, lotus-calyx-jewel light, starry-jewel light, great blazing jewel light, radiant jewel light, and the light of jewels like wreaths of lightning emitting great clouds of fragrance.

The park was also adorned by rain from ten hundred thousand great clouds of ornaments; ten hundred thousand sandalwood-scented clouds thundered; it was adorned by ten hundred thousand trailing clouds of garlands surpassing those in the heavens; ten hundred thousand clouds of varicolored cloths surpassing the celestials rained; it was adorned by ten hundred thousand clouds of ornaments surpassing those of the heavens; it was showered by ten hundred thousand celestial beings bowing their heads to see; it was showered by ten hundred thousand clouds of nymphs producing beings of their own kind who did the same things in the past, with bodies like their own; it was showered by ten hundred thousand clouds of enlightening beings who had come to hear the Teaching.

Innumerable living beings in all states of existence came from the ten directions to the laywoman Asha, who was seated on a golden throne, adorned with a net of pearls from the ocean, wearing a tiara, her wrists adorned with bracelets of gold more beautiful than that of the heavens, her arms resplendent with jewels of glorious light, wearing earrings of pure deep blue gems, her head adorned with a veil of all kinds of jewels, her neck draped with a string of wish-fulfilling jewels. Those who came to her, affected with various sicknesses, filled with various afflictions, immersed in various views, covered by obstructions caused by actions, had their sicknesses alleviated when they saw Asha. Their minds freed from the defilement of afflictions, the thorns of views removed, the mountains of obstructions disintegrated, they entered the sphere of unobstructed purity, in which sphere of purity all their roots of goodness were clarified, the sprouts of spiritual faculties grew, and they entered the ocean of principles of omniscience, they recited the ocean of all mystic spells leading to mental command, came face to face with the ocean of all concentration media, began all holy vows, set all means of practice into operation, purified the means of accomplishing all virtues, proceeded according to wisdom characterized by all higher knowledges with unregressing breadth of mind, and became physically unattached and unobstructed, able to go everywhere.

Then Sudhana entered the park, looking all over till he saw Asha sitting there. He went up to her, paid his respects, and said, "Noble one, I have set my mind on supreme perfect enlightenment, but I do not know how to learn and carry out the practice of enlightening beings. I hear you give instructions to enlightening beings, so please tell me how an enlightening being is to learn and carry out the practice of enlightening beings."

She said, "I have attained an enlightening liberation called 'characterized by sorrowless well-being.' It is definitely beneficial to see me, hear me, attend me, live with me, remember me. I am not visible to those who have not developed the bases of goodness, who are not under the tutelage of spiritual benefactors, who are not in the care of the perfect buddhas. Those who see me thereupon become irreversible in progress toward supreme perfect enlightenment. Furthermore, the buddhas of the ten directions come here and sit on this jewel seat and expound the truth to me. I am always seeing buddhas, hearing the truth, and meeting enlightening beings. The eighty-four thousand quadrillion beings who live here in this park are all irreversible in progress toward supreme perfect enlightenment, having performed the same practices as I have. Any others who live here too will all be irreversible in progress toward supreme perfect enlightenment, as enlightening beings of the same practice as I who have entered the community of those who cannot regress."

Sudhana said, "Noble one, how long ago did you set your mind on supreme perfect enlightenment?"

She said, "I remember a past state when I cultivated religious practice in the company of the buddha known as the Lamp, whom I served and from whom I received teaching. Before that was a buddha named Undefiled; I went forth from society into the tutelage of that buddha and held the wheel of teaching of that buddha. Before that was a buddha named Star; I propitiated that buddha. Before that was a buddha named Splendor of the Polar Mountain; before that was a buddha named Lotus Calyx; before that was a buddha named Illuminating; before that was a buddha named Universal Eye; before that was a buddha named Purified by Spiritual Knowledge; before that was a buddha named Diamond Navel; before that was a buddha named Deifying the Universe. Remembering back in this way lifetime to lifetime, age to age, as successive buddhas appeared in the world, I remember as many buddhas as grains of sand in thirty-six Ganges Rivers whom I propitiated, attended, served, and honored, from whom I heard spiritual teaching, under whose tutelage I carried out spiritual practice. Beyond this, only the buddhas know how many buddhas I propitiated. Enlightening beings are infinite because of the aspiration of enlightenment, because of pervading all universes; enlightening beings are infinite because of the guidance of great compassion, because of entry into the midst of all beings; enlightening beings are infinite because their great vows go to the end of all universes; enlightening beings are infinite because of great love, because of suffusing all beings with love; enlightening beings are infinite because of the practice of enlightening beings, because of entering into all ages in all lands; enlightening beings are infinite because of the power of concentration, because of not regressing on the path of enlightening beings; enlightening beings are infinite because of the power of mental command, because of attainment of the method of mystic spells able to hold the memory of truths for all beings; enlightening beings are infinite because of the power of the light of knowledge, because of retaining the realization of the knowledge and wisdom of past, present, and future; enlightening beings are infinite because of the power of mystic knowledge, because of ability to produce wheels of nets of light pleasing beings according to their mentalities; enlightening beings are infinite because of the power of intelligence, because of satisfying all beings with one utterance; enlightening beings are infinite because of purity of body, because of pervading all buddha-fields with their own body."

Sudhana said, "Noble one, when will you realize supreme perfect enlightenment?"

Asha said, "Enlightening beings do not aspire to enlightenment with the object of leading just one sentient being to perfection, nor for the sake of a hundred or a thousand or a million or a billion sentient beings, nor for any number of beings, nor for all the sentient beings in as many worlds as atoms in untold, inexpressibly vast numbers of billion-world universes. Enlightening beings aspire to enlightenment for the sake of all sentient beings in all worlds, to lead them to perfection. Enlightening beings do not aspire to enlightenment to propitiate, honor, and attend one buddha, or even as many buddhas as atoms in untold worlds, or to propitiate, honor, and attend the lineage of buddhas in one world or the lineage of buddhas in as many worlds as atoms in untold buddha-fields. Enlightening beings do not aspire to enlightenment to purify one buddha-land, or even to purify as many buddha-lands as atoms in untold, inexpressible numbers of worlds. Enlightening beings do not aspire to enlightenment to preserve the teaching of one buddha, or even to preserve the teachings of as many buddhas as atoms in untold, inexpressible numbers of worlds. Enlightening beings do not aspire to enlightenment to enter into the diversity of vows which are the point of departure of one buddha, nor even to enter into the diversity of vows which are the points of departure of as many buddhas as atoms in untold, inexpressible numbers of buddha-fields. Enlightening beings do not aspire to enlightenment to enter into the array of the buddha-field of one buddha, nor even to enter into the arrays of buddha-fields of as many buddhas as atoms in untold, inexpressible numbers of buddha-fields. Enlightening beings do not aspire to enlightenment to take part in the assembly of one buddha, nor even to take part in the assemblies of as many buddhas as atoms in untold, inexpressible numbers of buddha-fields. Enlightening beings do not aspire to enlightenment to preserve the wheel of teaching of one buddha, nor to preserve the wheels of teaching of even as many buddhas as atoms in untold, inexpressible numbers of buddha-fields. Enlightening beings do not aspire to enlightenment to penetrate the ocean of mind of one sentient being, nor to penetrate the oceans of mind of even as many sentient beings as atoms in untold, inexpressible numbers of buddha-fields. Enlightening beings do not aspire to enlightenment to know the sphere of faculties of one sentient being, nor to know the faculties of even as many sentient beings as atoms in untold, inexpressible numbers of buddha-fields. Enlightening beings do not aspire to enlightenment to penetrate the ocean of faculties of one sentient being, nor to penetrate the oceans of faculties of even as many sentient beings as atoms in untold, inexpressible numbers of buddha-fields. Enlightening beings do not aspire to enlightenment to enter into the succession of ages in one world, nor to enter into the succession of ages in even as many worlds as atoms in untold, inexpressible numbers of buddha-fields. Enlightening beings do not aspire to enlightenment to comprehend the continuity of actions and habits of the sentient beings in one world, nor to comprehend the continuity of actions and habits of the sentient beings even in as many worlds as atoms in untold, inexpressible numbers of buddha-fields. Enlightening beings do not aspire to enlightenment to comprehend the ocean of afflictions of sentient beings in one world, nor to comprehend the oceans of afflictions of the sentient beings even in as many worlds as atoms in untold, inexpressible numbers of buddha-fields. Enlightening beings do not aspire to enlightenment to comprehend the ocean of all actions of the beings in one world, nor even to comprehend the oceans of all actions of beings in as many worlds as atoms in untold, inexpressible numbers of buddha-fields. Enlightening beings do not aspire to enlightenment to comprehend the ocean of all modes of behavior of all beings in one world, nor even to comprehend the ocean of all modes of behavior of all beings in as many worlds as atoms in untold, inexpressible numbers of buddha-fields. Rather, enlightening beings aspire to enlightenment to lead all sentient beings without exception to full development— they wish to propitiate and honor and attend all buddhas, to propitiate and honor and attend the successions of buddhas in all worlds; they are determined to purify all buddha-lands; they strive to hold the teachings of all buddhas; they are zealously devoted to following the variety of vows which are the points of departure of all buddhas; they are determined to enter into the arrays of all buddha-lands; they wish to enter the oceans of assemblies of all buddhas; they seek to go deeply into the ocean of mind of all sentient beings; they wish to know the spheres of faculties of all sentient beings; they aspire to penetrate the ocean of faculties of all sentient beings; they wish to enter into the succession of ages in all worlds; they are inspired with courage to cut off the continuity of afflictions and habit energies of all sentient beings; their sun of knowledge rises to evaporate the ocean of afflictions caused by actions of all sentient beings; their light of wisdom becomes manifest to know the ways of behavior of all sentient beings; their cloud of great compassion gathers to extinguish the mass of fire of suffering of all sentient beings.

"To put it briefly, there are ten hundred thousand incalculable numbers of such aspects of the conduct of the practice of enlightening beings, which are to be accomplished by an enlightening being. Furthermore, the practice of enlightening beings enters into all things, for the attainment of knowledge; the practice of enlightening beings enters into all lands, to thoroughly purify them. Because of this vow of mine, when the purification of the realm of desire is finished, my commitments will be finished; when the purification of the world is finished, my commitments will be finished; when all sentient beings' propensities to continue afflictive habits are ended, my commitments will be ended."

Sudhana said, "What is the name of this liberation?"

Asha said, "This liberation is called 'characterized by sorrowless well-being.' I know this enlightening liberation, but how can I know the practice, tell of the virtues, convey the inconceivable enlightening skills, or show the infinite varieties of enlightening vows of the enlightening beings who have oceanic minds because of seeking all the buddha-teachings, who are like the polar mountain because of steadfast will, who are like the medicine 'good to see' because they free all sentient beings from the sicknesses of afflictions, who are like the sun because they eliminate the darkness of ignorance of all sentient beings, whose minds are like the earth because they are a refuge for all sentient beings, who are like air because they benefit all sentient beings, who are lamps producing the light of knowledge for all sentient beings, who are like clouds raining truth with a quiet sound, who are like the moon because they radiate a web of light beams of virtue, who are like gods because they protect all sentient beings?

"Go south—there is a district in Samudravetalya called Nalayur where a seer named Bhishmottaranirghosha lives. Go ask him, and he will instruct you in the practice of enlightening beings."

Then Sudhana left Asha, after paying his respects, reflecting on the extreme rarity of enlightening beings, on how hard it is to get on good terms with spiritual benefactors, on how very difficult it is to get to meet people of truth, on how hard it is to attain the faculties of enlightening beings, how hard it is to attain the purity of intent of enlightening beings, how hard it is to find colleagues, how hard it is to focus the mind accurately on enlightenment, how hard it is to apply the teachings leading to the state of freedom from distress, how hard it is to find ways to develop invincible goodness of mind, and how hard it is to get to see ways to quickly develop omniscience.

Bhishmottaranirghosha

Then Sudhana, his mind on the instruction of the enlightening being, his mind on the purification of the conduct of enlightening beings, his mind developing the power of virtue of enlightening beings, his mind lit by the energy of the vision of Buddha, with mental energy arising from receiving a treasury of teaching, his mental energy increased by the undertaking of great vows, all things apparent to his mind, his mind aware of the intrinsic essence of things, his mind free from all obstructions, his mind viewing the reality realm without obscurity, his pure will indestructible, his mind invulnerable and immune to the power of all demons, gradually made his way to Nalayur and sought out the seer Bhishmottaranirghosha.

At that time Bhishmottaranirghosha was sojourning in a retreat, a pleasant place with countless diverse trees and plants, shaded by the leaves of various trees, with flowering trees perpetually blooming in various colors and fruit trees perpetually bearing, the ground made of the finest jewel-fruits from various jewel trees, well distributed with great sandalwood trees, graced with fragrance constantly coming from pleasant aloeswood trees, adorned with trumpet-flower trees distributed in the four directions, with beautifully formed fig trees, with perpetually ripe fruits raining from rose apple trees, beautified by fresh water lilies and lotus blossoms.

Sudhana saw the seer Bhishmottaranirghosha wearing matted hair, sitting on a seat of bark, rags, fragrant grass, and antelope skin on a layer of straw in a hut built at the foot of a sandalwood tree, surrounded by ten thousand seers. Seeing Bhishmottaranirghosha, Sudhana went up to him, and thinking he had found a true spiritual benefactor, looking upon spiritual benefactors as the door to omniscience because they guide one on the true path, looking upon omniscience as coming from the teaching of spiritual benefactors because they lead to the stage of all-knowledge, looking upon omniscience as coming from the guidance of spiritual benefactors because they lead to the jewel land of the knowledge of the ten powers, looking upon omniscience as illumined by the torch of spiritual benefactors because they produce the light of knowledge of the ten powers, looking upon spiritual benefactors as the path to omniscience leading unbroken to the city of omniscience, looking upon spiritual benefactors as lamps on the way to omniscience because they show the level and the uneven, looking upon spiritual benefactors as a bridge to omniscience because the peril of falling is eliminated, looking upon spiritual benefactors as parasols of omniscience because they produce coolness by the power of great love, looking upon spiritual benefactors as streams of omniscience because they give rise to great compassion, looking upon the satisfaction of the vision of omniscience as coming from spiritual benefactors because they illumine the principle of the inherent nature of phenomena, Sudhana paid his respects to the seer and said, "Noble one, I have set my mind on supreme perfect enlightenment, but I do not know how an enlightening being is to learn and carry out the practice of enlightening beings. I have heard you give enlightening beings instruction; please tell me how an enlightening being is to learn and carry out the practice of enlightening beings."

The seer Bhishmottaranirghosha looked at the ten thousand people surrounding him and said, "This youth has set his mind on supreme perfect enlightenment and has invited all sentient beings to fearlessness. He is aiming for the welfare and happiness of all beings; he is facing the ocean of knowledge; he wants to spread the clouds of teaching of all buddhas; he wants to plunge into the ocean of all principles of the Teaching; he wants to live by the light of knowledge; he wants to bring the cloud of great compassion near; he wants to cause the rain of the great Teaching to shower; he wants to have the moon of great knowledge rise in the world and extinguish the burning of all afflictions; he wants to develop the roots of goodness of all sentient beings."

Then those ten thousand people scattered beautiful fragrant flowers over Sudhana, bowed to him, and circled him in respect, and said, "This person will be a savior; he will extinguish all the hellish torments of all beings, he will stop all brutish ways, he will get rid of the ways of the underworld, he will shut the door of all conditions inopportune for enlightenment, he will evaporate the ocean of craving, he will sever the bonds of craving, he will remove the mass of suffering, he will dispel the darkness of ignorance, he will surround the world with mountains of virtue, he will reveal the mine of jewels of knowledge, he will cause the sun of knowledge to rise, he will clarify the eye of truth, he will show what is good and bad in the world."

Then the seer Bhishmottaranirghosha said to those people, "Whoever aspires to supreme perfect enlightenment promotes the happiness of all sentient beings, carrying out the practice of enlightening beings, and will eventually attain omniscience. This youth has set his heart on supreme perfect enlightenment; he will fulfill the stage of complete buddhahood." Then the seer said to Sudhana, "I have attained an enlightening liberation called 'unsurpassed banner.'"

Sudhana said, "What is the scope of this liberation?"

Bhishmottaranirghosha stretched forth his right hand and rubbed Sudhana's head, then took Sudhana by the right hand. At that moment Sudhana saw in the ten directions as many buddha-lands as atoms in ten hundred thousand buddha-lands, and in them he perceived himself at the feet of as many buddhas as atoms in ten hundred thousand buddha-lands. He also saw the innumerable features in the pure adornments of those buddha-lands, and he saw the various arrays of the oceans of audiences surrounding the buddhas therein. He also saw the radiant mass of the marks and embellishments of the buddhas' bodies in the midst of the congregations. He also heard teaching from the buddhas without missing a single word, and he remembered the cycles of teachings of those buddhas in order without confusion, and he received the rain of those clouds of teaching as they showered on beings of various mentalities. He also entered the oceans of past vows of those buddhas, purified by zealous application of various kinds. He also entered oceans of past attainments of the buddhas, purified by oceans of various vows. He also saw the forms of buddhas manifested so as to please all sentient beings according to their mentalities. He also saw the nets of light rays of the buddhas, their various cool, pure halos. He also entered into those buddhas' powers by following the light of unobstructed knowledge. He seemed to be with one buddha for a day and a night, with another for seven days and nights, another for a fortnight, another for a month, another for a year, another for a century, another for a millennium, another for a hundred millennia, another for a million years, another for a hundred million years, another for a billion years, another for a hundred billion years, another for a trillion years, another for half an eon, another for an eon, another for a hundred eons, another for a thousand eons, another for a hundred thousand eons, another for a million eons, another for a hundred million eons, another for a billion eons, another for a hundred billion eons, another for a trillion eons, up to untold, inexpressible numbers of eons, or as many eons as atoms in the continent, or as many eons as atoms in untold buddha-lands. Thus did he perceive himself with the buddhas, illumined by the light of knowledge of the liberation "unsurpassed banner," imbued with the light of the concentration filled with sunlike radiance, reaching absorption in liberation of endless knowledge, imbued with the light of the mystic formulation of the structure of the universe, his mind illumined by the mystic formulation of the indestructible sphere, abiding in absorption in the realm of well-ordered bodies of knowledge, intent on the state of transcendent wisdom of the path of adornment of all planes, illumined by the light of concentration on the sphere containing the space of the enlightened, his mind illuminated by concentration on the circumference of the wheel of teaching of all buddhas, imbued with the light of absorption in the inexhaustible sphere of jewels of knowledge of past, present, and future.

Then the seer let go of Sudhana, who found himself once again standing before the seer Bhishmottaranirghosha. The seer said, "Do you remember?" Sudhana said, "I remember, noble one, by the empowerment of the spiritual benefactor."

Bhishmottaranirghosha said, "I know this enlightening liberation known as the unsurpassed invincible banner, but how can I know the practice, or tell the virtues, or accurately express the excellence of vows, or know the structure of the lands, or plunge into the sphere of knowledge, or enter into the realm of concentration, or attain the mystic powers, or attain to the freedom of liberation, or take up the various physical manifestations, or reveal the purity of voice, or show the light of knowledge of the enlightening beings who have attained absorption in the mystic knowledge supreme among all creatures, who are masters of all wheels of time, who are skilled in achievement of the knowledge of the characteristics of buddhas, who are supernal manifestations of the incarnation of the buddhas, who have comprehended the knowledge of all objects of past, present, and future as of one characteristic, whose bodies are distributed throughout all worlds, who are embodiments of knowledge in which all realms of reality are revealed, who appear to all sentient beings according to their inclinations, who benefit sentient beings according to their ways of thought and action, who glow with a brightness that illumines everywhere, who have purified the sphere of pure, vast, radiant knowledge?

"Go south to a land called Ishana, where there lives a priest named Jayoshmayatana. Go ask him how an enlightening being is to learn and apply the practice of enlightening beings."

Then Sudhana, pleased, uplifted, transported, overjoyed, happy, paid respects to the seer Bhishmottaranirghosha and departed, looking back at him again and again.

Jayoshmayatana

Then, illumined by the light of knowledge of the enlightening liberation "unsurpassed banner," directly witnessing the inconceivable miracles of the realm of buddhas, endowed with mystic knowledge directly aware of the inconceivable liberation of enlightening beings, his mind illumined by the inconceivable knowledge of concentration of enlightening beings, imbued with the light of knowledge of concentration comprehending all times at once, illumined by the realm of concentration comprehending that all is in perception, having attained the light of the highest knowledge in all worlds, approaching the state whose scope reaches everywhere in past, present, and future, intent on the knowledge showing nondual equality in differentiation, with the light of knowledge extending to all objects, with skillfulness rich in zeal for the purification of tolerance in the face of people's beliefs, having attained the light of certain knowledge of acceptance of things in terms of their inherent nature, his mind constantly involved in enlightening beings' practice of mystic knowledge reaching everywhere, which is meditation on inherent nature, his mind progressing rapidly and irreversibly toward omniscience, illumined by the lightning of knowledge of the ten powers, his mind tirelessly seeking the sound of the reality realm, determined to enter the realm of omniscience, intent on accomplishing the infinite array of practices of enlightening beings and purifying the infinite sphere of great vows of enlightening beings, his mind directed toward endlessly ongoing knowledge of the infinite network of all worlds, his mind not

shrinking from guiding infinite beings to complete development, beholding the infinite sphere of practice of enlightening beings, seeing the variety
of conditions in infinite worlds, seeing the variety of differentiations of infinite worlds, seeing infinite worlds within microcosms and macrocosms,
seeing the variety of the webs of perceptions and conceptions on which infinite worlds are based, seeing the variety of conventional terminology in
infinite worlds, seeing the variety of interests of infinite beings, seeing the
variety of differentiations of infinite beings, seeing the following of developmental teachings of infinite beings, seeing the variety in perceptions of
place and time of infinite beings, Sudhana, his attention on spiritual benefactors, gradually made his way to the priest Jayoshmayatana in the land of
Ishana.

At that time the priest was practicing an ascetic exercise of enduring fierce
heat, with his mind on omniscience; on four sides were huge bonfires like
mountains ablaze. Rising above appeared a great mountain precipice, a
razor-edge path.

Sudhana went up, paid his respects to the priest, and said, "Noble one, I
have set my mind on supreme perfect enlightenment, but I do not know
how an enlightening being is to learn and carry out the practice of enlightening beings. I hear you give enlightening beings instruction; please tell me
how to learn and carry out the practice of enlightening beings."

The priest said, "Climb this razor-edge-path mountain and jump from
there into the fire—thus will your enlightening practice be purified."

At that point Sudhana thought, "It is hard to avoid the situations that are
inopportune for enlightenment; it is hard to get to be human; it is hard to
remove error and doubt about the right opportunity; it is hard to find a buddha in the world; it is hard to have all one's faculties in order; it is hard to get
to hear the truth; it is hard to meet people of truth; it is hard to find genuine
spiritual benefactors; it is hard to get genuine guidance and instruction; it is
hard to live right in the human world; it is hard to carry out truth in all
respects. Might this not be a demon, or someone possessed by a demon, or a
cohort of the devil, or an imitation spiritual teacher, or a false enlightening
being, who has undertaken to impede my roots of goodness, who is out to
destroy my life? Does he not want to prevent me from reaching omniscience? Does he not want to lead me on a wrong path? Does he not want to
prevent me from attaining buddhahood?"

While he was involved in these thoughts, ten thousand Brahma gods
appeared in the sky and said to him, "Do not get fixed on such thoughts.
This sage has attained the light of the concentration of adamantine flame.
He has unrelenting energy and has begun the great undertaking of salvation.
He has set out to end the emotional attachments of all sentient beings. He is
striving to dissolve the webs of all views. He is determined to burn up the
deadwood of all afflictions and their actions. He is working to shed light in
the wilderness of all kinds of knowledge that is not conducive to enlightenment. He is resolved upon eliminating all beings' fears of old age and death.
He is intent on dispersing the darkness of past, present, and future. He has

undertaken to shine beams of light of all truths. As he mortifies himself with four fires under the blazing sun, even the Brahma gods, who think themselves creators and lords and supreme beings, and are engrossed in various views, do not take pleasure in their own states because of the light given off by this priest's peerless practice of heat austerity. Not enjoying the pleasure of meditation, they come to the priest, and he overwhelms them by mystic power, and through fierce austerity teaches them to get rid of all their views and destroy all pride and arrogance. He also teaches them so that they may suffuse all worlds with great love and compassion, make their will for enlightenment firm, enlarge their determination for enlightenment, turn to the vision of all buddhas, fully receive the voice of the buddhas, and hear the voice of buddhas everywhere without resistance or obstruction."

Ten thousand demons also stood in the sky, showered celestial jewels, and said, "The light emitted from the flames used by this priest in his heat mortification obscures our abodes, our ornaments, and our paraphernalia. Terrified, we and our cohorts go to the priest, who teaches in such a way that, coming to ourselves and getting back our right minds, we aspire to enlightenment and become irreversible on the way to supreme perfect enlightenment."

Also, ten thousand controlling gods, scattering celestial flowers, said, "While he is mortifying himself with four fires under the fiery sun, we find no pleasure in our own abodes. We and our cohorts go to him, and he teaches us so that we attain control of our own minds, control of afflictions, ability to be born in any state we wish, power to clear away obstructions caused by action, mastery of all concentrations, control of paraphernalia to purify our arrangements, and control conforming to our wishes."

Ten thousand gods of pleasant emanations also stood in the sky, presented sweet sounds of celestial music and song, and said, "The fire of the priest is producing such light that our palaces are glowing, being purified and becoming more radiant, and so are the decorations and nymphs here. We and our cohorts of godlings and nymphs no longer find pleasure in desires, and we do not enjoy sensual pleasures. Our minds and bodies cooled, we go to the priest, who teaches us so that our minds will be purified, so that our minds will be radiant, so our minds will be good, so our minds will be malleable, so we will become joyful, so we may purify the realization of the knowledge of the ten powers, so we may grow in enthusiasm for the great Teaching, so we may purify our bodies and produce measureless buddha-bodies, so we may purify our voices and attain the voice of Buddha, so we may purify our minds and attain omniscience."

Ten thousand gods of the heaven of satisfaction, along with their companies of celestial boys and girls, also stood in the sky, showered all kinds of fragrant powders, paying honor and respect, and said, "While he mortifies himself with fire there is no pleasure in our abodes. Being freed from attachment, we go to the priest and he teaches us so that we will be indifferent to all objects of sense, so that we will be perfectly and completely satisfied in mind, so that we will produce roots of goodness, so that we will aspire to enlightenment, and so that we will eventually fulfill all qualities of buddhas."

Ten thousand gods of the heaven of timely portion, along with their celestial sons and daughters, showered a rain of flowers and said, "While this priest is mortifying himself with fire, we have no pleasure in our celestial song. Freed from attachment, we go to the priest and he teaches us so that we will become detached from all sensuality and eventually attain all qualities of buddhahood."

Ten hundred thousand celestial beings of the thirty-three-fold heavens, each with thirty-two siblings, along with their celestial sons and daughters, showered rain from clouds of celestial cloths, jewels, ornaments, and flowers, then said, "While this priest is mortifying himself with fire, we have no pleasure in our palaces, parks, and groves, or in such enjoyments as music, dance, and song. Freed from attachment, we go to the priest, and he teaches us to remove all sensuality. He tells us this is all impermanent, unstable, bound to perish. He teaches us to thoroughly cut off all arrogance and heedlessness, to increase our desire for supreme enlightenment. Furthermore, at the sight of this priest, these peaks of the polar mountain quake. Terrified, we commit ourselves to reach omniscience, that we may be firm in our aspiration for omniscience."

Also, ten thousand rain spirits in the sky showered rain from clouds of celestial sandalwood, along with the sweet sounds of the songs of nymphs, producing clouds of celestial fragrance, and said, "The light emitted from this priest's fires, illumining the abodes of all the water spirits, removes fears of the hot rain of sand. It also extinguishes anger, and the water spirits become cool and clear in mind. Then, once our minds are clear, the priest teaches us to reject our low state as dragons and to stop all obstructive actions. Having taught us to overcome evil, he inspires us to supreme perfect enlightenment and leads us to omniscience."

Also, ten thousand spirit chiefs, standing in the sky, honored the priest Jayoshmayatana and the youth Sudhana with various offerings, then said, "Son, as this priest mortifies himself with fire, goodwill toward human beings is born in our minds, and all spirits, goblins, and demons also become benevolent. Benevolent, now harmless, they come to us; overcome by the dominant power of goodwill, we find no pleasure in our various estates. We all go with our respective companions to the priest; he radiates light from his body, which shines on us and fills our bodies with bliss. Our bodies and minds blissful, he teaches us in such a way that many spirits, goblins, demons, and ghosts are inspired to seek enlightenment."

Ten thousand chief celestial musicians also stood in the sky and said, "While we are in our abodes too, our abodes are illumined by the light of the priest's fires; touched by that light, we are filled with inconceivable bliss and we go to the priest, who then teaches us in such a way that we become irreversible in progress toward supreme perfect enlightenment."

Ten thousand titan kings rose from the ocean, knelt on their right knees, joined their palms in salutation, and said, "As this priest mortifies himself by fire, all our titan worlds, including the oceans, mountains, and land spheres, quake: we are all thereby divested of arrogance, heedlessness, and conceit; overwhelmed by the heat of his religious practice, we go to him, and he teaches us so that we may do away with all deceitfulness and guile, enter into acceptance of the profound truth, abide in the state of imperturbability, and perfect the knowledge of the ten powers."

Also ten thousand bird kings, assuming splendid human forms, said, "Son, the light from the flames of the priest's fires, shining on our abodes, causes them to quake. Frightened and agitated, we go to him, and by teaching us he exhorts us to great benevolence and compassion, he urges us to plunge into the ocean of mundane life to serve sentient beings sunk in the mud of desire, he urges us to purify our will for enlightenment, he exhorts us to keenness of wisdom and skill in means, and gets us to work at guiding sentient beings according to their maturity."

Ten thousand centaur kings also stood in the sky and said, "As this priest mortifies himself by fire, the voice of Buddha comes forth from the rows of palms, the trees hung with nets of bells, strings of jewels, garlands, and musical instruments, and the houses and furniture with all kinds of musical instruments and jewelry in our abodes as they are blown by the wind; the voice of the Teaching, the voice of the host of nonregressing enlightening beings, and the voice of the vows on which enlightening beings act also emerge, saying that in such-and-such a world the enlightening being so-and-so is vowing to attain enlightenment, in such-and-such a world the enlightening being so-and-so is giving up that which is difficult to give up, in such-and-such a world the enlightening being so-and-so is purifying the sphere of universally aware knowledge, in such-and-such a world the enlightening being so-and-so is going to the summit of enlightenment, in such-and-such a world the enlightening being so-and-so has conquered the demon hordes and is becoming supremely and perfectly enlightened, in such-and-such a world the buddha so-and-so is turning the wheel of the teaching, in such-and-such a world the buddha so-and-so has finished all the tasks of buddhas and is passing away into absolute nirvana. There may be an end to the particles of every tree and plant, limb and leaf, on this continent, but there is no end to those names of the buddhas and the vows of enlightening beings, the lofty points of departure of the conduct of enlightening beings, which are heard to sound from the rows of palms and all the musical instruments, jewelry, houses, and furniture in our abodes as they are blown by the wind, producing the voices of Buddha, the Teaching, and enlightenment. Ecstatically joyful at the sound of the names of the buddhas and the community of enlightening beings and the vows and practices they proceed upon, we go to the priest, and he teaches us so that we and the many beings around us become irreversible in progress toward supreme perfect enlightenment."

Innumerable gods of the realm of desire with magnificent appearances also stood in the sky, presented mental offerings, and said, "As this priest mortifies himself with heat, his bonfires give off such light that it illumines all the hells all the way to the uninterrupted hell, and the pains of all the creatures in hell cease. He also is visible to us by the same light. We above him, our minds clarified, have been born in the heavens of the realm of desire we wished for. Grateful to him, never tired of seeing him, we give up all sensuality and go to him, and he teaches us in such a way that innumerable sentient beings resolve to realize enlightenment."

Then Sudhana, pleased, enraptured, transported, overjoyed, happy, having heard this teaching, considered the priest Jayoshmayatana to be a true spiritual benefactor, and prostrated himself at the priest's feet and said, "I confess my error, noble one, in not recognizing you as a spiritual benefactor." Thereupon the priest spoke a verse to Sudhana:

> An enlightening being who follows instructions
> Has no doubts, his mind at one with the teachers.
> All benefits will be his, and they will be auspicious;
> Sure of buddha-knowledge too, he awakens at the foot of the enlightenment tree.

Then Sudhana climbed the path up the cliff of the mountain, a mass of razor edges, and threw himself into the fire. As he was falling he attained an enlightening concentration called "well established." On contact with the fire he attained an enlightening concentration called "mystic knowledge of the bliss of tranquillity." He said, "How wonderful is the pleasant feeling of this fire and this razor-edge mountain."

The priest said, "I have attained the enlightening liberation in which one is not overcome. I know this liberation, but how can I know the practice or tell the virtues of the enlightening beings whose resolve is like rays of fiery energy, determined to end all beings' afflictions and views, who are eminent leaders who never turn back, whose hearts are never exhausted or overcome, whose minds are never depressed, whose spirits never cringe or cower, whose resolve is adamant, who are never dejected in carrying out their great undertakings, who never slacken in their efforts, who are like whirlwinds, who work for the benefit of all beings, whose vigor never recedes?

"Go south, to a city called Simhavijurmbhita, where there lives a girl named Maitrayani, daughter of the rajah Simhaketu; go ask her how an enlightening being is to learn and carry out the practice of enlightening beings."

Then Sudhana paid his respects and left the priest Jayoshmayatana.

Maitrayani

Then, with inconceivable respect for spiritual benefactors, the great zeal purified, ready for the Great Vehicle, seeking enlightened knowledge, absorbed in the way to enlightenment, seeking association with spiritual friends, dwelling in the sphere of the Teaching, approaching unhindered knowledge, certain of the supreme truth, intent on ultimate knowledge, realizing that past, present, and future are ultimately one instant, aware of ultimate nonduality like space, sure of the ultimacy of nonduality, dwelling in the ultimate nondifferentiation of the reality realm, devoted to discipline whose goal is freedom from obstruction, intent on ultimate harmony in action, dwelling on the ultimate nondifference of those who realize Thusness, intent on the knowledge to tear apart the net of conceptions of all sentient beings, free from attachment to any land, his mind not attached to the congregations of the buddhas or to the purities of the buddha-lands, perceiving all sentient beings as void of self or inherent identity, realizing that all sounds are like echoes and eminently aware that all forms are like reflections, Sudhana gradually made his way to the city Simhavijurmbhita, looking for the girl Maitrayani.

He was told, "The girl Maitrayani, daughter of the rajah Simhaketu, with a retinue of five hundred girls, is up on the roof of a palace of radiant jewels, sitting on a seat set on sandalwood legs and draped with nets of strings of jewels and arrayed with celestial cloth, expounding spiritual teaching."

Hearing this, Sudhana entered the city, went to the house of the rajah, and stood at the outer foyer, desirous of seeing the girl Maitrayani. There he saw hundreds of thousands of people going in. He asked them where they were going and why they had come, and they told him they were going to Maitrayani to hear the Teaching. He thought to himself, "No one is prevented from going in." So he went in.

Having gone in, he saw the palace of radiant jewels set on a crystal base, with pillars of lapis lazuli and walls of diamond, ornamented with a hundred thousand projections of gold, furnished with countless jewel mirrors, arrayed with world-illumining jewels, spread with countless jewel nets, graced with inconceivable arrays of beautiful sounds from a hundred thousand golden bells shaken by the breeze. He also saw the girl Maitrayani, with dark eyes, black hair, and golden skin. Sudhana paid his respects to her and said, "Noble one, I have set my mind on supreme perfect enlightenment, but I do not know how an enlightening being is to learn and carry out the practice of enlightening beings."

She said, "Look at the adornments of my palace."

Looking all around, in each wall, each pillar, each mirror, each figure, each formation, each jewel, each golden bell, each jewel tree, each girl's body, each jewel necklace, he saw reflected images of the buddhas in the cosmos, with their first inspirations, spheres of practice and vows, manifestations of emergence in the world, mystical transformation on attainment of enlightenment, turnings of the wheel of teaching, and displays of ultimate extinction. This he saw in each and every object. Just as the sun, moon, and stars in the sky are seen reflected in a clear, limpid pool of water, so did all the buddhas of the cosmos appear reflected in each object of the luminous jewel palace, this as a result of the girl Maitrayani's past roots of goodness.

Having viewed this, holding in mind the features of this supernal array of visions of Buddhas, Sudhana joined his hands in a gesture of respect and turned his attention to Maitrayani's words. She said, "I have attained the means of access to perfect wisdom from the arrangement of the totality. I sought this from buddhas as numerous as grains of sand in thirty-six Ganges Rivers, and those buddhas introduced me to the means of access to perfect wisdom by way of the arrangement of the totality through various ways of entry into it, each different."

Sudhana said, "What is the sphere of this means of access to perfect wisdom by way of the arrangement of the totality?"

She said, "Focusing my attention on this means of access to perfect wisdom by way of the arrangement of the totality, meditating on it, following it, pondering it, contemplating it, making it familiar, keeping it in mind, putting it in order, putting it into effect, perfecting it, thoroughly examining it, I developed a mental control called 'facing in all directions,' in the sphere of which mental control incalculable tens of hundreds of thousands of media of the Teaching operate, assemble, become visible, become accessible, and develop—for example, the medium of buddha-lands, the medium of buddhas, the medium of doctrines, the medium of all beings, the medium of the past, the medium of the future, the medium of the present, the medium of the limit of duration, the medium of virtue, the medium of provisions of virtue, the medium of knowledge, the medium of provisions of knowledge, the medium of vows, the medium of differentiation of vows, the medium of practices, the medium of purification of practices, the medium of accumulation of practices, the medium of fulfillment of practices, the medium of actions, the medium of harmony of actions, the medium of streams of actions, the medium of performance of actions, the medium of fields of actions, the medium of rejection of evil actions, the medium of undertaking of proper actions, the medium of control of actions, the medium of morality, the medium of guidance to right ethics, the medium of concentration, the medium of practice pursuant to concentration, the medium of contemplation in concentration, the medium of spheres of concentration, the medium of emerging from concentration, the medium of mystic knowledge, the medium of the ocean of mind, the medium of ways of thought, the medium of clearing away entanglements of mind, the medium of illumining the obscure recesses of the mind, the medium of calming and clearing the pool of the mind, the medium of capacities of the mind, the medium of the actions of the mind, the medium of the occurrence of sentient beings' afflictions, the medium of defiling habit energies, the medium of the acting out of afflictions, the medium of interests, the medium of the conduct of sentient beings, the medium of the variety of conduct of sentient beings, the medium of the productions of the world, the medium of the inclinations of sentient beings, the medium of what is in the conceptions of sentient beings, the medium of places, the medium of the realms of phenomena, the medium of great compassion, the medium of great kindness, the medium of tranquillity, the medium of speech, the medium of reason, the medium of attainments, the medium of distinctions, the medium of unity, the medium of ultimate nonattachment, the medium of totality, the medium of the principles of buddhas, the medium of the principles of enlightening beings, the medium of the principles of disciples, the medium of the principles of individual illuminates, the medium of worldly principles, the medium of principles of formation of worlds, the medium of principles of disintegration of worlds, the medium of principles of the existence of worlds, the medium of purification of worlds, the medium of defilement of worlds, the medium of worlds with purity amid defilement, the medium of worlds with defilement amid purity, the medium of wholly defiled worlds, the medium of wholly pure worlds, the medium of levelness of worlds, the medium of inverted worlds, the medium of upside-down worlds, the medium of entry into the network of the cosmos in which everything is interrelated, the medium of revolving of worlds, the medium of being based on thoughts, the medium of the microcosmic found in the macrocosmic, the medium of the macrocosmic in the microcosmic, the medium of vision of buddhas, the medium of variety of embodiments of buddhas, the medium of variety of auras of buddhas, the medium of differences in the voices of buddhas, the medium of the production of the wheels of teaching of buddhas, the medium of the continuity of the wheels of teaching of buddhas, the medium of expressions of the wheels of teaching of buddhas, the medium of the turning of the wheels of teaching of buddhas, the medium of embodiments of buddhas, the medium of the audiences of buddhas, the medium of the differences in audiences of buddhas, the medium of entry into the oceans of audiences of buddhas, the medium of illumination of the powers of buddhas, the medium of concentrations of buddhas, the medium of mystic emanations from the concentrations of buddhas, the medium of the states of buddhas, the medium of the magic powers of buddhas, the medium of the projected forms of buddhas, the medium of buddhas' knowledge of what is on the minds of others, the medium of spiritual transformations of buddhas, the medium of abiding in the state of satisfaction, the medium of the works of buddhas up to the manifestation of ultimate extinction, the medium of works for the benefit of infinite beings, the medium of the profound doctrine of emptiness, the medium of various doctrines, the medium of forms of the practices of enlightening beings, the medium of the forms of the production of the aspiration for enlightenment, the medium of the forms of provisions of the aspiration for enlightenment, the medium of the forms of vows, the medium of the forms of practices, the medium of the forms of mystic knowledge, the medium of the forms of emancipation, the medium of the forms of purification of mental control, the medium of the forms of purification of the sphere of knowledge, the medium of the forms of purification of wisdom, the medium of the infinite forms of enlightenment, the medium of forms of purification of mindfulness.

"I know this means of access to perfect wisdom which is the array of total mindfulness; how can I know the practice or tell the virtues of the enlightening beings whose minds are like space, whose intellects are broad as the cosmos, whose mental flow is based on accumulated virtue, who have attained transmundane understanding, who do not practice worldly ways, who have attained the eye of the light of knowledge without obscurity, who clearly discern all realms of reality, whose awareness is infinite as space, whose eyes are mindful of all objects, who are filled with the light of the state of nonobstruction, who are skilled in analyzing all doctrines, meanings, and statements, who are not overcome by any world, who conduct themselves well according to worldly standards and are irreproachable in any worldly state, who are intent on the well-being of all worlds, who are a refuge for all beings, who know the manners and courtesies of speech of all worlds, who can give the appearances of dress and habitation of all worlds as they wish, and who are masters of all wheels of time?

"Go south, to the land called Trinayana, where a monk named Sudarshana lives. Go ask him how an enlightening being is to learn and carry out the practice of enlightening beings."

Then Sudhana paid his respects to Maitrayani and left.

Sudarshana

Then, contemplating the profound discernment of enlightening beings' knowledge, the profound attainment of the base of the reality realm, the profound knowledge of all subtleties, the profundity of the conceptuality of the world, the profundity of the base of nondoing, the profundity of the base of the mental stream, the profundity of the base of interdependent origination, the profundity of the plane of truth in terms of inherent nature, the profundity of the plane of truth in terms of the conventions of sentient beings, the profundity of the ground of adornment of the cosmos, the profundity of the plane of observation of the operation of the body, and the profundity of the ground of the world of action and thought, Sudhana made his way to the land of Trinayana.

Looking for the monk Sudarshana in towns and cities, marketplaces and villages, in herding stations, in hermitages, in the provinces, in mountains, caves, and forests, he saw Sudarshana walking around in a certain woods, young and handsome, with the physical marks and embellishments of a great man, his gaze steady, mindful, of vast intelligence, intent on the sphere of insuperable knowledge, his mind free from all vacillation, vain imagination, idle fancies, and false ideas, abiding in pure knowledge, aware of the vast range of enlightened knowledge, firmly resolved to guide all beings to full development, with a vast sphere of great compassion, aiming to bear the eye of the teachings of all buddhas, aiming to produce the light of knowledge in all sentient beings, ever-mindful of the way of the enlightened, treading it for the sake of all sentient beings, walking quietly and steadily, neither quickly nor slowly, dressed like the deities of the pure abodes, surrounded by all kinds of beings.

Furthermore, in front of Sudarshana as he walked were deities of direction who caused the world to turn; footstep-following deities received his steps on jewel lotuses; fire deities with inexhaustible spheres of light dispelled the darkness; forest deities showered rain of flowering plants; earth deities, the source of stability, revealed jewel mines; sky deities, their splendor illumining everywhere, adorned the sky; glorious ocean deities scattered great jewels over him; polar mountain deities, full of purity, folded their hands in respectful salutation; wind deities of unobstructed power gave off a fragrant flowery breeze; springlike night deities prostrated their beautifully adorned bodies in respect; ever-awakening daylight deities hovered in the sky holding banners of radiant jewels to produce light.

Sudhana went up to the monk Sudarshana, paid his respects, and said, "Noble one, I have set out for supreme perfect enlightenment and seek the practice of enlightening beings. I have heard you give enlightening beings instruction, and I ask you to tell me how an enlightening being is to learn and carry out the practice of enlightening beings."

Sudarshana said, "I am young, and have only recently become a monk. At that, in one life I have performed religious practice in the company of as many buddhas as grains of sand in thirty-eight Ganges Rivers. With some I performed spiritual practice for a day and a night, with some for a week, with some for a fortnight, with some for a month, with some for a year, with some for a century, with some for a millennium, with some for a hundred millennia, with some for a million years, with some for a trillion years, with some for untold, inexpressible numbers of years, with some for an intermediate eon, with some for half an eon, with some for an eon, with some for as long as untold, inexpressible numbers of eons, and from all those buddhas I heard explanation of the Teaching and received instruction. My vows were purified, my sphere of practice entering into the realm of realization was purified, the oceans of transcendent ways were fulfilled, I perceived their mystical transformations on attainment of enlightenment, I remembered their successive cycles of teaching without confusion, I realized the equality of their powers, and I preserved their instructions till the end of the right doctrine.

"I also realized all those buddhas' past vows for the purification of their buddha-lands, by the power of accomplishment of concentration on the sphere of vows. I also realized all those buddhas past enlightening practices for the purification of their own practice, by the power of attainment of concentration entering into all practices. I realized all those buddhas' purification of the transcendent ways, by the power of setting out on universally good practice.

"Furthermore, as I walk here, all realms flow toward me because of keenly observant knowledge being brought to the fore: all worlds flow away from me for the purification of passing over untold worlds in a single thought, by the power of accomplishment of great vows. In a single thought untold practical principles for sentient beings appear to me, for the fulfillment of the knowledge of the ten powers, by the power of carrying out the vows of practice of universally good enlightening beings. In a single thought the purities of visions of untold buddha-lands appear to me, so I may honor, attend, and serve as many buddhas as atoms in untold buddha-lands, by the power of carrying out the vow to serve former and future buddhas. In a single thought the teachings of untold buddhas occur to my mind, by the power of carrying out the vow to remember wheels of teaching accompanied by countless ways of proceeding with the teachings in action. In a single thought, untold oceans of enlightening practices appear to me, for the purification of all spheres of practice, by the power of carrying out the vow to fulfill the practices of enlightening beings, which are all interrelated. In a single thought, untold oceans of concentrations become manifest to me, for the purification of all spheres of concentration, by the power of carrying out the vow to comprehend all ways of concentration in one way of concentration. In a single thought untold oceans of faculties appear to me, for adaptation to all faculties and times, by the power of carrying out the vow to attain the faculty of ultimate mindfulness. In a single thought, untold wheels of time are manifest to me, for conveying timely teachings, by the power of carrying out the endless vow to continue till the end of sentient beings. In a single thought, untold oceans of all pasts, presents, and futures appear to me, for the definition of past, present, and future in all worlds, by the power of carrying out the vow for illumination of comprehensive knowledge.

"So I know the enlightening liberation 'the lamp of knowledge which is never extinguished.' How can I know the practice or tell the virtues of the enlightening beings with adamantine will, who are born in the families of all buddhas, who have undying life-roots, whose light of knowledge is never extinguished, who have indestructible bodies, whose magical forms are without end, who embody the principle of relativity, who appear to sentient beings according to their mentalities, whose bodies appear like those of all beings in color, form, and size, whose bodies are not harmed by fire, poisons, or weapons, whose beings are invulnerable as adamantine mountains, who vitiate the power of all demons and opponents, who shine like mountains of gold, whose bodies stand out among all beings, whose bodies are perceived by all beings, who are heard of everywhere, who are looked up to by all sentient beings, who are mines of the earth of all truths, who illumine all quarters, who are seen without opposition because they have destroyed the mountains of obstructions, who are seen as supreme heroes because they extirpate all roots of evil, who are a welcome sight because they are products of many virtues, who are like udumbara flowers because they very rarely appear?

"South of here, in the land of Shramanamandala, is a city called Sumukha, where a boy named Indriyeshvara lives. Go ask him how an enlightening being is to learn and carry out the practice of enlightening beings."

Then, intent on purifying attainment of the valor of enlightening beings, his mind illumined by the light of the power of enlightening beings, with the invincible energy of enlightening beings in his heart, his mind girded with the armor of the steadfast vows of enlightening beings, the breadth of the firm basis of intent of enlightening beings on his mind, determined to maintain the multitude of practices of enlightening beings, never tiring of the ways of enlightening beings, resolved to attain all qualities of enlightening beings, desiring to offer himself as a charioteer for all beings, desiring to bring all beings across the wasteland of the mundane whirl, never tiring of seeing, listening to, and attending spiritual benefactors, with immeasurable respect for the Teaching, Sudhana paid his respects to the monk Sudarshana and left.

Indriyeshvara

Thinking about the instruction of Sudarshana, applying it, passing it on, investigating it, talking about it, revealing it, contemplating it, approaching it, following it, reflecting on the principle of his teaching, entering into it, bringing it near, analyzing it, explaining it, elucidating it, pondering it, Sudhana, surrounded by celestial beings, spirits, and cherubim, made his way to the city of Sumukha in the land of Shramanamandala, looking for the boy Indriyeshvara.

Then, when Sudhana got to the city Sumukha, near a river junction, he saw Indriyeshvara, surrounded by ten thousand boys, playing in the sand. He went up to Indriyeshvara, paid his respects, and said, "Noble one, I have set my mind on supreme perfect enlightenment, but I do not know how an enlightening being is to learn and carry out the practice of enlightening beings."

Indriyeshvara said, "I have been taught writing and mathematics by Manjushri, and have been led into the door of knowledge encompassing higher knowledge of all practical arts. So I know all the various arts and crafts and sciences in the world dealing with writing, mathematics and symbols, physiology, rhetoric, physical and mental health, city planning, architecture and construction, mechanics and engineering, divination, agriculture and commerce, conduct and manners, good and bad actions, good and bad principles, what makes for felicity and what for misery, what is necessary for the vehicles of buddhas, disciples, and individual illuminates, what is necessary for buddhahood, and behavior linking reason and action. I know all these sciences, and I also introduce and teach them to people, and get people to study and practice them, to master and develop them, using these as means to purify, refine, and broaden people.

"I myself know enlightening beings' method of reckoning, which goes like this: a hundred hundred thousand is a koti; a koti squared is an ayuta; an ayuta squared is a niyuta; a niyuta squared is a bimbara; a bimbara squared is a kinkara; a kinkara squared is an agara; an agara squared is a pravara; a pravara squared is a mapara; a mapara squared is a tapara; a tapara squared is a sima; a sima squared is a yama; a yama squared is a nema; a nema squared is an avaga; an avaga squared is a mrgava; a mrgava squared is a viraga; a viraga squared is a vigava; a vigava squared is a samkrama; a samkrama squared is a visara; a visara squared is a vibhaja; a vibhaja squared is a vijangha; a vijangha squared is a vishoda; a vishoda squared is a vivaha; a vivaha squared is a vibhakta; a vibhakta squared is a vikhata; a vikhata squared is an ilana; an ilana squared is an avana; an avana squared is a thavana; a thavana squared is a viparya; a viparya squared is a samaya; a samaya squared is a viturna; a viturna squared is a hetura; a hetura squared is a vicara; a vicara squared is a vyavasta; a vyavasta squared is an abhyudgata; an abhyudgata squared is a vishishta; a vishishta squared is a nilamba; a nilamba squared is a harita; a harita squared is a vikshoba; a vikshoba squared is a halita; a halita squared is a hari; a hari squared is an aloka; an aloka squared is a drshvanta; a drshvanta squared is a hetuna; a hetuna squared is an ela; an ela squared is a dumela; a dumela squared is a kshemu; a kshemu squared is an eluda; an eluda squared is a bhaluda; a bhaluda squared is a samata; a samata squared is a visada; a visada squared is a pramatra; a pramatra squared is an amantra; an amantra squared is a bhramantra; a bhramantra squared is a gamantra; a gamantra squared is a namantra; a namantra squared is a nahimantra; a nahimantra squared is a vimantra; a vimantra squared is a paramantra; a paramantra squared is a shivamantra; a shivamantra squared is a delu; a delu squared is a velu; a velu squared is a gelu; a gelu squared is a khelu; a khelu squared is a nelu; a nelu squared is a bhelu; a bhelu squared is a kelu; a kelu squared is a selu; a selu squared is a pelu; a pelu squared is a melu; a melu squared is a sarada; a sarada squared is a bherudu; a bherudu squared is a kheludu; a kheludu squared is a maludu; a maludu squared is a samalu; a samalu squared is an athava; an athava squared is a kamala; a kamala squared is an agava; an agava squared is an ataru; an ataru squared is a helura; a helura squared is a mirahu; a mirahu squared is a carana; a carana squared is a dhana; a dhana squared is a pramada; a pramada squared is a nigama; a nigama squared is an upavarta; an upavarta squared is a nirdesha; a nirdesha squared is an akshaya; an akshaya squared is a sambhuta; a sambhuta squared is a mamama; a mamama squared is an avada; an avada squared is an utpala; an utpala squared is a padma; a padma squared is a sankhya; a sankhya squared is a gati; a gati squared is an upama; an upama squared is an aupamya; an aupamya squared is incalculable; an incalculable to the fourth power is measureless; a measureless to the fourth power is boundless; a boundless to the fourth power is incomparable; an incomparable to the fourth power is uncountable; an uncountable to the fourth power is unequaled; an unequaled to the fourth power is inconceivable; an inconceivable to the fourth power is immeasurable; an immeasureable to the fourth power is unspeakable; an unspeakable to the fourth power is unspeakably unspeakable; and unspeakably unspeakable squared is untold."

He counted out the grains of sand in the miles-wide mass of sand before him, telling how many grains of sand there were, and how many unspeakable numbers of grains of sand there were; then, having indicated this by these conventions of enumeration, he said, "This counting device serves enlightening beings for the succession of worlds; by this method of counting they count the multitudes of worlds in the ten directions. This method of counting serves enlightening beings in indicating the worlds in the ten directions in an orderly continuum. By this method of counting, enlightening beings count the string of names of the worlds in the ten directions. As in the case of indications of the string of names of worlds, in the same way this method of counting serves enlightening beings in indicating the successions of names of eons, buddhas, doctrines, sentient beings, actions, and indeed everything in the ten directions.

"I know this light of knowledge of enlightening beings which is characterized by higher knowledge of all arts and sciences. How can I know the practice, tell of the virtues, indicate the range, show the sphere, describe the power, show the will, elucidate the preparation, explain the commitment, show the conduct, illumine the purity of transcendent ways, expound the purity of accomplishment, tell of the sphere of concentration, or approach the light of knowledge of the enlightening beings who know the number of all worlds, who know the number of all modes of spiritual practice, who know the number of pasts, presents, and futures, who know the number of all sentient beings, who know the number of all bodies of doctrine, who know the number of enlightenments of all buddhas, and who command the wheel of names of all the teachings?"

"South of here is a city called Samudrapratishthana, where lives a lay devotee named Prabhuta. Go ask her how an enlightening being is to learn and carry out the practice of enlightening beings."

Having heard the words of the spiritual benefactor, Sudhana was thrilled and overjoyed; he paid his respects and took leave of Indriyeshvara, having obtained the treasure of will that is rare and most difficult to obtain, setting out to act benevolently toward all, freely able to perceive the succession of emergence of buddhas, intent on the wisdom to clarify the sphere of the Teaching, intent on showing the various means of emancipation everywhere, aware of past, present, and future without confusion, his mind an inexhaustible ocean of virtue, in control of the light of great knowledge, having broken open the doors of confinement in the city of mundane existence.

Prabhuta

Then, receiving the multitude of teachings of spiritual benefactors as the ocean receives torrential rains without being filled, the sprouts of his faculties raised from clear ground and developed by the rays of light of knowledge of sunlike spiritual benefactors, his body and mind cooled by the aura of light of teaching of the full moon of spiritual benefactors, having drunk the water of the teachings of spiritual benefactors like a herd of animals burnt by the heat of the summer sun, the lotuses of his mind opened like a blooming lotus pond by the instructions of spiritual benefactors like water flowing from the snowy mountains, his being illumined by the practice of the precious instructions of spiritual benefactors, like a treasure island covered with jewels, successful in accumulating knowledge and virtue according to the instructions of spiritual benefactors, like a great tree laden with flowers and fruits, having an abundant store of learning of instructions of spiritual benefactors, like a great cloud in the sky produced by the sport of dragons, a radiant mountain peak of various virtues arising from the instruction of spiritual benefactors like the wonderful peak of the world of the thirty-three heavens, full of pure qualities produced by the instructions of spiritual benefactors, overpowering and invincible like the god Indra surrounded by the deities of the thirty-three heavens who conquers the leaders and hordes of titans, Sudhana made his way to the city Samudrapratishthana, looking for the devotee Prabhuta. He was told by the people there that Prabhuta was in her house in the middle of town.

Sudhana went to Prabhuta's house and stood before the entrance with his hands joined in respectful salutation. He saw that her house was very large, covered with precious ornaments, with doors on all four sides, arrayed with countless jewels, the result of the development of inconceivable virtues. Entering the house and looking around, he saw the devotee Prabhuta in a jeweled chair, young, slim, fresh, in the blossom of youth, radiantly beautiful, her hair hanging loose, wearing no ornaments on her body, clothed in pure white garments. Except for buddhas and enlightening beings, no one came to that house whom she did not overwhelm by her appearance, her mastery of mind, her radiance, her voice, or her splendor. All who saw Prabhuta, whether human or celestial beings, thought of her as a teacher.

Also, in her house were arrayed ten million seats, superior to those of celestials and humans, perfected by the deeds of enlightening beings. There were no provisions of food or drink, or clothing or jewelry or other accoutrements to be seen in the house, except for a vessel placed before her. He also saw ten thousand ladies like goddesses standing before her, wearing celestial clothing and ornaments, with pleasing voices like goddesses. Those ladies, her attendants, responding to her word, waited on her, watched her, kept their attention on her, respectfully saluted her, looked at her, bowed to her, and expressed their reverence for her. The fragrance from their bodies perfumed the whole city, and all who smelled the fragrance became free from malice, free from hostility, nonviolent, free from envy and jealousy, free from guile and deceitfulness, disciplined, mentally unobstructed, free from depression and elation, even-minded, kind, altruistic, restrained in mind, charitable. And whoever heard their voices became happy, joyful, and humble in mind. And whoever saw them felt themselves freed of lust.

Then Sudhana paid his respects to Prabhuta and politely said to her, "Noble one, I have set my mind on supreme perfect enlightenment, but I do not know how to learn and carry out the practice of enlightening beings. I hear you give enlightening beings instruction, so I beg of you to tell me how an enlightening being is to learn and carry out the practice of enlightening beings."

She said, "I have attained an enlightening liberation which is an inexhaustible treasury of manifestations of good. From this one vessel I satisfy sentient beings of various tastes with food conforming to their wishes, with various sauces and spices, of various colors and aromas. From this one vessel I satisfy even a hundred beings with whatever food they wish, even a thousand beings, a hundred thousand, a million, a billion; I satisfy untold numbers of sentient beings of various tastes with whatever foods they wish, gratifying and pleasing them and making them happy—and yet this vessel does not diminish or run out. In this way, even if as many sentient beings as atoms in a continent, or four continents, or a thousand-world universe, or a million-world universe, or a billion-world universe, or even if as many sentient beings as atoms in untold buddha-lands come to me with various tastes, I satisfy, please, and delight them with foods according to their wishes, with various sauces, spices, colors, and aromas—yet this vessel never diminishes or runs out, it is never depleted or exhausted. Even if all the beings in all worlds in the ten directions, with various tastes and desires, should come to me, I would satisfy them all with whatever food they wished. And as with food, so also would I satisfy and please them with various kinds of drinks, various delicacies, various couches, various clothing, various flowers, various garlands, various fragrances, various incenses, various unguents, various aromatic powders, various jewels, various ornaments, various conveyances, various parasols, various banners, various pennants, and various kinds of utensils.

"Furthermore, any Buddhist disciples or individual illuminates in their last embodiment in one world in the east who attain the fruit of discipleship or individual illumination all do so after having eaten my food. And as this is true in one world in the east, so it is true in a hundred worlds, a thousand, a million, a billion, a trillion, a quadrillion, in as many worlds as atoms in a continent, as many worlds as atoms in four continents, as many worlds as atoms in a thousand-world universe, as many worlds as atoms in a million-world universe, as many worlds as atoms in a billion-world universe, up to as many worlds as atoms in untold buddha-lands—all those who realize the fruit of discipleship or individual illumination do so after having eaten my food. And as this is true in so many worlds to the east, so it is true in the worlds in all ten directions.

"The enlightening beings in one world in the east who are bound to attain enlightenment in one life all sit on the site of enlightenment, conquer the demons, and realize supreme perfect enlightenment after having eaten my food. The same is true of the enlightening beings to realize enlightenment in one life in up to as many worlds as atoms in untold buddha-lands in each of the ten directions—they all sit on the site of enlightenment, conquer the demons, and realize supreme perfect enlightenment after having eaten my food."

"Do you see these ten thousand women, my companions? Beginning with these, there are countless tens of hundreds of thousands of women whose practice is the same as mine, who are one in vows, one in roots of goodness, one in ways of emancipation, one in purity of devotion, equal in purity of mindfulness, one in purity of deportment, equal in infinity of understanding, equal in attainment of spiritual faculties, equal in pervasive awareness, equal in range of sphere of action, equal in penetration of spiritual principles, equal in ascertainment of meanings, equal in elucidation of doctrines and meanings, equal in purity of form, equal in infinity of power, equal in unsurpassed energy, equal in voicing truth, equal in purity of voice, equal in purity of qualities in all manners by manifesting infinite virtues, equal in purity of action by virtue of purity of results of irreproachable actions, equal in pervasive kindness by virtue of saving all sentient beings, equal in pervasive compassion by virtue of tirelessly developing all sentient beings, equally pure in physical action by virtue of appearing to all sentient beings in forms that please them, equally pure in speech in usage expressing the realm of realities, equal in going to the assemblies of all buddhas, equal in speeding to all buddha-lands to attend all the buddhas, equal in direct knowledge in understanding the principles of all doctrines, equal in purity of practice in attainment of all the stages of enlightening beings.

"These ten thousand women pervade the ten directions in a single instant to present food to the enlightening beings who are bound to become enlightened in one lifetime, giving them food from this same vessel. They pervade the ten directions to give food and drink to the saints and individual illuminates who are in their last existence. They go everywhere and satisfy all hungry ghosts with food. I also satisfy all the celestial beings with celestial food from this same vessel: I satisfy dragons with dragon food, spirits with spirit food, cherubim with cherub food, titans with titan food, birds with bird food, centaurs with centaur food, serpents with serpent food, humans with human food, and nonhumans with nonhuman food. Come here and in a moment you shall see with your own eyes."

No sooner had Prabhuta said these words than immeasurable numbers of such beings came in through the four doors of her house, invited by Prabhuta's standing vow. Prabhuta seated them in the places prepared and satisfied them with whatever kind of foods they wished, pleasing and delighting them. In the same way she also satisfied and pleased them with various drinks, delicacies, seats, couches, conveyances, clothes, flowers and garlands, perfumes and incenses, unguents and aromatic powders, ornaments, jeweled chariots, parasols, banners, pennants, and utensils. She satisfied all the various kinds of beings with their various kinds of food, yet the vessel was not depleted or exhausted; it never ran out.

Then Prabhuta said to Sudhana, "I know this enlightening liberation, which is an inexhaustible treasury of manifestations of good; how can I know the practice or tell the virtues of enlightening beings whose goodness is inexhaustible because of the endlessness of the ocean of good, who are like the sky in that they have produced a vast store of good, who are like wish-fulfilling jewels in that they fulfill the wishes of all sentient beings, who are mountains of good because they protect the roots of goodness of all beings, who are great clouds of good as they shower jewel rain on all beings, who are superintendents of the great treasury of good in that they open the door of the city of truth, who are great lamps of good in that they dispel the darkness of destitution for all sentient beings?

"South of here is a city called Mahasambhava, where a householder named Vidvan lives. Go ask him how an enlightening being is to learn and carry out the practice of enlightening beings."

Then Sudhana, paying his respects to the devotee Prabhuta, looking at her again and again without tiring of the sight of her, took his leave and departed.

Vidvan

Then, having gained the illumination of that enlightening liberation which is an inexhaustible treasury of goodness, reflecting on that ocean of good, gazing into that sky of good, climbing that mountain of good, gathering that mass of good, plunging into that stream of good, crossing that bridge of good, purifying that sphere of good, viewing that treasury of good, recalling that principle of good, contemplating that eye of good, purifying that multitude of good, Sudhana made his way to the city of Mahasambhava and looked all around for Vidvan, seeking a spiritual benefactor.

Looking for Vidvan, his whole being perfumed by the sight of spiritual benefactors, finding strength in spiritual benefactors, relying on spiritual benefactors, striving to follow spiritual benefactors, with tireless vigor in attending spiritual benefactors, all his roots of goodness due to spiritual benefactors, all his stores of virtue sustained by spiritual benefactors, his practice of skill in means developed by spiritual benefactors, all his roots of goodness growing by skill in attendance of spiritual benefactors without depending on others, his will for enlightenment becoming purified, his enlightening faculties developing, all his roots of goodness maturing, his accomplishments of great vows growing, his great compassion broadening, seeing himself near omniscience, receiving the light of teaching of all buddhas by the practice of Universally Good enlightening beings, the manifestations of the ten powers of buddhas increasing, Sudhana saw Vidvan at a crossroads in the middle of the city, on a seat on a high pedestal made of innumerable jewels, set on legs of diamonds and emeralds, with a web of white cowries on golden strings, set in pure jewels, with five hundred ornamental jewel figurines, arrayed with multicolored celestial cloth, with celestial banners and pennants flying above, covered with many nets of jewels, overspread with a great canopy of jewels, with garlands of gold and jewels hanging from it. A golden parasol with a handle of pure lapis lazuli was held over Vidvan, and he was being fanned by plumes made of pure white goose feathers while various incenses perfumed the air around him. He was attended by ten thousand people of equally virtuous past conduct, finer in appearance than celestials or humans, perfect in the will of enlightening beings, adorned with ornaments superior to those of the gods, playing music sweeter than that of the heavens to please all the people in the city, and showering celestial flowers.

Seeing Vidvan, Sudhana went up to him, paid his respects, and said, "Noble one, I have set out for supreme perfect enlightenment for the benefit of all beings—to extinguish the sufferings of all beings, to lead them to ultimate happiness, to rescue them from the ocean of the mundane whirl, to deliver them to the island of jewels of truth, to evaporate their cravings, to produce great compassion in them, to divert their craving for sensual pleasure and arouse in them craving for enlightened knowledge, to help them all cross over the wildness of the mundane whirl, to develop in them a taste for the way of buddhahood, to lead them out of the city of mundane states and lead them to the city of omniscience. But I do not know how an enlightening being is to learn and carry out the practice of enlightening beings. Noble one, I hear that you give enlightening beings instruction, so I ask you to tell me how an enlightening being is to learn the practice of enlightening beings, and how enlightening beings in the course of learning become a refuge for all sentient beings."

Vidvan replied, "It is good that you have aroused the aspiration for supreme perfect enlightenment. Rare are those who aspire to supreme perfect enlightenment, and rare are those who, having aspired to enlightenment, are tireless in seeking the practices of enlightening beings by meeting spiritual benefactors, who do not weary of going to spiritual benefactors, who are not pained by attendance on spiritual benefactors, who are not depressed by the difficulty of approaching spiritual benefactors, who do not give up seeking spiritual benefactors, who do not turn away from the sight of the countenance of spiritual benefactors, who do not get discouraged in the path taught by spiritual benefactors, who do not tire in the service of spiritual benefactors. Do you see my companions? I inspired them all to seek supreme perfect enlightenment; I caused them to be born in the family of buddhas; I nourished them by providing them with the ways of transcendence; I got them to live in good ways; I developed them in the ten powers of buddhas; I lifted them out of worldliness; I established them in the ranks of the enlightened; I removed them from the circle of mundane states; I started them in the cycle of enlightening teaching; I saved them from falling into bad conditions; I led them to realization of equality of things: for thus do enlightening beings become saviors of all sentient beings.

"I have attained good works produced from the treasury of mind: to those who need food I give food, to those who need drink I give drink, to those who need clothing I give clothing, to those who need flowers I give flowers, to those who want garlands I give garlands, To those who need perfumes or incenses I give perfumes or incenses, to those who need ornaments I give ornaments, to those who need jewels I give jewels, to those who need gold I give gold, to those who need silver I give silver, to those who need pearls I give pearls, to those who need chairs I give chairs, to those who need beds I give beds, to those who need means of transportation I give means of transportation, to those who need medicine I give medicine, and so on—whatever the needs, I provide them. Come here, and in a moment you will see for yourself."

As soon as Vidvan had spoken these words, innumerable beings gathered at his house, summoned by his past vows. They came from various regions, various nations, various cities, various towns, and various groups, of various conditions, various states of consciousness, various degrees of purity of sense, desiring various kinds of food, having various inclinations, needing diverse kinds of sustenance according to their states of being. They were invited by the vow of the enlightening being, by the power of the enlightening being, by the sounds of the drums of unattached giving; they came to Vidvan, looked at him, and made requests of him.

Seeing them gathered there begging, Vidvan thought for a moment, then looked at the sky. From the sky various kinds of food and drink streamed into his hand, and this Vidvan gave to the beggars according to their various tastes and desires, satisfying and delighting them with the food and drink they wanted, with the best kinds of all means of subsistence. Then, after satisfying them, he expounded the Teaching to them: that is, he elucidated means of accumulating a great store of knowledge, means of eliminating all poverty, means of producing all enjoyments, means of finding ways to knowledge of truth, means of accumulating a vast store of virtue, means of being able to feed on joy, means of attaining a body adorned with the marks and embellishments of greatness, means of attaining purity of invincible power, means of attaining knowledge of uninterrupted livelihood, and means of attaining inexhaustible good powers overcoming the power of all demons. As for those who came for food, once they were satisfied by the various foods from the sky, he taught them to attain intelligence for life, health, and strength. As for those who came for drink, once they were satisfied by the various fine, good, and pleasant drinks, he taught them to put an end to mundane cravings and develop craving for the pleasure of the way of enlightenment. Those who came for delicacies he satisfied with sweets, and then taught them to attain the refined characteristics of great people. Those who came for means of transportation he satisfied with gifts of various vehicles, then taught them to get on the Great Vehicle of universal enlightenment. Seeing those who came for clothing, he thought for a moment and looked at the sky: then from the sky immaculate clothes of various colors fell into his hand; giving them to the beggars, he taught them purification by attainment of buddhas' supreme golden complexion of modesty. Having provided each of the beggars with their needs, he taught them according to what they were fit for.

Having shown Sudhana the inconceivable scope of this enlightening liberation, Vidvan said to him, "I know the liberation of the capacity of the treasury of mind. How can I know the practice, tell the virtues, or show the miracles of the enlightening beings who have attained control over paraphernalia, who have treasure-producing hands, who cover all worlds with their hands, as treasuries of offerings to buddhas, and shower rain from clouds of various jewels in the assemblies of all buddhas, various clouds of ornaments, towers, clothing, celestial music and song, fragrances, incenses, unguents, aromatic powders, robes, parasols, banners, pennants, and all kind of paraphernalia, raining all kinds of offerings for buddhas, in the assemblies of all buddhas, in the abodes of all beings, to serve all buddhas and to develop and guide all sentient beings?

"South of here is a city called Simhapota. An eminent person named Ratnachuda lives there. Go ask him how to learn and carry out the practice of enlightening beings."

Sudhana, pleased, elated, uplifted, overjoyed, expressing his respect for the householder Vidvan as a disciple for a teacher, in honor of the Teaching, seeing all qualities of buddhahood as being fostered by him, seeing omniscience as coming from him, showing undying regard for spiritual benefactors, showing the inconceivability of unlimited knowledge in spiritual friends, acting in accord with the mastery of spiritual benefactors, heeding the instructions of spiritual benefactors, meditating on the faculty of faith deriving from spiritual benefactors, in quest of the instruction of spiritual benefactors, his mind on propitiation of spiritual benefactors, paid his respects to Vidvan and left.

Ratnachuda

Then, resorting to that water of goodness, watching that field of goodness, clearing off that mountain of goodness, plunging into that channel of goodness, opening that treasury of goodness, looking into that mine of goodness, clarifying that sphere of goodness, gathering that mass of goodness, generating that power of goodness, increasing that stream of goodness, Sudhana made his way to Simhapota city. Looking all over for the religious eminent Ratnachuda, he saw him in the middle of the marketplace. Sudhana went up to him, paid his respects, and said, "Noble one, I have set my mind on supreme perfect enlightenment, but I do not know how to learn or carry out the practice of enlightening beings. Please teach me the path of enlightening beings, on which path I may set out for omniscience."

Ratnachuda took Sudhana to his house and showed it to him, saying, "Look at my house." Looking it over, Sudhana saw that the house was radiant, made of gold, wide and high, surrounded by silver walls, adorned with crystal terraces, embellished with hundreds of thousands of lapis lazuli turrets, on coral pillars; there was a lion seat arrayed with red pearls, flying lion banners made of starry jewels, covered with a canopy of radiant jewels, draped with a net of wish-fulfilling jewels, arrayed with countless gemstones. There was a lotus pond, with cool water, made of emeralds. Surrounded by trees of all kinds of jewels, the house was large, ten stories high, with eight doors.

Entering the house, Sudhana looked around. On the first floor he saw supplies of food and drink being given away. On the second floor he saw all kinds of clothing being given away. On the third floor he saw all kinds of jewelry being given away. On the fourth floor he saw royal concubines, the most talented women on earth, being given away. On the fifth floor he saw a gathering of enlightening beings of the fifth stage, celebrating the Teaching in song, thinking and acting for the welfare and happiness of the world, practicing all sciences, putting into effect the method of mystic spells, the ocean of concentration, emergence from concentration, contemplation in concentration, and the light of knowledge. On the sixth floor he saw a gathering of enlightening beings who had attained transcendent wisdom, who had profound wisdom, who had mystic knowledge of the quiescence of all phenomena, who were completely familiar with the comprehensive method containing the method of concentration spells of the stages, whose sphere of action was unimpeded, who practiced nondualism, who were making songs of the Teaching following the process of transcendence by wisdom, analyzing and opening it up—a door of transcendent wisdom called matrix of equality, a door of transcendent wisdom called orderly analysis of the knowledge of all sentient beings, a door of transcendent wisdom called unmoving, a door of transcendent wisdom called light of dispassion, a door of transcendent wisdom called invincible matrix, a door of transcendent wisdom called world-illumining sphere, a door of transcendent wisdom called sphere of ways to attainment, a door of transcendent wisdom called oceanic matrix, a door of transcendent wisdom called attainment of equanimity of the universal eye, a door of transcendent wisdom called arrival at the inexhaustible treasure, a door of transcendent wisdom called ocean of all ways to truth, a door of transcendent wisdom called entry into the ocean of all beings, a door of transcendent wisdom called unobstructed intelligence, a door of transcendent wisdom called site of gradual descent of the clouds of the Teaching—he saw enlightening beings in untold numbers of orderly groups singing in chorus of countless tens of hundreds of thousands of such doors of transcendent wisdom. On the seventh floor he saw a gathering of enlightening beings who had attained acceptance of the fact that all sounds are like echoes, who were completely familiar with ascertainment of knowledge of means, and who took in the multitude of teachings of all buddhas. On the eighth floor he saw a gathering of enlightening beings who had attained undiminishing mystic knowledge, who observed all worlds, who were able to appear reflected in all communities, whose bodies were distributed evenly throughout all universes, who perceived the presence of all buddhas as a unified sphere, who were united with the body of all buddhas, who were chief interlocutors in the audiences of all buddhas. On the ninth floor he saw a gathering of enlightening beings who were to attain buddhahood in one lifetime. On the tenth floor he saw the oceans of first inspirations, practices, emancipations, and vows of all buddhas, mystic displays of all ways of enlightenment, the audiences of all buddhas, the sounds of the teachings of all buddhas, magical displays to edify all sentient beings.

Having seen this, Sudhana said to Ratnachuda, "Noble one, how did you achieve this? Where did you plant roots of goodness resulting in such an attainment?"

Ratnachuda said, "I remember that in the past, eons ago, more than as many eons ago as atoms in a buddha-land, in a world called Wheel of Many Colors, a buddha named King of Teaching Adorning the Cosmos with Infinite Rays of Light emerged in the world, tamer and leader of people, teacher of celestials and humans, accomplished in knowledge and action, blissful, supreme knower of the world, enlightened, blessed. Together with a billion disciples led by Radiance of Knowledge, and a trillion enlightening beings led by Energy of the Sun of Knowledge, he went to a royal park at the invitation of the king Master of the Law. I played music for that buddha in the middle of the marketplace of the city and burned one ball of incense as an offering to the buddha and the enlightening beings and disciples. By the burning of that one ball of incense, the whole continent was covered by infinitely various fragrant clouds in the forms of all sentient beings for seven days, and from those clouds emerged such sounds as these—'Inconceivable is the Buddha, possessed of a body of knowledge extensive as past, present, and future, omniscient, free from all obstructions, rid of all afflictions and habit energies, raised by all enlightened ones, sincere, giver of the fruits of measureless omniscience, concentration of all knowledge.' Such utterances came from the incense clouds by the power of Buddha to develop my roots of goodness to maturity and to rapidly generate roots of goodness in inconceivable numbers of beings. I dedicated the root of goodness in that miraculous vision of the Buddha's power to three points: to forever ending all poverty, to always hearing truth, and to meeting all enlightened and enlightening spiritual benefactors.

"I know this enlightening liberation of the supernal manifestation of the sphere of unobstructed vows. How can I know the practice or tell the virtues of enlightening beings who are mines of inconceivable, immeasureable virtues, who have entered the indivisible ocean of buddha-bodies, who take in the indivisible multitude of truths, who have attained an indivisible ocean of virtues, who have spread the net of the practice of universal good, who have entered the realm of indivisible absorption, whose roots of goodness are one with those of all enlightening beings, who abide in the pure nondiscrimination of buddhas, who have entered the indivisible equality of past, present, and future, who live continuously through all ages without tiring, who are in the stage of the sphere of the unfragmented universal eye?

"South of here is a land called Vetramulaka. A perfumer named Samantanetra lives in a city there called Samantamukha. Go ask him how an enlightening being is to learn and carry out the practice of enlightening beings."

Then Sudhana paid his respects to Ratnachuda and left.

Samantanetra

Immersed in the endless vision of buddhas, in communication with the endless congregation of enlightening beings, illumined by the endless means of the way of enlightening beings, his mind broadened and made sure by the endless principles of enlightening beings, pure in the endless path of devotion of enlightening beings, imbued with the infinite light of the faculties of enlightening beings, secure in the infinite willpower of enlightening beings, consciously following the infinite practice of enlightening beings, generating the infinite power of vows of enlightening beings, characterized by the infinite invincibility of enlightening beings, abiding in the infinite light of knowledge of enlightening beings, aware of the infinite law of enlightening beings, Sudhana made his way to the land called Vetramulaka, where he looked for the city Samantamukha, searching all over, here and there, in the highlands and the lowlands, over level and rough terrain; with tireless determination, unceasing, single-minded, with unflagging vigor and an inexhaustible mind, never forgetting the instructions of spiritual benefactors, wishing always to speak with spiritual benefactors, his senses fully aware, rid of all heedlessness, his eyes and ears open, he searched all over for the city of Samantamukha, and finally saw it, in the middle of the country of Vetramulaka, surrounded by ten thousand towns, with strong, high walls, adorned in forty-eight ways. He saw the perfumer Samantanetra in a perfumers' shop in the city.

Seeing Samantanetra, Sudhana went up to him, paid his respects, and said, "I have set my mind on supreme perfect enlightenment, but I do not know how an enlightening being is to learn and carry out the practice of enlightening beings."

Samantanetra said, "It is good that you aspire to supreme perfect enlightenment. I know the maladies of all sentient beings and how to cure those maladies. All who come to me from the ten directions, I cure of their maladies. Once they are cured, bathed, and anointed, I satisfy them with suitable ornaments, clothes, and food, and furnish them with immeasurable wealth. After that I teach them, presenting impurity to rid them of lust, praising great love to rid them of hatred, showing them analysis of elements to rid them of delusion. I teach them to get rid of the afflictions of action equally combining lust, hatred, and delusion by illuminating the ways to higher knowledge. I clarify the means of producing the determination for enlightenment by talking about the virtuous qualities of all buddhas. I elucidate the means of producing great compassion by showing the immeasurable miseries of the mundane world. I elucidate the means of attaining immeasurable virtuous qualities by describing the accumulation of vast stores of goodness and knowledge. I elucidate the means of producing the vows of the Great Vehicle by showing the development and guidance of all sentient beings. I elucidate the means of attaining the practice of universally good enlightening beings by spreading out the net of practice in all lands in all times. I elucidate the means of attaining a buddha-body of amassed distinguishing marks and embellishments by praising transcendent generosity. I elucidate the means of attaining buddhas' purity in all situations by explaining transcendent morality. I elucidate the means of producing the inconceivable purity of appearance of buddhas by explaining transcendent tolerance. I elucidate the means of producing the invincible body of buddhas by explaining transcendent vigor. I elucidate the unsurpassed purity of body of buddhas by explaining transcendent meditation. I elucidate the purity of the reality-body by explaining transcendent wisdom. I elucidate the purity of the body of Buddha appearing before all beings by explaining transcendent skill in means. I elucidate the purity of body involved in entering the minds of people in all eras and times by explaining transcendent commitment. I elucidate the purity of body appearing in all buddha-lands by explaining transcendent power. I elucidate the purity of body pleasing all sentient beings according to their inclinations by explaining transcendent knowledge. I elucidate the purification of the body of supremely pure appearance by explaining the removal of all unwholesome elements. Thus taking care of them with this giving of teaching, I provide them with the support of endless treasures and let them go.

"I also know how to compound all scents, incenses, perfumes, and unguents. Moreover, I know the ball of fragrance making offerings on meeting buddhas everywhere, pleasing to all beings. By this ball of fragrance all wishes are fulfilled; by it I produce multitudes of dwelling places, and so on, including multitudes of all kinds of offerings for buddhas. Whenever I want to make offerings to buddhas, I produce clouds of towers of fragrance and cause them to appear in all universes, in the assemblies of all buddhas. I adorn all universes with purification of buddha-lands, palaces of fragrance, walls of fragrance, turrets of fragrance, arches of fragrance, windows of fragrance, penthouses of fragrance, crescents of fragrance, parasols of fragrance, banners and pennants of fragrance, canopies of fragrance, webs of fragrance, lights of fragrance, immaculate adornments of fragrance, and rain showering from clouds of all fragrances.

"I know this medium of the Teaching, the ball of fragrance making offerings on meeting buddhas everywhere, pleasing all sentient beings; how can I know the practice or tell the virtues of the enlightening beings who are like great medicines, whom it is beneficial to see, to hear, to associate with, to remember, to follow, and to recall their names, with the sight of whom all sentient beings are relieved of afflictions, with the sight of whom sentient beings leave all evil ways, with the sight of whom sentient beings find a way to buddhahood, with the sight of whom the sufferings of sentient beings are relieved, with the sight of whom sentient beings are freed from fear of all mundane states, with the sight of whom sentient beings become fearless because of being near the abode of omniscience, with the sight of whom sentient beings no longer fall into the abyss of old age and death, with the sight of whom sentient beings attain the bliss of tranquillity through cosmic equanimity?

"South of here is a city called Taladhvaja, where there lives a king named Anala. Go ask him how to learn and carry out the practice of enlightening beings."

So then Sudhana paid his respects to the eminent perfumer Samantanetra and left.

Anala

Recalling those spiritual benefactors one after another, focusing his attention on the instructions of those spiritual benefactors, rejoicing in himself at being in the care of spiritual benefactors, reflecting that through the protection of spiritual benefactors he would never lose the way to supreme perfect enlightenment, Sudhana became joyful, serene, pleased, happy, calm, broadminded; he attained adornment of mind, nonattachment of mind, nonobstruction of mind, aloofness of mind, unification of mind, control of mind, extraordinary power of mind, mental conformity with the Teaching, mental pervasion of lands, mental beatification by the vision of Buddha, and constant mental focus on the ten powers.

He made his way from country to country, village to village, place to place, searching, till he came to the city of Taladhvaja, where he asked after the whereabouts of King Anala. He was told, "King Anala is on the throne carrying out his royal duties for the welfare of the populace. He governs the communities, punishes those who should be punished, promotes those who deserve promotion, chastises criminals, settles disputes, comforts and encourages the wretched and dejected, subdues the wild and arrogant; he puts a stop to the injury of living beings, theft, desire for others' spouses, falsehood, slander, harsh or violent talk, and divisive talk; he frees us from craving, malice, and false ideas."

Then Sudhana went to King Anala and saw him sitting on a great jeweled lion throne brilliant with diamonds, set on legs of countless varieties of luminous jewels, with beautiful figurines inlaid with jewels, arrayed with cowrie shells on golden threads, lit by many jewel lamps, in a lotus calyx made of magic gems, spread with many precious celestial robes, perfumed with various celestial incenses, embellished with a hundred thousand jeweled parasols, adorned with a hundred thousand jeweled banners, beautified by trailing flower garlands made of varicolored jewels, covered by a canopy of various celestial jewels. The king was young and handsome, with the marks and embellishments of a great man, wearing a crown of wish-fulfilling jewels, his forehead adorned with golden crescents, pure blue sapphire earrings hanging from his ears, a breastplate radiant with jewels on his chest, bracelets of the finest celestial gems on his arms, shaded by a large precious parasol with a cane of pure lapis lazuli and a thousand ribs of jewels with a gold covering, a wreath of jewel bells sweetly ringing, illumining all directions with its luster. The king had great regal power; his rule was invincible to enemy armies, his sovereignty was free of danger from enemy armies.

Sudhana saw ten thousand ministers gathered around the king conducting the affairs of state. He also saw ten thousand torturers before the king, looking like the warders of hell, of violent, terrifying appearance, holding swords, axes, spears, clubs, and impaling stakes, involved in punishing those to be punished. He saw criminals—thieves, bandits, murderers, troublemakers, rapists, and so on—brought bound before King Anala and saw the king deal out appropriate punishments: by the king's order, some had their hands and feet cut off, some had their ears and noses cut off, some had their eyes gouged out, some had their limbs or heads cut off, some had their whole bodies burnt by fire, some were being dismembered, crippled, burnt, sprinkled with acid. Sudhana watched them undergoing such harsh, injurious, and deadly punishments and saw a mountainous heap of rendered body parts on the execution ground and a tremendous torrent of blood. He also saw animals and birds eating the mutilated corpses there. He also saw some of the corpses hideously decomposing. He also heard the screams and cries of those being mutilated and killed, as terrifying as hell.

Seeing that dreadful, horrifying butchery, Sudhana thought, "I have set out for supreme perfect enlightenment for the sake of the welfare and happiness of all beings and am devoted to pursuing the practice of enlightening beings; I ask spiritual benefactors what good an enlightening being should do and what evil one should avoid. This King Anala, though, is devoid of goodness, an evildoer, malicious, a killer and oppressor, without regard for others, doomed to a miserable fate: so how can I hear about the practice of enlightening beings from him?"

As Sudhana was thinking this, concerned with saving all sentient beings, his mind full of compassion, celestial beings in the sky over his head called out, "Do you not remember the instructions of the seer Jayoshmayatana?"

Sudhana looked up and said, "I do."

The celestials said, "Do not give rise to doubt about the instructions of spiritual benefactors; they guide you on the right way. Indeed, the practical knowledge of skill in means of enlightening beings is inconceivable. The knowledge of how to take care of all sentient beings is inconceivable. The knowledge of how to benefit sentient beings is inconceivable. The knowledge of how to restrain sentient beings is inconceivable. The knowledge of how to further sentient beings is inconceivable. The knowledge of how to care for sentient beings is inconceivable. The knowledge of how to protect sentient beings is inconceivable. The knowledge of how to purify sentient beings is inconceivable. The knowledge of how to liberate sentient beings is inconceivable. The knowledge of how to perfect sentient beings is inconceivable. The knowledge of how to guide sentient beings is inconceivable. Go ask the king about the practice of enlightening beings."

Hearing the words of the celestials, Sudhana went to King Anala, paid his respects, and said, "Noble one, I have set my mind on supreme perfect enlightenment, but I do not know how to learn and carry out the practice of enlightening beings. I hear that you give instruction to enlightening beings; pray tell me how to learn and apply the practice of enlightening beings."

King Anala, having finished his duties, got off the throne and took Sudhana into the palace. Entering his own residence, the king seated Sudhana on a seat of honor and said to him, "Look at the furnishings of my house." Sudhana looked and saw that the house was large, with walls of seven precious substances, adorned with terraces of various jewels, embellished with hundreds of thousands of jewel towers, blazing with the radiance of inconceivable numbers of jewels, with pillars made of various jewels. In it were hundreds of thousands of variously adorned jewel lion chairs; jeweled regal banners flew overhead; it was covered with canopies of radiant jewels, draped with various webs of magical gems, decorated with countless ornaments of various jewels, complete with cool emerald lotus ponds, surrounded by rows of trees of all kinds of jewels. He also saw the king's hundred million ladies, all extremely beautiful, versed in all the arts, diligent, kindhearted, and attentive.

Then King Anala said to Sudhana, "What do you think—could such fruits of action come to a villain? Could a villain attain such a condition, with such a retinue, such riches, such power?"

Sudhana said, "No indeed, noble one."

The king said, "I have attained enlightening beings' magical liberation. The people in my realm are given to all sorts of evildoing—murder, theft, rape, falsehood, slander, vilification, divisive talk, covetousness, malice, false views, villainy, violence, cruelty. I am unable to turn them away from evildoing by any other means, so in order to subdue them, mature them, guide them, and secure their welfare, out of compassion I have illusory executioners kill and maim illusory criminals, making a display of intense suffering and pain; seeing this, the people in my realm become afraid to do evil. Seeing the people alarmed by this device, I have them give up evildoing and conduct themselves virtuously; then I establish them in ultimate security, the end of all suffering, the bliss of omniscience. I do not harm anyone by thought, word, or deed. I would sooner go to the deepest hell than so much as think of hurting even a dumb animal or an insect, much less a human being, who has potential for virtuous conduct. I do not do anything bad even in dreams, much less while awake.

"I have attained this magical enlightening beings' liberation. How can I know the practice or tell the virtues of the enlightening beings who have attained acceptance of the truth of nonorigination, who relate to all states of being as illusions, who understand that the practices of enlightening beings are like magical creations, who know that all worlds are like reflections, who comprehend that the nature of things is like a dream, who conform to the principle of the reality realm by nonattachment, who accomplish the network of interrelated practices, who are in the sphere of unimpeded knowledge, who know the way of universally comprehensive concentration, who are masters of endlessly progressing mental command, who are intent on the sphere of buddhahood?"

"South of here is a city called Suprabha, where a king named Mahaprabha lives. Go ask him how to learn and carry out the practice of enlightening beings."

So then Sudhana paid his respects and left King Anala.

Mahaprabha

Remembering that magic of knowledge, meditating on that magical liberation of enlightening beings, contemplating that magical nature, realizing the equality of the illusoriness of all actions, reflecting on the equal illusoriness of phenomena, following the equality of didactic developmental magical creations, remembering the inconceivable light born of knowledge, undertaking the magical performance of endless vows, purifying the magical nature of unattached conduct, thinking about the magical character of past, present, and future, Sudhana made his way from country to country, looking everywhere, high and low, over even and rough terrain, wet and dry places, mountains and valleys, villages, cities, towns, provinces, and capitals, tireless in body and mind, searching everywhere till he came to the environs of the great city Suprabha. He asked where King Mahaprabha was, and people pointed out the great city Suprabha and told him the king lived there.

So then Sudhana went to the city and was delighted upon seeing it. He thought, "Where does the spiritual benefactor live? I shall see the spiritual benefactor today and hear from him about the practice of enlightening beings, the way of emancipation of enlightening beings, the inconceivable nature of enlightening beings, the inconceivable range of virtues of enlightening beings, the inconceivable majesty of enlightening beings, the inconceivable concentration of enlightening beings, the inconceivable freedom of enlightening beings, and the inconceivable purity of accomplishment of great undertakings of enlightening beings." With these thoughts in mind Sudhana went into the great city Suprabha.

Once he was there, Sudhana looked around the city: it was beautiful, made of seven precious substances—gold, silver, lapis lazuli, crystal, red pearl, emerald, and coral. It was surrounded by deep moats made of the seven precious substances, with gold sand on the bottom, their surfaces covered with heavenly lotuses, and particles of sandalwood suspended in the water. The city was also surrounded by rows of palm trees made of the seven precious substances, and enclosed by walls made of seven kinds of diamonds—majestic, insuperable, indestructible, invincible, without obstacle, blazing with light, free from impurities. Each of the diamond walls was also inlaid with countless jewels, inset with gold posts and adorned with garlands of ivory and jewels. The gates of the city, at intervals of ten leagues on eight sides, were beautifully constructed of the seven precious substances. The city was large, a symmetrical octagon, set on a ground of blue lapis lazuli. There were ten million streets in the city, each one lined on both sides with hundreds of thousands of mansions made of various precious substances and adorned with arrays of many kinds of gems, flying jeweled banners and flags, fully furnished, with millions of people living in them. The city was also adorned with countless temples of gold and jewels, countless gold towers arrayed with innumerable jewels and covered with nets of lapis lazuli, countless silver towers arrayed with innumerable jewels and covered with nets of red pearls, countless lapis lazuli towers arrayed with innumerable jewels and covered with nets of varicolored jewels, countless crystal towers arrayed with innumerable jewels and covered with nets of diamonds, countless luminous jewel towers arrayed with innumerable jewels and covered with nets of sunny jewels, countless sapphire towers arrayed with innumerable jewels and covered with nets of radiant jewels, countless diamond towers arrayed with innumerable jewels and covered with nets of unsurpassed jewels, countless sandalwood towers arrayed with innumerable jewels and covered with nets of celestial flowers, countless towers of incomparable fragrances arrayed with innumerable jewels and covered with nets of heavenly flowers, all adorned with turrets of many jewels, encircled with balconies of seven precious substances, surrounded by rows of jewel trees. The turrets of the towers and the nets of jewels were also interconnected by jewel strings, and those strings were adorned with garlands of golden bells, to each of which were fastened strings of various jewels, from each of which hung circlets of small bells. Also the whole city was covered with countless nets of jewels, bells, celestial fragrances, heavenly flowers, and jewel figurines, with countless canopies of diamonds, various jewels, jeweled parasols, jewel pavilions, precious cloths, and jewel flower garlands, with variously jeweled banners and pennants flying overhead.

The house of King Mahaprabha was built in the middle of the city. It was four leagues wide on each side. Made of the seven precious substances, it was surrounded by arbors made of these seven precious substances in various combinations, decorated with nets of precious bells making pleasant sweet sounds. It was surrounded by seven rows of palm trees made of the seven precious substances and adorned with a hundred thousand towers made of inconceivable numbers of various jewels. The house was embellished with lotus ponds, made of jewels, their surfaces covered with celestial flowers, their floors spread with gold sand, with steps made of jewel bricks arrayed on four sides, graced with trees with jewel flowers and fruits. Pleasant sounds of birds warbling filled the air. It was like the palace of a celestial king. In the middle stood a tower of world-illumining jewels, wonderful, beautiful, brilliant with its inconceivable arrays of countless jewels, built by the King Mahaprabha as a treasury of good law.

Then Sudhana, not drawn by the jewel moats, not amazed by the jewel walls, not attracted by the jewel trees, not relishing the sound of the jewel bells, unattached to the sweet sounds of celestial songs, not paying any attention to the various precious furnishings of the apartments and towers, while in the midst of the joyful crowds of people enjoying the pleasure of the way of enlightenment, detached from pleasures of the senses, intent on contemplation of the truth, constantly asking everyone he met about spiritual benefactors, made his way to a crossroads in the city. Looking around at the crossroads, he saw King Mahaprabha there, not far from his venerable abode, seated on a magnificent throne. The throne had legs of blue lapis lazuli and was set on a lion made of white lapis lazuli. It was arrayed with nets of cowries on gold strings and varicolored precious cloths surpassing those of the gods, and ornamented with countless jewel figures. It was covered with a network of inconceivable numbers of jewels, and above was a beautiful gold silk canopy with multicolored decorations of celestial jewels. The throne of the great law was in the shape of the calyx of a lotus made of wish-fulfilling gems, and the king sat cross-legged thereon, graced with the thirty-two marks of a great person, adorned with the various embellishments of the virtuous. He was like a mountain of gold, brilliant as a mine of jewels, blazing with light like the orb of the sun, of placid appearance like the full moon, an oceanic accumulation of endless virtues of the profound Teaching, like a great cloud thundering the sound of inherent nature, like the sky studded with stars of maxims of the Teaching, like the polar mountain appearing to the minds of the ocean of sentient beings, like an island of jewels covered with various gems of knowledge. Sudhana also saw heaps of jewels, pearls, conch shells, camphor, coral, gold, and silver, heaps of celestial robes, heaps of celestial jewelry, heaps of food, and heaps of the finest delicacies arrayed before the king. He also saw millions of celestial chariots, celestial musical instruments, mounds of celestial incenses, many medicinal preparations, and many collections of all kinds of utensils, suitable and proper for people to enjoy as they wish. He also saw hundreds of thousands of milk cows with golden horns and hooves, provided to care for the poor. He also saw many millions of beautiful girls, adorned with all kinds of jewelry, dressed in heavenly clothes, limbs anointed with sandalwood perfume, versed in all the arts and skilled in all manners of love play. All the kinds of goods that were before the king were also set out in countless numbers on the street corners, in front of every house, along both sides of every street, to support the population, to make everyone happy, joyful, serene, and comfortable, to extinguish their afflictions, to introduce them to the meaning of the nature of all things, to get them all to have omniscience as their common aim, to rid them of malice toward others, to stop them from all evil action and talk, to extract the thorns of views, and to purify their course of action.

At that point Sudhana went up to King Mahaprabha, paid his respects, and said, "Noble one, I have set my mind on supreme perfect enlightenment, but I do not know how to learn and carry out the practices of enlightening beings. I hear you give enlightening beings instruction, and ask you to tell me how to study and accomplish the practice of enlightening beings."

The king said, "I purify and fulfill the enlightening beings' practice, which is characterized by great benevolence. This practice I have asked about, purified, ordered, observed, carried out, pursued, entered into, diversified, and expanded in the company of hundreds, thousands, millions— indeed, untold numbers—of buddhas. Based on this enlightening practice of great benevolence, I command kingship justly, I treat the world justly, I pass through the world justly, I lead the people justly, I bring justice to people and turn them to the sphere of right, I give them right guidance, I saturate them with justice, I direct them to attainment of what is right, I get them to contemplate the nature of things. I establish people in kindness, in the command of great kindness, in the power of kindness, in altruism, in goodwill, in sympathy, in friendliness, in hospitality, in determination to get rid of all suffering, in conduct conducive to ultimate happiness. I cool their minds and remove their mental tangles by producing the bliss of cessation. I divert their continuity of mind attached to delight in mundane routines and purify it in enjoyment of the pleasures of truth. I purify them of all unwholesome qualities and turn them away from what is not good. I turn back the flow of the mundane whirl. I destroy their ignorance in the ocean of principles of the reality realm, to cut off rebirth in all states of being. I inspire them to attain omniscience. I calm the ocean of their minds, to generate the indestructible power of faith. Thus do I govern righteously based on this enlightening practice of great benevolence.

"Furthermore, no one goes away from me intimidated, threatened, or frightened. If any poor people lacking in means of subsistence come to me seeking food or drink or clothing or any other need, I open the royal storehouse to them and allow them to take from there, or from the streets and crossroads of the city, whatever they need, things they would otherwise get involved in wrongdoing to get.

"All the inhabitants of this city are enlightening beings established in the Great Vehicle. They see this city according to the purity of their minds. Some see it small, some large; some see a ground of earth, some see a ground spread with lapis lazuli; some see clay walls, some see it surrounded by walls covered with the finest cloth, banners, and jewels; some see it full of gravel and sand, uneven, with a lot of ravines; some see the ground spread with large jewels, decorated and flat as the palm of the hand; some see it beautifully arrayed with mansions and palaces, with round windows, nets, crescents, jewels, and various other adornments. Even among those who live outside the city, those whose minds are pure, who have made roots of goodness, who have attended many buddhas, who are aiming for omniscience, and who make omniscience their ultimate goal, see it as made of jewels. Those whom I took care of in the course of past enlightening practice by means of charity, kindness, assistance, and cooperation see it this way, while others see it as made of clay.

"Whenever the inhabitants of my domain want to do anything wrong in the degenerate world, their natures disturbed by the times, in order to save them I go into an enlightening concentration guided by great benevolence called 'adapting to the faculties of the world,' whereupon their fears, misfortunes, animosities, quarrels, agitations, and hostilities cease. That happens as a matter of course by the achievement of the nature of the enlightening concentration adapting to the faculties of the world, which is guided by great benevolence. Come here and you shall see for yourself in a moment."

At that point the king entered that concentration, whereupon the whole city as well as the provinces of the kingdom quaked. As they shook, the jewel walls, jewel temples, jewel treasuries, jewel houses, jewel mansions, jewel palaces, jewel towers, jewel windows, jewel balconies, jewel arches, jewel crescents, jewel domes, jewel statues, jewel canopies, jewel bells, jewel banners, and jewel trees gave off beautiful, pleasant sounds and bowed toward King Mahaprabha. The inhabitants of the city Suprabha, ecstatic, prostrated themselves in the king's direction. The inhabitants of the rest of the domain, refreshed and joyful, bowed toward the king. Even the animals, in friendship and harmony with each other, bowed toward the king. Even the mountains and hills all bowed toward the king. All the trees and plants also bowed toward the king. All the lakes, ponds, streams, and rivers in the domain flowed toward the king. Ten thousand water spirits sent subtly aromatic rains from clouds of fragrant water, with thunder and lightning. Ten thousand celestial beings adorned the sky with countless clouds of celestial music, goddesses sweetly singing, clouds raining celestial jewel flowers, clouds raining various celestial fragrances, garlands, aromatic powders, jewelry, robes, parasols, banners, and pennants blazing with the radiance of jewels, presenting these to the king as tokens of respect. The chief of the water spirits also adorned the sky with a covering of countless clouds of celestial jewel lotuses, countless trailing ornaments of celestial jewel necklaces, streamers, garlands, ornaments, and leis, countless clouds of all-pervading celestial fragrances, countless clouds raining celestial cloths, incense balls, and aromatic powders, and countless clouds of nymphs playing sweet music and singing hymns of praise, producing these in the sky by the inconceivable power of the chief water spirit. Also, countless hundreds of thousands of sea and land goblins, malevolent beings who feed on flesh and blood and consume the vitality of fish, birds, animals, and humans, all became benevolent, placid, intent on not harming any creatures, and sympathetic to other beings; they joined their hands in respect and most joyfully bowed to the king, experiencing mental and physical bliss. Hundreds of thousands of other kinds of fiends and malevolent spirits, also becoming benevolent, placid, intent on not harming any creature, and sympathetic to other beings, joined their hands in respect and most joyfully bowed to the king, experiencing physical and mental bliss.

In this way all the fears, misfortunes, animosities, quarrels, agitations, and hostilities of all creatures on earth ceased. And as this happened on earth, so did it also happen throughout the galaxy, in as many as ten duodecillion worlds. This was by the achievement of the nature of the enlightening concentration adapting to the faculties of the world, which is guided by great benevolence.

Then King Mahaprabha came out of that concentration and said to Sudhana, "I know this medium of the light of knowledge of practice of enlightening beings which is characterized by great benevolence. How can I know the practice, tell the virtues, measure the mountain of merit, view the myriad stars of virtuous qualities, encompass the atmosphere of great vows, measure the power of impartiality toward things, clarify the forms of arrangements of the vehicle of universal salvation, express the excellences of the principles of universally good practice, open the doors of cultivation of great enlightening concentrations, or describe the clouds of great compassion, of the enlightening beings who are like immeasurable umbrellas of great benevolence, filling all beings with happiness; who are inseparable companions to all beings; who have set out to save all beings, working equally with the superior, inferior, and middling; whose benevolence is as impartial as the earth, supporting all beings; who are impartial as the full moon, shining the light of virtue and knowledge equally on all beings; who are impartial as the sun, illumining the world with knowledge of all that can be known; who are like great lamps, dispelling the darkness in the recesses of all beings' minds; who are like water-clarifying jewels, removing the turbidity of deceit and guile from the water of beings' minds; who are like wish-fulfilling jewels, fulfilling the aspirations of all beings; who are like a gale, driving all beings into the citadel of omniscience with its houses of concentration and equilibrium?

"South of here is a kingdom called Sthira where a devotee named Achala lives. Go ask her how to learn and carry out the practice of enlightening beings."

So Sudhana paid his respects to King Mahaprabha and left.

Achala

Then Sudhana left Suprabha city and shortly set forth on the road; reflecting on the teaching of King Mahaprabha, remembering the principle of enlightening practice of great benevolence, thinking of the light of that method of great concentration adapting to the faculties of the world, developing the inconceivable power commanding the goodness of the vows of enlightening beings, stabilizing the inconceivable wisdom of enlightening beings, knowing how to develop and perfect sentient beings, contemplating the inconceivable unique greatness of experience of enlightening beings, aiming for the inconceivable measurelessness of enlightening beings, remembering enlightening beings' inconceivable purity of development of sentient beings, thinking of the inconceivability of the purity of company of enlightening beings, focusing on enlightening beings' inconceivable way of considering and seeing what to do for sentient beings, Sudhana became joyful and happy, his mind became clear, light, steadfast, broad, and invincible. Weeping as he thought of his memories of spiritual benefactors, he thought, "Meeting spiritual benefactors is a mine of jewels of all virtues; it brings about the purification and fulfillment of all enlightening practices; it purifies the mindfulness of all enlightening beings; it purifies all enlightening beings' sphere of mental command; it generates the light of concentration of all enlightening beings; it fosters accomplishments of the vision of all buddhas; it causes the clouds of teachings of all buddhas to rain; it reveals the principles of the vows of all enlightening beings; it generates the inconceivable light of wisdom and knowledge; it strengthens and develops the sprouting faculties of enlightening beings. Spiritual benefactors save me from falling into evil ways; they guide me according to the principle of equality of things; they show me which paths are safe and which dangerous; they elucidate the way of universal enlightenment; they explain to me universally good enlightening conduct; they tell me the way to the citadel of omniscience; they lead me into the stronghold of omniscience; they plunge me into the ocean of principles of the cosmos; they illumine for me the way into the ocean of what can be known in past, present, and future; they show me the multitude of spheres of all goals; they cause me to develop all good qualities."

As Sudhana wept, a group of celestial enlightening beings in the sky, envoys of the buddhas who were always following Sudhana to inspire him, said, "The buddhas are pleased with an enlightening being who puts the instruction of spiritual benefactors into practice. An enlightening being who obeys the word of spiritual benefactors is close to omniscience. An enlightening being who does not doubt the word of spiritual benefactors becomes near to spiritual benefactors. An enlightening being who always pays attention to spiritual benefactors is within sight of all goals. Go to the devotee Achala in the kingdom of Sthira, and you will hear from her of the practice of enlightening beings."

Then Sudhana emerged from the light of concentration knowledge and made his way to the kingdom of Sthira, looking for the devotee Achala. People told him, "The devotee Achala is a girl living at home with her parents and relatives; she gives spiritual teaching to a large group of people." Filled with joy, Sudhana went to Achala's house. Standing in the door, he saw the whole house lit up with a soothing golden light. The moment Sudhana was touched by the light, five hundred subtle trances descended upon him, beginning with a trance characterized by power over all sensations, trance absorption in the realm of tranquillity, absorption in the welfare of all beings, absorption in the equanimity of the universal eye, and absorption in the matrix of realization of Thusness. The feeling of those trances was as subtle as the consciousness of a half-day old embryo.

He also smelled a scent more beautiful than that of any gods or goddesses or humans or any other creatures of the world, and there was to be found in all the world no one even equal to, much less more beautiful than, that girl Achala. The radiance of her complexion, the proportions of her body, and the magnificence of her aura were such that none in the world, save buddhas and coronated enlightening beings, even equaled, much less surpassed them. Her scent was unequaled and unsurpassed by any celestial, preternatural, or human beings. The furnishings of her abode were unequaled and unsurpassed in all the world, except by the accoutrements of buddhas and coronated enlightening beings. Her company was also unequaled and unsurpassed by any in the world, except for the companies of buddhas and coronated enlightening beings. There was no one in all the world who could look upon Achala with lust—there was no one in the world whose afflictions did not cease the moment he beheld her. Just as gods with controlling power who live in the realm of desire do not activate afflictions, similarly people who saw Achala did not act on afflictions. There was no one in the world who became satiated with the sight of Achala, except those who were sated with wisdom.

Then Sudhana, in an attitude of reverence, seeing Achala's inconceivable physical majesty, her inconceivable appearance, and her inconceivable aura of light, which could not be blocked by all the cities and mountains on the face of the earth, sensing the inconceivable beneficial fragrance coming from her pores, looking over her endless company of followers, noticing the matchless adornment of her abode, immersed in the measureless ocean of her virtues, eulogized Achala with this verse:

> Who keeps conduct pure,
> Develops great tolerance,

And makes vigor enduring as diamond
Stands out in the world like a mountain of light.

Then Sudhana said to her, "Noble one, I have set my mind on supreme perfect enlightenment, but I do not know how to learn and carry out the practice of enlightening beings. I hear that you give instruction to enlightening beings, so I ask you to tell me how an enlightening being is to learn and carry out the practice of enlightening beings."

In the affectionate, pleasing, charming words of an enlightening being, Achala greeted Sudhana and said, "It is good that you aspire to supreme perfect enlightenment. I have an enlightening liberation containing invincible knowledge, and I cultivate enlightening beings' way of practice of firm resolve. I have also attained mental command of the stage of equanimity in all things, and I am imbued with the light of knowledge to clarify the true state of all phenomena. I have also attained concentration of tireless search for truth."

Sudhana asked her about the sphere of these attainments, and she said her state was hard to believe. Sudhana urged her to tell him, assuring her that by the power of Buddha and the help of spiritual benefactors he would believe in it, enter into it, investigate, contemplate, follow, and cultivate it, and would not quarrel or make up arbitrary ideas or assumptions about it, but would strive to equal it.

Achala then said to Sudhana, "A long time ago, in a past eon called Undefiled Light, a buddha named Arms Extended Downward appeared in the world. I was the daughter of a king named Vidyuddatta. One quiet night, as my parents slept in the inner apartments of the palace, and the men and women of the court were fast asleep, and the sounds of music had all stopped, and my five hundred girl companions were all in bed, as I gazed up at the starry night sky I saw up there the Buddha, like the polar mountain, surrounded by many celestial beings, spirits, preternatural creatures, and countless enlightening beings, his body pervading everywhere with an aura of unobstructed light. From his pores came a fragrance that soothed my body and mind and made me happy. Getting up from bed, I saluted the Buddha; looking at him, I found I could not determine any limit to the extent of his height and breadth. As I reflected on his marks and embellishments of greatness, I thought, 'By performing what kind of action is such a body obtained? How are the marks and embellishments of greatness attained? How is the aura of light attained? How does the retinue of followers develop? How do the mentally produced dwelling and furniture appear? How is virtue developed? How is knowledge purified? How are the inconceivable meditative projections accomplished? How is mental command perfected? How is eloquence mastered?'

"Reading my mind, that Buddha said to me, 'Daughter, you should produce an invincible mind to destroy afflictions, an indomitable mind to get rid of all clinging, an intrepid mind to enter into the profound truth, a mind unshakable while descending into the whirlpool of the ocean of sentient beings who are attached to objects, a mind undeluded in the midst of all states of being, a mind tireless in seeking vision of all buddhas, a mind receiving the multitudes of teachings of all buddhas without complacence, a contemplative mind to attain the light of wisdom of all buddha-teachings, a retentive mind remembering the cycles of teaching of all buddhas, a mind free from forgetfulness even in regard to conventional terms, to say nothing of knowledge arising from the word of buddhas; and you should develop a mind of sharing, to distribute the jewels of the Teaching to all sentient beings according to their mentalities.'

"Having heard such principles of the Teaching from the Buddha, desiring omniscience, aiming for the development of the ten powers, seeking the eloquence of a buddha, wishing to purify in myself the aura of light of a buddha, wishing to perfect a body like a buddha, desiring the purity of marks and embellishments of greatness of a buddha, aiming to gain a congregation like a buddha, seeking purification of a buddha-land, wishing to accomplish the deportment of a buddha, wanting to attain the span of life of a buddha, developing a mind that neither afflictions nor anyone concerned with self-liberation alone could break down, like indestructible adamant, I do not remember the arising of a single thought of enjoyment of desires—much less engaging in sexual intercourse—for as many eons thereafter as atoms in this continent. I do not remember a single thought of anger toward my relatives, much less toward innocent others. I do not remember a single thought related to the idea of self, much less having considered anything my own. I do not remember any confusion, or any notion of difference, or yet any indifference, even while in the womb between death and birth, much less while focusing my attention. In all those eons I did not forget a single vision of a buddha, not even a dream vision, much less those appearing to the ten eyes of an enlightening being. Ever since that original inspiration I have been imbibing the ocean of the Teaching, contemplating and reflecting on every single statement, even in the context of worldly phenomena. There is not a single facet of the Teaching that I have not become absorbed in, even in the context of worldly arts and sciences. Ever since that first inspiration, while holding the wheel of teaching of the buddhas, I have never omitted even a single word as I learned it, even in following logic, except to regulate the guidance of others. There is not a single vow I have not undertaken in the presence of the buddhas I have met since then to purify the ocean of all sentient beings, even carrying out vows made to phantom buddhas. There is not a single enlightening practice from the ocean of past enlightening practices of the oceans of buddhas that I have not undertaken to purify my own practice. There is not a single sentient being I have seen since then that I have not established in the determination for supreme enlightenment. I do not remember even having a thought of individual liberation since then. I do not remember ever conceiving any doubt, any notion of duality, any false discriminations, any notion of variety, any idea of grasping or rejection, any concept of inferior or advanced, or any thought of attachment or resistance, in regard to so much as even a single word or letter of the Teaching, for as many eons as atoms in this continent.

"Ever since then I have never been apart from buddhas, enlightening beings, and true spiritual benefactors. I have always been hearing of the vows of buddhas, the practices of enlightening beings, the transcendent ways of enlightening beings, the light of knowledge of the stages of enlightening beings, the inexhaustible treasury of mental command and concentration of enlightening beings, the way to enter the infinite network of worlds, the original causes of the infinite realms of sentient beings. I have never left the light of knowledge removing the web of afflictions of all beings. I have always been acquiring knowledge of the productive causes of the roots of goodness of all beings. I have always been appearing to all beings according to their mentalities. I have always been purifying the verbal range to instruct all beings.

"Having attained this enlightening liberation containing invincible knowledge and this concentration of tireless searches for all truths, accumulating this enlightening way of practice of firm resolve, contemplating this method of mental command of the stage of equanimity in all things and this medium of the light of knowledge clarifying the basis of all things, I am capable of inconceivable miracles. Do you want to witness them?"

Sudhana said, "I do."

Then, as she sat there, Achala looked into, passed through, followed, and meditated on ten hundred thousand doors of concentration, beginning with the door of enlightening liberation containing invincible knowledge, the door of concentration of tireless searches for all truths, the door of concentration on the arrangement of the sphere of efficacy, the door of concentration on the sphere of the ten powers, and the door of liberation through concentration on the inexhaustible source of all buddhas. As soon as Achala had reach these concentrations, Sudhana saw as many worlds as atoms in ten inexpressible numbers of buddha-lands quaking, and appearing made of clear lapis lazuli. He also saw in each world a billion sets of four continents and a billion buddhas. He saw some of the buddhas in the heaven of satisfaction, some descending to be born on earth, some in the womb, some first-born, some leaving home for ascetic practice, some sitting under the tree of enlightenment, some defeating the demons, some realizing enlightenment, some teaching, some entering final extinction—this was because there was no obstruction to vision in the worlds made of clear lapis lazuli. He also saw the aura of light of each buddha pervading all universes, and he saw the orderly congregations of each buddha. He also heard the voice of the individual buddha communicating all the cycles of the Teaching to all sentient beings.

Then Achala emerged from concentration and said to Sudhana, "Did you see? Did you hear? Did you understand?"

Sudhana said, "I saw, I heard, I understood."

Achala said, "In this way, learning enlightening beings' practice of firm resolve, absorbed in tireless search for all truths, established in enlightening beings' way of liberation by invincible knowledge, I satisfy all sentient beings with good explanation by following mental command of the stage of equanimity in all things, using the skill of the light of knowledge of how to elucidate the basis of all things. How can I know the practice or tell the virtues of the enlightening beings who are imbued with inconceivable, measureless virtues, who are like eagles soaring independently through the sky, who plunge into the sea of sentient beings to take out the mature enlightening beings, who search the treasure island of omniscience for the jewels of knowledge of the ten powers, who go like strong fishers into the sea of the mundane whirl with the net of the Teaching to mature beings born amid craving and pull them out of it, who go like titan kings throughout all realms of existence quelling the titanic disturbances and agitations of afflictions, who rise like the sun in the sky of the reality realm to evaporate the water of beings' cravings and dry up the mud of afflictions, who rise like the full moon in the sky to awaken the water lilies of the minds of the teachable, who support all beings equally, whether friendly or hostile, high or low, to plant and grow the sprouts of roots of goodness in all sentient beings, who go everywhere unhindered like the wind to uproot the afflictions and views of all sentient beings, who go through the world like sovereigns uniting all beings with generosity, kindness, assistance, and cooperation?

"South of here is a city called Tosala in a land called Amitatosala. There is a mendicant named Sarvagamin living there. Go ask him how to learn and carry out the practice of enlightening beings."

So then Sudhana paid his respects to Achala and left.

Sarvagamin

His mind on the devotee Achala, remembering her teaching, absorbing what she had shown him, what she had told him, what she had described to him, what she had enjoined on him, what she had shared with him, what she had disclosed to him, what she had set forth to him, following it, reflecting on it, entering into it, cultivating it, embodying it, contemplating it, clarifying it, living up to it, Sudhana made his way from place to place, finally reaching the land of Amitatosala. There he sought out and found the city of Tosala.

Entering the city at sunset, he went from block to block, street to street, looking for the mendicant Sarvagamin. In the still of the night, he saw a mountain called Sulabha, north of the city. The mountain peak was adorned with thickets and groves of various plants and trees and was as bright as the sun. Seeing that light, Sudhana was ecstatic: he thought to himself, "I will undoubtedly see the spiritual benefactor on this mountaintop."

Sudhana went out of the city to the mountain and climbed to the shining peak, where he saw the mendicant Sarvagamin from afar. The appearance of the mendicant was superior to that of the great god Brahma, glorious and radiant; he was walking around surrounded by ten thousand brahmic gods.

Sudhana went up to Sarvagamin, paid his respects, and said, "Noble one, I have set my mind on supreme perfect enlightenment, but I do not know how an enlightening being is to learn and carry out the practice of enlightening beings. I hear that you give enlightening beings instruction, so please tell me how to learn and carry out the practice of enlightening beings."

Sarvagamin said, "It is good that you have set out for supreme perfect enlightenment. I am established in the enlightening practice of going everywhere, I have attained concentration of all-observing vision, and I am imbued with the light of knowledge of transcendent wisdom which distinguishes all planes of the cosmos without effort, based on nonbeing. In wandering through all worlds of living beings and inanimate objects, in wandering through the realms of existence of all beings, in the occasions of death of all sentient beings, in the occasions of birth of all sentient beings, in all kinds of conditions of existence, in the various places of birth, the worlds and abodes, of sentient beings of various appearances, forms, and sizes, bound to various kinds of existence, with various aims, wedded to various views and courses of action, believing in various forms of religion, I work for the benefit of sentient beings by various means and various applications of knowledge. Some I help by teaching various worldly arts, by means of the light of mental command of all kinds of arts. Some I help by charity, kindness, assistance, and cooperation, to lead them to omniscient knowledge. Some I help by describing the ways of transcendence, generating the light of knowledge of dedication to omniscience. Some I help by praising the aspiration for enlightenment, producing a basis for preservation of the seed of enlightenment. Some I help by describing all facets of the practices of enlightening beings, fostering the commitment to purify all buddha-lands and perfect all beings. Some I help by frightening them, showing them the misery and pain resulting from evil actions. Some I help by delighting them, telling them about the fruit of omniscience ultimately developing from giving gifts to all buddhas. Some I help by describing the virtues and qualities of all buddhas, to generate desire for the qualities of buddhas and determination for omniscience. Some I help by eulogizing the greatness of buddhas, to generate the desire to embody buddhahood and be constantly engaged in spontaneous, ceaseless buddha-work. Some I help by showing the mastery of buddhas, to generate the desire to attain supreme buddhahood.

"Furthermore, in every street, every block, every house, every district, every family and group, I assume forms like the men and women, boys and girls, and expound the Teaching to them according to their dispositions, aims, powers, and thoughts; they do not know who is teaching them or where I am from; they just practice truthfully what they have heard. And I go everywhere on this continent to those who are immersed in the views of false doctrines, in order to mature those who cling to various views. And just as I do so throughout the continent, so also do I work for the benefit of all beings on earth, in the galaxy, in the universe, in infinite worlds, in the paths of all beings, in the abodes of all beings, in the thoughts in which all beings rest, in the groups of all beings, in the masses of all beings, in all races of beings, among all types of beings, wherever they be, helping them according to their mentalities and inclinations, through various means, various methods, various approaches, various efforts, various devices, various expedients, various activities, assuming various forms, and speaking in various languages.

"I know this enlightening practice of going everywhere. How can I know the practice or tell of the virtues of the enlightening beings with bodies equal to all beings, who have attained concentration in which their own bodies and all bodies are indivisible, whose vast sphere of emanation adapts to all states of existence, who pass through existence in all worlds in their own bodies, who are intent on mystical projections pleasing to the sight of all beings, who appear to be born in all races, who carry out their vows unimpeded in all ages, who can manifest the interrelated cosmic network of practices, who are devoted to working for the welfare of all beings while living together with them without becoming defiled, who realize the basic equality of the worlds of past, present, and future, who are imbued with endless great compassion appearing in the realm of selfless knowledge, who aim to foster good in all beings?

"South of here is a land called Prthurashtra, where there lives an eminent perfumer named Utpalabhuti. Go ask him how to learn and carry out the practice of enlightening beings."

So Sudhana paid his respects to the mendicant Sarvagamin and left.

Utpalabhuti

Unconcerned with body and life, unconcerned with any material things, unconcerned with enjoyment of any people or places, unconcerned with objects of the senses, unconcerned with enjoying the experiences that go along with having followers, unconcerned with kingship, dominion, or power, concerned with developing, guiding, and purifying all sentient beings, with achieving supreme purity of a buddha-land, with tirelessly attending and serving all buddhas, with knowing and according with the inherent nature of all things, with permanently attaining the virtues of all enlightening beings, with carrying out the vows of enlightening beings through all ages, with entering the ocean of congregations of all buddhas, with entering all concentrations of enlightening beings in each particular mode of concentration by mystic transformation, with tirelessly receiving the light of knowledge of all truths through the cycles of teachings of all buddhas, pondering these and other virtues of all enlightening beings, Sudhana made his way to Prthurashtra, where he sought and found the eminent perfumer Utpalabhuti.

Seeing the perfumer, Sudhana went up to him, paid his respects, and said, "Noble one, I have set out for supreme perfect enlightenment, seeking the knowledge common to all buddhas, wishing to fulfill the vows fulfilled by all buddhas, wishing to see the embodiments of all buddhas, wishing to attain the reality body of all buddhas, wishing to know the body of knowledge of truths of all buddhas, wishing to purify all enlightening practices, wishing to manifest the sphere of concentration of all enlightening beings, wishing to master the sphere of mental command of all enlightening beings, wishing to disperse all obstructions, wishing to travel through all lands. But I do not know how an enlightening being is to learn and carry out the practice of enlightening beings. How does an enlightening being gain access to omniscience?"

Utpalabhuti said, "It is good that you aspire to supreme perfect enlightenment. I know about all fragrances—perfumes, incenses, ointments, and aromatic powders—and how they are compounded and used. I also know the sources of all fragrances. I know celestial fragrances, and I also know the fragrances of other types of beings, human and nonhuman. Indeed, I know various kinds of fragrances. I know fragrances that cure illness, I know fragrances that remove depression, I know fragrances that produce mundane joy, I know fragrances that incite passions, I know fragrances that extinguish passions, I know fragrances that produce pleasure in enjoyment of various created things, I know fragrances that produce rejection of all created things, I know fragrances that remove arrogance and heedlessness, I know fragrances that produce thoughts of Buddha, I know fragrances that accord with the principles of the Teaching, fragrances enjoyable to sages, the variety of fragrances of enlightening beings, and the fragrances of the arrangement of all stages of enlightening beings. I also know the external appearance of all these fragrances, as well as their source, production, manifestation, perfection, purification, removal, application, use, sphere of action, efficacy, nature, and root.

"In the human world there is a fragrance said to come from the agitation of water spirits: one grain the size of a sesame seed will cause this whole country to be covered with fragrant clouds that shower fine fragrant rain for seven days. Those on whose bodies or clothing that fragrant water falls become as brilliant as golden flowers, and any houses or buildings on which it falls become as brilliant as golden flowers. And any who smell the scent of that fragrant water wafting in on the breeze become ecstatic for seven days and experience many kinds of physical and mental pleasure and delight. Furthermore, no illness—whether due to constitutional upset or external trauma—occurs in their bodies, nor do they suffer any mental distress or depression, nor do they have any fear, anxiety, fright, agitation, or ill will. They become kind to one another, happy, and joyful. When they have become happy and joyful, I begin to purify their minds and teach them in such a way that they become certain of supreme enlightenment.

"There is a kind of sandalwood that comes from the mountains which will protect those anointed with its essence from burning even if they fall into a fire. The sound of kettledrums or conches smeared with it will drive away all enemy armies. There is a kind of aloe called 'lotus calyx' from the banks of the lake Heatless; a grain of it the size of a sesame seed will fill the whole continent with fragrance such that all who smell it gain a disciplined mind rejecting evil. There is a kind of fragrance from the Himalaya Mountains which is such that all who smell it become dispassionate; then I teach them in such a way that they attain a concentration called 'sphere of dispassion.' There is a kind of fragrance from the world of spirits called 'ocean storehouse' which is produced for the use of sovereign rulers; perfumed by it, the ruler and the ruler's armies stand in the sky. There is a kind of incense called 'beautiful array' originating in the celestial hall of the good doctrine; when it is burned, celestial beings gain awareness of the scent of enlightenment. There is a kind of incense from the pure treasuries in the palace of the heaven of timely portion; when it is burned, inhabitants of that heaven all go to the ruler of the heaven of timely portion, who then talks to them about the Teaching. There is a kind of incense in the heaven of satisfaction which, when burned before an enlightened being destined to become a buddha in one lifetime who is sitting on the throne of the Teaching, fills the whole cosmos at once with a great fragrant cloud and causes rain from the great cloud of the Teaching to shower in many arrays on the audiences of all buddhas. There is a kind of incense called 'fascinating' in the palace of the king of the heaven of beautiful emanations which, when burned, causes rain to shower from the cloud of the inconceivable Teaching for seven days.

"I know this art of perfuming. How can I know the practice, tell of the virtues, elucidate the method of purification of conduct, convey the irreproachable action, or explain the malice-free words, thoughts, and deeds of the enlightening beings who are free from foulness, who are void of lusts, who are free from the snares of the demon of afflictions, who have transcended all conditions of existence, who proceed with material form as being something in the magic of knowing, who are unstained by any world, whose way of life is free from attachment, who have purified the sphere of unobstructed knowledge, who are in the realm of unimpeded knowledge, who do not take refuge in any abode or rely on anything in existence?

"South of here is a city called Kutagara, where there lives a mariner named Vaira. Go ask him how to learn and carry out the practice of enlightening beings."

So then Sudhana paid his respects to Utpalabhuti and left.

Vaira

On the way to the city Kutagara, Sudhana observed where the road was variously low and high, even and uneven, dusty and dust-free, safe and perilous, impassable and unobstructed, crooked and straight. As he went along he thought, "My going to that spiritual benefactor will be a means of accomplishment of the path of enlightening beings, a means of accomplishment of the path of knowledge to assist sentient beings; it will be a means of accomplishment of the path of transcendence, a means of accomplishment of the path of knowledge to assist sentient beings. It will become a means of stopping all beings from falling into attachment and rejection, arrogance and servility; a means of turning all beings away from bad inclinations; a means of ridding all beings of the dust of afflictions; a means of removing the thorns and grit of wrong views from all sentient beings; a means of absorption in the unobstructed reality realm; a means of leading to the eternal citadel of omniscience. Why is that? Spiritual benefactors are mines of all that is good, sources of omniscience."

With these thoughts in mind, with a purpose rarely encountered, he made his way to Kutagara city looking for the mariner Vaira. When he got there, he saw the mariner surrounded by hundreds of thousands of merchants and hundreds of thousands of other people who wished to hear him talk, explaining to them the oceans of virtues of buddhas by talking about the ocean.

Sudhana went up to Vaira, paid his respects, and said, "Noble one, I have set my mind on supreme perfect enlightenment, but I do not know how to learn and carry out the practice of enlightening beings. I hear that you give enlightening beings instruction, and I hope you will tell me how one is to learn and carry out the practice of enlightening beings."

Vaira said, "It is good that you aspire to supreme perfect enlightenment and ask about the means of attaining great knowledge, about the cause of the various miseries of the mundane whirl, about the means of arriving at the island of omniscience, about the means of producing the indestructible vehicle of universal salvation, about the means of attaining the path leading away from the danger of falling into the state of individual liberation, about the source of the path of knowledge of the way to attain all kinds of tranquil concentrations, about the source of the unobstructed path of the chariot of vows carrying the practice of enlightening beings which goes everywhere, about the means of development and purification of the path guided by the nature of enlightening practice adorned with all waves of energy, about the means of development and purification of the endless path facing all things, the means of development and purification of the path into the ocean of omniscience.

"I live in this coastal metropolis of Kutagara, purifying enlightening practice characterized by great compassion. Observing those on this continent who are poor, I practice such spiritual exercises as will cause their wishes to be fulfilled: I will take care of their mundane needs, and I will satisfy them with spiritual enjoyments; I will teach them the way to accumulate virtue, I will foster knowledge in them, I will promote the growth of the power of roots of goodness, I will inspire them to seek enlightenment, I will purify their aspiration for enlightenment, I will firmly establish their power of great compassion, I will get them to extinguish the misery of the mundane whirl, I will firmly establish their power to act in the mundane world without tiring, and I will get them to care for all living beings. I will set them at the gate of entry into the ocean of virtue, I will produce in them the light of knowledge of the ocean of truths, I will turn them toward the ocean of all buddhas, and I will plunge them into the ocean of omniscience.

"With these thoughts in mind I roam this city on the edge of the ocean. Thus committed to the welfare and happiness of the world, I know all the treasure islands in the ocean. I know all the deposits of precious substances, all the types of precious substances, and all the sources of precious substances. I know how to refine, bore out, extract, and produce all precious substances, and I know all precious vessels, tools, and objects, and the light of all precious substances. I know the abodes of all water spirits, the agitations of all water spirits, the abodes of all sprites, the agitations of all sprites, the abodes of all goblins, how to alleviate the danger of goblins, the abodes of all ghosts, and how to put an end to obstacles caused by ghosts. I know how to avoid all the whirlpools and billows, and I know the colors and depths of all the waters. I know the cycles of the sun, moon, stars, and planets, and the lengths of the days and nights. I know when to travel and when not to; I know when it is safe and when it is dangerous. I know the performance and soundness of the hull and rigging of ships. I know how to control and steer ships, I know how to catch the wind, I know where the winds rise from, I know how to direct the ship and how to turn it around, I know when to anchor and when to sail.

"With this knowledge, always engaged in working for the benefit of beings, with a sturdy ship, safe, peaceful, without anxiety, I convey merchants to the treasure islands of their choice, pleasing them with spiritual conversation. Having enriched them with all kinds of jewels, I bring them back to this continent. And I have never lost a single ship. All who see me or hear my spiritual instruction are freed from all fears of sinking in the ocean of the mundane whirl; they become aware of the knowledge of how to go into the ocean of omniscience, they learn how to evaporate the ocean of craving, they are illumined with knowledge of the ocean of past, present, and future, they become capable of annihilating the ocean of suffering of all sentient beings, they undertake to clear the turbidity of the ocean of minds of all sentient beings, they begin the heroic effort to purify the ocean of all lands, they never turn back from going throughout the ocean of all places, they penetrate the variety in the ocean of faculties of all sentient beings, they adapt to the ocean of actions of all sentient beings, and they appear in the ocean of the world intentionally according to the mental set.

"I have attained this enlightening liberation which is characterized by great compassion and the sound of flowing water, and it is beneficial to see me, hear me, live with me, and remember my name; but how can I know the practice or tell of the virtues of the enlightening beings who traverse all the oceans of the mundane whirl, who are unaffected by the ocean of afflictions, who are free from the danger of being engulfed by the ocean of views, who travel the water of inherent nature of the ocean of all phenomena, who travel the ground of inherent nature of the ocean of all beings, who hold the net of means of salvation of all creatures from the oceans of the mundane, who abide in the ocean of omniscience, who pull all sentient beings out of the ocean of attachments, who remain continuously through the ocean of all times, who have true higher knowledge to perfect the ocean of all sentient beings, who do not miss the right occasions to guide the ocean of all sentient beings?

"South of here is a city called Nandihara. An eminent man named

Jayottama lives there. Go ask him how to learn and carry out the practice of enlightening beings."

Then Sudhana paid his respects and reluctantly left the mariner Vaira.

Jayottama

His mind filled with great love for the infinite realm of life, overflowing with great compassion, having amassed immense stores of virtue and knowledge, freed from the defilement of ignorance, passion, and all afflictions, realizing the equality of all things, proceeding equanimously on the path of omniscience, having eradicated the entryways into countless bad tendencies, proceeding heroically by the power of steadfast energy immune to all evils, filled with great calm by the inconceivable concentrations of an enlightening being, having thoroughly dispelled the darkness of ignorance by the light of the sun of wisdom, adorned with flowers of knowledge vivified by the moon of bliss and the breeze of means, according with the principles of knowledge of liberation through the ocean of great vows, imbued with knowledge pervading the reality realm unimpeded, facing the entrance of the imperishable city of omniscience, seeking the path of enlightening beings, Sudhana made his way to the city of Nandihara and sought out the eminent Jayottama, whom he saw in a grove at the eastern edge of the city, surrounded by thousands of elders, giving instructions regarding the various affairs of the city, in the course of which he was also talking about spirituality in order to get rid of all egoism, possessiveness, acquisitiveness, clinging to material things, dependency, binding cravings, impeding views, obscuring doubts, beclouding deceit and guile, defiling envy and jealousy, in order to clear and purify everyone's minds, in order to inspire them to delight in the vision of buddhas by fostering the power of pure faith in them, in order to get them to accept the buddha-teachings by bringing forth the powers of enlightening beings in turn, in order to generate the power of concentration of enlightening beings by revealing to them the practices of enlightening beings, in order to purify enlightening beings' power of recollection by showing them the power of wisdom of enlightening beings. Thus he was expounding the Teaching, to inspire them to seek enlightenment.

Sudhana went up to the grandee Jayottama, bowed to him, and with respect for the Teaching said, "I am Sudhana, O noble one, and I seek the practice of enlightening beings. Please tell me how to learn the practice of enlightening beings, how to orient myself to the disciplines that will perfect all sentient beings while I am learning, how to see all buddhas, how to hear the teaching of all buddhas, how to remember the multitudes of teachings of all buddhas, how to carry out the principles of the teachings of all buddhas, how to perform the practice of enlightening beings in all worlds, how to be indefatigable living in all ages by the practice of enlightening beings, how to perceive the transformation of all who have gone to Thusness, how to receive the empowerment of all buddhas, how to attain knowledge of the powers of all buddhas."

Jayottama said to Sudhana, "It is good that you aspire to supreme perfect enlightenment. I am purifying the method of enlightening practice that goes everywhere, by the power of attainment of nondoing based on nonbeing. By this method of purification of enlightening practice going everywhere, I expound the Teaching in all realms of being in the universe, I oppose untruth, I stop controversy, conflict, strife, combat, and hostility. I cut through bonds and break prisons apart. I eliminate fears. I put an end to evildoing, I turn people away from killing, stealing, sexual misconduct, falsehood, slander, harshness, divisive talk, longing, malice, and false views. I get them to stop all compulsive activity and to pursue all right and good actions. I teach everyone all arts and crafts that bring benefit to the world. I elucidate, articulate, explain, and promote all sciences for the happiness of the world. I go along with all false doctrines in order to develop the people involved in them. In order to show the excellence of higher knowledge, to put a stop to all views, to inspire interest in the teaching of all buddhas, I approach all the celestial beings in the realm of form all the way up to the world of Brahma and expound the Teaching to them. And as I teach in this universe, so also do I teach in as many worlds as atoms in ten unspeakable numbers of decillions of buddha-lands. I teach the ways of buddhas, the ways of enlightening beings, the ways of Buddhist disciples, and the ways of individual illuminates. I teach about the hells, what leads to hell, and the motives and actions of beings in hell. I teach about animality, the types who tend toward animality, what leads to animality, and the misery of animalistic life. I teach about the underworld, what leads to the underworld, and the misery of the underworld. I teach about heavens, what leads to heaven, and the enjoyments of heaven. I teach about the human world, what leads to the human world, and the variety of pleasant and unpleasant experiences in the human world.

"Thus I teach about the law of the world, the formation of the world, the decline of the world, the pain of the world, and emancipation from the world; I expound the Teaching in order to explain the path of practice of enlightening beings, to remove the ills of the mundane world, to show the virtues of omniscience, to extinguish the pain of infatuation with states of being, to elucidate the unimpeded nature of reality, to clarify the ordinary conduct of the world, to point out the happiness and misery of the conduct of all beings in the world, to show the notions on which all worlds are based, to elucidate the independent state of those who realize Thusness, to fend off all active afflictions, and to show the progress of the wheel of teaching of the enlightened.

"I know this method of purification of enlightening practice that goes everywhere, an undefiled manifestation of nondoing based on illumination. How can I know the practice or tell of the virtues of enlightening beings who have all mystic knowledges, who go throughout all lands with the body of knowledge of illusoriness, who have attained the stage of knowledge of the universal eye, who hear all utterances, who have attained control of the light of the way to truth that pervades past, present, and future, who are heroic masters of knowledge comprehending all things, who speak with the voice of totality communicating to infinite sentient beings according to their mentalities, who have phantom bodies the same as all enlightening beings pleasing to the masses of sentient beings with their various wishes, who are intent upon one and the same inconceivable body of all buddhas, whose body of knowledge pervades past, present, and future, whose sphere is as vast and measureless as the sky?

"South of here, in the land of Shronaparanta, is a city called Kalingavana, where a nun named Sinhavijurmbhita lives. Go ask her how to learn and carry out the practice of enlightening beings."

Then Sudhana paid his respects to Jayottama and left.

Sinhavijurmbhita

Then Sudhana made his way to the city called Kalingavana in the land of Shronaparanta, where he asked everyone he met the whereabouts of the nun Sinhavijurmbhita. As he was looking for the nun, everywhere he went hundreds of boys and girls came together from the streets and intersections and blocked the way. There were also hundreds of men and women, who told him, "the nun Sinhavijurmbhita is in this city, staying in Sunlight Park, which was donated by Jayaprabha, where she is expounding the Teaching for the benefit of countless beings."

So then Sudhana went to this Sunlight Park and looked all around. In the park he saw trees called "moon-risen," which were covered like pavilions, of flamelike color and blazing radiance, lighting up the space of a league all around. He also saw leafy trees called "completely covering," which are shaped like parasols, their clustered leaves providing shade, shining like blue crystal clouds. He saw flowering trees called "treasury of flowers," which had various pleasing forms like the Himalaya Mountains and showered endless streams of varicolored flowers, like the trees of paradise adorning the heavens. He also saw ever-ripe sweet fruit trees called "gathering of fruits of indescribable sweetness," which had the appearance of golden polar mountains and were always bearing fruit. He also saw jewel trees called "treasury of radiance," which looked like incomparable jewels and bore riches in buds producing garlands and ornaments of celestial jewels and wish-fulfilling gems, and were adorned by jewels of countless colors. He also saw trees of cloth called "soothing," from which hung precious celestial cloths of various colors. He also saw trees of musical instruments called "pleasing," which produced music more sweet and pleasant than that of the heavens. He also saw trees of fragrance called "gracing everywhere," which pervaded everywhere with all kinds of pleasing fragrances. There were also cool lotus ponds, with steps made of bricks of seven precious substances arrayed on four sides, surrounded by benches of various jewels painted with sandalwood fragrance, set in ground made of blue lapis lazuli, the bottom covered with gold sand, the ponds filled with water pleasantly scented with celestial fragrance, the surface of the water covered with varicolored lotuses of heavenly scent and texture, the air around them filled with the songs of birds, more lovely than the heavens, all surrounded by rows of beautiful trees of various celestial treasures.

At the foot of each of those treasure trees were arranged jewel lion seats of various pleasing forms, adorned with innumerable jewels of various kinds, spread with various precious celestial cloths, perfumed with incenses of all kinds of celestial fragrances, covered with canopies of various jewels hung with precious silks surpassing those of the heavens, enveloped in nets of gold adorned by various jewels, with circlets of bells giving forth pleasant sounds, surrounded by hundreds of thousands of celestial seats. At the foot of one precious tree he saw a lion seat in the calyx of a jewel lotus; at another, a lion seat in the calyx of a fragrant diamond lotus; at another, a lion seat in the calyx of a diamond lotus ornamented with dragons; at another, a lion seat in the calyx of a diamond lotus with clusters of jewel lions; at another, a lion seat in the calyx of a lotus of luminous jewels; at another, a lion seat in the calyx of a lotus of the finest diamonds; at another, a lion seat in the calyx of a lotus of world-illumining jewels; at another, a lion seat in the calyx of a lotus of jewels of white light.

He saw that the ground of the whole park was scattered with various jewels, just as the ocean is scattered with jewel islands. The earth, studded with blue lapis lazuli and inlaid with all kinds of jewels, was soft and pleasant to the touch, and would give way and spring back as one walked on it. The grounds were covered with diamond lilies, of pleasant texture and lovely scent. The sweet sounds of the calls of various birds were heard, and the park was graced with well-arrayed stands of heavenly precious sandalwood trees. There were endless streams of jewel blossoms raining from clouds of various jewel flowers in a magnificent array surpassing the pleasure garden of Indra, chief of gods. There were well-spaced towers with various incomparably fragrant incenses always burning, more magnificent than Indra's hall of justice, covered above with nets of various jewels surpassing those of the heavens, hung with garlands of pearl flowers spread all over with nets of shining gold arrayed with jewel bells. Trees of various musical instruments, jewel palm trees with nets of bells, played sweet music as they were stirred by the breeze, and the singing of goddesses was also heard. The park was splendidly adorned by rain from clouds of radiant celestial cloths, of infinite colors like the ocean, lovely to see. He saw Sunlight Park adorned with hundreds of thousands of towers arrayed with inconceivable, innumerable jewels, beautiful as the castle of the god Indra. It was adorned with arrays of all kinds of jewels, everywhere graced with arrays of beautifully formed parasols, always radiating pleasing light, like the abode of the god Brahma, shining with world-illumining light. It was as vast as a space that holds innumerable worlds. Sudhana saw this Sunlight Park by the strength of the mystic power of the nun Sinhavijurmbhita.

Sudhana looked all over and saw these magnificent adornments of the park, replete with infinite, inconceivable qualities, perfected by the maturation of the work of the enlightening being, born of vast supramundane roots of good, deriving from making offerings to inconceivably many buddhas, unsurpassed by all worldly goodness, sprung forth from the illusory nature of phenomena, composed of the results of extensive pure good works, without contamination, produced by the power deriving from the past virtuous actions of the nun Sinhavijurmbhita, unique, beyond the individually liberated, immune to the destructive influence of false teachers, imperceptible to maniacs and ignoramuses.

In all of those lion seats under the various precious trees he saw the nun Sinhavijurmbhita sitting, surrounded by a great company of followers, calm, composed, her senses and mind quiet, well controlled, her senses subdued, as restrained as an elephant, her mind pellucid and clear as a deep pool, granter of all desires like a wish-fulfilling jewel, unaffected by worldly things as a lotus is not clung to by water, fearless as a lion, with polished expertise, unshakable as a mountain, pure in conduct, soothing the minds of beings like intoxicating perfume, extinguishing the burning of afflictions like sandalwood from the snowy mountains, alleviating the pains of all sentient beings like the medicine "good to see," beneficial to all who behold her, producing the physical and mental bliss of quiescence like the light of a buddha free from the ills and delusions of passion, clearing the minds of sentient beings polluted by afflictions like the water-purifying crystal, promoting the growth of roots of virtue like a good field. He saw her sitting in those seats, with various audiences in the surrounding seats.

In one setting he saw the nun surrounded by gods of the heaven of pure abodes, expounding a doctrine called unity with endless liberation; in another he saw her surrounded by gods of Brahma's heaven, expounding a purity of the sphere of the voice called division of the universal ground; in another he saw her surrounded by gods and goddesses of the heaven of control of others' emanations, expounding a doctrine called array of powers of purification of mind of enlightening beings; in another he saw her surrounded by gods and goddesses of the heaven of enjoyable emanations, expounding a doctrine called pure array of all phenomena; in another he saw her surrounded by gods and goddesses of the heaven of satisfaction, expounding a doctrine called resorting to the treasury of one's own mind; in another he saw her surrounded by gods and goddesses of the heaven of timely portion, expounding a doctrine called endless array; in another he saw her surrounded by gods and goddesses of the thirty-three-fold heaven, expounding a doctrine called the method of rejecting; in another he saw her surrounded by water spirits, nymphs, and sprites, expounding a doctrine called array of lights of the sphere of buddhas; in another he saw her surrounded by demigods and demigoddesses and their children, expounding a doctrine called treasury of salvation of the world; in another he saw her surrounded by celestial musicians, expounding a doctrine called endless giving of delight; in another he saw her surrounded by titans, with their wives and children, expounding a doctrine called manifestation of power of reason in the knowledge of the reality realm; in another he saw her surrounded by fantastic birds, expounding a doctrine called the sphere of action concerned with alarming those in the ocean of existence; in another he saw her surrounded by centaurs expounding a doctrine called the range of manifestation of the action of Buddha; in another he saw her surrounded by great serpents, expounding a doctrine called production of the joy of the enlightened; in another he saw her surrounded by hundreds of thousands of women, men, boys and girls, expounding a doctrine called higher reaches of knowledge; in another he saw her surrounded by goblins, expounding a doctrine called production of compassion; in another he saw her surrounded by people devoted to the vehicle of listeners, expounding a doctrine called higher power of knowledge; in another he saw her surrounded by people devoted to the vehicle of individual illumination, expounding a doctrine called splendor of the illustrious virtues of buddhas; in another he saw her surrounded by people devoted to the Great Vehicle of universal enlightenment, expounding a medium of light of knowledge of concentration called door to totality; in another he saw her surrounded by enlightening beings who had just been inspired to seek enlightenment, expounding a medium of concentration called multitude of vows of all buddhas; in another he saw her surrounded by enlightening beings in the second stage, expounding a medium of concentration called sphere of dispassion; in another he saw her surrounded by enlightening beings in the third stage, expounding a medium of concentration called sphere of tranquillity; in another he saw her surrounded by enlightening beings in the fourth stage, expounding a medium of concentration called production of the field of action of the energy of omniscience; in another he saw her surrounded by enlightening beings of the fifth stage, expounding a medium of concentration called treasury of flowers of the tendrils of the mind; in another he saw her surrounded by enlightening beings in the sixth stage, expounding a medium of concentration called filled with light; in another he saw her surrounded by enlightening beings in the seventh stage, expounding a medium of concentration called adornment of the stage of totality; in another he saw her surrounded by enlightening beings in the eighth stage, expounding a medium of concentration called realm of the body distributed equally throughout the structure of the cosmos; in another he saw her surrounded by enlightening beings in the ninth stage, expounding a medium of concentration called array of the abode of the power of nonacquisition; in another he saw her surrounded by enlightening beings in the tenth stage, expounding a medium of concentration called sphere of nonobstruction; in another he saw her teaching an audience of thunderbolt bearers a doctrine called mighty array of thunderbolts of knowledge.

Thus he saw the mature, the teachable, the capable among those in all states of being gathered in this park, each type in a separate assembly, with various inclinations and interests, firmly intent and deeply faithful, with the nun Sinhavijurmbhita teaching them each in such a way that all became certain of supreme perfect enlightenment. How was that so? Because the nun Sinhavijurmbhita had gone into countless tens of hundreds of thousands of doors of transcendent wisdom, beginning with the equanimity of the universal eye, exposition of all buddhas' teachings, differentiation of the planes of the reality realm, dispersing all obstructions, production of good thoughts in all sentient beings, supreme adornment, matrix of the principle of nonattachment, sphere of the realm of reality, treasury of mind, and source of miracles pleasing to all. And all the enlightening beings and others who came to this park to see the nun Sinhavijurmbhita and hear her teach were guided by her, from the beginning accumulation of virtues, until she had made them irreversible on the way to supreme perfect enlightenment.

Then Sudhana, having seen the nun Sinhavijurmbhita with such an abode, such furnishings, such an audience, such mastery, such mystic power, and such eloquence, and having heard her teaching, his mind drenched by the immense cloud of the Teaching, his thoughts toward Sinhavijurmbhita pure, he prostrated himself and then circled her in respect hundreds of thousands of times. At that time the whole park and the congregations were suffused with a glorious light from the nun. Having made hundreds of thousands of circumambulations, he noticed that as he circumambulated he saw the nun whichever way he faced. He stood before her and said, "Noble one, I have set my mind on supreme perfect enlightenment, but I do not know how to learn and carry out the practice of enlightening beings. I hear you give enlightening beings instructions, so please tell me how to learn and carry out the practice of enlightening beings."

She said, "I have attained the enlightening liberation of removal of all vain imaginings." Sudhana asked her about the sphere of this liberation, and she said, "It is the light of knowledge whose nature is instantaneous awareness of the phenomena of past, present, and future." Sudhana asked about the compass of this light of knowledge, and she replied, "As I go in and out the door of this light of knowledge, there is born in me a concentration called 'possessed of all phenomena,' by the attainment of which concentration I go to all worlds in the ten directions with mentally produced bodies to present offerings as numerous as atoms in untold buddha-lands with bodies as numerous as atoms in untold buddha-lands to each of the enlightening beings in the heavens of satisfaction who are bound to attain buddhahood in one lifetime. In the forms of all sorts of beings, bringing all sorts of gifts, I go to make offerings to the enlightening beings in the heavens of satisfaction who are going to become buddhas in the next life, and I go to all the buddhas, be they in the womb, being born, at home, leaving home, going to the heights of enlightenment, at the pinnacle of enlightenment, having become supremely perfectly enlightened, gone to various realms of existence, or entering final extinction after having satisfied the minds of all beings, making such offerings with such mentally produced bodies. Those sentient beings who know my work of making offerings to buddhas all become certain of supreme perfect enlightenment. And to all those sentient beings who come to me I give instruction in this same transcendent wisdom.

"I see all beings with the eye of knowledge, yet I do not conceive any notion of 'sentient being,' and do not imagine so. I hear all beings' verbal signals, yet I do not imagine so, because I do not enter into the spheres of any discourses. I see all buddhas, yet I do not imagine so, because I know their body is reality. I remember the cycles of teachings of all buddhas, but I do not imagine so, because I am aware of the true nature of things. I pervade the cosmos in every moment of awareness, but I do not imagine so, because I know the nature of things as existing in illusion.

"Thus, I know the enlightening liberation of removal of all vain imaginings; but how can I know the practice or tell of the virtues of the enlightening beings who penetrate the infinite cosmos of realities, who are free from vain imaginings about all things, who pervade all realms of reality while sitting cross-legged in one body, who see all buddha-lands in their own bodies, who go to all buddhas in a single instant, in whose own beings the miracles of all buddhas are taking place, who lift up untold buddha-lands with a single hair, who show the eons of becoming and dissolution of untold worlds in their own pores, who in a single instant enter into the commonality of coexistence in untold eons, who enter untold eons in a single instant?

"South of here, in the land of Durga, is a city called Ratnavyuha, where Vasumitra, a worshiper of the god of light, is living. Go ask her how to learn and carry out the practice of enlightening beings."

So, paying his respects to the nun Sinhavijurmbhita, Sudhana left her and went on his way.

Vasumitra

His mind illumined by the lightning of great vision, meditating on the light of omniscience, observing the manifestation of power of essential nature, making firm the mnemonic command of the treasury of verbal communications of all beings, extending the mnemonic command to retain the cycles of teachings of all buddhas, establishing the power of great compassion as a refuge for all sentient beings, examining the power of omniscience which is the source of the means of perceiving the principles of all laws, following the purity of vows extending throughout the cosmos, clarifying the light of knowledge illumining all things, developing the power of mystic knowledge pervading all phenomena arraying the worlds of the ten directions, fulfilling the vow to remember, undertake, and accomplish all the deeds of enlightening beings, Sudhana made his way to the city of Ratnavyuha in the country of Durga, where he sought out Vasumitra.

People there who did not know of Vasumitra's virtues or the scope of her knowledge said to Sudhana, "What has someone like you—with senses so calm and subdued, so aware, so clear, without confusion or distraction, your gaze focused discreetly right before you, your mind not overwhelmed by sensations, not clinging to appearances, your eyes averted from involvement in all forms, your mind so cool and steady, your way of life profound, wise, oceanic, your mind free from agitation or despondency—what have you to do with Vasumitra? You should not have any lust for her, your head should not be turned by her, you should not have any such impure thoughts, you should not be ravaged by such desires, you should not be under the power of a woman, you should not be so bewitched, you should not enter the realm of temptation, you should not sink into the mire of sensuality, you should not be bound by the snares of the devil, you should not do what should not be done."

Those who knew the excellence of the virtues of Vasumitra, however, and who were aware of the scope of her knowledge, said, "Good, good! You have really made gain if you ask about Vasumitra. You surely seek buddhahood; you surely want to make yourself a refuge for all sentient beings; you surely want to extract the barbs of passion from all sentient beings; you surely want to transform the notion of purity. Vasumitra is in her house, north of the town square."

Hearing this, Sudhana was delighted. He went to Vasumitra's house and saw that it was surrounded by ten jewel walls, ten circles of jewel trees, and ten moats filled with fragrant water covered by celestial jewel lotuses of various colors, with gold sand spread on the bottom, the rippling waters producing an intoxicating fragrance, the banks adorned by many jewels. The house had well-arranged apartments and towers made of all kinds of precious substances; it had high arched doorways and circular windows, draped with nets and blazing with jewels. It was adorned with fences of countless various jewels, and its base was composed of masses of jewels studded with lapis lazuli. It was perfumed with all kinds of fragrant oils. The walls were studded with all kinds of jewels, and the roof was inland with various gems and covered with a gold net. A hundred thousand webs of gold bells gave off sweet, pleasant sounds as they rustled in the breeze. The house was adorned with sprays of jewel flowers from clouds of flowers of all kinds of jewels. The doors were decorated with multicolored banners of all kinds of jewels. The light of lamps of various jewels shone to an endless distance. The house had diamond beams made from the limbs of gigantic brilliant jewel trees, and it was an inexhaustible treasury of hundreds and thousands of riches in full view; it was also adorned with ten large gardens set around it.

There he saw Vasumitra, who was beautiful, with golden skin and black hair, her limbs and body well proportioned, more beautiful in form than all celestial and human beings in the realm of desire, her voice finer even than that of the god Brahma. She knew the language of all beings; she had a pleasant voice that could pronounce any sound, and was skilled in freedom of phonetic organization. She was well versed in all arts and sciences, she had learned to use the magic of true knowledge, and she had mastered all aspects of the expedient means of enlightening beings. Her beautiful body was decorated with assorted jewelry, draped with a radiant mesh made of all kinds of precious substances, shining with an array of countless celestial jewel ornaments. She wore a tiara of large wish-fulfilling gems, her waist was adorned with diamonds, and she had a lapis lazuli necklace on. She had a large, attractive retinue, all with the same virtues, the same practice, and the same vow. She was an inexhaustible treasury of goodness and knowledge. He also saw the whole house, with all its jeweled apartments and furnishings lit up by the lovely, refreshing, pleasant, blissful, enrapturing light that emanated from her body.

Sudhana went up to Vasumitra, paid his respects, and said, "Noble one, I have set my mind on supreme perfect enlightenment, but I do not know how to learn and carry out the practice of enlightening beings. I hear that you give enlightening beings instructions, and I hope you will tell me how an enlightening being is to learn and carry out the practice of enlightening beings."

She said, "I have attained an enlightening liberation called 'ultimately dispassionate.' To gods, in accord with their inclinations and interests, I appear in the form of a goddess of surpassing splendor and perfection; and to all other types of beings I accordingly appear in the form of a female of their species, of surpassing splendor and perfection. And all who come to me with minds full of passion, I teach them so that they become free of passion. Those who have heard my teaching and attain dispassion achieve an enlightening concentration called 'realm of nonattachment.'

"Some attain dispassion as soon as they see me, and achieve an enlightening concentration called 'delight in joy.' Some attain dispassion merely by talking with me, and achieve an enlightening concentration called 'treasury of unimpeded sound.' Some attain dispassion just by holding my hand, and achieve an enlightening concentration called 'basis of going to all buddha-lands.' Some attain dispassion just by staying with me, and achieve an enlightening concentration called 'light of freedom from bondage.' Some attain dispassion just by gazing at me, and achieve an enlightening concentration called 'tranquil expression.' Some attain dispassion just by embracing me, and achieve an enlightening concentration called 'womb receiving all sentient beings without rejection.' Some attain dispassion just by kissing me, and achieve an enlightening concentration called 'contact with the treasury of virtue of all beings.' All those who come to me I establish in this enlightening liberation of ultimate dispassion, on the brink of the stage of unimpeded omniscience."

Sudhana asked her, "Where did you plant roots of virtue, and what kind of deeds did you accumulate, that you got to be this way?"

She replied, "I recall that in a past age a buddha named Reaching the Heights appeared in the world. When the buddha went to the royal capital out of compassion for the people, as he crossed the threshold the whole city quaked and appeared to be vastly extended and made of jewels, adorned with the luster of many jewels, strewn with flowers of various jewels. A variety of celestial musical instruments played, and the sky appeared covered by high, immeasurable clouds of celestial beings. At that time I was the wife of a grandee. Impelled by the miracle of the buddha, I went with my husband in a state of exalted serenity and presented a coin to the buddha on the street. At that time Manjushri was an attendant of that buddha; it was by him that I was inspired to seek supreme perfect enlightenment.

"I know this enlightening liberation of ultimate dispassion, but how can I know the practice or tell the virtues of the enlightening beings who are endowed with the skill of endless means and knowledge, who are vast, inexhaustible treasuries of good, who are in the realm of invincible knowledge?

"South of here is a city called Shubhaparamgama, where a householder named Veshthila is presenting offerings to the shrine of the buddha Sandalwood Throne. Go ask him how to learn and carry out the practice of enlightening beings."

So Sudhana paid his respects to Vasumitra and left.

Veshthila

Then Sudhana went to Veshthila's house in the city of Shubhaparamgama. Paying his respects to the householder, he said, "Noble one, I have set my mind on supreme perfect enlightenment, but I do not know how to learn and carry out the practice of enlightening beings. I hear that you give enlightening beings instruction; please tell me how to learn and carry out the practice of enlightening beings."

Veshthila said, "I have attained an enlightening liberation called 'not ultimately exhausted.' To my way of thinking, no buddha in any world ever has, does, or will become finally extinct, except as a docetic device. When I opened the door of the shrine of the buddha Sandalwood Throne, I attained an enlightening concentration called 'manifestation of the endless lineage of buddhas.' I enter this concentration in each mental moment, and every moment understand many kinds of excellence."

Sudhana asked, "What is the sphere of this concentration?"

Veshthila replied, "When I am in this concentration, all the successive buddhas of this world-system—beginning with Kashyapa, Kanakamuni, Krakucchanda, Vishvabhuj, Shikhin, Vipashyin, Tishya, Pushya, Yashottara, and Padmottara—appear to me. In the continuity of vision of buddhas, by the continuity of the succession of buddhas, in one mental moment I see a hundred buddhas; in the next moment of awareness I find a thousand buddhas, then a hundred thousand buddhas, a million buddhas, a hundred million, a billion, a trillion, a quadrillion, a quintillion; I immediately become aware of the succession of appearance of untold numbers of buddhas, of as many buddhas as atoms in the continent, as many as atoms in untold buddha-lands. I also comprehend the order of preparations of those buddhas' initial aspiration, their spiritual transformation on achieving the aspiration for enlightenment, the purity of execution of their various vows, their purification of action, their fulfillment of the transcendent ways, their attainment of all the stages of enlightening beings, their perfection of attainment of tolerance, their conquering of demons, the supernal manifestation of their spiritual transfiguration on becoming perfectly enlightened, the variety of purity of their buddha-lands, the variety of their development of sentient beings, the variety of their audiences, the variety of their auras of light, the majesty of their teaching activities, and their accomplishment of the miracles of buddhas. I also distinctly remember their teachings, take them up mindfully, examine them in action, analyze them, follow them with discernment, and elucidate them with wisdom.

"I also perceive the successive buddhas of the future, beginning with Maitreya, seeing a hundred buddhas in a single mental instant, then a thousand, and so on, uninterruptedly seeing as many buddhas as atoms in untold buddha-lands. I also see the order of their aspiration and preparation and so on, and distinctly remember their teachings, take them up mindfully, examine them, follow them, and elucidate them. And just as I see the succession of past, future, and present buddhas in this world-system, so do I also comprehend the succession of all buddhas in as many past and future world-systems in the ten directions as atoms in untold buddha-lands. I also comprehend the order of the aspiration and preparations of those buddhas, and I comprehend the unbroken continuity of the successive incarnations of those buddhas.

"I am also aware of the succession of buddhas of the present in all worlds in the ten directions, beginning with Vairocana, incomparable, accessible to faith and the vigorous resolution of enlightening beings, increasing the energy of enlightening beings, unsurpassed by any worldlings, individual illuminates, or enlightening beings who have not reached that sphere. In a single mental instant I see a hundred buddhas; in the next instant of awareness I see a thousand buddhas, continuing thus without interruption until I meet as many buddhas as atoms in untold buddha-lands.

"I see whatever buddhas I wish, whenever I wish, and I hear all that has been, is being, and will be spoken by those buddhas I meet, and I take up what I hear, remember it, examine it in action, analyze it, follow it with discernment, and elucidate it with wisdom.

"I know this enlightening liberation of ultimate nonextinction; how can I know the practice or tell of the virtues of the enlightening beings who have attained instantaneous knowledge of past, present, and future, who dwell in all concentrations in the space of an instant, who are imbued with the light of those who realize Thusness, who realize the equality of all thoughts and imaginations, who are focused on the equality of all buddhas, who abide in the nonduality of self, sentient beings, and buddhas, whose realm is the manifestation of principles, whose nature is clarity, whose workings of knowledge pervade the network of worlds, who dwell unwavering on the seal of the teaching of all buddhas, who are in the range of knowledge making known all realms of reality, who are in the range of knowledge conveying the teachings of all buddhas?

"South of here is a mountain called Potalaka, where an enlightening being named Avalokiteshvara lives. Go ask him how to learn and carry out the practice of enlightening beings."

Then Veshthila said in verse,

Go, Sudhana, to Mount Potalaka in the ocean, a pure abode of the valiant,

Made of jewels, covered with trees, scattered with flowers, complete with gardens, ponds, and streams.

On the mountain the steady, wise Avalokiteshvara dwells for the benefit of the world.

Go ask him the virtues of the Guides—he will teach you great, wonderful means of attainment.

So Sudhana paid his respects to Veshthila and went on.

Avalokiteshvara

Reflecting on the teaching of Veshthila, entering the treasury of zealous application of enlightening beings, remembering the power of mindfulness of enlightening beings, remembering the power of the succession of enlightened guides, realizing the unbroken continuity of buddhas, remembering the progression of the hearing of the names of buddhas, following the principles of the teachings of the buddhas, entering into the array of collective practice of the buddha-teachings, intent on the the exclamation made by buddhas on becoming perfectly enlightened, focusing his attention on the inconceivable action of buddhas, Sudhana made his way to Mount Potalaka.

Climbing the mountain, he looked around for Avalokiteshvara and saw him on a plateau on the west side of the mountain, which was adorned with springs, ponds, and streams, sitting wakefully on a diamond boulder in a clearing in a large woods, surrounded by a group of enlightening beings seated on various jewel rocks, to whom he was expounding a doctrine called "light of the medium of great love and compassion," which concerns the salvation of all sentient beings.

Transported with joy on seeing Avalokiteshvara, his eyes fixed on him, his mind undistracted, full of the energy of faith in the spiritual benefactor, thinking of seeing spiritual benefactors as at once seeing buddhas, thinking of reception of the multitudes of all truths as originating in spiritual benefactors, thinking of the attainment of all virtues as deriving from spiritual benefactors, thinking of how hard it is to meet spiritual benefactors, thinking of spiritual benefactors as the source from which the jewels of knowledge of the ten powers are obtained, thinking of spiritual benefactors as the source of vision of inexhaustible knowledge, thinking that the growth of the sprouts of goodness depends on spiritual benefactors, thinking that the door of omniscience is revealed by spiritual benefactors, thinking that the way to enter the ocean of great knowledge is pointed out by spiritual benefactors, thinking that the accumulation of the store of omniscience is fostered by spiritual benefactors, Sudhana went up to Avalokiteshvara.

The enlightening being Avalokiteshvara, seeing Sudhana approaching in the distance, said, "Welcome, you who have set out on the incomparable, lofty, inconceivable Great Vehicle, intending to save all beings who are oppressed by various firmly rooted miseries and have no refuge, seeking to directly experience all the teachings of buddhas, which are beyond all worlds, incomparable, and immeasurable; you are filled with the energy of great compassion, determined to liberate all sentient beings, directed toward practice of the vision of universal good, intent on purifying the sphere of great vows, born of the ocean of knowledge of Manjushri, correctly proceeding on the instructions of spiritual benefactors, with the tireless will to build up roots of goodness, seeking to retain the multitudes of teachings of all buddhas; a mine of lotuses of virtue, fit to receive the empowerment of buddhas, imbued with the energy of the light of concentration, seeking to keep in mind the teachings of all buddhas, thrilled with the joy of the vision of buddhas, your mind expanded by the incalculable energy of achievement of virtue, wishing to reveal to others the power of the measure of omniscience to which you have access through your own mystic knowledge, determined to sustain the energy of light of knowledge of buddhas, firmly rooted in the power of great compassion."

Then Sudhana went up to Avalokiteshvara, paid his respects, and said, "Noble one, I have set my mind on supreme perfect enlightenment, but I do not know how to learn and carry out the practice of enlightening beings. I hear you give enlightening beings instruction, and I ask you to tell me how to learn and carry out the practice of enlightening beings."

Avalokiteshvara said, "It is good that you aspire to supreme perfect enlightenment. I know a way of enlightening practice called 'undertaking great compassion without delay,' which sets about impartially guiding all sentient beings to perfection, dedicated to protecting and guiding sentient beings by communicating knowledge to them through all media. Established in this method of enlightening practice undertaking great compassion without delay, I appear in the midst of the activities of all sentient beings without leaving the presence of all buddhas, and take care of them by means of generosity, kind speech, beneficial actions, and cooperation. I also develop sentient beings by appearing in various forms: I gladden and develop them by purity of vision of inconceivable forms radiating auras of light, and I take care of them and develop them by speaking to them according to their mentalities, and by showing conduct according to their inclinations, and by magically producing various forms, and by teaching them doctrines commensurate with their various interests, and by inspiring them to begin to accumulate good qualities, by showing them projections according to their mentalities, by appearing to them as members of their own various races and conditions, and by living together with them.

"Perfecting this practice of unhesitating compassion, I have vowed to be a refuge for all sentient beings, to free them from fears of calamity, threat, confusion, bondage, attacks on their lives, insufficiency of means to support life, inability to make a living, ill repute, the perils of life, intimidation by the crowd, death, miserable conditions, unknown hardships, servitude, separation from loved ones, living with the uncongenial, physical violence, mental violence, sorrow, and depression. I have undertaken a vow to be a refuge for all beings from all these fears and perils. I have also caused a way of remembrance to appear in all worlds, to extinguish the fears of all beings; I have caused my name to be known in all worlds to drive away the fears of all beings. I have caused the tranquillity of all beings, in endless forms, to appear in my body, to communicate to all beings individually according to the time. By this means I release beings from all fears, inspire them to seek supreme enlightenment, and cause them never to regress in the attainment of the qualities of buddhas.

"I have only attained this way of enlightening practice through unhesitating great compassion. How can I know the practice or tell of the virtues of the universally good enlightening beings, who have perfected the vows of all enlightened ones, who have gone the way of the practice of the universally good enlightening being, who are uninterrupted streams of performance of good works, who are always focused on the perception of the concentrations of enlightening beings, who continue their practice without deviation or regression through all ages, who continuously adapt to the times everywhere, who are familiar with the changing currents in all worlds, who continuously work to extinguish all sentient beings' bad thoughts and to increase their good thoughts, who continuously work to turn all sentient beings away from the repetitious circles of the mundane whirl?"

Then this was said:

> Having respectfully rendered honor and praise,
> Sudhana, well controlled, went south.
> On a cliff of a mountain he saw Avalokiteshvara,
> the seer who abides in compassion.

> On a diamond slope, adorned with jewels,
> Sitting on a lion seat in a lotus calyx, the Steadfast,
> Surrounded by various creatures and enlightening beings,
> Expounds the Teaching to them.

> Seeing this, Sudhana, his joy unequaled,
> Went and bowed to the feet of the Ocean of Virtue
> And said, "Teach me, noble one, with compassion,
> To attain this good conduct."

> Extending his undefiled arm of a hundredfold auspicious splendor,
> Radiating far-reaching pure light,
> Avalokiteshvara, the purified being, the sage,
> Laid his hand on Sudhana's head and spoke:

> "I know a gate of liberation, the embryo of knowledge
> Of clouds of compassion of all buddhas,
> Born of my own love and operating everywhere
> To protect and care for all beings.

"I protect all beings from many disasters;
Those caught in the grip of enemies,
Physically injured, and imprisoned
Are freed from their bonds on hearing my name.

"Arrows shot at the condemned do not wound them,
Weapons break and swords are deflected
If they remember my name.

"In disputes among kings, those who remember my name
Defeat their adversaries and gain what is good,
Increase in repute among friends and relatives,
And their property becomes inviolable.

"Any who remember my name
Go without fear
To forests infested with bandits and wild animals,
Conquering all enemies.

"For those who are thrown from a mountain into burning coals
By malefactors to harm them,
The flames become lotus sprouts in a pond of water
If they remember my name.

"Thrown into the sea, they will not die,
Nor will they be swept away by a river or burned in fire:
No harm will come to them, but rather benefit instead,
If they remember my name, even for a while.

"From fetters, chains, and beatings,
Scorn, humiliation, and constraint,
Abuse, whipping, threats, and scolding,
Those who remember my name will gain release.

"The inimical, faultfinders,
Those who always maliciously slander,
Become friendly on sight
When they hear my name remembered.

"Evil magicians trying to kill them are appeased,
And no poison can injure those who remember my name.

"Malicious spirits, fiends, demons, and goblins, life-sapping, dangerous,
Are all quelled, even in dreams, once my name is recalled.

"One will not be separated from family and friends

Or be joined with the unfriendly
Or become materially destitute,
If one remembers my name, even for a while.

"Those who remember my name will not go to hell
Or become animals or ghosts
Or fall into other unfavorable states;
They will be reborn as celestial or human, purified beings.

"People remembering my name will not
Be blind, deaf, or infirm;
They will not be violent, but friendly
And sound in mind and body for countless ages.

"Those who scatter a handful of flowers over me,
Calling my name, go to my refuge of bliss;
Those who give me offerings with a clear mind
Will be worthy of receiving offerings in my buddha-land.

"Purified beings, passing away, are born here,
Face to face with the buddhas of all worlds;
Those who remember my name see the buddhas
And hear their teaching.

"By this and infinite other means
I guide sentient beings in the world;
I have developed one liberation,
And cannot know all the virtues of the virtuous.

"Sudhana has attended spiritual benefactors
In the worlds of the ten directions
And has not tired of hearing the teaching of the offspring of Buddha;
Why would joy not arise while hearing the Teaching?"

At that moment an enlightening being named Ananyagamin descended from the eastern sky and stood on the top of the mountain range surrounding this world. As soon as he set foot on the mountain, the whole world quaked and appeared to be made of jewels. The body of that enlightening being gave off such a light that the sun and moon were overwhelmed, the lights of all realms of being, fire, jewels, and stars were obscured, the great hells were lit up, the dark recesses of the realms of animals and ghosts were illumined, all ills and miseries were allayed, sentient beings were not bound by afflictions, and all sorrows ceased. He also appeared to go to the buddha, causing clouds of all kinds of offerings—jewels, flowers, perfumes, garlands, robes, parasols, banners—to rain all over the buddha-land, and he also appeared reflected in the abodes of all beings, appearing to them so as to please them according to their inclinations, and he also appeared to have come to the enlightening being Avalokiteshvara on the peak of Mount Potalaka.

Then Avalokiteshvara said to Sudhana, "Do you see the enlightening being Ananyagamin in this assembly?"

Sudhana said, "Yes."

Avalokiteshvara said, "Go to Ananyagamin and ask him how to learn and carry out the practice of enlightening beings."

So then Sudhana paid his respects to Avalokiteshvara and went.

Ananyagamin

Then Sudhana, with Avalokiteshvara's verse of knowledge in mind, had not seen enough of Avalokiteshvara but obeyed his words and went to the enlightening being Ananyagamin. Paying his respects, Sudhana said, "Noble one, I have set my mind on supreme perfect enlightenment, but I do not know how to learn and carry out the practice of enlightening beings. I hear you give enlightening beings instruction, so please tell me how an enlightening being is to learn and carry out the practice of enlightening beings."

Ananyagamin said, "I have attained an enlightening liberation 'speeding forth in all directions.'"

Sudhana asked, "What buddha did you learn it from? How far away is that buddha's world, and when did you leave that world?"

Ananyagamin said, "This point is hard for celestial, human, and titanic beings, for monks and priests, to know, being the power of an enlightening being, the unregressing energy of an enlightening being, the accomplishment of the energy of an enlightening being. It cannot be heard or retained or believed in or comprehended by those who are not under the tutelage of spiritual benefactors, who are not under the attention of buddhas, who have no accumulated roots of goodness, who have not purified their intentions, who have not attained the faculties of enlightening beings, who do not have the eye of wisdom."

Sudhana said, "Please tell me, noble one—I will believe, I will have faith, by the empowerment of buddhas and the assistance of spiritual benefactors."

Ananyagamin said, "I come from the buddha-land of a buddha named Born of Universal Light in a world to the east called Full of Light. I attained the enlightening liberation 'speeding forth in all directions' at the feet of that buddha. As many eons as atoms in untold buddha-lands have passed since I left that world Full of Light. With each thought I take as many steps as atoms in untold buddha-lands, and with each step I pass as many buddha-lands as atoms in untold buddha-lands, in all of which are buddhas. I go to all those buddhas, and honor each buddha with the finest mentally produced offerings, stamped with the cosmic seal that has no formation, approved by the buddhas, pleasing to all enlightening beings. I also observe the oceans of sentient beings in all the worlds, penetrate their minds, discern their faculties, and appear to them bodily in accord with their inclinations and interests, speak of the Teaching, radiate auras of light, and provide them with various material necessities. I adapt my form for them, ceaselessly striving to guide them to perfection. And just as I proceed in the east, so do I also proceed in the south, west, north, northeast, southeast, southwest, northwest, the nadir and the zenith.

"I only know this enlightening liberation speeding in all directions. How can I know the practice or tell of the virtue of the enlightening beings who go everywhere, who face in all directions, who are in the realm of unfragmented knowledge, whose bodies are distributed evenly throughout all universes, who adapt their action to all sentient beings according to the inclinations and interests of those beings, whose bodies pervade all lands, who act in accord with the way things really are, who have realized the equality of past, present, and future, who accord with the equality of all places, who illumine the paths of all beings, who do not have arbitrary notions of buddhahood, who go along all paths without attachment or obstruction, who stand on the path of nonreliance?

"South of here is a city called Dvaravati, where the celestial Mahadeva lives. Go ask him how to learn and carry out the practice of enlightening beings."

So Sudhana paid his respects to the enlightening being Ananyagamin and went on.

Mahadeva

His mind following the far-reaching practice of enlightening beings, eager to embody the sphere of knowledge of the enlightening being Ananyagamin, seeing the excellence of the qualities of the realm of exercise of great mystic knowledge, girding himself with the armor of steadfast vigor, full of joy, his mind on the freedom of inconceivable liberation, accomplishing the virtues of enlightening beings, practicing concentration, establishing mental command, entering into vows, learning powers of analysis and expression, bringing forth power, Sudhana went to the city of Dvaravati and asked for Mahadeva.

The people of the city told Sudhana, "This Mahadeva is in a temple at a crossroads in the city expounding the Teaching in a giant body." Sudhana then went to Mahadeva, paid his respects, and said, "Noble one, I have set my mind on supreme perfect enlightenment, but I do not know how to learn and carry out the practice of enlightening beings. I hear that you give enlightening beings instruction, and wish you would tell me how to learn and carry out the practice of enlightening beings."

Then the celestial Mahadeva extended four hands in four directions, brought water from the oceans with extreme speed and washed his face; he scattered golden flowers over Sudhana and said, "Enlightening beings are hard to get to see, extremely hard to get to hear. They rarely appear in the world, being so exalted. They are supreme lotuses of humanity, saviors of the world, refuges for the world, reliances for the world. They are great suns, makers of light for sentient beings, the ones who show the path of safety and peace to those on the path of delusion. They are guides to the truth, leaders on the way to the citadel of omniscience. I think 'killer of wrong views' is the name for enlightening beings, in that they manifest themselves to those whose minds are undefiled, they appear before those whose deeds are pure, they imbue those who are free from evils of speech with the light of eloquence, and at all times they stand before those whose intentions are purified. Son, I have attained an enlightening liberation called 'cloud net.'"

Sudhana asked, "What is the sphere of this 'cloud net' liberation?"

At that moment the celestial Mahadeva manifested a heap of gold the size of a mountain before Sudhana, as well as a heap of silver, a heap of lapis lazuli, a heap of crystals, a heap of coral, a heap of emeralds, a heap of starry jewels, a heap of clear jewels, a heap of radiant jewels, a heap of jewels with facets facing in all directions, a heap of crown jewels, a heap of varicolored jewels, a heap of necklaces, a heap of earrings, a heap of bracelets, a heap of belts, a heap of anklets, a heap of various kinds of flowers, fragrances, incenses, garlands, unguents, aromatic powders, robes, parasols, banners, pennants, musical instruments, and all objects of desire. He then said to Sudhana, "Take of these and give gifts, do good works, make offerings to buddhas, take care of beings by generous giving, get them to practice transcendent relinquishment, teach the world by giving, show relinquishment, which is hard to do. In the same way as I give you all these goods, so also do I make relinquishment habitual in countless sentient beings whose sense of generosity is not repressed. Having gotten them to plant roots of goodness with the Buddha, the Teaching, and the Community, and spiritual benefactors, I get them to aspire to supreme perfect enlightenment.

"Furthermore, to those who are intoxicated with the enjoyment of objects of desire, who are very greedy for the enjoyment of objects, I make objects appear impure. To those filled with anger, those who are arrogant, conceited, proud, and haughty, those who should be led away from strife, I show terrors like fiends and ghouls who feed on flesh and blood, and show them that it is all the vehemence of arrogance. To those who are lazy and negligent I show the dangers of fire, water, kings, and brigands, to stir them to vigor and diligence. Thus with various appropriate means I turn them away from bad conduct and get them to develop good qualities, to destroy all impediments to the transcendent ways, to make the necessary preparations for the transcendent ways, to cross over all the precipitous paths on the mountains of barriers to enlightenment, and to enter the unobstructed state.

"I only know this 'cloud net' enlightening liberation. How can I know the practice or tell of the virtues of the enlightening beings who are like the celestial chief Indra, crushing the titans of affliction, who are like water, extinguishing the fire of suffering of all beings, who are like heat, evaporating the water of craving of all beings, who are like wind, shattering the mountains of all attachments, who are like thunderbolts, rending asunder the mountain of the congealed notion of self?

"South of here, at the site of enlightenment in the region of Magadha in Jambudvipa, lives an earth goddess named Sthavara. Go ask her how to learn and carry out the practice of enlightening beings."

So then Sudhana paid his respects to Mahadeva and went on.

Sthavara

Then Sudhana went to the earth goddess Sthavara at the site of enlightenment in Magadha. Ten hundred thousand earth goddesses said to one another, "Someone comes who will be a refuge for all sentient beings; a vessel of enlightenment comes who will break the shell of ignorance of all sentient beings; one who springs from the family of spiritual sovereigns comes who will put on the turban of unattached supreme purity of a spiritual sovereign; a hero bearing the mighty thunderbolt of knowledge comes who will destroy the weapons of all false teachers."

Then those earth goddesses, led by Sthavara, caused the earth to tremble, made the ocean roar, illumined the whole universe with a glorious light, and with bodies adorned with all kinds of jewelry, like bundles of lightning bolts descending from the sky, emerged from the surface of the earth, with all tree sprouts growing, all flowering trees blooming, all rivers flowing, all lakes and ponds rising, fragrant rains showering, great winds bearing flowers, billions of musical instruments playing, celestial palaces, ornaments, and tiaras appearing, bulls, elephants, tigers, and lions roaring, the lords of the gods, titans, serpents and spirits thundering, mountains crashing together, and hundreds of billions of treasuries surfacing.

Then the earth goddess said to Sudhana, "Welcome. This is a spot of ground where you have planted roots of goodness, which I have witnessed. Do you want to see the results in one place?"

Sudhana paid his respects to the goddess and said, "I do."

Then the goddess, touching the earth with the sole of her foot, caused it to appear adorned with hundreds of billions of deposits of countless jewels, and said to Sudhana, "These billions of treasuries of jewels accompany you and are at your service, to be used as you wish; they have been produced as a result of your good works and are preserved by the power of your good works. Take of them and do whatever should be done.

"I have attained an enlightening liberation, 'unassailable asylum of knowledge.' Having attained this liberation, I have constantly stayed by and protected the enlightening being Vairocana since the time of Dipankara Buddha. Since then I have observed the enlightening being's mental activity, entered his sphere of knowledge and all his vows, followed his purification of enlightening practice, gone along into all concentrations, pervaded the vastness of the mind of the mystic knowledges of all enlightening beings, and have comprehended, remembered, and taken in his mastery of the powers of all enlightening beings, his insuperability like that of all enlightening beings, his pervasion of the network of all lands, his reception of the prediction of enlightenment from all buddhas, his manifestation of attainment of enlightenment in all times, his way of activating all the cycles of the Teaching, the doctrines expounded in all the scriptures, his way of revealing the vista of the great Teaching, his way of knowing how to lead all sentient beings to perfection, and his way of manifesting all the miracles that buddhas perform.

"I attained this 'unassailable asylum of knowledge' enlightening liberation from the buddha Skillful Guide in the world Moon Banner eons ago, more eons than the number of atoms in the polar mountain, in an eon called Supernal Manifestation of Light. Going in and out of this 'unassailable asylum of knowledge' liberation and causing it to expand and broaden, I have always been seeing buddhas, continuing up to this eon of virtue in the present, and now I have propitiated as many buddhas as atoms in untold buddha-lands, and I have seen the spiritual transformations of all those buddhas when they came to the site of enlightenment, and I have witnessed all those buddhas' roots of goodness.

"I know only this enlightening liberation 'unassailable asylum of knowledge.' How can I know the practice or tell the virtues of the enlightening beings who attend all buddhas, who remember the tales of all the buddhas, who have entered the recondite knowledge of all buddhas, who speed throughout the cosmos in a moment of thought, who are physically equal to the buddhas, who are undefiled receptacles of the mind of all buddhas, who have always effected the birth of all buddhas, who are envoys physically indivisible from all buddhas?

"In this country Magadha in Jambudvipa is a city called Kapilavastu, where a night goddess named Vasanti lives. Go ask her how to learn and carry out the practice of enlightening beings."

So then Sudhana paid his respects to the earth goddess Sthavara and went on.

Vasanti

Then Sudhana went to the great city Kapilavastu, remembering the teaching of the earth goddess Sthavara, remembering that enlightening liberation "unassailable asylum of knowledge," extending the cultivation of that enlightening concentration, contemplating that enlightening doctrine, roaming in the freedom of that enlightening liberation, looking into the subtleties of knowledge of that enlightening liberation, entering into the ocean of knowledge of that enlightening liberation, focusing on the unity of the knowledge of that enlightening liberation, pursuing the accomplishment of the endless knowledge of that enlightening liberation, plunging into the ocean of knowledge of that enlightening liberation.

Going around the city from left to right, he went in by the eastern gate and stood in the middle of the crossroads of the city. Before long the sun set, and, skillfully grasping the instructions of spiritual benefactors, he longed to see the night goddess Vasanti, considering spiritual benefactors a sure source of attainment of enlightened knowledge, based concretely on the sphere of the eye of universal knowledge, turning in all directions, wishing to see the spiritual benefactor, thinking of her with great respect as the abode of knowledge, his eye of knowledge extending to all objects, looking over the ocean of all that is knowable with the eye of concentration reaching throughout the ocean of knowledge of principles of all reality realms, intent on extension of the eye of great knowledge. He saw the night goddess Vasanti in the sky over Kapilavastu, in a tower of brilliant, incomparable jewels, sitting on a great jewel lion throne in the calyx of a lotus of all the finest fragrances.

She was beautiful, with a golden complexion, soft, rich black hair, and dark eyes. Her body was adorned with all kinds of ornaments, and she was wearing a red robe. She wore a sacred crest adorned with the orb of the moon, and her body showed reflections of all the stars and constellations. He also saw in her pores all the sentient beings who had been liberated by her from the calamities of unfavorable circumstances, evils, and miserable conditions. He also saw in her pores all the sentient beings whom she had settled in heaven, and all whom she had perfected in the enlightenment of hearers and individual illuminates, and in omniscience. He also saw in her pores all the various means, embodiments, and appearances she assumed to perfect them. He also heard coming from her pores the various utterances she used to teach and develop them. He also perceived in her pores the timing, the adaptation to sentient beings' inclinations and interests, the enlightening practices, forceful means, ways of mystic transformation through concentration, powers, states, observations, contemplations, mystic projections, powerful expansions of the great person, and free masteries of liberation by which they were perfected.

Having seen and heard those oceans of teachings involving various means, Sudhana was transported with joy; he paid his respects to the night goddess Vasanti and said to her, "Noble one, I have set my mind on supreme perfect enlightenment. Seeing all qualities of buddhahood as based on spiritual benefactors, I rely on spiritual benefactors. Please show me the way of omniscience whereon an enlightening being sets forth to the stage of the ten powers."

Vasanti answered Sudhana, "It is good that you are so devoted to spiritual benefactors and desire to hear the words of spiritual benefactors. Carrying out the instructions of spiritual benefactors, you will surely arrive at supreme perfect enlightenment. I have attained an enlightening liberation, a means of guiding sentient beings by the light of truth, which dispels the darkness for all sentient beings. I am kind to the evil-minded, compassionate to evil-doers, pleased with those who do good, impartial toward the good and the bad; I am determined to purify the defiled, to set the misguided straight, to inspire higher aspirations in those with low aspirations, to increase the energy of those with inferior faculties, to free those attached to the mundane whirl from its repetitious circles, and to set those oriented toward the vehicles of individual salvation onto the path of omniscience. I am concentrating on these concerns and am imbued with the enlightening liberation through which I guide sentient beings with the light of truth that dispels the darkness for all sentient beings.

"Any people who travel on a dark night, where ghosts, thieves, and thugs lurk, when the sky is covered with black clouds, when it is misty, windy, and raining, when there is no moonlight or starlight, when there is no visibility, if they go on the sea, or on land, or in the mountains, or over deserts, or through forests, or through provinces or villages, or on the roads, if they are shipwrecked at sea or held up on land, or fall in the mountains or run out of provisions in the desert, or if they get stuck in the underbrush in the forest or run into trouble, or if they get scattered in the darkness, or if they get mugged in a town, or if they get lost or confused and cannot tell which direction they are going in, or if they run into disaster on the road, I rescue them by various means. For those traveling on the sea I quell hurricanes, get them past bad waters, stop unfavorable winds, quiet the raging billows, free them from the perils of whirlpools, clarify the directions, lead them on the right sea lanes, show them the channels, guide them to the isles of treasure, show them the way in the form of a navigator. Through various forms of being I act as a support and reliance. This root of goodness, furthermore, I dedicate in this way: 'May I be a refuge for all sentient beings, to put an end to all suffering.'

"For those on land on a dark night, where there are thickets and brambles, gravel and grit, on uneven terrain, battered by vicious wind and rain, painfully cold or hot, where savage beasts lurk, where killers and bandits roam, I save those who have lost their way on the earth, by means of the forms of the sun, the risen moon, meteoric showers, planets, the light of the stars, celestial beings, and enlightening beings. And I think: By this root of goodness may I become a savior of all sentient beings.

"For those on precipitous mountain paths, in danger of death, so that they may live, and for those who are dominated by the desire for fame, those who wish for renown, those who seek enjoyment, those who are avaricious, those who strive to get material things, those whose foremost desire is worldly success, those who are wrapped up in affection for their families, those who are lost in the jungle of views, and those who are oppressed by various miseries and fears, I become a refuge by various means: for example, by producing caves in the mountains for shelter, by producing fruits and roots for food, by producing streams for drinking water, by producing shelter against cold and heat, by showing the right path, by the songs of birds, by the luster of medicinal plants, by the glow of mountain spirits. I become a refuge for those in mountain caves and crevices, those oppressed by various pains, dispelling the darkness, producing level ground for them. And I resolve that just as I rescue these people in the mountains, so will I become a refuge for those fallen on the precipitous trails of the mountain of mundane existence, who are in the grip of old age and death.

"For those stuck in the jungle on a dark night, confronted with a vast expanse of trees, on roads blocked by grass and water, reeds, trees, and vines, in thickets of various trees and creepers, frightened by tigers roaring, their minds filled with what they have to do, plagued with various perils and misfortunes, not knowing the way out of the forest, I show the right way to go. And I resolve that by this root of goodness I will free those in the thicket of views, caught in the web of craving, oppressed by the various pains and perils of the mundane whirl, liberating them from all miseries.

"And as for those in the desert, in the darkness, by various means I comfort them, show them the way, and lead them to safety, resolving that by this root of goodness I shall liberate those who are in the desert of the mundane whirl, who have fallen into evil ways, freeing them from all suffering and setting them on the road of omniscience, where there is eternal safety.

"As for those in inhabited areas who are experiencing the trouble of owning a home, I draw them away from their attachments to their abodes by various means and resolve by this root of goodness to remove all sentient beings from attachment to the elements of body and mind and establish them in nonreliant omniscience.

"As for those in villages who are attached to their house and relatives, beset by various family troubles, their minds agitated by various anxieties, I take care of them by material gifts and please them in a proper manner, establish them in the state of nonattachment, and resolve by this root of goodness to remove those who cling to the village of their senses from the sphere of mundane objects and set them in the sphere of omniscience.

"As for those who lose their sense of direction on a dark night, who think level ground is uneven, who think high ground is low, who think low ground is high, I light the way for them by various means. To those who want to go out I show the door, to those who want to travel I show the road, to those who want to cross over I show the bridge, to those who want to go in I show the house, to those who want to look around I show the directions. I show the high and low ground, the smooth and rough terrain and its various formations. I show travelers the villages, cities, towns, provinces, and capitals. I show those who are hot and thirsty streams and ponds and groves and parks. To those grieving at separation from their loved ones I show their family and friends, advisers, acquaintances, and kin, and various pleasing forms. And I resolve that just as I light the way for those in the dark who cannot see and have lost their way, as I create light to make various forms manifest, in the same way I will use the light of great wisdom to destroy the darkness of ignorance of those in the long night of the mundane whirl, who have no sense of direction at all, who are in the darkness of ignorance, whose eye of knowledge is covered by the veil of nescience, who are perverted in concepts, thoughts, and views, who think the impermanent is permanent, who think the painful is painless, who think the selfless has self, who think the impure is pure, who cling to a definite self, being, life, soul, individuality, and personality, who are attached to sense faculties, sense consciousnesses, and sense data, who are confused about cause and effect, who do what is not good, who take life, who steal, who abuse sexuality, who tell lies, who slander others, who speak harshly, who sow dissension, who are covetous, who are malicious, who hold erroneous views, who do not honor their parents or mendicants or priests, who do not recognize the blameworthy or the good, who do not take pleasure in what is right, who are dominated by ill-gotten gain, who pervert what is right by erroneous views, who falsely impugn the enlightened, who try to suppress true teaching, who fly the banner of demons, who injure or kill enlightening beings, who are hostile to the Great Vehicle, who cut off the aspiration for enlightenment, who defame enlightening beings, who injure or kill their mothers, who are hostile, who revile the wise, who consort with the corrupt and unjust, who damage the relics of saints and the goods of the religious community, who oppose their parents, who act in hellish ways, who are on the brink of disaster—having destroyed the darkness of their ignorance by the light of great wisdom and directed them toward supreme perfect enlightenment, by the Great Vehicle of universal good I shall show them the path to the stage of knowledge of the ten powers; I shall show them the stage of the enlightened, the realm of the enlightened, the ocean of wisdom of omniscience, the sphere of enlightened knowledge, the consummation of the ten powers, the power of mental command of buddhas, and the unity of all buddhas. Having shown them this, I will establish them in the knowledge of equality of all buddhas.

"As for those who are sick, who are worn out from long illness, whose bodies are weakened, who have wasted away, those who have grown old and are overcome by old age, those who are wretched and poor, those who have come to the end of their lives, those who are in bondage, those who are being tortured, and convicts who have been imprisoned, I stand by them to save them from the danger of injury to their lives. I employ all means to remove the illnesses of those who are sick. Those who are wasted away and overcome by old age I take care of by constant attendance. I provide protection for the helpless, I enrich the poor, I take care of those who have fallen into misfortune by regarding their welfare as my own. Those abroad I lead to their own country, and those astray I lead in the right direction. Those in bondage I release from their bonds. Those who are being tortured I release from the pain of torture. I save the lives of convicts who have been handed over to the king for execution. I resolve that just as I am a refuge saving these beings from various perils and afflictions, so shall I take care of them with the supreme protection of the truth and liberate them from all mental afflictions. I shall enable them to transcend birth, old age, sickness, death, grief, lamentation, misery, depression, and mental disturbance. I shall free them from all fears of falling into bad conditions. I shall establish them in the care of spiritual benefactors. I shall take care of them by giving them jewels of true teaching. I shall get them to act impeccably. I shall direct them to the purity of the body of the enlightened. I shall establish them in the knowledge of the realm where there is ultimately no old age or death.

"As for those on wrong paths, those in the tangles of various views, those acting on erroneous conceptions, those doing evil in thought, word, and

deed, those uncontrolled in action, those devoted to various pious obser-
vances and ascetic practices, those who think the unenlightened are
enlightened, those who think the enlightened are unenlightened, those
who practice self-torture, those who worship bodies of water, mountains, or
particular places, and those who are under the control of bad companions, I
become a refuge for them by various means and thence turn them away from
evil, from immersion in views, from all bad conditions. I establish them in
right seeing in the world and place them in celestial and human states. I
resolve that just as I liberate these sentient beings from the miseries of such
bad behavior, so shall I establish all sentient beings in the transmundane path
of transcendence, make them irreversible in progress toward omniscience,
and lead them to omniscience by the great vow of universal good; and I shall
not fall from the stages of enlightening beings, while not turning away from
the realm of all sentient beings."

At that point, further revealing the realm of the enlightening liberation
which guides the world by the light of truth that dispels the darkness for all
sentient beings, the goddess looked over the ten directions by the power of
Buddha and spoke these verses to Sudhana:

This peaceful liberation of mind guides the world
To happiness in accord with the time
By producing the light of truth
To end the darkness of delusion and ignorance.

My kindness is vast and pure,
Developed over boundless eons past;
Dispelling evil, I illumine the world—
Realize this wisdom, O Sudhana, steadfast one.

Measureless is my ocean of compassion for the world;
Herein the buddhas of all times are born,
Hereby the pains of the world are soothed—
Realize this wisdom, O Sudhana, steadfast one.

Producing worldly happiness, both the joys
Which are conditional and those of the sages,
Thereby I am delighted, uplifted, pleased—
Realize this wisdom, O son of Buddha.

Forever turned away from the ills of the conditional,
As well as the knowledge and liberation of individual salvation,
Perfecting the power of buddhas—
Realize this wisdom, O son of Buddha.

Vast and pure is my eye, by which I see
The lands of the ten directions—

I see the buddhas in those lands
Sitting under the enlightenment tree.

I see thousands of buddhas with their circles,
The buddhas' bodies adorned with marks of greatness,
Emanating multifold glorious lights,
Radiating oceans of light from their pores.

I see the sentient beings in those lands,
How they die and are born;
I see the ignorant in the ocean of transmigration as they go
Round in circles experiencing the results of their own deeds.

My ocean of hearing is pure,
And all sounds enter therein:
Hearing the words of all sentient beings,
I keep them in mind.

The infinite expressions of the teachings of buddhas
I also hear and remember.

My sense of smell is far-reaching and pure,
Unobstructed in the midst of all things,
An entry into all states of liberation;
You should realize this wisdom.

My tongue is broad and long, coppery red,
Shiny like a jewel, pure;
With it I communicate to beings according to their mentalities:
You should realize this wisdom.

My reality body is transcendentally pure,
Omnipresent in all times;
The physical body beings see according to their mentalities,
By the power of their devotion.

My mind is free from attachment and taint,
Resonant with thunderous sound;
Therein are all buddhas assembled,
Yet I have no discrimination.

Innumerable are the beings on the face of the earth;
I know the oceans of their minds,
I know their faculties and inclinations,
But I have no discrimination.

My occult power is vast and consummate,
I shake innumerable worlds
And produce an aura of light
Whereby I tame the intractable.

My virtue is vast and pure,
An endless treasury, adorning everywhere;
With it I make offerings to buddhas
And sustain the life of all beings.

I have entered the ocean of buddhas,
Realizing the wisdom of all time,
And I enter into their vows—
This wisdom is peerless and perfect.

In every atom I see oceans of worlds
Of past, present, and future;
And I see oceans of buddhas therein,
And their universal ground of wisdom.

See Vairocana, enlightened,
Pervading all lands in the ten directions,
Sitting at the foot of the enlightenment tree
In each atom expounding the teaching of peace.

Then Sudhana said to the night goddess Vasanti, "How long ago did you set out for supreme perfect enlightenment? How long ago did you attain this liberation, by the attainment of which you have come to perform all beneficial actions in this way?"

Vasanti replied, "As many eons ago as atoms in the polar mountain, there was an eon called Tranquil Light, in which five billion buddhas were born. There was then a world system called Born of the Light of Jewels, in which there was a central world of four continents called Jewel Moon Lamp Light, the capital city of which was called Lotus Light. In that capital city was a king named Bridge of Good Law, who was a just ruler, a sovereign with all the attributes of kingship. He had conquered that trouble-free earth by justice and ruled it righteously.

"The king's wife was named Moon of Understanding of Right. She enjoyed herself making love in the first part of the night, and in the middle of the night, when the love play had ceased, she slept. At that time, in a forest called Source of Radiance of Peace, to the east of the city of Lotus Light, a buddha named Supreme Thunder of All Truths attained supreme perfect enlightenment at a great enlightenment site made of the finest jewels, with the lights of all supernal manifestations, radiating the lights of the magical displays of all buddhas. That buddha lit up the whole world-system Born of the Light of Jewels clearly with a great multicolored light.

"Also in that capital city Lotus Light was a night goddess named Pure Moonlight. She went to the wife of the king, awakened her by the sound of her jewelry jingling, and said to her, 'Know, O queen, that in the forest Source of Radiance of Peace, a buddha named Supreme Thunder of All Truths has attained supreme perfect enlightenment.' And she gave the queen an extensive explanation of the virtuous qualities of the buddha, the spiritual transformation of the buddha, and the vow practices by universally good enlightening beings. The queen, illumined by the light of the buddha, set out for supreme perfect enlightenment with overpowering resolve. She made great offerings to that buddha and to his group of enlightening beings and disciples.

"Do not suppose that queen was anyone other than me myself—I was that queen Moon of Understanding of Right in that time. By virtue of that aspiration, and the roots of goodness I planted with that buddha, I was not born in any bad states for as many eons as atoms in the polar mountain, nor did I have defective faculties, nor did I suffer. I always attained celestial greatness among celestials, and human greatness among humans, and never was apart from spiritual benefactors—that is buddhas and enlightening beings. I never came upon bad times. So I passed as many eons as atoms in the polar mountain happily, peacefully, safely, and rightly, planting roots of goodness with the enlightened: yet after all that time my enlightening faculties were not yet perfectly developed.

"After those eons had passed, ten thousand eons before this eon of Virtue, there was an eon called Sorrowless Dispassion, in a world called Blazing Light Undefiled by Passion. That world was both defiled and pure. Five hundred buddhas were born there. The first of those five hundred buddhas was named Light of Tranquil Eyes with Senses Like the Polar Mountain, accomplished in knowledge and action, gone to felicity, supreme knower of the world, guide of tractable people, teacher of celestials and humans, enlightened, blessed. I was an outstanding girl named Light of Wisdom, daughter of an eminent man named Resounding Fame, and I was beautiful and robust. The night goddess Pure Moonlight, by the power of a vow, became a night goddess named Light of Purified Eyes. In the still of the night when my parents were in bed, she made our house tremble, showed her body to me with a great light, told me about the qualities of the buddha, and then showed me the buddha sitting at the enlightenment site in the first week after his enlightenment.

"I went with my parents and a large group of relatives to that buddha, led by the night goddess Pure Moonlight. I made great offerings to that buddha, and when I saw the buddha, I attained a concentration called 'born of the world-guiding vision of Buddha,' and I attained a concentration called 'sphere of light of knowledge of the ground of past, present, and future,' whereby I remembered those eons as many as atoms in the polar mountain; and my aspiration for enlightenment came to the fore. Having heard the Teaching from that buddha, I attained this enlightening liberation called 'the means of guiding sentient beings by the light of truth which dispels the

darkness for all sentient beings,' by the attainment of which I physically pervade as many worlds as atoms in ten buddha-lands, and see the buddhas in
those worlds, and perceive myself at the feet of those buddhas. I also see all
the sentient beings in those worlds, and I know their vocal signals, and their
thoughts, inclinations, faculties, and interests, and their previous development under the tutelage of spiritual benefactors; and I manifest a body to
them which will please them according to their inclinations.

"Also, this liberation grows in each mental moment: in an unbroken succession of mental moments I pervade as many buddha-lands as atoms in a
hundred worlds, as many buddha-lands as atoms in a thousand worlds, as
many buddha-lands as atoms in a hundred thousand worlds; in each mental
moment I go on like this to pervade up to as many buddha-lands as atoms in
untold unspeakable numbers of worlds: and I see all the buddhas in those
lands, and I perceive myself in their presence, and I hear, take in, remember,
reflect on, and meditate on the teachings of those buddhas. I also enter into
the oceans of past vows of those buddhas, and the purifications of the
buddha-lands of those buddhas. I also undertake to purify a buddha-land. I
also see the sentient beings in those oceans of worlds, and I transform my
body to accord with the measures of the inclinations, faculties, and interests
of those sentient beings, in order to develop and guide them. Thus this liberation expands in each mental moment, by working to expand it to pervade
everywhere in the cosmos.

"I only know this enlightening liberation that is a method of guiding the
world by the light of the truth which dispels the darkness of all sentient
beings—how can I know the practice or tell of the virtues or comprehend
the sphere or show the freedom of liberation of the enlightening beings
who are completely versed in the infinite vow of enlightening practice of
universal good, who command the power to enter into every principle in the
ocean of the cosmos, who have mastered the adamantine concentration of
knowledge realized by all enlightening beings, who have undertaken the
vow to preserve the lineage of buddhas in all worlds, who have perfected
great goodness purifying all worlds in each mental moment, who command
the knowledge to develop and guide all universes in each mental moment,
whose eyes are suns that dispel the darkness of all obstructions for all sentient beings in all worlds, who strive to inform all sentient beings about the
Great Vehicle of universal liberation, who are moons of wisdom dispelling
the darkness of doubt and confusion for all sentient beings, whose pure
voices obliterate attachment to existence, who have the power to show miracles in each atom of all phenomena, who have unfragmented knowledge of
the ground of past, present, and future?

"In this very enlightenment site in Magadha lives a night goddess named
Samantagambhirashrivimalaprabha, who inspired in me the determination
for enlightenment and has encouraged me time and again. Go ask her how
to learn and carry out the practice of enlightening beings."

Then Sudhana praised the night goddess with these verses:

I see your body now, pure, with various characteristics,
Like the polar mountain.
Above the world, you illumine the world,
With a body like Manjushri.

Your reality body is transcendentally pure,
Equal in all times, without distinction:
Therein all worlds are gathered,
And form and dissolve without obstruction.

I see your body in all realms,
In a variety of manifestations:
And in your pores I see
The moon and stars.

Your mind is broad and pure, pervading
Like space in all directions;
Therein are assembled all buddhas,
Yet your knowledge is free from the taint of discrimination.

Brilliant clouds, as many as atoms in lands,
Issue from your pores;
They reach the buddhas in the ten directions,
Raining all kinds of ornaments.

Infinite bodies, as many as living beings,
Emerge from your pores;
They fill all the worlds in the ten directions,
And purify beings by various means.

I see inconceivably many lands in your pores,
Adorned in various ways,
Which you have purified,
Produced according to the minds of the beings.

Happy are those who hear your name,
Great is their gain;
And people who see you
Are near the path of enlightenment.

One should endure inconceivable eons of misfortune
In order to see you;
For those who are happy to hear of you,
You will extinguish their afflictions on sight.

Even if one were to speak

Of your qualities for as many eons
As atoms in a thousand lands,
There is no exhausting them.

Having praised the night goddess Vasanti with these verses, Sudhana paid his respects to her, looking at her again and again, never tired of attending spiritual benefactors, and left her.

Samantagambhirashrivimalaprabha

Realizing the purity of the sphere of the night goddess Vasanti's initial stage of determination to be an enlightening being, contemplating the origin of the embryo of enlightenment, entering into the ocean of vows of enlightening beings, purifying the path of transcendent ways of enlightening beings, going into the sphere of stages of enlightening beings, extending the sphere of practice of enlightening beings, remembering the ocean of ways of emancipation of enlightening beings, looking over the vast ocean of light of omniscience, extending the cloud of great compassion of enlightening beings intent on the salvation of all sentient beings, putting Vasanti's vow of practice of universally good enlightening action into effect throughout all lands forever, Sudhana went to the night goddess Samantagambhirashrivimalaprabha, paid his respects to her, and said, "Noble goddess, I have set my mind on supreme perfect enlightenment, but I do not know how an enlightening being acts in the stage of enlightening practice, or how one proceeds, and how one perfects it."

She said, "It is good that, aspiring to enlightenment, you ask how to proceed and how to fully accomplish the stages of enlightening beings. By the fulfillment of ten things is the practice of enlightening beings accomplished: by purification of attainment of concentration in which all buddhas are seen face to face; by purification of the eye viewing the infinite body of all buddhas resplendent with marks of distinction; by entering into the manifestation of the infinite ocean of qualities of buddhas; by realizing the cosmic dimensions of the ocean of spheres of the infinite manifestations of the teaching of buddhas; by entering the emanation of multitudes of beams of light, as many as beings, from the pores of all buddhas, aiding sentient beings in various ways; by seeing oceans of flames the colors of all jewels coming from each pore; by penetrating the mystical manifestation of oceans of emanations of buddhas pervading all universes and guiding sentient beings in each mental moment; by penetrating the sounds of thunder of all the scriptures proclaimed in the past, present, and future cycles of teachings of the buddhas, using the myriad languages of all sentient beings; by entry into the infinite ocean of buddha-names; by penetrating the guidance of sentient beings by manifestation of inconceivable miraculous transformations of buddhas. By attainment of these ten things, enlightening beings become fully accomplished in enlightening practice.

"I have attained the enlightening liberation 'bliss of tranquil meditation boldly going everywhere.' By this I see the buddhas of past, present, and future, and enter into their oceanic congregations, their oceanic projections by concentration, their oceanic efforts in the past, and the oceans of their names. I also comprehend the differences of the teaching cycles of those buddhas, the variety of their life spans, the differences in their voices, and their embodiment of the infinite realm of reality. Yet I do not become attached to those buddhas in terms of state of being. Why? Because those buddhas do not go, having stopped all worldly courses of action; they do not come, because of the nonbecoming of intrinsic nature; they are not present, being physically equal to the unoriginated nature of reality; they are not extinct, being characterized by nonorigination; they are not real, because they convey the vision of phenomena as in illusion; they are not false, because of accomplishing the welfare of all beings; they do not pass from one condition to another, because they are free from death and birth; they do not perish, because of the imperishable nature of things; they are uniform, because they are beyond all manner of speech; they are formless, because of being done with the forms and natures of things.

"Furthermore, while thus understanding all buddhas, by the light of the sphere of meditation of buddhas I expand this enlightening liberation 'bliss of tranquil meditation boldly going everywhere'; I extend it, enter into it, follow it, live up to it, accomplish it, make it consistent, delve into it, develop it, meditate on it, contemplate it, internalize it, make it my sphere of action, stabilize it, make it manifest, illumine it, order it, analyze it, fulfill its requirements, and effect it.

"Therein, based on great compassion without any false conceptions, to focus my mind solely on carrying out the salvation of all beings, I cultivate the first stage of meditation. To cease all mental action and focus my mind solely on joy and happiness in taking care of all sentient beings with the power of knowledge, I cultivate the second stage of meditation. To realize the purity of inherent nature of all beings with equanimity detached from the mundane world, I cultivate the third stage of meditation. To extinguish the burning of the pain of afflictions of all sentient beings I cultivate the fourth stage of meditation. To extend the sphere of the vow for omniscience, for skill in producing the ocean of all concentrations, to enter the means of access to the ocean of liberation of all enlightening beings, to know the science of occult powers of all enlightening beings, to effect the mystic projection of practices of all enlightening beings, I cultivate the enlightening liberation that goes everywhere through tranquil meditation, purifying the knowledge that enters into every realm of reality.

"Furthermore, as I cultivate this liberation, I develop sentient beings to maturity by a variety of means. In people engrossed in sex play in the still of the night I induce the thought of impurity, the thought of disappointment, the thought of weariness, the thought of trouble, the thought of bondage, the thought of bedevilment, the thought of impermanence, the thought of pain, the thought of selflessness, the thought of ownerlessness, the thought of offense, the thought of old age and death, and the thought of indifference to all objects of desire. And those people, developing this state of mind, indifferent to all pleasures, coming to enjoy spiritual pleasure, go forth from home to homelessness. When they have gone into the forest and are following spiritual principles, I foster faith in them. I cause a lull in all disturbing, frightening, loud sounds, and in the quiet of the night I reveal to them the profundity of the buddha-teaching. I provide them with circumstances conducive to effort, open the door of renunciation, show the path, provide light, dispel darkness, put a stop to fear, praise renunciation, speak of the qualities of the Buddha, the Teaching, and the Community, and of spiritual benefactors, and praise going to spiritual benefactors.

"As I cultivate this liberation, I put a stop to sentient beings' wrong passions and wrong feelings and thoughts. I put a stop to the ideas and thoughts of those dominated by wrongful gain, those who act on false notions. I see to it that evil does not arise in those in whom it has not yet arisen, and that the false conceptions of those in whom evil has arisen are stopped. For those in whom thoughts of roots of goodness have not yet arisen, I motivate thoughts of the ways of transcendence, spiritual practice, achievement of the aspiration for omniscience and release, the principle of kindness, suffusing all sentient beings with great compassion, and producing the various bases of celestial and human happiness. For those to whom such thoughts already occur, I provide various means of guidance. I motivate all the appropriate thoughts and intentions until they are in accord with the way to omniscience.

"I know only this enlightening liberation of the bliss of tranquil meditation boldly going everywhere. How can I know the practice or tell of the virtues of the enlightening beings who are completely conversant with the vows of practice of universally good enlightening beings, who have attained knowledge of the cosmos with its endless forms, in whose minds all roots of goodness are developed, who have attained awareness of the knowledge and powers of all buddhas, whose minds abide in the sphere of all buddhas, whose minds are unhindered wherever they may be, who have fulfilled the resolve for omniscience, whose minds have entered the ocean of all lands, whose minds see all buddhas and take in the teachings of all buddhas, who dispel the darkness of all ignorance, whose minds generate the light of omniscience as the way to effect the final destruction of craving for repetitious mundane enjoyment?

"Right by me, on the right side of the site of enlightenment of Vairocana, there lives a night goddess named Pramuditanayanajagadvirocana. Go ask her how an enlightening being should work on the deeds of enlightening beings."

Then the night goddess Samantagambhirashrivimalaprabha spoke these verses to Sudhana, further revealing the enlightening liberation of the bliss of tranquil meditation boldly going everywhere:

The buddhas, supreme in all times,
Appear to those with faith.

Their eye is vast and pure;
Thereby they enter the oceans of buddhas.

See the undefiled body of Buddha,
Beautifully adorned with distinctive marks;
And see the miracle of the Buddha
Pervading the cosmos in every moment.

The felicitous one Vairocana has become enlightened
Sitting at this enlightenment tree;
Throughout the vast cosmos,
He teaches according to mentality.

The Buddha has realized true nature
As bodiless, utterly quiet, nondual;
His physical body, adorned with marks of distinction,
He manifests throughout the world.

The body of Buddha is vast, inconceivable,
Filling the entire cosmos:
It is seen everywhere equally,
Showing all the buddhas everywhere.

The Buddha's auras of light,
Numerous as atoms in all lands,
Reflecting each other's radiant colors,
Pervade the cosmos every moment.

Inconceivable, vast clouds of light
Stream endlessly from the Buddha's pores;
They pervade all worlds and extinguish
The heat of afflictions of all beings.

Infinite oceans of emanations of Buddha,
Emerging from Buddha's pores,
Go throughout the cosmos and stop the suffering
Of all miserable states of being.

Buddha's voice thunders pleasantly,
And the light of the ocean of good sayings
Showers the widespread rain of truth
And produces the will for enlightenment in sentient beings.

Those who have been guided by him in the past
And practiced the ways of enlightenment for eons
See Vairocana Buddha's features

Reflected in all lands.

The Buddha, appearing in all worlds,
Stands before all beings:
I cannot know all
Their various realms of attention.

All the exalted enlightening beings
Are together in one pore of Buddha:
That way of liberation, which is inconceivable,
I cannot know in full.

My neighbor goddess
Stands rapt before the Buddha,
Her eyes like starry fire—
Go ask her how to practice enlightenment.

Then Sudhana paid his respects to the night goddess Samantagambhi-rashrivimalaprabha and took leave of her.

Pramuditanayanajagadvirocana

Immersed in the teachings of the spiritual benefactors, with practice of the words of the spiritual benefactors in mind, desirous of the sciences of spiritual benefactors, his attention focused without distraction by seeing spiritual benefactors, his mind illumined through seeing spiritual benefactors with a light that destroys all obstructions, his mind immersed, through seeing spiritual benefactors, in the ocean of great compassion that saves all beings, his mind illumined, through seeing spiritual benefactors, by the light of knowledge of the ocean of principles of the cosmos, Sudhana went to the night goddess Pramuditanayanajagadvirocana.

The goddess, in order to further mature the development of Sudhana's roots of goodness based on visiting spiritual benefactors, showed him visiting spiritual benefactors as made possible by great provisions of virtue and knowledge, as great heroic effort, as energy that is hard to attain, as long-term perseverance, as entry into infinite realms, as connected with long association, as connected with manifestation of fulfillment of endless tasks, as undertaking the provision of the endless equipment of the path, as made possible by indomitably going everywhere, as coming and going without departure.

Then Sudhana went to the night goddess in the manner of one going to a spiritual benefactor energetically proceeding to provide for omniscience, striving to carry out the ocean of great vows, determined to endure endless suffering for the sake of even one single sentient being, proceeding with perseverance to traverse the cosmos in a single atom wearing the armor of great energy, speeding everywhere in all directions, associating with the practice of enlightening beings of endless eons at a single point, every moment of thought in enlightening practice entirely based on omniscience, determined to tread the path mystically projected by the buddhas of all times, treading the path flowing through all spheres of reality, keeping the attention on the principles of all realms of reality, pervading the whole cosmos of reality.

He saw the night goddess sitting in a lion seat in a flower calyx in the circle of the Buddha, in an enlightening concentration characterized by the vast, pure energy of the joy of universal good. He also saw emerging from all her pores multitudes of emanations illumining all sentient beings, making all sentient beings happy, showing the practices of the transcendent ways according to the vision of all sentient beings, pleasing to the sight of all sentient beings. He saw multitudes of emanations showing the practice of giving in accord with the mentalities of all sentient beings, using their own languages to communicate with them, to detach all sentient beings from their attachments, by indifference to material things, giving impartially to all sentient beings without neglecting any, impartial toward all sentient beings, not disrespecting or disregarding any sentient beings, relinquishing all things internal and external, showing the relinquishment of that which is very hard to give up, showing the practice of giving to sentient beings in all worlds according to their mentalities. He saw multitudes of emanations projecting the difficult act of relinquishment practiced by the enlightening beings of past, present, and future emerge and appear to all sentient beings in all worlds in the ten directions, by attainment of the inconceivable mystic power of enlightening beings.

He saw multitudes of projected bodies in the forms of all sentient beings emerge from every pore of the goddess, appearing before all sentient beings in all worlds, showing them unshakability in all aspects of self-control, illustrating as many forms of austerity as there are living beings, showing independence from all worlds, disregard of all objects, indifference to all mundane abodes, showing that celestial and human prosperity and decline, happiness and suffering, are all inextricably intertwined, showing impurity and putting an end to the false notion of purity in the world, revealing the nature of things as impermanent, unstable, and changing, showing the nature of all conditioned states as painful and selfless, promoting the appeal of living constantly in the realm of the enlightened, directing sentient beings to the ultimate purity of the way of life of the enlightened, teaching the practice of discipline using expressions adapted to the mentalities of all sentient beings, showing the grace of ethical conduct pleasing all sentient beings, developing all sentient beings to maturity.

He also saw emerging from all the goddess's pores multitudes of projected bodies with various appearances showing sentient beings' patient endurance of mutilation and dismemberment, patient endurance of beatings, patient endurance of unjust abuse, reproof, contempt, degradation, beatings, and threats, showing unshakability, showing kindness to all beings without hauteur or servility, showing freedom from conceit, showing inexhaustible knowledge of the inexhaustibility of tolerance of the true nature of all things, showing the practice of forbearance to destroy all afflictions of all sentient beings, turning sentient beings away from all warped conditions, praising the supreme purity of the enlightened, developing sentient beings to maturity.

He also saw emerge from all the pores of the goddess multitudes of projections of the forms of various kinds of beings, the same as all beings in appearance and size, showing all sentient beings, according to their mentalities, the exertion of energy to store the great knowledge and virtue needed for omniscience, showing the energy to destroy all demons, the energy to work for enlightenment without being disturbed or deflected, the energy to lift all sentient beings out of the sea of the mundane whirl, the energy to get rid of all paths leading to falls into miserable conditions, evils, and states inopportune for enlightenment, the energy to pulverize the mountain of nescience, the energy to serve all buddhas tirelessly, the energy to receive and hold all buddha-teachings, the energy to cut through and shatter the mountains of all obstacles to enlightenment, the energy to develop and guide all sentient beings tirelessly, the energy to purify all buddha-lands, and the supreme purity of the energy of the enlightened, thus developing sentient beings to maturity.

He also saw multitudes of projected bodies emanate from the goddess's pores producing joy in sentient beings by various means, removing depression, wary of all sensuality, promoting modesty in the world, directing sentient beings to guard their senses, praising unexcelled religious practice, portraying the realm of desire as a perilous realm of demons, showing the realm of enjoyment of all worldly desires even to those free from sensuality, establishing sentient beings in enjoyment of truth, step by step producing the bliss of the attainments of meditation and concentration, praising conscious contemplation of all the afflictions of all sentient beings, showing the magical creativity of the ocean of concentrations of all enlightening beings, showing the majesty of the miracles of the mystic knowledges of enlightening beings, making sentient beings joyful and happy, removing melancholy, bringing goodness of mind, producing cleverness and activity of mind, purifying the mind, clarifying the senses, producing physical bliss, promoting the growth of the energy of the joy of truth, thus developing sentient beings to maturity.

He also saw multitudes of bodies in the forms of all sentient beings emanate from all the goddess's pores, appearing agreeably to all sentient beings in all lands, showing them tirelessness in going to all spiritual benefactors, showing tirelessness in attendance on all mentors and spiritual benefactors, showing tireless energy in taking in and holding in mind the operations of the cycles of teachings of all buddhas, investigating the oceans of all approaches to the truth, describing the way to enter the ocean of all buddhas, elucidating the teaching of the characteristics and nature of all phenomena, showing the door of concentration, showing the thunderbolt of wisdom which breaks through the mountain of views of sentient beings, by continuous mental application showing the rise of the sun of wisdom dispelling the darkness of ignorance of all sentient beings, developing sentient beings in omniscience while engendering joy in all sentient beings.

He also saw multitudes of projected bodies, equal to all sentient beings, with splendid, inconceivably various appearances, emanate from the goddess's pores and appear before all sentient beings in accord with their inclinations and interests, using various languages to reveal higher knowledge of all worldly good, explaining the excellence of the path of omniscience by doing all that should be done in the world, by showing the issue of all states of existence, by describing the way out of conditioned existences, and by showing the way out of the wilderness of all views, showing transcendence of the paths of individual salvation, showing absence of attraction or aversion toward the created or the uncreated, showing nonattachment to the pleasures of mundane life or nirvana, showing unceasing progression from the heaven of satisfaction, showing unceasing attainment of enlightenment at the pinnacle of enlightenment, showing the realm of wisdom to guide all beings out of the sea of doubt, illumining omniscience for sentient beings.

He also saw as many multitudes of projected bodies as atoms in all lands emanate from each pore of the goddess and stand before all sentient beings praising the vow of practice of universally good enlightening beings, praising the excellence of the vow to ultimately purify all universes, praising purification of all worlds in each moment of thought, praising persistence in entering the powers of buddhas in each moment of thought, showing ceaseless entry into the ocean of principles of the cosmos—equal to the number of atomic particles in all oceans of worlds—in every single moment of thought, praising ceaseless elucidation of purification of the path of omniscience in all lands throughout all time, showing ceaseless entry into the ocean of past, present, and future means of guidance, showing ceaseless manifestations of all magical powers of enlightening beings, leading all sentient beings to omniscience by showing the practice of the vows of enlightening beings.

He also saw multitudes of projected bodies as numerous as the minds of all beings emanate from each of the goddess's pores and stand before all sentient beings, showing them the endless power of the provisions for omniscience, showing the unbreakable, invincible, indestructible power of the will for omniscience, showing the nonregressing, irreversible, sustained, ceaseless power of accomplishment of the supreme practice of all enlightening beings, praising enlightening beings' power to remain unaffected by the ills of mundane life, showing enlightening being's power to destroy all demons, showing enlightening beings' power of great compassion tirelessly carrying out enlightening actions throughout all ages, showing enlightening beings' power to shake all buddha-lands and please all beings, showing enlightening beings' power to crush all demons and false teachers, to nurture the power of knowledge to turn the wheel of the great teaching in the world, elucidating omniscience for all sentient beings.

He also saw multitudes of projected bodies in endless forms, presented to the minds of all sentient beings, emanate from each pore of the goddess, filling the endless realms of sentient beings in the ten directions, showing beings, according to their mentalities, the energetic activity of the knowledge of the practice of enlightening beings, showing knowledge comprehending all realms of sentient beings, showing knowledge comprehending all sentient beings' minds, showing knowledge thoroughly aware of the faculties of all sentient beings, showing knowledge comprehending all sentient beings' actions, showing knowledge of proper timing in developing and guiding all sentient beings, showing the knowledge to echo the languages of all realms of existence, showing knowledge pervading the ocean of ways to knowledge of all phenomena in each moment of thought, showing knowledge of the formation and disintegration of all worlds, showing knowledge of the differences in basis, form, and arrangement of all worlds, showing the knowledge to go to buddhas with magical offerings, serve the buddhas, and receive their teachings, thus producing joy in sentient beings by showing the practice of the transcendent way of knowledge, soothing their minds, producing joy and happiness, getting rid of melancholy, purifying the mind, leading to goodwill, clarifying the senses, producing the power of resolution, making sentient beings irreversible on the way to omniscience.

Just as he saw her proceeding to develop sentient beings in the world by demonstrations of the practices of the transcendent ways, he saw multitudes of bodies of beings of various forms emanate from each of the goddess's pores with the thunder of the laws of all enlightening beings, the preparations of the goddess's first inspiration, propitiation of spiritual benefactors, going to buddhas and attending them, the practice of virtuous conduct, the relinquishment of what is hard to give up in the course of practicing transcendent giving, the purification of transcendent discipline, the abandonment of rulership and retinue and going forth from society, the exercise of forbearance in austerities difficult to practice in the world, unshakability in the application of the vows undertaken by enlightening beings, the oceans of practices of steadfast resolutions of enlightening beings, the endurance of suffering which is impossible, unspeakable, unthinkable to all worldly beings, the endurance of physical and mental harassment, acceptance of the nonperishing nature of deeds, earnest acceptance of all truths, contemplative acceptance of the nature of all things, energy in undertaking to become omniscient, energy in accomplishing all aspects of buddhahood, all practices of transcendent energy, the preparations for transcendent meditation, energetic efforts in transcendent meditation, practices purifying the attainments of transcendent meditation, mystical powers attained by enlightening beings through concentration, entries into the ocean of mediums of concentration, practices of transcendent meditation, the preparations for transcendent wisdom, the clarification of the sun of great wisdom of enlightening beings, the issue of great masses of wisdom, the treasures of wisdom, applications of the ways of contemplation of the ocean of great wisdom, applications of the principles of great skill in means, embodiments of the transcendent vows of enlightening beings, achievements of great transcendent vows, practices of transcendent commitment, past efforts involved in great transcendent vows, great resources for the attainment of transcendent power, cooperating circumstances of transcendent power, oceans of principles of transcendent power, indications of transcendent power, past efforts involved in transcendent power, principles of transcendent knowledge, applications of transcendent knowledge, methods of purification of knowledge, realms of knowledge, attainments of knowledge, ranges of knowledge, integration of principles of knowledge, methods of communicating knowledge, consequences of the courses of knowledge, suffusions of knowledge, expansions of knowledge, embodiments of knowledge, principles of the ocean of knowledge, past efforts involved in the accomplishment of knowledge, attainments made possible by ascertainment and entry into the modes of practice of knowledge, attainments of knowledge involved in the method of total integration of perfect knowledge, attainments of knowledge of truth comprehending right and wrong, attainments of knowledge of actions, of lands, of ages, of past, present, and future, attainments of knowledge of the emergence of buddhas, attainments of knowledge of buddhas, attainments of knowledge of enlightening beings, attainments of knowledge originating in the mind of enlightening beings, attainments of knowledge of the particular states of enlightening beings, attainments of knowledge of the origins of enlightening beings, attainments of knowledge of the orientation of enlightening beings, attainments of knowledge of the vows of enlightening beings, attainments of knowledge of the cycles of teaching of enlightening beings, attainments of knowledge of enlightening beings' ascertainment of what is right, attainments of knowledge of principles of the ocean of practice of enlightening beings, attainments of knowledge of the multitude of enlightening beings' doctrines, their spheres, their hidden resources, and their courses of action—all the principles of enlightening beings connected with consummate knowledge of infinite objects, Sudhana saw being embodied by emanations from the goddess to develop sentient beings to maturity. He saw multitudes of embodiments of the forms of all kinds of beings emanating from the goddess, filling the cosmos, appearing before all sentient beings, and developing them to maturity.

He also saw projections of the streams of good thoughts rising in the goddess's past lives, beginning with the preparations of her initial aspiration, the continuing successions of commendations of aspiration to enlightenment, the continuous successions of death and rebirth, the continuous successions of incarnation, the continuous successions of names, the continuous successions of visits to spiritual benefactors, the continuous successions of harmonizations with buddhas, the continuous successions of absorption of every sentence and syllable of the teachings of buddhas, the continuous successions of states of mind in carrying out the path of enlightening beings, the continuous successions of attainment of concentrations, the continuous successions of pervasion of vision of all lands, the continuities of the circles of knowledge of the succession of ages, the continuous succession of penetrating knowledge of the cosmos, the continuous succession of knowledge observing the realms of sentient beings, the continuous succession of knowledge of individual deaths and rebirths, penetrating the ocean of principles of the cosmos, the continuous successions of contemplative knowledge purifying the celestial ear, the continuous successions of media of access of wisdom observing the minds of all sentient beings, the continuous successions of media of initial access of the celestial eye, the continuous successions of initial perceptions of the celestial ear, the continuous successions of initial knowledge of others' thoughts, the continuous successions of initial recollections of the past states of self and others, the continuous succession of the initial circumstances of attainment of uncontrived mystic powers based on nonbeing, the continuous succession of pervading everywhere by exercise of great mystic powers, the continuous succession of attainments of liberations of enlightening beings, the continuous successions of comprehension of the inconceivable principles of the ocean of liberations of enlightening beings, the continuous successions of mystic transformations of enlightening beings, the continuous successions of procedures of enlightening beings, the continuous successions of attainments of enlightening beings, the continuous successions of impressions of enlightening beings, the continuous succession of entries into the path of enlightening beings, and so on, including the night goddess's continuous successions of entries into the most subtle knowledge of enlightening beings. He saw projected bodies emanate from each pore of the goddess, expounding the Teaching to sentient beings, elucidating, clarifying, demonstrating, discussing, analyzing, extending, categorizing, explaining, communicating, and conveying it to them.

He saw some teaching with the sound of wind, some with the sound of water, some with the sound of fire, some with the sound of the ocean, some with the sound of earth quaking, some with the thrilling sound of mountains crashing together, some with the sweet sound of celestial cities trembling, some with the sound of celestial palaces crashing together, some with the voices of celestial beings, some with the voices of various fantastic beings and entities, some with the voices of human chiefs, some with the voices of Brahma chiefs, some with the songs of nymphs, some with celestial music, some with the sound of jewels, some with the voices of all living beings, explaining the sphere of the night goddess's liberation to sentient beings. Thus he saw the range of the night goddess's liberation, with the attainment of perfection proceeding from her first aspiration, including her sport in liberation, being communicated to all sentient beings by means of multitudes of embodiments of enlightening beings, various utterances of enlightening beings, multitudes of emanation bodies of buddhas, and various utterances of buddhas.

He saw untold buddha-lands in the ten directions being purified in each instant of thought by each of her hosts of projected bodies; he saw infinitely varied oceans of sentient beings being liberated from all ills and miseries; he saw infinitely varied sentient beings being led to celestial and human states; he saw infinitely varied multitudes of sentient beings being led to the stages of individual liberations. In each moment of thought Sudhana saw infinite masses of sentient beings going through the ten stages; he listened, reflected, investigated, discerned, contemplated, approached, followed, entered, and made himself equal thereto, by the mystical power of the night goddess's enlightening liberation characterized by the immensity of the inconceivable joy of universal good, by the development of inconceivable roots of goodness through having performed the same practices in the past and having been empowered by the support of the enlightened, and by having become a vessel of universally good enlightening practice.

Then Sudhana, imbued with the light of the ocean of ecstasy of enlightening beings, empowered by the buddhas of the ten directions, stood reverently before the night goddess Pramuditanayanajagadvirocana and sang her praises in such terms:

For measureless eons you have studied
The profound nature of the buddhas,
Progressively extending throughout the worlds of the ten directions,
Appearing according to the minds of the beings therein.

Knowing them to have no self, no master,
To be always confused by untruth and false ideas,
By occult powers you manifest many kinds of bodies
And guide sentient beings.

Infinite, tranquil, the reality-body
Is nondual and pure:
Sentient beings clinging to duality
You guide by myriad emanations.

While you have no attachment
To mind or matter,
You guide the world
By emanation of perfect forms.

Detached from the internal and the external,
Having left the ocean of mortality,
You manifest infinite reflections
In the states of mundane existence.

You have no vacillation,
No vain imaginations or false ideas;
To the ignorant attached to falsehood you show
The inherent nature of things to guide them.

Single-minded for many eons
On the states of the ocean of all concentrations,
To make offerings to buddhas everywhere, you send forth
Multitudes of emanations from your pores.

You enter the way to the powers of buddhas
In every moment of thought:
Striving to save all beings,
You show them incarnations like themselves.

Observing the ocean of being,
Its variety of actions and various forms,
Showing the path of nonobstruction by things,
You purify sentient beings.

Your body, of splendid appearance,
Is purified by the practice of universal good:
In command of the minds of beings,
You manifest the form of a goddess in the world.

Having praised the goddess with these verses, Sudhana said to her, "How long have you been devoted to supreme perfect enlightenment, and how long ago did you attain this enlightening liberation characterized by the immense pure energy of the joy of universal good?"

The goddess answered him, "I remember, many eons ago, past as many eons as atoms in the world, the land Blissful Light of Jewel Radiance, in the eon Silent Sound, filled with a hundred duodecillion sets of four continents, in the center of which were four beautiful continents, extending as far as the light of a mountain of jewels, filled with a hundred duodecillion royal cities, in the center of which was a delightful city Fragrant Banner, radiant with jewels: therein lived a wise king named Lord of the People, a world ruler, adorned with the thirty-two marks and eighty embellishments of great people, born spontaneously from a lotus calyx, his body shining gold, his light filling the continent all at once, spreading through the sky. He had a thousand sons, all with the constitution of heroes, ten million ministers, learned, intelligent, wise, and ten million concubines, beautiful as goddesses, expert in the arts of love, affectionate, altruistic, kind, attentive to the king. That king ruled the whole four continents and enriched them by the power of justice. I was the main wife of that king, with a clear voice and a pleasing body; my aura of pure golden light extended a thousand leagues. One night as the king, his sons, and his retinue slept, the sounds of singing ended, and as I was peacefully asleep in bed, in the middle of the night a buddha appeared in the world and filled the ten directions with infinite mystic projections, pervading everywhere with various magical bodies imbued with glorious oceans of light, as many as atoms in all lands. The earth, including the mountains, quaked, announcing the appearance of the buddha; gods, titans, humans and spirits, were all thrilled at the emergence of the buddha. The buddha's emanations came forth from every pore; pervading the worlds of the ten directions, they taught according to people's mentalities. The buddha showed me all those infinite manifestations in a dream: hearing those profound teachings, I was joyful while dreaming. Ten thousand night goddesses stood in the sky above me, describing the buddha in celestial tones and telling me to wake: 'Arise, O queen, a buddha has appeared in your realm, hard to meet in a hundred oceans of eons; those who behold him are happy and purified.' I became joyful, and on awakening I saw an immaculate light. Seeing this light, immediately I beheld the buddha at the enlightenment tree, adorned with the thirty-two marks, oceans of lights streaming from his pores, rising above all like the polar mountain. Seeing him, I joyfully wished to become like that; I made this vow upon seeing the grandiose manifestation of Buddha. I woke the king and his concubines, and when they saw the light of Buddha they were thrilled. I went to the buddha with my husband, accompanied by millions of people and troops. I made offerings to the buddhas for twenty thousand years, giving precious substances, the earth, and its seas. The buddha expounded myriad scriptures, multitudes of virtues, an ocean of vows, and the adornments thus produced, explaining the origins of all buddhas according to mentalities in this world. That night goddess awakened me for my benefit, and then I was inspired with compassion, eager to become like this and then awaken the heedless. This was my first aspiration to supreme enlightenment, and while coming and going in the oceans of being, I have never lost this resolve.

"I served ten decillion buddhas with faith while desiring celestial and human enjoyments in the mundane. The first buddha was Ocean of Glory, next was Lamp of Virtue, third was Jewel Brightness, fourth was Spacelike Wisdom, fifth was Flower Calyx, sixth was Moon of Unattached Intellect, seventh was Power King of the Moon of Truth, eighth was Light of the Sphere of Knowledge; ninth was Jewel Flame Mountain Lamp, and tenth was Light and Sound of All Times. I served all the buddhas, beginning with these, but had not yet attained the eye to enter this ocean of wisdom.

"After that a land called Jewel Light came into existence; the age was called Celestial Glory, and five hundred buddhas emerged therein. The first buddha was Light of the Lunar Sphere, second was Solar Lamp, third was Star Banner, fourth was Jewel Mountain, fifth was Flower Flame Ocean Lamp, sixth was Blazing Glory, seventh was Filled with Heavenly Glory, eighth was Shining King, ninth was Radiant Clarity, and tenth was King of Light of Universal Knowledge. Beginning with these ten, I served all those buddhas, but I was still attached to body and mind, my intellect dwelling on what really has no abode.

"After that there was a world named Myriad Lights of the Lamp of Truth; the world was beautiful, the age was called Light of Brahma: the buddhas in that world were numberless, and I served them and their retinues, and reverently heard the teachings of all those buddhas. The first buddha was Jewel Mountain, second was Ocean of Virtues, third was Clarity of the Cosmic

Voice, fourth was Roar of the Ocean of Truth, fifth was Banner of Truth, sixth was Energy of Mystic Spells, seventh was Light of the Power of Truth, eighth was Spacelike Awareness, ninth was Light of the Peak of the Polar Mountain of Flames of Truth, and tenth was Massive Radiance; beginning with these ten, I served all those buddhas, yet I did not awaken to the real nature whereby I could enter the ocean of buddhas.

"After that was a buddha named Sun Lamp Brilliance; the land was called Enlightened Mind, and there was an age there called Glory of Soma. Therein were eight hundred octillion buddhas whom I served, with an endless variety of fine offerings. First was King of Celestial Musicians, second was Tree King, third was Polar Mountain of Virtue, fourth was Jewel Eye, fifth was Array of Shining Lights, sixth was Radiance of the Ocean of Truth, seventh was Lord of the World, eighth was Blazing Glory, ninth was Virtuous, and tenth was King of Light of All Laws; beginning with these ten, I served all those buddhas, yet still did not attain the knowledge to enter the ocean of truth.

"After that there was a pure land of indestructible energy, Omnipotent Cloud of Light, arrayed with various adornments; therein were many purified beings, mostly healthy, with few afflictions. In the age Energy of the Tranquil Mind, a thousand buddhas came forth: the first was Diamond Navel, second was Bearer of Unattached Power, third was Reflection of the Cosmos, fourth was King of Light Illumining All Quarters, fifth was Energy of Compassion, sixth was Ocean of Vows, seventh was Lamp of the Sphere of Patience, eighth was Light of the Sphere of Truth, ninth was Array of Oceans of Light, tenth was King of Tranquil Light. Beginning with these ten, I served all those buddhas, yet I did not awaken to the real nature which is spacelike, inherently pure, based on which I could carry on spiritual practices in all lands.

"Then there was a pleasant land called Radiance of a Multitude of Fragrant Lamps, both defiled and pure, where there was an age called Good Possibility, in which one hundred trillion buddhas appeared, by whom it was adorned for ten eons; I held in memory the teachings spoken by those Guides. The first one was Vast Renown, second was King of Powerful Radiance of the Ocean of Truth, third was Sovereign of Truth, fourth was Voice of Virtue, fifth was Glory of Truth, sixth was Celestial Crown, seventh was Radiance of Energy of the Flame of Knowledge, eighth was Sound of the Sky, ninth was Lamp Appearing Everywhere, and tenth was Mind of Light Radiating from the Brow. I served all those buddhas, but did not purify the unhindered path.

"After that was a land called Supreme Mind, constructed of jewels, in fine arrays, well proportioned; in the age Luminous there, five hundred buddhas emerged. I honored all those buddhas, seeking this liberation: Host of Virtues was first, second was Silent Sound, third was Oceanic Glory, fourth was Sun Energy, fifth was Mountain King, sixth was Thunder on a Polar Mountain of Distinctive Marks, seventh was King of Law, eighth was King of Virtues, ninth was Mountain of Merit, and tenth was King of Silent Light; I served all those buddhas, beginning with these ten, but though the path of the buddhas, into which all buddhas enter, was purified, I still had not attained the forbearance to enter into this way of the buddhas.

"After that was a land of beautiful light called Mind Wreathed with Silent Sounds; that world was inhabited by purified beings with little affliction. In the age called Delightful Pleasure there were eight hundred octillion buddhas; I attended and served them all and clarified the path of the supreme buddhas. The first buddha was Mass of Flowers, second was Ocean Womb, third was Mountain of Being, fourth was Crest of the Lord of Gods, fifth was Jewel Matrix, sixth was Gold Mountain, seventh was Heap of Gems, eighth was Banner of Justice, ninth was Glory of Speech, tenth was Mind of Knowledge; beginning with these ten, I served all those buddhas.

"After that was a land called Lamp Emblematic of Beautiful Creations; in the age called A Thousand Glories were one hundred decillion buddhas: Quiescent Star of Tranquility, Supreme Glory of Myriad Silent Lamps, Illuminating King, Trailing Cloud, Solar Radiance, Light of the Lamp of Truth, Flaming Brilliance, Filled with Celestial Glory, Lamp of Wisdom Roaring Like a Lion; beginning with these ten, I served all those buddhas, but did not attain the forbearance to enter this ocean of wisdom.

"After that was a land called Splendor of Universal Light, in an age called Independent Array, in which were twenty-six octillion buddhas: first was Mass of All Virtues, then Spacelike Mind, Array of Good Capacities, Thunder of the Ocean of Truths, Voice of the Cosmos, Blissful Light of Myriad Emanations, Universal Energy, Sound Born of the Ocean of Truths, Mountainous Lamp in an Ocean of Virtues; and the last of them I propitiated was Paragon of Virtue Radiant As a Jewel. When that buddha emerged in the world, I was a queen, Moonlike Face, going to honor the buddha. He expounded a scripture on the supernal manifestations originating in an ocean of independent vows, which I listened to and remembered. I attained tranquil concentration of broad vision, and the power of mental command. I see oceans of buddhas in one land after another, from moment to moment. I have borne a cloud of universal light from the womb of compassion by means of kindness, a will for enlightenment as vast as space, with the measureless light of the powers of buddhas.

"Seeing the world in error, engrossed in the glitter of permanence and pleasure, shrouded in the darkness of delusion and ignorance, filled with afflictions, thinking falsely, given to views, wandering in obscurity, controlled by craving and evildoing, accumulating a variety of deeds in mundane conditions, going from one state to another, suffering the physical and mental pains of birth, old age, and death, I have therefore wished above all for their welfare and happiness: in all places where there were buddhas, I produced a multitude of vows, to be as a source of happiness for all beings, with endless preparation and development according to the myriad methods of the path; and I emanated vast multitudes of projections of the transcendent ways throughout the cosmos, speeding to gladden the beings in all paths of existence. Progressing through the stages with great speed into the wisdom of all times, traversing the stages unhindered, I went to all buddhas in a moment of thought; and having entered the practice of universal good, I realized the myriad principles of the differentiations of the ten universes.

"That king named Lord of the People, the world ruler who was determined to prevent the dying out of the lineage of buddhas, was none other than Manjushri, who had become a king, successful in perpetuating the family of buddhas. The night goddess by whom I was awakened was emanated by the enlightening being Universally Good. The wife of the king was me. When I was awakened by the night goddess, I was caused to see Buddha; this was when I first aspired to enlightenment. Ever since that inspiration, for as many eons as atoms in a buddha-land, I have never fallen into bad states but have always wound up in celestial and human states. Wherever I have been, I have never been apart from the sight of buddhas; then when I saw the buddha Paragon of Virtue Radiant As a Jewel, I attained this enlightening liberation characterized by the immense pure energy of the joy of universal good, by the attainment of which I have come to develop and guide all sentient beings in this way.

"I just know this enlightening liberation characterized by the immense pure energy of the joy of universal good. How can I know the virtues or tell of the practice of the enlightening beings who have attained the ocean of great speed setting out for omniscience in the presence of all buddhas in each instant, who enter unceasingly into the ocean of great vows at every moment in the beginning of all undertakings, who are skilled in carrying out a multitude of practices in every moment of thought over endless eons in the ways shown by the ocean of all vows, and who are skilled in producing in each practice as many bodies as atoms in all buddha-lands, and who pervade the systems of all universes with each body, and who are skilled in demonstrating practices according to the mentality of sentient beings in each universe, and skilled in comprehending the ocean of ways of transformation of all buddhas of past, present, and future?

"There is a night goddess named Samantasattvatranojahshri who lives right here in the Buddha's circle. Go ask her how an enlightening being is to enter and purify the sphere of practice of enlightening beings."

So then Sudhana paid his respects to the night goddess Pramuditanayanajagadvirocana and left her.

Samantasattvatranojahshri

Entering with intense absorption into the night goddess Pramuditanayanajagadvirocana's liberation of immense pure energy of the joy of universal good, understanding it, plunging into it, penetrating it, following it throughout its full range, going along with it, cultivating it, accomplishing it, encompassing it, carrying out the instructions of the spiritual benefactors, recollecting the teachings projected by the night goddess Pramuditanayanajagadvirocana for the continuity of teaching and instruction, with all faculties turned in all directions following the sight of spiritual benefactors, with the intention to get to see spiritual benefactors, free from all conceits, with attention focused on seeking spiritual benefactors, with determination to develop the great provisions of virtue and knowledge, with vigorous initiative to harmonize with spiritual benefactors, with all roots of goodness one with those of spiritual benefactors, firmly intent on the practice of all skill in means of spiritual benefactors, having generated an ocean of energy fostered by spiritual benefactors, Sudhana went to the night goddess Samantasattvatranojahshri.

When Sudhana came to her, the night goddess, in order to show him the majesty of the endless enlightening liberation manifesting guidance for sentient beings in all works, showed him a body replete with beautiful features and embellishments, and emanated a light from the circle of hair between her brows called "emblem of pure stars of the lamp of flames of universal knowledge," with infinite light beams; the light illumined the whole world, then descended into Sudhana and pervaded his entire body. As soon as Sudhana was touched by the light, he attained a concentration called "sphere of ultimate dispassion," whereby he saw as many worlds as atoms in a buddha-land forming and dissolving in each particle of fire, water, earth, diamond, various jewels, flowers, perfumes, incenses, arrays of gems, and all objects in between the night goddess Pramuditanayanajagadvirocana and the night goddess Samantasattvatranojahshri. He also saw clusters of water, fire, air, and earth, and the sentient beings in all the worlds, with the various abodes they dwell in and the various arrays of the lands—various mountain ranges, rivers, lakes, oceans, heavens, trees, adornments of the skies, adornments of the habitations of all kinds of beings, the realms of hells, animals, ghosts, the realms of death and birth among humans, all the various conditions of existence being interconnected, infinite different courses of being interrelated. He also saw the difference in those worlds—he saw some worlds to be defiled, some pure, some wholly defiled, some with purified states of being, some with purity in the midst of defilement, some with defilement in the midst of purity, some wholly pure, some level, some inverted, some askew.

He saw the night goddess Samantasattvatranojahshri in all realms of being in those worlds, facing every sentient being capable of being guided; by seeing all worlds together at once, he saw her standing, without division, before all sentient beings, adapting to their life spans, their various spheres of belief, their physical forms, their conventions of verbal communication, and their mastery, in order to guide them to full development. That is to say, he saw her standing before all sentient beings without division to free beings in hells from the pains and fears of hell, to free beings in brutish states from the perils of mutual predation, to free beings in the realm of ghosts from the pains and perils of hunger and thirst, to free beings in the realm of dragons from all the pains and perils of the dragon realm, to free all beings in the realm of desire from all the pains and perils of the realm of desire, to free all beings in the human realm from all the fears and perils of darkness, to free beings from all fear of ill repute, to free beings from intimidation by groups, to free beings from fear of death, to free beings from fear of falling into states of misery, to free beings from fear of not being able to make a living, to free beings from fear of loss of virtue, to free beings from fear of loss of the determination for enlightenment, to free beings from the danger of association with bad companions, to free beings from fear of separation from spiritual benefactors, to free beings from fear of falling into the stages of individual salvation, to free beings from fear of suffering the pains of the various mundane states, to free beings from fear of all association with the uncongenial, to free beings from fear of coming on bad times, to free beings from fear of being born among bad people, to free beings from fear of doing evil, to free beings from fear of obstruction by deeds, to free beings from fear of bondage by attachment to various notions.

That is to say, he saw her confronting the purification of all lands by undertaking the vow to save all beings, whether corporeal or incorporeal, thinking, nonthinking, and neither thinking nor nonthinking, by the immense power of the vigorous exercise of the energy of concentration of enlightening beings, by exertion of the power of the great mystic knowledges of enlightening beings, by the power of execution of the vow to practice the conduct of universally good enlightening beings, by having generated the energy of the ocean of means of great compassion, to suffuse all beings with desireless universal love, to increase the energy of joy, which is the origin of happiness for all beings, to apply the knowledge of how to take care of all beings, by embodiment of the vast spiritual power of enlightening liberation. He saw her confronting realization of knowledge of all things, attendance of all buddhas, preservation of the teachings of all buddhas, accumulation of all roots of goodness, development of all enlightening practices, unhindered penetration of the minds of all beings, maturation of the faculties of all beings, purification of the ocean of interests of all beings, removal of obstructing elements for all beings, dispersal of the darkness of nescience of all beings, and the implementation of all good, to generate the light of omniscience.

Then Sudhana, having seen this inconceivable manifestation of the night goddess's enlightening liberation showing guidance for beings in all worlds, prostrated himself before her, enraptured. At that point the night goddess stopped assuming the adornments of the forms of enlightening beings and continued to produce all the mystical manifestations by means of the form of a night goddess. Then Sudhana stood respectfully before her and spoke these verses to her:

> I have seen your immense body,
> Of excellent appearance, adorned with jewels,
> Variously beautified by embellishments
> As the sky is by the stars.
>
> Your aura of light, the sublime radiance of your body,
> Is equal to the atoms in endless lands;

Like various kinds of matchless colors,
It pervades everywhere endlessly.

From every pore you radiate nets of light,
As many as minds of beings;
On a beautiful lotus in each ray of light
Stands an emanation of you, extinguishing pain in the world.

You emit fragrant clouds of light
In the forms of all beings, all pure,
Showering flowers everywhere,
On all the buddhas in the cosmos.

Your multitude of lights, vast and pure,
Is like a mountain radiant with jewels;
With it you illumine all worlds
And remove the darkness of delusion.

Myriad pure suns emerge
From your mouth;
Your sunlight shines throughout
The vast realm of Vairocana.

Pure moon and star lights
Radiate from your eyes in great numbers
And pervade the ten directions,
Illumining the world and destroying darkness.

From your features come myriad emanations
In the forms of all beings;
They go throughout the cosmos
Developing the countless masses.

Your body appears before all beings
Everywhere, creating joy;
You put an end to measureless dangers—
From kings, brigands, fire, and floods—guiding beings.

As directed, I have come to you,
Observing your qualities;
A pure aura of light beams
Emanated from between your brows,
Illuminating all places,
Producing great light in the world;
Having shown many various wonders,
It descended into my body.

When the light descended on me,
I experienced a marvelous, supreme happiness;
I was imbued with mental command, a hundred concentrations,
And I saw the infinite buddhas everywhere.

I knew the number of atoms
In the ground where I walked,
And saw in each atom
As many lands as atoms in lands.

In an atom are hundreds
Of various mixed-up, defiled lands,
Where the beings suffer pains
And weep and wail.

There are also many lands with purity amid defilement,
Where the happiness is little and the suffering much,
Where the compassionate buddhas,
Their disciples, and the self-enlightened gather.

There are also lands with defilement amid purity,
Where many enlightening beings are assembled,
Beautiful lands graced with men and women,
Where the family of buddhas abides.

Oceans of lands, vast and pure,
Are in an atom, or an even plane,
Purified over long eons past
By the action of Vairocana.

In every land buddhas appear
At the enlightenment tree;
Having attained enlightenment,
They teach and guide the world.

I see you in the vast realm of Vairocana,
Honoring all the infinite buddhas.

Then Sudhana said to the night goddess, "It is wonderful how deep your enlightening liberation is. What is this liberation called? How long ago did you attain it? How does an enlightening being practice so as to purify this liberation?"

She replied, "This state is hard for celestials, Buddhist disciples, and individual illuminates to arrive at. Why? Because this is the realm of enlightening beings who follow the commitment to the practice of universally good enlightening beings; it is the sphere of enlightening beings imbued with great compassion who have undertaken the salvation of all sentient beings, who have undertaken the purgation of all unfavorable and unhappy states, who have undertaken the perpetuation of the lineage of buddhas in all buddha-lands, who have undertaken to preserve the teachings of all buddhas, who have plunged into the ocean of great vows to continue enlightening practice through all ages, who have undertaken to clarify the light of unobscured knowledge of the ocean of all phenomena, who have attained the state of the light of instantaneous knowledge of the ocean of wisdom of past, present, and future.

"Now, then, by the empowerment of Buddha I will tell you: in the past, as many eons ago as atoms in a buddha-land, there was an age called Sphere of Dispassion in a world called Sunny Brilliance; as many buddhas as atoms in the polar mountain arose in that age. That world, furthermore, was arrayed with multitudes of all kinds of jewels and adorned with palaces and mansions made of diamond. Now, that world rested on an ocean of all kinds of jewels of pure light and was itself made of all kinds of fragrant jewels. It was perfectly round and pure, with some defilement. It was covered with canopies of all kinds of ornaments, and surrounded by a thousand peripheral mountain ranges, circles of jewels in all arrays. It had millions of sets of four continents, some of which were inhabited by beings whose actions were defiled and beings whose actions were undefiled, some of which were inhabited by beings whose actions were a mixture of defilement and purity, some of which were inhabited by beings who were mostly pure with some defilement, beings of refined virtues, beings with little in them that is blameworthy; and some were inhabited by wholly pure enlightening beings.

"In the eastern part of that world, at the border of the peripheral mountains, was a set of four continents called Jewel Flower Lamp Banner. The land was pure, with some defilement. There was an abundance of food without plowing or sowing, and there were dwelling places resulting from the maturation of past deeds. There were wish-fulfilling trees everywhere, trees of various fragrances always emitting clouds of perfume, various garland trees constantly showering garlands, various flower trees raining multitudes of flowers of inconceivable colors and scents, trees of aromatic powders of various qualities continually giving forth a rain of powder of fragrant jewels, various jewel trees shining with light from their jewel buds, and trees of various celestial instruments that filled the air with beautiful sounds produced when stirred by the breeze. The sun and moon shined pleasantly day and night, and jewels shone everywhere.

"At that time there were millions of capital cities on those four continents, each of which was surrounded by a thousand rivers. Each of those rivers carried various celestial flowers and produced celestial music; the banks were lined with trees of various jewels, and those who traveled by boat on the rivers enjoyed various delights to their hearts' content. Between the river were built millions of cities, each surrounded by millions of towns. In all the cities and towns were many heavenly parks, palaces, and mansions.

"In the middle of the southernmost of those four continents was a central capital city called Jewel Flower Lamp Banner, which was prosperous and peaceful, with a large population of virtuous people. The king in that city ruled the four continents; spontaneously born in the calyx of a lotus, he had the thirty-two marks of a great man and was a just ruler. He had a thousand sons, valiant, strong, destroyers of enemy armies. He also had millions of concubines who were products of the same virtues as was the king, carried out the same practices, and were noble-minded. They were as beautiful as goddesses, with golden complexions, celestial fragrances and auras of pure light emanating from their bodies. He also had millions of ministers, superlative advisers.

"The king also had a beautiful wife, whose aura constantly suffused a thousand leagues all around her with multicolored light of celestial fragrance. That queen had a daughter by the king who was so beautiful that no one ever tired of looking at her. Just as no one was ever tired of the sight of the sovereign, in the same way no one was ever sated with the sight of the princess, except those sated with wisdom.

"At that time the life span of the beings in that world was measureless— there were none with fixed life spans and no untimely deaths. Also at that time the variety of forms of sentient beings was known, as was the variety of their colors, voices, names, families, life spans, physical sizes, abilities and strengths, agreeable and unpleasant affairs, and higher and lower inclinations. There, those with better appearances and more confidence, who were physically perfect and good-looking, proclaimed their superiority to others; and those with well-formed bodies looked down on all those with ill-formed bodies. Then, because of the evil of mutual contempt, they lost their span of life, physical appearance, strength, and happiness—all was lost.

"There was an enlightenment tree north of the city called Sound of Clouds of Teachings Illumining All. Its strong roots were made of indestructible diamonds that showed the arrays of the enlightenment sites of all buddhas in every moment; its trunk was a mass of all kinds of jewels, high and wide; its foliage, flowers, and fruits were made of all kinds of jewels. It was perfectly formed, well proportioned everywhere, its foliage equally distributed, with endless adornments throughout, flashing with all kinds of jewel lights radiating in all directions, producing sounds of magical displays of the spheres of all buddhas.

"In front of that enlightenment site there was a pond of fragrant water called Sound of Clouds Thundering Teachings with Jewel Flower Lightning, surrounded by millions of jewel trees. Each of those trees was formed like the enlightenment tree. The banks of the pond were made of well-distributed collections of all kinds of gems, hung with strings of all kinds of jewels, graced with arrays of mansions made of pure jewels, adorned with pure arrays of all kinds of ornaments. The whole enlightenment site was also surrounded by countless jewel towers in lotus calyxes with inconceivable adornments. In the middle of the pond appeared a great ruby lotus called

Array of Clouds of Light Rays Flashing Lightning from Between the Leaves Illumining the Sphere of the Buddhas of Past, Present, and Future.

"In that lotus appeared a buddha named Paragon of Virtue Radiant with the Light of Universal Knowledge, who was the first of as many buddhas as atoms in the polar mountain to attain supreme perfect enlightenment in that eon. Having developed sentient beings for thousands of years by hearing the Teaching, he prepared them by manifestation of lights for ten thousand years for the appearance of the buddha in ten thousand years: there emanated from that great lotus a light called 'spotless lamp of all beings,' and the beings touched by that light became aware that the buddha would emerge in ten thousand years. They realized that the buddha would emerge in nine thousand years as a light called 'full of undefiled radiance' emanated from the enlightenment tree, and the beings touched by the light perceived all subtle forms. Realizing that the buddha would emerge in eight thousand years as a light called 'voice of the results of the deeds of all beings' emanated from the enlightenment tree, the beings touched by the light comprehended the oceans of their own doings and gained recollection and knowledge of their deeds. Realizing that the buddha would emerge in seven thousand years as a light called 'voice produced by all roots of goodness' emanated from the enlightenment tree, the beings touched by the light gained completeness of all their faculties. Realizing that the buddha would emerge in six thousand years as a light called 'sound of revelation of the inconceivable sphere of buddhas' emanated from the enlightenment tree, the beings touched by the light were transformed into higher states. Realizing that the buddha would emerge in five thousand years as a light called 'conveying the dramatic mental impression of the purity of all buddha-lands' emanated from the enlightenment tree, the beings touched by the light saw all aspects of the purity of buddha-lands. Realizing the buddha would emerge in four thousand years as a light called 'lamp of the unity of the realm of buddhas' emanated from the enlightenment tree, the beings touched by the light comprehended the omnipresent miracle of the buddha. Realizing the buddha would emerge in three thousand years as a light called 'lamp in the presence of all beings' emanated from the enlightenment tree, the beings touched by the light were engrossed in the sight of the buddha right before them. Realizing the buddha would emerge in two thousand years as a light called 'lamp of lightning of knowledge of past, present, and future' emanated from the tree of enlightenment along with the voice of the past efforts of the buddha, the beings touched by the light put faith in and entered into the oceans of past efforts of the buddha. Realizing the buddha would emerge in a thousand years as a light called 'lamp of realization of suchness of unobscured knowledge' emanated from the enlightenment tree, the beings touched by the light gained the power of the universal eye to see the miracles of all buddhas, the buddha-lands, and all sentient beings. Realizing the buddha would emerge in a hundred years as a light called 'product of virtues of all beings resulting from seeing buddhas' emanated from the enlightenment tree, the beings touched by the light got an impression of the emergence of Buddha. Realizing the buddha would appear in seven days as a light called 'sound producing happiness and joy in all sentient beings' emanated from the enlightenment tree, the beings touched by the light developed the energy of the great joy of seeing Buddha.

"Having thus developed beings for ten thousand years by means of such measureless lights, when the seven days were up he shook that whole world with infinite means of shaking it and made it completely pure, as the buddha-lands of all buddhas in the ten directions are pure—and in each moment of thought he showed the various inconceivable arrays of all those buddha-lands. And in those final seven days all the beings in that world who were ripe for the sight of Buddha stood facing the site of enlightenment.

"Then the supremacy of the realm of all buddhas was proclaimed from every single object in that world—from all the peripheral mountains, all the polar mountains, all the other mountains, all the rivers, all the seas, all the trees, all the land masses, all the cities, all the walls, all the buildings, all the clothing, ornaments, and paraphernalia, all the music and song, and all the created adornments—emanating clouds of all kinds of fragrant smoke, clouds of lusters of all jewels, clouds of all kinds of precious clothing and jewelry, clouds of mountains of all kinds of jewel flowers, clouds of all kinds of aromatic powders, clouds of light rays of all buddhas flashing, clouds of auras of all buddhas, clouds of oceans of sayings of all buddhas, clouds of glorious manifestations of the marks and embellishments of all buddhas, manifesting the signs that a buddha is about to appear in the world. Around the great ruby lotus Array of Clouds of Light Rays Flashing Lightning from Between the Leaves Illumining the Sphere of the Buddhas of Past, Present, and Future, there stood as many ruby lotuses as atoms in ten buddha-lands, on which appeared as many jewel lion seats, on which appeared as many enlightening beings sitting cross-legged.

"As soon as that buddha, Paragon of Virtue Radiant with the Light of Universal Knowledge, had realized supreme perfect enlightenment, the buddhas in all worlds in the ten directions attained supreme perfect enlightenment and set in motion the wheel of teaching for sentient beings in accordance with their mentalities: thereby innumerable sentient beings in that world were thenceforth freed from the calamities of all states of misery, innumerable sentient beings were led to heaven, innumerable beings were led to the stage of saints, innumerable beings were led to the stage of individual enlightenment, innumerable beings were developed to the point of enlightenment in which emancipation is realized by way of intense illumination, innumerable sentient beings were developed to the point of enlightenment characterized by pure exertion, innumerable sentient beings were developed to the point of enlightenment in which emancipation is realized through the efficacy of purification of the senses, innumerable sentient beings were developed to the point of enlightenment in which emancipation is realized through pursuing conduct consonant with the powers of knowledge, innumerable sentient beings were led to enlightenment in which emancipation is made possible by conveyance to the precincts of the citadel of truth, innumerable sentient beings were led to enlightenment in which emancipation is realized by means of integration of efforts in practice, innumerable sentient beings were led to enlightenment in which emancipation is realized through methods of concentration, innumerable sentient beings were led to enlightenment in which emancipation is realized through means of purifying all objects, innumerable sentient beings were inspired to the enlightenment of enlightening beings, innumerable sentient beings were set in the path of enlightening beings, innumerable sentient beings were led to the purification of the path of transcendent ways, innumerable sentient beings were led to the first stage of enlightening beings; in the same way, as the buddha turned the wheel of teaching by his inconceivable spiritual power, in each moment of consciousness innumerable sentient beings were led to the second, third, fourth, fifth, sixth, seventh, eighth, ninth, and tenth stages; innumerable sentient beings were introduced to the practice of enlightening beings based on the most excellent vows; innumerable sentient beings were led to the purification of commitment to the conduct of universally good enlightening beings. Thus, as the buddha turned the wheel of teaching by his inconceivable spiritual power, he succeeded in guiding innumerable sentient beings in each moment of consciousness, and all the sentient beings in that world, according to their mentalities, perceived the Teaching through various bodies expediently projected by the buddha.

"At that time, furthermore, in order to discipline the beings in the city who were intoxicated with enjoyment of forms and colors and who were contemptuous of each other, the enlightening being Universally Good magically assumed a body of superlative appearance and went to the city. His glorious light illumined the city so that the lights of the king and queen, the lights of the jewel trees and the precious stones, even the lights of the sun, moon, planets, and stars, and all the lights of the whole continent, could not be perceived. Just as when the sun rises the darkness disappears and the moon, planets, and stars cannot be seen, in the same way all the lights of the continent, overwhelmed by the light of Universal Good, could not be seen. Just as a mass of carbon black does not look beautiful or shine or seem bright or lustrous in the presence of pure gold, in the same way the bodies of those beings did not look beautiful or shine or seem bright or lustrous in the presence of the universally good enlightening being Samantabhadra. They thought, 'Who might this be, a god, or Brahma, before whom we do not appear beautiful, do not shine, do not glow, have no radiance or luster? We cannot grasp his appearance.'

"Then Universally Good stood in the sky above the palace of the king in the middle of the city and said to the king, 'Know, O king, that a buddha, a perfectly enlightened one, has arisen in the world. He is in this very realm of yours, at the enlightenment site Emblem of the Sound of Clouds of Teaching Revealing Universal Truth.'

"Now, the daughter of the king, seeing the form-body and the supernal manifestation of light of the enlightening being Universally Good, and hearing the sound of his ornaments, was enraptured and was inspired with this thought: 'Whatever basic goodness I have accumulated, may I thereby attain such a body, such adornment, such features, such deportment, such mystic power. Just as he generates light in the dark night of sentient beings and announces the emergence of a buddha, in the same way may I also dispel the darkness of nescience in sentient beings and produce the light of great knowledge. Wherever I may be born, may I never be apart from this spiritual benefactor.'

"Then the king, along with his armies, his concubines, his sons, his ministers, and the inhabitants of the city, left the city and rose a league in the air by the magic power of the king, who filled the four continents with a great light, and who, in order to get all sentient beings to see the buddha, manifested his reflection in all the jewel mountains, stood before all the sentient beings in the four continents, and praised the sight of buddha in verse:

> Buddha has appeared in the world,
> Savior of all living beings;
> All should get up and go
> To see the guide of the world.

> Buddhas appear once
> In millions of eons
> And teach the truth
> For the benefit of all beings.

> Seeing the world in error,
> Shrouded by the darkness of nescience,
> And oppressed by the pains of life and death,
> Buddhas conceive great compassion.

> For countless millions of eons
> They have practiced enlightenment
> To perfect sentient beings
> And extinguish all suffering.

> They have given up
> Their hands and feet, ears, noses, and heads
> For endless eons, to attain
> The immortality of enlightenment.

> It is hard to find a guide of the world,
> Even in millions of eons;
> To listen to them, meet them, and associate with them
> Cannot but be fruitful.

This supreme teacher is to be seen
Sitting on the seat of enlightenment,
Having conquered the demon armies
And realized the highest awakening.

Behold the body of Buddha,
With an endless array of lights,
Emanating various glows
Which soothe the world.

Countless multitudes of light beams
Emanate from the Buddha's pores;
Those on whom they shine
Feel incomparable joy.

Honor the guide of your own will—
Muster great energy and go to him.

"Then the king, having exhorted the inhabitants of his domain with these verses, showering the whole enlightenment site with offerings from ten thousand clouds of offerings developed from the roots of goodness of the ruler, went to the buddha, covering the sky with clouds of parasols of all jewels and canopies of clouds of all kinds of flowers, adorning the sky with cloud covers of all kinds of robes, clouds of nets of jewel bells, clouds of fragrant flames given off by an ocean of all kinds of scents, clouds of chairs made of all kinds of jewels, magically adorning the sky with clouds raining all kinds of presents. Having gone to the buddha and paid his respects, the king sat before the buddha in a throne of great jewels flashing light in all directions.

"At that point the daughter of the king took off all her jewelry and scattered it over the buddha; the jewelry formed a parasol over the buddha's head and stayed there, covered all around with nets of various jewels, held by the chief water spirits, the whole body of jewelry forming a perfect circle surrounded by ten jewel parasols, all completely pure, in the shape of a tower, variously arrayed, covered by clouds of all kinds of jewel ornaments, covered by arrays of diamond trees, adorned with the finest pearls from all the fragrant seas. In the middle of that she saw a great enlightenment tree called 'draped with foliage of all jewels produced by the cosmos of realities,' with infinitely various adornments, displaying various auspicious supernal manifestations. There she saw a buddha named Vairocana surrounded by as many enlightening beings as atoms in untold buddha-lands, all of whom had undertaken the vows of practice of universally good enlightening beings and dwelt in the inconceivably various total unity of all enlightening beings. She also saw the leaders of all worlds in the presence of the buddha.

She saw the infinitely various projections of Vairocana Buddha and perceived the successive ages of his past enlightening practice. She also perceived that world's ages of formation and disintegration, and the succession of past buddhas in that world. She also saw the universally good enlightening being Samantabhadra in that world, and saw him in the presence of all buddhas, honoring the buddhas and guiding all sentient beings to full development. She also saw all the enlightening beings reflected in the body of Universal Good, and saw herself there too in the presence of all the buddhas, in the presence of all the enlightening beings reflected in the body of Universal Good, in the abodes of all sentient beings. In each of those worlds she also saw as many worlds as atoms in a buddha-land, with their boundaries, bases, forms, masses, and various purities of adornment, covered by clouds of various supernal manifestations, with various names and numbers of ages, various lineages of buddhas appearing, various temporal locations, various spatial locations, belonging to various phenomenal realms within various planes of the cosmos, situated in various planes of space, with various arrays of enlightenment sites, various lights projected by buddhas, various buddhas' lion thrones, various oceanic audiences of buddhas, various circulations of the audiences of buddhas, various clarifications by the skill in means of buddhas, various buddhas' ways of turning the wheel of teaching, various sayings of buddhas, various indications of oceans of ways of expressing thought, and enunciations of multitudes of various scriptures.

"Seeing all these, she was all the more enraptured. The buddha expounded to her in her rapture a scripture called Voice of the Cycles of Teaching of All Buddhas, along with as many accompanying scriptures as atoms in ten buddha-lands. When she had heard these scriptures, ten hundred thousand kinds of concentration entered into her, subtle and pleasant, like the consciousness of an embryo on the first day in the mother's womb, like the commencement of activity in beings, like the impulse of the sprout in the seed of a tree on the day it is planted—this is how subtle and full of potential those concentrations were. Ten hundred thousand concentrations descended into her, beginning with such concentrations as one called 'face-to-face communication with all buddhas,' one called 'illumination of all lands,' one called 'penetrating the principles of all pasts, presents, and futures,' one called 'voice of the teaching activity of all buddhas,' one called 'communicating the ocean of vows of all buddhas,' one called 'communicating the voice of all means of emancipation from all suffering and torture of the mundane whirl,' one called 'manifestation of the vow to dispel the darkness of all sentient beings,' one called 'determination to release all sentient beings from suffering' one called 'source of achievement of happiness for all sentient beings,' one called 'source of tireless developmental guidance for all sentient beings,' one called 'characterized by entry into the path of all enlightening beings,' and one called 'supernal manifestation produced by entry into the stages of all enlightening beings.'

"With her mind subtly concentrated, unwavering, joyful, refreshed, unpreoccupied, in harmony with the wise, focused on profound omniscience, swelling with oceanic love, free from all attachments, not dwelling on any worldly objects, entering the sphere of those who arrive at Thusness, aware of the appearances of all buddhas, unperturbed, unagitated, unobstructed, unfragmented, neither excited nor depressed, tireless, unretreating, undiscouraged, meditating on the inherent nature of all things, realizing the ocean of principles based on the inherent nature of all things, following the principles of investigation of all things, plunging into the ocean of all sentient beings, determined to save all worldlings, illumined by the vast ocean of buddhas, plunging into the ocean of vows of all buddhas, breaking through all obstructions to enlightenment, gathering great stores of virtue, on the verge of attainment of the ten powers of buddhas, aware of the realms of all enlightening beings, amassing the provisions of all enlightening beings for the path of enlightenment, her mind reaching everywhere to take up the great vow of universal good, by as many oceans of vows as atoms in ten buddha-lands she undertook the past vow of all buddhas for the purification of their own buddha-lands. That is, by guiding all sentient beings to perfection, to know all ways to the realm of reality, to enter the ocean of all ways to the realm of reality, to enter enlightening practice in all buddha-lands forever, to live in the sphere of the practices of all enlightening beings forever, to visit all buddhas, to associate with all spiritual benefactors, to fully honor and serve all buddhas, to continue with each moment of consciousness the practice of enlightening beings which increasingly becomes aware of omniscient knowledge. She undertook the vow of universally good enlightening practice by means of as many oceans of ways of undertaking vows as atoms in ten buddha-lands, beginning with such vows as these.

"Then the buddha Paragon of Virtue Radiant with the Light of Universal Knowledge made her aware of his past roots of goodness and inspired her to achieve them—he made them clear to her, revealed them, described them, analyzed them, and explained them; he strengthened them to endure without perishing, extended them to great range, and firmly established them so as to make them equal to the measure of omniscience, so she would apprehend, from the first determination for enlightenment, the incalculable past vows of the enlightened.

"Ten eons before that, in the world Light Shining from a Jewel Sun and Moon, in which the teaching of the buddha Moonlike Brilliance was preserved, that same woman, instructed by the enlightening being Universally Good, repaired a ruined image of the Buddha seated on a lotus, painted it, and adorned it, having gone to Universally Good with the aspiration for enlightenment. Because of that root of goodness, she never fell into misfortune and always was born in celestial or human families and was always beautiful. She always saw buddhas and associated with the enlightening being Universally Good, and in every life was developed, inspired, and caused to be mindful by that spiritual benefactor. At this time, furthermore, Universally Good was thoroughly pleased with her.

"Who do you think the king of that time was? It was none other than the enlightening being Manjushri, the Glorious One, who was the king. And do not suppose that it was anyone else but the night goddess

Prashantarutasagaravati, who is seated here near me, who was the queen. And do not think it was anyone but I who was the daughter of the king and queen, who in the time of the teaching left by the buddha Moonlike Brilliance repaired a ruined image of the Buddha on a lotus. That became a determining factor for me all the way to supreme enlightenment. And when I was directed by the enlightening being Universally Good toward supreme perfect enlightenment, I first aroused the determination for enlightenment. Then, when I went to the buddha Paragon of Virtue Radiant with the Light of Universal Knowledge and cast my jewelry over him, saw the buddha's miraculous power, and heard the Teaching from him, I attained this enlightening liberation showing guidance to all sentient beings. And I propitiated all those buddhas, numerous as atoms in the polar mountain, and honored them with all kinds of offerings. And I listened to all their teachings, and put their instructions into practice; and I gained such intense respect for those buddhas that in a single moment of thought I would see all those buddhas, their circles of enlightening beings, and their buddha-lands.

"When that world Radiant Brilliance had passed away and the age Sphere of Dispassion was over, there followed a world called Magnificent Array Brilliantly Adorned with Jewel Discs, and an age called Great Light; five hundred buddhas emerged therein, and I propitiated them all. The first buddha in that age was named Representative of Great Compassion; when he was leaving home, I, who had become a night goddess, made offerings to him. After him, a buddha named Adamantine Paragon of Man arose; I, at that time a ruler, made offerings to him, and he expounded to me a scripture called Source of All Buddhas, accompanied by as many scriptures as atoms in ten buddha-lands, which I listened to and took up. After that a buddha named Magnificent Array of Lights of a Mountain of Blazing Fire appeared; at that time the daughter of a grandee, I made offerings to him, and he expounded to me a scripture called Containing the Manifestations of Past, Present, and Future, accompanied by as many scriptures as atoms in the continent, which I listened to and took up. After that a buddha named King of Energy Risen Above the Ocean of All Phenomena appeared in the world; at that time a titan chieftain, I made offerings to him, and he expounded to me a scripture called Analysis of Knowledge of the Planes of All Reality Realms, accompanied by five hundred scriptures, which I listened to and took up. After that a buddha named Light of the Ocean of Splendor of the Profound Doctrine appeared; at that time the daughter of a chief water spirit, I honored him with a shower of wish-fulfilling jewels, and he expounded to me a scripture called Light of Reason in the Ocean of Reality Realms, accompanied by as many scriptures as atoms in ten buddha-lands, which I listened to, took up, and memorized. After that a buddha named Splendor of the Multitude of Manifestations of the Ocean of Virtue appeared; at that time a seer with five kinds of occult knowledge, I went to him by magical power with a company of six thousand seers and honored him with incense and flowers. He expounded to me a scripture called Lamp of Independence, accompanied by six thousand scriptures, which I listened to and took up. After that a buddha named Imbued with Sunny Radiance appeared. At that time I was an earth goddess named Source of Common Weal; accompanied by countless earth goddesses, I went to that buddha showering jewel flowers and garlands from trees of all jewels as tokens of honor. He expounded a scripture called Womb of Knowledge from Which All Buddhas Are Born, along with countless scriptures, which I listened to and remembered permanently.

"The last of those five hundred buddhas was named Lamp Radiant As a Mountain Peak of Jewels Filling the Space of the Cosmos. At that time I was a dancing girl named Radiantly Beautiful Face. When the buddha came into the city, I began to dance and by the power of the buddha rose into the air and went to the buddha, praising him with a thousand verses. He illumined my whole body with a light called Array of Cosmic Lightning, which emanated from the circle of hair between his brows; and as soon as that light touched me I attained a liberation called 'offspring of contemplation of the principles of the reality realm.'

"Thus I associated with and honored all the five hundred buddhas of that age in that world, and I remember everything they taught me, forgetting nothing, not even a line or letter. Also, as I went to each buddha, I benefited innumerable beings by describing the ways of buddhas. Also, from each buddha I obtained illumination by the lightning of omniscience, called 'womb of knowledge of past, present, and future, extensive as the cosmos,' which is the oceanic body of the reality realm, containing at once all the practices of universal good. Now I perceive infinite buddhas in each mental moment, and from seeing those buddhas, flashes of light of omniscience which I have not previously apprehended or seen enter into my mind, and I do not fall away from the practice of universally good enlightening beings. Why? Because apprehending these flashes of light of omniscience is endlessly and infinitely revealing and instructive."

Then the night goddess Samantasattvatranojahshri spoke these verses to Sudhana, further elucidating the enlightening liberation showing guidance for beings in all worlds:

> Listen, Sudhana, as I tell
> Of what is deep, hard to see, hard to fathom:
> Means of distinction of the planes of all times,
> Total illumination of the appearances of things.

> Listen to me explain how I first aspired to enlightenment
> In quest of the qualities of buddhas,
> And how I attained
> This liberation of awareness.

> More eons ago than atoms in a buddha-land,
> There was a land called Radiant Brilliance, vast and pure,
> Where there was an age called Sphere of Dispassion,
> During which there was an unbroken succession of buddhas.

As many buddhas as atoms in the polar mountain, free from evil,
  appeared:
The first was Paragon of Virtue Radiant with the Light of Univer-
  sal Knowledge;
Then Banner of Truth, Polar Mountain of Light, and Lion of Virtue;
King of Peace, Continual Life, Lofty Renown, Glory of Supreme Virtue,
Light Maker, Moon Face—these were the first ten buddhas there.

Vault of the Sky, Universal Light, Omnipresent, Source of the Sea
  of Mindfulness,
Exalted, Summit of Glory, Light of Lofty Flames of Truth,
Lotus Born, The Compassionate, and Flower of the Cosmos—
These were the second ten, lighting the ocean of buddhas.

Mind of Foremost Light, Mind of Knowledge, Manifold Benefits,
  Glory of Indra,
Celestial Intellect, Mind of Supreme Energy, Splendor of Knowledge,
Brilliance of the Best of Lights, Mighty Celestial Stride, Lotus of
  the Cosmos—
These were the third ten buddhas, revealing this vast teaching.

Splendor of a Mountain of Jewel Lights, then Radiant Ocean of Virtues,
Light of Truth, Lotus-Born Glory, Moonlike Eye of the World, Fra-
  grant Light,
Brilliant As a Mountain of Jewels, Radiant King in the Form of a
  Celestial Musician,
Full of Glorious Light of the Finest of Jewels, and tenth was Physi-
  cally Calm.

After that were Vast Awareness, Jewel Luster, Splendor of Clouds in
  the Sky,
Superb Appearance, magnificent, and Sphere of Holy Practices, radiant,
Living Like Primeval Man, Splendid As the Polar Mountain, King
  Resplendent with Virtue,
Paragon of Invincible Resolve, and Lofty Tree the tenth of them.

Imbued with the Splendor of the King of Trees, Reflection of the
  Bodies of the
Leaders of the Worlds, Superlative Radiance, Spotless Light, Bril-
  liance of the
Energy of Earth, Glory of the Supreme Virtues of the Profound Teaching,
Knowledge of the Sound of the Ocean of Truths, Pole of the World,
  Radiant Mind, Diamond Light.

Light of Brahma, Sound of Space, Splendor of Reflection of the Cosmos, Sphere

Of Lights, Brilliant Mind with the Ten Powers of Knowledge, Lamp
  of Space,
Beautiful Splendor, Glory of Sunlight, Light of Virtue, Tranquil
  Radiance, and
Beauty of Clouds of Compassion, were the next ten buddhas.

Mindful of the Light of Power Born of Thusness, Appearing to All Beings,
Exalted Light, Embodiment of Impartiality, Born of Truth, Swift As
  the Wind,
Paragon of Heroism, Jewel Body Luster, Light Appearing in All Times—
These were the next ten buddhas.

Shining Light of the Ocean of Vows, Splendor of the Mountain of
  Adamantine Will,
Exalted Brilliance, Paragon of Mindfulness, Aware of Truth, Lamp
  of Wisdom,
Radiance of the Most Excellent Light, then Vast Intellect,
Following the Course of Knowledge of the Principles of the Cosmos,
  and Light of Knowledge of Oceanic Awareness.

Sublime Giver of Jewels of Truth, Clouds of Glory of Mountains
  of Virtue,
Light of the Lamp of Peace, Light of Fiery Energy, Voice of Cessation,
Paragon of Tranquillity, Radiant Lamp of the World, Energy of
  Great Vows,
Invincible Power, Radiant Sea of Lights of Knowledge.

Spiritual Master, Unattached Mind, Understanding the Speech of
  All Beings,
Articulate in All Languages, Resolved to Sacrifice Willingly, Appearing to All
Beings Everywhere, Adopting Forms Congenial to All Beings, Living Together
for the Benefit of Others, Embodiment of Nature, and the Buddha Good:

Beginning with these, I served as many buddhas, light-makers,
As atoms in the polar mountain.
And I served all the buddhas who appeared
In as many eons as atoms in the buddha-lands,
And entered this ocean of liberation.
I have practiced and developed this liberation for infinite eons;
Having heard it and put it into practice,
You will accomplish this teaching soon.

"I know only this enlightening liberation showing guidance to beings in
all worlds. How can I know the practice or tell the virtues of the enlighten-

ing beings who live by various resolutions in the infinitely varied ocean of enlightening practices, who manifest various minds and bodies, who have perfected oceans of various faculties, who have carried through the various vows of enlightening beings?

"In this same enlightenment site is a night goddess named Prashantarutasagaravati, who sits next to me on a lotus seat, in a calyx adorned with starry diamonds, surrounded by countless tens of hundreds of thousands of night goddesses—go ask her how to learn and carry out the practice of enlightening beings."

So Sudhana paid his respects to the night goddess Samantasattva-tranojahshri and left her.

Prashantarutasagaravati

Then Sudhana, cultivating that enlightening liberation of the night goddess Samantasattvatranojahshri, showing guidance to beings in all worlds, entering into it, becoming absorbed in it, plunging into it, expanding it, spreading it, extending it, mastering it, making it manifest, attaining it, went to the night goddess Prashantarutasagaravati. He paid his respects to her and said, "With the help of spiritual benefactors I am learning the practice of enlightening beings, entering into the practice of enlightening beings, carrying out the practice of enlightening beings; having undertaken the practice of enlightening beings, I want to become thoroughly familiar with omniscience. So please tell me, noble goddess, how an enlightening being is to learn and carry out the practice of enlightening beings."

The goddess said, "It is good that you seek the ocean of practices of enlightening beings by relying on spiritual benefactors. I have attained an enlightening liberation of supernal manifestations of a moment of consciousness producing floods of immense joy."

Sudhana said, "What is your activity, your sphere of action, your means of practice, your contemplation? What is the scope of this liberation?"

She said, "I have attained equanimity through purification of the ocean of mind. I have attained indestructible adornment undefiled by the taint of all worldly passion. My mind is unregressing and unswerving from its object. My mind is unshakable, adorned with virtues like a mountain of jewels. My mind is not fixed on anything, not dependent on anything. My mind is intent on serving all beings. My mind is tireless in seeing all buddhas. My desire for the powers of all enlightening beings is pure. My mind dwells in the ocean of mindfulness of the manifestations of great knowledge. I have set out to overcome the sorrows of all beings and am devoted to removing the suffering and sadness of all beings. I have undertaken to stop all beings' preoccupation with objects of sense. I have undertaken to extinguish beings' suffering caused by separation from loved ones and contact with the uncongenial. I am intent on stopping all the sufferings of beings that come from delusion arising from their relations to objects. I am a refuge for all fallen beings and am engaged in showing all beings means of emancipation from the miseries of the mundane whirl. I have undertaken to stop all sentient beings' sadness, lamentation, suffering, depression, and mental disturbance occasioned by birth, old age, and death. I have undertaken to produce the supreme felicity of the enlightened in all beings. I find satisfaction in presenting my services for the happiness of beings in all abodes, and I see to their spiritual protection, and I gradually develop them to omniscience. That is to say, I produce detachment in beings who live in great palaces and mansions, and I remove their various melancholies, and in order to put an end to all attachments, I teach them to realize the intrinsic nature of all things. I teach those who have long-standing ties of affection with their families and relatives in such a way that they may get to meet and associate with buddhas and enlightening beings. Those who are involved with their spouses and children I teach in such a way as to extinguish their craving for mundane enjoyments and so that they will become impartial toward all and will come to have great compassion. Those in the marketplaces I teach in such a way that they will enter into association with the community of sages and get to meet enlightened people. Those who are obsessed with consumer goods I teach in such a way that they acquire transcendent forbearance. Those who take pleasure in music, song, and dance, I teach the way to enjoy spiritual pleasures. Those eagerly desirous of enjoyment of sense objects I teach in such a way that they may arrive at the realm of the enlightened. Those who are filled with anger I teach in such a way as to lead them to transcendent tolerance. Those who are lazy I teach in such a way as to purify transcendent vigor. Those whose minds are confused I teach to attain the transcendent meditation of those who arrive at Thusness. Those lost in a tangle of views, fallen into the darkness of ignorance, I teach in such a way as to lead them out of the tangle of views and the darkness of ignorance. Those who are stupid I teach in such a way that they may acquire transcendent wisdom. Those attached to the realms of desire, form, or formlessness, I teach in such a way that they may escape from the sufferings of the mundane whirl. Those with low aspirations I teach in such a way that they may fulfill the vow of enlightenment. Those intent on their own benefit I teach in such a way that they may fulfill the vow to bring benefit to all beings. Those with weak wills I teach in such a way that they may perfect the transcendent power of enlightening beings. Those in misery I teach in such a way as to enable them to attain the felicity of omniscience. Those who are sick I teach in such a way that they may develop the reflectionlike bodies characteristic of enlightening beings. Those attached to various pleasures I teach in such a way that they may acquire delight in the practices of enlightening beings. Those who are destitute I teach in such a way that they may obtain the spiritual treasury of enlightening beings. Those who resort to parks and gardens I teach in such a way that they are motivated to seek the way to enlightenment. Those who are on the road I teach in such a way that they set out on the road to omniscience. Those in villages I teach in such a way that they may be emancipated from everything in the realms of desire, form, and formlessness. Those in communities I teach in such a way as to lead them beyond the paths of those who strive for individual salvation and set them on the way to buddhahood. Those in cities I teach in such a way as to reveal the city of the supreme truth. Those in the intermediate directions I teach in such a way that they may attain knowledge of the equality of past, present, and future. Those in the four quarters I teach in such a way that they may realize higher knowledge of all things. Those whose behavior is governed solely by lust I teach to stop their craving for all mundane pleasures by means of contemplation of impurity. Those who act on hatred I teach in such a way that they many enter the ocean of universal love. Those who act on delusion I teach in such a way that they may realize higher knowledge with analytic comprehension of all things. Those who act equally on lust, hatred, and delusion I teach in such a way that they may rise above them through the ocean of means of the undertakings of all vehicles of emancipation. Those who are inclined to enjoyment of evanescent mundane objects I teach in such a way as to lead them away from attachment to transient mundane objects. Those who are touched by all the miseries of the mundane whirl I teach in such a way that they may be unaffected by the woes of life and death. Those who are susceptible to guidance by the enlightened I teach in such a way as to elucidate unborn birth. Those who are attached to physical and mental elements I teach in such a way that they may abide in nonreliance. Those who are cowardly I teach in such a way as to reveal the excellence of the adornments of the path of enlightenment. To those who are conceited I elucidate acceptance of the equality of all things. To those who are prone to deceit and guile I explain the purity of intention of enlightening beings.

"In this way I take care of all sentient beings by giving teaching. Leading them away from all miseries and paths leading to unhappiness, showing them the happiness of human and celestial states, freeing them from the dominion of the realms of desire, form, and formlessness, leading them to omniscience, developing them to maturity by various means, I rejoice, exult, become glad at heart, having achieved manifestation of the ocean of energy of great joy.

"Furthermore, as I observe the oceans of assemblies of enlightening beings in all directions, I generate oceans of energy of various joys in the enlightening beings carrying out various vows, enlightening beings with variously purified bodies, with various auras of light, radiating auras of light beams of infinite colors, illumined by knowledge penetrating oceans of various ways to omniscience, plunged into oceans of various concentrations, manifesting various occult powers, speaking in various languages, variously adorned, plunged into various principles of buddhahood, gone to various lands, seeing various multitudes of buddhas, imbued with oceans of various intellectual capacities, aware of the sphere of knowledge of various liberations of buddhas, encompassing oceans of various knowledges, dwelling in various methods of concentration, freely employing various doctrines, liberations, and disciplines, entering various doors to omniscience, variously adorning the sky of the cosmos, filling the sky with clouds of various supernal manifestations, observing various communities, gathered joyfully in various worlds, gone to various buddha-lands, assembled in various places, sent forth by buddhas, leaving the presence of various buddhas in company with groups of enlightening beings, showering rain from clouds of various adornments, entering into the systems of various buddhas, contemplating the oceans of teachings of various buddhas, plunged into various oceans of knowledge, sitting in the midst of various magnificent arrays. Those enlightening beings, filled with various joys, enter the oceans of assemblies of buddhas, see them, and contemplate them; as they meditate on the infinity of the powers of buddhas, floods of great joy arise in them.

"Furthermore, perceiving the inconceivable purity of the form body of Vairocana Buddha, adorned by the marks of greatness, I experience exalted joy and serenity. Observing his array of lights, vast as the cosmos, moment to moment manifesting an infinitely varied ocean of colors, in each moment of consciousness I experience floods of great joy.

"Also, seeing as many oceans of great beams of light as atoms in infinite buddha-lands emanate from each pore of Vairocana Buddha's body, each beam of light accompanied by as many oceans of light beams as atoms in infinite buddha-lands, pervading all buddha-universes and extinguishing the suffering of all beings, in each moment of consciousness I experience floods of great joy.

"Also, seeing massive clouds of lights the color of all jewels, as many as atoms in all buddha-lands, emerging from Vairocana's head moment to moment, pervading all universes, I experience great floods of joy.

"Also, seeing multitudes of various fragrant lights, as numerous as atoms in all buddha-lands, emanating from each pore of Vairocana's body in each moment of thought, I experience great floods of joy.

"Also, as I observe Vairocana's body, seeing multitudes of images of Buddha, adorned with the marks of greatness, as numerous as atoms in all buddha-lands, emanating from each of the Buddha's marks of greatness in each moment of thought, I experience great floods of joy.

"Also, seeing multitudes of mystically projected bodies of Buddha, shining with the eighty embellishments of greatness, as numerous as atoms in all buddha-lands, emanating from each of the Buddha's physical embellishments in each moment of thought, I experience great floods of joy.

"Also, as I observe Vairocana's body, seeing multitudes of Buddha's spiritual manifestations, as numerous as atoms in untold buddha-lands, emanate from each pore in each moment of thought, including manifestations of the Buddha's first inspiration, purification of the six transcendent ways, and progress through the stages of enlightenment, I experience great floods of joy.

"Also, as I watch Vairocana's body, seeing multitudes of all kinds of beings, celestial, preternatural, and human, as numerous as atoms in untold buddha-lands, emanating from each of Vairocana's pores in each moment of thought, along with their characteristic atmospheres of projected auras, going throughout all worlds, appearing to those sentient beings who are suited to being guided by manifestations of such and such particular forms of being, and expounding the Teaching to them, I experience great floods of joy.

"And as I watch Vairocana's body, seeing multitudes of Brahma gods, as numerous as atoms in untold buddha-lands, emanating from each pore in each moment of thought, along with the miraculous projections of Brahma gods, appearing to sentient beings in all universes who are suited to being guided by manifestations in the form of Brahma gods and expounding the Teaching to them with the voice of Brahma, in each moment of awareness I experience great floods of joy of cosmic dimensions concomitant with all-knowledge.

"And so I attain what I have never attained before, understand what I have never understood before, penetrate what I have never penetrated before, pervade what I have never pervaded before, see what I have never seen before, and hear what I have never heard before. Why? All things are to be completely known by the nature of things as being of one characteristic at all times, while yet manifest in an endless variety as all things.

"This is the range of the ocean of means of the enlightening liberation of supernal manifestations of a moment of thought producing immense floods of joy. This liberation is infinite because it goes into the ocean of principles of the cosmos. This liberation is inexhaustible because it is inseparable from the determination for omniscience. This liberation is endless because it is perceived by the eye of enlightening beings. This liberation is peerless, because it pervades the total cosmos. This liberation is all-sided, because it encompasses all miracles in a single object. This liberation is unfailing, because of practicing the nonduality of all bodies of reality. This liberation is unborn, because its practice is like magic. This liberation is like a reflection, because it arises as a reflection of the vow for omniscience. This liberation is like an emanation, because it emanates the practices of enlightening beings. This liberation is like earth, because it is the refuge of all sentient beings. This liberation is like water, because it rains great compassion on all sentient beings. This liberation is like fire, because it ends the cravings of all sentient beings. This liberation is like wind, because it directs all sentient beings to omniscience. This liberation is like the ocean, because it is a repository of ornaments of virtues for all sentient beings. This liberation is like the polar mountain, because it rises out of the ocean of jewels of knowledge of all things. This liberation is like the sky, being the space in which the miracles of the buddhas of past, present, and future take place. This liberation is like a great cloud, showering the rain of the cloud of the Teaching on all sentient beings. This liberation is like the sun, dispelling the darkness of nescience of all sentient beings. This liberation is like the moon, imbued with an ocean of goodness and knowledge. This liberation is like arrival at Thusness, reaching everywhere. This liberation is like one's own reflection, being produced by rightness of action. This liberation is like an echo, thundering the voice of all truths in accord with inclinations. This liberation is like a reflection, communicating to all sentient beings according to their mentalities. This liberation is like a great tree, flowering with the miracles of all buddhas. This liberation is like diamond, its nature unbreakable. This liberation is like a wish-fulfilling jewel, accomplishing an endless variety of miracles. This liberation is like a flawless jewel, showing the miracles of the buddhas of past, present, and future without interference. This liberation is like a jewel of happiness, equally producing the voice of the teachings of all buddhas. This liberation is illustrated by countless such similes."

Then Sudhana asked the night goddess, "How did you manage to attain such a liberation?" She replied, "There are ten great provisions of enlightening beings, great accomplishments, great encompassing practices, great illuminations, great manifestations of power, great good fortunes, great heritages, great capacities, great powers, by the practice of which enlightening beings attain this liberation. What are the ten? Enlightening beings' great encompassing practice of giving, devoted to satisfying all sentient beings according to their wishes; enlightening beings' great encompassing practice of appropriate conduct, devoted to embodying the virtues of all buddhas; enlightening beings' great encompassing practice of forbearance, devoted to contemplating the nature of all things; enlightening beings' great encompassing practice of vigor, devoted to undertaking the attainment of omniscience without turning back; enlightening beings' great encompassing practice of meditation, devoted to extinguishing the fire of afflictions of all sentient beings; enlightening beings' great encompassing practice of wisdom, devoted to higher knowledge of all things; enlightening beings' great encompassing practice of skill in means, devoted to guiding all sentient beings to perfection; enlightening beings' great encompassing practice of vows, going to all lands to go into the practice of enlightening beings for all time in all lands; enlightening beings' great encompassing practice of power, going to all universes to ceaselessly manifest realization of enlightenment in each instant in all lands; enlightening beings' great encompassing practice of knowledge, intent upon the powers of all buddha-lands in those oceans of structures of all realms of reality. And in each of those buddha-lands I see Vairocana Buddha at the pinnacle of enlightenment manifesting the miracle of perfect enlightenment in each moment of consciousness, pervading the oceans of structures of all reality realms with each miraculous display of enlightenment. I also perceive myself in the presence of each of those buddhas and listen to what the buddhas in those worlds teach. And as multitudes of emanations of all those buddhas come forth from all their pores, proclaiming myriad teachings and showing various miracles, and turn the wheel of teaching in all realms by mastery of sentient beings' minds, using various ideas, I remember, apply, and contemplate it all. I pick it up by mental command, able to swiftly grasp all meanings and expressions, clarify it by wisdom penetrating the inner sanctum of purity of all realities, follow its course by higher knowledge investigating the ocean of all realities, encompass it by awareness as vast as past, present, and future, balance it by wisdom conforming to the equality of those who arrive at Thusness. I carry out all the principles of the Teaching, I bring forth multitudes of scriptures from all the clouds of teaching, I arrange oceans of doctrines in all the multitudes of scriptures, I gather cycles of doctrine in all the oceans of doctrines, I find oceanic floods of spiritual joy in all the waves of doctrine, I produce momentum in attainment of the stages of enlightenment in all the oceans of spiritual joy, I produce momentum in attainment of oceans of concentration in the momentum through all the stages, I attain oceans of visions of buddhas in all the multitudes of oceans of concentration, I attain oceans of awareness in all the oceans of visions of buddhas, I order the stages of knowledges of past, present, and future in all the oceans of awareness; by concentration on pervading the endlessly variegated ocean of realms, by concentration on comprehending the ocean of past practices of infinite buddhas, by concentration on the range of knowledge of the ocean of past efforts of infinite buddhas, by concentration on attainment of the light of knowledge of infinite buddhas, by concentration on perception of the purity of conduct of infinite buddhas, by concentration on perfection of the stage of forbearance of infinite buddhas, by concentration on attainment of the scope of knowledge of the mighty effort increasing the great force of energy of infinite buddhas, by concentration on attainment of perception of the efforts to purify the ocean of contemplative attainments of the meditations of infinite buddhas, by concentration on the perception of the purity of the ocean of means of consummation of transcendent wisdom of infinite buddhas, by concentrating on penetrating the ocean of ways of consummation of transcendent skill in means of infinite buddhas, by concentration on comprehending the ocean of ways of consummation of transcendental vows of infinite buddhas, by concentration on attainment of knowledge of increasing and perpetuating the good and wise transcendent power of infinite buddhas, by concentration on attainment of contemplation of the ocean of principles of the perfect knowledge of infinite Buddhas, by concentration on attainment of the scope of knowledge of infinite buddhas's past progress through the stages of enlightening beings, by concentration on infinite buddhas' past entry into the spheres of the stages of enlightening beings, by concentration on infinite buddhas' abiding in the stages of enlightening beings, by concentration on infinite buddhas' perfection of the stages of enlightening, by concentration on contemplation of the ocean of knowledge of infinite buddhas, by concentration on attaining manifestation of the knowledge of infinite buddhas, by concentration on communication of all meetings and association with past buddhas on the part of infinite buddhas when they were enlightening beings, by concentration on attainment of the scope of knowledge of infinite buddhas' productions of bodies going throughout all lands in the past when they were enlightening beings, by concentration on infinite buddhas' extension of their past enlightening practices throughout all universes, by concentration on the manifestation of infinite buddhas' past practices as enlightening beings using various methods to develop and guide all sentient beings, by concentration of infinite buddhas' pervasion of all realms with their light, by concentration on infinite buddhas' demonstration of miracles to sentient beings, by concentration on the scope of knowledge of infinite buddhas' ascent through the stages of enlightenment, by concentration on attainment of the scope of knowledge of the miracle of perfect enlightenment of infinite buddhas, by concentration on receiving and holding all the doctrines preached by infinite buddhas, by concentration on attainment of knowledge of the oceans of marks of distinction manifested by infinite buddhas, by concentration on awareness of infinite buddhas' oceans of embodiments representing practices, by concentration on attaining the scope of knowledge of the vast realm of infinite buddhas, in every moment of thought I comprehend everything about those buddhas from their first determination to the cessation of their true teaching.

"If you ask also how long ago I attained this enlightening liberation of supernal manifestations in a moment of thought producing great floods of joy, when I was an enlightenment tree goddess named Exemplary Light Serving As a Beacon of Good in the world Pure Golden Radiance as many eons ago as atoms in a buddha-land, I first aspired to enlightenment on hearing the teaching of the buddha Unremitting Voice of the Reality Realm, and after having carried out the practice of enlightening beings for as many eons as atoms in a buddha-land, I was born in this world and propitiated the buddhas of the eon of Virtue from Krakucchanda to Shakyamuni. And I will propitiate and honor all the buddhas yet to come, in this world and in all worlds. Even now that world of Pure Golden Radiance still exists, and the lineage of the buddhas there is unbroken. So you should apply yourself to this doctrine with the great strength of enlightening being."

Then the goddess further explained her liberation to Sudhana in verse:

> Listen to me tell, O Sudhana,
> How I attained this pure liberation.
> Hearing this and generating the power of joy,
> Enter this way of liberation.

> I practiced for many eons past
> And purified my mind;
> Generating great momentum of zealous application,
> I came into the presence of the citadel of omniscience.

> Hearing of the buddhas, supreme in all times,
> And developing great faith in them,
> I served them and their retinues for hundreds of eons
> With all that is pleasing.

> Seeing the buddhas of the past,
> I honored them for the benefit of all beings;
> And I heard their incomparable teaching,
> Generating immense power of joy.

I always paid respect to my parents and elders,
Taking pleasure in their welfare;
I served them and honored them,
While entering this liberation.

Many people who were old, infirm, poor,
Handicapped, suffering, helpless,
I made happy, rich, and protected,
Over hundreds of lifetimes.

In my past practice I rescued those
In the sea of existence from various perils—
From the perils of kings and robbers,
Fire and water, wild beasts and enemies.

I saved those always burning with afflictions in the world,
Made that way by impure deeds,
In dangerous straits in the mundane whirl,
Born in the paths of existence.

The terrors of the calamities in the woeful states of misery
Are harsh and violent, continuous and manifold;
The terrors of birth, old age, death and sickness in the world
I put an end to entirely.

Stilling the intense pains of the mundane world,
Producing all happiness in sentient beings,
Producing the ultimate bliss of the enlightened,
For endless eons—this is my vow.

"I only know this enlightening liberation of supernal manifestations in a moment of thought producing vast floods of joy—how can I know the practice or tell the virtues of the enlightening beings who have plunged into the ocean of all principles of the cosmos of reality, who are freed from all internal and external suffering, who know all eons are in the thoughts, who are versed in the knowledge of the becoming and dissolution of all worlds?

"At this same enlightenment site, in the circle of Vairocana Buddha, is a night goddess named Sarvanagararakshasambhavatejahshri—go ask her how an enlightening being is to learn and carry out the practice of enlightening beings."

Then Sudhana spoke these verses to the night goddess Prashantarutasagaravati:

Instructed by a spiritual benefactor,
I came to you, O goddess;

I see you sitting on your seat
Of infinite height.

Those whose minds are on appearances,
Who cling to existence or conceptualize being,
And the low-minded with false views,
Cannot know this realm of yours.

No worldly or celestial beings can know
The features of your appearance and form,
Even if they look for endless eons—
So endless is the sight of your form.

You are free from dependence on the body-mind clusters,
And you do not rest on the sense media either;
Gone beyond the world and transcended desire,
You appear in the world, transforming.

You have attained immovability, faultless and unattached,
You have clarified the eye of higher knowledge;
In every atom you see as many buddhas as all atoms
Magically transforming.

Your body contains the body of truth,
Your mind is made of knowledge, unhindered.
Illumined by universal light,
You produce endless light in the world.

You produce endless deeds from the mind,
So all worlds are adorned by your deeds;
Knowing that worlds are mental in nature,
Your manifest yourself in bodies
Equal to beings.

Knowing this world is like a dream
And all buddhas are like reflections
And all phenomena like echoes,
You live in the world without clinging to anything.

In each moment you show yourself
To the beings of past, present, and future,
Yet there is no inclination to dualism in your mind,
And thus do you expound the Teaching in all realms.

The oceans of beings are as infinite
As the endless oceans of atoms,

And infinite too are the oceans of Buddha—
All are the sphere of your practice of liberation.

Then Sudhana paid his respects to the night goddess and left her.

Sarvanagararakshasambhavatejahshri

Then, contemplating that enlightening liberation of supernal manifestations in a moment of thought producing floods of joy, fostering it and making it manifest, remembering the instruction of the night goddess Prashantarutasagaravati, absorbing it, keeping in mind knowledge of the principles inherent in it, a measureless repository of many principles to be found in each statement, fixing it in memory, examining it intellectually, putting it into practice, consciously extending it, physically feeling and dwelling in it, entering into it, Sudhana made his way to the night goddess Sarvanagararakshasambhavatejahshri.

He saw the night goddess sitting on a great lotus seat full of diamonds illumining the dwelling places in all cities, accompanied by untold numbers of night goddesses, with a body appearing to the beings in all realms, with a body equal in form to all beings, with a body appearing to all beings, with a body unstained by all worlds, with a body equal to all beings in number of manifestations, with a body transcending all worlds, with a body adapted to developing and guiding all beings, with a body proclaiming the truth in all realms, with a body reaching everywhere, with a body ultimately freed from obstructions, with a body of the essence of those who arrive at Thusness, with a body guiding all beings to ultimate perfection.

Sudhana, enraptured upon seeing the night goddess, paid his respects to her and said, "O goddess, I have set out for supreme perfect enlightenment; please tell me how an enlightening being is to be a benefactor to others while carrying out enlightening practice, and how an enlightening being is to take care of sentient beings with the highest protection and care, and how an enlightening being, engaged in the work of enlightening beings by the assent of the enlightened, is to approach the seat of a spiritual sovereign?"

The night goddess replied, "It is very good that you ask about the way of practice of distributing teachings to sentient beings according to their mentalities, to attain the goal of guiding all sentient beings to perfection, to attain the goal of the effort to preserve the family of all buddhas, to apply all-pervasive knowledge, to confront entry into the ocean of means leading to all realms of reality, to penetrate all knowables by knowledge boundless as space, to receive and hold the teachings of all buddhas.

"I have attained an enlightening liberation, 'entry into the profound miracle of pleasing sound.' Having attained this liberation, engaged in preaching the great Teaching, free from attachment, dedicated to dissemination of the treasury of teachings of all buddhas, imbued with the power of great compassion and goodwill, set on working for the welfare of all sentient beings to inspire them to seek enlightenment, set out to become a leader of all sentient beings to ceaselessly accumulate stores of virtues in determination for enlightenment, engaged in producing clouds of teaching and suns of teaching in all worlds to guide all sentient beings on the path of omniscience, ceaselessly reaching out impartially to all sentient beings to illumine all worlds so as to produce infinite roots of goodness, applying a purified mind to practical knowledge of sustaining the performance of good works of all sentient beings, set out to lead all sentient beings to accord with all paths of good action, engaged in the work of directing all sentient beings in good ways, engaged in showing all sentient beings the way to peace and security, set out to lead all sentient beings to emancipation, engaged in directing all sentient beings to all good practices, set out to serve all spiritual friends uninterruptedly, engaged in directing all sentient beings to the teaching of the enlightened, engaged in undertaking all pure and good practices such as giving, firmly resolved to realize omniscience, with a broad mental sphere firmly focused on the powers of buddhas, I stay by the spiritual benefactor, determined to shatter the mountains of afflictions and obstructions to enlightenment caused by actions, undertaking the preparations for omniscience, engaged in developing all good qualities, engaged in application of thought to the infinite variety of objects confronting omniscience.

"Furthermore, as I purify this medium of light of the Teaching, communicating to all sentient beings, accumulating roots of goodness, I observe, approach, and proceed through the reality realm in terms of ten aspects. What are the ten? I realize that the reality realm is immeasurable, by gaining vast vision of knowledge. I realize that the reality realm is infinitely various, so as to perceive the miracles of all buddhas. I realize that the reality realm is endless, so as to fulfill travel to all buddha-lands and service of buddhas. I realize that the reality realm is boundless, so as to show the practice of enlightening beings in all oceans of worlds. I realize that the reality realm is uninterrupted, so as to enter the sphere of unfragmented knowledge of those who arrive at Thusness. I realize that the reality realm is one, so as to enter the sphere of the voice of those who realize Thusness, which communicates to all sentient beings according to their mentalities. I realize that the reality realm is inherently pure, so as to realize the ultimate end of the past vow to guide all sentient beings to perfection. I realize that the reality realm is equal in all worlds, so as to enter the range of the practice of universal good. I realize that all realms of reality are adorned with one adornment, so as to comprehend the adornment of the miracle of the universally good enlightening being. I realize that the reality realm is imperishable, because of the imperishable nature of the purity of all good pervading the reality realm. Thus do I observe, approach, and proceed through the whole reality realm in terms of ten aspects, to accumulate all roots of goodness, to realize the greatness of buddhas, to arrive at the inconceivable sphere of buddhas.

"Furthermore, I expound the Teaching to sentient beings by means of the operation of ten thousand spheres of mental command, with the attention on the greatness of Buddha in this way. I expound the Teaching to sentient beings by means of the operation of ten thousand spheres of mental command, beginning with the sphere of mental command called absorption in the ocean of all truths, the sphere of mental command of light of remembrance of all buddhas, the sphere of mental command containing light illumining the ocean of deeds of all sentient beings, the sphere of pure mental command of absorption in the ocean of all means of liberation, the sphere of mental command uttering the names of all buddhas, the sphere of mental command of absorption in manifestation of the ocean of past vows of all buddhas, the sphere of mental command of swift turning of the attention to all truths, and the sphere of mental command called light of absorption in omniscience.

"Moreover, I teach sentient beings with wisdom consisting of learning, wisdom consisting of thinking, and wisdom consisting of practice. I teach sentient beings about the process of one existence, and I teach sentient beings about the processes of all existences. I teach about the ocean of names of one buddha, I teach about the oceans of names of all buddhas. I teach about one ocean of worlds, I teach about all oceans of worlds. I teach about the ocean of predictions of enlightenment of one buddha, I teach about the oceans of predictions of enlightenment of all buddhas. I teach about the ocean of audiences of one buddha, I teach about the oceans of audiences of all buddhas. I teach about the cycle of teachings of one buddha, I teach about the oceans of cycles of teachings of all buddhas. I teach about one scripture, I teach about the scriptures containing the cycles of teachings of all buddhas. I teach about one gathering of an audience of a buddha, I teach about the oceans of audiences of all buddhas. I teach about one thought of omniscience, I teach about the oceans of all elements of determination for enlightenment. I teach about one vehicle of emancipation, I teach about the oceans of all vehicles of emancipation. I teach sentient beings in untold ways such as these.

"Entry into the oceans of those who arrive at Thusness, identical to the structures of the reality realm, taking care of sentient beings in the highest spiritual way of expounding the Teaching to them, living by the practice of universally good enlightening beings for endless eons, I cultivate this enlightening liberation of entry into the profound miracle of pleasing sound, by expanding it in every moment of consciousness, by the means of actualizing the sphere of liberation; and I pervade all realms of reality in every moment of thought with each means of actualizing the sphere of liberation."

Sudhana said, "This enlightening liberation is marvelous. How long ago did you attain it?"

The goddess said, "Many eons ago there was world called Multitude of Cities of Spiritual Lights, set on a network of lofty fragrant jewel mountains, as many as atoms in four continents, arrayed with lotus flowers intoning the past vows of all buddhas, composed of multitudes of jewels produced by the deeds of all sentient beings, shaped like a huge lotus, pure with some defilement, encircled by as many masses of flowers as atoms in a mountain, adorned by lofty polar mountains of fragrant jewels, as many as atoms in a polar mountain, and with as many sets of four continents as atoms in a polar mountain. On each continent were untold trillions of cities.

"In that world there was an age called Pure Light, in which there arose as many buddhas as atoms in a polar mountain. In the middle of the world was a set of four continents called Resplendent Banner, in the middle of which was a metropolis called Omnipresent Jewel Flower Light, not too far from which was an enlightenment site called Image of the Abode of a Spiritual Sovereign. At that site a buddha named Illuminating King Voicing the Ocean of All Truths arose, the first of the buddhas of that age. At that time there was a monarch named Radiantly Pure Countenance, who received from that buddha a scripture called Ocean of All Truths and followed it.

"After that buddha passed away, the king left home and preserved the buddha's teachings. At the time of the ending of the teaching, when it was divided into a thousand sects, with a thousand different explanations of the doctrine, and uninterrupted degeneracy of the age was imminent, in order to shake up the people shrouded by the barriers of afflictions and contentious quarrelsome mendicants, who were not seeking the virtues taught by the buddha but were wholly devoted to enjoyment of sense objects, addicted to talk of kings and thieves, addicted to talk of women, lands, and seas, addicted to materialistic thought and conversation, the renunciant king, a true follower of the religion, warned them, 'Alas! The torch of the great teaching, which was developed over many eons, is going to die out.' Then he rose into the sky to the height of seven palm trees, emanated clouds of flames of infinite colors, produced great networks of multicolored lights from his body, extinguished the burning of afflictions in the world with multicolored light, and directed infinitely many sentient beings toward enlightenment. The buddha's teaching was thereby rekindled and remained in the world for another sixty thousand years.

"At that time there was also a nun named Light of Projections of the Wheel of the Teaching. She was the daughter of that king Radiantly Pure Countenance, and she had a retinue of a hundred thousand nuns. Hearing that rousing speech and seeing that great miraculous performance, she and her retinue had been inspired to seek enlightenment. Furthermore, those hundred thousand nuns became irreversible in progress toward supreme perfect enlightenment: they attained a concentration called 'coming into existence in the presence of those who have arrived at Thusness,' and they attained a mental command called 'adamantine light of the teachings of all buddhas,' and a perfection of wisdom called 'entry into the principles of the ocean of all truths.' The nun Light of Projections of the Wheel of the Teaching attained a concentration called 'lamp illumining the source of the teachings of all buddhas,' as well as this subtle, gentle enlightening liberation 'entry into the profound miracle of pleasing sound,' after which all the miracles of the buddha Illuminating King Voicing the Ocean of All Truths became visible to her.

"What do you think—was the king of that time, who went forth into the teaching of the buddha Illuminating King Voicing the Ocean of All Truths, followed the buddha's teaching, sustained the teaching after the buddha's demise when it was dying out, and kindled the torch of the teaching, anyone else? You should not see it this way. It was none other than Samantabhadra, the universally good enlightening being, who was that king Radiantly Pure Countenance. And do you think the king's daughter, who became a nun, accompanied by a hundred thousand nuns, was anyone else? Do not see it that way. It was I myself who was that nun at that time. I preserved the teaching of that buddha, and I made those hundred thousand nuns irreversible in their progress toward supreme perfect enlightenment, I established them in the concentration 'coming into existence in the presence of those who have arrived at Thusness,' I established them in the mental command 'adamantine light of the teachings of all buddhas' and the perfection of wisdom 'entry into the principles of the ocean of all truths.'

"After that I learned from a buddha named Light of the Peak of Knowledge of the Mountain of the Undefiled Teaching, then Crest of Light, then Multitudes of Lights of the Sun of the Teaching, then Sound of Explanation of the Ocean of the Teaching, then Light of the Sphere of Knowledge of the Sun of the Teaching, then Cloud of Banners Marked by the Flowers of the Teaching, then Supreme Brilliance of the Mass of Lights of the Teaching, then Moon of Light of the Depth of the Principles of the Teaching, then Mine of All Images Arising from Knowledge of the Teaching, then Crowned with the Treasury of Knowledge, then King Imbued with the Glory of the Highest Mountain, then Paragon of Universal Knowledge, then Paragon of Energy in All Good Practices, then Multitude of Lights of Spiritual Jewel Flowers, then Supreme Depth of the Light of Peace, then Moon Radiating Images of Eyes of Light, then Ocean of Brilliance of the Flames of Knowledge, then Sphere of Skill of Universal Knowledge, then Light of Knowledge of the Nadir and Zenith, then Lamp Blooming with Flames, then Supreme Lion of Knowledge, then Supreme Light of the Universal Sun, then Lofty Mountain Adorned with Precious Characteristics, then Complete Reflection of the Course of the Sun, then Radiant Moon of Awareness of the Nexus of Realities, then Multitude of Beauties of the Blossoming of the Lotus of the Teaching, then Universal Light of the Solar Orb of the Marks of Distinction, then Glorious Voice of the All-Illumining Teaching, then Adamantine Lion of Practical Wisdom, then Heroic Paragon of Universal Knowledge, then Embodiment of the Flowering of the Lotus of the Teaching, then Ocean of Splendor of Flowers of Virtue, then Mass of Light from the Pinnacle of Spiritual Treasures, then Multitude of Lights from the Summit of Knowledge, then Light of Jewels Bearing All Facets of the Teaching, then Glorious Moon of Awareness at the Pinnacle of Enlightenment, then Moon Glowing with the Fire of the Torch of the Teaching, then All-Reflecting Crown, then Lamp Emblematic of the Body of the Teaching, then Multitude of Representations of the Adamantine Ocean, then Clouds of Glory of Lofty Repute, then Radiant Moon of Sandalwood, then Fiery Light of Flowers of Universal Beauty, then Light Shining on All Beings, then Beautiful Calyx of the Lotus of Virtue, then

King Shining with Fragrant Flames, then Lotus of Logic, then Shining with Magnificent Marks of Greatness, then Universally Renowned, then Polar Mountain of Light of Impartial Knowledge, then Glory of Light of the Citadel of Religion, then Majestic As a Forested Mountain, then Shining Clarity of Universal Light, then Sound of the Ocean of the Teaching, then Energy Arisen from the Undertaking of All Spiritual States, then Foremost Light of Universal Knowledge, then Resplendent with Superior Qualities, then Represented by the Lance of Spiritual Power, then Brilliant Sound of the Wheel of the Teaching, then Light of Knowledge and Wisdom Crowned with Radiant Virtue, then Glorious Moonrise of the Wheel of the Teaching, then Enlightened Paragon Illumining the Lotus of the Teaching, then Jewel Lotus Full of Light, then Lamp of Myriad Peaks of Jewel Radiance, then Flower of Pure Knowledge of Universal Vision, then Vast Treasury of Lights, then King Crowned with a Halo of Light Beams, then Crested with Myriad Virtues, then Mass of Manifestations of the Pinnacle of Religion, then Energy of Enormous Virtue, then Lamp of Myriad Suns of Truth, then King Acclaimed As a Source of Teaching, then Multitude of Sets of Teachings, then Light Representative of the Awareness of Enlightened Knowledge, then Radiant Moon Aware of the Sphere of Realities, then Magnificent As a Mountain of Gold and Jewels, then Topknot of Myriad Spheres of Light of All Truths, then Flaming Light of the Wheel of Teaching, then Lofty Majesty, then Myriad Lights of the Torch of All-Sided Energy, then Light of Vast Crowning Wisdom Sealed by Concentration, then Beautiful Jewel Light, then Voice of Arrays of Jewels from the Light of the Teaching, then Powerful Light in the Sky of Reality, then Moon Adorned with Marks of Greatness, then Flashing Cloud on a Mountain of Light, then Light in the Unobstructed Sky of Reality, then Body Blossoming with the Beauty of the Marks of Greatness, then Supreme Splendor and Voice of the World Ruler, then Light and Sound of Concentration on All Truths, then Mine of Initiatory Sounds, then Sound of the Ocean of Blazing Flames of the Teaching, then Light of Reflections of the Appearances of Past, Present, and Future, then Shining Light of the Highest Splendor of the Sphere of the Teaching, then Powerful Light in the Realm of Reality, then Lion Manifesting the Ocean of All Concentrations, then Light of Total Knowledge, then Lamp of the City of Reality with the Light of Universal Wisdom.

"In that age Pure Light, as many buddhas as atoms in the polar mountain appeared, beginning with these. The last of them was a buddha named Supreme Lamp of Knowledge Lighting the City of the Reality Realm. I served all those buddhas, from the first to the last, and I listened to their teachings, and left society to delve into all their teachings. I kept all their instructions in mind, and from all of them I attained this enlightening liberation of entry into the profound miracle of pleasing sound, by various methods of attainment, and I matured infinitely many sentient beings in the presence of all those buddhas. Since then I served all the buddhas that have emerged in as many eons as atoms in a buddha-land by putting their teachings into practice. Thenceforth I have been awake in the midst of beings asleep in the slumber of nescience during the night of mundane routines; I have guarded the city of their minds, removed them from the city of the triple world, and settled them in the city of the way of omniscience.

"I just know this enlightening liberation of entry into the miracle of pleasing sound, which stops mixed-up worldly talk and does not use duplicitous speech, ultimately leading to truth. How can I know the practice or tell of the virtues of the enlightening beings who have unobstructed knowledge of the essential nature of all speech, who command awareness of all realities in each moment of thought, who comprehend the utterances of all beings, who are familiar with the patterns of thought of all beings, who know the ways of classification and naming of all things, who are masters of the ocean of mental command of all truths, who are skilled in producing teachings adapted to the mentalities of all beings, who endeavor to guide all beings to perfection—how can I know their accomplishment in taking care of all beings, or know their efforts applied to undertaking the supreme works of enlightening beings, their attainment of subtle knowledge of enlightening beings, their multifaceted powers of the mine of practice of enlightening beings, or their accession to the lion throne of those who tell of the deeds of enlightening beings? Why do I say this? They are people of truth who have entered mental command of all stages of the Teaching.

"Right here in the presence of Vairocana Buddha there is a night goddess named Sarvavrikshapraphullanasukhasamvasa, who is sitting next to me. Ask her how an enlightening being is to learn omniscience and how one is to practice so as to lead all sentient beings to omniscience."

Then the night goddess Sarvanagararakshasambhavatejahshri spoke these verses to Sudhana, further illustrating the enlightening liberation entering into profound miracles of pleasing sound:

> Profound and hard to see is the liberation of enlightening beings,
> Like space, entering everywhere;
> They see the buddhas of all times,
> Infinite, throughout the cosmos.

> They attain endless liberations born of virtue and knowledge,
> Of inconceivable nature, immeasurable:
> Increasing unimpeded momentum in all directions,
> They plunge into the paths of benevolence in all times.

> Many eons ago there was a world
> Called Cities of Spiritual Lights:
> In that glorious world
> Was a brilliant age called Pure Light.

> In that age was an unbroken succession of buddhas,
> As many as atoms in the polar mountain.

Illuminating King Voicing the Ocean of All Truths
Was the first buddha of the age,
Supreme Lamp of Knowledge Lighting the City of the Reality Realm
Was the last of those buddhas:
I visited and served them all,
And joyfully heard their teachings.

I saw the golden light of the first buddha,
Illuminating King Voicing the Ocean of All Truths,
Like the polar mountain resplendent with the thirty-two marks,
And seeing him I determined to become a buddha.

As soon as I saw that buddha there arose
My first aspiration to buddhahood, full of power,
By means arising from the progress of omniscience,
As pure as space, of the nature of Thusness.

Thenceforth seeing all the buddhas throughout all times,
And all the multitudes of enlightening beings,
And all the myriad worlds and sentient beings there,
I produced an ocean of ambrosia of goodwill.

I determined to pervade all lands,
Showing my body differently to sentient beings according to their
    mentalities,
To illumine and stir all the lands
And develop the beings to maturity.

I went and saw the second buddha,
And the buddhas in the oceans of lands in the ten directions,
In as many lands as atoms in an ocean of lands,
And finally saw the last buddha of that age.

I went and served all the buddhas,
Lamps of the world, that appeared
In as many ages as atoms in all worlds,
That I might purify this liberation.

Then, having attained this enlightening liberation of entry into the profound miracle of pleasing sound, having entered an ocean of infinitely
various media of concentration, his mind having developed an immense
ocean of means of sustained attention, illumined with the great mystic
knowledge of enlightening beings, having entered an ocean of great joyful
intelligence, his mind expanded with a vast ocean of ecstasy, Sudhana
praised the night goddess with these verses:

Vast is your wisdom, coursing in the ocean of truth,
And you have traversed the infinite sea of existences.
Long-lived, without affliction, an embodiment of beneficent
    knowledge,
Your presence illumines this assembly, O goddess.

Aware of the nature of things, like the sky,
You enter unhindered into all times;
In an instant of consciousness without discriminatory thought
You assess all objects, inconceivable as they are.

With the eye of knowledge you see into the beingless nature,
While by compassion you enter infinite oceans of beings.
Deliberately plunging into most profound liberation,
You guide and develop innumerable beings.

You know how to analyze all states of being,
And are aware of the way to penetrate the essence of things:
You practice the undefiled path of all sages;
You will liberate all beings, purifying them.

You are an unexcelled leader of beings, O goddess,
As you acquire omniscient knowledge throughout the universe,
You expound the Teaching to all beings therein,
And extinguish all fears in the world.

You go by way of the path of Vairocana's vows,
With unhindered, vast, undefiled understanding;
Everywhere practicing the powers of the enlightened,
You witness the miracles of buddhas in all lands.

Hard to accomplish is a skylike mind such as yours,
Free from the taints of the afflictions;
Therein are all lands in all times,
All buddhas, enlightening beings, and all living creatures.

Day and night, instants and moments, seasons, fortnights, months,
And years, along with their passing away and imagined
    discriminations,
And the waves of eons, with their enumerations of myriad names,
The oceans of concepts of sentient beings, all you see in an instant.

The deaths and births of beings in the ten directions,
With form or without, thinking and thoughtless,
You comprehend according to their conventional truth,
And show them the way to supreme enlightenment.

Born of the family of the network of Vairocana's vows,
Having become one with all buddhas,
Your spiritual body pure, your mind unobstructed,
You appear to beings according to their minds.

Having eulogized the goddess with these verses, Sudhana paid his respects and went on.

Sarvavrikshapraphullanasukhasamvasa

Then Sudhana, further cultivating, fostering, and expanding the enlightening liberation of entry into the profound miracle of pleasing sound, went to the night goddess Sarvavrikshapraphullanasukhasamvasa. He saw her sitting on a lion throne of jewel tree shoots inside a tower of branches of jewel trees of all fragrances, surrounded by ten thousand night goddesses. He went up to her, paid his respects, and said, "Noble goddess, I have set my mind on supreme perfect enlightenment, but I do not know how an enlightening being is to carry out and learn the practice of enlightening beings. Please tell me how to perform and learn the practice of enlightening beings, and how to act and learn so as to arrive at omniscience."

The goddess said to Sudhana, "By my power, when the sun goes down, the blooming lotuses become highly fragrant; all the men and women sporting in the parks decide to go home; the highly conscious beings on the roads and paths in the night head for the protection of all beings: those who live in mountain caves go into the mountain caves, those who lie in trees head for the trees, those who live in caves go into their caves, those who live in villages, cities, or towns go into their villages, cities, and towns, those who live in water go down in the water, those who live in other abodes go to their respective dwelling places, to spend the night comfortably.

"Furthermore, to the young men and women intoxicated with the joy of youth, reveling in music and song and intent on sensual pleasures, I praise the effort to produce roots of goodness as an antidote to the fears of the darkness of birth, old age, and death. I enjoin giving on those who are greedy and lead the ill-behaved to discipline. To those who are hostile I praise kindness, and I lead those agitated in mind to patience. I lead the lazy to undertake the vigorous effort of enlightening beings. Those whose minds wander I establish in meditation. I furnish the stupid with transcendent wisdom. Those who are interested in the Lesser Vehicle I establish in the Great Vehicle. Those who are attached to the world, who act within the sphere of attachment to the conditions of existence, I lead to the transcendent commitment of enlightening beings. Those who are overcome by obstructions, tormented by afflictions in their actions, lacking in the power of virtue and knowledge, I lead to the transcendent power of enlightening beings. Those bound up in the darkness of nescience, in the darkness of the ignorance characterized by egoism and possessiveness, I lead to the transcendent knowledge of enlightening beings.

"Furthermore, I have attained the enlightening liberation 'manifestation of contentment with the treasure produced from great joy.'"

Sudhana said, "What is the sphere of this liberation?"

The goddess said, "The scope of this liberation is the knowledge and means to take care of sentient beings by the goodness of those who arrive at Thusness. How is that? Whatever well-being sentient beings experience is all due to the power of the goodness of the enlightened, due to the path of the teaching of the enlightened, due to putting the word of the enlightened into practice, due to learning from the enlightened, due to the support of the enlightened, due to practicing the path of knowledge of the enlightened, due to planting roots of goodness like the enlightened, due to the true teaching of the enlightened, due to the illumination of the sun of knowledge of the enlightened.

"Indeed, the happiness of beings comes from the light of the sphere of pure deeds of the family of the enlightened. How do I know? As I enter into this enlightening liberation of the manifestation of contentment with the treasure produced from great joy, and recall and plunge into the ocean of Vairocana Buddha's past practices as an enlightening being, thus do I know and understand—as the Buddha was concentrating on the stages of enlightenment in the past, seeing sentient beings caught up in egoism and possessiveness, in the darkness of ignorance, gone into a tangle of views, dominated by craving, bound by the fetters of desire, hostile and malevolent, continuously pursuing delusions, wrapped up in envy and jealousy, their minds crowded with afflictions, experiencing the great misery of the mundane whirl, tormented by the pains of poverty in the mundane whirl, deprived of the sight of the enlightened, there appeared in the Buddha a mind of great compassion, a mind to take care of all sentient beings materially for their benefit, a mind to produce means of worldly support for all sentient beings, a mind free from attachment to all things, a mind without acquisitiveness for any objects, a mind not dwelling on any pleasures, a mind free from grasping for any material goods, a mind not seeking rewards for giving, a mind not eager for existence in any world, a mind not confused about causal relations, a mind contemplating the truth after thorough investigation, a mind to provide refuge for the welfare of all living beings.

"Having comprehended the essence of all things as it really is, having impartial goodwill toward all sentient beings, working to fill all worlds with great compassion, covering all worlds with the canopy of the great Teaching, holding the thunderbolt of great knowledge, which shatters the mountain of afflictions of all sentient beings, his mind growing in satisfaction through the welfare of all sentient beings, determined to effect the ultimate happiness of all sentient beings, wishing to provide all sentient beings with everything they need, working impartially without abandoning any sentient beings, wishing to satisfy all sentient beings with the wealth of sages, determined to attain the jewel of knowledge of the supreme ten powers, empowered with the mystic knowledges of enlightening beings, pervading all worlds throughout the space of the entire cosmos with a multitude of various enlightening manifestations, appearing before all sentient beings, swirling a great cloud of all manner of objects and showering a rain of all kinds of precious ornaments, he undertook to give infinite various articles to all sentient beings for their use as appropriate, to perform innumerable services, to strive to provide care by all sorts of charity, giving away many kinds of things, to construct arrangements of myriad benefits, services, and useful articles, to practice various forms of giving, satisfying sentient beings according to their mentalities by endless giving, to make uninterrupted effort to save all beings from the miseries of the mundane world, without desiring the gratitude of anyone, impartial toward all beings, purifying the mind-jewel of all beings, increasing the flood of the ocean of wealth of all-knowledge for all beings produced from the ocean of roots of goodness at one with those of all buddhas, engaged in taking care of all beings by providing for their needs, undertaking all this continuously, from moment to moment, to develop and guide all sentient beings and gradually purify them.

"He undertook to adorn every land as a supreme pure buddha-land in every moment of thought, to purify the practice of the ocean of methods of the Teaching in every moment of thought, to fulfill the means of knowledge pervading all of space in every moment of thought, to purify the means of knowledge of how to tame all sentient beings in every moment of thought, to bring to light the knowledge of how to guide all worldlings in every moment of thought, to always teach in a manner appropriate to the time in every moment of thought, to be a benefactor to all beings by showing the skillfulness to support all knowledge in each moment of thought, carrying out the practice of enlightening beings in each moment of thought in all kinds of worlds, in various forms, by various means, having entered the way of enlightening beings, to suffuse the worlds with various manifestations of the practice of enlightening beings, to show the bodies of all the buddhas of past, present, and future to other beings according to their mentalities in each moment of thought, increasing the flood of the ocean of wealth of all-knowledge for all beings.

"Thus as Vairocana Buddha was carrying out the practice of enlightening beings in the past, he aroused great compassion for those without virtue or knowledge, those attached to the world, ungrateful, wrapped up in the darkness of nescience, egotistical and possessive, shrouded by the darkness of ignorance, immersed in unreasonable thought, lost in the wilderness of views, heedless of cause and effect, dominated by afflictions in action, fallen into a pit of suffering in the wasteland of the mundane whirl, experiencing the misery of various kinds of want; producing vast multitudes of practices of the ways of transcendence, praising the firm foundation of roots of goodness, removing the pain of mundane want from all sentient beings, fostering the growth of great stores of virtue and knowledge, clarifying the realm of causes, enlightening them on the consistency of deeds and states, showing the origin of all beings and lands, involving them in the continuation of the family of buddhas, getting them to remember the teachings of all buddhas, turning them away from all evil, describing the preparations for omniscience, producing a great multitude of transcendent practices filling all realms of beings, he established sentient beings in the care of the ultimate Teaching, satisfying them according to their mentalities. He directed them in preparation for omniscience, he introduced them to the great transcendent ways of enlightening beings, he got them to support themselves on the wealth of sages, he got them to increase their roots of goodness by the momentum of the joy of omniscience. Introducing them to the miracles of all buddhas, taking them into ultimate unattached bliss, showing them the greatness of the enlightened, he led them to enlightening beings' knowledge of means of salvation."

Sudhana said, "How long ago did you set out for supreme perfect enlightenment?"

The goddess said, "This is hard to reach, hard to know, hard to believe, hard to penetrate, hard to say, hard to understand. Neither celestial nor human beings can comprehend it, nor can any listeners or individual illuminates comprehend it, except those who, by the empowerment of Buddha, by the help of spiritual benefactors, by the mind being stabilized on great stores of virtue and knowledge, by purity of intention, by the mind being buoyant, undisturbed, straightforward, unimpaired, open, unobscured, by the mind being illumined by the light of universal knowledge, by the mind being dedicated to the welfare and happiness of all beings, by the mind being invulnerable to the afflictions of all demons, by the mind being within range of attainment of omniscience, thus do not seek any mundane pleasures, are focused on the pleasure of the enlightened, have undertaken to put an end to the suffering and misery of all beings, are headed into the ocean of virtues of the enlightened, are in the realm of the space of meditation on the intrinsic nature of things, have purified the path of higher aspirations, have turned away from the flow of the mundane whirl, are turned toward the ocean of knowledge of the enlightened, are certain to arrive at the citadel of omniscience, proceed energetically into the sphere of those who arrive at Thusness, advance boldly toward buddhahood, are headed toward complete fulfillment of the powers of omniscience, and will ultimately attain the ten powers—such people can penetrate, believe in, grasp, follow, and know this matter. Why? Because this matter is the sphere of buddhas—not even enlightening beings can reach it, much less others. Now, with the support of the Buddha I will tell you, for the sake of the correct purification of the minds of those capable of learning, so that those who practice good can master their minds, and so that you may have an explanation of what is on your mind."

Then the goddess, further elucidating what she meant, looked over the realm of the buddhas of past, present, and future and spoke these verses:

> Profound, infinite, is the sphere of buddhas,
> Of which you now ask, O child of Buddha.

Even in eons as many as atoms in inconceivable lands
It could not be fully told.

The peaceful nature of the buddhas cannot be known
By the covetous or the malevolent,
Or by those shrouded in the darkness of delusion,
Or those whose minds are defiled by hypocrisy and conceit.

This sphere of buddhas cannot be known
By those ruled by envy and jealousy,
Or those whose minds are polluted by guile and deceit,
Or those enshrouded by barriers of action based on afflictions.

Buddhahood cannot be known
By those who depend on mental or material elements,
Or those attached to the body as real,
Or those with false views and ideas.

Hard to know is the tranquil realm of buddhas,
Which is inherently pure and nonconceptual—
This reality cannot be truly known
By those attached to life and being.

Those who are born in the family of buddhas,
Who are empowered by all the buddhas,
Who preserve the lineage of the enlightened,
Are the knowers of this sphere.

Those who are tireless in good practices
And are helped by spiritual benefactors,
With their minds focused on the powers of sages,
They attain peace on perceiving this.

This is the sphere of the undefiled
Whose minds are pure, without false ideas,
Like the sky in all directions,
Lamps of wisdom who have dispelled darkness.

Those who pervade all worlds
Of all times with compassion
And are benevolent to all beings
Enter the way of the buddhas.

This is the stage of those without grasping,
The happy ones without attachment

Who always gladly give all there is
Impartially to all beings.

This is the sphere of the undefiled,
Whose minds are unafflicted and conduct impeccable,
Whose minds are ultimately free from regret,
Who apply themselves to practice of Buddha's teaching.

This is the liberation of the inexhaustible
Whose minds are unshakable, imperturbable,
Whose minds are focused on the essence of things,
Whose minds are unhindered by the oceans of actions.

This is the sphere of the disciplined,
With indefatigable and nonregressing minds,
With strength, vigor, and control,
With endless energy in preparing for omniscience.

This is known to those gone to peace,
With tranquil minds, concentrated,
Ultimately calm and cool,
Practitioners of all the branches of meditation.

This is known to the lamps of wisdom,
Whose minds are liberated from all attachments
And have penetrated the essence of things,
Who have gone the way into the reality realm of the enlightened.

This is the liberation of those who know the path,
Whose minds have penetrated the essence of beings,
Whose minds are not imprisoned in the sea of existence,
Who are moons reflected in the minds of beings.

This is known to the universally good,
Who are born from the ocean of vows
Of the buddhas past, present, and future,
And carry them out forever in all lands.

This is the liberation of those who penetrate all oceans of worlds
By means of the oceans of principles of the reality realm
And see their ages of becoming and decay without discrimination.

This is known to those of unobstructed vision
Who see the buddhas under the enlightenment trees,
As many as atoms in all lands,
Teaching after having realized enlightenment.

You have come after many eons
Of serving spiritual benefactors
In quest of the Teaching, seeking tirelessly;
Having heard it, you can remember it.

To purify your mind
I will tell you freely
Of the infinite realm of Vairocana
By the inconceivable power of Buddha.

The goddess continued, "Long ago, past eons as many as atoms in an ocean of worlds, there was an ocean of worlds called Sun on the Summit of a Mountain of Gold and Jewels. Therein, furthermore, was a buddha called Supreme Light Illumining the Realm of Truth at the Summit of Knowledge, who purified that ocean of worlds while carrying out the practice of enlightening beings in the past. In that ocean of worlds were as many world systems as atoms in all the mountains on earth, each system containing as many worlds as atoms in a galaxy. In each world there were as many sets of eons as atoms in a world, each containing many eons, in each of which there were many events, including buddhas appearing in the world and displaying miracles. Each buddha that appeared expounded as many scriptures as atoms in a world, in each of which scriptures were outlined as many instructions for enlightening beings as atoms in the world, with infinitely various indications of how to guide sentient beings, operated by the principles of various vehicles of liberation, guided by the buddhas' various mystic powers of perception and prescription.

"Within that ocean of worlds was a central world-system called Array of Markers of Doors Facing All Directions, in which there was a world called Ubiquitous Light the Color of All Jewels. The borders of that world were arrayed with jewels reflecting images of the enlightenment sites of all buddhas; it rested on an ocean of flowers made of all kinds of jewels, it was composed of jewels showing the appearances of emanations of all buddhas, it was shaped like a celestial palace, and it was pure with an admixture of defilement. Furthermore, in that world there were as many world-regions with four continents as atoms in the polar mountain; at the center was a set of four continents called Mountain Peak of All Jewels, whose four continents were innumerable hundreds of thousands of leagues in extent. On each continent were ten thousand great cities. In the middle of the southern continent was a great metropolis called the Light of Myriad Arrays of Jewel Trees, surrounded by ten thousand cities. On that continent, furthermore, the life span of the people was ten thousand years. The king in that metropolis was named Encompassing Sound of the Proclamation of All Laws, a sovereign ruler. The king had five hundred ministers, six thousand concubines, and seven hundred sons all of whom were brave and manly, well built and handsome, dignified and strong. The whole continent was under the protection of that king, and he had no enemies or opponents.

"At that time the end of the eon was approaching in that world; the five corruptions were in evidence, people had stopped acting virtuously and had taken to bad ways, most of them were headed for misery. Because of their wrongdoings their lives were short, they had scanty means of subsistence, they were ugly, they experienced little pleasure and much pain, they were in the habit of argument and dissent, they were given to foul and incoherent speech, they were overcome by acquisitiveness, they were corrupt in mind and thought, they were lost in the jungle of various views. As they were obsessed with unreasonable desires and dominated by unwholesome acquisitiveness, the rain that would cause the crops to grow did not fall in the proper season. For that reason, furthermore, with all the vegetation withered, the people suffered from various diseases and scattered to the eight directions, without resort. They all went to the capital city Light of Myriad Arrays of Jewel Trees, surrounded it, and with various gestures of supplication raised a great outcry to the king—'We are oppressed, abandoned, tormented by hunger and thirst, dismayed and distressed, without any savior, without refuge or resort, in a cage of suffering; our livelihood is threatened, and we are on the brink of death.' The people in the city who were suffering from hunger and thirst, who were naked and homeless, who were in misery, despondent, and depressed, also were sick and tired of suffering. They betook themselves to the king as a man of great knowledge and a protector, thinking they had found a source of comfort, happiness, and livelihood, a guide to the way out, a great ship, an island of jewels of knowledge, a great benefit, thinking they had found all the delights of heaven.

"The king, hearing their outcry, was filled with countless tens of hundreds of thousands of facets of great compassion. Meditating on the principle of great compassion, in a moment he became single-minded and uttered ten statements of great compassion: 'Alas, these people, without support, have fallen into the great pitfall of the mundane whirl—how can I be a refuge for them, leading them to the state of repose of the enlightened? Alas, these people have no savior and are oppressed by all kinds of afflictions—how can I become their savior, leading them to impeccable behavior? Alas, these people have no refuge in the world and are terrorized by old age and death—how can I become a refuge for them, removing all their fears of life and death? Alas, these people have no resort and are oppressed by various kinds of worldly distress—how can I become a resort for them, leading them to ultimate safety on the path of omniscience? Alas, everyone is in the darkness of ignorance, shrouded in the darkness of uncertainty and doubt—how can I become a light, dispelling the darkness of ignorance for them? Alas, these people are without illumination—how can I spread the light of great knowledge, showing them all the way into unobscured knowledge? Alas, the world of these people lacks the light of knowledge, and their minds are polluted by envy, jealousy, guile, and deceit—how can I produce the light of supreme knowledge, leading them all to cultivate purity? Alas, the world is without a guide and has plunged into a dangerous current in the ocean of the mundane whirl—how can I become a guide, to show them what to do? Alas, everyone lacks a teacher, all are misguided—how can I become a teacher for everyone, with the proper timing commanded by a buddha to guide people to complete maturity in all qualities? Alas, everyone lacks a leader, all are as though blind—how can I become a leader, to lead everyone on the way to unobstructed omniscience?'

"Having made these expressions of compassion, the king announced that he would undertake a great sacrifice, that he would satisfy everyone, giving them whatever they needed. With that the storehouses in every city and town on the continent were opened and all kinds of goods were placed on the streets, all the necessities of life were set out, all treasuries were opened, all stores of valuables were displayed; and the king projected a likeness of himself to every house to fulfill their wishes.

"Having arranged this act of giving things away, he had a great place of sacrifice prepared east of the city, in front of the city gate called Jewel Mountain Light. That place was equal in length and width, covering a most extensive area. It was level and clean, without potholes, clear of brambles, dust, and gravel. It was made of all precious elements, and the surface was spread with jewels. It was adorned with many arrays of jewels and strewn with flowers of various jewels. There was an abundance of all the finest aromatic powders, and it was perfumed with all kinds of scents. There were lamps giving off jewel lights, and the sky was covered with radiant clouds of incense. The place was adorned with orderly rows of trees of all kinds of jewels as well as various mansions, palaces, and towers. Overhead were parasols, banners, and pennants, flashing with trailing strings of various jewels. It was covered with nets of various jewel flowers, encircled with parasols made of webs of fragrant jewels. Jewel bells on nets of gold rang. It was shaded by canopies shining with various jewels, spread with aromatic powders of all the finest fragrances, and beautifully strewn with flowers made of all kinds of jewels, while pleasant music sounded from innumerable instruments. It was purified with arrays of various ornaments of all kinds of jewels, produced as a result of the deeds of enlightening beings.

"In the middle was a great lion throne, standing on a surface made of a variegated collection of ten kinds of jewels, surrounded by shining railings made of ten kinds of jewels, beautified with trees of ten kinds of jewels arrayed evenly between the railings, its feet firmly set on unbreakable diamond. The throne was set with jewel figurines and was adorned with hundreds of jewel protuberances. It was embellished with variegated arrays of jewels, jewel banners and streamers were raised all around it, and it was covered with nets of jewel bells, nets of celestial jewels, and nets of jewel flowers. It gave off clouds of fragrance and was arrayed with many-colored cloths of pleasant texture, finer than those of the heavens. Sweet music and song were heard all around. There were stairs of various jewels, arrayed with banners and railings, and shining jewel statues depicting various spiritual transfigurations. Here the king sat, handsome, serene, endowed with the pure marks of a great man, strong, robust, good, kind, and virtuous in all ways, endowed with all the best qualities, born of a line of great rulers, in command of all goods, pure in control of the law, master of his own mind, eloquent, endowed with unshakable knowledge, correctly applying well-constructed laws, showing endless virtues.

"Furthermore, as the king sat there, in the sky above him there appeared a great parasol, on a long, brilliant jewel pole, its hundred thousand ribs made of all kinds of jewels, brilliantly adorned with blazing lights, covered with lustrous gold, arrayed with nets of jewels, hung with bells of gold and jewels on strings of jewels, adorned with garlands of jewels twirling all around, producing sweet heavenly sounds, the ringing of the bells urging all beings to act virtuously. The king, moreover, fanned with jewel wisp fans, shone with a splendor surpassing that of the king of gods. As soon as the king sat on this throne, all the people stood before him with their palms joined and paid their respects.

"Then, seeing the assembly of countless petitioners, with various needs and desires, from various places, speaking various languages, all looking up to the king as the pole of prosperity, each thinking of him as a man of great knowledge, looking up to him as a great man of goodness and charity, considering him to have undertaken the vows of enlightening beings, the king felt as if he were seeing good friends and was flooded with immense compassion. There arose in him the dauntless energy to satisfy all petitioners forever and the all-pervasive will to give to everyone impartially.

"Furthermore, when the king saw all those petitioners, he became happier than if he had acquired rule over the galaxy for boundless eons, more than if he had acquired the throne of lordship over the gods for countless eons. His joy upon seeing those petitioners was as that of someone in the wilderness, long separated from family and friends, upon being united with them. His mind was filled with happiness, he was uplifted with joy and flooded with delight. The power of his faith in the enlightenment of buddhas increased, his budding faith in omniscience grew, the power of his purity of determination for all the qualities of buddhahood swelled, his faculties as an enlightening being became fit for use, he was flooded with a feeling of contentment and well-being, and by the force of great joy his senses and will as a benefactor became flexible. Why? Because the king, who was intent on omniscience, had betaken himself to the nature of omniscience, stood before the door to the path of omniscience, had engaged his attention on the satisfaction of all living beings, was on the verge of entry into the ocean of all enlightened virtues, was intent on shattering the mountains of obstructions caused by demons, actions, and afflictions, was absorbed in properly taking up the instructions of all buddhas, was endeavoring to embody all roots of goodness, was free from all attachments, was unattached to any objects in the world, and realized that all things are in essence like space, thought of all those petitioners as like an only son, as like his parents, as worthy of gifts, as spiritual benefactors, as precious, as doers of what is difficult, as useful in many ways, as supreme benefactors, as supporting the path of enlightenment, as guides and teachers.

"The king then fulfilled the needs and wishes of all the petitioners with unmitigated kindness, without turning his back on anyone, giving impartially to everyone, according to their needs. He gave away whatever he had to whoever required it, impartial toward all living beings.

"At that time, in that gathering at the sacrificial ground, there was a grandee's daughter, named Jewel Light, with a retinue of sixty girls. She was beautiful, with a clear, healthy complexion, dark hair and eyes, a pleasant scent, and a clear voice. She was well dressed and wore fine ornaments. She was alert and intelligent, modest, stable, and well behaved. She was respectful to the worthy, most circumspect and clear-headed in conduct, profound in action, endowed with wisdom. She had already accomplished basic skills involved in grasping, practicing, and realizing enlightening teachings, and she had attained clarity and serenity through the teachings. Her intentions were pure and good, and she was dedicated to the welfare of others. She was aiming for the vision of Buddha and was seeking omniscient knowledge. She stood near the king's throne in an attitude of respect, but she did not take anything from among the goods the king was distributing. Just standing there, she thought, 'I have gained a true boon in getting to see such a spiritual friend as this.' Thinking of the king as a spiritual friend, a sympathizer, a protector, and an enlightened one, with a mind free from deceit or guile, flooded with supreme joy and happiness, she took off her jewelry and tossed it before the king, so that it lay on the ground between the railings around the throne. Having scattered her jewelry, she made these vows: 'Just as the king Encompassing Sound of the Proclamation of All Laws is a refuge for leaderless people in the dark, so may I also become one such in the future. The reality he knows, may I also know. By the means through which he attains emancipation, may I also be emancipated. The path he practices, may I also practice. Just as he is fair to behold, has endless wealth and assistants, and is invulnerable and invincible, may I also become like this. Wherever he is born, may I also be born.'

"Perceiving her involved in such thoughts, the king looked at her and said, 'Take what you need. I am giving away all I have to satisfy everyone.' Made this offer by the king, she gained even more faith; with a serene mind, energized by lofty, far-reaching virtue, she spoke these verses to the king:

> Before you were here in this city, great king,
> It was joyless, lifeless, horrible as the realm of ghosts.

> People were murderous, thieving, unrestrained,
> Deceitful, harsh, and foul in speech.

> They were covetous, malicious, and opinionated;
> By their wrongdoing they fell into states of woe.

> Because of the ills of the views of these unjust, ignorant people,
> For many years there was no rain.

Because of drought the seeds died, crops and trees did not grow:
Lakes and streams dried up, plants and forests withered.

The rivers all went dry, the parks were like deserts;
Before you appeared, clear-eyed, the earth was strewn with bleached
    bones.

Now you have joined with the needy, and all are satisfied—
Coming forth, you shower gifts on the four quarters, fulfilling all, low
    and high.

There are no more thieves, mercenaries, or frauds—no one is killed
    or injured;
None go hopelessly to death, the world is leaderless no more.

People who like to kill used to drink the blood of their victims—
Those who used to eat each other's flesh have become kindly due to
    your charities.

People used to wear rags and leaves,
And were hungry and homeless.

With you here, the grains grow by themselves and the trees give forth
    their bounty;
Wise women and men appear too, now that you have been born,
    leader of the world.

Those who were formerly all on wrong paths
Are now well adorned and dressed, sporting like gods in paradise.

Men were wrongly obsessed with desires, delighting in unruly passion,
Given to raping women and girls in their own care and the care of others.

Now, though others' wives be like goddesses, well dressed, adorned,
    and perfumed,
When men see them they are satisfied with their own wives, as in the
    heaven of content.

People used to be deceitful, cruel, coarse, and dishonest in speech;
Having given this up, now they act justly, freed from wrong views.

No music or celestial song, nor even the voice of Brahma or the sing-
    ing of birds
Can match your voice, O leader.

Above you stands a jewel parasol with webs of gold,
On a jewel cane, radiant, with nets of jewelry all around.

The notes of its bells surpass all sounds in the world:
Like the tones of Buddha's voice, they intone the tranquil sound of truth.

Those in all lands who hear this put an end to afflictions,
Hearing the names of the buddhas over the ages and the oceans of
the wise.

By your power the bells bespeak the successive lands since the past,
The names of the lands, and the cycles of true teaching everywhere.

The sound of the bells, liquid, free-flowing, rings throughout the
continent,
Telling of the manners of action of the gods and the lords of the worlds.

Hearing the bells tell of the accumulations of their deeds, gods and people
Give up evil, practice good, and rely on the enlightenment of the buddhas.

Your father was Starlight, the king, your mother queen Lotus Light;
You were born in a corrupt age and acquired the rulership.

There was a large park, arrayed with flowers and precious lamps,
Adorned with five hundred lotus ponds, and surrounded with hundreds of trees.

On the bank of each pond was a villa, with a thousand pillars,
Resplendent with a thousand balustrades, with radiant nets and crescents all around.

When it had not rained for years, with lawlessness prevailing everywhere,
The water in the ponds evaporated and the trees withered.

Seven nights before your birth there were innumerable wonders,
Convincing all who saw them that a savior was surely to be born.

In the middle of the night the earth quaked,
And a light like the sun appeared in the pond called Impeccable.

Thereupon the five hundred ponds were filled with pure water,
The trees flourished, and flowers and fruits were filled with life.

The ponds, filled with water, refreshed the whole grove;
By the streams flowing from them the whole continent was replen-
ished with moisture.

The herbs, crops, and greenery growing, the trees flowered and
   fruited;
All the seeds in the earth sprouted, moistened by the water.

Every place on earth was equally watered then,
And all places low and high became level.

Ravines and rugged terrain then became instantly level;
Brambles, gravel, and the like disappeared, replaced by beautiful jewels.

All the people exulted, like the thirsty drinking water,
And celebrated this park, saying, "By whose power is this felicity?"

Then the king Starlight, with his wife, son, and ministers,
Surrounded by millions of people, went to enjoy the park.

In the middle was the pond Impeccable, filled with fragrant water;
There the king stood, up in its villa, a temple of truth.

It had been seven nights since the water had appeared;
Again the whole earth trembled, with all its mountains and abodes.

In the middle of the pond a thousand-petaled lotus appeared,
Shining like a thousand suns, suffusing the peak of the polar mountain
   with light.

Its stem was diamond, its calyx the essence of beauty, its clean
   broad leaves
Diamond, its pericarp of finest gold, its filaments radiant, with
   superb fragrance.

On that pericarp the Guide was born, sitting up straight, cross-legged;
You shone, your body resplendent with the marks of greatness,
   attended by celestial beings.

Descending from the temple, the king took you in his arms, delighted,
And handed you to the queen, saying "This is your son—be of
   good cheer."

Millions of hidden treasuries appeared, the trees of plenty released
Their goods, and the air was filled with music as you were born, leader
   of the world.

All those living on the continent looked up to you, trusting—
Respectfully they said, "This is the leader of the leaderless."

The light emanating from your body illumined the whole earth;
Dispelling the darkness of the world, it put an end to all ailments.

All malevolent creatures, the venomous and harmful,
Became inactive then.

Frustration, censure, ill-fame, pain, misfortunes, illness, accidents—
These all ended, fortune came, and everyone became joyful.

Everyone loved one another, and all became kind;
Free from animosity, nonviolent, they set out on the path of knowledge.

The righteous king shut off the evil ways, opened the way to heaven,
And showed the way to omniscience—you have done a great service to
the world.

We benefit further from seeing you, oceanic giver; after long absence,
A leader of the helpless is born in the world—you are a rare guide.

"Having thus eulogized the king, the girl Jewel Light then paid her
respects to him and stood there reverently. Looking at her, the king said,
'Rare are those who appreciate the virtues of others. For the ignorant, the
ungrateful, the undiscerning, the agitated, the disturbed, the muddled
thinkers, the deranged, the backsliders, those who do not realize the excellence of others' virtues, it is impossible to comprehend or even conceive of
the virtues of the enlightened, or to realize the excellence of knowledge of
all virtues. Without a doubt you have set out for enlightenment, since you
have understood such virtues of enlightening beings. Our efforts for the care
of beings have not been fruitless, as you, endowed with such knowledge,
have appeared in our kingdom, by virtue of the higher knowledge of superior people.'

"Then with his own hand the king gave her a priceless robe, radiant with
sparkling jewels, and also gave a precious robe to each of her companions.
He said, 'Take this and put it on.' Jewel Light then knelt on the ground,
picked up the robe in both hands, lifted it to her head, and put it on. Her
companions likewise each put on their robes. Having put on the robes, the
girl and her companions circled the king in respect, with the reflections of
all the stars glittering in their robes. Seeing this, the people said, 'You are
beautiful, young lady, with your companions, adorned with stars like a night
goddess; surrounded by them, you sparkle most brightly.'"

Then the night goddess Sarvavrikshapraphullanasukhasamvasa said to
Sudhana, "You should realize that it was none other than the buddha
Vairocana, who at that time was the king Encompassing Sound of the Proclamation of All Laws, and the queen Lotus Light, wife of the king Starlight
and mother of the king Encompassing Sound of the Proclamation of All
Laws, was none other than Queen Maya; Maya was the queen Lotus Light at
that time, by whom the spontaneously born child was carried at the hip. And

the king father, the elder king Starlight, was none other than King Shuddhodana. And you may think the girl Jewel Light of that time was someone else, but you should realize that she was none other than I—I myself was that girl Jewel Light in that time. As for the people of that time who were taken care of by the king Encompassing Sound of the Proclamation of All Laws by means of generosity, kindness, charitable works, and sympathy, you might think they were other people, but you should not see it that way—they are now the enlightening beings gathered here in the audience of the Buddha, standing on the ground of enlightening beings, irreversibly determined to reach supreme perfect enlightenment, some in the first stage, some in the second, some in the third, some in the fourth, some in the fifth, some in the sixth, some in the seventh, some in the eighth, some in the ninth, some in the tenth stage, who have attained by various different vows, various approaches to omniscience, various preparations, various accomplishments, various ways of emancipation, various purifications of manifestations of the path, various mystic powers, and various manifestations of the path, and, by various states of liberation, abide in various spiritual abodes in this assembly."

Then the night goddess spoke these verses to Sudhana, further revealing the enlightening liberation of manifestation of satisfaction by treasure produced from great joy:

> Broad is my vision, with which I observe everywhere, vast oceans
> Of lands of many kings, and oceans of beings in a whirl.

> In all lands buddhas sit at enlightenment trees, dispassionate,
> Pervading everywhere by mystic powers and always teaching and
>   guiding beings.

> My hearing is perfectly clear, and I hear all sounds thereby;
> I hear all the teachings of the buddhas and am extremely joyful.

> My knowledge, nondualistic, unhindered, penetrates the spheres of
>   others' minds;
> The vast ocean of minds of the world I comprehend in an instant.

> I remember the past by the power of recollection and concentration,
> Know oceans of eons, the many hundreds of oceans of lives of myself
>   and others.

> I know in an instant as many eons as atoms in an ocean of lands,
> The beings transmigrating, the buddhas and their projections.

> I also remember the initial vow of the buddhas, and those who attained,
> Having accomplished their practice, by many means appropriate to
>   their undertaking.

The attainments to the stage of coronation of the oceans of lofty
   virtue,
And their many ways of awakening, I comprehend in an instant.

I know the methods by which they taught in the world, their measureless virtues
In nirvana, and how long their teachings remained.

The pure principles of their myriad vehicles and extensive guidance
   of beings
Shown in the world, I know in particular, in countless various ways.

This way of liberation, witnessing the wealth of satisfaction produced
   from the treasury of joy,
I have cultivated over many hundreds of eons, and you too should
   enter this way.

I know only this enlightening liberation of manifestation of satisfaction
by treasure produced from great joy. How can I know the practice or tell of
the virtues of the enlightening beings in the presence of all buddhas who
have plunged into the ocean of commitment to omniscience, who have fulfilled the vow to accomplish the myriad past vows of all buddhas, who have
the mighty knowledge to enter all stages of enlightening upon entering one
stage of enlightening, who have purified the practice of the vow to comprehend all practices of enlightening beings in one practice, who are masters of
the state of comprehension of the whole ocean of all enlightening liberations in each enlightening liberation?

"In this same enlightenment site there is a night goddess named
Sarvajagadrakshapranidhanaviryaprabha, in the presence of the Buddha; go
ask her how an enlightening being is to develop sentient beings to supreme
perfect enlightenment, purify all buddha-lands, serve all buddhas, and practice all buddhas' teachings."

Then Sudhana paid his respects to the night goddess Sarvavrikshapraphullanasukhasamvasa and went on.

Sarvajagadrakshapranidhanaviryaprabha

Then Sudhana went to the night goddess Sarvajagadrakshapranidhanaviryaprabha and saw her sitting, in that same assembly, on a seat
of jewels reflecting the abodes of all beings; her body was covered with a net
of jewels reflecting the principles of the cosmos. Her body showed reflections of all moons, suns, stars, and planets; she appeared to sentient beings
according to their mentalities, she manifested her own body in forms like
those of all beings; her body manifested infinitely various appearances; her
body manifested the principles of the states of all modes of bearing; her body
appeared to be present everywhere; her body appeared to sentient beings

everywhere to mature them; her body appeared to all beings, pervading everywhere with various projections proclaiming the truth; her body descended from the sky to meet the needs of beings at all times; her body was bowing at the feet of all buddhas; her body was leading all sentient beings in accumulating roots of goodness; her body was facing all buddhas, receiving their teachings and remembering them, heedfully minding and retaining them in fulfillment of her vows; her body was filling all directions with infinite various manifestations; her body was radiating the light of the lamp of truth dispelling darkness for all beings; her body showed the embodiment of pure knowledge of the illusoriness of things; her body showed the embodiment of spirituality free from ignorance and passion; her body was born of the magical nature of reality; her mind was aware of the nature of reality; she was illumined with the light of impartial knowledge; her mind and body were ultimately free from irritation and inflammation; she had come from the indestructible realm of the body of reality; her body was a pure embodiment of the nature of things, inherently undefiled, naturally unafflicted, empowered by the realization of Thusness, not fixed or dependent. Sudhana, seeing her, bowed his head; remembering as many ways of seeing her as atoms in a buddha-land, he prostrated himself on the ground for a long time.

Finally rising from the ground, in a reverential attitude Sudhana gazed at the body of the night goddess, and as he did so he attained ten purities of thought, whereby he gained communality with all spiritual friends. What were those ten? He thought of spiritual friends as his own mind, to associate with them in all situations in the effort to attain omniscience. He thought of them as the pure essence of the development of his own actions, to accomplish the attainment of extensive roots of goodness to please spiritual friends. He thought of them as adorning the practice of enlightening beings, to associate with them in carrying out adornment by all spiritual vows. He thought of them as bringing him to all aspects of buddhahood, to practice the paths taught by all spiritual friends. He thought of them as the state of comfort, to manifest the abode of the supreme state of the realm of all buddhas. He thought of them as the one way of emancipation, to purify the practice of the commitment of emancipation by the vehicle of universal good. He thought of them as oceans of virtues of omniscience, to increase the production of all good qualities. He thought of them as fulfilling, increasing, and preserving all consummate good, to increase the force of energetic effort for total knowledge of complete enlightenment. He thought of them as fulfilling all roots of goodness, to fulfill the aspirations of all beings. He thought of spiritual friends as fulfillers of all aims, to establish the mastery of all acts of enlightening beings. He attained these ten purities of thought, whereby he attained communality with the night goddess and enlightening beings as numerous as atoms in a buddha-land.

That is, he attained communality of recollection, in remembering all buddhas of all times and places; communality of intellect, in unconfused ascertainment of the principles of the ocean of all truths; communality of course, in familiarity with the principles of clear distinction following the courses of the teachings of all buddhas; communality of enlightenment, so as to realize the ocean of all principles of all times by spacelike awareness; communality of purity of faculties, so as to realize the knowledge of the ocean of faculties of all enlightening beings; communality of mental purity, so as to accomplish the path of adornment achieving the virtues of the path of enlightening beings adorned by the protection and care of living beings in all ways; communality of sphere, so as to attain the scope of the sphere of knowledge of those who have arrived at Thusness; communality of following principles, so as to gain the light of the path of entry into the ocean of principles of complete omniscience; communality of comprehension of meaning, so as to attain comprehension of knowledge of the nature of all things; communality of spiritual abode, so as to shatter the mountains of all obstructions; communality of purity of the physical body, so as to attain physical purity resplendent with the marks and embellishments of greatness, appearing to sentient beings variously according to their dispositions; communality of power, so as to increase focus on omniscience in which all powers of enlightening beings are consummated; communality in expertise in all spiritual methods, so as to make the mind clear as space; communality of energy, so as to be capable of tireless perseverance in enlightening practices through all ages; communality of eloquence, so as to illumine unobstructed knowledge of all things; communality of insuperability, so as to purify the body beyond all worldlings; communality of noble-minded, nondepressive, intrepid speech, for purity of good relations with all groups; communality of voice, for enunciation of all truths; communality of purity of articulation, in respect to the myriad principles of conventions of expression of the languages of all beings; communality of purity of virtue, in respect to purities of accomplishment of virtues taught by the buddhas; communality of harmonizing with the tradition of principles and actions of buddhas, for purity of consequences of blameless action; communality of devotion to truth, so as to turn the wheels of teaching of all buddhas who appear in the world; communality of religious practice, so as to dwell in the knowledge of the realm of all buddhas; communality of great kindness, so as to pervade the ocean of all beings in every moment with the various aspects of kindness; communality of entry into the ocean of great compassion, so as to rain teachings for the salvation of all beings; communality of physical action, for equality in application of means to perfect all beings; communality of purity in verbal action, in respect to seeking modes of expression of all truths; communality of mental action, for production of focus on omniscience in the minds of all beings; communality of adornment of all kinds, to approach all buddhas in all buddha-lands; communality of visitation of all buddhas appearing in the world; communality of seeking the teachings of all buddhas; communality of service, to serve all buddhas at all times; communality of leading beings to full development, in all realms of beings; communality of attainment of illumination of all methods of teaching sentient beings; communality of attainment of concentration, in all methods of concentration; communality of universal pervasion, so as to pervade all buddha-lands with projections of practices of enlightening beings; communality of states of enlightening beings, in the oceans of means of miracles of all enlightening beings; communality of associates, associating with all enlightening beings in practice; communality of entry, entering the most suitable aspects of all worlds; communality of mental distinction of the extent of all buddha-lands; communality of differences in approach, according to differences in entering the ocean of all buddha-lands; communality of thorough penetration of the entire range of reason, in representations of endless knowledge of differentiations of all buddha-lands; communality of emergence in all buddha-lands; communality of nonregression, never to regress in penetrating and comprehending all realms; communality of dispelling darkness, so as to illumine the sphere of knowledge of all buddhas awakening at the site of enlightenment; communality of arrival in the oceans of audiences of all buddhas; communality of pervasion of the network of all buddha-lands, in efforts to serve the buddhas in untold buddha-lands; communality of direct knowledge of the connections of all principles of the Teachings; communality of application, in undertaking all the principles of the Teaching in order; communality of seeking, to purify intensive seeking for truth; communality of purity, in accumulating the adornments of enlightened virtues of physical, verbal, and mental action; communality of goodness of mind, to purify the sphere of knowledge of all things and the sphere of mind without evil thoughts; communality of vigor, in efforts to fulfill the undertaking of collection of all roots of goodness; communality of arrays of practices, in accomplishments of all enlightening practices; communality of unhindered state, in understanding the characteristics of all things; communality of skill in means, in mystical displays of the knowledge of each spiritual state; communality of purification of senses, in assumptions of suitable appearances according to the mentalities of sentient beings; communality of attainment of the concentration methods of enlightening beings, in cultivation of all enlightening teachings; communality of base, in the abodes of all buddhas; communality of accession to the stages of enlightenment, in attainments of all stages of buddhas and enlightening beings; communality of standpoint, in all states of enlightening beings; communality of instruction, in receiving the instructions of all buddhas; communality of concentration, entering the ocean of all concentrations at once; communality of differentiation of concentrations, in the context of various buddha-works; communality of mindfulness, of all points to remember; communality of conduct of enlightening beings, continuing to perform the tasks of enlightening beings through all times; communality of pure faith, to expand the ocean of energy of joy of devotion to infinite enlightened knowledge; communality of destruction of all obstructions to enlightenment; communality of nonregressing knowledge, to produce endless stores of enlightened knowledge; communality of emergence at appropriate times to guide all sentient beings to full development; communality of abode on the ways to omniscience; communality of sphere, entering the sphere of the majesty of the design of the cosmos; communality of independence, so as to be mentally free of all dependence; communality of teaching of all truths, realizing knowledge of the equality of all things; communality of exertion, so as to embody the power of all buddhas; communality of higher knowledge of means of accomplishing communication with all beings; communality of attainment of uncontrived mystic powers, entering the oceans of lands in all directions; communality of the stage of mental command, so as to gain the illumination of the ocean of all concentration spells; communality of penetration of the secrets of all the buddhas' teachings in the doctrines of all the scriptures; communality of entry into profundity, in realizations of the principle of all things being like space; communality of range, coursing through all worlds; communality of splendor, appearing to beings according to their mentalities; communality of shaking, showing beings changes in the basis of the world; communality of fruitful action, edifying all who see, hear, or remember them; communality of emancipation, so as to awaken to the knowledge of the ten powers, to fulfill all vows.

Thus did Sudhana, by attainment of ten purities of thought while gazing at the night goddess, gain communality with the night goddess in as many such ways as atoms in a buddha-land. Then, having seen the night goddess in as many ways as atoms in a buddha-land, having attained an infinite variety of purity of perception of spiritual friends and entered into as many aspects of communality with them as atoms in a buddha-land, Sudhana bared one shoulder, bowed to the goddess, and spoke these verses:

> As the power in my own mind, my will
> For enlightenment is firm and unbending;
> As in your mind, O goddess, so in mine
> This determination now spontaneously arises.
>
> All evils are cleared away,
> And resplendent good is developed:
> From witnessing your beauty
> Endless goodness is born in me.
>
> My mind is adorned with myriad virtues,
> Each to the benefit of living beings;
> Adorned thereby, I carry on practice
> In all lands for all time.
>
> You have taught me the consummation
> Of all the teachings to aid me:
> For my benefit, thinking to assist me,
> You present supreme spiritual instruction.
>
> You have blocked the path to woe and calamity

And shown the way to felicity;
You have also shown the way to omniscience,
Followed by all enlightened ones.

I think of you as a vehicle
Of emancipation, incomparable, rare;
Like space, undefiled, infinite,
Pure is the door to omniscience.

I think of you as a pure,
Immeasurable mine of omniscience;
Oceans of virtues, vast as the sky,
Arise in my mind every moment.

Guide me by the transcendent ways
And nourish me with inconceivable virtues;
Fully developed by pure virtues, before long
I will gain the turban of omniscience.

I always think of spiritual friends
As fulfillers of the path of omniscience;
Therefore I think by serving them all,
Good can be quickly developed.

All advantages come from that,
And achievement of good qualities;
Having honored this infinite group,
I will tell the world of the path of all knowledge.

You are my mentor, of measureless virtue,
My guide on the way of omniscience;
Even in countless millions of eons
I could never thank you enough, O sage.

Having spoken these verses, Sudhana said to the night goddess, "You have shown me the sphere of this inconceivable enlightening liberation; tell me, what is this liberation called? How long ago did you set out for supreme perfect enlightenment? When will you realize supreme perfect enlightenment?"

The goddess replied, "This liberation is called 'made of roots of goodness fostering the development of all beings.' Imbued with this liberation, realizing the equality of the essence of all things, comprehending the nature of all things, going to refuge in the independent state, passing away from all worlds, comprehending the differentiations in forms of things yet realizing the nature of things is without difference, without variation or distinction in appearance, not blue, yellow, red, or white, I manifest different bodies, of many appearances—of varying appearance, of nonvarying, undifferentiated appearance, neither colored nor colorless, of many appearances, infinite appearances, pure appearance, appearing to emanate all sorts of supernal manifestations, appearing to be visible everywhere, appearing to be the same as all beings, transcendent appearance manifest to all beings, appearance of light reflected everywhere, nonoffensive appearance, appearance beautified with the marks and embellishments of greatness, appearance resplendent with impeccable behavior, appearance manifesting the exertion of great power, appearance of unapproachable profundity, appearance unsurpassed in all worlds, appearance varying from moment to moment, appearance manifesting multitudes of different forms, appearance of various physical forms, appearance manifesting infinite miraculous displays, appearance as an eloquent speaker, appearance of all beautiful forms, appearance adapted to development of all beings, appearance of consummate good manifest to those who are teachable according to their mentalities, appearance reflected everywhere without obstruction, pure, untainted, serene, radiant appearance, healthy, beautiful appearance of an indestructible body, appearance of cultivation of inconceivable spiritual methods, superlative appearance overwhelming all, appearance without darkness or obscurity, appearance dispelling all darkness, appearance imbued with all good qualities, appearance of an ocean of virtues of a great soul, appearance attained by honoring the worthy in the past, appearance of supreme vastness of a mind clear as the sky, appearance revealing an ocean of indestructible, inexhaustible virtues, appearance free from all worldly attachments, appearance freely pervading everywhere, appearance instantly manifesting a multitude of different appearances in untold myriads of realms, appearance increasing floods of great joy in all sentient beings, appearance to protect all beings, appearance emanating multitudes of manifestations of all virtues of buddhahood from every pore, appearance purifying the wills and aspirations of all sentient beings, appearance showing determination of the meanings of all spiritual teachings, appearance radiating a network of varicolored lights, appearance of pure light as vast as the sky, appearance contained in the light of the untainted essence of pure jewels, appearance reflecting the undefiled real nature of things, incomparable appearance, appearance reflecting the variety of the ocean of means of liberation, appearance of ubiquitous light, appearance manifest to the world according to the time without fragmentation, appearance originating in the realm of tranquillity and restraint, appearance quelling all afflictions, appearance revealing a field of blessing for all sentient beings, appearance producing calm by all means, appearance fruitfully manifest throughout the world, appearance revealing the exertion of great knowledge, appearance of an unobstructed all-pervasive body, appearance of a universally supreme body manifest in ways beneficial to all beings, appearance embodying an ocean of great love, appearance embodying a mountain of great virtue, appearance reflected in all states of being while independent of all worlds, appearance purifying the power of great knowledge, appearance coexisting with the memory of all worlds and beings, appearance of light of all jewels, appearance showing the matrix of the source of light, appearance corresponding to the faith of all beings, appearance actualizing expression of all knowledge, appearance with laughing eyes cheering the world, appearance of light of the finest arrays of all jewels, appearance without grasping yet not turning away from sentient beings, unfixed, uninvolved appearance, appearance manifesting mystical powers, appearance showing all kinds of miracles, appearance of revealing the roots of goodness of the enlightened, impeccable appearance arising from the ocean of principles of all realms of reality, appearance as reflections going to the assemblies of all buddhas, appearance perfecting all kinds of forms, appearance resulting from good action, appearance adapted to guide those to be taught, appearance that all beings never tire of seeing, appearance radiating multicolored lights, appearance showing the ocean of forms of past, present, and future, appearance radiating lights of all colors, inexpressible appearance, appearance showing a variety of meanings in halos of light, appearance transcending all worlds, appearance manifesting as many suns as atoms in untold buddha-lands in each pore, appearance magically producing multitudes of forms like the clear moon, appearance emanating multitudes of mountains of flowers of infinite colors, appearance emanating garlands of all kinds of adornments, appearance manifesting multitudes of lotuses of all jewels, appearance filling all universes with clouds of incense of all fragrances; in each moment of consciousness producing clouds of treasuries of all kinds of fragrant powders and pervading all universes in the ten directions, I show all this to sentient beings who can be guided by seeing, those who can be guided by hearing, those who can be guided by remembering, those who can be guided by production of emanations of teaching cycles, those who can be guided when the time is ripe, those who can be guided by seeing physical bodies, those who can be guided by service, those who can be guided by comprehension, those who can be guided by manifestation of various miraculous effects, those who can be guided by manifestation of inconceivable miraculous effects, by mastery of minds, by mastery of timing, by mastery of prevention of evil deeds, by mastery of promotion of good deeds, by mastery of accomplishment of past great vows, by mastery of momentum toward omniscience, by mastery of the means of attainment of the immense miracles of the liberations of enlightening beings, by mastery of the source of power of great compassion accomplishing the salvation of all beings, by mastery of the will producing purity of the ocean of great love, empowered by the enlightened.

"Thus, based on this enlightening liberation, fostering roots of goodness according to sentient beings' mentalities for their development, realizing the undifferentiated essence of reality, manifesting an infinite variety of physical forms, projecting visions of an infinite variety of multitudes of appearances from each body representing practices, radiating an infinite variety of multitudes of light beams from each appearance of action, showing reflections of buddha-lands, showing infinite buddhas emerging from each beam of light in each buddha-land, showing the infinite variety of projections of each buddha, I vivify past roots of goodness, develop new roots of goodness, increase existing roots of goodness, and enhance developed roots of goodness; and in each mental moment I establish infinite beings in the stage of nonregression, where they will not retreat, advancing toward supreme perfect enlightenment.

"Also, you ask how long ago I set out for supreme perfect enlightenment, and how many eons I have been carrying out enlightening practice. I will tell you this, too, by the power of Buddha.

"The sphere of knowledge of enlightening beings is not in the realm of thought, conception, or imagination. It cannot be known in terms of length or brevity of life, or in terms of defilement or purity of ages, or in terms of brevity or length of ages, or in terms of multitude or variety of ages, or in terms of variation or differentiation of ages. Why? Because the sphere of knowledge of enlightening beings is utterly pure in its essential nature, it is outside the net of all conceptions, it is beyond the mountains of all obstructions. It appears in the mind and sheds light on beings who can be guided, according to their mentalities, when the time is ripe for their development.

"It is like the sun: there is no reckoning of day and night on the sun, but when the sun has gone down that is known as the night, and when it has come up that is known as the day. In the same way, in the nonconceptual sphere of knowledge of enlightening beings there are no thoughts or conceptions of imaginations, or notions of cycle or duration or time frames: but when the will of enlightening beings arises, then by the light of the sphere of nonconceptual knowledge, and by mastery of timing in development of all sentient beings, conceptual calculations of ages, duration, and cycles are distinguished; in the sphere of nonconceptual knowledge, conceptual calculations of passage of time in past and future ages are distinguished.

"It is like the orb of the sun in the sky: it is perceived reflected in all jewel mountains, in all jewel trees, in all jewels, in all jewel treasuries, in all oceans, in all springs and streams, in all vessels of clear water, and in the minds of all beings; it appears to all beings, and is seen reflected in each particle of all the jewels—the sun does not originate in the jewel mountains, does not enter the jewel trees or particles, is not in the crystals, does not come to the jewel treasuries, does not enter the oceans, does not enter any bodies of water—yet it is seen within them all. In the same way a great enlightening being, leaving the ocean of existence, risen into the sky of the reality realm of the enlightened, dwelling in the realm of the sky of the essence of things, abiding in the sky of peace, is seen in all realms of existence in forms similar to all sentient beings, for the development and civilization of sentient beings: yet the enlightening being is not stained by the ills of the mundane whirl, is not burnt by the suffering of death and birth, does not live by concepts and imaginations, and has no notion of length or brevity of the age. Why? The enlightening being is ultimately beyond all errors of mistaken conceptions, thoughts, and views, sees with accurate knowledge of all worlds as dreamlike, realizes all worlds are like magic, has attained knowledge of the realm devoid of beings, sees things as they are, and yet by control of great vows of the sphere of vast compassion appears to all sentient beings to guide them to perfection.

"Just as a boatman is always at work on the rivers to ferry people over, never ceasing, all his life never dwelling on the near shore or on the farther shore, and not remaining in midstream either, in the same way the enlightening being undertakes to save sentient beings from the current of the mundane whirl by the power of the boat of the transcendent ways; the enlightening being does not fear the near shore, does not think of the farther shore as safety, and yet is always engaged in ferrying sentient beings over. Though the enlightening being enters the variety of ages by persisting in enlightening practice through all ages, beyond measure, yet the enlightening being does not carry on enlightening practice within notions of passage and length of ages.

"Just as space, extensive as the cosmos, is without discrimination whether worlds become, decay, or disappear, is by nature pure, undefiled, neither turning back nor tiring, not long or short, eternally supporting all lands, in the same way the space of the will and knowledge of the enlightening being, with the whirlwind of great vows, never tires in keeping sentient beings from falling into all states of misery, has no fear in leading them to the paths of felicity, is not exhausted in setting them on the ways to omniscience, does not follow afflictions, and is not stained by the ills of the mundane whirl.

"Just as a magically produced man has all his limbs and body parts but lacks ten physical elements—inhalation and exhalation, coolness and warmth, hunger and thirst, joy and sorrow, the pains of birth, old age, sickness, and death—in the same way, in the enlightening being whose form is born of the magic of knowledge, whose body is one with the cosmos, who appears in all states of existence to perfect sentient beings, who lives through all ages, ten things are not to be found: desire for the mundane world, rejection of life in the mundane, currying of enjoyment of objects, malevolence, desire for enjoyment, the burning of afflictions, experiences of painful feelings, fear of difficult situations, desire for existence, and attachment.

"I will tell you more, by the power of Buddha, to increase the power of vows of enlightening beings of the future.

"In the very remote past there was a world called Jewel Light. In that world was an age called Beautiful Light. In that age ten thousand buddhas appeared. The first of those buddhas was one called King Illumining Space with the Voice of Truth, who was one of those who has arrived at Thusness, perfectly enlightened, consummate in knowledge and action, arrived at felicity, supreme knower of the world, tamer of humans, teacher of humans and gods, a blessed buddha.

"That buddha appeared not far from a capital city called Array of Delights, in the middle of the four continents of the world. East of that city was a forest called Beautiful Light, in which there was an enlightenment site called Cloud of Jewel Flowers. At that site a lion throne in the calyx of a lotus of radiant jewels appeared, and this is where that buddha realized supreme perfect enlightenment.

"At that time the human life span was ten thousand years. Now, there being many who were set in evil ways—killing, stealing, raping, lying, foul and harsh in speaking, divisive, covetous, malicious, and deluded—the buddha sat at the site of enlightenment for a full thousand years and taught enlightening beings, world leaders, and people who had served past buddhas, in order to mature people's existing roots of good.

"At that time there was a king called Victorious Light in that capital city Array of Delights. He had thrown many hundreds of thousands of criminals and evildoers into prison to discipline them—thieves, killers, rapists, liars, abusive and violent people, troublemakers, greedy people, malicious people, people obsessed with aberrant ideas, people addicted to unlawful pleasures, people overcome by desire for ill-gotten gains, people involved in false cults, evildoers, people who had committed violence, people who had done no good, people who had neglected to come to the aid of those in danger and fear, people without respect for their parents or for mendicants, priests, and holy people.

"The king had a son named Conqueror, who had twenty-eight of the marks of a great man, and lived in the palace surrounded by many graceful women. He heard the frightful cries of those who were bound up in prison; agitated and upset by these cries, moved with compassion, he left the palace and went into the prison, where he saw those people cast into the dungeons, bound by all sorts of fetters and shackles, chained together and thrown into the darkness, shrouded in smoke, exposed to unhealthy drafts, emaciated, hungry and thirsty, naked and homeless, filthy and unkempt, being subjected to various tortures, screaming in pain.

"Seeing the prisoners, the prince was inspired with great compassion and an unprecedented determination to help others. He comforted the prisoners, intending to deliver them from their bonds. Giving them assurance, he went to the king and said, 'Know, O king, that I have given assurance to the people in prison. Please set them free.'

"The king called his five hundred ministers together and asked them what they thought about this. They said, 'These people are plunderers of the royal treasuries, attackers of the king, arrested entering the royal palace; they should be executed. Furthermore, anyone who wants to save them is also guilty of crime against the king.'

"The prince, overwhelmed with great compassion, said to those ministers, 'Let it be as you say. Just release these convicts—I can endure all pains for their sake. Whatever you would do to them, do to me. To free them from bondage I will undergo all kinds of torture and give up my body and life. Why? If I cannot liberate these people from bondage, how can I liberate those who are bound to the world, who are tied up by the ropes of craving, who are in the abyss of ignorance, who are cast into the darkness of delusion, who suffer the pains of poverty, who have fallen into the depths of evil ways, who act senselessly, whose minds are confused, who see no way to emancipation, who are without illumination, who are attached to the world, who lack virtue and knowledge, who have lost their faculties of knowledge, whose minds are tainted with various afflictions, who are flung in the mud of suffering, who are under the control of demons, who are tormented by birth, old age, death, grief, lamentation, misery, depression, and sorrow?'

"Then the prince released all those prisoners from their bonds, by giving up himself, his whole retinue, and all his wealth. Freeing them, he removed all that was torturing them once and for all. At that point the five hundred ministers, up in arms, went to the king and said, 'Know that the law of the king has been broken by the will of the prince, and all of our lives are uncertain. If you do not punish the prince, your own life will not last long.'

"The king, enraged, set out to kill his son and those convicts as well. The queen, hearing of this, was very upset: her hair undone, her jewelry and makeup removed, she went to the king with a thousand of her ladies, beating her breast and throwing dust on her head, weeping and wailing; she said to him, 'Let the prince go free, let him live.' The king turned to the prince and said, 'Give up on these criminals. If you do not, you will die for their sake.'

"The prince, facing death, was not fazed, being focused on omniscience, dedicated to the welfare of others, guided by great compassion. The queen, his mother, asked the king to allow a fortnight for observation: 'Let the prince give people whatever they need for half a month; then do whatever you want with him.' The king agreed to this.

"North of the city there was a large park called Sunlight that had been made in the past as a sacrificial ground. The prince went there and gave to anyone who asked whatever they needed. Thus for half a month he freely gave away various goods—food, clothing, utensils, and so on—to whoever needed them.

"Then, on the last day of the fortnight, the whole population gathered—the king, his ministers, his women, the grandees, the landlords, the townspeople, and all the religious impostors. Now the buddha-king Illumining Space with the Voice of Truth, realizing it was an opportune time to teach people, went to that sacrificial ground, respectfully surrounded by celestial and spiritual beings. The crowd of people, and the prince, saw the buddha coming from afar, serene, pleasant to see, senses calm, mind quiet, self-controlled, master of his faculties, tranquil as an elephant, clear as a pool of water, purified, undefiled, miraculously radiating light by the great power of a buddha, overpowering with the mastery of a buddha, shining with the magnificence of a buddha, adorned with the marks and embellishments of a buddha, pervading all worlds with the light of his aura, illuminating them with rays of light, emanating orbs of fragrant jewel fire from every pore, causing all worlds to quake with the quaking of a buddha-land, destroying all beings' afflictions, coming forth as a buddha raining multitudes of all kinds of supernal manifestations, bearing himself as a buddha, increasing the flow of joy in all beings, conveying the power of the sight of a buddha. Seeing the buddha thus, everyone's mind became clear and serene.

"Then the prince and the people, going out to meet the buddha, their minds clear, prostrated themselves before the buddha, made offerings of many kinds, and said, 'Welcome, welcome, Blessed One; the Buddha has turned his attention to us, the Buddha has bestowed his favor on us.' Then the prince pointed out a seat of honor to the buddha and said, 'Please sit down, O Blessed One—this seat has been prepared.' Then, as the buddha approached, the gods of purity, by the power of the buddha, changed it into a calyx of a lotus of fragrant diamonds. The buddha sat on it, and enlightening beings sat on surrounding seats. As soon as they saw the buddha, everyone in the assembly was relieved of afflictions and obstruction and disturbance, and became fit vessels for the holy teachings.

"Then the buddha, knowing that those people had become capable of receiving the Teaching, gave them a systematic talk. He expounded to them a scripture called *Illumination of the Multitude of Causes*, including all elements of the Teaching, which he spoke in the languages of all people. At that, eighty million people in that crowd attained dispassionate, pure, objective vision of things. Many millions reached the stage beyond learning. Ten thousand were led to the Great Vehicle, introduced to the way of fulfillment of the great vows of universally good enlightening action. Thus as the buddha turned the wheel of teaching by the great miraculous power of buddhas, as many beings as atoms in a hundred thousand buddha-lands in the ten directions came to the guidance of the Great Vehicle. An infinite variety of beings in the interrelated buddha-lands in the worlds of the ten directions put an end to evil. Countless beings were established in the way to paradise. And as for the prince, he attained this enlightening liberation made of roots of goodness fostering the perfection of all beings according to their mentalities.

"Now then, you may think that the prince in that time, who gave up his body and life, his wealth and retinue, and all human pleasures, in order to liberate those people from bondage, was somebody else. Who was it who made that great sacrifice without reservations, who won the favor of the buddha of that time, who resolved to attain perfect enlightenment when he saw the buddha, who attained this enlightening liberation made of roots of goodness fostering the development of all beings according to their mentalities? It was none other than I myself who was that prince in that time. As that prince, overwhelmed by great compassion, set on the welfare of all beings, unattached to the things of the world, desiring only perfection, with no wish for glory, fame, or repute, not elevating myself, not degrading others, unattached to things, without any notion of existents, without desire for anything in the world, material or immaterial, indifferent to the pleasures of the world, attentive to the sphere of the enlightened, purely intent on enlightenment, having developed an indomitable will, benevolent toward all living beings, compassionately resolved to quell the suffering of all beings, intent on the power of the enlightened, purifying the path of enlightenment, preparing the paths of emancipation of the Great Vehicle, contemplating the path to omniscience, I did these difficult deeds. This is how long ago I attained this liberation.

"And who do you think those five hundred ministers were, who unjustly incited the king to execute me? They were none other than five hundred people whom Devadatta incited to kill the Buddha. The Buddha subsequently guided them and foretold their enlightenment, predicting that in the future, after as many eons as atoms in a polar mountain, in an age called Good Light, there would be five hundred buddhas, with buddha-lands of various qualities, born of various races, tribes, and families, showing various miracles at birth, undergoing various spiritual transmutations on leaving society, manifesting various lights at the tree of enlightenment, approaching the pinnacle of enlightenment in various ways, showing various ways of destroying demons, showing various miracles on attainment of enlightenment, articulating various terms for the principles of their teachings, expounding various scriptures, speaking various languages, surrounded by various audiences, emanating various auras of light, having various life spans, their teachings to remain for various lengths of time, their teachings variously circulating, and their names to be various, all embodiments of great compassion. The first buddha of the age to attain supreme enlightenment in the world Jewel Light would be one named Great Compassionate One, the second would be named Moon of Commitment to the Welfare of All Beings, the third would be Lion of Great Compassion, the fourth would be Desirous of the Welfare of All Beings, and the last one would be Supreme Healer.

"Who do you think those criminals of that time were, doomed to die, whom I released from bondage by sacrificing my life? They were none other than the buddhas of the present age, Virtue, beginning with Krakucchanda, and countless millions of other enlightening beings who were inspired to seek enlightenment by seeing the buddha Resolution Born of the Glory of the Proclamation of Endless Power, and are now carrying out enlightenment practice throughout the universe, and are cultivating and extending this enlightening liberation born of roots of goodness aiding the development of all beings according to their mentalities.

"Who do you think the Victorious Light of that time was? It was none other than the great debater Satyaka. And who do you think were the retinue and servants of the king, but the sixty thousand philosophers whom Satyaka brought to the buddha to debate and whom the buddha predicted would become enlightened and appear in the world as buddhas, with variously arrayed buddha-lands, in various ages, with various names.

"To continue, the prince, Conqueror, given permission by his parents, after having released the prisoners, gave up his great wealth and family and went to the buddha. For five thousand years thereafter he cultivated spiritual practice, during which time he perfected ten thousand concentration methods, attained ten thousand ways of mental command, entered into ten thousand channels of mystic knowledge, attained ten thousand great treasuries of enlightening beings, produced ten thousand currents of momentum toward omniscience, purified ten thousand facets of tolerance, carried out ten thousand contemplations, developed ten thousand bodies of power of enlightening beings, entered ten thousand doors of knowledge of enlightening beings, produced ten thousand ways to transcendent wisdom, became aware of ten thousand channels of conscious vision of thousands of buddhas, and accomplished ten thousand vows of enlightening beings. With these realizations, in each mental moment he went to ten thousand buddha-lands in the ten directions, and in each moment of thought remembered ten thousand buddhas past and future in each world; and he perceived ten thousand multitudes of emanations of those buddhas radiating throughout the ten directions. In each moment of thought he saw all the beings in ten thousand buddha-lands, passing away and coming to life in various states, undeveloped and developed, felicitous and miserable, of good and bad appearance, following their desires; and he understood the passing away and coming to life of those beings, as well as the revolving of their minds, the conduct of their minds, the continuity of their thoughts, the variety of their inclinations, the multitude of their faculties, the courses of their endeavors, their habits of action, and the proper timing to develop and guide them.

"Subsequently the prince passed away from there and was reborn in the same city Array of Delights, in the same royal family, and attained sovereign rulership. As the king, following the demise of the buddha-king Illumining Space with the Voice of Truth, he propitiated a buddha named Glorious King Risen in the Sky of Truth. After that, at that same enlightenment site, having become a chief god, he propitiated a buddha named Sanctuary of Celestial Rulers. After that, in the same world, having become a celestial chief of the heaven of timely portion, he propitiated a buddha named Fiery Energy of the Radiant Mountain of Mental Command. After that, having become a celestial chief of the heaven of satisfaction in the same world, he propitiated a buddha named King Proclaiming the Light of the Wheel of the Teaching. After that, having become a celestial chief of the heaven of good emanation in the same world, he propitiated a buddha named King Like the Moon in the Sky. After that, having become a celestial chief of the heaven of command of others' emanations in the same world, he propitiated a buddha named Paragon of Indestructible Power. After that, having become a chief Brahma god in the same world, he propitiated a buddha called Sound of Projections of the Wheel of Teaching Reflected Everywhere. Beginning with these, ten thousand buddhas emerged in the age Beautiful Light in the world Jewel Light, all of whom were propitiated by the prince Conqueror.

"Following that age Beautiful Light was an age called Subtle Light; in that age I was a king called Great Wisdom. As a king, I propitiated a buddha named Glorious Mountain of Marks of Greatness. Next, in the same age, as a householder I propitiated a Buddha named Restrained in Body and Mind. Next, in the same age, as a government minister, I propitiated a buddha named Undefiled Child. Next, in the same age, as a titan chief, I propitiated a buddha named Holder of Energy. Next, in the same age, as a tree spirit, I propitiated a buddha named Polar Mountain of Marks of Greatness. Next, in the same age, as a caravan leader, I propitiated a buddha named Undefiled Arms. Next, in the same age, as a city spirit, I propitiated a buddha named

Walking Boldly As a Lion. Next, in the same age, as a god of riches, I propitiated a buddha named Crown of the Lord of Gods. Next, in the same age, as a celestial musician, I propitiated a buddha named Spiritual Renown. Next, in the same age, as a goblin chief, I propitiated a buddha named Crown of Light.

"In this way, I propitiated sixty million buddhas in the age of subtle light, beginning with these ten. I honored and served those buddhas in various forms of existence, and as I went to each buddha I matured countless beings for supreme perfect enlightenment. And as I went to each buddha I attained various concentrations, various mental commands, various accomplishments, various types of specialized knowledge, various perspectives on truth, various operations of knowledge, various perceptions of the totality of realms, various awarenesses of the totality of lands, various perceptions of the totality of visions of Buddha; all these I entered into, purified, enlarged, and devoted my attention to from start to finish.

"And just as I propitiated the buddhas in the age of Subtle Light, so did I propitiate all the buddhas who arose in as many eons as atoms in all oceans of worlds and came from other worlds and taught, and I listened to their teaching and remembered it. I have retained all their teachings, and from all of those buddhas I got this enlightening liberation born of roots of goodness aiding the development of all beings according to their mentalities, by various means of attainment and by various ways of liberation."

Then the night goddess spoke these verses to Sudhana elucidating this liberation:

> This supreme liberation is inconceivable;
> Resolute, you ask me about it.
> Listen as I tell you all,
> By the power of the Buddha.
>
> Endless, vast, inconceivable eons ago,
> Countless worlds away,
> There was a pleasant world
> Called Jewel Light.
>
> There was an age called Beautiful Light
> In which numberless buddhas emerged;
> I propitiated those supreme sages
> As I cultivated this liberation.
>
> There was a great and glorious metropolis there
> Called Array of Delights
> In which there lived both
> Pure-minded people and evildoers.
>
> The king there was Victorious Light,

Who ruled his people justly;
His son was called Conqueror,
A fine man with the marks of greatness.

Thousands of offenders had been
Condemned to death by the king;
Seeing them, the prince was seized with compassion
And asked the king to release them.

Hearing this, the king called his ministers
And told them all about it:
They all said, bowing to the king,
"He is out to destroy you."

Incited by the ministers, the king
Hastened to kill the prince.
Undismayed, indifferent to his own death,
The prince did not abandon the convicts.

Grieved to hear the prince was condemned,
The queen and the palace ladies asked the king
To free the prince for a fortnight
To give all kinds of gifts to the people.

Granted permission by the king, the prince
Made gifts of all that was asked for,
Day and night, for half a month,
Giving charity to all who came.

Whatever the needy required,
That he gave them, prepared for death;
The whole population of the city came out,
Lamenting the fate of the prince.

Then the buddha at the enlightenment tree,
Illumining Space with the Voice of Truth,
Realizing people's faculties were ripe,
Went to that sacrificial ground out of compassion.

Going there, the buddha
Produced a miraculous display
And expounded a scripture,
The voice of the Teaching as myriad lamps of truth.

Countless people were edified,
And the buddha foretold their enlightenment;

The prince Conqueror, enraptured,
Set out for supreme enlightenment.

The prince gave the buddha
Many offerings and joyfully said,
"May I become a guide, savior, refuge,
And resort for the people of the land."

He left home to join the buddha,
Seeking the path of perfect enlightenment;
He spent hundreds of eons
Thoroughly investigating the essence of things.

Pitying all the helpless ones
Fallen into the sea of suffering,
Having cultivated the path of enlightenment,
He attained this liberation.

All the buddhas in that age
He propitiated with pure faith;
He made great offerings to them
And kept their teachings in mind.

After that, for eons numerous
As atoms in oceans of lands,
He propitiated and made offerings to
All the buddhas that arose.

I was the prince Conqueror,
Who, seeing people imprisoned,
Gave up my body to free them
And thus attained this liberation.

I cultivated it for eons as many
As atoms in oceans of lands,
Expanding it moment by moment
Through endless incomparable means.

From all the buddhas I saw
I gained some realization
And was shown this liberation
By a succession of means.

From them I learned the inconceivable
Reality of liberation over countless eons,
Imbibing all at once the multitude of teachings

Projected by the buddhas when established therein.

Those established therein
Go everywhere without attachment,
Instantly comprehending the countless
Names and groups of past, present, and future.

They appear before all the multitudes
Of buddhas of all times,
Manifesting themselves in the presence
Of those buddhas as reflected images.

They go everywhere and appear
Before all the buddhas,
Showering all kinds of ornaments
As offerings to the buddhas.

Then they ask the myriads of buddhas
Multitudes of questions
And remember the infinite teachings
Poured forth by the buddhas.

They go to the circles of buddhas everywhere,
As far as they can see,
Sitting on seats of many forms,
Manifesting various miracles.

With bodies of infinite appearances,
They fill all realms, by the thousands;
They show an endless, endless variety of forms,
And all those forms in one.

From each pore they emanate countless
Multitudes of light rays
And extinguish the fire of afflictions
Of all beings by various means.

In this state, emanating myriad projected bodies
From each and every pore,
They pervade all realms with them
And guide beings with rain from the ocean of truth.

This way of enlightenment, with inconceivable forms,
Is the resort of all enlightening beings;
Based on this they carry out practices
In all lands for all time.

Expounding the Teaching according to mentalities,
They remove the web of views;
Dwelling in ultimate felicity,
They show people the stage of omniscience.

With inconceivably many bodies of endless forms
In all states of existence,
They teach according to mentality,
Their forms reflections of all beings.

So many and infinitely more,
As inconceivably many as atoms in all lands,
Are the oceans of manifestations of the fearless ones
When they have attained this peaceful liberation.

The goddess continued, "I know only this enlightening liberation born of roots of goodness fostering the development of all beings according to their mentalities. How can I know the practice, or comprehend the oceans of virtues, or completely know the power of knowledge, or know the realm of thought, or understand the mastery of concentration, or recognize the miracle of liberation, of the enlightening beings who have transcended all worldly courses, who appear as reflections in all states of being, who are intent on shattering the mountains of barriers to omniscience, who know the nature and characteristics of all things, who are engaged in dispelling the darkness of all barriers caused by afflictions, who are skilled in carrying out a thorough investigation of all things, who actually realize the knowledge of selflessness, who ceaselessly develop and guide all sentient beings, who really know the principle of the nondual reality realm, whose intellects encompass the ocean of all manners of verbal expression?

"In the Lumbini grove, here on Jambudvipa, there lives a goddess of the Lumbini grove named Sutejomandalaratishri. Go ask her how enlightening beings are born in the family of buddhas, how they become light-makers for the world, and how they carry on the practice of enlightening beings forever without wearying."

Then Sudhana paid his respects to the night goddess Sarvajagadrakshapranidhanaviryaprabha and left.

Sutejomandalaratishri

Remembering the instruction of the night goddess Sarvajagadrakshapranidhanaviryaprabha, cultivating and extending the enlightening liberation born of roots of goodness fostering the development of all beings according to their mentalities, Sudhana made his way to the Lumbini grove. When he got to the Lumbini grove he circled it, looking for the goddess Sutejomandalaratishri. Finally he saw her sitting on a jewel lotus calyx lion seat in a tower made of encircling branches of trees of all jewels in the

Lumbini grove, surrounded by twenty million billion wood goddesses, teaching them, expounding to them a scripture called Exposition of the Ocean of Lives of All Enlightening Beings, born in the family of buddhas, increasing the flood of the ocean of virtues of enlightening beings. Seeing the goddess, Sudhana went up to her, paid his respects, and said, "I have set my mind on supreme perfect enlightenment, but I do not know how enlightening beings get to be born in the family of buddhas, or how, carrying out the practice of enlightening beings, they become light-makers for sentient beings."

The goddess replied, "There are ten kinds of birth by which enlightening beings become born in the family of buddhas. Enlightening beings who have accomplished these develop correctly by means of the skills of enlightening beings, without stopping, without becoming exhausted, without regressing, without giving up, without wearying, without becoming discouraged, without becoming confused, without tarrying, without becoming afraid, without waning away. They follow the way to omniscience and remember the principle of the realm of reality; they become ripe for the enlightenment of buddhas and broaden the determination for enlightenment. They grow by means of all the transcendent ways, they withdraw from all worldly ways, and progress into the stage of those who realize Thusness. They refine mystic knowledge, become aware of all principles of enlightenment, and accord with the realm of omniscience. What are these ten kinds of birth of enlightening beings? The first is called the birth of enlightening beings as offspring of the undertaking of the vow to serve all buddhas. The second is the birth of enlightening beings as offspring of consummation of all elements of the determination for enlightenment. The third is the birth of enlightening beings as offspring of meditation on the principles of the Teaching. The fourth is the birth of enlightening beings as offspring of purification of the intent in viewing past, present, and future. The fifth is the birth of enlightening beings as offspring of the light of universal awareness. The sixth is the birth as enlightening beings as offspring of the family of all buddhas. The seventh is the birth of enlightening beings as offspring of the array of lights of the manifestation of powers of buddhas. The eighth is the birth of enlightening beings as offspring of consummation of contemplation of the way to omniscience. The ninth is the birth of enlightening beings as offspring of manifestation of emanations throughout the cosmos. The tenth is the birth of enlightening beings as offspring of momentum going into the stage of the enlightened.

"What is the first birth of enlightening beings, as offspring of the undertaking of the vow to serve all buddhas? Here the enlightening beings, honoring, respecting, serving, attending, and pleasing all buddhas just as when they first made offerings in service of a buddha, never tire of seeing the enlightened; their minds expanded by floods of joy from the buddhas they honor, they are flooded with well-being by the sight of buddhas. Gaining virtue with unwavering faith, tireless, they ceaselessly work to bring offerings to all buddhas. This is enlightening beings' first kind of birth, as offspring of the undertaking of the vow to serve all buddhas, which is conducive to the production and acquisition of roots of goodness in preparation for omniscience.

"What is enlightening beings' birth as offspring of consummation of all elements of the determination for enlightenment? Here enlightening beings arouse the will for supreme perfect enlightenment: that involves the will of great compassion to save all beings; the will to please all buddhas ultimately; the will to seek all ways of enlightenment, to be equanimous toward all things; the will for the greatest of undertakings, to head for omniscience; the will of great kindness, to treat all beings with care; the will not to abandon any beings, to be firmly equipped for omniscience; the will to avoid deceit and falsehood, to attain the light of truthful knowledge; the will to act in accord with one's speech, to carry out the path of enlightening beings; the will not to disappoint the buddhas, to keep the vows of all buddhas; the will for the great undertaking of omniscience, to ceaselessly guide and perfect all beings that will ever be. When enlightening beings have fulfilled as many such elements of the determination for enlightenment as atoms in a buddha-land, then they are born in the family of buddhas.

"What is enlightening beings' birth as offspring of meditation on the principles of the Teaching? Here the enlightening beings' minds are turned to meditation according all the principles of the teaching, dedicated to fulfilling all aspects of the path of omniscience, intent on practicing impeccable actions, bent on purification of the ocean of all concentration methods of enlightening beings, determined to practice and perfect all qualities of enlightening beings, intent on accomplishing all elements of the path of enlightening beings, energetically striving for omniscience, like the fire that burns ceaselessly through an eon of destruction, determined to accomplish the infinite variety of practices of enlightening beings aimed at guiding all sentient beings to perfection; in terms of all practical techniques and accomplishments of perfect qualities of enlightening beings they enter into the means of realization of all methods of cultivation and meditation.

"What is enlightening beings' birth as offspring of purification of the intent in viewing past, present, and future? Here enlightening beings become pure in the element of intent; they come into the range of the enlightenment of buddhas; they enter the ocean of methods of enlightening beings; their minds are firm, governed by an intent as strong as steel; they are aloof from all forms of existence; they are attentive to the accomplishments of miracles of all buddhas; they gain higher direction so as to increase the keenness of awakening faculties; they become noble-minded, so that their will becomes clear; they become unshakable, so that they develop their firm great vows; they are kept in mind by the buddhas, so that they break through all barriers; they become refuges relied upon by all sentient beings.

"What is enlightening beings' birth as offspring of the light of universal awareness? Here the enlightening beings become fully engaged in the effort to guide all sentient beings to perfection. They become free from any notion of things, having let go and relinquished all. They become perfectly pure and self-controlled, dwelling in the sphere of those who arrive at Thusness. They become tolerant, having attained the light of acceptance of all teachings of buddhas. They become greatly energetic, accomplishing right emancipation everywhere. They become released through meditation, having purified the sphere of knowledge of all-sided concentration. They become radiant with the energy of transcendent wisdom, having attained awareness of all truths. They become unimpeded in vision, perceiving the manifestations of the ocean of vision of buddhas. They manifest the total potential of the reality of all things, satisfying all beings. They become engrossed in the attainment of truth.

"What is enlightening beings' birth as offspring of the family of all buddhas? Here the enlightening beings are born in the family of buddhas, born into the lineage of buddhas. They become accomplished in the methods of all buddha teaching and pure in the great vows of the buddhas of past, present, and future. Their roots of goodness become one with the roots of goodness of all buddhas, and they become one body with all buddhas. They go beyond the world by pure qualities. They come to abide in the state of a great being, in absorption in the sight of the power of buddhas. They carry out the means of purifying beings according to the time and are tireless in answering questions about the ways of enlightenment.

"What is enlightening beings' birth as offspring of the array of lights of the manifestation of powers of buddhas? Here enlightening beings, within range of entry into the powers of buddhas, do not regress in their travels to buddha-lands, and do not backslide in their approach to the ocean of various virtues of enlightening beings. They are not frightened by the knowledge that all things are really illusory, and they know all worlds are like dreams. They effect the magical manifestation of all forms, like reflections, and they attain mastery of the miraculous effects of mystic knowledge, like emanations. They show their faces like shadows or reflected images in all states of being. They know all buddhas' teachings are like echoes, and they attain supreme perfection of explanation of the principles of the reality realm, teaching through the use of various meanings and methods.

"What is enlightening beings' birth as offspring of consummation of contemplation of the ways to omniscience? Here the enlightening beings, like children, become established in the state of enlightening beings, where they contemplate the way to omniscience. In each medium of the way of knowledge they will travel for measureless eons defining the infinite realm of enlightening beings, and they become masters of all concentrations of enlightening beings, attaining supreme perfection. In each and every moment of awareness they appear in the presence of the buddhas in untold buddha-lands in the ten directions. They attain holistic concentration on differentiated objects, and show mastery of distinct knowledge of inseparable things. They enter the realm of no object in boundless objects. They enter the stage of endless definition of minute objects, and they know the immeasurable nature of things as small or large. They realize all worlds are equally definitions of consciousness, and they understand all objects and all modes of making them known, by means of meditation.

"What is enlightening beings' birth as offspring of manifestation of emanations throughout the universe? Here the enlightening beings set up variously arrayed buddha-lands everywhere in an instant of thought. They become perfectly expert in creating emanational beings, skilled in producing emanational buddhas, and expert in creating projections of the Teaching. Their sphere of action is the unobstructed cosmos of realities; they become able to produce manifestations of all kinds of bodies according to the mentalities of those they are dealing with, and arrive at the skill to guide unthinkable numbers of sentient beings. They show enlightenment through various practices, are skilled in accomplishing the unobstructed path of omniscience, and thereupon demonstrate the ability to turn the wheel of the Teaching. They become skilled in accomplishing an infinite variety of means of guiding sentient beings; they are able to guide sentient beings with proper timing, and are always absorbed in the mother lode of illuminating knowledge.

"What is enlightening beings' birth as offspring of momentum going into the stage of the enlightened? Here enlightening beings are initiated into the realm of oneness of all buddhas of all times, and they enter into the perspective of continuity of all worlds. They know the continuous generation of mind of all beings in their past and future goings and comings. They know the continuum of action and knowledge of all enlightening beings, they know the continuum of enlightenment of all past, future, and present buddhas, and they know the continuum of skill in use of all the teachings. They know the continuum of all past, future, and present ages of formation and disintegration, as well as their names and features. They effect the knowledge underlying showing sentient beings the realm of awakening to the manifestation of enlightenment according to their development, at the appropriate times, and they show the continuity of the means of turning the wheel of teaching leading to realization of enlightenment applied by all buddhas who appear in the world, by skill in carrying out techniques of guiding endless numbers of beings.

"These are enlightening beings' ten births as enlightening beings, in which they are born, come into existence, form and develop, are fulfilled and completed; they magically produce offerings of adornments in a single array for awakening in all lands; they produce magical powers for endless eons to guide sentient beings ceaselessly; they awaken to the stream of the endless succession of teachings in the multifaceted succession of particularizations of the various objects of sense in the ocean of all actualities; they show the inconceivable majesty of buddhas throughout the space of the cosmos; they show the operation of the Teaching in the context of the immeasurable oceans of varieties of actions of sentient beings, to develop and guide and care for them; they cause all worlds never to be deprived of the presence of a buddha; they convey the multitudes of all teachings, the purity of the ocean of their innumerable utterances, in all objects of sense; having

reached the state of unobstructed infinitude, they produce spheres of
enlightening beings beautifully arrayed with all realities; they expound the
infinitely various treasury of the Teaching, pursuant to infinite
buddhahood, for the purpose of perfecting all beings, expounding it to all
beings in accord with their mentalities."

Then Sutejomandalaratishri, goddess of the Lumbini grove, looking over
the ten directions by the empowerment of Buddha, spoke these verses to
Sudhana, shedding light on the meaning of the ten kinds of birth of enlightening beings:

Those who behold the buddhas
With pure, untainted minds never weary:
Undertaking endless offerings to all buddhas,
They are established in the first birth, wise.

Extending to all lands in all times,
All things, and all buddhas,
Minds equipped with the vow to liberate beings,
This is called the second birth of the inconceivable.

Those who tirelessly imbibe the Teaching,
Contemplative and unattached,
Equanimous in mind and body, pure as space,
Attain the third peerless birth.

Those who enter the ocean of great compassion
With wills as firm as a diamond mountain,
Plunging into the ocean of means of omniscience,
Theirs is the fourth birth of the best of people.

Those who carry out the oceans of pure transcendent ways,
Suffusing all worlds with love,
Developing beings by the lights of truth,
Theirs is the fifth birth of great people.

Knowing the nature of things, unhindered in mind,
Born in the family of the peerless buddhas of all times,
Those who enter the ocean of the reality realm
Attain the sixth great birth of sages.

Those whose spiritual body is pure and mind unattached,
Who pervade all lands with their own bodies,
And enter into all powers of buddhas,
Attain the seventh inconceivable birth of the enlightened.

Those who have mastered the ocean of knowledge,

Contemplate the way to omniscience,
And enter the ocean of all ways of concentration
Attain the eighth birth of those abiding in Thusness.

Those who purify spiritual realms,
Engaged in perfection of all beings,
And show the miraculous effects of buddhas,
Attain the ninth birth of the great-minded.

Those who enter the power of the conquerors,
Developing the immense force of omniscience,
With unhindered knowledge of the differentiation of the cosmos,
Attain the tenth birth of the offspring of buddhas.

"By these ten births enlightening beings are born in the family of buddhas and become light-makers for sentient beings.

"Also, I have attained an enlightening liberation of vision of the birth of enlightening beings in all objects for incalculable eons."

Sudhana asked, "What is the scope of this liberation?"

The goddess said, "I have perfected a vow to go to see all manifestations of birth of enlightening beings. Indeed, I have entered the immense ocean of births of the blessed Vairocana—perceiving the births of the enlightening being in this billion-world universe, when the Blessed One was to manifest birth here in the Lumbini grove, I appeared here by my past vow and stayed here cultivating recollection of the enlightening being's births, and as I did so I realized that the Blessed One would descend to earth from the heaven of happiness in one hundred years.

"Then ten omens appeared in this Lumbini grove. What ten? The whole grove became level, without uneven terrain, without any pitfalls; this was the first omen to appear. Then the whole grove became clear of gravel and brambles, and the ground became diamond, strewn with jewels; this was the second omen to appear. Then the whole grove was adorned with rows of trees of all kinds of jewels; this was the third omen to appear. Then the whole grove was arrayed with adornments set on tree roots made of figurines of fragrant jewels, sending forth sprouts more fragrant than celestial perfumes, growing from mines of aromatic powders, producing multitudes of all kinds of banners and pennants; this was the fourth omen to appear. Then the whole grove was filled with all kinds of arrays of garlands of various celestial flowers; this was the fifth omen to appear. Then great treasuries of jewels opened up in all the trees in this grove; this was the sixth omen to appear. Then in all the lotus ponds in the grove, all kinds of jewel lotuses sprang up from the earth in bud and emerged on the surface of the water; this was the seventh omen to appear. Then the various beings of the realms of desire and the realm of form in this world all stood reverently here in this grove; this was the eighth omen to appear. Then the females of all the various kinds of beings came here joyfully with all kinds of offerings and bowed before the holy fig tree; this was the ninth omen to appear. Then lights called "lamp of the magical manifestations of birth of enlightening beings" emanating from the navels of all the buddhas of the ten directions appeared in this grove; and in all the beams of light, reflections of the magical manifestations of births of all the buddhas were seen, and the sounds of the voices of buddhas telling of the virtues of enlightening beings magically born were heard emanating from the light beams. This was the tenth omen to appear. These ten omens appeared when the time of the enlightening being Vairocana's birth was near, and because of the appearance of these omens the thought occurred to all world leaders that the enlightening being would be born. And I, for my part, was flooded with inconceivable joy from seeing those omens.

"Then, as Lady Maya (mother of Vairocana-Shakyamuni Buddha) went out of the city of Kapilavastu, ten omens of great light appeared in this Lumbini grove, by the appearance of which the fervor of joy of vision of the teaching of omniscience grew in countless beings. What were the ten? Light appeared in the chambers of all the jewel towers on the ground level; light appeared in the buds of all the fragrant flowers; light appeared in the blossoming buds of all the jewel lotuses, coming from all the petals, and sweet, agreeable sound flowed from them. Also, the light of the first inspiration of the enlightening beings of the ten directions appeared, illumining this Lumbini grove. Also, the mystical manifestation of light of the enlightening beings of the ten directions entering all the stages of enlightening beings appeared in this grove. Also, the light of the attainment of knowledge on consummation of all the transcendent ways by the enlightening beings of the ten directions appeared in this grove. Also the light of knowledge controlling all vows of the enlightening beings of the ten directions appeared in this grove. Also the light of all enlightening beings' knowledge of developmental disciplines appeared in this grove. Also the light of all enlightening beings' attainment of knowledge of the principles of the reality realm appeared in this grove. Also the light of all enlightening beings' attainment of knowledge of buddhas' projected birth, leaving society, and realization of enlightenment appeared in this grove. These ten omens of light appeared, by which the darkness of the recesses of the minds of infinite enlightening beings were lit up.

"Then, as Lady Maya leaned against the holy fig tree, all the world rulers, the gods and goddesses of the realm of desire, the gods and goddesses of the realm of form, and all the other beings who had gathered there to make offerings to the enlightening being were bathed in the glorious radiance of Maya's body, and their arrays of offerings were also illumined thereby; and all the lights in the billion-world universe were eclipsed by Maya's light. The lights emanating from all her pores, not repelled by other lights, unobscured, unobstructed, pervaded everywhere, extinguished all the pains of the hells, the animal realms, the ghost realms, and the pains and afflictions of the beings in all states of existence, then remained, shining, illuminating. This was the first miracle attending the birth of the enlightening being in the Lumbini grove.

"Then everything in this universe was seen reflected in the abdomen of Lady Maya, and in all the worlds in the universe, at the foot of trees in groves in the capitals of the southern continents Lady Maya appeared just as she did in the Lumbini grove, surrounded by all the world leaders as she was about to give birth to the enlightening being, by the miracle of knowledge which gives birth to enlightening beings. This was the second miracle attending the birth of the enlightening being in the Lumbini grove.

"Then, from every one of Lady Maya's pores came visions of how the Blessed One had served buddhas as he carried out enlightening practice in the past, and the teachings expounded by those buddhas were also heard in the buddhas' voices coming from her pores. Just as the sun, moon, stars, planets, and thunderclouds are seen reflected in a lake, in a piece of gold, in a mirror, or in crystal-clear water, in the same way the past emanations of the buddhas, thundering with exposition of all the teachings, were seen in the pores of Lady Maya. This was the third miracle attending the birth of the enlightening being in the Lumbini grove.

"Then, from each of Maya's pores appeared visions of all the universes, all the worlds, all the lands, and all the places the Blessed One had carried on enlightening practices, all the features of the lands, the means of salvation being taught, the names and numbers of the ages, the buddhas there, the pinnacles of purification, the life span of the beings of those ages, the enlightening being's births in the worlds, the people he associated with, the spiritual benefactors he followed, the good practices he applied himself to, the principles he put into action, the buddha-lands in which he carried out enlightening practice, the bodies in which he performed enlightening practice and attained nonregression, and what his appearance, surroundings, and pleasant and painful experiences were in his successive lifetimes—all was seen in each of Maya's pores. And in each of those lifetimes, Lady Maya was the mother of the enlightening beings. And all the bodies of the enlightening being were seen as a magical reflection in the pores of Lady Maya. This was the fourth miracle attending the birth of the enlightening being in the Lumbini grove.

"Then the physical forms, the means of subsistence, the pleasures and pains, and the life cycles through which the Blessed One performed enlightening practice in the past were all seen reflected in all the pores of Lady Maya's body. This was the fifth miracle attending the birth of the enlightening being in the Lumbini grove.

"Then the difficult sacrifices the Blessed One made in the course of his past enlightening practice, relinquishing everything inside and outside himself, the appearances of the enlightening being as a donor, the appearances of those who received his gifts, the gifts themselves, the circumstances of the giving, and the company of the enlightening being, were all seen reflected in the pores of Lady Maya. This was the sixth miracle attending the birth of the enlightening being in the Lumbini grove.

"Then manifestations of the lands, the groves, the raiment, the flowers and garlands, perfumes and incenses, banners, pennants, and parasols, all the precious adornments, and the sublime sounds of the music and singing of the times when all the buddhas of the past descended into their mother's womb, appeared in this grove for all to see and hear. This was the seventh miracle attending the birth of the enlightening being in the Lumbini grove.

"Then all the furnishings of the enlightening being, surpassing those arraying the abodes of the celestial chiefs and the abodes of the chiefs of all other realms of being—diamond towers, diamond mansions, diamond nets, diamond statues, diamond ornaments, all the finest fragrances, and all kinds of beautiful objects—emerged from Lady Maya's abdomen and arrayed this Lumbini grove. This was the eighth miracle attending the birth of the enlightening being in the Lumbini grove.

"Then as many enlightening beings as atoms in untold millions of buddha-lands, all of the same appearance as the blessed Vairocana, adorned with similar marks and embellishments of greatness, with similar auras, emanating similar lights, with similar deportment, projecting similar radiance, with similar retinues, and similar adornments, emerged from Lady Maya's abdomen first, extolling the myriad qualities of the Blessed One. This was the ninth miracle attending the birth of the enlightening being in the Lumbini grove.

"Then, when the time for the birth of the enlightening being had come, the diamond ground in front of Lady Maya split and a great jewel lotus called Calyx Arrayed with All Jewels emerged. Its calyx was unsurpassed diamond, surrounded by all the finest jewels in a dazzling array. It had as many petals as atoms in ten buddha-lands, all evenly arrayed, made of various jewels fringed with pure wish-fulfilling gems, lined with innumerable filaments the colors of all jewels, draped with nets of countless jewels, covered with heaps of indestructible diamonds, surrounded by celestial chiefs, sprinkled by showers from fragrant clouds by the water spirits, surrounded by the chief demigods clasping celestial flowers in their hands, with the chief celestial musicians appearing singing eulogies of the enlightening being's past service of buddhas, the chief titans prostrating themselves in respect, freed of arrogance, pride, and conceit, the chief birds trailing jewel streamers, adorning the sky, the chief celestial choristers looking on joyfully singing songs encouraging the enlightening beings, the chief serpents showering adornments, proclaiming their joy. This was the tenth miracle attending the birth of the enlightening being in the Lumbini grove.

"After these ten miracles had appeared, the enlightening being, manifesting an effusion of inconceivable, measureless light, emerged from Lady Maya's abdomen, like the sun from the horizon, like lightning from the clouds, like the diffusion of the dawn from the mountains, like a great torch from the darkness. Thus did the enlightening being manifest emergence from the abdomen of Lady Maya, by the nature of manifestation of illusory form, by the nature of noncoming, by the nature of manifestation of appearance to the world without origin or extinction.

"Thus did I perceive the oceans of miracles attending the birth of the Blessed Vairocana as I sojourned here in the Lumbini grove. And just as I perceived the oceans of miracles attending the birth of this Vairocana in this world, in the same way I perceived the oceans of miracles attending the birth of Vairocana Buddha in all worlds in this universe. And just as I perceived the billions of miracles attending the birth of Vairocana Buddha in all worlds in this universe, so also did I perceive, in each mental moment, with each penetration of consciousness, as many miracles attending the birth of Vairocana Buddha as atoms in a buddha-world, in the worlds within all the atoms in all universes accessible to knowledge penetrating the atoms in all buddha-lands. In the next moment I perceived, in each of the buddha-lands in the atoms of a thousand buddha-lands, an equal number of miracles attending the birth of the enlightening being. In this way, in each of the buddha-lands in the atoms of each buddha-land, I perceived all the miracles attending the birth of the enlightening being, without reaching their end. I did not reach the end of the succession of buddha-lands in each and every atom, or of the miracles attending the birth of the enlightening being in each and every one of those buddha-lands. And just as I perceived all the miracles attending the birth of the enlightening being in this world, so also did I perceive, in each moment of consciousness, all aspects of all the miracles attending the birth of the enlightening being in infinitely many worlds in the ten directions, by application of unceasing power."

Then Sudhana asked the goddess, "How long ago did you attain this enlightening liberation of vision of the miracle of birth of enlightening beings in all objects over incalculable eons?"

She replied, "In the past, as many eons ago as atoms in ten million buddha-lands and even more, there was a buddha named Invincible Paragon of Virtue who emerged in a world called Ubiquitous Jewels in an age in which eighty decillion buddhas appeared. In that world there was a central group of four continents called Dazzling Array of Lights, in the southern continent of which was a capital city called Lofty Banner of Pure Adornments, where there was a king named Jewel Flame Eye Light, whose wife was named Queen of Joyous Light. Just as Maya is the mother of the Buddha Vairocana here, that queen was the mother of that buddha Invincible Paragon of Virtue in that world at that time, the first of the eighty decillion buddhas of the age. When the time for the birth of the enlightening being came, the queen went to a park called Circle of Lights of Golden Flowers, accompanied by twenty decillion women, and there gave birth to the child Invincible Paragon of Virtue, by the inconceivable miracle of the birth of an enlightening being. In the middle of that park was a tower called Brilliant Heap of Pure Jewels, and this was where that queen gave birth to that buddha, holding on to the limb of a wish-fulfilling tree.

"At the time of the buddha's birth there was a wet nurse named Light of Purity standing by, and as soon as the buddha was born, the world leaders bathed him with fragrant water, presented countless suitable offerings of the finest quality, then handed him over to the nurse Light of Purity. As soon as she took him into her hands, the nurse was flooded with great joy and attained an enlightening concentration called 'sphere of the universal eye,' by the attainment of which she saw countless buddhas in various worlds in the ten directions, and this enlightening liberation of vision of the miracle of birth of enlightening beings in all objects over countless ages subtly entered into her, just as the consciousness of the embryo enters the abdomen of the mother on the day of conception. By attaining this liberation, she accomplished the great vow to see the miracle of birth of all buddhas.

"Now, who do you think the enlightening being's nurse Light of Purity at that time was? It was none other than I myself who was the nurse Light of Purity. And who do you think the twenty decillion women were? They were none other than the twenty decillion goddesses who live here in the Lumbini grove, my companions. And who do you think was Queen of Joyous Light, mother of the child Invincible Paragon of Virtue? It was none other than Lady Maya here. And who was the king Jewel Flame Eye Light? It was none other than this king Shuddhodana. From that time on I was never separated from the Blessed Vairocana, by entry into the ocean of miracles of his births as an enlightening being, and entry into the ocean of miraculous manifestations of his power to guide sentient beings, in every moment of awareness.

"Furthermore, just as in this world I perceived the oceans of lands of Vairocana and the buddhas born of the ocean of the totality of great vows in every moment of thought in all atoms by the eye of knowledge penetrating all atoms, and perceived the ocean of manifestations of buddhas in those lands, and perceived the ocean of miracles of births of those buddhas as enlightening beings, in the same way, in every mental moment I perceived the oceans of miracles of births as enlightening beings of infinite buddhas in the ten directions. And just as in this universe, by successive penetration of all atoms, I perceived the buddha-qualities of complete perfect buddhas as they were being born as enlightening beings, in the same way I perceived oceans of lands in the atoms of untold decillions of buddha-lands in the ten directions, and perceived the vast oceans of buddhas therein, saw those buddhas as they were miraculously being born as enlightening beings, paid reverence to them as buddhas, listened to those buddhas' teachings, and practice in accord with their teaching."

Then Sutejomandalaratishri, goddess of the Lumbini grove, elucidating this enlightening liberation of vision of the miracle of birth of enlightening beings over countless eons, looked over the ten directions by the power of Buddha and spoke these verses:

Son of Buddha, listen respectfully
To what I say to your question:
The realm of buddhas, silent and hard to see,
I explain in terms of cause.

I remember unthinkable eons ago, past as many eons

As atoms in a hundred million lands,
An age in which there were
Eight decillion buddhas.

Invincible Paragon of Virtue
Was the first of those buddhas;
I saw him being born
In the wonderful park of golden flowers.

I was then his wet nurse,
By the name of Light of Purity, wise;
The world guardians put him in my arms
When he was born, shining with golden light.

Taking that supreme person in my arms,
I could not see the top of his head;
Looking at his inconceivable body,
I could not see any bounds.

Adorned by marks of greatness, pure,
His body was beautiful to behold;
Seeing him, like a jewel figurine,
Incomparable joy welled up in me.

Thinking of his measureless virtues,
An infinite sea of felicity grew in me;
And seeing his ocean of miracles,
I was inspired to seek enlightenment.

Seeking the oceans of qualities of buddhas,
My ocean of vows grew;
All lands were purified,
And all paths of miserable states were closed.

To serve the inconceivable buddhas
To come in all lands,
And to liberate suffering beings,
My ocean of vows emerged.

Hearing the teachings of those saviors,
I attained this excellent sphere of liberation,
Having carried out practice to purify enlightenment
For as many eons as atoms in a hundred million lands.

I served all the buddhas
Who appeared over the ages,

And remembered their teachings,
Purifying this ocean of liberation.

There were as many buddhas in the past
As atoms in a hundred million lands;
Remembering their cycles of teaching,
I developed this sphere of liberation.

Seeing all atoms
In a buddha-land,
In every atom I see oceans of lands
Purified by the Buddha.

In those lands I see Guides
Being born in the best of groves,
In an instant manifesting
Inconceivable vast miracles.

I see the leaders, in whatever land,
Seeking supreme enlightenment,
Living in heaven, or appearing to be born,
In inconceivable decillions of lands.

I see them being born with great miracles,
In hundreds of oceans of lands,
Attended by the best of women,
Expounding the Teaching.

I see as many buddhas as atoms in a hundred million lands
In one moment of consciousness,
Showing the world in many ways
Tranquillity in an instant.

I see all the births of buddhas,
Looking into the oceans of lands in an atom;
In life after life, in millions of bodies,
I arrive at compassion in their service.

In inconceivable oceans of lands,
In the endless realms where they appeared,
In all those worlds I appear before them
And make the clouds of Teaching rain.

Child of Buddha, I know
This inconceivable, exalted liberation,

Which could not be all seen
Even in inconceivable decillions of eons.

"I just know this enlightening liberation of vision of the miracles of birth of enlightening beings in all objects over countless ages—how can I know the practice or tell the virtues of the enlightening beings whose minds are the sources of all eons from moment to moment of consciousness, who manifest birth by meditation on all the principles of the Teaching, who are determined to serve all buddhas, who are intent on realizing all buddha-teachings, who are like reflections appearing to be born in all races, who are born spontaneously in lotus calyxes in the presence of all buddhas, who have higher knowledge of proper timing in developing all beings, who manifest miracles of birth oriented toward guiding all beings, who show multitudes of miracles in all lands, who are reflected in all conditions and classes and families of beings?

"In the city of Kapilavastu lives a girl of the Shakya clan named Gopa. Go ask her how an enlightening being should live in the world for enlightening development."

Then Sudhana paid his respects and left the goddess of the Lumbini grove.

Gopa

Then Sudhana left the Lumbini goddess and went to the city of Kapilavastu; cultivating that enlightening liberation of vision of miracles of birth of enlightening beings in all objects over countless ages, entering into it, expanding it, practicing it, purifying it, mastering it, contemplating it, examining it, he made his way to the meeting hall of enlightening beings reflecting the cosmos. When he went there, a goddess of the enlightening beings' meeting hall named Sorrowless, together with ten thousand house goddesses, appeared before Sudhana and said to him, "Welcome is the great person with wisdom, knowledge, and courage, who roams the grounds of the vast palace of reality intent on cultivating the inconceivable liberations of enlightening beings, in the presence of the city of truth, ceaselessly entering into the endless methods of enlightening beings, attaining manifestation of the ocean of virtues of those who realize Thusness, aiming for the knowledge of how to act and speak so as to mature all people, acting and speaking according to knowledge of the behavior of all people, mind oriented toward spiritual practice, committed to increasing the flood of the ocean of joy in the feelings of all beings, on the path of knowledge of the Teaching of all those who arrive at thusness. As I see you, with steady gaze on the pure realm of conduct of profound spiritual practice, before long you will attain perfection of the supreme ornaments of body, speech, and mind of the enlightened, and will act in the world with a body adorned with the marks and embellishments of greatness and a mind adorned with the light of knowledge of the ten powers. As I see your steadfast, energetic exertion, before long you will be furnished with all the requisites for manifesting your being in the presence of all buddhas of past, present, and future; receiving their teachings, experiencing the delight of the tranquil palace of spirituality, with all the meditations, liberations, concentrations, and attainments of enlightening beings, you will see into the profound liberation of buddhas. That is because you do not tire, do not regress, do not feel pain in going to spiritual benefactors, meeting them, associating with them, receiving instructions, and applying the ways to virtue; and you are not overcome by any interference or barrier or obstacle, or by any demon or deity. Therefore you will soon become a source of joy for all beings."

Then Sudhana said to the goddess Sorrowless, "May it be as you say—I would find supreme joy in extinguishing the burning of all beings' afflictions, in stopping the development of their evil deeds, in making them all happy, in getting them to act impeccably. Whenever sentient beings are involved in evil deeds and afflictions, with scattered minds, fall into painful or pleasurable states, and experience various forms of physical and mental distress, enlightening beings become most unhappy at that. Just as a doting parent would love its only child and would be most distressed at seeing the child be dismembered, in the same way a practicing enlightening being is most unhappy to see people fallen into miserable states because of compulsion by afflictions in action. Whenever sentient beings live in felicity because of good thoughts, words, and deeds, and experience physical and mental pleasures in celestial and human realms, enlightening beings are delighted and become happy and joyful.

"Furthermore, enlightening beings do not seek omniscience for their own sake, nor to produce mundane enjoyments and pleasures, nor in search of the various enjoyments of the realm of desire, nor under the compulsion of errors of conception, thought, and view. They live and work in the world without being controlled by fetters, bonds, propensities, or obsessions, without being controlled by craving or views, without their minds being bound up in ideas of mundane enjoyments, without being taken with the taste of pleasure of meditation, without being blocked by mental barriers.

"Furthermore, enlightening beings, giving rise to great compassion for sentient beings suffering immeasurable miseries in the ocean of existence, undertake a great vow to care for all beings. They appear carrying out the practice of enlightening beings in the mundane whirl, engaged in the development and guidance of sentient beings, by the force of the power of carrying out the vow of great compassion. They undertake a vow to serve all buddhas in quest of thoroughly unobstructed omniscience for all sentient beings. By mastery of the vow to serve buddhas, they do not tire in enlightening practice. While they carry on enlightening practice, seeing defiled lands they undertake a vow to purify all buddha-lands. While purifying oceans of lands, observing the variety of beings' states, they undertake a vow to purify the undifferentiated supreme reality body. Seeing sentient beings' acts, words, and thoughts defiled, they undertake a vow to purify sentient beings' acts, words, and thoughts. Seeing sentient beings with incompletely purified senses and minds, they carry on enlightening practice tirelessly, completely purifying the mental behavior of all sentient beings.

"Thus enlightening beings are indefatigable in carrying out the infinitely various practice of enlightening beings. Practicing in this way, they become ornaments of heaven and earth, by producing human and celestial welfare. They become parents, because they bring enlightening beings into existence. They become nurses, leading into the path of enlightening beings. They become guardian spirits, giving protection from the danger of falling into bad ways. They become great mariners, ferrying beings across the ocean of the mundane whirl. They become refuges, eliminating the dangers of all demons and afflictions. They become resorts, leading to the ultimate state of coolness. They become landings leading into the ocean of enlightenment. They become guides, leading to the island of spiritual jewels. They become flowers, their minds blooming with the virtues of all buddhas. They become adornments, radiating the light of great virtue and knowledge. They become sources of supreme joy, pleasing in all ways. They become worth visiting, because they act impeccably. They become universally good, perfecting themselves in all respects. They become an ever-welcome sight, never appearing disagreeable. They become light-makers, emanating light beams of knowledge. They become illuminators, holding the lamp of truth. They become radiant, purifying the will for enlightenment. They become warrior chiefs, stopping the acts of demons. They become suns, radiating webs of light rays of wisdom. They become moons, the moon of awareness rising in the sky. They become clouds, showering the Teaching on all beings. Thus do enlightening beings become a joy to all living creatures as they carry out enlightening practice."

Then Sorrowless, goddess of the hall of assembly of enlightening beings, with those ten thousand house goddesses, showered Sudhana with a rain of mentally created flower garlands, aromatic powders, perfumes, and jewelry, all superior to those in the heavens; then, surrounding him, they sang these verses in his praise as he entered the abode of enlightening beings:

Buddhas emerge in the world at times,
Producing the light of knowledge,
Resolved on perfect enlightenment
Out of compassion for the world.

Hard to get to see
Even in millions of eons,
You are a sun of knowledge
For the world in the darkness of ignorance.

Seeing the world in error,
Shrouded in the darkness of nescience,
Conceiving great compassion
You've set out for independence.

With pure intention you seek

The enlightenment of buddhas;
You serve spiritual benefactors
Without concern for yourself.

You are not attached to the world,
You are independent and aloof;
You do not dwell in the defilement of the world,
Your mind is free as the sky.

You practice lofty deeds of enlightenment,
Beautiful light of virtues;
You appear in the world
Radiating lights of knowledge.

You do not leave the world,
Nor are you stained by worldly things;
You traverse the world unattached,
Like the wind through the sky.

Just as the holocaust
Burns constantly,
With energy like fire
You carry on enlightening practice.

Lionlike, great hero,
Progressing boldly with steadfast vigor,
Imbued with the power of knowledge,
You practice undaunted.

All the oceans
Of principles in the cosmos
You will enter, O Hero,
By serving true benefactors.

Then the goddess Sorrowless, having eulogized Sudhana, followed him as
he went on, bound to him by love for truth. Sudhana went into the meeting
hall of enlightening beings which shone with reflections of the cosmos and
looked around, desirous of seeing the Shakyan girl Gopa. He saw her in the
middle of the hall sitting on a seat of jewels which reflected the abodes of all
enlightening beings, surrounded by eighty-four thousand maidens, all of
royal lineage, who had equally established good foundations of the practice
of enlightening beings, who had been won over by her generosity in the
past, who practiced gentle, pleasing speech, who were taken with the happiness of approaching the goal of omniscience, who were thoroughly
absorbed in the common purpose of complete knowledge of buddhas and
enlightening beings, who were sustained by the loving care guided by great

compassion, who had purified great kindness, who had already developed the inconceivable skill in means of enlightening beings. All of those eighty-four thousand women were irreversible in progress toward supreme perfect enlightenment; they had comprehended enlightening beings' means of transcendence, and needed no one's guidance in the studies of enlightening beings. Their minds were free from all attachments and aloof of all mundane pleasures. They had cleared the way to the unobstructed cosmos and their minds were rapidly approaching omniscience. They were free from the web of all obstacles and barriers, and transcended all attachments. They acted as positive emanations of the body of reality, dedicated to leading all beings to perfection. Their minds sprang from a vast ocean of virtue, and they carried out the vow of the practice of universal good. They had developed tremendous energy in powers of enlightening beings, and the light of their minds was as a sun of knowledge.

Then Sudhana went up to Gopa, paid his respects, and said, "I have set my mind on supreme perfect enlightenment, but I do not know how enlightening beings act in the midst of the mundane whirl without being stained by its ills; how they realize the equal essence of all phenomena without staying in the stage of personal liberation alone; how they manifest the qualities of buddhas without stopping the practice of enlightening beings; how they remain in the stage of enlightening beings yet show the sphere of all buddhas; how they transcend all worldly states yet act in the midst of worldly states; how they achieve the reality-body yet produce endless physical manifestations; how they resort to the formless reality-body yet manifest bodies like all beings; how they comprehend all the inexpressible truths, yet expound the truths to sentient beings in all languages; how they know there are no beings in the elements of existence, yet do not give up efforts to guide all beings; how they realize all phenomena are unoriginated and unperishing, yet do not give up the effort to serve all buddhas; how they realize there are no results of action in phenomena, yet do not give up the effort to perform good deeds."

Gopa said to Sudhana, "It is very good that you think it fit to ask about the nature of this kind of practice of enlightening beings, as this is the question of one who is set on practicing the vow of universal good. So listen well and think carefully, for I will tell you, by the power of Buddha.

"There are ten things by which enlightening beings fulfill this kind of enlightening practice, the light of total knowledge, like the cosmic net of interrelation of all things. What are the ten? Association with superior spiritual friends; attainment of enormous devotion; purity of lofty good will; a state of mind founded on oceanic virtue and knowledge; listening to the great teaching of buddhas; associating with thought devoted to the buddhas of past, present, and future; equally following the practices of all enlightening beings; gaining the empowerment of all buddhas; purity of intent, greatly compassionate in nature; attainment of the basic power of mind to stop all vicious circles. Having attained these ten things, enlightening beings fulfill this kind of enlightening practice, like the cosmic net of inter-relation of all things, radiating total knowledge.

"Then enlightening beings with unrelenting vigor, having attained these things, developing and expanding them by putting them into practice in endless ways, propitiate spiritual benefactors in ten ways: by indifference to themselves, by not seeking worldly goods, by realizing the equality of essence of all things, by not turning back from the commitment to omniscience, by observing all the principles of the cosmos, by being mentally free of all existents, by independence in the space of truth where there is nothing to depend on, by freedom from obstruction in the undertaking of all enlightening beings, by entering all lands, by perfect clarification and purification of the unobstructed sphere of knowledge of enlightening beings."

Then, by the empowerment of Buddha, looking over the ten directions, Gopa uttered these verses illustrating what she meant:

Those who set out for vast pure wisdom for the welfare of others
And serve true benefactors honestly
With tireless vigor, seeing them as teachers,
Carry out practice in the world like the cosmic net.

Those whose devotion is vast as the sky,
Embracing all worlds of past, present, and future,
All lands, beings, phenomena, and buddhas—
Theirs is this practice, producers of the light of knowledge.

When the will is infinite as the sky,
Supremely pure, free from the taint of afflictions,
Therein arise the virtues of all buddhas,
Concentrating the whole variety of the cosmic net of practice.

The wise who rest on great oceans of virtue,
Inconceivable, infinite, vast as omniscience,
As pure offspring of the body of all virtues
They act in the world unstained by the filth of the world.

Those who listen to the teaching of buddhas
And tirelessly catch every nuance
Are lamps shining with wisdom in accord with truth;
Theirs is this practice which lights the world.

Those who perceive in an instant of awareness
The infinite buddhas everywhere, interrelated,
Contemplate the ocean of all buddhas;
This is the way into the mind of the enlightened.

Those who see the vast audiences of the buddhas

Enter the ocean of their meditations
And their infinite ocean of vows;
This is the practice of those like the cosmic net.

Those empowered by all the buddhas
Practice universal good for endless ages,
Reflected in all lands;
This is the practice of the lights of truth.

The suns of compassion and knowledge emerge, steadfast,
Seeing the misfortune of the world,
And disperse the darkness of delusion with the light of truth;
This is the practice of those like the sun.

Seeing people revolve in the rut of existence,
The wise stand opposed to the flow of the mundane whirl;
Developing the measureless wheel of true teaching,
They practice universal higher goodness and wisdom.

Those who learn these infinite principles,
Appearing in the world according to people's mentalities,
With their own bodies like reflected images,
Develop people in the oceans of being.

Suffusing the world with myriad expressions of love,
Showing spiritual practice to people of various interests,
Teaching them according to their mentalities,
The steadfast lead billions to enlightenment.

Then Gopa said to Sudhana, "I have attained an enlightening liberation whose sphere is observation of the ocean of concentrations of all enlightening beings."

Sudhana asked, "What is the scope of this liberation?"

Gopa replied, "Having attained this liberation, I penetrate as many ages in this world as atoms in untold buddha-lands, and I know all the beings in all conditions of existence therein, and I know all the deaths and births of those beings, their developments, their accomplishments, the variety of results of their actions; I know their undertakings—good, bad, liberative, nonliberative, certain, uncertain, wrongly fixated, compulsive, noncompulsive, based on good, not based on good, fostered by good, fostered by evil, fostered by good and evil, good by development, bad through neglect.

"I know the oceans of names of all the buddhas in those ages as numerous as atoms in untold buddha-lands; I know the oceans of initial inspirations of those buddhas, the ways they set out for omniscience, their undertakings of the oceans of all vows, their heading for previous buddhas, their oceans of efforts in the service of previous buddhas, their oceans of fulfillment of past enlightening practices, their oceans of arrangements of means of emancipation. I also know the oceans of those buddhas' development and guidance of sentient beings, and I know their oceans of attainment of enlightenment, their majestic displays of mystic power in turning the wheel of the teaching, and their oceans of miraculous displays of all buddhas. I also know the differences in the audiences of those buddhas, and I know the methods of emancipation of the listeners in those audiences, as well as their past roots of goodness, the variety of their cultivation of the path, and the difference in the purity of their attainment of knowledge. I also know the sentient beings who have been led to individual enlightenment by those buddhas, and I know the past roots of goodness of those individual illuminates, as well as their attainments of individual enlightenment, the doors of liberation mystically developing in their peaceful states, their various spiritual transformations, their development of others, their teachings, and the various freedoms of liberation in their infinite states of concentration. I also know the ultimate extinction of those buddhas.

"I also know the oceans of enlightening beings surrounding those buddhas, and I know those enlightening beings' first cultivation of roots of goodness, their first inspirations and vows, the variety of their vows, the variety of their production of arrangements of vehicles of emancipation by all the practices of enlightening beings, the variety of their perfection of provisions for the path of transcendence, the variety of the manifestations of their practices of the path of enlightening beings, the variety of their provisions for advancing through the states of enlightening beings, the variety of the speed of their advance through the states of enlightening beings, the variety of their spheres of concentration in the stages of enlightening beings, the spiritual manifestations of their advance through the states of enlightening beings, their spiritual states during their progress through the states of enlightening beings, their footholds in the stages of enlightening beings, their practices cultivating the states of enlightening beings, their methods of purifying the stages of enlightening beings, their abodes in the stages of enlightening beings, their characteristics in the stages of enlightening beings, their mastery of the stages of enlightening beings, their science of entry into the stages of enlightening beings, the enlightening beings' science of salvation, the enlightening beings' science of development, the different states of enlightening beings, the mystic projections of enlightening beings' practices, the oceans of concentrations of enlightening beings, the oceans of methods of liberation of enlightening beings. I also know those enlightening beings' attainments of oceans of various concentrations in each moment of consciousness, their discoveries of the range of omniscience, their tremendous flashes of omniscience, their means of attainment of the forbearance of enlightening beings, their plunges into omniscience. I also know those enlightening beings' travels to oceans of lands, their penetrations of the principles of oceans of phenomena, the variety of characteristics of all things, the mystic projection of the designs of all states of enlightening beings, the oceans of principles of various vows, and the variety of oceans of miracles.

"Just as I penetrate the various oceans of ages past in this world, in the same way I know the endless unbroken succession of ages of the future; and just as I know all this in this world, so do I know it in all the worlds within this world. And just as I know this in all the worlds within this world, so do I know it in all the worlds in the atoms of this world. And just as I know it in all the worlds in the atoms of this world, so do I know it in the worlds in the ten directions contiguous with this world. And just as I know it in the worlds in the ten directions contiguous with this world, so do I know it in all the worlds in the ten directions surrounding this world. And just as I know it in all the worlds in the ten directions surrounding this world, so do I know it in all the worlds in the radiant world system of Vairocana. And just as I know it in all the worlds in the radiant world system of Vairocana, I know it in all the worlds surrounding the radiant world system of Vairocana. And just as I know it in all the worlds surrounding the radiant world system of Vairocana, I know it in all the places in the worlds in the oceans of worlds in the masses of worlds in this whole flower treasury universe, and in all the structures and features of the worlds.

"And as in this flower treasury universe, so also in all universes in the endless cosmos, throughout space, I know, comprehend, and recall the oceans of past vows of Vairocana, his oceans of past efforts, oceans of past attainments, persistence in enlightening practice through infinite ages, methods of purifying lands, means of serving past buddhas, ways of receiving the teachings of past buddhas, methods of attaining enlightening concentrations in the past, means of attaining control over utensils, ways of practicing the oceans of virtues of past buddhas, oceans of ways of perfecting giving, methods of effecting the purification of the conduct of an enlightening being, means of attaining the forbearance of an enlightening being, oceans of force of the vigor of an enlightening being, oceans of methods of fulfilling all elements of meditation, oceans of ways of purification of the sphere of wisdom, means of manifesting reflections of life in all worlds, ways of purification of the sphere of vows of practice of universal good, pervasion of all worlds, oceans of means of purification of all lands, oceans of light of knowledge of all buddhas, oceans of spiritual manifestations of accession to the enlightenment of all buddhas, means of attainment of the range of knowledge of all buddhas, oceans of mystic manifestations of attainment of enlightenment, oceans of ways of free exercise of the majestic power of turning the wheel of teaching, oceans of various audiences, the past roots of goodness of all the enlightening beings in all those audiences, their oceans of initial vows, their oceans of methods of developing and guiding sentient beings, the oceans of sentient beings matured by the Buddha as he carried out enlightening practice in the past, those enlightening beings' oceans of means of causing roots of goodness to grow in every moment of consciousness, their oceans of ways of attaining concentration, oceans of means of attaining total mental command, oceans of means of purification of the sphere of expository knowledge, oceans of mystic manifestations of accession to all stages of enlightenment, oceans of means of effecting the network of practice, oceans of gradual refinement, oceans of knowledge of gradual attainment entering all worlds, and oceans of all faculties, powers, elements of enlightenment, meditations, liberations, concentrations, attainments, and spiritual transformations.

"And just as I comprehend, know, and realize the oceans of enlightening practice of Vairocana Buddha in this whole cosmos, so also do I comprehend, know, and realize the indivisible oceans of enlightening practice of all buddhas in all oceans of worlds throughout the cosmoses throughout all space. In this way I comprehend the entry into the indivisible totality of all enlightening beings' practices, entry into the infinite web of illusion, infinite cosmic pervasion, infinite instruction, and indication of entry into the basis of endless eons, of all buddhas in all oceans of worlds throughout the cosmos, to the furthest reaches of space. Why? Because this is the scope of the enlightening liberation whose sphere is observation of the ocean of concentrations of all enlightening beings; having attained this, I know the patterns of mental behavior of all beings, the accumulations of goodness of all beings, the means of purgation of defilements of all beings, the variety of deeds of all beings, the doors of concentration of all buddhas' disciples, the stage of concentration of all buddhas' disciples, the tranquillity, liberation, and mystic transformation of all individual illuminates, the methods of the oceans of concentrations of all enlightening beings, the ocean of ways of liberation of all enlightening beings, and the ocean of ways of liberation of all buddhas."

Then Sudhana asked Gopa, "How long ago did you attain this liberation?"

She replied, "As many eons ago as atoms in a hundred buddha-lands, there was a world called Producing Fearlessness. In that world was an age called Superior Conduct. In the middle of that world was a set of four continents called Safe. On the southern continent was a metropolis called Magnificent Trees, the greatest of eighty-four billion cities. Each of the cities was built on a ground of blue lapis lazuli and was surrounded by walls made of seven precious substances and seven moats of fragrant water with gold sand on the bottom, covered with red, white, and blue lotuses as big as cartwheels radiating brilliant webs of light and beautiful scents. They were also surrounded by seven networks of railings made of jewels and seven rings of palm trees, and abounded in groves of trees made of seven precious substances. Above, they were covered with networks of clouds. The grounds of the cities were like jeweled checkerboards, the plots evenly divided by arrays of various jewels. Groups of mystic adepts lived and roamed there, and birds filled the air with pleasing song. The cities were adorned with millions of parks, and they were prosperous and wealthy. Hundred of thousands of happy men and women populated them. There were constant showers of beautiful flowers, stirred by the wind. Hundreds of thousands of earth spirits lived in them. Furthermore, from the golden nets of wind chimes adorning all the trees came happy voices saying, 'Bathe, drink, eat, practice the Teaching, arouse the determination for enlightenment, realize mastery of the stage of nonregression; happiness to you!'

"At that time, in the capital city Magnificent Trees, there was a king named Lord of Wealth, ruler of the region. He had eighty-four thousand women in his palace. He also had five hundred ministers, and also five hundred sons, all of whom were brave, powerful warriors, handsome and well built. His queen, the foremost of the eighty-four thousand women, was named Lotus Born. She had a son named Lord of Glory, who was very handsome and bore the thirty-two marks of a great man, pleasing to the sight of all.

"Once, as a youth, this prince went, with the permission of his father and mother, to go see one of the parks of the city, called Clouds of Light on a Mountain of Fragrant Plants. He went together with twenty thousand girls, projecting a great aura of felicity, glory, energy, splendor, and beauty, admired by men and women all around. They got into a golden vehicle with four huge diamond wheels and unbreakable diamond axles set in the finest sandalwood. It was ribbed with well-arranged diamonds of all fragrances, splendidly adorned with flowers of all jewels, draped with nets of all jewels, with a lion seat set in the middle of the interior, arrayed with great jewels. The reins, strings of jewels, were held by five hundred girls, and it was drawn by a thousand thoroughbred horses fleet as the wind. Overhead was a beautiful sloping canopy made of white lapis lazuli, with a flawless, immeasurable luster, supported by tall poles of blue lapis lazuli, adorned with all kinds of arrays of rare jewels, held by hundreds of thousands of people surrounding the vehicle, singing and playing music, scattering flowers and burning incense. The eight-lane road was level and free of gravel, set on a bed of all precious substances, spread with gold sand, decorated with flowers of various jewels, lined on both sides with rows of jewel trees and railings of various gems. Above, it was covered with nets of golden bells, adorned with canopies of various jewels, and arrayed with many thousands of jeweled banners, pennants, and streamers. Rows of jewel buildings were arrayed on either side.

"In some of those buildings were precious vessels filled with various jewels, to be given to those in need. In some buildings were all kinds of precious ornaments, for those in need of ornaments. In some buildings were wish-fulfilling jewels, to fulfill the wishes of all beings. In some buildings were vessels filled with all kinds of food and drink, to be given to whoever needed them. In some buildings were celestial foods of all the most pleasant appearances, fragrances, savors, and textures. In some buildings were various delicious celestial fruits. In some buildings were millions of fine celestial garments, for those in need of clothing to use as they wished. In some buildings were all kinds of the finest celestial fragrances, for those who wanted perfume, to use at will. In some buildings were all kinds of utensils for people to use as they wished.

"At that time there was a courtesan named Beautiful in that metropolis, with whom the king consorted. She had a lovely daughter named Splendor

of Delight in Virtuous Conduct, who was neither too tall nor too short, neither too stout nor too lean, neither too heavy nor too light. She had black
hair and eyes, a pleasant face, and a clear voice. She spoke sweetly and kindly,
she was wise, versed in all arts and sciences, clever and diligent, dignified and
serene, kind-hearted and gentle, always pleasant to be with. She had scarcely
any desire, aversion, or folly; she was modest and conscientious, soft and sincere, free from guile and deceit, self-controlled. She and her mother,
accompanied by many girls, got in a jeweled chariot and rode out of the city
before the prince Lord of Glory. Looking for the prince, going according to
the king's directions, when she saw the prince she became greatly enamored
of him. Bound by the excessive affection she conceived for the prince,
unable to control herself, she said to her mother, 'If you do not give me to
the prince Lord of Glory, I will die or suffer torment equal to death.' Her
mother said, 'Do not think this way. This prince has the marks of a supreme
ruler, and it is obvious that after his father passes away he will succeed to the
throne and become king. At that time a special woman will appear from the
sky. Furthermore, we prostitutes give pleasure to everyone; we do not serve
one person all our lives as a rule. We have set out to attend the prince Lord of
Glory at the command of the king Lord of Wealth. Do not hold fast to this
wish of yours, for it is unattainable.'

"Now, at that time a buddha named Supreme Sun was appearing in the
world, a saint, perfectly enlightened, complete in knowledge and conduct,
gone to felicity, supreme knower of the world, tamer of humans, teacher of
celestials and humans, awake, blessed. He was at an enlightenment site
called Light Emerging from the Cloud of Teaching in the park Cloud of
Light on a Mountain of Fragrant Plants, where he enjoyed his first seven
days since attaining enlightenment.

"The girl, who was reclining in the chariot, saw that buddha in a dream.
When she awoke, a goddess who had been a relative in a past life told her
that the buddha was in the park, in his first week of enlightenment, surrounded by a group of enlightening beings, before a crowd of all kinds of
spirits, and that all the deities of earth, space, water, fire, wind, oceans, rivers, mountains, night, dawn, forests, trees, plants, grain, cities, foot tracks,
sanctuaries, bodies of light, habitations, the sky, and all directions had gathered to see the buddha Supreme Sun.

"Emboldened by seeing the buddha and hearing of the buddha's virtues, finding a favorable opportunity, the girl then spoke these verses
before the prince:

> I am known in the world for beauty,
> Renowned everywhere for virtues.
> None compares to me in the power of knowledge;
> I know all arts, amusements, and magic.
>
> Hundreds, thousands of men
> Look on me with lust,

But I have no desire
For people of the world.

I have no ill-will,
Neither am I pleased by anyone.
I have neither anger nor hatred;
I delight in the welfare of all.

When I saw you, young man, excellent
In form and strength, endowed with virtue,
All my senses were delighted,
And immense joy arose in me.

Your complexion is like a pure shining jewel,
Your hair is black and curly,
You have a fine brow and nose;
I offer myself to you.

You have excellent features.
Resplendent, you are like a mountain of gold.
In your presence I do not shine;
I am like a pile of charcoal.

Your eyes are large and dark,
Your jaw is like a lion's, your face like the full moon.
The fine sound of your voice is irresistible;
Please take me in.

Your tongue is long and broad,
Coppery red, soft, shining like a jewel;
With your superb, clear voice
You delight people when you speak.

Your teeth are even, shining white,
Clean and well spaced;
When you show them as you smile,
You delight people, O hero.

Your body has the thirty-two marks
Of greatness, brilliantly shining, pure.
Adorned with them, you will become
A sovereign ruler of men.

"Then the prince Lord of Glory said to the maid Splendor of Delight in

Virtuous Conduct, 'Whose daughter are you, whose ward? I cannot make
another's ward my own.' Then he spoke these verses:

> O lovely one, endowed with beauty of form,
> With fine features and a pure body,
> I ask you to tell me this—
> Whose ward are you?

> Have you father or mother,
> Brother, husband, or master,
> Or someone else who thinks of you
> As his, treating you kindly?

> I hope you are not vicious,
> Do not steal,
> Are not promiscuous,
> And do not lie.

> I hope you do not cause discord,
> Do not slander others,
> Do not covet others' goods,
> And are not hostile toward anyone.

> May you not stand on the wasteland of views;
> Let your intelligence not be taken away by habits;
> May you not exert bad influence on people
> By guile or deceit.

> Do you love and respect your parents,
> Relatives, friends, and elders?
> Does your heart reach out
> To give to the poor to help them?

> Are you well disposed toward spiritual benefactors
> Who tell you about religion at the appropriate time?
> Are you truly healthy and capable
> In body and mind?

> Do you respect the buddhas
> And love the enlightening beings?
> Do you know the supreme Teaching
> From which the enlightening beings are born?

> Can you abide by the supreme religion
> And not do any wrong?

Do you have higher love and respect
For the infinite ocean of virtues?

Are you kind
To the helpless and lost?
Are you really compassionate
Toward evildoers?

Are you most happy
To see the success of others?
Are you indifferent, by the power of wisdom,
To those who annoy you for no reason?

Seeing people in the slumber of ignorance,
Do you firmly seek supreme enlightenment?
Would you not weary of endless ages
Of spiritual practice?

"Then the supreme courtesan Beautiful, mother of the maid Splendor of Delight in Virtuous Conduct, said to the prince Lord of Glory, 'This daughter of mine, who was spontaneously born from within a lotus, has never before gone out of the house.' Then she spoke these verses:

Listen to what I say, O prince,
About my daughter, of whom you ask.
I will tell you of her birth
And how she grew up.

On the very same morn as your birth,
My daughter too was born,
Generated spontaneously in the calyx of an undefiled lotus,
All her limbs complete, with nice big eyes.

In springtime, the best of seasons,
When the crops and herbs are growing,
In my beautiful grove of sal trees
I utterly forgot myself.

The branches were blooming with most beautiful flowers,
The fruiting trees were like dense clouds;
Amid the trees with singing birds
I roamed, joyful, free from care.

I was with eight hundred girls,
Adorned with garlands of flowers,
Wearing various precious cloths,
Well versed in song and speech.

I sat on the bank of a pond
Filled with lotuses of various scents;
The area around, strewn with flowers,
Was filled by those well-cultivated girls.

In the middle of the water appeared
A supremely fine lotus with a thousand petals;
Its stem was lapis lazuli, its petals were diamond,
Its pericarp was pure gold.

It had a multitude of stamens of the finest fragrant jewels
And had a brilliant golden sheen:
The people were confused—
How could the sun rise at night?

Then, the night ended, from the rising sun,
Stimulating with its glow,
There emanated light and sweet sounds,
Foretelling the birth of this girl.

Then this precious girl appeared in the human world,
Pure in the best of conduct.
No deed is lost to the doer; she was the fruition
Of good actions in the past.

With dark hair, lotus-blue eyes,
A clear voice and golden complexion,
Finely clad in garlands, she emerged
From the lotus, resplendent as pure light.

Her limbs are bright, her body evenly balanced;
Her limbs are complete, her body well proportioned:
She shines like a golden statue adorned with jewels,
Illumining all directions.

The finest fragrance of sandalwood wafts from her body,
Filling the air around her;
As she speaks, with celestial sweetness,
A scent like blue lotus comes from her mouth.

Whenever she smiles,
Heavenly music plays;
This treasure of a woman should not be abandoned
To the control of the vulgar.

In the world of men no one can be found

Who is worthy to be her husband, except you,
A resplendent figure with the marks of greatness—
Therefore, please accept this girl.

For she is not short or too tall,
Not stout or too thin;
She is slender at the waist, full-breasted,
Suitable for you, with an impeccable body.

She has perfect knowledge of calculation,
Writing, symbology, and technical literature;
She has mastered all the arts and crafts
In the whole world.

She is expert in archery
And always hits her mark;
Pacifying opponents by her power of attraction,
She is ultimately successful everywhere.

All her limbs are like pure jewels;
She radiates an aura of light.
Adorned by the virtues she has accomplished,
She is fit to be your companion.

She knows the cause of all illnesses
That afflict living beings,
And she is able to cure them
By correct use of medicines.

She has mastered all the different languages
Of the people on the continent
And the variety of customary usages
Of society everywhere.

She knows the articulation of sounds
And the means of differentiation among them,
And she is expert in all
The songs and dances in the world.

She is not jealous or envious,
She is not lustful or ill-tempered;
She is taciturn, honest, and gentle,
Free from anger and harshness, very intelligent.

She is diligent, well behaved, not argumentative,
Always obedient to the worthy;

She is respectful, seeking to do whatever is good.
She will do as you ask.

She is always compassionate toward the elderly,
Toward the sick and the poor,
Toward the suffering, the blind,
And toward the helpless.

She is always thinking of the welfare of others,
And never thinks of benefit for herself;
Seeking the welfare of the whole world,
She is adorned with superior virtues of mind.

She is never careless, always mindful and aware,
Whether standing, sitting, reclining, or walking,
Whether silent or speaking;
She is always remembered and honored.

This virtuous one shines in all ways,
And is always loved by people;
None would tire of looking at her,
But she has no attachment to the world.

Respectful of spiritual friends,
She wants always to see you;
This far-seeing, uncorrupted lady has a pure mind,
Stable as the polar mountain.

Ever-adorned with her own virtues,
She has no enemies at all;
She has no peer in knowledge.
She is fit to be your bride, O prince.

"Then the prince, having entered the park, said to the maid in the presence of her mother, 'I have set out for supreme perfect enlightenment, whereby I may gather the infinite stores of omniscience, cultivate the practice of enlightening beings for infinite eons and perfect all the transcendent ways, serve the buddhas for endless eons, uphold the teaching of all buddhas, purify all buddha-lands, perpetuate the lineages of all buddhas, develop all groups of sentient beings to maturity, stop the pains of the mundane whirl for all sentient beings, lead sentient beings to ultimate bliss, clarify the eye of knowledge in all sentient beings, strive for the attainments of all buddhas and enlightening beings, abide in the equanimity of all enlightening beings, accomplish all the stages of enlightening beings, purify all sentient beings, cultivate total giving to put an end to poverty for all sentient beings, practice transcendent giving for endless eons and satisfy all sentient beings with gifts of food and drink, and satisfy all beggars by giving away all goods. As I practice total relinquishment, everything internal and external is to be given away—I am to give away my sons, daughters, wife; I am to relinquish my eyes, head, hands and feet, all my limbs. You will hinder my giving, you will become unhappy at the relinquishment of beloved children, you will feel much physical and mental pain, you will resent my determination to give up everything. When I cut off my limbs to give them to beggars, you will be pained and grieved. And there will come a time when I leave you to go forth into the tutelage of a buddha; at that time you will be unhappy.' Then the prince spoke these verses to the maid:

> I am going to fulfill the immeasurable ocean
> Of provisions for perfect enlightenment;
> Therefore, with compassion for all,
> I have set forth forever for enlightenment.
>
> For infinite eons, measureless as air,
> I will purify my vow;
> For endless eons I will perform the preparations
> Of the initial stage of the buddhas.
>
> I will learn the paths of transcendence
> From the buddhas of past, present, and future
> And perfect the path of supreme enlightenment
> By the great means of unexcelled knowledge.
>
> I will purify all
> Defiled lands everywhere;
> I will remove all difficulties
> And evil ways from all worlds.
>
> I will purify all beings
> Who are wrapped up in afflictions, blind with delusion;
> Developing them by various means,
> I will bring them into the path of omniscience.
>
> I will accomplish the unobstructed stages
> And serve the buddhas for myriad eons;
> Generating kindness toward the world,
> I will give all gifts.
>
> As I am engaged in giving all
> To beggars who come,
> Do not become depressed
> Or sad or unsympathetic.

Seeing benefit for one who wants my head,
A wise person would delight in lofty conduct;
You would be tormented,
So hear my purpose and become firm.

You would be grieved at my giving
My severed hands and feet to beggars
And speak bitterly, faint and distressed;
So hear my purpose and think about it.

I will give away my prized possessions,
Even my children, yet I want you;
Hear my aim and if you do not despair,
All shall be as you wish.

"The maid replied to the prince, 'Let it be as you say. I will do as you wish.
I am at your service and will accompany you wherever you want to go. I will
always stay with you and be diligent in all tasks. I will behave as you wish. I
will exert myself properly and act in harmony with you." Then she spoke
these verses to the prince:

Even if my body should be burnt to death
In the fires of hell,
I would endure it for myriad lifetimes
As your companion in practice.

Even if life after life for endless lives
My body were cut asunder,
I would endure it with a steadfast mind
If you were my husband.

Even if the mountains should crush
My head for endless ages,
I would endure it unfazed
If you became my husband.

In infinite lifetimes you may cut off
Your own limbs and give them to others;
Lead me to control of my thoughts
And make me firm in my duty.

I give you my body completely,
O prince of men;
Performing spiritual practice for myriad ages,
Give me to whoever wants me, and I will be happy.

You have set out for supreme enlightenment,
With infinite compassion for beings;
Having taken all beings into your care,
Take me in too with compassion.

It is not for enjoyment
Or wealth or sensual pleasure
That I want you, best of men, for my husband,
But to share the same spiritual practice.

You look upon all beings
With clear eyes and kind heart;
Being compassionate with undefiled mind,
You will surely become a king of sages.

As you walk along, a jewellike glow
From your footsteps remains on the earth, pure;
Endowed with the marks of greatness,
You will surely become a sovereign king in the human world.

In a dream I saw the enlightenment site
Illumined by clouds of true teaching in this kingdom;
With the buddha sitting at the foot of the best of trees,
In the company of many enlightening beings.

That exalted buddha Supreme Sun
Is like a mountain of finest rose gold;
In my dream he patted my head,
And I awoke then, full of joy.

A pure-bodied goddess named Light of Delight,
Who had been a companion in the past,
Told me the buddha was here,
Staying at the supreme site of enlightenment.

I had been thinking before that I wanted
To see the prince Lord of Glory,
And I was told by the goddess
I would see the prince soon.

Now I have seen the buddha in a dream,
And have seen you, the perfect man;
My wish is fulfilled, and I am happy;
With you now I will honor that supreme sage.

"Then the prince, having heard the name of the buddha Supreme Sun and having thus gotten the opportunity to see the buddha, became very joyful; he showered the maid Splendor of Delight in Virtuous Conduct with five hundred jewels, gave her a shining crown of jewels, and covered her with a precious robe the color of fire blazing with jewels. And she, thus honored, neither rejoiced nor wept, nor did anything but gaze steadily at the prince with palms joined in respect.

"Then the prominent courtesan Beautiful spoke these verses to the prince:

> For a long dark time I have wished
> To give this girl to you;
> Now this beautiful maiden
> Of virtue and quality is yours.
>
> There is no girl in the world
> Equal to her, much less superior;
> By virtue of her conduct, intellect, and other qualities,
> She is the best of women in the world.
>
> Born of a lotus, there is no question of her class;
> She cannot be called impure.
> Her mind is free from the taint of all faults;
> She is capable of sharing your practice.
>
> Her limbs are extremely soft,
> Conveying the finest pleasures of touch;
> The sick are instantly cured
> By her touch.
>
> The pure fragrance of her body
> Excels all the finest perfumes;
> All men who smell it
> Become pure in conduct.
>
> Her body shines like gold,
> Undefiled like a lotus;
> Angry and cruel people
> Become kind when they have seen her.
>
> She speaks kindly, sweetly, pleasantly,
> A delight to people who hear;
> When they have heard her, the darkness of evil disperses,
> And none wants to do anything bad.
>
> Her mind is pure, her heart untainted;
> There is no guile at all in her.

What she says is just what she thinks,
And thus she makes people happy.

She does not fool anyone by deceit,
Nor does she lead people on for gain;
She is modest and discreet,
Always respectful to old and young.

She is not fascinated by class
Or looks or followers.
She has no conceit or arrogance;
She is always humble toward all.

"Then the prince and the maid, with her retinue of twenty thousand girls, left the park and went to the site of enlightenment where the buddha was, to see, pay respects to, make offerings to, and attend the buddha. Going by vehicle as far as the vehicle would go, the prince got off the vehicle and approached the buddha on foot; even at a distance he saw that the buddha was serene, a sight to behold, senses tranquil, mind quiet, senses under control, like a tame elephant, his heart like a clear, still pond. When he saw the buddha, the prince's mind became settled, and with a clear mind he developed great joy, well-being, and energy that derives from seeing a buddha. With his mind full of great joy, energy, serenity, and rapture, he paid his respects to the buddha, and together with his whole company, including the young woman, covered the buddha with five hundred thousand great jewel lotuses, and made five hundred sanctuaries of jewels for the buddha and adorned each one with five hundred thousand diamonds.

"Then the buddha, knowing the prince's strong determination, expounded a scripture called Lamp at the Door of the Universal Eye, upon hearing which the prince attained ten oceans of concentrations absorbed in all principles of the Teaching: he attained ways of concentration such as those called 'light produced from the oceans of vows of all buddhas,' 'path of illumination of past, present, and future,' 'going forth into the circle of all buddhas,' 'entry into the highest range of awareness of all beings,' 'attainment of the scope of knowledge of the causes that produce all worlds,' 'lamp illumining the oceans of faculties of all beings,' 'cloud of knowledge to save all beings,' 'lamp leading to the development and emancipation of all beings,' 'communicating the cycles of teaching of all buddhas,' and 'multitude of undertakings to purify the practices of universal good.' Beginning with these, the prince attained ten oceans of concentrations absorbed in all the principles of the Teaching. The young woman attained a meditation called 'filled with an ocean of invincible knowledge' and became irreversible in progress toward supreme perfect enlightenment.

"Then the prince, paying respects to the buddha, left the presence of the buddha with the young woman and the rest of the company and went to his father, the king, in the city. Greeting the king respectfully, he informed him that the buddha Supreme Sun had appeared in the world and was staying in the king's realm, having recently attained enlightenment. The king then asked the prince who had told him so, and he replied that it had been the young woman Splendor of Delight in Virtuous Conduct.

"Then the king, hearing of the emergence of the buddha, felt that he had gained a great treasure, felt that he had found the rare jewel of Buddha; he considered the sight of a buddha to be the end of the danger of falling into evil ways; he felt he had found a great physician who could heal all afflictions. He thought of the buddha as a liberator from all the sufferings of the mundane whirl, as one who leads to ultimate peace and felicity, as one who reveals the unobscured light of knowledge. He thought of the buddha as the appearance of a great torch dispelling the darkness of ignorance, and felt that he had found a spiritual guide for a world with no guide, thinking of the buddha as a leader to omniscience for the leaderless.

"Hearing of the emergence of the buddha with great joy, the king Lord of Wealth gathered together all the warriors, priests, townspeople, ministers, family priests, princes, and governors, as well as the gatekeepers and courtiers, and abdicated the throne in favor of his son Lord of Glory, who had brought the joyous news of the appearance of the buddha. Then, having crowned the prince as king, he went together with ten thousand people to the buddha, paid his respects, and sat with his retinue before the buddha.

"Then the buddha, looking at the king and the whole assembly, emitted a light from the curl of hair between his brows, a light called 'lamp of the minds of all beings,' which illumined all worlds in the ten directions, then stopped in front of all the world leaders, displayed inconceivable buddha-projections, clarified the minds of those beings who could be taught by the buddha, and then, by the inconceivable mastery of Buddha, by means of embodiment of Buddha appearing in all worlds, speaking all languages in the voice of Buddha, expounded a medium of mental command called 'unshaded lamp of meaning of all things,' which was accompanied by as many media of mental command as atoms in a buddha-land. The king Lord of Wealth, hearing of this medium of mental command, gained an immense spiritual perspective on all things. As many enlightening beings there as atoms in the continent attained the mental command of the unshaded lamp of meaning of all things. Sixty million people, freed from contaminations, were mentally liberated. Ten thousand people became dispassionate and untainted, and their objective vision of things was clarified. An immense number aspired to supreme perfect enlightenment for the first time. Infinitely many beings in the ten directions, by seeing the inconceivable mystic displays projected by the buddha, reached liberation by way of the Three Vehicles.

"The king Lord of Wealth, having gained great illumination from the Teaching, thought, 'I cannot apply myself assiduously to such a teaching or accomplish such knowledge while living at home; let me leave home to be with the buddha.' Then he told the buddha he wanted to receive the precepts from the buddha and leave home to become a mendicant. The buddha assented to this.

"So then the king and ten thousand of his people left home to follow the buddha. Not long after leaving home, he accomplished the mental command of the unshaded lamp of meaning of all things, along with its subsidiaries, and attained that many concentrations. He also attained ten mystic knowledges of enlightening beings and plunged into infinite oceans of analytic knowledge. He also attained a purity of body called 'unhindered sphere of action' in going to see the buddhas of the ten directions. He received the teaching of the buddha, preserved it, and preached it, having become a great spiritual preacher and a practitioner of the teaching. By the power of attainment of mystic knowledge, he pervaded the whole world, appearing to people according to their mentalities, telling them of the emergence of the buddha, illuminating the nature that produces all buddhas, explaining the accomplishment of the past practices of the buddha, praising the miraculous power of the buddha, supporting the buddha's teaching.

"As for the new king, the son of Lord of Wealth, on that very day, the time of the full moon, he obtained the seven treasures of kingship. As he was sitting in the upper palace surrounded by a group of women, there appeared a great disc called 'unobstructed momentum,' adorned with a hundred thousand jewels, made of gold, shining all over, perfectly formed. There also appeared a great elephant named Diamond Mountain Blaze. There also appeared a horse named Swift As the Wind in the Mountains. There also appeared a great jewel called 'supreme cluster of sunlight.' There also appeared the young woman Splendor of Delight in Virtuous Conduct, to be his treasure of a wife. There also appeared a treasurer named Mass of Abundant Wealth. There also appeared a military leader, the seventh treasure, called Untainted Eye. Endowed with these seven treasures, he became king, sovereign, ruler of the four continents, just, commander of the law, victorious, with the power and vigor of the people. He also had a full thousand sons, strong and valiant, destroyers of enemy armies. Under his just rule the earth was free from war, free from evil, free from calamity, prosperous, peaceful, pleasant, and well populated.

"In each of the eighty-four thousand main cities on the continent, he had five hundred sanctuaries built, complete with all the finest features, equipped with all utensils, supplies, and facilities, adorned with gardens, buildings, promenades, and delightful groves. In each sanctuary he also had buddha-memorials built, high and wide, adorned with many arrays of jewels. And he invited the buddha Supreme Sun to all those cities, where he presented the buddha with inconceivable offerings of all kinds. The miracle of the entry of the buddha into the cities fostered virtue in innumerable people, and all those with disturbed minds attained tranquillity, while those with calm minds developed the intense joy of seeing the buddha; those who were full of joy attained purity of will for enlightenment, while those whose will for enlightenment was pure developed great compassion; those of goodwill became involved in the quest for all buddha-teachings, while those who knew the principles of the buddha-teaching set their minds to meditation on the intrinsic nature of all things; those who had realized the equality of things set their minds on realizing the equality of past, present, and future; those who had attained the scope of knowledge of past, present, and future entered into the light of knowledge of the succession of all buddhas, while those who had entered the knowledge of various manifestations of buddhas set their minds on the salvation of all sentient beings; those engaged in the salvation of all beings vowed to complete the path of enlightening beings, while those who had realized the equanimity of the path generated the light of knowledge to bring forth the cycles of teaching of all buddhas; those who were ready for the guidance of the ocean of teachings set their minds on pervading the network of all lands with their own bodies, while those who realized the equality of lands undertook to know the faculties of all sentient beings, and those engaged in consideration of the faculties of all sentient beings in accord with their inclinations purified the determination to reach omniscience. Entering into the fulfillment of such benefits for such people, the king Lord of Glory had the buddha Supreme Sun enter all the cities, to develop and guide those people by the inconceivable vision of the miracles of the Buddha.

"Now, who do you think that prince Lord of Glory was? You should see him as none other than this buddha Shakyamuni, who at that time was a prince named Lord of Glory, who attained kingship, and was on good terms with the buddha Supreme Sun. And who do you think the king Lord of Wealth, father of Lord of Glory, was? You should see him as none other than the buddha Jewel Flower Light, who at that time was a king named Lord of Wealth, who attained supreme perfect enlightenment at an enlightenment site symbolized by reflection of the moon and expounded the Teaching surrounded by as many enlightening beings as atoms in untold buddha-lands in a world called Shining Lamp of the Aura of Buddha in a world system called Family Born of a Diamond Reflecting Past, Present, and Future in the center of an ocean of worlds called Multitude of Reflections in the Space of the Cosmos of Realities, which was to the east past as many oceans of worlds as atoms in a world. Furthermore, that ocean of worlds, Multitude of Reflections in the Space of the Cosmos of Realities was purified by that buddha Jewel Flower Light in the course of his past practice as an enlightening being, and all the past, present, and future buddhas in that ocean of worlds were ripened for supreme perfect enlightenment by that buddha Jewel Flower Light as he carried out the practice of enlightening beings.

"Now then, who do you think was the queen Lotus Born in that time, mother of the prince Lord of Glory, foremost of the eighty-four thousand women? You should see her as none other than Lady Maya, mother of the Blessed Buddha, progenetrix of the enlightening being Vairocana, established in unobstructed liberation of universal light, direct witness to the appearance of the countless multitude of all buddhas, who knows the manner of manifestation of birth of all enlightening beings.

And who do you think was the great courtesan Beautiful? You should see her as Sunetra, wife of Dandapani of the Shakya clan, who is my mother.

And who was her daughter, Splendor of Delight in Virtuous Conduct? You should see her as me.

"Who do you think were the retinue of the king Lord of Wealth? They were these enlightening beings seated here in this assembly, guided by the Buddha to the fulfillment of the vows of universally good action, with a body reflected in all worlds, mind unadulterated and unfragmented in all concentration states of enlightening beings, eyes seeing the being and countenance of all buddhas, ears hearing the utterances of all buddhas, breath in control of all spiritual stations, voice going to all buddha-lands, the body of an enlightening being ceaselessly going to the audiences of all buddhas, entering the network of all places by production of embodiments suitable to develop and guide according to the mentalities of those to whom the enlightening beings appear, arriving at fulfillment of the vows of practice of universal good unbroken throughout the ages.

"The king Lord of Glory and I, furthermore, attended the buddha Supreme Sun as long as he lived, providing him with the necessities of life. After that buddha passed away entirely, a buddha named Pure Body emerged, in that same world, and we honored and served him. After that we served, in succession, buddhas named Moon Reflecting Knowledge in All Limbs, King of Golden Light, Adorned with Marks of Greatness, Moon Blazing with a Web of Brilliant Light Beams, Paragon of Observant Knowledge, King Illumined with Great Knowledge, Adamantine Energy, Invincible Power of Knowledge, All-Observing Knowledge, Cloud of Pure Light, Crown Blazing with Lights of Knowledge, Banner of Lights of Virtue, Energy of the Sun of Knowledge, Limbs Like Blooming Jewel Lotuses, Lamp of Felicity, Radiance of Multitudes of Rays of Knowledge, Moon Shining Everywhere, Powerful Lion Illumined by Universal Knowledge, Moon of Cosmic Mind, Reflection in the Spacelike Mind of Beings, Tranquil and Well Balanced, Ubiquitous Sound of Silence, Cluster of Images in a Network of Light Rays of Stable Knowledge, Radiance of the Mountain of Immortality, Thunder of the Ocean of Truths, Crown of Light in the Sky of Buddhas, Moon of Light Beams, Face of Complete Knowledge, Luster of Flowers of Pure Knowledge, Glorious Light of a Mountain of Jewel Flowers, Light of Myriad Stars of Virtue, Knowledge Emerging from the Heights of Concentration, Jewel Moon, Circle of Flames, Sublime Jewel Radiance, Unhesitating in Practice of Universal Knowledge, Blazing Lamp Topped with a Sea of Flames, King Proclaiming the Mansion of Truth, Famed for Peerless Virtue, Moon Reflecting Past Vows, Lamp of Meaning with Spacelike Knowledge, Lord of the Sky, Born of Truth, King Filled with Shining Light, Paragon of Spirituality, Chief in Knowledge, Lotus in the Ocean of Truth. Beginning with these, there were sixty decillion buddhas in that world whom we honored, served, and provided with food and clothing, medicine and furniture.

"The last of those sixty decillion buddhas was one named Energy Born of Great Zeal for Truth. When that buddha came to town, I, as wife of the king, together with my husband, made all kinds of offerings and then heard an exposition of the Teaching from the buddha called 'lamp produced by the emergence of all those who arrive at Thusness,' on hearing which I attained the eye of knowledge, and attained this enlightening liberation whose sphere is observation of the oceans of concentrations of all enlightening beings.

"Cultivating this liberation for as many eons as atoms in one hundred buddha-lands, carrying out enlightening practice with the enlightening being Vairocana, I associated with countless buddhas during those many eons. In an eon I might serve one buddha or two, up to an inexpressible number of buddhas; some eons I served as many buddhas as atoms in a buddha-land. Yet never did I know the size of the enlightening being's body or what it looked like; nor did I know the enlightening being's physical, verbal, or mental actions, nor his knowledge and vision, his range of knowledge, or his realm of concentration of knowledge. As for those who, seeing the enlightening being carrying out the practice of enlightening beings, developed pure faith through various associations, all of them were taken care of by the enlightening being by various worldly and transmundane means, and became associates of the enlightening being. Associating with the enlightening being as he carried on enlightening practice, they never regressed on the way to supreme perfect enlightenment.

"Having attained the enlightening liberation whose sphere is observation of the oceans of concentrations of all enlightening beings when I saw the buddha Energy Born of Zeal for Truth, as I cultivated this liberation along with the enlightening being for as many eons as atoms in a hundred buddha-lands, I propitiated, served, and attended all the buddhas who emerged in those ages and heard, took up, and remembered their teachings; and I attained this liberation from all those buddhas, by various methods, by various enunciations of principles and systems of scriptures, by various bodies of liberation, by various doors of liberation, by various liberative meditations and procedures, by various ways of access, by entry into various oceans of buddha-lands, by various visions of oceans of buddhas, by entry into various buddhas' assemblies, by various paths following the oceans of vows of enlightening beings, by carrying out various paths following the oceans of vows of enlightening beings, by carrying out various practices of enlightening beings, by accomplishing various practices of enlightening beings, by various manifestations of the scope of the endeavor of enlightening beings: yet I still did not enter the enlightening being's universally good liberation. Why? Because the ways of liberation of the universally good enlightening beings are infinite as space, infinite as the thoughts of all sentient beings, infinite as the ocean of time periods of past, present, and future, infinite as the ocean of places, infinite as the ocean of structures of the cosmos; indeed, the ways of liberation of the universally good enlightening beings are equal to the sphere of buddhahood.

"For as many eons as atoms in a buddha-land I gazed at the enlightening being, never tired of seeing him. Just as countless illogical thoughts and illusions rise in the minds of a woman and man full of passion when they get together, as I watched the body of the enlightening being, in every moment of consciousness I perceived infinitely various indications from each of his pores—the range of world systems, their various foundations, various con-joining arrangements, various configurations, various mountain ranges, various arrays of the ground, various arrays of clouds in the sky, various names and numbers of eons, emergence of various buddhas and formation of lineages of buddhas, various adornments of enlightenment sites, various occult powers involved in the buddhas' teaching procedures, various arrays of buddhas' audiences, various enunciations of scriptures, productions of various vehicles of emancipation, and various manifestations of pure light, the like of which I had never seen before. By ceaseless effort, from each of his pores I saw in each moment of consciousness infinite oceans of buddhas, various adornments of enlightenment sites, various mystic operations of the Teaching, and various miraculous proclamations of scriptures. From each of his pores I saw, in each moment of consciousness, infinite oceans of beings, various houses, gardens, mountains, palaces, rivers, seas, and dwellings, vari-ous physical bodies, various goods, various actions and efforts, and various forms of development of faculties. From every one of his pores infinitely various ways of entering past, present, and future became perceptible; infi-nitely various oceans of vows of enlightening beings were purified, infinite oceans of differences of the practices of the stages of enlightening beings became perceptible, the infinitely various purities of the transcendent ways of enlightening beings became perceptible, infinitely various oceans of past efforts of enlightening beings became perceptible, infinitely various oceans of ways of purifying buddha-lands became perceptible; infinitely various oceans of the universal love of enlightening beings, oceans of universal love for all beings, and oceans of heroic efforts to develop and guide all beings descended into the world, infinite oceans of the universal compassion of enlightening beings arose, infinite oceans of the great joy of enlightening beings grew, and in every moment of consciousness infinitely various oceans of efforts to take care of all sentient beings were accomplished.

"In each moment of consciousness through those eons numerous as atoms in a hundred buddha-lands, I perceived oceans of principles of the Teaching from each pore of the enlightening being, and never reached the end, even though I did not go into what I had already gone into, and did not attain what I had already attained. This I did by going into the ocean of various ways of liberation of the enlightening being, even when he was the prince Siddhartha in the royal palace surrounded by women; I perceived infinitely various oceans of principles of past, present, and future through each of his pores, by penetrating the oceans of ways into the realm of reality.

"I only know and have attained this enlightening liberation whose sphere is observation of the oceans of concentrations of all enlightening beings. How can I know the practice, tell of the qualities, or show all the oceans of virtue of the enlightening beings who have gone into the infinitely various oceans of liberative means, who purposely appear physically like all beings, who appear to act in accord with the mentalities of all beings, who emanate infinitely various appearances from all their pores, who realize the purity of essence and nature of all bodies, who are free from discriminatory thought because of awareness of the spacelike quality of the nature of beings, whose intellect reaches everywhere with certain discernment, occupied with spiritual powers equal to those who arrive at Thusness, who produce miraculous displays of infinite spheres of liberation, who have mastered the state where they can enter the vast cosmos of realities in a thought, who roam freely in the ocean of liberation of the all-sided stage of all truths?

"Go to Lady Maya, mother of the enlightening being, who is sitting on a great jewel lotus seat near the Blessed Vairocana. Go ask her how enlightening beings become undefiled by the taint of worldly things while they are carrying out the practice of enlightening beings, how they become unflagging in serving all buddhas, how they become undeviating from the ends of the actions of enlightening beings, how they become free from all hindrances to entry into the liberations of enlightening beings, how they become unfixed to all states of enlightening beings, how they come into the presence of all buddhas and do not stop their efforts to take care of all sentient beings, do not cease enlightening practice for all time, do not regress from the undertaking of the Great Vehicle of universal enlightenment, and do not become discouraged in maintaining and increasing the roots of goodness in the world."

Then, by the empowerment of Buddha, Gopa spoke these verses illustrating this way of liberation:

> Those who see the best of people
> Engaged in the practice of perfect enlightenment
> All go to join him,
> Be they friendly or inimical.

> I remember as many eons as there are atoms
> In a hundred lands;
> There was an excellent world of outstanding light,
> With an age of supreme magnificence.

> In that age, in that world,
> Were sixty decillion buddhas;
> The last of them, best of sages,
> Was a lamp of the world, Spiritual Paragon.

> At the time of that buddha's demise
> There was a glorious king
> Who had conquered all enemies,
> A king of kings with unobstructed knowledge.

> He had five hundred sons
> Who were heroic, brave, and handsome,

Physically perfect and pure,
Adorned with unexcelled splendor.

The king and his sons had faith in Buddha
And made great offerings to the enlightened;
They always followed the true teaching
And were unshakable in application of its practice.

The king had a brilliant son,
A pure being,
Adorned with the thirty-two
Marks of a great man.

Giving up his kingship, he left home
Together with five million people;
Having gone forth, he worked with firmness and energy
To preserve the teaching of the Buddha.

There was a city full of trees,
Best of a billion cities;
There was a forest there of various trees,
Quiet and most beautiful.

There the king's son sojourned,
Experienced, intelligent, clear-minded;
He elucidated the Buddha's teaching
To purify the spirit of defiled beings.

Gathering wise people, he entered the city,
Composed, of noble mien and serene appearance,
His gaze steady, mindful, aware,
His action profound, walking steadily.

There was an excellent town, Banner of Joy,
And a grandee there named Resounding Fame;
I was his beloved daughter,
Named Shining Light, more beautiful.

I saw the shining prince and his retinue
As I stood in the door of my house;
He was handsome, with the marks of greatness,
And I became very happy on seeing him.

When he passed my door,
I put a pearl in his bowl;

Then, taking off all my jewelry,
Full of love I gave it to him.

With an impassioned heart
I made a gift to that enlightening being,
And for two hundred and fifty eons
Did not fall into evil states.

I was born among celestials,
Or as a human princess,
And in endless forms
I always saw the prince.

Then I was born to a courtesan,
Saw the prince and fell in love,
Made myself known to him,
And became his obedient wife.

He and I together made offerings
To the sage Supreme Sun with pure faith,
And having seen that buddha,
I was inspired to seek supreme enlightenment.

During that eon sixty decillion
Buddhas emerged in the world:
The last of those buddhas
Was Energy of Zeal for Truth.

Then my objective eye was clarified
And I became aware of the essence of things;
My continuous errant conceptions were silenced,
And I attained this illumination thenceforth.

After that I observed the stage
Of concentration of enlightening beings;
In a mental instant I see unthinkable
Oceans of lands in the ten directions.

And I see in all directions
Various pure worlds, infinitely wondrous;
Seeing them, my mind does not cling to them,
Nor is it repelled by defiled lands.

I also see the enlightenment sites in those lands
And all the buddhas there,
And I behold in one thought
Their measureless oceans of light.

In the same way I see their oceanic congregations
In an instant of awareness, unimpeded,
And know all their concentrations,
And all their immeasurable liberations.

I also keep their myriad practices in mind,
And penetrate all the principles of the stages;
And in each and every instant I enter
Into the countless oceans of their vows.

Observing the body of the True Man for endless eons
And carrying out his practice,
I have never seen an end to the mystic projections
Emanating from his every hair.

And I see oceans of lands beyond number
On the tip of a single hair,
With their masses of air and water, fire and earth,
On various foundations, with different forms,
And diverse patterns of structure,
Of various types, according to distribution of elements,
With an endless variety of adornments.

I see each of the untold realms
In the measureless oceans of lands,
And I see the buddhas therein
Guiding people by articulating truth.

I do not understand his activities,
His speech, his mind, or its action,
Or his mystic powers and miracles, or great sublime practice,
Though I have been working at this for eons.

Then Sudhana paid his respects and took leave of Gopa.

Maya

Then Sudhana, turning to go to Lady Maya, having attained knowledge from investigation of the sphere of buddhahood, thought to himself, "How can I meet, associate with, and learn from spiritual benefactors whose senses are detached from all worlds, who do not abide anywhere, whose bodies are beyond all attachments, who have set out on the unimpeded path, who have purified the spiritual body, who skillfully project bodily forms by the illusion of physical action, who observe the world as being within the illusion of knowledge, who are physical embodiments of vows, whose bodies are made of mind by the power of Buddha, whose bodies are not born and do not perish, whose bodies are neither real nor unreal, whose bodies neither come nor go, whose bodies neither become nor disintegrate, whose bodies are of one form which is formless, whose bodies are nondual and freed from attachments, whose bodies have no resting place, whose bodies have no extinction, whose bodies are like reflections and have no difference, whose bodies are like dreams in action, whose bodies are like images in a mirror, whose bodies stand tranquilly everywhere equally, whose bodies are emanations pervading all directions, whose bodies are continuous through past, present, and future, whose bodies are neither physical nor mental and are indivisible, whose bodies are beyond the range of vision of all worldlings, whose secret being can only be known to the vision of the eye of universal good, whose realm of action is unobstructed like space?"

As he was engaged in such thoughts, a city goddess named Jewel Eyes, surrounded by a group of sky goddesses, showed herself in the sky, her body adorned with various adornments, holding a basket of celestial flowers of many shapes and colors, and spoke to Sudhana in these terms as she scattered them before him: "You should guard the city of mind, by not dwelling on enjoyment of mundane objects. You should adorn the city of mind, by concentrating on the ten powers of the enlightened. You should clean the city of mind, by getting rid of jealousy, envy, and guile. You should extinguish the burning of the city of mind, by meditating on all truths. You should expand the city of mind, by increasing the flow of great energy in preparing for omniscience. You should protect the dwellings, storehouses, and facilities of the city of mind, by command of the vast spiritual palace of all concentrations, attainments, meditations, and liberations. You should illumine the city of mind, by absorbing universal transcendent wisdom in the assemblies gathered around all buddhas. You should make the city of mind firm, by putting the paths of means produced by all buddhas into the city of your own mind. You should build strong walls about the city of mind, by purification of mind in carrying out the vow of practice of universal good. You should make the city of mind invincible and impregnable, by being invulnerable to all afflictions and bad influences. You should light up the city of mind, by illumining all beings with the knowledge of the enlightened. You should irrigate the city of mind, by receiving the clouds of teaching of all buddhas. You should firmly brace the city of mind, by absorbing into your own mind the oceans of virtues of all buddhas. You should broaden the city of mind, by suffusing all beings with great love. You should provide shelter, by producing the shield of all good ways in the vast canopy of the Teaching. You should water the city of mind, by feeling great compassion for all beings. You should open the doors of the city of mind, by giving of yourself and giving goods to all beings. You should purify the city of mind, by turning away from passion for ephemeral things. You should make the city of mind steadfast and strong, by excluding all unhealthy elements from your body-mind continuum. You should energize the city of mind, by maintaining the energy to produce the provisions for omniscience. You should illuminate the city of mind, by the illumination of recollection of the spheres of the buddhas of past, present, and future. You should know how to stock the city of mind, by examination, learning, and higher knowledge of the various doors of truth in the scriptures of the cycles of teaching of all buddhas. You should know how to govern the city of mind, by showing all beings the path of entries into omniscience in various ways. You should know how to support the city of mind, by perfection of accomplishment of the vows of all buddhas of past, present, and future. You should know how to increase the power to provide for the city of mind, by increasing the great stores of virtue and knowledge from all realms of truth. You should know how to emanate light throughout the entire city of mind, by higher knowledge of the science of stripping away defilements from the minds, senses, and interests of all sentient beings. You should know how to control the city of mind, by embracing all the principles of the realm of reality. You should make the city of mind light, by the light of mindfulness of all buddhas. You should know the essence of the city of mind, by penetrating the principle of nonsubstantiality of all things. You should observe the illusoriness of the city of mind, by going to the spiritual city of omniscience.

"By thus purifying the city of mind, an enlightening being can produce all good. Why? Because no obstacles stand before an enlightening being whose mind-city is thus purified—no obstacles to seeing buddhas, or obstacles to hearing the Teaching, or obstacles to serving buddhas, or obstacles to efforts to save sentient beings, or obstacles to purifying buddha-lands. Spiritual friends are easily perceptible to an enlightening being looking for spiritual friends when the mind is free from obstacles; and omniscience for enlightening beings comes through the help of spiritual friends."

Then a goddess, Spiritual Lotus, surrounded by innumerable goddesses radiant with modesty and beauty, came forth from the enlightening site praising Lady Maya and stopped in the sky in front of Sudhana, each goddess emanating webs of light of many jewel colors, colors of pure flames of incense of many fragrances, colors soothing the mind, colors increasing the flow of joy in the mind, colors cooling the fever of the body, colors showing physical purity, webs of light produced by the motion of unattached, unimpeded bodies. Illumining a multitude of lands, revealing to Sudhana the forms of all buddhas everywhere, the lights then circled the whole world and descended into Sudhana's head, and from his head entered into all of his pores.

As soon as the light rays of the goddesses touched Sudhana, he acquired an eye called 'dispassionate light,' with which no darkness can coexist; he acquired an eye called 'unobscured,' whereby he saw the essence of beings; he acquired an eye called 'dispassionate sovereign,' whereby he viewed the sphere of essence of all phenomena; he acquired an eye called 'pure state,' whereby he viewed the nature of all lands; he acquired an eye called 'shining light,' whereby he viewed the reality body of those who arrive at Thusness; he acquired an eye called 'universal light,' whereby he viewed the inconceivable perfection of the physical embodiment of those who arrive at Thusness; he acquired an eye called 'unobstructed light,' whereby he viewed the becoming and disintegration of worlds in all universes; he acquired an eye called 'total illumination,' whereby he observed the manner of extraction of the principles of the scripture in the teachings of all buddhas; he acquired an eye called 'universal scope,' whereby he viewed the infinite variety of mystic powers used by buddhas to guide beings; he acquired an eye called 'all-seeing,' whereby he observed the emergence of buddhas in all lands.

Then a supernatural being named Fine Eye, doorkeeper of the hall of assembly of enlightening beings, at the head of ten thousand supernatural beings, together with his wife and son and clan, sprinkled Sudhana with flowers of various colors and pleasant fragrances, and said, "An enlightening being imbued with ten qualities can approach all spiritual friends. What are these ten? A pure mind free from guile and deceit; great compassion taking in all beings as a whole; meditation on the unreality of self-existence of all beings; the willpower to proceed unswervingly toward omniscience; the power of attention to the spheres of all buddhas; clear perception of the purity of essence of all phenomena; great kindness to all beings as a whole; the light of knowledge that dissolves all barriers; the great body of teachings that acts as a shield against the miseries of the mundane whirl; the eye of knowledge of all currents of reality, directed toward the path of spiritual friends.

"Having attained these ten things, enlightening beings can approach all spiritual friends; and by observation through ten ways of concentrated meditation they can come face to face with all spiritual friends. What are the ten? Meditation on the purity of the sky of reality; meditation viewing the ocean of all realms; meditation without discrimination or thought of any objects; meditation on the appearance of the multitudes of buddhas of all realms; meditation on the multitude of virtues of omniscience; meditation with every thought constantly on spiritual friends; meditation on the virtues of all buddhas deriving from spiritual friends; meditation on being with all spiritual friends forever; meditation on always going to all spiritual friends everywhere equally; meditation devoted to tireless application of the techniques of all spiritual friends. The enlightening being who has accomplished these ten kinds of concentrated meditation comes face to face with all spiritual friends and attains a liberation through concentration called 'enunciation of the teachings of all buddhas by spiritual friends,' practicing which the enlightening being realizes the indivisible sameness of all buddhas and finds spiritual friends everywhere in contact."

Having been told this by the supernatural being, Sudhana looked up to the sky and said, "Bravo, O noble one, sympathetic one; you are trying to help me and show me spiritual friends. Tell me, in the right way, how to proceed; where should I go? Where should I search? What should I meditate on to see spiritual friends?"

The supernatural being said, "One may go into the presence of spiritual friends by an attitude of universal respect, by mental focus on remembering spiritual friends in all things, by concentration speeding everywhere by dreamlike speed of mind, by realizing mind and body as like reflections."

Then Sudhana, practicing as he had been taught by the supernatural being Fine Eye, saw a great jewel lotus spring up from the ground in front of him. In the heart of the lotus he saw a tower called 'chamber containing the cosmos,' beautifully made of gold and jewels. Inside the tower he saw a lotus calyx throne made of wish-fulfilling jewels, set on jewel figurines of the chiefs of all realms of being, arrayed with many kinds of precious adornments and bells which emanated sounds telling of the principle of universal love, the names of the buddhas of past, present, and future, the teachings of all buddhas, and the vows of all enlightening beings. It was also arrayed with rows of jewels which reflected the manifestations of buddhas and the succession of births of all buddhas of past, present, and future, rows of radiant jewels showing the lights of the activities in all buddha-lands throughout space and the effecting of all miracles, emanating the auras of light of all buddhas, emanating apparitions like the chiefs of all worlds making offerings to buddhas, and jewels filling the cosmos in every moment with the mystic projections of the universally good enlightening being. Every object on the throne of inconceivable qualities emanated celestial eulogies of the enlightened. The throne was also surrounded by an inconceivable number of seats arrayed with jewels.

Sudhana saw Lady Maya sitting on that throne, her physical form transcending all in the triple world, having gone beyond all states of being; facing all beings, appearing according to their mentalities; unstained by any world, being made of myriad virtues; in the likeness of all beings, appearing in such a way as to please all beings; adapted to develop and guide all beings, descending into the presence of all beings; appearing continuously to beings at all times like the sky, appearing to all beings to be permanent; not going anywhere, not passing away from all worlds, not coming anywhere, not coming into existence in any world; unoriginated, absorbed in the equanimity of nonorigination; unextinguished, involved in the affairs of all worlds; not real, having attained suchness; not false, appearing in accord with the world; not in motion, being divorced from death and birth; not annihilated, because of the nonannihilation of the nature of reality; undefinable, being beyond any manner of speaking; uniform, her auspicious characteristics issuing from indefinability; like a reflection, appearing according to the minds of all beings; like magic, made of the magic of knowledge; like specks of light, moment to moment sustained by the thoughts of beings; like a shadow, bound to all beings by commitment; dreamlike, appearing to beings according to their mentalities without being mixed up; reaching throughout all universes, being in nature pure as space; issuing from universal compassion, engaged in the protection of the community of beings; issuing from the door of nonobstruction, pervading the cosmos in each instant; infinite, dwelling in all worlds without defilement; measureless, transcending all manner of verbal expression; nondwelling, manifesting to guide all beings; unfixed, appearing magically in the body of a living being; not really existing, made by the magic of aspiration; unsurpassed, being beyond all worlds; unreal, being a manifestation of tranquillity; unproduced, connected to beings according to their acts; like a wish-fulfilling jewel, fulfilling the commitment to satisfy the wishes of all beings; without discrimination, based on the thoughts of all beings; beyond conception, unknowable to all beings; based on resolve, never leaving the mundane; pure, nonconceptual like Thusness.

In this form did Sudhana see Lady Maya, manifesting a physical body that was not form, being a reflection of form; not feeling, being the ultimate cessation of painful feelings of the world; outside the thoughts of all beings, but appearing in their thoughts; issuing from the unfabricated nature of reality, detached from illusory action; transcending the sphere of discriminatory consciousness, born of the knowledge of vows of enlightening beings; having no intrinsic essence, being beyond the range of all verbal expression; free from the burning of the mundane whirl, having arrived at the state of supreme coolness of the reality-body—she was appearing physically to beings in accord with their minds by mastery of their minds, appearing in forms resembling all beings but superior to the physical forms of all beings. Some beings saw her in the form of a devil woman, with a form superlative among devil women; some saw her in forms superlative among the goddesses of various heavens; some saw her in forms superlative among the females of the various kinds of beings; some saw her in the form of a most beautiful human princess.

Then Sudhana, emptied of notions of the forms of all beings, penetrating the minds of other beings, saw Lady Maya in the minds of all beings, her virtue sustaining all beings, her body an accumulation of the virtues of omniscience; she was engaged in nondiscriminatory perfect giving, impartial toward all beings, having united all beings in the fellowship of universal compassion; she had set out to actualize the virtues of all buddhas; she had entered the ocean of all ways of tolerance; her mind was expanded with a flood of energy of omniscience; she was indefatigable in clarification of all spheres of truth; she was adept in meditation on the essence of all things; her mind was accomplished in all branches of meditation; she was engaged in all branches of meditation without confusion and had perceived the unique sphere of meditation of those who arrive at Thusness; she was intent on various meditations to evaporate the ocean of afflictions of all beings; she knew how to analyze the teachings of all buddhas; she had the wisdom to consider all the designs of reality; she gazed tirelessly on all buddhas; she ceaselessly observed the succession of buddhas of past, present, and future; she faced the door of vision of all buddhas; she knew the variety of techniques to perfectly accomplish the path of attainment of all buddhas; she coursed in the space of all who realize Thusness; she knew how to take care of all beings; she appeared in an infinite variety of reflections to develop and guide beings according to their mentalities; she comprehended the variety of purities of all buddha-bodies; she had vowed to purify all lands; she had perfected the vow to guide all beings to ultimate liberation; her mind pervaded the spheres of all buddhas with respect; she had the energy to produce all the miracles of enlightening beings; she had purified the supreme spiritual body; she manifested infinite physical bodies; she crushed the power of all demons; she was imbued with the power of great roots of goodness; with intellect born of the power of truth she perceived the power of buddhas; she had perfected all powers of mastery of enlightening beings; she was flooded with the power of omniscience; her wisdom was illumined by the lightning of the knowledge of all buddhas; her knowledge contemplated the infinite ocean of minds of beings; she comprehended the myriad mentalities of beings; she was expert in knowledge of the differences in faculties of others; she was skilled in knowledge of the differences in interests of infinite beings; her body pervaded infinite oceans of lands in the ten directions; she was expert in knowledge of the differences in all worlds; she was skilled in the means of knowing the junction and disjunction of all lands; she saw throughout all realms by knowledge; she was aware of all times; she bowed to all buddhas; her mind was directed toward reception of the ocean of all buddha-teachings; she was engaged in accomplishing fulfillment of all qualities of buddhas; her intellect was applied to the production of all the provisions for enlightenment; she boldly considered and carried out all the undertakings of enlightening beings; she had completed all the elements of development of the will for enlightenment; she was engaged in protecting all beings; she undertook to be the mother of all enlightening beings and buddhas.

Beginning with these, Sudhana saw Lady Maya in as many ways as atoms in the continent: seeing her, he magically made his body as extensive as Lady Maya, and with this omnipresent body bowed to the ubiquitous Maya. As he was bowing, an infinite variety of concentrations entered into him. Observing those concentrations, making them externally undetectable, cultivating them, mastering them, remembering them, making them all-pervasive, expanding them, watching them, increasing them, accomplishing them, and fixing their impression, he rose from those concentrations and circled Lady Maya, her retinue, her abode and seat, and then stood respectfully before her and said, "Noble one, Manjushri inspired me to seek supreme perfect enlightenment and directed me to attend spiritual benefactors. So I have been approaching spiritual friends, benefactors, and in the course of doing so I have come to you. Now please tell me, noble one, how an enlightening being may achieve omniscience while carrying out the practice of enlightening beings."

She said, "I have attained an enlightening liberation, 'magical manifestation of knowledge of great vows.' Imbued with this liberation, I am the mother of all the enlightening beings in their final existence in all the worlds in this world-ocean where Vairocana Buddha's miraculous manifestation of birth as an enlightening being in the final existence takes place. All those enlightening beings grow in my belly and come forth from my right side. So here too in this great city of Kapilavastu, as wife of the king Shuddhodana, I became the mother of the enlightening being Siddhartha, by the great inconceivable miracle of the birth of an enlightening being.

"At that time I was in the house of king Shuddhodana, and when the time of the enlightening being's descent from the heaven of contentment had arrived, from every pore the enlightening being emanated as many rays of light as atoms in untold buddha-lands, arrayed with the qualities of the birth of all enlightening beings, known as the light originating from the qualities of birth of all buddhas; those rays of light illumined the whole world, then descended on my body and entered into every pore of my body, beginning with my head. As soon as those light rays of the enlightening being, with various names, emanating magical projections of the various miracles attending the birth of an enlightening being, had entered me, they caused the spheres of light at the front of the enlightening being's light rays to be manifest in my body, and the supernal manifestations of miracles attending the birth of all enlightening beings were visible. And as soon as those light rays of the enlightening being had entered my body, I saw all the enlightening beings whose birth-miracles were shown in the spheres at the front of the enlightening being's light rays, as they sat on the Buddha's lion throne at the site of enlightenment, surrounded by congregations of enlightening beings, honored by the leaders of the worlds, turning the wheel of the teaching. I also saw all the buddhas with whom those buddhas associated as they carried out enlightening practices in the past. I also saw mystical projections of their initial inspiration, attainment of enlightenment, turning of the wheel of the teaching, final extinction, and the pure arrays of all buddha-lands, as well as the multitudes of emanations of those buddhas pervading the cosmos in each moment of consciousness. When those rays of light of the enlightening being entered my body, my body outreached all worlds, and my belly became as vast as space, and yet did not go beyond the human physical size. The supernal manifestations of the enlightening beings' abode in the womb everywhere in the ten directions all appeared in my body.

"Upon the appearance in my body of the furnishings of the enlightening being's abode in the womb, the enlightening being, together with as many enlightening beings as atoms in ten buddha-lands, all with the same vow, the same practice, the same roots of goodness, the same state of liberation and the same stage of knowledge, adept at the same mystic projection, having accomplished the same endeavor, adept at the same practice, having purified the same spiritual body, able to assume an infinite variety of physical forms, expert in the projection of the endeavors of universally good enlightening beings, respectfully attended by chiefs of all worlds, descended from the heaven of contentment by the great miracle of enlightening beings; appearing to pass away from all heavens of contentment, appearing to become regenerated in all worlds, from each heaven of contentment to early existence, following skill in means of developing inconceivable numbers of sentient beings to maturity, alerting all intoxicated, deluded beings, detaching from all attachments, emanating a great network of light beams dispelling the darkness from all worlds, stopping all evils and miseries, putting an end to all hellish ways of being, making all beings aware of their past deeds, rescuing all beings, appearing in the presence of all beings, he descended from the heaven of contentment with his retinue and entered my belly.

"Once all of them were in my belly, they walked around in strides as big as a billion-world universe, even as big as worlds as numerous as atoms in untold buddha-lands. Also all the untold congregations of enlightening beings at the feet of all buddhas in all worlds in the ten directions entered my belly in every moment of thought to see the miracle of the enlightening being's dwelling in the womb. The chief gods of all the heavens also came to the enlightening being in the womb, to see and honor him, to listen to the Teaching and hear his discourse. Yet even though it took in all those multitudes, my belly was not enlarged, nor did this body of mine become any more than a human body. Yet it received so many multitudes; and all the celestials and humans saw the various pure arrays of the enlightening beings' surroundings. Why was this? Because of the development of this enlightening liberation of the magic of knowledge of great vows.

"Just as I received the enlightening being in my belly in this world, so did I likewise do so in all worlds in the billion-world universe, and with this same miraculous manifestation; yet this body of mine is neither dual nor nondual, neither single nor multiple; this is because of the development of this enlightening liberation of the magic of knowledge of great vows. And just as I was the mother of this buddha Vairocana, so was I the mother of infinite buddhas before. Whenever an enlightening being was spontaneously born in the calyx of a lotus, there I became a lotus-pond goddess and received the enlightening being, and the world recognized me as the progenetrix of the enlightening being; in whatever buddha-land an enlightening being appeared, I became an enlightenment-site goddess there: thus in whatever ways enlightening beings manifested birth in the world in their final existence, in so many ways did I become the mother of the enlightening beings.

"Just as I was the mother of this buddha in this world in all his manifestations of miracles of birth as an enlightening being, so was I the mother of the buddhas Krakucchanda, Kanakamuni, and Kashyapa; and so will I be the mother of all the buddhas of this eon.

"When the time comes for the enlightening being Maitreya, now in the heaven of contentment, to manifest descent from heaven, and emanate the lights of the manifestation of the miracles of enlightening beings abiding in the womb whence they are born, I will see all realms in all universes which are illumined thereby, where Maitreya will be born in a royal family in the human world and will guide sentient beings, and everywhere therein I will be the mother of the enlightening being.

"And just as I will be the mother of Maitreya, so will I be the mother of all buddhas in this eon in this universe, and in all universes of the ten directions, penetrating endless universes. And just as I will be the mother of Maitreya, by untold virtues, so shall I be the mother of all the buddhas in this eon, and in endless billions of eons in all the worlds in all world systems in this flower treasury ocean of worlds, I will be the mother of all the buddhas of the future when they are enlightening beings, carrying on the practice of universally good enlightening beings, establishing guidance for the perfection of all beings in all ages."

Then Sudhana asked Lady Maya, "How long ago did you attain this enlightening liberation of magical manifestations of knowledge of great vows?"

Maya replied, "Inconceivable eons ago, beyond the range of mind, beyond conscious calculation, there was an age called Pure Light. In that age of Pure Light there was a world called Elevated, which was pure with some defilement, made of many jewels, with surrounding mountains, polar mountains, and oceans, containing realms of celestials, humans, animals, ghosts, and hells, variegated and pleasant to see. In that world were a billion sets of four continents, in the middle of which was a group of four continents called Supreme Lionlike Majesty, in which there were eighty billion metropolises, among which was one called Possessed of the Best of Banners. There in that metropolis was a king called Great Energetic Power, a sovereign ruler. There was also an enlightenment site in that metropolis called Conspicuous Rays of Light, wherein there was a deity called Radiant Eyes. Furthermore, at that enlightenment site an enlightening being named Pure Standard sat, to attain omniscience. A demon named Golden Light, along with a great army of cohorts, had come invisibly to prevent the enlightening being from attaining omniscience; but the king Great Energetic Power, who had attained the mastery which enlightening beings realize, issued a great magical projection, producing a great army, more numerous than and superior to that of the demons, to surround the enlightenment site and fight off the demon army. The demon army was thereby scattered, and the blessed Pure Standard realized perfect enlightenment.

"The goddess of the enlightenment site, Radiant Eyes, looking upon the king as her son, then prostrated herself before the buddha and made a vow: 'Wherever I may be born, may the king Great Energetic Power be my son; and when he attains supreme perfect enlightenment, I will be his mother then too.' Having made this vow, she attended ten decillion buddhas at that enlightenment site during that eon.

"Now, who do you think that goddess was? It was I myself who was the enlightenment-site goddess Radiant Eyes at that time. As for the king Great Energetic Power, who had the mastery of an enlightening being and destroyed the demon army by means of a magical projection, it was none other than this present buddha, the blessed Vairocana, the saint, the perfectly enlightened one, who was at that time the king Great Energetic Power. Ever since then, wherever I have been, he has come as my son, carrying out the practice of enlightening beings in all buddha-lands, in all states of being, in all lifetimes, based on all that is good, in all undertakings through which enlightening practice is carried out. Wherever he emerged to develop and perfect sentient beings, there I was his mother, and in his final existence too, I was his mother, everywhere. In all modes of birth as an enlightening being, moment to moment, however many miracles of birth as an enlightening being he displayed, in every case I was his mother. In the same way I was the mother of infinite buddhas of the past, and I am mother to the infinite buddhas of the ten directions in the present. And all the buddhas I was mothers to in their last existence as an enlightening being emanated lights from their navels and illumined this great body and this seat.

"I only know this enlightening liberation of magical manifestation of knowledge of great vows—how can I know the practice or tell of the virtues of the enlightening beings who are filled with great compassion, who never tire of guiding to perfection of omniscience, who are able to display projections of the miracles of all buddhas from every pore?

"In the thirty-three-fold heaven of this world is a goddess named Surendrabha, who is the daughter of a god named Smrtimati. Go ask her how to learn and carry out the practice of enlightening beings."

So then Sudhana paid his respects and left Lady Maya.

Surendrabha

Then Sudhana went to the thirty-three-fold heaven, and went to the goddess Surendrabha. Paying his respects to the goddess, Sudhana stood before her and said, "Noble one, I have set my mind on supreme perfect enlightenment, but I do not know how to learn and carry out the practice of enlightening beings. I hear you give instruction to enlightening beings, so please tell me how to learn and practice."

Surendrabha replied, "I have attained an enlightening liberation called pure manifestation of unimpeded recollection. I am aware that there was an age called Flowering, in which I served as many buddhas as there are grains of sand in the Ganges River. When they went forth from their customary surroundings, I protected them, provided for them, and made parks for their use. And all the developmental guidance of sentient beings performed by those buddhas—while they were enlightening beings, while in the womb of the mother, while being born, while taking seven steps, while roaring the lion's roar, during childhood, during life at home, when leaving home, when awaking at the site of enlightenment, while teaching, while displaying the miracles of buddhas—all that, from their first inspiration to the final ending of their true teaching, I know and remember, recall and keep in mind, reflect on and follow.

"There was an eon called Well-Being, in which I served as many buddhas as sand grains in ten Ganges Rivers; there was an eon called Good Fortune, in which I served as many buddhas as atoms in a buddha-land; there was an eon called No Attainment, in which I served eighty-four thousand duodecillion buddhas; there was an eon called Beautiful Light, in which I served as many buddhas as atoms in this continent; there was an eon called Peerless Light, in which I served as many buddhas as sand grains in twenty Ganges Rivers; there was an eon called Blazing Glory, in which I served as many buddhas as sand grains in the Ganges River; there was an eon called Sunrise, in which I served as many buddhas as sand grains in eighty Ganges Rivers; there was an eon called Victorious March, in which I served as many buddhas as sand grains in sixty Ganges Rivers; there was an eon called Beautiful Moon, in which I served as many buddhas as sand grains in seventy Ganges Rivers.

"In this way, I remember as many eons as sand grains in the Ganges River, during which I was always with buddhas, and I heard of this enlightening liberation of pure manifestation of unimpeded recollection from those buddhas, and practiced it as they told me. Thus, constantly engrossed in this liberation, I recollect, remember, keep in mind, reflect on, and recall the supernal manifestations of all those buddhas from their stages of enlightening to the end of the duration of their true teachings, by means of this enlightening liberation of pure manifestation of unimpeded recollection.

"I only know this enlightening liberation—how can I know the practice, or tell the virtues, of the enlightening beings who are free from all obscurity and darkness, who light up the night of the mundane whirl, who are rid of all obstacles, who do not slumber, who are rid of apathy and indolence, who have stopped compulsive actions based on conditioning, who have purified awareness of the essence of all things, who awaken others to the purity of the ten powers?

"In the city of Kapilavastu there lives a boy named Vishwamitra who is a teacher. Go ask him how to learn and carry out the practice of enlightening beings."

Then Sudhana paid his respects and left the goddess Surendrabha.

Vishwamitra

Descending from the thirty-three-fold heaven, Sudhana made his way to Kapilavastu, where he went to see the young teacher Vishwamitra. Paying his respects, he stood before the teacher and said, "Noble one, I have set my mind on supreme perfect enlightenment, but I do not know how to learn and carry out the practice of enlightening beings. I hear you give enlightening beings instruction, so please tell me how to learn and practice."

Vishwamitra said, "I learned the science of writing from a young enlightening being named Shilpabhijna. Go ask him and he will tell you how the practice of enlightening beings is to be learned and carried out."

Shilpabhijna

Then Sudhana went to the youth Shilpabhijna, paid his respects, and said to him, "Noble one, I have set my mind on supreme perfect enlightenment, but I do not know how to learn and carry out the practice of enlightening beings. I hear you give enlightening beings instruction, so please tell me how an enlightening being is to learn and carry out enlightening practice."

Shilpabhijna said, "I have attained an enlightening liberation with higher knowledge of arts. In uttering the phonemes, as I pronounce *A*, by the associative power of an enlightening being I enter a door of transcendent wisdom called sphere of totality; pronouncing *Ra*, I enter a door of transcendent wisdom called differentiation of infinite levels; pronouncing *Pa*, I enter a door of transcendent wisdom called differentiation of levels of the cosmos of realities; pronouncing *Cha*, I enter a door of transcendent wisdom called analysis of the universal sphere; pronouncing *Na*, I enter a door of transcendent wisdom called independence; pronouncing *La*, I enter a door of transcendent wisdom called unattached; pronouncing *Da*, I enter a door of transcendent wisdom called unregressing effort; pronouncing *Ba*, I enter a door of transcendent wisdom called adamantine sphere; pronouncing *Da*, I enter a door of transcendent wisdom called universal sphere; pronouncing *Sa*, I enter a door of transcendent wisdom called ocean womb; pronouncing *Va*, I enter a door of transcendent wisdom called branching out everywhere; pronouncing *Ta*, I enter a door of transcendent wisdom called sphere of light; pronouncing *Ya*, I enter a door of transcendent wisdom called multitude of mixtures; pronouncing *Shta*, I enter a door of transcendent wisdom called light extinguishing all burning; pronouncing *Ka*, I enter a door of transcendent wisdom called unified multitude; pronouncing *Sha*, I enter a door of transcendent wisdom called directed rain; pronouncing *Ma*, I enter a door of transcendent wisdom called crest of various currents of great force; pronouncing *Ga*, I enter a door of transcendent wisdom called extending to all levels; pronouncing *Tha*, I enter a door of transcendent wisdom called unified womb of Thusness; pronouncing *Ja*, I enter a door of transcendent wisdom called plunging into purification of the mundane whirl; pronouncing *Swa*, I enter a door of transcendent wisdom called supernal manifestation of recollection of all buddhas; pronouncing *Dha*, I enter a door of transcendent wisdom called contemplative investigation of truths; pronouncing *Sha*, I enter a door of transcendent wisdom called light of the wheel of teaching of all buddhas; pronouncing *Kha*, I enter a door of transcendent wisdom called womb of knowledge of the causal ground of accomplishment; pronouncing *Ksha*, I enter a door of transcendent wisdom called investigation of the treasury of the ocean in which all actions are stilled; pronouncing *Sta*, I enter a door of transcendent wisdom called light of purity dispelling all afflictions; pronouncing *Na*, I enter a door of transcendent wisdom called access to worldly knowledge; pronouncing *Tha*, I enter a door of transcendent wisdom called sphere of knowledge of the cycles of the mundane whirl; pronouncing *Bha*, I enter a door of transcendent wisdom called array of manifestations of spheres of existence; pronouncing *Chha*, I enter a door of transcendent wisdom called division of the encompassing sphere of practice applied to development; pronouncing *Sma*, I enter a door of transcendent wisdom called turning to face all directions to see all buddhas; pronouncing *Hwa*, I enter a door of transcendent wisdom called matrix of power to observe what all sentient beings cannot; pronouncing *Tsa*, I enter a door of transcendent wisdom called plunging into practice of the ocean of all virtues; pronouncing *Gha*, I enter a door of transcendent wisdom called strong oceanic vessel holding the multitude of all teachings; pronouncing *Tha*, I enter a door of transcendent wisdom called going in the direction of the vows of all buddhas; pronouncing <u>Na</u>, I enter a door of transcendent wisdom called voicing the millions of configurations of the wheel of phonemes; pronouncing *Pha*, I enter a door of transcendent wisdom called sphere of the ultimate development of all sentient beings; pronouncing *Ska*, I enter a door of transcendent wisdom called suffusion of the sphere of light of unimpeded intellectual powers contained in the stages of enlightenment; pronouncing *Sya*, I enter a door of transcendent wisdom called sphere of exposition of all buddha-teachings; pronouncing *Shcha*. I enter a door of transcendent wisdom called thunder of truth filling the sky of beings; pronouncing <u>Ta</u>, I enter a door of transcendent wisdom called lamp of the ultimate consummation of selfless work for the benefit of sentient beings; pronouncing <u>Dha</u>, I enter a door of transcendent wisdom called matrix of the distinction of cycles of the Teaching.

"As I pronounce the phonemes, I enter immeasurable, innumerable doors of transcendent wisdom, beginning with these forty-two. I have attained this enlightening liberation with higher knowledge of arts, and it is this I know. How can I know the practice or tell the virtues of enlightening beings who have attained perfection of all mundane and transcendental arts, inasmuch as they have no barrier, no doubt, no confusion, no uncertainty, no hesitation, no ignorance, no difficulty, no impairment, no frustration, no lack of knowledge, and no misunderstanding in regard to the subject matters of all arts—all writing and mathematics, all applied sciences of spells and herbs, all the bases of obsession, psychotherapy, epilepsy, lameness, and insanity, the science of compounding medicines, chemistry, mineralogy, the making of parks, groves, villages, towns, and cities, knowledge of the vicissitudes of the world through astronomy, physiognomy, geomancy, meteorology, agronomy, and prediction of trends of events, and the analysis, communication, understanding, and actualization of all transmundane phenomena.

"In the city of Vartanaka, in the region of Kevalaka, in this same country of Magadha, there lives a laywoman named Bhadrottama. Go ask her how an enlightening being is to learn and carry out the practice of enlightening beings."

So Sudhana paid his respects and left the noble youth Shilpabhijna.

Bhadrottama

Then Sudhana went to Vartanaka city in the region of Kevalaka, where he called on the laywoman Bhadrottama. Paying his respects to her, he said, "Noble one, I have set my mind on supreme perfect enlightenment, but I do not know how an enlightening being is to learn and carry out the practice of enlightening beings. I hear you give enlightening beings instruction, so please tell me how to learn and practice."

She said, "I know and teach a doctrine called 'baseless sphere' and have attained a concentration of mystic empowerment. In that concentration there is no foundation of any phenomenon whatsoever. Therein is produced the mystical empowerment of the eye of omniscience, the mystical empowerment of the ear of omniscience, the mystical empowerment of the nose of omniscience, the mystical empowerment of the tongue of omniscience, the mystical empowerment of the body of omniscience, the mystical empowerment of the mind of omniscience, the mystical power of the waves of omniscience, the mystical power of the lightning of omniscience, the mystical power of the flood of omniscience, spheres illumining the world.

"It is this doctrine of the baseless sphere that I know. How can I know all the unobstructed, unattached practices of enlightening beings? Go south—there is a city called Bharukaccha, where there lives a goldsmith named Muktasara. Go ask him how an enlightening being is to learn and carry out the practice of enlightening beings."

So then Sudhana paid his respects, took his leave, and departed.

Muktasara

Then Sudhana made his way south, to the goldsmith Muktasara in the city of Bharukaccha. Paying his respects to Muktasara, Sudhana said, "Noble one, I have set my mind on supreme perfect enlightenment, but I do not know how an enlightening being is to learn and carry out the practice of enlightening beings. I hear you give enlightening beings instruction, so please tell me how to learn and practice."

Muktasara said, "I know an enlightening liberation called supernal manifestation of unobstructed mindfulness, and I ceaselessly seek the Teaching at the feet of all buddhas in the ten directions. I only know this enlightening liberation. How can I know the practice or tell the virtue of the enlightening beings who roar the fearless roar of the lion, who are grounded on great virtue and knowledge?

"There is a householder named Suchandra living in this city, whose house is always illuminated; go ask him how to learn and carry out the practice of enlightening beings."

So Sudhana paid his respects, took his leave, and departed.

Suchandra

Then Sudhana went to the householder Suchandra, paid his respects, and said, "Noble one, I have set my mind on supreme perfect enlightenment, but I don't know how to learn and carry out the practice of enlightening beings. I hear you give enlightening beings instruction, so please tell me how an enlightening being is to learn and practice."

Suchandra said, "I have attained an enlightening liberation called light of undefiled knowledge. I only know this liberation. How can I know the practice or tell of the virtues of the enlightening beings who have attained infinite liberation? South of here is a city called Roruka, where a householder named Ajitasena lives. Go ask him how to learn and carry out the practice of enlightening beings."

So Sudhana paid his respects and left.

Ajitasena

Then Sudhana made his way to the city of Roruka, where he called on the householder Ajitasena. Paying his respects, Sudhana said, "Noble one, I have set my mind on supreme perfect enlightenment, but I do not know how an enlightening being is to learn and carry out the practice of enlightening beings. I hear you give enlightening beings instruction, so please tell me how to learn and practice."

Ajitasena said, "I have attained an enlightening liberation called inexhaustible appearance, with the attainment of which I obtained an inexhaustible treasury of vision of buddhas. South of here is a village called Dharma, where there lives a brahmin named Shivaragra. Go ask him how an enlightening being is to learn and carry out the practice of enlightening beings."

So then Sudhana paid his respects again and left.

Shivaragra

Then Sudhana made his way to Dharma village and called on the brahmin Shivaragra. Paying his respects, he said, "Noble one, I have set my mind on supreme perfect enlightenment, but I do not know how an enlightening being is to learn and carry out the practice of enlightening beings. I hear you give enlightening beings instruction, so please tell me how to learn and carry out the practice of enlightening beings."

Shivaragra said, "I act on a vow of truth, that as by truth, by speaking truth, there has never been, is not now, and never will be, a single enlightening being who has turned away from supreme perfect enlightenment, who is turning away, or who will turn away, by that vow of truthful speech this work of mine may succeed. So whatever I wish comes to fruition. By this vow of truth, I accomplish all my tasks. It is this vow of truth that I know. How can I know the practice or tell the virtues of the enlightening beings whose words and deeds mutually accord in truth?

"South of here is a city called Sumanamukha, where there live a boy named Shrisambhava and a girl named Shrimati. Go ask them how an enlightening being is to learn and carry out the practice of enlightening beings."

Then, with great reverence for the Teaching, Sudhana paid his respects to the brahmin Shivaragra and left.

Shrisambhava and Shrimati

Then Sudhana went to the city of Sumanamukha, and there he called on the boy Shrisambhava and the girl Shrimati; paying his respects to them, he said, "Noble ones, I have set my mind on supreme perfect enlightenment, but I do not know how an enlightening being is to learn and carry out the practice of enlightening beings. I hear you give enlightening beings instruction, so please tell me how to learn and carry out the practice of enlightening beings."

They said to him, "We have attained and experienced an enlightening liberation called 'illusory.' Having realized this liberation, we see all worlds as illusory, being produced by the illusion of causes and conditions. We know all beings are illusory, by knowledge of the illusion of afflictions in action. We see all worldlings as illusory, born of the illusion of ignorant craving for existence. We see all phenomena as illusory, arisen from the illusion of mutual conditioning. We see the whole triple world as illusory, produced by the illusion of misunderstanding. We see all sentient beings, afflicted by birth, old age, death, grief, lament, suffering, and sorrow, as illusory, born of the illusion of untrue ideas. We see all lands as born of illusion, produced by the delusion of ideas of substance of existence in the illusions wrongly seen by the conceiving mind. We see all hearers and individual illuminates as illusory, born of illusory thoughts of knowledge and effort. We know the succession of all enlightening beings' practices, vows, and developmental guidance of sentient beings as illusory, being essentially illusions of action and teaching created from illusion. We see the circle of all buddhas and enlightening beings as illusory, being essentially illusions of the inconceivable realm, produced by the illusions of vows and knowledge.

"We know this enlightening liberation of illusoriness. How can we know the practice or tell of the virtues of the enlightening beings who follow the extensive network of the endless illusion of action?"

Then the boy and girl, having showered Sudhana with an inconceivable stream of virtue and told him of their own range of liberation, said to him, "Go south, to a place called Samudrakaccha. There is a park called Great Array there, wherein there is a great tower called Chamber of Adornments of Vairocana, which has been produced by the maturation of roots of goodness of enlightening beings, originating from the thoughts of enlightening beings, arisen from the vows of enlightening beings, based on the masteries of enlightening beings, created by the power of mystic knowledge of enlightening beings, made of the skill in means of enlightening beings, completed by the power of virtue and knowledge of enlightening beings, showing enlightening beings' great compassionate guidance of sentient beings, built of arrays of spiritual powers of enlightening beings, adorned by the states of inconceivable liberation of enlightening beings. There an enlightening being, a great being named Maitreya, lives for the purpose of benefiting the people of his native land, developing his parents and relatives to maturity, making those there who carry out the same practices firm in the Great Vehicle, to develop the roots of goodness of other beings according to their states, to show how to enter this liberation, to cultivate the power of an enlightening being to be born anywhere and travel about, appearing in all states of being, to perfect those beings, to develop the power of universal compassion of enlightening beings in the desire to benefit all beings, to become aware of the state of enlightening beings, which is detached from all abodes and locations, and to appear to live in all states of existence while being ultimately unattached.

"Go to Maitreya and ask how an enlightening being is to seek the practices of enlightening beings, clarify the path of enlightening beings, carry out the studies of enlightening beings, purify the aspiration for enlightenment, accomplish the vows of enlightening beings, establish the provisions of enlightening beings, enter the stages of enlightening beings, fulfill the transcendent ways of enlightening beings, persist in the tolerances of enlightening beings, stabilize the qualities of achievement of enlightening beings, and attend spiritual benefactors.

"Why? Because the enlightening being Maitreya has entered into all practices of enlightening beings; he has reached the goal of aspirations of all enlightening beings; he has comprehended the actions of all beings; he has confronted the developmental guidance of all beings; he has fulfilled all the transcendent ways; he has been through all the stages of enlightening beings; he has attained all the tolerances of enlightening beings; he has attained the certainty of enlightening beings; he has received all the predictions of buddhahood; he has roamed in all the liberations of enlightening beings; he has held the empowerments of all buddhas; he has been anointed by all buddhas with the consecration of the realm of omniscience. As a spiritual benefactor, he will nourish your roots of goodness, increase your determination for enlightenment, make your will firm, purify all your roots of goodness, increase the powers of your enlightening faculties, show you the realm of nonobstruction, bring you into conformity with the stage of universal goodness, introduce you to the means of carrying out all the vows of enlightening beings, describe to you the perfection of the virtues of the practical undertakings of all enlightening beings, and tell you about the practice of universal good.

"You should not develop just one virtue, nor concentrate on clarifying just one doctrine, nor be satisfied with just one practice, nor concentrate on carrying out just one vow, nor take up just one instruction, nor rest in completion, nor think of attaining the three tolerances as ultimate, nor rest upon fulfillment of the six transcendent ways, nor stop on attainment of the ten stages, nor vow to encompass and purify a finite buddha-land, nor be content with attendance on a limited number of spiritual benefactors.

"Why? Because an enlightening being should gather infinite roots of goodness, assemble infinite provisions for enlightenment, produce infinite bases of aspiration for enlightenment, learn infinite principles, extinguish the afflictions of infinite beings, penetrate the minds of infinite beings, know the faculties of infinite beings, work for the emancipation of infinite beings, be aware of the conduct of infinite beings, create guidance for infinite beings, destroy infinite afflictions and their consequences, clear away infinite obstacles caused by actions, put a stop to infinite views, remove infinite mental afflictions, produce infinite mental purities, destroy infinite miseries, evaporate infinite oceans of beings' cravings, dispel infinite ignorance, bring down infinite mountains of pride, remove infinite bonds of the mundane whirl, evaporate the infinite ocean of birth, cross over infinite torrents of existence, extricate infinite beings stuck in the mud of desire, emancipate infinite beings from the dungeon of the triple world, place infinite beings on the path of sages, extinguish infinite lust, hatred, and delusion, rise above infinite nets of demons, purify infinite will of enlightening beings, increase infinite effort of enlightening beings, produce infinite faculties of enlightening beings, purify infinite resolutions of enlightening beings, enter infinite equanimity of enlightening beings, pursue infinite practices of enlightening beings in their entirety, purify infinite qualities of enlightening beings, fulfill infinite practices of enlightening beings, accord with infinite worldly practices, show infinite adaptations to the world, produce infinite power of faith, stabilize infinite power of vigor, clarify infinite power of mindfulness, purify infinite power of concentration, arouse infinite power of wisdom, stabilize infinite power of resolution, produce infinite power of virtue, expand infinite power of knowledge, establish infinite power of enlightening beings, fulfill infinite power of buddhas, ascertain infinite ways to truth, enter infinite realms of truth, clarify infinite doors to truth, produce infinite lights of truth, create infinite perspectives on truth, illumine infinite groups of faculties, clear away infinite afflictions, collect infinite spiritual medicines, cure sentient beings of infinite sicknesses caused by afflictions, collect infinite stores of immortality elixir, enter infinite buddha-lands, honor infinite buddhas, enter infinite assemblies of enlightening beings, remember infinite instructions of buddhas, endure infinite maliciousness from sentient beings, cut off infinite paths of misfortune, give infinite happiness to sentient beings, create infinite benefit for sentient beings, purify infinite methods of mental command, carry out infinite vows, cultivate infinite powers of universal love and compassion, persist in infinite endeavors in search of truth, pursue infinite powers of meditation, develop infinite mystic knowledge, purify infinite lights of knowledge, go the ways of infinite beings, encompass infinite becoming, appear in infinite different forms, know infinite different languages, comprehend infinite differences in the minds of beings, enter the vast realm of action of enlightening beings, live in the vast palace of enlightening beings, observe the profound state of enlightening beings, awaken to the mysterious realm of enlightening beings, reach the difficult goal of enlightening beings, sustain the hard-to-attain energy of enlightening beings, enter the difficult-of-access certainty of enlightening beings, be aware of the varied practice of enlightening beings, show the ubiquitous miracle of enlightening beings, receive the united multitudes of teachings, spread the infinitely varied network of practices of enlightening beings, fulfill the endless ways of transcendence, receive infinite directions for the future, enter countless doors of tolerance, purify countless stages of enlightenment, purify innumerable ways of access to truth, purify untold buddha-lands, put on spiritual armor for endless eons, serve infinite buddhas, accomplish the undertakings of inconceivable vows.

"In short, the practice of enlightening beings is to perfect all sentient beings, to live in all ages, to manifest birth everywhere in all conditions, to awaken to knowledge of all times past, present, and future, to practice all truths, to purify all lands, to fulfill all vows, to provide for all buddhas, to be one with all enlightening beings in aim, to attain rapport with all spiritual friends.

"Therefore you should not tire of seeking spiritual friends and benefactors, should not weary of meeting spiritual friends and benefactors, should not become complacent about questioning spiritual friends and benefactors, should not give up the determination to contact spiritual friends and benefactors, should not cease striving to respectfully attend spiritual friends and benefactors, should not misconstrue or resist the advice or instruction of spiritual friends and benefactors, should not be irresolute in acquiring the qualities of spiritual friends and benefactors, should not doubt the ways of emancipation shown by spiritual friends and benefactors, should not malign the acts of spiritual friends and benefactors adapting to the world to expedite their work, should not give up increasing pure faith in spiritual friends and benefactors.

"What is the reason for this? It is from spiritual benefactors that enlightening beings learn the practice of enlightening beings; it is through spiritual benefactors that all enlightening beings' virtues are perfected; spiritual benefactors are the source of the streams of all enlightening beings' vows; the roots of goodness of all enlightening beings are produced by spiritual benefactors; the provisions for enlightenment are produced by spiritual benefactors; all enlightening beings' perceptions of truth derive from spiritual benefactors; the purification of all ways to enlightenment derives from spiritual benefactors; the accomplishment of all studies of enlightening beings depends on spiritual benefactors; the virtuous qualities of all enlightening beings are based on spiritual benefactors; the purification of all enlightening beings' wills is rooted in spiritual benefactors; the steadfastness of determination of all enlightening beings is born of spiritual benefactors; the light of the oceanic mental command and intelligence of all enlightening beings derives from the guidance of spiritual benefactors; the treasuries of ways of purification of enlightening beings are sustained by spiritual benefactors; the lights of knowledge of all enlightening beings are generated by spiritual benefactors; the excellence of vows of all enlightening beings is in the hands of spiritual benefactors; single-mindedness is led by spiritual benefactors; the faith characteristic of the attainment of all enlightening beings has its source in spiritual benefactors; the secrets of all enlightening beings are in the treasury of spiritual benefactors; spiritual benefactors are mines of principles of enlightening beings; the sprouts of power of the faculties of all enlightening beings are fostered by spiritual benefactors; the oceans of knowledge of all enlightening beings are expounded by spiritual benefactors; the treasuries of all enlightening beings are guarded by spiritual benefactors; the accumulations of virtues of all enlightening beings are protected by spiritual benefactors; the purities of life of all enlightening beings are generated by spiritual benefactors; the multitude of teachings for all enlightening beings come from spiritual benefactors; the entries into the paths of emancipation of all enlightening beings are in the keeping of spiritual benefactors; the enlightenment of all buddhas is attained by association with spiritual benefactors; the practice of all enlightening beings is governed by spiritual benefactors; the developments of virtues of all enlightening beings are illumined by spiritual benefactors; the directions followed by all enlightening beings are shown by spiritual benefactors; the greatness of will of all enlightening beings is described by spiritual benefactors; the power of universal love of enlightening beings derives from spiritual benefactors; the power of universal compassion of enlightening beings is generated by spiritual friends; the masteries of all enlightening beings are governed by spiritual benefactors; all elements of enlightenment are produced by spiritual benefactors; the charitable works of all enlightening beings originate from spiritual friends.

"Sustained by spiritual benefactors, enlightening beings do not fall into bad ways; supported by spiritual benefactors, enlightening beings do not fall away from the Great Vehicle; minded by spiritual benefactors, enlightening beings do not overstep the precepts of enlightening beings; guarded by spiritual benefactors, enlightening beings do not come under the sway of bad influences; protected by spiritual benefactors, enlightening beings do not deviate from the laws of enlightening beings; aided by spiritual benefactors, enlightening beings go beyond the stage of sentient beings; taught by spiritual benefactors, enlightening beings do not drop into the fall of those who seek individual liberation alone; hidden by spiritual benefactors, enlightening beings rise above the world; developed by spiritual benefactors, enlightening beings are unstained by mundane things; attended by spiritual benefactors, enlightening beings become heedful and alert in all their practices; roused by spiritual benefactors, enlightening beings do not give up their undertakings; assisted by spiritual benefactors, enlightening being become invulnerable to active afflictions; based on the power of spiritual benefactors, enlightening beings cannot be crushed by any demons; in association with spiritual benefactors, enlightening beings develop all the elements of enlightenment.

"What is the reason for this? Spiritual benefactors are those who clear away obstructions, restrain us from evil, teach us what is not to be done, extricate us from folly, dispel ignorance, break the bonds of views, emancipate us from the mundane whirl, cut off attachments to the world, free us from the nets of demons, extract the barbs of suffering, liberate us from the thicket of nescience, convey us across the desert of views, ferry us over the torrents of existence, pull us out of the mud of desire, extricate us from false paths, show the path of enlightening beings, enjoin on us the undertaking of enlightening beings, establish us in spiritual practices, lead the way to omniscience, clarify the eye of wisdom, strengthen the determination for enlightenment, foster universal compassion, tell about enlightening practices, give instruction in the ways of transcendence, direct us into the stages of enlightenment, impart tolerance, engender all roots of goodness, produce all preparations for enlightenment, bestow all virtues of enlightening beings, deliver us to the presence of all buddhas, show all virtuous qualities, inspire us to our goals, enhance efforts and attainments, show the ways to emancipation, protect us from the paths of destruction, illumine the ways to perceive truth, shower multitudes of teachings, extinguish all afflictions, stop the formation of views, and introduce us to all aspects of enlightenment.

"Moreover, spiritual benefactors are mothers, giving birth to the family of buddhas; they are fathers, producing great benefit; they are nurses, protecting us from all evils; they are mentors, elucidating the learning of enlightening beings; they are guides, leading us into the path of transcendence; they are physicians, relieving us of the maladies of afflictions; they are like the Himalaya Mountains, growing the herb of knowledge; they are heroic warriors, protecting us from all perils; they are ferrymen, ferrying us across the torrents of the mundane whirl; they are helmsmen, delivering us to the treasure island of omniscience.

"Therefore, thinking in this way, you should continue to approach spiritual benefactors, with a mind like the earth, bearing all burdens unbendingly; with a mind like adamant, having an unbreakable will; with a mind like a mountain range, impenetrable to all miseries; with a mind like a servant, doing whatever is bidden; with a mind like a student, following all instructions; with a mind like a slave, willing to take on all tasks; with a mind like a nurse, not overcome by afflictions; with a mind like a servant, taking up any task obediently; with a mind like a street cleaner, getting rid of pride and conceit; with a mind like the full moon, appearing at the proper times; with a mind like a good horse, avoiding all unruliness; with a mind like a vehicle, carrying a precious cargo; with a mind like an elephant, tame and docile; with a mind like a mountain, unshakable; with a mind like a dog, not getting angry; with a mind like an outcaste youth, free from arrogance and egotism; with a mind like a bull with its horns cut off, stripped of all haughtiness; with a mind like an apprentice, free from inflated ideas of your own worth; with a mind like a ship, coming and going tirelessly; with a mind like a bridge, crossing over with the directions of spiritual benefactors; with a mind like a good son, looking up to the countenance of spiritual benefactors; with a mind like a prince, carrying out the directives of the spiritual king.

"Think of yourself as sick, and think of spiritual benefactors as physicians; think of their instructions as medicines, and think of the practices as getting rid of disease. Think of yourself as a traveler, and think of spiritual benefactors as guides; think of their instructions as the road, and think of the practices as going to the land of your destination. Think of yourself as crossing over to the other shore, and think of spiritual benefactors as boatmen; think of their instructions as a ford, and think of the practices as a boat. Think of yourself as a farmer, and think of spiritual benefactors as water spirits; think of their instructions as rain, and think of the practices as the ripening of the crops. Think of yourself as a pauper, and think of spiritual benefactors as the givers of wealth; think of their instructions as wealth, and think of the practices as getting rid of poverty. Think of yourself as an apprentice, and think of spiritual benefactors as mentors; think of their instructions as arts, and think of the practices as accomplishments. Think of yourself as fearless, and think of spiritual benefactors as heroic warriors; think of their instructions as attack, and think of the practices as vanquishing enemies. Think of yourself as a merchant, and think of spiritual benefactors as ship captains; think of their instructions as treasure, and think of the practices as obtaining treasures. Think of yourself as a good son, and think of spiritual benefactors as parents; think of their instructions as the family business, and think of the practices as the perpetuation of the family business. Think of yourself as a prince, and think of spiritual benefactors as the chief ministers of a spiritual king; think of their instructions as the precepts of kingship, and think of the practices as putting on the turban of truth adorned with the crest of knowledge and overseeing the capital of the spiritual sovereign.

"You should approach spiritual benefactors with these thoughts in mind. Why? With their attitude toward spiritual benefactors purified in this way, practicing the instructions of spiritual benefactors, enlightening beings grow in goodness, like plants, bushes, and trees growing up the mountains; they become vessels of all buddha-teachings, as the oceans are of water; they become repositories of all virtues, as the seas are of pearls; they purify the determination for enlightenment, as fire does gold; they rise above the world, like the polar mountain over the sea; they become unstained by things of the world, like a lotus in water; they reject all bad actions, as the ocean throws up a corpse; they increase in good qualities, as the moon grows brighter as it waxes; they illumine the reality realm, as the sun does the earth; they grow the bodies of vows of enlightening beings, just as children grow in the care of their parents.

"In short, enlightening beings who have put the instruction of spiritual benefactors into effect embody untold virtues, purify untold resolutions, develop untold enlightening faculties, purify untold mystic powers, perfect untold worthy practices, get beyond untold demons, abide by untold ways to truth, fulfill untold ways of purifying virtue and knowledge, fulfill untold deeds, purify untold modes of conduct, carry out untold vows.

"In sum, all practices of enlightening beings, all transcendent ways of enlightening beings, all stages of enlightening beings, all concentrations of enlightening beings, all mystic knowledges and spiritual powers of enlightening beings, all manifestations of mental command and intellectual power of enlightening beings, all knowledge of dedication and infinity of superknowledge of enlightening beings, all accomplishments of vows of enlightening beings, and all perfections of attainments of all aspects of buddhahood, derive from spiritual benefactors, are rooted in spiritual benefactors, are born of spiritual benefactors, are fostered by spiritual benefactors, are based on spiritual benefactors, are caused by spiritual benefactors, are produced by spiritual benefactors."

Now Sudhana, hearing about the virtues and qualities of spiritual bene-

factors, about the infinity of practice of enlightening beings, and the vastness of the buddha-teaching, was thoroughly delighted and uplifted in
mind. He then paid his respects again to the boy Shrisambhava and the girl
Shrimati and took his leave.

Maitreya

Then Sudhana, his mind enriched by the instructions of spiritual benefactors, went to the region of Samudrakaccha, contemplating that instruction
in the conduct of enlightening beings, strengthening his body by thinking
of past activities inconsistent with proper conduct, controlling his thoughts
by thinking of past mundane mental behavior not conducive to purification
of body and mind, contemplating the greater common weal in the present
by thinking of the vanity of past involvement in harmful mundane activities, establishing the power of forming correct ideas of the practice of
enlightening beings by thinking of former untrue notions based on mere
fancy, strengthening the will based on the excellence of striving for the welfare of all beings by thinking of the ills of past striving for his own personal
benefit, increasing the energy of his faculties with great inspiration to strive
to attain all elements of buddhahood by thinking of past indulgence in
pleasure seeking; purifying his being with the vow of enlightening beings
connected with correct perception in the present free from delusion by
thinking of past endeavors made up of error inextricably bound up with
delusion; unifying body and mind with great vigor in action by thinking of
past accomplishment of tasks through exertion of great vigor and striving
for the attainment of complete buddhahood in the present; developing great
joy and happiness by thinking how it would be to go on forever as in the
past—helpless amid the ills of unenlightened life—and instead dedicating
himself to the aid and benefit of all beings by establishing all the teachings of
enlightenment, developing energy in his faculties rooted in inconceivable
good by seeing this present life as a cause of old age, sickness, death, and
grief, an abode of assemblage and disintegration, and yet the basis and condition of carrying out the practice of enlightening beings forever, absorbing
the buddha-teachings that mature sentient beings, seeing the buddhas and
going to all their lands, attending all teachers of truth, keeping the instructions of all buddhas, seeking all truths, meeting all spiritual friends,
realizing all elements of buddhahood, and embodying the vows of enlightening beings.

In this frame of mind, with these thoughts, engaged in such reasoning,
with faith in the grace of all enlightening beings, with admiration for the
determination of all enlightening beings, with respect for the determination
of all enlightening beings, with reverence for the purity of the senses of all
enlightening beings, with the powers of purity of sense derived from
attentiveness to the teachings of all enlightening beings, with clarity of
mind deriving from respecting all enlightening beings, with provisions of
roots of goodness deriving from faith in all enlightening beings, with varie-

ties of offerings deriving from the accomplishments of all enlightening beings, with expressions of respect made equally to all enlightening beings, with observations of the variety of eyes developed in the bodies of all beings, with productions of arrays of descriptions of the conceptual worlds of all beings made with the clarity of expression of all enlightening beings, with perception of the state of presence in the abodes of all buddhas by fulfillment of the mystic power of all enlightening beings of past and present, with awareness of the miracles of buddhas and enlightening beings everywhere, following the all-pervasiveness of the bodies of all buddhas and enlightening beings in every single point, with perception of the light of superknowledge of the purity of vision of all enlightening beings, with a mind sense comprehending the network of all places as a whole, pervading all levels of the cosmos, with the power of accomplishment of vows, extending everywhere throughout the entirety of space, continuous through past, present, and future, ceaselessly penetrating all truths, entering all areas illumined by the instructions of all spiritual benefactors, by the penetrating power of faith and resolve, Sudhana, his mind pursuing such thoughts of respect, reverence, honor, submission, regard, empowerment, and determination, with the eye of knowledge intent upon the ground of the realm of such infinite knowledge, prostrated himself in front of the door of the great tower, chamber of the adornments of Vairocana, the illuminator.

Contemplating such application of accomplishment for a while, by the power of effectuation of resolute vows, deriving from intense faith, Sudhana projected himself continuously into the presence of all buddhas, and likewise into the presence of all enlightening beings, to the abodes of all spiritual benefactors, to all monuments of buddhas, to all statues of buddhas, to the abodes of all enlightening beings and buddhas, to the locations of all treasures of true teaching, to the presence of all monuments to saints and individual illuminates, to the vicinities of all groups of sages, worthies, and parents: he continuously projected himself into the presence of all beings, by entering into the totality of the body of knowledge, extending everywhere, by focusing attention through knowledge of control of formation of mental images.

And just as he prostrated himself before the great tower of the chamber of the adornments of Vairocana, in the same way he prostrated himself before all the aforementioned beings and objects throughout the cosmos.

"In this way, continuously mystically manifesting the eons of the endless future, by equanimity like the infinity of space, equanimity like the nonobstruction of the reality realm, equanimity toward the omnipresent ultimate limit of reality, the equanimity of absence of false notions in those who realize Thusness, the pervasiveness of perceptions of reflectional knowledge, equanimity toward thoughts as being like dreams, equanimity toward the representations of all worlds as being like reflections, equanimity toward conditional origins being like echoes, equanimity toward nonorigination, equanimity toward formation and disintegration, and equanimity toward the evolution of causal conditions as being equal to nonexistence, believing that development takes place according to actions, believing that results come about according to causes, believing that all Three Vehicles come to be according to accumulation of spiritual practices, believing that the appearance of all buddhas comes from faith, believing that all creations of offerings to buddhas come from devotion, believing that all projections of buddhas derive from respect, believing that the nature of all buddhas derives from the accumulation of virtues, believing that all arrays of mental adornments derive from wisdom and technique, believing that all buddha-teachings derive from vows, believing all the arrays of adornments spreading throughout the realm of realities, the sphere of omniscience, by the practices of all enlightening beings, derive from dedication; and by elimination of nihilism by knowledge of dedication, by elimination of the notion of permanence by knowledge of nonorigination, by elimination of erroneous views of causality by knowledge of causality, by elimination of false views by independent knowledge, by elimination of notions of self and others by knowledge of interdependence, by elimination of views attached to extremes by knowledge of the reality realm without extremes or mean, by elimination of the notion of transmigration by knowledge of the equal extinction of all abodes, by elimination of notions of becoming and decay by knowledge of nonorigination and nonextinction, by elimination of all views by knowledge of the nonorigination of emptiness, by dealing with the nonindependent nature of things with the power of knowledge of how to accomplish vows, by detachment from all notions of appearances by knowledge of the signless ultimate, due to the nature of things being unperishing like seeds producing sprouts, due to the nature of things being like the impression of a stamp, due to the nature of things being like seeing reflected images, due to the nature of things as being represented by sounds that are like echoes, due to the nature of things as arising from acts that are like illusions, due to the nature of things as rousing the formless world of mind, due to the nature of things as results conforming to the accumulation of causes and conditions, due to the nature of things as like developments according to accumulation of acts, due to the nature of things as outgrowths of skill in means, due to the nature of things as flowing into the transcendent equality of reality and unreality—with conscious thought accomplishing entry into knowledge thus, Sudhana prostrated himself before the great tower, the chamber of adornments of Vairocana.

After a long while, his being flooded by the energy of inconceivable roots of goodness, his body and mind refreshed, he rose from the doorstep of the tower, gazed with unblinking eyes at the great tower containing the adornments of Vairocana, circled it respectfully hundreds of thousands of times, and voiced these thoughts: "This is abode of those who dwell in the state of emptiness, signlessness, and wishlessness; this is the abode of those who dwell in the state of nonconceptualization of all things, those who dwell in the state of the unity of the cosmos, those who dwell in the state of ungraspability of the realm of beings, those who dwell in the state of the nonorigination of all things, those who dwell in the state of nonattachment to all worlds, those who dwell in the state of nonreliance on what all worldlings rely on, those who dwell in the state of having shed everything, those who dwell in the state of independence from all supports, those who dwell in the state of independence of all bodily existence, those who dwell in the state of annihilation of all afflictive notions, those who dwell in the state of the essence of all things, those who dwell in the state of freedom from false imaginings, those who dwell in the state of detachment from all thought, those who dwell in the state of neither entering nor leaving all perceptions, those who dwell in the state of entry into profound transcendent wisdom, those who dwell in the state of capacity to penetrate the realm of reality in all its aspects, those who dwell in the state of ability to extinguish all afflictions, those who dwell in the higher state of wisdom free from all views, cravings, and conceits, those who dwell in the state of freedom arising from higher knowledge of all meditations, liberations, concentrations, and spiritual attainments, those who dwell in the state of development of all spheres of concentration of enlightening beings, those who dwell in the state of presence with all buddhas. This is the abode of those who dwell in the state where one eon enters all eons and all eons enter one eon; those who dwell in the state of the totality of one land and all lands as one land; those who dwell in the state where one thing and all things, all things and one thing, harmonize without conflict; those who dwell in the state of the unity of one being and all beings as one being; those who dwell in the state of nonduality of one buddha and all buddhas, all buddhas and one buddha; those who dwell in the state of instantaneous penetration of all meanings; those who dwell in the state of going to all lands in a single mental pulse; those who dwell in the state of appearance in the abodes of all beings; those who dwell in the state of willing welfare and happiness for all beings; those who dwell in the state of attainment of complete independence.

"This is the abode of those who have dropped all attachments to the world yet appear in the abodes of all beings in order to develop them to maturity; those who are not attached to any land but travel in all lands in the service of buddhas; those who travel in all lands to encompass the arrangement of all buddha-lands, without leaving where they are; those who are in the presence of all buddhas while free from attachment to the conception of Buddha; those who continue to associate with spiritual friends, even though they have no peer in any world in terms of knowledge; those who dwell in the abodes of all demons while yet being detached from passion; those who dwell in the state of comprehension of all ideas while their minds are clear of all ideas; those who adapt to all beings without duality between self and other; those who are physically present in all worldly realms without being cut off from the realm of reality; those who vow to remain in the world for all time without dwelling on the idea of long or short periods; those who appear in all worlds without moving from one spot.

"This is the abode of those who abide in the state of entering everywhere into the recondite realms of truth; those who dwell in the state hard to know; those who dwell in the profound state; those who dwell in the nondual state; those who dwell in the signless state; those who dwell in the unopposed state; those who dwell in the ungraspable state; those who dwell in the nonconceptual state; those who dwell in the state inconceivable to all individual illuminates; those who dwell in the state that is beyond the sphere of all demons; those who dwell in the state that is undefiled by any worldly objects; those who dwell in the state of the transcendent ways of enlightening beings; those who dwell in the state of conformity to the state of all buddhas.

"This is the abode of those who dwell in the state that is void of signs yet do not enter the unchangeability of individual illuminates; those who dwell in the abode of nonorigination of all things and yet do not fall into the condition of nonorigination; those who dwell in contemplation of impurity yet do not make the condition of dispassion their final realization, nor do they live with elements of passion; those who dwell in the state of love, their minds not stained by hatred; those who dwell on interdependent origination, ultimately free from delusion in regard to all things; those who dwell in the four meditation states, yet do not come under the sway of meditation; those who dwell on the four immeasurables, yet do not go to the world of pure form, so that they may develop all sentient beings; those who dwell in the states of the four formless attainments, yet do not go to the formless world, because of universal compassion; those who dwell in the state of tranquillity and insight, yet do not realize knowledge and liberation for themselves alone, so that they may develop all sentient beings; those who dwell in the state of universal equanimity, yet do not abandon the realm of sentient beings; those who dwell in the state of emptiness yet do not stick to it as a view; those whose sphere is not in appearances yet who confront the guidance of beings who act on appearances; those who have no wishes at all, yet do not give up the vows of enlightening beings; those who can control all active afflictions, yet for the sake of developing sentient beings appear to act under the influence of afflictions; those who have ended death and birth by perfect knowledge, yet appear to be born and die; those who are detached from all conditions of existence, yet go into all conditions of existence by the power to guide all beings; those who dwell in love but have no emotional attachment; those who dwell in compassion but show no hesitation; those who dwell in joy but are always grieving because they watch all who are suffering; those who dwell in equanimity while working for others; those who dwell in the attainments of the nine successive stages of meditation, yet do not disdain the realm of desire; those who are independent of all becoming yet do not dwell in the experience of the absolute; those who dwell in the three liberations but do not dwell in the feeling of liberation of individual saints; those who observe the four holy truths but do not dwell in the experience of the result; those who dwell in profound contemplation of interdependent origination but do not dwell in attachment to the ultimate; those who practice the eightfold holy path but do not dwell in ultimate emancipation; those who transcend the states of sentient beings but do not dwell in attachment to individual liberation; those who have perfect knowledge of the five grasping clusters but do not dwell in ultimate extinction of the clusters; those who are beyond the four demons but do not dwell on the idea of demons; those who have transcended the senses yet do not remain ultimately inoperative; those who dwell in Thusness, but do not dwell in the absolute limit of reality; those who show all vehicles of emancipation but do not leave the Great Vehicle—this is the abode of those who abide in all virtues."

Then Sudhana spoke these verses:

Here is the compassionate, pure-minded Maitreya,
Radiant with love, striving for the good of the world;
At the stage of coronation, heir of the buddhas,
He dwells in contemplation of the enlightened realm.

This is the realm of great knowledge
Of the illustrious offspring of buddhas, secure in liberation;
This is the abode of those unrivaled ones
Who travel the realm of reality without attachment.

This is the abode of those risen from the power of discipline, generosity, patience, and vigor,
Who have reached perfection of the power of mystic knowledge by meditations,
Who are firm in wisdom, technique, resolve, and power,
Who have reached the goal of the Great Vehicle.

This is the abode of those of unobstructed intellect and broad mind,
Enjoying the realm of space, free from dependence,
Penetrating all times, free from obstruction,
Clearly perceiving all being and becoming.

Those who understand the principle of nonorigination of all things
Realize the nature of things as of the essence of space;
They do not rest on anything, like a bird in the sky—
This is the abode of those who are perfect in knowledge.

Those who, knowing the nature of passion, hatred, and delusion
As unreal, evolving from thoughts,
Go to dispassion, free from conception—
This is their abode, who have realized peace and tranquillity.

Investigating the doors of liberation, the truths, their meanings,
The path, the clusters, the senses, beings, and relativity,
Those who do not become attached to quiescence,
Who have wisdom and skill in means—this is their abode.

This is the abode of those who have entered the realm of unobstructed knowledge,

In whom vain imaginings and false thoughts of lands and beings
    have ceased,
Who have abandoned the notion of self-existence of things,
Do not grasp things, and are filled with peace.

Those who traverse this cosmos unattached and unhindered
Roam free of existents, like the wind in the sky;
Free from all dependence, acting independently,
This is their abode, those of independent wisdom.

This is the abode of the compassionate ones
Who radiate love to extinguish all the ills
Of all beings in the miserable states of views
Suffering grievous pains.

In the confines of the mundane whirl, having lost the path of the wise,
Like a troop of people born blind without a guide;
Those who see the world like this and guide them to the path of liberation,
Like the leader of a caravan—this is their abode.

This is the abode of those invincible warriors
Who see the world in the snare of demons,
Mastered by birth, sorrow, old age, and death,
And lead the way to safety, peace, and emancipation.

Seeing this world afflicted, diseased,
They gather the medicines of immortal knowledge
And foster release, with great compassion;
This is the abode of those like master physicians.

This is the abode of those like mariners
Who make a ship of good ways
To save those fallen in the sea of death, a mass of sorrows,
Soothing troubled, helpless beings.

Those of pure minds devoted to omniscience
Who relieve beings in the sea of affliction,
Cross the ocean of existence and pull them out—
This is their abode, who are like fishers.

This is the abode of those like giant birds
Who watch the abodes of all beings
With love and compassion, based on great vows,
And pull beings out of the sea of existence.

This is the abode of those who course in the sky of reality,
As suns and moons illumining the abodes of beings,
With the orb of vows and rays of knowledge
Lighting up the world.

This is the abode of the steadfast
Who remain for eons to develop even one being,
And as for one do the same for all,
As refuges for the world.

This is the abode of those of adamant will
Who spend endless ages in a single land
Working tirelessly for the benefit of the world,
And as in one land, do the same everywhere in the ten directions.

This is the abode of those like oceans of intellect
Who imbibe the multitudes of teachings of buddhas
In the ten directions at a single sitting
And continue forever, alert and never complacent.

This is the abode of those unobstructed in action
Who go forth to untold oceans of lands,
Enter the assemblies of the Guides,
And serve the buddhas in various ways.

This is the abode of the mines of all virtue
Who have entered the infinite ocean of practice,
Steadfast, plunging into the ocean of vows,
Acting for the weal of the world for myriad eons.

This is the abode of those with unobstructed eyes
Who perceive infinite lands, buddhas, beings,
And ages, in a single point, going in and out
Without encountering any boundaries.

This is the abode of those exalted in perfection of virtue
Who perceive myriad eons, lands, buddhas, and beings
In a single moment of awareness,
Based on unobstructed knowledge.

This is the abode of those unattached and unhindered in action
Who carry out as many vows
As atoms in all lands
And drops of water in the oceans.

They enter holy undertakings, mnemonic powers, concentrations,

Meditations, liberations, and vows,
Practicing these for endless eons;
The mindful offspring of Buddha are in here.

Here abide the offspring of Buddha, various, diverse;
They carry out many instructive talks,
And, considering arts and sciences beneficial to the world,
They dwell here, in the abode of the wise.

Here they dwell, in knowledge of means of supercognition,
Of all the different patterns of existence everywhere;
They see births and deaths everywhere,
While grounded in liberation within illusion, unhindered in action.

Abiding here, from their first determination,
They show spiritual practice based on the good;
Filling the cosmos with multitudes of emanations,
Thus they show hundreds of miracles.

Those who awaken to enlightenment in an instant of awareness
Enter an endless variety of acts of knowledge;
This is the abode of those who have reached what is hard to attain,
Such that the thought of it would drive the worldling mad.

This is the abode of those whose minds are unhindered,
Who course in the unobstructed reality realm,
Whose sphere is that of nongrasping,
Whose will and intellect are pure.

This is the abode of the peerless ones
Who live and act in all worlds
Without attachment, who abide
In knowledge of nonduality.

This is the abode of the dispassionate
Who realize phenomena are like space in essence,
Without any basis, quiescent,
And live among them as in space.

Here abide the merciful
Who see the world injured by pain and sorrow
And concentrate on the welfare of the world,
Filled with great compassion.

Here the infinitely liberated
Appear in the abodes of all beings

Like the sun and moon,
Free from the snare of the mundane whirl.

Here the offspring of Buddha stay,
Yet in the presence of all buddhas,
Appearing in all lands,
Throughout endless eons.

While here they pervade all directions
With multitudes of emanations,
As many as the bodies of all enlightening beings,
Equal to the universe.

The valiant ones are all in here
Examining the sphere of the enlightened;
They abide for countless eons
Yet never become surfeited.

Here, in each instant awakening
To untold millions of concentrations,
They reveal the realm of buddhahood
In accord with the concentration they enter.

Those of vast perception here
Instantly gain access to
Eons, lands, and buddha-names,
Throughout measureless eons.

Here they enter infinite eons
In a single thought,
Free of false ideas,   ·
By control of thoughts of the world.

Here, in the abode of concentration,
They see past, present, and future,
Pinpointed on each instant,
As they roam in the palace of liberation.

While here in this abode,
Sitting cross-legged, without disappearing
They simultaneously appear
In all lands, everywhere.

Abiding here, these mighty ones
Drink of the ocean of buddhas' teachings,

Having gone into the sea of knowledge
And reached the other shore of inexhaustible virtue.

Here, with unobstructed thought,
They think of the number of all buddhas,
The number of all lands and ages,
And the number of all phenomena as well.

Staying here, the offspring of buddhas
Instantly discern the formation and decay
Of all the lands there be
In past, present, and future.

Here, in the palace of enlightening beings,
They observe in all their difference
The action of the buddhas,
The aspirations and faculties of beings.

In a single atom they see
Congregations, lands, beings, and ages,
As numerous as all atoms,
All there without obstruction.

In the same way
They see in all atoms
Congregations, lands, beings, and ages,
All clearly defined.

Here they discern the essence of things,
Of all lands, ages, and buddhas,
As without inherent existence,
Through the principles of nonbecoming.

Here they observe the equality
Of beings, phenomena, and buddhas,
And discern the equality of lands and endeavors
Of past, present, and future.

The steadfast ones here in this best of abodes
Guide millions of other beings,
Glorify millions of buddhas,
And also contemplate phenomena.

In millions of eons I could not tell
The scope of the undertakings and knowledge
Of the wise, beyond thought,
So endlessly vast is it.

I bow in respect to the abode
Of the blameless ones in the realm of nonobstruction
And to the noble Maitreya, best of enlightening beings,
Unhindered in action, incomparably pure in mind, always aware.

Having praised and honored the enlightening beings dwelling in the great tower of the chamber of adornments of Vairocana in this way with innumerable eulogies of enlightening beings, Sudhana stood at the foot of the tower wishing to see the great enlightening being, desirous of meeting Maitreya. Then he saw Maitreya outside the tower, coming from somewhere else, followed by a great number of beings, respectfully flanked by the gods Indra, Brahma, and the world guardians, surrounded by many relatives and priests, coming toward the great tower of the chamber of the adornments of Vairocana. Seeing Maitreya, Sudhana was uplifted in mind, very happy and joyful, and prostrated himself before Maitreya from afar.

Now Maitreya, seeing Sudhana, pointed him out to the crowd with his right hand and spoke these verses eulogizing the virtuous qualities he had actualized:

Look at Sudhana, pure in mind, born of enduring riches;
Seeking the practice of supreme enlightenment, this wise one has
    come to me.

Welcome, son of compassion and love, universally kind;
Welcome, tranquil eyes; do not flag in practice.

Welcome, pure of heart, tireless in mind;
Welcome, buoyant in sense; do not flag in practice.

Having set out to contemplate all truths, guide all beings,
And follow all spiritual benefactors,
You are welcome, with your unshakable, steadfast resolve.

You are welcome, having come by a good path, on the path of virtue;
You are welcome, having set forth on the path of the Victors;
May you succeed, never stopping.

Welcome, full of virtue, enriched by goodness;
Your scope of action is endless; it is rare to see such as you in the world.

You consider gain and not gaining equal, you are beyond censure,
Misery, and ill repute; like a lotus, unstained by worldly things,
You are undistracted in mind.

Your heart is pure, free of guile and deceit, a good receptacle,

Free from pride and conceit; free from anger, not arrogant,
You are a welcome sight.

Attentive to all fields of awareness, born of the treasures of every
   dimension,
Developing the treasuries of all buddhas; welcome, indefatigable one.

Aware of past, present, and future, absorbed in the reality realm,
Born of the womb of virtues of all buddhas; welcome, tireless hero.

Sprung from the ground of Manjushri's knowledge, grown by the
   watering
Of Meghashri, having sought out all enlightening beings, come—
I will show you the unimpeded realm.

See this net of vows, pervading the cosmos, inconceivable;
Spreading it, drawing forth the path of enlightening practice,
   Sudhana has come.

Seeking the realm of the Victors, pursuing the practice of the undefiled,
Inquiring into the ocean of vows, this indefatigable one has arrived.

Asking where the past guides have studied, what the future ones
   will learn,
And what the present ones practice, he has come here.

He comes with the thought of spiritual teachers,
Guides to the realization of all truths,
Teachers of the path of enlightening practice—
Thus he has come here.

He comes with these thoughts: "Enlightening beings increase my wisdom
And grant me enlightenment, they are praised by the buddhas.

"They are my parents, my wet nurses of virtue, always protecting
my limbs of enlightenment, keeping me free from all harm.

"As physicians they release me from old age and death,
As celestial beings they shower the ambrosia of immortality;
They are like the moon, clear and full, like the sun,
Showing the way to peace.

"They are like polar mountains, impartial to friend and foe,
Like oceans, unshakable in mind, like pilots and protectors.

"They are valiant givers of fearlessness, reliable caravan leaders,

guides who give me well-being"—with these thoughts he serves the
Friends.

"They always show all spheres of truth,
Showing the virtue and knowledge of all buddhas;
Removing the ills of all states of woe,
They show me what is good.

"They bestow the treasures of buddhas,
They guard the treasuries of the Victors;
They are holders of the secrets of the buddhas"—
Thus this wise one follows the Friends.

See this wise one of lofty aspiration serving the Friends;
You should study as he indicates.

By virtue of past goodness he saw Manjushri and set out for
enlightenment,
Acting on Manjushri's instructions; observe his perseverance.

Having given up all comforts, home, family, and wealth, like an immortal,
He attends the Friends as a servant.

Having purified his mind and relinquished his body, this wise one
Will see the abode of all buddhas and henceforth develop this fruit.

Seeing people afflicted with sickness, beings tortured by a hun-
dred pains,
Burning with the fears and sorrows of birth and death,
He compassionately acts for their benefit.

Seeing the world beaten by the mechanisms of suffering,
In the repetitious circle of conditioning,
He seeks the adamantine knowledge
That breaks the mechanism of suffering and the circle of
conditioning.

Aiming to clear all lands of the weeds and brambles of lust and hatred,
Infestations of clinging to views, sprouts of harm,
He seeks the strong plow of wisdom.

The mind of the world is thick with delusion and ignorance,
Bereft of the eye of wisdom, without a guide;
He will become a leader of the world,
Showing the way to the abode of safety.

He will be a conveyor of tolerance and liberation,

Assailing the enemy afflictions with the sword of knowledge,
Heroic bestower of freedom from fear, teacher of the world.

He is assembling the ship of the Teaching,
Having learned the route of the ocean of knowledge;
He is a helmsman on the sea of existence,
Leading to the treasure island of peace.

This buddha-sun will rise in the sky of reality, a great light,
An orb of vows with rays of knowledge, illumining the abodes of
    all beings.

This buddha-moon will rise, a full orb of virtues
Equally cooling with higher love, exquisite light impartial toward all.

Based on a firm ground of will, enlightenment practice gradually rising,
He will become an ocean of knowledge, mine of all spiritual jewels.

Born of the dragon of the mind of enlightenment, ascended into the
    sky of reality,
Raining the teachings everywhere, he fosters all good fruits.

He will light the lamp of truth, the pure wick,
Dispelling the darkness of defilement,
The lamp in a strong vessel of love and awareness,
Glowing with the pure flame of the spirit of enlightenment.

From the embryo of the aspiration for enlightenment, compassion,
    and love,
Gradually developing the limbs of enlightenment, this baby buddha
    is growing.

He will develop the embryo of virtue and clarify the path of knowledge;
He is recognized as an embryo of knowledge, developed in accord
With the womb of vows.

One like this, girt with compassion and love,
An altruist determined to liberate beings,
Is hard to find in the world, celestial or human,
So pure is his mind.

Based on good roots of mind, grown through steadfast effort,
Shading the three realms of being—such a fruit-bearing tree of knowledge
Is hard to find.

Aiming to develop all virtues, inquire into all truths,

And break through all doubts, he serves the Friends with diligence.

Destroying the afflictions of demons, clearing away views, defilement, and craving,
Intent on freeing all beings, he has learned to do what is best.

He will clear away the states of woe and show heaven; he will lead the world
On the road of liberation, on which virtuous path he stands.

He will become a destroyer of conditioned existence,
Cutting through the net of all states of being,
Liberating beings in all states from misery
And giving them well-being.

He will free them from the straits of views,
Cut through the entanglements of the web of craving,
Clear away blameworthy passions,
And become a guide on the path for the world.

He will be a refuge for the world, providing light for all beings,
A guide in the three realms of existence, knowing becoming and decay everywhere.

He will purify people asleep in affliction, wisely pulling them from the mud of lust,
Freeing them from clinging to notions, liberating them from bondage.

Rejoice, Sudhana, for you will illumine the various aspects of reality,
Illumine the various aspects of the world,
And reach the goal of the various aspects of all truths.

As your behavior is mild, as your faith is impeccable,
As your intention is virtuous, you shall fulfill them all.

You will see all buddhas soon, you will soon go to all lands,
You will soon know all truths—such good have you done on your own.

You will purify many lands and liberate masses of beings;
You will fulfill myriad practices—such are your many attainments.

You will be a vessel of virtues, a source of good;
You will be equal to the offspring of buddhas, in accord with your devotion.

You have conquered the demons and purified your actions;

You have cleared away the afflictions in accord with your vows.

You will clear the path of knowledge and realize the path of truth;
Before long you will halt the course of the mechanism of suffering,
Which is due to afflictions in action.

You will turn the supreme wheel of truth, breaking the cycle of suffering
Of all beings, which is based on the routines of the world,
The circle of becoming, gone astray in repetition of mundane states.

You will preserve the lineage of buddhas, purify the lineage of the
     Teaching,
Support the spiritual Community, and become a source of treasures.

You will remove the web of craving and the dense net of views,
You will free the world from the net of suffering,
Having purified such a network of vows.

You will perfect beings, purify the world, and establish
The realm of knowledge—such is your intention.

You will bring greater felicity, beneficially gladdening sentient beings,
Gladdening the family of enlightening beings, satisfying the wishes of
     all buddhas.

You will be a buddha clearly seeing the abodes of all states of being,
Seeing reflections of all lands and the scope of all truths.

You will be a light illumining the reality realm,
Extinguishing all states of woe, bringing felicity to existence.

You will show the door of heaven and open the door of enlightenment
     in the world;
You will lead the world to the door of liberation, the doorway you
     have cleared.

You will lead away from false paths into the path of sages;
You will humbly follow the path of enlightenment, resolute and diligent.

Intent on freeing beings in the sea of existence from suffering,
You will save the world from the sea of existence—
Become such an ocean of virtue.

You will evaporate the sea of afflictions of beings
With the transcendent lights of the sun of knowledge;
Introducing them to the ocean of spiritual practice,

You will lead them into the ocean of knowledge.

You will increase the ocean of understanding
And purify the ocean of practice;
Soon you will plunge deep into the ocean
Of the vows of all buddhas.

You will view many oceans of lands and see the oceans of congregations therein;
By the power of the ocean of understanding, you will imbibe the ocean of teachings.

You will see multitudes of buddhas and will make myriads of offerings;
You will hear millions of truths—such are the vows you make.

You will go to the abodes of all lands, to all the abodes of beings,
And will observe the abodes of all buddhas—this is the direction you are taking.

You will observe the abode of concentration and tell of the abodes of liberation;
You will dwell in spiritual powers, grounded in the reality realm.

You will rise over the abodes of all beings, like the light of sun and moon,
And ascend to the presence of the buddhas—such is your climb on the great path.

You will walk in the realm of good, in the realm unattached to any world,
And attain supreme peace—such is your realm of higher knowledge.

The differentiations of the cosmic network,
And all the differentiations of the network of lands,
Soon you will see, pervading, like the wind unhindered in the sky.

You will see the extent of the reality realm,
You will go to the reaches of the worlds,
You will see all buddhas of all times;
So rejoice, Sudhana.

Do not be downhearted, be happy and content,
In that you have seen, see, and will see yet such liberation as this.

Sudhana, you are a good vessel of virtues, following the instructions of Buddha;
You are fit to bear this Teaching—by it you see this wonder.

Such as are hard to see in millions of eons, much more to reveal their virtues,

You have seen carrying out good practice, enlightening beings
In the realm of nonattachment.

You are welcome in the human world; inconceivably great is your gain,
That you have seen Manjushri face to face and made such a vessel
of virtue.

You have left all states of woe, cleared away the misfortune of situations
Inopportune for attaining enlightenment, transcended all evil things—
Do not be weary or distressed.

You have left the stage of the ignorant and are firmly grounded
In the virtues of enlightening beings; having fulfilled
The greatest knowledge, soon you will attain buddhahood.

Enlightening practice is like an ocean, enlightened knowledge is
like space,
The ocean of vows is equally vast—you should be happy with these.

The Friends are indefatigable, firm in will, and sure in application;
Those who follow such Friends as these will soon become guides
themselves.

Seeing how various are the many practices of enlightening beings
To educate sentient beings, do not become perplexed
About enlightenment practice that confronts all realities.

Your achievement of virtue is inconceivable;
You are useful, righteous, virtuous, and faithful.
By this accomplishment today you see such enlightening beings.

See how great is your gain in seeing enlightening beings continuously;
They each show you your vows, and you follow them all.

Hard to find even in hundreds of lifetimes
Is such a participant in the practices of enlightening beings;
Therefore the enlightening beings, one after another,
Show you their ways of liberation.

People live with enlightening beings for millions and billions of ages
Yet do not know of their state, nor make themselves vessels of virtue.

You hear this teaching, and see what is hard to find in the world,
The spiritual manifestation of greatness of enlightening beings—
You should be uplifted in mind.

All the buddhas are minding you, the enlightening beings are caring
  for you,
And you are grounded in their teaching—bravo, Sudhana, you live a
  good life.

You live according to the principles of the family of enlightening beings,
And learn the qualities of the offspring of buddhas;
You will prolong the lineage of buddhas—you should be most joyful.

All buddhas are your peerless parents, all enlightening beings your siblings;
The elements of enlightenment are all your relatives—
Nobly born are you, as an offspring of the buddhas.

Sustainer of the lineage of spiritual sovereigns,
Prolonger of the lineage of enlightening beings,
You will attain buddhahood soon, so be happy, Sudhana, full of joy.

Soon you will receive the supreme marvelous coronation of all buddhas
And become equal to the peerless heirs of the Victors.

As a man sows a seed, so shall he reap the fruit;
Today I bring you glad tidings, that you may find inconceivable joy.

Even unthinkable millions of enlightening beings
Who have carried out this practice for millions of eons
Have not attained such accomplishment
As you have realized in one lifetime.

This is all the fruit of devotion and firmness and vigor of will;
Those who admire this practice should take up what Sudhana has done.

All practice derives from vows, all qualities derive from application;
Sudhana, you have accomplished this, forever the best course of conduct.

The extent to which the dragons will is the extent to which rain is
  produced;
The extent of the scope of vows and knowledge is the extent of pervasion
Of enlightenment practice.

This should be shown to you, Sudhana, by the practice of the good;
Once one realizes this, one will be serving the Friends thereby.

Remember the millions of bodies past that you squandered uselessly
  for lust;
Now pursuing the path of enlightenment, this body, well disciplined,
Should be critical.

Over millions of eons past you experienced all miseries in conditioned
    states;
Having turned away from myriad buddhas, you did not hear such a
    doctrine as this.

Now you have got your chance as a human, in the presence of Buddha,
With such spiritual friends; how could one not be purified
when one has heard of the practice of supreme enlightenment?

Even if there are buddhas existing and the Teaching is heard
From spiritual friends and benefactors,
If one does not listen to this doctrine one's mind will not be purified.

By it an attitude of faith and devotion is produced, supreme respect;
Getting rid of desire, views, and lassitude, listen to this Teaching more
    and more.

Hearing of such an entry into practice, whoever accomplishes this
    undertaking
Makes a supreme gain, inconceivable—this human life is worthwhile.

For one whose mind is thus purified, the buddhas are not hard to find,
The enlightening beings are all friends, and there is no more doubt
    of enlightenment.

One who has entered such a teaching keeps all the precepts,
Abandons all causes of misery, and embraces all virtues.

Soon, relinquishing this body, you will go to a buddha-land, purified;
You will see the abode of enlightening beings and behold the bud-
    dhas everywhere.

You have completed a set of past causes, Sudhana, based on your devotion;
You serve the Friends with the highest aim, thereby growing like a
    lotus in water.

Intent on rapport with all spiritual friends and with all buddhas,
Intent on seeking out all truths, arise, well disciplined, and do not weary.

Set out to apply all truths and follow all the paths; offspring of Buddha,
Grounded on vows, arise, vessel of all virtues.

Through such perfect devotion you have paid this honor to me;
Soon you will come into the presence of the assemblies of all buddhas.

Bravo, Sudhana, buoyant in mind, conscious of the vows of all

buddhas;
Firm in resolve, you soon will reach the perfection of virtue of buddhas.

Ask Manjushri about ultimate liberation in the realm of knowledge;
He will initiate you into the highest practice of good in your final
    existence.

Thus Maitreya, seeing Sudhana arrive, imbued with virtues, in the realm
of nonobstruction, revealed him to the assembly, speaking of his treasury of
qualities. Sudhana, hearing such supreme direction and instruction, was
flooded with joy and burst into tears. His hair stood on end and he sighed
with delight. He rose and paid his respects to Maitreya. Then, by the mental
power of Manjushri, there appeared in his hands beautiful flower garlands
and jewels, produced by the vows of enlightening beings; blissfully, Sudhana
showered these on Maitreya. Then Maitreya patted him on the head and
said, "It is good that you are so indefatigable, Sudhana; you will be a vessel of
virtues, like Manjushri and me."

Hearing this, Sudhana disclosed the joy of his heart: "It is hard to find,
even in hundreds of lifetimes, such Friends as these whom I have now met. It
is good for me to have come here today. By the direction of the honorable
Manjushri, perfect in true virtue, I have found this rare Friend. I should
quickly meet Manjushri himself."

Then Sudhana stood respectfully before Maitreya and said, "Noble one, I
have set out for supreme perfect enlightenment, but I do not know how an
enlightening being is to learn and carry out the practice of enlightening
beings. It has been predicted by all the buddhas that noble Maitreya will
become supremely perfectly enlightened in one lifetime; and one who is
sure of supreme perfect enlightenment in one lifetime has gone beyond all
the stations of enlightening beings, entered the certainty of enlightening
beings, fulfilled all the transcendent ways, entered all doors of tolerance,
attained all states of enlightening beings, mastered all ways of liberation,
perfected all concentrations, reached the goal of all courses of action of
enlightening beings, attained all powers of memory, intellect, and methods
of elucidation, mastered all powers of enlightening beings, gathered all provisions of enlightening beings, mastered the methods of wisdom and skill in
means, developed the illumination of higher knowledge, mastered all learning, purified all practices of enlightening beings, accomplished all methods
of carrying out vows, received the directions of all buddhas, comprehended
all vehicles of liberation, taken on the empowerment of all buddhas,
embraced the enlightenment of all buddhas, preserved the treasuries of all
buddhas, stored the secrets of all buddhas, gained leadership of the esoteric
circle of all enlightening beings. Such a one is a hero in all assaults against
afflictions, a guide to those in the wilderness of the mundane whirl, a physician for those sick with afflictions, a chief of all beings, a leader, preeminent
among all noble people, highest of all saints, a pilot for those in the sea of the
mundane whirl; such a one draws the net of means to guide sentient beings,

observes the faculties of people who have matured, is united with all sentient beings, is engaged in protecting all enlightening beings, is in concert with all the works of enlightening beings, is in the circles of all buddhas, is reflected in the abodes of all beings, is unstained by the things of the world, is beyond the reach of all demons, is in accord with the realm of all buddhas, has attained nonobstruction in the sphere of all enlightening beings, is engaged in the service of all buddhas, is one with all enlightened qualities, wears the turban of coronation, sits on the throne of spiritual sovereignty, is initiated into the realm of omniscience, is a source of all enlightened teachings, has attained enlightenment and mastery of omniscience.

"So please tell me, noble one, how an enlightening being is to learn and carry out the practice of enlightening beings, by which practice an enlightening being attains enlightenment and understands all enlightened teachings, responds when called upon, rescues sentient beings, fulfills the commitment to carry out the practice of enlightenment, comforts and inspires people, keeps true to one's word, ascertains all the myriad buddha-teachings, sustains the lineage of buddhas and enlightening beings, and preserves the eye of enlightenment."

Then the enlightening being Maitreya, looking over the whole crowd, pointed out Sudhana and said, "Good people, look at this fine young man, who asks me about the perfection of the virtues of enlightening practice. With this diligence, this purposefulness, this zealous commitment, this steadfast will, this unflagging vigor, this thirst for enlightened teaching, this excellent questing, this burning urgency, this desire to meet spiritual friends and benefactors, this indefatigability in attendance on spiritual friends and benefactors, he left his city in search of spiritual benefactors at the direction of Manjushri and traveled south, inquiring of a hundred and ten spiritual benefactors, until finally he has come to me, his mind thoroughly unwearied.

"Good people, it is hard even to get to hear of the name of those like this who have set forth on the Great Vehicle of universal enlightenment, who have undertaken the great vow, who are resolute in the great endeavor, who are girt with great compassion, who are intent on saving sentient beings with great love, who act with transcendental energy, who are engaged in protecting the great caravan of beings, who are carrying beings across the ocean of the mundane whirl, who are on the road to omniscience, who are engaged in assembling the spiritual ark, who are determined to assemble the great wealth of the treasures of the Teaching, who are engaged in assembling the preparations for the great spiritual activity—it is hard to even hear their names, to see them in person, to associate with them, or to share in their practice.

"Why is this? This sincere good person has set out to save all beings, undertaken to liberate all beings from misery, to evaporate all bad tendencies, to put an end to all states that are inopportune for attaining enlightenment, to block off all perilous roads, to dispel all darkness of ignorance, to cross all the wastelands of the mundane whirl, to stop all vicious circles, to get beyond the reach of all demons, to remove all attachment and dependence, to rescue people from the mire of lust, to abandon passion for joy, to remove the fetters of views, stop attachment to the body as real, cut through the snare of conception, stop the pursuit of error, to pluck out the thorns of delusion, to break through obstacles, to shatter the mountains of obstructions, to remove the net of craving, to dissolve the bonds of ignorance, to illuminate existence, to do away with guile and deceit, to clear mental disturbance, to remove doubt and confusion, to get out of the current of ignorance and delusion, to repel all the ills of the mundane whirl.

"Indeed, good people, this worthy wishes to assemble the ship of the Teaching, a precious gift, to rescue beings from the four torrents. He wishes to set up the great bridge of the Teaching for those sunk in the morass of views. He wishes to produce the light of knowledge for those in the darkness of delusion. He wishes to point out the path of sages to those lost in the wilderness of the mundane whirl. He wishes to dispense the medicine of the teaching to those suffering from the illness of afflictions. He wishes to give the element of immortality to those assailed by birth, old age, and death. He wishes to cool those burning with the three fires by means of the water of tranquillity. He wishes to give great comfort to those suffering from sorrow, grief, misery, and depression. He wishes to give those bound in the prison of existence the knowledge of how to break out. He wishes to give the sword of wisdom to those tied up in the bonds of views. He wishes to show the door of liberation to those locked in the city of the triple world. He wishes to show the direction of safety to those headed in dangerous directions. He wishes to comfort those suffering from the joint operation of afflictions. He wishes to lend a hand to those terrorized by the perils of falling into states of woe. He wishes to show the citadel of nirvana to those struck by the murderous clusters. He wishes to tell those surrounded by the serpents of the elements how to escape. To those loitering in the ghost town of the sense media, he wishes to show the way out by the light of wisdom. Those on wrong paths he wishes to lead into the right path. To the friendless he wishes to show true spiritual friends. Those clinging to the realm of the infantile unenlightened condition he wishes to initiate into the teachings of sages. Those clinging to the city of the mundane whirl he wishes to lead away into the city of omniscience.

"Thus, for the salvation of sentient beings, this worthy, ceaselessly pursuing the complete purification of the aspiration for enlightenment, is tireless in mastering the Great Vehicle, never complacent in seeking all means of conveying truth, constantly engaged in fulfilling all the provisions for enlightenment, always bearing the responsibility of clarifying all avenues of truth, carrying out all practices of enlightening beings with vigor, not stopping anywhere, carrying out all vows with unbending effort, meeting all spiritual benefactors without complacence, tireless in attendance on all spiritual benefactors, properly following the advice and instruction of all spiritual benefactors.

"In all the world it is hard to find people who aspire to supreme true enlightenment; it is even harder to find those who set out for supreme true enlightenment, who master the teachings of buddhas with such diligent application, seek the path of enlightening beings with such ardor, purify the practice of enlightening beings with such purposefulness, attend spiritual benefactors with such diligence, follow the knowledge of spiritual benefactors with such urgency, carry out the instructions of spiritual benefactors with such unbending determination, assemble the elements of enlightenment with such correct understanding, be so indifferent to gain, honor, and praise as not to ruin the will appropriate to an enlightening being, seek the Great Vehicle of enlightening beings with such detachment from home and family, comforts, enjoyments, and material goods, and seek omniscience with such indifference to joy and life. Other enlightening beings will not, in millions of eons, attain the fulfillment of the practice and vows of enlightening beings, abide in enlightenment, purify a buddha-land, guide sentient beings, know the reality realm, attain the transcendent ways, extend the network of practices, fulfill the undertakings of vows, transcend the works of demons, develop rapport with spiritual friends, perfect all the practices of enlightening beings, or accomplish the power to carry out the practice of the universally good enlightening being, to the extent that this Sudhana will achieve these things in one lifetime."

Then Maitreya, having eulogized the true virtues of Sudhana, and thereby strengthened the determination for enlightenment in hundreds of thousands of people, said to Sudhana, "It is good that you have set your mind on supreme perfect enlightenment for the welfare and happiness of all worlds, for the salvation of all beings, for the attainment of all enlightened qualities. You have made a great gain, and your existence amid humanity is indeed welcome. You live the good life among the living and have satisfied the purpose of the emergence of Buddha in the world. You have met the benefactor Manjushri and have made yourself a worthy vessel of truth. You have been nourished with virtues and stabilized on good qualities. You have purified high resolve and good intention. You are minded by all buddhas, and you are in the care of all spiritual friends. By this intent of yours you have developed the determination for supreme perfect enlightenment.

"What is the reason? The determination for enlightenment is the seed of all elements of buddhahood; it is like a field, growing good qualities in all beings; it is like the earth, being a support for all beings; it is like water, washing away all afflictions; it is like wind, unattached to all worlds,; it is like fire, burning up the deadwood of clinging to views; it is like the sun, illumining the abodes of all beings; it is like the moon, fulfilling the sphere of all good qualities; it is like a lamp, producing spiritual light; it is like an eye, seeing the even and the uneven; it is like a road, leading to the city of omniscience; it is like a passageway, leading away from all wrong paths; it is like a vehicle, carrying all enlightening beings; it is like a door, leading into all the practices of enlightening beings; it is like a mansion, because of determination to abide in concentration; it is like a park, because of experience of spiritual pleasures; it is like a home, protecting all beings; it is like a basis, being the practice of all enlightening beings, it is like a father, protecting all enlightening beings; it is like a mother to all beings; it is like a nurse, protecting in every way; it is like a king, overwhelming the mentality of all individually liberated ones; it is like an overlord, because of the excellence of all vows; it is like the ocean, containing all jewels of virtue; it is like the polar mountain, being impartial toward all beings; it is like the surrounding mountains, being a refuge for all beings; it is like the Himalaya, growing the herb of knowledge; it is like intoxicating fragrance, being the seat of all scents of virtue; it is like the sky, because of the great extent of its virtue; it is like a lotus, unstained by any things of the world; it is like an elephant, patient and noble; it is like a horse of good breed, free from all unruliness; it is like a charioteer, being the driver of the Great Vehicle; it is like medicine, curing the ills of afflictions; it is like a pit, because in it all bad qualities disappear; it is like a thunderbolt, penetrating all things; it is like a chest of incense, producing the aroma of all virtues; it is like a great flower, pleasant to the sight of all beings; it is like cooling sandalwood, cooling off the burning of passion; it is like the moon, pervading the cosmos; it is like the medicine 'good to see,' obliterating all ills due to afflictions; it is like an extracting drug, as it extracts the arrows of evil propensities; it is like a chief of gods, because of mastery of all the faculties; it is like the god of wealth, because it puts an end to all poverty; it is like the goddess of beauty, being adorned with all virtues; it is like jewelry, gracing all enlightening beings; it is like the conflagration that ends an eon, burning up all evildoing; it is like medicine for underdevelopment, because it increases the growth of all enlightened qualities; it is like a dragon pearl, repelling the poison of all afflictions; it is like a water-clearing jewel, because it removes all turbidity and pollution; it is like a wish-fulfilling jewel, granting success in all aims; it is like the horn of plenty, fulfilling all wishes; it is like the desire-granting tree, as it showers the ornaments of all virtues; it is like a goose-feather robe, as it does not absorb any of the ills of the mundane whirl; it is like cotton fiber, being soft in nature; it is like a plow, clearing the mind-field of sentient beings; it is like a warrior, striking down the self; it is like an arrow, piercing its target of suffering; it is like power, overcoming its enemy, afflictions; it is like armor, protecting logical thought; it is like a scimitar, cutting off the head of affliction; it is like a sword blade, slashing through the armor of pride, conceit, and arrogance; it is like a razor, slicing off compulsive propensities; it is like the banner of a hero, bringing down the banner of pride; it is like a machete, felling the tree of ignorance; it is like an ax, cutting through the tree of suffering; it is like combat, being a savior from all attacks; it is like hands, protecting the body of the transcendent ways; it is like feet, being the base of all virtue and knowledge; it is like a surgical probe, cleaning away the covering of the sheath of ignorance; it is like an extracting instrument, extracting the thorn of the notion of self; it is like a hoe, dragging away the thorns of propensities; it is like a benefactor, freeing you from the bonds of the mundane whirl; it is like wealth, rejecting all that is useless; it is like a teacher, knowing the way to carry out all enlightening practices; it is like a mine, having inexhaustible blessings; it is like a fountain, having inexhaustible knowledge; it is like a mirror, showing the reflection of all ways into truth; it is like a white lotus, free from defilement; it is like a great river, carrying forth the streams of the ways of transcendence and the ways of integration; it is like the chief water spirit, causing the clouds of the Teaching to shower; it is like the root of life, sustaining the universal compassion of all enlightening beings; it is like the elixir of immortality, bringing you to the deathless realm; it is like an all-encompassing net, taking in all beings who can be guided; it is like health, producing endless health; it is like an antidote to poison, vitiating the poison of desire; it is like a spell, destroying the poison of all folly; it is like wind, removing all barriers and obstacles; it is like an island of jewels, being a mine of the spiritual jewels of all the limbs of enlightenment; it is like a family, producing all good qualities; it is like a home, being the abode of all virtuous qualities; it is like a market, attended by all enlightening 'merchants'; it is like liquid metal, clearing all obstructions caused by actions and afflictions; it is like a honeybee, filling the stores of provisions for omniscience; it is like a road, whereby all enlightening beings approach the city of omniscience; it is like a vessel, holding all pure qualities; it is like rain, settling the dust of afflictions; it is like a basis, defining the respective stations of all enlightening beings; it is like a magnet, unaffected by individual liberation; it is like a jewel, inherently pure; it is like an emerald, being totally beyond the knowledge of all individual illuminates and worldlings; it is like the drum that sounds the hour, because it wakes up beings sleeping in affliction; it is like still, clear water, being pure; it is like an ornament of the finest gold, obscuring all collections of virtue in the conditioned realm; it is like an enormous mountain, being invulnerable to anything in the triple world; it is like a savior, not abandoning any who take refuge in it; it is like motivation, because it draws you toward your aim; it is like intelligence, because it creates contentment of the heart; it is like sacrifice, because it satisfies all beings; it is like understanding, because it is what is best in the minds of all beings; it is like a treasury, preserving all enlightened qualities; it is like a summary, containing all the practices and vows of enlightening beings; it is like a protector, protecting all beings; it is like a guardian, repelling all evils; it is like the net of Indra, rounding up the titans of afflictions; it is like the snare of the sky god, rounding up the teachable; it is like the fire of Indra, burning up all habitual propensities and afflictions; it is like a monument for the world. In sum, the virtues of the determination for enlightenment are equal to all the qualities and virtues of buddhas. Why? Because it is the source of all the practices of enlightening beings, and from it come all buddhas of past, future, and present. Therefore, whoever has aroused the determination for supreme perfect enlightenment becomes imbued with measureless virtues because of being absorbed by the will for omniscience.

"Just as there is a medicine called 'fearless' that prevents five perils—one is not burned by fire, not affected by poison, not wounded by weapons, not swept away by water, not suffocated by smoke—in the same way, an enlightening being who has taken the medicine of the will for omniscience is not burned by the fire of passion, not affected by the poison of objects, not wounded by the weapons of afflictions, not swept away by the torrent of existence, not suffocated by the smoke of false discrimination.

"Just as there is a medicine called 'liberated' that frees one from fear of attack, in the same way an enlightening being who has taken the medicine of knowledge of aspiration for enlightenment has no fear of being impinged upon by the mundane whirl.

"Just as there is an herb whose scent repels all poisonous snakes, in the same way the scent of the determination for enlightenment wards off the vipers of afflictions.

"Just as a person who has taken the herb of invincibility is victorious over all enemies, the enlightening being who has taken the herb of invincibility of the will for omniscience is invulnerable to all opposing demons.

"Just as there is a medicine called 'extracting' that removes all barbs, so all barbs of passion, hatred, delusion, and views drop out of the enlightening being who has taken the extracting medicine of the determination for enlightenment.

"Just as there is a medicine called 'good to see' that cures all illnesses, the enlightening being who has taken the good-to-see medicine of the aspiration for enlightenment is cured of all the illnesses of afflictions and ignorance.

"Just as there is a medicinal tree called 'continuity' whose bark heals all wounds and ulcers upon application and which itself regrows as it is stripped, the tree of continuity of omniscience, which grows from the seed of the essence of enlightenment, heals the wounds and ulcers of actions and afflictions of the faithful on sight, and the tree of omniscience cannot be exhausted or killed by all beings.

"Just as there is a kind of herb that promotes growth, by the efficacy of which all the trees in the continent grow, similarly by the efficacy of the growth-promoting drug of the will for enlightenment, the saints and enlightening beings all grow.

"Just as there is an herb called 'attainment of pleasure,' which when applied to the body produces physical and mental health, in the same way the 'attainment of pleasure' herb of the aspiration for omniscience produces physical and mental health in enlightening beings.

"Just as there is an herb called 'gaining memory' that purifies the conscious memory, in the same way the memory herb of the aspiration for enlightenment produces in enlightening beings purity of unhindered memory of all buddha-teachings.

"Just as there is an herb called 'great lotus' by which one may live for an eon, the enlightening being who keeps taking the great spiritual medicine of the will for enlightenment becomes able to live for countless eons.

"Just as there is an herb of invisibility that renders one invisible to any humans or nonhumans, the enlightening being under the protection of the invisibility herb of the will for enlightenment, who is assured of buddhahood, cannot be seen in the range of all demons.

"Just as there is a great jewel in the ocean called 'totality of all jewels,' which is such that it is impossible for all the eonic fires to evaporate even a drop of the ocean where it is, in the same way it is impossible that enlightening beings whose mental course is imbued with the 'totality of all jewels' gem of the determination for omniscience could lose even one virtue dedicated to omniscience; whereas if they abandon the determination for omniscience, all of their roots of goodness would evaporate.

"Just as there is a great jewel called 'collection of all lights,' which in a necklace obscures all jewelry, in the same way an enlightening being wearing the ornament of the 'collection of all lights' mind-jewel of the aspiration for enlightenment is unsurpassed by all aspirations to individual salvation.

"Just as there is a water-clarifying jewel that will clear all turbidity and foulness from water in which it is placed, in the same way the water-clarifying jewel of the determination for enlightenment clears all the murk and turbidity of afflictions.

"Just as fishers wearing the water dwelling gem do not die in water, in the same way an enlightening being protected by the water-dwelling gem of the will for omniscience does not die in the sea of the mundane whirl.

"Just as there is a jewel called 'dragon scale gem,' with which fishers and others who live from the sea enter the abodes of the dragons without being attacked by dragons or sea serpents, in the same way an enlightening being holding the spiritual jewel of the dragon of knowledge of the determination for omniscience enters the abodes of the realm of desire without being harmed.

"Just as the chief of gods overwhelms other gods when wearing the jewel of lordship, in the same way the enlightening being wearing the crown of vows with the regal jewel of the aspiration for omniscience overwhelms all in the triple world.

"Just as someone with a wish-fulfilling jewel does not fear poverty, the enlightening being with the wish-fulfilling jewel of the aspiration for omniscience has no fears about livelihood.

"Just as a 'sun beauty' jewel emanates fire when exposed to the sun, in the same way the sunny jewel of the will for omniscience emanates the fire of knowledge when touched by the light rays of the jewel of wisdom.

"Just as the moon beauty jewel emits water when touched by moonlight, in the same way the moon beauty jewel of the aspiration for enlightenment emits the water of commitment to all good when touched by the light of the moon of dedication of roots of goodness.

"Just as great elephants wearing a crown of wish-fulfilling jewels have no fear of attack, in the same way those wearing the crown of wish-fulfilling jewels of great compassion of the aspiration for enlightenment have no fear of the ills of the state of misery.

"Just as a jewel called 'repository of the adornments of the world' fulfills the wishes of all beings without ever being exhausted, in the same way the aspiration for enlightenment, the great jewel containing the adornments of all worlds, is never exhausted because of fulfilling the undertaking of enlightenment, which is the wish of all beings.

"Just as the great jewel of a sovereign king dispels darkness and lights up the palace, in the same way the royal jewel of the aspiration for omniscience dispels the darkness of ignorance in all states of being and radiates the great light of knowledge in the realm of desire.

"Just as everything bathed in sapphire light becomes blue, wherever the sapphire of the aspiration for omniscience is taken, and whatever roots of goodness are dedicated by the will for omniscience, all become the color of the jewel of omniscience.

"Just as a jewel in a shower of filth does not absorb any foul odors, in the same way the jewel of the aspiration for enlightenment is not defiled though in the realm of desire, because it is essentially pure.

"Just as the jewel 'pure light' outshines all other jewels, in the same way the jewel of ultimately pure light of the aspiration for omniscience is not overcome by the accumulated virtues of all ordinary people, or all learners, saints, and solitary illuminates.

"Just as one fiery jewel disperses all darkness, in the same way one fiery jewel of the aspiration for omniscience, coupled with objective observation and correct thought, dispels the darkness of ignorance.

"Just as a priceless jewel in the hand of a merchant in a boat on the sea is superior in beauty and value to hundreds of thousands of crystals in town, in the same way the priceless jewel of the aspiration for omniscience, even in the ocean of the mundane whirl, in the boat of vows, in the determination of an enlightening being who has just aspired to enlightenment for the first time, even though not having yet reached the city of omniscience, is still superior to the crystals of all hearers and individual illuminates in the town of liberation.

"Just as the jewel known as the 'powerful king,' even when on the surface of the earth, shows the arrays of appearances of the abodes on the far-distant sun and moon, in the same way the powerful king jewel of the aspiration for omniscience, in which all virtues are purified, even while in the mundane whirl shows the arrays of appearances of the spheres of all buddhas in the great sun and moon of knowledge of those who realize Thusness in the reaches of the sky of the cosmos of reality.

"Just as all the wealth, jewels, silver, gold, flowers, perfumes, garlands, clothes, and furnishings there are as far as the sun and moon shine do not match the worth of the powerful king jewel, in the same way, all the virtues of celestials and humans, all Buddhist disciples and self-illuminates, tainted or untainted, as far as the scope of the reality-realm reveals, do not match the worth of the powerful king jewel of the determination for enlightenment.

"Just as the jewel known as 'containing the arrays of the oceans' shows the arrays of all oceans, in the same way the determination for enlightenment shows the array of the ocean of the scope of all-knowledge.

"Just as nothing surpasses celestial gold, with the exception of a wish-fulfilling jewel, there is nothing except the wish-fulfilling jewel of omniscience, which surpasses the celestial gold of the aspiration for enlightenment.

"Just as a master snake-catcher can place all serpents under his control, the enlightening snake-catcher who has mastered the will for enlightenment can place all the serpents of affliction under control.

"Just as an armed warrior is invulnerable to enemy troops, the enlightening being armed with the determination for omniscience becomes invulnerable to the enemy troops of afflictions.

"Just as one handful of celestial serpent sandalwood powder perfumes a thousand worlds, and three thousand worlds full of jewels cannot match the worth of an ounce of it, in the same way one element of the celestial serpent sandalwood of the aspiration for omniscience perfumes the whole cosmos with virtue and surpasses the minds of all learners, those who are beyond learning, and self-illuminates.

"Just as the precious snowy sandalwood stops all burning and cools the whole body, in the same way the snowy sandalwood of the aspiration for omniscience stops the burning of all afflictions, false notions, lust, hatred and delusion, and cools the body of knowledge.

"Just as all who come to the polar mountain become one color, gold, in the same way all who approach enlightening beings who are entirely dedicated to omniscience become one color, the color of omniscience.

"Just as the bark of a tree of paradise emits a fragrance that is not found in all the flowers on earth, in the same way the fragrance of the bark of virtue and knowledge of the tree of vows grown from the seed of enlightening beings' determination for omniscience is not found in any of the flowers of hearers and individual illuminates, who have lesser roots of goodness, in their untainted discipline, concentration, wisdom, liberation, and knowledge and vision of liberation.

"Just as it can be known of a budding tree of paradise that it will produce hundreds of thousands of blossoms, in the same way it can be known that the paradise tree of the aspiration for omniscience budding with roots of goodness will produce countless flowers of enlightenment, imperfect and perfect, in celestials and humans.

"Just as the fragrance of cloth or oil perfumed for one day with paradise tree flowers is not to be found in cloth or oil perfumed for a hundred thousand days with jasmine flowers, in the same way the fragrance of enlightening beings' virtue and knowledge, of the mind and body infused for one lifetime with the determination for omniscience, wafts to the presence of all buddhas in the ten directions, and is not to be found in the fragrance of untainted virtue and spiritual knowledge of those infused for a hundred thousand eons with the aspirations of those who seek individual salvation.

"Just as there is a kind of tree that grows in an ocean, on all of which, from its roots to its flowers and fruits, all beings are at all times living, in the same way the world is sustained by the process of enlightening, growing from the root of vows based on great compassion, from the initial aspiration for omniscience through the duration and ending of the true teaching.

"Just as there is an ointment called 'golden light,' one ounce of which will make a thousand ounces of copper gold, while those thousand ounces of copper cannot appropriate the ounce of ointment and make it copper, in the same way the one element of the essence of the aspiration for omniscience, concentrated by knowledge of dedication of roots of goodness, takes away the copper of the barriers caused by actions and afflictions and makes them into the color of total knowledge of all things, and the essential element of the aspiration for omniscience cannot be defiled or appropriated by any actions or afflictions.

"Just as even a little bit of fire will produce as much flame as the amount of fuel it gets, in the same way even a little bit of the fire of the determination for omniscience, because of mixing with objects, will increase in its production of flames of knowledge to the extent of the provisions it is supplied with.

"Just as millions of lamps can be lit from one lamp, without the one lamp being exhausted or diminished by all the lamps taking their flame from it, in the same way from the one lamp of the aspiration for omniscience the lamps of aspiration for omniscience of all buddhas of past, future, and present are lit, yet the one lamp of aspiration for omniscience is not exhausted, and shines undiminished by the lights of the lamps of aspiration to omniscience proceeding from it.

"Just as when a lamp is put into a room, even a thousand years of darkness immediately vanishes and it lights up the place, in the same way when the lamp of the aspiration for omniscience enters the room of the mind of sentient beings, dark with ignorance, immediately untold eons of darkness caused by the obstruction by afflictions is dispelled, and the lamp produces the light of knowledge.

"Just as a lamp makes light according to the condition of its wick, and burns as long as there is a supply of oil, in the same way the lamp of the aspiration for omniscience lights up the realm of reality according to the excellence of the wick of vows of the enlightening being, and as long as there is a supply of the oil of the practice of universal compassion, so long will there be the power for the buddha-tasks of guiding sentient beings and purifying lands.

"Just as celestial gold ornaments on the head of the king of gods of control over others' emanations cannot be outshone by any of the celestials in the realm of desire, in the same way the celestial gold ornament of the aspiration for omniscience, set on perfected virtue and fastened on the head of universal vows of nonregressing enlightening beings, cannot be outshone by ordinary people or by learners or attainers of individual liberation.

"Just as lion cubs thrive on the roar of the lion, king of beasts, while the other animals all hide, in the same way by the roar of omniscience of the Buddha, the human lion, extolling the determination for enlightenment, the lion-cub beginning enlightening beings thrive on the enlightened teachings, while all grasping, clinging people hide.

"Just as the strings of all instruments snap at the sound of an instrument strung with lion sinew, in the same way at the virtue-extolling sound of the instrument strung with the sinew of the aspiration for enlightenment of the buddha-lion whose body is the transcendent ways, the strings of the lute of sensuality snap and the songs of praise of the virtues of the individually liberated fade out.

"Just as a drop of lion milk in an ocean of cow milk causes all the milk to separate and does not mix with it, in the same way the ocean of milk of acts and afflictions accumulated over hundreds of thousands of eons is destroyed by putting into it one drop of the milk of the determination for omniscience of the Buddha, the human lion, and it does not mix with the liberation of those who are only enlightened for themselves alone.

"Just as the extraordinary power of the cry of a kalavinka chick still in the shell is not found in any of the birds of the mountains, even when they are full grown, in the same way the extraordinary power of the cry of universal compassion of the aspiration for enlightenment of a fledgling enlightening being still in the shell of the mundane whirl is not found in the individually liberated.

"Just as the wing flapping power and clear vision of a newborn garuda is not found even in fully grown birds of other species, in the same way the power of the determination for enlightenment and the purity of the mind of compassion in a beginning enlightening being born in the family of the buddhas is not found even in seekers of individual liberation and self-illuminates who have been practicing for a long time.

"Just as a spear in the hand of a powerful man can pierce any armor, however strong it is, in the same way the spear of the determination for omniscience, in the hand of an enlightening being of steadfast vigor, pierces the armor of all views and propensities.

"Just as a mighty man full of wrath cannot be defeated by any man on earth as long as there are eruptions on his forehead, in the same way a mighty enlightening being filled with universal love and compassion cannot be overcome by any devils or actions in any world as long as the eruptions of the determination for omniscience do not disappear from the face of will.

"Just as the special strength of application to technique of a student of archery is not found in a teacher of archery who has already learned it all, the special strength of zealous practice of beginning enlightening beings is not found in those who seek and attain personal salvation without the aspiration for universal enlightenment.

"Just as the first step in learning archery is to learn the stance, in the same way for an enlightening being learning about omniscience is the first step to understanding all the buddha-teachings in the act of setting out with the determination for omniscience.

"Just as when a magician is going to make a display of magical effects, all the effects are accomplished by first thinking of the magical formula, in the same way when manifesting the spheres of buddhas and enlightening beings, the establishing of the spheres of buddhas and enlightening beings takes place by first evoking the vow to accomplish enlightenment.

"Just as all magical formulas are formless and invisible but produce magical phantoms with form by mental activity, in the same way the determination for omniscience is formless and invisible, yet it fashions all spiritual realms with arrays of ornaments of all virtues merely by control of mental activity.

"Just as all rats and mice take cover as soon as they see a wildcat on the prowl, in the same way all conditioning and affliction flee just from the proceeding of application of intense determination for omniscience.

"Just as when one puts on an ornament of the finest gold it outshines all bangles, in the same way the enlightening being wearing the gold ornament of the determination for omniscience outshines the ornaments of virtue of all hearers and individual illuminates.

"Just as even the smallest bit of the most powerful magnet can burst strong chains asunder, in the same way even the smallest bit of aspiration for omniscience with powerful determination can burst asunder the chains of views, ignorance, and craving.

"Just as wherever a magnet is used, all metals that it expels are repelled and do not remain there or join with it, in the same way wherever the determination for omniscience is used, whether in the midst of actions or afflictions or the liberation of hearers and individual illuminates, those actions and afflictions and individual liberation are expelled and do not remain or join with it.

"Just as a fisher with knowledge of sea monsters is free from fear of any creatures of the sea and is safe from harm even in the mouth of a whale, in the same way the enlightening being with the knowledge of the powerful determination of the aspiration for enlightenment is free from fear of all the actions and afflictions of the mundane whirl and cannot be annihilated even in the midst of realization of individual liberation, because of not falling into the extinction produced by witness of ultimate reality.

"Just as one who has drunk the elixir of immortality does not die from the attacks of others, in the same way the enlightening being who has drunk the immortality elixir of the aspiration for omniscience does not die in the stages of learners of individual salvation and does not cease acting on the vow of universal compassion of enlightening beings.

"Just as a man who has perfected the ointment of invisibility can wander through people's houses unseen by anyone, the enlightening being grounded on the wisdom and commitment of the determination for enlightenment can roam in the realms of all demons without being seen by any demons.

"Just as a person who cleaves to a great king does not fear ordinary people, the enlightening being who cleaves to the spiritual king of the determination for omniscience does not fear any obstacles, hindrances, or states of misery.

"Just as someone in water is in no danger from fire, the enlightening being who is soaked in the virtue of the aspiration for enlightenment is in no danger from the fire of knowledge of individual liberation.

"Just as a person who cleaves to a heroic warrior does not fear enemies, the enlightening being who cleaves to the heroic warrior of the determination for omniscience does not fear the enemies that are evil actions.

"Just as the king of gods with the thunderbolt weapon crushes all the titans, the enlightening being with the thunderbolt of the steadfast will of the aspiration for omniscience crushes all the titans of demons and false teachers.

"Just as a person who takes the elixir of life lives for a long time and does not grow weak, the enlightening being who uses the elixir of the aspiration for omniscience goes around in the mundane whirl for countless eons without becoming exhausted and without being stained by the ills of the mundane whirl.

"Just as in all compounds of herbal extracts potable water is primary, never spoiling, in the same way in the application of preparations of all enlightening beings' practices and vows the determination for omniscience is primary, never becoming corrupt.

"Just as in all of a person's doing the faculty of life is the primary necessity, for an enlightening being to absorb the buddha-teachings the aspiration for enlightenment is the primary necessity.

"Just as a person who has lost the faculty of life has no way to live, being unable to do anything for his people, in the same way an enlightening being without the life root of the determination for omniscience has no way to live, being unable to obtain enlightened knowledge for all beings.

"Just as the ocean cannot be ruined by any poisons, the ocean of aspiration for omniscience cannot be ruined by any of the poisons of compulsive actions, afflictions, or aspirations for personal liberation alone.

"Just as the sun is not outshone by the lights of all the stars, the sun of aspiration to omniscience is not outshone by the taintless virtues of those who are personally liberated.

"Just as a newborn prince is not inferior to fully grown ministers, because of his superior birth, a beginning enlightening being, born in the family of the enlightened spiritual kings, is not inferior to Buddhist disciples with long experience in religious practice, because of the superiority of universal compassion of the aspiration for enlightenment.

"Just as a minister, no matter how old, should pay respect to a prince, no matter how young, and a prince need not honor a minister, in the same way Buddhist disciples and self-illuminates, no matter how long they have performed religious practice, should pay respect to even a beginning enlightening being, and the enlightening being need not honor those who are enlightened only for themselves.

"Just as a prince, without any power yet never without the character of royalty, is not equaled even by the ministers who have gained eminence, because of his superior birth, in the same way a beginning enlightening being, no matter how much under the sway of action and affliction, is never without the character of the aspiration for omniscience, and is not equaled even by eminent Buddhist disciples and self-illuminates, because of being of the family of enlightened ones.

"Just as a clear jewel appears impure to a clouded eye, the inherently pure jewel of the aspiration to omniscience is perceived as impure by those whose eye of unbelief is beclouded by ignorance.

"Just as a body of medicine endowed with all medical knowledge and medicinal herbs cure the diseases of sentient beings by sight, contact, and association, in the same way the body of vows and knowledge of enlightening beings, sustained by the knowledge and medicine of wisdom and means assembling all roots of goodness, endowed with the will for enlightenment, cures sentient beings' diseases of afflictions by hearing, seeing, association, recollection, and application.

"Just as a goose-feather robe is not stained by any dirt, the goose-feather robe of the aspiration for enlightenment is not stained by the dirt of afflictions of the mundane whirl.

"Just as a wooden figure held together by the main pin does not fall apart and can perform any kind of movement, in the same way the body of the vow and knowledge of omniscience, held together by the main pin of the vow of enlightenment, can perform the tasks of enlightening beings, and does not fall apart as the embodiment of the vow of omniscience.

"Just as a machine without its pins cannot work, even though the parts are the same, similarly, the enlightening being without the commanding will of the aspiration to omniscience cannot attain buddhahood, even though the preparations of the parts of enlightenment be the same.

"Just as a sovereign ruler has a precious incense by the perfume of which his four armies are levitated into the air, in the same way the roots of goodness of an enlightening being, perfumed by the incense of the determination for omniscience, leave the mundane and end up in the unconditioned realm of the sky of enlightened knowledge.

"Just as diamond comes from nowhere else but a jewel mine, from a diamond or gold mine, in the same way the diamondlike aspiration for omniscience comes from nowhere else but the jewel mine of roots of goodness in sentient beings' minds, from the diamond mine of universal compassion saving all beings, or from the gold mine of concentration on omniscience.

"Just as there is a kind of tree called 'rootless' whose roots cannot be found, yet branches, leaves, and flowers appear luxuriantly on the tree, in the same way the root of the aspiration for omniscience cannot be found, yet it appears in all worlds, blooming with all virtues, knowledge, and mystic capacities, forming a web of vows.

"Just as a diamond does not shine beautifully in another kind of vessel, and cannot be held in an imperfect, perforated vessel, only in a perfect vessel, in the same way the diamond of the aspiration for omniscience does not shine in the vessels of people with inferior resolutions, in the envious, in the immoral, in the mentally corrupt, in the lazy, in the heedless, or in the stupid, and it cannot be held by a vessel of a wavering, inconstant mind with defective will, only in the precious vessel of the powerful will of an enlightening being.

"Just as diamond pierces all jewels, the diamond of the determination for omniscience pierces the jewels of all truth.

"Just as adamant splits all mountains, the adamant of the aspiration for omniscience splits the mountains of all views.

"Just as even a cracked diamond is better than an ornament of gold, the finest of precious metals, in the same way the diamond of the aspiration for omniscience is better than the gold ornaments of the virtues of hearers and individual illuminates, even if the will is broken by adversity.

"Just as a diamond, even if cracked, relieves poverty, in the same way the diamond of the determination for omniscience, even if split, relieves the poverty of the mundane whirl.

"Just as a diamond, however little, breaks all gems and stones, in the same way the diamond of the aspiration for omniscience, focused on however small an object, breaks all ignorance.

"Just as a diamond does not come into the hands of an ordinary man, the diamond of the determination for omniscience does not come into the hands of those of low intentions and poor roots of goodness.

"Just as someone who has no knowledge of gems does not recognize the qualities of diamonds or understand their excellence, in the same way a stupid person does not know the qualities of the diamond of wisdom of the aspiration for enlightenment and does not understand its excellence.

"Just as a diamond cannot be worn out, the diamond of the aspiration for enlightenment, the basis of omniscience, cannot be worn out.

"Just as the thunderbolt weapon cannot be held even by a strong man unless he has superhuman strength, likewise the thunderbolt of the aspiration for enlightenment cannot be held even by the mighty saints and sages, only by the great enlightening beings with great illumination, excelling in the superhuman might of infinite roots of goodness based on the power of the cause of omniscience.

"Just as a thunderbolt can prevail where all other weapons cannot, and will not be destroyed, in the same way where the weapons of vows and knowledge of all Buddhist disciples and self-enlightened ones cannot prevail, in developing and guiding people or living through the toils of practice through the ages of past, present, and future, there the enlightening being who holds the great thunderbolt weapon of the determination for omniscience, indefatigable, prevails unharmed.

"Just as adamant cannot be held on any spot on the earth except on an adamantine surface, in the same way the adamant vows of emancipation of enlightening beings cannot be held by those whose goal is personal salvation only; it can only be supported by the adamantine ground of the resolute determination for universal enlightenment.

"Just as the ocean does not leak any water because it is a solid container with an unyielding ground, in the same way the roots of goodness of an enlightening being, grounded on adamant, solid, unyielding dedication to enlightening, do not die out in any states of existence.

"Just as earth set on an adamantine base does not collapse or sink, in the same way the vows of enlightening beings, grounded on the adamantine base of the determination for enlightenment, are not rent apart and do not collapse in any mundane realm.

"Just as a diamond does not rot in water, the diamond of the aspiration for enlightenment does not decompose or soften even though it remain in the water of action and affliction for all ages.

"Just as a diamond is not burnt or heated by fire, the diamond of the determination for omniscience is not burnt by the fires of suffering of the mundane whirl and is not heated up by the fires of afflictions.

"Just as the seat of buddhas sitting on the site of enlightenment battling the devil and awakening to omniscience cannot be supported by any spot on earth except the earth surface of the adamantine center of the universe, in the same way the great force of power of the roots of goodness of enlightening beings aspiring to perfect enlightenment, carrying out the practice, fulfilling the transcendent ways, entering into tolerance, attaining spiritual station, dedicating roots of goodness, receiving assurance of buddhahood, providing the necessities for the path of enlightening beings, and holding the multitudes of teachings of all buddhas, cannot be sustained by mind other than the mind set on omniscience, the adamantine core of all vows and knowledge.

"The aspiration for omniscience has these and untold other extraordinary virtues; and those who have set their minds on supreme perfect enlightenment are, have been, and will be endowed with such virtues. Therefore you have made a great gain in having aspired to supreme perfect enlightenment and seeking the practice of enlightening beings, because of attainment of these virtues.

"Also, you ask how an enlightening being is to learn and carry out the practice of enlightening beings. Go into this great tower containing the adornments of Vairocana and look—then you will know how to learn the practice of enlightening beings, and what kind of virtues are perfected in those who learn this."

Then Sudhana respectfully circumbulated the enlightening being Maitreya and said, "Please open the door of the tower, and I will enter." Then Maitreya went up to the door of the tower containing the adornments of Vairocana, and with his right hand snapped his fingers; the door of the tower opened, and Maitreya bade Sudhana to enter. Then Sudhana, in greatest wonder, went into the tower. As soon as he had entered, the door shut.

He saw the tower immensely vast and wide, hundreds of thousands of leagues wide, as measureless as the sky, as vast as all of space, adorned with countless attributes; countless canopies, banners, pennants, jewels, garlands of pearls and gems, moons and half moons, multicolored streamers, jewel nets, gold nets, strings of jewels, jewels on golden threads, sweetly ringing bells and nets of chimes, flowers showering, celestial garlands and streamers, censers giving off fragrant fumes, showers of gold dust, networks of upper chambers, round windows, arches, turrets, mirrors, jewel figurines of women, jewel chips, pillars, clouds of precious cloths, jewel trees, jewel railings, jeweled pathways, jeweled awnings, various arrays of the floor, chambers of jewels, jeweled promenades, rows of golden banana trees, statues made of all kinds of jewels, images of enlightening beings, singing birds, jewel lotuses, lotus ponds, jewel stairways, ground of masses of various jewels, radiant gems, arrays of all kinds of jewels. Also, inside the great tower he saw hundreds of thousands of other towers similarly arrayed; he saw those towers as infinitely vast as space, evenly arrayed in all directions, yet these towers were not mixed up with one another, being each mutually distinct, while appearing reflected in each and every object of all the other towers.

Then Sudhana, seeing this miraculous manifestation of the inconceivable realm of the great tower containing the adornments of Vairocana, was flooded with joy and bliss; his mind was cleared of all conceptions and freed from all obstructions. Stripped of all delusion, he became clairvoyant without distortion, and could hear all sounds with unimpeded mindfulness. He was freed from all scattering of attention, and his intellect followed the unobstructed eye of liberation. With physical tranquillity, seeing all objects without hindrance, by the power of production everywhere he bowed in all directions with his whole body.

The moment he bowed, by the power of Maitreya, Sudhana perceived himself in all of those towers; and in all those towers he saw various diverse inconceivable miraculous scenes. In one tower he saw where the enlightening being Maitreya first aspired to supreme perfect enlightenment, what his family was, what his basic goodness was, how he was inspired, how he was encouraged by spiritual friends, how long he lived, what age he lived in, what buddha he met, what land he adorned, what assembly he was in, and what kind of special vows he undertook. He also perceived the length of life of the beings and the buddha of that time, and saw himself in the presence of that buddha, and saw all of his works.

In one tower he saw where Maitreya first attained absorption in love, whence came his name, "The Loving One." In another he saw where he carried out spiritual practice; in another, where he fulfilled the transcendent ways; in another, where he attained acceptance of things as unoriginated; in another, where he was assured of supreme perfect enlightenment, how he was assured, by whom, and how long it was predicted it would be before he was enlightened.

In one tower he saw Maitreya as a sovereign king directing people to virtuous action; in another he saw Maitreya as a world guardian bestowing well-being and happiness on the world; in another he saw Maitreya as Indra, fostering detachment in those obsessed with pleasure; in another he saw Maitreya as Brahma, describing to people the measureless pleasure of meditation; in another he saw Maitreya as the chief of the gods of timely portion, describing to people the virtues of attentiveness and diligence; in another he saw Maitreya as the chief of the heaven of contentment, revealing the virtues of enlightening beings bound to become buddhas in one lifetime; in another he saw Maitreya as a king of the heaven of good emanations, showing a company of celestials the array of emanations of all enlightening beings; in another he saw Maitreya as a lord of the heaven of control, explaining to the gods control over all phenomena; in another he saw Maitreya causing the devil to act, showing the gods the impermanence of all states of being; in another he saw Maitreya born in the palace of titans, teaching the titans truth so that they might do away with all conceit, pride, and arrogance, plunge into the ocean of knowledge, enter the ocean of spiritual knowledge, and attain the magic of knowledge of truth.

In one tower he saw the underworld and saw Maitreya illumine the great hells with light and relieve the hellish pains of the beings in hell. In another tower he saw the ghost world and saw Maitreya giving much food and drink to the ghosts, relieving their hunger and thirst. In another tower he saw Maitreya guiding the beings in the animal realm.

In one tower he saw Maitreya expounding the Teaching to world guardians in an assembly of celestial kings; in another he saw him in a group of chief gods of the thirty-three-fold heavens; in another he saw him in a group of chiefs of the heaven of timely portion; in another he saw him in a group of lords of the heaven of contentment; in another he saw him in a group of chiefs of the heaven of good emanations; in another he saw him in a group of kings of the heaven of control; in another tower he saw Maitreya as a Great Brahma in a group of Brahma lords, expounding the Teaching.

In one tower he saw Maitreya in a group of dragons and serpents; in another, in a group of goblins and fiends; in another, in a group of titans and demons; in another, in a group of giant serpents; in another, in a group of human chiefs; in another tower, he saw the enlightening being Maitreya in a group of gods, dragons, goblins, fiends, cherubs, titans, birds, minotaurs, serpents, humans, and nonhumans, expounding the Teaching to them.

In one tower he saw Maitreya in a group of hearers; in another, in a group of individual illuminates; in another, in a group of enlightening beings; in another tower, he saw Maitreya expounding the Teaching to beginning enlightening beings who had just set their minds on enlightenment. In another tower he saw Maitreya extolling the excellences of the stages to those who had undertaken practice; in another, to those who had attained tolerance and were irreversible; in another, to those bound to be enlightened in one lifetime who had attained coronation; in another tower, to enlightening beings in the first stage.

In another tower he saw Maitreya with enlightening beings in stages up to the tenth, extolling the excellence of all the stages. In another tower he saw Maitreya speaking of the infinity of fulfillment of the transcendent ways; in another, of impartiality in approaching and entering into all studies; in another, of breadth of entry into concentration; in another, of depth of liberation; in another, of pervasion of the realm of higher knowledge of quiescent meditation, concentration, and trance; in another, of entry into the methods of guidance in enlightening practice; in another, of breadth of performance of vows; in another tower he saw Maitreya with a group of enlightening beings engaged in the same practice as he, speaking of the relevance of providing for the welfare and happiness of all beings, of the various arts and sciences to be employed for the benefit of the world.

In another tower he saw Maitreya with a group of enlightening beings bound to be enlightened in one life, telling them about coronation with the knowledge of all buddhas. In another tower he saw Maitreya perambulating ceaselessly for hundreds of thousands of years; in another, he saw him engaged in recitation; in another, engaged in contemplation of doctrine; in another, engaged in exposition of doctrine; in another, engaged in writing down the Teaching; in another, absorbed in concentration on universal love; in another, absorbed in all the meditations and immeasurables; in another, absorbed in the points of totality and the liberations; in another tower he saw Maitreya absorbed in the practice of bringing forth the higher knowledge of enlightening beings.

In one tower he saw enlightening beings absorbed in an enlightening concentration which emanated phantoms, and saw multitudes of all kinds of emanations coming from every pore of their bodies. From the pores of some he saw multitudes of celestial hosts emerging; from some he saw multitudes of dragons, goblins, cherubs, titans, birds, minotaurs, serpents, Indras, Brahmas, world guardians, and emperors; from some he saw multitudes of princes; from some he saw multitudes of grandees, ministers, and gentlemen; from some he saw multitudes of hearers, individual illuminates, and enlightening beings; from some he saw multitudes of buddha-bodies; from the pores of some he saw measureless multitudes of phantoms of all sentient beings emerge. He heard various aspects of the Teaching being broadcast from the pores of some of the enlightening beings—teachings of the virtues of enlightening beings, transcendent generosity, discipline, tolerance, vigor, meditation, wisdom, methods, vows, power, knowledge, the means of integration, the immeasurables, concentrations, trance, superknowledge, mystic spells, intellectual powers of analysis and exposition, tranquillity and observation, means of liberation, interdependent origination, the reliances, summarization of teachings, the points of mindfulness, the right efforts, the bases of mystic powers, the religious faculties and powers, the limbs of enlightenment, the paths, explanation of the vehicle of hearers, explanation of the vehicle of individual illuminates, explanation of the Great Vehicle, the stages, tolerances, practices, and vows—in this way he heard voices expressing all the ways into the Teaching being broadcast.

In another tower he saw gatherings of the audiences of buddhas, as well as the various differences among those buddhas, their different families, the infinite variety of their physical adornments, the variety of their life spans, the differences in their lands and eras, the variety of their teachings, the variety of the outwardness of their projected manifestations, the differences in the duration of their true teachings, and all the differences in their assemblies.

In the middle of the great tower containing the adornments of Vairocana he saw one tower which was bigger than all the others and arrayed with adornments surpassing all the other towers. In that tower he saw a billion-world universe, in which he saw a hundred million sets of four continents, with a hundred million Jambudvipas and a hundred million heavens of contentment. In those Jambudvipa continents he saw the enlightening being Maitreya being born in a lotus calyx; he also saw Maitreya taking seven steps as Indra and Brahma watched, looking over the ten directions, making the lion roar, showing all the stages of childhood, in the palace, out in the garden, setting out for omniscience, appearing to undertake ascetic practice, finally eating food, going to the site of enlightenment, conquering the devil, awakening to enlightenment, steadily gazing on the tree of enlightenment, being asked by Brahma to teach, and turning the wheel of the teaching, going into the celestial abodes, with various different manifestations of enlightening teaching, using various names of eras in different ways, with various different spans of life, various different arrays of gatherings, with various demonstrations of ways of purification of lands, carrying out various practices and vows, with various structures of teaching used as means to develop and mature all concerned, showing various distributions of relics and bases of maintaining the teachings. And everywhere there Sudhana perceived himself at Maitreya's feet.

In all those assemblies, in all the manifestations of works, in the varieties of spans of life, by means of the knowledge based on clear recollection, standing on the ground of knowledge, sure to reach omniscience, Sudhana heard, from all the objects in all those towers, the nets of bells and chimes, the drums and songs, and so on, and from the beings therein, the thunder of inconceivable multitudes of voices. From some he heard of the variety of aspirations for enlightenment; from some, about the variety of offerings to buddhas; from some, about the variety of arrays of buddha-lands; from some, about the infinite variety of teachings of buddhas—thus he heard the voices of all the teachings as they had been expounded in the past.

He also heard about setting out for omniscience—in such-and-such a land the enlightening being so-and-so aspired to enlightenment, heard such-and-such a teaching, was inspired by the spiritual benefactor so-and-so, went to such-and-such a congregation at the foot of the buddha so-and-so in such-and-such a land in such-and-such an age, planted such-and-such roots of goodness, heard about such-and-such qualities of buddhahood, undertook such-and-such a variety of vows with such-and-such an intention, will realize supreme perfect enlightenment in so many eons after having carried out practice for so many eons, will be named so-and-so, will live so long, in a buddha-land with such-and-such qualities, with such-and-such higher commitments, such-and-such guidance of beings, such-and-such a congregation of disciples, individual illuminates, and enlightening beings, the true teaching to last for so many ages after the death of the Buddha, with such-and-such benefits.

He heard another voice saying that in such-and-such a world the enlightening being so-and-so makes so many hundreds of difficult sacrifices in the practice of transcendent giving; the enlightening being so-and-so keeps the precepts, cultivates tolerance, acquires vigor, attains meditations, engages in the investigation of wisdom; the enlightening being so-and-so, in search of truth, relinquishes kingship, wealth, family, hands and feet, eyes and head, and practices self-mortification by fire; the enlightening being so-and-so, advanced in the teaching of those who arrive at Thusness, works as a spiritual preacher, giving the gift of religion, performs the service of religion, raises the banner of religion, beats the drum and blows the horn of religion, showers the rain of religion, preserves the teaching of the enlightened, adorns monuments to the enlightened, has images of buddhas made, comforts beings, and guards the treasury of truth.

He heard another voice say that the buddha so-and-so now is in such-and-such a world, currently existing and expounding the Teaching, with such-and-such an initiation, in such-and-such an assembly in such-and-such a land in such-and-such an age, with such-and-such a life span, with such-and-such a doctrine guiding people in such-and-such a way, realizing such-and-such vows.

In this manner, from each object Sudhana heard articulations of an infinite variety of aspects of the Teaching, and by listening to all those voices he heard those facets of the Teaching with a mind flooded with joy. From some he got facets of mental command; from others, facets of commitment, tolerance, conduct, transcendence, higher perceptions, mystic knowledge, liberation, and concentration.

He also saw measureless arrays of reflections in the mirrors, reflections of assemblies of buddhas, circles of enlightening beings, congregations of disciples, groups of self-illuminates, defiled lands, pure lands, defiled and pure lands, reflections of all buddhas in one world, worlds with buddhas, small worlds, large worlds, subtle worlds, gross worlds, worlds in the cosmic net of Indra, inverted worlds, level worlds, worlds of hells, animals, and ghosts, worlds full of celestials and humans.

He also saw countless enlightening beings on the promenades or sitting on their seats, engaged in various activities. Some were walking around, some were doing spiritual exercises, some were practicing observation, some were projecting universal compassion, some were working on various sciences having to do with the welfare of the world, some were instructing, some were reciting, some were writing, some were asking questions, some were engaged in ripening conduct, concentration, and knowledge, some were undertaking vows.

He saw webs of jewel lights coming from the pillars, some sapphire, some topaz, some ruby, some white, some crystal, some golden, some emerald, some diamond, some rainbow, some the colors of all lights, delightful to the body and mind, supremely pleasant to the eye.

He also saw the golden statues of women and all the jewel statues with their hands extended downward, holding myriads of flowers, garlands, parasols, banners and pennants, incense and perfume, various jewels on gold strings, various pearl necklaces, garlands of various jewels, holding all kinds of ornaments in their hands. He saw some figures bowing, crowned with jewels, with steady gaze, palms joined, in gestures of respect. He also saw delicate clouds of pure water imbued with all fragrances coming from the pearl necklaces, and saw long streams flowing from the webs of strings of lapis lazuli. He also saw all the jewel parasols embellished with all kinds of ornaments, and he saw the inner chamber adorned with jewel bells, sets of chimes, silk streamers, strings of bells, slivers of jewels, and heaps of various gems. He saw countless superb red, blue, and white lotuses growing in the lotus ponds, some a foot across, some a fathom across, some as big as a wagon wheel; and in them he saw arrays of various figures—figures of women, men, boys, girls, Indra, Brahma, the world guardians, gods, dragons, goblins, cherubs, titans, birds, centaurs, serpents, sages, saints, and enlightening beings—bodies in the forms of all living beings, various in appearance, joining their palms and bowing in gestures of respect. He also saw figures of buddhas adorned with the thirty-two marks of great people, sitting in the lotus posture.

Also, on the checkerboard lapis-lazuli surface of the ground, he saw inconceivable reflections in each square; here he saw the reflection of a land, there the reflection of a buddha. All the arrays of adornments in those towers he saw reflected in each of the squares.

Also, in all the flowers, fruits, and buds of the jewel trees he saw golden busts of all kinds of beings—buddhas, enlightening beings, gods, dragons, goblins, cherubs, titans, birds, serpents, Indras, Brahmas, the world guardians, human emperors, princes, grandees, ministers, women, men, boys, girls, monks, nuns, male and female devotees, some with flower garlands hanging from their hands, some with strings of jewels hanging from their hands, some holding all kinds of ornaments, some bowing with their palms joined and gaze steady, paying respect, some singing hymns of praise, some in trance, some with a golden luster, some with a silver luster, some with a frosty luster, some with a sapphire luster, some with a shining jewel luster, some shining with the colors of all jewels, some with a saffron luster, some shining like bodies of light, some with bodies adorned with the marks of greatness.

From the crescents adorning the towers he saw reflections of countless moons, suns, stars, and planets emerge and illumine the ten directions.

He also saw the walls of the palatial towers resplendent with checkerboards of all jewels, and in all of the jewel square he saw Maitreya carrying out all the practices of enlightening beings, as he had done while performing enlightening practice in the past: in one square he saw Maitreya giving away his head; in another, giving away clothing; in another, giving away his topknot jewel; in another, giving the crown jewel of truth; in another, giving away his teeth; in another, giving away his tongue; in another, giving away his ears and nose; in another, giving away his heart; in another giving away his marrow and flesh; in another, giving away his blood; in another, giving away his skin; in another, giving away his limbs; in another, giving away his body; in another, giving away his sons, daughters, and wife; in another, giving away heaps of jewels; in another, giving away village, town, city, and country; in another, giving away the continent; in another, giving away four continents; in another, giving away all powers of rulership; in another, giving away the throne; in another, giving away servants; in another, giving away the palace and harem; in another, giving away parks and retreats; in another, giving parasols, banners, and pennants; in another, giving garlands and perfumes; in another, giving medicines; in another, giving all kinds of food and drink; in another, giving all kinds of implements; in another, giving all kinds of furniture, cushions, and shelters; in another, giving precious copper vessels; in another, giving excellent vehicles; in another, freeing those in bondage; in another, freeing the condemned; in another, giving medical care to the young; in another, showing the right path to those on the path of destruction; in another, navigating the rivers as a boatman; in another, as a wonder horse, rescuing people on the isle of demons in the ocean; in another, as a great seer, practicing the sciences; in another, as a ruler, leading people into the paths of righteous conduct; in another, as a physician, engaged in treating the sick; in another, serving his mother and father; in another, listening to spiritual benefactors; in another, in the form of a Buddhist disciple, engaged in teaching people; in another in the form of a self-illuminate, in another in the form of an enlightening being, in another in the form of a buddha, engaged in teaching people; in another, manifesting existence as paragons of types of beings, developing beings to maturity; in another, as a religious preacher expounding experience of the teachings of buddhas, reciting the teachings, reflecting deeply on them, decorating monuments of buddhas, having statues of buddhas made, enjoining people to honor the buddhas, giving out perfumes, making all kinds of offerings to buddhas, leading people into paths of actions based on virtuous ways, directing people to the precepts, to refuge in the Buddha, the Teaching, and the Community, to listening to the Teaching, to discussion, recital, and profound contemplation of the Teaching, sitting on the lion seat to talk of the Teaching, revealing the enlightenment of buddhas. Thus Sudhana saw Maitreya's practices of the six ways of transcendence over countless eons, projected from each of the squares of the checkerboard walls. In one tower he saw magical arrays of all the spiritual benefactors whom Maitreya attended, and he perceived himself in the presence of all those spiritual benefactors, being welcomed and told not to be weary, to behold this wonder of the enlightening being.

So Sudhana saw these and other inconceivable projections of magnificent scenes from each of the towers and each object in the towers. By the power of unwavering mindfulness, by all-encompassing purity of vision, by unobstructed knowledge of observational skill, by attainment of control over the basis of knowledge of enlightening beings, standing on the ground of knowledge issuing from the perceptions of enlightening beings, he saw this whole endless manifestation of marvelous scenes.

It was like someone asleep seeing various things in a dream—nice houses and mansions, charming villages, towns, and cities, agreeable clothing, food and drink, or delightful performances of music, song, and dance; or as one might see pleasant parks, gardens, and retreats, trees, rivers, lotus ponds, and mountains, or perceive oneself together with family and friends, or as one might see the ocean, or the polar mountain, or the celestial abodes on the highest mountains, or the whole continent, or perceive oneself to be many miles tall, in which case one would see one's house and surroundings as enormous; one sees all the elements arrayed together, as if it were daytime, and one does not know the length or brevity of the night, nor realize one is asleep. If one sees oneself in a pleasant situation, one's body will be at rest, one will be free from torpor and drowsiness, with all attachments removed, feeling great joy and bliss; it will seem to last long—a day, a week, a fort-night, a year, a century, or even more—and when one awakes, one will remember it all. In the same way Sudhana, by the power of the enlightening being, by the knowledge of the collection of dreams that constitutes the world, the notion of smallness gone from his mind, abiding in the immensely vast unobstructed perception of enlightening beings, with the mental scope of enlightening beings, his intellect having entered into the inconceivable wisdom of enlightening beings, saw the whole supernal man-ifestation, was perfectly aware of it, understood it, contemplated it, used it as a means, beheld it, and saw himself there.

It was like the case of a dying man hovering in his final mental state, on the brink of the mental state immediately preceding rebirth, faced with the state of being which is caused by his actions, as a result of the accumulation of whatever actions he has done; he will see hell if he has done evil, or the state of animals, ghosts, or the underworld, and may see angry, abusive henchmen of the underworld carrying weapons, and hear the cries of lament and anger of the beings in hell. He will also see the great hells burning, blaz-ing masses of flames, and will see the copper cauldrons and the tortures being carried out, and will perceive those undergoing them. He will also see and feel the pains of the burning of the fires of hell. But by accumulation of good actions one will see heaven, and will see the assemblies of gods and goddesses and all the magnificent arrays of heaven; one will see and experi-ence the enjoyments of the parks, palaces, rivers, lotus ponds, mountains of jewels, and wish-fulfilling trees. At the end of one's life one will feel one has passed away from this world and been reborn in the next, even though one has not yet died; thus by the wonder of the mental realms caused by actions one will see and experience these events. In the same way Sudhana, by the wonder of the states caused by the actions of an enlightening being, saw that whole supernal manifestation of the tower of Vairocana.

Just as a man possessed by a spirit sees various things, and tells of what he is asked about, in the same way Sudhana, by the power of knowledge of an enlightening being, saw all those arrays.

Just as a man who has entered the abode of water spirits, by entering into the perception of water spirits, thinks a day or a week or a fortnight or a month or a year or a century has passed, merely in his perception, and when leaving the perception of water spirits for the perception of humans sees that it was only a short time, in the same way, with the mindfulness of the perception of an enlightening being, by the power of Maitreya, in that short time Sudhana had the sense of the passage of billions of eons.

There is a celestial mansion called "chamber of the finest ornaments of all worlds," wherein the whole universe is seen by reflection, with all objects clearly defined; in the same way Sudhana saw all those arrays, unconfused, reflected in all the objects.

Just as a monk in the trance of absorption in one of the points of totality is single-minded and undivided whether walking, standing still, sitting, or reclining, and sees and experiences the whole world through entry into the sphere of total absorption in whatever point of totality he is focused on, by the marvel of meditation, in the same way Sudhana saw all those arrays whatever object he immersed himself in.

Just as all the adornments of the cities of celestial musicians are visible in the sky, without constituting a barrier to anyone, just as human abodes within demonic abodes, each distinct within the demonic abodes, are visible according to the purity of the objects of desire, just as reflections of the worlds of the universe are seen in the ocean, just as a magician sees all forms and activities by the power of spells and drugs, in the same way Sudhana, by the inconceivable direction of the magic of the enlightening mystic knowledge of Maitreya, saw all those miraculous displays, by bringing forth the power of magic of knowledge of truth, by the power of mystic knowledge mastered by the enlightening being.

Then the enlightening being Maitreya, entering the tower and relaxing his magical force, snapped his fingers and said to Sudhana, "Arise. This is the nature of things; characterized by nonfixity, all things are stabilized by the knowledge of enlightening beings, thus they are inherently unreal, and are like illusions, dreams, reflections."

Then, at a finger snap, Sudhana emerged from that trance and Maitreya said to him, "Did you see the miraculous display of the magical power of enlightening beings? Did you see the results of the power of enlightening beings' preparations for enlightenment? Did you see the creations of the vows and knowledge of enlightening beings? Did you see the practices and attainments of enlightening beings? Did you hear the enlightening beings' ways of emancipation? Did you see the infinity of adornments of buddhalands? Did you see the excellence of the vows and expertise of buddhas? Did you realize the inconceivability of the liberation of enlightening beings? Did you experience enlightening beings' bliss of absorption?"

Sudhana said, "I saw, noble one, by the empowerment and spiritual force of the benefactor. And what is this liberation called?"

Maitreya said, "This liberation is called the sanctum of supernal manifestations of unconfused recollection entering into knowledge of all objects of past, present, and future. And an enlightening being assured of enlightenment in one lifetime attains untold liberations like this."

Sudhana said, "Where has that magnificent display gone?"

Maitreya said, "Where it came from."

Sudhana said, "Where did it come from?"

Maitreya said, "It came from the effectuation of the magical power of knowledge of enlightening beings, and it resides in that very magical power. It does not go or come at all, it is not an aggregate or an accumulation, it is not uniform and unchangeable, it is not abiding or fixed in existence, it is not located in any place. It is like the network of clouds of the water spirits which do not appear from body or mind and yet are indeed seen in masses; by the mental power of the water spirits measureless clouds emerge, by the wonder of the realm of the water spirits. In the same way, those supernal manifestations are not internal or external, yet it is not that they are not seen, by the magical power of the enlightening being, and because of your own capacity.

"Just as the illusions of a magician manifesting illusory objects do not come from anywhere or go away, nor are they in transit, yet they appear by the power of spells and drugs, in the same way those supernal arrays have never gone or come, nor accumulated, but they appear by proper learning of the inconceivable magic of knowledge of enlightening beings, by mastery of knowledge empowered by past vows."

Sudhana said, "From how far away do you come?"

Maitreya said, "In the state where there is no coming; the state of enlightening beings is the state of neither motion nor stasis, the state of no support or abode, the state of no passing away or rebirth, the state neither static nor transient, the state of no stirring or arising, the state of no concern or attachment, the state of no deeds or fruition, the state of no origination or destruction, the state of no annihilation or eternity. Furthermore, great compassion is the state of enlightening beings, as they attend to sentient beings who can be guided; great kindness is the state of enlightening beings, as they rescue suffering beings; discipline is the state of enlightening beings, as they become reconstituted according to will; commitment is the state of enlightening beings, based on past vows; spiritual power is the state of enlightening beings, as they manifest all that is pleasant; nondoing is the state of enlightening beings, as they do not leave the presence of all buddhas; neither grasping nor rejecting is the state of enlightening beings, as they are not obsessed with body or mind; wisdom and means is the state of enlightening beings, as they adapt to sentient beings, manifesting emanations is the state of enlightening beings, their bodies being equivalent to reflected images.

"And you ask how far away I come from—I come here from the village of Kuti in the territories of the Malada people, land of my birth. There is a gentleman there named Gopalaka, who guides people into the buddha-teachings, teaches the native people according to their capacities, and establishes family and relatives, priests and householders, in the Great Vehicle."

Sudhana asked, "What are the native lands of enlightening beings?"

Maitreya said, "There are ten native lands of enlightening beings. What are they? The arousal of the aspiration for enlightenment is a native land of enlightening beings, causing one to be born in the family of enlightening beings. Strong will is a native land of enlightening beings, causing one to be born in the family of spiritual friends. The stages are a native land of enlightening beings, causing one to be born in the family of the transcendent ways. Carrying out vows is a native land of enlightening beings, causing one to be born in the family of sublime acts. Universal compassion is a native land of enlightening beings, causing one to be born in the house of means of salvation. Profound contemplation is a native land of enlightening beings, causing one to be born in the house of transcendent wisdom. The Great Vehicle is a native land of enlightening beings, causing one to be born in the house of skill in means. Educating sentient beings is a native land of enlightening beings, causing one to be born in the house of buddhas. Knowledge and means is a native land of enlightening beings, causing one to be born in the house of tolerance of things as unoriginated. Practicing and realizing all truths is a native land of enlightening beings, causing one to be born in the house of all buddhas of past, future, and present.

"Transcendent wisdom is the mother of enlightening beings, skill in means is the father of enlightening beings, transcendent generosity is the milk of enlightening beings, transcendent discipline is their nurse, transcendent tolerance is their adornment, transcendent vigor is what makes them grow, transcendent meditation purifies their practice, spiritual friends teach them, the elements of enlightenment are their companions, all enlightening beings are their siblings, the determination for enlightenment is their family, practice is the rule of their family, the stages are their residence, attainment of tolerance is birth in the family, carrying out vows is acquisition of the knowledge of the family, purity of conduct is following the rule of the family, promoting the Great Vehicle is preserving the continuity of the family, consecration as one bound to attain buddhahood in one life is princehood among spiritual kings, and the attainment of all who arrive at Thusness is complete purification of the family.

"Thus the enlightening being has gone beyond the stage of the ignorant and has entered the certainty of enlightening beings, has been born in the family of buddhas, has been established in the lineage of buddhas, has become capable of perpetuating the three treasures, has become involved in protecting the family of enlightening beings, has become socially pure and impeccable, blameless among all people, has become well born in the highest family of buddhas, the body a repository of great vows.

"Enlightening beings who have succeeded in being born in the family this way do not shrink away from existence in any world, because they realize all things are like reflections; they are not defiled by life in any state of existence, because they realize birth in all states of being is phantomlike; they are tireless in guiding and perfecting all beings, because they are aware all is selfless; they never cease taking care of all beings, because they embody universal love and compassion; they do not fear living through all ages, because they believe the mundane whirl is like a dream; they are not afflicted by the appearance of birth and death, because they realize the clusters of mental and physical elements are illusory; they are not injured in the midst of all objects, because they realize they are of the nature of the reality realm; they are not deluded by any of the states of the mundane whirl, because they have thoroughly realized they are like mirages; they are unaffected by any bedeviling objects because they are familiar with the illusoriness of all things; they are incapable of being deceived by any afflictions, because they have mastered the spiritual body; they reach their goal in all states of being, because they have attained control over becoming.

"With a body existing in all worlds, in forms like all beings, with different powers, with distinct forms of speech like those of all beings, with modes of conduct like those approved by all beings, with adaptations to the world as extensive as the precepts of all beings, appearing to be born in families consonant with all kinds of purity, by entries into the perceptions and ideas of all beings through engagement in activity, by powers of physical manifestation equal to the creations of vows of all enlightening beings, I pervade all universes, and arrived here in the south, in the village of Kuta in the Malada region, in order to develop to maturity those who carried out the same practices as I in the past but have lost the aspiration for enlightenment, and to manifest birth on this continent, to guide parents and relatives born in the priestly caste, and to generate the family of enlightened ones so as to free them from the pride and conceit of the superiority of the priestly caste.

"Here in the south, by that means guiding beings according to their mentalities and according to their capacity for being taught, I live in this tower containing the adornments of Vairocana. When I have passed away from here, I will manifest birth in Tushita, the celestial abode of happiness and contentment, in order to adapt to beings according to mentality, and to mature the celestials of that heaven engaged in the same practice, to manifest supernal arrays of emanations of the virtue and knowledge of enlightening beings beyond all realms of desire, to dispel all craving for sensual enjoyment, to make it clear that all mundane routines are impermanent, to show that all celestial existence ultimately declines and passes away, to join with the enlightening beings bound for buddhahood in one life in proclaiming the teaching of great knowledge called 'appearance of descent from heaven into rebirth on earth,' to take care of those matured together in that state of existence, and to enlighten those sent forth by Shakyamuni when the time comes to be guided. At that time I will realize omniscience, the fulfillment of my aspiration; and when I have attained enlightenment, you will see me again, with the spiritual benefactor Manjushri.

"Now go back to Manjushri and ask him how an enlightening being is to learn and carry out the practice of enlightening beings, enter the sphere of universally good practice, undertake and carry it out, expand it, follow it, purify it, enter fully into it, and fulfill it. He will show you the real benefactor. Why? The best of vows of decillions of enlightening beings is Manjushri's; vast is the outcome of the practice of Manjushri; measureless is the accomplishment of vows of Manjushri; ceaseless is Manjushri's achievement of the best of virtues of all enlightening beings; Manjushri is the mother of decillions of buddhas; Manjushri is the teacher of decillions of enlightening beings; Manjushri is engaged in the perfection of all beings; widespread is the name of Manjushri in all worlds of the ten directions; Manjushri is the interlocutor in the assemblies of untold buddhas; Manjushri is praised by all buddhas; abiding in the knowledge of profound truth, Manjushri sees all things according to their true significance; Manjushri has ranged far into all modes of liberation; he is immersed in the practice of universally good enlightening beings. He is the progenitor of spiritual benefactors, who makes you grow in the family of the enlightened, causes you to establish roots of goodness, shows you the provisions for enlightenment, introduces you to true benefactors, immerses you in all virtues, establishes you in the network of universal vows, causes you to hear of the accomplishment of all vows, shows the secrets of all enlightening beings, and has similarly practiced the wonder of all enlightening beings together with you in past lives.

"Therefore when you go to Manjushri, do not be faint-hearted, do not become weary in receiving instruction in all virtues. Why? All the spiritual benefactors you have seen, all the ways of practice you have heard, all the modes of liberation you have entered, all the vows you have plunged into, should all be looked upon as the empowerment of Manjushri; and Manjushri has reached the ultimate perfection."

Then Sudhana paid his respects to Maitreya the enlightening being and went on.

Manjushri

Then Sudhana, passing more than one hundred and ten cities, went to Sumanamukha and stayed there thinking about Manjushri, wishing to see and meet with Manjushri. Then Manjushri extended his hand over a hundred and ten leagues and laid it on the head of Sudhana, who was standing in the city of Sumanamukha, and said, "Good, good! Those without the faculty of faith, those who are weary or sluggish in mind, those who have not accumulated efforts, those whose vigor recedes, those who are satisfied with meager virtues, those imbued with only one root of goodness, those unskilled in carrying out practical vows, those who are not in the care of spiritual benefactors, those who are not minded by the buddhas, cannot know this true nature, this principle, this sphere, this abode—they are unable to know, to fathom, to penetrate, to believe, to conceive, to know exactly, or to attain."

Having caused Sudhana to see by means of his spiritual talk, having directed him, inspired him, gladdened him, imbued him with countless facets of truth, illumined him with the great light of infinite knowledge, led him into the endless mental command, presence of mind, concentration, and superknowledge of enlightening beings, plunged him into the sphere of universally good practice, and established him in his own place, Manjushri left the presence of Sudhana.

Then Sudhana, attending as many spiritual benefactors as atoms in a billion-world universe, his mind having accumulated the provisions for omniscience, acting on the instructions of all spiritual benefactors with correct understanding, his mind equally attentive to all spiritual friends, his intellect in harmony with all spiritual friends without emotion, following the ocean of principles of the advice and instruction of all spiritual friends, filled with universal compassion, illumining all beings with universal love, physically blissful, abiding at peace in the vast liberation of enlightening beings, his equanimous vision attentive to all dimensions, having accomplished the ocean of virtues of all buddhas, on the path of resolve of all buddhas, strengthened by the energy of vigor of preparation for omniscience, his mind thoroughly dedicated to the will of all enlightening beings, comprehending the succession of all buddhas of past, present, and future, awake to the ocean of principles of all enlightened teachings, following the ocean of principles of the wheels of teaching of all buddhas, in the realm of manifesting reflections of life in all worlds, immersed in the principles of the vows of all enlightening beings, set out to carry on enlightening practice throughout all ages, seeing the realm of omniscience, having developed all the faculties of enlightening beings, aware of the path of omniscience, his intellect focused on all the principles of the reality realm, illumining the principles of all lands, following the course of beneficial action extending to all beings, shattering the precipitous mountains of spiritual impediments, according with the unimpeded nature of reality, abiding at peace in the liberation of enlightening beings containing the universal reality realm, investigating the realm of all buddhas, empowered by all buddhas, stood contemplating the realm of the enlightening being Universally Good.

Having heard the name of the enlightening being Universally Good, his practice of enlightenment, the excellence of his vow, the excellence of basing his undertaking on the provisions for enlightenment, the excellence of his expertise in accomplishment, his conduct in the stage of universal good, his preparations for the stages, the excellence of his attainment, the speed of his attainment of the stages, his entry into the stages, his stabilization in the stages, his progress through the stages, his importance in the stages, his mastery of the stages, and his abiding in the stages, Sudhana, eager to see the enlightening being Samantabhadra, Universally Good, sat on a lotus seat of jewels facing the lion throne of the Buddha on the enlightenment site there filled with oceans of diamonds, with a mind as vast as space and free from all attachments, with perception of all lands well developed, with a mind having transcended all barriers and clingings, with a mind unimpeded, in the realm of nonobstruction in the midst of all things, with a mind freely pervading everywhere without hindrance, with a pure mind entering the realm of omniscience, with a well-ordered mind purified by observing the ornaments of the site of enlightenment, with a broad mind immersed in the ocean of all enlightened teachings, with a vast mind pervading all realms of beings to guide them to perfection, with an immeasurable mind purifying all buddha-lands, with an infinite mind reflected in the circles of all buddhas, abiding indefatigably for all ages, until the ultimate realization of the power, expertise, and unique qualities of all buddhas.

Furthermore, to Sudhana, engaged in these meditations, there appeared ten signs prefiguring the vision of the enlightening being Universally Good, by virtue of the empowerment of all buddhas having nourished his past roots of goodness, and by virtue of having past roots of goodness equivalent to those of the enlightening being Universally Good. What were those ten signs? All buddha-lands were purified by purification with the adornments of the sites of enlightenment of all buddhas. All buddha-lands were purified by removal of all evils and miserable states and conditions inopportune for enlightenment. All buddha-lands were purified by purification of buddha-lands with arrays of spiritual lotus ponds. All buddha-lands were purified by cooling and refreshing the bodies and minds of all beings. All buddha-lands were purified by becoming made of jewels. All buddha-lands were purified by all the beings becoming adorned with the marks and embellishments of greatness. All buddha-lands were purified by formation of masses of all adornments. All buddha-lands were purified by all the beings becoming kind, benevolent, and friendly to each other. All buddha-lands were purified by becoming arrayed with the adornments of sites of enlightenment. All buddha-lands were purified by all the beings becoming consciously absorbed in mindfulness of Buddha. These ten signs appeared foreshadowing the vision of the great enlightening being Universally Good.

After that, ten great lights appeared, foreshadowing the manifestation of the great enlightening being Universally Good. What were the ten? In each atom of all worlds the network of all buddhas shone. The auras of light of all buddhas emanated from each atom of all worlds, with hundreds of thousands of various colors, and pervaded the whole cosmos. Clouds of jewels manifesting reflections of all buddhas emanated from each atom of all worlds and pervaded the cosmos. Multitudes of circles of flames of all buddhas emanated from each atom of all worlds and pervaded the cosmos. Multitudes of all kinds of fragrant flowers, garlands, perfumes, and incenses emanated from each atom of all worlds and pervaded the cosmos radiating the light of the enlightening being Universally Good. Multitudes of lamps in the forms of all beings emanated from each atom of all worlds and pervaded the cosmos. Multitudes of figures of light beams in the forms of the bodies of all buddhas emanated from each atom of all worlds and pervaded the cosmos showing the basic vows of all buddhas. Oceans of multitudes of reflections of enlightening beings of all forms and appearances, representations of phantom bodies of all beings, fulfilling the wishes of all beings, emanated from each point of all worlds and pervaded the cosmos. These ten great lights appeared foreshadowing the manifestation of Universally Good.

Then Sudhana, having seen these ten foreshadowing lights, had the opportunity to see the enlightening being Universally Good, supported by the power of his own roots of goodness, a living manifestation of all buddha-teachings, empowered by all buddhas, immersed in the vows of the enlightening being Universally Good, in the presence of the realm of all buddhas, having the power of certainty of the lofty realm of enlightening beings, perceiving the attainment of the light of omniscience in the sight of the enlightening being Universally Good, his senses directed toward vision of the enlightening being Universally Good, flooded with great energy for the vision of the enlightening being Universally Good, striving unremittingly in the search for the enlightening being Universally Good, with the sphere of his senses turned to all directions, with the body of an enlightening being entering the sphere of the eye of universal good, with a mind directed toward all buddhas and aware of the enlightening being Universally Good in the presence of all buddhas, with a will seeking unremittingly for the enlightening being Universally Good, inwardly perceiving the vision of the enlightening being Universally Good in all objects, with the eye of knowledge on the path of the enlightening being Universally Good, with a mind as vast as space, with a powerful resolve supported by indestructible universal compassion, with a vow to accompany the enlightening being Universally Good throughout all time, with purity of manner equally following the practice of the enlightening being Universally Good, abiding in knowledge based on the state of the enlightening being Universally Good, dwelling in the sphere of all those who realize Thusness, he saw the enlightening being Universally Good sitting on a lion seat in the calyx of a great jewel lotus in front of Vairocana Buddha, the perfectly enlightened one, in an ocean of enlightening beings, his body standing out among the whole assembly, unexcelled by any worldlings, looking over all the enlightening beings, his knowledge endless, his range insuperable, his sphere inconceivable, having arrived at equality of past, present and future and attained equality with all buddhas.

He saw clouds of light rays as numerous as atoms in all buddha-lands emanate from each of Universally Good's pores and illumine all worlds throughout the space of the cosmos, relieving the pain of all beings. He saw as many auras of light as atoms in all buddha-lands emanate from Universally Good's body, increasing the ecstasy of all enlightening beings. He saw clouds of fragrant flames of various colors emanate from Universally Good's head and pores, pervading the audiences of all buddhas and showering on them. He saw as many clouds of all kinds of flowers as atoms in all buddha-lands emanate from each of Universally Good's pores, filling the audiences of all buddhas and showering on them. He saw as many clouds of all kinds of fragrant trees as atoms in all buddha-lands emanate from each of Universally Good's pores, adorning all universes throughout space with fragrant trees budding with inexhaustible aromatic powders and oils, showering on the audiences of all buddhas. He saw clouds of all kinds of cloth emanate from every pore, covering all universes throughout space and decorating them. He saw clouds of streamers, ornaments, strings of pearls, and wish-fulfilling jewels, numerous as atoms in all buddha-lands, emanate from every pore, filling the assemblies of all buddhas and showering on them to fulfill the wishes of all beings. He saw clouds of jewel trees, as many as atoms in all buddha-lands, emanate from every pore, filling all universes in space, adorning them with blooming jewel trees and showering great rains of jewels on the audiences of all buddhas. He saw multitudes of embodiments of celestial beings, as many as atoms in all buddha-lands, emanate from every pore, filling all worlds praising the enlightening being. He saw multitudes of phantom embodiments of the celestial beings in all the brahma-worlds emanate from every pore, asking the enlightened buddhas to turn the wheel of the teaching. He saw multitudes of embodiments of all the celestials in the realm of desire emanate from every pore, receiving the cycles of teaching of all buddhas. He saw multitudes of all buddha-lands of past, present, and future, as many as atoms in all buddha-lands, emanate from each pore in each mental moment, pervading all universes throughout space as places of rest, salvation, and refuge for beings with no place of rest, no savior, no refuge. He saw multitudes of all buddha-lands, as many as atoms in all buddha-lands, filled with congregations of inspired enlightening beings, emanate from every pore, pervading all universes throughout space, conducive to the purification of beings of lofty resolve. He saw multitudes of pure lands with defilement, as many as atoms in all buddha-lands, emanate from every pore in each moment of thought, pervading all universes throughout space, conducive to the purification of defiled beings. He saw multitudes of defiled lands with mental purity, as many as atoms in all buddha-lands, emanate from every pore in each moment of thought, pervading all universes throughout space, conducive to the purification of wholly defiled beings. He saw multitudes of embodiments of all enlightening beings, as many as atoms in all buddha-lands, emanate from every pore in each instant of consciousness, pervading all universes throughout space, adapting to the conduct of all beings and developing all beings to supreme perfect enlightenment. He saw multitudes of embodiments of enlightening beings, as many as atoms in all buddha-lands, emanate from every pore in each mental moment, pervading all universes throughout space, invoking the names of all buddhas in order to increase the roots of goodness of all beings. He saw multitudes of embodiments of enlightening beings, as many as atoms in all buddha-lands, emanating from every pore, pervading all universes throughout space, in all buddha-lands presenting the accomplishment of all roots of goodness of all enlightening beings, from the first arousal of the aspiration for enlightenment. He saw as many multitudes of enlightening beings as atoms in all buddha-lands emanate from every pore, in each and every buddha-land illustrating the oceans of vows of all enlightening beings for the perfection of the practice of universally good enlightening beings. He saw as many clouds of practices of the enlightening being Universally Good as atoms in all buddha-lands emanate from every pore, raining showers fulfilling the wishes of all beings, increasing the flood of joy of attainment of omniscience. He also saw as many clouds of perfect enlightenment as atoms in all buddha-lands emanating from every pore, showing perfect enlightenment in all buddha-lands, increasing the great spiritual energy of attainment of omniscience.

Then Sudhana, having seen this manifestation of Universally Good's mystic power, happy, fulfilled, enraptured, uplifted, delighted, joyful, contemplated the body of Universally Good further and saw, from every part of his body and every pore, the billionfold world, with its masses of air, earth, and fire, its oceans, continents, rivers, jewel mountains, polar mountains, peripheral mountains, villages, cities, towns, communities, districts, forests, dwellings, populations, hells, animal realms, underworlds, realms of titans, dragons, birds, humans, and celestials, realms of desire, formless realms, its bases, foundations, and forms, its clouds, lightning, stars, nights, days, and fortnights, half years and years, intermediate eons and eons. And as he saw this world, in the same way he saw all the worlds to the east, and as in the east he saw all the worlds in all directions, in the south, west, north, northeast, southeast, southwest, northwest, the nadir and the zenith. By way of reflections he saw the emergence of all buddhas, along with their circles of enlightening beings, as well as other beings, and he saw the succession of all worlds in past eons in this world, all that in one mark of greatness of the body of Universally Good—the emergence of all the buddhas, the circles of enlightening beings, the sentient beings, the abodes, the days and nights, the ages. In the same way he also saw all the buddha-lands of the future. And just as he saw the succession of past and future worlds in this world, in the same way he saw the successions of all past and future worlds in all worlds in the ten directions, through each mark of greatness and each pore on the body of the enlightening being Universally Good, all in perfect order, not mixed up with one another.

And just as he saw the enlightening being Universally Good sitting on a jewel lotus calyx lion seat before Vairocana Buddha displaying this miracle, likewise he saw him displaying the same miracle in the world Padmashri of Bhadrashri Buddha in the east; and as in the east, he also saw the enlightening being Universally Good sitting on a jewel lotus calyx lion seat in the presence of all buddhas in all worlds everywhere displaying this same miracle, and from each individual body of Universally Good he saw all objects of past, present, and future appearing in reflections, and likewise saw all lands, all beings, all buddhas emerging, and all congregations of enlightening beings appearing as reflections; and he heard the voices of all beings, the voices of all buddhas, the turning of the wheel of teaching of all buddhas, the presentation of all advice and instruction, the attainments of all enlightening beings, and the mystic powers of all buddhas.

Having seen and heard this inconceivable miracle of the enlightening being Universally Good, he attained ten states of consummation of knowledge. What were these ten? He attained the state of consummation of knowledge physically pervading all buddha-lands in a moment of thought. He attained the state of consummation of holistic knowledge going to the presence of all buddhas. He attained the state of consummation of knowledge serving all buddhas. He attained the state of consummation of knowledge asking about the Teaching and receiving answers from each and every buddha. He attained the state of consummation of knowledge of meditation on the cycles of teaching of all buddhas. He attained the state of consummation of knowledge of the inconceivable miracles of buddhas. He attained the state of consummation of knowledge to expound one expression of truth forever by means of inexhaustible specific knowledge of all truths. He attained the state of consummation of direct knowledge of the ocean of all truths. He attained the state of consummation of knowledge of all principles of the realm of reality. He attained the state of consummation of knowledge to live together with the thoughts of all beings. He attained the state of consummation of knowledge of instantaneous direct witness of the practice of the enlightening being Universally Good.

To Sudhana, who had realized these states of consummate knowledge, Universally Good extended his right hand and laid it on his head. With Universally Good's hand on Sudhana's head, as many concentrations as atoms in all buddha-lands entered into Sudhana, and by each concentration he entered into as many oceans of worlds as atoms in all buddha-lands; as many hitherto unseen provisions for omniscience as atoms in all buddha-lands accrued to him; as many origins of elements of omniscience as atoms in all buddha-lands became manifest to him; he rose up for as many great undertakings for omniscience as atoms in all buddha-lands; he entered into as many oceans of vows as atoms in all buddha-lands; he went forth on as many emancipating paths of omniscience as atoms in all buddha-lands; he was involved in as many practices of enlightening beings as atoms in all buddha-lands; he was boosted by as many floods of omniscience as atoms in all buddha-lands; he was illumined by as many lights of knowledge of all buddhas as atoms in all buddha-lands.

Just as in this world, in the presence of Vairocana Buddha, the enlightening being Universally Good extended his right hand and laid it on Sudhana's head, in the same way Universally Good sitting at the feet of all buddhas in all worlds extended his right hand and laid it on Sudhana's head. In the same way, sitting at the feet of all buddhas in all worlds within the atoms of all worlds Universally Good extended his right hand and laid it on Sudhana's head. And just as facets of truth entered Sudhana as he was touched by the hand of Universally Good at the feet of Vairocana Buddha, likewise facets of truth entered Sudhana in various ways as he was touched by the multitudes of hands extended from the bodies of all the Universally Goods.

Then the great enlightening being Universally Good said to Sudhana, "Did you see my mystical projection?"

Sudhana said, "I saw, noble one. But only a buddha could understand such an inconceivable mystical projection."

Universally Good said, "I practiced for as many eons as atoms in untold buddha-lands, seeking the mind of omniscience, and in each immense eon I associated with as many buddhas as atoms in untold buddha-lands, to purify the aspiration for enlightenment. And in each immense eon I made great sacrifices, giving away everything, announced in all worlds, fulfilling all beings, storing virtue for omniscience. And in each immense eon I made as many great sacrifices as atoms in untold buddha-lands, extreme sacrifices, seeking the qualities of omniscience. And in each immense eon I gave up my body untold numbers of times, and I gave up kingships, villages, cities, towns, counties, and communities, and I gave up dearly beloved companions, so hard to give up, and I gave up spouses and children. I gave away the flesh of my own body and gave blood from my own body to beggars, and I gave away my bones and marrow. I gave away my limbs, my ears and nose, my eyes and tongue, caring only for buddha-knowledge and not for my physical life. In each immense eon I gave away as many of my own bodies as atoms in untold buddha-lands, seeking from my own bodies the unsurpassed head of omniscience which rises beyond all worlds. And as I did in each immense eon, so also did I do in oceans of great eons as numerous as atoms in untold buddha-lands. In each immense eon I honored and served as many buddhas as atoms in untold buddha-lands, providing food and clothing, shelter, furniture, medicine, and other necessities. And I went forth into the tutelage of each buddha, applied the instructions of all buddhas, and I hold their Teaching.

"I do not know of a single thought in all those oceans of eons in which I neglected the instructions of the buddhas. I am not aware of having had a single malicious thought in all those eons, or an egotistic thought, or a selfish thought of possession, or a thought of difference between self and others, or a thought of parting from the path of enlightening beings, or a thought of weariness at staying in the world, or a thought of depression, or a thought deluded by hindrances, or any thought apart from the aspiration for enlightenment, the invulnerable asylum of invincible knowledge, directed toward preparations for omniscience.

"All oceans of eons would be exhausted in telling of my past efforts to purify buddha-lands, my compassionate efforts to save, develop, and purify all beings, my efforts to serve buddhas, my efforts in listening to teachers in quest of truth, my self-sacrifice for the sake of absorbing truth, my sacrifice of life to protect truth. Of all the oceans of teachings, there is not a single statement that I did not get by giving up rulership, that I did not get by giving up all that exists, by undertaking the salvation of all beings, by contemplating my own being, by undertaking to attain higher states ahead, by undertaking to produce the light of all worldly knowledge, by undertaking to produce the light of all transmundane knowledge, by undertaking to produce mundane happiness for all sentient beings, by undertaking to tell of the virtues of all buddhas. Thus it would take up as many eons as atoms in untold buddha-lands to tell of the accomplishment of my past endeavors.

"By such power of preparation, power of accomplishment of assemblage of root causes, power of lofty resolution, power of accomplishment of virtues, power of contemplation of all truths as they are, power of the eye of wisdom, power bestowed by buddha, power of great vows, power of great compassion, power of thoroughly purified mystic knowledge, power of the care of spiritual benefactors, I attained the ultimately pure body of reality, which is continuous and unfragmented throughout past, present, and future. I also purified an unexcelled physical body, beyond all worldlings, appearing to all beings according to their mentalities, omnipresent, in all buddha-lands, abiding everywhere, showing all kinds of mystical projections everywhere, visible in all worlds.

"Look at this body I have achieved, produced over endless multitudes of eons, hard to get to appear even in decillions of eons, hard to get to see. Beings who have not planted roots of goodness cannot even hear of me, much less see me. There are beings who become irreversible on the way to supreme perfect enlightenment just by hearing my name; there are those who become irreversible just by seeing me, those who become irreversible just by contact with me, those who become irreversible just by following me, those who become irreversible just by associating with me, those who become irreversible by seeing me in a dream, and those who become irreversible on the way to supreme perfect enlightenment by hearing my name in a dream.

"Some beings become mature by remembering me for a day and a night; some become mature remembering me for a fortnight, some a month, some a year, some a century, some an eon, some a hundred eons, and some up to as many eons as atoms in untold buddha-lands. Some become mature remembering me for one lifetime, some a hundred lifetimes, some up to as many lifetimes as atoms in untold buddha-lands. Some become mature by seeing my radiance, some by seeing emanation of light beams, some by feeling the earth quake, some by seeing my physical form, some by being encouraged. Thus beings become irreversible toward supreme perfect enlightenment through as many means as atoms in a buddha-land. Furthermore, whoever hears of the purity of my buddha-land shall be born in pure buddha-lands, and whoever sees the purity of my body will be born in my body. Behold the purity of this body of mine.

Then Sudhana, contemplating the body of the enlightening being Universally Good, saw in each and every pore untold multitudes of buddha-lands filled with buddhas. And in each buddha-land he saw the buddhas surrounded by assemblies of enlightening beings. And he saw that all those multitudes of lands had various bases, various forms, various arrays, various perimeters, various clouds covering the skies, various buddhas appearing, various enunciations of cycles of the Teaching. And just as he saw this in each pore, so also in all pores at once, in all the marks of greatness, all the embellishments, all the limbs and parts of the body; and in each he saw multitudes of lands, with as many multitudes of projected bodies of buddhas, as atoms in all buddha-lands, emerging and filling all worlds in the ten directions developing beings toward supreme perfect enlightenment.

Then Sudhana, edified by the advice and instruction of the enlightening being Universally Good, entered into all the worlds within the body of Universally Good and developed the beings toward maturity. Furthermore, the light of knowledge and roots of goodness accumulated by Sudhana in going to, meeting, and attending as many spiritual benefactors as atoms in a buddha-land did not amount to even a minute fraction, not to any calculable fraction, of his accumulation of roots of goodness concomitant with seeing Universally Good. As many successive buddha-lands as he had entered from his first determination up to his seeing Universally Good, he entered more, successive oceans of buddha-lands, with attributes as numerous as atoms in untold buddha-lands, in a single pore of Universally Good in each moment of thought. And as in one pore, so in all pores; in each moment of thought passing as many worlds as atoms in untold buddha-lands, passing the worlds of endless eons at a step, he still did not come to the end—he did not come to the end of the successions of oceans of lands, of the matrices of oceans of lands, of the differentiations of oceans of lands, of the interpenetrations of oceans of lands, of the origins of untold oceans of buddha-lands, of the dissolutions of oceans of lands, of the arrays of oceans of lands, of the matrices of oceans of appearances of buddhas, of the interpenetrations of oceans of appearances of buddhas, of the origins of oceans of appearances of buddhas, of the dissolutions of oceans of appearances of buddhas, of the oceans of congregations of enlightening beings, of the successions of oceans of congregations of enlightening beings, the matrices of oceans of congregations of enlightening beings, the differentiations of oceans of congregations of enlightening beings, the unity of oceans of congregations of enlightening beings, the formations of oceans of congregations of enlightening beings, the dissolutions of oceans of congregations of enlightening beings, the entrances of realms of sentient beings, the entrances of instantaneous knowledge of faculties of sentient beings, the penetrations of knowledge of sentient beings' faculties, the developmental guidance of sentient beings, the profound states of occult powers of enlightening beings, or the multitudes of enlightening beings' accessions to and supercessions of the stages.

He traveled and contemplated in a land for an eon, in another for up to as many as eons as atoms in untold buddha-lands, without moving from that land. In each moment of consciousness he entered infinite oceans of lands and developed sentient beings toward supreme perfect enlightenment. This continued as he gradually attained equality with Universally Good in terms of the ocean of vows of practice of the universally good enlightening beings, equality with all buddhas, equality of pervasion of all lands, equality of fulfillment of practices, equality of manifestation of the miracle of attainment of enlightenment, equality of turning the wheel of teaching, equality of purity of intellect, equality of voice and articulation, equality of power and expertise, equality of the enlightened state, equality of universal love and compassion, equality of the spiritual metamorphoses of the inconceivable liberation of enlightening beings.

Then the great enlightening being Universally Good, thus explaining courses of eons, as many eons as atoms in the untold buddha-lands in the succession of worlds, went on to make a vow:

As many buddhas as there may be in any world

Throughout the ten directions, throughout past, present, and future,
I honor them all, without exception,
Pure in body, speech, and mind.

With as many bodies as atoms in all lands
I bow to all buddhas,
With a mind directed to all buddhas,
By the power of the vow of the practice of good.

In a single atom, buddhas as many as atoms
Sit in the midst of enlightening beings;
So it is of all things in the cosmos—
I realize all are filled with buddhas.

I laud all the buddhas therein,
Expounding in all languages
The qualities of all buddhas,
With endless oceans of manifestations.

With the finest flowers, garlands,
Musical instruments, perfumes and parasols,
The finest lamps and incenses,
I make offerings to those buddhas.

With the finest clothes, fragrances,
And mountainous baskets of aromatic powders,
With the finest of all kinds of adornments
I make offerings to those buddhas.

Whatever be the best of offerings,
I produce them for all buddhas;
By the power of devotion to the practice of good,
I honor and serve all buddhas.

Whatever evil I may commit
Under the sway of passion, hatred, or folly,
Bodily, verbally, or mentally,
I confess it all.

And whatever the virtue of beings everywhere,
Hearers, saints, self-conquerors,
Enlightening beings and buddhas,
In all that I do rejoice.

And all the Lamps of the Worlds in the ten directions
Who have realized enlightenment and attain nonobstruction

I seek as guides, that they may turn
The supreme wheel of teaching.

And those who wish to manifest extinction
I petition respectfully to remain
For eons as many as atoms in the land
For the welfare and happiness of all beings.

By honor, service, and direction,
By appreciating, seeking, and requesting teachings,
Whatever good I have accumulated,
I dedicate it all to enlightenment.

May the buddhas of the past be honored,
As well as those now in the worlds of the ten directions,
And may those of the future be at ease,
Filled with joy, having realized enlightenment.

May all the lands of the ten directions
Be purified, supreme, and filled
With buddhas and enlightening beings
At the tree of enlightenment.

May all beings in the ten directions
By happy and well;
May all beings' righteous aim be successful,
May their hope be realized.

As I am carrying out enlightenment practice,
May I recall my lives in all states;
In every lifetime, as I die and am reborn,
May I always transcend the mundane.

Learning from all buddhas,
Fulfilling the practice of good,
I will practice pure conduct,
Always free from defect.

I will expound the Teaching
In the languages of gods and dragons,
In the languages of demons and humans,
And of all living beings.

May those engaged in the ways of transcendence
Not stray from enlightenment;
And may all evils to be inhibited

Be thoroughly extinguished.

I will traverse the paths of the world
Free from compulsion, affliction, and delusion,
Like a lotus unstained by water,
Like the sun and moon unattached in the sky.

Extinguishing all the miseries of bad states
And bringing all beings to happiness,
I will act for the welfare of all beings
In all lands everywhere.

According with the conduct of sentient beings
While fulfilling the practice of enlightenment,
And cultivating the practice of good,
Thus will I act throughout future eons.

May I always be in communion
With those who share my practice;
Physically, verbally, and mentally,
I will carry out vows as one practice.

And may I always be with my benefactors,
Who teach me the practice of good;
May I never displease them.

May I always see the buddhas face to face,
Surrounded by enlightening beings;
I will make fine offerings to them
Forever, unwearied.

Preserving the true teaching of buddhas,
Illumining the practice of enlightenment,
And purifying the practice of good,
I will practice for all future eons.

Migrating through all states of being,
Having acquired inexhaustible virtue and knowledge,
May I become an inexhaustible treasury of wisdom and means,
Concentration, liberation, and all virtues.

As I carry on the practice of enlightenment,
May I see the inconceivable buddhas sitting among enlightening beings
In the lands as numerous as atoms
That are in each atom.

Thus may I perceive the oceans
Of buddhas and lands of all times
In each point in the ten directions
As I practice for myriad eons.

May I ever penetrate the eloquence of buddhas,
The voices of all buddhas which adapt to mentalities,
The purity of articulation of all buddhas,
By the sounds of the ocean of tones in a single utterance.

Into those infinite voices
Of all buddhas of all times
May I enter by buddha-power,
Turning the wheel of teaching.

May I enter all eons
Of the future instantly,
And may I act in all eons
Of all times within an instant.

May I see all buddhas of all times
In one instant
And always enter their sphere
By the magical power of liberation.

May I produce the arrays of all lands
Of all times in an atom,
May I thus perceive all the arrays
Of buddha-lands in all the ten directions.

Learning the teachings of
The Lamps of the Worlds to come,
I visit all the Guides
Who have passed away to eternal rest.

By occult powers, swift in all ways,
By the power of knowledge, all-sided,
By the power of practice, with all virtues,
By the power of universal love,
By the power of goodness, all pure,
By the power of knowledge, unobstructed,
Gathering the power of enlightenment,
Clearing away the power of acts,
Destroying the power of afflictions,
Vitiating the power of demons,
May I fulfill all powers

Of the practice of good.

Purifying oceans of lands,
Liberating oceans of beings,
Observing oceans of truths,
Plumbing oceans of knowledge,
Perfecting oceans of practices,
Fulfilling oceans of vows,
Serving oceans of buddhas,
May I practice, untiring, for oceans of eons.

The lofty vows of enlightenment practice
Of the buddhas of past, present, and future
May I fulfill completely,
Practice what is good, and realize enlightenment.

All who share in the practice
Of the sage of Universal Good,
The foremost offspring of all buddhas,
I name them good.

Pure in body, speech, and mind,
Pure in conduct, with a pure land,
As the sage is named Good,
May I become thus equally.

May I carry out the vow of Manjushri
To totally purify the practice of good;
Tireless through all future ages,
May I fulfill all those tasks.

May there be no limits to practice,
And no limit to virtues;
Persisting in infinite practices,
I know all their miraculous creations.

As long as the earth exists,
As long as all beings exist,
As long as acts and afflictions exist,
So long will my vow remain.

Let me give the buddhas all worlds
In the ten directions adorned with jewels,
Let me give celestials and humans supreme happiness
For eons as many as atoms.

Those who develop respect and devotion
On hearing this supreme dedication,
Seeking supreme enlightenment,
Will be most blessed.

They will have abandoned all evils
And all bad associates
And will quickly see Infinite Light,
If they have this vow of enlightening practice.

Great is their gain, worthwhile their life,
Auspicious their birth as humans;
They will soon be like
The universally good enlightening being.

Those who have committed hellish crimes
Under the sway of ignorance
Will quickly put an end to them all
When this practice of good is expounded.

Endowed with knowledge, distinction, and nobility,
Invulnerable to false teachers and demons,
They will be honored
By all in the triple world.

They will quickly go to the
Tree of enlightenment
And sit there for the benefit
Of all living beings;
They will realize enlightenment,
Turn the wheel of teaching,
And conquer the devil
And all its cohorts.

Buddha knows those who hold this vow to practice good,
Who cause it to be told of and taught;
The fruit of this is supreme enlightenment—
Do not entertain any doubt.

As the hero Manjushri knows, so too does Universal Good;
As I learn from them I dedicate all this virtue.
By the supreme dedication praised by the buddhas of all times
I dedicate all this virtue to the practice of highest good.

Acting in accord with the time, may I remove all obstructions,
May I see Infinite Light face to face and go to the land of bliss.

There, may all these vows be complete;
Having fulfilled them, I will work for the weal of all beings in the world.

Let me abide in the circle of that buddha, born in a beautiful lotus,
And receive the prophecy of buddhahood there in the presence
Of the buddha of Infinite Light.

Having received the prophecy there, with millions of emanations
I will work for the weal of beings everywhere, by the power of Buddha.

By whatever virtue I accumulate, having invoked the vow to practice good,
May the pure aspiration of the world be at once all fulfilled.

By the endless surpassing blessing realized from dedication
To the practice of good,
May worldlings submerged in the torrent of passion
Go to the higher realm of Infinite Light.

The Buddha said, "Sudhana, those enlightening beings led by Manjushri, the monks developed by Manjushri, Maitreya, and all the enlightening beings of the age of virtue, the great enlightening beings gathered in various worlds, as numerous as atoms, led by Universally Good, appointed inheritors of spiritual sovereignty, the great disciples led by Shariputra and Maudgalyayana and their circle, as well as celestial and human beings, were elated and they applauded what the blessed enlightening being Universally Good had said."

APPENDIX 1
Technical Terminology and Symbolism in *The Flower Ornament Scripture*

Appendix 1

The Flower Ornament Scripture is written without much abstruse technical vocabulary, and to the extent that it does use such terminology, it also provides its own explanatory and descriptive material to convey its intent. Nevertheless, in presenting this scripture in English, in which there do not presently exist firmly established conventions or familiar cultural bases for expressing Buddhist ideas, it may be helpful to the understanding of the scripture in translation to discuss some basic terms.

Due to the volume of the scripture, footnoting individual occurrences of technical terms would call for a great deal of cross-referencing. This would swell the bulk of each volume, and might well produce a situation of chaos rather than order in locating definitions. Furthermore, the virtually constant interruption of the text would likely prove distracting, disrupting the continuity of what is designed to be recited and should be read in a flowing manner, gradually building up a total picture through a succession of impacts, images, and ideas. For these reasons, the main terms in which the fundamental points of the teachings of the scripture are cast will be presented summarily in this introduction for easy reference. Other terms that are not so critical will be dealt with in the glossary. The abstract philosophy of the school based on this scripture is presented elsewhere,[1] and only the essential points which bear directly on the structure and content of the scripture itself will be introduced here.

Throughout the text of the scripture the terms "sentient beings" and "living beings" are frequently to be met with. These terms, which are used synonymously, require some explanation. Here "sentient" or "living" contrasts to "enlightened" or "enlightening" beings, but does not imply that the latter are literally insentient or not living. The implication of "sentient" and "living" is reference to the condition of being dominated or compelled by senses, feelings, emotions, thoughts; of being imprisoned, so to speak, by mundane life, at the mercy of its vicissitudes, without self-mastery or ability to transcend compulsive preoccupation

1. Thomas Cleary, *Entry into the Inconceivable: An Introduction to Hua-yen Buddhism* (Honolulu: University Press of Hawaii, 1983).

with external and/or internal phenomena. It is a fundamental task of enlightening beings to rise above, and help others to rise above, the fetters of mundane life and sense experience.

There are numerous categories of "sentient beings," several of which attract attention as being of frequent occurrence, used to describe basic unwholesome psychological elements or conditions. The states referred to as hells, hungry ghosts, and animals, are collectively called the three evil ways or states of woe or courses of misery. "Hungry ghosts" represent craving and greed, "animals" represent ignorance and folly, and "hells" represent states dominated by ignorance, greed, and hatred. Sometime the states of misery or evil ways are also said to be four, the fourth being the realm of "titans," who symbolize anger, resentment, jealousy, and hatred.

In connection with sentient beings, the common term "birth-and-death" is also important. This refers to the impermanence of all things and beings. It also refers to the virtually constant fluctuation in the mental states of sentient beings. That is to say, for example, in a moment of anger one is "born" as a titan; in a moment of craving one is "born" as a hungry ghost; in a moment of folly one is "born" as an animal. Every phase of psychological or social development, every shift in interest, attention, or mood, every physiological change, even every passing thought are all examples of "birth-and-death." Emancipation from birth and death, a prime objective of enlightening endeavor, refers to not being submerged in or dominated by such changes; a traditional metaphor for this is that of the mirror, which is not itself affected by the flux of images it reflects.

The condition of sentient beings is said to be one of affliction, and the term "afflictions" is met with throughout the scripture. In Buddhist psychology there are often said to be several major afflictions: greed, anger, ignorance, conceit, envy, jealousy, doubt, and wrong views. The first three of these are especially singled out and called the "three poisons," which stultify the mind and prevent if from realizing its enlightenment potential, causing instead the accumulation of suffering.

Ignorance, or folly, or delusion, is sometimes referred specifically to ignorance of cause and effect, by which one falls into vicious circles without a clue of how to escape. Causality means that no condition is in itself inevitable, and ignorance is also understood to refer to ignorance of the real nature of things—that is, lack of awareness of the conditional nature of phenomena. This forms the basis for desire, which in its compulsive form is the poison of greed or covetousness. Ignorance is thus also referred to as the notion that there is something to gain or possess.

Greed, craving, covetousness—these terms basically refer to attachment to things, feelings, thoughts, to emotional involvement in things, possessiveness and acquisitiveness. These terms also refer to psychological greed—for praise, approval, recognition, attention. Contention, conflict, and frustration occasioned by covetousness in turn underlie anger and hatred.

The poison of anger, hatred, resentment, may again be a reaction to frustration or competition involving more abstract psychological desires, such as self-esteem, as well as material and sensual desires. This poison represents the drawing of boundaries and definition of individual (or group) self-interest as opposed to the interests of others. Only by awareness of interrelatedness, the ultimate unity of being, is the false premise of the self-other dichotomy exposed so that this poison can be extirpated.

The affliction of conceit involves self-importance, pride, seeking to put oneself above others, to surpass others, and having false imaginings of one's worth or achievements. In this same general vein are also defined four fundamental afflictions in relation to the illusion of self, or the ego: ignorance of the real nature of self; the idea of the real existence of a self; pride in the self; and self love.

The affliction of doubt refers to unwillingness to recognize truth, or indulgence in vain speculation. It is not to be confused with doubt used to pry the mind from fixed conceptions. Compulsive doubt and hesitation to accept truth is seen as an extension of self-importance.

Wrong views are usually said to have five archetypes: the notion of a truly existent corporeal self; extreme views, which cling to ideas of permanence or total annihilation; false views, meaning denial or disregarding of causality, or arbitrary superstitious conceptions of causality; attachment to opinions and views; and attachment to rituals or rules, particularly with the idea that enlightenment can be obtained by mechanical adherence to forms. Attachment to rituals also refers to sacrificial and propitiatory ceremonies thought to bring benefits or avert calamity; these are considered a mundane fetter, and were originally not part of Buddhism.

These afflictions are not looked upon as sins or moral defects but as illnesses and sources of suffering. They are not considered a necessary part of the human condition. Various exercises, such as contemplation of impermanence, remembrance of death, evoking of love and compassion, and many other concrete and abstract practices are prescribed as specific cures for the various afflictions.

Higher states of sentient beings, which are still worldly or mundane, are represented by celestial realms. These generally represent states of satisfaction or felicity or psychic power, or comparatively refined mental conditions experienced in meditation and trance. Many gods and celestial realms of Indian mythology were employed by Buddhists for symbolic or metaphorical purposes, sometimes in a very general way to show that mundane happiness, power, and even the most exalted formless trances, are still not liberation. Although a number of these realms are mentioned in *The Flower Ornament Scripture*, on the whole they do not play a very important part, and specific notes on these realms will be deferred to the Appendix.

In addition to these beings, there are also mentioned a number of other mythological creatures from ancient Indian lore. For the most part these are of little symbolic value, except perhaps to represent diversity. They seem to appear simply as stock items of the cosmology of the civilization in which the scripture was written down.

Turning to what are sometimes called the sanctified realms, or realms of sages, we come first to what are known as the two vehicles, or the small vehicle(s). The term "vehicle" means a vehicle or method of liberation, a course of understanding and application by which emancipation from mundane bondage may be realized. "Two vehicles" refers to what are known in Sanskrit as shravakas and pratyekabuddhas. Shravaka means "hearer" or "listener" and refers to a follower or disciple of a Buddha, usually thought of particularly as a renuciant mendicant disciple. These "listeners" concentrate on the realization of selflessness, dispassion, and the consequent freedom from craving, cares, and personal suffering.

Listeners, Buddhist disciples, are divided into four grades, each grade being also divided into those striving to attain that state and those who have realized the fruit. The four grades are: stream-enterers, who are for the first time disengaged from mental preoccupation with the world; once-returners, who come back to mundane life once before final liberation; nonreturners, who never return to the mundane flow; and saints, who have attained nirvana, a tranquil, dispassionate state of extinction of afflictions. The first three are called learners, while the saints are called nonlearners once they have realized liberation, because they no longer need to learn anything or strive for their own emancipation.

Pratyekabuddha means "enlightened for one" and refers to an individual illuminate, a self-enlightened one, who attains liberation without a teacher. Another implication of the name is that an individual illuminate supposedly does not teach others directly. Self-enlightened ones are also called those who are enlightened by awareness of conditioning. They contemplate impermanence and observe that vicious circles, anxieties, and vexations, which are conditioned by striving, clinging, and craving, derive from basic ignorance of the illusory nature of the ego and the ephemeral nature of the world. Individual illuminates therefore root out the notion of self and put an end to desires, so that they attain serenity.

The two vehicles of disciples or listeners and self-enlightened ones or individual illuminates are called the small or lesser vehicles because of primary focus on individual liberation, concentration on one teacher or path, and lack of flexibility and compassion to teach people of different temperaments. In these senses they are contrasted to the so-called great vehicle of the bodhisattva or enlightening being, which is concerned with universal liberation and consequently involves greater variety and flexibility of approach. In *The Flower Ornament Scripture*, it is stated that the so-called lesser vehicles may be demonstrated by enlightening beings when they are conducive to the liberation of people with whom the enlightening beings happen to be dealing. The ways of disciples, self-enlightened ones, and enlightening beings are collectively called the three vehicles; in this scripture the term great vehicle is used to refer to the vehicle of buddhahood, of which the three vehicles might be preparations or partial, provisional techniques. The great vehicle of buddhahood is also referred to as the one vehicle, because it is based on the unity of being and comprehensiveness of approach.

The career of the enlightening being is of particular significance in *The Flower Ornament Scripture*, and much of the scripture is devoted to describing practices of enlightening beings. The enlightening being is dedicated to universal enlightenment, at once realizing enlightenment and enlightening others. Although the deeds and practices of enlightening beings are described in elaborate terms in the scripture, in general they are said to be based on ten ways of transcendence, or transcendent ways. Also called the perfections of enlightening beings, these are means of transcending the world, and are also ways of transcendent action in the world; in terms of *The Flower Ornament* doctrine of simultaneity of cause and effect, both aspects are included at once.

The first way of transcendence is giving or generosity. This may be giving of material things, of security, or of liberating teaching. Second is morality, or self-control, or discipline, living according to ethical principles, abiding by certain precepts such as injunctions against killing, stealing, falsehood, slander, and so on. This morality also involves living by general ethics of altruism, and acting in ways conducive to liberation in situations that are not defined by formal standards. Third is forbearance, patience, or tolerance; this involves not only tolerance of people and their doings, but also acceptance of truth without fear. Fourth is energy or effort, meaning indomitability in carrying out enlightening practices in the world. Fifth is meditation or concentration, by which the mind is taken off the realm of desires, attention is mastered, and understanding is empowered. Sixth is wisdom or transcendental knowledge; this refers to nondiscursive knowledge of the emptiness of inherent nature of things, which enables one to be ultimately unattached without dependence on control or concentration. Sometimes it is said to include discursive and analytic knowledge as well as insight or intuitive knowledge.

The first five of these ways of transcendence are sometimes referred to as the treasury or store of virtue, and the sixth is referred to as the treasury of knowledge. These six items, especially wisdom or nonconceptual knowledge, are in some form common to listeners, individual illuminates, and beginning enlightening beings; beyond these six are four more transcendent ways, which are more directly applied to the enlightenment of others, and are in the sphere of more advanced enlightening beings.

Seventh is means, which includes skill in application and direction of the elements of enlightening practices and skill in means of liberating other people.

Eighth is vows, involving the determination of commitment to seek complete perfect enlightenment and to help others realize enlightenment.

Ninth is power, referring to powers of mental cultivation and powers of ascertainment.

Tenth is knowledge, including mystical knowledge of the ranges of awareness of Buddhas and practical knowledge of the sciences of developing and maturing people.

The ways of transcendence may be presented as a progression, but they can only be completed and perfected in conjunction with each other; this is an important aspect of the Flower Garland doctrine of interdependence and totality.

In conjunction with these ways of transcendence, enlightening beings also cultivate what are known as the four immeasurable minds or four pure abodes. These terms refer to immeasurable kindness, immeasurable compassion, immeasurable joy, and immeasurable equanimity. "Immeasurable" means that these feelings or attitudes are extended to embrace all beings, overcoming emotional biases or discriminations between friends and enemies, relatives and strangers.

Also mentioned as basic types of practice of enlightening beings are what are called the four means of salvation or four means of integration. These consist of charity or giving, kind speech, beneficial action, and cooperation. The hallmark of the enlightening being is to be in the world yet at the same time beyond the world. These are means by which the enlightening beings integrate with society in order to carry out their work.

The primary object of the Buddhist teachings as a whole may be said to be buddhahood. The term "Buddha" means enlightened, and as such refers to the fully awake, fully realized, complete human being; what is perhaps more outstanding in *The Flower Ornament Scripture*, however, is the universal or cosmic sense of Buddha. The scripture explicitly states that "Buddha" is to be seen in all lands, all beings, and all things. This is a basic premise of the scripture's grandiose descriptions of the scope of buddhahood; the individual human Buddha may be said to be one who is open to this level of awareness.

Buddha is said to have many dimensions of embodiment. The multiplicity of Buddha-bodies at times may refer to all things or beings, or to the potential or realization of full awakening in individual human beings. The "body" of Buddha, which is often mentioned in connection with the omnipresence of Buddha, is the so-called body of reality. This reality-body is defined in many ways: it may sometimes be said to be identical with all phenomena, or it may be said to be the pure mind, or it may be said to consist of "thusness and the knowledge of thusness," or it may be referred to as the universal qualities of buddhahood, such as the "ten powers."

Mention has already been made of "thusness" or "suchness." This term also can have several nuances. In one sense it simply means "everything," without arbitrary conceptual glosses. Sanskrit terms for "thusness" include such expressions as *bhutatathata*, "the thusness of what is", *yathabhuta*, "as is"; and *tathata*, "the quality of being such." The implication of the terms "thus" or "such" that no specific notion can truly define being as it really is; the term "thusness" hence can refer specifically to the inconceivable real nature of things, which is also called "emptiness" to allude to the lack of intrinsic meaning of signs and names by which particular things are discriminated and defined. Also, thusness can refer to the pure nature of the mind; when the mind is clear and this inherently pure nature is unobscured, reality as it is becomes apparent. Thusness is sometimes spoken of as "pure" and "defiled," or "unchanging" and "going along with conditions;" the first item of each pair refers to the unique real nature which is equal in everything, or emptiness, inconceivability, while the second refers to apparent reality, the realm of myriad differentiations. Thusness is also equated with "buddha-nature" and the "realm of reality," which includes both absolute and ordinary reality.

Among the qualities that constitute the reality-body of Buddhas in the sense of a universal spiritual body which all Buddhas develop are what are called the ten powers, the four fearlessnesses, and the eighteen unique qualities of Buddhas. The ten powers, which are powers of knowledge, are especially frequently mentioned.

The ten powers are defined as knowledge of what is so and what is not so, knowledge of the deeds of beings and the consequences of those deeds, knowledge of all states of meditation, concentration, and liberation, knowledge of the faculties of others, knowledge of the inclinations and understandings of beings, knowledge of the characters of beings, knowledge of where all paths lead, knowledge of past lives, clairvoyance, and knowledge of having extirpated all contaminations from the mind. These may be enumerated and defined in somewhat different ways in different Buddhist literature. The "beings" known to the Buddhas may of course be understood as the various conditions of human beings, though not necessarily limited thereto. The ten powers of knowledge of Buddhas are considered vestigial or latent powers in all humans, and some of them may be more or less developed in individuals. Some of these powers can be awakened and cultivated to some extent through awareness and attention in everyday life, while access to some psychic powers is possible only through intense meditation. Knowledge of past and future may be usefully understood as profound understanding of causes and effects, insight into psychological, social, and other developmental processes over a span of time; this type of knowledge is said to include, however, capacities of recollection and reception that generally remain undeveloped and unknown to ordinary people. In Buddhism it is accepted that intuitive knowledge and direct perception can be awakened and can do what discursive knowledge cannot do, so the operation of certain psychic powers is not accessible to conceptual knowledge.

The four fearlessnesses of Buddhas are the fearlessness of omniscience, the fearlessness of having put an end to all mental contamination, fearlessness in explaining things which hinder enlightenment, and fearlessness in explaining ways to end suffering. Fearlessness here means that the Buddha's knowledge is certain and free from doubt and hesitation. The meanings of omniscience or universal knowledge, which underlie fearlessness, will be taken up along with consideration of the so-called body of knowledge of Buddhas.

The eighteen unique qualities of Buddhas are: freedom from error; freedom from clamor; freedom from forgetfulness; freedom from distraction or fragmentation of mind; freedom from the notion of manifoldness; conscious equanimity; no loss of will; no loss of energy; no loss of memory; no loss of concentration; no loss of wisdom; no loss of liberation; no loss of knowledge and insight of liberation; always acting in accord with knowledge and wisdom; always speaking in accord with knowledge and wisdom; always thinking in accord with knowledge and wisdom; unimpeded knowledge of the past; and unimpeded knowledge of the present.

Buddhas' body of knowledge, in its broadest sense, may be said to contain all knowledge, and in the scripture innumerable spheres of knowledge are mentioned. Overall, however, the body of knowledge is often defined in terms of four kinds of knowledge, from which all other proceed. The first knowledge is called the mirrorlike knowledge, or great round mirror. Clear, nondistorting, nondiscursive awareness is likened to a mirror that reflects things objectively and impartially, without discrimination or attachment. This is also called the mind's aspect of true thusness. Next is knowledge of equality, of the equal nature of all things, referring to the relativity and inherent emptiness of phenomena. Knowing the essential emptiness of things is also referred to as universal knowledge or general omniscience. The third Buddha-knowledge is called subtle observing or analytic knowledge; this is knowledge of particulars, knowledge of characteristics and differentiation. While knowledge of equality deals with the "emptiness" side of the relativity = emptiness equation, analytic knowledge deals with the "relativity" side. Together they realize the mutual noninterference of equality and distinction, forming, with the underlying mirrorlike knowledge, the basis for the fourth Buddha-knowledge, called the knowledge of practical accomplishment. This refers to acting in the world, in harmony with essential emptiness-equality and with concrete conditions.

Omniscience, or all-knowledge, or universal knowledge, is said to be of three types. One is the aforementioned general aspect of omniscience, which refers to knowledge of emptiness. Beyond this is knowledge of modes of the path, which is knowledge of types of people and various means whereby they may be liberated. The former knowledge is common to saints, self-enlightened ones, and enlightening beings, while the latter is in the realm of enlightening beings. The consummate omniscience of Buddhas, containing the ten powers, is knowledge of all particulars of causality and the overall and specific means of enlightenment.

Considering the matter of the scripture's frequent references to the Buddha's innumerable "spiritual" or "mystic" powers being revealed everywhere, from the point of view of the scripture, all things, all beings, mind, and space itself are bodies of Buddha, so the miracle of awareness and existence—the ultimate causes of which are beyond the power of conception to grasp—are "miracles" of Buddha. They are constantly edifying in the sense that, as the scripture says, all things are always teaching. The miraculous transformation performed by the Buddha for the enlightenment of sentient beings is, from this perspective, the shifting of the mental outlook to experiencing everything as a learning situation. This vision of life as a whole as the scene of enlightenment is one of the major themes of *The Flower Ornament Scripture*, and is a basic meaning of the statement that there is ultimately only one vehicle of enlightenment.

Mention of the doctrine of "only mind" may be called for to clarify statements in the scripture to the effect that all things are creations of mind. This does not mean creation in the sense of creating something out of nothing. This doctrine means that practically speaking the world only "exists" as such because of our awareness, and that what we take to be the world in itself is our experience and inference based thereon. The conceptual order which is taken to be characteristic of objective reality is, according to this doctrine, a projection of the mind, a description that filters and shapes experience in accord with mental habits developed throughout the history of the species, the civilization, and the individual. Techniques of visualization, meditation, concentration, and trance are used in part to detach the mind from fixation on a given conceptual and perceptual order through cultivation of other ways of perceiving and conceiving, and through experience of other spheres, which are equally real to the senses. By mastering attention and realizing the relativity of world and mind through actual experience as well as reasoning, one may then gain freedom while in the midst of the world, having, as scripture says, mastered mind rather than being mastered by it.

In Huayan Buddhism, the school whose philosophy is based on *The Flower Ornament Scripture*, the cosmos, or realm of reality, is a central idea, one which may be used to clarify certain features of the scripture. The cosmos, as the term is used here, includes the entirety of conventional (mundane) and absolute (transcendental) reality. The term from which the notion of cosmos or reality realm derives (Sanskrit: *dharmad-*

hatu) can be used to refer to phenomena, individually or collectively, to universes as defined by certain laws or states, to realms of existence and principles defined by the teachings of Buddhism, and also to the realm of nirvana. The Chinese philosophers of the Huayan school distinguished four general reality-realms in which everything, the cosmos, is included: the realm of phenomena, the realm of noumenon, the realm of noninterference or integration of noumenon and phenomena, and the realm of mutual noninterference among phenomena.

The realm of phenomena refers to all things and events. The realm of noumenon refers to the essence of things in themselves, the principle of voidness or emptiness—the lack of inherent nature or intrinsic reality in conditional, dependent things. The realm of mutual noninterference of noumenon and phenomena means that since phenomena are products of causes and are interdependent and have no absolute individual existence, therefore they are all empty or void of intrinsic nature. Hence their conditional existence does not interfere with their absolute emptiness, and vice versa. Their interdependent existence and emptiness of own being are two sides of the same coin. The realm of noninterference among phenomena is based on the same principle: whatever their apparent differences, phenomena are the same in the sense of being dependent and hence void of absolute identity. The noumenal nature, or emptiness, of one phenomenon, being the same as that of all phenomena, is said to at once pervade and contain all phenomena; and as this is true of one, so it is true of all. Furthermore, the interdependence of phenomena means that ultimately one depends on all and all depend on one, whether immediately or remotely; therefore, the existence of all is considered an intrinsic part of the existence of one, and vice versa.

The realms of noninterference between noumenon and phenomena and noninterference among phenomena are represented symbolically in *The Flower Ornament Scripture* by such images as Buddha's pores each containing innumerable lands, with each atom in those lands also containing innumerable lands, each land containing innumerable Buddhas, and so on, ad infinitum. This illustrates the infinite mutual interrelation of all things. The principle of all things reflecting or "containing" one another is also symbolized by the so-called "Net of Indra," which is an imaginary net of jewels that reflect each other with the reflections of each jewel containing reflections of all the jewels, ad infinitum.

A further illustration of the principle of interdependence and interrelation is afforded by the formation of assemblies in the scripture. To give a simplified example, let us take a group of one hundred individuals: singling out one, we could say this individual is surrounded or accompanied by ninety-nine people; adding the totality of the ninety-nine, the group, as one more (a typical Huayan accounting method based on the interdependence of individuals and sets), this means one individual is accompanied by one hundred. In the same way each individual may be selected as the focus and considered to be accompanied by one hundred.

Hence there are a hundred people each accompanied by a hundred people: viewed as discrete individuals, there are only one hundred, but seen in terms of their interrelation there are basically ten thousand, and this latter figure could be multiplied indefinitely to account for complex relations. All beings and phenomena, being relative, are looked upon in this way in Huayan philosophy: based on the same principle, a person or thing may be seen as multiple when considered in terms of relationships, being in a sense a different person or thing in terms of each different relationship. In reference to the enlightening being, who consciously adopts different guises and deals with people in different ways, this is represented as multiplication of the body of projection of myriad different bodies.

Like many popular Buddhist scriptures, *The Flower Ornament Scripture* is rich in imagery and symbolism. While certain images may at times be taken literally, there are numerous specific symbolic connotations assigned to particular items in the text of the scripture itself as well as in traditional exegesis. Some consideration of the metaphorical language of the scripture is therefore called for to gain access to the inner meanings.

At various points throughout the text are elaborate descriptions of a multitude of adornments. In general, these symbolize virtues, teachings, and also qualities of the world as perceived by a pure mind. The term virtue is often used in the scripture in a very broad sense to include all beneficial and liberating acts as well as wholesome qualities, spiritual faculties, and powers of knowledge.

Jewels and precious substances symbolize enlightening teachings; their variety represents the multitude of doctrines expounded by enlightening beings and Buddhas in adapting to different situations and audiences. Rain is also used as a metaphor for teaching; showering rains of all manner of jewels and ornaments and other beautiful things refers to the exposition of many principles and teachings.

Flowers may be used to represent the mind or mental factors or states, particularly the development of wholesome qualities and the unfolding of knowledge. Flowers are also used to symbolize practices employed to further spiritual evolution, and fruits symbolize the results of those practices.

Canopies or parasols represent protection from afflictions, inclusion in a sphere of activity or enlightenment, compassion, breadth of mind, and universality of knowledge.

Seats, thrones, and residences represent spiritual states, stability, or spheres of awareness and action.

Banners and pennants stand for virtues, outward manifestations of qualities or realizations, excellences of character; they also stand for symbolism and representation in general.

Personal ornaments such as garlands and jewelry represent virtues, knowledge, skills, or cultivation of one's faculties.

Oceans and clouds represent clusters or groups. Oceans are also used to symbolize immensity, depth, immeasureability.

Light symbolizes knowledge or awareness; variegated light represents differentiating knowledge, different kinds of knowledge, or knowledge of different spheres. Lights, particularly jewel lights, also can represent the experience of a certain kind of meditation in which the attention is focused only on colors, not on things as usually conceived; the colors seen in this kind of concentration are called jewel lights. While fire can be used to represent passion and afflictions, flames are also used to represent wisdom, the destruction of ignorance and folly; lamps and torches are associated with light and flames, representing awareness, knowledge, and wisdom.

Buddha-lands, or buddha-fields, have several levels of meaning. They are spheres of enlightenment, or spheres of action of Buddhas; they may be thought of as actual lands with inhabitants, as communities or societies, or as spheres of awareness. Each realm of sense is a buddha-land, and so is every particle of matter. A human being can be looked upon as a buddha-land of sight, a buddha-land of hearing, a buddha-land of taste, a buddha-land of smell, a buddha-land of feeling, and a buddha-land of thought. As a unit of measurement, a buddha-land or buddha-field is represented as a universe or system of a billion worlds.

APPENDIX 2
Amplifications of Book 39

Appendix 2

There are a number of passages, some quite long, to be found in Prajna's forty-scroll translation of the *Gandavyuha*, which are not in either of the earlier Chinese translations, nor in the Sanskrit original. It is probably fair to assume, therefore, that these are additions made by Prajna or his committee of assistants. Indeed, some of them appear to be of the nature of explanations of or amplifications on the text; some seem to go off a bit excessively on tangents. The following excerpts present a selection of those additions which seemed in my opinion to be worth translating. —THOMAS CLEARY

Instructions of Muktaka

The accumulation of illusions from action is called mind; intellect thinks and assesses, and the ideational consciousness discriminates. The five sense consciousnesses discern the differences in objects. Ignorant people are unable to realize this, so they fear old age, sickness, and death, and seek nirvana. They do not know either birth and death or nirvana, and create arbitrary and false notions about objects. Also, the ignorant think that the future perishing of objects of sense from the faculties is nirvana. When buddhas and enlightening beings themselves realize enlightenment, they overturn the repository consciousness and realize the knowledge of basic awareness. All ordinary ignorant people misunderstand the Buddha's expedient means and cling to the existence of Three Vehicles. They do not realize that the world is produced from mind and do not know that all elements of buddhahood are the direct experience of one's own mind. They see sense data without and cling to them as really existing. Just like oxen or goats, they are unable to wake up and know, so they have no way to escape the whirl of birth and death.

Buddhas say that all things have no origin or extinction, no past, present, or future. Why? Because as one's own mind manifests sense data, objects fundamentally have no existence; because all things, existent or not, have no origin and are like the horns of a rabbit. The realm of sages' own enlightenment is like this. The ignorant arbitrarily create false ideas, taking the nonexistent as existing and the existent as not existing. They grasp the various manifestations of action of the repository consciousness and fall into the

1535

two views of origin and extinction. Not understanding their own minds, they create false notions.

Instructions of Shilpabhijna

Sudhana said, "O sage, how does one practice so as to attain this liberation? Shilpabhijna replied, "If enlightening beings practice ten things and completely fulfill them, then they can attain this enlightening liberation of higher knowledge of the arts. What are the ten? Sufficiency of knowledge, diligently seeking good associates, intense vigor, removing obstructing delusions, purity of correct practice, respecting correct teaching, observation of the inherent emptiness of phenomena, destroying false views, practicing the right path, acquisition of true knowledge. If enlightening beings can fulfill these ten things, they can rapidly attain this liberation. Why? By sufficiency of knowledge, enlightening beings diligently seek good associates; seeing them, they approach them, happily respect them, and think of them as buddhas. By associating with them, they are constantly being taught, so they are able to apply intense vigor to difficult practices. Having attained vigor, they can use good qualities to destroy what is not good. By destroying what is not good, they enable all good qualities to reach fulfillment. Once goodness is fulfilled, then they can get rid of all obstructing delusions. By getting rid of obstructions, they cause body, speech, and mind to attain great purity, in accord with correct practice. By this purity, they are able to respect the teachings of all buddhas, enlightening beings, and spiritual benefactors. Because of this respect for the teaching, they diligently seek to observe the emptiness of all phenomena. Having realized that all phenomena are empty, their minds are unobstructed wherever they turn. Deeply realizing interdependent origination, they get rid of the notion of causelessness, extinguish the mind of false views, and practice the right path. Having entered the right path, they attain true knowledge. By attaining true knowledge, they attain this liberation and witness the profound reality realm."

Sudhana then said, "What is this truth called?"

Shilpabhijna replied, "These words are called truth."

Sudhana said, "What words are called truth?"

Shilpabhijna replied, "Words that do not deceive are called true."

"What are words that do not deceive?"

"They speak of the eternal constancy of the essence of truth, it being ever of one nature."

"What is the unchanging nature?"

"It is understood through personal realization of the essence of things."

"What is the essence of things like? Are that which understands and that which is understood one or two?"

"The reality that is personally realized by enlightening beings is neither one nor two. By this power it is possible to equally benefit self and others. Just as the earth can produce everything without discrimination, so it is with the minds that benefit and are benefited. But the essence of things neither has form nor is formless. It is like space. It is hard to know, hard to understand. This truth is subtle, beyond verbalization. Why? Because it transcends the sphere of all verbal expression, it transcends all possible ranges of speech, it transcends the range of description, discrimination, and thought, it transcends the sphere of all reflection and assessment, it transcends all realms known to ignorant sentient beings, it transcends all realms of bedevilments connected with afflictions, it transcends all spheres of mind and consciousness. It has no 'this' or 'that,' no signs or signlessness; it is beyond all illusory realms. It abides in no abode, and is the sphere of tranquil sages. The realm of personal realization of those sages has no formal characteristics, no defilement or purity, no grasping or rejection, no pollution or confusion. Its clarity is supreme, its essence is eternal and unperishing. Whether or not buddhas appear in the world, the essence of the reality realm is always one and the same. It is for this truth that enlightening beings carry out countless difficult practices; having attained realization of this truth, they can benefit all sentient beings and enable sentient beings ultimately to abide in this truth. This is really true, this is unchanging, this is ultimate reality, this is the body of all knowledge, this is the inconceivable reality realm, this is the nondual reality realm."

Instructions of Suchandra

Suchandra said, "If enlightening beings can practice ten things, they can fully attain this liberation. What ten? Never leaving spiritual benefactors; never giving up remembrance of vision of buddhas; never giving up listening to true teaching; never giving up honoring and serving buddhas, enlightening beings, and spiritual benefactors; never abandoning learned and wise companions and teachers who are able to expound the Teaching; never giving up listening to talk of all the practices of the transcendent ways; never giving up hearing about all the elements of enlightenment; never giving up the three doors of liberation; never giving up the four immeasurables; never giving up the body of all knowledge. If enlightening beings do not give up on these ten things, they can attain this liberation of light of undefiled knowledge."

Sudhana asked, "How can this liberation be experienced in the present?"

Suchandra said, "In the present one should make transcendent wisdom and the mind unite as far as possible; then one can enter this liberation whatever one perceives and cognizes."

Sudhana asked, "Is it realized by hearing talk about transcendent wisdom?"

Suchandra said, "No. Why not? Because transcendent wisdom is realized by seeing the true essence of things."

Sudhana asked, "Is it not a fact that hearing can produce knowledge, and then by thinking about the nature of knowledge one can get to see True Thusness and personally realize enlightenment?"

Suchandra said, "No, it is not so. It is impossible to personally attain enlightenment by hearing and thinking. Let me give you a simile. Suppose someone is traveling from west to east through a desert in the summer heat, and he meets a man coming from the east and asks, 'I am thirsty and hot—where is there water and shade? I want to quench my thirst and rest and cool off.' The man knows, and tells him, 'Go east. There will be two roads, one to the left, one to the right. Take the one to the right, and if you keep traveling on it, you will eventually reach a sweet spring and trees giving shade.' Now, do you suppose that this person who is hot and thirsty can quench his thirst or cool off simply by hearing about the spring and trees and thinking about going there? Of course not. It is necessary to go by the road pointed out, to get to the oasis, bathe, and drink; only then will he be able to quench his thirst and cool off. So it is with enlightening beings: they cannot enter the doors of the Teaching only by the understanding that comes from hearing and thinking. In this simile, the desert is birth and death, the one coming from the west is sentient beings, the heat is delusions, and thirst is craving. The one from the east who knows the road is the buddhas and enlightening beings who abide in all knowledge and realize the equal real meaning of the true essence of things. Finding pure water and being free from heat and thirst stands for personally realizing real truth.

"Let me give you another simile. Suppose the Buddha lived for an eon and in various ways eloquently told people on earth about heavenly ambrosia, its various qualities, its wonderful texture, its beautiful color and fragrance and wonderful flavors. Do you think the people would know what the celestial food tasted like when they heard about it and thought about it? Of course not. And in the same way, one cannot realize the essence of transcendent wisdom just by hearing and thinking about it."

Sudhana said, "How do enlightening beings skillfully explain so as to enable people to really attain experience?"

Suchandra said, "The true essence of transcendent wisdom experienced by enlightening beings is the definitive, proper basis of their explanation. It is because of having attained this liberation that they can skillfully explain for people.

"Furthermore, enlightening beings attain this liberation by fulfilling ten things: getting rid of all unwholesome qualities, not deviating from the precepts of Buddha, getting rid of all envy, serving all enlightened ones, diligently practicing all beneficial works, acquiring wisdom, acquiring skill in means, acquiring great determination, acquiring detachment, acquiring vigor. If enlightening beings fulfill these ten things, they will realize this liberation."

Instructions of Shivaragra

Sudhana said, "Noble One, the true power of this liberation is called the speaking of a vow of truth; what does this mean?"

The brahmin said, "Speaking a vow of truth means suchness as is, unchanging, nondual, ultimate truth, and the substance of the body of reality of the enlightened ones of past, present, and future."

Sudhana said, "How can all enlightening beings practice so as to attain this reality body?"

He replied, "If enlightening beings can cultivate ten things to fulfillment, they will attain this reality body. What ten? The body of equality, the body of purity, the body of tranquillity, the body of space, the body of sublime knowledge, the body of infinity, the body of practice, the body of the essence of things, the body of detachment from rumination, the body of inconceivability. If enlightening beings have these ten bodies, they attain the pure reality body of the enlightened."

Sudhana said, "At what state do enlightening beings in this liberation attain these ten bodies?"

The brahmin said, "Enlightening beings in the first stage who dwell in this liberation attain the body of equality, because they realize the essence of things, get rid of all deviation, and see the equality of phenomena. Enlightening beings in the second stage who dwell in this liberation attain the body of purity, because they get rid of the defilement of immorality and are always pure in respect to the essence of all the precepts. Enlightening beings in the third stage who dwell in this liberation attain the body of infinity, because they get rid of unwholesome elements such as craving, anger, and envy, and abide in higher concentrations. Enlightening beings in the fourth stage who dwell in this liberation attain the body of practice, because they always diligently practice to assemble all the elements of enlightenment. Enlightening beings in the fifth stage who dwell in this liberation attain the body of the essence of things, because they observe and become aware of all true principles and realize the essence of phenomena. Enlightening beings in the sixth stage who dwell in this liberation attain the body of freedom from rumination, because they observe the principle of interdependent origination, which is difficult to understand, difficult to know, not in the sphere of rumination. Enlightening beings in the seventh stage who dwell in this liberation attain the body of inconceivability, because they assemble the skillful techniques of the buddhas' teachings and their knowledge and activity is fulfilled. Enlightening beings in the eighth stage who dwell in this liberation attain the body of tranquillity, because the afflictions are no longer active and they are detached from worldly descriptions. Enlightening beings in the ninth stage who dwell in this liberation attain the body of space, because their physical forms are boundless, pervading everything. Enlightening beings in the tenth stage who dwell in this liberation attain the body of sublime knowledge, because the sublime realm of omniscience is completely assembled."

Sudhana asked, "How is the spiritual body of buddhas different from these ten kinds of spiritual bodies of enlightening beings?"

He replied, "The essence of the spiritual body is not different; the only difference is in the power."

Sudhana went on, "What does that mean?"

He replied, "It means the spiritual reality-bodies of buddhas and enlightening beings are equal, without difference. Why? Because the essence and characteristics of all phenomena are equal, being one and the same body. So it is that ordinary people and sages, delusion and enlightenment, causes and effects of defilement and purity, going and coming, advancing and retreating, are all the same one form. Now, when I say there is a difference in power, I mean that the properties of the body of buddhas are completely developed and have superior power, unlike the enlightening beings. Let me give you a simile to illustrate this. Suppose there is a jewel that has not yet been cut and polished and so does not sparkle; the ordinary people would not care for it. Once it is cut and polished so that it sparkles and shines, people value it. There is no difference in the substance of the jewel, but the appearance is different. Although enlightening beings are the same as buddhas in essence, which is called the reality-body or spiritual body in both cases, it cannot be said that they are the same as buddhas in terms of inconceivable pure qualities such as knowledge and spiritual powers. Why? Because the buddhas have purified all sublime qualities over countless eons to ultimate perfection so that they are infinite as space, filling the worlds in the ten directions, sublimely pure, free from the stain of delusion, with immense light that illumines every place and extraordinary power that aids sentient beings everywhere. Though enlightening beings have the spiritual reality-body, its qualities are not yet perfected, and there is residual defilement; so they are like the waxing moon, which is the same in name and substance, but changes in light and appearance as it waxes because there is a difference in fullness. So it is with enlightening beings and buddhas in respect to their spiritual reality-bodies; in the former it is not full, whereas in the latter it is full. The body of enlightening beings is like the moon from the first to the fourteenth of the lunar month, when its light cannot shine around, whereas the reality-body of buddhas is like the moon on the fifteenth, when it is full, its light shining everywhere without boundary or obstruction. Yet the ten kinds of spiritual body of enlightening beings are the same in essence as the body of buddhas, without duality, though they cannot be said to be one because of the difference in their cultivated qualities. Therefore, if enlightening beings dwell in this liberation and fulfill the ten bodies, then they can realize the complete reality-body of buddhas in which all qualities are perfected.

"Furthermore, enlightening beings attain an indestructible adamantine body in ten respects: they are invulnerable to the poison of all afflictions, craving, anger, and folly; they are invulnerable to pride, envy, false views, and delusions; they are invulnerable to the suffering and oppression of bad states; they are invulnerable to profit, loss, censure, praise, fame, slander, pain, and pleasure; they are invulnerable to birth, old age, sickness, death, grief, and lament; they are invulnerable to false philosophies; they are invulnerable to the demons of afflictions, the clusters, and death; they are invulnerable to celestial demons and their cohorts; they are invulnerable to all hearers and individual illuminates; they are invulnerable to all attractive objects in the world. If enlightening beings can embody these ten meanings, they will attain the indestructible adamantine body of buddhas.

"Furthermore, there are ten kinds of correct path of skill by which one can know teaching that has no error in it. What are the ten? One is when the path of the vehicle of enlightening beings is taught to those who are to be harmonized with the Great Vehicle, rather than the path of the vehicle of hearers. Second is when the path of the vehicle of hearers is taught to those who are to be harmonized with the vehicle of hearers, rather than the path of the vehicle of enlightening beings. Third is when the path of omniscience of buddhas is taught to those who are to be harmonized with the buddha-vehicle, rather than the vehicle of individual illuminates. Fourth is when the vehicle of individual illuminates is taught to those who are to be harmonized with the vehicle of individual illuminates, rather than the path of omniscience. Fifth is when people who are attached to self and phenomena are taught selflessness and the emptiness of phenomena rather than the path of artificial self and phenomena, which deals with self, person, being, life, and personality. Sixth is when people who cling to being or nonbeing are taught the middle way beyond extremes, and are not taught doctrines of being and nonbeing that fall into extremes. Seventh is when people whose minds are scattered are taught calm cessation and observation, and are not taught methods that will distract them. Eighth is when people who are infatuated with mundane things are taught the path of knowledge of Thusness, which is beyond the world, and are not taught the paths of the ignorant and infantile. Ninth is when people who like to be in birth and death are taught the path to nirvana beyond birth and death, and are not taught to stay in the world teaching people. Tenth is when people who cling to the emptiness of things and do not practice the right way are taught the right way, on which there are no brambles, and are not taught false and dangerous paths fraught with brambles. If enlightening beings enter the true path in these ten ways and are able to know how to teach without error, what they say is true."

APPENDIX 3
Commentary on Book 39 by Li Tongxuan

Translator's Introduction

ACCORDING TO BUDDHIST LEGEND, the fullest extent of consciousness available to humankind was rediscovered by Gautama Buddha thousands of years ago and summarized in the monumental discourse known as *The Flower Ornament Scripture (Avatamsaka Sutra)*. Finding this statement of complete enlightenment beyond even the most advanced minds of his time, the Buddha spent the rest of his life teaching people how to prepare themselves for this comprehensive understanding. At every step of the way, there were those who succeeded in absorbing, utilizing, and finally superseding each stage of preparation, as well as those who took the part for the whole, assumed they had realized all there was to know, and fell by the wayside.

After the disappearance of Gautama Buddha, those among his mendicant followers who had attained a certain stage of individual enlightenment gathered together to recite and systematize what they had learned from their teacher. Since the Buddha's teachings were adapted to the specific needs of individuals and groups according to their stage of evolution, the result was a vast amount of material, a highly complex body of principles and practices.

Not yet having reached the full consciousness of the Buddha, however, these mendicants were unaware of the teachings beyond their own range, and some of them assumed that they had recorded the full dispensation of their master, even though all of them refused to say they had attained all that the teacher had attained. Eventually the followers of the followers of these mendicants, imagining themselves to be the elite of a new religion holding the authentic teachings of the Buddha, not only rejected the more versatile and expansive teachings left among certain lay adepts and communities but even organized themselves into more than a dozen competing sects, each with its own proprietary interest in what it considered truth.

According to *The Scripture of the Great Ultimate Extinction,* the fragmentation of the Buddha's teaching, with different factions using parts of the teaching as claims to their own authority, was to be expected as a characteristic degeneration. *The Scripture on Unlocking the Mysteries,* revealing certain advanced teachings, represents this as already happening to mentally isolated Buddhist groups in the time of Gautama Buddha and explains its technical inefficiency.

Legend has it that the comprehensive teaching of *The Flower Ornament Scripture* was under these conditions withdrawn for a time, until the advent of a major renewer, the great Nagarjuna, who studied all aspects of Buddhist learning and recovered the teaching of *The Flower Ornament Scripture* "from the ocean." Consistent with his role in revitalizing the comprehensive teaching, Nagarjuna is also regarded as ancestor of all the major branches of East Asian Buddhism, including the Zen, Pure Land, and Tantric schools.

Turning from legend to history, it must be admitted that the terrestrial source of *The Flower Ornament Scripture* is unknown. This is a characteristic it has in common with the other great scriptures of the universalist Buddhist tradition, but the range of this scripture and the multitude of far-flung branches of the school it comprehends places it in a class by itself. It appears to be the product of an esoteric association like the later Sarmoun "Bees" who are said to traverse the world gathering the "honey" of knowledge from relict deposits.

The Sarmoun is the inner branch of the Designers, recognized for the last five hundred years as the most comprehensive school of Sufism. Teachings projected by the Designers and their associates have been outwardly connected by observers, and inwardly connected by practitioners, with every major religion in the world, a phenomenon easily understood in reference to the activities of the Bees. The idea of restoration of lost knowledge parallels the legend of the recovery of *The Flower Ornament Scripture*, and the connection with all religions also parallels the claim of the scripture that true teaching has been represented in all cultures and in all faiths.

When Buddhism began to filter into China to revitalize that delapidated civilization in the early centuries of the common era, *The Flower Ornament Scripture* was among the first sources of study materials in translation. At first only a limited number of ideas from the great body of the Teaching were introduced to broaden the mental horizons of the Chinese, but by the early fifth century a nearly complete translation was available. Some two centuries later a more comprehensive version was produced, not only adding teachings missing from the earlier work but also rendering the text in a far more skillful and readable translation.

Unifying the scattered lore of complete Buddhism, *The Flower Ornament Scripture* presents a scheme of fifty-two stages of enlightenment in five or six ranks. The five ranks are known as the ten abodes, the ten practices, the ten dedications, the ten stages, and universal enlightenment. The designation of six ranks adds to this the final rank of sublime enlightenment.

During the early absorption of Flower Ornament teachings in China, special attention was given to the ten stages, which are described in a book of the scripture that traditionally circulates as a single volume and was separately translated into Chinese at least five times. The book on the ten stages is without a doubt one of the key sections of the scripture, one of only two that still exist in the Sanskrit language from which so many Buddhist scriptures were translated.

The other book still extant in Sanskrit is the thirty-ninth book of *The Flower Ornament Scripture*, the *Gandavyuha*, or *Garland Scripture*, known in the comprehensive Chinese edition as *The Book On Entry into the Realm of Reality*. This final book, of unparalleled beauty and grandeur, recapitulates the entire scheme of the fifty-two stages in the tale of a pilgrimage reflecting the total effort of the original recollectors of the comprehensive teaching of *The Flower Ornament Scripture*. It is this book that is the subject of the present volume, a commentary on the *Gandavyuha* composed by the great Li Tongxuan, a distinguished eighth-century Chinese Buddhist.

There are two major Chinese commentaries on the complete translation of *The Flower Ornament Scripture*, the one by Li Tongxuan, a layman, and one by his contemporary Zhengguan, a monk. Zhengguan's commentary, which also includes a subcommentary on the commentary, is largely done from the point of view of what is known as the School of Characteristics, and is typically encyclopedic and astonishingly detailed. In contrast, Li's commentary, *Huayan helun*, is done from the point of view of what is known as the School of Essence and places tremendous emphasis on sudden enlightenment.

When I translated the complete version of *The Flower Ornament Scripture* into English years ago, I used both Li's and Zhengguan's commentaries. No one who reads the latter could fail to be impressed by Zhengguan's colossal scholarship; more difficult than the scripture itself, that commentary is a tour de force ranging over the enormous domain of Buddhist psychology and philosophy. A Western scholar once assured me that Zhengguan had wasted his time writing his commentary because no one would ever read it; and while I deeply lament this attitude, it is not difficult to understand it as an affirmation that the current state of Buddhist scholarship in the West is insufficient to make Zhengguan's work comprehensible to the average reader of the present day.

Li's commentary, on the other hand, without the intensive detail that characterizes Zhengguan's work, demonstrates the expansive embrace, vibrant aliveness, and sensitivity to symbolism typical of Chan Buddhism. Li emphasizes the point that *The Flower Ornament Scripture* is directed at ordinary people, and his commentary renders the scripture even more accessible to the nonspecialist. Nevertheless, produced as it was from a background of extensive learning in Buddhist teachings, it contains a great deal of material that makes sense only to someone similarly well versed in the whole range of Buddhist scriptures. For this reason I have chosen to use a Ming dynasty (14th–17th centuries C.E.) distillation of Li's original commentary, adapted after the fashion of the time to present the essential teachings in a manner accessible to the nonspecialist.

In recapitulating the teachings of *The Flower Ornament Scripture*, the *Gandavyuha, The Book on Entry into the Realm of Reality,* uses the format of a journey for knowledge. Sudhana, the inspired young pilgrim of the story, visits fifty-three teachers to learn the conduct of the bodhisattva, the enlightening being dedicated to liberation of the hidden resources of humanity. Quite out of keeping with the modern myth that the inner circle of living Buddhism was traditionally a male monkish elite, the story represents a small minority of the teachers as monks, and nearly half as females.

The first ten teachers visited by Sudhana teach him the so-called ten abodes, which are explained in quite different terms in the fifteenth book of *The Flower Ornament Scripture*. The first abode, called the abode of inspiration or initial determination, is a preliminary stage in which the aspirant sets his or her mind on the comprehensive knowledge that characterizes fully awakened buddhas. In this abode practitioners serve buddhas, remain willingly in the world, guide worldly people to reject evil, instruct people in the Teaching and encourage them to practice it, learn the virtues of enlightenment, enter the company of the enlightened, teach tranquil concentration as an expedient, encourage detachment from compulsive routines, and provide protection for those who are suffering.

The second abode, called the abode of preparing the ground, requires certain attitudes towards others: altruism and compassion, desire to give happiness and security, pity and concern, the desire to protect, identification, and the willingness to learn from everyone. Practitioners in this abode encourage and study formal learning, calmness, association with the wise, kind speech, timely speech, fearlessness, understanding, action in accord with the teaching, avoidance of folly and delusion, and stability.

The third abode, called the abode of practice, involves contemplation of phenomena in certain specific ways: as impermanent, as irritating, as empty of ultimate reality, as selfless, as having no creation, as senseless, as not corresponding to the names conventionally given to them, as having no locus, as being beyond conception, and as lacking stable solidity. Here practitioners observe the realms of sentient beings; the realms of phenomena and principles; the realms of the world; the material elements; and the realms of desire, form, and formlessness.

The fourth abode, called the abode of noble birth, is characterized by permanent access to the presence of the enlightened; deep and pure faith; careful examination of things; and knowledge of beings, lands, worlds, actions, consequences, birth and death, and nirvana. Practitioners in this abode endeavor to learn, practice, develop, and fulfill the teachings of past, present, and future buddhas; and they realize that all buddhas are equal.

The fifth abode, called the abode of full equipment with skill in means, calls for practitioners to cultivate virtues for the salvation and benefit of others, to free others from trouble, to free others from the miseries of compulsive routines, to inspire pure faith, to harmonize and pacify others, and to enable others to experience perfect peace. In this abode practitioners learn that beings are infinite, inconceivable, and identityless; create nothing; and possess nothing.

In the sixth abode, called the abode of the correct state of mind, the practitioners' minds are unwavering regardless of whether they hear praise or vilification of buddhas, buddhas' teachings, or enlightening practices. Their minds are also unwavering regardless of what they hear about sentient beings—that they are finite or infinite, defiled or undefiled, easy or hard to liberate. Practitioners are also undisturbed in mind regardless of what they hear about the origin or end of the universe or the existence or nonexistence of the universe. In this abode they learn in what respect all things are signless, are insubstantial, are impossible to cultivate, lack ultimate existence, lack true reality, are empty of absoluteness, have no identity, are like illusions, are like dreams, and cannot be apprehended conceptually.

In the seventh abode, the abode of nonregression, the practitioner is firm and does not backslide, regardless of what is said about the existence or nonexistence of buddhas, of truth, of enlightening beings, or of the practices of enlightening beings. Similarly, the practitioner is undaunted by whatever may be said about whether enlightening beings do or do not attain emancipation; whether or not there were, are, or will be buddhas in the past, present, or future; whether buddhas' knowledge is finite or infinite; or whether past, present, and future are uniform or not. Here the practitioner learns in what respect one is many and many are one, how expression accords with meaning and meaning accords with expression, how nonexistence is existence and existence is nonexistence, how formlessness is form and form is formless, how nature is natureless and naturelessness is nature.

The eighth abode, called the abode of youthful nature, or innocence, is characterized by flawless thought, word, and deed. The practitioner takes on new modes of life at will; knows people's various desires, understandings, realms, and activities; knows how worlds come into being and pass away; and is able to travel freely by psychic projection. Topics of study in this abode include knowledge, activation, maintenance, observation, and visitation of fields of enlightenment.

In the ninth abode, the abode of the spiritual prince, practitioners know how people are born, how afflictions arise, how habits continue, and what techniques are to be employed to liberate people. They know innumerable teachings and understand manners. They know the differentiations of the world, they know past and future events, and they know how to explain both conventional and ultimate truth. In this abode they also study the skills, manners, contemplations, power, fearlessness, and repose of spiritual monarchs.

In the tenth abode, the abode of coronation, the spiritual monarchs analyze, illumine, support, visit, and purify countless worlds; they observe and teach countless people, knowing their faculties, and cause countless people to strive for enlightenment and realize peace and harmony. The practitioners promote the knowledge that is proper to buddhas; knowledge of past, present, and future; knowledge of all worlds; knowledge of all beings; knowledge of all things; and knowledge of all buddhas.

The next ten teachers instruct the pilgrim Sudhana in the ten practices, which are described in the twenty-first book of *The Flower Ornament Scripture*. The first one, called the practice of joy, or giving joy, is based on transcendent generosity. The practitioner is magnanimous in giving, without any concept of person, personality, human being, giver, or receiver. Exercising generosity in this way, the practitioner observes only the infinity of reality and the realm of beings and sees them as empty, signless, insubstantial, and indeterminate. In this way the practitioner develops pure generosity without taking pride in it.

Second is what is known as beneficial practice, based on transcendent morality. The practitioner maintains pure discipline and self-control, free from attachment to material senses, without seeking power, status, wealth, or dominion. By knowing all things are unreal, practitioners are able to master life, death, and nirvana; to liberate themselves and others; to attain tranquillity, security, purity, dispassion, and happiness; and to foster these attainments in others. Practitioners aspire to follow the enlightened; to detach from mundane activities; to fulfill the qualities of buddhahood; to remain supremely equanimous and be impartial towards all; to understand objective reality clearly; to eliminate error; to cut through conceptualization; to abandon attachment; to achieve emancipation; and to abide mentally in supreme wisdom.

The third, the practice of nonopposition, is based on

transcendent tolerance. Practitioners develop humility and forbearance, refraining from harming others. Not seeking personal prominence or material gain, practitioners resolve to expound the Teaching to others so that they may get rid of all evil and put an end to greed, hatred, folly, pride, hypocrisy, possessiveness, jealousy, obsequiousness, and dishonesty. They transcend suffering by reflecting on the ultimate unreality of the body, detaching from the idea of self and all that pertains to it.

The fourth, the practice of indomitability, is based on transcendent energy. Practitioners become free from mental poisons and direct their energy towards ending psychological afflictions; uprooting confusion; eliminating the compulsion of habit; and learning all about people, phenomena, time, and the powers and qualities of the enlightened.

The fifth, the practice of nonconfusion, is based on transcendent meditation. Practitioners develop perfect mindfulness, so that their minds become undistracted, imperturbable, pure, open, and free from confusion. With this mindfulness they are able to hear and remember enlightened teachings and put them into practice without confusion. They are also able to change from one state of being to another without mental disturbance and to enter into all sorts of meditation states, realizing that they are all of the same essence. Practitioners attain true knowledge of phenomena and develop an increasingly vast sense of compassion.

The sixth, called the practice of good manifestation, is based on transcendent wisdom. Here practitioners are pure and nonacquisitive in thought, word, and deed, realizing that thoughts, words, and deeds have no absolute existence. Free from falsehood, they are accordingly freed from bondage; they abide in the absolute essence of reality yet appear in life expediently, having no retribution for their actions. Practitioners realize the transcendental truth of emptiness, the inconceivability of reality; yet they never give up the will to enlighten others and always expand their sense of compassion.

The seventh, the practice of nonattachment, is based on

transcendent skill in means. Practitioners neither form attachments to the sacred nor feel aversion towards the mundane, holding the Teaching without proprietary sentiments and teaching people without emotional involvement. By virtue of their great commitment and will power, practitioners remain secure while teaching others, not becoming disturbed or discouraged, having attained nonattachment and independence.

The eighth, the practice of the difficult-to-attain, is based on transcendent vows. Here practitioners perfect virtues that are difficult to attain and never abandon or weary of the vow of universal salvation. They understand that people do not really exist, yet they do not abandon them; they do not remain in the mundane world yet do not remain in transcendental nirvana either, always traveling back and forth to deliver others from the mundane to the transcendental. Practitioners observe all things to be ungraspable yet not nonexistent; they see things as they are, without neglecting their work of demonstrating the practices of enlightening activities wherever they are.

The ninth, the practice of good teaching, is based on transcendent power. Here practitioners attain inexhaustible intellectual powers and boundless versatility in teaching, their compassion extending to all beings. They adapt to the faculties, natures, and inclinations of the people they address, and respond inexhaustibly to whatever questions or difficulties people bring them. Practitioners of good teaching are able to do this by discovery of the boundless resources of the potential of enlightenment, by attainment of the light of all truths, and by fulfillment with universal knowledge. They are void of worldliness yet enter into all worlds, acting as refuges, lights, and guides for others, revealing the powers of the enlightened.

The tenth, the practice of truth, is based on transcendent knowledge. Here the practitioners develop knowledge of what is so and what is not so; knowledge of consequences of past, present, and future actions; knowledge of faculties, realms, and understandings; knowledge of where all paths lead; knowledge of defilement or purity and proper or improper timing of all meditations, liberations, and concentrations; knowledge of past abodes in all worlds; knowledge of clairvoyance; and knowledge of the end of all taints. Practitioners preserve the right teachings of the buddhas of all times for the benefit of all people and reach the source of the reality of the teachings of buddhas. Through the influence of the practitioners those who associate with them attain understanding, joy, and purity.

From the next ten teachers Sudhana learns the ten dedications, extensively described in the massive twenty-fifth book of *The Flower Ornament Scripture*. The first is called dedication to saving all beings without clinging to any image of beings. Practitioners of this dedication cultivate transcendent generosity, discipline, patience, energy, meditation, and wisdom; and they dwell in great compassion, kindness, joy, and equanimity. They dedicate these virtues to the benefit of all people to enable everyone to be purified, to reach the ultimate realization of enlightenment, and to be forever freed from the suffering and affliction of miserable states.

The second is called indestructible dedication. Practitioners of this dedication attain indestructible faith in buddhas and bodhisattvas, in the qualities and teachings of buddhas, in pure ways of life, in the path of dedication to enlightenment, in teachers of ways of enlightenment, in spiritual powers of buddhas, and in the practice of expedient means of enlightenment. Practitioners amass virtues, develop them, concentrate on them, contemplate and analyze them, find joy in them, and live by them; they set their minds on dedication in accord with the essential nature of things, dedication entering into uncreated truth yet perfecting created expedients, dedication of techniques discarding attachments to concepts of phenomena, and dedication of expedient application of practices without clinging to forms.

Third is dedication equal to all buddhas. Practitioners of this dedication do not conceive either like or dislike for any perceived objects; their minds are free, pure, joyful, flexible, and without sorrow or trouble. They vow to increase the bliss of the enlightened, the bliss of the unconceivable abode of buddhas, the bliss of the matchless concentration of buddhas, the bliss of unlimited compassion, the bliss of liberation, the bliss of immeasurable power, and the bliss of tranquillity detached from cognition. Practitioners dedicate their virtues to enabling others to fulfill their vows, perfect transcendent practices, stabilize an indestructible determination for enlightenment, give up conceit, and attain the clear, sharp senses of the enlightened.

Fourth is dedication reaching all places. Practitioners of this dedication intend the power of their virtues to reach all places, all things, all worlds, all beings, all lands, all space, all time, and all speech; they pray that their virtues may include all truths, all enlightening practices, all enlightened spiritual powers, all enlightening methods of meditation, all educational activities, and all ways of adaptive response to others. Practitioners are able to develop people to maturity; beautify and purify lands; avoid spoiling works; understand all things; comprehend ultimate reality apart from desire; achieve pure faith; and have clear, sharp faculties. They are able to appear responsively in all worlds, expound truth in all places, travel psychically in response to others' minds, attain comprehensive recollective and explanatory powers, and attain instantaneous universal perception reaching all places.

Fifth is dedication of infinite stores of virtue. The infinite stores, or treasuries, of virtue dedicated by the practitioners are attained by repentance and removal of obstructions caused by past actions, by paying respect to all the enlightened, by requesting the enlightened to teach, by listening to the teachings and putting them into practice, and by rejoicing at the virtues of all buddhas and all people in all times. These practitioners are aware that all things are like phantoms and illusions, yet they cultivate the pure deeds characteristic of the enlightened; they enter into inconceivable freedom yet employ skill in expedient means to perform the work of the enlightened and illumine the world. They dedicate all their virtues to all fields of enlightenment, to all those working for enlightenment, to all the enlightened, to enlightenment itself, to all universal vows, to all essential ways of emancipation, to purifying all realms of being, to seeing the enlightened appear in all worlds, to seeing the life of the enlightened as infinite, to seeing the enlightened teaching throughout the cosmos, and to assuring the development of all people.

Sixth is dedication that stabilizes all roots of goodness, causing them to endure. Practitioners exercise all manner of generosity, including the giving of right teachings and the giving of protection. As they exercise this generosity, the practitioners develop mental control by which they practice dedication, controlling the body and controlling sensation, conception, action, and consciousness. When they give material things to people, they pray that people may attain corresponding qualities: for example, when they give clothing, they pray that people may develop a sense of shame and conscience; when they give flowers, they pray that people may become pleasing to all they meet; when they give perfumes, they pray that people may become generous; when they give bedding, they pray that people may become wise; when they give shelter, they pray that people may become peaceful; when they give lamps, they pray that people may become illuminated; when they give medicines, they pray that people may become mentally as well as physically healthy.

Seventh is dedication according to all sentient beings. Practitioners of this dedication cultivate virtues by the power of pure determination for enlightenment and give people what they need without any psychological artifice, without expectation, without desire for reputation, without regret, without irritation; they extend compassion and mercy to all unremittingly, not letting conditions stop their generosity and never growing weary of it. Through this generosity they develop an unattached mind, an unfettered mind, a liberated mind, a strong mind, a profound mind, a concentrated mind, a nonsubjective mind, a controlled mind, an undistracted mind, an understanding mind, a dedicated mind, a penetrating mind. In dedicating their virtues, they pray that people may lack nothing material or moral, experience peace and happiness, get rid of confusion and delusion, attain pure impartial minds, and attain all knowledge without difficulty.

Eighth is dedication characteristic of true Thusness. Practitioners of this dedication attain clear and perfect recollection and get beyond confusion and disturbance. They vow to attain freedom of thought, word, and deed so as to carry out enlightening practices; they vow to develop infinite generosity, to cultivate all enlightening practices, to master all the teachings, to arrive at the realm of universal knowledge, to remember the buddhas of all times, to live in the world unwearied to edify others, and to activate countless liberative techniques of thought and wisdom. Practitioners dedicate these virtues without clinging to the world or to people, not relying on anything, free from discriminatory views, in accord with all impartial truths.

Ninth is dedication without bondage or attachment. Practitioners of this dedication honor and respect emancipation from compulsive routines, embodiment of all virtues, repentance of past acts, moral support of virtues, and expressions of respect for the enlightened. They dedicate their virtues with an unbound, unattached, liberated mind, to accomplish universally good thought, word, and deed without forming arbitrary notions of worlds or worldly things, of enlightenment or enlightened beings, of enlightening practices or ways of emancipation, of buddhas or their teachings, of training or not training people, of virtue or dedication, of self or others, of gifts or recipients, or of truth or knowledge. They do not become proud or conceited, yet they are not self-demeaning either; the virtues they cultivate are for the benefit of all conscious creatures, dedicated to the most honorable human state, the state of buddhahood.

Tenth is infinite dedication equal to the cosmos. For practitioners of this dedication, the giving of teaching is paramount, establishing the will for enlightenment in others. They are impartial, tireless in practicing good works, pure of heart, independent in knowledge. They vow to develop the ability to perfect all perspectives of universal freedom; the ability to absorb, retain, and expound true teachings; and to cultivate enlightening practice for the benefit of one and all. They also vow to fulfill the practice of unalloyed morality, nonreliance, nonacquisitiveness, nonattachment, noncontention, stabilization of good will, incomparable compassion, immutable joy, and undisturbed equanimity.

The next ten teachers represent to Sudhana the ten stages, which are expounded in the twenty-sixth book of *The Flower Ornament Scripture*. The first stage, the stage of joy, is characterized by calmness, happiness, ebullience, exaltation, delight, vigor, geniality, and freedom from anger. The practitioners of this stage become extremely joyful thinking of the enlightened ones and their teachings, of those working for enlightenment and their practices, of the ways of transcendence, and of the ability to help people. They become free from all fear by transcending the very idea of self, so they cannot be coerced by fear of ill repute, fear of death, fear of misery, or intimidation by crowds. Practitioners in this stage also make a preparatory study of the indications of all the stages, becoming versed in the problems and solutions of the stages, the attainments and cultivation of the stages, and the step-by-step progression through the stages. No longer interested in mundane satisfactions, practitioners attain a special power that fosters in them the elements that purify the stages: faith, compassion, kindness, relinquishment, indefatigability, knowledge of the teachings, knowledge of the world and humanity, modesty and conscience, stability, and association with the enlightened.

Second is the stage of purity, which is sought by way of ten dispositions of mind: honesty, gentleness, capability, docility, tranquillity, goodness, purity, nonattachment, broadmindedness, and magnanimity. In this stage practitioners naturally avoid killing, stealing, sexual misconduct, false speech, coarse speech, useless speech, covetousness, malevolence, and erroneous views.

Third is the stage of refulgence. Practitioners enter this stage by consciously focusing their minds on purity, stability, freedom from illusion, dispassion, nonregression, steadfastness, ardor, tirelessness, high-mindedness, and magnanimity. In this stage they also examine the impermanence, painfulness, impurity, unreliability, destructibility, instability, and momentariness of all that is conditioned, thus causing their minds to become yet more liberated from conditioned things and directed towards enlightened knowledge. Practitioners cultivate nine levels of meditation, up to the stage of neither perception nor nonperception, and experience many kinds of miracles and extradimensional powers, such as clairvoyance, clairaudience, knowledge of the past, and ability to go in and out of extraordinary states without falling under the sway of those states.

Fourth is the stage of blazing radiance. Practitioners attain this stage by entering into the radiance of the Teaching through ten ways of contemplation: contemplation of the realms of beings, of the realms of the world, of the realms of phenomena and principles, of the realm of space, of the realm of consciousness, of the realm of desire, of the realm of form, of the realm of the formless, of the realm of high-minded devotion, and of the realm of inclinations of the magnanimous mind. Practitioners at this stage examine inner and outer phenomena with precise awareness, getting rid of worldly desire and dejection; they strive for the development, enhancement, and preservation of good states and for the lessening, elimination, and prevention of bad states. They also develop the bases of spiritual powers, the elements of the path to liberation, and the various branches of enlightenment.

Fifth is the stage difficult to conquer. Practitioners enter this stage by impartial attention to purity of the teachings of past, present, and future buddhas; to purity of conduct, to purity of mind; to purity of removal of opinion, doubt, uncertainty, and perplexity; to purity of knowledge of what to apply and what to relinquish; to purity of the final discernment and realization of all the elements of enlightenment; and to purity of perfecting all people. They attain unwavering attention and become familiar with both conventional and ultimate truths. As they meditate on all truths, practitioners also develop skills in practical arts and sciences, according to the needs of the people of the time.

Sixth is the stage of presence. Practitioners enter this stage by observing phenomena in terms of their equality in having no ultimate definition, in having no fixed origin, in being apart from any concept or notion of things, in being primordially pure, in neither coming nor going, in being existent in some sense and nonexistent in another, and in being like dreams or reflected images. They observe the formation and disintegration of worlds, they realize that the origins of worldly ways are all rooted in attachment to self. This leads them to a thorough examination of the process of conditioning, followed by liberating absorption in emptiness, signlessness, and wishlessness. Practitioners in this stage furthermore develop unbreakable intent and become immune to delusive influences.

Seventh is the stage of going far, in which practitioners are proficient in concentration on emptiness, wishlessness, and signlessness; enter into selflessness and transcend ideas of personality; yet still accumulate virtue and knowledge and do not give up practicing infinite kindness, compassion, joy, and equanimity. They detach from the world yet work to beautify the world; whereas practitioners arrive at extinction in the sixth stage, in the seventh stage they plunge into extinction and emerge from it in each mental instant, without being overcome by extinction. They live in the world by willpower for the sake of others, without being stained by the ills of the world; they become calm and serene, yet they can be passionate as an expedient without, however, becoming inflamed by passion.

Eighth is the stage of immovability. In this stage practitioners fully realize that all things are nonconceptual, accessible to nonconceptual knowledge. They become wholly detached from mind, intellect, consciousness, thought, and ideation and thus become free from all striving in thought, word, and deed; no actions based on views, passions, or intentions become manifest in them. Nevertheless, even though they have attained peace and liberation, practitioners in this stage who are supported by their past vows of complete enlightenment do not become complacent but are further inspired to seek infinite knowledge. By means of the knowledge they develop, they are able to distinguish many paths in the world, show all aspects of virtue, control their own resolution, know the past and future, repel deluding influences, and carry out enlightening activities in endless contexts without regression.

Ninth is the stage of good mind. Practitioners in this stage gain accurate knowledge of good, bad, neutral, mundane, and transmundane actions. They also know how people get entangled in afflictions, acts, senses, resolutions, dispositions, inclinations, propensities, and habits; and they know what is beneficial or not. Practitioners also know all about the compartmentalization of mind, the complexity of mind, how the mind becomes defiled, how the mind becomes bound and liberated, and how it creates illusions. Learning to become expert teachers, practitioners in this stage develop analytic knowledge of principles, meanings, expressions, and elocution; and they attain mental command of the teachings through concentration spells, learning to teach in accord with the dispositions, faculties, and inclinations of the people with whom they are working.

Tenth is the stage of cloud of teaching, emblematic of the ability of practitioners to teach like clouds showering rain. In this stage—which is also called the stage of anointment or coronation, symbolizing anointment or coronation with the crown of all knowledge—practitioners attain incalculable numbers of special concentrations and gain access to the higher knowledges characteristic of the enlightened. They attain inconceivable liberation; infinite powers of recollection; and ability to receive, absorb, and hold the revelations of the mysteries of complete enlightenment.

The next ten teachers after this represent the eleventh stage, the practice of Universal Good. Universally Good, the name of the supernal bodhisattva Samantabhadra, who represents the active manifestation of the totality of all enlightening practice, is the fifty-third and final benefactor visited by the pilgrim Sudhana in the tale of the *Gandavyuha*. These teachers of the eleventh stage transmit ten major aspects of this totality: producing knowledge from compassion, consistently remembering all truths through mastery of knowledge and compassion, teaching worldly principles everywhere, penetrating the mysteries of writing and higher knowledge of arts, helping people by both conventional and mystical arts and sciences, pure liberation by being in the world without clinging thoughts, illumination by pure knowledge working in the world, finding infinite forms in formlessness, speaking so as to reveal truth, and living in the world with complete knowledge and compassion.

The fifty-first teacher is Maitreya, the Loving One, who is thought of as the Buddha of the Future. The Heaven of Satisfaction, where the higher personality of Maitreya awaits incarnation on earth, is extensively described in the twenty-third and twenty-fourth books of *The Flower Ornament Scripture*, and the encounter between the pilgrim Sudhana and an earthly personality of Maitreya is now described in similar grandeur and detail. Maitreya opens the door to a building of cosmic proportions, the inner dimensions of which Sudhana finds even greater, containing infinite numbers of buildings of equal size. In these buildings Sudhana sees the entire panorama of Maitreya's career, feeling the passage of eons in a short period of time, learning the way to enlightenment in one lifetime.

Maitreya finally sends Sudhana back to Manjushri, who first sent him on his journey for knowledge and who now becomes his fifty-second benefactor. Manjushri in turn, reaching out to Sudhana beyond time and space, illumines him with the light of infinite knowledge and leads him into endless mental command, presence of mind, concentration, and higher knowledge, plunging him into the sphere of practice of Universal Good.

The vision of Samantabhadra, the Universally Good bodhisattva, finally ushers the pilgrim Sudhana into the ultimate range of the enlightenment experience. Samantabhadra is introduced as a prototype of the bodhisattva effort in the third book of *The Flower Ornament Scripture*, in terms similar to the Sufis' global Assembly of Saints and the Taoists' Celestial Government: "Universal Good always fills the universe with various bodies flowing everywhere, with concentration, psychic power, skill and strength, teaching widely without hindrance in a universal voice." Then the final chapter of the final book of the scripture describes the cosmic vision of Universal Good and the merging of the pilgrim with the total being of Universal Good and the final realization of enlightenment.

Entry into the Realm of Reality

The Guide

THE INHERENT BASELESSNESS of physical and mental objects is called reality. The interpenetration of one and many, the disappearance of the boundaries of the real and artificial, of affirmation and negation, is called the realm.

Also, the realm that is purely concomitant with knowledge and not with emotional perceptions is called the realm of reality.

Furthermore, actually to realize that the seeds of unenlightened consciousness are purely functions of knowledge and are not subsumed by delusion is the sphere of independent knowledge and is called the realm of reality.

What is more, since the substance of knowledge has no abode and is all-pervasive, one sees the absolute and the mundane to be totally inconceivable. In the infinite realm where all beings and objects reflect one another, buddha-lands are multiplied and remultiplied, sages and ordinary people are the same whole, and the forms of objects interpenetrate. This is called the realm of reality.

And when one subtle sound pervades the universe, a single hair measures infinity, views of great and small disappear, others and self are the same body, conditioned consciousness and feelings are gone, and knowledge pervades without obstruction, this is called entry into the realm of reality.

1565

This is the eternal goal of all buddhas of all times, without beginning or end. The progressive practices of the preceding stages all have this as their substance. At this point practice is complete; allowing knowledge to act, it returns to its original state—fundamentally there is no change.

As to the setting of this scripture, it takes place in the human world to illustrate that the garden of the human world is the very garden of the reality realm, that the nature of living beings is the nature of the reality realm, and that the world of living beings is the world of true awakening.

Manjushri, the spirit of wisdom, wanted to induce the pilgrim Sudhana to trust in the fundamental unshakable knowledge that is inherently pure and has no origin or extinction, no cultivation or witness, to induce him to become a bodhisattva, an enlightening being, of the stage of faith. So Manjushri explained enlightened teachings for Sudhana, to inspire the thought of enlightenment in him.

Since the thought of enlightenment is not learned or cultivated, the thought of enlightenment is always clearly self-evident as long as we carry out enlightening practices to quell habit energy.

It is as when clouds disperse in the sky; the sky is itself clear, so there is no further search for clear sky.

Just carry out the myriad practices of compassion and wisdom as means of stabilizing enlightenment. If any practice is not understood or not carried out, or if there is any grasping and rejecting, then there is an obstacle, and so the thought of enlightenment is not in its complete state, since enlightening action is itself the thought of enlightenment.

So once Sudhana had awakened the thought of enlightenment, he asked Manjushri how to learn to act as an enlightening being and practice the path of enlightening beings—he asked no more about the thought of enlightenment.

Because the methods of progress expounded in the previous assemblies of the *Avatamsaka Sutra* had not yet been realized by an ordinary human being, in the *Gandavyuha* Manjushri wants to make Sudhana a signpost for later generations of seekers.

Also, the names of the teachers and their abodes—people holy and ordinary, spirits, royalty, mendicants, lay people, non-Buddhists, humans, celestials, males and females—represent certain principles.

Furthermore, the South, the direction of Sudhana's pilgrimage, is used to stand for truth, clarity, and openness. When you arrive at open, clear, true knowledge without subjectivity, then everywhere is the South.

Therefore Manjushri sent Sudhana south to call on spiritual friends and benefactors, each of whom sends him onwards that he may progress and not dawdle over past learning. This is why the friends always praise the virtues of those Sudhana has yet to meet.

In the realm of principle, Manjushri stands for knowledge of the fundamental. Samantabhadra stands for knowledge of differentiation, and Maitreya stands for the uncreate realization within Manjushri and Samantabhadra.

These three principles are all in the fifty spiritual friends—representing the five ranks of enlightenment—that Sudhana meets on his pilgrimage, so there are fifty-three teachers.

Since the fifty teachings of the spiritual friends each has cause and effect—as in other books of the *Avatamsaka Sutra,* where there are ten bodhisattvas and ten buddhas to represent cause and effect—this makes one hundred. Add to this the basic ten ways of transcendence and this makes one hundred and ten, the number of cities Sudhana is said to have passed through.

The Fifty-three Teachers

1. MEGHASHRI

First Sudhana climbed the Mountain of Marvelous Peaks, saw the monk Meghashri ("Glorious Clouds"), and realized the abode of inspiration.

Clouds have four meanings. They are everywhere, repre-

senting concentration. They bear moisture, representing virtue.
They shade and cover, representing compassion. They shower
rain, representing knowledge. Hence the name *Glorious Clouds*.

The significance of monkhood is the cessation of opinionated argument. The word used means "stopping contention."
When one is without thoughts, still and quiet as a mountain,
then formless subtle principles become evident.

Sudhana climbed the mountain to its furthest reach and
looked all over for Meghashri. This symbolizes use of the power
of calm observation to gain access to the abode of the enlightened.

Sudhana saw Meghashri on a separate peak. This symbolizes going through expedient meditation methods to get into
the original state where there is neither concentration nor
distraction.

Meghashri was walking slowly, symbolizing being undisturbed. Walking around represents not lingering in concentration trance.

Meghashri saw all living beings as the body of enlightenment and saw the mundane world as like light, like a reflection,
neither real nor false, inherently undefiled. He maintained the
integrity of ordinary vision, so he saw living beings. He maintained the integrity of objective vision, so for him all objects
were insubstantial. He maintained the integrity of the vision of
knowledge, so he could magically produce objects. He saw the
body of buddhas to be free of both being and nonbeing.

Therefore Meghashri told Sudhana that he always saw
infinite buddhas of the ten directions and knew the teaching of
universal vision through the light of knowledge attained by
recollection of the realm of buddhas.

2. SAGARAMEGHA

Next Sudhana went to the country of Sagaramukha
("Ocean Door"), saw the monk Sagaramegha ("Ocean
Cloud"), and realized the abode of preparing the ground.

Spontaneous discipline is like the ocean. Not retaining the corpse of birth and death is the ocean door. Because he was able to make the ocean of birth and death itself into the ocean of great knowledge and always benefit people with this principle, the monk was called Ocean Cloud.

Having attained the light of highest knowledge, using it to observe current subjective and objective worlds to develop all knowledge, he knew that the ocean of ignorance and pain caused by the twelvefold process of conditioning is wholly the vast ocean of essence of the buddhas of all times, and that there is no place to attain buddhahood outside the ocean of birth and death. Therefore Ocean Cloud said he had been living in that country for twelve years.

Because this ocean of essence is not finite and is full of knowledge and virtue, Ocean Cloud said the ocean was very deep and very wide and adorned with many treasures.

In ordinary people, the seven conditions of ignorance, restlessness, self-consciousness, name and form, sense receptors, contact, and reception are currently active, so they cling greedily and obstinately, thus forming the three conditions of craving, grasping, and becoming. From these three conditions develop the conditions of birth, aging, sickness, and death.

Being tossed about on the waves of pain in an endless circle, temporary students of individual liberation reject this in disgust and do not conceive great compassion. Therefore Sagaramegha directly used basic intuitive insight to illumine all at once the intrinsic baselessness of the substance and forms of conditioned production, all at once transforming it into an ocean of great knowledge.

This ocean produced a huge lotus, symbolizing the action of knowledge without taint. Because enlightened action is always in accord with knowledge, the flower covered the whole ocean.

When titans stand in the ocean, the water only comes up to their waists; because wise action does not sink into the ocean of birth and death, the lotus stem was held by titans.

As knowledge gives natural discipline to wash away mental defilement, water spirits showered fragrant water.

As objectless compassion responds without contrivance, the spirits bowed in reverence.

As knowledge is invincible, the embodiment of the buddha sitting on the lotus blossom was immensely tall. The function of knowledge is represented by the buddha extending his right hand. The reflection and combination of knowledge and action is represented by the buddha's laying his hand on Sagaramegha's head.

Knowledge of the fundamental is represented as the universal eye, knowledge of differentiation is represented as a scripture. Teachings are set up in consideration of people's faculties and states, and so, as people are infinite, the teachings are infinite.

So Sagaramegha said there was a buddha on the flower whose height reached to the summit of existence and that the buddha had reached out with his right hand, laid his hand on Sagaramegha's head and expounded the universal eye scripture, which is so vast that an ocean of ink and a brush made of mountains could not write out even a little of one statement of one doctrine of one book of the scripture. Sagaramegha said he had been keeping the scripture for twelve hundred years, alluding to the use of knowledge of expedients to overturn the twelve hundred afflictions and be liberated from them all.

3. SUPRATISHTHITA

The Sudhana went to a village on the seashore of Lanka, where he saw the monk Supratishthita ("Well Established") and realized the abode of practice.

Having contemplated the twelve links of conditioning, Sudhana reexamined current habit energies of discrimination active in his senses and found that they had all become seeds of knowledge, so he no longer lingered over them.

The mountain of Lanka is in the south seas, so high and

steep that it is nearly impossible to climb. Now that the ocean of birth and death had turned into the ocean of knowledge, Sudhana had found the way of ascent and rested peacefully in patience, not deluded by the bedevilments of birth and death. Therefore Sudhana saw the monk Supratishthita walking in the sky; because he dwelt neither in the world nor beyond the world, he "traveled in the sky."

Because the voice of the teaching had universal influence and the light of knowledge destroyed illusion, therefore the rain spirits produced thunder and lightning as offerings to the monk.

Because of his practical knowledge and compassion, his humility and self-discipline, bird maidens surrounded the monk respectfully.

Because of his mastery of use of the ten transcendent ways to benefit beings, the monk was honored by ten kings.

Because he had entered the door of freedom through great knowledge, the monk was unhindered by barriers of defilement and purity; all false states of existence melted away on contact, to become like the sky.

Therefore the monk said he had found the door of unob-structed liberation, swiftly serving buddhas everywhere, going throughout the ten directions in an instant of thought, going through walls, penetrating the earth, and walking on water, as if they were all space.

4. MEGHA

Then Sudhana went to the Dravidian city of Vajrapura, saw the grammarian Megha, and realized the abode of noble birth.

The significance of Dravidia is the melting away of mis-taken understandings by the teaching of sages. *Megha* means "Cloud," representing one who contains life-giving moisture and showers the rain of the teaching.

Sudhana saw Megha in the middle of the city, surrounded by thousands of people, expounding ways into truth through arrays of revolving letters.

The preceding teachers were all mendicants: Megha is a layman, to represent the fact that when transcendence of the world is achieved, transcendent knowledge is not divorced from the world. He was in the world yet unaffected by it, so he was "in the middle of the city." His knowledge body was free, interchanging with society, so he was "surrounded by thousands of people."

Revolving means turning completely. Since the fact that an individual word or sound has no inherent identity underlies infinite words and sounds, infinite words and infinite sounds are one word and one sound. Therefore one and many revolve around and embellish each other. All mundane phenomena are transmundane phenomena, and all transmundane phenomena are mundane phenomena.

When it is said that phenomena exist, each one is inherently empty; when it is said that phenomena do not exist, that does not destroy appearances. Therefore the absolute and the mundane, existence and nonexistence, completely change into each other and embellish each other. Since the totality, individuality, sameness, difference, integration, and disintegration of all phenomena simultaneously revolve around each other in an interrelated array, this is called the method of arrays of revolving letters.

Megha is personally a layman, while the spirit of enlightenment is an absolute principle. Mundane truth should obey absolute truth, so when Megha heard that Sudhana had awakened the thought of enlightenment, he immediately got down from his seat and bowed.

Because he wanted to inspire Sudhana to further progress, Megha told him that he only knew this teaching method of concentration spells of subtle sound.

5. MUKTAKA

Next Sudhana went to Vanavasin ("Forest Dweller"), saw the distinguished man Muktaka ("The Liberated One"), and realized the abode of full equipment with skill in means.

Muktaka was in the midst of the mundane, the same as Megha. The wise use places where there are many beings living and dying for meditation communities, and meditation communities are called forests, so Megha had indicated a community in the South called Forest Dweller.

Indicative of the fact that the twelve links of conditioning—ignorance, restlessness, self-consciousness, name and form, sense receptors, contact, reception, craving, grasping, becoming, birth, aging and death—are the substance of meditation, Sudhana traveled for twelve years to get to Vanavasin.

Before, with Sagaramegha, he had observed the twelve links of conditioned life and attained transmundane awareness; here he neither destroys conditioned life nor clings to conditioned life. Traveling means not dwelling.

When Sudhana saw Muktaka he threw himself bodily on the ground, because the essence of the body-mind cluster is itself meditation; he also joined his palms, symbolic of the nonduality of the absolute and mundane.

Because the subject of trance is immensely deep, all-pervasive, and completely fulfilling, Muktaka entered absorption into a concentration formula for the whirlpool of boundless buddha-fields, whereat there appeared in the ten directions the enlightenment sites of buddhas as numerous as atoms in ten buddha-fields.

The whirlpool has the meaning of depth, the number ten has the meaning of fulfillment. In absorption, the buddhas resulting from his own knowledge and his own causal practices appeared in profound stillness, so Muktaka said that when he entered absorption in trance he saw ten buddhas in the ten directions, with their ten chief assistants.

Because buddha is the accord of the inner mind with reality, therefore one thought in harmony is a moment of buddhahood, while a continuum of thoughts in harmony is a continuum of buddhas.

There is no country outside mind, no buddha outside mind, so the Liberated One Muktaka said that if he wanted to see buddhas such as the Buddha of Infinite Light in the World of Bliss, he could see them as soon as he thought of them.

Because the whole realm of the infinite compassionate acts of all knowledge is a meditation community, inherently unimpeded, Muktaka said he had only delved into the ins and outs of this way to liberation through unimpeded manifestation.

6. SARADHVAJA

Then Sudhana went to the tip of the continent, saw the monk Saradhvaja, and realized the abode of the correct state of mind.

Because Saradhvaja had reached the ultimate boundary of transmundane knowledge, he "lived on the tip of the continent." Because he had only attained the great compassion by which worldlings transcend the world and had not attained the great compassion by which to enter the mundane and share its confinements, he was a "monk." Because his oceanic knowledge could smash through delusion, he was called Ocean Banner.*

Sudhana saw Saradhvaja by the side of a place for walking meditation. A place for walking represents function, concentration in quiescence. This represents having tranquillity based on function. That Saradhvaja was sitting by the side of the promenade represents not dwelling in quiescent function, being spontaneous and free. He was detached from his breathing, representing tranquillity and function in accord with inner reality, since essence is inherently omnipresent and is not going in or out.

So Sudhana saw Saradhvaja in a trance next to a promenade detached from his breathing.

Grandees, householders, and Brahmins are worldly people who practice virtue, while feet are means of travel; so Sudhana saw grandees, householders, and Brahmins issuing from Saradhvaja's feet and traveling throughout the ten directions.

---

*Chinese translates the name as if it were Sagaradhvaja.

Warriors are a governing class, Brahmins are a priestly class. Knees are joints that bend and extend freely. Because of Saradhvaja's freedom of pure knowledge, warriors and priests issued from his knees.

The midsection is the place of worldly desires, and wizards are people without desire. By knowledge Saradhvaja magically produced actions similar to those of sentient beings yet was without desire himself, so wizards as numerous as sentient beings issued from his waist.

Water spirits symbolize the rain of the Teaching enlivening beings, and the sides of the body are covered, so a multitude of water spirits issue from Saradhvaja's sides.

The heart has the meaning of bravery, the auspicious symbol on a buddha's heart has the meaning of endless purity of conduct. Titans represent not sinking in the sense of not sinking into the ocean of birth and death because of diligence in all practices. Therefore a multitude of titans issued from the auspicious symbol on Saradhvaja's heart.

Because the practices of all vehicles are not left out in the development of sentient beings yet the two vehicles of individual liberation turn their backs on the great function of the compassion and knowledge of buddhas, multitudes of followers of the two vehicles of individual liberation issued from Saradhvaja's back.

The shoulders have the sense of bearing burdens, while fearsome supernatural beings have the sense of protection. Because they bear the great work and protect sentient beings, therefore a multitude of supernatural beings issued from Saradhvaja's shoulders.

Celestial musicians are the spirit of music, and the abdomen represents the containing of myriad truths. Since they always sing praises of enlightening truths, celestial musicians issued from Saradhvaja's abdomen.

An emperor signifies the turning of the wheel of the Teaching, so a multitude of emperors issued from Saradhvaja's face.

The sun breaks through the darkness, so suns issued from Saradhvaja's eyes.

In the midst of birth and death, practical wisdom is foremost, so enlightening beings issued from Saradhvaja's head.

Because their knowledge is most elevated, buddhas issued from the crown of Saradhvaja's head.

This all illustrates the use of knowledge of emptiness to produce various bodies, creating multitudes of emanations filling the ten directions, developing, educating, and adorning sentient beings while in essence being like space, completely free from cogitation. Therefore Saradhvaja produced the appearances of these multitudes of beings in the midst of trance.

Sudhana also saw Saradhvaja producing countless light beams from his pores—his whole body was the unimpeded light of truth of the body of reality.

Sudhana stood there for a day and a night, two days and nights, seven days and nights, a fortnight, a month, finally six months and six days, until Saradhvaja emerged from trance. One day and one night represents the fulfillment of generosity. Seven days and seven nights represent the seven branches of ethics. The full fortnight represents the fulfillment of forbearance (a fortnight is half a month, and forbearance is a half in the sense of only benefiting oneself and not actively benefiting others). One month symbolizes the fulfillment of diligence. Six months represent the sixth abode, the correct state of mind. The six days represent the fulfillment of the sixth transcendent way, that of wisdom.

Because he had only attained the pure love of unaffected action and had not yet attained the great compassion and skill in means to cooperate with sentient beings, Saradhvaja said he had only attained this method of absorption in transcendent wisdom.

7. ASHA

Next Sudhana went to Samudravetali, saw Asha, and realized the abode of nonregression.

Samudravetali ("Keeper of the Ocean Door") is the tide. This represents reality adapting to evolve sentient beings in a timely manner.

Asha was in a park called Samantavyuha, which is translated as "Ubiquitous Adornment." This represents countless practices taking place in life and death constituting a ubiquitous array of adornments.

Being greatly compassionate yet unaffected, Asha was a lay devotee. Being gentle and of good will, she appeared as a woman, though she was not conscious of being a woman.

Sudhana saw the park and its buildings, ponds, and other features as being adorned with jewels and saw Asha's features to be ineffably beautiful, because they were an environment and a person produced by respect for the enlightened and service to life, the countless practices of knowledge and compassion.

Because of the combining of compassion and knowledge, Asha said that the buddhas of the ten directions all came to explain truths to her. She also said that the eighty-four quadrillion beings living in the park carrying out the same practices as she were all irreversible in progess towards supreme perfect enlightenment, because she used the eighty-four thousand afflictions to appear to be like them in order to meet and guide them, so that they had arrived at the original unity of the essence of life and death and enlightened knowledge.

As she would enter into life and death to educate sentient beings—while realizing that life, death, sentient beings, and the teaching activity are all nirvanic processes that neither come into nor go out of existence, and are ultimately peaceful—she said she had attained this state of sorrowless well-being.

8. BHISHMOTTARANIRGHOSHA

Then Sudhana went to the land of Nalayur on the coast, saw the seer Bhishmottaranirghosha, and realized the abode of youthful nature, or innocence.

The seer lived on the seacoast because he had used transcendent vows to initiate works of wisdom to complement his compassion, merging them into one, and only thus had attained effortless great function, benefiting multitudes without even thinking about it, like the ocean tide thundering and washing effortlessly.

The land of Nalayur is called Not Lazy, in the sense of the homeland of the seer being the use of effortless knowledge to help beings tirelessly.

Bhishmottaranirghosha is called He Who Utters A Fearsome Sound, in the sense that when he spoke he crushed followers of aberrant doctrines. Because he used knowledge to adapt to different religions without having different views, he is represented as a seer.

Because he had both knowledge and compassion, the virtues that protect beings, the seer was seen in a grove variously adorned. The seer himself was sitting on an antelope hide spread on some grasses, symbolizing a state of few desires.

Because the seer had myriad practices in him, he is represented as having ten thousand followers, wearing deerskin.

Because the realms of the "dusts"—sense experiences—all return to the "ground" of knowledge, Sudhana cast his body on the ground.

Because effortless knowledge is unshakable, the seer said he had attained a liberation called "unsurpassed banner," emblematic of invincibility.

Because the seer's union of knowledge and environment was comprehensive, when he took Sudhana's hand the pilgrim saw himself going to buddhas in the ten directions as numerous as atoms in ten buddha-fields.

The gesture of taking the hand represents mystic empowerment: because the eighth stage is the beginning of effortless knowledge, people at this stage may linger in quietude and be unable to let knowledge and compassion work spontaneously. Then it is necessary for sages to add support and promote inspiration. Thus when the seer took his hand, Sudhana was helped and supported by the sage in his entry into reality.

Once one has entered reality, one is always thus of one's own power, just as one does not carry a boat about after crossing a river in it. Therefore when the seer let go of his hand, Sudhana returned to where he had been before.

9. JAYOSHMAYATANA

Then Sudhana went to Ishana, saw Jayoshmayatana, and realized the abode of the spiritual prince.

Ishana is called Long and Straight, symbolizing the use of inclusive teaching to extend the straight path, making one's abode in having no false pretenses.

Jayoshmayatana the Brahmin is called Overcoming Heat because he used knowledge to adapt to falsehood, his power able to overcome the poisonous heat of emotional afflictions; entering into spiritual function, he appeared to be like a Hindu ascetic, roasting his body with fires all around under the burning sun, yet in reality he was leading aberrant cultists back to right knowledge.

There was a razor mountain there, symbolizing the razor of truth cutting through confusion. Below was a bonfire, representing the light of adamantine knowledge. Because he understood inherent liberation and could use his energy freely, he had no fear and could show and remove the emotional afflictions of beings in the long night of ignorance; so the Brahmin climbed the razor mountain and threw his body into the bonfire.

Because it is ordinarily unthinkable to contravene the objective order, when Jayoshmayatana urged Sudhana to climb the razor mountain and jump into the fire, Sudhana hesitated.

Because this inconceivable realm of energy use must be entered into experientially, celestial spirits appeared in the sky and sang praises of Jayoshmayatana's virtues, urging Sudhana not to doubt.

When his knowledge meshed with the total event, Sudhana entered in experientially; so he climbed the razor mountain and leaped. Before he was even halfway down he attained well-established mental focus, and the moment he hit the fire he also attained mental focus on the bliss of tranquillity.

Because he used this one practice to show endless different practices according to people's different inclinations, Jayoshmayatana said he had attained liberation into an inexhaustible sphere.

10. MAITRAYANI

Then Sudhana went to the city of Simhavijurmbhita, saw the girl Maitrayani, and realized the abode of coronation.

As she was spontaneously compassionate yet unaffected by the habits of attraction that result in bondage to existence, Maitrayani is represented as a girl. As her compassion was born of knowledge and she was independent and fearless, her father was a king called Lion Banner.

In this abode of coronation, knowledge and compassion completely include the knowledge and compassion of the five ranks, with no different road, so Maitrayani is portrayed as having a retinue of five hundred girls.

As she was able to abide in the abode of buddhas, containing the causes and effects of buddhahood through the five ranks, she lived in a palace of radiant jewels. As she used the practice of great compassion based on all knowledge to expound the five-part body of reality, the pure teaching covering sentient beings, she sat on a seat set on sandalwood legs, draped with nets of gold strings and arrayed with celestial cloth.

Since all beings entered this chamber of compassion in this palace of knowledge and the enlightening beings of the five ranks all sojourned there, Sudhana saw countless people going in the royal palace.

The crystal base of the palace stands for the clear purity of the body of reality. The lapis lazuli pillars stand for maintenance of pure conduct. The diamond walls stand for protection by knowledge. The golden fences stand for outward strictness in discipline. The bright windows stand for illumination of the ordinary world by the light of the Teaching.

Because her heart was undefiled, Maitrayani was born with golden skin; because she covered living beings with knowledge, she was born with jet-black eyes and hair.

So Sudhana saw the objects and person in the palace thus magnificently adorned.

And since each principle contains all principles, and they interpenetrate simultaneously, so knowledge and objects interpenetrate on infinite levels; therefore when the girl had Sudhana look at the palace, he saw the features of the realms of all the buddhas contained in each wall, each pillar, and each mirror image.

The girl said this was the medium of wisdom in the total array, which she had learned from buddhas as numerous as grains of sand in thirty-six Ganges rivers, entering into a different aspect of it with each buddha.

The medium of the total array refers to one rank including all ranks. The ten abodes, ten practices, and ten dedications are three decades; the ten beliefs, or ten stages of faith, are faith in these three teachings. The ten stages and the eleventh stage are also just developments of these three teachings, involving no new principles. So these three teachings produce the six ranks; this is the reason for the number thirty-six.

The six ranks are included in this abode, and each rank has inexhaustible practical undertakings; though the characteristics of the practices are different, the principles are not different— this is the significance of entering into different aspects of the Teaching with each of the buddhas, who are as numerous as grains of sand in thirty-six Ganges rivers.

Summary of the First Ten Teachers

1. Meghashri elucidated the way of meditation to bring out the buddha-knowledge in one's own mind and see the realms of the buddhas everywhere.

2. Sagaramegha elucidated the way to contemplate the twelve conditioning links in the ocean of birth and death as the fundamentally pure ocean of buddha-lands.

3. Supratishthita elucidated the way to emerge unimpeded into the ordinary world with the freedom of the knowledge of reality.

4. Megha elucidated the way to live in the ordinary world and cultivate worldly letters and penetrate all they imply.

5. Muktaka elucidated the way of spontaneous meditation on the body containing the countless realms of buddha-fields.

6. Saradhvaja elucidated the way to the unimpeded spiritual power of tranquil function freed from bondage.

7. Asha elucidated the way to live in the world to develop and extend great compassion.

8. Jayoshmayatana elucidated the way of asceticism to contact aberrant cultists.

9. Bhishmottaranirghosha elucidated the way to appear similar to misguided people by means of effortless knowledge.

10. Maitrayani elucidated the way of simultaneous completeness of knowledge and compassion, including all ranks when knowledge is fulfilled and compassion complete.

The next ten teachers represent the ten practices for self-help and helping others. It is not that the ten abodes do not include self-help and helping others, but the polish of the teachings of the ten practices is necessary lest one be incapable of autonomy in the different realms of the world.

11. SUDARSHANA

Next Sudhana went to Trinayana, saw the mendicant Sudarshana, and realized the practice of joy.

Trinayana means "Three Eyes." The eye of knowledge observes faculties, the objective eye knows principles, and the eye of wisdom distinguishes right from wrong. These three are originally one, which is given three names according to function.

If one lacks these three eyes, one is also deluded already and so cannot help others. Therefore the name of the land is Three Eyes.

Sudhana sees a mendicant for the first of the practices because it is possible to enter the world and integrate illumination beneficially for others, inducing them to end contention, only when one's own mind is unattached to the world.

The practices involved in adaptation to the world are many, as many as trees in a forest. Their purpose is to enter birth and death to liberate beings from birth and death—and also to induce beings to make compassionate commitments to go back into birth and death to liberate yet others, going on and on in this way, like one lamp lighting a hundred thousand lamps so that all darkness is illumined and the light never ends. This is the meaning of going and returning. Thus the story says Sudhana saw the mendicant walking around in a forest, emblematic of this process.

The mendicant's appearance as a young man signifies ability to carry out practical actions. His handsome features stand for correctness of action. His hair curled regularly to the right, symbolizing his action in accord with the Way. He had a topknot of flesh on top of his head, symbolizing loftiness of knowledge and fullness of virtue. His skin was golden, symbolizing clarity of heart and purity of intellect. His forehead was broad, flat, and square, symbolizing breadth of knowledge and vision. His lips were red and clean, symbolizing skillful explanation of the principle of emptiness. He had an auspicious sign on his chest, symbolizing clarity and coolness of wise action. His fingers were webbed, symbolic of using the Teaching to scoop sentient beings up out of the ocean of suffering.

Because his practice of saving beings was universal, he was surrounded by celestial spirits. Because he could adapt the Teaching to people's faculties, his method being without fixed method and his teaching being without fixed dogma, spirits of direction guided him whichever way he turned. Because his conduct was undefiled, footstep-following spirits held lotuses for him to walk on.

As he used meditation to manifest the production of knowledge and wisdom, so the earth spirits revealed jewel mines to him. Because he was elevated yet humble, the polar mountain spirits bowed to him. He spoke elegantly, causing others to admire him; breeze signifies verbal teaching, and flowery fragrance signifies appreciation, so the wind spirits gave off a flowery fragrant breeze.

Because he was at the beginning of the ten practices, he is represented as young. He included the three teachings of the ten abodes, ten practices, and ten dedications all in one practice without leaving the eightfold correct path, and this lifetime was a lifetime without before or after, beginning or end; so Sudarshana said he was young and had only recently left home, but he had in this lifetime cultivated pure conduct in the company of as many buddhas as sand grains in thirty-eight Ganges rivers.

Because the moment delusion disappears an instant and all time interpenetrate, there being no far or near in knowledge, each atom containing oceans of lands, Sudarshana said he had cultivated pure conduct with some buddhas for a day and a night, with others up to untold eons.

12. INDRIYESHVARA

Then Sudhana went to Sumukha, saw the boy Indriyeshvara by a river, and realized beneficial practice.

The land symbolizes the fragrance of morality scenting everywhere, the river symbolizes the undefiled discipline to enter the world autonomously, eventually to enter the ocean of knowledge, just as rivers flow to the sea.

Because play is buddha-work, Sudhana saw the boy playing in the sand.

For him the substance of discipline was in using practical and artistic genius to enter the world and yet go beyond the world, just as for Sagaramegha the substance of discipline was in identifying the ocean of birth and death with the ocean of knowledge.

For the boatman, a later teacher, the substance of discipline was in carrying people across, not staying on this shore or on the further shore. For the night goddess of joyful eyes, another teacher, the substance of discipline was great compassion.*

According to the rank, progress is not the same; but when knowledge penetrates, every rank is included. Therefore the boy said he knew the teaching of higher knowledge of all practical arts and knew about writing, printing, analysis, medicine, industry, agriculture, commerce, and alchemy.

13. PRABHUTA

Then Sudhana went to Samudrapratishthana, saw the laywoman Prabhuta, and realized the practice of nonopposition.

The city where Prabhuta lived was called Ocean Foundation because her tolerance was like the ocean admitting a hundred rivers. Prabhuta was called Perfected because she perfected all practices through patience and tolerance.

Because of her patience, Prabhuta is depicted as physically beautiful, clothed in pure white, her hair hanging down. Because of her fulfillment of myriad practices, she is depicted as being surrounded by ten thousand maidens.

By means of the distribution of the cosmic network of knowledge of the real universe, the small contains infinity; and by the great heart of willpower of knowledge of the real universe, Prabhuta could satisfy the hunger of all living beings with a tiny morsel of food, yet without diminishing the food.

Because a single morsel of food is as extensive as the universe—food unlimited to inside or outside, center or extremes—Prabhuta said she had attained a way of liberation that was an infinite treasury of blessings and could feed an unlimited number of beings with a small vessel of food and drink.

Countless beings entered Prabhuta's home by its four

---

*See nos. 22 and 33.

doors, because they were received by the four infinite minds—infinite love, infinite compassion, infinite joy, and infinite equanimity.

14. VIDVAN

Then Sudhana went to Mahasambhava, saw the householder Vidvan, and realized the practice of indomitability.

Because his diligence produced great benefit, Vidvan's city was called Great Production; and because he observed faculties and examined phenomena, Vidvan was called the Knower. He is represented as a householder because he stayed in society to improve customs and morals.

As he used the practices of the four integrative methods and seven branches of enlightenment to live on the road of life and death unwearied, Vidvan was seen at a crossroads in the city, sitting on a pedestal made of seven precious substances.

Using diligence to equip himself with blessings and virtues and to eliminate suffering and poverty, Vidvan said he had attained a way of liberation that enabled him to produce treasuries of blessings at will.

Since both material and metaphysical generosity are produced by knowledge of emptiness and baselessness, therefore when countless beings came from various lands seeking from him what they desired, Vidvan looked up to the sky, and all they wanted descended from the sky; and he taught them truths according to their faculties.

In the first abode, one begins to understand the wisdom of buddha, and one is born in the home of the enlightened. In the fourth abode one quells worldly delusions, pure buddha-knowledge appears, and one is born in the home of the enlightened. In the eighth abode one is born in the house of the effortless knowledge of the enlightened. In the tenth abode, knowledge and compassion help everyone, one ascends to the rank of coronation, and one is born in the house of the enlightened.

Now in the fourth practice, by using the approach of

contemplating the emptiness of phenomena, this understanding produces liberation and quells remaining worldly habits; knowledge of the reality body appears, and one is born in the home of the enlightened. Thus Vidvan said that his companions had already been reborn in the family of buddhas.

15. RATNACHUDA

Then Sudhana went to Simhapota, saw the eminent Ratnachuda, and realized the practice of nonconfusion.

The city was called Lion Foundation to represent the fearlessness attained through meditation. The body of concentration pervades all practices: just as Muktaka in the fifth abode contained innumerable lands in himself and took for his meditation the provenance of objects from the body, here in the fifth practice the body is in function; so countless objects are all included in one meditation, reaching the crown of the Teaching—therefore Ratnachuda is called Jewel Topknot.

The silent function of the body of practice is always concentrated, undiminished in the midst of the marketplace of life and death; so Sudhana saw Ratnachuda in a marketplace.

Ratnachuda used meditation to embody the ten transcendent ways and the eight-fold right path, so he is represented as living in a building with ten stories and eight doors.

On the first floor of the building, food was being distributed, representing generosity. The other floors each represent one transcendent way; finally the top floor was filled with buddhas, representing knowledge. These ten floors completely take in the five ranks and include buddhahood. Since the substance was independent meditation in the real universe, the stories of the building were adorned by the ten transcendent ways within meditation.

Ratnachuda said that in the remote past he had played music and burned a ball of incense in offering to a buddha who came to the city and dedicated the merit to three points; and that for this he had been rewarded with such an abode.

The remoteness of that past event symbolizes the trancendence of feelings and entry into concentration. The music symbolizes explanation of truth. This represents producing insight through concentration.

The ball of incense represents one kind of "scent"—concentration—including the five kinds of "scent," the fivefold spiritual body consisting of discipline, concentration, insight, liberation, and the knowledge and vision of liberation.

The three points are always seeing the enlightened, always hearing truth, and always being free from poverty and misery. The message is that the substance or body of concentration has already been attained in the ten abodes, and now, in the meditational aspect of the ten practices, independence of tranquil function is attained. Ratnachuda's attainment of liberation of the treasury of infinite blessings means fulfillment of myriad practices within meditation.

16. SAMANTANETRA

Then Sudhana went to Vetramulaka, saw the perfumer Samantanetra, and realized the practice of good manifestation.

The land was called Reed Roots, because wisdom is deep and stable, penetrating to the wellspring of truth, just as reed roots reach deeply into the water table.

Samantanetra was called Universal Eye because he knew all through wisdom.

Because the gates of wisdom are manifold, lofty, and hard to enter, the city where Samantanetra lived was seen to have high walls. Because insight into emptiness has no boundaries, the streets were wide and even.

Samantanetra said he was skilled in curing diseases, meaning that he had learned conventional medicine; this also represents the Teaching. For example, illnesses associated with wind represent people who think too much, an affliction cured by counting breaths. Jaundices represent people with too much desire, an affliction cured by contemplation of impurity. Inflammatory illnesses represent people with too much foolishness, an affliction cured by contemplation of conditioning. Mental illnesses represent people who cling to subtle forms and are not free from bewilderment and extraordinary perceptions, an affliction cured by contemplation of the emptiness of phenomena. Illnesses caused by toxins represent the way possessiveness can produce binding and harmful actions. Illnesses associated with water represent craving, illnesses associated with fire represent anger. All these illnesses can be treated by the Teaching.

Samantanetra also said he was skilled at compounding perfumes. This means he practiced worldly arts, and it also represents the Teaching, as wisdom skillfully expounds the Teaching, whose fragrance perfumes the odors of evildoing to turn them into the scent of knowledge.

Samantanetra said he knew how to induce sentient beings to see buddhas everywhere and rejoice, using wisdom to cause all realms to enter the realm of buddhahood.

17. ANALA

Then Sudhana went to Taladhvaja, saw the king Anala, and realized the practice of nonattachment.

Taladhvaja is called Bright and Clean, because the bright and clean knowledge and wisdom that goes beyond the world also enters the world to practice compassion, observing people's faculties so as to be able to harmonize with them, not contacting people randomly—hence the name of the city.

King Anala is called Tireless because he helped beings masterfully and never tired of helping them. Because King Anala used myriad activities to enter the world, Sudhana saw him surrounded by ten thousand ministers, collectively ordering the affairs of state.

Anala used his knowledge of skill in means to manifest the appearance of horrifying scenes in order to govern, so there were ten thousand fierce soldiers cutting off the heads of criminals, or gouging out their eyes, or any number of similar horrors.

The king had Sudhana enter his palace and look at its superlative adornments; then he said he knew magical liberation, explaining that these punishments, the criminals, and the soldiers, were all magical projections of great compassion to frighten actual people into giving up evil. In reality, not even a single gnat or a single ant was harmed, much less any humans. This was why he had been rewarded with such splendor, to make it clear that he would, on the contrary, have been doomed if he had been torturing people intentionally because of his own subjective feelings.

18. MAHAPRABHA

Then Sudhana went to Suprabha, saw the king Mahaprabha, and realized the practice of the difficult-to-attain.

The city is called Beautiful Light to represent the subtle function of differentiation within effortless knowledge.

King Mahaprabha is called Great Light to represent fundamental effortless independent knowledge.

One gains access to effortless, subtle function only when one has remedied the unfulfilled knowledge and compassion of earlier stages and balanced them masterfully; thus in the story Sudhana wandered through the human world, eventually to make his way to the city of Beautiful Light.

Effortless knowledge and compassion are difficult to attain; even though Sudhana looked around, he still sought certainty through direction. So when he had reached the city he inquired further of the longtime inhabitants.

Because Sudhana had embodied a variety of practices of knowledge and compassion, he saw the ground, trees, buildings, terraces, and flower ponds of the city to be all adorned with jewels.

The story says the city was octagonal, with ten leagues to a side, and also that it had ten million streets, on each of which lived countless beings. Ten million streets could not fit into a ten-league octagon; these are not worldly measurements, but representative of the great metropolis of fundamental knowledge, with streets representing the infinity of interactions of the ten ways of transcendence.

Therefore beings saw the city differently, according to their faculties and their ways of acting—some saw it as large, some as small, some as clean, some as polluted, and so on. In this way the king of knowledge showed everyone the laws of reality.

When one uses independent knowledge to enter into minds as many as beings and identify with them, there is no separate nature—the sentient and insentient are of one nature, and all are transformed according to knowledge into agents of buddha-work.

In the world when a national leader is enlightened, even the animals dance, and phoenixes appear. When ordinary people are perfectly filial, they also experience phenomena like finding leaping fish in frozen ponds and bamboo shoots sprouting in winter. How much the better when knowledge penetrates the fountainhead and practice is equal to the real world—kindness takes in all beings, spirituality gathers all awarenesses; one has no subjective mind but takes to heart the minds of all beings, just as a clear jewel may take on all colors.

As the king had entered the door of absorption in great kindness adapting to the world, so the people, birds, and animals of the city and its environs all came to pay him respect. The trees and grasses of the mountains and plains all bowed towards him; the lakes, springs, rivers, and seas all flowed towards him; and the celestial spirits showered him with gifts.

The reason that the seventh and this eighth practice are both represented by kings is to illustrate that while the power and function of compassion and knowledge differ according to the rank, there are not two paths. Therefore the seventh and eighth abodes are both represented at the seashore, and the seventh and eighth dedications are represented in the same assembly. The appearance of the teachers as various persons in various walks of life symbolizes the differences in power and function.

19. ACHALA

Then Sudhana went to the kingdom of Sthira, saw the devout woman Achala, and realized the practice of good teaching.

The location is called a kingdom to represent mastery of teaching, the devout woman is called Immovable because of her spiritual power to remain unaffected.

Protected by the mother of knowledge and the father of skill in means, the mind is not influenced by objects; to represent this and the compassion of humility, Achala is said to be a young woman in the care of her mother and father.

When Sudhana went into her house, upon contact with the golden aura of the house he attained five hundred trances; illumined by the edifying light of the chamber of compassion, he gained access to five hundred entryways into the five ranks. The trances were subtle as the consciousness of a new embryo, because when knowledge enters compassion, it is harmonized and becomes comfortable.

No one who saw this young woman became enamored of her; because her behavior was unaffected by emotional love, her body was not erotic but caused the minds of all who saw her to become upright and correct.

Achala said that long ago in the time of an ancient buddha she had been a princess, daughter of a king named Vidyuddatta, called Lightning-bestowed. At that time she was inspired with the thought of enlightenment on seeing the magnificence of the buddha, and in all the eons since that time she had not so much as had a lustful thought, let alone acted on lust.

The buddha of that time was called Arms Extended Downward, representative of carrying out transcendent vows from effortless knowledge to guide sentient beings. The king was called Lightning-bestowed because knowledge sees the path of enlightenment quickly. Achala was a princess because from knowledge she cultivated kindness.

Before the eighth practice one is still affected by the habit of sadness; here in the ninth there are no ingrained habits. That is why Achala said she had no lust. In the rank of teacherhood one overcomes obstacles to mastery of teaching, requiring tireless effort; so she said she had attained absorption in tireless search for all truths.

20. SARVAGAMIN

Then Sudhana went to Tosala, saw the mendicant Sarvagamin, and realized the practice of truth.

Tosala is called Production of Happiness, to represent the use of ubiquitous physical manifestation through fulfillment of transcendent knowledge in order to benefit ordinary people and make them happy.

Sarvagamin is represented as a mendicant because his knowledge was equal to a buddha's. He is called Going Everywhere because he appeared to assimilate to false ideas and to the three vehicles of Buddhism. The Confucian and Taoist sages were also in this category.

Ordinarily, learners are called outsiders as long as they have not yet entered into the real universe, where there is interpenetration of noumenon and phenomena, of bodies and lands. In this case, Sarvagamin appeared to be an outsider, helping beings according to type, yet in reality he was not an outsider.

In the middle of the night Sudhana saw the flora on the mountain east of the city of Tosala radiate light like the rising sun, representing the sun of great knowledge in the middle of the night of birth and death.

Sudhana saw Sarvagamin walking around on the flat mountaintop: the mountaintop symbolizes the lofty supremacy of knowledge, the flatness symbolizes the evenness of compassion.

Walking around illustrates not dwelling partially on either knowledge or compassion.

Sarvagamin said he knew the enlightening practice of going everywhere; by means of knowledge he penetrated all existences, and appeared in corresponding physical forms, as echoes respond to sounds without there being any substance coming or going.

After this the ten dedications are set up. By means of the ten practices one can perfect worldly arts of government and education, yet one is still unable to remain in the ocean of birth and death, neither emerging nor sinking, based on unobstructed action in the real universe by the universally good practice of inherent buddhahood. Therefore the ten dedications are needed.

21. Utpalabhuti

Then Sudhana went to Prthurashtra, saw the eminent perfumer Utpalabhuti, and realized dedication to saving all beings without clinging to any image of beings.

The land is called Vast Territory to represent far-ranging vows. Utpalabhuti's being a perfumer symbolizes the combining of knowledge and compassion, noumenon and phenomena, nirvana and samsara, and ideas of defilement and purity all into one ball while still freely totalizing or distinguishing them. He is a layman on account of his great compassion, entering birth and death without being affected.

The nature of fragrance rests on nothing, yet it radiates good and extinguishes bad; this symbolizes great vows that rely on nothing yet radiate deeds that benefit beings.

The regal fragrance of fundamental knowledge emerges within ignorance, the fragrance of differentiating knowledge emerges within myriad objects; so the eminent said he knew where the king of fragrances came from and knew how to compound fragrances.

According to Utpalabhuti there is in the human world a fragrance that comes from the struggle of water spirits and that causes those anointed with it to become golden in color. This represents the first abode, in which tranquillity and insight struggle with conditioning, producing the fragrance of knowledge; those who enter thereupon attain true awakening.

Also, there is a kind of sandalwood whose essence will protect people from burning by fire. This represents the abode of preparing the ground, in which the body of discipline is anointed with the principle of essencelessness so that it can enter the fire of the three poisons without being burned.

In the ocean there is a fragrance called invincible, which, when painted on drums, causes even brave opponents to retreat on hearing the sound of the drums; this represents the development of acceptance of reality in the abode of practical cultivation, causing evils to withdraw spontaneously.

Ten kinds of fragrance are mentioned, representing the ten abodes; by combining the two aspects of the ten abodes and ten practices—the absolute and the mundane, knowledge and compassion—causing them to be free, the method of dedication is created.

Because this dedication first enters the ocean of great compassion, one might leave out the awareness of knowledge; so ten fragrances are used to symbolize the principle of the ten abodes. Because one principle contains all the principles, this is represented by compounding fragrance.

22. Vaira

Then Sudhana went to the city of Kutagara, saw the mariner Vaira, and realized indestructible dedication.

Kutagara is called the City of High Houses, the high houses representing knowledge. Vaira is called Independent, because he used natural discipline and great compassion to go into the ocean of birth and death while remaining free.

Vaira is represented as a mariner, for he was like a ship that does not stay on the near shore, does not stay on the farther shore, and does not stay in midstream, but carries people across. He ferried people over the ocean of birth and death by means of myriad principal and satellite practices within discipline, so he was seen on the seashore surrounded by hundreds of thousands of merchants.

Being profoundly calm and unshakable in the middle of the ocean of birth and death, Vaira said he knew all the treasure islands in the ocean.

Knowledge of the locations of precious substances refers to the empty and nonempty matrices of enlightenment. Knowledge of categories of precious substances refers to countless natural virtues. Knowledge of types of precious substances refers to the realization of buddha-nature. Knowledge of precious vessels refers to understanding of beings' faculties. Extraction of precious substances refers to setting up teachings according to faculties in order to bring out knowledge and virtue.

Part of the enlightening beings of the pure lands are free like dragons; when purity and pollution have not been forgotten, this is the danger zone of the dragon abodes. Listeners can empty the three poisons; this is the danger zone of demons. Conditional illuminates dwell in the ocean of nirvana, so buddha-knowledge does not appear; this is the danger zone of goblins. Since the ocean of birth and death becomes a way of access to the real universe, Vaira said he avoided all such danger zones.

Knowing whirlpools, depths, and shallows refers to knowing the workings of craving, grasping, and becoming. The ranges of ocean waves refer to the quantity of thoughts in emotive consciousness. The good and bad colors of the waters refer to the joy and anger of the clinging mind.

Vaira also knew the movements of the sun, moon, and stars, meaning that he understood the mysterious signs of yin and yang in the world and used this to help people. It also represents the methods and guidelines for developing maturity according to faculties by different teachings and practices.

Vaira also knew about the soundness of ship hulls and how well their machinery worked, emblematic of his knowledge of the degree of maturity of faculties and capacities, of whether or not people's minds were transformed, and of whether or not they could enter birth and death.

Vaira brought merchants to treasure islands so that they could collect jewels, then brought them back to the continent; this symbolizes passing through the various ranks and their teachings, and then, when the ten stages are fulfilled, in the eleventh stage going back to live as before in the ocean of birth and death to carry out the practice of Universal Good.

Vaira said he had attained practice characteristic of great compassion, meaning that the natural discipline of great compassion is indestructible.

23. Jayottama

Then Sudhana went to Nandihara, saw the eminent Jayottama, and realized the dedication equal to all buddhas.

Nandihara was called the City of Happiness because the eminent grandee Jayottama skillfully settled people's affairs and because he skillfully examined truths, to the delight of the people.

Jayottama was called Supreme Victor because of the supremacy of his practice of patience. He was seen in a grove of "sorrowless" trees east of the city lecturing to a group of innumerable businessmen and city elders: *east of the city* symbolizes development of goodness by knowledge; the grove of "sorrowless" trees represents protection from anxiety through patience; the businessmen symbolize exchanging ignorance for knowledge, bad for good; the city elders represent education of the populace by means of virtue.

Jayottama said he knew the pure method of cultivating enlightening practices everywhere, because the practice of dedication equal to all buddhas reaches everywhere.

The reason these last three teachers are lay people is to represent dedication directed from the absolute to the mundane.

24. SINHAVIJURMBHITA

Then Sudhana went to the city of Kalingavana in the land of Shronaparanta, saw the nun Sinhavijurmbhita, and realized dedication reaching all places.

The land was called Brave, the city called Struggle, emblematic of energetically entering the ordinary world to stop the struggle between the two views of absolute and mundane, pure and defiled.

Sinhavijurmbhita was called Lion Stretch to symbolize the tirelessness of her practice of kindness. She is portrayed as a nun because in this rank, like the fourth abode and fourth stage, one leaves the bonds of the world and is born in the family of the enlightened. Her mendicancy represents patience by abandonment of superficial adornments, and her femaleness represents kindness.

She was in the park of the king Victorious Light. Kingship symbolizes knowledge; this means that in this rank of energy and diligence one combines patience, knowledge, and kindness to comprehend the practices of the five ranks in one spiritual realm.

The park was magnificently adorned, illustrating environmental perfection as a result of spiritual development. Sudhana saw the nun sitting on various seats lecturing to various groups, symbolizing her integrative educational activities, including those in all the stages up to the eleventh, which borders on buddhahood.

This is the teaching of the infinite cosmic network, in which one rank pervades all ranks, and each rank pervades the spiritual cosmos, all refining one another, forming fifty-three teachings and one hundred and ten cities as a totality, as individually distinct, as the same, as different, as integrated, and as disparate, all freely interacting.

25. VASUMITRA

Then Sudhana went to the land of Durga, saw the woman Vasumitra, and realized dedication of infinite stores of virtue.

This woman was settled in a polluted, fearsome realm, making it hard for people to believe in her; so the land was called Danger. By means of meditation she entered into defiled realms and turned them all into spheres of knowledge; by virtue of great compassion she remained in the ordinary world, and by virtue of knowledge she remained unaffected, so her city was called City of Jewel Arrays.

The name *Vasumitra* means "Friend of the World," meaning that she was a teacher and friend to people. Her femaleness represents being in the absolute without being absorbed by it, while being in the midst of bondage without being affected by it. She gave the appearance of impassioned behavior, yet her heart was dispassionate. She appeared to be a woman, yet in ultimate reality one is neither male nor female; she is just portrayed as a female to represent the compassion of the real universe.

In the realm of the magic of knowledge of Universal Good one's own body is like a magical effect, the world is like a projected image; with no mind influenced by objects, there are no objects that can influence the mind. The mind having no nature of its own, objects are also basically nonexistent. This is inconceivable to common sense and inaccessible to the folly and confusion of subjective views. It is necessary that knowledge penetrate the true source and that practice match the real universe before one can embody this Way.

This woman was living in her house north of the town square; this means that the dangerous road of folly in the long night of birth and death is the house of enlightening beings, and that they have no other house.

Vasumitra said she had attained the liberation of ultimate dispassion, because by means of the supreme knowledge of the real universe she lived in the midst of pollution without becoming defiled. One attains the joy of meditation just by believing in this, so Vasumitra said that anyone who looked at her became free from desire and attained absorbing joy. Because insight produced from concentration understands the nature of sound, she said that anyone who conversed with her for a while attained mastery of sound.

Vasumitra went on to speak of holding her hand, getting up on her couch, gazing at her, embracing her, and kissing her. Holding her hand means seeking salvation. Getting up on her couch means ascendancy of formless knowledge. Gazing at her means seeing truth, embracing her means not departing from it. Kissing her means receiving instruction.

This illustrates how all who come near enter a door of total knowledge, unlike those who only seek to get out of bondage and do not arrive at the ultimate dispassion—supreme knowledge of the real universe that remains in the polluted world without being defiled, freely helping the living, neither bound nor freed.

Vasumitra also said that in the time of a past buddha, Manjushri had fostered her inspiration to enlightenment; and that upon her inspiration with the thought of enlightenment she had distributed all of her wealth and thereby attained this liberation. The encouragement of Manjushri represents producing concentration from knowledge, the wealth represents the ability of concentration to permeate everything totally.

Inspiration with the thought of enlightenment is detachment from lust, giving of wealth is detachment from greed. A single coin may not be much money, but if the mentality of ability to give up what is valued is the same as when giving a lot of money, then this is what is called infinite stores of virtue.

26. VESHTHILA

Then Sudhana went to Shubhaparamgama, saw the householder Veshthila, and realized dedication adaptively stabilizing all roots of goodness.

Veshthila is called the Embracer, illustrating the vastness of his knowledge and wisdom, which embraced all things. This layman had before him a shrine where there was placed a sandalwood throne without an icon on it; the idea is to illustrate how buddhas and sentient beings have no sign of origination and destruction, using the shrine with the sandalwood throne as a device to indicate this symbolically, to inform us that our own essence and manifestations are like the original formless Buddha on the throne.

When you understand that essence is spacelike and find that appearances are like projections, you open up enlightened knowledge and vision; then there is no beginning and no end, no present and no past. Thus Veshthila said that when he opened the shrine he attained liberation without complete extinction, absorbed in the infinity of the lineages of buddhas.

27. AVALOKITESHVARA

Then Sudhana went to Mount Potalaka, saw the enlightening being Avalokiteshvara, and realized dedication according to all sentient beings.

Potalaka is a mountain where many small white flowers grow; this represents the modesty and compassionate behavior of the enlightening being.

Avalokiteshvara represents living in the ocean of birth and death, helping beings compassionately. This is one of the three laws that make up the virtues of Vairocana, the Illuminator Buddha; the other two are the subtle principle of the spiritual body represented by Manjushri and the myriad acts of the body of knowledge represented by Samantabhadra.

Avalokiteshvara lives on a mountain of little white flowers to show people they should not do even a little wrong and should not abandon even a little good.

Sudhana saw Avalokiteshvara on a plateau on the west side of the mountain, which was adorned with shining springs and streams, thick woods, and soft fragrant plants spiraling to the right covering the ground. West is the direction associated with killing and punishment, meaning a place calling for the practice of compassionate education. The great compassion of the enlightening being is paramount, intent on the benefit of beings and not dwelling on personal rewards, so he lives in the material world of sentient beings, represented by the mountainside. The springs and streams represent the clear shining of the heart of compassion, the woods represent the dense shade of works of kindness. The fragrant plants represent fine words that please people, while spiraling to the right symbolizes sentient beings going along with the teaching.

Sudhana saw Avalokiteshvara sitting on a diamond boulder, surrounded by countless enlightening beings sitting on jewel rocks. This symbolizes adamantine knowledge going along with compassion, their subtle functions meshing without disturbance.

The enlightening being said he had perfected liberation of great compassionate action, showing how Avalokiteshvara represents the universal compassion of buddhas of all times. Therefore from here on, even to the tenth stage, all levels are associated with great compassion, but in this rank one enters the ordinary world and great compassion becomes fulfilled; so Avalokiteshvara says he has perfected it.

Then the enlightened being Ananyagamin came from the sky and stood atop the mountain range surrounding the world, causing the earth to quake and radiate light so brilliant it obscured the lights of all the celestial bodies. Ananyagamin came from the sky because true knowledge has no resting place. The surrounding mountains are the deluded attachments of sentient beings to conditioned realms; the earthquakes represent the disappearance of delusion on the appearance of knowledge. The light outshining the sun, moon, and stars is the light of uncontaminated knowledge that cannot be reached by the lights resulting from worldly actions. Ananyagamin coming to where Avalokiteshvara was represents great knowledge coming back to compassion.

28. ANANYAGAMIN

Then Sudhana saw the enlightening being Ananyagamin and realized dedication characteristic of true Thusness.

As knowledge and compassion are not two separate entities, Ananyagamin, called He Who Proceeds Directly, was also on the mountain of little white flowers, the same as Avalokiteshvara.

Ananyagamin said he had come from the East, from a world pregnant with subtle marvels, where he had associated with a buddha born of universal light, and thus attained liberation enabling him to speed forth in all directions.

One's own treasury of knowledge of subtle inner designs is always producing without producing anything—this is the eastern world pregnant with subtle marvels.

From fundamental knowledge are produced differentiated magical knowledge-bodies, which echo throughout the ten directions without traveling in essence; this is the liberation enabling one to speed forth in all directions, attained in the company of a buddha transcending all.

It had already been eons since Ananyagamin had left that world, and in each instant he took as many steps as atoms in untold buddha-fields, with each step passing as many buddha-fields as atoms in untold buddha-fields, honoring each of the buddhas in those fields with subtle offerings.

Because the essence of knowledge is inherently omnipresent and all-inclusive, it extends without actually speeding, transcending sensual or intellectual assessments; therefore Ananyagamin passed so many buddha-fields in a single instant of thought. By the unfabricated seal of knowledge he mastered the magical function of acts, so that they succeeded effortlessly, becoming subtle offerings.

29. MAHADEVA

Then Sudhana went to Dvaravati, saw the celestial Mahadeva, and realized dedication without bondage or attachment.

Dvaravati means "Having a Door," the name of the place deriving from the fact that in the rank of teacher there is a great door of truth that opens up to enlighten sentient beings.

Mahadeva ("The Great God") had knowledge like the celestials, showing signs of good and evil, rewarding and punishing in a timely manner, always responding spiritually to myriad beings, yet without deliberate contrivance. This is why he is portrayed as a celestial spirit. All nature spirits are reflections of enlightening beings, beyond the psychic power of mundane ghosts.

Mahadeva extended four hands, brought water from the four oceans, and washed his face. This symbolizes using the four integrative methods to receive sentient beings with careful consideration.

Mahadeva said he had attained "cloud net" liberation, showering teaching as rain from clouds of great compassion and rescuing sentient beings as with a net.

Mahadeva manifested heaps of gold, silver, and jewels, then gave them to Sudhana for him to practice giving to others. This illustrates how the function of acts is inexhaustible with the magical great compassion born of uncontrived knowledge.

30. STHAVARA

Then Sudhana saw the earth goddess Sthavara at the site of enlightenment and realized infinite dedication equal to the cosmos.

In this rank, the five realities of enlightenment, inner design, knowledge, kindness, and compassion are united into one and all fulfilled as the site of enlightenment.

Because kindness and compassion underlie and produce the various teachings and methods, supporting and nurturing living beings, Sthavara is represented as an earth goddess.

The sky god Mahadeva represented the subtle function of pure knowledge; this earth goddess represents the substance of great compassion. The substance is always functioning yet always tranquil, so the earth goddess is called Stable.

Sky moves, earth is still; this symbolizes the protection and support of knowledge and compassion.

Sudhana saw Sthavara with a million earth goddesses, all radiating light and causing the earth to tremble; this illustrates how compassion and knowledge are completely fulfilled at this point, so habits that defile purity disappear.

Sthavara touched the ground with her foot, whereupon countless deposits of jewels spontaneously gushed forth: this represents the way great compassion can clearly reveal the hidden resources of the mind-ground, having full use of the spirit without overt effort.

Sthavara said she had attained liberation through an indestructible store of knowledge; since compassion arises from knowledge, nothing can destroy it, and since in action in the real universe no knowledge is not included and no compassion not fulfilled, it is called a store, or mine.

The goddess also said she had attained this liberation eons before in the service of buddhas; because great compassion is limitless, even enlightenment and final extinction are all beginningless and endless household affairs.

31. VASANTI

Then Sudhana went to the city of Kapilavastu, saw the night goddess Vasanti, and realized the stage of joy.

Kapilavastu is called the Yellow City, representing knowledge uniting with the middle way. Yellow is the color associated with the center and with felicity.

Vasanti is said to be in charge of spring growth, symbolic of the production of myriad practices in the first stage. She is a night goddess to represent great knowledge in the night of birth and death.

The next ten teachers beginning with this night goddess are female, emblematic of the great compassion of enlightening beings, like a mother begrudging no effort to raise her children. As they are in the spiritual ranks—in charge of protecting and helping the world—even though they do not physically leave the Buddha's assembly, they still can project their appearances throughout the ten directions.

The night goddess wore a red robe, a sacred crest, and pearl necklaces; all the stars and constellations shone on her body. This represents how the first stage includes the laws of all the stages, so the awareness of great compassionate differentiating knowledge is comprehensive.

The goddess said she had attained the liberation of the light of truth that dispels the darkness of ignorance in all sentient beings and was able to be a guide or make shelter, passage, and light on dark, stormy, and dangerous nights to free beings from fear of the darkness. This shows how the practice of great compassion is detailed and comprehensive. She also said she had always been a woman for countless eons, practicing this teaching, showing how great compassion is so deep that it does not seek to leave the world, for in the original real universe there is no world to leave.

32. SAMANTAGAMBHIRASHRIVIMALAPRABHA

Then Sudhana saw the night goddess Samantagambhira-shrivimalaprabha at the site of enlightenment and realized the stage of purity.

Great compassion in the ordinary world is not separate from fundamental awareness, so this scene also takes place at the site of enlightenment.

The night goddess said she had attained liberation through the bliss of tranquil meditation going everywhere. This is because the fundamental meditation underlying discipline, spontaneous meditation on the essence of all objects, is by nature inherently omnipresent.

She said that while she focused her mind wholly on the salvation and protection of living beings, she practiced the various stages of meditation up to the extinction of irritation and affliction in sentient beings. This shows how the substance of discipline of the spiritual body is always spontaneously in a state of concentration yet always functions along with compassion, teaching in accord with the faculties of the learners; all is an aspect of meditation. Though this meditation is the same as what is practiced in the meditation heavens, there is not the same attitude of attraction to meditation and enjoyment of tranquillity.

33. PRAMUDITANAYANAJAGADVIROCANA

Then Sudhana saw the night goddess Pramuditanayanajagadvirocana on the right side of the enlightenment site and attained the stage of refulgence.

The right is the position of compassion; this represents initiating action by enlightenment and developing tolerance and kindness. The goddess is called Joyful Eyes Illumining the World; joyful eyes represent tolerance and kindness, illumining the world means not abandoning sentient beings.

From every pore of her body the night goddess emanated countless multitudes of projected bodies, filling the ten directions and expounding the practical aspects of the ten ways of transcendence; this illustrates how the work of the teaching reaches everywhere.

She also emanated multitudes of bodies like various beings and multitudes of bodies like human and celestial rulers, pervading the ten directions, adapting and assimilating everywhere to liberate others.

The night goddess said that in the distant past she was the wife of a king who was in fact Manjushri, the spirit of wisdom, and that she was awakened by a night spirit emanated by Samantabhadra, the spirit of Universal Good. This represents how activation of complex functions based on fundamental knowledge and practice of great compassion are not limited by time; this is because cultivation of world transcendence shows up in an instant, while practice of great compassion goes on forever.

34. SAMANTASATTVATRANOJAHSHRI

Then at the same assembly Sudhana saw the night goddess Samantasattvatranojahshri and realized the stage of blazing radiance.

In this rank knowledge and compassion are completed and one is born in the house of the enlightened, never parting from enlightenment; hence the goddess was in this assembly at the Buddha's site of enlightenment.

Sudhana saw the goddess in all worlds, in all states of being, in all times, liberating sentient beings by techniques adapted to their languages, behaviors, and understandings. This was because she had attained the freedom to appear in all worlds to civilize beings.

The goddess said that in a past eon called Sphere of Purity there appeared as many buddhas as particles in a polar mountain; in that time a king was born spontaneously from a lotus, and the king had a daughter, who was none other than the night goddess herself. The name of the age is based on the roundness and purity of the body of knowledge. The buddhas as numerous as particles represent different fruits of knowledge realized in the course of progressive practice. The king being born from a lotus represents knowledge being undefiled. The princess being the night goddess herself stands for the merging of knowledge and compassion.

The goddess said she had attained her liberation from one hundred and ten buddhas in the past, and she also said she followed buddhas numerous as atoms in lands. The interpenetration of the causes and results of the ten and eleven stages make a hundred and ten buddhas. When knowledge is complete and praxis comprehensive, one's own mind is like buddha, all acts are like buddha, all insights are like buddha, nothing in all worlds in the ten directions is not buddha—this is "buddhas numerous as atoms in lands." To see any thing or any being as other than buddha is a false view.

The goddess also said that in such and such ages, in the time of such and such buddhas, she had been a night spirit, an emperor, and other beings, including an entertainer. Entertainment represents delight in truth. These incarnations all represent practices according to rank within the realization of enlightenment.

Therefore when practice and realization reach each other, the buddhas spontaneously respond. If you see anything apart from your own practice and own realization, this is not true seeing. Even if you get visions by forced seeking, these are only temporary hallucinations, not real buddhas.

35. PRASHANTARUTASAGARAVATI

Not far from here Sudhana saw the night goddess Prashantarutasagaravati and realized the stage difficult to conquer.

In this stage one uses meditation concentration to cultivate worldly arts and crafts. As one has these skills without becoming alienated from the essence of enlightenment and the practice of diligence, the goddess's place is said to be "not far from here."

The goddess is called Possessed of an Ocean of Tranquil Sound. Tranquillity is concentration, while the ocean of sound is function. This illustrates how the body of concentration is uncontrived yet its response is universal. This night goddess was the mother of the night goddess of universal salvation, representing the ability of the body of concentration to produce energetic action. Unless all practices are based on concentration, one will become fatigued at some time.

The goddess said she had attained liberation of supernal manifestations producing floods of joy in each instant of thought. This illustrates the all-pervasiveness of the joy of meditation, the mutual adornment of principle and practice, the vastness of benefit to the living. She also said she would serve all the future buddhas of this eon, as well as the future buddhas of all worlds in all eons, illustrating how the essence of meditation is complete, in the sense that past, present, and future form one time, like a mirror containing multiple images.

36. SARVANAGARARAKSHASAMBHAVATEJAHSHRI

Then in the Buddha's assembly Sudhana saw the night goddess Sarvanagararakshasambhavatejahshri and attained the stage of presence.

This goddess represents protection of the minds of sentient beings and increasing the power of knowledge and insight in the mind. She said she had attained liberation of extremely profound, free, subtle sound, illustrating the single "sound" that is everywhere in the universe, without substance, without discrimination, able to express all truths, teach sentient beings, and manifest all knowledge freely.

The goddess said she had attained this liberation eons in the past. The first buddha in her recollection was called the Illuminating King Voicing the Ocean of All Truths; after that buddha's demise, a certain king left home to preserve the buddha's teachings. The countless eons refer to the ability to turn the countless expressions of the sentient beings of all worlds into a total ocean of expressions of insight. The first buddha stands for fundamental knowledge, and the buddha's name represents freedom in expounding truth and breaking delusion.

The demise of the buddha represents the attainment of knowledge free from bondage and the disappearance of trapped attention and reflection. The king leaving home stands for knowledge of emptiness. Since wisdom activates transcendent compassion, the king's daughter also became a nun.

By the time the buddha's teaching was about to die out, there were a thousand sects that often engaged in disputation and quarrel and were on the verge of destroying Buddhism. This illustrates insight into emptiness that is not yet equipped with the great compassion to enter the ordinary world.

The goddess also mentioned one hundred buddhas and said she had served them all: this represents cultivating the fruits of interdependent progress of all ten stages within the sixth stage. The reason she did not reach the manifestation of the fruits of the eleventh stage is that insight into emptiness is not yet the practice of Universal Good that enters into bondage. It is for this same reason that in the book on the ten concentrations the thirty enlightening beings with insight into emptiness all entered the stage of coronation yet did not see the body of Universal Good.

37. SARVAVRIKSHAPRAPHULLANASUKHASAMVASA

Then, in the Buddha's assembly, Sudhana saw the night goddess Sarvavrikshapraphullanasukhasamvasa and realized the stage of far going.

This goddess symbolizes using expedients in the midst of freedom from birth and death to enter into birth and death and carry out practices everywhere.

The goddess said she had attained liberation producing the light of great joy, meaning that she had clearly penetrated the four integrative methods and the four infinite minds.

She also said that in the remote past there had been a king named Encompassing Sound of the Proclamation of All Laws, who had five hundred ministers, six thousand concubines, and seven hundred sons. The king set up a great charitable event, which a young woman named Jewel Light, daughter of a grandee, attended with sixty maids.

The king was Vairocana and the young woman Jewel Light was the night goddess; this represents the stage of practical compassion in a bad time when there is a lot of suffering. The king represents knowledge, the five hundred ministers represent the five ranks being practiced in concert, the six thousand concubines represent compassion pervading the six realms of being, the seven hundred princes represent the practices of the seven limbs of enlightenment, the woman Jewel Light represents compassion, the sixty maidens at the assembly represent the compassion of the six ranks combining with knowledge. That the king was Vairocana Buddha represents knowledge being the fruit of action in the ordinary world.

38. SARVAJAGADRAKSHAPRANIDHANAVIRYAPRABHA

Then at the site of enlightenment Sudhana saw the night goddess Sarvajagadrakshapranidhanaviryaprabha and realized the stage of immovability.

The spirit, whose name means "Light of Energy of the Vow To Protect All Beings," represents total absorption in helping living beings, using effortless knowledge to let the power of the fundamental vow do its work.

Sudhana saw the spirit sitting on a seat of jewels reflecting the abodes of all beings; this represents how the pure function of knowledge in effortless knowledge appears in all places.

The body of the night goddess showed reflections of the sun, moon, and stars; and she appeared to sentient beings everywhere in the forms of various bodies, according to the mentalities of those beings. This represents the body of knowledge appearing in context.

The night spirit said she had attained liberty to teach beings in ways that promoted goodness. When knowledge of the essence of nonbeing is realized, all faculties of goodness develop.

Certain metaphors are raised here, such as that of the orb of knowledge of enlightening beings being like the sun traversing the sky, having itself no day or night; or like a phantom in the world, having no joy or sorrow. The goddess uses them to answer the question of how long it has been since she has been inspired to seek enlightenment, making it clear that enlightening liberation cannot be measured in temporal terms.

The goddess related that in the remote past there had been a buddha named King Illumining Space with the Voice of Truth, who sat on the enlightenment site for a full hundred years. The king of that time and place, called Victorious Light, had a son, the crown prince Conquerer, who had twenty-eight of the thirty-two marks of a world ruler. After releasing people from prison, the prince led a holy life for five hundred years.

The buddha represents effortless knowledge, like an echo, everywhere aware yet not based anywhere. The hundred years represent the hundred transcendent ways of the full ten stages practiced in one stage. The king represents knowledge, the prince represents practical kindness, the prison represents the sphere of operation of kindness. Leading a holy life for five hundred years after renunciation stands for leaving the home of effort and penetrating the five ranks in effortlessness. The prince only had twenty-eight of the marks of greatness, lacking four, because in the eighth stage one lacks the causes and effects of the ninth and tenth stages.

39. SUTEJOMANDALARATISHRI

Then Sudhana saw the night goddess Sutejomandalaratishri in the Lumbini grove and realized the stage of good mind.

Lumbini is the garden where Buddha was born, called Supreme in Pleasure because of the bliss produced in people by the Teaching.

In the stage of good mind, subtle insight and intellect are completed, and one is good at explaining teachings; hence the spirit is called Glory of the Sphere of Good Power.

The goddess explained ten kinds of birth by which enlightening beings are born in the family of buddhas and said she had countless eons since attained liberty to be freely reborn. This means that having attained effortless knowledge and being on the verge of rising to receive a buddha's work, in this stage one studies buddhas' powers of elucidation—this is called being reborn.

The goddess said she had purposely been reborn in the Lumbini grove, where she realized the Buddha would be born in a hundred years. The Buddha also appeared to be born in each Lumbini grove in the billion-world universe and in each atom of all worlds in the ten directions. The ascent from this stage to the tenth stage is referred to as a hundred years; being born in all places means that since unfabricated knowledge is like space, like magic, even a single moment of the descent of the spirit pervades the real universe, without any here or there, coming or going, or interruption in time. Goddesses bearing gifts awaited the birth of the Buddha, illustrating the ancient saying, "Sages act, and all beings observe."

The night goddess recounted the story of a past age in

which eighty decillion buddhas were born. A royal queen, accompanied by twenty decillion ladies-in-waiting, went to a park of golden flowers, and there, as she held onto a tree, she gave birth to an enlightening being. The wet nurse at that time was none other than the night goddess herself.

The number of buddhas in the eon, eighty decillion, represents the issue of the effortless knowledge of the eighth stage. The number of ladies with the queen, twenty decillion, represents the fulfillment of joy in truth produced by the buddhas' twin practice of compassion and knowledge. That the queen gave birth while holding onto a tree represents the development of great knowledge through focus on great compassion. The role of the wet nurse also symbolizes compassion.

40. GOPA

Then Sudhana saw the girl Gopa in Kapilavastu and realized the stage of clouds of teaching.

The setting symbolizes the essence and function of knowledge and compassion reaching everywhere, immaterial yet nurturing and supporting all beings. The setting is the same as that of the first stage (represented by the night goddess Vasanti, the thirty-first benefactor) because knowledge and compassion are simultaneous.

Gopa's name has the sense of watching over, or protecting, representing the preservation of the ground of great compassion.

According to the story, Gopa was the wife of Buddha in a past life, representing kindness, compassion, and delight in truth. She also is said to have been wife to Buddha for eons, symbolizing the inseparability of knowledge and compassion.

Knowledge attuned to reality is omnipresent; it cannot be discussed in terms of matter, cannot be understood in terms of form or appearance. It manifests similarity to humans and demonstrates humanlike laws, it manifests similarity to celestials and demonstrates celestial ways; it is variegated according to the species to which it appears; it cannot be known by one practice, cannot be understood by one body. This is because that is the nature of the body of practices of Universal Good.

The qualities of knowledge are briefly described in ten ways. First, the body of knowledge rests on nothing, manifesting characteristics according to the subject. Second, appearances of knowledge are like reflections in essence, without any material conventionality. Third, reflections of knowledge originally do not exist; the subject appears according to the mind. Fourth, knowledge has no "here" or "there"—it responds to objects like an echo. Fifth, sentient beings see it falsely, but that is not the doing of knowledge itself. Sixth, knowledge makes nothing but arises according to illusions. Seventh, magical birth does not involve thoughts of desire. Eighth, the spacelike power of intention appears responsively throughout the ten directions. Ninth, uncontrived, great compassion pervades the ordinary world to benefit beings. Tenth, knowledge is common to all conscious beings, so observation of the ordinary is always real. These ten aspects of the Teaching are Gopa's practice.

At that time there was in the hall of universal reflections of the light of truth a goddess named Sorrowless who came with ten thousand house goddesses to welcome Sudhana. Ten thousand symbolizes myriad practices, the house goddesses represent the shelter of kindness and compassion. Welcoming represents knowledge and kindness meeting.

Sudhana saw Gopa surrounded by eighty-four thousand maidens of royal lineage, representing the eighty-four thousand afflictions. All of them were engaged in the same practice, through kindness and compassion; and compassion is born of knowledge.

Gopa said she had once been the bride of a prince, who was a previous manifestation of the present Buddha; she and her husband went together to see the buddha of their time and hear the Teaching. This symbolizes the inseparable union of knowledge and compassion in this stage.

She added that she had attained liberty to observe the

concentrations of all enlightening beings, yet even after eons she did not completely know the practices of enlightening beings, because the practice of Universal Good is infinite.

The ten teachers who follow Gopa represent the practice of Universal Good in the eleventh stage.

41. MAYA

Then Sudhana saw Lady Maya in this world and realized the method of magical attainment of enlightenment by producing knowledge from compassion.

"This world" symbolizes the realm embraced by great compassion, without distinctions of far and near, inside and outside. Lady Maya represents the effortless great compassion that is always in the world. The fact that she is the mother of Buddha symbolizes great compassion magically producing great knowledge.

A city goddess named Jewel Eyes exhorted Sudhana to guard the citadel of mind, a goddess named Spiritual Lotus eulogized Lady Maya, lights entered Sudhana's head, and a goblin guarding the teaching hall instructed Sudhana to view body and mind as like dreams or reflections as he sought teachers.

Jewel Eyes represents the eye of knowledge within compassion, the lights symbolize teaching, and the goblin represents devouring the poisons of ignorance. These three principles constitute expedients on the threshold of the eleventh stage, ushering one into the great practice of Universal Good.

When Sudhana put these teachings into practice, he saw a jewel lotus spring up from the earth, with Maya sitting on it manifesting countless incarnations in conformity with the doings of sentient beings. This illustrates the absence of inherent identity of body and mind—this is seeing bodies magically produced by compassion and knowledge.

Maya said that her body, even though in its original state, contained oceans of enlightening beings who traveled freely within her belly, crossing a billion-world universe in a single step. This means that the ocean of great compassionate practices of Universal Good is endlessly vast, like space.

Maya said she was the mother of all buddhas of all times, meaning that the knowledge to help beings spontaneously is all born of the mother of great compassion.

Maya also said she had attained this liberation of the magic of knowledge inconceivable eons before, making it clear that it is not possible to calculate in ordinary relative terms—it is necessary that calculation be forgotten, feelings end, and knowledge become manifest before one could know how long it had been since she had attained this liberation. Therefore only buddhas could know how many eons it had been.

42. SURENDRABHA

Then, in the thirty-three-fold heaven, Sudhana saw the goddess Surendrabha, daughter of the god Smrtimati, and realized unfailing mindfulness of all truths through mastery of knowledge and compassion.

The god Smrtimati ("Mindful") appeared in an earlier book of *The Flower Ornament Scripture*, and here is called a king, who also has a daughter. This represents spontaneous wisdom and compassion without thought, spiritual teaching without fixed convention; this freedom is represented as divinity and kingship, which thus do not refer literally to a specific realm or status.

The goddess said she had attained liberation of unimpeded recollection, meaning that the extent of the eons of past, present, and future was perfectly clear to her, manifest in the immediate present. This is natural, by knowledge without thought.

The goddess said that she served all the buddhas in countless eons. This is a description of temporal relativity within the absolute where there is no temporal relativity. Because the timeless realm of knowledge is instantly all-pervasive, this is not a result of fabrication.

After this the teachers are lay people, not presented as supernatural, to show that the Way of transcendence is fulfilled, but there may be lack of breadth of freedom in helping living beings. There is no more will to seek liberation apart from defilement and purity: there is only riding on the ship of the essence of reality and hoisting the sail of great compassion, with great knowledge as the captain, following the wind of the fundamental vow, casting the net of transcendent ways, traveling the ocean of birth and death, hauling out "fish," those with attachments, and placing them on the shore of independent knowledge, to dwell in the precious hall of the real universe, like the tower of Maitreya described hereafter.

43. VISHWAMITRA

Then Sudhana saw the young teacher Vishwamitra in the city of Kapilavastu and realized how to be a teacher of worldly principles everywhere.

Vishwamitra did not tell Sudhana anything but sent him to see Shilpabhijna, illustrating the rule for teacher-exemplars, which is properly not to instruct personally but to leave this to assistant mentors, just answering questions about unresolved matters. This represents the fact that the virtuous are never alone, always having associates to assist in the development of education.

44. SHILPABHIJNA

Then Sudhana saw Shilpabhijna and realized universal knowledge of writing.

Shilpabhijna was a student of Vishwamitra. He said he had attained liberation with higher knowledge of arts. Constantly reciting forty-two phonemes, he entered into countless facets of transcendent wisdom. Because these phenomena include all writings, to hold one in mind is to hold all in mind, and to hold all in mind is to hold one in mind—this is the portal of wisdom.

For example, in reciting *A,* he entered the facet of transcendent wisdom in which there are no distinctions in the power of enlightening beings. *A* is the negative prefix: realizing the truth that all is empty and not really existent is the realm of nondifferentiation in the power of enlightening beings. Pronouncing *Ra,* he entered the facet of transcendent wisdom in which there are infinite differentiations, as *Ra* represents the realm of differentiated knowledge and practice of Universal Good.

45. BHADROTTAMA

Then Sudhana saw the Buddhist laywoman Bhadrottama and realized how to help people by conventional and mystical arts and sciences.

Bhadrottama is called Best of the Good because she understood all principles. Because she was in the material world helping beings, sometimes she was a diviner, sometimes a curer, sometimes an appraiser of jewels, sometimes a writer.

Understanding all genius and effective knowledge, able to control all pernicious influences, containing the ocean of knowledge of Universal Good, equaling the spiritual body of Manjushri, embodying buddhahood, spiritualizing myriad beings, reaching everywhere and performing all practices, in accord with the saying that buddhas have reality for their body, only when one arrives at all realities and knows all truths can one be a teacher of gods and humans.

But reality has no place of abode, so the body also has no anchor—though it pervades myriad existences, it has no substance itself. Therefore Bhadrottama said she had only realized liberation of the baseless sphere.

46. MUKTASARA

Then Sudhana saw the goldsmith Muktasara in the city of Bharukaccha and realized the way to pure liberation by being in the world without clinging thoughts.

Adorn thoughts with formless knowledge and thoughts will naturally not cling to phenomena. This is liberation.

47. SUCHANDRA

Then Sudhana saw the householder Suchandra in the same city and realized the way to illumination by pure knowledge working in the world.

The practical great compassion represented in this meeting is one with the formless liberation of the preceding meeting, so it takes place in the same city. In the ten abodes, ten practices, ten dedications, and ten stages, the seventh and eighth steps merge into each other; in this eleventh stage, the sixth and seventh grades are one body. Using the light of great compassion to break through the confusion of sentient beings is liberation of the illumination of pure knowledge.

48. AJITASENA

Then Sudhana saw the householder Ajitasena in the city of Roruka and realized the method of finding infinite forms in formlessness.

The city Roruka represents the great vows that produce spiritual practices. The householder Ajitasena represents victory over the demons of birth and death.

The totality of states of mind are the infinite forms of buddha. These are the infinite forms in formlessness.

49. SHIVARAGRA

Then Sudhana saw the Brahmin Shivaragra in Dharma village and realized the way of speaking in such a manner that truth is revealed.

Dharma village represents the rank of a teacher of Dharma whose village is the real universe. The Brahmin Shivaragra represents transcendent power—in the ordinary without being ordinary, in the clamor without making clamor.

The liberation of speech revealing truth is attained by realization that the essence of all words and speech is inherently real and that persons and things are all thus—so there is no empty talk.

50. SHRISAMBHAVA AND SHRIMATI

Then Sudhana went to the city of Sumanamukha, saw the boy Shrisambhava and the girl Shrimati, and realized illusoriness, living in the world with complete knowledge and compassion.

The city represents subtle practice within knowledge, the boy and girl represent desireless, unaffected gentility and humility, with equal knowledge and compassion.

The boy and girl said they had attained the liberation of illusoriness, meaning they had realized that the realms of buddhas and sentient beings are both illusory products of knowledge.

In the illusory state, there is neither real nor false; mind and objects merge, essence and appearance do not interfere: the body and the environment interpenetrate, their radiance and reflections multiply ad infinitum. The being pervading the sacred and the profane, the essence complete through all time, they abide in the world permanently yet without resting on anything. Therefore they said that the essence of illusory states in inconceivable.

After this they directed Sudhana to see Maitreya, who is to fulfill buddhahood in one lifetime. This one lifetime is the birthless lifetime, not a lifetime in the temporal order. The three principles represented by Maitreya, Manjushri, and Samantabhadra are the body of all causes and effects of the fifty ranks, not principles that exist outside the fifty ranks.

51. MAITREYA

Shrisambhava and Shrimati used the inconceivable power of faculties for goodness to make Sudhana feel at ease and aglow, then directed him to the great building called chamber of adornments of Vairocana in the Great Array Park in Samudrakaccha, at the edge of the ocean, where he saw the enlightening being Maitreya and realized the way to buddhahood in one lifetime.

The seashore represents gradually ascending progress to buddhahood in one lifetime, facing the shore of the ocean of birth and death. The Park of the Great Array symbolizes adornment of buddhahood with the knowledge and compassion to enter birth and death.

The name *Vairocana* includes both the meaning of differentiated light, symbolizing knowledge of distinctions, and ubiquitous illumination shining everywhere, symbolizing fundamental knowledge.

The building represents the universally enlightening knowledge of the substance and function of the real universe, working in various ways for the maximum benefit of living beings. Therefore its size is equal to space, so that all worlds and their beings are living in it—though unaware of each other—as told in detail in the scripture, represented by the various worlds seen by Sudhana in the tower.

The building was made by the great compassion of the ocean of enlightened knowledge, the great vow to help the living, and it was situated in the park of birth and death of all sentient beings. Therefore Maitreya said its manifestation is produced from skill in means, from virtue and knowledge; it comes from nowhere and goes nowhere. These are all characteristics of presence in the midst of origination and destruction with knowledge of illusoriness. It is like the power of actions of sentient beings, which arises and disappears without any graspable substance or appearance of coming and going.

Maitreya is the Loving One, of whom buddhahood in the next lifetime was foretold. In the realm of knowledge of illusory states in the real universe, in every particle of every land there are infinite oceans of buddhas, but their unique enlightenment is always as is, without origin or disappearance, without past, future, or present. It is only through the great practice of Universal Good that there are manifestations of attainment of buddhahood, nirvana, and giving instructions for the future, according to what is timely and appropriate for sentient beings. That is why Maitreya appears to be in the position of successorship before the present buddha's mission is ended, while in reality Maitreya is already equal to the buddhas.

Shrisambhava and Shrimati extolled the virtues of Maitreya at length to induce Sudhana to approach and attend Maitreya, and warned him not to try with a limited mind to practice the six ways of transcendence, dwell in the ten stages, purify a buddha-field, or serve teachers. This makes it clear that the six transcendent ways and the ten stages are not yet free from the transcendental partial view of purity; do not yet fully embody the practice of Universal Good; and are not the same as the body of virtues of the ocean of fruits of rewards of Vairocana Buddha, the ocean of blessings represented as flower crowns, necklaces, bracelets, and so on. Through them one only attains equality with the emanation buddhas transcending the world, giving up the mortal body that likes and dislikes.

Therefore when the eleventh stage is fulfilled, the Teaching leads into the real universe, to merge with the complete embodiment of the fundamental root and arrive at the realm of the great knowledge of the real universe that originally underlies unawareness, thus naturally to be rewarded with boundless virtues.

In addition, the infinitely adorned body of enjoyment developed by the differentiating knowledge of the ocean of practical vows of Universal Good would not allow Sudhana to stick to limited practices projected to inspire ordinary people.

Now Sudhana prostrated himself in front of the building, using various modes of praise to extol this building as the abode of great sages with measureless virtues. This illustrates the fruits of buddhahood as being such that they can never be fully described.

The enlightening being Maitreya came from elsewhere and

lauded Sudhana's virtues to the crowd, then extolled at length the virtues of the thought of enlightenment. "Coming from elsewhere" means that when adapting to conventions in order to teach people, one does not dwell on one's own rewards. The process of using all spiritual capacities, enlightenment power, and the myriad practices of enlightening beings to turn the ocean of afflictions into the ocean of all knowledge is all based on the thought of enlightenment.

The thought of enlightenment is independent, and knowledge is also independent, so all that is done is without dependence or obsession—myriad practices are like projections, helping the living is like magic, spiritual capacities and enlightened powers are like the moon in the sky appearing in waters everywhere. All these are functional capacities of the thought of enlightenment. Anything attained through any agency but the thought of enlightenment is not natural law, so the virtues of the thought of enlightenment are inconceivable.

Maitreya made a sound by snapping his fingers, and the door to the building opened up. Snapping the fingers has the meaning of dismissing material sense, sound has the meaning of stirring awake. When material sense is removed and attachment gone, the door of knowledge spontaneously opens.

Once Sudhana had entered the building, the door then reclosed. Opening means the disappearance of delusion and the appearance of knowledge. Reclosing means that in knowledge there is no inside or outside, no exiting or entering, no delusion or enlightenment. This means wholly returning to the source.

Sudhana saw the interior of the building to be infinitely vast as space. This represents the infinity of the realm of knowledge. The ornaments were all made of precious substances, representing the value of practical acts of kindness and wisdom.

In the building Sudhana saw spiritually projected scenes: the past, present, and future practices of Maitreya, as well as the buddhas with whom he worked and his spiritual friends, who also expounded various truths to Sudhana. Because the realm of knowledge of the body of reality is by natural law always so, no thing is not spiritual, no phenomenon is not wonderful—these are spiritual scenes. Because past, present, and future are not beyond a moment, Sudhana saw events of all times. Because the nature of past, present, and future is perfect, they clearly always teach—so Sudhana heard past buddhas teaching.

When Maitreya withdrew his spiritual force, the scenes that had been manifested now disappeared. This is because the identities of phenomena are like dreams, like illusions, like shadows, like reflections, always there and yet always gone, always one and yet always different. Maitreya let Sudhana know the essence of true Thusness, naturally going along with conditions yet naturally reverting to essence.

52. MANJUSHRI

Then Maitreya sent Sudhana back to see his first benefactor Manjushri, showing that the ultimate result is the same as the cause, because the way into eternity of the silent function of universally illumined knowledge is not of the past, present, or future and has no beginning or end, no exit or entry.

Sudhana traveled through a hundred and ten cities to see Manjushri, representing simultaneous certainty of the principles he had practiced. The unity of all buddhas and sentient beings in the same one real unverse is the place where Manjushri is seen.

Manjushri reached out over a hundred and ten leagues to lay his right hand on Sudhana's head, praising his ability to set out on these practical undertakings and be received by spiritual friends. Then he had Sudhana fulfill countless teachings, and had him enter the sphere of the practice of Universal Good. Laying the hand on the head symbolizes mutual identification of cause and effect. The hundred and ten leagues symbolize having passed through the causes and effects of the five ranks. Introduction to the realm of practice of Universal Good means introduction to perpetual practice of Universal Good after the fruition of buddhahood.

After establishing Sudhana in his own place, Manjushri disappeared, illustrating how after the fruition of buddhahood one is not different from when one was among ordinary mortals. After one attains buddhahood, buddha is basically nonexistent, so Manjushri "disappeared."

Sudhana saw as many spiritual benefactors as atoms in a billion-world universe, in the sense that knowledge of the body of reality pervades the real universe evenly, so he saw everything everywhere as no different from the body of Manjushri, the personification of wisdom.

53. SAMANTABHADRA

Finally, in front of the Buddha's seat at the diamond mine site of enlightenment, Sudhana escalated his awareness to the vastness of space, whereupon he saw Samantabhadra ("Universally Good"), sitting on a jewel lotus in front of the Buddha. This means that the aftermath of the fruition of buddhahood is ultimately not apart from the subtle principle of enlightenment, the diamond mine of knowledge, in the first attitude of faith, yet it activates the cosmic network of perpetual practice.

Samantabhadra extended his right hand and lay it on Sudhana's head, whereupon Sudhana attained as many concentrations as atoms in all buddha-fields. And just as Samantabhadra lay his hand on Sudhana's head here, so did each Samantabhadra before every buddha in every atom of every world in the ten directions also lay his hand on Sudhana's head, and Sudhana attained the same spiritual experience. This illustrates the eternal buddhahood of the real universe and its eternal practice of Universal Good; only upon reaching and according with these do you realize the buddhas are already enlightened and Universal Good is already in action. It also illustrates how the fulfillment of practice is not apart from cause—time does not shift, knowledge does not alter.

With each step in the buddha-fields in the pores of Universal Good, Sudhana crossed untold worlds, but even traveling thus throughout the eons of the future one could not know the limits of the order of succession of oceans of lands in a single pore of the matrices of oceans of lands, of the differences in oceans of lands, of the interpenetration of oceans of lands, or of the formation and disintegration of oceans of lands; one could not know the limits of the oceans of buddhas or the oceans of congregations of enlightening beings. This is because such is the reality of the vast realm of infinite practice of Universal Good.

Then Sudhana attained the ocean of practical vows of Samantabhadra, equal to Universal Good and equal to the buddhas, filling all worlds with one body, equal in sphere, equal in practice, equal in true awareness, equal in spiritual powers, equal in teaching, equal in kindness and compassion, equal in the freedom of inconceivable liberation. This illustrates how the ocean of infinite practices is carried out by all buddhas of all times and places. This is the ultimate enlightenment, in which there are no more ideas of attaining buddhahood or not attaining buddhahood.

GLOSSARY

Glossary

absolute state—Nirvana.

action—As "karma" refers to doings that are conditioned by past habits and also condition future habits and states of development.

adornment—All manifestations, all phenomena, may be referred to as "adornments." The features of the world may be called adornments of space. Also, qualities are adornments of essence; specifically, virtue and knowledge are adornments of persons; beauty and harmony are adornments of worlds.

anointed—Means "crowned," based on the ancient Indian coronation ceremony of anointing the crown prince with the waters of the surrounding oceans; in this scripture it means anointment with the "elixir" of true knowledge. This is the highest of the ten abodes of enlightening beings (see Book 15), in which the knowledge of all aspects of enlightening practices is consummated; it is also used to describe the highest of the ten stages of enlightening beings (see Book 26), in which the ten powers of buddhahood are developed.

Aparagodaniya—The western of the four continents of Indian Buddhist geography.

bases of mystic powers—Four bases of spiritual powers: will, effort, concentration, and meditation.

birthless—Refers to emptiness of absolute existence or individuality; as things have no independent individual existence or absolute reality, they are said to have no origin—the "origin" or "birth" of something specific is a point of definition conceived by the mind of the perceiver, not an inherent property of objects. From the point of view of relativity and continuity, as all things are part of one whole and have no separate existence, these are ultimately no boundaries or demarcations, no beginnings, so individual things have in themselves no point of origin as discrete entities outside of projected definitions.

Brahma—Refers to a class of gods; or, as a proper name of an individual god, it refers to the god Brahma, associated with knowledge and creativity.

Brahma heavens—*See* heavens.

celestial devil—The ruler of the sixth heaven in the realm of desire, the heaven of control of or free enjoyment of others' emanations; "others' emanations" means the experiences of the senses, and the celestial devil is the grasping aspect of the cognitive faculty, which conceives attraction and repulsion and thus acts as a compulsive force and a source of confusion.

celestial ear—Supernormal hearing, of extraordinary range and acuity.

celestial eye—Clairvoyance, ability to see things and events at great distances; also referred specifically to seeing the births and deaths of sentient beings everywhere.

child of Buddha—Or "offspring of Buddha"—an epithet of enlightening beings.

compounded—Conditional, made up of elements, not having independent discrete existence; usually it is said that all things are compounded except space and nirvana.

conqueror—An epithet of a Buddha, referring to the victory over oneself; also the term Victor is used.

definitive marks of all things—(1) All actions are impermanent; (2) all actions involve suffering; (3) all things are selfless; (4) nirvana is ultimately tranquil.

demons—Any attachment or obsession, anything that obstructs wisdom, is called a demon. Any delusion or force of distraction is called a demon. The so-called four demons are the demon of afflictions, the demon of the five clusters (q.v.) or mental and physical elements, the demon of death, and the Devil or the Most Evil One, the king of the heaven of free access to or control of others' enjoyments, the highest of the heavens in the realm of desire, symbolic of the conceptual or cognitive mind commandeered by desire.

Devadatta—Arch villain of Buddhist myth, renegade from the original Buddhist order, said to have attempted to kill the Buddha.

diamond realm—Existence seen as identical to emptiness and therefore indestructible.

discriminatory thought—Thinking of percepts and concepts as objective realities, discrete and definitive; fixation on appearances while ignorant of essence. Discrimination is commonly used in the sense of false or arbitrary discrimination, notions not true to reality; it may also be used, however, in the sense of nonemotive, unbiased discernment. Context makes it clear which of these meanings is intended. Also, discrimination in the sphere of relative mundane truth may be temporarily suspended for the purpose of focusing the attention on absolute truth, then resumed with greater clarity, precision, and detachment in order to function in the ordinary world after the awakening of transmundane insight.

dusts—The material world; used specifically to refer to sense data.

eight difficult situations—Conditions in which it is difficult to be able to hear the teaching of enlightenment: hells, the state of hungry ghosts, the state of animals, earthly paradise, the heaven of long life, the conditions of deafness and blindness, the condition of intellectual brilliance in terms of worldly knowledge, and in times before and after the existence of a Buddha in the world.

eight liberations—(1) Contemplating external form while still having internal images of form: this means looking at or contemplating "impure forms" such as decomposing corpses to inhibit the arising of physical desires and eliminate attachment to the body; (2) contemplating external form without internal images of form: this means observing impure external forms even after attachment to the body is quelled, in order to strengthen this detachment; (3) fulfilled stage of physical realization of pure liberation: this refers to observing "pure forms" which means only seeing light and color; "physical realization" means at this stage the body is filled with bliss; (4) absorption of the mind in the infinity of space; (5) absorption in the infinity of consciousness; (6) absorption in nothingness; (7) neither perception nor nonperception; (8) cessation of sensation and perception.

eightfold path of sages—An ancient formulation of eight elements of the way to liberation: right seeing, right thinking, right speech, right action, right livelihood, right effort, right recollection, right concentration. "Right" here means conducive to liberation.

eighteen elements—Six sense faculties, six associated sense consciousnesses, and six fields of sense data—in combination these are the elements of experience.

end of the right doctrine—It is said that spiritual teachings go through three stages: the first is when the genuine teaching is operative and there is practice and realization; second is a period of imitation, where there is practice but no true realization; third is the ending period, when the teaching is vitiated and has become an inoperative relic.

enter—This word is commonly used in the sense of intellectual penetration, experiential understanding, realization, insight, vision.

essence—Emptiness, or the conditional nature of things.

field of blessings—Saints, enlightening beings, and Buddhas are called fields of blessings because of their beneficial effect on the world, and because giving to them produces blessings and felicity. Also, all beings may be called fields of blessings, for the reason that giving to others is productive of blessings or worldly happiness as well as furthering human development through nonpresumptuous generosity.

five clusters—Components of living beings: matter (physical form), sensations, perceptions, (mental) conformations, consciousness. Traditionally this analysis is made for contemplation purposes, especially to convey the sense that the psychophysical being is not an irreducible unity, and to provide a framework for meditation on the emptiness of the ideas of self, soul, person, and individual life. They are called "grasping clusters" as long as they are characterized by clinging and attachment.

five eyes—Five levels of perception: the physical eye, the celestial eye (clairvoyance), the eye of wisdom (perceiving emptiness of absolute reality), the objective eye (seeing things in the relative world as they are in fact, without subjective projection), and the Buddha-eye (including all of the preceding four eyes).

five faculties—Faith, energy, recollection, concentration, awareness.

five powers—Full development of the five faculties.

five precepts—Basic precepts forbidding killing, stealing, sexual misconduct, lying, and drinking alcohol.

flower ornament meditation—Observation of the "net of Indra" principle, seeing all things as interrelated, seeing the unity of being.

four bases of spiritual powers—(1) Will, or desire; (2) energetic effort; (3) concentration; (4) meditation. These are bases of higher psychic developments.

four demons—Major sources of distraction and delusion: the demon of afflictions, the demon of the clusters, the demon of death, and the "celestial demon" of the conceptual faculty controlled by desire.

four fearlessnesses—Four kinds of expertise, or infallibility, or confidence peculiar to Buddhas. In the Chinese tradition these are understood as freedom from fear of contradiction, or confidence, in realizing all truths; in awareness of extinction of all contaminations; in definitive description of all obstacles to enlightenment; and in accuracy of realization of all ways to emancipation. Indian tradition refers to these as types of expertise. There are also four kinds of expertise proper to enlightening beings: expertise in memory and explanation of teachings heard; expertise in protecting others by virtue of purity of thought, word, and deed, with nothing in one's conduct harmful to others, this being attained as a result of realization of selflessness; rightly taking up the Teaching without heedlessness, attaining ultimate wisdom and skillfulness, liberating sentient beings, causing joy to all who see the enlightening being, and clearing away obstructions to enlightenment; and never forgetting the thought of omniscience, not seeking emancipation by any other way, attaining full mastery and benefiting sentient beings in all ways. (Also *fourfold fearlessness*)

four formless concentrations—Absorption in the infinity of space, the infinity of consciousness, the infinity of nothingness, and in neither perception nor nonperception. (Also *four formless attainments*)

four fruits of ascesis—The four stages of the vehicle of listeners; stream-enterers, once-returners, nonreturners, and saints.

four gross physical elements—Earth, water, fire, air; these represent the material body and are used in contemplation of physical disintegration, to view the body as an object rather than a self, to develop dispassion.

four immeasurable states of mind—Immeasurable kindness, compassion, joy, and equanimity; cultivated by enlightened beings.

four intellectual powers—Knowledge of doctrines (or phenomenal facts and principles), meanings, phraseology, and appropriate expression. Also called the four powers of understanding and the four special knowledges, these are analytic and expository powers exercised in preaching and teaching. The four general aspects of enlightened knowledge are: mirrorlike knowledge (unbiased perception of things as they are, like a mirror that reflects impartially without grasping or rejecting); knowledge of essential equality (realization of the emptiness of absolute reality of all things); differentiating knowledge (distinguishing the relative characteristics of things); practical knowledge (involved in the accomplishment of tasks).

four means of integration—Generosity, kind speech, beneficial action, cooperation; also called means of salvation, these are means by which enlightening beings integrate with the world and also integrate people into a buddha-land.

four meditations—Four stages of meditation, each having several characteristic elements: (1) focused awareness, precise thought, joy, bliss, single-mindedness; (2) inner purity, joy, bliss, single-mindedness; (3) equanimity, mindfulness, precise knowledge, bliss, single-mindedness; (4) neither pain nor pleasure, equanimity, mindfulness, single-mindedness.

four points of mindfulness—Contemplation of the body as impure, sensation as irritating, mind as impermanent and unstable, and things as ungraspable and identityless, these are used to develop detachment.

four powers of understanding—*See* four intellectual powers.

four right efforts—(1) Eliminating unwholesome states; (2) preventing further arising of unwholesome states; (3) developing good states; (4) increasing good states.

four special knowledges—*See* four intellectual powers.

four torrents—Desire, becoming, views, ignorance; currents that sweep the mind away from enlightenment and hold it in bondage by compelling force.

freedom from birth—Detachment from the world.

gandharva—A demigod; mythical celestial musician.

gandharva city—A mirage or illusion.

garuda—A fantastic birdlike creature.

gate—A method, a means of access to understanding, a facet or aspect of experience; commonly used to refer to a way of entry into truth, a specific teaching or practice, or a particular perspective.

gods—Representations of higher psychic faculties or meditative states without enlightenment.

Guide—An epithet of Buddha.

heavens—These are classified as belonging to the realm of desire, the realm of form, or the formless realm.

> *Brahma heavens*—or heavens of purity—are in the realm of form, free from lust, tranquil; there are three divisions—Brahma hosts or pure hosts, Brahma assistants, and great Brahmas. Brahma is the creator god of Hindu mythology.
>
> *heaven of enjoyment of emanations*—In the realm of desire; the inhabitants enjoy themselves by emanating sense experiences with which they amuse themselves.
>
> *heaven of free access to, or control of, others' enjoyments or emanations*—Highest of the heavens in the realm of desire, where the inhabitants enjoy the emanations of other heavens in the realm of desire.
>
> *heaven of good manifestation*—In the fourth meditation.
>
> *heaven of good sight*—In the fourth meditation.
>
> *heaven of great freedom*—The realm of Maheshvara, the Great Lord, at the summit of the realm of form, presiding over the world system.
>
> *heaven of infinite light*—In the realm of form, perceived in the third meditation.
>
> *heaven of infinite purity*—In the realm of form, perceived in the third meditation.
>
> *heaven of little light*—In the realm of form, perceived in the second meditation.
>
> *heaven of minor purity*—In the realm of form, perceived in the third meditation.
>
> *heaven of minor vastness*—In the fourth meditation.
>
> *heaven of no heat*—In the fourth meditation.
>
> *heaven of no troubles*—In the fourth meditation, the abode of nonreturners.
>
> *heavens of the four world guardians*—Abodes of guardian deities of the four quarters.
>
> *heaven of the ultimate of form*—Highest of the heavens in the realm of form, at the peak of the fourth meditation.
>
> *heaven of thirty-three celestial realms*—Or thirty-three heavens; in the realm of desire, ruled by Indra, envisioned as atop the polar mountain Sumeru, with the thirty-three realms of celestial cities surrounding Indra's palace.
>
> *heaven of universal purity*—In the realm of form, perceived in the third meditation.
>
> *heaven of vast results*—In the realm of form, perceived in the fourth meditation.
>
> *heaven of vastness*—In the fourth meditation.
>
> *light-sound heaven*—Also called heaven of ultimate light purity; in the realm of form, there is no sound and speech is done by means of light.
>
> *Suyama heaven*—The "heaven of timely portion," in the realm of desire, representing knowledge of suitable time and amount of enjoyment.
>
> *Tushita heaven*—The "heaven of happiness" or contentment, in the realm of desire, said to be the abode of the buddha-to-be.

Honored One—An epithet of Buddha.

Human Tamer—An epithet of Buddha, as a teacher.

immortality—Refers to nirvana, freedom from bondage to life and death.

indestructible body—Refers to the realization of the identity of existence and emptiness, and to the unity of being, transcending ephemeral particulars.

Indra—A particular god, ruler of the gods of the thirty-threefold heaven, sometimes called the king or emperor of goods.

invisible crown—Refers to the inconceivability of the ultimate realization of enlightenment.

Jambudvipa—The southern of the four continents of Indian Buddhist geography, sometimes identified with India.

kalavinka—A mythical bird with a beautiful voice.

kinnara—A fantastic creature with a human body and a horse head.

knot of flesh on the head—One of the supposed physical marks of Buddha.

limbs of enlightenment—Seven aspects of enlightenment: discrimination of true and false, energy, joy, ease, relinquishment, stability, mindfulness.

lion—A term used to refer to Buddhas as the best of humans.

lion throne/seat—Seats of honor for Buddhas and enlightening beings.

lion's roar—The realization or explanation of the ultimate emptiness of conditional things.

Maheshvara—"Great Lord," applied to Indra and other gods.

mahoraga—A great serpent; a fantastic creature.

methods of fostering the path—Thirty-seven aids to enlightenment, consisting of the four points of mindfulness, four right efforts, four bases of spiritual powers, five faculties, and five powers (all of the foregoing are glossed separately), the seven branches of enlightenment (analysis of things, vigor, joy, ease, equanimity, stability and concentration, and mindfulness), and the eightfold path (right seeing, thinking, speech, action, livelihood, effort, recollection, and concentration).

moon—A symbol of truth or reality, being reflected everywhere while itself remaining undivided.

most honorable human—Buddha.

naga—A mythical creature; a "dragon" or rain spirit.

nature—Sometimes used in the conventional sense of character or quality, more usually refers to absolute or intrinsic nature, which is naturelessness or emptiness.

nature of things—Emptiness, or relativity.

nine successive stages of meditation—These consist of the four basic stages of meditation, the four formless attainments, and the stage of passing away of all sensation. (Cf. "The Ten Stages," Book 26)

oceanic reflection concentration—A metaphor for holistic awareness; the mind is likened to an ocean which, when the waves are stilled, clearly reflects everything at once. *The Flower Ornament Scripture* supposed emerges from the oceanic reflection concentration.

one sound—Or "one voice," refers to universal truth, such as the truth of the relativity of all conditional things.

other shore—Transcendence, or ultimate perfection or consummation.

path of ten virtues—Not killing, not stealing, not committing adultery, not lying, not speaking divisively, not slandering others, not speaking frivolously, not being greedy, not being moved to anger or hatred, not entertaining false views.

perdurance—Refers to unity of emptiness and existence, so that there is really nothing which disintegrates, having no independent reality to begin with.

points of mindfulness—Mindfulness of the body, sensations, mind, and phenomena; these are basic meditation practices.

points of totality—Yogic practices involving total absorption in ten objects of concentration, which are expanded to cover the total field of awareness: absorption in the color blue, the color yellow, the color red, the color white, earth, water, fire, air, space, and consciousness.

principles of great people—Having few desires, being content, enjoying peace and quiet, being vigorous in effort, being heedful and mindful, cultivating meditation concentration, cultivating knowledge and wisdom, and not indulging in idle speculation.

purity—Essential purity means emptiness; relative purity means purity as opposed to defilement. Asking about purity is part of the ordination ceremony and refers to asking the novice whether he is pure, or innocent, in regard to the precepts.

Purvavideha—The eastern of the four continents of Indian Buddhist geography.

quakes—Representation of the "shaking" or breaking down of fixed views, the shattering of the habitual world view.

rakshasa—A fantastic creature, may refer to evil goblins or to benevolent demigods.

real character—The identity of emptiness and existence.

reliances—Four basic principles for understanding Buddhism: rely on the teaching, not on the person; rely on the meaning, not on the letter; rely on the complete teaching, not on partial teaching; rely on knowledge, not on conditioned consciousness.

religious faculties and powers—Faith, vigor, recollection, concentration, discernment. (Also *five faculties, five powers*)

roots of goodness—Also bases of goodness, foundations of goodness; refers to virtues firmly established in one's character, or to virtues in general, or good deeds, or higher developments of human faculties.

seven branches of enlightenment—Factors involved in attaining enlightenment: discernment, energy, joy, comfort, recollection, concentration, equanimity.

seven jewels of awakening—The seven branches, or limbs, of enlightenment. *See* thirty-seven aids to enlightenment.

seven kinds of wealth—The spiritual wealth of sages—faith, discipline, learning, conscience, shame, detachment, and wisdom.

seventh sage—The historical Buddha Shakyamuni was said to be the seventh of a succession of ancient Buddhas.

shrouds—Another term for afflictions or hindrances to enlightenment; also refers to obstructions to meditation such as agitation and torpor, anxiety and craving.

six dispositions—The states of being of heavens, hells, animals, ghosts, humans, and titans; a way of referring to the mundane existence in general and in particular.

six paranormal powers—Six spiritual powers: psychic travel, or projection of awareness; clairvoyance (celestial eye); clairaudience (celestial ear); mental telepathy or mind-reading; recollection of past states; awareness of the ending of mental contaminations.

six principles of harmony and respect—Six bases of organization of a religious community: the same acts of devotion, the same recitations, the same faith, the same precepts, the same views, and the same livelihood.

six principles of steadfastness—Steadfastness in faith, steadfastness in the midst of phenomena, steadfastness in practice, steadfastness in virtue, steadfastness in highest attainment, and steadfastness in awareness.

six thoughts—Thought of Buddha, of the Teaching, of the spiritual Community, of discipline, of charity, and of heaven.

sixfold respect—Principles for a spiritual community—respect in behavior, speech, and thought; sharing the same ethics, the same views, and the same material goods.

sixteen knowledges of refined meditation—This refers to the so-called eight recognitions and eight knowledges, which are recognition of and knowledge of the four holy truths as they apply to the realm of desire, and as they apply to the realms of form and formlessness.

sixty-two views—This refers to all the various opinions and doctrines of the philosophers of India, and by extension to all dogmas and fixed ideas.

sweet dew—Or ambrosia, or elixir; the elixir of immortality, an epithet of nirvana, by which one overcomes the dread and sorrow of death; also used generally for realization of eternal truth.

teacherless path/teacherless knowledge—Autonomous knowledge or inherent knowledge which cannot in itself be taught or learned, but is to be awakened from latency.

ten eyes—The physical eye, the celestial eye, the eye of wisdom, the objective eye, the Buddha-eye, the eye of knowledge, the eye of light, the eye leaving birth and death, the unobstructed eye, the eye of omniscience.

Ten Powered—An epithet of Buddhas.

ten powers—These are ten kinds of enlightened knowledge. One description of the ten powers according to the Chinese tradition is given in the Introduction to this volume. They are also described as knowledge of the following ten things: (1) what is so and what is not so; (2) results of actions; (3) various interests; (4) various realms; (5) higher and lower faculties; (6) all destinations; (7) all states of meditation and concentration, how they are defiled, how they are purified, and how to emerge from them; (8) past states of being; (9) the conditions of death and birth of other beings; (10) the end of contamination. These ten kinds of knowledge power are sometimes equated with the comprehensive omniscience of Buddhas, the knowledge of all particulars. The term "ten powers" typically refers to these ten powers of Buddhas, but there are also ten powers of enlightening beings: (1) resolution; (2) deliberation; (3) becoming; (4) patience; (5) knowledge; (6) extirpation; (7) concentration; (8) presence of mind; (9) virtue; (10) action. Another enumeration of the ten powers of enlightening beings gives (1) intent; (2) will; (3) application; (4) wisdom; (5) commitment; (6) means; (7) practice; (8) magic; (9) awakening; (10) teaching.

ten universes—Prototypes of existence: realms of animals, ghosts, hells, titans, humans, celestials, hearers, individual illuminates, enlightening beings, and buddhas.

tenfold knowledge—Knowledge of facts, inferential knowledge, knowledge of others' minds, knowledge of the world, knowledge of the Four Truths (of the existence of suffering, the cause of suffering, the end of suffering, and the way to end suffering), knowledge of extinction, and knowledge of nonorigination.

thirty-seven aids to enlightenment—Elements of the Path of enlightenment—four points of mindfulness (mindfulness of the body, sensations, mind, and phenomena); four right efforts (to eliminate existing bad states, prevent future arising of bad states, foster good states, and further develop existing good states); four bases of psychic powers (desire, effort, concentration, contemplation); five faculties and five powers (faith, perseverance, mindfulness, concentration, precise awareness); seven branches of enlightenment (discernment, diligence, joy, alleviation, relinquishment, stability, attention); the eightfold right path (right insight, right thought, right speech, right action, right livelihood, right effort, right recollection, right meditation).

thirty-two marks—An ancient Indian idea that a great man has thirty-two special physical features was also applied to the idealized image of Buddha; here they are symbols of qualities attained by cultivation of good practices.

three doors of liberation—See three liberations.

three fires—The fires of craving, hatred, and folly.

three kinds, or bodies, of pure precepts—Discipline or self-control developed in the realm of desire, discipline arising from meditation, and discipline arising from entry into uncontaminated concentration. Also, precepts designed to get rid of evil, precepts designed to embody virtue, and precepts related to helping others.

three levels of truth—Imaginary or mentally constructed truth; relative truth, or the conditional, interdependent existence of things; and absolute truth, the ultimate emptiness of the imagined and relative truths.

three liberations—Liberation through realization of signlessness, wishlessness, and emptiness; that is, by realizing that things are not as they appear, have no inherent aim, and have no inherent existence.

three modes of conduct—Behavioral discipline, discipline concomitant with concentration, and discipline concomitant with the path of enlightenment.

three spheres pure—Emptiness of absolute existence of subject, object, and medium; usually applied specifically to giving without attachment to the giver, the receiver, or the gift.

three superknowledges—Knowledge of past states of self and others; seeing the future life and death of self and others; and knowledge of the end of afflictions and contaminations.

three times—Past, present, and future.

three tolerances—Tolerance of opposition and injury, tolerance of suffering, and tolerance of truth.

Three Treasuries—The Buddha, the Teaching, and the religious community.

Three Vehicles—Vehicles of salvation: the vehicle of "hearers" or disciples; the vehicle of individual illuminates; the vehicle of enlightening beings. The first two, called the small or lesser vehicles, culminate in lesser nirvana, or dispassion; the third, called the Great Vehicle, includes both self- and other-enlightenment, and both mundane and transmundane welfare.

three worlds/triple world—The realms of desire, form, and formlessness. The realm of desire is the realm of passion of the ordinary person. The realm of form is the realm of the four meditations (q.v.). The formless realm is the realm of the four formless concentrations (q.v.). These realms are psychically, not spatially, distinct; they are usually cited together as the totality of the mundane, and emancipation is referred to as liberation from, or nonattachment to, any of these realms.

threefold repetition—This refers to repetition during the ceremony of ordination and giving monastic precepts, where the novice is required to affirm his commitment three times.

titan—A kind of being, representing anger, jealousy, pride, and arrogance.

torrents—The four torrents are the torrent of passion, involving great anger, folly, and suspicion, in the realm of desire; the torrent of existence, involving greed and pride in the form and formless realms; the torrent of views, involving delusive views; and the torrent of ignorance.

twelve sense media—The six sense faculties and six fields of sense data.

two kinds of nirvana—Nirvana with remainder, being the extinction of afflictions and views while in this life; and nirvana without remainder, being final extinction upon physical death.

uncreated—This means void or empty of absolute inherent nature; it is also used of what are known as uncompounded phenomena (space and extinction), but again corresponds as well to the uncompounded or uncreated essence—emptiness—within the compounded.

universal tongue—Refers to the expounding of universal truth or all-pervasive principles such as emptiness.

Uttara—The northern of the four continents of Indian Buddhist geography.

walking seven steps—This refers to the myth of the birth of the Buddha, who is said to have walked seven steps in each direction upon coming into the world.

water of eight qualities—The ideal water of pure lands, which is cool, clear, sweet, soft, lustrous, settled, nourishing, and able to allay hunger and thirst.

wish-fulfilling gem—A mythical jewel that grants all wishes; used as a symbol of the mind, especially in terms of its powers of adaptation.

yaksha—A kind of being, sometimes thought of as a ghost or spirit, sometimes benign, sometimes malignant.

Also by Thomas Cleary